1999 Behavioral Outcomes & Guidelines Sourcebook

FAULKNER & GRAY

1999 Behavioral Outcomes & Guidelines Sourcebook

A Practical Guide to Measuring,
Managing and Standardizing
Mental Health and Substance
Abuse Treatment

1999
Behavioral Outcomes & Guidelines Sourcebook

Copyright © 1999

Faulkner & Gray, Inc.
Eleven Penn Plaza
New York, NY 10001
http://www.FaulknerGray.com/health

ALL RIGHTS RESERVED

Except as permitted under the United States Copyright Act of 1976, no part of this publication may be reproduced in any form, whether by photostat, microfilm, or any other means, or incorporated into any information retrieval system, electronic or mechanical, without the prior written permission of the copyright owner.

For permission, contact Linda Ragusin at
(630) 305-7251 or FAX to (630) 305-7313

ISBN: 1-57987-091-0

Published by Faulkner & Gray's
Healthcare Information Center

Material in this book is provided for information only and may not be construed as advice. While reasonable attempts have been made to publish all information as accurately as possible, the publisher shall not be liable for any special, consequential, or exemplary damages resulting, in whole or in part, from the readers' use of, or reliance upon, this material.

PRINTED IN THE UNITED STATES OF AMERICA

1999 Behavioral Outcomes & Guidelines Sourcebook

Kenneth M. Coughlin, MA
Editor

Laura Herold
Anne Lewis
Monica Payne
Project Editors

Bob Cooper
Production Director

Beth Rosenthal
Managing Editor

Ed Dwyer
Publisher

Contributors

Astrid Beigel, PhD
Los Angeles County
Department of Mental Health
Los Angeles CA

Julie Boyle
Evanston IL

Richard Camer
Silver Spring MD

Les DelPizzo
CMHC Systems
Dublin OH

Jon Hamilton
Bellingham WA

Christine Kilgore
Falls Church VA

John S. Lyons, PhD
Department of Psychiatry
and Behavioral Sciences
Northwestern University Medical School
Chicago IL

John J. McGinley, MS
New York NY

Joseph P. Naughton-Travers, EdM
Behavioral Health Advantage
Greensboro NC

Jordan A. Oshlag, MSW, LICSW
Sudbury MA

Joan Retsinas, PhD
Providence RI

Martin Sipkoff
Gettysburg PA

Linda Wasmer Smith
Albuquerque NM

Christine Torre
Los Angeles County
Department of Mental Health
Los Angeles CA

Cynthia Washam
Jensen Beach FL

Table of Contents

Chapter 1: Outcomes Measurement Now: Building Reliable and Valid Bridges to 21st Century Care

Managing Care With Outcome Data: New Hopes, New Responsibilities
 (*Behavioral Healthcare Tomorrow*)..2
The Evolving Role of Outcomes in Managed Mental Health Care
 (*Journal of Child and Family Studies*) 8
Outcome Measures for Individuals With Severe and Persistent Mental Illness
 (*Behavioral Healthcare Tomorrow*)..14
Measuring Outcomes and Costs for Major Depression (*Psychopharmacology Bulletin*) 19

Chapter 2: The Mechanics of Measurement

The Technology of Survey Administration: An Exploration of Your Options,
 From Paper-and-Pencil to IVR (Joan Retsinas, PhD)..28
Who Gets the Results? (Linda Wasmer Smith) 34
New Perspectives On Quality Management Training: Increasing the Effectiveness of Outcome
 Measurement Systems Through High-Quality, Ongoing Training (Christine Torre and Astrid
 Beigel, PhD)..39
How To Involve Staff in Developing an Outcomes-Oriented Organization
 (*Behavioral Healthcare Tomorrow*)..45
Implementing Cost-Effective Information Technologies for Outcomes Management
 (Les DelPizzo) 50
Principles for Assessment of Patient Outcomes in Mental Health Care (*Psychiatric Services*)......55
Protecting Client Confidentiality and Improving Provider Relations Through a New Form of
 Managed Care: Collaborative Care Management (Access Measurement Systems, Inc.)..................61
Laying the Groundwork (Joseph P. Naughton-Travers, EDM,
 and Jordan A. Oshlag, MSW, LICSW)..66
Implementing Outcomes in the Real World of Clinical Service Delivery
 (John S. Lyons, PhD, and Zoran Martinovich, PhD)..75

Chapter 3: Case Studies: Leading Outcomes Measurement Initiatives

The Outcomes Measurement Project: A Massachusetts Provider Group Embraces Outcomes
 Assessment—and Survives (Richard Camer) 84
Outcomes News: A Monthly Newsletter for Mental Health Corporations of Massachusetts Members
 • September 1997 88
 • January 1998 92
Taking Outcomes Measurement Statewide (Julie Boyle) 95
Four Winds-Saratoga: Improving the Care Provided to Children and Adolescents in an Acute Care
 Setting (Joint Commission on Accreditation of Healthcare Organizations) 100
Outcomes Management for Acute Psychiatric Services (John S. Lyons, PhD)....................111

Assessing the Effectiveness of Mental Health Care in Routine Clinical Practice
(*Evaluation & the Health Professions*) 118
Client Outcome Data: An Emerging Force in Managed Care (Rex S. Green) 127

Chapter 4: Client Satisfaction Ratings: Too Much of a Good Thing?

Assessing Client Satisfaction: Attend to Design, Implementation, Analysis in Your Plans
(*Behavioral Health Outcomes*) 130
Satisfaction Ratings: Meaningful or Meaningless? (*Behavioral Healthcare Tomorrow*) 133
Asking the Right Questions (*1999 Medicaid Managed Behavioral Care Sourcebook*) 136
Clinical Outcome, Consumer Satisfaction, and Ad Hoc Ratings of Improvement in
Children's Mental Health (*Journal of Consulting and Clinical Psychology*) 144
Behavioral Healthcare Rating of Satisfaction™ (BHRS™)
(Michael G. Dow, PhD, and John C. Ward, Jr., PhD) 158

Chapter 5: Measuring the Outcome Of Addictions Treatment

Fee-for-Good-Service: A California County Has Begun Reimbursing SA providers Based on
Performance (Christine Kilgore) 162
Hazelden: Using Outcomes Measurement To Improve Chemical Dependency Treatment (Joint
Commission on Accreditation of Healthcare Organizations) 168
Making the Case With Public Stakeholders To Support SA Treatment
(*Behavioral Health Outcomes*) 171
Gambling Treatment Outcome Monitoring System (TOMS) (Randy Stinchfield, PhD) 173
Treatment Outcome Study (TOS) Baseline Design (New York State Office of Alcoholism and
Substance Abuse Services, Health and Planning Services Division, Evaluation and Program
Monitoring Unit) 175

Chapter 6: Children and Adolescents: Different Needs, Different Tools

The Santa Fe Summit on Behavioral Health, Final Report: A Special Section Which Addresses
Outcomes Measurement for Children and Adolescents With Serious Emotional Disorders
(American College of Mental Health Administration) 188
Use of the Child and Adolescent Functional Assessment Scale (CAFAS) as an Outcome
Measure in Clinical Settings (*The Journal of Mental Health Administration*) 193
Fifth National Roundtable on Outcomes Measures in Child Welfare Services: Summary of
Proceedings (American Humane Association)
• Emerging Trends in Child Welfare and Challenges Related to Outcome Measurement 205
• Examining Outcome Across Service Systems and the Community 213
Multiagency Outcome Evaluation of Children's Services: A Case Study
(*The Journal of Behavioral Health Services & Research*) 220
Managing What You Measure: Creating Outcome-Driven Systems of Care for Youth With Serious
Emotional Disturbances (*The Journal of Behavioral Health Services & Research*) 233

Measuring Treatment Outcome and Client Satisfaction Among Children and Families:
  A Case Report (*Professional Psychology: Research and Practice*) 248
Measuring Outcomes in Children's Services: Appendix (Manisses Communications Group, Inc.)...253

Chapter 7: Setting and Meeting Performance And Accreditation Requirements

Uncertain Outcome: Behavioral Health Care Organizations Are Viewing
  JCAHO's ORYX Initiative With Apprehension (Martin Sipkoff)..264
New JCAHO Sentinel Event Policy Change Raises Concerns
  (*Briefings on Behavioral Health Accreditation*) 269
Performance Measures Applicable to Behavioral Health Care Settings [excerpt]
  (Joint Commission on Accreditation of Healthcare Organizations) 271
PERMS 2.0: A Step Toward Core Behavioral Measures? (*Medical Outcomes & Guidelines Alert*)....281
The Santa Fe Summit on Behavioral Health: Preserving Quality and Value in the Managed Care
  Equation: Final Report (The American College of Mental Health Administration):
  • Section II: The Key Indicators 284
  • Section V: Measures..289
  • Section VI: Measures and Indicators 293
  • Appendix 1, Comparison of Performance Indicators:
    NCQA/BHMAP-ACMHA-NASMHPD/NASADAD/APWA...294
  • Appendix 2, ACMHA Process Group Indicators and Proposed Measures............................296
  • Appendix 4, Mental Health Statistical Improvement Program (MHSIP) 298
Quality According to QISMC (*1999 Medicaid Managed Behavioral Care Sourcebook*) 300
Performance Indicator Measurement in Behavioral Healthcare [excerpt]
  (Institute for Behavioral Healthcare Council)..303
State Mental Health Directors Adopt a Framework of Performance Indicators for
  Mental Health Systems (National Association of State Mental Health Program Directors)..........318
An Instrument To Evaluate the Process of Psychiatric Care in Ambulatory Settings
  (*Psychiatric Services*)..320

Chapter 8: Outcomes Management in the Public Sector

Help From Uncle Sam: A Federal Center Is Striving To Standardize
  And Improve Outcomes Measurement for the Public and Private Sectors (Jon Hamilton)..........326
Development of Outcome Indicators for Monitoring the Quality of Public Mental Health Care
  (*Psychiatric Services*)..330
Implementing a Statewide Outcomes Management System for Consumers of Public
  Mental Health Services (*Psychiatric Services*) 341
Michigan's Mission Based Performance Indicator System
  (Michigan Department of Community Health) 348
A Multistakeholder-Driven Model for Developing an Outcome Management System
  (*The Journal of Behavioral Health Services & Research*) 353
Risk-Adjusting Mental Health Outcomes: Access and Quality Applications
  Under Managed Care (Association for Health Services Research, 15th Annual Meeting)............364

Chapter 9: Selecting Meaningful Yardsticks

Guide to Behavioral Outcomes and Client Satisfaction Measurement Instruments 374
A "Global" Look at BASIS-32 (*McLean Reports*) 551
Validation of the Panic Outcomes Module (*Evaluation & the Health Professions*) 555
A Consumer-Constructed Scale To Measure Empowerment Among Users
    Of Mental Health Services (*Psychiatric Services*) 563
Use of a New Outcome Scale To Determine Best Practices (*Psychiatric Services*) 571

Chapter 10: Practicing What You Preach: Creating and Implementing Behavioral Guidelines

Devising Depression Guidelines for Primary Care Physicians (Cynthia Washam) 578
A Decisive Year Ahead for the Practice Guidelines Coalition
    (*1999 Medical Outcomes & Guidelines Sourcebook*) 582
Practice Guidelines Coalition: Administrative Framework for Practice Guideline
    Development and Approval (*Practice Guidelines Coalition*) 587
Ethical and Political Issues in Practice Guidelines Implementation: A Dialogue
    (*Behavioral Healthcare Tomorrow*) 591
At Issue: Translating Research Into Practice: The Schizophrenia Patient Outcomes Research Team
    (PORT) Treatment Recommendations (*Schizophrenia Bulletin*) 599
Addressing Issues of Face Validity in the Application of a Clinical Guideline (*Evaluation Review*)... 611
Routine Treatment of Adult Depression (*Psychiatric Services*) 616
Directory of Behavioral Practice Guidelines 618

Chapter 11: Recent Mental Health and Substance Abuse Research Findings

Review of Recent Outcomes Literature (John J. McGinley) 628

Appendices:

Appendix A
Selected Instruments
- MHSIP Consumer Survey (The American College of Mental Health Administration) 645
- Mental Health Statistical Improvement Program (MHSIP) Consumer Survey
  (Short Version) (The American College of Mental Health Administration) 647
- Solution-Focused Recovery Scale for Abuse Survivors (Yvonne Dolan, MA) 648
- Children's Functional Assessment Rating Scale™ (CFARS™)—Florida Version
  (Michael G. Dow, PhD, and John C. Ward, Jr., PhD, the University of South Florida,
  And the Florida Department of Children and Families) 649
- Functional Assessment Rating Scale™ (FARS™)—Florida Version
  (Michael G. Dow, PhD, and John C. Ward, Jr., PhD, the University of South Florida,
  And the Florida Department of Children and Families) 651
- Child and Adolescent Strengths Assessment (John S. Lyons, PhD) 653
- McLean Hospital Outpatient Perceptions of Care (McLean Hospital) 655
- Rhode Island Outcome Evaluation Instrument
  (Rhode Island Department of Mental Health, Retardation, and Hospitals) 657

Appendix B
Outcomes Measurement System Vendors
- Access Measurement Systems, Inc. 662
- AdvantaCare, Inc. 664
- BHOS, Inc. (formerly Behavioral Health Outcomes Systems) 666
- Corporation for Standards & Outcomes (CS&O) 668
- DeltaMetrics 670
- HCIA's Response 672
- Integra, Inc. 674
- Mental Health Outcomes, Inc. 676
- OQ Systems, Inc. 678
- Parrot Software 679
- Performance-Based Outcomes, Inc. 680
- Strategic Advantage Systems Corporation 681
- Velocity Healthcare Informatics 683

Appendix C: Behavioral Benchmarks
- OMP Has System for Comparing Provider Outcomes (*Behavioral Health Outcomes*) 684
- Behavioral Benchmarks: Results From the National Outcomes Management Project (Center for Quality Innovations & Research, Department of Psychiatry, University of Cincinnati) 687

Appendix D: Sources 700
Appendix E: Other Resource Organizations and Periodicals 705
Appendix F: Further Reading 712
Appendix G: Key Internet Resources 718
Appendix H: Acronyms 721

Preface

Keeping Pace With a Maturing Field

For growing numbers of behavioral plans and practices, "outcomes measurement" and "guideline implementation" are no longer simply buzzwords but day-to-day realities. As the field matures, the focus of interest is slowly shifting from the "whys" and "wherefores" of setting up an outcomes or guidelines program to the finer points of implementation. At the same time, more and more providers have systems in place and experiences to share.

This, the fifth edition of the *Behavioral Outcomes & Guidelines Sourcebook*, reflects this maturation. A major focus of this year's volume is on issues and problems that surface only after the commitment to accountable treatment is made and an instrument or guideline has been selected. The outcomes portion of the book addresses such critical questions as, How do you interpret results to clinicians? What, if any, data should be shared with clients? How can you improve your batting average in collecting follow-up data? What new data-gathering and scoring technologies are available?

We also relay lessons learned from some of the leading outcomes measurement initiatives, including the Mental Health Corporations of Massachusetts' Outcomes Measurement Project, which has been tracking individual patient progress as well as assembling data by mental health provider or site since March 1997. (We also reprint some recent editions of the group's exemplary outcomes newsletter.) Also highlighted is the Santa Clara County (California) Department of Alcohol and Drug Services' groundbreaking outcomes program, which now pegs part of providers' pay to a "quality achievement score"—a measurement of how well providers adhere to certain length-of-stay and efficiency guidelines.

Outcomes results cannot exist in a vacuum; to be placed in the proper context, they must be compared with the results of other providers. This is the premise behind the Outcomes Management Project (OMP), which coordinates and analyzes data from 20 participating group practices and integrated delivery systems. The OMP and the Center for Quality Innovations & Research at the University of Cincinnati's Department of Psychiatry generously permitted us to share some of the OMP's recent behavioral benchmarking data so that others who employ their widely used instruments can see how they stack up (see Appendix C).

As the field develops, new or refined tools continue to emerge. Once again, the *Sourcebook* presents a survey of major outcome and satisfaction measurement instruments, which we modestly believe remains the most comprehensive such roundup available. This year's survey encompasses 108 instruments and is based on questionnaires sent to instrument developers seeking key data to assist users in the instrument selection process. Developers of instruments included in last year's survey were invited to update their information, and more than 20 new instruments have been added to the guide, including the Severity of Psychiatric Illness, the Adolescent Treatment Outcomes Module, the Multnomah Community Ability Scale, and the Panic Outcomes Module.

A number of these instruments are reprinted in their entirety in Appendix A, including the "Florida versions" of the Children's Functional Assessment Rating Scale (CFARS) and the Functional Assessment Rating Scale (FARS), and the new "short form" MHSIP (Mental Health Statistics Improvement Program) Consumer Survey.

Another exciting development in the past year was the release of the American College of Mental Health Administration's Final Report on its first "Santa Fe Summit." Leaders from all sectors of the mental health and substance abuse field were invited to attend a working meeting in March 1997 in an effort to reach a consensus on core performance measures for mental health and substance abuse care. The fear is that the continued proliferation of measures will drain precious energy and resources. The Final Report, much of which appears in these pages, presents a group of provisional indicators and other material that lays a solid groundwork for basic performance criteria.

In the guidelines arena, we look at how HMOs are adapting the Agency for Health Care Policy and Research's depression guidelines for primary care physicians and update the important work of the Practice Guidelines Coalition, which is trying to achieve the same kind of consensus in the area of guidelines that the American College of Mental Health Administration is hoping to effect for performance measures. We also direct you to the "Key Internet Sites" in the appendix for information on the Texas Algorithm Project, which is evaluating the impact of medication algorithms in public sector patients with severe and persistent mental illness. (Because details of the Project's findings to date are still under review or are in press elsewhere, they could not be reproduced here.) Finally, we again proudly present our updated Directory of Behavioral Practice Guidelines, which we believe to be the most inclusive survey of its kind.

As always, important developments emerged too late for inclusion here. We recently learned that the ValueOptions, the nation's second largest managed behavioral health care company, is establishing a Center for Behavioral Health Outcomes at the University of Virginia. The Center, which is the first such collaboration between an MBHO and a major university, will evaluate the effectiveness of managed behavioral health care and offer suggestions on how it can be improved. In these efforts, the Center will be in the enviable position of drawing from ValueOptions' data on its more than 20 million covered lives. The Center's initial focus will be on public-sector programs, which we hope to investigate further in next year's edition.

Also, as of this writing, The Evaluation Center@HSRI (Human Services Research Institute) was poised to release a long-awaited toolkit to help organizations implement the Mental Health Statistics Improvement Program (MHSIP) Consumer-Oriented Mental Health Report Card, which is currently being tested in a number of states. (See page 298.) The toolkit will include assistance on planning and organizing, design and methods, managing and analyzing data, and reporting results.

Once again, there are many whose help was crucial to the final product. Particular thanks go to John S. Lyons, PhD, John C. Ward, PhD, and David Kraus, PhD, for their generous contributions of material in the face of many follow-up calls and e-mails. In addition, the Institute for International Research's May 1998 conference in Boston on behavioral outcomes measurement proved to be an invaluable resource.—K.M.C.

Chapter 1

Outcomes Measurement Now: Building Reliable And Valid Bridges to 21st Century Care

Managing Care With Outcome Data: New Hopes, New Responsibilities

MARK MORAN

For managed behavioral healthcare organizations, outcome measurement may turn out to be the proverbial "tail that wags the dog."

After a decade of trimming costs and altering clinical practice in ways that have garnered the animosity of clinicians, behavioral managed care organizations are now being required to demonstrate a commitment to quality by generating outcome data. Meeting this requirement is a challenge that calls for cooperation from those same clinicians, already overburdened with demands from case managers (and receiving less money for their work)—a challenge that leaders in the field say will require a radical change in the way providers and managed care companies work together.

If companies are truly committed to quality, not merely to talking about it, it is a challenge that must necessarily transform the managed behavioral healthcare industry itself, moving it away from oversight of clinical decision-making into a partnering relationship with providers. In its most visionary form, the accelerating push for outcome measurement—in combination with advances in information technology could help to realize the long-deferred promise of managed behavioral healthcare: matching patients' unique needs with statistically derived "best practices" for high-quality, cost-effective treatment.

"Our roles are shifting," said Paul McCarthy, PhD, vice president for quality assurance and outcome management at Green Spring. "A constellation of trends is shaping the industry today, moving us away from micromanagement and toward the delegation of care management to providers. Outcome data and very well developed clinical practice guidelines, coupled with advances in information systems that allow for rapid feedback of data to providers, really constitutes an evolving disease management system that should allow us to specify the best provider-treatment match for any given patient."

A Field in Its Infancy

While a handful of companies are pushing the envelope of innovation in outcome management, the industry as a whole remains far behind that visionary goal, and interviews with industry leaders suggest that many organizations fall well short of their own professed intentions.

"There is a lot of variability in the field," said Jeb Brown, PhD, director of quality management at Human Affairs International (HAI). "I would say the field is in its infancy when it comes to realizing the potential of outcome measurements. Most companies know they have to have outcome data, but only a few have gone beyond conceptualizing it and really integrated it into how they do business."

Eric Anderson, PhD, president and chief executive officer of Integra, said that most of what passes for "outcome data" among managed behavioral healthcare companies are post-treat-

---

Source: Reprinted with permission by Manisses Communications Group, Inc. Originally published in Behavioral Healthcare Tomorrow June 1998; 7(3): 21-24, 40.

Mark Moran is a writer for Medical Worlds News and has been on staff with Psychiatric News.

ment, narrative reports on patient satisfaction, which he termed, "relatively meaningless." Said Anderson, "If that's what people are doing, then the state of outcome measurement in the industry is abysmal."

Far more rare, he said, is the use of well-designed instruments that yield statistically valid data. Yet behavioral managed care companies may soon find that they have no choice but to get up to speed. Both the National Committee for Quality Assurance and the Joint Commission on Accreditation of Healthcare Organizations have established regulations requiring companies to demonstrate a commitment to quality through the use of outcome measures.

An even more decisive pressure is coming from purchasers themselves, who are now demanding accountability for the services offered by managed care companies. The days of attracting purchasers simply by promising to cut costs may be over, industry experts say.

"We have definitely seen a commodification in the marketplace," said Zachary Meyer, MHA, vice president of quality management systems at MCC. "The price differential between one company and another has begun to narrow so that purchasers are naturally looking at other attributes to help drive the purchasing decision. If price alone isn't going to be the key driver, then inevitably purchasers will be looking at quality."

Yet leaders in the field cite a number of interrelated barriers and obstacles to realizing the potential of outcome management, even among those companies that are using scientifically valid instruments. Not least among these obstacles has been the resistance of providers to cooperate in using outcome measurements with their patients.

Meyer and others say this problem is related less to intransigence on the part of therapists, than to the failure of managed behavioral care organizations' care managers to settle on a standard, provider-friendly instrument. With scores of companies each using different instruments, and with providers already overburdened by demands for justification of treatment, asking a therapist to complete still another form is no small request.

"Look at it from a provider's perspective," Meyer says. "If we try to say to them, 'We're going to pay you less, but we want you to complete this additional tool that will take another twenty minutes of your time,' providers are invariably going to push back."

Robert Fusco, MD, corporate medical director at Managed Health Network (MHN), said that inevitably the managed behavioral healthcare industry must settle on a standardized measure of outcomes. "For the industry at large this whole process has not been a coordinated effort," he said. "There has been a fragmentation of the delivery system, and competition among the various managed care organizations rather than cooperation."

Shorter Is Better

So what does the optimal outcome measurement instrument look like? On this question, leaders in the field are unanimous: shorter is better.

Measurement tools should require no more than five minutes of a provider's time to complete, and no more than twenty minutes of a patient's time. Industry experts cite four features of a data collection tool that make for easy administration and scoring: concise questions, a Likert scale rating system, a simple check box or fill-in bubble for scoring, and use of a computer-scannable response form. Questions should measure the success of treatment in three broad areas: symptom severity; patient functioning at home, school or work; and overall quality of life, especially satisfaction with interpersonal relationships.

Even more vital than the brevity of the instrument, leaders agree, is integration of the measurement tool into the regular flow of patient care and communication between providers and managers of care. It is the seamless use of measurement as a part of everyday business, they say, that will ultimately allow companies to seize on the full potential of outcome data while responding to providers' demands for a quick and painless instrument. In this regard, companies will be assisted by rapidly evolving information systems technology, allowing for almost instantaneous transmission of information between providers and managers of care.

Beyond that, outcome experts at managed behavioral healthcare organizations appear to agree on only one other thing: whatever their company is doing is the best in the field. It is a pride of ownership that belies the professed desire for cooperation in the interest of quality outcome.

Moreover, interviews with industry leaders reveal a tension between conflicting goals of scientific rigor, on the one hand, and broad applicability and easy integration into work flows on the other. Some companies are using established tools long recognized for validity and reliability which have proven successful in studies involving small numbers of patients and providers. Others have developed their own instruments; these have found broad applicability across thousands of cases, albeit with less scientifically elegant results, in a way that integrates the measurement tool into the regular flow of patient care and communication between provider and managed care company.

Nuts and Bolts

So which companies are doing what, precisely?

HAI uses the OQ-45, a forty-five item questionnaire developed by researchers at Brigham Young University. Brown, of HAI, reports that the tool is now in use with just 2,000 of the company's 14,000 network providers—a relatively small rollout that he qualifies by noting that more than 50 percent of the company's referrals now go to those providers using the instrument.

Likewise, McCarthy, of Green Spring, reports using the Basis-32 and the SCL-90R, two symptom checklists developed at Johns Hopkins University. These instruments have been employed by Green Spring in studies and projects with a small subset of network providers involving not more than 300 to 400 patients, and sometimes as few as 50 to 60 patients.

In contrast, MCC, Integra, and MHN have crafted their own instruments for broad-based use. Fusco, of MHN, says his company's instrument measures symptom severity, functional impairment, and overall quality of life, and is completed by both patient and provider at the beginning of treatment and at the end. The instrument includes six domains of functioning rated on a 9-point scale, as well as an 11-point problem resolution scale.

He emphasized that the broad applicability of the tool allows it to be integrated into established protocols of communication between the company and its providers. "We have been able to embed our measures in the collection of data, as part of our case management process, pre- and post-treatment, and to some degree during the course of treatment," Fusco said. "We have accomplished this by integrating the tool into the information that providers return to us when they complete our case management assessment form and request for recertification."

Similarly, MCC has developed a combined mental health and substance abuse measurement that can be completed by both the patient and provider as part of an initial 50-minute assessment. When the forms are complete, the provider faxes them back to the managed care company, where the information is instantly read into a database using optical character recognition (OCR) technology. The data is then used to assemble a patient profile report which can be faxed again to the provider with three essential components: a case history summary, a score for severity of symptoms, and an outcome prediction that is derived from a growing database of cases. Follow-up questionnaires are completed after six months and twelve months, Meyer said.

Meyer concedes the process is not flawless. OCR technology is far from perfected, he said, and still requires a considerable degree of manual oversight to ensure accurate reading of patient and provider reports. Yet he believes the advantages of using an instrument that is broadly applicable, rather than symptom-specific, are borne out in everyday practice. The patients whom clinicians see on a regular basis present with a range of unique mental health and substance abuse problems that may not be easily encompassed by brand-name tools designed for assessing specific conditions, Meyer said.

"We tend to take standardized instruments off the shelf and apply them in clinical settings that don't naturally fit, or that are even an incredible burden to the provider and patient, he said. "We need to develop very broad-based assessment tools that we can operationally integrate into the way we do business."

Anderson, of Integra, concurs. Integra's "Compass" instrument comprises several questionnaires ranging in length from 30 to 130 items, developed under a grant from the National Institutes of Mental Health, that measure patient status across three broad domains: symptoms, well-being, and functioning. These domains correspond broadly to a theory of mental health put forward by Ken Howard, PhD, professor of psychology at Northwestern University, demonstrating a dose-response relationship between treatment and improvement in any one of the three categories. While there has been some dispute about the ability to generalize the patient sample from which Howard derived the dose-response relationship, Integra's effort nevertheless represents a statistically driven approach to titrating psychotherapy that is unique in the behavioral managed care field.

A distinguishing feature of the company's effort, Anderson says, is its use of the "Compass" tool concurrent with treatment, not just at the beginning and end. As treatment progresses, rates of change—as measured against baseline scores—are compared with a dose-response curve generated from the company's database of more than 50,000 cases. Plotting the patient's progress on that curve allows the case manager and provider to determine together whether more intensive treatment is indicated or whether the benefits of continued treatment are reaching the stage of diminishing returns.

The company's process is also distinguished by the use of computer-based technology for rapid transfer of information between provider and managed care company. Anderson describes the following process: Providers enter outcome data they collect from patients on a desktop computer using software that links the provider to a network databank; the information is then electronically transmitted to the network, where it is instantly translated into a treatment algorithm and fed back to the provider again, who can use the information to shape an effective treatment.

At this level of sophistication, Anderson says, the role of the behavioral managed care company really begins to change from that of cost-conscious oversight manager to unobtrusive supplier of information—what Anderson calls "a back room support" partner—helping to shape clinical care according to statistically derived best practices.

"We want to refine how we deliver managed behavioral healthcare to the point where we are re-engineering ourselves, Anderson said, "Ultimately, we envision ourselves as a partner to large provider organizations who want some of the capability of a managed care company, but don't want the intermediary."

How Information Shapes Treatment

For most companies, such visionary ideals are barely on the horizon. Fusco, of MHN, emphasizes that until the industry settles on a standard, provider-friendly instrument for collection of data, the potential for outcome measurement will be dormant.

"The industry has to mature to the point where time and experience have demonstrated the validity of measures so that we are all using them regularly and routinely, and we all know them and understand what to do with the information," he said.

What companies do with the information, Fusco said, could change the way patients in behavioral managed care are treated. The optimal uses of outcome information include the development of statistically derived "best practices," as well as processes of continuous quality improvement arrived at by sharing information across network providers about what works and what doesn't. Ultimately, information might be used to shape the structure of benefits, and guide the development of health systems, Fusco said.

Here, too, the gulf between vision and reality is only too apparent. Most companies are using what little data they have for provider profiling—a practice that is not without potential for improving quality, but that is also fraught with controversy. Though companies uniformly insist that they do not use negative outcome data to drop providers from a network, all of them say they will use the information in referral decisions.

That will be cold comfort, surely, for clinicians who are not likely to appreciate the distinction—if there is one—between being dropped from a network and being blackballed. Therapists who have been using outcome measurements in their networks acknowledge a trend toward making instruments more provider-friendly, but say they still remain wary that the results may be used as a tool for punishment. At the same time, therapists do not yet find the information they are getting from their companies very helpful.

"Outcome information is not yet really useful to the frontline clinician," said one clinician, who noted that the transfer of information between treatment professionals and care managers still needs to be refined. Electronic transfer from a laptop computer is ideal, she said, but the technology is still too expensive for most providers to take advantage of it.

The ability to adjust outcome results for differences in the severity of cases seen by clinicians is critical to provider profiling, but it is not clear that behavioral managed care organizations have yet achieved the necessary sophistication required to disaggregate data. Several companies say they address case-mix severity through the use of more generic measurement tools: By measuring improvement in functioning, rather than changes in symptomatology, one can compare providers who are treating patients with conditions in a specified range of severity, they say.

While that approach may account for differences in the severity of patients with acute illness, it does not address the problem of chronicity, and begs the question: How will managed behavioral healthcare organizations use outcome measurement with clinicians who are treating patients with severe and persistent mental illness?

Yet in some areas companies are making creative use of information gleaned from outcome measurement. Meyer reported that MCC's outcome data has begun to yield important information about how the structure of a benefit may affect the course of treatment. One critical finding has been an association between higher co-payments and a tendency on the part of patients to disengage from treatment. "We know now that when the co-payment is greater than twenty dollars, the patient is one-and-a-half times less likely to engage in treatment," he said.

Meyer said the company's efforts are also yielding information about how to titrate the intensity of treatment in outpatient substance abuse programs. When comparisons are made of programs that offer very intensive, multiple-session treatment in a short period, against those that offer less intensive treatment extended over a longer period of time, Meyer reports that the latter produce significantly better outcomes.

On the clinical level, Brown said that HAI's data has been used for early identification of patients who are likely to drop out of treatment. "If we could teach providers to pay attention to the instrument, they could target patients at risk for premature termination without waiting for me to feed the information back to them," he said.

Most promising, perhaps, for really transforming the relationship between providers and managed care, is the use Integra is making of its data to establish a dialogue with clinicians about the course of individual patients.

Typically, Anderson notes, case managers at managed care organizations make determinations about authorizing sessions on the basis of written reports. Those determinations are bound to be more or less arbitrary, he said, to the consternation of providers who are liable to view the process as a game that is rigged against them.

In contrast, Integra uses the "change scores" derived from use of the "Compass" tools to begin a conversation with the clinician about the best way to proceed with a particular case: "Patient A appears to be falling behind the expected score at this stage of therapy. What needs to happen in treatment to bring the score up?"

Said Anderson, "We think our system transforms what is perceived by many as an arbitrary administrative process into a discussion about the clinical status of the patient, which is really at the core of what providers would like to do anyway—develop treatment plans based on the needs of the patient."

Follow the Data: Variability in Outcome

Faced with demands for outcome measurement, managed behavioral healthcare organizations uniformly profess a faith in scientifically valid data. But will they follow that data where it leads them, and not just where they want it to go?

Brown, of HAI, noted that experiments with treatment protocols tend to give weight to very well-designed studies, a devotion to scientific rigor that everyone in the behavioral managed care industry applauds. The problem, he said, is that these studies may not reflect the actual day-to-day experience of clinicians and their patients

"When you start to look at real data from the real world, it may not behave the same way that experiments in the laboratory do," he said.

Brown claims that HAI's accumulating outcome data is yielding a surprising finding: Variability in outcome data appears to be less related to treatment protocols or types of psychotherapy, and more to characteristics unique to the clinician-patient interaction.

"I can't find a lot of difference in outcome due to the different psychotherapies," he said. "In fact, when I control for patient characteristics, I can't find any difference at all."

Far more important, he said, are factors that should be common across all the psychotherapies: Does the patient feel hope? Does the patient feel understood? Does the patient trust the therapist? These characteristics will be determined by the clinician's ability to establish rapport, as well as by any number of external factors that the patient brings to therapy.

And therein lies the future challenge of outcome measurement for behavioral managed care companies: refining the analysis of outcome data to account for the myriad variables that define the patient who walks in the door, and the clinician who greets him or her in a therapeutic encounter. The very weight of these variables appears to confound attempts to restrict treatment to a "cookbook" approach, he says.

"The really interesting issue in the future for all of us is how much variability is out there in outcomes," Brown said. "We all still have a long way to go in finding out what truly makes a difference in treatment."

The Evolving Role of Outcomes In Managed Mental Health Care

JOHN S. LYONS, PHD

In the 30 years prior to this decade, most negotiations regarding the nature and duration of mental health care occurred between the consumer and the provider. In many situations, where consumers were unsophisticated about their options, the provider had near carte blanche for directing treatment. In contrast, during this same period, negotiations about payment for services generally occurred between the provider and a third party payor. This bifurcated negotiation process, whereby the provider first determines type and duration of treatment with the consumer and then determines payment with a third party insurer, has been identified as one of the causes of the dramatic increase in the costs of mental health care (and health care in general) from 1960 through the early 1990s.

Perhaps it should be surprising that it took the government and insurance industry 30 years to realize that the inherent design of fee-for-service health benefits was flawed. However, powerful historical factors were rooted in the decision to leave treatment decisions predominantly in the hands of providers. At times, providers have resisted efforts to "second guess" treatment decisions, even opposing peer review. Also, there was little consensus among mental health professionals regarding which interventions worked for whom or, in some cases, whether interventions worked at all. Perhaps the strongest reason for resistance, however, arose from a hesitancy to disrupt the "doctor-patient relationship." While this was a concern throughout health care, it was of particular concern to mental health providers because the predominant theory of treatment emphasized the sanctity of the therapist-client relationship.

As health care costs continued to rise much more rapidly than inflation in the 1980s, the urgency of addressing the system of care increased to the point of action. The first successful model for containing costs was prospective payment, specifically Medicare's Diagnosis-Related Groups (DRG). By dictating the duration of hospital stays that would be covered prior to the onset of services, DRGs had a dramatic effect on reducing hospital lengths of stay. Managed care interventions, from utilization management to risk sharing Health Maintenance Organization (HMO) models followed rapidly on the heels of this success.

Managed Care And Outcomes

The function of managed care, regardless of the specifics of its design, is to insert the payor into the negotiation regarding the nature and duration of services provided to the consumer. Early managed care efforts focused on benefit limits (e.g., 10 sessions only) and aggressive utilization management. This sometimes led to rather draconian policies that prevented consumers from receiving

---

Source: Lyons JS. The Evolving Role of Outcomes in Managed Mental Health Care. Journal of Child and Family Studies 1997; 6(1):1-8. Copyright 1997 Plenum Publishing Corporation. (Reprinted with permission.)

John S. Lyons, PhD, is Director, Mental Health Services and Policy Program, Northwestern University Medical School, Chicago, Illinois. Correspondence should be directed to John S. Lyons, Department of Psychiatry and Behavioral Sciences, Northwestern University Medical School, Ward Building 9-200, 303 East Chicago Avenue, Chicago, IL 60611-3008.

needed treatment. It has become increasingly recognized that, as managed care evolves, efforts must be placed on efficiently matching the needs of the consumer with the services provided. To accomplish this goal however, it becomes necessary to articulate and measure actual mental health need. Measuring service utilization is relatively straightforward, but it is only one half of the puzzle. Ensuring that the consumer receives the service that he or she needs, but no more than that, requires measurement of both clinical need and an assessment of the clinical benefit received from services provided. It is in this environment that outcomes have arisen as an important objective in service delivery and administration.

In many ways, the recent focus on outcomes does not represent anything new. The Community Mental Health Acts in the 1960s mandated evaluation as an ongoing function of service delivery. Despite spawning a generation of evaluation scientists, these mandated evaluations generally had little effect on the process of service delivery. Based on this experience there may be some healthy skepticism about the latest upsurge in interest in outcomes. However, there are several reasons why the assessment of outcomes in the mid-1990s can be expected to have greater impact on service delivery compared to earlier efforts.

First, there has been a shift away from a culture of evaluation in which the evaluator is external and information is viewed as a form of power to a learning organization culture in which performance data are seen as an integral management tool. In a learning organization, information is not to be controlled but rather to be shared to stimulate performance enhancements. This cultural shift, which is manifest in Deming approaches and Total Quality Management, represents an important difference in how organizations view information. Second, computer technology has improved dramatically. Powerful, easy to use systems are readily available. Almost everyone has some computer experience. Thus, the capacity for information management is greatly enhanced. Finally, there is a much greater demand for accountability, not only from payors but also from activist consumer groups as well. Given these new circumstances, mental health service providers find themselves in a position in which outcomes become a value-added part of their business operation rather than an unenforced mandate.

Outcome Methodologies

There are at least four different methodologies that have been used to approach the measurement and management of outcomes (Lyons, Howard, O'Mahoney, & Lish, 1997). Each of these will be reviewed below.

Change Analysis

The goal of change analysis designs is to estimate the amount of benefit received from a treatment. There are a variety of different specific techniques that have been used with this goal in mind. The most common has been called "*static estimation.*" Static estimation is the primary methodology of consumer satisfaction surveys. In this approach, a single assessment is taken in which the consumer is asked to estimate how much benefit he/she received from a treatment episode. The advantage of this method is that it is the least expensive measurement strategy. The disadvantage is that it does not necessarily provide valid information about actual benefit. For example, we have found that the timing of these surveys has enormous effects on consumers' ratings of their experience of therapy. As a person gains more distance from the time at which they initiated treatment, the perception of his/her distress at the start of treatment increases. Thus, a survey at six months might show more benefit than one at six weeks, but this difference may only reflect a modified perception of well-being at the start of treatment (e.g. "I never knew how badly off I was until I got into therapy").

A somewhat more sophisticated approach to change analysis involves the estimation of clinical benefit prospectively. *Prospective change* analysis requires the measurement of clinical status on at least two occasions, usually at the beginning and end of treatment. The change from start to finish provides a more direct estimate of the actual clinical benefit of the treatment. However, as Cook and Campbell (1979) pointed out, this type of design does not allow a causal inference that the treatment had anything to do with any observed change. As such, a richer approach to change analysis requires *disaggregation*. Disaggregation, or the breaking of the sample into smaller, more homogeneous groups can be a powerful strategy for investigating outcomes associated with a particular service or program.

Chapter 1: Outcomes Measurement Now

Perhaps the most common form of disaggregation involves studying the 'dose-response' relationship. The logic of this strategy is that in circumstances where a service is effective, more of that service (at least to a point) should be more effective than less of the service. Howard, Kopta, Krause, and Orlinksy (1986) were the first to demonstrate a dose-response relationship in psychotherapy. Similar findings have been reported for other services (e.g., Lyons, Howard, O'Mahoney, & Lish, 1997). Finding a reliable dose-response relationship can be fairly compelling indirect evidence for the effectiveness of a particular treatment. Other variables can be used to disaggregate as well. For example, compliance with practice guidelines can be used as a disaggregation variable. Cases that follow guidelines should be expected to have better outcomes than those which do not.

Decision Analysis

Readers who are familiar with quality assurance case review know that when something goes wrong in a case, it is often possible to trace problems back to faulty decision making. In fact, service providers have the greatest control over the decisions that they make. As such, these decisions offer fertile ground for quality and outcome improvement activities. Decision analysis approaches to outcomes focus on identifying the clinical characteristics that should lead to specific decisions (e.g., to hospitalize or not) and then developing either clinical or statistical prediction models that define the optimal likely decision given the consumer's current clinical characteristics.

For example, psychiatric hospitalization is a risk management intervention. In the presence of significant risk of harm to self and others, hospitalization can be a valuable strategy for managing that risk. Elsewhere, we have built risk-based prediction models to define the likelihood of hospital admission (Lyons, Stutesman, Neme, Vessey, O'Mahoney, & Camper, in press). Once defined, these models can be used to identify deflections (i.e., high risk/not hospitalized), risk-inappropriate admissions (low risk/hospitalized) as well as risk-appropriate hospitalizations (i.e., high risk/hospitalized). Such information can be quite valuable for improving decision making in crisis settings. The same logic applies to any other decision in the service system (e.g., initiation of treatment, alteration of medication dosage).

It is also possible to use advanced statistical techniques to model decision-making in order to inform quality improvement efforts. For example, we have used Optimal Discriminant Analysis (ODA, Yarnold & Soltysik, 1991) to model hospitalization decisions. Figure 1 presents one such model for a private managed care firm. This model uses the Severity of Psychiatric Illness scale (Lyons et al., in press) and can be interpreted as follows. If the person manifests profound Self Care Impairment (a score of 3) the decision tree goes right and if he or she has no substance use or are subthreshold on a substance-related disorder (a score of 0 or 1), he or she is hospitalized 13 of 13 times. On the other hand, if the person has profound Self Care Impairment and a substance-related disorder (score of 2 or 3) then he or she is as likely to be hospitalized as not (2 of 4).

Looking at the left branch of the decision tree, a person with no profound Self Care Impairment (score of 0, 1, or 2), with a recent hospitalization, tends to be rehospitalized (11 of 13). This is a clear quality improvement issue. It appears that in this program having a recent prior hospitalization is a very strong marker for hospitalization. In a well functioning system of care, discharged patients should be linked to services that could prevent future hospitalizations. For those persons without profound Self Care Impairment and no recent hospitalization (Premorbid Dysfunction 0, 1 or 2), if they are acutely Suicidal (a score of 3) they are hospitalized (17 out of 20). The remaining individuals tend not to be hospitalized.

Outcome Prediction

Perhaps the most sophisticated outcomes strategy involves the process of predicting the trajectory of clinical recovery for a given consumer based on his/her characteristics and the type of service provided. Individual cases can then be evaluated based on their progress compared to the expected trajectory of improvement. Groups of consumers can be compared on their relative improvement correcting for expected rates of improvement. Ken Howard and his colleagues have accomplished this task for outpatient psychotherapy

(Sperry, Brill, Howard, & Grissom, 1996). Figure 2 provides an example of a case performing above expected levels of improvement.

Successful outcome prediction models require a substantial database to allow for model building. They also require the measurement of those outcomes which one would expect to change. For example, Howard's COMPASS system combines subjective distress, symptoms, and functioning into a Mental Health Index in order to capture change on three primary outcomes of psychotherapy (Sperry et al., 1996). To date the necessary data is unavailable to allow for the application of this approach to other services.

Needs-Based Planning

We are in a climate of rapid change in the design of mental health service systems. Optimally, any changes should be guided, at least in part, by the needs of the consumers served by the system of care. Needs-based planning is a form of outcomes methodology with this objective. The process of needs-based planning can build on any one or all three of the above methodologies. The focus, however, in this strategy is less on any given case or provider, but rather on the functioning of a system of providers.

As an example, I have been involved in a needs-based planning process in the State of Illinois Department of Children and Family Services (DCFS). DCFS spends more than $400 million on mental health services for its 50,000 wards. By far, the largest proportion of these expenditures is on residential services. This expense prevents the funding of creative community-based alternatives. As such, it became a priority to identify whether or not some children were

Fig. 1. Optimal Data Analysis of Decision-Making Regarding Psychiatric Hospitalization in a Managed Care Environment

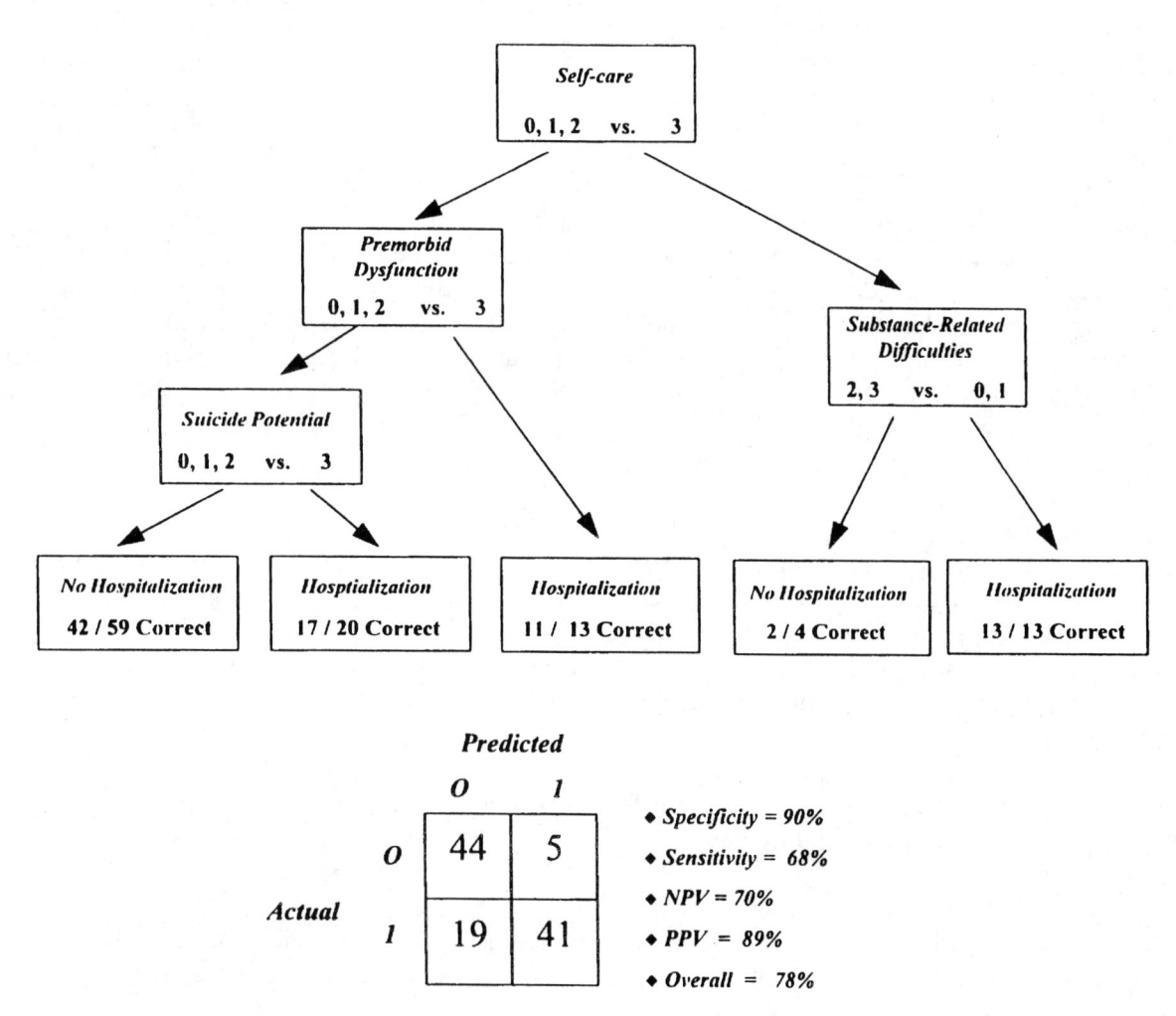

Self-care
0, 1, 2   vs.   3

Premorbid Dysfunction
0, 1, 2   vs.   3

Substance-Related Difficulties
2, 3   vs.   0, 1

Suicide Potential
0, 1, 2   vs.   3

No Hospitalization	Hospitalization	Hospitalization	No Hospitalization	Hospitalization
42 / 59 Correct	17 / 20 Correct	11 / 13 Correct	2 / 4 Correct	13 / 13 Correct

Predicted

		0	1
Actual	0	44	5
	1	19	41

- *Specificity = 90%*
- *Sensitivity = 68%*
- *NPV = 70%*
- *PPV = 89%*
- *Overall = 78%*

Chapter 1: Outcomes Measurement Now

Fig. 2. Outcome Prediction Methodology Predicting the Rate of Recovery, As Measured by the Mental Health Index, of a Person Receiving Psychotherapy

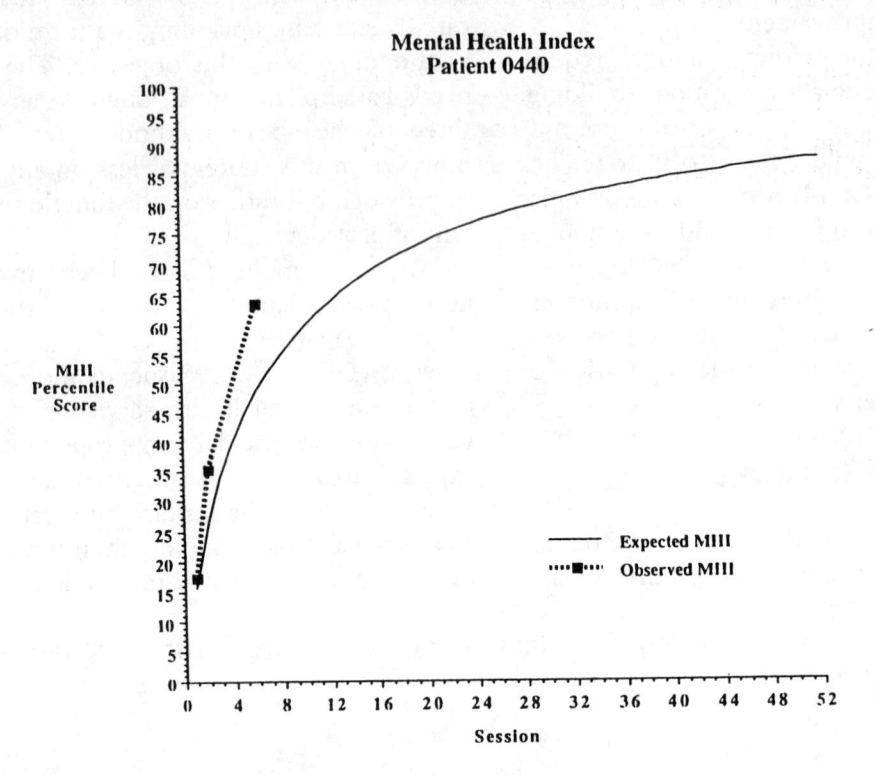

being served in residential settings who could be better served in community settings.

Using the Childhood Severity of Psychiatric Illness scale, we surveyed a stratified random sample of 333 children currently in residential placements. On average these children had been in residence for one year. About 20% of the sample failed to meet diagnostic criteria for a serious emotional disorder. Furthermore, nearly 16% of the sample had never engaged in any of the following risk behaviors—suicidality, dangerousness, runaway, crime or delinquency or sexual aggression. Age was the only predictor of who these children who were placed in residential treatment without significant need. Older adolescents were particularly likely to receive inappropriate residential placement. The results of this study suggested an opportunity to step down a significant number of children who were not at risk into community placements. Consistent with the reform plan, savings from this stepdown process could be sufficient to be reinvested in community-based services with some rapid impact.

In the evolving world of managed mental health care, outcomes have the potential of playing a very important role in ensuring that consumers with mental health needs receive effective, efficient, and high quality care. By no means do outcomes represent a panacea for the problems and challenges that mental health service providers face during the coming decades. However, these strategies represent an important advance in our efforts to demonstrate the value of mental health services to skeptics and advocates alike while providing information that can be used by clinicians and administrators to improve the quality of service delivery.

References

Cook, T., & Campbell, D. (1979). *Quasi-experimentation in the design of field research*. Houghton-Miflin, New York.

Howard, K. I., Kopta, M., Krause, M. S., & Orlinsky, D. E. (1986). The dose-effect relationship in psychotherapy. *American Psychologist*, 41, 159-164.

Lyons, J. S., Howard, K. I., O'Mahoney, M. T., & Lish, J. (1997). *Measuring and managing clinical outcomes in mental health*. New York: Wiley.

Lyons, J. S., O'Mahoney, M. T., Doheny, K. M., Dworkin, L. N., & Miller, S. I. (1995). The prediction of short-stay psychiatric inpatients. *Administration and Policy in Mental Health, 23,* 17-25.

Lyons, J. S., Stutesman, J., Neme, J., Vessey, J. T., O'Mahoney, M. T., & Camper, H. J. (in press). Predicting psychiatric emergency admissions and hospital outcomes. *Medical Care.*

Sperry, L., Brill, P., Howard, K. I., & Grissom, G. (1996). *Treatment outcomes in Psychotherapy and psychiatric interventions.* New York: Brunner/Mazel.

Yarnold, P. R., & Soltysik, R. C. (1991). Theoretical distributions of Optima for Univariate discriminant of random data. *Decision Sciences, 22,* 739-752.

Outcome Measures for Individuals With Severe and Persistent Mental Illness

LAURA BLANKERTZ, PHD, JUDITH COOK, PHD, SALLY ROGERS, PHD, AND RUTH HUGHES, PHD

In a time when mental health service providers are cutting costs and services, stakeholders need adequate information in the form of outcome measures to evaluate services based on quality. Outcome measures are particularly important for high-risk populations, where severe and persistent mental illness results in serious functional impairment of daily life. A client oriented method of gauging rehabilitation of real-world behavior over the long term, as well as the short-term, and which allows for comparison with other programs, must be developed. Lack of agreement on the domains to be measured, however, has hindered the development of common standards, making it difficult to track accountability and service effectiveness. Four authors provide a framework to help organizations choose and develop appropriate outcome measures, as well as core data suggested to measure longitudinal changes in rehabilitation.—Eds.

Mental health service providers—managed care organizations and individual providers—exist in an environment of economic constraint. This milieu increases demands for accountability of economic resources and demonstrations of service effectiveness. Funders, policymakers, and the public want to know what outcomes or results they can expect for the money invested, not only what kind of services will be provided. They want this information in order to compare the effectiveness of different organizations. Without outcome measures, organizations have no means of defending themselves from cost-cutting efforts, attempts to shorten lengths of stays, or cost comparisons with other programs. If outcome measures with comparable, common elements are not developed and adopted, funders and policymakers will be left to evaluate services on the basis of cost, not quality.

Collecting outcome measures can have other benefits for an organization besides proof of effectiveness. First, outcomes are an important aspect of continuous quality management, indicating areas of poor performance and providing a means of monitoring changes that might improve performance. Second, outcomes can improve staff morale and job satisfaction by providing positive feedback for work well done. Third, the tracking process puts a positive focus on the attainment of good outcomes—higher quality work.

Fourth, as an important element of program evaluation, results can answer such questions as: Is the program reaching the targeted clients? Is the program delivering appropriate services? Are services having the right impact?

Outcome measures are especially important for the people who have a severe and persistent mental illness which results in serious functional deficits in daily life—a high-cost, high-risk population. Through years of experimentation and innovation, the public mental health sector has learned that

---

Source: Reprinted with permission by Manisses Communications Group, Inc. Originally published in Behavioral Healthcare Tomorrow August 1997: 62-67.

Laura Blankertz, PhD, is the director of research for the Matrix Research Institute located in Philadelphia.

Judith Cook, PhD, is the director at the University of Illinois/Chicago National Research and Training Center on Psychiatric Disability.

Sally Rogers, PhD, is the director of research for the Boston University Center for Psychiatric Rehabilitation.

Ruth Hughes, PhD, is the executive director of the International Association of Psychosocial Rehabilitation Services (IAPRS), headquartered in Columbia, Maryland

attention to functioning is as important as treatment of the symptoms of an illness. The emerging new generation of medications, which began with clozapine and risperdal, has resulted in dramatic improvement for many with psychotic disorders. The combination of drug treatment and psychiatric rehabilitation may lead to recovery for a significant segment of the high-risk population. However, the outcomes of interventions for severe and persistent mental illness are inherently more difficult to document than physical health disabilities. Mental illness is multifaceted. Not only does it have positive (and sometimes negative) symptoms as a direct manifestation of the disorder, but it can produce impairment in many areas of life, such as social, educational, and vocational. Tracking progress in these areas may be more useful than measuring physical symptom reduction. Due to the changes, recovery, not maintenance, is the goal for those who serve persons with severe and persistent mental illness.

Currently, no set of client-level outcome measures can be adopted as a common instrument for community mental health treatment and rehabilitation services. Researchers, consortiums of managed care, government officials, behavioral healthcare companies, and providers all seek to develop standard outcome measures. There is not only lack of agreement on the domains to be measured, but on what to measure in each domain, and from whose perspective? With the plethora of outcome measures being generated, agencies and organizations need helpful criteria to locate methods that accurately measure long-term as well as short-term results of their activities of interest, and those that allow comparisons with other programs. Here we discuss a framework to help organizations choose appropriate outcome measures by reviewing literature on principles for their development and proposing general criteria to be considered. In addition, this paper suggests a minimum core data set to collect comparable data on long-term rehabilitation changes.

Principles of Outcome Measures

For the last two decades, outcome measures have been recognized as important for mental health research and service delivery. The number of performance measures and report cards has multiplied rapidly in the last several years, due to the mandate to evaluate managed care organizations and the providers of services with whom they subcontract. A wide variety of outcomes instruments are currently available, with many more under development. This range of measures perhaps explains why recent work in the field has often revolved around development of principles for this emerging field.

The Outcomes Roundtable, a group focusing on developing outcome measures for individuals who suffer from mental and addictive disorders, has listed principles of consumer assessment. These include: appropriateness of the measure for the specific activity to be measured; demonstration of validity and reliability of the measure; inclusion of consumer perspectives; minimal response burden; general health status questions; consumer evaluation of treatment and outcomes; quantification of type and extent of treatment; prognostic information that can be predictive of outcomes; areas of personal functioning; and reassessment at clinically meaningful intervals. From a pragmatic point of view, Newman and Ciarlo (1994) list 11 principles for outcomes selection, with some overlap of the Round Table list. Outcome measures should:

- Be relevant to the target group
- Have a simple, teachable methodology
- Use objective (observable) referents
- Use multiple respondents
- Identify outcomes that are the result of rehabilitation processes
- Have solid psychometric data
- Have low implementation cost
- Be understandable by a nonprofessional audience
- Involve easy feedback and uncomplicated interpretation
- Be useful in clinical services
- Be compatible with clinical theories and practices

The National Institute of Mental Health (NIMH) listed seven areas of outcome measurement research that overlap to some extent with Newman and Ciarlo's, but are more technical in nature. They require:

- Including multiple domains of outcome, with development of instruments in areas usually unmeasured

- Consensus on a basic set of measures to be used in clinical and community settings that balance cost and value of information
- Testing, within the mental health field, the validity and reliability of instruments used outside the mental health field
- Identifying appropriate instruments for longitudinal studies, taking into account the inherent stability of mental illness
- Developing analytic techniques that account for difficulties in analyzing data collected at different points over time (such as missing data)

The Five "Cs" of Choice

All of these principles offer guidance, but several additional concepts should be kept in mind when choosing instruments to record outcomes for rehabilitation and treatment services to individuals with severe and persistent mental illness. These concepts are consistent with the principles already listed, and augment them to include criteria that reflect current pressures to compare programs, and reflect the true cost and benefits of rehabilitation processes.

Changes

First, outcomes should measure changes in real-world behaviors, activities, or social status. Many have called for more real-world means of actual objective changes in clients' lives that result from rehabilitation. The outcomes should encompass clients' skills acquired in the rehabilitation process beyond the training environment, as well as any resulting change in functional status.[1] Measurement of consumer perspective on services, or changes in symptoms or dysfunctional behavior, is important; a change in real-life status or activities should also be recorded, or there will be no way to determine objective change in the disabilities and handicaps caused by mental illness over time.

Clinicians often perceive symptoms to be the major indicators of a patient's well-being. This perception is based on clinical outcome used as a feedback mechanism for clinicians, not on what is valued by consumers. Consumers are often more concerned about their living situations, interpersonal relations, and having productive vocational roles; true recovery improves social functioning and minimizes psychopathology.

Measures of change should represent the longitudinal basis of the rehabilitation process. Most outcome measures being developed assess the immediate impact of rehabilitation services (immediate reduction in the presenting problems, higher level of functioning, or lower symptomatology). Severe mental illness is chronic; services should include interventions that maximize long-term outcomes. Ideally, a set of outcome measures would be administered when a client first enters a program, then again after a set time interval in a program (outcome measures can also be initiated on clients already in a program). A time period long enough to permit change should be selected. Many researchers in the field suggest six-month intervals. These measures should assess changes that occur over longer periods of time, such as housing or vocational status, rather than measures affected by repeated testing. Longitudinal measures assess long-term changes that can lag behind services, and are sensitive to the variable course manifested by different forms of mental illness.

Constant

Outcome measures should remain constant during each administration if they are to measure true changes. Clinicians may be tempted to change measures over time, as they read or hear about new instruments. This situation is exacerbated by the lack of a common framework by which to evaluate new measures. Using different outcome measures at different time periods means that comparisons of behaviors, activities, or functional status cannot be made. If it is necessary to change or add outcome measures, change should be made incrementally, so that new data can be benchmarked against existing information.

Comparable

Outcome measures used by one agency should be comparable with measures used by other agencies. That is, all agencies should use at least a core group of measures that all other agencies use. Organizations often include outcome measures that have the greatest affinity with their mission, goals, and client population. The result is that each organization uses a different measure. Measures that include common core questions at the same level of specificity are necessary if funding sources are going to choose the most effective programs on the basis of outcomes, rather than on the basis of cost. Comparable measures make it possible for consumers to choose among the various agencies or managed healthcare alliances.

Using comparable measures does not mean that all measures collected by all agencies must be the same. Each agency will devise its own set of measures that best reflects its own mission and the interests of its stakeholders. All agencies should ask one or two questions in the areas of the rehabilitation process that are shared, in addition to intensive and numerous questions in rehabilitation areas of particular interest to them.

Outcome measures should include basic data for each client that provide demographics as well as level of severity (days of hospitalization, time in community mental health services, or level of functioning, for example), so groups as a whole can be characterized and described before being compared to other groups. It makes no sense to compare outcome measures for very different types of clients.

Client-Oriented

Outcome measures should be client-oriented. That is, the unit on which information is collected should be the individual client. Outcome measures should be those considered most useful by consumers and family members, as well as by providers and funders. They should collect information directly from the client, for example, assess client satisfaction with the services provided at a minimum.

Earlier measurements of quality focused on organizational activities, resources, and services. This focus limits conclusions based upon individual progress. Collecting individual-level data provides maximum flexibility for future data analysis and utilization.

Consequences

Outcome measures should reflect the consequences of mental illness and rehabilitation in many areas of a client's life. Mental disabilities are often multifaceted. That is, they affect many areas of life, such as social, residential, and vocational aspects, and have a direct impact on symptoms. As the underlying nature of mental health disabilities varies, changes can occur in some areas, but not others. Rehabilitation efforts in any one life area can affect functioning in other areas positively or negatively, in an anticipated or unanticipated fashion. Outcome measures should gauge basic functioning in areas like financial, legal, educational, residential, vocational, hospitalization, quality of life, and the impact in other areas of the mental illness not directly targeted by the program. These long-term, secondary outcomes may be just as important as the short-term, primary outcomes—especially in terms of total cost of care. If measures of secondary outcomes are not included, the results may reflect temporary gains that do not accurately depict the client's status.

Choosing Specific Outcome Areas

Faced with an abundance of measures, agencies and organizations need practical strategies to decide what to focus on in data collection. Each agency should collect outcome measures that represent the main focus of its activities. Agencies may want to compile extensive outcome measures in their areas of focus but collect simpler outcome measures in other areas of rehabilitation that mark general client movement that are comparable with other agencies. How does an agency decide the main focus of their activities? To attain comprehensive outcome measures, an agency should consider the activities and goals most valued by the stakeholders and include these as outcome domains. Stakeholders are groups and individuals that have a vested interest in, or are affected by, an agency. For a rehabilitation agency, these might include clients, funders, administration, staff, family, and the community at large. For example, clients might value quality of life, empowerment, and jobs. Funders may value cost effectiveness. Administrators may favor provision of the least restrictive services.

A second approach is to use the mission statement of the agency as a resource. A mission statement is a brief paragraph that describes the overall purpose of the agency, and its philosophy. For example, the mission of agency A is to increase vocational outcomes and community integration of its clients through client choice and empowerment. The three focal elements are: vocational outcomes (jobs and job training); community integration (participation in community activities); and client empowerment. Agency B's goal is to maintain clients in the community (out of the hospital) by providing them with skills and support needed in the environments of their choice. The focal elements are: days in the community, social, vocational, and residential skills, and empowerment. A third approach is to look at the array of services and determine in what areas the majority are offered. These areas should correspond to the domains derived from the mission statement. Sometimes, however, mission statements become outdated or do not reflect the actual activities of the organization. Measures should always reflect services actually delivered.

Choosing a Comparative Measure

Organizations can choose from many different kinds of outcome instruments and measures. Individual measures focus on clinical symptoms, quality of life, level of functioning, or perceived progress in treatment. Some measures look at problem behavior in a variety of areas. Additional questions measure client satisfaction. None of these inventories contains any one instrument that captures outcomes, reflecting rehabilitation outcomes in many different areas of a client's life, and that can be used as a core set of comparable measures to capture changes over the long run.

Conclusion

Organizations that work with individuals with severe and persistent mental illness must develop client-level outcome measures. Such measures allow the various stakeholders of an organization—consumers, staff, and funders—to judge the services offered. If outcome measures influence decisions about organizations or agencies, these measures must reflect changes in real-world behaviors, remain constant, permit comparison between agencies on core data, be client-oriented, and reflect the impact of mental illness on many different areas of a client's life. Such measures should reflect principles most mentioned in the field (minimal response burden, inclusion of consumer perspectives, validity and reliability, easy feedback, and uncomplicated interpretation) and identify which outcomes are direct results of treatment and rehabilitation processes. Functional measures capture behaviorally-based changes in various life areas and do not depend upon clinical reports. Such measures can assess which gains are part of the recovery process of the many clients who seek help from modern medications and rehabilitation interventions.

References

1. Attikisson, C., et al. Clinical services research. *Schizophrenia Bulletin* 18(3), 561-526.

Measuring Outcomes and Costs for Major Depression

BRENDA M. BOOTH, PHD, MINGLIANG ZHANG, PHD, KATHRYN M. ROST, PHD, JAMES A. CLARDY, MD, LESLIE G. SMITH, MD, AND G. RICHARD SMITH, MD

Abstract
This article addresses briefly the measurement of multidimensional outcomes and costs for major depression. We emphasize the importance of measuring outcomes in a variety of domains, including the broader issues of improvement or decline in functioning and impairment based on domains known to be affected by major depression. We emphasize the importance of measuring the economic costs of illness, both the direct total health care costs and indirect costs. Direct costs include mental health treatment costs and all other health care costs. Indirect costs include such varied factors as lost wages for the depressed individual and caregiver burden. We demonstrate the usefulness and importance of using these measures with several examples from our own research.

Introduction

This article is written from our perspective as mental health services researchers in which we generally focus on what is happening in the "real world" of mental health care rather than on the carefully controlled settings of clinical trials. Mental health services researchers are concerned with what is effective in mental health care, in contrast to pharmaceutical clinical trials that address issues of medication efficacy (Heithoff & Lohr 1990). In contrast to the general practice in pharmaceutical drug clinical trials, we measure outcomes in a variety of domains in mental health services research, not just in terms of symptoms. In effectiveness studies, therefore, we are frequently concerned with the broader issues of improvement or decline in functioning and impairment based on domains known to be affected by the disorder under investigation.

Mental health services researchers often include a measurement of costs so that policy issues related to health care costs and cost-effec-

---

Source: Booth BM, Zhang M, Rost KM, Clardy JA, Smith LG, and Smith GR. Measuring Outcomes and Costs for Major Depression. Psychopharmacology Bulletin 1997; 33(4):653-658.

Brenda M. Booth, PhD, Centers for Mental Healthcare Research, University of Arkansas for Medical Services, Little Rock, AR and VA HSR&D Field Program for Mental Health, Little Rock, AR. Mingliang Zhang, PhD, Centers for Mental Healthcare Research, University of Arkansas for Medical Services, Little Rock, AR and VA HSR&D Field Program for Mental Health, Little Rock, AR. Kathryn M. Rost, PhD, Centers for Mental Healthcare Research, University of Arkansas for Medical Services, Little Rock, AR and VA HSR&D Field Program for Mental Health, Little Rock, AR. James A. Clardy, MD, Centers for Mental Healthcare Research, University of Arkansas for Medical Services, Little Rock, AR. Leslie G. Smith, MD, Centers for Mental Healthcare Research, University of Arkansas for Medical Services, Little Rock, AR. Richard G. Smith, MD, Centers for Mental Healthcare Research, University of Arkansas for Medical Services, Little Rock, AR and VA HSR&D Field Program for Mental Health, Little Rock, AR.

This work was supported by USPHS Grant P50 MH-48197 (all authors), MH-55297 (KMR & MZ), and MH-54444 (KMR) from the National Institute of Mental Health and by the VA HSR&D Field Program for Mental Health (all authors).

Reprint requests: Dr. Brenda M. Booth, Centers for Mental Healthcare Research, Dept. of Psychiatry, University of Arkansas for Medical Sciences, 5800 West 10th Street, Suite 605, Little Rock, AR 72204.

tiveness can be examined. In terms of cost, there is an emphasis on the importance of measuring the economic costs of illness, both the direct total health care costs and indirect costs. Direct costs include mental health treatment costs and all other health care costs. Indirect costs include such varied factors as lost wages for the depressed individual and care-giver burden.

This article addresses briefly the measurement of multidimensional outcomes and direct and indirect costs for major depression. It demonstrates the usefulness and importance of using these measures with several examples from our work at the Centers for Mental Healthcare Research at the University of Arkansas for Medical Sciences and the Little Rock Department of Veterans Affairs Medical Center.

Measurement of Outcomes

Our choice of outcomes domains for outcomes assessment reflects the World Health Organization (WHO) definition of health as "a state of complete physical, mental, and social well-being and not merely the absence of infirmity" (WHO 1948). From this perspective, remission of an episode of major depression, while necessary, is not generally sufficient as an outcomes measure. We would argue that even in a pharmaceutical clinical trial, optimum outcomes should be defined in this larger definition of health in addition to remission of major depression or reduced depression symptoms. For example, patients may assert that they have not necessarily achieved an optimum outcome if they are still unable to work, even though their depression has been resolved according to *DSM-IV* criteria. In depression as in other psychiatric disorders, the important outcomes to measure are defined by the areas of functioning that are most affected by the disorder. For major depression, it is generally clear what areas of functioning are affected and which measures to use to evaluate improvement in functioning. Consumer groups are frequently as concerned about measures of improved functioning as they are about improved clinical status (National Institute of Mental Health 1980).

In general, it is critical to measure "disorder-specific outcomes" in addition to measuring general health and general mental health outcomes. These disorder-specific outcomes domains vary amongst disorders. Important disease-specific outcomes for major depression are clearly different from those for panic disorder and alcohol abuse. It is generally agreed that bed-disability is a critical outcome measure for depression because this kind of activity restriction is common in many depressed individuals (Broadhead et al. 1990). However, bed-disability is rarely a measure indicating substantial impairment in individuals with alcohol disorders. Criminal justice involvement is a critical outcomes domain for substance use disorders (Collins & Schlenger 1988) but not for major depression or panic.

On the other hand, certain generic measures of functioning such as physical and social health are common to all disorders. Indeed, it is often helpful to have a common measure so that comparisons can be made across disorders. We generally recommend the Medical Outcomes Study SF-36 (Ware, Jr. & Sherbourne 1992), a 36-item self-report multi-dimensional measure of a range of health-related functioning or quality of life from physical health to social health and mental health symptoms. However, it is important to caution that the SF-36 may not be an appropriate measure of health-related quality of life in chronic mental illnesses (e.g., "compared to your normal activity") such as schizophrenia (Dickey et al. 1996; Fischer et al. 1997). The problem primarily is one of comparability of points of reference for those with and without chronic thought disorders.

In major depression, therefore, it is important to define a minimum set of patient outcomes domains in order to understand how patients progress toward the WHO definition of health. We have a substantial amount of research information that can be used in determining which outcome domains to measure beyond symptoms and this research indicates substantial impairment and functional limitations associated with major depression (Hays et al. 1995; Rost et al. 1992; Wells et al. 1989). For example, depressed primary care patients have functional outcomes similar to or worse than those of chronic medical illnesses (Hays et al. 1995). These limitations are not just in traditional mental health domains such as role limitations due to emotional problems but also in physical dimensions including role limitations due to physical health (Hays et al. 1995). Depressed patients frequently have comorbid medical conditions (Coulehan et al. 1990) associated with a more difficult course of illness (Keitner et al. 1991). In a multisite study of medically hospitalized veterans, we found that patients with co-occurring *DSM-III-R* diagnoses of depression or dysthymia experienced substantial decrements in functioning compared to patients without depression diagnoses (Booth et al., in press).

Once these domains are identified, the next issue is how to measure these domains. Outcomes domains can be grouped into disorder-specific outcomes and general measures of health status (Smith et al. 1997). Disorder-specific outcomes measures for major depression include depression severity, preferably a measure with a scoring capability to determine whether the patient meets criteria for a major depressive episode. Disorder-specific outcomes measures for major depression should also capture the disabilities or impairment commonly associated with the disorder such as days in bed, restricted activity days, and days worked. From the perspective of return to our ideal of health, improvements in disability or impairment should be major outcomes to be assessed during a pharmaceutical trial or in any other study in which depression outcomes are to be measured.

Casemix or prognostic variables are patient factors known to be associated with outcome. Casemix variables allow investigators to compare outcomes in observational studies between groups who get different treatments. They describe patient presenting factors at the time of initial assessment and include comorbid conditions identified by psychiatric epidemiology as common in the disorder under evaluation. These casemix variables need to be controlled for in analysis because of their known associations with outcomes. In a randomized clinical trial, we assume that such prognostic factors are equalized among groups by virtue of random assignment. However, in observational studies, which are generally the case in health services research, groups to be compared may differ in these critical variables. In major depression, key casemix variables include substance use and abuse, chronic medical conditions, prior psychiatric hospitalizations, and family history of depression (Rost et al. 1992; Smith et al. 1996). But it is important to note that if groups are widely divergent in these casemix variables or sociodemographic characteristics, controlling for casemix in outcomes analysis may not be realistic. For example, casemix adjustment to compare a largely female Medicaid client population with a generally male employee group would probably not be feasible because the two populations would undoubtedly differ on many unmeasured variables that affect outcomes.

One useful generic measure of health status, or health-related quality of life, is the Medical Outcomes Study (MOS) SF-36. This 36-item instrument is particularly appropriate in studying major depression because this disorder was one of the tracer conditions followed in the MOS (Tarlov et al. 1989). There are a variety of population norms on the SF-36 (Ware, Jr. et al. 1993) against which to measure cohorts with psychiatric disorders. The SF-36 has been used not only in the Medical Outcomes Study but also in a wide variety of studies in mental and medical health (Ware, Jr. et al. 1993). Scoring programs are publicly available and the SF-36 also lends itself well to scoring to reflect two health dimensions: physical functioning and mental/emotional functioning (Ware, Jr. et al. 1994).

One promising tool for measuring multidimensional disease-specific outcomes in a pharmaceutical clinical trial is the Depression Outcomes Module (DOM) which was developed by our research group (Rost et al. 1992; Smith et al. 1996). This instrument was designed to measure disorder-specific and generic outcomes, casemix characteristics, and services use (Table 1) in a brief yet reliable and valid manner (Rost et al. 1992). We also encourage users of the DOM to add or expand on critical areas for their particular use; for example, an implementation of the DOM in an employee assistance program might include aspects of work performance as outcomes measures.

The DOM was recently accepted by the Foundation for Accountability (Smith et al. 1996) and the Joint Commission on Accreditation of Healthcare Organizations (1997) as meeting their standards for a performance measurement system. It assesses initial patient status (baseline) to measure the critical disorder-specific outcomes domains for major depression including severity of depression and functional impairment or disability. Casemix variables are also briefly assessed. The outcomes domains are included also in a patient followup assessment that could readily be incorporated into a standard clinical trial followup

Table 1

Measures Included in the Depression Outcomes Module

OUTCOMES MEASURES
Severity of depressive symptoms
Remission of episode
Suicidality
Social functioning
Bed days
Disability days
Work disability
Mortality

CASEMIX MEASURES
Severity of depressive symptoms
Psychiatric comorbidities
Dysthymia
Alcohol disorder
Drug disorder
Medical comorbidities
Family history of depression or alcoholism
Previous psychiatric hospitalization
Number of previous depressive episodes
Social support
Age at onset

TREATMENT AND SERVICES
Treatment
Current psychotropic medication
Antidepressant Rx
Compliance
Psychotherapy
Type
Number of visits
Electroconvulsive therapy

Setting
Outpatient care
General medical visits
Mental health visits
Emergency room care
Partial hospitalization/day treatment
Inpatient care
Hospital admissions
Total length of stay

appointment. At baseline, there is also a brief clinician review of diagnostic criteria for major depression, and at followup there is a brief medical record review that assesses dimensions of care for concordance with practice guidelines (Depression Guideline Panel 1993). The DOM has excellent psychometric properties in terms of construct validity and test-retest reliability (Rost et al. 1992). The SF-36 is also included in the DOM as a generic measure of health status.

The advantages of implementing multidimensional outcomes assessment are apparent from a recent administration of the DOM in the public mental health sector in Arkansas. A cohort of clients in crisis with depression presenting to the Arkansas Community Mental Health Centers is being followed longitudinally. The sample has received a range of initial treatment services, from none beyond the initial evaluation to hospitalization for depression. Based on 4-month followup data, we found that 78 percent at baseline and 62 percent at followup met *DSM-IV* diagnostic criteria. Even though a McNemar's test identified a significant reduction in the diagnosis of depression ($p<.05$), it could be argued that remission of major depression is certainly not as frequent as would be found in controlled clinical trials (Depression Guideline Panel 1993). On the other hand, the baseline casemix analysis indicates that this group has a number of indicators of poor outcomes including frequent family history of depression or alcoholism (80%) and previous psychiatric hospitalizations (61%). Further analysis will help to determine whether unremitted major depression is associated with these indicators.

Furthermore, this project is as concerned about functioning as about more clinical issues and we found major improvements in functioning over time. On average, the number of restricted activity days in the past 4 weeks decreased substantially (6 days) between baseline and followup ($p<.001$). In other words, even though just over half the sample reported sufficient depression symptoms to meet *DSM-IV* criteria at 4 months after the initial assessment, the sample's functioning improved considerably during the same time interval.

Measurement of Costs

For many psychiatric disorders including major depression, it is critical to identify total health care costs, not just depression treatment costs. Recent estimates of costs of treatment for depressive disorders range from $12.4 billion (Greenberg et al. 1993) to $19.2 billion (Rice & Miller 1993) per year in 1990 dollars. Depression treatment costs represent, however, only a small portion of the total health care costs for depressed individuals. In a longitudinal community study of depressed Arkansans, we found that costs for depression treatment represented on average only 5.5 percent of subjects' total health care expenditures. Even amongst those subjects who received depression treatment, treatment costs were only 8.1 percent of total health care costs.

Measurement of total health care costs is also important because of the possibility that, in the long run, mental health treatment may reduce general medical expenditures. This concept is called the "offset effect" of mental health treatment (Hankin et al. 1983; Holder & Blose 1992) and is often used to justify providing insurance coverage for mental health and substance abuse treatment. Especially in cases where treatment costs are small relative to total health care costs, it is likely that treatment may be effective in reducing general medical expenditures.

Lack of treatment for depression results in large costs to society (Hirschfeld et al. 1997). In fact, conservative estimates of costs due to mortality and morbidity alone (disability and lost productivity) range from $11.2 billion (Rice & Miller 1993) to $31.3 billion (Greenberg et al. 1993) in 1990 dollars. Clinical trials represent a unique opportunity to measure whether new treatments reduce total health care and indirect costs as well as mental health care costs. This issue is particularly important when evaluating the high costs of new medications and justifying their use.

In prospective studies, we use a multi-informant strategy to measure the total direct health care costs of psychiatric disorders such as depression (Smith et al. 1986). Subjects are interviewed to obtain information regarding their total health care use from all locations, including hospitals, emergency rooms, and outpatient settings, and from all types of providers including medical/surgical physicians, psychiatrists, pharmacists, and chiropractors. With signed release of information from subjects, we obtain copies of medical records and billing information from these providers and locations. New providers identified from these records are also contacted. Insurance records are also obtained for information regarding charges and to identify other providers. Once it is believed that all provider and cost information is complete, the medical records are abstracted to determine charges and diagnoses.

For projects in which it is not possible to obtain this level of detail, we are frequently able to obtain administrative data regarding health services use. These administrative databases include private insurance claims records, claims records of public payors such as Medicaid and Medicare, and health care utilization databases such as those maintained by the Department of Veterans Affairs (Booth et al. 1997). Access to these databases varies and may require signed release of information from research subjects. Measurement of costs through administrative databases is less generally complete than through the multi-informant strategy because the databases usually lack either "out of plan use" or some dimensions of health care use. For example, a database maintained by a behavioral health care organization will lack information on medical care utilization and costs.

Patients' time to seek and receive treatment (and potentially time of their companion as well, if relevant) is another component of treatment costs. Although time costs are usually ignored in most studies for various reasons, this source of treatment cost can be an important component in many evaluations (Jagannath et al. 1997; Zhang et al. 1996). Time costs can be estimated in several ways using the human capital approach and willingness-to-pay methods. In the first approach, the patient's wage rate may be used to approximate his/her time costs, although many patients, including homemakers, the elderly, children, and the unemployed, may not be labor market participants. In willingness-to-pay estimates, individuals are asked to place a monetary value on an hour of time. These figures are used to estimate time costs.

When economic evaluations are conducted, an economist may also estimate the indirect costs of disease or treatment. In many serious disorders, indirect costs such as criminal justice costs are substantially greater than the direct health care costs (Rice et al. 1990). Some indirect costs that are important to measure for major depression include: lost wages, lost productivity, caregivers' costs, lost leisure time, lost household production, the cost of early mortality, and pain and suffering. Measurement or estimation of indirect costs may be critical because the economic advantages of treatment may show up in reducing indirect costs rather than reducing direct costs. Therefore, even if an offset effect of treatment is not found for health care expenditures, substantial economic returns may be identified in terms of the indirect costs of depression.

There are multiple approaches to measuring/estimating indirect costs. Data on costs of the criminal justice involvement may be obtained from agencies in the judicial system. Missing work and bed-disability days may be approximated by wage rates using the human capital approach or estimated using the willingness-to-pay approach (Drummond et al. 1987). Because of the complexity in measuring/estimating indirect costs, we usually make a number of assumptions. Therefore it is essential to perform sensitivity analyses of alternatives by changing the parameters of the major assumptions. Such analyses provide a greater level of confidence about the robustness of the indirect cost estimates.

In a study of depressed Arkansans, we measured the economic return of depression treatment in terms of lost wages. This analysis compared the cost of depression treatment to changes in lost earnings. Preliminary analysis under a variety of scenarios found that provision of depression treatment was associated with a net positive economic return in the form of a reduction in lost earnings (Zhang et al. 1997).

Economic Evaluations: Cost-Effectiveness And Value

The final advantage of measuring both functional outcomes and cost is that economic evaluations can be conducted to compare the relative cost-effectiveness and cost-benefits of two or more treatments (Drummond et al. 1987). This kind of evaluation may be particularly important when comparing two treatments that vary widely in treatment costs or even in total health care costs. To illustrate, a new antidepressant may be very expensive in terms of pharmacy costs compared to a less expensive medication but, because of lower hospital readmission rates, may be associated with lower total health care costs for similar outcomes. Newer medications are also often associated with greater adherence because of lower side effects. In these cases, the improved outcomes (i.e., greater effectiveness) can compensate for higher medication costs. A different type of analysis looks at the long-term costs of treatment compared to quality of life gained or lost (Zhang et al. 1996). Economic analyses can provide important additional information when evaluating new medications or for justifying new medications being placed in hospital formularies.

We have also been developing a provisional formulation within which to view the relationship between outcomes and costs that we call "value." In this definition, value is calculated from the perspective of a purchaser of care, such as a large employer group or state Medicaid authority. We have defined the value provided by a health care system, from the purchaser's perspective, as the change in patients' health status for a severity-adjusted tracer condition (Kessner et al. 1973) divided by the expenditures for those patients (Smith 1996). A tracer condition is a single condition for which patients are followed, or "traced," through an organization in order to understand its workings (Kessner et al. 1973). The tracer condition is assumed to be generalizable to the system of care or service delivery. If the tracer condition is major depression, which would be an appropriate mental health tracer condition for primary care or a private psychiatric practice, the value provided by a health care system would be defined as the change in the patients' health status for major depression divided by the expenditures for those patients (Smith 1996). This arithmetic formulation is the inverse of the traditional cost-effectiveness ratio. The advantage of our formulation is that patients are placed in the numerator so that the metric is in terms of outcomes rather than cost. In other words, value lets us know how much health status is improved for a particular unit of cost.

We examined two systems of care for major depression, one predominantly fee-for-service and one a managed-care organization. When we calculated health status profiles of health-related quality of life, measured by the SF-36, we found the change in health status looked very similar for both systems of care. However, when we calculated the value, or improvement in health status per unit of expenditures, we found that one group delivered more "bang for the buck" in that the improvement in health status per unit cost was significantly greater for one system of care on almost all SF-36 subscales. The value varied because expenditures for treatment of depression were substantially different between the two groups. In other words, one system of care delivered the same level of outcomes for lower cost.

Conclusion

We strongly advocate measuring multi-dimensional outcome domains for major depression and other mental disorders. It is important to do so because the goal of treatment should be to return the patient to a high level of overall functioning, not just to reduce symptoms. Additionally, a critical dimension of outcomes assessment should be economic evaluation, both in terms of measuring total health care costs and the indirect costs of illness. These outcome domains are particularly important once a medication has been shown to be efficacious. At that point we need to know that it is effective in general clinical settings and also that its use is cost-effective.

References

Booth, BM; Blow, FC; and Cook, CAL. Functional impairment and co-occurring psychiatric disorders in medically hospitalized men. *Arch. Int. Med.*, in press.

Booth, BM; Blow, FC; Cook, CAL; Bunn, JY; and Fortney, JC. Relationship between inpatient alcoholism treatment and longitudinal changes in health care utilization. *J. Stud. Alcohol* 58(6):625-637, 1997.

Broadhead, WE; Blazer, DG; George, LK; and Tse, CK. Depression, disability days, and days lost from work in a prospective epidemiologic survey. *JAMA* 264(19):2524-2528, 1990.

Collins, JJ, and Schlenger, AT. Acute and chronic effects of alcohol use on violence. *J. Stud. Alcohol* 49(6):516-521, 1988.

Coulehan, JL; Schulberg, HC; Block, MR; Janosky, JE; and Arena, VC. Medical comorbidity of major depressive disorder in a primary medical practice. *Arch. Intern. Med.* 150:2363-2367, 1990.

Depression Guideline Panel. *Depression in Primary Care: Volume 2. Treatment of Major Depression. Clinical Practice Guideline, Number 5.* Rockville, MD: U.S. Department of Health and Human Services, Public Health Service, Agency for Health Care Policy and Research, AHCPR Pub. No. 93-0551. April 1993.

Dickey, B; Wagenaar, H; and Stewart, A. Using health status measures with the seriously mentally ill in health services research. *Med. Care* 34(2):112-116, 1996.

Drummond, MF; Stoddart, GL; and Torrance, GW. *Methods for the Economic Evaluation of Health Care Programmes.* New York: Oxford University Press, 1987.

Fischer, EP; Owen, RR; and McCracken, WA. "Outcomes Assessment in Schizophrenia Using the SF-36." Presented at the Annual Association for Health Services Research meeting, Chicago, IL, June 1997.

Greenberg, PE; Stiglin, LE; Finkelstein, SN; and Berndt, ER. The economic burden of depression in 1990. *J. Clin. Psychiatry* 54:405-418, 1993.

Hankin, JR; Kessler, LG; Goldberg, ID; Steinwachs, DM; and Starfield, BH. A longitudinal study of offset in the use of nonpsychiatric services following specialized mental health care. *Med. Care* 21(11):1099-1110, 1983.

Hays, RD; Wells, KB; Sherbourne, CD; Rogers, W; and Spritzer, K. Functioning and well-being outcomes of patients with depression compared with chronic general medical illnesses. *Arch. Gen. Psychiatry* 52:11-19, 1995.

Heithoff, KA, and Lohr, KN. Promise and limitations of effectiveness and outcomes research: Summary statement of the IOM Core Committee. In: Heithoff, KA, and Lohr, KN, eds. *Effectiveness and Outcomes in Health Care: Proceedings of an Invitational Conference by the Institute of Medicine.* Washington, DC: National Academy Press, 1990. pp. 8-18.

Hirschfeld, R; Keller, MB; Panico, S; Arons, BS; Barlow, D; Davidoff, F; Endicott, J; Froom, J; Goldstein, M; Gorman, JM; Guthrie, D; Marek, RG; Maurer, TA; Meyer, R; Phillips, K; Ross, J; Schwenk, TL; Sharfstein, SS; Thase, ME; and Wyatt, RJ. The National Depressive and Manic-Depressive Association Consensus Statement on the Undertreatment of Depression. *JAMA* 277:333-340, 1997.

Holder, HD, and Blose, JO. The reduction of health care costs associated with alcoholism treatment: A 14-year longitudinal study. *J. Stud. Alcohol* 53(4):293-302, 1992.

Jagannath, S; Vesole, DH; Zhang, M; Tricot, G; Copeland, N; Jagannath, M; Bracy, D; Jones,

R; and Barlogie, B. Feasibility and cost effectiveness of outpatient autotransplants in multiple myeloma. *Bone Marrow Transplantation*, in press, 1997.

Joint Commission on Accreditation of Healthcare Organizations. *ORYX Outcomes: The Next Evolution in Accreditation*. Oakbrook Terrace, IL: Joint Commission on Accreditation of Healthcare Organizations, 1997.

Keitner, GI; Ryan, CE; Miller, IW; Kohn, R; and Epstein, NB. 12-month outcome of patients with major depression and comorbid psychiatric or medical illness (compound depression). *Am. J. Psychiatry* 148(3):345-350, 1991.

Kessner, DM; Kalk, CE; and Singer, J. Assessing health quality: The case for tracers. *N. Engl. J. Med.* 288(4):189-194, 1973.

National Institute of Mental Health. *A Client-Oriented System of Mental Health Service Delivery and Program Management: A Workbook and Guide*. NIMH Series FN No. 4. Washington, DC: U.S. Government Printing Office, Superintendent of Documents, DHHS Publication No. (ADM) 80-307. Printed 1980.

Rice, DP; Kelman, S; Miller, LS; and Dunmeyer, S. The economic costs of alcohol and drug abuse and mental illness: 1985. Report submitted to the Office of Financing and Coverage Policy of the Alcohol, Drug Abuse, and Mental Health Administration, U.S. Department of Health and Human Services, San Francisco, CA: Institute for Health and Aging, University of California, 1990.

Rice, DP, and Miller, LS. The economic burden of affective disorders. *Adv. Hlth. Econ. Hlth. Serv. Res.* 14:21-37, 1993.

Rost, K; Smith, GR; Burnam, MA; and Bums, BJ. Measuring the outcomes of care for mental health problems: The case of depressive disorders. *Med. Care* 30(5):MS266-MS273, 1992.

Smith, GR. How to measure the value of behavioral healthcare: Adding the patient to the equation. *Behav. Healthcare Tomorrow* 5:43-47, 1996.

Smith, GR; Mosley, CL; and Booth, BM. Measuring health care quality: Major depressive disorder. *Major Depressive Disorder, Discussion Papers*. Rockville, MD: Department of Health and Human Services, Public Health Service, Agency for Health Care Policy and Research. AHCPR Pub. No. 96-NO23. Printed 1996.

Smith, GR; Rost, KM; Fischer, EP; Burnam, MA; and Burns, BJ. Assessing the effectiveness of mental health care in routine clinical practice: Characteristics, development, and uses of patient outcomes modules. *Evaluation and the Health Professions* 20:65-80, 1997.

Smith, GR, Jr; Monson, RA; and Ray, DC. Psychiatric consultation in somatization disorder: A randomized, controlled study. *N. Engl. J. Med.* 314:1407-1413, 1986.

Tarlov, AR; Ware, JE, Jr; Greenfield, S; Nelson, EC; Perrin, E; and Zubkoff, M. The Medical Outcomes Study: An application of methods for monitoring the results of medical care. *JAMA* 262(7):925-930, 1989.

Ware, JE, Jr; Kosinski, M; and Keller, SD. *SF-36 Physical and Mental Component Summary Measures: A User's Manual*. Boston: New England Medical Center, The Health Institute, 1994.

Ware, JE, Jr, and Sherbourne, CD. The MOS 36-item short-form health survey (SF-36): I. Conceptual framework and item selection. *Med. Care* 30(6):473-483, 1992.

Ware, JE, Jr; Snow, KK; Kosinski, M; and Gandek, B. *SF-36 Health Survey Manual and Interpretation Guide*. Boston: The Health Institute, New England Medical Center, 1993.

Wells, KB; Stewart, A; Hays, RD; Burnam, MA; Rogers, W; Daniels, M; Berry, S; Greenfield, S; and Ware, J. The functioning and wellbeing of depressed patients: Results from the Medical Outcomes Study. *JAMA* 262(7):914-919, 1989.

World Health Organization. Constitution of the World Health Organization. *World Health Organization: Basic Documents*. Geneva: World Health Organization, 1948.

Zhang, M; Owen, RR; Pope, SK; and Smith, GR. Cost-effectiveness of clozapine monitoring after the first six months. *Arch. Gen. Psychiatry* 53:954-958, 1996.

Zhang, M; Rost, KM; Fortney, JC; and Smith, GR. "Economic Returns on Treatment for Depression." Poster presented at the 15th Annual Meeting of the VA HSR&D, Washington, DC, February 1997.

Chapter 2

The Mechanics of Measurement

The Technology of Survey Administration

An Exploration of Your Options, From Paper-and-Pencil To IVR

JOAN RETSINAS, PHD

Writing about the technology of behavioral health assessments in 1998 is like writing about transportation in 1920. While few families had one car, let alone two, and most people relied on their feet or trolleys, you suspected that eventually the car would eclipse both feet and trolleys, and that the airplane—a rarity—might eclipse them all. But since you couldn't plot "the future," you wrote about the status quo, even while anticipating its demise.

Behavioral health assessment is a transport system, although the cargo transported, befitting America at the millennium, is not goods but information—specifically, information about patients' mental well-being. Imagine a network, beginning with the patient, who "loads" the information. That information goes to a central station for "processing." Processing can be simple: the patient's responses are tabulated and analyzed. Or processing can be complex: software charts the results as the patient takes the assessment instrument over time. Sophisticated programs compare the patient with his counterparts, yielding profiles and baselines and, sometimes, "red flags" for treatment. That processed information—the tables, scores, graphs, profiles—goes to clinicians. It also goes to managed care planners, utilization reviewers, and outcomes researchers, whose feedback returns to clinicians.

The "raw material" of this transport system—and a key diagnostic tool in mental health—is the patient's responses to a standardized assessment instrument. Where laboratory and radiological tests gauge a patient's physical well-being (or at least the well-being of internal organs), these question-and-answer instruments can gauge the patient's mental or emotional status. Managed care reviewers, moreover, use these instruments to evaluate treatment. And the aggregate responses from thousands of patients help researchers judge the effectiveness of different strategies. Understandably, the transport system is crucial.

In behavioral health transport—as in the transport of all information—the key criteria are:
- ease of "loading" the information,
- speed of delivery,
- quality of the transport, and
- costs.

An ideal system will be easy to load, allowing most patients to assess their emotions, their functioning, and their social relationships in a format that a computer can process. It will deliver the information rapidly. Just as a neurologist needs to see the MRI when evaluating a patient's palsy, a mental health clinician needs assessment information during the office visit—in what psychologist William Berman calls "real-time turnaround of individual patient data." "Post-visit" data may satisfy accreditation requirements, and may help managed care reviewers and outcomes researchers, but will not help clinicians draft care plans. The ideal system will not skew, or lose, information in transit from patient to computer. The analysis will include not just the patient's score, but the comparison of that patient against a population of similar patients: the larger the "database" of patients, the more the clinician can trust the predictive power of the analysis. Finally, this system will cost little in time or money.

The transport of information begins with the patient. Most commonly, the patient is given a standardized questionnaire and marks responses with a pencil on a paper answer sheet. Less commonly, the patient will sit down at a computer terminal to enter responses directly into the system. Rarest of all, the patient will punch answers into a telephone. Yet, like the airplane glimpsed through 1940's lenses, today's rare telephone-entry system may someday dominate.

Paper-and-Pencil Assessments

The "status quo" of behavioral health transport, circa 1998, begins with a pencil and paper. Typically, the patient, sitting in the waiting room, fills out an "instrument" that may take from 5 to 20 minutes. By checking off boxes, circling letters, or filling in blank spaces, the patient describes his symptoms, functioning, relationships.

This is the most common way of "loading" information: the patient, accustomed to filling out insurance forms, fills out yet another form. Grant Grissom, vice president for research and development at Field Diagnostic Services, Inc., notes that today's patients expect to fill out forms. "Loading" can happen anywhere: in a rural mental health clinic, in a large group practice, in a solo clinician's office. In a crowded waiting room, everyone can fill out forms at the same time. By now patients are not surprised—and may even expect—to confront a self-assessment questionnaire, which managed care companies increasingly require.

As for the validity and reliability of the patient's information, clinicians caution that the attitude of the clinician, and of staff, may influence the patient's willingness to fill out the form, if not the seriousness with which he or she completes it. Curtis Reisinger, senior vice president of American Professional Credentialling Services, warns that a clinician who presents the assessment with disdain ("Here, take this silly old thing," or "The Managed Care Company is making me do this") will bias the response. If a harried receptionist shoves the instrument to the patient with a stack of insurance forms, that too may bias responses. If staff must elaborate on questions, that elaboration clouds the standardization of the instrument. Finally, if patients do not take the test themselves, but answer questions read by a staff person, that also can detract from the standardization.

Yet the "loading" of information does not stop with the patient. The information goes to a central processing station, to be analyzed, and then disseminated to clinicians, managed care reviewers, and researchers. The paper and pencil form cannot go instantly to the computer, but must be delivered—stage 2 of "loading."

Stage 2 "loading" can consist of direct entry via keyboard to computer, optical scanning, and fax.

Keyboard Loading

To enter the patient's responses into a computer, a staff person must translate each mark into a keyboard stroke. This is time-consuming for staff. It also is not particularly accurate: each form must be verified to ascertain mistakes the patient made filling out the form, as well as mistakes the data-entry person made at the keyboard. Most critically, however, the "keyboard" step precludes rapid delivery of results. Although the method works well with a one-time, small-sample research survey, it works poorly for larger patient cohorts. William Berman, who is CEO of BHOS, an outcomes measurement company, gives this method "a two-to-three-year lifespan."

Optical Scans

Optical scans upgrade the pen-and-paper instrument. The patient still marks answers on paper forms, but a machine "reads" the forms. Some scans resemble college admission SATs; in others, the machine reads characters and numbers.

Scannable forms are easier to score than simple pencil-and-paper forms. A staff person feeds the form into a machine, which then processes the information.

Scannable forms are also more accurate. The error rate from the keyboard transfer of paper/pencil drops substantially with scans. Machines range in complexity: the more sophisticated will read both sides of the paper, as well as detect errors. Dennis Morrison of the Center for Behavioral Health, a group practice in Bloomington IN, estimates that a quality scan machine will detect 30 percent of errors, meaning that staff would need to verify 30 percent of the response sheets. This consumes less staff time than the pencil-and-paper method, where staff must verify all responses.

With a scanner, the information can go quickly to the clinician, the managed care reviewers, and the outcomes researchers. Yet the scanner

Chapter 2: The Mechanics of Measurement

itself will not aggregate data, develop baselines, create normal curves, or chart a patient's responses over time. For that, data must go to a computer for processing. And that feedback—of "processed" data—may take from minutes to hours to days, depending on the system. In systems where patients take the assessment instrument days before their meeting with the clinician, the clinician may have the information on hand before the visit.

Indeed, many managed care companies recognize that "real-time turnaround" is crucial. Zachary Meyer, vice president at MCC Behavioral Care, notes that MCC clinicians see the results of the patient's assessment before the patient walks into the office. At the time of the office visit, the clinician also fills out a standardized instrument. Two days later MCC will fax back to the clinician a detailed analysis, including benchmarking data and "red flags."

Faxes

Here, a staff person faxes the completed the answer sheet to a central processing machine for analysis. Theoretically this allows for rapid feedback to the clinician. If a patient comes early enough to the waiting room, the clinician could have the completed test results by the time of the encounter. (Admittedly, not every patient comes early.) In short, the feedback is as rapid as the fax and the computer allow. And the machines are standard office fare.

Consumer Loading Via Computer

Computer loading of behavioral assessment data is rapid, efficient, and feasible—yet rarer than paper-based loading. Curtis Reisinger estimates that sales of paper-based (primarily scans and faxes) transport outnumber electronic transport by 10 to one.

Computer loading saves on staff time because the patient, sitting at a terminal, directly enters the data. Using a mouse, a keypad, or a touchscreen, the patient answers the questions. (If a patient cannot read, or requires voice cues, a computerized voice can ask the questions. The technology also exists to allow the patient to speak responses.) Staff are not central to this method, although staff may need to instruct patients. Computer loading allows for almost instant feedback—clinicians can have the results as quickly as they can touch a few computer keys. Computer loading may even yield more accurate responses. Geoffrey Gray, president of OQ Systems, the firm that markets the OQ-45 outcomes instrument and its variations, suggests that some patients, such as those with substance abuse, reply more candidly to a machine than to a person. Computer-loading can certainly yield more complete responses: systems can be designed to encourage the patient to answer all questions and not to leave spaces blank.

Yet many patients—as well as health care systems—are not ready for computer entry.

In this era of the Internet, some patients are computer-illiterate. Dennis Morrison estimates that 20 percent of patients will adapt immediately to the computerized assessment; 60 percent will need some instruction, and 20 percent will fail their mini-tutorial. Curtis Reisinger concurs: "Some people are not yet comfortable with computers."

Some health care organizations, too, are not yet ready. The logistics of the waiting room may be a barrier. Do patients get escorted to a small booth? If so, how many booths? How many machines? As many people as are sitting in a crowded waiting room can simultaneously complete paper assessments, but not everybody in a crowded room can sit at a computer at the same time. Small hand-held computers may solve the space problem, but in turn present problems of access and security. If the system uses hand-held computers, does everybody get one? If so, theft may be a concern. Kurt Strosahl, research evaluation manager at Group Health Permanente Medical Group, notes that when Group Health considered hand-held computer entry, decision-makers discussed inventory control—attaching to every computer a beeper that would sound when it crossed the threshold, much as a department store marks its inventory. (The Group ultimately opted for integrated voice response technology; see below.) Some small practices may not have computers; and when they investigate purchasing one, they learn that there is no one standard computer technology—Macintoshes, IBMs, and their clones do not readily connect.

Grace Rowan-Szal works with DATAR, a Texas project focused on methadone maintenance clinics. DATAR is in its second five-year grant cycle; in the last few months, it switched in some settings from pencil and paper "keyboard" instruments to optical scans combined with faxes. Two years ago DATAR also piloted computer-screen entry of data in a few settings, but Rowan-Szal notes that since "community-based treatment programs may not have computers," the fax is a center's best recourse.

In short, the computer—particularly linked to the Internet—may be far more efficient than paper-and-pencil-based transport, even ones that use fax machines. Yet much of behavioral health has not made that progression. Nor is it likely to in the immediate future.

Integrated Voice Response

The newest, most exciting transport system in the world of behavioral health assessment is integrated voice response (IVR) technology. It is also the rarest.

With IVR, the patient answers the standardized assessment instrument's questions via the telephone.

American business has discovered IVR transport. Consumers—of banks, airlines, and retail stores—are rapidly learning the IVR drill: dial an 800 number, and, in response to questions posed by an automated voice, punch in numbers. Those numbers, entered as data from the person's telephone, allow for aggregation, profiles, and breakdowns. Although only a sliver of American business now uses IVR systems, developers expect usage to soar (as it has for automatic voice mail). Jerry Mahoney of International Voice Technology stresses that an IVR system is "simple to develop," and simple to link to a database, like Microsoft Access or Oracle. In the world of commerce, IVR grows more prevalent.

To date, only a few behavioral health systems have bought IVR systems; but if enthusiasm translates into sales, IVR may become the norm of the next decade. Its technology leapfrogs over the key problems of the other systems. Briefly, a patient, at home, dials a number (even a local number), then enters a multi-digit access code that will (1) steer the patient to the appropriate assessment instrument, (2) identify the clinician who will receive the data analysis, and (3) identify the patient.

The Burden on Staff

Transport based on paper forms, as well as on computer entry, generally takes place in the crowded waiting room, and generally presupposes that the administrative staff will present the instrument to the patient. Kurt Strosahl calls this "putting the burden on lowest-paid staff in highest-stress positions." This paper-based transport also presumes that patients will arrive on time to fill out the form, even though, as Strosahl notes, up to 60 percent of patients may arrive late.

IVR bypasses the waiting room dilemma. With IVR, the patient is told to call from home a few days before the scheduled visit. The office staff is not involved. From the vantage of William Coleman, of Montana Community Partners, a public sector HMO for Medicaid patients, IVR solved a major hurdle. On the one hand, Montana Community Partners wanted outcomes data. On the other hand, clinicians did not want to spend time gathering data. They saw the instruments as a burden without any therapeutic benefits. And they simply were not complying with outcomes assessment data-gathering. In late July 1998 Montana Community Partners piloted three projects using the YOQ, the Ohio Youth Score, and the CAFAS, with the first two using IVR. (The state hopes to translate the CAFAS into an IVR model too). Where earlier transport systems had left "everyone dissatisfied," the "IVR match seemed perfect."

Indeed, it makes the intake "capital equipment" a non-issue. Clinicians don't need to debate the purchase of optical scanners versus faxes versus computers—the intake equipment is already in the patient's home.

The Burden on Patients

The patient can complete the assessment instrument at home, at a convenient time, before the clinical visit. Since most people are familiar with a telephone, the "acceptance" of this technology is high. Geoffrey Gray found that the "hang-up" rate of the IVR version of the OQ-45 and SF-12 was 7 percent. IVR is, as Coleman notes, "consistent with what people do—talk on the phone."

Chapter 2: The Mechanics of Measurement

Unlike the Internet, which speaks to a computer-literate and relatively elite population, the telephone is part of most Americans' landscape. Admittedly, some American consumers have not yet encountered IVR; but, as the technology escalates, permeating commerce, more people will know the drill.

Therapeutic Input

The point of the behavioral health transport system is to help patients. And to help patients, clinicians need to see the data when they see the patient, so they can use the data to determine a therapeutic regimen. While systems that give clinicians late data may satisfy accreditation requirements (or help managed care reviewers and outcomes researchers), they do not help clinicians treat patients. Faxes, scans, computer-entry—all can theoretically deliver pre-visit feedback; but equipment glitches, late patients, and harried staff all work against speed.

IVR permits the kind of rapid feedback that makes the information from standardized assessment instruments useful to clinicians. Washington State's Group Health Permanente Medical Group has 460,000 consumers and 120 FTEs in seven Mental Health Centers (as well as a network model of clinicians). Now that it has started using IVR, Kurt Strosahl, who oversaw the introduction of this technology, likens the previous debates of scans over keyboards to "an elephant over the woolly mammoth."

Standardization

IVR systems feature standardization. The same automated voice, the same questions, the same protocol will happen for all patients, without the influences of staff or clinician. The system, moreover, can be designed to encourage patients to answer all questions. It can also be designed to give patients flexibility (How many days of work did you miss in the past month? Type a number).

Disentangling the Costs

When a managed care organization or practice buys an outcomes assessment system, it is buying access to the assessment instrument, the technology to enter the patient's responses into a mode for "processing," and the "processing," followed by the report back to the purchaser. "Processing" will yield two products: first, the patient's scores (and the patient's scores over time, if the patient is taking the same instrument repeatedly); second, the comparison of the patient against a population of similar patients with similar diagnoses/symptoms. The comparison depends upon access to a database of patients: the larger, the more inclusive, the database, the more rigorous and useful the analysis. As Benjamin Brodey, MD, psychiatrist and director of research at Medassure IVR Systems notes, "the score itself is meaningless." Although the purchaser is buying a physical item (a computer, a software package, a scanner), he or she is getting a mixture of access to intellectual property and a mechanical transport system for data.

The Behavioral Health Assessment Instrument

Many instruments, are in the public domain, and the clinician may use them at no charge (e.g., the Beck Depression Inventory). Others are proprietary (e.g., the Shedler QPD screening tool for depression). Costs to use a proprietary instrument vary: Point of View, for instance, will sell its hand held computer, programmed with the Shedler QPD, plus one "processing station," for $2,400, with a $700 fee for use of the instrument.

Loading the Information Into The "Processing" Computer

Pen-and-paper questionnaires, scanned questionnaires, faxed questionnaires—all must go to a central computer for processing. If a staff person types the patient's responses into a computer (the pencil/paper model), the "loading costs" will include that staff time. If an employee paid $25,000 a year spends half his/her time entering data, the office will be paying $12,500 for "loading." An office that uses scanned forms will need to buy a scanner (from $400 to $1000, with more sophisticated scanners able to detect more errors). For faxed forms, an office may need a dedicated fax machine. Both scanned and faxed forms will consume staff time, but far less than keyboard entry.

When the patient enters the information directly into the computer, the office time drops. The key expense is for leasing or buying the equipment. Martin Nankin, CEO of Field Diagnostic Services, Inc., estimates a purchaser can buy one hand-held computer for approximately $350. (In 1996, Kaiser Permanente bought from Point of View hand-held computers, programmed with different assessment instruments, to use as a screening tool in primary care clinics.)

With telephone-based loading systems, Medassure IVR will install a PC-based IVR system for $6,000, "loading" four assessment instruments onto the system, enabling the purchaser to use four phone lines for incoming calls (one for faxing back information). There is no office expense for staff time.

Processing of Patient Responses

In the final report, the purchaser wants not just the patient's scores, but the context of similar patients with similar diagnoses. (How does this 35-year-old single parent with four children on this regimen for depression line up with comparable patients?) In short, the purchaser is buying access to a database. In assessing "processing" costs, the buyer must weigh:
- the number and kinds of assessment instruments to be processed,
- the number of patients,
- the requested analyses, and
- the size and inclusivenss of the database.

For a paper instrument, a buyer can pay a fee per patient: OPTAIO, for instance, charges from 55 cents (Brown Attention Deficit Disorder Scale) to $7.50 (Butcher Treatment Planning Inventory).

A buyer with many patients may opt to purchase the software for "processing." The cost will depend in part on the database. A firm eager to build up its database may distribute the software free so that the buyer's clients can be added to its database. Another firm may charge for the software. Martin Nankin will sell a client the computer, monitor, and printer for $1,500 (at cost), and he is considering the strategy of providing the software at no additional charge.

With IVR systems, costs of "processing" also include phone charges. Medassure has installed systems that run on local phone exchanges. If a system runs on an 800 line, the costs will five to 10 cents/minute (an average survey might take 10 minutes). (The cost of scoring and interpreting is included in the $6,000 fee.) At present, notes Geoffrey Gray, "people don't have benchmarks on pricing." A company that goes out to bid for an IVR system might get bids that range from below $6,000 to $50,000.

A Footnote on Costs

Both computers and IVR systems are not only more efficient and faster, but generally cheaper than the older, more labor-intensive transport, which often fails to deliver the product quickly enough to be useful. (And IRS regulations allow buyers to amortize capital costs over three years.) Ultimately the market should prevail; and the "best" transport will predominate, growing even more affordable.

Computers and IVR systems, however, are simply the vehicles. The buyer is purchasing access to information about a patient, in relation to comparable patients. Since the predictive power of data grows as the size and the quality of the base grow, "users" gain from a burgeoning, inclusive database. This is true in retail marketing, in mortgage finance, and in behavioral health assessments. In short, the "best" assessment system of the future will be the one with the best database.

The Future

Futurists describe paradigms: horse-and-buggies giving way to automobiles, automobiles giving way to airplanes, airplanes ceding to space capsules.

In behavioral health transport, the dominant paradigm is the paper form, entered by scan or fax into the computer. New technologies, however, allow patients to enter information directly into transit—sitting at computer terminals or holding hand-held computers. "Computer telephony" marks an extension of technological wizardry.

In a decade or so, this technological wizardry may be commonplace. And the behavioral health writer, entering a historical footnote on pen-and-paper instruments, will focus on the "commonplace" IVR systems that foreshadowed a still newer paradigm just over the horizon.

Who Gets the Results?

When and How To Report Outcomes Results Back To Clinicians and Clients

LINDA WASMER SMITH

The nuts and bolts of doing studies that measure the outcomes of mental health and substance abuse treatment continue to vex behavioral health providers. Two issues that still arise are: With whom should you share the data that have been collected? And how should you go about doing this? Here's expert advice on when and how to report outcomes results back to clinicians and clients.

The Whys and Wherefores

Once upon a time, outcomes data were used largely for marketing purposes. Today, however, most people realize that outcomes information is also a powerful tool for improving clinician performance. "My view is that the whole goal of doing outcomes studies is to change clinician behavior, and that's pretty hard to do if you don't give the outcomes data back to the clinicians," says Dennis Morrison, CEO of the Center for Behavioral Health in Bloomington IN. "Ideally, what you want to say is: 'Here are some data that can help you become a better clinician tomorrow than you are today. We believe that's something you want to do.'"

"What you don't want to say is: 'Here are some data, and if you don't clean them up, you're out of a job,'" adds Morrison. In fact, the fear that data will be used in a punitive fashion is one of the major stumbling blocks to outcomes research. "Remember, these folks are well versed in psychometric technology," says Morrison. "If you try to beat them up with numbers, they will quite naturally respond defensively." They may fail to cooperate fully with data collection, or they may even cheat to skew the results in their favor. Therefore, it not only matters that you share results with clinicians; it also matters that you do so helpfully rather than harmfully.

Another reason clinicians may fail to cooperate with outcomes research is because they see nothing in it for them. "Many clinicians view an outcomes survey as just another piece of irritating paperwork," says Bill Berman, president and CEO of BHOS, Inc., an outcomes services and products company in Mamaroneck NY. "These are the folks who are collecting your data, and unless they see the value in it, they're not going to collect it well." Providing prompt feedback that helps clinicians make real-world decisions can help overcome such resistance.

Fast-Track Facts

"If a client has completed a clinical questionnaire as part of an outcomes study, you should score it immediately or at least within the next day or so, then get that information back to the clinician so that it can be used as part of treatment planning," says Gayle Zieman, cofounder of the National Outcomes Management Project. "This goes a long way toward making clinicians feel as if the outcomes project is relevant and valuable to them and their clinical practice."

The Treatment Outcomes Package, marketed by Access Measurement Systems of Ashland MA, is one example of a system that offers such speedy feedback. A client fills out an assessment form prior to starting therapy. The form is immediately faxed to the company, where it is scored by a computer. It is then faxed back to the provider agency within 15 to 30 minutes, so that the clinician can use it during the first session. "It certainly expedites the clinical process to have this information available before you ever go into therapy," says

> ## The National Outcomes Management Project
>
> The National Outcomes Management Project is based on the belief that it is not the methodology that sets apart outcomes systems, but rather how the data are used for quality improvement. This project, established in 1995, is housed at the University of Cincinnati Department of Psychiatry. It now includes 17 participating clinics, group practices, and behavioral health delivery systems in 12 states. All of the participants have a managed care orientation. In three metropolitan areas—Cincinnati, Albuquerque, and Minneapolis—major competitors are involved.
>
> The project's standardized outpatient methodology is typical of the way data are collected and shared by the best outcomes systems.
>
> - Clients are assessed prior to their first appointment. This may occur in the waiting room before the first appointment, or the clients may receive the assessment forms by mail with instructions to return the completed forms at the first appointment.
> - Clients are assessed again at specific follow-up points. Clients receive the assessment forms by mail at three months and sometimes also six months after the initial assessment, regardless of whether they have remained in treatment or not. If they don't return the completed forms promptly, they get a phone or mail reminder.
> - Individual client reports are sent back to the clinician at each assessment point. These reports are placed in the clinical record.
> - Chart audits are performed at six months to gather information on diagnoses, medications, psychotherapy, and adverse incidents.
> - Participating clinics and groups upload their encrypted outcomes data to the University of Cincinnati every quarter.
> - In-depth quarterly reports on the aggregate data are sent back to the participating clinics. An annual meeting is also held.
>
> For more information, contact Gayle Zieman [and see Appendix C].

Jeanne Crawford, associate vice president of Access Measurement Systems.

Some clinicians may initially feel that asking clients to fill out a form right off the bat is an unwelcome intrusion. "But once they get used to doing it, my experience is that clinicians don't want to go into that first therapy session without this information in hand," says Crawford. "It's like a physician trying to diagnose a medical patient without knowing the results of relevant blood tests."

"In addition, clients are sometimes more honest on a paper-and-pencil form than they are face-to-face with a clinician," Crawford says. "Plus, we get anecdotal reports back from clinicians who say, for instance, that they didn't realize a client was suicidal until they looked at the form. One of the wonderful things about using a clinically rich outcomes measurement system is that it can provide helpful information that the clinician may otherwise not be privy to." When you add follow-up data, it can also give insight into a client's progress over a period of time.

Apples and Apples

Feedback can take the form of information on specific clients, but it can also focus on particular clinicians or clinics. There are two basic kinds of comparisons that can be drawn: you can compare several different time points for one clinician or clinic, or you can compare several different clinicians or clinics to each other. In making the latter kind of comparison, of course, it's important to have good norms against which to measure a given therapist or agency.

Whatever type of data you're presenting, you should always aim to be clear and concise. In general, says Morrison, graphs tend to convey information more efficiently than text or tables. Since your audience usually has limited time, the goal is to present the data in a form that is quickly grasped.

So do most organizations share their outcomes data in some form with clinicians? "Our company operates in about 75 facilities nationwide, and I think it varies dramatically," says Bill Edell, a senior vice president at Mental Health Outcomes in Lewisville TX. "Some facilities have big presentations for the clinicians with lots of hoopla about the results." Others share little or no data.

Increasing Follow-Up Response Rates

Outcomes research often involves an initial assessment with follow-up assessments at set times down the road, when a client may have already left treatment. Getting clients to respond to follow-up forms can be quite a challenge. "You can generally assume that people have 150 things they'd rather be doing more than filling out your forms," says BHOS' Bill Berman. Here are some pointers for improving your batting average when collecting follow-up data:

- **Don't skimp on spending.** Berman estimates that it costs $25 to $40 per patient per time point to do good follow-up research. This adds up quickly, but if you try to cut corners, you may wind up with shoddy data.

- **Target your population carefully.** "Since it's usually too expensive to follow up with everybody, you need to decide who offers the best potential payoff for your organization," says Berman. "If your organization is particularly good with certain clients, then you might want to demonstrate your expertise by collecting data on them." Examples of typical target populations include adolescent substance abusers and people with recurrent major depression.

- **Give clients advance warning.** "Early on, we get permission from our clients to follow them up. That way, it's not a complete surprise when they get a call three months or six months later," says Bill Edell of Mental Health Outcomes.

- **Build a personal relationship.** "You have to know how to talk to people and enlist their assistance," says Berman. Always treat clients with respect and courtesy, and make sure they understand what you're doing.

- **Assure clients of confidentiality.** If clients have concerns, reassure them with an explanation of how their privacy will be protected. Remember that many people are sensitive about behavioral health treatment.

- **Don't rely only on mailings.** "What most people do is send out a mailing with a questionnaire, saying, 'Please send this information back to us.' If there is no response, they send another mailing, and that's it. But that's just not enough," says Berman. To get a high response rate, you'll probably need to supplement mailings with phone calls or even on-site visits. "Nobody I know who is using mailings alone has gotten better than a 25 percent response rate, and most have gotten substantially below that," says Berman. However, in a recent study at Fordham University, Berman achieved a 70 percent response rate at six months and 55 percent at one year by combining regular phone calls and multiple mailings.

- **Consider offering incentives.** Money is one way to motivate clients to cooperate. "But you have to be careful that it's not coercive," says Berman. "I would offer no more than a few dollars to cover their time."

- **Respect clients' right to say "no."** Be sensitive to the fact that many people are quite uncomfortable discussing their treatment for behavioral health problems. "They simply may not be willing to discuss their treatment now," says Berman. "If any clients say, 'I don't want to talk about this,' you should accept their wishes. It's their decision about whether or not to participate."

- **Develop good phone skills.** "One of the things we stress with our follow-up people is that they aren't to be clinicians over the phone," says Edell. They should avoid giving clinical advice or making value judgments during phone contacts. "When clinical issues do arise," says Edell, "we encourage the clients to contact their local clinician or behavioral health facility to get help."

- **End each contact gracefully.** Yes, manners do still count. "With many clients, the problem isn't getting them on the phone. It's getting off the phone, because they're often lonely and want to talk," says Edell. Be firm but tactful when saying good-bye. Adds Edell, "It also might not hurt to encourage such clients to reach out to community resources such as support groups."

Until recently, the lack of national norms has posed a major problem in outcomes research. "This problem arose because many of the early outcomes measurement systems were proprietary," says Zieman. "Today, however, some of the national vendors that sell outcomes products maintain a full database. Those who use the product are required to send their data to a central location, where all data are pooled and analyzed to establish benchmarks across settings." Assuming you've selected an outcomes measurement tool for which national normative data are available, you may want to let clinicians know how their clinic stacks up against others in the country.

The Whodunit Story

Just as important, however, may be letting clinicians know how they compare to other clinicians in their agency. Typically, this is done by presenting a graph in which individual clinicians are identified only by numbers, to preserve anonymity. Although clinicians know their own numbers, they don't know each others' numbers, at least in theory. In practice, though, people talk. A conversation or two in the break room may be all it takes to figure out who is who on the graph.

Says Morrison, "When clinicians are given data in an environment that is not punitive, some research shows that the folks at the worst end of the continuum tend to find out who the folks at the best end are, then seek them out and ask them what they're doing." Although this may lead to positive changes in behavior, it can also create potential embarrassment for the bottom performers. The motivation may be stronger for people who aren't doing as well to seek out those who are doing better, rather than the reverse. Yet malicious gossip still occurs.

To reduce the wear and tear on professional relationships, Zieman suggests that this type of data only be presented for relatively large groups of clinicians. "In our experience, when we provided this kind of data for a large group of staff—say, 18 or 20 people—they didn't spend a whole lot of time trying to figure out who was who because the graph looked fairly complex. But this sort of graph probably isn't appropriate for groups of fewer than eight or 10 people."

One way to handle the situation is to publish the names of the top two or three performers, while keeping the other names anonymous. This is a variation of the practice used by real estate companies that put the names and photos of their best salespeople in newspaper ads. "It's a way of rewarding your best people," says Morrison. At the same time, it highlights the top performers so that others can easily seek them out for guidance without having to first guess their identities.

Feeding Back Facts

Whatever approach you take, it's crucial to reassure clinicians about how outcomes data will be used if you want to enlist their full support. Let them know in advance how their anonymity will be protected, for example. In addition, "you may have to train folks to understand the value of quantification," says Edell. "The fact is, many people choose to become psychologists or social workers because they don't want to get into quantifying performance. They may need to undergo a mind shift away from the purely subjective and more into numbers."

Another issue to address up front with clinicians is the method of risk adjustment. Once again, says Edell, "it's an educative process." Clinicians need reassurance that any head-to-head comparisons will be made fairly. Therapists are savvy enough to know that, if Clinician A treats chronic schizophrenics and Clinician B treats neurotic patients, Clinician A will always have worse outcomes, even if he or she is a better therapist. What they may not understand is how statistics can be used to take such differences in patient population into account. Learning more about how the outcomes data will be risk adjusted may help allay clinician concerns.

Finally, you might want to acknowledge to clinicians that the state of the art in outcomes research is still imperfect. For example, existing tools often understate symptom severity for schizophrenic and other seriously mentally ill clients. Clinicians may be relieved to know that such shortcomings are widely recognized. While no one would suggest that outcomes measurement is a perfect science, clinicians can learn to make the most of existing outcomes tools.

Q&As for Clinicians

In summary, sharing outcomes data with clinicians, if done appropriately, can help them answer questions such as these:

Individual Case Data

- How is an individual client functioning at a given time?
- How is an individual client progressing over time?

TIP: Data should be presented in the clearest, most concise form.

TIP: Feedback from individual client assessments should be provided very quickly, so that the information can be used in treatment planning.

Aggregate Data

- How does a particular clinician compare to others in the clinic?
- How does a particular clinician or clinic compare to national norms?

TIP: Graphs are often quicker and easier to read than text or tables.

TIP: Data on how particular clinicians compare to others in their clinic should only be published for large groups, to protect the clinicians' anonymity.

TIP: Top clinicians can be identified by name, if desired, to offer recognition and encourage the worst clinicians to seek out the best for guidance.

TIP: Risk adjustment, if needed, is important for ensuring that you are comparing apples and apples, rather than apples and oranges.

TIP: Outcomes measurement tools that provide national norms for comparison have a big advantage over other competing products.

Sharing Data With Clients

Experts agree that outcomes data in some form should be shared with clinicians. More controversial is the notion of sharing certain data with clients as well. However, Access Measurement System's Crawford believes there are several benefits to giving clients some of their own individual case data. In fact, when Access faxes back a scored assessment form, it includes a page that is meant to be photocopied and given to the client to take home.

Over the years, Crawford has noted several advantages to this type of approach. "During the course of therapy, the clients might say, 'I saw when we did the initial assessment that I showed a lot of problems in X area, and I'm not sure we're working on that enough.' Or, at the start of therapy, they might say, 'Look, this shows me on paper that I'm really feeling as bad as I thought I was.' It turned out to be a very empowering and validating experience for many clients."

One concern is the possibility that a given client's data might show little or no progress. "But don't you think clients deserve to know that as well?" asks Crawford. "Besides, clients on some level already know when they're not getting better. They should be able to see the documentation of that, just as they could look at an X-ray to see that a broken bone hadn't knit." For most clients, though, this shouldn't be an issue. The bulk of the evidence from outcomes research shows that a large majority of clients do fairly well, usually within a short period of time.

Of course, there are some clients with whom data probably shouldn't be shared. For example, "sharing data might be inappropriate if a client is really disorganized, agitated, or in some other way unable to process the information," says Crawford. Another no-show situation might be if a client is very depressed and the clinician believes that seeing the data would only make things worse.

The Last Word

Clinicians are notoriously afraid of outcomes data, fearful that they will be harshly judged and penalized on the basis of numbers alone. Clearly, feedback is going to be most effective in a situation where people are not afraid of failing to get a raise or losing a contract. In the right environment, though, feedback can help both clinicians and clients focus on problem areas and set therapeutic goals. Getting the maximum benefit from sharing data, however, takes time and effort from clinicians as well as funding and training from managers and health care purchasers.

It's worth the bother, according to these experts. "My view is that we should be generating outcomes data to change clinician behavior or at least to help clinicians know better how to deal with different clientele," says Morrison. "But data generated for these purposes still hold robust marketing information." That's double the reason to enlist the support of clinicians and clients in outcomes research.

New Perspectives on Quality Management Training

Increasing the Effectiveness of Outcome Measurement Systems Through High-Quality, Ongoing Training

CHRISTINE TORRE AND ASTRID BEIGEL, PHD

Introduction

Quality management in behavioral health is rapidly emerging as a multidisciplinary field of its own. Although the assessment of results is not new, the current emphasis on outcome measurement is an integral part of the new quality management field. Consistent with this, much has been written regarding the planning of programs, selection of measures, technology, and implementation. Interestingly, little attention has been paid to training and its importance in the success of any system.

Training is necessary for all levels of participants, from clinicians and other service providers to managers, administrators, and policymakers. While a basic context is helpful to understand quality management, each separate group requires specific training geared to its part in the quality management process. Because the field is constantly evolving, training cannot be static but must accommodate frequent change.

This article reviews the need for training in general, presents the authors' work in the area as an example, and uses the resulting data to develop a comprehensive framework with general applicability for training. The framework is intended to be used as a guide to develop training after final decisions have been made as to the design, methodology, measures, indicators, technical specifications, and other details of an outcome measurement system. The framework is useful across the public and private sectors, large and small agencies/organizations, and provider disciplines. (See Table, "Conceptual Training Framework.")

Underlying Realities

Several issues underlie the way in which mental health service agencies or providers function that must be considered before results can be measured. First, the new emphasis on quality management and outcome (results) appears to be here to stay (Sperry, 1997). Managed care contracts are rarely written without specific references to quality improvement and the demonstration of the effectiveness of services provided. There is little choice for most systems/agencies in whether or not they will incorporate outcome measurement of some sort into their everyday operations. Secondly, any successful quality management program has an associated cost, which must include the training component.

Planning for this cost is part of the new way of doing business. It must be calculated in establishing a per-client cost, just as with other indirect costs such as space, equipment, etc. In designing a training program in any organization it is critical to recognize that the quality of the information collected will have a direct impact on the usefulness and relevance of the findings. If results are used as intended, i.e., for decisionmaking at various levels, there is at least an ethical responsibility for payers and managers to ensure the accuracy of the findings since they will impact clients and service providers.

Christine Torre is Manager and Astrid Beigel, PhD, is Chief of Quality and Outcome Bureau at the Los Angeles County Department of Mental Health. They are leaders in the quality management field in California and nationally. They have been influential in shaping the direction of outcome measurement in California at the state and local levels and have written and presented extensively on the topic.

Conceptual Training Framework

AREA	TRAINEES	TRAINERS	CONTENT	TIMING*
General Overview (Includes all areas)	All Participants: Managers, Providers, Clients, Special Groups	Quality Management Experts	All Areas: General Applicability & Orientation	Beginning of Project, Periodically
Clinical Applications	All Service Providers, Supervisors	Clinicians, Service Providers, *Mentors*, Specialists	Clinical Uses, Integration into Assessment/Treatment Process	Immediately before Project Starts, Periodically
Data Collection & Reporting	Quality Management Staff	Quality Management Experts	Presentation & Formatting of Information	After Project Begins, Before First Reporting Period, Periodically
Data Interpretation	Service Providers, Managers, Administrators, Clients, Policy Makers	Quality Management Experts	Usefulness & Application of Information, Basic Methodology, Ethical Uses of Data	Beginning of Project, When Data become Available, Ongoing Support
Continuous Quality Improvement	All Participants: Managers, Providers, Clients, Special Groups	Quality Management Experts	Ongoing Process to Improve Service Provision & Results	Before Project Begins, Periodically
Technology	Technical Staff, Data Entry Staff, Computer Operators, Statisticians	Technical Experts	Specific Applications, Uses of Hardware & Software	Immediately before Project Begins, Ongoing Support

* All training must be flexible to accommodate change and be available to new participants in the process.

Torre/Beigel 1998.

The Los Angeles County experience is not unlike the observations of others and quite consistent with the literature in the field. In brief, for a quality management system to be successful, higher management as well as subordinate managers must be committed to the endeavor and recognize its value, rather than merely giving pro forma support. Clearly, this commitment requires financial resources to train all those in the organization who are either involved or affected by various aspects of quality management and outcome assessment.

First and foremost, management commitment involves a recognition that outcome measurement is critical, if for no other reason than it is here to stay and will affect funding in the future. Hopefully, there will be a belief that the information derived will add value to the treatment process and benefit service recipients. Thus, a first step is for managers and decisionmakers at all levels to become involved in the process. Managers must realize that the money invested in training will benefit the process, make the system more cost-effective and increase efficacy. Once managers recognize the potential usefulness of the outcome data for quality management and understand how to use it, they will likely set the tone for others in the organization, i.e., service providers, support staff, technical staff, etc., to become partners. When management provides the demonstrated leadership, others will be empowered (Torre, et al., 1997)

Setting the Context for a Multidisciplinary Field

The field of outcome measurement is multidisciplinary. People from a variety of disciplines and backgrounds are being brought together. In many cases their roles are similar but their perspectives, training, and experience differ. This is the case even within clinical disciplines. However, each participant may be called upon to administer the same measures. The situation becomes further complicated regarding data use and interpretation, which then involves an even broader spectrum of participants. Unifying the approaches and maximizing the skills of each person in the process is the challenge of a quality management training agenda. Training must begin by setting the context within which the outcome measurement system lies. The concepts of accountability, continuous quality improvement, effectiveness, and ethics must be shared with all participants in the process, along with basic information on specific areas of the system such as measures and indicators, technology to be used, and resulting products.

Formal and Informal Training

Initial training to introduce participants to the system must be formal, often provided in group settings using credible, knowledgeable trainers. These sessions should present an overview and broad-based conceptual information to set the stage for the implementation of the specific components of the system. At this point, the tentative nature of what is known about outcome measurement must be emphasized, preparing participants for eventual refinement of the processes as more experience is gained. Therefore, it is critical to stress that change and flexibility are productive and necessary rather than arbitrary.

Formal but more focused and specific training must also be conducted with separate groups (clinicians, technical staff, managers, etc.) on the detailed information needed to perform their specific tasks in the process. At this point, training materials such as handbooks and guidelines are introduced and widely distributed. Adequate time must be allowed for questions, discussion, and examples of hands-on situations and vignettes. This portion of the training is best conducted immediately before implementation of the outcome measurement process so that content of the training is quickly put to use and not lost.

Training in this new field is not a one-time occurrence. The process will be greatly enhanced by ongoing, less formal opportunities to refine skills and review changing protocols and procedures. Broad-based sessions are necessary to introduce contextual information, and small group sessions that meet the specific needs of different groups are vital in transmitting detailed, procedural information. In addition, there is a need for supportive sessions to enhance initial training and allow participants to share experiences that lead to refinement of the process. These sessions may become less frequent over time as participants become more comfortable with the new processes.

Trainers

It is critical that training be of high quality and relevant to the group being trained. It is evident the credibility of the trainer is related to how the training will be viewed by the audience. These factors must be considered when selecting either outside experts or on-site agency staff to provide training.

Quality training can be defined as well presented information that is relevant and appropriate to those being trained. Thus, the presenter must be knowledgeable and credible in the content area. Outside experts or someone of the same discipline as his or her audience are often perceived more favorably. In Los Angeles County, for example, the training of psychiatrists in quality management was far more effective when someone of the same discipline (a psychiatrist) who is an expert in the field with name recognition was retained to provide training, in contrast to another time when training was provided by an equally well-qualified expert from another discipline.

Another example revealed that it is key that the trainer be viewed as someone with line experience in training service providers and not as an individual from an outside agency in an administrative or oversight position and without related background. Again, in the Los Angeles County experience, even if such persons were technical experts, their ideas were less valued and, therefore, less influential due to perceived lack of credibility. Further, it must be emphasized that trainers who have oversight roles are often seen as insufficiently neutral to allow training to be received objectively.

With the emergence of quality management as a new multidisciplinary specialty area, quality management experts now exist. One type of trainer can be a quality management expert from outside or within the organization. Such experts may come from any of several backgrounds with respect to education and experience (e.g., service providers, administrators, etc.). What they have in common is experience in conducting and developing quality management programs. These quality management experts can provide an integrated overview of the programs, measures, applications, etc.

The second type of expert is one who can instruct appropriate staff regarding the use of technology. All programs in any organization, now or in the near future, will use measures, instruments, or indicators that require the use of technology and computer skills at some level.

A third group of experts includes those who are viewed as discipline/specialty experts, e.g., psychiatrists, statisticians, administrators, etc. As noted, this group can be particularly important because the audience often perceives them as highly credible.

In addition, both formal and informal training is conducted on an ongoing basis by quality management experts within the organization as well as by mentors, i.e., those of like discipline/job duty who are more experienced but have similar responsibilities. These can be service providers, administrators, managers, technical staff, etc., who become internal experts and teachers (see "Mentor Program" below).

There must be a balance in training between the use of outside experts, experts from within the organization, and mentors. The use of outside experts in the field is an important component of an effective training program when their expertise is introduced at key points in the process. While experts can offer contextual and "big picture" information, however, they may not be as effective when imparting information about the specific process to be employed in a given program or system. The experts must, however, have credibility relating to their own experience in similar settings, not mere titles or authority.

Mentor Program

When a new program is being implemented, the most valued sources of information often are respected peers who have already experienced the change or innovation. This realization prompted the establishment of a Clinical Mentor Program in Los Angeles as a highly effective approach to one aspect of training and ongoing support. It was hypothesized that, both within a particular program/agency or in others beginning to implement quality management programs, it would be valuable to identify line clinicians (service providers) to act as guides/teachers to peers, to be available to peers within and outside of their own organizations on an informal basis, and to provide formal training both for new and refresher orientation.

The goal of the Clinical Mentor Program is to reinforce the point that the clinician (line provider) is central to obtaining data and information for any quality management system. More specifically, the more this group values the process and contributes to it, the more effective the program will be. Thus, shortly after the inception of a pilot program in Los Angeles County, a minimum of two Mentors at each participating facility were identified, met regularly as a clinical support group, received special formal training from outside expert trainers, and themselves engaged in both formal and informal training in their own organization. Thus, the intent was to live up to the true definition of mentor by having this group of interested, practicing line clinicians act as guides to peers less experienced in the quality management process. Their particular contribution is to be available to other clinicians at their own or other facilities for presentations, telephone consultation, clinical forums, and on-site demonstrations and instruction. Ideally, Clinical Mentors are staff who, in addition to their line clinical duties, voluntarily take on mentoring activities because of their particular interest. Of course, management support and sanction is critical, but Mentors should not be management's designees.

The core group of Mentors was established as the pilot programs were initiated and will be expanded as additional programs and organizations become participants in the quality management process. Ideally, there will always be a body of well-trained service providers to consult, support, and train, and to make ongoing contributions to the refinement of the quality management system in Los Angeles County, or wherever such programs are implemented.

The Clinical Mentor Program represents one mentoring model. It is anticipated similar programs will be developed for other groups involved in quality management, e.g.; managers, payers, technical experts, etc.

Introducing Technology

Most outcome systems involve the use of new technology. At the service provider level, many behavioral health systems are not equipped with the latest technology and system personnel are not familiar with computerized systems to scan, analyze, and report data. This presents an additional training challenge. Typical of large organizations, Los Angeles County staff assigned to manage the new technology at program sites often did not possess even rudimentary knowledge of computer operation. When this is the case, it is critical that staff first be given the opportunity to learn basic computer applications; otherwise, the risks of lost or damaged data are increased exponentially. In addition, many agencies are choosing to purchase packaged software/hardware systems that may not be compatible or easily integrated with existing computer/MIS systems. Experienced MIS staff may also require training to become familiar with the new technology and maximize its utility.

Along with initial, technical training, ongoing support is crucial. Questions and problems needing immediate attention frequently arise and rapid access to knowledgeable assistance is vital. In Los Angeles, central staff have developed expertise in using the outcome technology and are available by telephone to assist as needed. Support groups for technical staff also can provide shared experience and solutions. The Los Angeles Technical Support Group meets at least quarterly with central technical staff to discuss problem areas, develop solutions, and recommend refinements to the system. When new staff are hired at program sites, they can be oriented more quickly since they immediately become part of the group.

Developing Training Materials

Effective materials and protocols are critical to successful training. They must be clear, concise, and well organized. Handbooks or manuals must be prepared so that they can be easily revised and also tailored to specific programs or specific users. Information must be available to all users. An example of an effective manual, designed to meet these criteria is the *Clinician's Handbook* developed for use in the implementation of the pilot project in Los Angeles (Nelson, et al., 1997). The *Handbook* provides an overview of quality management and outcome assessment, describes the Los Angeles pilot project, gives detailed information about the measures and instruments used with administration protocols and scoring criteria, and includes recommendations for clinical uses. The *Handbook* was prepared in a looseleaf format to allow for updating and adding information and includes sections where site-specific information can be inserted. It has a section for vignettes and frequently asked questions. The *Handbook* was used in formal training sessions and then distributed to all clinicians/service providers and others involved in the outcome pilot at 12 program sites. Since its initial distribution, the *Handbook* has been modified for use in other outcome projects by inserting appropriate sections and deleting irrelevant information.

Assessment of the Los Angeles Experience

As the Los Angeles County Department of Mental Health has worked diligently to implement uniform outcome measurement systems throughout its programs, training has emerged as one of the most important aspects of the process. Staff initially spent considerable time developing and preparing training protocols and other materials prior to the implementation of each phase of the project. Some of the efforts have proven to be more useful than others. The model presented in this article is a result of periodic refinements and adjustments. (See Table, Conceptual Training Framework.") Clearly, there is room for further improvement over time. The components of training that have proven to be most valuable have been the use of outside experts where appropriate, the development of training materials such as the *Clinician's Handbook*, and the use of mentors.

The areas that have emerged as particularly problematic include the difficulties in engaging managers at certain levels and the perceived lack of administrative support by those at the top of the organization. In the future, these challenges will be approached directly with more effort focused on demonstrating to managers the usefulness of the outcome information in their quality improvement process. This should result in greater administrative support of the quality management effort and modify staff perception of management's investment.

Contextual Framework: A General Model For Training

One key to the design and development of a successful quality management/outcome measurement system is the use of a contextual framework that defines the various aspects of training. Actual experience has contributed to the development of the Training Framework, which serves as a conceptual model for designing training to meet the specific needs of any group, e.g., public or private sector, different disciplines, large or small organizations, etc.

The Conceptual Training Framework (see Table), developed by the authors, is a flexible model for use in the development of a training protocol for implementing an outcome measurement system in any setting. The framework includes the major areas to be addressed (general overview, clinical applications, collection and reporting data, data interpretation, continuous quality improvement, and technology); who should be trained (from clients to administrative staff and policymakers); who should train (internal staff, outside experts, etc.); content areas (general to specific); and timing of training. The framework can be adjusted to be workable for any type of outcome system, from basic collection of existing administrative data to more complicated client-level measurement. The framework provides a simple way to conceptualize the components needed to provide high quality, comprehensive and ongoing training. It allows training developers to consider the major needs, materials, and approaches. It focuses on the idea that training is ongoing and that there can never be too much training. This emphasis will increase the probability of obtaining meaningful results, which will be used to provide the best possible services to clients.

References

Nelson D, Torre C, Beigel A, and Peyton D. *Clinicians Handbook: Using Clinical Inventories for Assessment, Treatment Planning, Monitoring and Evaluating Progress.* Los Angeles County Department of Mental Health, 1997.

Sperry L.. Treatment Outcomes: An Overview. *Psychiatric Annals* 1997:95-99.

Torre C, Clark W, Beigel A, and McConnell W. Strategies for Successfully Implementing a Technology Based Quality Management System in Public Sector Mental Health. Albert E. Treischman Center, 6th Annual Clinical Technologies Conference, "Tools for the Trade," 1997.

How To Involve Staff in Developing An Outcomes-Oriented Organization

J. RANDY KOCH, PHD, JUNE M. CAIRNS, MSW, LSW, AND MOLLY BRUNK, PHD

> *Outcomes management requires the active participation of clinical staff and/or network providers to succeed. They form the bedrock of the system, since they are the ones who most typically administer the outcomes assessment questionnaires to consumers, encourage them to complete them, and respond to questions and complaints about them. Resistance from clinicians can cause even the most well-designed outcomes management system to fail. Yet with the application of several basic principles, organizations can maximize active participation from its clinicians to operate a dynamic outcomes management system. The authors of this article describe the principles involved, and the action steps necessary to implement them. These principles include: articulate the value of the outcomes management system, involve clinical staff in its design, make it relevant to treatment goals, assure clinicians the system will not be used punitively, show them how it will be used to improve treatment, obtain staff feedback routinely on how the system is working, and demonstrate how the organizational culture from top management down uses the outcomes information to make decisions.*—Tom Trabin, PhD, MSM

Movements to improve the quality of services and increase accountability of behavioral healthcare providers are encouraging many organizations to develop outcomes measurement systems (OMS) to support the management of care. The April 1997 issue of *Behavioral Healthcare Tomorrow* provided an overview of current report card initiatives (such as PERMS, MHSIP, and HEDIS) being developed by private and public behavioral healthcare organizations. Each report card incorporates slightly different indicators of outcomes, but they are all innovations with potential to affect participating organizations in profound ways.

In the past the organizational culture of behavioral healthcare and social services providers has been oriented towards reimbursement, and the amount was only indirectly related to outcomes. Implementation of an OMS will require fundamental organizational transformation to produce its intended benefit. Should it fail to do so, organizational analysts may attribute the cause to a failure in implementation, not to a failure in the original idea.[1,2,3,4]

For any innovation to be implemented effectively, it must have a "good fit" with the users' values.[3] All stakeholders in the organization should be involved in the initial planning to ensure that the OMS measures indicators are significant to the users of the information. Assessment of outcomes must be perceived as consistent with the values of the organization and its members. Effective implementation of an OMS relies on staff who have direct contact with con-

---

Source: Reprinted with permission by Manisses Communications Group, Inc. Originally published in Behavioral Healthcare Tomorrow June 1998; 7(3): 29-31, 62.

J. Randy Koch, PhD is the director of research and evaluation for the Virginia Department of Mental Health, Mental Retardation and Substance Abuse Services.

June M. Cairns, MSW, LSW is the executive director for the Children, Youth and Family Council of Delaware Valley, Virginia.

Molly Brunk, PhD is a senior research associate for the Center for Public Policy, Virginia Commonwealth University and senior research associate in the office of Research and Evaluation, Virginia Department of Mental Health, Mental Retardation and Substance Abuse Services.

sumers, that is, service providers who collect data, recruit consumer participants, and use the information to improve services. Unfortunately, it is often the same group who values assessment of outcomes the least. Service providers frequently report that they do not need an assessment to know if a consumer has improved.

Special steps must be taken to facilitate their active support for the OMS or the outcomes data produced will be of questionable quality. The following suggestions for obtaining the committed involvement of service providers in the process of developing an outcomes-oriented organization are based on the authors' experiences implementing performance and outcomes measurement systems in both the private and public sectors.

Advantages of Involving Staff in the Design Phase

Service providers who have direct input in the design of the outcomes management system to be used in their organization will provide feedback that can produce a better system, use the output to improve their practice, and eventually, value the assessment of outcomes. They benefit by gaining greater understanding of the purpose, goals, and operation of an OMS. When service providers understand an OMS, they are less resistant and more able to identify potential problems, which can then be resolved prior to full implementation. The expertise of service providers is needed in the following areas:

Selection of Relevant/Useful Indicators—Service providers understand what the treatment is designed to accomplish and are best able to define those outcomes most relevant to their program. For example, for a child with low self-esteem who is experiencing depression that interferes with successful completion of schoolwork, brief treatment might focus on reducing the symptoms of depression and helping the child function better at school, but may have no immediate effect on self-esteem. Measuring self-esteem is not a relevant outcomes measure in this case.

Development of Practical and Efficient Procedures—People who are not involved in the day-to-day processes of providing services may not be aware of the most practical strategies for implementing an outcomes system.

Data Collection Procedures—At a state hospital for adolescents, the management group (for example) developed a plan to have the primary clinician treating the patient be responsible for collecting several self-report measures from the youth and the family. The assumption was that the primary clinician is the one most likely to contact the patient after discharge. This hospital, however, is part of a larger continuum of care and once the patient is connected with an outpatient therapist, the hospital's primary clinician no longer has contact with the youth. The primary clinicians were focused on patients currently in the hospital. They were able to come up with an alternative procedure that was more practical and efficient: admissions staff could collect the required information since they were the ones who continued to serve as liaisons with people outside the hospital. Admissions staff and the primary clinicians submitted a proposal that the primary clinicians would take on the caseload responsibilities of the admissions staff, and thereby free up admissions staff time to respond to requests for admissions and obtain assessment information.

Information Application Procedures—Service providers are more likely to use information that they perceive as relevant to treatment goals. In one public community mental health center, supervisory staff wanted to shift the organizational culture from a focus on past issues to current behaviors that can be affected by treatment. They perceived that the outcomes instrument being used to evaluate youth could help them to accomplish this goal. By focusing team discussions on the behavioral functioning measured by the OMS rather than on the patient's history, they were able to change the culture of the team.

If staff perceive the indicators to be useful, and not burdensome to collect, and actually use the information in their practice, they will have a greater investment in the success of the system. Their investment in the OMS will have a direct impact on their ability to (a) produce a higher quality of data, (b) submit data in a timely fashion, and (c) encourage others to make use of the OMS and expand to additional programs.

Methods for Overcoming Staff Resistance

Even with the best planning and the most participatory approach, those who manage outcomes measurement systems must be alert to ways in which staff limit full implementation of the system. Their behaviors can threaten the quality of the outcomes data and the integrity of the entire effort. It is critically important to take proactive steps to build staff commitment to the collection, analysis, and use of outcomes data. Some suggestions follow.

Recognize Staff Concerns

Staff often have legitimate concerns about measuring consumer outcomes. These should be identified and actively addressed. Some of the more common concerns are included here.

- *Takes time away from direct service*—Clinicians chose this field because they want to work directly with consumers. Anything—particularly paperwork—that takes time away from direct services, is not typically well received. Staff need to be shown how the OMS will help them to better serve their consumers. Their help should be enlisted to make the data collection processes most efficient so that it takes as little time away from direct services as possible.
- *Fear that results will be used against staff*—While not often mentioned by staff, we suspect that a typical reason for staff resistance is their concern that the OMS will be used against them, perhaps as a tool for personnel evaluation. To address this concern, staff must be involved in defining the purpose of the OMS initially, and the information that is gathered must be used constructively to improve services, not to identify "bad" clinicians.
- *Consumer confidentiality*—Staff are rightly concerned about protecting consumer confidentiality and must be involved in developing appropriate safeguards.
- *Not a "value-added" activity*—It is often difficult for staff to understand the value in the collection of data; they do not see how it will help them or improve services.

Unfortunately, those who have conducted program evaluations in the past, or who have recently developed performance measurement systems, have contributed to this problem by not reporting information back to staff in a timely and useful manner, if at all. Information must be reported back to staff; in fact, it is best to wait to collect data until the system is well prepared to report the information in a timely fashion.

Begin With Education And Discussion

Staff should be involved from the very beginning by educating everyone as to what an OMS is and is not, and what it can and cannot do. Clarify the purpose and goals of the OMS, and how the information will be used. It may be helpful to bring in other service providers who have participated in a similar OMS, who can describe how the system has been helpful to them.

Management Support

Upper and middle management must state their commitment to the OMS and express their enthusiasm. They should also recognize the validity of staff concerns, while stressing the value of measuring consumer outcomes.

"Walk the Walk"

It is not enough for management to simply tell staff that measuring consumer outcomes is valuable; they must back it up with action. Management must invest the time and resources to develop a good system, and model the behavior they expect from their staff by using outcomes information to make decisions. When staff sees that management is committed to investing resources to have a high-quality OMS and uses the information that is collected to improve services, staff is more likely to be committed to the same goals.

Start Small

No matter how well planned, implementing an effective and efficient OMS is a challenging effort.

No doubt, mistakes will be made and necessary refinements will have to be identified. Given this, it is best to start small and build. An ideal strategy is to implement a small pilot project from which staff can learn and improve. In such situations, mistakes (and there will be some) will be relatively small, and won't affect the entire agency or network of providers. It is important that your first attempt be successful; a bad experience will make it more difficult to obtain staff support for further efforts.

Start With Volunteers

As part of the strategy of starting small, perhaps select a small number of staff who volunteer to participate. In all organizations, some staff members will enthusiastically embrace change and try a new way to do business. These individuals can be recruited first to participate in the initial phases of a new OMS. If successful, they will be the best "salespeople" to help convince staff who are skeptical.

Provide Incentives

Management can demonstrate support for an OMS by "valuing" data collection activities as an integral part of providing services. Simple acknowledgment of effort is usually not sufficient to maintain the OMS over a long period of time. For example, time spent completing assessments can be counted towards productivity goals.

Reduce Burden on Staff

Participation in an OMS does add work for staff. To the extent possible, steps should be taken to minimize the burden. Data collection required by the OMS should be carefully examined to make sure that other data collection and reporting requirements are not being duplicated. Redundant data should be eliminated. (In general, it is important to integrate the OMS into the current operations of an organization, rather than making it an "add-on.") We have found that instruments used to conduct baseline outcomes assessments can often be substituted for traditional agency intake assessments, and components of the outcomes assessment process can be integrated with existing treatment planning/monitoring procedures, thus reducing redundancy and streamlining the system. It is also critical to provide the necessary technical and human resource support (in areas such as forms preparation, data entry, and scheduling of assessments), to reduce the burden on direct service staff.

Provide Timely And Useful Feedback

As noted earlier, it is critical that staff get something back for their effort, especially timely and "user-friendly" reports. Given that most systems rely on direct service staff to collect the vast majority of data, summary information about individual consumers should be readily available to use to review progress, develop treatment plans, and update referral sources. As partnerships between the public and private sectors increase, these reports can provide objective information about consumer outcomes that will facilitate clear communication among direct service staff in different sectors.

Use the Results To Improve Services

Using the information to improve services is, of course, the primary purpose of the OMS. It is important that data be used in a highly visible manner so staff can see how their contribution enhances the effective operation of the whole agency; such use also reinforces the need to provide accurate and timely data.

Monitor for Signs Of Staff Resistance

Organizations are always implementing "innovative" practices, and often staff believe that if they "wait it out," the need to change will go away. Some people will not change behavior willingly, preferring to do what is familiar (a.k.a., "if it's not broken, don't fix it"). Supervisors should ensure that staff implement the OMS correctly before they are allowed to judge value.

Solicit Staff Feedback

Once an OMS has been implemented, seek continual staff feedback on its operation. Schedule regular "feedback sessions" where the strengths and weaknesses of the system and problems that need to be addressed can be identified. Then follow through by making the necessary adjustments.

Critical Steps for Obtaining Staff Involvement

In larger agencies, a broad range of staff will participate in the development of an OMS, including clinical service providers, program managers, administrators, clerical workers, and board or community advisory committee members. All staff should be involved in the following critical steps:

Define the Purpose and Goals Of the System

This step should focus on describing the values of the organization, the type of OMS that will mesh with those values, and how the information will be used to meet the needs of everyone involved.

Select Domains and Indicators

Review with staff more than one OMS currently in development. This can provide the basis for a discussion of which domains and indicators would be consistent with the values identified in the first step.

Select Measures

A review of the literature can help to identify potential measures of the selected indicators. Staff should determine the criteria against which these are evaluated: for example, is ease of administration or cost the more important factor? The measures that score the highest on staff-defined criteria can be used in a field test to make the final determination. A field test provides staff with "hands-on" experience with the measures; if the measures they recommend are selected, it will be evidence of management's commitment to staff involvement.

Develop Efficient Data Collection Procedures

Involvement of a broad range of staff can be particularly helpful in developing procedures for data collection and management that are consistent with current procedures; for example, integration with intake procedures.

Provide Opportunities For Feedback

Information should be provided to staff in a way that allows them to interpret and use the results. Their feedback about the OMS and the information it produces can be obtained through regular meetings of work groups or through focus groups, and the suggestions these generate may be used to refine the system.

Summary and Conclusion

In response to increased demand for greater accountability and improved quality, many behavioral healthcare organizations are implementing systems to measure the outcomes of services. Staff at all levels of the provider organization must be committed to the success of the OMS to ensure the collection of reliable and valid data that can be used for clinical and management decision making.

This article has provided a variety of suggestions for involving staff in the design and implementation of an OMS to ensure that the vision of an outcomes-oriented organization can be successfully realized.

References

1. Hackman, J.R., & Wageman, R. 1995. Total quality management: Empirical, conceptual and practical issues. *Administrative Science Quarterly*, 40, 309-342.
2. Klein, K.J., & Ralls, R.S. 1995. The organizational dynamics of computerized technology implementation: A review of the empirical literature. In L.R. Gomez-Mejia & M.W. Lawless (Eds.), *Implementation Management of High Technology*. Greenwich, CT:JAI Press, 31-79.
3. Klein K.J., & Sorra, J.S. 1996. The challenge of innovation implementation. *Academy of Management Review*, 21, 105 5-1080.
4. Reger, R.K., et al. 1994. Reframing the organization: Why implementing total quality is easier said than done. *Academy of Management Review*, 19, 565-584.

Implementing Cost-Effective Information Technologies For Outcomes Management

Les DelPizzo

There are several important assumptions that underlie any discussion of cost effective information systems, and I want to make them very explicit. The first is that, on an internal basis, any outcomes system should focus on a most scarce resource: the attention of your staff, both your management staff and your clinical staff. You know what it is like; you are deluged with work every day, so you need to create an effective outcomes system by integrating it into whatever is important to your staff. You have to find out where the "leverage points" are in your organization.

From an outside perspective, this is so easy to forget, because we generally enter the picture at the "how to" level. But let's back up a bit and ask ourselves, why we are even bothering to do outcomes in the first place? The reason you need to do this is to demonstrate relative value; that's why you go into outcomes.

And you cannot prove relative value with clinical data alone; you cannot do that with financial data alone; you cannot do that with demographic data alone. You need that "bucket" of information coming from all those sources. You may have heard about the concept of "data pools," whereby you combine those data flows into single indicators, or into suites of indicators, to begin conveying the relative value—how much change occurred for this population, or you are saving this much money, etc. To measure relative value, you have to have more than one indicator, one element. This is the second assumption.

The final assumption that permeates this discussion is that the measure of outcomes must be integrated into all critical workflow processes. What I think has to be avoided is the perception or the reality that generating outcomes is some kind of overlay that is somehow being placed on top of your system, is intruding on your system or is something different from what day-to-day work is. It is not different from day-to-day work.

Marrying Outcomes Data And the MIS System

I have given a number of presentations that talk about enterprise report cards, which are based on the whole idea that CQI—continuous quality improvement, which is essentially what the accrediting bodies are trying to formalize—is the kind of reflective practice you should really be trying to create. Those are the workflows that create the feedback loop in your organization, where you plan to do something, you do it, you check your results, and you keep that iteration going. And in that loop is where outcomes should be plugged.

The implications of this approach are that outcomes data should be integrated into standard reports. Think about the reports in your system that people pay attention to: the balance sheet and other financial reports as well as reports used for utilization review. You have to begin looking at ways to integrate outcomes data into those reports. Alternatively, you can create an enterprise report card—some kind of outcome-oriented report that then becomes part of a suite of reports

---

Les DelPizzo is vice president of marketing at CMHC Systems, located in Dublin OH. This article is adapted from DelPizzo's presentation at the Behavioral Health Outcomes Management Forum, which was sponsored by the Institute for International Research, May 7-8, 1998, in Boston MA.

that all key, critical managers see, and perhaps even share, with staff. There is a big movement in some parts of the management world right now to share financial data with everybody. There is some research that shows that firms that do this have better business performance than firms that don't. I would submit to you that the same would hold for any kind of outcomes system you would want to name. You have to share this information; you have to get your staff's attention. But you also have to have standardized reports into which you are putting this information.

The other implication, which I've really made explicit, is that outcomes data includes a full range of information—it's not just claims; it's not just administrative or financial; it's all of those. Those become components that you use, almost like Lego blocks, to put together these indicators reports. Too often we tend to stop at the clinical.

Another important point is that the workflow should equal information flow. For any of you who are process engineers or workflow engineers, this is a given. But creation of outcomes data should be everybody's job. Every part of everybody's work, even the client's. So if you, even for a moment, imagine your enterprise as a set of flowing information streams, each with a receiving node and a generating node, then you have to start asking yourself: How do I begin to integrate an outcomes management process? What kinds of information are generated here, and where does it go? And how does it flow into the standardized reports and come back into the feedback loop?

One of the conclusions I've reached, partly from laboring under this set of assumptions, is that what really matters is not "whether" but, rather, "how" to integrate your outcomes system into your regular information system process. I don't think you have a choice; I don't think it is possible to create a true outcomes management system unless you accept the idea that you have this flow of information in your enterprise right now, and that everybody is both a generator and receiver of information. Instead of trying to lay on another process over that, you need to integrate very organically how you are going to create the outcome indicators out of that information that is being generated and received. If you are going to do that, then you might as well put it into your existing information system. The alternative is to buy your information system with the idea that you are eventually going to do this, so it becomes part of the specification that has to be there before you purchase the system. And finally, you need to bring technology to the workflow process.

The benefits of integrating outcomes measurement into your information system is that there is full integration into both your normal data collection processes and your reporting. The other thing—and I should have labeled this an assumption—is that my company, CMHC Systems, sells information technology. Very often, in the first three years of implementation for most of our customers, many just take their existing work processes and automate them into the new technology. That's satisfactory—it's adequate—but it means that they get about 30 percent of the power and the push that they can get from having an automated information system, because they haven't backed up and asked how they can change their work processes now that they have this tool.

One of the problems, of course, is that everybody has to have the tool for awhile before that sinks in. So we have a whole generation of customers now who are re-implementing, because they finally got the idea that having this technology means they can do work differently. As you have that "Aha!," that's when you can begin integrating the kinds of information you need to build these indicators into your normal work processes.

If you integrate this into your information system, then you have an ongoing, organic indicator system that continuously measures relative value as you combine information from these different data pools, and you have a graph—a report card element—that you can track over time.

The Risks of Integration

Having said all of this, let me mention some of the risks of using your information system as your vehicle for outcomes management. One of the problems is if the information system itself is badly engineered—i.e., if customers just took the new bottle and put the old wine in it. If your information is flawed—has holes in it—then, first of all, the information system is not valued by most of the staff, and grafting the outcomes system onto that is just adding another problem to an already problematic situation. The other risk here is that it really requires a certain kind of holistic thinking and acting to do this sort of integration. That kind of thinking is in short supply. What we are finding out, for instance, as a software vendor is that our implementations are a function of the system manager—the person who puts the system together—and that type of creative person who really understands information is in short supply. And the smaller the agency, the lower the probability that you are going to have people who can really do this, so that is a real risk.

Finally, you have to have an information system that is up to the task. That's a whole other subject, but to deal with certain kinds of clinical data, let me give you just one example of the kind of robustness you need to have. If you are going to have your system be the automated medical records system, or if you are trying to maintain certain kinds of clinical data, then your system has to be able to handle multiple layers—and layers within layers—because you are going to have a record for your agency, a layer that just deals with a certain program perhaps, and within that program you are going to have a treatment plan, and within that treatment plan you are going to have objectives, and so on. And each of those can change as you go down—a person may move from program to program. Even within a program, you want a history of a treatment plan. Then, if you are keeping outcome records, there is layer upon layer of information within each of those treatment plans, because you want that longitudinal history of indicators. So you want to have a very robustly constructed MIS (management information system) to do that, and you are going to run into this problem whether you buy just an outcomes system or whether you truly try to integrate this into your MIS. There are not a lot of MISs out there right now that really deal well with clinical data, and that's the reason; it's a very tough problem. There are some, however, and I'm not talking just about ours; there are other good systems out there.

Betting the Farm On the Web

This brings us to the crux of this discussion. At the workflow node, who is generating what information where? Let's focus first on a client or patient. What you are trying to do here is create a very permeable boundary, so that information from the client comes easily into your system. I'm assuming you've already solved the problem of where to put it in your information system. You want the client to reach out and touch you without your spending a lot of money, time and attention. And the technology you employ to do that is going to depend on who your client population is.

Let's talk about some of these technologies. I am convinced—and to a certain degree my company is betting the farm—on the fact that the Web is going to become one of the primary media of information communication everywhere. It's already becoming ubiquitous, and it will only become more so. And we're going to find that, as Web development tools become more sophisticated, the technology becoming more and more robust, it's going to be a fragmented and crazy market for awhile. The tools are all out there, however.

What these tools can mean is that for a fairly sophisticated population of clients and commercial accounts, etc., there is no reason why an enterprise cannot begin the assessment process well before the client or patient ever comes in the door. And I'm not talking about using the phone. Once a customer is granted access to a phone triage system, and once the person on the other end of the line knows that they are an eligible member and determines that somebody needs to be called, the next thing they can do is give that patient a password for them to get into an Internet connection, and they can do all of the assessment by themselves via the Web. Why would anybody want to do that? There is a significant body of information saying that people are more truthful when talking on the phone or using the computer than they are when communicating face-to-face with a clinician. I've never seen one study that says that's not true, although it may exist—I'm not a researcher by trade. The other reason is that it is very cheap. The permeability of that is almost *100 percent*.

One issue that does come up when talking about the Web is security. I don't think it is such a big problem at this point. In fact, I'm less concerned about security than about responsiveness on the Web, because it is a public utility. But by using a password system, you can almost do this as an extranet. It also depends on where you set this thing up. If someone is dialing in from home, then their response time may be low, but because they are sitting at home, they may not mind it. If, on the other hand, somebody is in your office and trying to respond to an assessment, then they may want to have faster response time, and you can do that, because you are probably running an intranet where you are using Web technology to run your own network.

People often ask me whether public clients will be able to access and use the Web. The answer is, absolutely. This country is spending billions of dollars a year to provide Internet access in every library, and some social service agencies are also doing it. Public populations do have access to the Net, and, believe me, the learning curve for using this technology is extremely low. For young kids in Medicaid populations, it's probably five minutes tops, and they can teach Grandma how to do this in no time; it's just not that tough. I truly believe that the Web represents an enormous possibility for lowering the bar for making the information generation process extremely permeable for clients at all levels.

Other Technological Alternatives

Then there is the phone. There are interactive voice recognition systems on the market today. CMHC Systems sells a speech recognition system for clinicians called SpeechWriter, and my company has a relationship with Philips Electronics, which is one of the biggest purveyors of electronics in the world. They have a system running in Germany right now where you can call the national railroad and find out what train is running on what day to Düsseldörf and make your reservation without ever talking to a human.

Now you may ask, how can that be? There are a couple of things you need to know about speech technology, for those of you who are even remotely "techie." The problems with speech technology is that when you try to deal with a very large vocabulary, it's very hard to get high recognition. And to get anywhere near high recognition, you have to have the speaker trained. But with the small vocabulary needed to fill out an assessment form or to move money from your checking to savings account, for example, the system is voice or speech independent.

So the technology already exists. It is pricey now, but you know what happens with technology: the prices are being driven down. These systems require very heavy CPUs in computers, but these things used to be all hardware-dependent. The first version of SpeechWriter we wrote had to have a very expensive speech recognition board in the computer; version two, which came out six months later, was totally software—there wasn't even a board with it, and it worked better. Something to keep in mind when you look at the cutting edge.

With touch systems and voice systems, you can have the computer in a carrel next to a waiting room and have people begin entering data while they wait. Yes, you will need a data editor somewhere, but, believe me, there is no more cost-effective way than making technology permeable.

There are also special appliances for data entry. There is, for example, a little box that one company has called Point of View. Perhaps you have seen Bill Berman's BHOS system at various trade shows. It's basically a computer, but you'd never know it; it has a big screen on top, and it's programmed to produce Bill's assessment instrument. You can choose which one you are going to use and use a touch-screen for data entry. When you are done you hit "Submit," or you just put the device back into a docking terminal, and it uses wireless technology—infrared—to send the information back into the computer. Those kinds of devices are going to become more and more common.

When we start now to talk about computers that are libretto-size or palm-size, the ability to have people engage your information system will become easier and easier. Early on they'll be costly, but they will get cheaper as they become more common.

Finally, there are options such as scanning. People can write out their information and put it on bubble paper. The technology for getting scanned information into information systems is already there. We must have five scanners on our authorized equipment list that we can sell to any customer, and so does every other software vendor. It is very inexpensive to do that.

The Cost of the Web

Returning to the subject of Web technologies, let's talk about cost for a minute. You will need a pretty good server and probably need someone to run your network. Those of you who are in proactive agencies are already setting up your intranet. If you are not doing it now, then you will be doing it shortly.

The bottom line on this whole technology thing is for your staff. Basically, you want to have easier ways for them to input information into your point-of-service recording system, which frankly should be your integrated MIS. If they are using an MIS, then have them put their clinical and point-of-service information right into the MIS.

One thing about that, however: you've heard about thin client computers, network computers, etc. The beauty of going into a browser-based world is that you only have to put on a clinician's desk a system that can run Windows and have a browser on it; it doesn't even matter which browser you use. You can have a system like that for $500 today, and they have the world at their fingertips, including your management information system. It is enormously powerful. The problem is that to get the service staff tapped into it, you have to have the automated clinical reporting process, so maybe it is better for you to spend some time thinking about how you are automating your clinical reporting process before you even get to outcomes. And, finally, you have to have a robust, multilayered clinical database to receive that information, so that you can report on it as data.

Principles for Assessment of Patient Outcomes in Mental Health Care

G. RICHARD SMITH, JR., MD, RONALD W. MANDERSCHEID, PHD, LAURIE M. FLYNN, AND DONALD M. STEINWACHS, PHD

With the dramatic changes that are occurring in mental health and substance abuse treatment systems, it is imperative that the field keep its focus on the patient and the patient's outcomes of care. Outcomes management systems that measure the processes of care, the patient's characteristics, and the patient's outcomes of care can be helpful in maintaining this focus. To facilitate the development of these systems, the Outcomes Roundtable, a group of mental health consumer, professional, service, and policy-making organizations, has articulated a set of 12 broadly applicable principles of outcomes assessment. The principles call for outcomes assessments that are appropriate to the question being answered, that use tools with demonstrated validity and reliability and sensitivity to clinically important changes over time, and that always include the consumer perspective. In addition, the principles recommend outcomes assessments that create minimal burden for respondents and are adaptable to different health care systems, that include general health status as well as mental health status, and that include consumers' evaluation of treatment and outcomes. Outcomes assessment tools should quantify the type and extent of treatment, should include generic and disorder-specific information, and should measure areas of personal functioning affected by the disorder. Outcomes should be reassessed at clinically meaningful points in time. Outcomes assessment should use appropriate scientific design and representative samples and should examine outcomes of consumers who prematurely leave treatment as well as those who continue in treatment.

Our nation is experiencing a dramatic restructuring of private and public mental health and substance abuse treatment systems. This process reflects a combination of changes in political philosophy, escalating treatment costs, and the development of new service delivery systems. The treatment programs of this nation may change more in the next five years than they did over the past 40 years, a period that has included the community mental health center movement, the deinstitutionalization process, and the development of neuroleptic medications. In this time of change, it is imperative to focus explicitly on the person who should be the center of all treatment efforts—the person with mental illness or substance abuse problems or both. Specific concentrated effort needs to be directed toward ensuring that, in the midst of change, the patient receives the highest quality care.

One approach to keeping the focus on the person with mental illness and on the quality of

---

Source: Smith GR, Manderscheid RW, Flynn LM, and Steinwachs DM. Principles for Assessment of Patient Outcomes in Mental Health Care. Psychiatric Services August 1997; 48(8):1033-1036. (Reprinted with permission.)

Center for Outcomes Research and Effectiveness (CORE), University of Arkansas for Medical Sciences. For fee information related to Outcomes Measurement Tools, contact CORE at (501) 660-7550.

The authors are members of the steering committee of the Outcomes Roundtable, a multi-disciplinary group whose purpose is to develop outcomes measures that will improve care for persons with mental and addictive disorders. Dr. Smith is affiliated with the Center for Mental Healthcare Research at the University of Arkansas for Medical Sciences, 5800 West Tenth Street, Suite 605, Little Rock, Arkansas 72204. Dr. Manderscheid is chief of the survey and analysis branch in the division of state and community systems development at the Center for Mental Health Services in Rockville, Maryland. Ms. Flynn is executive director of the National Alliance for the Mentally Ill in Arlington, Virginia. Dr. Steinwachs is professor and chair of the department of health policy and management at Johns Hopkins University in Baltimore.

treatment has been the rapidly developing field of patient outcomes assessment. The technology of this field assesses changes in health status, in its broadest context, over time and the relationship of those changes to the care provided to patients. This information is then used to modify services and treatments to improve the outcomes of care. Systems that generate these types of data are referred to as outcomes assessment systems or outcomes management systems.[1]

Recently this focus on patient outcomes assessment has been widely advocated.[2,3] For a variety of reasons, however, few clinical organizations have implemented outcomes assessment systems. In fact, in a recent national search for effective outcomes management systems in mental health and substance abuse settings, only five such systems could be identified.[4]

This lack of effective systems is further complicated by the increasing demand for such systems by accrediting bodies and policy advocacy groups. The Joint Commission on Accreditation of Healthcare Organizations is in the process of making outcomes assessment an essential part of a facility's quality improvement program required for accreditation.[5] Further, the Foundation for Accountability, a coalition of major public and private purchasers of health care, including the Health Care Financing Administration and Fortune 100 companies, and consumer groups, including the National Alliance for the Mentally Ill, among others, are embarking on an aggressive agenda to encourage purchasers to require that their providers present evidence of the outcomes that their care produces.[2]

These developments, coupled with the proliferation of commercial vendors who sell outcomes assessment services, make it imperative that the field move toward some consensus about how outcomes assessment should be accomplished. To facilitate a consensus, this paper proposes a set of principles for outcomes measurement and outcomes assessment systems for mental health and substance abuse treatment. These principles can be used to create and implement outcomes assessment systems and to determine whether existing systems meet important basic criteria. To date, not enough attention has been paid to the development of appropriate outcomes protocols. This inattention to the development of the outcomes measurement field has impeded assessment of the quality of care and efforts to improve care, thus limiting the benefit of such technologies for people with mental disorders and substance abuse problems.

These principles for outcomes assessment were developed by a task force of the Outcomes Roundtable. The Outcomes Roundtable is jointly sponsored by the Johns Hopkins University and the National Alliance for the Mentally Ill with additional sponsorship by several other organizations (listed in the acknowledgments section at the end of the paper). The principles represent the first product of the Roundtable, which will also conduct demonstration projects and provide communications to the field about outcomes assessment.

These principles derive from a long history of measurement science, psychometrics, and health services research. They are not unique to this document. However, these concepts have not previously been compiled or modified specifically for clinical outcomes assessment, and they are not widely used at present in our health care systems.

Principles of Patient Outcomes Assessment

Outcomes Assessments Should Be Appropriate to the Application Or Question Being Answered

There are at least two different groups of applications for which outcomes assessment tools can be used, and each requires different types of tools. One application is to understand the relationship between patients' health status (outcomes), disease status, and treatment (processes of care). For this application, disorder-specific assessment tools are needed.

A second task is to more broadly understand the general health status, symptoms, mental health status, or global well-being of groups of patients. For this application, generic assessment tools not tailored for specific disorders may be appropriate.

Among the outcomes that can be assessed are symptoms; functioning, including physical, mental, and social functioning; global well-being; and health-related quality of life. Different instruments exist to measure these different outcomes.[6]

Tools for Assessing Outcomes Should Have Demonstrated Validity and Reliability and Must Be Sensitive to Clinically Important Change Over Time

Validity is a property of the assessment tool that indicates that the instrument assesses the true state of the phenomenon being measured.[7] Reliability is whether the assessment is reproducible.[7] Sensitivity to clinically important change over time indicates that as patients experience clinically significant changes in their condition or conditions, the assessment tools will be able to detect the changes.[7] Another important aspect of an instrument's validity is its ability to convey similar meaning to groups of people with different social, ethnic, and cultural backgrounds and with different languages.[8]

Unless a tool has demonstrated validity and reliability, the user of the tool can have no confidence in its ability to provide meaningful information. Similarly, if an assessment tool cannot help to distinguish clinically important changes, such as the cessation of panic attacks among patients with panic disorder, the tool has little utility.

Outcomes Assessments Should Always Include the Patient's Perspective; Outcomes Assessments Obtained from Providers and Family Members May Enhance What Is Learned

High quality care is person-centered care and always includes the patient's perspective.[2] The patient's perspective is even more important for outcomes assessment because many important outcomes can be determined only by asking the patient. The perspectives of providers and family members are also important, because each may emphasize different dimensions of outcomes than will the patient.

Determining whether an adolescent with depression has had an increase or decrease in acting-out behavior can be assessed by asking the adolescent directly. However, at times, the provider or family members may note a substantial change in behavior even though the adolescent does not report it. In a similar fashion, assessment of changes in quality of life should be addressed primarily to the patient. Often the provider may have little or no insight about the quality of a patient's life; the family may have considerably more insight.

Outcomes Assessment Systems Should Place Minimal Burden On the Respondent and Have The Ability To Be Adapted to Different Health Care Systems

Burden for the respondent consists of the time and effort required to complete the assessment tool.[9] Finishing the assessment should not be an onerous task, or the completeness and accuracy of the information may be jeopardized. Furthermore, outcomes assessment tools that can be used only in unique health care settings have limited utility. A long-term objective of outcomes assessment is to compare the outcomes of patients in different health care settings using the same tools.[1]

Outcomes assessment systems that consume too much of the clinician's or the patient's time are wasteful and unnecessary because the primary focus of the treatment setting should be treatment, not measurement. An outcomes assessment system that is unique to a particular program is less helpful than systems that share several data elements. Systems that share elements provide the opportunity to compare outcomes between treatment settings and provide the basis for quality improvement efforts.

Outcomes Assessments Should Include General Health Status As Well as Mental Health Status

General health status usually includes physical, mental, and social functioning, as well as self-reported perceptions of overall health.[10] Just as mental health issues are often neglected in general health settings, mental health settings, at times, overlook the patient's general health.[11] General health is vital to overall health and therefore needs to be a part of outcomes assessment.

The physical capacity to work and engage in social activities may be as important to the patient as his or her mental capacity for these activities. Therefore, it is important to keep the focus on the entire person.

Outcomes Assessments Should Include Measures of the Patient's Evaluation of Treatment and Outcomes

One measure of the success of the treatment system in focusing on the needs of the patient is the patient's evaluation of the care being provided and the outcomes of that care. This information can be used in modifying treatment programs to be more helpful and responsive to patients.

For example, if mothers in a mother-child cocaine treatment program say that individual psychotherapy sessions are not as helpful as group psychotherapy sessions, the treatment providers would be well advised to consider restructuring the program. Such consideration would be especially important if patients perceive that the outcomes of the group therapy program are better than the outcomes of the individual psychotherapy program.

Outcomes Assessment Tools Should Quantify the Type and Extent of Treatment the Patient Receives (the Process of Care) For the Target Condition in Order to Understand the Clinical Relationship Between the Outcomes Of Care and Treatment

If an outcomes assessment system is intended to help reveal the relationship between treatment process and the outcomes of treatment, then measures of the content of treatment for each patient are needed.[8] Efforts to improve the quality of mental health care require both treatment process and outcomes information.[6]

For example, in a state substance abuse treatment system that is interested in the relationship between treatment and outcomes, it is likely that the system manager will want to know whether patients who attend 12-step programs have better outcomes than those who do not. If 12-step programs are found to be helpful, the state system may choose to encourage more frequent provision of 12-step programs.

Outcomes Assessment Tools Should Include Generic and Disorder-Specific Information That Is Predictive of Expected Patient Outcomes; This Prognostic Information May Include Case Mix and Severity Characteristics That Are Associated With Choice Of or Success of Treatment

Generic prognostic characteristics are those such as socioeconomic status and social support that are known to affect outcomes for most health problems.[6] Groups of patients with higher socioeconomic status will generally have better outcomes than those with lower socioeconomic status.[12] Disorder-specific prognostic characteristics are usually related to disease severity and are known to affect outcomes for a particular disorder, such as substance abuse by a person with major depression or the loss of family support by a patient with alcohol dependence.

When groups of patients are compared, the issue of one group's being more ill than the other group frequently arises. Use of prognostic characteristics (severity adjustment) permits the analyst to adjust for these differences between groups.[13] For example, if a large group practice is seeking to understand how the outcomes of psychotherapy compare with those of medication in treating panic disorder, the group practice will need to know whether the severity of illness of patients receiving psychotherapy is similar to that of patients receiving medication.

Outcomes Assessments Should Include Areas of Personal Functioning Affected by The Condition or Conditions Of Interest

Disorder-specific functioning is a concept that recognizes that different health problems or disorders have different effects on functioning.⁶ For example, geographic limitations are important to patients with panic disorder but are not particularly relevant to patients with bipolar disorder. Disease-specific functional limitations should be included in outcomes assessments.

For a person with schizophrenia, the ability to live independently is an important and relevant outcome. On the other hand, the functional limitation of the ability to live independently does not occur frequently enough among people with major depression for the question to be asked routinely in assessing the outcomes for this disorder.

Outcomes Should Be Initially Assessed and Reassessed at Clinically Meaningful Points In Time Given the Course Of the Disorder

Outcomes assessment should occur at time intervals that have clinical meaning, when sufficient time has elapsed between assessments to note important events such as remission, relapse, or other clinical changes.⁶ Outcomes assessment that is simply convenient for assessors will have little clinical utility.

Outcomes assessment is frequently accomplished at admission to and discharge from the hospital. If outcomes are assessed only at those points, little is gained by the discharge assessment because the vast majority of patients will be improved at discharge. Follow-up at some time after discharge, if it is feasible within a system of care, will provide more meaningful information.

Outcomes Assessments Should Use an Appropriate Scientific Design and Representative Sample

This recommendation is made to ensure the generalizability, or external validity, of the data to patients from the treatment program of interest.⁷ Unless all patients or a representative sample of patients are assessed, the outcomes and treatment data will be of little use in understanding the outcomes of care. Even worse, the data could be seriously misleading due to the selection of an inadequate or inappropriate sample.

For example, if follow-up assessments are made entirely by telephone to the first 50 people who can be reached, two sources of bias are introduced. First, only people of higher socioeconomic status who can afford telephones, and who are likely to have better outcomes, will be assessed. Second, those who are at home and not at work will be assessed. It is likely that those at home will have poorer outcomes. Thus such a research strategy will result in confusing and perhaps misleading or meaningless information about the group of patients receiving treatment.

Assessing Outcomes of Patients Who Prematurely Leave Treatment Is as Important as Assessing Outcomes of Those Who Are Still in Treatment at The Time of Follow-Up

It is usually easier to obtain follow-up outcomes assessment from patients who are still in treatment than from those who have completed treatment or who have dropped out. Those who have successfully completed treatment will likely have better outcomes than those still in treatment, and those who have dropped out of care may have worse outcomes. To obtain the clearest picture of how treatment is affecting patients in the system, those who have left treatment must be included in the assessment.

In some treatment programs, dropout rates are substantial because patients have lost eligibility or insurance coverage, or because patients do not believe they are benefiting from care. However, dropouts from treatment should be included in outcomes assessment, or the results will not reflect what is actually happening in the program.

Conclusions

The steering committee of the Outcomes Roundtable endorsed these principles and encourages their adoption and application by all organizations providing services to persons with mental illnesses and substance abuse disorders. Without better information on patients' outcomes and what treatments work for whom, and under what circumstances, we cannot expect to improve the

Chapter 2: The Mechanics of Measurement

quality of care and the quality of the lives of persons who suffer from mental illnesses and substance abuse.

The implementation of outcomes assessment systems is a complex organizational task[14] over and above use of these principles. Careful attention to implementation is needed if patient outcomes assessment is to become a routine aspect of health care, analogous to the use of the laboratory in internal medicine practice. The steering committee of the Outcomes Roundtable believes that these efforts will be well worth the resources expended as we work to improve the outcomes of treatment for our patients.

Acknowledgments

Additional sponsors for the Outcomes Roundtable are the American Psychiatric Association, the Center for Mental Health Services, Eli Lilly and Company, the National Depressive and Manic-Depressive Association, the National Institute on Alcohol Abuse and Alcoholism, the National Institute on Drug Abuse, the National Institute of Mental Health, and the Washington Business Group on Health. In addition to the authors, the members of the task force to develop principles for outcomes assessment were Jean Campbell, PhD, Robert F. Cole, PhD, Juliann DeStefano, RN, MPH, Susan Dime-Meenan, Bill Edell, PhD, Richard K. Fuller, MD, Laura A. Genduso, PharmD, Florence Gonzales, Eric Goplerud, PhD, J. Rock Johnson, JD, Anthony F. Lehman, MD, Brenda W. Lyles, PhD, Steven M. Mirin, MD, Lloyd Sederer, MD, Rona Purdy, and David L. Shern, PhD.

References

1. Ellwood PM: Outcomes management: a technology of patient experience. *New England Journal of Medicine* 318:1549-1556, 1988
2. Ellwood PM, Lundberg GD: Managed care: a work in progress. *JAMA* 276:1083-1086, 1996
3. Steinwachs DM, Fischer EP, Lehman AF: Outcomes assessment: information for improving mental health care. *New Directions for Mental Health Services*, no 71:49-57, 1996
4. Dialogue on Outcomes on Mental and Addictive Disorders. Arlington, Va, *National Alliance for the Mentally Ill Outcomes Roundtable*, Winter 1997
5. O'Leary DS: Quality drivers for the millennium. *Joint Commission Perspectives*, Jan-Feb 1996, pp 2-3
6. Smith GR, Rost K, Fischer EP, et al: Assessing the effectiveness of mental health care in routine clinical practice: critical components, administration, and application of outcomes modules. *Evaluation and the Health Professions* 20:65-80, 1997
7. Fletcher RH, Fletcher SW, Wagner EH: *Clinical Epidemiology: The Essentials*, 3rd ed. Baltimore, Williams & Wilkins, 1996
8. Burnam MA: Measuring outcomes of care for substance use and mental disorders. *New Directions for Mental Health Services*, no 71:1-24, 1996
9. Patrick DL, Erickson P: *Health Status and Health Policy: Quality of Life in Health Care Evaluation and Resource Allocation*. New York, Oxford University Press, 1993
10. Ware JE, Brook RH, Davies-Avery A, et al: Conceptualization and Measurement of Health for Adults in the Health Insurance Study: Vol 1. *Model of Health and Methodology*. Santa Monica, Calif, Rand, 1980
11. Koran LM, Sox HC Jr, Marton KI, et al: Medical evaluation of psychiatric patients: I. results in a state mental health system. *Archives of General Psychiatry* 46:733-740, 1989
12. Pappas G, Queen S, Hadden W, et al: The increasing disparity in mortality between socioeconomic groups in the United States, 1960 and 1986. *New England Journal of Medicine* 329:103-109, 1993
13. Smith GR: State of the science of mental health and substance abuse patient outcomes assessment. *New Directions in Mental Health Services*, no 71:59-67, 1996
14. Smith GR Jr, Fischer EP, Nordquist CR, et al: Implementing outcomes management systems in mental health settings. *Psychiatric Services* 48:364-368, 1997

Protecting Client Confidentiality and Improving Provider Relations Through A New Form of Managed Care: Collaborative Care Management

DAVID R. KRAUS, PHD, AND FREDERICK P. HORAN, PHD

Abstract
This article details a new type of working relationship between providers and managed care organizations (MCOS) called Collaborative Care Management (CCM). This model is more provider friendly, protects patient confidentiality, introduces important quality management tools to the provider's practice, improves working relationships between payors and providers and is less costly to administer as well. Rising behavioral health care expenses with little demonstrable connection between costs and quality or even the necessity of care have led to the rapid growth of managed behavioral health care. However, traditional managed care techniques are often arduous and time consuming, as well as requiring the release and review of very personal patient information. Legislation limiting managed care organization (MCO) access to confidential information is becoming popular, requiring new strategies to manage benefits. The CCM system uses benchmarks to set mutually agreeable utilization targets, and a comprehensive outcome and patient satisfaction tool to monitor quality of care indicators. The quality management tools described here are empirically based, validated on a diverse population and processed by a neutral third party to control for bias. Providers are allowed to make their own decisions about benefit management as long as they stay within agreed upon utilization and quality parameters. Only aggregate data is provided to the MCO. The system may eliminate the need for pre-certifications and many case reviews. Patients' confidentiality is more secure and most providers will benefit from reduced management oversight.

Controlling the costs of mental health treatment while ensuring that patients receive high quality care is now a major focus of employers, care managers, and providers of clinical services. MCOs are routinely required by employers and other payors to show how they will manage costs while demonstrating positive clinical outcomes and maintaining high levels of patient and provider satisfaction. Providers are being asked to demonstrate the necessity of treatment, the utility and quality of their services, and their ability to provide care in a cost-effective manner. This can be difficult as many practices, and even some large facilities, lack the expertise and user friendly tools to develop adequate internal quality management programs that will satisfy the demands of MCOs.

This paper describes a model of provider and MCO relationship that is evolving in Massachusetts between Medicaid providers of behavioral health care and the Mass. Behavioral

---

Source: Kraus DR and Horan FP. Protecting Client Confidentiality and Improving Provider Relations Through a New Form of Managed Care: Collaborative Care Management. 1997. (Reprinted with permission.)
  David R. Kraus, PhD, is President of Access Measurement Systems, Inc. Frederick P. Horan, PhD, is Senior Vice President of Quality Management, Access Measurement Systems, Inc.

Health Partnership which manages the care for the vast majority of MA Medicaid recipients. The goal of this new relationship is to improve provider/MCO relations while providing each party with the tools and information needed to continually improve the quality of care.

On the surface, MCOs and providers would seem to share a common goal of ensuring that patients receive high quality cost-effective care. What this actually means and how it is demonstrated are where the two groups frequently diverge. Providers often complain of micromanagement and unrealistic demands to produce sophisticated quality management data that may seem irrelevant to the business of treating patients. MCOs in turn are often reluctant to allow providers greater freedom in managing the care of their patients, fearing that clinicians are not willing, or equipped to contain costs or objectively demonstrate the quality of their services. In the midst of these struggles, traditional managed care techniques have raised concerns over patients' rights to confidentiality. Legislation recently enacted in Massachusetts limits insurance access to confidential information during the first $500 of mental health benefits. Other states have either enacted or are considering similar restrictions. While this type of legislation may offer some protection against potentially improper use of personal patient information, MCO supported quality management activities such as outcomes and patient satisfaction evaluations can be seriously compromised unless alternatives that are more responsive to patients' needs are developed.

This paper offers a new strategy for managing behavioral health care benefits. This system suggests ways in which the two general functions that MCOs have assumed—ensuring quality of care and containing costs—can, to a great degree, be returned to the provider. In this plan, the role of the MCO is to be an administrative support and quality management collaborator, as opposed to being actively involved in the day-to-day care decisions of patients. The biggest stumbling block to such a scheme in the past has been a lack of provider expertise in quality management and cost containment along with the dearth of adequate tools to accomplish these goals. This system offers a solution to these problems. It combines a new user-friendly patient evaluation, outcome, and satisfaction system that provides objective assessment and quality management data yet allows providers to maintain the confidentiality of their patients. It is designed to be useful in practices and facilities that are relatively new to the quality management arena, as well as in sites where QM has been a way of life. This system combines these tools with the concept of "benchmarking", which allows a practice or facility to develop its own internal cost controls. The system, which we have called Collaborative Care Management (CCM) has some essential features that are described below.

Quality Management Data Collection

Anyone who has ever been an administrator in a hospital or managed care organization knows what a daunting task it is to develop meaningful quality management programs. Most outpatient practices (and many hospital) still either have no such programs, or only rudimentary systems that provide little useful information that can actually help improve patient care. In developing the CCM concept, it was clear that the system would require the use of a comprehensive assessment tool that was empirically validated, easily administered, low cost, and that could quickly assess problems and progress across a wide range of diagnostic categories. If these criteria were not met, the likelihood of the instrument gaining enthusiastic acceptance with clinicians and MCOs would be small. In addition, it needed to be demonstrably objective and free from provider bias that would render the outcome and satisfaction results open to question. The system also had to provide clinically useful information immediately to providers. If the time and effort were to be taken to systematically evaluate patients, the results had to be integrateable into the treatment planning process in order to provide the greatest benefit to the patient and provider. Finally, the use of a neutral third party data collection service was considered essential. Those with vested financial interests in outcome results should not handle or report these data, as these results would be received with understandable skepticism. For the system to work, both MCO and provider needed to have a high level of confidence in the data and results generated.

As we were unable to find an instrument that could meet all of these criteria, we (Access Measurement Systems) spent four years developing our own which we call the TOP (for Treatment Outcome Package). This package consists of a computer scanable and scoreable assessment tool, which has been empirically designed and validated on a range of clinical populations including Medicaid consumers. The initial assessment portion of the TOP is designed to be filled out by the patient in a waiting room in about twenty minutes. It is then faxed to a computer center where it can be immediately scored twenty-four hours a day. A computer-generated report is returned to the clinician within fifteen minutes so that it is available before the patient leaves the initial session. The report provides information relating to patient demographics, the type and severity of presenting problems, functional and symptom levels, the patient's goals for treatment, medical concerns, previous psychiatric history, and possible diagnoses. At the end of the treatment episode, the instrument is again administered, along with the patient satisfaction portion of the TOP. Together these make up the outcome report.

Feedback

Part of the difficulty that practices and facilities experience in implementing quality management programs is that clinicians typically experience few direct benefits from the efforts that they put into supporting the program. Often, results are only reported sporadically and their relevance to the practicing clinician is questionable. The information that is collected by the TOP has several uses that make it attractive to clinicians, practice managers, payors, and MCOs. As the initial assessment is scored and returned within fifteen minutes, results can be used as the basis for the initial treatment plan as well as a springboard for further exploration of critical issues disclosed by the patient that may not have come up during the clinical interview. This feature is most attractive to clinicians who see the instrument as a helpful tool rather than an additional burden. Outcome data can be reported not only for an individual patient, but by therapist, practice, or facility (see the appendix for sample reports). This allows clinicians to monitor an individual patient's progress and use this information to inform further treatment planning decisions. It also helps clinical supervisors tailor training and supervision to specific clinician's needs. Equally important, it allows facilities, networks, and MCOs to demonstrate with empirical and objectively scored data, that they are delivering high quality care.

Patient Confidentiality

In response to the growing concerns about the integrity of computerized record keeping from a confidentiality perspective, the TOP utilizes a patient coding system that leaves all identifying information in the hands of the provider. In a CCM system, the MCO receives aggregate data in most cases, unless clinical concerns such as the need for extended benefits or a more in depth review becomes apparent. Individual patient data is not routinely needed in this system (and may violate confidentiality laws in a growing number of states). An added benefit of this process is that it allows patients to be more honest and accurate in their reporting on questionnaires. When individual patent data is returned to the MCO, many patients either worry about their benefits being denied and therefore exaggerate symptoms, or they worry about their confidentiality being violated and minimize symptoms. Therefore, this system can dramatically improve the accuracy of data, and in turn, the usefulness of the system.

CCM and Benchmarking

It may sometimes appear to providers that MCOs, especially those with risk-based (capitated) contracts, are tying case management decisions to reach specific, short term utilization objectives. In many managed care companies where utilization targets are generated and posted on a daily basis, the clinical staff may feel pressure to do just that. This type of short term goal setting sometimes results in inconsistent case management decisions in an effort to reach utilization targets, which can create anger and frustration on the part of the providers and can possibly lead to less than optimum patient outcomes. A growing trend in the industry is toward the use of "benchmark" utilization goals. In the CCM system, frequent MCO micromanagement of cases is replaced with these broader utilization goals that must be met by the practice or facility to avoid more intensive scrutiny (or sometimes financial penalties) by the MCO. Although the CCM system places more responsibility for the management of care with the provider, it is not so "hands off" a strategy as is found in a capitated system. Quality management mechanisms must be in place and the practice must be able to demonstrate the efficacy of their services along with high levels of patient satisfaction as opposed to just an ability to cut costs. With collaborative care management, under-utilization is no more desirable than over-utilization, as the result of either may be increased MCO case management.

Utilization Parameters

In order to begin CCM, there must be an agreed upon means of establishing appropriate utilization objectives (benchmarks) for the particular patient population to be treated in a given practice or facility. This is an inexact science at best and requires ongoing dialogue between the MCO and provider so that reasonable adjustments can be made that reflect the true clinical needs of a given panel of patients. This process is helped by the objective assessment data collected with the TOP that support the clinician's assertions regarding the level of acuity of a given group of patients, as well as outcome data that demonstrate the value of a given course of treatment in improving patients' health status.

Participation

Participation in the system must be mandatory for both patient and provider unless there is some overwhelming clinical reason why this is not possible. The TOP has been successfully used with a wide range of patients in both acute and subacute settings. In certain cases, such as when used with children or severely impaired patients, the manner of administration may be adapted (the questionnaire can be used as a structured clinical interview), but in all cases the instrument should be used. Patients are rarely resistant to the assessments when informed by their provider that the process is a necessary and useful part of their treatment process, that their answers are not released to the insurance company, and that their benefits are not related to how they answer the questionnaire.

Internal Care/Duality Management

A benchmarking case management system requires that provider groups and facilities have their own internal care review and quality management capabilities. By monitoring their own practice patterns and implementing peer review procedures as soon as data indicate that this may be warranted, increased oversight by an MCO will usually be avoided. In addition, by establishing continuous quality improvement mechanisms based on the outcome and satisfaction measures, a practice or facility can enhance patient care and confidence in its services. With a system that meets the above criteria, most providers can be exempt from many of the tedious procedures imposed by traditional managed care. Their interest in becoming "unmanaged" helps to generate the enthusiasm necessary to implement and continue the system.

Scientific Advisory Board

The core of the CCM approach rests on scientifically valid results that both provider and MCO can trust. In addition to the neutrality of a third party data collection and reporting service, the providers represented by their trade organization, Mental Health Corporations of MA, the payor MBHP, and AMS have created a scientific advisory board that will be chaired by David Barlow, Ph.D., a leading national outcome expert. The role of the advisory board will be to help set benchmarks for various patient populations and oversee the ongoing scientific merit of the project.

Implementing Collaborative Care Management

In general, after six months to a year of using the TOP, providers will have generated enough data to document their need (or lack thereof) for further management oversight Those providers above the mean on managing both cost and quality of care can be exempt from prior approvals, case reviews, and additional benefit requests. Those providers who fall below a predetermined cut-off score on quality and cost management may continue with some form of care management either by the practice or the MCO. In the CCM system, the goal of care management is to help clinicians make changes that bring them within an acceptable range as established by the agreed upon utilization and outcome benchmarks. In very rare cases, providers who consistently fall below the mean may be considered for disciplinary action including contract termination. This is done using the peer review process in conjunction with the objective measures, as it is an inappropriate use of an outcome system to determine that a provider is providing low quality service based purely on a below average statistical profile. The outcome profile should simply help to alert the MCO and practice/facility management to the need for more rigorous oversight and review.

Additional Benefits

The savings to an MCO in reduced oversight costs is more than enough to pay for the assessment/outcome system such as the TOP. The system is ideal for helping to move provider contracts towards shared financial risk. Finally, the collaborative care management system helps to improve the nature of the relationship between provider and MCO, as there are more opportunities to become collaborators rather than adversaries.

References

Bilbery, J & Bilbery, P (1995) "Judging, Trusting, and Utilizing Outcome Data: A Survey of Behavioral Healthcare Payors," *Behavioral Healthcare Tomorrow*, 4(4), 62-65.

Nash DB & Markson, LE (1991) "Managing Outcomes: The Perspective of the Players," *Health Service Management*, 8(2),3-51.

Nelson, DC; Hartman, E; Ojemann, PG; & Wilcox M (1995) 'Breaking New Ground: Public/Private Collaboration to Measure and Manage Medicaid Patient Outcomes." *Behavioral Healthcare Tomorrow*, 4(4), 31-37.

Kraus, DR & Jordan, JR (1996) "Validation of a Treatment Outcome and Assessment Tool: The Treatment Outcome Package," *Professional Psychology: Research and Practice*. Submitted for publication.

Laying the Groundwork

Operational Recommendations for Integrating Guidelines And Outcomes Into Clinical Practice

JOSEPH P. NAUGHTON-TRAVERS, EdM, AND JORDAN A. OSHLAG, MSW, LICSW

Pressure continues to mount on behavioral health providers to measure outcomes and implement clinical treatment guidelines. This pressure is applied both internally and externally. Internally, clinicians, consumers, and advocates need proof that what they are doing works. Externally, payment sources are demanding evidence that treatment is effective and cost efficient.

Both outcomes measurement and treatment guidelines are critical tools for improving the quality of care, not just controlling the cost of service delivery. However, integrating these tools into an agency's workflow can be extremely challenging. A number of operational changes must be made:

- develop an on-going staff education program;
- perform an analysis of your current client population and treatment practices;
- ensure that clients are accurately diagnosed at the time of admission;
- centralize management of intake, case assignment, and utilization management functions;
- develop written procedures and quality assurance measures for all operational functions;
- put in place a nimble management information system with up-to-date client and service data; and
- develop information resource management skills.

Develop an On-Going Staff Education Program

Staff education is critical to successful implementation and usage of clinical guidelines and outcomes. An education program should be developed for both clinical and administrative staff, and this program should be on-going.

Inform clinical staff about health insurance, managed care models, and current public sector managed care projects. No longer can we separate fiscal and business office matters from clinical service delivery. Clinicians should have an understanding of insurance coverage and the basic information and procedures required to collect payment. They should understand the various measures used by payers to manage the cost of service delivery (e.g., preferred provider networks, service authorizations, reduced fee arrangements, treatment protocols, and perfor-

---

Joseph Naughton-Travers, EdM, is the founder of Behavioral Health Advantage, a Greensboro NC-based company offering training and consulting services to behavioral health providers. He has presented both regionally and nationally on outpatient practice analysis and data collection, provider profiling, data warehousing, and using technology to improve care delivery.

Jordan A. Oshlag, MSW, LICSW, is manager of Implementation and Special Projects at Hill Associates Healthcare Management Systems in Sudbury MA. In addition to his work at Hill Associates, Oshlag is a nationally recognized presenter in Solution Focused Brief Therapy and has had extensive clinical experience working with adolescents and adult populations in a variety of settings. He is the author, with Susan Lee Tohn, of Crossing the Bridge: Integrating Solution Focused Therapy Into Clinical Practice *(Solutions Press, 2nd edition, 1997).*

mance specifications) and receive detailed training on the operational and paperwork requirements of the payers that affect their clients. Build consensus with clinical staff by focusing on using guidelines and outcome measures to *improve care delivery*, not just to manage cost or comply with payer requirements.

Develop in-service training about clinical guidelines, specialty treatments, and outcome implementation projects. Most clinical staff have had little formal training in these issues. Teach clinical staff using information gathered from conferences, professional journals, and experts in the field. Inform them about additional treatment models that can improve care delivery, such as Solution Focused Brief Therapy, and innovative interventions with specific client populations (e.g., the latest medication therapies). Include clinical staff in the development of outcome implementation plans by reviewing the experiences of other agencies and focusing on how the results will benefit clients.

Instruct clinical staff in how to analyze client populations and clinical practice patterns. Clinical guidelines are "...intended to augment, not supplant, the clinician's decisionmaking process" (Brown & Kornmayer, p. 31). Your staff should be able to step back from the details of their daily clinical work to analyze and evaluate their clinical practice. Presentations about the agency's client demographic and diagnostic mix, length of treatment by diagnosis, and client satisfaction and outcome data by client type are excellent tools for fostering discussion about treatment practices and care improvement. This is particularly effective when the agency focuses on the *processes* of providing care, not on the performance of individual clinicians.

Teach administrative staff the reasons for guidelines and outcome measures and train all staff in how to educate clients about their purpose and benefits. Reception and office staff often answer client questions about the agency and may be involved in administering satisfaction or outcome instruments. It is important that they understand that these tools will be used to improve the quality of care. All staff members should be comfortable answering basic questions from clients. It may be helpful to prepare a "fact sheet" so that there is a consistent message from the agency. It could answer such questions as:

- Why do I answer questionnaires and tests prior to receiving treatment?
- Are my results kept confidential?
- What does the agency do with my opinions and test results?
- How will these tests benefit me?
- Do I have to take these tests?
- Will my therapist see this?
- Can someone help me fill these out?
- Will I get to see the test results?

Have regular meetings to share and discuss data with clinical staff. Feedback about service delivery and effectiveness can be useful only if it is immediate. As data about treatment practices and effectiveness emerge, present it to clinical staff for discussion. Discussion points can include:

- Does the information make sense for our client population, or does it appear that something is missing?
- Do we need more information?
- Does the information suggest ways that we might improve care?
- If so, how do we implement the changes, and test them?
- Might additional staff training be helpful?
- What are we doing right with those cases that are successful?

Perform an Analysis of Your Current Client Population's Demographics and Your Treatment Practices

This seems fairly straight forward, but proves to be difficult for many organizations. It is common to hear program managers unable to get reports on basic information such as a current caseload or client diagnosis list.

Basic client demographic and treatment information is vital to understanding outcome measures (Naughton-Travers and Oshlag, 1997). If you are measuring progress on clients' basic functionality, knowing whether your population includes 5 or 25 percent severely and persistently mentally ill clients is crucial. A diagnostic mix report will quickly tell you whether the overall profile matches your expectations of the population makeup. Additionally, knowing the diagnostic profile of your agency helps in selecting appropriate clinical guidelines.

Chapter 2: The Mechanics of Measurement

Minimally, your analysis should yield the following information:
- number of active clients,
- gender mix,
- age mix,
- percentage of identified severely and persistently mentally ill clients,
- primary payer mix,
- diagnostic mix (primary diagnosis by DSM IV categories),
- service modality mix (procedure by DSM IV categories),
- medication usage by diagnosis,
- average length of treatment (sessions by DSM IV categories), and
- treatment intensity (session by time period).

Share the demographic information with clinical staff and watch for changes over time. This is probably the most important step. Clinical staff can only help to improve care delivery and manage cost if they understand who their clients are and how they are treating them. This also involves them in the management of service delivery and helps them to develop their practice analysis and utilization management skills.

Ensure That Clients Are Accurately Diagnosed At the Time of Admission

The clinical diagnosis is a critical component of most treatment guideline mechanisms, outcome measurement, and expert systems. In fact, some consider it *the* key component. Given its importance, how the diagnosis is formulated, tracked, and changed over time when necessary are critical operational issues. Organizations should have procedures in place to monitor this critical function. The diagnosis can affect a number of important factors, including, but not limited to: whether treatment itself is paid for, the number of sessions authorized by the managed care organization, the treatment modality and philosophy, the expected length of treatment, what medications may be warranted, the rate of reimbursement in capitated payment arrangements, and even the type of clinician assigned to the case.

In the past decade, technology has greatly expanded the ways to arrive at an initial diagnosis. Traditional methods have been augmented by an explosion of expert systems that assist clinicians in formulating the initial diagnosis as well as provide the clinician other valuable information.

Use your most experienced clinicians to conduct intakes and review diagnostic formulations. Some agencies use "intake" staff (interns or less experienced clinicians) to conduct the initial evaluation, sometimes assisted by level-of-functioning measurement tools such as the BASIS-32 (Eisen, Dill, and Grob, 1994), TOPS (Access Measurement Systems), and the Beck Depression Scale (Beck, 1978). Because of the critical role the diagnosis plays in formulating treatment plans, managing utilization, and determining reimbursement, we believe that this approach is no longer sufficient. For example, psychological testing can be helpful in completing differential diagnoses and should be readily available. Instruments include the Minnesota Multiphasic Personality Inventory (MMPI-2), the Symptom Checklist 90-Revised (SCL-90-R) and the Personality Assessment Inventory (PAI) (Hays, 1995; Moreland, 1996). Another advantage of using your most experienced clinicians to conduct intakes is the higher possibility that clear, well-formed goals will be drawn up during the diagnostic interview, thus shortening therapy (Tohn and Oshlag, 1995).

Get the right diagnosis into your MIS and keep it up to date. Coinciding with the rapid increase in the methods and tools used to formulate diagnosis are the opportunities for this process to go awry. For example, one ambulatory provider with whom we have worked routinely assigned the same diagnosis to all clients upon initial intake. This diagnosis was later changed in the medical record to the correct one, but was never changed in the management information system. Another oft-heard complaint among billing staff is the complete absence of the diagnosis by clinical staff; billing staff are often given permission to input a default diagnosis in order to bill claims. In the 1998 Massachusetts Data Warehouse project (Naughton-Travers and Oshlag, 1998), we discovered that 9.6 percent of the population of 193,884 clients had no diagnosis recorded at all.

Instruct your clinical staff that it is no longer appropriate to give clients a "light" diagnosis. Some clinicians will give a client a less "severe" diagnosis in an effort to protect the client. Although it is true that certain diagnoses can negatively affect clients—e.g., by falling into the hands of a life insurance company (Sykes Wylie, 1995; Cohn, 1998)—the practice of under-diagnosing is misguided. It is essential for outcomes and expert systems, not to mention good treatment, to accurately diagnosis each client. If a clinician assigns an adjustment disorder with depressed mood (309.0) and not a Major Depressive Disorder, Single Episode (296.2x) (APA, 1994), the entire treatment protocol may be altered and potentially misdirected.

Given the potential for misdiagnosing, not diagnosing at all, or not getting this information to the proper people, organizations should have solid and reliable protocols and procedures for gathering and disseminating diagnostic information.

Centralize Management of Intake, Case Assignment, And Utilization Management Functions

In order to effectively utilize the guidelines and outcome measures in which an agency invests, the organization should develop an efficient method for integrating information into daily practice. Integration can occur in the following main areas: intake, case assignment, on-going treatment planning, and utilization management. In addition to integration, each of these areas provides additional information that must be continuously fed back into the process. (See Exhibit 1.) A paradigm to frame this feedback loop is what Bologna and Feldman (1995) describe as treatment redesign and system redelivery:

> Treatment redesign refers to changes in the specific interventions and treatment techniques that comprise the client's full episode of care; the initial interview, the therapy and the medications. System redelivery refers to change in the operational and administrative structures that support gradual transitions in the treatment path.

In today's market, agencies have multiple product lines and sites that often make it unfeasible to truly centralize the intake, case assignment, and utilization management functions. However, centralization of the *management* of these functions is essential for integrating guidelines and outcomes.

It is crucial for an organization to determine what information is vital to gather at the point of intake. This will vary depending on the population served, funding sources, goals of the organization, and intake method used. Intake methods generally fall into one of two categories described in Exhibit 2. Each starts with a phone call and then a face-to-face interview. Most phone procedures include collecting basic client demographic information, determining if the client has been seen by the organization in the past, services being sought, the appropriateness of the referral, the client's current level of functioning, and payer information. Although the initial assessment interview varies greatly from organization to organization, it is crucial that the approach used *within* an organization be consistent.

Outcomes and guidelines can be utilized in a variety of ways at this stage. As Panzarino (1996) points out, "Pretreatment measures should provide predictive data to identify high risk or non-compliant patients" (p. 70). Outcomes results can assist in developing the initial diagnosis, establish baselines of functionality (e.g., the GAF, TOPS), and provide valuable information to both clinician and client.

If an organization has predetermined what information is important to gather at the initial stage of treatment, it becomes possible to collect consistent data from clients. Another advantage of centralizing the intake process is the ability to detect and gather missing data as early as possible in treatment (Berman & Hurt, 1996).

Centralizing the management of the case assignment function allows an organization to employ outcomes and guidelines in guiding case assignment, thus improving treatment. *What is the best treatment for a 27-year-old female presenting with depression and possible post-traumatic stress? If the client prefers a female therapist and is not appropriate for group therapy, which of the clinicians on staff can provide the most clinically sound and cost effective treatment?* Hand-in-hand with case assignment is centralized appointment scheduling. This allows the most timely assignment of cases because the scheduler knows all available appointments in clinicians' schedule.

Chapter 2: The Mechanics of Measurement

Exhibit 1.

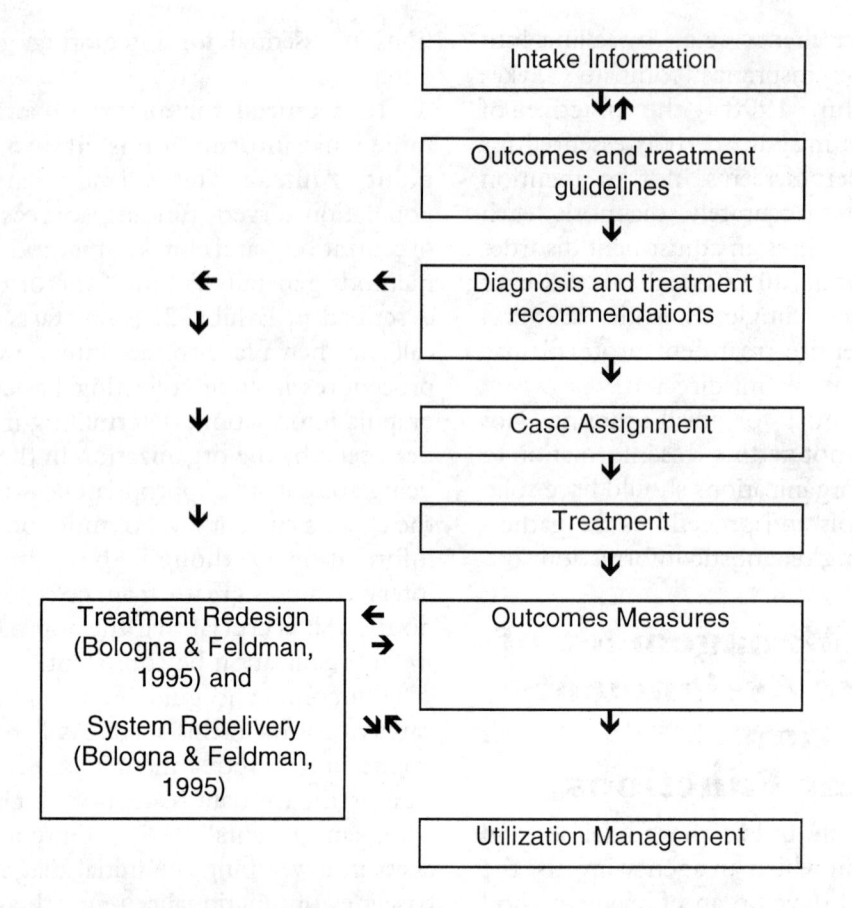

```
                    ┌─────────────────────────┐
                    │   Intake Information    │
                    └─────────────────────────┘
                              ↓↑
                    ┌─────────────────────────┐
                    │ Outcomes and treatment  │
                    │       guidelines        │
                    └─────────────────────────┘
                              ↓
         ←        ← ┌─────────────────────────┐
         ↓          │ Diagnosis and treatment │
                    │     recommendations     │
                    └─────────────────────────┘
                              ↓
         ↓          ┌─────────────────────────┐
                    │     Case Assignment     │
                    └─────────────────────────┘
                              ↓
         ↓          ┌─────────────────────────┐
                    │        Treatment        │
                    └─────────────────────────┘
                              ↓
┌─────────────────┐         ┌─────────────────────────┐
│Treatment Redesign│   ←    │    Outcomes Measures    │
│(Bologna & Feldman│        │                         │
│     1995) and    │   →    │                         │
│                  │        └─────────────────────────┘
│ System Redelivery│  ↘↖              ↓
│(Bologna & Feldman│
│      1995)      │         ┌─────────────────────────┐
└─────────────────┘         │  Utilization Management │
                            └─────────────────────────┘
```

Use outcomes and guidelines information to modify treatment plans over time. If outcome or level-of-functioning measures are periodically recorded during the treatment process, they can be used to modify the treatment if it is proving ineffective. It is vital that this information be fed back to both the clinician and client when appropriate.

Utilization management is the focal point for clinical guidelines and outcome usage. Whether your agency is using a simple measure of client progress (such as the Solution Focused Progress Scale (Tohn & Oshlag, 1995)) or a more sophisticated outcome measure (such as the TOPS), centralized utilization management allows controlled and purposeful application of outcomes and guidelines. By analyzing data trends, organizations can determine what is working and what needs improvement. As Berman and Hurt (1996) emphasize, it is critical to focus attention on the process, not the people. Things can backfire if clinicians believe they are the "target" of outcomes (e.g., measuring productivity, progress, and client satisfaction).

Exhibit 2. Intake Methods

Intake Method	Description
Dedicated Intake Staff	Basic information is gathered over the phone to determine the appropriateness of the referral to the system of care, level of functioning, and an initial interview is scheduled. This information is often gathered by non-clinical staff. After the initial interview is conducted, and the case is assigned a therapist.
Direct Clinician Assignment	Detailed information is gathered over the phone and based upon it, a clinician is assigned. The clinician completes the intake interview and continues as the primary therapist unless treatment factors dictate changing therapists.

The centralized utilization management staff is also responsible for disseminating the information to clinical staff for discussion and analysis. As an agency becomes more proficient at implementing these tools, it can also benefit from pooling data with other providers, creating data warehouses as a way to establish benchmarks and provide comparisons to a larger population. For example, for a given type of client it is useful to know what the average number of sessions is, the average client satisfaction, and what treatment guidelines result in the best treatment outcome. A data warehouse uses more information to generate this "best practice" data and gives agencies an exceptional marketing tool if they can demonstrate equally effective treatment at lower cost than can other providers.

Develop Written Procedures and Quality Assurance Measures for All Operational Functions

To successfully integrate outcomes and treatment guidelines into practice, data integrity must be maintained. Although time-consuming, creating written procedures for all aspects of data collection and analysis is well worth the time invested. Procedures should cover the following areas: initial data collection, case assignment, outcomes, medication, treatment plan variations, and information dissemination. Below is a partial list of the information necessary in each procedural area:

- **Initial data collection**. Is the information being gathered in a timely fashion? Do paper forms and data-entry function flow smoothly and ensure that all elements are recorded? How are missing data elements tracked and handled? Do quality assurance functions ensure that the information is as complete and accurate as possible? How are changes in client information recorded in a timely manner?
- **Case assignment**. Are the guidelines functional? Can clinicians be assigned by gender, language, location, areas of expertise (as defined by training and historical outcome analysis), and ability to bill the payer? How do the procedures ensure rapid access to care? How is the case assignment process modified based on ongoing utilization and outcome analysis?
- **Outcomes**. Are outcomes instruments administered at the proper time periods? What percentage of post-treatment measurements are obtained? What efforts are made to increase this number? Are there procedures to analyze the reasons for non-participation by staff or clients?
- **Medication**. What medications (dosage and frequency) are clients taking? How are changes in medication tracked? What procedures are in place to report current medication information to clinicians and psychiatrists for review?
- **Treatment plan variations**. Based on the guidelines, how are variations from the treatment plan reported and evaluated? How are modifications in treatment plans processed and recorded?
- **Information dissemination**. How and when is utilization and outcome information disseminated to staff? Is it provided in a useful format? How is it integrated into practice? What procedures are in place to ensure that feedback about the usefulness of the information is received and processed? How are requests for details or further analysis handled?

Put in Place a Nimble Management Information System With Up-To-Date Client and Service Data

One of the greatest challenges that providers face is finding and effectively utilizing a client information system. The search process can be time-consuming and expensive. Monica Oss of the Gettysburg PA-based behavioral consulting firm Open Minds estimates that between 3 and 7 percent of the budgets of agencies with less than $10 million in annual revenue is likely to be spent on technology-related functions (Oss, 1997, p.6). While it is beyond the scope of this work to detail all of the selection criteria for a software system, we will highlight the critical functions and operational obstacles.

The MIS must contain online, real-time information about all clients and service delivery. Part of this is simply a matter of how the software works. *Do staff have access to the most recently entered data, or is there an "update" process that must be run before this can occur?* Operationally, providers must build processes that ensure that data entry occurs rapidly. *Are new clients registered in the MIS at the time of service, or days later? Are rendered services recorded immediately?*

Having both software functionality and operations that ensure up-to-date information is critical for managing care and cost. This allows the centralized intake, case assignment, and utilization management staffs to analyze and use the information immediately. In addition, they can quickly identify cases that are outliers to guidelines or care protocols, they have up-to-date information about outcomes for case assignment and treatment plan modification, and they can share information with clinicians about their treatment practices and effectiveness immediately, not weeks or months after service delivery.

The information must be accurate, and available at the point-of-service. As mentioned, a system must be in place to ensure that information is accurately recorded. Additionally, both clinical and administrative staff must have access to the information at their work locations. Historically, computer access to the MIS has only been available in business and clerical offices. This is insufficient to meet the needs of today's providers.

The system must have flexibility to accommodate changes. A "nimble" management information system allows a reasonable amount of flexibility for adding new data requirements or developing new reports. The system does not have to be 100 percent customizable, nor should providers expect the software to last for a decade. Rather, it should be flexible enough to accommodate moderate changes in information needs in a timely manner.

For example, when a provider decides to begin recording outcome measures over time, there must be a way to record and report the information. If the utilization management staff needs to track medication and dosage information for clients for quality review purposes, there must be a way to customize the software so that it contains the list of medications and possible dosages.

The information must be easily accessible by staff. Obviously, all of the information is useless if the provider has no way to access it. A "good enough" MIS is one that has a report generator that accesses all of the data fields in the software. The ideal one (which we have not yet located) has a brilliant, easy-to-use interface that leads novice users through the process of gathering the information they need. The more common and currently available option is to train staff about basic reports and report generation functions, and to have software experts available to assist them.

But we believe that the greater challenge lies not in the MIS software itself, but in the developing skills necessary for staff to use the information for managing their daily work.

Develop Information Resource Management Skills

As systems of care become more sophisticated in their usage of clinical guidelines and outcomes, it becomes increasingly critical that all levels of staff become literate in the acquisition and usage of information about clients and service delivery. It will no longer be sufficient to refer questions to the resident "MIS expert"; rather, individual clinical and administrative staff must become more self-sufficient in obtaining and using information in their daily work.

John Diebold describes this information literacy as "...basically a matter of making users aware of the potential of the information resource, and then teaching them how to utilize it most effectively to meet their individual needs" (Diebold, 1985, p. 42). He describes this new way of thinking about information usage as "Information Resource Management"—that is "...managing information as a resource in much the same way as other...resources are managed" (Diebold, 1985, p.41). This means that staff must not only understand what information is available and how to access it, but they must be sensitive to the cost and process of acquisition. For example, tracking 100 different demographic factors about clients may be helpful to both marketing and utilization management staff, but the cost of obtaining and accurately recording it may be prohibitive. The key is to find a balance between the cost and potential yield and for staff to understand how to sort through the choices.

So what does this mean for an individual behavioral health provider? What are the information resource management competencies that they should have in place?

We start with the basics. **All clinical and administrative staff should have access to, and a basic understanding of, the agency management information system.** The ideal scenario is one of desktop access with basic, real-time reporting. This also means that agencies must invest a significant amount of time and money in training staff about the management information system.

Clinical staff must have immediate and up-to-date access to information about their current clients. For example, they should be immediately able to report the number of active clients, the dates of service and services provided, significant clinical events, medications, level-of-functioning and outcome measures, compliance with protocols and guidelines, and authorization requirements. Utilization management staff must quickly be able to access length of treatment information and to identify cases that are outliers to clinical guidelines and treatment plans.

The clerical administrative staff should be able to access appointment information, medical records requirements and reminders, and client-care provider information. Frequently, they must be familiar with overall MIS reporting capabilities because they are used as an informal software "help desk" by all other staff.

How do I get a list of clients on Prozac? Where do we enter the BASIS-32 scores? How do I find out which of my clients need additional authorization for services? How do I make this report stop running? These are examples of the countless questions that clerical staff encounter from clinicians and managers alike.

Executive and financial administrative staff need daily access to summary service delivery, financial, and quality information. For example, agencies should be able to easily report up-to-date productivity and revenue numbers, capitated contract usage information in summary format, and overall outcome and satisfaction information. Cases that are high-risk clinically and financially should be able to be flagged and managed. Managerial staff usually need to access and understand the more sophisticated query capabilities of the management information reporting system in order to analyze service delivery and the cost and effectiveness of treatment.

Agencies must designate an Information Resource Manager to be a resource for managerial staff. This is a high-level manager who understands what information is collected by the agency and the operational processes for gathering and reporting it. This is not the "computer repair" specialist or clerical help desk position found at most agencies. Rather, the Information Resource Manager (or Chief Information Officer that many companies now have) is available to advise management staff about access and usage of information.

For example, suppose a managed care payer institutes a number of performance specifications for its provider network—care access guidelines, clinical guidelines and protocols, and detailed case management reporting for high utilizing clients. The Information Resource Manager should be available to review the requirements, determine data tracking and reporting needs, and recommend operational procedures that will be efficient and cost-effective. The skills required for this position are difficult to find—a blend of clinical, fiscal, and operational knowledge combined with overall computer and software literacy.

Summary

These operational recommendations will be daunting for some providers. They involve great investments of time and money and are system-wide in nature. Successful integration requires a constant and clear vision from executive staff about the benefit of implementing outcomes results and treatment guidelines, with a watchful eye to the continuing changes in the industry.

Bibliography

Access Measurement Systems, Inc., 1996. [P.O. Box 365, Ashland MA 01721.]

American Psychiatric Association. *Diagnostic and Statistical Manual of Mental Disorders*, Fourth Edition. Washington DC: American Psychiatric Association, 1994.

Beck AT. *Depression Inventory*. Philadelphia: Philadelphia Center for Cognitive Therapy, 1978.

Chapter 2: The Mechanics of Measurement

Berman W, Hurt S.. Talking the Talk, Walking the Walk: Implementing an Outcomes Information System. *Behavioral Healthcare Tomorrow* June 1996:39-43.

Bologna N and Feldman M. Using Outcomes Data and Clinical Process Redesign: Improving Clinical Services. *Behavioral Healthcare Tomorrow* November/December 1995:59-61.

Brown GS and Kornmayer K. Expert Systems Restructure Managed Care Practice: Implementation and Ethics. *Behavioral Healthcare Tomorrow* 1996; 5(1):31-34.

Cohn J. Mangling Care. *The New Republic* 1998; 219(6):15-16.

Diebold J. *Managing Information: The Challenge and the Opportunity.* New York: AMACOM—A Division of the American Management Association, 1985.

Eisen S, Dill D, and Grob M. Reliability and Validity of a Brief Patient-Report Instrument for Psychiatric Outcome Evaluation. *Hospital and Community Psychiatry* 1994; 45:242-247.

Hays L.. Relating Psychological Testing to Prognosis and Outcomes. *Behavioral Health Management* September/October 1995:21-25.

Kraus D and Horan F. Outcomes Roadblocks: Problems and Solutions. *Behavioral Health Management* September/October 1997:22-25.

Moreland K. How Psychological Testing Can Reinstate Its Value in an Era of Cost Containment. *Behavioral Healthcare Tomorrow* February 1996:59-61.

Naughton-Travers J and Oshlag J. *Analyzing Outpatient Practice Patterns: The Massachusetts' Data Pool.* Company Report: Hill Associates Healthcare Management Systems, 1997.

Naughton-Travers J and Oshlag J. *The Massachusetts' Data Warehouse: 1995 to Early 1998.* Company Report: Hill Associates Healthcare Management Systems, 1998.

Naughton-Travers J and Oshlag J. Executive Decision Making Through Data Warehousing. *Behavioral Health Management* 1998; 18(1):23-26.

Oss M. Information Technology: At the Heart of Change. *Behavioral Health Management* January/February 1997:6.

Panzarino P. Outcomes Management Makes Strides in Quality Accountability. *Behavioral Healthcare Tomorrow* 1996; December:69-71.

Sykes Wylie M. Diagnosing For Dollars? *The Family Therapy Networker* May/June 1995:23-33.

Tohn S and Oshlag J. *Crossing the Bridge: Integrating Solution Focused Therapy Into Clinical Practice.* Natick: Solutions Press, 1995.

Implementing Outcomes in the Real World of Clinical Service Delivery

JOHN S. LYONS, PHD, AND ZORAN MARTINOVICH, PHD

"Make no small plans."
—Daniel Burnham

While Daniel Burnham's grand advice has been credited with establishing the beautiful lakeside city parks that dramatically enhance the quality of life in Chicago, it is probably not the way to conceptualize an outcomes management project. The single most challenging aspect of successful outcomes management, even more than measurement and analytic design issues, is ensuring that outcomes management is successfully implemented and embedded into clinical operations. Starting small and emphasizing feasibility are important guiding principles in this regard.

Behind the concept of feasibility is the ideal of fitting the collection of outcomes data into the ongoing, standard operations of clinical service delivery. At a minimum, the collection of these data should not burden service delivery. In the best case, collection of outcomes data might be used to reduce other paperwork or improve the process of communication within the clinical operation. If outcomes data collection does burden service delivery, it is absolutely essential that the information collected be used in a way that serves the clinical enterprise; either through quality improvement reports or funding justification.

Thus, in many ways decisions about implementing any outcomes management initiative have greater implications than any decisions about what measures to use or what methodology to employ. In fact, these decisions should be informed by any impact that they might have on issues of implementation. This article is an attempt to discuss some of the most salient challenges to the effective implementation of an outcomes management project. The article is divided into two sections. The first reviews some of the common challenges facing outcomes management and opportunities to address these challenges. The second discusses an eight-stage implementation plan.

Challenges and Opportunities

Addressing Ethical Issues

The introduction of outcomes management approaches into behavioral health care service delivery forces us to confront a series of novel ethical issues. There are two levels of ethical concern. First, data collection must follow reasonable ethical strictures. Second, the use of outcomes data must conform to a different set of ethical standards.

The ethics of data collection. Three core principles should inform the ethics of collecting outcomes data: informed consent, choice, and the minimization of any risk of harm resulting from the data collection process. Informed consent requires that you notify service recipients and other respondents regarding the collection of relevant outcomes data and the implications of this process for the delivery of services. At minimum, informed consent requires the service recipient to be notified as to what data are to be collected and how they will be used.

John S. Lyons, PhD, is the director of the Mental Health Services and Policy Program of the Institute for Health Services Research and Policy Studies at Northwestern University. He is an associate professor of Psychiatry and Medicine.

Zoran Martinovich, PhD, is an assistant professor of Psychiatry at Northwestern University Medical School.

Choice requires that the service recipient is given the decision as to whether or not he or she will actively participate in the outcomes measurement process. This choice and its implication for treatment (if any) should be disclosed to the recipient.

Any potential risks of participation should be disclosed. The most common risk is the emotional upset that can come from describing problems in structured interviews or on written forms. Efforts should be made to ensure that outcomes measures are respectful to the service recipient and his or her families. For example, one well-known instrument assessing symptoms of depression in older adults includes an item that asks, "Do you feel particularly helpless the way you are now?" A notable minority of respondents experience this question as insulting.

The ethics of data use. Once data are collected it is important that their use be guided by reasonable ethical standards. Gellman & Frawley (1996) have identified eight common principles of information practices that can be used to guide decisions regarding the use of outcomes data. These principles can be found in Table 1.

In order to ensure that your organization meets these ethical standards, it is recommended that a data committee be established that has the responsibility for the oversight of outcomes management practices. This committee should be comprised of representatives from each of the major stakeholders, including service recipients and their families. Also, use of common identifiers (e.g., social security number) as the unique identifier in an outcomes management project should be minimized. Confidentiality is better protected through using unique identifiers that are not traceable to other common databases.

Table 1. Principles of Ethical Information Management Practices Adapted From Gellman & Frawley (1996).

1.	**Openness.** Whenever data are collected, the subjects of these data should be notified of the existence of data, the purpose for which the data are collected, and their range of use.
2.	**Individual participation.** All subjects of data collection should have the right to view any record of data about themselves. In addition, they should be allowed the opportunity to correct or delete any data that are not timely, accurate, relevant, or complete. This allowance is unnecessary for data that cannot be traced to a specific individual.
3.	**Collection limitation.** When appropriate, prior consent should be obtained from the subject of any data collection. In addition, limits should be established with regard to the amount and type of personal information that can and should be collected from individual subjects.
4.	**Data quality.** The entity collecting data has the responsibility to ensure that all data are accurate, complete, timely, and relevant to the purposes for which they are used. Allowing inaccurate information to inform decisionmaking is unethical.
5.	**Use limitation.** Clear limitations should be established for the use of individual data within any organization. Not all members of the organization have a right to access personal information.
6.	**Disclosure limitations.** No communication of individual data that has any potential, no matter how remote, of being traced back to that individual should occur outside of the organization collecting data without the written consent of the subject of that data or his/her guardian or another responsible legal authority.
7.	**Security.** Reasonable security precautions should be taken to ensure that individual data is protected against the risks of loss, unauthorized access, destruction, modification, and disclosure by parties both within and outside of the agency collecting the data.
8.	**Accountability.** Individuals within the organization collecting data should be held accountable for adhering to the above principles of ethical information management.

Building in Service Recipient Involvement

One of the more exciting advancements in outcomes management in the past several years has been the growing inclusion of service recipients, their families, and advocates in the process of measuring and managing outcomes. This participation can occur at a number of different levels.

The lowest level of consumer involvement is as respondents in outcomes measurement. This is a recommended standard except in those situations where it is clinically inappropriate to attempt to obtain recipient measures. An example of such a situations would include crisis and inpatient admission assessments, where the individual service recipient may be experiencing a high level of emotional upset.

Beyond simply obtaining the recipient perspective through measurement, there are a variety of other models of consumer involvement in outcomes management initiatives. This involvement can include the planning phase, the operational phase, or the interpretative phase of outcomes projects.

Organizational Issues

Over the past several decades quality assurance, improvement, and management requirements have led nearly all mental health service organizations to develop some organizational capacity that can be used for outcomes projects. Often, however, the style with which these organizations empower quality management committees has a dramatic impact on the meaningfulness of the effort.

At the one extreme, some organizations view quality efforts as a necessary process to ensure funding and/or accreditation but as irrelevant to service delivery. In these organizations outcomes measurement and management initiatives are seen as a nuisance forced onto the organization by external authorities. Quality committees have essentially no power as change agents within the organization and membership is seen as a responsibility, perhaps even a chore. At the other extreme, some organizations take outcomes and other quality data as a critical source of information for management decisions. In these organizations, the quality process is embedded in normal organization structures (i.e., it is not an add-on) and compliance with the requirements of external accrediting and funding agencies is simply a process of documenting and communicating normal business processes.

Clearly, organizations that value data will have greater success implementing outcomes management projects. If the organizational culture suggests that the project is a nuisance, it will be difficult to overcome the many operational and psychological barriers to implementation. On the other hand, even in organizations that value outcomes data, it is still necessary to create an organizational culture that views data as an opportunity for learning rather than a threat to personal autonomy. Creating a learning organization culture (e.g., Senge, 1990) is an important organizational priority that can spur successful outcomes management projects.

Nuts and Bolts: Fitting Outcomes Measurement To Operations

As mentioned earlier, fitting outcomes management to the clinical service delivery operations is a critical issue in effective implementation. Failure to accomplish a good fit will result in operational friction that can easily lead to incomplete or expensive data collection that over the long run will result in the failure of the project.

There are several key principles for addressing operational issues. These are summarized below:

1. **Keep data collection short and simple**. Excessive paperwork slows down the process of completing forms and can delay service delivery operations. It has been our experience that clinicians are willing to do no more than three to five minutes of extra paperwork in order to cooperate with an outcomes project. Service recipients often are willing to invest more time, but data collection that takes more than 10 to 15 minutes is likely to be too much.

2. **Schedule data collection consistent with service delivery. Data collection should flow with service delivery**. If a service recipient undergoes an intake interview, this is an appropriate time to collect demographic, case-mix, and baseline outcome data. Providers of outpatient

services seldom know when the last session will occur. Therefore, collection of outcome data at multiple time points over the course of treatment is needed to ensure that end-of-treatment outcomes can at least be estimated.

3. **Have a single person responsible for monitoring data collection compliance.** It is essential for the success of any outcomes project to have a "persnickety"—someone who is watching carefully to monitor the completeness and timeliness of data collection. This person must have the authority (or, at least, access to authority) to hold respondents accountable for participation in data collection.

4. **Hold respondents accountable for complete and timely data.** It is generally necessary to make respondents accountable for participation. This is difficult for service recipient measures, although incentives for participation serve the same purpose. For clinician measures, it is often necessary to make compliance with outcomes measurement a clearly defined aspect of good job performance.

5. **Use the information at all levels of the organization within a reasonable time frame.** The more meaningful the outcomes information becomes to all stakeholders within an organization, the more successful an outcomes management project will become. Timeliness is an important aspect of use; therefore, speedy turnaround of outcomes data for feedback to participants is important. Computers make nearly instantaneous feedback possible.

Building Enthusiasm, Overcoming Resistance

Beyond establishing organizational support for outcomes management, which generally is an issue of leadership, it is similarly important to create some enthusiasm for these efforts at all layers of an organization. Since outcomes management tools can be viewed as a new technology, it is useful to apply some of the research on technology innovation to this issue. One can generally expect three basic classes of reaction to any technological innovation:

Technophiles: These staff love new innovations. They buy new technology as it becomes available and love to be the first to try anything. The challenge of managing these staff is to keep things interesting. While they eagerly adopt new technology they just as easily get bored with existing tools.

Ambivalents: These staff will use new technology once you demonstrate its usefulness to them. They will not be interested in being the first, but as soon it is clearly in their best interests, they will willingly adopt new technology.

Technophobes: These staff will resist any new technology, often to extremes. This resistance can take any form, from passive sabotage to active hostility. It is generally very difficult to get these individuals to change their habits and participate in any innovation. Threatened job action is commonly needed for compliance within this group.

It is often useful to build on the enthusiasm of "technophiles" in the early stages of implementation. However, one should be careful to include strong representatives from the larger class of "ambivalents" to ensure that the utility of participation becomes known within the larger organization culture. The "ambivalents" often have the greatest credibility in presenting the utility of new tools. Sometimes it is possible to "marginalize" the negative impact of particularly vocal or influential "technophobes" by including them in the planning process. Be careful, though; they can derail the entire enterprise.

Guidelines for Implementation

Stage 1. Assessing Organization Needs and Priorities

The first step in implementing an outcomes project is to undertake an organizational review to determine what the organization's needs and priorities are with regard to outcomes. Either external factors or internal organizational considerations, or some combination of both, might drive both needs and priorities. The different implications for implementation of externally- versus internally-driven priorities are significant.

As an example of external pressure for outcomes, an accreditation body or third-party payer might be requiring that the organization implement an outcomes management effort. These entities may specify what outcomes to measure or may provide a limited set of measurement choices. For example, the Joint Commission on Accreditation of Healthcare Organizations' ORYX initiative provides a list of outcomes measures that have been approved for use. The advantage of externally motivated outcomes management is that it is often easier to implement because the organization must. The disadvantage of these projects is that they often end up as somewhat trivial efforts to "document" outcomes rather than learn from them.

Internal needs often create a very different type of pressure for outcomes management. These needs include factors such as the interest of a particular staff member(s) in pursuing outcomes management, or a service-delivery problem identified within the organization for which clear information was lacking. Without external pressure, motivating the organization becomes somewhat more difficult. The enthusiasm of the parties with interest in the project become a critical driving force in getting things done. On the other hand, the use of information collected in these types of projects is often much more dramatic than for outcomes management projects whose primary intent is to appease some external monitoring body.

Given the above considerations, it is important to initially establish the reasons that an outcomes management project should be initiated and the goals it is intended to achieve. These reasons and goals likely will be multiple. After the project has been fully implemented, it is instructive to return to these reasons and goals to evaluate the success of the implementation process.

Stage 2. Selecting Measures And Methods

Once organizational needs and priorities are established, the second step of implementation is to decide what measures to use. Table 2 presents eight primary principles of outcome measurement selection. Clearly, if some external entity specifies the choice of measures, this imposes certain constraints. However, even in these circumstances, it might be worth considering adding an additional measure or measures if there is concern that the required measures will fall short of the goals of

Table 2. Principles of Outcome Measurement (Adapted from Lyons, Howard, O-Mahoney & Lish, 1997)

What To Measure
I. Define the goals and objectives of the service(s) for which outcomes should be measured. Ensure that selected measures are consistent with these goals and objectives
II. Involve all stakeholders in the process of determining outcome priorities. This should include payers, providers, administrators, service recipients, and advocates.
III. Determine what is possible and practical to measure. It may be necessary to measure only certain outcomes and not others or to use multiple phases of a project with different measures.

How To Measure
IV. Use or build on existing measures. There are more than 1,400 different outcome measures available.
V. Design methodology (who uses measures when) based on the nature of the intervention and the operations used to provide it.
VI. Choose measures that are reliable, valid, brief, and easy-to-use.

When To Measure
VII. Begin measurement at the earliest possible time.
VIII. When the end of treatment is unknown, always measure on a fixed schedule that ensures that most cases will receive multiple assessments so that change can at least be estimated.

good outcome measurement. The most common shortcomings of required outcomes measures are that they are too long to be practical (e.g., the Addiction Severity Index), or they measure a construct that is not clearly the correct outcomes goal (e.g., Family Empowerment Scale), or they cannot be used reliably in unstructured clinical settings (e.g., the Global Assessment Scale or Global Assessment of Functioning).

Reliability in outcomes management projects is a somewhat complicated consideration. For rating scales, inter-rater reliability (e.g., kappa coefficient) is a conservative but reasonable requirement. A minimum kappa of 0.70 should be required at training. Inter-rater reliability should be periodically monitored to protect against "reliability decay" (see below).

When an outcome measure involves the assessment of a subjective internal state, reliability becomes difficult to prove. Test-retest reliability makes little sense for states that show substantial individual differences in change across instrument administrations. In such a case, rank ordering of scores may change substantially from administration to administration, yielding a low test-retest reliability even if the scale accurately and precisely measures individual differences. The standard psychometric approach in these circumstances is to use internal consistency reliability (e.g., Cronbach's alpha). These statistics assess whether or not the items in a scale "hang together." For high internal consistency reliability, there needs to be multiple items that measure the same construct. However, this requires more items than are ideal in clinical operations, where time is of the essence. You may find yourself sacrificing demonstrable reliability for self-report measures, as is routinely done in consumer satisfaction measurement, in order to assess a wider range of potentially valid outcomes. In cases where outcomes data are intended to be evaluated at an aggregated level (averaging across persons), reliable estimates of averages are possible even when reliabilities for individual scores are limited. In the case where outcomes data have direct applications to the individual clinical case, however, less than ideal reliabilities may be dealt with by repeatedly measuring the same person across occasions (cf., Howard, Moras, Brill, Martinovich, and Lutz, 1996).

Stage 3. Working The Organization

This stage involves preparing the organization for action. One of the first activities at this stage is describing the measures and methods to the parties involved and giving them an opportunity to comment on the proposed project. Even if most do not take this offer and actually provide input, it provides a context in which later complaints have a lower chance of sabotaging the implementation. In many cases good advice informs changes in the outcomes management protocol.

Another step at this stage is to make it clear to all stakeholders that the organization's leadership supports the project. Such support from leadership is critical to successful implementation. Documentation of this support can be accomplished in many ways. Memoranda of support or having leadership mention the project in meetings are useful strategies.

A third activity that facilitates implementation is to generally talk up the project, particularly with individual staff members who may be less supportive of the effort. There are almost always some individuals who threaten to sabotage organizational innovations. Generally you know who they are prior to any implementation. Be sure to talk up the project with them and try to get a public, verbal commitment from them in support of the project.

Once the project is implemented, it is absolutely essential that all participants receive feedback on the results. If the project is an individual case-level outcomes management intervention, then this feedback takes care of itself. However, if it is a change analysis focused on documenting program effectiveness to an external audience, then it is necessary to make sure that internal audiences receive the information as well.

Stage 4. Pilot Testing

There are several reasons why pilot testing is an important step in implementing any outcomes management project. First and foremost, you do not want errors in measurement and design to go forward and waste everyone's time. It is generally impossible to anticipate every reaction or potential point of friction. Pilot testing allows you the opportunity to debug methods and measures. There are political advantages to pilot testing as well. Sometimes proponents of outcomes management projects must talk up the advantages of a project in order to "sell" it to the organization.

Stage 5. Training and Initiation

Perhaps it goes without saying, but all participants should be trained prior to the full implementation of the project. This might include training to some reliability criteria on rating measures. Training should always include training in the protocol so that the information is collected consistently and processed efficiently.

The actual initiation of the project should begin on a set date that has been announced at least several weeks ahead of time. The level of monitoring the project in the first few weeks should be intensive. This is necessary to ensure that the protocol becomes an efficient part of standard operating procedures. An individual (or individuals for some multiple-site projects) should have responsibility for the successful initiation of the project. This individual does not have to be senior in the organization management, but he or she should be persistent with good interpersonal skills. This person should also report to someone who is senior in the organization so that leadership leverage can be used if problems should ensue. The most likely problem is staff resistance or sabotage.

Stage 6. Maintenance And Management

There are a set of priorities for the ongoing maintenance of an outcomes management project. First, it is important to maintain the reliability of measures. Rating scales in particular are subject to what is often called 'reliability decay'. Without attention, raters tend to forget criteria and training and develop idiosyncratic ways of using measures. Reliability can be maintained by periodic monitoring and/or retraining.

Second, as mentioned above, it is important that information is processed quickly and accurately. Use of information in a timely manner is a central mechanism of project maintenance. Particularly with rapidly changing service systems, outcomes data can fall out of date fairly rapidly. Also, if participants believe that the information is not used, then compliance with measurement protocols begins to decline. This decline can escalate quickly to make projects irrelevant.

Third, some attention must be paid to the potential of "gaming" the system. Gaming refers to efforts to misrepresent clinical information in an effort to achieve some secondary goal. There are three ways to minimize these effects:

1. Use of multiple informants. Different stakeholders have different secondary goals, so measuring across stakeholders provides some balance to the misrepresentation of any single participant.
2. Use of independent raters. This is the most expensive solution to the problem of gaming. It is possible to hire raters that have no potential conflict of interest and would, therefore, be assumed to be less likely to misrepresent clinical status. This solution is sometimes useful for a subset of cases just to see whether any evidence of gaming exists.
3. Audit of ratings. We have used this technique, in which measures are completed retrospectively based on clinical record information and then compared to the forms completed prospectively. Simply letting raters know that an audit is possible is a useful deterrent to gaming.

Stage 7. Analysis And Interpretation

The nature of the analysis will depend on the questions being addressed. For widest consumption, simple analyses are more desirable than complicated ones. Graphic presentations of findings generally communicate more rapidly than do numeric. Statistical testing is relevant only to a subset of likely audiences.

When more sophisticated analyses are warranted some interesting options exist. For decision analysis projects, logistic regression and Optimal Data Analysis techniques can be powerful statistical approaches for modeling decisions. For example, we have used logistic regression to build prediction models of psychiatric hospitalization (Lyons, Stutesman, et al., 1997). Feedback to the provider is kept simple, as a probability of admission or as a decision that does not fit the data (e.g., hospitalized when predicted not to be).

Interpretation of findings depends on the target audience. If the audience is primarily external, then the organization is going to want to develop and present an interpretation of the findings. On the other hand, if the audience is primarily internal, then it often is useful to simply present the data and have interpretations generated by stakeholders. Combining groups of providers and service recipients in interpretation sessions is a novel and powerful technique to stimulate behavior change through outcomes.

Stage 8. Re-Engineering

Outcomes management projects should be subjected to the same level of scrutiny and accountability as the services that they are designed to monitor. The process of re-engineering should be managed within the context of the ongoing oversight of the outcomes management project. For example, if the quality assurance committee has authority over the outcomes management project, then it also should be responsible for deciding on changes in the measures or the project procedures.

There is an interesting tension that can impede needed re-engineering. In order to compare data historically, it is necessary to have comparable measures and methods. This can lead to significant inertial force to not change anything. On the other hand, measures "wear out" like anything else. Factors like changes in language, service design, and case-mix can require changes in outcomes measurements or procedures. The introduction of new computer systems provides opportunities for change as well. In general, it is better to evolve an outcomes management project to keep it current and relevant than to have a great deal of historical data for comparison. Sometimes it is sufficient to keep a few key items over time to achieve this goal without limiting re-engineering.

Summary

Implementing outcomes management projects is the hard part of successfully using outcomes to improve performance of mental health services. Organizational, political, and operational consideration all rightfully influence planning decisions. In implementing an outcomes management project, no detail is too small. Careful planning, including the involvement of all stakeholders and careful pilot testing to ensure that the measures and methods make sense in the clinical operation, are important aspects of the implementation process. Equally important, once implemented the outcomes should be used to understand service delivery and this understanding should be shared with all participants. Only by making outcomes management a vibrant activity within an organization can it become a valued tool in administration and service delivery.

References

Gellman R and Frawley KA. The Need To Know Versus the Right to Privacy. In: T Trabin, ed. *The Computerization of Behavioral Healthcare. How To Enhance Clinical Practice, Management, and Communications.* San Francisco: Jossey-Bass, 1996; pp. 191-212.

Howard KI, Moras, Brill P, Martinovich Z, and Lutz J. Evaluation of Psychotherapy: Efficacy, Effectiveness, and Patient Progress. *American Psychologist* 1996; 51:1059-1064.

Lyons JS, Howard KI, O'Mahoney MT, and Lish J. The Measurement And Management of Mental Health Services. New York: John Wiley & Sons, 1997.

Senge P. *The Fifth Discipline: The Art and Practice of the Learning Organization.* New York: Doubleday/Currency, 1990.

Chapter 3

Case Studies: Leading Outcomes Measurement Initiatives

The Outcomes Measurement Project

A Massachusetts Provider Group Embraces Outcomes Assessment—and Survives

RICHARD CAMER

Mention outcomes measurement and you probably think: large managed behavioral health care company, treatment management, unhappy providers, and clinicians. Now consider an innovative outcomes measurement project in Massachusetts, where an association of mental health providers has persuaded its members that collecting outcomes data is in their best interest.

"It's a survival strategy," says Elizabeth Funk, executive director of the Mental Health Corporations of Massachusetts (MHCM), an association representing more than 90 mental health provider organizations across the state. "If we didn't feel threatened, we probably wouldn't have been able to pull it off."

What MHCM did was to find an outcomes measurement tool that met its providers' needs and persuade nearly half of them to integrate data collection into their regular patient-care routine. The resulting Outcomes Measurement Project has been up and running full force since March 1997 and can track individual patient progress as well as assemble data by mental health provider or site.

"The intent was for us to sort of take the initiative and not wait until we were required and be stuck with something we didn't [like]," says Raymond Brien, director of Mental Health and Substance Abuse Services (MHSA) of the Berkshires, a provider with 140,000 covered lives in western Massachusetts. "If payers, even if they're not requiring it, look favorably on you for just measuring clinical outcomes, never mind what your results are, then it's worth doing."

Over the last year and a half, adult acute outpatients have completed an assessment form at their initial visit and a follow-up form at their fourth visit or within eight weeks, whichever is soonest. Clinicians receive individual patient reports within 15 minutes of faxing it to the outside vendor, making it possible to discuss results during the patient's visit. The outside vendor also regularly prepares aggregate reports on treatment outcomes for each of the participating mental health providers, as well as cumulative data for MHCM.

The most contentious element of outcomes measurement—stratifying outcomes data by individual clinician—will only be broached after clinicians accumulate sufficient numbers of patient encounters and after the MHCM membership can agree on the scope and use of such data.

"We wanted to protect our providers from ruthless application of premature and maybe inappropriate data in network management," Funk says. "We're going to hold our members harmless...until we are confident clinically that what we get from this project is in fact the kind of information that we can use to develop practice patterns and service protocols."

Selection Team Chooses Access' TOP Instrument

Owning and managing the release of treatment outcomes data was one goal established early in a lengthy development process that began more than five years ago, says Jeanne Crawford, MPH, former deputy director of MHCM. During that time association officials met with numerous providers as well as public and private payers in the Commonwealth to assess the state of the art in outcomes measurement and the goals and expectations of all who would be affected. They also reviewed more than a half dozen available instruments and pilot-tested the SF-36 and the BASIS-32.

They decided that whatever outcomes measure they chose needed to have "face validity" for both clinicians and patients, be capable of measuring small improvements in a seriously and persistently mentally ill patient population, and be scored by an independent entity that had no stake in the data. It also had to be reasonably priced, since providers were to pay the cost themselves.

"We wanted to work with a company that would do the whole job: not only score individual forms, but provide data back to providers in a format that was user friendly," Crawford says. "Most of the [available] instruments don't do this at all, and you have to buy some kind of software or contract with some other vendor."

MHCM finally settled on the Treatment Outcomes Package (TOP) developed by Access Measurement Systems (AMS) in Ashland MA. The TOP instrument assesses patient functioning in 15 domains, including quality of life, levels of depression and anxiety, and social relations. In addition, the instrument records factors known to correlate with mental health outcome, including medical illness, stressful life events, and patient satisfaction with treatment.

Measurement of these "confounding" factors is one feature that distinguishes TOP from other outcome measurement tools, says David Kraus, president of AMS and a clinical psychologist. "If you don't measure that and control for those variables, you've lost the ability to demonstrate...that the reason the outcome went the way it did was not related as much to the therapy as it was to some important event."

One "very powerful" factor that most instruments do not control for is the payer, which can account for 20 percent of the variance in outcome, Kraus says. "If your payer is denying you benefits or you are not happy with the package of services you are receiving, you are going to take that out on how you feel about the provider and the treatment process," he says.

Another factor assessed by the TOP instrument, stressful life events, has a profound effect on outcomes, Kraus says. "The amount of stress that somebody has coming into treatment, or the amount they have at the end of treatment, isn't as important as the difference between intake and follow-up," Kraus says company research has found.

Real-Time Capabilities

AMS was created in 1992 by Kraus and two other clinicians. "We were interested in moving forward as providers ourselves in terms of finding out what we should be doing in the outcome field, and we realized the state of the art was very limiting," Kraus recalls. AMS first developed its TOP for adult outpatients and has since created separate measures for children, substance abuse patients, and those in residential settings.

In addition to its work with MHCM, Kraus says the company is working with the American Psychological Association, the National Council for Community Behavioral Health Care, and counties in California and Georgia. "We're now the largest provider of psychiatric outcomes in the country," Kraus says.

AMS is unusual in its ability to provide "real-time" reports to clinicians on individual patients. After the patient completes the TOP form at the beginning of the initial visit, the provider faxes it to AMS for scoring. (MHCM recommends a two-hour session for the initial visit to allow sufficient time to complete the TOP and any other paperwork.) A two-page report containing demographic information, scores on 15 clinical domains, and suggested diagnoses is faxed back within 15 minutes—making it possible for the clinician to discuss the results with the patient during that visit. The second page of the report can even be photocopied, where appropriate, for patients to take home.

"Handing people a report makes it feel more real and validates their feelings," says Crawford, who once ran a behavioral medicine clinic at Yale University and is now an associate vice president at AMS.

"Clients also like to do it," says Brien of MHSA of the Berkshires. "They feel it means you care about them and take their treatment very seriously."

Brien says that resistance to the outcomes project from his 100 or so clinicians has all but dissipated and many are beginning to "learn stuff" from the process. "The reports on individual clients are indeed useful," he says. "You get some things to consider. It doesn't diagnose for you—we'd be very upset if it attempted to. But it helps you focus brief, time-limited treatments more quickly," he says.

Resistance from provider groups and clinicians was a significant hurdle to overcome, says Crawford, who participated in numerous meetings with provider CEOs and went with AMS personnel during training sessions with clinicians and support staff.

"Mental health people have never been evaluated in this way," Crawford says, so it took a lot of education and a lot of support to address their concerns.

Highest among the concerns was the potential for misuse of the data. As a safeguard, MHCM does not receive treatment outcome data by individual provider but only in aggregate form for all providers who participate. Individual providers get their own data and may make it available to payers or others at their discretion.

Clinicians also have been assured that, at least initially, they have no reason to fear the collections of outcomes data.

"The places where it has gone the best have been where the CEOs have really been behind it and have been very reassuring to the staff that...personnel decisions are not going to be based on this initial first year of data," Crawford says.

Kraus says he discourages clients from using clinician profiling data in any way that is punitive, "because the chances of them being wrong in their assessments are very high." He believes an accurate profile can come only after each clinician has data on 30 to 40 patients in every diagnostic category. "How many years will it take somebody to develop that kind of profile?" he asks.

Another key concern was whether patients would be willing or able to complete the TOP, which is longer than many other available instruments, Crawford says. But that hasn't been the case. Fully 85 percent of patients complete the form on their own, most in 20 to 25 minutes, she says.

"Almost no one needs assistance because it's pretty easy to fill out," Brien adds.

Cost was also an important issue, as each provider pays for its own evaluations. AMS's price structure is based on volume, with an up-front cost ranging from $3 to $7 per patient depending on the total number of patients evaluated and a cost of $1.50 for each administration of the form. Because of the size of its client base, MHCM was able to negotiate for its members a total fee of about $6 per patient for two administrations and scoring of the test.

Other costs are more difficult to quantify, Brien says. Aside from a facsimile machine, there are no other equipment or software costs. But someone at each site has to make sure the process happens—greeting patients, giving them the form, and offering them help when needed. There are also training costs, "not so much the cost of the trainer, but the cost of having people doing this and not engaged in some income-producing stuff," Brien says. The hardest costs to quantify are "administrative and clinical time—looking at the results, using them, so on," he says.

Since March 1997, MHCM members have administered initial forms to more than 5,500 patients and conducted follow-up evaluations on about 550, Funk says. "There are lots of reasons that we have found why people don't do follow-up," she says. Frequently, it is because the patient is not seen for a fourth visit, when the follow-up administration is usually conducted.

"Somebody comes two or three times and feels satisfied," Funk says. "It's extremely difficult to engage them after they've gone."

Brien believes low follow-up is more related to how well the second test is integrated into routine practice. Conducting the initial evaluation is relatively straightforward, but making sure patients are flagged to complete the instrument at their fourth visit, which does not necessarily occur four weeks later, presents a challenge. Then someone needs to remind the clinician about the follow-up, and he or she must remember to tell the patient at the end of the session.

"So people forget, people are rushed, they haven't planned two hours (for the session)," Brien says. "So we have to refine how we do the second instrument."

Improvement Across The Board

Nevertheless, MHCM, Brien, and others appear excited about the results of the outcomes measurement project that they have seen thus far. "When you look at the whole data set, our clients do remarkably well," Crawford says. "There is not one domain where our clients aren't showing improvement."

Greatest improvement has been seen in the clinical domains of "temper" and "anxiety"; the least improvement was seen in "social functioning," Crawford says. "That's where we are seeing the highest severity initially as well."

The demographic information collected has also helped to better identify the patients being served. "Some of the CEOs say they now have a true picture of their client population for the first time," Crawford says. No one had previously documented the severity of illness among these patients. "This is information that was not available before," she says.

Brien says he has been able to show that his clients have a much higher incidence of medical problems, substance use, and life stressors compared with the general population. But after four sessions of treatment, they display statistically significant improvements in all 15 clinical domains measured by the TOP instrument. And on measures of patient satisfaction (the TOP includes a separate mail-in survey administered at the follow-up), they surpass national norms.

MHCM has engaged noted anxiety disorders researcher David Barlow, of Boston University, to conduct ongoing analyses of the project's aggregate data. Brien says that in a preliminary analyses, Barlow and his research team are finding that patients' rating of their clinicians' skills and warmth are among the factors that correlate most highly with positive clinical outcomes.

Brien says he is a few months away from getting outcomes data broken down by individual clinician. "I think we have to learn a whole lot more about what [the data] mean before we begin to use it both clinically, and for evaluation purposes," he says.

In the year ahead, Funk says MHCM will work with members to help them improve their consistency and follow-up rate on the TOP instrument. "We never dreamed it would be so complicated," she says. "Some [of our members] have 30 sites with one manager. Some have one site with one manager. Some have their own research." MHCM also publishes a newsletter on the OMP (see following pages).

The group recently completed pilot testing of a child and adolescent version of TOP and hopes to introduce that as well soon. "That means finalizing the instrument and one whole heck of a lot of training, education, getting people to sign on, having a clean roll-out process," Funk says.

Treatment outcomes measurement projects for the chronically mentally ill, substance abusers, and those in residential settings are also in the works, she adds.

All this activity may be very well-timed, Crawford says, noting that the Health Care Financing Administration is "talking about" mandating outcomes measures for their Medicaid behavioral health care carriers. "When that happens, and it is coming, it will be a real change in how mental health services are given and how we look at them," she says.

That prospect may seem scary, but it also presents opportunities. "There has been such a steep drop in the financial resources devoted to behavioral health, but only with data can we show there is a need for some of that to come back to us."

Outcomes News: A Monthly Newsletter For Mental Health Corporations of Massachusetts Members

SEPTEMBER 1997

Welcome

The first issue of *Outcomes News* is intended for management, clinicians, support staff, and any other personnel involved in the process of collecting outcomes data as part of the MHCM Outcomes Measurement Project (OMP). This newsletter is designed to serve as a forum for your questions about the OMP as well as a place to share solutions to the problems that many of you have faced with this project.

OMP Update

The MHCM OMP is now several months old, and we are learning a considerable amount about the process of how to collect outcomes data. Since March MHCM Deputy Director Jeanne Crawford has had the opportunity to visit several sites that have enrolled in the project, and she has come to appreciate some of the complex issues that many of you are facing. Jeanne has also had the exciting experience of seeing talented people devise creative solutions to complicated issues around the process of conducting outcome measurement. Some problems still exist, but many have been solved. In the spirit of not reinventing the wheel, we want to provide you with the answers to some frequently asked questions.

Why Should We Measure Outcomes?

Outcome measurement in mental health is here to stay. The days when behavioral therapy was conducted without any form of accountability are long gone. The advent of managed care has hastened the need for outcome measurement, but even without managed care, we, as behavioral health practitioners, need to assess what we do in order to provide more responsible therapy. In addition, according to national experts, reimbursement for mental health services will continue to plummet until we comprehensively measure and deliver quality data demonstrating how these cost reductions affect patient care. Clients and providers need outcomes!

Why Is MHCM Sponsoring An Outcomes Measurement Project?

The only program of its kind, the OMP is designed to assess the outcomes of treatment on all outpatient adult clients in the MHCM network. Although there are other outcomes measurement projects in place across the country, most are being implemented by managed care companies, governmental agencies, or basic researchers. As a result, the needs of providers (and consumers) have often been left out of the measurement loop. This has led to the creation of instruments that are not user friendly or capable of measuring the great wealth of clinical skill brought to each therapeutic contact, do not adequately measure change in the seriously and persistently mentally ill, and do not recognize the multiple risk factors that affect our client base. In many cases, outcomes measurement has had more to do with the financial needs of payers than with the clinical needs of the consumers. (For instance, in another state, Medicaid network management

---

Source: Reprinted with the permission of Mental Health Corporations of Massachusetts, Inc.

decisions are being made based on a single administration of an eight-question instrument with a 30 percent response rate.) The MHCM approach gives providers the opportunity to take a front seat in the management of therapeutic outcomes and clinical practices.

Why Are We Using the Treatment Outcome Package (TOP)?

MHCM staffed an outcomes committee that spent three years looking at ways to collect outcomes information. The committee evaluated at least 50 different systems and conducted a small pilot study of the SF 36 and the Basis 32. We chose the TOP for the following reasons:

- *Clinically useful information.* It gives scores in multiple domains as well as a list of possible DSM IV diagnosis. It also provides a list of clinically significant responses.
- *Easy scoring.* The MHCM membership wanted an instrument that could be easily and quickly scored. With a fax machine, scores can be back in clinicians' hands in about 15 minutes.
- *Useful and timely data.* The membership of MHCM wanted to work with a company that would be able to provide quarterly reports to each agency and aggregate data to MHCM. Access Measurement Systems (AMS), the company that created the TOP, is able to do that as part of the fee for instrument use.
- *Lowest cost.* The price of the TOP was acceptable. Many instruments are very costly, and even instruments that were free had a hidden cost for scoring and aggregating the data. AMS gave us the best price of any company.
- *Flexibility.* We wanted to work with a company that would allow us to have input into further development of the assessment tool. AMS has been extremely responsive to the input of providers, and has made many changes to the instrument based on your feedback.
- *Client satisfaction.* The TOP contains a client satisfaction questionnaire which was important to the MHCM membership. It also measures clients' satisfaction with their third-party payers. In addition, the satisfaction questions are separate from the main body of the TOP and presented in such a way as to provide for client anonymity.
- *Confidentiality.* Client confidentiality is assured in the TOP which does not use the client's name or social security number as a client identifier.

All of This Sounds Good, But the TOP Is Just Too Long.

Too long for what? We know that collecting outcome measures using an instrument that is eight items long or even 50 seems like it would be much easier. But the feedback that we have gotten from agencies that are actually using the TOP does not support this belief! Most clients are able to complete the TOP on their own in 15 to 45 minutes. A smaller group of clients has difficulty completing the TOP, but it appears that they would have difficulty completing any questionnaire, even if it was significantly shorter.

OK, But Even 15 to 45 Minutes Is a Long Time.

True, but do we really want to manage ourselves and ultimately be managed based on a very brief set of questions that doesn't even begin to address the complexities of the clients that we see? The TOP provides useful clinical information that we wouldn't get from a very brief questionnaire. Also, when we conducted a pilot test using a shorter questionnaire, we were told that the clients felt that the questions were not relevant to their situations.

Why Don't We Use More Well Known Instruments Like the Beck Depression Scale or the Hamilton?

We needed a broad-based tool that covered multiple domains. The Beck or the Hamilton, for example, are wonderful tools, but don't give us enough information on their own. In addition, those tools are not designed to take into account all of the risk factors that make treating your clients more complex.

Increase in Clients Using TOP: Percentage Change

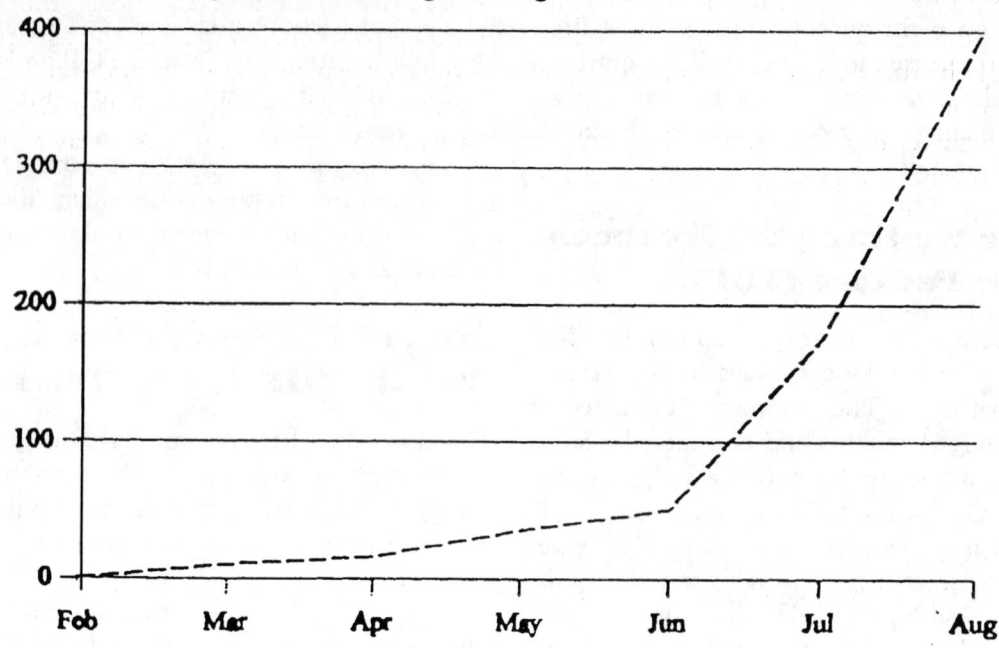

How is the Data Going To Be Used?

Initially, the data will primarily be used to understand the process of collecting outcomes data. Because this project is new and innovative, the initial data will have to be studied for a long time before we can fully understand its meaning. Once we have a thorough understanding of what we have, we will be able to use the *aggregate* data from across the state in making policy decisions about behavioral health care throughout the Commonwealth with DMA, DMH and various MCOs. And of course, agencies will be using their data to evaluate their own programs.

Ideas From Around the State

MHCM and AMS are in the process of developing a manual and a training video for administering the TOP. In the meantime, there are several procedural issues that have been handled effectively by agencies across the Commonwealth.

When scheduling an initial intake appointment, tell the client that the appointment is two hours long as opposed to asking them to come an hour early.

- Clients are accustomed to filling out paperwork and usually do not object to the time spent filling out the TOP.
- Clients usually see the value of filling out the TOP because its face validity is strong. This can be reinforced by reviewing the TOP with the client and allowing the client to take home a copy of the second page of the faxed back report. (AMS redesigned the fax-back form at MHCM's request so that a copy of the second page could be given to the client when appropriate.)
- If you are uncomfortable explaining the TOP to your clients the first few times you administer it, share the information with the client at the beginning of the second session (rather than the first), giving yourself time to become accustomed to it.
- Consider posting a sign in the waiting room asking clients to remind staff to administer the follow-up questionnaire. Many clients find the TOP useful, and are interested in the results of the follow-up questionnaire.
- Many clients need a certain amount of privacy to fill out the TOP, but do not want to be ignored. Asking the client how they

are doing is often reassuring. Unless it is unavoidable, don't leave clients in a closed room by themselves to complete the questionnaire.
- Remember to program the CSID on your fax machine. It prints the "banner" on the top line of your taxed pages. Without it, AMS may not be able to call you if there is a problem with transmission. Call AMS at 617/881-4777 if you need help (and have your fax manual handy).

Research Plans

MHCM has created an advisory council with broad representation from consumer groups, state agencies, academia, and participating providers. The first meeting of the full advisory council will take place on October 23. At that time, the group will begin to discuss the way the aggregate data is to be shaped and used. In addition, each participating organization is going to have a large data set to examine. If you have ideas about creative ways to look at the data, contact Jeanne Crawford at MHCM.

Feedback

Please send your questions, comments, complaints, and compliments to:
Jeanne Crawford
MHCM
59 Temple Place, Suite 662
Boston, MA 02111
617/451-9635; fax 617/451-3287
mhcm@wn.net

Outcomes News: A Newsletter For Mental Health Corporations Of Massachusetts Members

JANUARY 1998

OMP Update

As we move into the New Year, it is a good time to assess what we have accomplished with the MHCM Outcomes Measurement Project (ONP) and where we are going. As of the end of December, we have administered about 5,000 Adult TOPs. Thirty-seven MHCM agencies are participating in the adult project, with 88 sites enrolled.

A pilot-test of the Child TOP has been completed, resulting in a revised and shortened version of the instrument for children. Under the direction of Sylvia Perlman, PhD, the new version will be tested at the beginning of 1998. If you have questions about the outcomes measurement project for children, please contact Sylvia through the MHCM office.

Also in the testing phase is the Residential Outcomes Toolkit developed by the MHCM Residential Committee. For more information about the work of the Committee in this area, please contact Jeanne Crawford.

The OMP Road Show

Jeanne Crawford and Outcomes Committee chair Sy Friedland (Executive Director of Jewish Family and Children's Service) have presented on the development and progress of the OMP at a number of national conferences over the past several months. Two important conferences included the International Congress on Performance Measurement and Improvement in Health Care (co-sponsored by the Joint Commission on Accreditation of Healthcare Organizations) and the Alfred E. Trieschman Center Conference, Tools for the Trade: Information Systems to Measure and Improve Behavioral Health Outcomes. Feedback from participants in Chicago, Orlando, Cambridge, and Raleigh has been enthusiastic and positive: leaders from other states and regions are taking note of the structure, management, and initial results of the OMP.

OMP Advisory Committee

The Outcomes Advisory Committee, held its first meeting on October 23 at Boston University. David Barlow, Chair of the Advisory Committee, Elizabeth Funk, Jeanne Crawford, and Sy Friedland presented an overview of the history and development of the OMP. David Kraus and Fred Horan, President and Vice President of Access Measurement Systems (AMS), provided background information about AMS and the TOP.

David Barlow then led the Committee in a discussion of next steps for the project. At the recommendation of the group, MHCM staff and members are preparing to examine the data from the following perspectives:

- *Demographic and Descriptive Factors*: What does the presenting population "look" like? Can we begin to develop a picture of the age, gender, ethnicity, income status, presenting problems and diagnosis, housing status, treatment status, substance abuse history and medical status of our consumers, as well as the ways that these factors are related?
- *Dosage Effects*: Does timing of clinical sessions have an impact on ultimate outcome by diagnosis or demographic (risk) factor or any other clinical variable?
- *Timing of Clinical Effects*: Do clinical improvements (or lack thereof) in one

---

Source: Reprinted with the permission of Mental Health Corporations of Massachusetts, Inc.

domain correlate with improvement in another? Can we use improvement or lack of improvement as a predictor of future change?
- *Risk Factors and Outcomes*: What risk factors correlate with positive and negative outcomes, dropout status, and client satisfaction?

Initial Findings

What follows are some initial demographic characteristics and outcomes findings. This information was tabulated in October based on about 2,000 administrations. While still preliminary, the data provide a fascinating look at the people we serve. As the graph illustrates, clients are showing improvement in all domains.

Demographic Factors
- 6.4% of clients are homeless
- 60.9% are female
- 62.8% are Christian
- 73.4% are Caucasian
- 58.0% have a family income less than $20,000
- 90.8% have a high school diploma or less
- 39.9% are unemployed
- 37.4% are employed full time

Medical Status
- 32.4% report fair to poor health
- Average PCP visits in past two months: 1.9
- Average number of prescriptions: 2.1
- Average number of medical hospitalization days in last year: 1.4
- 39.8% are nonsmokers
- 22.7% have had back problems in the last year
- 12.3% have asthma
- 10.4% have ulcers
- 7.0% have anemia

Stressful Events
- Average stress severity level: 26.3 (General population mean is 11.4)
- 39.3% report financial problems in the last year
- 38.4% report social support problems
- 37.3% report relationship problems
- 28.7% report work problems
- 25.5% have ended a relationship
- 22.7% report an illness of someone in their life
- 18.6% report a death of an important person

Treatment and Substance Abuse
- Average previous psychiatric hospitalizations: 1.7
- Average number of therapists seen: 2.5
- 13.6% report someone worrying about substance abuse
- 8.9% report at least one DUI
- 58.3% report no substance use in past month
- 34.8% report use of alcohol
- 11.0% report use of marijuana
- 2.9% report use of cocaine
- 0.8% report use of hallucinogens

Food for Thought: Variables Related To Improvement

Based on your experience and knowledge, do you think the following characteristics correlate positively or negatively with improvement as measured on the TOP?

1. Years of school
2. Number of cigarettes smoked in a typical day
3. Social functioning score
4. Impulsivity score
5. Depression score

Answers: 1. negative; 2. negative; 3. positive; 4. negative; 5. Negative.

Questions and Answers

Is the MHCM OMP a Basic Research Project?

No. The collection of any kind of data involves asking and answering questions; so it is with the MHCM OMP. Project participants are collecting information on outcomes so they can manage themselves better clinically and administratively. Without hard data, it is impossible to demonstrate with any certainty that treatments are effective and that staff and financial resources are being

Adult Summary Scores: Intake and Follow-up TOP

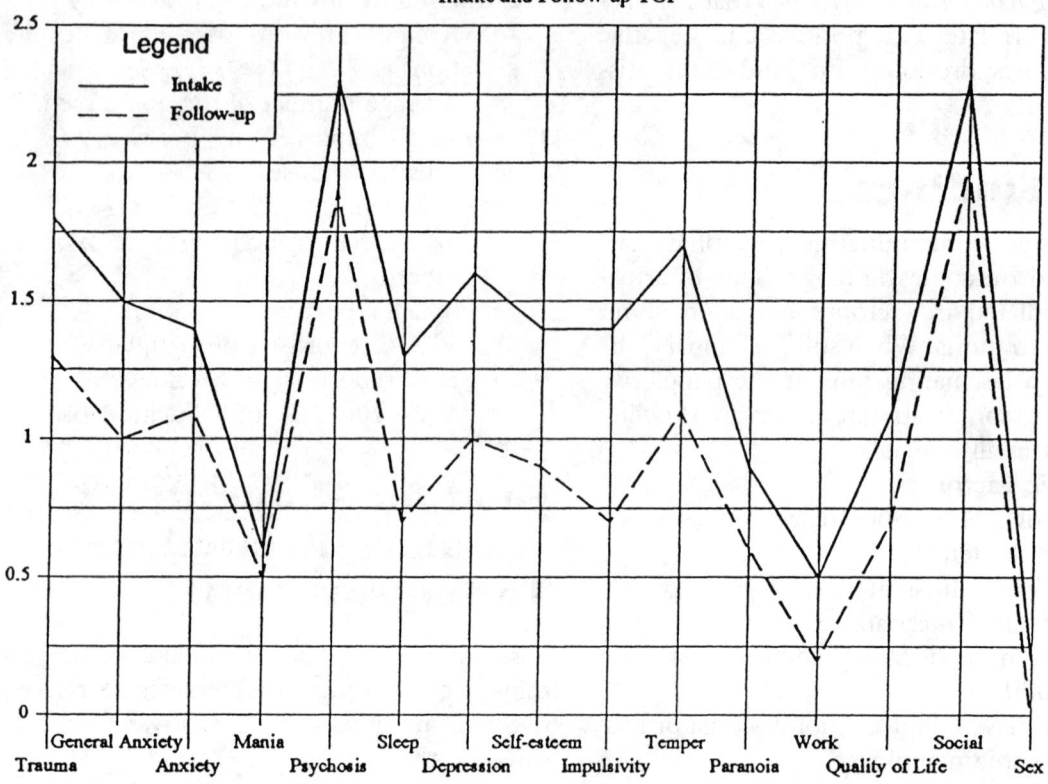

Adult Summary Scores
Intake and Follow-up TOP

(Line graph showing Intake and Follow-up scores across categories: Trauma, General Anxiety, Anxiety, Mania, Psychosis, Sleep, Depression, Self-esteem, Impulsivity, Temper, Paranoia, Work, Quality of Life, Social, Sex)

allocated appropriately. As participants collect more data, they will be able to specifically pinpoint what works well, and what doesn't. The goal of our data analysis is to allow members to make better treatment decisions and to provide better clinical services for clients.

How Can I Better Integrate the Information From the TOP Into My Clinical Work?

Being able to use the information from the initial and follow-up TOP in your clinical work is of paramount importance. To facilitate this process, MHCM, in conjunction with AMS, will be holding a series of regional training sessions for clinicians and clinical directors in the beginning of February. We will send an announcement of the dates, times, and locations of these important trainings in the very near future.

What Other Changes Have Been Made to the TOP for Adults?

Thanks to the comments of one of our members, the wording on a question referring to immune function has been reformatted to avoid any appearance of intruding into areas of client confidentiality.

Feedback

The comments we have received on this newsletter have been very positive. Please let us know how we can make it even more useful to you. Call Jeanne Crawford at the MHCM office (617/451-9635).

Taking Outcomes Measurement Statewide

Two Years in the Planning, Ohio's Ambitious Initiative Is About To 'Go Live'

JULIE BOYLE

In one of the more ambitious outcomes efforts to date, the state of Ohio is introducing an initiative that will gather standardized outcomes data for nearly all adults and youth served by the state's $1 billion public mental health system. After nearly two years of planning, a pilot of the outcomes measurement approach is being launched in fall 1998, with statewide rollout to the system's 51 county-level boards expected to begin mid-summer 1999. The anticipated results: a wealth of benchmarking data, a greater level of accountability for providers, and better treatment for patients.

Ohio's outcomes effort got rolling three years ago as the state began to gear up for an anticipated Medicaid waiver that would bring managed care to the mental health sector in the state. While those plans have stalled due to the defeat of enabling legislation and pending an appeal of a federal judge's overturning of the state's contract award, the outcomes project has proceeded full steam ahead.

Its progress has been slow but steady as every effort has been made to incorporate the views of consumers, providers, family members, university researchers, the state, and county-level mental health boards. Steering the initiative has been a 42-member task force representing all of these varied constituents.

The task force met monthly for 16 months to identify the outcomes the public mental health system wants to achieve, as well as the tools with which to measure them. According to Dee Roth, chief of program evaluation and research at the Ohio Department of Mental Health, the group's first challenge was to articulate the goals it wanted to attain for clients. "When you ask people to name outcomes, 80 percent of the stuff you get at first are performance measures," she says. "It's much easier to think about how to monitor an agency or a service than to express exactly what you're trying to accomplish," she says.

After several brainstorming sessions, the group settled on four domains for outcomes measurement: clinical status; functioning; quality of life; and safety and health, a category that includes issues such as suicidal thoughts and housing stability.

Intent upon capitalizing as much as possible on the work of others, the task force then collected outcomes tools for evaluation. "We sifted though every existing instrument in the western world," says Roth. "Each was put through a filter to see how well it met our criteria." Among those criteria: reasonable cost, low burden on providers, strong psychometric properties, cultural sensitivity and consistency with identified desired outcomes, particularly consumer recovery and empowerment.

The task force also defined four distinct population groups for the purposes of its work:
1. adults with severe mental disabilities,
2. other adults served by the system,
3. youth with serious emotional disturbances, and
4. other youth.

As it examined outcomes instruments, the task force also wrestled with the issues of who should be surveyed, how often, and how to achieve consistent, reliable results from a statewide, culturally diverse population. It set as a goal to have each consumer surveyed by only one key provider at intervals that would be specified according to the different population groups.

"It was a long and thorny process," says Roth. "For kids, there are fewer instruments available and virtually all are proprietary. For adults, there

Consumers Steer Quality Improvement Study

In another collaborative effort to improve its mental health system, Ohio's Department of Mental Health is using teams of interviewers to gather information about the quality of its services from those whose opinion matters most: the clients themselves.

According to program development specialist Abdin Noboa, these Consumer Quality Review Teams (CQRT) have been working for the past two years to gather and analyze data from more than 2,000 in-depth interviews. Currently there are three teams operating in the state: one aimed at children in Hamilton county; and two that target adults, one in the Akron area and another in the state's western half.

Guided by the department's office of consumer services, these consumer-led teams have been involved in every phase of the project, including instrument development, identifying interviewees, conducting the interviews, turning the responses into statistical form, data analysis, formulation of recommendations, and, finally, advocacy. "This project is consumer-driven in its scope, its aim, its purpose, and its implementation," says Noboa.

Noboa says that the teams are focusing on what the department refers to as the "four As" of service improvement: availability, accessibility, acceptability and appropriateness. Each interview lasts approximately 90 minutes and requires two CQRT members: one to interview and one to record. While the instruments vary depending upon the interview subject and the services he or she is receiving, each includes a number of questions designed to elicit reflective responses. Says Noboa, "We want to get at how they feel about the system, and about the process of recovery itself."

The result of this approach has been a goldmine of data that has sometimes been difficult to sift, according to Noboa. "It's been somewhat of a challenge to turn qualitative responses into quantitative data," he says. Nevertheless, he adds, "The data collection has been extremely rich. We have enough for five dissertations."

While not all of this data will be used as the CQRTs formulate recommendations for the local mental health boards, Noboa believes none of it will go to waste. "Because these consumer-led teams have taken the time to do these lengthy, door-to-door, face-to-face interviews, they've become extremely well-informed," he says. "They can be considered experts."

With most of the interviews completed, and data analysis well under way, Noboa anticipates that reports will be finalized and distributed to the local mental health boards in the CQRTs' three areas by the first quarter of 1999. He hopes that, in addition to resulting in system improvement across the state, the CQRT's efforts will yield an even deeper change. "As consumers learn that their views and thoughts matter and will be used for their benefit, they'll grow empowered to have a greater voice in shaping the system," he says.

---

are many, but they tend to be fairly narrow in focus and few include the kinds of safety and health outcomes that we wanted to measure, particularly the negative ones."

To achieve the comprehensive outcomes assessment it desired, the task force adopted several instruments in their entirety, pulled elements from others and generated a few questions of their own. After months of review and discussion, as well as a pre-test, the task force settled on the following sets of instruments and survey intervals for the various consumer groups:

Adults With Severe Disabilities

- Symptom Distress Scale (Mental Health Statistics Improvement Program (MHSIP) Task Force on Consumer-Oriented Mental Health Report Card).
- Making Decisions empowerment scale (Rogers, Chamberlin, Ellison and Crean).
- Items from the Quality of Life Interview (Lehman), the Quality of Life Questionnaire (Greenly, Greenberg and Brown), and the HAPI-A (Hoosier Assurance Plan Instrument-Adult).

- Modified items from the Multnomah Community Ability Scale.
- Items generated by the task force.

Baseline data for these adults is to be collected at admission, after six and twelve months, and annually thereafter.

Other Adults

- Symptom Distress Scale (Mental Health Statistics Improvement Program (MHSIP) Task Force on Consumer-Oriented Mental Health Report Card).
- Items from the Quality of Life Interview (Lehman), the Quality of Life Questionnaire (Greenly, Greenberg and Brown), and the HAPI-A (Hoosier Assurance Plan Instrument-Adult).
- Items generated by the task force.

Baseline data is to be gathered at admission and again at the estimated 3/4 point of treatment to avoid losing the opportunity to collect additional data from the many consumers of this type who simply stop seeking care, rather than plan termination of their treatment.

Children and Adolescents

- CAFAS (Child and Adolescent Functional Assessment Scale).
- FES (Family Empowerment Scale).
- BERS (Behavioral and Emotional Rating Scale).

For children and adolescents with serious emotional disturbances, the task force recommended measurement at intake, then every three to six months, and again at termination of treatment. For other children/adolescents, it called for measurement at intake and at the three-quarter point of treatment. According to Roth, the task force has established an advisory group that is further refining the issue of data collection for children/adolescents. "Because it can be hard to make the distinction at the outset between a child who is a long-term care client and a clinic client, we're taking a closer look at how to define and deal with these kids," she says.

While the task force is confident in the validity of the instruments it has chosen, at least one member is concerned that they may meet with some skepticism from providers. Sean Hill, manager of quality management, at Eastway Corporation, a Dayton-based provider, says, "Because we've changed the form of some of these instruments, there may be some worry that they may not be as reliable as they were if they hadn't been broken apart and used piecemeal."

Trial Run Set For Fall 1998

Because of this kind of concern, as well as the sheer complexity of the initiative, the outcomes project will be pilot-tested in two community mental health systems beginning in October 1998. As an implementation work group struggles to put together the implementation plan, Roth says that the broader task force's earlier work is looking like a cakewalk in comparison. "The mechanics of implementation is a mind-bending challenge," she says. "We're dealing with a system that has local boards, who in turn contract with local agencies, each of which differs from the other. Just trying to figure out the data flow is a nightmare."

A statewide data system that has been in development for several years will lend significant support to the data component of the outcomes initiative. The Multi-Agency Comprehensive Information System (MACSIS) will contain all the outcomes data specified by the task force, as well as event-level data for community services, including event-level billing of services and behavioral health information on clients, housing status and clinical characteristics. State law prohibits MACSIS from collecting name-identified outcomes data and therefore won't be able to support care management at the local agency level. However, agencies will be able to link event-level outcomes data to service utilization and billing data for use in care management. Masked individual-level data will be available at state and local levels through a central data warehouse.

"MACSIS will enable us to emerge with a data warehouse, coded and encrypted for privacy, that will contain an enormous wealth of information," says Roth. She says the state is looking at software options that will allow providers and administrators to access the data and produce both paper and electronic reports for staff.

With data collection at the pilot sites slated to begin in October, Roth expects the pilots to run through the end of June 1999, with the project being phased in gradually throughout the state beginning July 1999.

Providers Wary But Ready

Although the vast majority of the work on the outcomes initiative up until this point has been done by the state and its task force, the rest of the burden will fall squarely on the shoulders of the state's mental health providers, and, to some extent, on consumers and family members. However, Roth points out, these are the groups that stand to benefit the most from the effort. "We've spent most of our time discussing how to make this information useful at the individual provider level," she says. "Everyone has agreed that if this information can't be used at all levels, including the consumer, provider, and the state, then we're wasting a bunch of time."

Roth believes that most providers are wary, but resigned to the fact that a more comprehensive and thorough outcomes effort is necessary. "Most realize that outcomes are becoming the way of the behavioral health world," she says.

Collecting their own outcomes data will equip providers to better compete with the for-profit companies trying to break into the state market, she points out. "The belief here has been that these for-profits don't really have the expertise to deal with the severely mentally disabled population, yet they have been collecting outcomes data that we just don't have," Roth says. "Our providers need to be able to prove that they can do it better."

Tom Lambric, a consumer advocate with the Stark County Community Mental Health Board, who was a task force member, concurs that some providers are complaining. "The cry from providers is that it will be an administrative burden, especially at the clinician level," he says. "As a result, there has been a call for regulatory relief that I believe both the community boards and the state are trying to respond to."

In fact, the outcomes task force did recommend in its report to the director of the Ohio Department of Mental Health that the state eliminate existing regulatory requirements that do not support or that duplicate the new outcomes program. The task force has also stated its wish to link with the Joint Commission on Accreditation of Health Organizations (JCAHO) to gain deemed status for using the outcomes program to meet JCAHO's impending outcomes requirements, known as ORYX.

Providers also have voiced concerns about comparisons that may be drawn from outcomes data. "This will introduce an accountability that wasn't there before," says Lambric. "But the task force has strongly stated that no comparisons should be made with the data until we have a firm handle on the information we have."

Roth believes that, while the state does have normative data on several of the instruments, the more useful comparisons will come from data generated within the state. "We should be able to identify differences by client gender, race, and age; by regions of the state; and by urban versus rural areas."

While some providers may quake a bit at the prospect of data-based comparisons, others welcome the opportunity for state-level benchmarking, Eastway's Hill believes. "Once the data starts coming in and we build in the parameters to ensure safe benchmarks, we'll have an enormous amount of data fairly quickly for benchmarking," he says. "Most people in the state are hungry for that; they're looking forward to there being a unified system."

Consumer advocate Lambric is eager for the statewide outcomes initiative to begin producing data that will shed some light on the issue of empowerment and its impact on recovery for mental health clients. "I'm not sure what's going to happen, but at some point we may finally start confirming the belief that people who are more empowered are functioning better," he says.

Such a discovery, while it will validate Lambric's and others' view that empowerment is an essential element of treatment, may ultimately be frustrating, he points out. "With Medicaid's guidelines on reimbursement for medically necessary treatment, we may find that these outcomes are valuable, but we can't necessarily afford to provide them," he says. "This could lead to a shift away from traditional case management so that clients can access some services outside the system."

It's this potential for discovery and change that makes the outcomes initiative so exciting, Lambric believes. "As we change the way we measure what's going on in the state and for the first time have a place to benchmark from, we'll have a way to challenge how we're doing, and what we're doing."

The Outcomes Implementation Pilot's Web site can be found at: **http://www.mh.state.oh.us/initiatives/outcomes/pilot.html**

Four Winds-Saratoga: Improving the Care Provided to Children and Adolescents in an Acute Care Setting

What Is Four Winds-Saratoga?

Four Winds-Saratoga is an acute care psychiatric health system located in Saratoga Springs, New York. It offers a comprehensive range of specialized evaluation and treatment services for children, adolescents, adults, and older individuals, as well as for parents and families. Treatment programs are organized by age and level of intensity. Four Winds-Saratoga features an 83-bed inpatient service, as well as partial hospital, intensive outpatient, and outpatient services available across the developmental continuum.

What Does Performance Improvement Mean at Four Winds-Saratoga?

The leadership at Four Winds-Saratoga is strongly committed to continuous efforts to improve the quality of care delivered to clients. A central mission of the organization is to provide all clinical care staff with the data, knowledge, and skills needed to effect improvements in both the processes and outcomes of care on a continual basis. Core to this mission are ongoing outcomes studies (initiated in 1991) of the hospital's programs and services. These studies have provided methodically collected data to assess performance and decision making.

Four Winds-Saratoga has adopted the FOCUS (Find-Organize-Clarify, Understand-Select)-PDCA (Plan-Do-Check-Act) performance improvement methodology. Performance improvement, including performance measurement, is seen as part of the daily work of all staff throughout the organization. To build organizational capability for measurement and improvement, Four Winds-Saratoga employs two full-time staff responsible for quality management and outcomes assessment. In addition, two consultants assisted in the design and implementation of outcomes assessment and performance improvement initiatives, provided data analysis support, and offered staff development opportunities essential for successfully implementing improvement projects.

The Child and Adolescent Outcomes Study

What Were the Project Goals?

In July 1994, the Four Winds-Saratoga Child and Adolescent Outcomes Study was initiated. The purposes of this two-year project (phase 1) were to
- provide clinical and social functioning profiles of child and adolescent inpatients from multiple perspectives;
- permit comparison of data on Four Winds patients to normed data; and
- examine patterns of change during and after hospitalization.

These clinical performance data were then used to help make decisions about high-impact improvement opportunities.

Source: Using Performance Measurement to Improve Outcomes in Behavioral Health Care. Oakbrook Terrace IL: Joint Commission on Accreditation of Healthcare Organizations, Copyright 1998, pages 88-97. Reprinted with permission.

How Were Data Collected?

Clinical and social functioning assessments were collected from clients ages 8 through 17, their parents, and clinicians at three points in the treatment process: admission, discharge, and one month after discharge. Instruments used for data collection included the following:

- Piers-Harris Children's Self-Concept Scale (PHCSCS), which is completed by the client at admission, discharge, and follow-up;
- Child and Adolescent Adjustment Profile (CAAP), which is completed by the client's parent at admission and follow-up;
- Child and Adolescent Functional Assessment Scale (CAFAS), which is completed by the clinician at admission;
- Patient Satisfaction Survey, which is completed by the client at discharge; and
- Parent Satisfaction Survey, which is completed by the client's parent at discharge.

To be eligible for inclusion in this study, parents and/or clients were required to sign informed consent statements, have lengths of stay of seven days or longer, and complete the data collection instruments at the prescribed times. If an individual had participated in the study and was readmitted to the facility during the two-year study period, readmissions were included as follow-up data and the individual was not reassessed for subsequent admissions. Follow-up PHCSCS and CAAP surveys were mailed to clients and their parents one month after discharge. One reminder letter was sent to nonresponders.

Upon completion of phase I (June 30, 1996), the study design was modified to

- collect data on each admission of individual clients, rather than the initial admission only; and
- administer the CAFAS at follow-up as well as at admission.

How Were the Data Analyzed?

Data analysis was ongoing, with reports on data completion and client satisfaction rates communicated to the units monthly and summary reports on outcomes reported quarterly. The data set included demographic and diagnostic information about the clients, as well as individual and subscale scores for the various measurement tools. Data analysis included comparisons across groups and over time. Data summaries were presented in simple line graphs, bar graphs, and tables.

What Did the Data Show?

Data generated from this Study were primarily examined in three ways. First, children and adolescents receiving inpatient treatment at Four Winds-Saratoga were compared with similar groups in outpatient mental health programs, probation programs, and the public school system. Second, the problems reported by the children and adolescents receiving treatment as inpatients at Four Winds-Saratoga were examined from three perspectives: child or adolescent, parent, and staff. Finally, change in the child or adolescent over the course of inpatient treatment was examined.

The findings of the comparison of the PHCSCS scores and CAAP ratings of Four Winds-Saratoga children and adolescents with the comparison groups were as expected. The child and adolescent inpatients had greater difficulties in social functioning and with symptoms than did the children and adolescents in the outpatient, probation, and public school samples. Initial CAAP ratings for children and adolescents admitted as inpatients to Four Winds-Saratoga were also lower than the ratings for the children and adolescents admitted to the outpatient mental health program.

Upon the children's and adolescents' admission to inpatient treatment, the clients, their parents, and the clinical staff used the PHCSCS, CAAP, or CAFAS, respectively, to record their perceptions of each child's or adolescent's problems at time of admission. Clinical ratings given by staff on the CAFAS revealed moods/emotions, role performance, and peer relations to be the predominant categories in which clients experienced moderate to severe difficulties. Correspondingly, client self-reports on the PHCSCS indicated greatest difficulty on the behavior and happiness scales. Similarly, on the CAAP parents rated their children lowest on the peer relations, hostility, and withdrawn scales.

The outcomes analyses most useful for quality improvement efforts are those documenting change over time. Changes in the child or adolescent were examined in several ways.

Chapter 3: Case Studies: Leading Outcomes Measurement Initiatives

Clients' self-ratings on the PHCSCS were documented at admission, discharge, and follow-up (one month after discharge). Total scores on the PHCSCS improved from admission to discharge for 77% of the patients (see Table 1). Further, the improvements in percentile ranks of PHCSCS ratings from admission to discharge were statistically significant across all subscales and were sustained through the follow-up period (see Figure 1).

Table 1. Percentage of Child and Adolescent Inpatients at Four Winds-Saratoga Whose PHCSCS* Scores Improved From Admission to Discharge

Subscale	Percentage Improved
Behavior	62%
Intellectual status	60%
Physical appearance	59%
Anxiety	65%
Popularity	62%
Happiness	65%
Total score	77%

* PHCSCS = Piers-Harris Children's Self-Concept Scale.

The CAAP was completed by parents at the time of their children's admission and during the follow-up period. In confirmation of the self-ratings of their children, the parents' CAAP ratings also showed improvement over time. Table 2 illustrates improvement rates in the children and adolescents from their parents' perspective (as reported on the CAAP) from admission to follow-up. Between 51% and 68% of the clients were rated as improved on the domains measured by the CAAP. Specifically, parents of Four Winds inpatients reported significant improvement ($p < .05$ or better) on all CAAP subscales except dependency, with the greatest change recorded in the hostility and behavior categories. By the time of discharge, the profiles of child and adolescent inpatients at Four Winds-Saratoga mirrored the admission profiles of the children and adolescents receiving treatment in the outpatient clinic.

Additional data analysis examined patterns of change during and after hospitalization by gender, age, and diagnosis. Highlights of those analyses included the following:

1. Although there were no significant gender-related differences in the percentage of clients reporting improvement from admission to follow-up (80% of the females, 72% of the males), the pattern of change seemed to differ by sex. Girls rated

Figure 1. Percentile Ranks Based on Piers-Harris Self-Reports

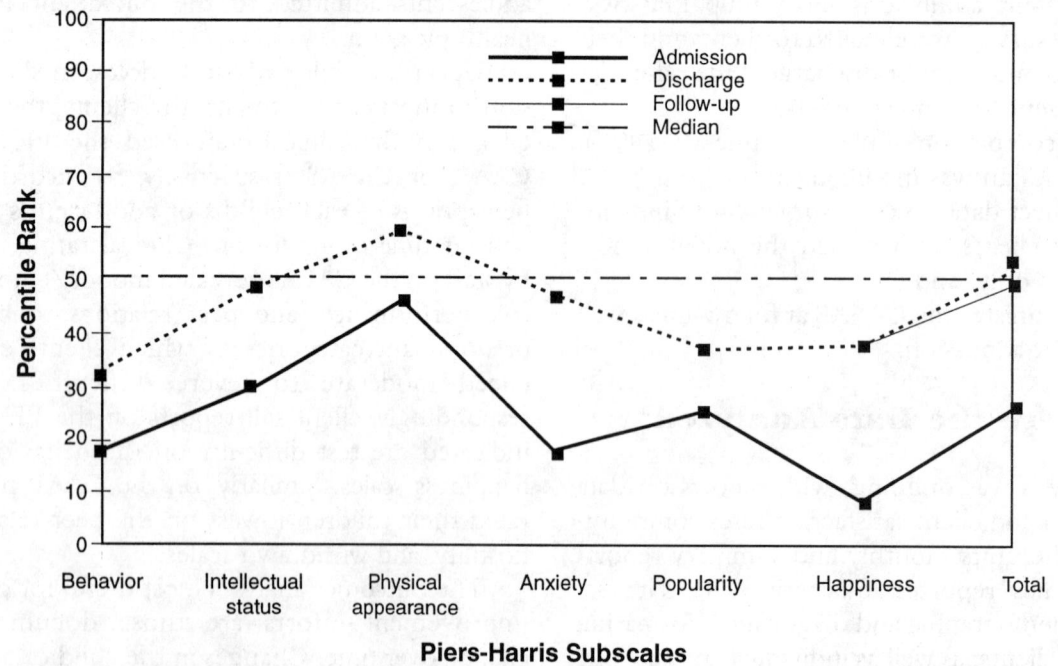

n = 94; 7/94-6/96

Table 2 Percentages of Improved CAAP* Scores From Time of Inpatient Admission To Follow-up

CAAP Subscale	Total (n = 55)	Mood (n = 35)	Behavior n = 15)	Boys (n = 25)	Girls (n = 30)
Peer relations	60%	54%	49%	67%	55%
Dependency	51%	49%	60%	54%	48%
Hostility	58%	54%	60%	67%	52%
Productivity	60%	59%	64%	61%	60%
Withdrawal	68%	65%	80%	75%	63%

CAAP = Child and Adolescent Adjustment Profile

themselves the same or lower than boys on all dimensions of the PHCSCS at admission, reported greater improvements in the hospital compared with boys, and at follow-up reported very similar levels of adjustment.

2. Older adolescents (13 to 18 years) rated themselves significantly lower at admission on all subscales of the PHCSCS than did younger clients, and they showed a greater degree of improvement during hospitalization. At follow-up, however, they reported some deterioration on the intellectual, happiness, and overall scores. In contrast, the gains accrued by the younger clients during hospitalization were sustained or improved at follow-up.

3. The PHCSCS differentiated clients by diagnostic category at admission in predicted directions. Compared to clients with mood disorders, clients with conduct disorders were less likely to sustain improvements accrued during hospitalization at follow-up. This finding, in combination with other observed patterns in responsiveness to treatment of clients with conduct disorders, prompted the performance improvement initiative described in the following section.

How Was This Outcomes Measurement Project Used To Improve Performance?

In addition to generating excellent descriptive data about clients' responses to treatment, this outcomes study became the springboard for selected performance improvement initiatives. These included a project to improve the treatment provided to children and adolescents with disruptive behavior disorders and a project to provide staff development opportunities to participate in the outcomes study.

Table 3 presents the improvement project report for the effort to improve the treatment of children and adolescents diagnosed with disruptive behavior disorders.

The staff development initiative is still under way. It focuses on three key changes: Improve overall client and parent response rates to the outcomes assessments instruments, introduce a clinical assessment at follow-up, and initiate a treatment intervention capability after discharge. A summary intermediate report of this project is presented in Table 4.

Table 3. Four Winds-Saratoga Performance Improvement Project, Initiated June 1996

Method: FOCUS (Find-Organize, Clarify, Understand, Select)-PDCA (Plan-Do-Check-Act)

- Find a process to improve
- Organize a team that knows the process
- Clarify current knowledge of the process
- Understand sources of process variation
- Select the process improvement: plan, do, check, act

Step 1: Find a Process to Improve

Process targeted for improvement: Treatment of children/adolescents with disruptive behavior disorders

Background: During the second quarter of 1995, child and adolescent services staff noted an increase in disruptive behaviors among particular groups of clients. The disruptive behaviors led to more frequent use of physical interventions (restraints, seclusions, holds) with these clients. Data from the Master Patient Index and Incident Management database were analyzed and confirmed the following:

- An increase in the number of clients admitted with diagnoses of attention deficit hyperactivity disorder and intermittent explosive disorder and conduct disorder, collectively described as disruptive behavior disorders.
- A trend (since the second quarter of 1994) toward an increase in the use of physical interventions with this group of patients.

Data from the client outcomes study compared clients who required physical interventions because of disruptive episodes with clients who did not. Four findings emerged:

- Clients requiring physical interventions were more likely to have diagnoses of behavior disorders than mood or anxiety disorders.
- Clients requiring physical interventions had been rated by their parents at admission (on the hostility subscale of the Child and Adolescent Adjustment Profile) as being particularly troubled.
- Clients requiring physical interventions showed less overall improvement in their self-ratings on the Piers-Harris Children's Self-Concept Scale (PHCSCS) than did patients not requiring intervention.
- Fewer clients with behavior disorder diagnoses reported improved PHCSCS scores from admission to discharge than did the clients in the other diagnostic groups.

Pecentage of Clients Improved by Diagnosis from Admission to Discharge (1/95–9/95)

Condition	Mood %	Anxiety %	Behavior %	Total %
Worse	25	9	37	28
Same	3	—	5	3
Improved	72	91	58	69
Total	100	100	100	100
(n)	[71]	[11]	[43]	[125]

These data confirmed the clinical staff's impression that successful treatment of this client population required the development of different strategies.

Step 2: Organize a Team Knowledgeable of the Process

A performance improvement team was organized with representation from nursing, direct care staff, medical staff, administration, and support services.

Step 3: Clarify Current Knowledge of the Process

The performance improvement team studied the process of how these clients were evaluated and treated at the hospital. These individuals underwent the routine assessment and treatment planning process used for all clients, and they were incorporated into the standard milieu and treatment program of the units. In the event that they exhibited disruptive behavior, staff responded as they did to all clients based on techniques learned in behavior management training.

Step 4: Understand Sources of Variation/Breakdown In the Process

1. This diagnostic configuration was one not previously encountered by the staff. Although clients with behavior disorders had always been treated at the hospital, they had never before constituted such a large segment of the client population. Clearly, staff needed additional training to successfully work with these clients.
2. The treatment planning time frames and treatment protocols in use had been developed at a time of significantly longer lengths of stay and were not well suited to the current shorter lengths of stay.

Year	Average Length of Stay (in Days)
1990	87.5
1991	69.4
1992	50
1993	45
1994	42
1995	30

Development of the comprehensive treatment plan occurred seven days after admission, resulting in delayed strategizing for this client population.

Reliance on a positive peer culture-based milieu in which stabilized clients were able to support and serve as models for those in their acute phase was not feasible because of shorter lengths of stay. Clients were in an acute phase for much of their hospitalization.
3. Significant variation was discovered in the use of medications with these clients, particularly regarding the timing of clients being started on medication. This time frame for initiation of medications typically ranged from 7 to 21 days following admission, which was more aligned with previous longer lengths of stay.

Table 3. Four Winds-Saratoga Performance Improvement Project, Initiated June 1996 (continued)

4. The physical environment of the units was not sufficiently supportive of this client population. The space was inadequate for physical/recreational activities.
Furthermore, incidents occurred during which clients used furniture in their rooms to barricade themselves, thereby creating unsafe situations.

Step 5: Select the Process Improvements

In response to the identified issues, the following initiatives were taken:
1. *Staff education and training.* Education and training for staff working with this client population was set as a high priority by leadership.
Education efforts included
    - on-site expert consultation regarding behavioral and cognitive treatment planning and interventions; and
    - technical assistance by a special education consultant regarding programming for clients with concomitant learning disabilities.
2. *Benchmarking.*
    - A literature search was conducted and a resource library was developed to identify and incorporate best practices in the treatment of disruptive behavior disorders.
    - Three reports on restraint/seclusion by the New York State Commission on Quality of Care were reviewed and their recommendations regarding best practices were endorsed. These recommendations emphasized strong administrative oversight, staff training, and a positive therapeutic environment.
    - A number of innovative programs in the Northeast were visited to further identify best practices in assessment, treatment, and management techniques.
3. *Practice guidelines for prescribing medication.*
The medical staff analyzed the variation in initiation of mood-stabilizing medications for this client population. After extensive review, they endorsed a more aggressive approach for those clients with significant histories of violent/disruptive behaviors. Rather than waiting for several days of evaluation before beginning medications, physicians began utilizing focused assessment techniques, as well as historical data regarding aggression, violence, and explosiveness, to determine the appropriateness of earlier initiation of medications. Medications are now typically introduced on approximately the fourth day after admission.
4. *High-risk protocol.*
Child and adolescent services developed a color-coding system for medical records and kardexes to identify clients assessed as being at high risk for disruption or explosiveness. This system permits easy identification of clients with potential for disruptive episodes, thereby allowing staff to make quick decisions in complicated situations.
5. *Revisions to milieu and treatment planning.*
In response to the recommendations of a focus group consisting of staff, consultants, and former clients, the milieu program was changed to include a "welcoming period" immediately following admission. This structure intensifies staff-client contact via a staff mentor and dilutes client-client contact for the first three days of treatment. Thus, staff-client relationships are solidified before clients are introduced to their peer culture. The last two days of client stays are also highly structured and include reflective assignments and feedback from staff and peers.

The treatment-planning process was amended to support more immediate strategizing for these clients. Instead of reliance on development of the comprehensive treatment plan beginning on the seventh day, greater emphasis was placed on developing a strong initial treatment plan within the first 24 hours after admission so as to quickly initiate and guide the course of treatment.

6. *Physical environment.*
Child and adolescent services modified the therapeutic environment to improve spaces for the expression of anger, including expanded quiet or time-out rooms. They incorporated an intercom stereo system to provide soothing music or sounds at appropriate times. In addition, a ropes course was constructed to permit expression of physicality in appropriate ways. Also, furniture in designated rooms was secured to the walls or floor.

Current Status

The process improvements discussed in the preceding section were implemented during the fourth quarter of 1995 and throughout 1996.

Outcomes Study Results

Data for the first four months of 1997 showed improved outcomes for this population. Of the patients with behavior disorders, 79% showed improved PHSCS scores from admission to discharge in this time period compared with 58% during the preproject period.

Incident Management Database

Changes in both clinical policy and clinical practice have shifted the distribution of restraint versus seclusion versus holds across child and adolescent services. Restraint is still used very infrequently. Brief (five- to ten-minute) therapeutic holds, the least intrusive approach, have now become the most frequently used physical intervention.

	Use of Physical interventions		
Date	Restraint	Seclusion	Hold
Second quarter 1995	4%	46%	50%
Second quarter 1 997	4%	17%	79%

Staff Feedback

Child and adolescent services staff report feeling more confident and supported in their treatment of these clients. Their knowledge and skills have been enhanced and leadership has demonstrated clear support for staff working with a challenging client population.

Table 3. Four Winds-Saratoga Performance Improvement Project, Initiated June 1996 (continued)

Figure 2 Children and Adolescents with Disruptive Disorders (Admissions 1993-1995)

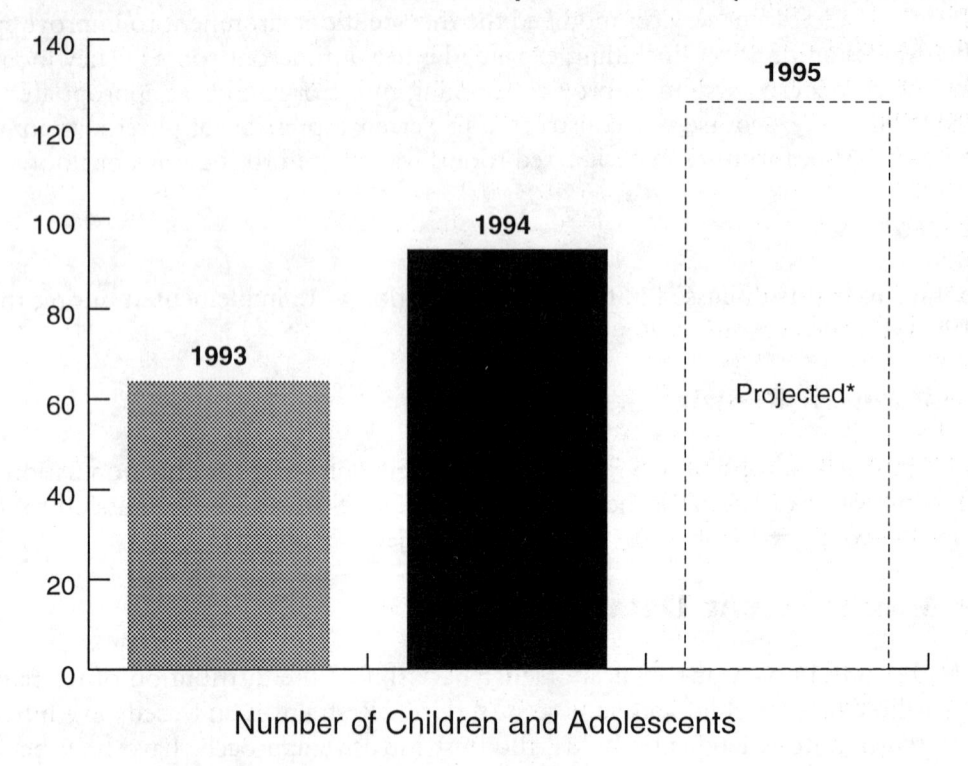

Number of Children and Adolescents

*Based on data through June 1995

Figure 3 Physical Interventions for Children and Adolescents With Disruptive Disorders (1994-1995)

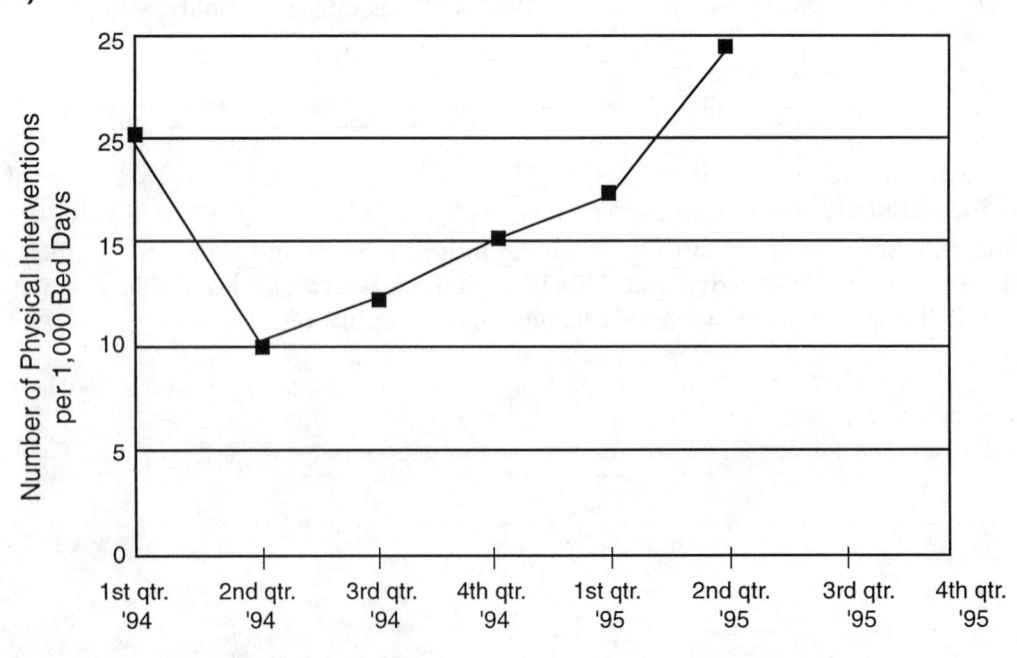

Table 4. Four Winds-Saratoga Summary Intermediate Report Child and Adolescent Staff Development Initiative

In the first phase of the child and adolescent outcomes study, 53% of patients completed the Piers-Harris Children's Self-Concept Scale (PHCSCS) at admission and discharge. Of these patients, 24% completed the mailed follow-up survey. Because the original study design did not include a follow-up clinical assessment, change measures from a clinical perspective were unavailable. In fall 1996, a staff development process was initiated with staff from child and adolescent services to accomplish three goals: improve overall client and parent response rates to the outcomes assessment instruments, introduce a clinical assessment at follow-up, and initiate a treatment intervention capability after discharge.

As the result of fluctuating and inconsistent participation in the outcomes study and satisfaction surveys, two staff persons (mental health worker, unit clerk, or teacher) from each of the child and adolescent units were recruited to serve as outcomes study assistants. The hospital supported this project by motivating the outcomes Study assistants with an additional $.50 an hour to add this component of data collection to their role responsibilities. Assistants received approximately eight hours of training in Child and Adolescent Functional Assessment Scale (CAFAS) assessments and were tested to establish scoring reliability.

In the first phase of the project, the assistants were asked to complete CAFAS assessments at admission, thus relieving the research assistant of that role. Their performance goal was to improve the PHCSCS completion rate to 80%. Before the project, participation rates for completion of the client self-report assessments at admission and discharge had been below 55%. By the third quarter of 1996 (after implementation), the rate of participation improved to 77%. By the first quarter of 1997, the participation rate reached an all-time high of 88%.

As a result of the success in meeting the first-phase goals, the second phase of the project was launched. Follow-up phone interviews were initiated in April 1997 to permit repeat CAFAS assessments one month after discharge, encourage parent and child completion of the Child and Adolescent Adjustment Profile (CAAP) and PHCSCS at follow-up, and provide clinical referral or assistance if requested. Interview formats were scripted by the research staff. Outcomes study assistants were trained to conduct the phone interviews. Initially, every third discharged client was chosen for a follow-up call. After successful interactions with clients and their families in the first set of phone interviews, that rate was increased to every other client.

In May 1997, the outcomes study assistants completed 15 of 17 interviews attempted, resulting in a CAFAS response rate of 88% (one client had been rehospitalized and another could not be located). The assistants reported positive responses from families to the interviews, as well as some requests for assistance. For example, one family requested adjustments in the medication schedule prescribed at discharge, which was unnecessarily complicated and caused missed medications. The problem was referred to the psychiatrist, who adjusted the medication regimen.

This initiative has not been in place long enough to establish improved rates of response to the follow-up PHCSCS and CAAP instruments; however, the initiative has clearly been very successful in the following respects: generating follow-up clinical assessments, providing opportunities for clinical intervention at a critical stage in the client's return to the community; and offering staff meaningful roles in clinical assessment, outcomes measurement, and performance improvement.

Lessons Learned at Four Winds-Saratoga as a Consequence of Conducting Outcomes Assessment and Performance Improvement Activities

Four Winds-Saratoga learned five lessons as a result of these outcomes assessments and performance improvement activities:

1. Meaningful performance improvement can occur only in an environment in which leaders develop a culture committed to continuously improving the clinical care services delivered to clients. This expectation of continuously striving for excellence is the cornerstone of performance improvement.
2. Outcomes measurement must be linked to outcomes management, which is a critical performance improvement initiative. The purpose of generating outcomes data is to facilitate sound decision making about where to focus improvement efforts. The aim of these improvement efforts is to achieve better outcomes by maximizing the effectiveness and efficiency of key practices and processes.
3. It is worthwhile to offer incentives to staff to encourage participation in high-priority performance improvement projects. Incentives may include continuing education and professional development, enhanced professional responsibility, organizational recognition, and financial remuneration.
4. All staff, especially middle-level managers, must develop critical thinking skills, an understanding of data interpretation, and the mind-set to make data-based decisions in combination with professional experience and judgment.
5. Clinical care practices should be examined and modified in the context of changes in the current health care environment. Creative solutions are required to manage the challenges of shorter lengths of stay and decreasing reimbursement rates.

Outcomes Management for Acute Psychiatric Services

John S. Lyons, PhD

With the increasing emphasis on outcomes in behavioral healthcare, there has been a growing call for standard outcomes approaches that can be used across the available array of mental health services. At the same time, that array has been expanding. If one considers this array of available services as a continuum, acute psychiatric services are at one extreme. The mental health needs of recipients of these services are both more immediate and intense than other mental health interventions. As such, the goals of these services are rather different from the goals of other, nonacute behavioral healthcare interventions. Given this reality, the application of outcomes management techniques to acute psychiatric services poses unique challenges. While the federal government has remained relatively uninterested in the outcomes of acute psychiatric services, managed care firms, managed provider organizations, third party payers, and accreditation entities have shown a great deal of interest. Acute psychiatric services, and in particular hospitalization, remain the most expensive segment of the mental health service system. Increasing the urgency to implement outcomes management tools, the Joint Commission on Accreditation of Healthcare Organizations has targeted inpatient psychiatry programs as among the first mental health services required to implement outcomes approved through their ORYX program.

Given the unique role of acute psychiatric services within the larger service system, it is necessary to differentiate outcomes management approaches for such services. One of the primary principles of outcomes management is that outcomes measurement design should be based on the specific goals and objectives of the service (Lyons, Howard, O'Mahoney, and Lish, 1997). Decisions regarding the choice and timing of measures should be made in accordance with an understanding of the desired impact of the service. In the absence of such direction, outcomes management approaches risk the untoward consequences of providing false information about the effectiveness (or lack thereof) of the target service. This is a critical issue in acute psychiatric services since the goals of crisis assessment, stabilization and triage are very different from the goals of mental health treatments such as psychotherapy, medication or rehabilitation. The starting point of all outcomes management projects is to first define and understand the services for which outcomes are to be measured.

Defining the Array Of Services

Crisis Assessment

The primary objective of crisis assessment service is to provide the appropriate referral and triage to need mental health services. Thus, the primary outcome of the crisis services involves a decision regarding the setting and nature of services needed. Crisis assessment services are generally provided at hospital emergency departments. Assessment in these situations is face-to-face and allows a good opportunity for comprehensive assessment. However, the service recipient is often very distressed or is cognitively impaired due to acute psychotic symptoms. Thus, the ability to obtain

---

John S. Lyons, PhD, is the director of the Mental Health Services and Policy Program of the Institute for Health Services Research and Policy Studies at Northwestern University. He is an associate professor of Psychiatry and Medicine.

valid historical data is somewhat limited at least for some cases. The primary outcome of crisis assessment is safety and triage to an appropriate treatment and setting.

Clearly the most important outcome of crisis assessment is that nothing bad happens following the decision regarding appropriate service. The problem with this outcome is that more restrictive settings always ensure better outcomes. Thus, the movement in crisis assessment is toward studying the decisionmaking within the context of the level of risk that each case presents.

Acute Inpatient Hospitalization

Inpatient psychiatric hospitalization services have changed enormously over the past decade. While the number of admissions continues to rise, the average length of stay has plummeted from several weeks to less than six days. As such, the objectives of inpatient services have shifted from the treatment to crisis stabilization and resource mobilization. It is probably naïve to assume that much effective treatment can occur with highly distressed individuals over very brief periods of time. Certainly the expectation of significant functional change borders on the absurd.

Inpatient programs have historically been quite different from outpatient services. As such linkage between these two services is an important outcome. Holding inpatient programs accountable for successful referral to outpatient follow-up is a common performance management strategy. Given inpatient programs' new role as crisis stabilization and resource mobilization interventions, greater attention to the objective of successful referral to outpatient follow-up is warranted. Hospitals often remain focused on the internal clinical states of the individual patients without addressing their post-hospitalization ecological needs.

Acute Partial Hospital

With the consequent reduction in inpatient length of stay, there was an increase in the use of acute partial hospital programs. In their initial manifestation, partial hospital programs functioned like the daytime programming on inpatient units. All that was missing was the overnight stay. In fact, often the same staff provided services in both programs or partial hospital patients were allowed on the inpatient units during the day. Thus, partial programs inherited the treatment component of traditional inpatient programs. As such, the goals and objectives of these programs include a treatment component. However, there has been increasing pressure to force acute partial hospitals to behave like current inpatient programs, which focus more exclusively on crisis stabilization.

Acute partial hospital programs should be distinguished from similarly named but different partial hospital programs that are long-term group interventions. These traditional partial programs have very different treatment goals than do acute partial programs. Traditional partial programs are generally designed for persons with severe and persistent mental illness or debilitating personality disorders.

Intensive Outpatient

The common criticism of both inpatient and partial hospital programs is that there is a set service package that everyone participates in without regard to the individual's specific clinical status. More recently, there has been pressure to provide individualized service packages to recipients. The traditional model of serving everyone with exactly the same services has been replaced with efforts to provide intensive services that match the individual recipient's needs. Intensive outpatient services is a term generally reserved to described individualized service plans that include aggressive medication management, frequent psychotherapeutic contact, and the use of specialized group interventions when indicated. Unlike partial hospital programs in which all recipients work the same basic program, intensive outpatient interventions are less programmatic and should be more flexible to address the individual needs of the recipient. Intensive outpatient programs also include crisis psychotherapy interventions in which the individual may attend daily individual sessions during a period of acute distress.

Acute In-Home Services

Another innovation of the past decade has been the use of in-home services to address acute psychiatric needs. In-home services are particularly appealing for adolescent or geriatric cases in which a caregiver is living in the home with the primary service recipient. When barriers to the management of a case in the community arise from the recipient's living environment, it can be useful to insert services into that environment to help address those barriers. For example, some youth with behavioral disorders are exhausting to parents who may lack the capacity to provide a sufficient level of supervision. In-home services that provide such supervision and teach the parent how to address the youth's behavior can be effective in maintaining a youth in his or her family home. These types of services are a hallmark of the "wraparound" service movement in children's mental health.

Objectives—Defining Outcomes in Acute Settings

Since the dramatic changes in the mental health service system brought on by managed care and other purchaser reforms, the nature of acute psychiatric services has evolved. No longer is psychiatric hospitalization considered a treatment opportunity. Even partial hospital programs are seen as primarily involved in crisis stabilization. These changes have created unique challenges to outcomes management in the acute care setting.

Decisionmaking—Level of Care

One area that sometimes is not included in generic discussion of outcomes management is the management of decisionmaking. Using decision analysis strategies (Lyons, et al., 1997), it is possible to improve the quality of care through enhancing decisionmaking. Nowhere is this opportunity more salient than in acute psychiatric settings because a primary objective of crisis assessment services is to determine the optimal treatment *and* setting for a specific recipient. As such, decisionmaking is a primary objective of acute services.

There are a variety of tools that have been used for decision support and analysis applications. The LOCUS (American Association of Community Psychiatrists, 1996) measure can support psychiatric level-of-care decisionmaking. The American Academy of Child and Adolescent Psychiatry has recently come out with guidelines that form the basis of a decision support tool. We have created two tools, one for adults and one for children and adolescents that have been used for these purposes. The Severity of Psychiatric Illness has three items that have been shown to reliably predict both hospitalization and hospital outcome (Lyons, Stutesman, et al., 1997). This prediction model has been replicated across diverse environments, including both private and public mental health systems of care. In terms of outcomes, more risk-appropriate hospitalizations have better clinical outcomes. An example of an application of the Child and Adolescent version of this measure is described below.

Decision analysis allows for the application of sophisticated statistical modeling. We have used logistic regression for some applications and Optimal Discriminant Analysis (ODA; Yarnold, et al., 1994) for others. Logistic regression allows one to predict a decision, build a statistical model based on the behavior of clinicians in the field, and standardize that model. In this way, individual decisionmakers can be compared to normative decisions. ODA allows for the representation of the most probable decision tree. Figure 1 presents a partial ODA model based on hospital decisions for children and adolescents. Note how concerns about placement safety modify the level of suicide risk associated with a decision to hospitalize. This model is accurate for 81 percent of the cases.

Clinical Outcomes

As mentioned previously, clinical outcomes of acute services likely do not correspond to clinical outcomes of other mental health services. The standard triad of subjective well-being, symptoms, and functioning are likely to be too broad to capture the specific effects of acute services. Also, recipients of acute services are generally extremely distressed at the initiation of services so significant relief from crisis levels of distress can be expected to occur naturally regardless of the intervention. Crisis services generally do not attempt to address all symptoms, only those that represent an immediate risk to the recipient, his or her family, or the community. There is seldom an opportunity to have a significant impact on functioning in the short time frames in which acute services are delivered. Instead, clinical outcomes in these settings should focus on the reduction of risk-

Figure 1. Psychiatric Hospital Decisions for Children and Adolescents in Child Welfare. An Optimal Data Analysis

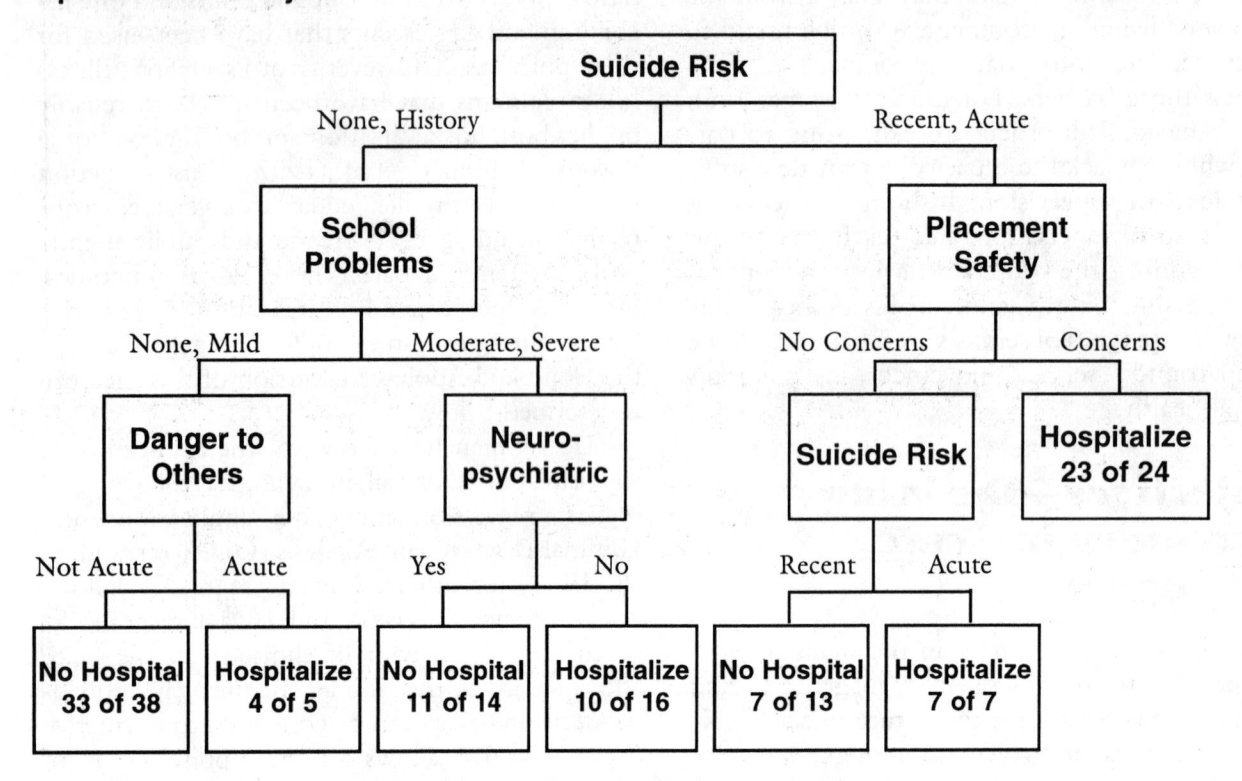

```
                              Suicide Risk
              None, History /              \ Recent, Acute
                           /                \
                   School                    Placement
                   Problems                  Safety
          None, Mild /    \ Moderate, Severe    No Concerns /    \ Concerns
                    /      \                               /      \
           Danger to        Neuro-                  Suicide Risk   Hospitalize
           Others           psychiatric                            23 of 24
       Not Acute / \ Acute    Yes / \ No           Recent / \ Acute
                /   \             /   \                  /   \
        No Hospital  Hospitalize  No Hospital Hospitalize  No Hospital Hospitalize
        33 of 38     4 of 5       11 of 14    10 of 16     7 of 13     7 of 7
```

related symptoms (e.g., suicidality, aggression, agitation, impaired judgment, or reality assessment) and reduced need for monitoring. Resource mobilization is a potentially important outcome of acute services that has received little attention.

Utilization Outcomes

Despite the dramatic reductions in hospital lengths of stay, admissions remain fairly high in most service systems and, overall, the costs of acute psychiatric services remains among the most expensive components of the mental health service system. As such, utilization outcomes are important economic performance indicators. In some cases, utilization outcomes may also reflect upon the quality of care. Table 1 provides a summary of some common utilization outcomes.

A primary advantage of utilization outcomes is that they are easy to measure and uniformly available, making data collection cheaper and more complete. The disadvantage of utilization outcomes is that they generally have clear-cut economic implications, but their implications with regard to quality of care and clinical outcome may be far from direct. For example, a project is described below that demonstrates that even rapid readmissions to a hospital may be unrelated to the clinical outcomes of the hospital episode.

Unique Implementation Challenges

Probably the greatest challenge to outcomes management in acute psychiatric settings is that it is very difficult to obtain consistent and reliable self-

Table 1. Common Utilization Outcomes in Acute Psychiatric Services

Admissions (per 1000 members)
Re-admissions
30-days
90-days
1 year
Length of stay
Annual hospital days
Emergency room visits
Crisis calls
Outpatient visit following discharge
7-days
30-days

report data at the initiation of acute services. In the emergency department or in the first few hours of a psychiatric hospitalizations, the service recipient's level of distress and/or mental status make use of standardized self-report instruments difficult, at least for a substantial proportion of cases. Persons experiencing acute psychotic reactions cannot reliably complete outcomes measures. Persons in the throes of a suicidal depressive episode may not be inclined to do so. For some of these individuals, the level of distress is sufficiently high as to make requests for self-report borderline unethical.

A second unique challenge of outcomes management in acute care settings involves the time frame over which services are provided. Generally, crisis services whether they are provided in inpatient, partial, or outpatient settings, occur over the span of only a few days. Given this shortened time frame, acute psychiatric services will have dramatically different goals and objectives compared to any other mental health services. As such, it is not reasonable to use outcome measures for acute services that are applicable elsewhere in the service system.

The third unique challenge of acute psychiatric services is that the goals of these interventions are quite different from those of other mental health services. As mentioned above, attempts to use measures that are standards of outpatient care can result in misleading outcomes data. This provides a challenge to systems of care that are attempting to use comparable outcomes throughout.

Examples of Outcomes Management Projects In Acute Psychiatry

The Use of Psychiatric Hospitalization in Child Welfare

Over the past two years, the Mental Health Services and Policy Program at Northwestern University has been operating an outcomes management system for the Illinois Department of Children and Family Services (DCFS) crisis assessment services. In this project, all workers complete a Childhood Severity of Psychiatric Illness rating form (CSPI, Lyons, 1998) at all crisis screenings. In addition to service use and volume, on a monthly basis we report back to each agency with regard to their hospitalization decision making.

The CSPI is not used as a decision support tool in that workers are not given any decision guidelines to be used during their crisis assessment and triage. Rather the tool is used for decision analysis; the hospitalize/deflect decision in each case is compared to a model generated from statewide data. Thus, crisis workers' decisions are compared to their peers.

In the model, three variables are used to predict the decision to admit-Suicide Potential, Dangerousness to Others, and Impulsivity. These three four-point scales from the CSPI reliably predict about 78 percent of all decisions to admit (even on cross validation with an independent sample, Leon, Uziel-Miller, Lyons, Tracy, 1998). Interestingly, the prediction of deflections is more accurate (84 percent) than hospitalizations (70 percent) based on a sample of 2,205 crisis screenings. This is due to the fact that crisis workers tend to hedge risk by choosing to hospitalize when in doubt.

When we first began to provide feedback to workers on their decisions, there was a general suspicious response. One agency thought that they should change how the completed the CSPI so that it justified hospitalization rather than explore their clinical approach to crisis triage. However, with time and a consistent message, most agencies and workers have come to understand this feedback as a learning and quality improvement opportunity.

One of the unique aspects of this project is that we have implemented an audit process to ensure that the CSPI remains a reliable and valid representation of the needs of the child or youth rather than a document justifying a decision. Annually, a random sample of case records are selected from each agency and reviewed by independent trained raters. This is possible because the CSPI was designed to be used either prospectively or retrospectively with equal reliability and validity. Our first year's experience with this process suggests that the clinical ratings are reliable with no systematic biases (e.g., overrating the severity of hospitalized cases).

Readmission as a Hospital Quality Indicator

A standard performance indicator for psychiatric hospitalization has been readmission to the hospital. The logic of this indicator is compelling. If a hospital does a good job of solving the psychiatric crisis that perpetuated the hospitalization then there should be no need for further hospitalizations following discharge. In this model a re-hospitalization represents a clear-cut failure of the hospital episode.

In a study of 255 psychiatric hospital cases from a regional Midwestern managed care firm, readmissions within 30 days and six months were compared to cases in which no readmission occurred (Lyons, O'Mahoney, et al., 1997). The Severity of Psychiatric Illness (SPI) was used as the measure of case-mix and the Acuity of Psychiatric Illness (API) was used as the measure of clinical outcome (Lyons, 1998).

The readmitted cases were more severely ill as measured by the SPI and more acutely ill (API) at hospital admission. However, at discharge the cases who were readmitted were at the same clinical status as cases who were not readmitted. Case-mix differences at admission reliably classified about 83 percent of readmissions. Controlling for length of stay it was possible to also demonstrate that early discharge (e.g., sicker and quicker) did not contribute to readmission.

The clear implication of this finding is that it would be a strategic error to hold hospitals accountable for readmission rates. The unintended consequence of such a performance management intervention is that hospitals would be discouraged from taking on the hospital care of persons with severe and persistent mental illness. While it may be that readmissions reflect upon the quality of systems of care, based on these data they do not appear to reflect upon the performance of individual hospitals. Interestingly, there appears to be significant between-hospital differences in their threshold for admitting patients. Some admit significantly lower-risk patients than others. This contributes to somewhat differential readmission rates but not because of anything that happens during the hospitalization.

Outcomes From an Older Adult Partial Program

Over the past two decades partial hospitals have sprung into prominence among acute psychiatric service options and then begun to decline. In response to the dramatic escalation in the use of psychiatric hospitals, partial hospital programs initially represented a low-cost alternative to treatment in 24-hour settings. If a person had sufficient support in his or her living environment, there was no need to require an overnight hospital stay. In the absence of such support, however, hospitalization was still indicated.

Because of the reliance on in-home support to managed overnight risk, partial hospital programs have been particularly popular for addressing the acute psychiatric needs of adolescents and older adults. Both of these populations tend to have primary caregivers who are available for providing supervision or monitoring in the evenings and at night. When supervision is not available, acute inpatient services are more likely to be required.

As a part of an effectiveness evaluation for a national chain of partial hospital programs for older adults, we studied clinical outcomes associated with six different programs. Approximately 25 recipients were recruited from each site, resulting in a sample of about 150. In order to balance credibility with efficiency we used a data collection strategy that combined staff reported data with clinical interviews completed over the phone with independent interviewers. Data was collected at admission, discharge, and approximately one month following discharge. Interview and staff ratings were positively correlated, indicating agreement between staff and recipients on clinical status.

Results of this study, demonstrated that the program was reliably effective with older adults. A dose-response relationship was observed which allowed us to estimate the amount of service (Howard, et al., 1986). According to the statistical model, 50 percent of recipients would achieve reliable clinical improvement if they received 16 days of treatment. Eighty percent of recipients would achieve reliable clinical improvement if they received 22 days of treatment. However, nearly half of the participants failed to achieve a sufficient dose of treatment. Transportation, physical health, and resistance to participation all contributed to lower-than-desired lengths of participation.

Interestingly, both older adults with primary depressive symptom presentations and those with more agitated, cognitive impairment presentations appeared to reliably benefit from the intervention. The clinical improvement in the former group was manifest by reduced depression and suicidal ideation. The clinical improvement in the second group was manifest by reduced agitation. It also appeared that caregiver burden was diminished for the more cognitively impaired older adults. Thus, it appeared that partial hospital programs can serve an important clinical role in the management of acute episodes among older adults with mental illness.

Summary

Acute psychiatric services are a unique portion of the mental health service system that requires a somewhat different approach to outcomes management. It is difficult to obtain self-report data from much more than a slim majority of recipients. One cannot expect dramatic symptom or functioning improvement over the short term of service delivery. Assessment of risk is more important than with other services, and decision analysis has many potential applications. Given these circumstances, it is difficult to generalize outcomes management approaches that have been successful in outpatient settings to these services. Remaining focused on whether the outcomes are consistent with the goals and objectives of the service is the single most important consideration in the design of outcomes management projects for these services.

References

American Association of Community Psychiatrists (1996). *LOCUS. Level of Care Utilization System for Psychiatric and Addiction Services.* Adult Version.

Howard KI, Kopta M, Krause MS, and Orlinsky DE. The Dose-Response Effect Relationship in Psychotherapy. *American Psychologist* 1986; 41:159-164.

Leon SC, Lyons JS, Christopher NJ, and Miller SI. Psychiatric Hospital Outcomes of Dual Diagnosis Patients Under Managed Care. *American Journal of Addictions* 1997; 7:81-86.

Lyons JS, Howard KI, O'Mahoney MT, and Lish J. *The Measurement and Management of Clinical Outcomes in Mental Health.* New York: John Wiley & Sons, 1997.

Lyons JS, O'Mahoney MT, Miller SI, Neme J, Kabat J, and Miller F. Predicting Readmission to the Psychiatric Hospital in a Managed Care Environment: Implications for Quality Indicators. *American Journal of Psychiatry* 1997; 154:337-340.

Lyons JS, Stutesman J, Neme J, Vessey JT, O'Mahoney MT, and Camper HJ. Predicting Psychiatric Emergency Admissions and Hospital Outcomes. *Medical Care* 1997; 35:792-800.

Lyons JS. *The Severity and Acuity of Psychiatric Illness.* San Antonio TX: The Psychological Corporation, Harcourt Brace, 1998.

Yarnold PR, Soltysik RC, and Martin GJ. Heart Rate Variability and Susceptibility for Sudden Cardiac Death: An Example of Mutivariable Optimal Discriminant Analysis. *Statistics in Medicine* 1994; 13:1015-1021.

Assessing the Effectiveness Of Mental Health Care In Routine Clinical Practice

Characteristics, Development, and Uses Of Patient Outcomes Modules

G. RICHARD SMITH, JR., KATHRYN M. ROST, ELLEN P. FISCHER, M. AUDREY BURNAM, AND BARBARA J. BURNS

The health care delivery system faces continually increasing pressure to be accountable for the historically unparalleled amount of resources it utilizes. This article discusses one set of recently developed tools known as outcomes modules that are used to assess how treatment affects outcomes in patients with a given disorder. These tools currently are being used to inform administrative decisions about how to improve the quality of care, and can potentially influence decisions by patients, providers, and payers of care as well. The critical components of outcomes modules, as well as their administration and applications are described, using modules for psychiatric conditions as examples.

Consider the following scenarios:

The director of a large multisite community mental health care program is concerned that the organization may not be providing high quality care to all its patients. A mechanism is needed to routinely monitor and evaluate the effectiveness of care in the program and to compare effectiveness among sites.

Budget cuts are forcing the chief of staff and the chief of psychiatry at a major medical center to reduce services. To reach a rational decision about which services to cut, the administrators need systematic data on the relative effectiveness of individual therapy, group therapy, and day treatment in their organization.

A large purchaser of care is attempting to decide whether to pay for psychotherapy for many mental health conditions where its efficacy has not been rigorously tested. The purchaser must decide within the next 6 months which benefits to offer in next year's plans.

The common thread in these vignettes is the need for tools to permit health care professionals to assess the results of services delivered in routine clinical practice (Mirin & Namerow, 1991). Patient outcomes modules[1] are standardized sets of validated instruments designed to facilitate the systematic gathering of data on patient response to treatment for a particular condition. These

---

Source: Smith GR, Rost KM, Fischer KM, Burnam MA, and Burns BJ. Assessing the Effectiveness of Mental health Care in Routine Clinical Practice. Evaluation & the Health Professions March 1997; 20(1):65-80. Copyright (c) 1997. Reprinted by permission of Sage Publications, Inc.

Authors' Note: This work was supported in part by the NIMH Center for Rural Mental Healthcare Research (P50 MH48197); a grant for the Department of Veterans' Affairs HSR&D Service (HFP 90-019); and contracts from InterStudy, Excelsior, MN, and the Upjohn Co., Kalamazoo, MI. Dr. Smith is also supported by a NIMH Research Scientist Development Award, Level II (K02 MH00843). Address correspondence and requests for reprints to G. Richard Smith, MD; Department of Psychiatry and Behavioral Sciences, University of Arkansas for Medical Sciences, CORE 5800 West 10th Street, Suite 005, Little Rock, AR 72204, (501) 660-7505.

tools currently are being used by health care administrators to monitor clinical performance. They can be used also to provide critical and previously unavailable information to inform the decisions made by patients, providers, and payers.

Patient outcome modules for physical conditions such as hip replacement, cataracts, and hypertension are being developed and validated under the leadership of the Health Outcomes Institute, formerly InterStudy[2] (Ellwood, 1988). The Centers for Mental Healthcare Research (CMHR) at the University of Arkansas for Medical Sciences has taken an active role in the development of outcome modules for psychiatric conditions in collaboration with the Department of Veterans Affairs and InterStudy. Outcomes modules for alcohol dependence, panic disorder, and major depression have been field tested and validated; modules for drug abuse disorders and schizophrenia, as described in articles by Hollenberg, Rost, Humphrey, Owen, and Smith and Cuffel, Fischer, Owen and Smith appearing in this issue of *Evaluation and the Health Professions*, currently are undergoing validation.

Initially, researchers were the primary consumers of outcome modules. Increasingly, numerous organizations providing capitated mental health services have integrated specific modules into routine clinical care to monitor outcomes for a given diagnosis or tracer condition. This article will describe the components of outcomes modules for mental health disorders that we view as critical and the uses that we envision for such modules.

Critical Components Of a Mental Health Care Outcomes Module

The goal of an outcomes module is to measure the impact of treatment on the outcomes of care adjusting for prognostic characteristics in a diagnostically similar patient population. To develop an outcomes module for each of five psychiatric conditions, we convened separate five- to nine-member multi-institutional expert panels. Each expert panel was charged with advising us on the relevant clinical and methodologic issues in creating a module for each condition with the following critical components: (a) ability to verify that patients participating in the protocol met diagnostic criteria for the condition under study, (b) ability to provide valid and reliable data about salient outcomes from both the patient's and provider's perspective, (c) ability to measure prognostic variables to permit comparisons across groups, and (d) ability to assess the type and extent of treatment the patient received for the target condition across various health care delivery settings.

Following each expert panel meeting, the research team drafted a module reflecting the direction provided by the panel. We incorporated measures, scales, or items tapping the constructs of interest adapted from previously developed measurement work whenever possible, giving credit in the user's manual that accompanies each module to the scale's original developer. Where no appropriate scales existed, we developed new items (Rost, Smith, Burnam, & Burns, 1992) or modified existing items. The expert panel then reviewed the prototype and made suggestions on the protocol for field testing. Following its field test, each module was revised to remedy addressable problems. The following sections discuss the four critical components (verification of diagnostic criteria, reliable and valid outcomes measures, prognostic variables to compare outcomes across groups, and measurement of the type and extent of treatment) of outcomes modules, and give examples of how the modules we have developed address each component.

Verification of Diagnostic Criteria

The modules collect information about diagnostic criteria for the condition of interest from the patient and/or treating clinician to establish the appropriateness of the module for the patient in question. The diagnostic component of each module has been designed to provide a brief diagnostic assessment that provides the highest possible sensitivity and specificity compared to a gold standard research diagnosis. The higher the sensitivity, the greater the proportion of true positives the diagnostic component will identify for inclusion in the protocol. The higher the specificity, the greater the proportion of true negatives the diagnostic component of the module will exclude. An additional measure of the success of the diagnostic component is the kappa statistic, which reflects the degree of concordance between the diagnostic module and gold standard research diagnosis adjusted for chance. Kappa statistics from .80 to 1.0 are considered excellent, kappa statistics from .60 to .80 are considered good, and kappa statistics from .40 to .60 are considered fair. In alcohol dependence, patient reports about diagnostic criteria from the modules show better agreement with structured interviews than clinician reports (Dawes, Frank, & Rost, 1993). The patient-derived diagnosis in the Alcohol Outcomes Module has a 100% sensitivity in an alcohol dependent patient population and a 76% specificity in a non-alcohol-dependent, drug-abusing patient population (both groups included patients who did not have the diagnosis) to the structured interview diagnosis of current alcohol dependence ($\kappa = 0.81$). In panic disorder, clinician reports about diagnostic criteria show better agreement with structured interviews than patient reports (Owen et al., in press). Clinician assessment of diagnostic criteria has a 79% sensitivity and a 92% specificity to the structured interview diagnosis of current panic disorder ($\kappa = 0.61$). In major depression, combining clinician and/or patient reports about diagnostic criteria shows the best agreement (Rost et al., 1992). This strategy results in 100% sensitivity and 78% specificity to the structured interview diagnosis of major depression ($\kappa = 0.84$).

Reliable and Valid Outcomes Measures

Modules also monitor how symptoms of the disorder change over time. Outcomes in each of the modules include not only clinical symptoms associated with the condition of interest, but indicators of functioning as well. Although the former is often of primary concern to the clinician, the latter may be of greatest importance to the patient. In terms of clinical symptoms, the alcohol dependence module measures the extent of alcohol consumption in the past month, the panic outcomes module measures the number of panic attacks in the past month, and the major depression module measures the severity of depression symptoms in the last 2 weeks.

In terms of general functioning (Ware & Sherbourne, 1992), measures of physical, mental, and social functioning are monitored using the SF-36 (also known as the Health Status Questionnaire) (Ware, Snow, Kosinski, & Gandek, 1993), as well as the module itself. The SF-36, with scales assessing functioning role (physical and emotional), bodily pain, general health, vitality, social functioning, mental health, and reported health transitions, permits comparisons of outcomes across and within different physical and mental health conditions (Ware et al., 1993). Each outcomes module supplements the SF-36 by measuring particular aspects of functioning that are relevant for the mental health condition of interest. For example, because panic disorder often limits patients from participating in the range of social activities they would otherwise pursue, the panic outcomes module supplements the measure of social functioning in the SF-36 with measures of several distinct types of social impairment often seen in panic disorder.

Validation studies indicate that the relatively short scales included in the outcomes modules provide reliable and valid measures of a range of relevant outcomes. A detailed description of the psychometric performance of the major outcomes constructs in the three modules validated to date appears in Table 1. Interested readers are encouraged to contact the authors for copies of more extended descriptions of the methodology and findings of each validation study.

Ideally, the modules could be used to provide data to clinicians on individual patients and about the patients' clinical change over time. Two problems limit this ability. The first is measurement precision. As can be seen in Table 1, the reliability of all of the outcomes measured by the modules discussed in this manuscript allows for group rather than individual comparisons. However, there is not sufficient precision of the scales to allow individual patient level interpretation. The second problem involves the heterogeneity of patients, where patients with more favorable case-mix/prognostic factors would be expected to make greater gains than those with poorer prognosis, irrespective of treatment. Both problems may be solved, in the future, with better assessment approaches. Because there is a great demand for a "hemoglobin equivalent" in mental health that would provide standardized feedback to clin-

Table 1. Reliability and Validity of Key Outcomes Measures

	Reliability	Validity
Alcohol[a]		
Alcohol consumption in past month	.87[b]	.74[c]
Physical consequences	.88[d]	.55[c]
Emotional consequences	.85[d]	.40[c]
Social consequences	.72[d]	.42[c]
Panic[e]		
Frequency of panic attacks	.96[b]	.71[c]
Anticipatory anxiety	.82[b]	.61[c]
Avoidance/distress	.89[b]	.62[c]
Suicidality	.80[b]	.56[c]
Depression[f]		
Severity of depressive symptoms	.85[b]	.63[c]
Suicidality	.70[b]	.42[b]

a. Data taken from Mental Health Outcome Module Development and Testing: Validation of the Alcohol Outcomes Module (Rost, 1993).
b. k or intraclass correlation.
c. Pearson correlation between module measure and gold standard.
d. Cronbach's alpha.
e. Data taken from Mental Health Outcome Module Development and Testing: Validation of the Panic Outcomes Module (Rost et al., 1994).
f. New measure of severity was developed to keep the module in the public domain, Data taken from the Process and Outcomes of Care for Major Depression in Rural Family Practice Settings (Rost et al., 1995).

icians on the mental health of their individual patients, further measurement work in this area would be very welcomed.

For outcomes modules to be useful, they must be sensitive to clinically important changes in outcomes over time. With regard to alcohol, patient reports about any drinking at follow-up on the Alcohol Outcomes Module demonstrate good agreement (κ = 0.83) with the Structured Clinical Interview for DSM-III-R (SCID) (Spitzer, Williams, Gibbon, & First, 1992). Similarly, patient reports about changes in physical, emotional, and social problems related to drinking within the Alcohol Outcomes Module show strong correlations ($r > 0.65$) to SCID judgments about changes in severity between baseline and follow-up. In panic, there is good agreement between patient reports on the Panic Outcomes Module about change in the frequency of panic attacks between baseline and follow-up and structured interviewers' determinations of the same constructs ($r = .47$). We also observe good agreement between patient reports on change in anticipatory anxiety and structured interviewers judgments ($r = .59$). In depression, studies in both the general medical setting and the specialty care setting have found that patient reports about change in severity of depressive symptoms, as measured on early versions of the Depression Outcomes Module, significantly differ between patients who receive pharmacologic intervention concordant with recently released guidelines (Depression Guideline Panel, 1993a; Depression Guideline Panel, 1993b) and patients who do not[3] (Rost et al., 1992; Rost, Wherry, Williams, & Smith, 1995).

Prognostic Variables to Compare Outcomes Across Groups

Prognostic characteristics known to be associated with choice and/or success of treatment also are included in the modules. These variables, sometimes referred to as case-mix variables, allow analysts to more confidently interpret relationships between treatment and observed outcomes in studies where patients are not randomly assigned to the treatment conditions. They are particularly important when comparing outcomes across sites because they potentially allow analysts to adjust for preexisting differences in prognosis that would otherwise confound the comparisons. Even with the best adjustments, caution should be taken when interpreting differences observed between patient groups in nonexperimental designs.

Although the conclusiveness of the literature admittedly varies across conditions, there appears to be sufficient evidence that clinical variables like disease severity, duration, and comorbidity have an important impact on outcomes for the psychiatric conditions of interest. Outcomes modules also measure a second group of demographic and social factors that affect outcomes, such as age, education, and social support.

Our approach to validating this component of the module has been to demonstrate that the clinical prognostic measures we include in each module (severity, duration, and comorbidity) are reliable and show good concurrent/criterion validity to structured interviews or other widely utilized gold standard measures. In alcohol, the module's measures of disease severity, duration, and comorbidity demonstrated acceptable test-retest reliability: The alpha coefficient for the severity scale was 0.71, the intraclass correlation coefficient for duration was 0.81, and the kappa coefficients for indicators of three psychiatric comorbidities ranged from 0.56 to 0.79. The measure of disease severity and duration in the Alcohol Outcomes Module also showed good concurrent/criterion validity, correlating 0.48 and 0.58, respectively, to structured interview measurements of the same constructs. However, the module's measures of comorbidity showed unacceptable agreement with structured diagnostic interviews, and work is currently underway to improve the module's measurement strategy in that area.

In panic, protocol constraints prohibited us from collecting test-retest information on case-mix variables; however, we were able to examine criterion validity. The module's measure of disease severity showed weak agreement with a structured interviewer's judgment of severity ($r = .27$). In contrast to alcohol, Panic Outcomes Module measures of psychiatric comorbidity showed good agreement with structured interview diagnoses of agoraphobia, depressive disorders, and alcohol/drug disorders ($\kappa = 0.55$ or greater). No gold standard measure was available to test the validity of the module's measure of duration. In depression, limited information is available on the reliability or validity of prognostic characteristics included in the module; however, because all prognostic measures in the Depression Outcomes Module were borrowed directly from previously validated instruments, we do not anticipate significant problems with this component of the module.

Considerably more theoretical and empirical work needs to be undertaken to determine how completely the prognostic variables are able to level the playing field in analyses comparing outcomes across nonexperimental groups. Until further evidence accumulates demonstrating that statistical adjustment for differences in these measured prognostic variables sufficiently controls for sample heterogeneity, comparisons of outcomes between nonexperimental groups should be made cautiously, understanding that initial differences between groups can lead to outcome differences irrespective of treatment.

Measurement of the Type And Extent of Treatment

A careful and comprehensive description and quantification of the services a patient receives is essential to understanding how the provision of care influences outcomes. This component of the module has been designed to measure the types of treatment received for the condition of interest (e.g., pharmacotherapy, individual therapy, group therapy, or electroshock therapy), the extent (e.g., dose, frequency, duration, or number of sessions) of each treatment received, and the setting in which the treatment is delivered (e.g., primary care, specialty care, emergency room, day treatment, or hospital). The modules have been explicitly designed to measure both treatment provided by the system (or payer) as recorded in medical records, as well as treatment received outside the system as reported by patients. Our initial work has not focused on establishing the psychometric precision of treatment received within the system largely because the validity of administrative databases will undoubtedly vary across organizations. Although there are few alternative sources to collect information about out-of-system use, the precision of patient reports about out-of-system use also needs to be more extensively investigated.

Although outcomes modules have been carefully crafted, they are not static instruments. The modules described here are merely first-generation tools, and as such, are open to improvement.

The modules will need to be modified on an ongoing basis to reflect changes in knowledge and clinical practice.

Administration of Outcomes Modules

To conduct outcomes monitoring, an organization needs to choose a target diagnosis or tracer condition of particular interest. We generally recommend that patients enter the outcomes monitoring protocol when their clinicians diagnose the disorder of interest at the initial visit for the condition or for a new episode of the condition. Patients complete the Patient Baseline Assessment of the relevant outcomes module, the SF-36, and the Personal Characteristics Form when they enter the protocol.[4] Clinicians complete the Clinician Baseline Assessment of the relevant outcomes module when patients enter the protocol. It is critical to recruit as high a proportion as possible (> 90%) of patients (or a probability sample of patients) with the diagnosis of interest into the protocol, including patients from clinicians who are less than enthusiastic about outcomes monitoring: Without high participation rates, the findings will not be generalizable to all patients with the tracer condition who received care in the organization.

Information from the Patient Baseline Assessment and the Clinician Baseline Assessment is examined to determine whether patients meet diagnostic criteria to continue in the outcomes monitoring protocol. Those patients who do not meet diagnostic and other minimal eligibility criteria detailed in the users' manuals are excluded from outcomes monitoring.[5]

However, for conditions like major depression or alcohol disorders that are highly prevalent and often underdiagnosed (Bush, Shaw, Cleary, Delbanco, & Aronson, 1987; Wells, Hays, Burnam, Rogers, Greenfield, & Ware, 1989), we have developed a modified strategy to identify a representative cohort of patients with the condition of interest. Patients who are at high risk for the condition can be identified by administering a brief screener to all patients before their visit or in a yearly mail survey (Rost, Burnam, & Smith, 1993). Clinicians and patients complete the baseline portion of the module on all patients who screen positive. Patients who do not meet diagnostic criteria or other minimal eligibility criteria in the baseline component of the module do not proceed further with the protocol. This strategy allows users to examine the outcomes of a representative group of patients with a particular tracer condition in their practice, even when clinicians fail to diagnose sizable proportions of patients with the condition of interest.

We recommend that organizations collect outcomes data on each patient eligible for follow-up at either 4- or 6-month intervals from baseline until remission of the episode. Patients complete the Patient Follow-up Assessment and the SF-36 at follow-up. Data collection from the administrative databases using the Medical Record Review is conducted when patients complete follow-up. Follow-up intervals are chosen by the organization to (a) provide sufficient time for clinical change to occur, (b) be short enough to be responsive to the needs of the organization for information, and (c) to not overwhelm the patient or the organization with work. It is critical to follow as high a proportion as possible (> 80%) of patients who were recruited into the protocol and remained eligible after completing the baseline assessments to avoid selection bias. It is important to follow those who dropped out of treatment, as well as those who remain in treatment. Information on respondent burden, follow-up rates, and missing data for the three mental health outcomes modules we field tested are included in Table 2. The reader is cautioned that these estimates may vary across organizations. For example, our follow-up rates reflect that patients were paid to complete the outcomes module as part of a 4-hour battery of validation instruments.

Application of Outcomes Modules

To date, outcomes modules for mental health conditions have been used primarily for evaluating the effectiveness of routine clinical interventions. Administrators who are charged with improving the quality of care have chosen a tracer condition; provided the necessary training to clinical and administrative staff on protocol implementation; identified personnel to conduct recruitment and follow-up; and made arrangements for data entry,

Table 2. Missing Data and Response Burden in Outcomes Modules

	Percentage Missing Data Mean (SD)	Estimated Minutes to Completion[a]
Alcohol[b]		
Patient Baseline Assessment	1.2 (1.7)	20
Clinician Baseline Assessment	1.3 (2.6)	6
Patient Follow-Up Assessment	7.0 (9.7)	14
Panic[c]		
Patient Baseline Assessment	1.1 (2.9)	18
Clinician Baseline Assessment	0.7 (2.0)	5
Patient Follow-Up Assessment	4.8 (2.1)	20
Depression[d]		
Patient Baseline Assessment	2.3 (3.6)	20
Clinician Baseline Assessment	NA	3
Patient Follow-Up Assessment	2.6 (3.3)	20

NOTE: NA = not available
a. These estimates are derived from subtracting subject's recorded stop time from recorded staff time and proportionately reducing the difference to reflect items that were discarded from the module after validation.
b. Data taken from Mental Health Outcome Module Development and Testing: Validation of the Alcohol Outcomes Module (Rost, 1993). .
c. Data token from Mental Health Outcome Module Development and Testing: Validation of the Panic Outcomes Module (Rost et al., 1994).
d. New measure of severity was developed to keep the module in the public domain. Data taken from the "Process and Outcomes of Care for Major Depression in Rural Family Practice Settings" (Rost et al., 1995).

management, and analysis. It is not yet possible to draw definitive conclusions about the impact of outcomes monitoring because even the first organizations to undertake this effort are just now completing data collection. However, even at this early stage, outcomes monitoring has had some expected, as well as some unexpected, consequences for the organizations involved. One expected consequence was the identification of treatment non-adherence and drop-out rates that were higher than administrators expected, although not necessarily higher than the literature suggested. A second expected consequence was the discovery that extended hospitalizations for major depression produced outcomes similar to shorter hospitalizations that was not explainable by differences in patient severity. Administrators responded to these findings by conducting concerted quality improvement programs to address these problems. Unexpected (yet not undesired) consequences included the (a) departure of a small number of clinicians (< 5%) who were not willing to make practice changes necessary to become goal-congruent with the organization, and (b) the discovery that many clinicians in the organization failed to assign even a tentative diagnosis at the first visit, which resulted in nonreimbursement for thousands of dollars worth of services provided!

We expect that organizations that undertake outcomes monitoring will discover substantial levels of unintended variation in clinical practice, which consumes enormous resources without improving outcomes. These variations can provide a rational basis for identifying and correcting quality of care problems in even the best run organization.

We also anticipate that outcomes modules have other important applications for patients, providers, and payers in the health care system. For patients, outcomes monitoring can provide graphic displays to inform the decisions they make about treatment and treatment compliance, as is currently being done with patients deciding about hip replacement surgery. In the mental health field, clinicians can show patients with panic disorder how the frequency of panic attacks and social functioning is expected to change over time if they continue behavioral therapy and/or psychotropic medication.

For individual providers, the use of aggregate-level information to improve clinical decision making such as how to better match patients to alternate treatment protocols may provide substantial help. For large group providers, merging the results of outcomes monitoring across several practices can provide a sufficiently large cohort to identify treatment modalities that produce consistently good outcomes in the routine care of the patients they treat. These treatment modalities then may be formally tested in controlled clinical trials. We expect that outcomes monitoring may provide clinicians evidence that supports their clinical decisions about which treatments work, to inform decisions about service cutbacks. As measurement precision continues to improve in subsequent generations of outcomes modules, clinicians may be able to rely on outcomes monitoring to monitor progress in individual patients.

For purchasers of mental health services, outcomes monitoring will provide valuable information on differences in outcomes among provider organizations that, complemented by cost data, can help them judge the value of the services they are purchasing.

Discussion

Among the principal advantages of developing outcomes modules is that they provide an approach to outcomes monitoring that is standardized, comprehensive, adaptable, and relatively low burden for patients and clinicians. At present, researchers and program evaluators use a wide assortment of instruments, which makes it difficult, if not impossible, to make meaningful comparisons across studies. The time required to complete the extensive existing research batteries often limits their use to specialized research settings with limited generalizability. By consolidating relevant items from the most robust instruments into a single, brief yet comprehensive tool, we hope to encourage adoption of a standardized measurement package that will permit increasingly meaningful and informative comparisons of the results of independently conducted efficacy and effectiveness assessments.

Utilization of outcomes modules in routine care also will facilitate the introduction of continuous quality improvement into clinical practice. Continuous quality improvement is a process employed by industry to enhance the caliber of its product by monitoring production performance, altering procedures to rectify observed problems, and evaluating the results of such changes on an ongoing basis. This process of performance, outcomes, or effectiveness management is eminently applicable to health care. Until recently, however, the tools necessary to implement it have been largely lacking. Outcomes modules help to fill this gap and offer an opportunity to test whether rational choices can in fact be made when needed data are available and whether, as a result, the average effectiveness of health services in the organizations using the modules will increase.

The most interesting question, and the greatest challenge for the future, is whether outcomes modules will be used in ways that facilitate and promote more effective care and better patient outcomes. There is a potential for outcomes data to be used to patients' detriment if they are interpreted simplistically or invoked to merely limit coverage or to otherwise reduce access to care for seriously ill, high-risk, or high-cost individuals. The potential is also clearly there for clinicians to use outcomes data to optimize treatment and for managers of health care organizations to identify and provide the most effective forms of care to improve the health status of patients.

Notes

1. Because the term *measure* usually refers the assessment of a single construct, and understanding the outcomes of care requires the measurement of multiple constructs, we refer to these sets of instruments as outcomes modules rather than outcomes measures.
2. The modules described in this article axe available for unlimited public use. Please contact Suzanne McCarthy, CORE, 5800 West 10th Street Suite 605, Little Rock, AR 72204.
3. Because copyright restrictions are forcing us to develop a new measure of depression severity to keep the Depression Outcomes Module in the public domain, further psychometric testing will have to be performed to verify the module's measurement of depressive symptoms.
4. Future modules for schizophrenia and adolescent disorders may supplement patient reports

with information from a family member or other appropriate informant when the patient cannot or will not provide valid data.

5. Minimal eligibility criteria (e.g., sufficient cognitive functioning, in the judgment of the treating clinician, to report about life experiences during the past 6 months) were put in place to assure the validity of self-reported data without crippling the generalizability of the sample recruited into the protocol.

References

Bush, B., Shaw, S., Cleary, P., Delbanco, T. L., & Aronson, M. D. (1987). Screening for alcohol abuse using the CAGE questionnaire. *American Journal of Medicine*, 82, 231-235.

Dawes, M. A., Frank, S., & Rost, K. (1993). Clinician assessment of psychiatric comorbidity and alcoholism severity in adult alcoholic inpatients. *American Journal of Drug and Alcohol Abuse*, 19, 377-386.

Depression Guideline Panel (1993a). *Depression in primary care: Vol. 1. Detection and diagnosis* (Clinical practice guideline, No. 5; AHCPR Publication No. 93-0550). Rockville, MD: US Department of Health and Human Services, Public Health Service, Agency for Health Care Policy and Research.

Depression (Guideline Panel. (1993b). *Depression in primary care: Volume 2. Treatment of major depression* (Clinical practice guideline, No. 5; AHCPR Publication No. 93-0551). Rockville, MD: US Department of Health and Human Services, Public Health Service, Agency for Health Care Policy and Research.

Ellwood, P. M. (1988). Outcomes management: A technology of patient experience. *New England Journal of Medicine*, 318, 1549-1556.

Mirin, S. M., & Namerow, M. J. (1991). Why study treatment outcome? In S. M. Mirin, J. T. Gossett, & M. C. Grob (Eds.), *Psychiatric treatment: Advances in outcome research* (pp. 1-14). Washington, DC: American Psychiatric Press.

Owen, R. R., Rost, K., Hollenberg, J., Humphrey, J. B., Lazoritz, M., Bartlett, J., & Smith, G. R., Jr., (in press). Effectiveness of care for panic disorder. *Evaluation Review*.

Rost, K., Smith, G. R., Jr., Burnam, M. A., & Burns, B. J. (1992). Measuring the outcomes of care for mental health problems: The case of depressive disorders. *Medical Care*, 30, MS266-MS273.

Rost, K., Wherry, J., Williams, C., & Smith, G. R., Jr. (1995). The process and outcomes of care for major depression in rural family practice settings. *Journal of Rural Health*, 11, 114-121.

Rost, K. M. (1993). *Mental health outcomes module development and testing: Validation of the alcohol outcomes module, Final report* (SDR Grant #91.005.A). Washington, DC: Department of Veterans Affairs.

Rost, K. M., Burnam, M. A., & Smith, G. R., Jr. (1993). Development of screeners for depressive disorders and substance disorder history. *Medical Care*, 31,189-200.

Spitzer, R. L., Williams, J.B.W., Gibbon, M., & First, M. B. (1992). The structured clinical interview for DSM-III-R (SCID): I. History, rationale and description. *Archives of General Psychiatry*, 49, 624-629.

Ware, J. E., Jr., & Sherbourne, C. D. (1992). The MOS 36-item short-form health survey (SF-36): I. Conceptual framework and item selection. *Medical Care*, 30, 473-483.

Ware, J. E., Jr., Snow, K. K., Kosinski, M., & Gandek, B. (1993). *SF-36 health survey manual and interpretation guide*. Boston: The Health Institute, New England Medical Center.

Wells, K. B., Hays, R. D., Burnam, M. A., Rogers, W., Greenfield, S., & Ware, J. E. (1989). Detection of depressive disorders for patients receiving prepaid or fee-for-service care: Results from the Medical Outcomes Study. *Journal of the American Medical Association*, 262, 3298-3302.

Client Outcome Data: An Emerging Force in Managed Care

REX S. GREEN

Our annual APHA Sunday seminar last November emphasized the role tracking outcomes of clients plays in managed care settings. Surely the importance of tracking client outcomes grows as health plans trim costs and restrict care to meet financial goals. Our speakers shared their latest insights on how to collect and utilize client outcome data to address these issues.

Rex Green recommended applying statistical process control (SPC) methods to track client outcomes in an ongoing manner. After providing an introduction to some of the basic SPC techniques, he described how he applied these methods to previously collected ratings of functioning. He elected to combine ratings across three scales and over time to estimate the rate of change each client experiences during an episode of service. Positive change was expected for these data, since they were collected every visit from newly admitted outpatients at a community mental health center. An Xbar, R-chart was selected to summarize the results. The plot of means for both three successive and five successive discharges from outpatient service revealed wide variations for about the first 50 percent of discharges, then small variation for the remainder of the data. The level of change declined slightly over time. The process of delivering outpatient services was not under statistical control, since one or more points on the plot of the ranges exceeded the upper control limit. The amount of change being 1-3 units per week range on a scale of 0-100 was assumed to be smaller than had been targeted by the programs providing the services, because typical episodes of 3-5 weeks would yield on average only a 15 point change or less.

Gary Bond argued that the assessment of program fidelity is critical to the success of assertive community treatment (ACT), or any mental health service. He reviewed the history of the development of fidelity scales and described how they are applied. Staff or trained interviewers rate the degree of implementation of key characteristics of ACT. Areas covered by the scales include staffing, organization, services, and a summary score. Even using multiple raters, levels of reliability tend to fall below .50, except for the total score, leading him to conclude that additional work should be done on scale development. As part of a formal study of the fidelity scales, scores on the fidelity of program implementation were correlated with reduction in psychiatric hospitalization days. Across 11 programs fidelity correlated .55 with reductions in days. This and other results indicate the presence of some concurrent validity for fidelity scales.

Next, Frederick Newman provided an update on the development and application of outcome assessment tools being employed by the State of Indiana to monitor the effectiveness of mental health services under managed care. Since initiating this development process in 1995 following a 9-step plan, steps 1-7 and parts of step 9 have been completed. The Hoosier Assurance Plan Instrument (HAPI) for adults is a staff rating instrument containing 16 items loading on four factors, symptoms, community functioning, social skills, and risk/substance abuse behaviors, plus

---

Source: Contact Rex S. Green at (408) 255-0671 or e-mail: rsgreen@worldnet.att.net (Reprinted with permission.)

two items covering health status and reliance on services. Results from confirmatory factor analyses and concurrent validity with DSM Axis V ratings were presented. The four-factor structure was supported across several samples of data. Correlations with Axis V ratings were higher for the first three factors, generally above .30, across samples. Correlations with risk behaviors were lower or not significant. These findings are consistent with earlier research on underlying dimensions of functioning. The Child and Adolescent Functional Assessment Scale (CAFAS) was adopted for monitoring outcomes of care provided to children and adolescents. Two confirmatory factor analyses strongly supported the seven-factor structure of the instrument—school, home, substance abuse, emotions, self-harm, thinking, and environment. The results of studies of internal consistency of the subscales and interrater agreement indicated which subscales performed better on this population. Levels of reliability were good, except for ratings of substance abuse among younger children. Composite scores for both measures are being reported in the Provider Profile issued annually.

Richard DeLiberty, who is a Deputy Director of the Indiana Division of Mental Health, shared a pre-release copy of the latest Hoosier Assurance Plan Provider Profile Report Card with our group. Because our meeting occurred in Indianapolis, he had time to pull the latest draft, which is the second annual report on service providers participating in the managed care project. Following an introduction to the results, each provider's services and annual results are summarized in about one page. Tables at the end of the report provide comparisons among providers. The topics describing each provider include their approach to providing services, a list of special services, accessibility of support groups, and utilization review procedures. The performance indicators are graphed in a standardized score format, with 50 representing the overall mean across providers. Some of the indicators are time needed to obtain a first appointment, appropriateness of services, competency of services, degree of help received, and quality of the personal relationships. The pattern of dots is easy to interpret, given the standardized scoring. In addition, comments about the utility of the report were added by several directors of provider agencies who attended the seminar.

Frances Hoffman, a professor at the University of Missouri in St. Louis, presented three examples of outcome improvement projects at an adolescent inpatient psychiatric facility in New York State. She discovered that for ongoing performance improvement efforts, the quality of the assessments interacts with the quality of care and the switch to managed care. Data for these studies were obtained by applying three measures of symptomatology and functioning to tap the perspectives of patient, parent, and clinician at admission, discharge, and one month following discharge. Patient and parent satisfaction with services were also assessed. Participation in the study increased from 61 to 81 percent during a 12-month period. Outcomes improved somewhat following efforts to improve services from the perspective of patients and parents. In other studies of a similar nature, targeting the improvement of response rates for completing the assessments also improved client outcomes, and monitoring LOS for managed care led to clarification of treatment goals and changes in the collection of client outcomes.

Marcia Kauffman reported the results of her doctoral study that focused on whether therapists could improve their ability to form therapeutic alliances and thus enhance client outcomes by monitoring and reflecting on certain therapeutic behaviors. She provided our group with examples of how the self-monitoring occurred and presented the results of her study. Given the volunteer nature of participation, she concluded that the absence of significant effects did not suggest the absence of a relationship between self-monitoring and improved alliances or client outcomes. She anticipates pursuing further studies of her hypothesis.

Due to the informal nature of our meetings, even more was learned during lunch and on breaks about the results of each other's projects. We hope you have the opportunity to join us next November 15 in Washington, when the topic of our forum will be "Outcome Management for Behavioral Healthcare: An Eye to the Future." Anyone wishing to present a paper should contact Rex S. Green at 408-255-0671 or RSGreen@worldnet.att.net.

Chapter 4

Client Satisfaction Ratings: Too Much of a Good Thing?

Assessing Client Satisfaction: Attend To Design, Implementation, Analysis In Your Plans

A workshop at the Clinical Technologies conference at the Albert Trieschman Center in Cambridge, Mass., last fall focused on the struggles of one small agency to design and implement valid patient satisfaction outcomes.

David Coleman, PhD, executive director of The Center for Children's Services in Danville, Ill., began the workshop by stressing the difficulty of getting significant person-related variables. Nevertheless, he said, the "demand for client-centered outcomes has been pronounced."

"Client satisfaction makes a difference in how closely you can match what the client wants with what you offer," said Coleman, "and it is vital to set up a system that allows clients to tell you what they want."

Coleman outlined 10 steps that agencies should take to produce a meaningful, workable system for collecting patient input and producing relevant reports.

1) Ask the Right Questions

The first step, said Coleman, is to decide what information you want to get—i.e., feedback on clinical staff, other staff, the facility, procedures, etc.—and who will be providing you with the data—e.g., will you use self-report, behavioral indicators, correlates. Unless you have done this step carefully, you will waste your efforts.

2) Ask Questions The Right Way

Do you want to elicit the feedback verbally, through a paper and pencil survey or interactive computer program, or perhaps via videotape? Each method has its strengths and weaknesses that include cost and ease of administration.

The voice and tone of your questions are important as well. Coleman recommends that you start your survey with the simplest questions—e.g., how happy are you with the way things are?—and go from there.

3) Choose Your Sample Carefully

It often is impractical to survey all your patients, so you may need to sample. When choosing a sample, Coleman stressed the importance of making it representative—e.g., consider factors such as sex, age, diagnosis. Also look at variables such as mandated treatment and any other factors that could bias the results.

4) Assess Validity

Coleman recommended that you ensure that the data are:
- accurate—e.g., by using validation groups/methods; and

Source: Reprinted with permission by Manisses Communications Group, Inc. Originally published in Behavioral Health Outcomes *February 1998; 3(2):1-3.*

For more information, contact Dr. Coleman at: (217) 446-1300.

For more information on the CSQ, which is copyrighted, address correspondence to: Dr. Attkisson, Department of Psychiatry, BOX CPT, University of California, San Francisco, CA 94143-0984; or to Dr. Greenfield, Senior Scientist, Alcohol Research Group, Ste. 300, 2000 Hearst Ave., Berkeley, CA 94709-2176.

- representative—considering differential response rates, etc.

Agencies new to patient satisfaction may want to use an already published tool since results can be compared to normative data. At Coleman's agency they decided to base their system on *The Client Satisfaction Questionnaire (CSQ) Scales*—authored by C. Clifford Attkisson, PhD, and Thomas K. Greenfield, PhD—a brief 8-question tool that is easy to use and adapt.

5) Identify Possible Confounders

Coleman said that you may get confusing or erroneous results if there are unaccounted for confounders such as:
- self-selection by participating clients; and
- self-selection by method—e.g., mail-in and telephone biases. Mail may not get through if clients move frequently, not everyone will have a telephone, depending on class, type of client.

6) Consider Your Process For Collecting Surveys

If you use only a walk-in sample, you don't address closed cases. Likewise, telephone and mail samples are renowned for their poor response rates.

Decide when you want to administer the form. "We did it every six months by selecting a two-week period and asking everyone who came in to complete the form, regardless of where they were in treatment," said Coleman. Each group needs to tailor this process to meet agency needs.

7) Deal With Low Response Rates

"We decided to use a reward system," said Coleman, "which we needed because human service satisfaction survey response rates are traditionally very poor—around 1%." Your reward system must have broad-based appeal, he added. For example, thank you letters, tickets, a lottery of $250, produced different success rates. Also

---

Technical Tips on Surveying Customer Satisfaction

Designing consumer survey instruments is fraught with pitfalls. Tone, language style, and formatting all affect the way repondents perceive a survey, and thus the way they respond to them.

The usual advice is to rely on a standardized instrument that has been field tested. But in the area of patient satisfaction, there are few to rely on and they may not elicit the information you want about your particular program and clients.

One possibility is to work with a professor or advanced graduate student at a nearby college or university. Preferably you would try to identify someone experienced in opinion and/or satisfaction surveys who is familiar with behavioral health treatment approaches and environments.

But even if you had the best client satisfaction instrument possible, you still face the problems of poor response rates and of limiting the things you can learn from consumers. To get around those, you might want to try talking with fewer people to get more in-depth feedback.

Mario Hernandez, Ph.D., who is research associate professor at the University of South Florida, suggests using focus groups and case studies. Not only do you have more control over who is in your sample, you also can use open-ended questions that allow you to learn some things you didn't already know—or think to ask about.

But you'll want to be careful who conducts your focus groups and how. Provider representatives may find it difficult to stay objective and open to the criticisms and suggestions being made. On the other hand, if an outsider facilitates such sessions, it is important to establish limits that protect individual clinicians and other staff from being publicly singled out.

Some programs depend on well trained consumers to conduct focus groups and have been satisfied with the results that tell them what patients and/or their families:
- like about the program;
- think are barriers or problem areas; and
- suggest be changed to improve their satisfaction and outcomes.

remember to consider concerns about survey confidentiality—e.g., use two envelopes.

"Taking data on how well the reinforcers work depending on when offered, how, and who to, is also a necessary part of developing and refining your system," said Coleman. This enables you to redesign your system to reflect the results you get. "For example, he added, "the group we offered tickets and money to immediately produced the best response rate for us."

8) Use Technological Aids

With the volumes of information that providers are expected to collect, it is becoming increasingly necessary to use whatever technological aids are available to us, said Coleman. "We need all the help we can get to make data collection more efficient," he added, "and using bar codes and the latest computer software can ease the process along."

9) Interpret the Results

Just reporting results doesn't really help; you need to do something with the data. Coleman suggested:
- comparison with published norms—i.e., if you have used a known scale, it may be possible to match your data with results that have been published with a comparable subject group;
- comparison with prior data you have collected at your agency; and
- analysis of subgroups—e.g., voluntary vs. involuntary clients, diagnostic category, parents vs. children.

10) Correlate Satisfaction Outcomes With Other Data

To conduct complete analyses and produce meaningful reports on patient satisfaction, Coleman recommended tying satisfaction results to other characteristics, such as:
- formal/informal outcome measures;
- personality scale scores;
- impact on service delivery; and
- impact on funding.

"Patient satisfaction data can enable you to look at particular treatment strategies—i.e., early or late client engagement—to see what seems to work," said Coleman.

It is also important to check data over a period of time to see whether they are stable, and to see whether client feedback is being heard and heeded.

"Track any changes in client satisfaction," Coleman added, "to see whether you are making a difference to people."

This information is useful for QA and to payers to check whether you are doing what you say you are doing. More importantly, though, is to use it to improve client satisfaction.

Satisfaction Ratings: Meaningful Or Meaningless?

KIRK M. LUNNEN, MS AND BENJAMIN M. OGLES, PHD

The measurement of consumer satisfaction with behavioral healthcare services is increasing with market and regulatory requirements. Some organizations refer to the results of their measures as outcomes. Some confusion and debate has consequently arisen as to the meaning of consumer satisfaction and its relationship to other types of outcomes. In this article, Lunnen and Ogles refer to existing research to clarify these meanings and relationships.

Measures of consumer satisfaction are collected in a wide variety of settings. The advantages of satisfaction surveys are both obvious and numerous. Such data are relatively easy to collect, inexpensive, have strong validity, and are understandable to non-psychometrically sophisticated individuals. Their use is fairly widespread across mental health institutions, businesses, and other service organizations to gauge the extent of consumer satisfaction with the goods or services provided. Satisfaction is also an essential component of many managed healthcare quality assurance programs. In fact, there are numerous cases in both published research as well as clinical practice where satisfaction is used as the primary outcome indicator. The instruments used range from thrown-together, homemade tests to lengthy, psychometrically sophisticated devices.

Despite their popularity, increasing evidence suggests that clients' reports of satisfaction are not an accurate indicator of meaningful changes in symptoms or functioning. A wealth of clinical research indicates that the correlations between satisfaction data and other outcome variables are generally quite low, usually falling between the zero to .40 range. We will first refer to findings from two recent studies to highlight this and to suggest that satisfaction is not as valuable an outcome indicator as previously suspected.

The Meaningfulness of Satisfaction Reports

Post-therapy scores on specific outcome measures must be similar to the scores of non-symptomatic or healthy individuals on the same instrument. Also, the amount of change (from pre- to post-treatment) must be significant to be statistically reliable. Pekarik and Wolff concluded:

> The fact that this study used stricter criteria (clinical significance) to define and separate those who were therapeutic successes from those who had failed and still found little in the way of significant relationships between outcome and satisfaction provides stronger evidence than previously available of the negligible relationship between satisfaction and outcome. The clinical-significance definitions clearly produced extreme groups of successes and failures, yet even these were not related to satisfaction. This strongly suggests that satisfaction is not meaningfully related to traditional client measures of outcome.[1]

We conducted a similar analysis of satisfaction from the clients' point of view and added an evaluation from the perspective of clients'

Source: Reprinted with permission by Manisses Communications Group, Inc. Originally published in Behavioral Healthcare Tomorrow *August 1997:49-51.*

Kirk M. Lunnen, MS, is a doctoral candidate in the clinical psychology program at Ohio University. Benjamin M. Ogles, PhD, is an associate professor in the Department of Psychology at Ohio University.

spouses/significant others. Clients at a rural community mental health center were administered the Outcome Questionnaire (OQ-45) at intake, and before each subsequent session of therapy.[2] When an individual client demonstrated large enough changes on the instrument to be considered statistically reliable, the client, along with their spouse/significant other, was asked to complete a satisfaction survey. Reliable changes were separated into two groups: 1) those who showed symptomatic improvement ("improvers"), and 2) those who showed symptomatic deterioration ("deteriorators"). Data from a group of subjects who did not make reliable improvement or deterioration ("non-changers") were also gathered.

By client report we found that satisfaction levels for the improvers were not significantly higher than non-changers, but were significantly higher than the deteriorators. From the spouse/significant other perspective, there were no differences in the level of satisfaction across the three client groups. Only one of six comparisons was significant, suggesting minimal concordance between symptom change and satisfaction.

Together, these two recent studies suggest that the satisfaction level of clients who can be classified as clinically improved do not differ from clients who make little or no symptomatic improvement. Why might satisfaction and symptomatic improvement be unrelated?

The Relationship Between Satisfaction and Symptoms

A variety of reasons may explain why satisfaction is not necessarily related to improvement in symptoms:

1. It is conceivable that clients have rated their degree of satisfaction on the basis of something other than their satisfaction with the symptom or presenting problem change. Several factors independent of symptomatic change, such as likability of the therapist, availability of services, pleasantness of the clinic environment, etc., may contribute to clients' ratings of satisfaction.
2. There is also a lack of variability in satisfaction ratings in most studies. Evidence indicates that clients tend to report high satisfaction regardless of outcome. This restriction of range may attenuate the relationship between satisfaction, and symptomatic improvement.
3. Clients may be willing to report negatives about themselves, while they are reluctant to report dissatisfaction with the service provider. As a result, their level of distress may actually increase while they report continuing satisfaction with treatment. In many instances, clients recognize that their changes in symptoms are unrelated to the effort of the treatment provider; an oncologist may provide state-of-the-art quality care, yet the client may still die as a result of cancer.
4. There is also some question as to whether current instruments actually provide an appropriate range of items reporting dissatisfaction. Pekarik and Wolf suggest that "Future research could address this by generating satisfaction items that...assess a wider range of clinical phenomenon. For example, rather than simply ask about satisfaction with the therapist, items could assess specific aspects of therapist behavior (e.g., therapist advice on how to cope with problems outside the session)."
5. Another common problem with client satisfaction ratings is low return rates. In many agencies questionnaires are mailed to individuals some time after the completion of treatment. Response rates for these surveys are notoriously low. For example, in the 1995 *Consumer Reports* survey of attitudes toward psychotherapy 22,000 (12%) of 180,000 readers responded to the survey. However, only 7,000 (31% of the responders) answered questions relevant to mental health. Of the 7,000, only 4,100 answered the questions with a mental health professional in mind. The other 2,900—less than three percent of the readership—answered relative to discussing problems with friends, clergy, or family. Any of these reasons, among others, may contribute to the incongruence between satisfaction ratings and clinical outcome.

What should we conclude from these findings? It is not our purpose to deride satisfaction assessment as an irrelevant and useless method. Because they appear to be independent of clinical improvement, some may argue that satisfaction ratings provide a unique piece of information. As a result, it may be even more important to assess satisfaction as a way of measuring client reactions to treatment incidentals. Perhaps the best option is to include the assessment of both satisfaction and changes in symptoms or functioning.

One example of this type of assessment strategy involves Our own efforts to develop brief, practical measures of outcomes for children and youth with severe emotional disorders (The Ohio Scales). The Ohio Scales were initially developed for tracking the effectiveness of cross-system services for children and youth in the public sector. Areas of assessment include four specific content areas: problem severity, level of functioning, hopefulness, and satisfaction with services.[3] We feel strongly that both clinical changes and satisfaction are important areas to assess when evaluating individual or system success. Within the public sector there is a strong move toward including clients and families in all parts of treatment planning, and delivery. Collecting data regarding their satisfaction with services, in addition to clinical change, is one way to keep track of their reactions to the system. Within the current consumerism movement it seems apparent that client satisfaction will continue to be an important component of any service evaluation.

The larger question for organizations and administrators who want to assess treatment effectiveness may be whether to rely exclusively on satisfaction ratings. Many organizations are scrambling to find useful methods of assessing treatment outcome as the healthcare market changes. Because client satisfaction measures are easy to implement, some agencies are turning to them as the foundation of their outcome assessment package. In some cases, it may be the only outcome indicator. Although client satisfaction may provide useful information, it is important to note that clinical improvement may not be related to it. The bottom line is that agencies who wish to ascertain the clinical effectiveness of their interventions must consider using other sources of data.

References

1. Pekarik, G. & Wolff, C.B. (1996). Relationship of satisfaction to symptom change, follow-up adjustment, and clinical significance. *Professional Psychology: Research and Practice*, 27, 202-208.

2. Lambert, M.J., Lunnen, et al. (1994). *Administration and Scoring Manual for the Outcome Questionnaire* (OQ-45.1). Salt Lake City, UT: IHC Center for Behavioral Healthcare Efficacy.

3. Ogles, B.M., Lunnen, K.M., et al. (1996). Conceptualization and initial development of the Ohio Scales. In C. Liberton, K. Kutash, & R. Friedman (Eds.), *The 8th Annual Research Conference Proceedings, A System of Care for Children's Mental Health: Expanding the Research Base* (pp. 33-37). Tampa, FL: University of South Florida, Florida Mental Health Institute, Research and Training Center for Children's Mental Health.

Asking the Right Questions

A Rational Approach To Measuring Client Satisfaction

ASTRID BEIGEL, PHD, AND CHRISTINE TORRE

Abstract: Client satisfaction surveys generally show a preponderance of high satisfaction ratings with little variability across populations, which is probably an accurate reflection of clients' perceptions, rather than an instrument problem. This interpretation is based on theoretical and empirical studies and surveys demonstrating ratings of services are related to expectations and clients generally get at least what they expect. The authors speculate that the right questions are not being asked to solicit clients' suggestions for service improvements. It is proposed the latter must be measured separately and distinctly from satisfaction to adequately and accurately answer both questions.

Determining consumer or client satisfaction with services, products, activities, and events of all kinds has become paramount in our society. In health care in general, and behavioral health in particular, the shift to managed care has accelerated the importance of measuring client satisfaction with services. Satisfaction has been accepted as one of the cornerstones of quality management in the behavioral health care field. Directives to measure satisfaction are part of the quality management guidelines and provider requirements set by managed care companies, administrative service organizations, provider groups and public agencies. In the public sector, including the Medicaid population, the emphasis on client participation has increased exponentially.

As a result of this emphasis on client satisfaction assessment, a plethora of client satisfaction instruments and measures have emerged, developed by a range of interested parties, including hospitals, consumer groups, and providers. There is little uniformity or standardization among these measures, and questions often are included to meet criteria that seem important to the developers and give the appearance of measuring what they are intended to measure. Standardized measures also have been created based on empirical research and validated on groups using services.

But these satisfaction instruments, including the standardized ones, have led to frustration because of a lack of variation in satisfaction ratings, which generally are overwhelmingly positive. Such results have proven insufficient for program evaluation and continuous quality improvement. Adopting longer measures in an effort to increase variability does not appear to affect the results.

This article addresses the issue of client satisfaction measurement from a practical point of view and reviews traditional speculations and findings, including the authors' own study. It proposes a new approach which distinguishes between client satisfaction with services and clients' views on how to improve services by "asking the right questions." Specifically, it is suggested that satisfaction with services and ways of improving services are separate constructs/questions. While the focus of this article is on the public sector, the approaches are equally applicable to other settings.

What Is Satisfaction?

The measurement of satisfaction is one component of a comprehensive quality management system and is distinct from other components such as outcome, compliance with standards, and process factors (Beigel & Torre, 1996). While the dictio-

---

Biegel A and Torre C. Asking the Right Questions. In: 1999 Medicaid Managed Behavioral Care Sourcebook, K Coughlin, ed. New York: Faulkner & Gray, 1998, pp. 359-367.

Astrid Beigel, PhD, is chief, and Christine Torre, is manager of outcome programs, in the Quality and Outcome Bureau, the Los Angeles County Department of Mental Health. They are leaders in the quality management field in California and nationally. They have been influential in shaping the direction of outcome measurement in California at the state and local levels and have written and presented extensively on the topic.

nary defines *satisfaction* as meeting or exceeding expectations or needs, Hunt (1977) concludes that satisfaction is an evaluative reaction resulting from the interaction of the product or situation with the individual's expectations. In behavioral health, this refers to clients' perceptions of the services provided. Presumably, if clients' needs and expectations are met, they are satisfied.

How Satisfaction Is Typically Measured

The standard approach to measuring satisfaction with behavioral health services has been to use a client-completed survey of some sort. All such instruments, regardless of how they were developed, have some things in common. The instruments typically consist of a number of questions ranging from a few to as many as 40 or 50. Usually, the responses are rated on scales of from four to 10 or more points, with anchors that differ markedly, e.g., "strongly agree" to "strongly disagree"; "very satisfied" to "very dissatisfied"; "delighted" to "terrible" etc. The questions vary considerably in such areas as content, specificity, and value judgment. What appears consistent is that the respondents tend to be persons receiving services *at the time* they express their opinions. The results consistently reveal high levels of satisfaction, frequently more than 90 percent, with very little variability.

Several types of instruments have emerged over the years, including global measures of satisfaction with specific services and multi-dimensional measures attempting to assess various elements of satisfaction (Attkisson & Greenfield, 1998), sometimes combined with questions related to outcome, access, and appropriateness of services (Task Force on Consumer Oriented Report Card, 1996). Various approaches have been taken to the administration of measures, including programs that employ consumer interviewers (Kennington, 1996), telephone contacts, surveys by mail, and touch-screen technologies (Dow, et al., 1996).

Some of the most notable research on satisfaction has taken place at the University of California San Francisco, where over the past two decades the Client Satisfaction Questionnaire-8 (CSQ-8) and the Service Satisfaction Scale-30 (SSS-30) have been developed, studied, and refined. Both instruments were designed to be direct measures of a client's experience with a specific service, and they are widely used in a range of behavioral health and medical agencies in both the public and private sectors (Attkisson & Greenfield, 1998).

Client involvement in the development of consumer-oriented measures of satisfaction also has been increasing. The Mental Health Statistics Improvement Program (MHSIP) Consumer Survey is an example of an instrument developed with considerable client involvement. The MHSIP Consumer Survey, which is beginning to gain wide acceptance, was developed by a MHSIP task force under the federal Center for Mental Health Services as part of an effort to design a consumer-oriented report card. The instrument is multi-dimensional in that it is intended to measure the domains of access, appropriateness, outcomes, and prevention, as well as satisfaction with services. The total survey is 40 items, although the first 25 items have been used in a number of settings as a satisfaction instrument (Koch & Harlow, 1997). The developers' intent, however, was to include satisfaction items within the other domains. The instrument begins with several general satisfaction items and scatters others throughout the survey (Task Force on Consumer Oriented Report Card, 1996).

The Behavioral Healthcare Rating of Satisfaction (BHRS), developed at the University of South Florida with client participation, is being used throughout the Florida State behavioral health system. A 26-item measure designed specifically for persons with severe mental illness, the BHRS has undergone several revisions and continues to be modified (Dow & Ward, 1996).

Why So Little Variation?

The reasons for the general lack of variation in responses—regardless of instrument, administration method, or population—continue to be debated (Larsen, et al., 1979), and have raised professional suspicions about the use of such measures in program evaluation (Greenfield, 1983). Debates are also ongoing about the validity of self-report/client perception and the lack of correlation of satisfaction with treatment outcome. There does seem to be agreement that satisfaction measurement is one aspect of service assessment, independent of treatment outcome and other aspects of program evaluation, and is therefore not a substitute for other indicators (Attkisson & Greenfield, 1998).

A Comparison of Satisfaction Measures: An Exploratory Study

In order to address some of the concerns about client satisfaction, including instrument selection, length, content, and structure of measures, the authors conducted a study, with all of the problems inherent in field investigations. The study compared three satisfaction measures: the CSQ-8 (Nguyen, et al., 1983); the BHRS (Dow & Ward, 1996); and the 25 items of the MHSIP (excluding outcome items) that have been used in other studies to measure satisfaction (Koch & Harlow, 1997).

The participants in the study were drawn from four Los Angeles County outpatient psychiatric mental health clinics that serve severely and persistently mentally ill adults. Two clinics are directly operated by the Los Angeles County Department of Mental Health and the other two are private agencies under contract to the county.

The study was intended to be nonintrusive and, as a result, did not meet all of the desirable methodological criteria. However, there was substantial uniformity across clinics, and the findings yield significantly more information than mere speculation and contribute to substantiating the general hypotheses presented in this article.

During a two-month period, each of the four clinics included in the study was instructed to provide one of the three client satisfaction surveys to

Table 1. Item-Means and Item-Totals, for Individual Providers
MHSIP and BHRS scores also transformed to be comparable with CSQ-8 scores

		CSQ-8 raw	MHSIP raw	trans.	BHRS raw	trans.
Provider A	n=128	45	34		49	
	mean item-mean	3.5	4.0	3.2	5.2	3.5
	stdev	0.54	0.58	0.44	0.52	0.31
	mean item-total	28.3	99.8		134.7	
	stdev	4.35	14.56		13.60	
Provider B	n=137	46	43		48	
	mean item-mean	3.5	4.2	3.4	5.2	3.5
	stdev	0.47	0.49	0.37	0.58	0.35
	mean item-total	27.9	104.5		133.8	
	stdev	3.79	12.22		15.09	
Provider C	n=108	48	16		44	
	mean item-mean	3.5	4.1	3.3	4.8	3.3
	stdev	0.43	0.48	0.36	0.94	0.56
	mean item-total	27.9	102.0		125.2	
	stdev	3.43	11.96		24.34	
Provider D	n=171	55	43		73	
	mean item-mean	3.2	3.0	2.5	4.5	3.1
	stdev	0.53	0.68	0.51	1.01	0.61
	mean item-total	25.9	75.3		117.4	
	stdev	4.26	16.96		26.26	
	total n=544	194	136		214	

all clients presenting themselves for services until the supply they were given was depleted. (It was considered unrealistic to have the same client complete all three instruments.) The surveys were completed by adults (18 and over) receiving services at the time (except those attending a first session) who were able to respond to the English language versions. The surveys were distributed by a range of nonclinical staff, usually support staff (never the client's own clinician), and assistance was offered if needed. The surveys were completed and returned the same day. All surveys were anonymous and no other identifying or demographic data were collected.

In addition, to assess perceptions of an instrument's usefulness, clients were asked to choose one of the following:
- I like this instrument. It should be used.
- I have mixed feelings. It doesn't matter if you use it or not.
- I don't like it. It should not be used.

For analytic purposes, surveys were excluded if: (1) any of the eight items on the CSQ-8 were not completed, or (2) if four or more items were missing from the 25-item MHSIP or the 26-item BHRS. Further factor and cluster analyses used only those surveys that had no missing items.

The findings are based on a total sample of 544 clients. The MHSIP was completed by N = 136; CSQ-8, N = 194; BHRS, N = 214. Table 1 shows the distribution of the number of responses by provider/clinic for each instrument, including means and standard deviations.

The instruments vary in their rating scales with respect to anchor designations and number of points on the scale. The CSQ-8 consists of four-point rating scales with anchors that vary, depending on the question. It also varies scale direction from positive to negative and negative to positive. The BHRS item ratings are on a six-point scale, ranging from "Disagree Strongly" to "Agree Strongly." The MHSIP is rated on a five-point scale, ranging from "Strongly Disagree" to "Strongly Agree," with a neutral point, i.e., "I Am Neutral." In addition, "Not Applicable" can be selected as an alternative.

Although all three measures differ in ratings, the scoring methodology is similar, i.e., the score is either a total (the sum of the individual item ratings) or the mean of the individual item scores (the sum of the item scores divided by the number of questions, i.e., mean item mean). To make meaningful comparisons among the three measures, the scores on the BHRS and MHSIP were statistically transformed so they could be more readily compared to the CSQ-8. Thus, comparisons are made as if all three measures were based on four-point scales. (For purposes of comparison with other studies, nontransformed data are also included in Tables 1 and 2.)

Figure 1 summarizes the study's major findings. These data, in combination with the findings presented in Tables 1 and 2, substantiate the hypotheses that satisfaction with services is a relatively unidimensional construct and different from the construct relating to other service-relat-

Table 2. Item-Means and Item-Totals, for Four Providers Combined
MHSIP and BHRS scores also transformed to be comparable with CSQ-8 scores

	CSQ-8 raw	MHSIP raw	trans.	BHRS raw	trans.
n=514	194	136		214	
mean item-mean	3.4	3.8	3.1	4.9	3.3
stdev	0.51	0.77	0.57	0.86	0.52
mean item-total	27.4	93.8		126.6	
stdev	4.07	19.13		22.39	
number of points in scale	4	5		6	
maximum item-total	32	125		156	

ed variables such as the presence or absence of events, or services or activities that are deemed to be values, such as the notification of rights and waiting time (for example, items 7, 15, and 17 on the MHSIP (7: "Staff returned my call within 24 hours"), (15: "I was given information about my rights"), and (17: "Staff told me what side effects to watch for"). Therefore, it is not surprising the MHSIP (even excluding the "outcome" items) differs from the CSQ-8 and BHRS, since it was designed to measure areas such as access and appropriateness, in addition to satisfaction.

The findings of this study are similar to those reported by Koch and Harlow (1997) regarding the MHSIP and to those reported by the developers of the BHRS (Dow & Ward, 1996; Dow, 1997). All studies used very similar populations—severely and persistently mentally ill adults receiving services in public sector outpatient settings.

The most important findings are: (1) clients report being generally satisfied; (2) there is little variability among satisfaction measures; (3) there is high consistency in responses across similar measures; (4) more than two-thirds of the respondents reported "liking" the instrument they rated; (5) the MHSIP, which measures more than satisfaction, behaves differently than the BHRS and CSQ-8, which are intended to be satisfaction measures; and (6) negatively worded items cluster together, suggesting a method (wording artifact) variable.

This last finding is substantiated in the work of Koch (1998) and others, which have found that when the items are reversed (worded positively), they no longer cluster together as a factor. That is, the factor disappears and the items cluster with others in the scale. (For example, the negatively worded "I was unable to get the services I thought I needed" can be rephrased as "I was able to get the services I thought I needed.") This suggests the wording is confusing (greater variability) rather than demonstrating the existence of a separate construct. As a result, the MHSIP has been revised and in the new version the negatively worded items are stated positively (Koch, 1998).

The Impact of Expectations On Satisfaction

The findings above, along with the earlier work of other authors, suggest client satisfaction ratings are relatively constant regardless of factors such as

---

Figure 1. Study of Three Client Satisfaction Instruments

Design
- Four Sites
- Three instruments/sample size
  Mental Health Statistics Improvement
  Program (MHSIP)   N = 136
  Client Satisfaction Questionnaire
  (CSQ-8)   N = 194
  Behavioral Healthcare Rating of Satisfaction
  (BHRS)   N = 214

Major Findings
- All three instruments are equally and highly internally consistent, i.e., items within each instrument measure the same thing (coefficient $\alpha = .90$ or above)
- All three instruments have basically one general factor/cluster. However, on the BHRS and MHSIP, which have some negatively worded items, the negative items cluster on a factor of their own, i.e., negative items cluster.
- BHRS and CSQ-8 behave very similarly; MHSIP somewhat differently with respect to variability on individual item ratings, distribution, etc., consistent with the fact that it is intended to measure domains other than satisfaction.
- When comparisons are made between sites, there are statistically significant differences between sites, regardless of the instrument used. This suggests site, rather than instrument, differences. Ratings are on the "satisfied" end of the continuum.
- When comparisons are made between instruments, regardless of site, there are statistically significant differences between the BHRS and MHSIP, and between the CSQ-8 and MHSIP, but not between the CSQ-8 and BHRS. This suggests the MHSIP measures something other than satisfaction.
- All ratings are generally highly positive, i.e., high satisfaction.
- When respondents were asked to rate their "liking" of the instrument, ratings of preference were not significantly different and were generally high; 76% for CSQ-8; 69% for BHRS; and 64% for MHSIP.
- Findings are consistent with other studies.

instrument used, item wording, or content of the measures.

An extensive body of empirical and theoretical research, much of it founded in social psychology, demonstrates that expectations influence perceptions (Beigel, 1973; Kincade, 1996). Studies have found a generally positive relationship between clients' expectations and results of treatment in behavioral health (Bloch, et al., 1976; Friedman, 1963; Goldstein & Shipman, 1961; Karzmark, et al., 1983; Lipkin, 1954; Sotsky, et al., 1991; Tollinton, 1973; Uhlenhuth & Duncan, 1968). More specifically, an extensive body of empirical research substantiates the theory that initial expectations about services (treatment) are a major determinant of satisfaction with those services (Frank, 1968; Kincade, 1996; Oliver, 1977; Oliver, 1980; Ross, et al., 1981; Ross et al., 1994). Initial expectations interact with subsequent experiences, influence the perception of those experiences, and result in the range of satisfaction ratings. Thus, there is a strong positive relationship between expectations and satisfaction, whether these expectations are explicit or implicit.

A tentative explanation for typically positive satisfaction ratings on a continuum from "very satisfied" to "very dissatisfied" in behavioral health is that clients appear to define expectations that are subsequently met. Thus, when rating satisfaction with services, clients assess globally against a standard set by themselves. This standard-setting process takes various factors into consideration and makes comparative judgments.

For example, when satisfaction ratings are requested at a fast-food restaurant, it is not necessary to explicitly state that the rater should consider a variety of factors in making the judgment. Expectations are implicitly different from those that would apply when rating a gourmet restaurant. While there may be considerable variation in quality and ambiance between the two eating establishments, the ratings could easily be, and often are, the same, because the expectations are different.

Our expectations form an implicit standard, and it is possible to have "better" services rated lower if the initial expectations are higher. The auto mechanic who promises the car at 2:00 p.m. and delivers it at 3:00 p.m. is more likely to encounter dissatisfaction than if the car is promised at 4:00 p.m. and is delivered at 3:00 p.m.

Given this expectation hypothesis, it is not surprising that satisfaction ratings are generally high. The research suggests that in behavioral health, people usually get what they expect (although not always; about 10 percent of the ratings are in the "dissatisfied" range). Further, it must be noted that generally only those who are receiving services at the time the rating is made are included in most surveys. The opinions of those who have already left due to displeasure (or another reason) are not heard. This, of course raises questions of generalizability, and this group requires further study in any service satisfaction assessment process. However, those surveyed at the time they are receiving services appear to believe they are getting what they bargained for.

The premise that explicit or implicit expectations influence perceptions (in this case, satisfaction ratings) raises important questions in comparing satisfaction ratings. Clearly, such ratings can be influenced by manipulating or defining expectations, i.e., the premise can be modified. For example, it is possible to design programs that are innovative, where promises are great and beyond those usually made to clients, and garner satisfaction ratings that are less positive than for the usual programs where the "promise" is less (Torre, 1997). Obviously, care must be taken in interpreting findings.

Conclusion: Ask the Right Questions

Clearly, to help providers or programs develop services that are more responsive to client wishes or needs, or to distinguish among providers regarding their service delivery, it is necessary to have "better" and more pertinent information.

It is frequently concluded that instruments are not adequate because they appear not to give the desired results, i.e., at minimum, more variability in responses and a higher percentage of "unfavorable" ratings. But it can be asked, "Is a good instrument merely one that gives us the answers we want, or do we also have to *ask the right questions?*" A concerted effort must be made to design instruments that will elicit the information we want. "Is the client satisfied with services?" is an entirely different question than "What can be done to improve services?" Different measures with different questions must be developed, validated, and administered to address each of these issues separately.

It is the contention of these authors that *satisfaction with services*, i.e., whether expectations are met, is a different question from *service enhancement*, i.e., quality improvement. Service enhancement is the desire for additional or different services, and questions about it must be asked separately. Therefore, it is proposed that service enhancement be determined in separate surveys with questions addressing particular service improvement issues. Such surveys are proposed in addition to client satisfaction surveys, not in lieu of them. The important point is that *service improvement/enhancement* is a different construct from satisfaction and requires *asking the right questions*.

Finally, in either case (satisfaction or quality enhancement/improvement) it is critical that those who have discontinued services be located. The opinions of this group, representing a different population, must be solicited in order to obtain the full range of information for both service satisfaction and quality improvement surveys.

Acknowledgments

The authors express their appreciation to Gerald (Jay) Sumner, PhD, statistical consultant for data analysis and consultation, and wish to acknowledge his sage advise, critique, and support. We also thank Janet McLeod for invaluable editorial assistance and insightful suggestions.

References

Attkisson, C.C., Greenfield, T.K. The UCSF Client Satisfaction Scales: I. The Client Satisfaction Questionnaire-8. Forthcoming chapter in M.A. Maruish (Ed.). *The use of psychological testing for treatment planning and outcome assessment.* (2nd Ed.). Mahwah NJ: Lawrence Erlbaum Associates; 1998.

Beigel, A. Resistance to change: differential effects of favourable and unfavourable initial communications. *British Journal of Social and Clinical Psychology*, Great Britain; 1973; 12:153-158.

Beigel, A., Torre, C. Building partnerships: the road to meaningful outcome measurement. 11th WICHE Decision Support Conference; Reno NV; 1996.

Bloch, S., Bond, G., Qualls, B., Yalom, I., Zimmerman, E. Patients' expectations of therapeutic improvement and their outcomes. *American Journal of Psychiatry*; 1976; 133:1457-1460.

Dow, M.G. Personal communication; 1997.

Dow, M.G., Ward, J.C. Jr. Program Evaluation and Outcome Assessment Project. HRS District 7, Phase Three Summary, Fiscal Year 1995-1996. Contract #GH324. Department of Community Mental Health. Florida Mental Health Institute. University of South Florida, Tampa FA; 1996.

Dow, M.G., Ward, J.C. Jr., Thornton, D.H. User friendly assessments of consumer satisfaction: touch screen and scanning methods for the BHRS. National Association of State Mental Health Program Directors (NASMHPD), Washington DC; 1996.

Frank, J.D. The influence of patients' and therapists' expectations on the outcome of psychotherapy. *British Journal of Medical Psychology*; 1968; 41:349-356.

Friedman, H.J. Patient-expectancy and symptom reduction. *Archives of General Psychiatry*; 1963; 8:61-67.

Goldstein, A.P., Shipman, W.G. Patient expectancies, symptom reduction and aspects of the initial psychotherapeutic interview. *Journal of Clinical Psychology*; 1961; 17:129-135.

Greenfield, T.K. The role of client satisfaction in evaluating university counseling services. *Evaluation and Program Planning*; 1983; 6:315-327.

Hunt, H.K. Overview and future research directions in H.K. Hunt (Ed.) *Conceptualization and measurement of consumer satisfaction and dissatisfaction.* Cambridge MA: Marketing Science Institute; 1977.

Karzmark, P., Greenfield, T., Cross, H. The relationship between level of adjustment and expectations for therapy. *Journal of Clinical Psychology*; 1983; 39:930-932.

Kennington, P. The GEST model: consumer and family impact on continuous quality improvement. Managed Public Mental Health Care: A Blueprint for Change, San Diego CA; 1996.

Kincade, L.E. Development of an expectancy scale with EAP population: Implications for quality improvement and consumer outcome satisfaction. Unpublished doctoral dissertation. California Coast University; 1996.

Koch, J.R. Personal communication, January 1998.

Koch, J.R., Harlow, J.Y. Statewide consumer satisfaction survey for mental health and substance abuse outpatient and psychosocial services. Virginia Department of Mental Health, Mental Retardation, and Substance Abuse Services. National Association of State Mental Health Program Directors (NASMHPD), Arlington VA; 1997.

Larsen, D.L., Attkisson, C.C., Hargreaves, W.A., Nguyen, T.D. Assessment of client/patient satisfaction: development of a general scale. *Evaluation and Program Planning*; 1979; 2:197-207.

Lipkin, S. Clients' feelings and attitudes in relation to the outcome of client-centered therapy. *Psychological Monographs*; 1954; 68.

Nguyen, T.D., Attkisson, C.C., Stegner, B.L. Assessment of patient satisfaction: development and refinement of a service evaluation questionnaire. *Evaluation and Program Planning*; 1983; 6:299-314.

Oliver, R.L. Effect of expectation and disconfirmation on post exposure product evaluation: an alternative interpretation. *Journal of Applied Psychology*; 1977; 62:480-486.

Oliver, R.L. A cognitive model of the antecedents and consequences of satisfaction decisions. *Journal of Marketing Research*; 1980; 17:460-469.

Ross, C., Wheaton, B., Duff, R.S. Client satisfaction and the organization of medical practice: why time counts. *Journal of Health and Social Behavior*; 1981; 22:243-255.

Ross, C., Frommelt, G., Hazelwood, L., Chang, R.W. The role of expectations in patient satisfaction with medical care. *Healthcare Marketing: A Foundation for Managed Quality*. Gaithersburg MD: Aspen Publishers; 1994: 55-59.

Sotsky, S.M., Glass, D.R., Shea, M.T., et al. Patient predictors of response to psychotherapy and pharmacology: findings in the NIMH Treatment of Depression Collaborative Research Program. *American Journal of Psychiatry*; 1991; 148:997-1008.

Task Force on Consumer Oriented Report Card. *The MHSIP Consumer Oriented Mental Health Report Card*. Rockville MD: Center for Mental Health Services; April 1996.

Tollinton, H.J., Initial expectations and outcome. *British Journal of Medical Psychology*; 1973; 46:251.

Torre, C. Summary of results: consumer satisfaction questionnaire (CSQ-8) PARTNERS program. Los Angeles County Department of Mental Health internal report; 1997.

Uhlenhuth, E., Duncan, D., Subjective change in psychoneurotic outpatients with medical student therapists: some determinants of change. *Archives of General Psychiatry*; 1968; 18:532-540.

Clinical Outcome, Consumer Satisfaction, And Ad Hoc Ratings of Improvement In Children's Mental Health

WARREN LAMBERT, MARK S. SALZER, AND LEONARD BICKMAN

Mental health clinics and managed care organizations assess treatment effectiveness with consumer satisfaction measures and ad hoc measures of improvement obtained from a single informant; some of these measures are as simple as asking clients whether they improved during treatment. In the present correlational study of 199 treated adolescents, we used a multitrait-multimethod analysis to examine psychometrically measured pathology change (pre- and postassessment of symptoms and functioning), consumer satisfaction, and perceived improvement reported by multiple informants. Confirmatory factor-analytic results indicate that (a) outcome variance due to multiple informants cannot be ignored, (b) consumer satisfaction is unrelated to pathology change, and (c) parent-reported perceived improvement ratings are more akin to satisfaction than to pathology change.

In recent years, concerns about the effectiveness of mental health services have been widely expressed. The cost-containment strategies used by managed care organizations raise consumer fears about a possible decline in the quality of care. Managed care companies (behavioral healthcare organizations; BHOs) wish to show purchasers that their services are effective. Perhaps the only thing that consumers, corporations, and government agree on is the need for mental health agencies and providers to measure the effectiveness of their services.

Mental health professionals can point to meta-analyses of studies as evidence that therapy is beneficial (e.g., Casey & Berman, 1985; Smith, Glass, & Miller, 1980; Weisz, Weiss, Alicke, & Klotz, 1987). However, recent distinctions between lab-based findings (efficacy) and field-based findings (effectiveness) have been sobering. Results of laboratory studies of manualized interventions in ideal treatment conditions may not apply to therapy delivered in the average practice (see Hoagwood, Hibbs, Brent, & Jensen, 1995; Weisz, Donenberg, Han, & Weiss, 1995). Excluding the Consumer Reports (CR) survey results ("Mental health," 1995; Seligman, 1995), the effectiveness of psychological therapy in the field has not been demonstrated for either adults or children and adolescents (Weisz, Weiss, & Donenberg, 1992).

Source: Lamber W, Salzer MS, and Bickman L. Clinical Outcome, Consumer Satisfaction, and Ad Hoc Ratings of Improvement in Children's Mental Health. Journal of Consulting and Clinical Psychology April 1998; 66(2):270-279. Copyright (c) 1998 by the American Psychological Association. Reprinted with permission.

Warren Lambert, Mark S. Salzer, and Leonard Bickman, Center for Mental Health Policy, Vanderbilt University.

This research was supported by the U.S. Army Health Services Command (DA-DA10-89-C-0013) as a subcontract from the North Carolina Department of Human Resources/Division of Mental Health, Developmental Disabilities and Substance Abuse Services, and Grant R01MH-46136-01 from the National Institute of Mental Health.

Correspondence concerning this article should be addressed to the authors at Center for Mental Health Policy, Vanderbilt University, 1207 18th Avenue South, Nashville, Tennessee 37212. Electronic mail may be sent to lambertuansv5.vanderbilt.edu.

However, few field-based studies have been conducted (Bickman, 1997).

Purchasers, managed care providers, and consumers need to assess the effectiveness of a particular managed care plan or provider. As a result, outcome assessment is becoming a common practice for mental health service providers. Just as the clinical researchers before them, evaluators in the field struggle with methodological problems, such as the problem of confounding traits with assessment methods.

The target of most clinical outcome evaluation is pathology change, such as change in symptoms over time. Repeated measurements of symptoms and functioning are used to evaluate the clinical benefit of a particular program or intervention. Clinical effectiveness is determined by (a) the extent to which symptoms decrease and functioning increases, and (b) whether scores for a treated group are significantly better than scores for a comparison group. Unfortunately, repeated measurements are financially expensive and may require more time and effort than clients are willing to provide.

An inexpensive approach to outcome evaluation can be seen in the CR mental health service outcome survey of over 4,000 CR readers ("Mental Health," 1995). Seligman (1995) praised this survey as an ideal study of the effectiveness of psychotherapy. A composite of three items was used to assess clinical effectiveness: (a) satisfaction ("Overall, how satisfied were you with this therapist's treatment of your problems?"); (b) specific improvement ("How much did treatment help with the specific problem that led you to therapy?"); and (c) global improvement (how informants described their "overall emotional state" at the time of the survey compared with the start of treatment). The constructs assessed in the CR survey are satisfaction with treatment (first question) and perceived improvement (second and third questions).

Both satisfaction and improvement have gained popularity in assessments of the effectiveness of mental health services. A recent survey (Bilbrey & Bilbrey, 1995) indicates that over 90% of BHO representatives view customer satisfaction as an important outcome, and of all methods used to evaluate outcome, BHO representatives consider satisfaction to be the most helpful. The Collection of satisfaction data has become a high priority for BHOs and mental health agencies and providers (Bilbrey & Bilbrey, 1995; Daniels, Kramer, & Mahegh, 1995; Trabin, Freeman, & Pallak, 1995). The American Managed Behavioral Healthcare Association (AMBHA) has developed a performance measurement system (PERMS 1.0) that includes numerous indicators related to satisfaction with services (Ross, 1997).

Although satisfaction and service effectiveness are often equated, research examining their relationship has been mixed. One study found a moderate correlation ($r = -.30$) between satisfaction and self-reported pathology change, but no correlation with therapist-rated outcomes (Attkisson & Zwick, 1982). Another study (Deane, 1993) found a moderate correlation between therapist-rated outcomes and satisfaction. Conflicting results were found in two studies measuring symptom change using the Reliable Change Index (Jacobson & Truax, 1991). Ankuta and Abeles (1993) reported greater client satisfaction ratings for those in the clinically significant change group, whereas Pekarik and Wolff (1996) reported no such relationship. Others reported minimal to no relationship between satisfaction ratings and pathology change (Campbell, Ho, Evenson, & Bluebird, 1996; Cauce et al., 1996; Eisen, 1996; H. Mark, personal communication, May, 1996; Ries, Jaffe, Comtois, & Kitchell, 1996) or quality of life (Minsky, 1997).

Typical client satisfaction surveys include items inquiring about the extent to which the consumer perceives that clinical improvement occurred as a result of treatment. We refer to these items as perceived improvement. Perceived improvement involves symptom and functioning areas that are most relevant to each particular client. The measurement of satisfaction and perceived improvement has practical advantages over the measurement of change in pathology. The surveys take little time to complete and are administered only once. The assessment of satisfaction and perceived improvement is considered an inexpensive, yet valid approach to assess overall changes in symptoms and functioning.

A second issue in outcome assessment concerns which data collection methods are used, such as self-report, interview, or behavioral observation, and which informants are asked to assess each outcome trait. Including the informant in an outcome assessment model acknowledges that each respondent has a particular viewpoint; the parent and adolescent surveys are not parallel forms of the same test. If viewpoints were not distinct, asking the parent, "Is your adolescent difficult?" would be the same as asking, "Are you a difficult adolescent?"

The assessment of interrater agreement, especially therapist-client agreement, has a long history in psychotherapy research. One recent literature review (Weiss, Rabinowitz, & Spiro, 1996) showed that the level of agreement between therapist and client ratings of therapy varied greatly across studies. In an extensive review of informant issues in child and family mental health, Northrup (1995) found that the agreement between multiple informants rating child psychopathology is low to moderate (Achenbach, McConaughy, & Howell, 1987; Kazdin, 1994). These interrater discrepancies have led to suggestions that differences in perception among various stakeholders (i.e., clients, therapists) should be studied in their own right rather than disregarded as measurement error (Northrup, 1995; Weiss et al., 1996).

Method variance due to multiple informants may be a source of erroneous results in outcome studies. Large systematic differences between respondents are treated as error, or shared method variance may inflate positive correlations between measures assessing two seemingly independent traits. Without multiple informants it is unclear whether the relationship is due to shared method variance (i.e., single informant) or traits that are truly correlated. Method variance might account for some moderate correlations between pathology change and client satisfaction.

Campbell and Fiske (1959) clarified the requirements for construct validity by distinguishing between trait variance and method variance. In the present study, traits (constructs of interest) are symptom change and satisfaction with services. Methods (operations used to measure the constructs of interest) include self-ratings by the adolescent client, ratings by a client's parent, and ratings by a trained interviewer. Campbell and Fiske (1959) used the distinction between traits and methods to list a number of requirements for validity. For example, they wrote, "A third common-sense desideratum is that a variable correlate higher with an independent effort to measure the same trait than with measures designed to get at different traits which happen to employ the same method" (p. 83). With this criterion (and others), Campbell and Fiske (1959) strove to protect researchers from misinterpreting method-based correlations as a link between traits. Campbell and Fiske's original article showed how inspecting a multitrait-multimethod (MTMM) matrix of correlations could help determine whether the requirements for convergent and discriminate validity were met, but better methods are available now to replace the inspection of correlation matrices. Confirmatory factor analysis (CFA), also called structural equation modeling (SEM), offers a more objective way to evaluate correlation matrices, to define hypotheses, and to determine which hypotheses offer a better fit to the data. Byrne (1994) and Byrne and Goffin (1993) showed how to program the MTMM in Bentler's (1992) EQS or in Jöreskog's LISREL (Byrne, 1989).

The present study uses data from the Fort Bragg Evaluation Project (FBEP), a study of treated children and adolescents in two contrasting systems of mental health care. The FBEP was designed to see whether an experimental continuum of care produced better outcomes and client satisfaction, as well as lower costs, compared with traditional services at two comparison sites. In the FBEP, closely matched groups of clients were treated in the demonstration, a continuum of care, or comparison sites in a quasi-experimental design. Informants included the client, a parent, and a trained interviewer, with additional data from teachers and providers. For the present study, only adolescent clients were used because younger children did not fill out self-reports. The results of the FBEP (Bickman, 1996a; Bickman, 1997; Bickman et al., 1995) and the methods (Bickman, 1996b) of the FBEP appear elsewhere. In the present study, we examine relationships among pathology change (as reported by adolescents, parents, and trained interviewers), client satisfaction (as reported by adolescents and their parents), and perceived improvement (reported by parents). An assumption of this research, one that will be tested empirically, is that the most valid outcome measurement model must include multiple outcome traits (constructs of interest) and multiple methods (multiple informants). We tested three hypotheses: (1) CFA models that distinguish different informants will provide a better fit to the data than those that do not; (2) satisfaction measures and symptom change measures are distinct; and (3) parent-reported perceived improvement will resemble measures of satisfaction more than measures of pathology change.

Method

Research Participants

The FBEP research sample is described in detail elsewhere (Bickman et al., 1995). The FBEP evaluated the outcome, utilization, and dollar cost of treatment for children ages 5 to 17 who received mental health treatment through the Civilian Health and Medical Program for the Uniformed Services (CHAMPUS). Children were treated in an innovative continuum of care demonstration at Fort Bragg or in traditional reimbursed care at Fort Campbell or Fort Stewart.

The total sample included 498 adolescents from $N = 984$ children of all ages. Cases with any missing parent or child mental health data were excluded from the present study. The overall rate of participation in clinical data collection at Wave 2 was 84% (Bickman et al., 1995, Table 3.13). Although this rate of participation by voluntary subjects is acceptable, a pre-post study using multiple informants makes severe demands on data completeness because a difference score is missing if either the pre- or postmeasure is missing. After dropping cases with incomplete mental health scores, a study sample of 199 adolescents remained. The size of the present sample is adequate by Breckler's (1990) criterion ($N > 100$), and close to the median ($N = 198$ subjects) reported by Breckler's (1990) meta-analysis of published CFA articles. Sample characteristics appear in Table 1.

Categorical data in Table 1 shows a middle class sample with many two-parent homes, a sample different from indigent cases in single-parent homes. Clinical characteristics of the sample appear in Table 2. Presenting problems in this sample most often concern behavior or mood, and the majority have serious emotional disturbance (diagnosis plus impairment).

The average adolescent in the sample had a total problem score in the low-clinical range on the parent-reported Child Behavior Checklist (CBCL; Achenbach,

Table 1
Characteristics of the 199 Adolescents Studied

Category	% of 199 adolescents
Male	50.3
Race	
White	64.3
African American	21.1
Two parents in home	84.4
Serious emotional disturbance (diagnosis + impairment)	62.3
Medicated for behavior or emotion	27.9
Parent reports previous child problems	78.1
Parent reports previous child treatment	62.0
Parent reports abuse or violence in home	10.6
Adolescent picked up by police	24.6
Highest parental education included some college	85.4
Site	
Fort Bragg demonstration	52.8
Comparison	47.2
Household income <$15,000	9.8
Presenting problem conduct or behavior	35.5
Presenting problem anxiety or mood	24.9

1991). The sample's mean CBCL total was 64 on a scale in which nonclinical samples have a mean of 50 and standard deviation of 10. Adolescent self-descriptions on the Achenbach's Youth Self-Report (YSR; Achenbach & Edelbrock, 1987) appeared less pathological than the parent descriptions, as did teacher reports, which were missing too often to be used in the present study. The average adolescent in the sample received substantial treatment, with an average of 14 outpatient sessions and 6 hospital days (positively skewed). When service utilization was followed for a year after intake, the average length of treatment extended over 227 days until termination.

Table 2
Clinical Characteristics of the Adolescents Studied

Clinical characteristic	M	SD
Achenbach CBCL total problem t score	64.48	10.08
Achenbach CBCL internalizing t score	61.99	11.37
Achenbach CBCL externalizing t score	64.36	11.07
Achenbach YSR total problem t score	57.51	10.77
Achenbach YSR internalizing t score	55.69	12.26
Achenbach YSR externalizing t score	58.62	10.29
No. of outpatient sessions	14.02	12.90
No. of days in hospital	6.18	16.62
Length of treatment in days	226.77	130.19

Note. CBCL = Child Behavior Checklist. YSR = Youth Self-Report.

Measures

Mental health symptom change and consumer satisfaction were assessed by three kinds of measures: (a) mental health symptom scores, (b) adolescent and parent reports of satisfaction with treatment, and (c) a simple parent-reported perceived improvement scale. A total of 14 variables were used, 7 measuring symptoms, 7 measuring satisfaction. A summary of these measures appears in Table 3.

Symptom change. The symptom scores included assessments of behavior problems, *Diagnostic and Statistical Manual of Mental Disorders*, third edition, revised (*DSM-III-R*; American Psychiatric Association, 1987) psychopathology, and impairment in functioning. In addition to self-reports, trained interviewers rated clients in the FBEP. Interviewers were project employees. Interviews were videotaped, and a sample re-rated; if an interviewer's reliability decreased, they were re-trained.

Included in the assessment of symptoms were (a) self-report checklists by the parent (CBCL; Achenbach, 1991) and by the adolescent client (YSR, Achenbach & Edelbrock, 1987); (b) ratings of symptoms by trained interviewers based on parent report (Parent-Reported Child Assessment Schedule, PCAS; Hodges, McKnew, Cytryn, Stem, & Kline, 1982) or adolescent report (Child Assessment Schedule, CAS; Hodges, Kline, Stem, Cytryn, & McKnew, 1982; Hodges, McKnew et al., 1982); (c) ratings of functioning impairment by trained interviewers (Child and Adolescent Functioning Assessment Schedule, CAFAS, and General Level of Functioning; GLOF; Hodges, 1990; Hodges & Gust, 1995); and (d) a parent-reported rating of caregiver strain resulting from the adolescent's problems (Burden of Care Questionnaire, BCQ; Brannan, Heflinger, & Bickman, 1997). Each of the symptom measures was administered at intake and again at 6 months for all clients, whether or not they were still in treatment.

To measure improvement with the pathology measures, difference scores were used. Difference scores were defined so that for all measures[1] of pathology, a large difference score is good, and a negative difference score means the adolescent's score became worse. Difference scores have been criticized (Cronbach & Furby, 1970) and defended (Newman, 1994); certainly multiwave longitudinal models (Diggle, Laing, & Zeger, 1994) are better than two-wave difference scores for evaluating a clinical trial. However, the present study required a simple operational definition of improvement, and for this purpose, difference scores are adequate.

Measures of client satisfaction. In addition to the symptom remission scores listed in the top half of Table 3, the FBEP evaluated parent and adolescent satisfaction with treatment (Brannan, Sonnichsen, & Heflinger, 1996). These measures appear in the lower half of Table 3 (Satisfaction, V8-V14). The first six measures (V8-V13) were taken from the FBEP satisfaction scales. The last measure (V14, perceived improvement) is a mea-

Table 3
Fourteen Measures of Symptoms, Satisfaction, and Perceived Improvement

Type of measure	Name	Content	Occasions	Respondent	Type of validity
Symptom outcome	V1. CBCL total problems	Behavior problems	Pre-post	Parent	Extensive criterion-related validity
	V2. PCAS total pathology	DSM-III-R symptoms	Pre-post	Parent	Recent criterion
	V3. Parental burden	Family difficulties from treated child	Pre-post	Parent	Some criterion
	V4. Youth Self-report	Behavior problems	Pre-post	Adolescent	Extensive criterion
	V5. CAS total pathology	DSM-HI-R symptoms	Pre-post	Adolescent	Recent criterion
	V6. CAFAS impairment	Functioning	Pre-post	Interviewer	Some criterion
	V7. GLOF level	Functioning	Pre-post	Interviewer	Extensive criterion
Satisfaction	V8. Global satisfaction	Treated well?	Post only	Parent	Face validity
	V9. Clinic helpful?	Worthwhile to go?	Post only	Parent	Face validity
	V10. Improvement	Child got better?	Post only	Parent	Face validity
	V11. Global satisfaction	Treated well?	Post only	Adolescent	Face validity
	V12. Clinic helpful?	Worthwhile to go?	Post only	Adolescent	Face validity
	V13. Improvement	Child got better?	Post only	Adolescent	Face validity
Perceived improvement	V14. Perceived improvement	How much better?	Post only	Parent	Face validity

Note. CBCL = Child Behavior Checklist; PCAS = Parent-Reported Child Assessment Schedule; CAS = Child Assessment Schedule; CAFAS = Child and Adolescent Functioning Assessment Schedule; GLOF = General Level of Functioning; Pre-post = preassessment to postassessment; *DSM-III-R* = *Diagnostic and Statistical Manual of Mental Disorders.*

sure of overall outcome similar to that used by CR. The placement of V14 with satisfaction measures reflects our hypothesis that perceived improvement is more similar to satisfaction scales than to symptom scales, an assumption that will be tested later. In the present study, overall measures of satisfaction were based on averages of the service-specific satisfaction scales so that satisfaction scores estimate satisfaction on all services received from intake to 6-month follow-up. Three aspects of satisfaction were used: (a) global satisfaction averaged over all global satisfaction items and all services, (b) "helpfulness" assessed how helpful the informant felt the component of treatment was, and (c) "improved" measured how much the informant felt the adolescent improved during the treatment. Item 3 (improvement items taken from satisfaction scales) will be tested to see if it belongs with satisfaction items, or with mental health symptom changes. The FBEP "perceived improvement" scale was selected for special study because it resembles scales used in the CR study. Its five items simply asked whether the adolescent had improved; the total score was the average of all five items[2]

The first seven measures (V1-V7) were difference scores based on measures of pathology. Six of the seven (V1, V2, V4-V7) are established measures backed by extensive research. One measure (V3, parental burden) is a new instrument developed in the FBEP. Burden (V3) and CAFAS Functioning Impairment (V6) are the best predictors of future service utilization in the FBEP.

The satisfaction measures (V8-V13) were taken from the FBEP's satisfaction study (Bickman et al., 1995, p. 121). These items are typical of those included in client satisfaction measures. The last measure (V14, perceived improvement) is a five-item scale asking the parent whether the adolescent improved; this scale resembles the assessment method used in the CR study. One of the main purposes of the present study is to observe whether perceived improvement behaves more like a measure of symptom change or of satisfaction.

Procedure

In the FBEP, research volunteers were recruited at intake from the population of all children and adolescents treated at the demonstration continuum of care or the comparison's traditional mental health care. Every case received an extensive evaluation including self-report forms and a clinical interview at intake (Wave 1) and 6 months after intake (Wave 2), regardless of whether they were still in treatment. Subjects were the treated adolescent and a parent, often the mother.

Results

Univariate Correlations

Before testing the MTMM hypothesis, simple univariate correlations between measures of symptom change and global satisfaction were examined without factor analysis. First, descriptive statistics for the 14 variables were checked for restriction of range; all variables had ranges in excess of three standard deviations (*SD*s).

The correlations appear in Table 4. For the parent, the correlation between clinical change on standardized instruments and satisfaction with treatment was 0.38, a moderate correlation consistent with the literature. For the adolescent the correlation was lower but still significant, r (symptom change, satisfaction) = .18. More thorough analyses presented later, however, will suggest that these correlations between satisfaction and symptom change are artifacts of method variance.

Table 4

Correlations Between Summary Measures of Satisfaction and Symptom Change

Correlation	1	2	3	4	5	6
Parent satisfaction (V8 + V9 + V10)	—					
Parent symptom report (V1 + V2 + V3)	0.38**	—				
Adolescent satisfaction (V11 + V12 + V13)	0.29**	0.14[a]	—			
Adolescent symptoms (V4 + V5)	0.08	0.19**	0.18**	—		
Interviewer rated functioning (V6 + V7)	0.22**	0.24**	0.18**	0.28**	—	
Parent-reported perceived improvement (V14)	0.65**	0.44**	0.23**	0.13	0.30**	—

[a] $p = .06$, nonsignificant.
*$p < .05$. **$p < .01$.

The bottom row of Table 4 shows the correlation of the perceived improvement scale with other measures of symptom change and satisfaction. Parent-reported perceived improvement shows significant correlations with many items, including parent-reported satisfaction and symptom change, and adolescent reported satisfaction. In Table 4, V14 (parent perceived improvement), correlates significantly with everything but adolescent reported symptom change. A superficial description of this result might be "a simple perceived improvement scale, correlating with both measures of symptom change and satisfaction, had concurrent validity as a measure of both clinical improvement and satisfaction." The confirmatory factor analysis that follows will examine critically this simplistic interpretation of correlations among measures of satisfaction, clinical change, and perceived improvement to see how well this explanation fits the data.

A matrix of correlations among all 14 variables was calculated using Bentler and Wu's (1993) EQS, a confirmatory factor analysis program. Standard scores with a mean of zero and a standard deviation of one based on the $N = 199$ sample were used to make different units comparable, and all variables were standardized such that a high score was good (much improvement, high satisfaction). Some variables had statistically significant departures from the normal distribution, according to Shapiro and Wilk's W (Shapiro & Wilk, 1965); therefore Satorra-Bentler robust statistics were used, including the robust corrected fit index (CFI*; Byrne, 1994, p 88.). Robust estimates measure the departure from normality and scale parameters and alpha levels accordingly. EQS provides two measures of comparative fit, CFI (normal) and CFI* (robust). EQS made it possible to hypothesize a number of models describing the relationships among clinical difference scores, measures of satisfaction, and perceived improvement and then assess how accurately each model fits the observed correlations. The confirmatory factor analytic models that follow will test whether the superficial conclusions based on Tables 2 and 3 can withstand rigorous examination in a more comprehensive explanatory model.

Byrne (1994, Chapter 6) presented a confirmatory factor analysis model for multitrait-multimethod problems, illustrated with both the popular LISREL model of Jöreskog (Byrne & Goffin, 1993) and Bentler's (1992) EQS. The present study uses Byrne's EQS version as the starting point for analysis. This analysis makes three assumptions: (a) The 14 measures reflect two constructs ("traits"): mental health symptom change and consumer satisfaction, (b) methods include the three informants: parent, adolescent, and trained interviewer, and (c) a satisfactory model could be used to test two hypotheses: (1) Perceived improvement (V14), and the two improvement items from the satisfaction scales fit better with measures of consumer satisfaction than with measures of mental health symptom change, and (2) Symptom reduction and consumer satisfaction are orthogonal (uncorrelated), not oblique (correlated).

Confirmatory Factor-Analytic Models

Because the hypothesized multitrait-multimethod model is complicated, we tested more parsimonious models first. A complicated model is justified only if it offers a significantly better fit than simpler models. Table 5 shows the results of testing five hypothesized models to account for the correlations among the 14 measures. Once an adequate model is found, specific hypotheses can be tested within it.

Model 1: Outcomes (symptom change and satisfaction) are one. This common factor model states that all 14 measures assess one common factor or construct. This model is used in studies that treat mental health outcome and client satisfaction as "proxies," meaning that if one is expensive you can measure the other instead. In this model, there is only one point of view (usually the parent's). This model is theoretically the most parsimonious model. Unfortunately, Table 5 (row 1) shows that this model has an extremely poor fit with the data. Its robust comparative fit index (CFI*) is only 0.19 on a 0 to 1 scale in which 0.90 is adequate. Model 1 is inaccurate; it must be rejected.

Model 2: Two constructs, symptom change and satisfaction. Model 2 posits a distinction between symptom change and satisfaction but ignores differences among informants. As models in Table 5 add parameters, their fit necessarily improves. In each step an incremental χ^2 was calculated by subtracting the model's total misfit χ^2 from the χ^2 for the preceding step. In Table 5, the misfit χ^2 went down from 463 in row 1 to 412 in row 2. Degrees of freedom decreased from 79 to 78. This leaves an incremental χ^2 difference of 51 with $df = 1$. Because a χ^2 (1) of 3.85 is significant, the incremental χ^2 difference of 51 is not due to chance. Thus, for Hypothesis 2 we conclude that the fit is significantly better than the fit of Hypothesis 1, but, with a robust CFI* of only 0.29, that the fit is still unacceptable.

Model 3: No traits, three methods. In a systematic approach to building a satisfactory model in methodical steps, Hypothesis 3 had to be tested, although it is theoretically unsatisfactory. This hypothesis states that the correlations among the 14 variables can be explained by who reported the data, without considering what they were trying to report. Model 3 fits significantly better than Model 2, showing that method variance makes a contribution, but the model's fit is inadequate. Thus it can be rejected on both empirical and theoretical grounds.

Model 4: One trait, three methods. This model admits that the informants could have different distinct points of view, and it assumes that symptom change and consumer satisfaction are the same. This model offers a much better fit than any before it, with a CFI* = 0.86, but that degree of fit is marginal, because the robust comparative fit index is less than 0.90 (satisfactory).

Model 5: Two traits, three methods. The classical MTMM in Figure 1 has adequate fit (CFI* = 0.92). The MTMM model had a significantly better fit than all the simpler models, as shown in Table 5. Figure 1 shows the MTMM model. The model's structure is a smaller version of Byrne's (1994) MTMM model based on four traits and four methods (self, teacher, parent, and peer). Figure 1 has two traits (symptom change and satisfaction) and three methods (parent, adolescent, and trained interviewer).

Description of the MTMM model. In the initial MTMM model, there are seven measures of symptom change and seven measures of satisfaction. (Treating perceived improvement measures as satisfaction is a hypothesis that will be tested later.) All significant parameters were positive, as expected. The three informants have a modest correlation among them (0.25 to 0.37), suggesting that they are describing the same thing to a limited extent. However, most of what each informant reports is not shared by other informants.

As this study hypothesized, symptom change and satisfaction were not significantly correlated (normal distribution $r = .06$, $p = .53$, *ns*; robust $r = .10$, $p = .59$). For brevity, only robust estimates will be presented here. The nonsignificant correlation between symptom change and satisfaction suggests that they are distinct and unrelated[3] and that satisfaction could be equally high regardless of whether the adolescent's symptoms got better or worse. This finding answers the first question of the present study: Are satisfaction and symptom change correlated in this sample? The answer is no.

Role of perceived improvement. In the MTMM model in Figure 1, there were two forms of improvement perceived by the parent. One (V14)

Table 5
Accuracy Estimates From Confirmatory Factor Analysis, Most Parsimonious First

Model	Theory	Normal compar. fit index (CFI)	Robust compar. fit index (CFI*)	Robust $x^2(df)$	Incremental significance (First step)	Result
Common factor ("It's all one")	All 14 variables are aspects of the same thing. Methods (raters) have negligible differences.	0.46	0.19	463 (79)		Extremely poor fit
Two traits, ignore methods	Satisfaction and clinical outcome are distinct. Methods (raters) have negligible differences.	0.53	0.29	412 (78)	$p < .001$	Very poor fit
Result	Raters have distinct viewpoints. Model includes methods only, no traits.	0.76	0.60	331 (77)	$p < .001$	Poor fit
One trait, three methods	Outcome and satisfaction are not distinct. Raters have distinct viewpoints.	0.90	0.86	143 (60)	$p < .001$	Marginal fit
Two traits, three methods (multitrait multimethod)	Outcome and satisfaction are distinct; raters have distinct viewpoints	0.95	0.92	96 (59)	$p < .001$	Good fit

Note. Bentler and Byrne suggest that CFI values less than 0.90 are inadequate. Incremental significance shows whether each step down the table improves the model's fit significantly based on robust chi-square differences from the previous model. Compar. = comparative.

Figure 1.
The multitrait multimethod (MTMM) model. CFI = comparative fit index; CBCL = Child Behavior Checklist; PCAS = Parent-Reported Child Assessment Schedule; YSR = Youth Self-Report; CAS = Child Assessment Schedule; CAFAS = Child and Adolescent Functioning Assessment Schedule; GLOF .= General Level of Functioning; Sat. = satisfaction; Subj. = subject; Sig. = significant.

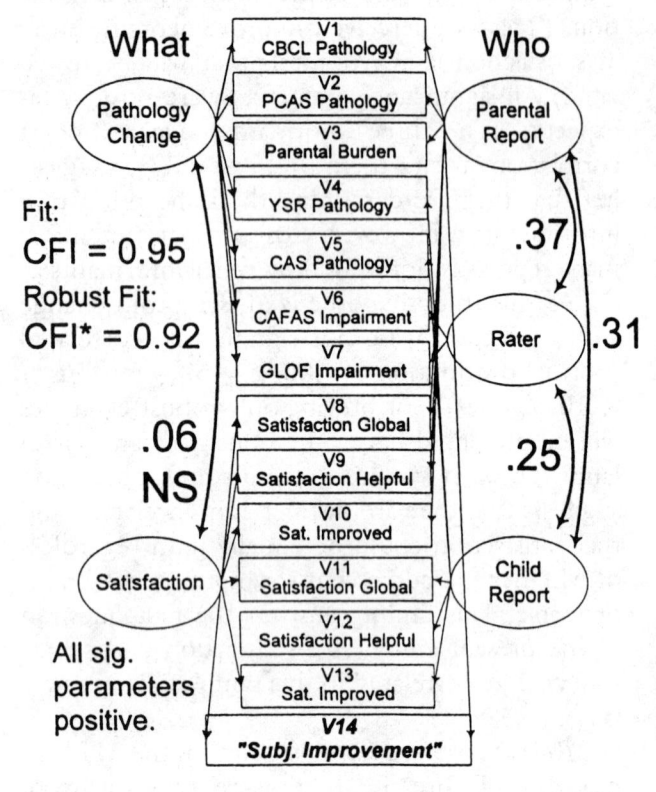

[Diagram: MTMM model showing "What" factors (Pathology Change, Satisfaction) connected to variables V1-V14, and "Who" factors (Parental Report, Rater, Child Report). Fit: CFI = 0.95; Robust Fit: CFI* = 0.92. Path between Pathology Change and Satisfaction: .06 NS. Correlations: .37, .31, .25. All sig. parameters positive.

Variables:
V1 CBCL Pathology
V2 PCAS Pathology
V3 Parental Burden
V4 YSR Pathology
V5 CAS Pathology
V6 CAFAS Impairment
V7 GLOF Impairment
V8 Satisfaction Global
V9 Satisfaction Helpful
V10 Sat. Improved
V11 Satisfaction Global
V12 Satisfaction Helpful
V13 Sat. Improved
V14 "Subj. Improvement"]

was a five-item scale asking the parent whether the adolescent got better or worse over 6 months after intake into treatment. Another (V10) was a similar item from the parent satisfaction scale, with scores averaged over services if there was more than one. In the MTMM model, the five-item perceived improvement scale had a large loading on the parent factor (β = .82, z = 10, p < .01); however, improvement perceived by the parent was not significantly related to the satisfaction factor (β = .18, z = 1.6, p > .05). Unlike the five-item perceived improvement scale, the improvement item on the satisfaction scales did load significantly on the satisfaction factor (β = .20, z = 2.0, p < .05). These loadings are much smaller than those between parent-reported global satisfaction and the satisfaction factor (β = .79, z = 7.74, p < .01). Although perceived improvement may sometimes be a statistically significant measure of consumer satisfaction, it is not a very good one.

Perceived improvement and outcome. The MTMM model in Figure 1 does not prove that perceived improvement is not a measure of symptom change; perhaps treating improvement both as symptomatic outcome and as satisfaction would improve the model's fit. To test this hypothesis, the MTMM model in Figure 1 was revised. Perceived improvement (V14) was treated as both a symptomatic outcome and as a measure of satisfaction. In Figure 1, an arrow would be drawn connecting V14 to both the pathology change and satisfaction factors. This change did not improve the overall MTMM model's fit, χ^2 (1, N = 199), = .03 ns. Furthermore, the loading of parent-perceived improvement on symptom change was only 0.02 (z = .22, p > .05): this negligible loading offers no support at all for the hypothesis that the parent's perceived improvement scale is a measure of symptom change.

This test of perceived improvement could be extended to all three measures of perceived improvement, two from satisfaction scales (V10, parent-reported, V13, adolescent-reported) and one from the CR-like perceived improvement scale (V14, parent-reported perceived improvement scale). In Figure 1, arrows could connect V10 (parent-reported improvement), V 13 (adolescent-reported improvement), and V14 (parent-reported perceived improvement scale) both to pathology change and satisfaction. Having three more parameters added negligibly to the CFI* (.922 to .926), and the Sotorra-Bentler robust χ^2 improvement from these added parameters was nonsignificant, χ^2 (3, N = 199) = 5.1, ns. Again, there was no empirical support for the idea that treating perceived improvement as symptom change improved the model.

There was one unexpected finding in the last model. Both parent-reported satisfaction-scale measures of perceived improvement loaded significantly on the satisfaction factor (β_{V10} = 22, z = 2.2, β_{V14} = .22, z = 2.1). In contrast, the adolescent-reported measure of perceived improvement from the satisfaction scales, surprisingly, loaded significantly on symptom change and nonsignificantly on satisfaction, r (V13, symptom change) = .22, z = 2.46; r (V13, satisfaction) = -.04, z = -.5 ns; these significant loadings were much lower than those for adolescent reported symptom changes (for the YSR, β_{V4} = .56; for the CAS, β_{V5} = .61). These results present evidence, admittedly serendipitous, that adolescent-reported perceived improvement may be a measure of symptom change (but not a good one), and that parent-reported improvement may be a measure of satisfaction (but not a good measure of satisfaction either).

A further test of the hypothesis that parent-reported perceived improvement represents satisfaction whereas the same report by an adolescent may represent symptom reduction was tested in another modification of the MTMM model. This modification placed both satisfaction-improvement items (V10, parent; V13 adolescent) in the model in Factor 1, symptom change. For the parent, the resulting loading was nonsignificant, but for the adolescent, it was significant (z = 2.23, p < .05). This unanticipated finding, suggesting that adolescent-reported perceived improvement was a measure of symptom change, inspired further post hoc analysis.

Post hoc analysis of adolescent-reported perceived improvement. In response to the preceding results, a new variable (V15) was added to the study's MTMM model, namely the perceived improvement scale as reported by the adolescent (parent version = V14; adolescent version = V15).

When adolescent-reported perceived improvement was added to the MTMM model as a measure of satisfaction, the fit of the MTMM model became significantly worse (($\chi^2 \Delta$ = 59.3, df = 12, p < .001). When adolescent-reported perceived improvement was treated as both symptom change and satisfaction in the MTMM model, the model's fit improved (($\chi^2 \Delta$ = 14.6, df = 1, p < .001). In this "both" model, the loading of V15 on symptom change was significant, and the loading on satisfaction was nonsignificant. Dropping V15 as satisfaction led to no loss of fit (($\chi^2 \Delta$ = 0.2, df = 1, p > .05). In these new 15-variable post-hoc analyses, the correlation between the satisfaction factor and the symptom change factor remained nonsignificant (r = -.02, p > .05, ns). It appears that adolescent-reported perceived improvement behaves empirically as a measure of symptom change and not as a measure of satisfaction. This last result may be left as a hypothesis for further research, namely, that self-reported perceived improvement may, for adolescents, be a statistically significant measure of clinical symptom change.

Discussion

The present study had three main findings. First, simplistic models did not fit the data. Adequate fit required distinguishing symptom reduction from client satisfaction, and also recognizing that adolescents, parents, and trained interviewers have separate points of view. These results support the first two hypotheses stating that multiple traits and multiple methods must be distinguished. Second, although parent-reported perceived improvement has face validity as a measure of symptom change, empirically, the scale behaves more like a measure of client satisfaction. The third result suggested that when satisfaction scales asked adolescents whether they improved, answers were significantly correlated with symptom change. When parents answered the same question, their response correlated with client satisfaction and not with symptomatic change. This last result, found serendipitously, should be tested in further research.

Our data suggest that errors may result from ignoring method (informant) variance in outcome measurement. For example, a statistically inadequate model showed a moderate correlation between parent-reported satisfaction and parent-reported pathology change (r = .38); this moderate correlation disappeared (r = .06) in the MTMM model. Without the MTMM model, it would have been impossible to determine whether the correlation was due to methods of measurement or due to traits of interest. This result is consistent with the low correlations between informants found in ratings of child pathology (Achenbach et al., 1987; Kazdin, 1994) as well as historic adult studies (e.g., Edwards, Yarvis, Mueller, & Langsley, 1978; Garfield, Prager, & Bergin, 1971) showing low to moderate correlations between therapist and client ratings of success.

The lesson of the MTMM model might be summarized as symmetry, meaning that ideal evaluations should cross each trait with every method in a balanced design. Having multiple informants and multiple measures is feasible in research funded by large grants, but the requirement of symmetry may seem excessive to those evaluating large caseloads in community settings without external funds. A practical solution may be a new breed of assessment tools so inexpensive they can be given to large numbers of cases and informants at a low cost, such as Bickman, Lambert, and Karver's (1997) brief functioning measure. The need to use multiple informants may be affected by the purpose of the measurement. Thus, if the need is to predict service use in program evaluation, fewer informants would be required than in basic research, where a symmetric design may be required to reveal the whole picture.

In the present study, we found no correlation between satisfaction and pathology change, which is similar to findings from many studies (Campbell et al., 1996; Cauce et al., 1996; Eisen, 1996; H. Mark, personal communication, May, 1996; McLellan & Hunkeler, in press; Ries et al., 1996) but not all (e.g., Ankuta & Abeles, 1993; Attkisson & Zwick, 1982). An implication of these results is that satisfaction cannot be used as a proxy for change in psychopathology. This result does not imply that satisfaction scales are without value; the assessment of satisfaction is a reasonable response to demands for a consumer voice in health care evaluations. Unfortunately, current satisfaction scales may be weak in construct validity (Lebow, 1982; Williams, 1994) and may give only the illusion of consumerism (Salzer, 1997; Williams, 1994). More work needs to be done to determine what satisfaction measures assess before satisfaction data would have construct validity.

The conclusions from this study apply to children's mental health services and included three informants (parent, adolescent, and trained interviewer) that are not available in studies involving adults. It would take an adult study using multiple methods, such as reports by client, spouse, and trained interviewer, to reveal whether the *Consumer Reports* surveys measure satisfaction or pathology change. Because the present study is apparently the first one that attempted to validate the use of satisfaction and perceived improvement, it is possible that perceived improvement behaving as a measure of satisfaction, not psychopathology change, would not be confined to studies of children's mental health.

The *Consumer Reports* survey with face valid ad hoc measures has obvious appeal. To run such a study, the evaluator writes some items, such as "How much did you improve?" On termination, or at a haphazardly chosen time, some clients answer the questions. Unlike other clinical assessments, scores can be tallied without evidence of reliability or validity. Unfortunately, the measurement of clinical effectiveness, with its demands for ratings of multiple traits by multiple informants, may not be easy. A multitrait multimethod longitudinal outcome evaluation may be too expensive for clinics struggling to survive. The present study does not suggest that simple ad hoc measures should never be used, but it does suggest that there is a difference between the results of simple ad hoc perceived improvement-satisfaction surveys and longitudinal studies of clinical outcomes. Users of homespun surveys supported by face validity should acknowledge this limitation in their reports. Those constructing face-valid questionnaires for program evaluation are not relieved of the obligation to present "evidence of the validity and suitability of tests for the purpose of the evaluation and the populations involved" (Standard 12.1, "Program Evaluation," American Educational Research Association, American Psychological Association, and National Council on Measurement in Education, 1985).

Footnotes

1. Low GLOF scores indicate poor functioning. However, for consistency, GLOF difference scores were reversed so that a large positive score indicates improvement.

2. This scale asked the parent five questions about his or her son or daughter's improvement from intake to 6-month follow up. The first item was "Thinking back to the reasons that brought your child to services, about how much do you think he/she has changed, overall, in the last 6 months? [much better, a little better, stayed the same, a little worse, much worse]." The next four items asked: "...would you say his/her behavior has changed?,...you think your child would say,...how...your child is feeling?, child would say he/she is feeling...?"

3. This lack of correlation is not due to the fact that most children improved during the 6 months after intake. Difference scores had variance, were only moderately skewed. All had ranges greater than five standard deviations. The fact that the average difference

score was above zero does not impair the ability of difference scores to correlate with other variables if an empirical connection exists.

References

Achenbach, T. M. (1991). *Manual for the Child Behavior Checklist/4-18 and 1991 Profile.* Burlington: University of Vermont, Department of Psychiatry.

Achenbach, T M., & Edelbrock, C. (1987). *Manual for the Youth Self-Report and Profile.* Burlington: University of Vermont, Department of Psychiatry.

Achenbach, T M., McConaughy, S. H., & Howell, C. T (1987). Child/ adolescent behavioral and emotional problems: Implications of cross-informant correlations for situational specificity. *Psychological Bulletin,* 101, 213-232.

American Educational Research Association, American Psychological Association, and National Council on Measurement in Education. (1985). *Standards for educational and psychological testing.* Washington, DC: American Psychological Association.

American Psychiatric Association. (1987). *Diagnostic and statistical manual of mental disorders* (3rd ed., rev.). Washington, DC: Author.

Ankuta, G. Y., & Abeles, N. (1993). Client satisfaction, clinical significance, and meaningful change in psychotherapy. Professional Psychology: Research and Practice, 24(1), 70-74.

Attkisson, C. C., & Zwick, R. (1982). The client satisfaction questionnaire: Psychometric properties and correlations with service utilization and psychotherapy outcome. *Evaluation and Program Planning,* 5, 233-237.

Bentler, P. M. (1992). *EQS: Structural equations program manual.* Los Angeles: BMDP Statistical Software, Inc.

Bentler, P. M., & Wu, E. J. C. (1993). *EQS/Windows user's guide.* Los Angeles: BMDP Statistical Software, Inc.

Bickman, L. (1996a). A continuum of care: More is not always better. *American Psychologist,* 51(7), 689-701.

Bickman, L. (1996b). Methodological issues in evaluating mental health services [Special issue]. *Evaluation and Program Planning,* 19(2).

Bickman, L. (1997). Reactions to Fort Bragg findings: New directions for mental health services research. *American Psychologist,* 52, 562-565.

Bickman, L., Guthrie, P. R., Foster, E. M., Lambert, E. W., Summerfelt, W. T., Breda, C. S., & Heflinger, C. A. (1995). *Evaluating managed mental health services: The Fort Bragg experiment.* New York: Plenum.

Bickman, L., Lambert, E. W., & Karver, M. (1997). *A low-cost index of child functioning for predicting service use.* Manuscript submitted for publication.

Bilbrey, J., & Bilbrey, P. (1995, July/August). Judging, trusting, and utilizing outcomes data: A survey of behavioral health care payers. *Behavioral Health Care Tomorrow,* pp. 62-65.

Brannan, A. M., Heflinger, C. A., & Bickman, L. (1997). The Caregiver Strain Questionnaire: Measuring the impact of living with a child with serious emotional disturbance. *Journal of Emotional and Behavioral Disorders.*

Brannan, A. M., Sonnichsen, S., & Heflinger, C. A. (1996). Measuring satisfaction with children's mental health services: Validity and reliability of the satisfaction scales. *Evaluation and Program Planning,* 19(2), 131-141.

Breckler, S.J. (1990). Applications of covariance structure modeling in psychology: Cause for concern? *Psychological Bulletin,* 107, 260-273.

Byrne, B.M. (1989). *A Primer of LISREL: Basic applications and programming for confirmatory factor analytic models.* New York: Springer Verlag.

Byrne, B. M. (1994). *Structural equation modeling with EQS and EQS/Windows.* Thousand Oaks, CA: Sage.

Byrne, B. M., & Goffin, R.D. (1993). Modeling MTMM data from additive and multiplicative covariance structures: An audit of construct validity concordance. *Multivariate Behavioral Research,* 28, 67-96.

Campbell, D. T., & Fiske, D. W. (1959). Convergent and discriminant validation by the multi-trait multi-method matrix. *Psychological Bulletin,* 56, 81-105.

Campbell, J., Ho, L., Evenson, R. C., & Bluebird, G. (1996, February). Consumer satisfaction and treatment outcomes. Paper presented at the Sixth Annual National Conference on State Mental Health Agency Services Research and Program Evaluation, Arlington, VA.

Casey, R.J., & Berman, J. S. (1985). The outcome of psychotherapy with children. *Psychological Bulletin, 98*(2), 388-400.

Cauce, A. M., Dyck, D., Hendryx, M. Srebnik, D. Caverly, S., & Setevenson, J. (1996). *Evaluation of SSB6547 Progress Report: Substituting outcomes for process regulations.* Report prepared for the Washington State Division of Mental Health.

Cronbach, L.J., & Furby, L. (1970). How should we measure "change"—or should we? *Psychological Bulletin, 74,* 68-80.

Daniels, A., Kramer, T. L., & Mahesh, N. M. (1995, July/August). Quality indicators measured by behavioral group practices. *Behavioral Health Care Tomorrow,* pp. 55-56.

Deane, F. P. (1993). Client satisfaction with psychotherapy in two outpatient clinics in New Zealand. *Evaluation and Program Planning, 16,* 87-94.

Diggle, P., Laing, K. Y., & Zeger, S. L. (1994). *Analysis of longitudinal data.* New York: Oxford University Press.

Edwards, D. W., Yarvis, R. M., Mueller, D. P., & Langsley, D. G. (1978). Does patient satisfaction correlate with success? *Hospital and Community Psychiatry, 29*(3), 188-190.

Eisen, S. V. (1996, August). Client satisfaction and clinical outcomes: Do we need to measure both? *Behavioral Healthcare Tomorrow,* pp. 71-73.

Garfield, S.L., Prager, R.A., & Bergin, A. E. (1971). Evaluation of outcome in psychotherapy. *Journal of Consulting and Clinical Psychology, 37*(3), 307-313.

Hoagwood, K., Hibbs, E., Brent, D., & Jensen, P. (1995). Introduction to the special edition: Efficacy and effectiveness studies of child and adolescent psychotherapy. *Journal of Consulting and Clinical Psychology, 63,* 683-687.

Hodges, K. (1990). *The Child and Adolescent Functional Assessment Scale (CAFAS)*. Unpublished manuscript.

Hodges, K., & Gust, J. (1995). Measures of impairment for children and adolescents. *Journal of Mental Health Administration, 22*(4), 403-413.

Hodges, K., Kline, J., Stem, L., Cytryn, L., & McKnew, D. (1982). The development of a child assessment interview for research and clinical use. *Journal of Abnormal Child Psychology, 10,* 173-189.

Hodges, K., McKnew, D., Cytryn, L., Stem, L., & Kline, J. (1982). The Child Assessment Schedule (CAS) Diagnostic Interview: A report on reliability and validity. *Journal of the American Academy of Child and Adolescent Psychiatry, 21,* 468-473.

Jacobson, N. S., & Truax, P. (1991). Clinical significance: A statistical approach to defining meaningful change in psychotherapy research. *Journal of Consulting and Clinical Psychology, 59*(1), 12-19.

Kazdin, A. E. (1994). Psychotherapy for children and adolescents In A.E. Bergin & S. L. Garfield (Eds.), *Handbook of psychotherapy and behavior change.* New York: Wiley.

Lebow, J. (1982). Consumer satisfaction with mental health treatment. *Psychological Bulletin, 91,* 244-259.

Mental health: Does therapy help? (1995, November). *Consumer Reports,* pp. 734-739.

McLellan, A. T., & Hunkeler, E. (in press). Is patient satisfaction related to patient outcome in alcohol and drug abuse treatment? *Psychiatric Services.*

Minsky, S. (1997, February). *The relationship between a self-report quality of life instrument and a consumer satisfaction survey.* Paper presented at the Seventh Annual National Conference on State Mental Health Agency Services Research and Program Evaluation, Arlington, VA.

Newman, E L. (1994). Criteria for selecting statistical procedures for progress and outcome assessment. In M. E. Maruish (Ed.), *Use of psychological testing for treatment planning and outcome assessment* (pp. 111-134). Hillsdale, NJ: Erlbaum.

Northrup, D. A. (1995). *The relationship between adolescent and parent reports about family issues.* Unpublished doctoral dissertation, Vanderbilt University, Nashville, TN.

Pekarik, G., & Wolff, C. B. (1996). Relationship of satisfaction to symptom change, follow-up adjustment, and clinical significance. *Professional Psychology: Research and Practice, 27*(2), 202-208.

Ries, R. K., Jaffe, C., Comtois, K. A., & Kitchell, M. (1996). *Patient satisfaction and outcome with outpatient integrated dual diagnosis treatment.* Unpublished manuscript.

Ross, E. C. (1997). Managed behavioral health care premises, accountable systems of care, and AMBHA's PERMS. *Evaluation Review, 21,* 318-321.

Salzer, M. S. (1997). Consumer empowerment in mental health organizations: Concepts, benefits, and impediments. *Administration and Policy in Mental Health, 24,* 425-434.

Seligman, M. E. P. (1995). The effectiveness of psychotherapy: The Consumer Reports study. *American Psychologist, 50*(12), 965-974.

Shapiro, S. S., & Wilk, M. B. (1965). An analysis of variance test for normality (complete samples). *Biometrika, 52,* pp. 115-124.

Smith, M. L., Glass, G. V., & Miller, T. I. (1980). *Psychotherapy.* Baltimore, MD: Johns Hopkins University Press.

Trabin, T., Freeman, M. A., & Pallak, M. S. (Eds.). (1995). *Inside outcomes: The national review of behavioral health care outcome programs* (Revised and expanded edition). Tiburon, CA: Centralink Publications.

Weiss, I., Rabinowitz, J., & Spiro, S. (1996). Agreement between therapists and clients in evaluating therapy and its outcomes: Literature review. *Administration and Policy in Mental Health, 23,* 493-511.

Weisz, J. R., Donenberg, G. R., Han, S. S., & Weiss, B. (1995). Bridging the gap between laboratory and clinic in child and adolescent psychotherapy. *Journal of Consulting and Clinical Psychology, 63*(5), 688-701.

Weisz, J. R., Weiss, B., Alicke, M. D., & Klotz, M. L. (1987). Effectiveness of psychotherapy with children and adolescents: A meta-analysis for clinicians. *Journal of Consulting and Clinical Psychology, 55*(4), 542-549.

Weisz, J. R., Weiss, B., & Donenberg, G.R. (1992). The lab versus the clinic: Effects of child and adolescent psychotherapy. *American Psychologist, 47,* 1578-1585.

Williams, B. (1994). Patient satisfaction: A valid concept? *Social Science and Medicine, 38*(4), 509-516.

Behavioral Healthcare Rating of Satisfaction™ (BHRS™)

(Please use a number 2 pencil.)

This section should be completed by staff of this provider agency before giving out the form.

Purpose of Evaluation:
○ 3 months after admission to provider
○ 6 months after admission to provider
○ Annual evaluation
○ Planned discharge from provider
○ A.M.A./A.W.O.L. discharge from provider
○ Other (see other agency options on back)

Substance Abuse Certification:
(Mark only if applicable)
○ Parents putting children at risk
○ Dually diagnosed
○ Involved in criminal justice system
○ Intravenous (IV) drug user
○ Other substance abuse

Current Level of Care from this Provider:
(Mark only one)
○ Crisis Stabil./Inpatient
○ Residential
○ Partial Hospitalization
○ Day Treatment
○ Outpatient
○ Detox
○ Case Management
○ Intensive Case Mgmnt.
○ Vocational
○ State Hospital
○ Other
○ None

[PROVIDER AGENCY TAX ID#] [SITE CODE] [DISTRICT CODE] [OPTIONAL CODE]

Instructions:

Please answer each question below by filling in the appropriate circle with a number 2 pencil.

USE NO. 2 PENCIL ONLY
EXAMPLES
CORRECT MARK ○ ● ○   INCORRECT MARKS ✓ ✗ ○

How many years of education do you have?
○ ○ ○ ○ ○ ○ ○ ○ ○ ○ ○ ○ ○ ○ ○ ○ ○ ○ ○ ○
1 2 3 4 5 6 7 8 9 10 11 12 13 14 15 16 17 18 19 20

(Fill in the circle referring to the last grade you completed. A high school degree or GED would be 12, technical school beyond high school would be 13 or 14, an Associate's degree would be 14, a Bachelor's degree would be 16, a Master's degree would be 18, a Ph.D. would be 20, an MD would be 20, etc.)

To what extent did you choose to become involved in the program? (Mark only one circle.)

○ I decided to come to this program.
○ I was encouraged to come here by others, but I agreed to give it a try.
○ I was forced to come into this program against my will.

Sex: ○ Male   ○ Female

[SOCIAL SECURITY NUMBER] [DATE OF BIRTH MO. DAY YR.] [TODAY'S DATE MO. DAY YR.]

Please help us by answering some questions about the services you have received. We really want to know what you think of this program—whether positive or negative. For each statement, please fill in the circle that best describes your opinion (ignore the numbers within the circles). Your answers will be kept confidential. Thanks for your help.

	Disagree Strongly	Disagree	Disagree A Little	Agree A Little	Agree	Agree Strongly
1. The staff member I work with most closely seems qualified to help me.	①	②	③	④	⑤	⑥
2. The program has helped me improve the way I deal with my problems.	①	②	③	④	⑤	⑥
3. I am satisfied with this program.	①	②	③	④	⑤	⑥

(Over)

Copyright © 1994, 1996, 1997 M. Dow & J. Ward, USF, FMHI

Source: Behavioral Healthcare Rating of Satisfaction™ (BHRS™). Psychological Assessment Resources, Inc. Copyright Michael G. Dow and John C. Ward. (Reprinted with permission.)

	Disagree Strongly	Disagree	Disagree A Little	Agree A Little	Agree	Agree Strongly
4. The building and facilities have usually been clean.	①	②	③	④	⑤	⑥
5. The program is helping me.	①	②	③	④	⑤	⑥
6. I learned things in this program that will help me.	①	②	③	④	⑤	⑥
7. This program is too controlling.	⑥	⑤	④	③	②	①
8. I would recommend this program to other people who need help.	①	②	③	④	⑤	⑥
9. I did not get enough attention from the staff.	⑥	⑤	④	③	②	①
10. The treatment methods do relate to my problems.	①	②	③	④	⑤	⑥
11. The services focus on what I want from treatment.	①	②	③	④	⑤	⑥
12. I am meeting my goals in treatment.	①	②	③	④	⑤	⑥
13. The services focus on my needs.	①	②	③	④	⑤	⑥
14. The clinical staff person I worked with most closely has been helpful.	①	②	③	④	⑤	⑥
15. The building and furniture are comfortable.	①	②	③	④	⑤	⑥
16. This program has improved my ability to function.	①	②	③	④	⑤	⑥
17. This program taught me how to communicate better with others.	①	②	③	④	⑤	⑥
18. I am treated with respect by the staff.	①	②	③	④	⑤	⑥
19. Some staff at this program have blamed me for my problems.	⑥	⑤	④	③	②	①
20. The staff cares about whether I get better.	①	②	③	④	⑤	⑥
21. The program has helped me improve the quality of my life.	①	②	③	④	⑤	⑥
22. If I were to have problems, I would return to this program.	①	②	③	④	⑤	⑥
23. My situation improved because I came here.	①	②	③	④	⑤	⑥
24. I don't trust the staff.	⑥	⑤	④	③	②	①
25. I was able to talk with staff when I needed to do so.	①	②	③	④	⑤	⑥
26. I am pleased with this program.	①	②	③	④	⑤	⑥

If "Other" is marked for Purpose of Evaluation (on front of form), staff should mark one of the following agency options:

○ 6 months after admission to specific program   ○ Discharge from specific program
○ 12 months after admission to specific program   ○ None of the purposes listed here

CP97-0828 (C3.F3)   Printed in U.S.A.   0987654321   Copyright © 1994, 1996, 1997 M. Dow & J. Ward, USF, FMHI

Chapter 5

Measuring the Outcome Of Addictions Treatment

Fee-for-Good-Service

A California County Has Begun Reimbursing SA Providers Based on Performance

CHRISTINE KILGORE

Providers who contract with the Santa Clara County Department of Alcohol & Drug Services in San Jose in CA knew for some time that the way in which they were reimbursed and assessed was to change dramatically. But starting in July 1998, all the notification and anticipation was transformed into a stark reality.

Fifteen percent of the providers' pay now hinges on their ability to achieve what the county has labeled a "quality achievement score"—a measurement of how well providers adhere to certain length-of-stay and efficiency guidelines. In time, after the county's fiscal year is over in July 1999 and after the county finishes evaluating various tools, the providers' score—and thus their reimbursement—will also reflect clinical outcomes measures.

The county's intention, at least over the next several years, is to focus its development of an outcomes measurement program not on clinicians' reports but on the use of patient self-report tools that can be employed to measure the status of substance abusers at intake into the system, during treatment, at discharge, and, hopefully, well after discharge. In a trial run of sorts, providers are now employing a range of questionnaires, including the SF-12 and BASIS-32.

A Dramatic Change

For providers, the county's new system for performance-based contracting and outcomes-linked reimbursement represents a dramatic change. For years, they'd been reimbursed based on fixed costs, with little attention paid to performance. The system has already caused some shuffling and withdrawals within the provider community, and there's general uneasiness among the providers about whether they'll be fairly reimbursed.

But, at least among some providers, there's also an element of trust. The providers have been integrally involved in the development of the county's broader managed care system and, in particular, its new reimbursement system. It was a small committee of providers that actually developed the performance measures and the basic system of scoring and payment. County officials tweaked and adjusted the measures, but the crux of the system, by all parties' accounts, is the providers' doing.

"The county wanted to stay out of the process [of developing the performance measurement system]," says Martha Beattie, a consultant who helped facilitate the committee's work. "They wanted the providers to own it."

The system of performance-based contracting and reimbursement is a major element—and the most striking one, Department leaders say—of a broader overhaul of alcohol and drug services in Santa Clara County.

Planning for a new system of managed care began in the spring of 1993 when the Department faced severe budget reductions, saw that private health care organizations were starting to compete for public dollars, and decided it needed to better manage its adult treatment services. A hard look at the system and a review of residential and outpatient utilization data deepened the Department's realization that services for its pool of about 400,000 potential patients were decentralized and uncoordinated, and that there wasn't any true system of care. Patients and referral agencies had to negotiate with each provider separately to gain access to services, and each provider used its own patient assessment and intake process. The result was that patients wasted time and energy and often ended up with services that didn't meet their needs. High-cost services—particularly residential treatment—were often misused, and referrals in general were frequently inappropriate. The Department, meanwhile, had no clear performance expectations and no way to assess the quality of care.

The Department decided to focus its energy on the development of a central intake unit—a gatekeeping unit, or single point of contact for patients and referring agencies—that would control access to the system and reduce inappropriate referrals. It formed a steering committee and applied for a federal Target Cities Grant that was funding some of these central intake units. The county didn't qualify for funding, but it didn't let that stop them.

The Department convened a new Managed Care Steering Committee to build on the work of this initial planning process and outline preliminary steps for a managed care system. About two years later, in summer 1995, the Department expanded the committee—comprised of representatives from the county, providers, and labor organizations—and charged it with developing a full-fledged proposal for a system of managed care.

The following spring, in 1996, the county Board of Supervisors approved the committee's plan. Its main goals: a single point of contact and clear standards of accountability; a system that is client-focused and outcomes-driven; and a contract and reimbursement system that supports performance and outcomes measurement.

Raising the Bar, But Slowly

The man leading the call for a new reimbursement system—long before the Managed Care Steering Committee issued its plan—was Bruce Copley, deputy director of the Department of Alcohol & Drug Services.

"We had a fairly typical arrangement with community providers that was based on cost reimbursement. It was more of a fee-for-service arrangement, where providers just needed to keep [facilities or programs] full and they got reimbursed," he says. "We realized early on that without the concept [of performance-based reimbursement], we weren't going to be able to move the system where we wanted it to go."

Copley says he knew that providers couldn't be pushed toward too much change too fast, and that the Department has been flexible and understanding of providers' concerns throughout the process. "We needed to not have people go over the cliff," he says. "We're dealing with many traditional nonprofit corporations that are used to slow, incremental change"

Yet he still took a firm, direct approach to, as he says, "lifting the bar." During a one week strategic planning meeting in summer 1996, and in subsequent monthly meetings comprised largely of county officials and providers, Copley facilitated a critical evaluation of the system and told providers that their relationship with the Department—and the way in which they were paid—would change. "I told them, 'You can't rely on us solely as your source of revenue,' which was in some ways debunking the traditional way nonprofits work with their employers," he says. "We looked at all our internal arrangements, the environment, the strengths and weaknesses, and where we needed to go. I told them, 'You have to help figure out how to get there.'"

Providers were required contractually to attend the monthly planning meetings and participate in what the Department labeled "hot groups," or five-to-seven-person committees charged with developing solutions on issues such as paperwork simplification, high-end users, and "rapid repeater" patients. "We weren't just talking about the problems. It broke down the cat-and-mouse games that can go on with counties and providers," says Copley, who speaks often of counties "taking control."

One of the "hot groups"—this one comprised solely of providers—was charged with developing the performance measures on which a chunk of their reimbursement would hinge. They worked over several months with Martha Beattie, an alcohol and drug researcher in Berkeley who was attempting to compare alcohol and drug services in several counties and was acutely interested in Santa Clara's proposed provider reimbursement system. She served as a sort of facilitator, helping the providers through a process of logically assessing how treatment was delivered in each of the three main treatment modalities (residential, detoxification, and outpatient), what desired outcomes should be, and how they should be measured.

"We asked things like, how do we know clients are learning anything? How can we measure that? We developed quizzes and things we need to put in place," says Lee Bennett, program director for Horizons South, a detox and residential facility for men in San Jose. "The process was underscored by a very cautious approach to performance-based reimbursement."

The Measures Take Shape

What the providers ended up with is the crux of the performance measures that are being used to calculate 15 percent of their reimbursement this fiscal year. The vast majority of the measures—11 measures each for residential and outpatient treatment services, and eight for detoxification services—deal with length of stay or treatment, with completion of the treatment and recovery process, and with procedural issues like getting patients to complete full assessments and orientations and having them sign treatment plans within designated periods of time. A few measures deal with an actual reduction or elimination of substance abuse. Each of the three sets of measures also includes one stating that 95 percent of clients must be satisfied with the program.

The measures for residential treatment services, for instance, say that 90 percent of clients who stay three days or more will sign an initial treatment plan within nine days of admission; that clients shall receive an average of 45 days of ser-

---

Performance Measures FY 1998/1999

Rev. 7/7/98

Residential Treatment Services

1. 98% of clients will complete a full assessment: Level of Care (LOC) Assessment, SASSI-3 & Treatment Assessment. (rank: 1)*
2. 98% of clients will sign the Comprehensive Orientation Summary to program treatment services and rules within 9 days of admission. (rank: 1)
3. 90% of clients are given an orientation to Managed Care Continuum within 9 days of admission. (rank: 4)
4. 90% of clients who stayed 3 days or more will sign the initial treatment plan within 9 days of admission. (rank: 1)
5. 90% of clients staying 9 days or more discharged with satisfactory progress. (rank: 3)
6. 90% of clients staying 9 days or more will discharge within 60 days of admission. (rank: 4)
7. 90% of clients staying 9 days or more and discharged within 60 days will have a continuing care plan begun at least 14 days prior to discharge. (rank: 5)
8. 90% of clients staying 9 days or more will have continued abstinence or reduced AOD use at discharge. (rank: 3)
9. Clients shall receive an average of 45 days of service. (rank: 4)
10. Clients staying 9 days or more will complete an outpatient intake appointment. (rank: 5)
    65% 1st qtr.   75% 2nd qtr.   80% 3rd qtr.   85% 4th qtr.
11. 95% client satisfaction with the program. (rank: 2)

   *Measures based on a scale of 1-5, with 1 having lowest ranking and 5 having highest.

Outpatient Treatment Services

1. 98% of clients will complete a full assessment: Level of Care (LOC) Assessment, SASSI-3 & Treatment Assessment. (rank: 1)*
2. 98% of clients who stay 2 or more hours will sign the Comprehensive Orientation Summary to program treatment services and rules. (rank: 1)
3. 90% of clients will be given an orientation to the Managed Care System continuum within 4 hours of service. (rank: 4)
4. 80% of clients will sign the initial treatment plan by the second treatment session. (rank: 1)
5. Clients who sign the initial treatment plan will stay in treatment 4 hours or more. (rank: 5)

vice; and that 90 percent of clients staying nine days or more will have continued abstinence or reduced alcohol and drug use at discharge.

Each measure is ranked based on a scale of one to five, so that certain measures hold more weight than others in determining final scores. Programs are expected to achieve certain minimum, or benchmark, scores in order to receive the full 15 percent of payment. If providers score less, their payment will be proportionally reduced.

Staff in the Department's new Quality Improvement/Managed Care Coordination (QI/MCC) Office will monitor the performance measures, at least for now, chiefly by assessing the utilization data that providers routinely enter into the Department's management information system and by reviewing treatment plans and other documents contained in patients' records. Both providers and county officials will be assisted in their respective efforts to meet and assess performance measures through a one-sheet checklist that can be stapled onto the front of each patient's chart. The worksheet lists the performance measures and provides space for providers or counselors to indicate where in the chart the supporting documentation can be found.

Both Copley and Ida Santos, the quality assurance manager, view the current performance measures as a work in progress and the first part of a two-step process. "The measures we have now are geared toward how well systems operate. Before we even worried about client outcomes, we needed to ensure that clients moved through [the system], that services actually got taken off the shelf and delivered," says Copley. "Until we do that, other outcomes measures aren't very useful—they wouldn't help you make fundamental shifts in system design."

65% 1st qtr.   75% 2nd qtr.   80% 3rd qtr.   85% 4th qtr.

6. 90% of clients who stayed 4 hours or more will begin the continuing care plan at least 14 days prior to discharge. (rank: 5)
7. 85% of clients staying 4 hours or more will have continued abstinence or reduced AOD use at discharge. (rank: 3)
8. Clients shall receive an average of 20 hours of service. (rank: 4)
9. Clients shall remain in treatment an average of 80 days. (rank: 4)
10. 70% of clients who transfer from residential treatment will stay in outpatient treatment a minimum of 8 hours or more. (rank: 5)
11. 95% client satisfaction with the program. (rank: 2)

*Measures based on a scale of 1-5, with 1 having lowest ranking and 5 having highest.

Detoxification Services

1. 90% of clients will complete the full assessment: CIWA, Level of Care (LOC) Assessment & SASSI 3. (rank: 1)*
2. 85% of clients will complete detox treatment satisfactorily. (rank: 3)
3. 90% of clients will stay 1 day or more. (rank: 3)
4. Clients shall receive an average of 3.2 days of service (rank: 4)
5. 85% of clients completing the detox process will be given an orientation to the Managed Care Continuum. (rank: 4)
6. 55% of clients staying one day or more will accept a referral for additional treatment in the Managed Care system. (rank: 5)
7. 75% of clients staying 1 day or more who accept a referral will keep the initial intake appointment with the Managed Care treatment provider. (rank: 2)
8. 95% client satisfaction with the program. (rank: 2)

*Measures based on a scale of 1-5, with 1 having lowest ranking and 5 having highest.

Source: Santa Clara County, Santa Clara Valley Health & Hospital System, Department of Alcohol and Drug Sevices (Reprinted with permission.)

Chapter 5: Measuring the Outcome of Addictions Treatment

Act Two: Outcomes

Santos' task now is to move into the next phase by implementing and evaluating various patient self-report tools that can be used to measure patient status and recovery. At the time of this writing, she was planning to require that providers, starting in fall 1998, routinely administer the SF-12, a general measure of health status and functioning, and the BASIS-32 (Behavior and Symptom Identification Scale), a rating scale in which patients report their degree of difficulty with a range of symptoms and problems, including alcohol and drug abuse.

Santos also planned to require use of the GAF (Global Assessment of Functioning) scale, which measures overall psychosocial functioning, and unlike the others, is strictly clinician-administered. And she was considering mandating the use of a modified version of the GAIN (Global Appraisal of Individual Needs), which assesses patients' perception of alcohol and drug use. Each of the tools had undergone pilot testing by several providers. If implementation throughout the county is successful and the tools yield useful data, they will be incorporated into the performance-based reimbursement system, Santos says.

Providers started using the CSQ-8 last summer to measure overall patient satisfaction as part of the performance-based reimbursement system.

Both Santos and Beattie say the goal is to choose patient self-report tools—standard or homegrown—that can be administered at intake, at designated points during treatment, at discharge, and hopefully, in phone interviews conducted well after discharge. (None of the measures being tested are used post-discharge, but each is used both at entry and exit from treatment.)

They realize the enormity of their post-discharge goal, since patients in the public sector, particularly drug and alcohol abusers, are widely known to be mobile and extremely hard to follow. Bennett says he's tried through "various efforts" to keep in touch with patients who've left and has found that "it's very difficult." Such long-term assessments are "in their infancy, and the success rate isn't that high. If after six months you're able to contact 40 percent, you're extremely lucky," he says. "But we need to know, 'What's the payback?' for our services. The only way to tell that is through outcomes assessment, and the longer-term, the better."

Santos envisions client self-reports as being at the heart of the outcomes criteria that the Department plans to make part of its performance measurement system. The county has purchased a computerized system for outcomes data collection and database management from HCIA-Response in Waltham MA that it hopes will help officials reach that goal. But Santos also plans to investigate other potential measures of the success of alcohol and drug treatment. "We want to look, for instance, at [patients'] legal status, or criminal activity, at discharge," she says. "If a person was on probation when he or she came in, what is their status when they leave?"

Santa Clara's new managed care system already has prompted some reorganization and shifting of alliances within the provider community, according to Copley. "We've lost a couple of residentials, and have gotten some new outpatient programs," he says. "There were also a few attempted mergers between outpatient and residential programs—some earnest talk."

It's unclear how much of this change is a response to the county's new reimbursement system and how much is a response to its broader effort to shift resources from residential treatment toward a wider continuum of services, including many new ancillary services. What is clear, however, is that providers—even those who have been integrally involved in the development of performance measures—are anxious about their new performance- and outcomes-linked pay.

"It's OK to have performance contracting if the system is operating efficiently, but if it's not the providers could be hurt, and not by their own doing," says Bennett. "The discomfort I have now is that the system might not be working efficiently enough yet for me to feel comfortable with performance-based reimbursement. If [performance] measures state, for instance, that the average length-of-stay in a detox facility should be 3-1/2 days and we have to keep someone for 12 days because the rest of the system can't accommodate him, we're responsible...even though we're not really responsible. All the assurances in the world don't make that worry go away."

Copley says the Department has been responsive to providers' concerns, partly by phasing in at-risk payment more slowly and in a different manner than it had planned. Copley originally wanted to measure achievement scores—and pay providers accordingly—strictly on a quarterly basis. He later decided that, at least for the fiscal year starting last July 1998, scores would be measured quarterly but averaged over the year, with payment reconciled at the end. "This way, you're not as likely to put people over the edge," he says.

The Department also had planned to put 5 percent of pay at risk during a "phase-in" period in the fourth quarter of the last fiscal year. It ended up implementing the new system at only 2 percent, after recognizing that the providers needed more time to adjust and realizing that some of the performance measures as they were originally developed by the provider "hot group" needed some fine-tuning. Copley also says that the 15 percent portion of reimbursement that's now at-risk (the other 85 percent will be paid on a cost basis) is significantly less than what he and others in the Department had originally planned. "Our intent," he says, " was to get at the 50 percent level."

According to Bennett, one of the providers' disappointments is that they can't earn extra compensation for exceeding the benchmarks. "There's no incentive money for improving," he says. Copley says the county is still "struggling with" the issue of moving more toward incentive-based reimbursement and will "be working on that this [fiscal] year." If budgets allow it, he hopes to end up with an "enterprise fund" that will award superior programs and enable them to enhance their services.

Bennett says he doesn't think "Santa Clara County is ready for that yet" but he's hopeful that the new system will spur positive change overall. "We still have some problems with it, but the fact is that we're all part of the system. We all have a say on what goes on, and the county has understood our difficulties with [the new reimbursement system,]" he says. "It's a matter of trust...I trust the county wants this thing to succeed."

Hazelden: Using Outcomes Measurement to Improve Chemical Dependency Treatment

What Is Hazelden?

Founded in 1949, Hazelden is an internationally recognized provider of comprehensive recovery services for alcoholics and addicts. Its treatment milieu consists of a unique and intensive integration of educational and therapeutic services. At its main facility, which is located on 488 acres of woods, hills, and lakes in Center City, Minnesota, Hazelden provides:

- primary residential services, including detoxification, group therapy, individual counseling, topic-focused information and education, recreation therapy, and other therapeutic activities;
- an outpatient recovery program, which is a five-week, structured program consisting of 15 evening sessions covering topic-focused information and group therapy;
- extended rehabilitation therapy, which includes group and individual counseling; and
- a family program, which is a three- to five-day residential program available to family members or friends of people with chemical dependencies, regardless of whether they are in treatment at Hazelden.

What Does Performance Improvement Mean at Hazelden?

At Hazelden, performance improvement is defined as an active learning process. As a result, staff are always striving to monitor the quality of services provided, the outcomes clients achieve, and ways to make service delivery more effective. Measurement, which produces performance data, is the linchpin in Hazelden's improvement efforts.

Hazelden has a documented measurement plan with three main components. The first component identifies the following five key processes that define its core work:

1. Preentry (the client's first contact and request for help);
2. Admission (the client's actual physical arrival);
3. Assessment and treatment planning;
4. Provision of care, services, and treatment; and
5. Ongoing recovery and continuing care.

Performance measurement initiatives attempt to interpret these five key processes from multiple perspectives. The viewpoints of the client, family members and friends, payers, purchasers, accreditors, and regulators are of particular interest. Process performance is measured in a concurrent fashion, primarily through survey-based data collection. Specific performance reports are generated for various audiences monthly and quarterly. In these reports, statistical process control techniques and qualitative approaches are used to paint a descriptive picture of the performance of each of the key processes. In addition, a comparative analysis of the performance of key processes is conducted.

The second component of the measurement plan is the client profile. A clinical picture of Hazelden clients is created by using instruments with demonstrated reliability and validity. Special

---

Source: © Using Performance Measurement to Improve Outcomes on Behavioral Health Care. Oakbrook Terrace IL: Joint Commission on Accreditation of Healthcare Organizations, copyright 1998, pages 127-129. Reprinted with permission.

attention is given to understanding clients' addictions, psychiatric diagnoses, and medical problems. The Addiction Severity Index (ASI), Behavioral and Symptom Identification Scale (BASIS-32), Global Assessment of Functioning (GAF), and Medical Outcome Study Health Survey SF-36 are being incorporated into the assessment process to evaluate life functioning, behavioral problems, family environment, severity, and risk factors. The client profile is a concurrent clinically descriptive client database.

The third component of the measurement plan addresses the evaluation of key operational (nonclinical) processes. Indicators in this section of the plan track financial performance, monitor key human resources variables, and assess critical aspects of the environment of care.

Hazelden's Withdrawal From Benzodiazepines Study

What Was the Project Goal?

Withdrawal from benzodiazepines presents a series of clinical challenges. First, the process, which involves tapering the medication dosage, is lengthy. Second, the withdrawal period is typically characterized by significant signs and symptoms of anxiety. Third, the anxiety often causes clients to be psychologically unavailable for talking therapies. Staff at Hazelden wondered if the addition of complementary therapies to the treatment plan might ease client distress during this difficult withdrawal process. The specific goal of the study was to discover whether acupuncture, head and neck massage, or routine treatment led to better outcomes for clients withdrawing from benzodiazepines.

How Were Data Collected?

A multidisciplinary team consisting of a chemical dependency counselor, registered nurse, psychologist, physician, member of the clergy, family therapist, and recreation therapist was established. All team members independently created a flowchart that depicted their own understanding of the steps in the process of benzodiazepine withdrawal. These flowcharts were compared and discussed. That discussion led to the definition of benzodiazepine withdrawal as a process consisting of four phases: entry into treatment, drug withdrawal, end of treatment stay, and end of primary treatment/early recovery. Team members brainstormed a number of questions about the client's experiences in each of the four phases of treatment. Those questions became the framework for the series of data collection instruments used by clients and staff.

After examining their benzodiazepine withdrawal treatment process and considering state-of-the-art treatment for benzodiazepine addiction, the team also generated a list of clinical milestones that clients should achieve while in treatment. Ultimately, these milestones will be incorporated into a benzodiazepine withdrawal clinical pathway that will be developed as a consequence of this measurement project.

Next, to gain an increased understanding of the relationship between the variety of therapeutic interventions and recovery from benzodiazepine addiction, the team completed a diagram. Six main contributors to recovery were identified: assessment, detoxification, therapy, behavior/lifestyle changes, education, and spirituality. Next, to create a comparative database, the team worked for about six months to collect baseline data on 30 clients undergoing standard benzodiazepine. withdrawal treatment. The Beck Anxiety Inventory (BAI) was used to assess somatic, cognitive, and affective symptoms of anxiety, severity of anxiety symptoms, behavioral problems, and risk factors for anxiety. For the assessment to include all symptoms specified in the *Diagnostic and Statistical Manual of Mental Disorders*, 4th edition (DSM-IV), the team added five additional items that evaluated insomnia, seizures, agitation, hallucinations, and overall level of anxiety.

Next, using the framework developed as a part of the analysis of the benzodiazepine withdrawal process, the team developed a series of checklists (data collection tools) to be completed by the client, addictions counselor, nurse, and recreation therapist. Consumers, counselors, and nurses filled out surveys at four points in time: the beginning of withdrawal or "early treatment," middle of withdrawal or "midtreatment," and end of withdrawal or "end of primary treatment." The recreation therapy staff completed a single assessment at the end of treatment. Finally, the client was queried about how the benzodiazepine withdrawal process could be made more comfortable.

When the baseline data had been collected, the experiment was initiated. All clients admitted for benzodiazepine withdrawal were eligible to participate in the study. At the time of their admission, the clients were told of the study examining the effect of acupuncture, head and neck massage, and routine treatment on benzodiazepine withdrawal. To match the comparative group, a sample of 30 clients each would be included in the acupuncture, head and neck massage, and routine treatment groups. Clients had to give informed consent before they could participate in the study. Clients in the acupuncture group receive acupuncture treatments from a certified acupuncturist five times each week for the duration of their treatment. Individuals in the head and neck massage group receive five massage treatments per week throughout their treatment. Clients in the routine treatment group participate in the usual treatment, which includes relaxation techniques, meditation, recreation, and group and individual therapy. Staff anticipated completing data collection by mid-December.

How Were Data Analyzed?

Because this study is still in progress, data analysis has not been completed. However, the plan is to examine the client outcomes (dependent variable) in relation to the various treatment approaches (independent variable). Tracked client outcomes include the following: progress in treatment, as measured by the various surveys; length of withdrawal; length of treatment; satisfactory completion of treatment; use of medications, such as over-the-counter analgesics; and abstinence at 1, 6, and 12 months. Treatment approaches include standard treatment, acupuncture, and head and neck massage.

What Did the Data Show?

As of press time, no data analysis has been conducted.

How Was This Measurement Project Used To Improve Performance?

Because this study was still in progress, no specific improvement actions have been taken. It is anticipated, however, that the data generated from this measurement project will be used in two fundamental ways. First, staff plan to use the data to help identify milestones of recovery, which will then be used as critical components for the development of clinical pathways/practice guidelines. Second, depending on the final study results, alternative treatment models for benzodiazepine withdrawal may be institutionalized.

Lessons Learned at Hazelden as a Consequence Of Conducting This Outcomes Measurement Activity

Although this project was still under way at press time, several lessons can be learned from this outcomes measurement activity:

1. The multidisciplinary team approach to performance improvement really works. Team members bond through their shared focus on critical clinical issues. They quickly commit to the common goal of measuring and improving key clinical processes and outcomes.
2. Serving on a performance improvement team provides a rich opportunity for professional growth and development. Although individual team members may have varying levels of knowledge and skills related to performance measurement and improvement, staff quickly develop the understanding and competencies necessary to systematically measure, assess, and improve performance.
3. Comprehensive, meaningful outcome/process studies require more time and resources than originally anticipated. However, improved performance is worth the investment.

Making the Case With Public Stakeholders To Support SA Treatment

A vital component of any outcomes system design is to identify all your stakeholders to make sure that you measure the outcomes that they expect. The three most obvious groups you answer to are your funders/payers, board of directors, and client-consumers. But what about the public at large?

The ongoing debate about parity legislation demonstrates that we are not assured of universal support for equitable behavioral health benefits. Public support for treatment of addiction appears to be even weaker than for mental illness, as evidenced by its exclusion from the Federal parity measure adopted this past year.

This suggests that addiction treatment providers—and their clients—would benefit from considering taxpayers as stakeholders and thus, make sure to measure and report outcomes that the public expects.

Deni Carise, PhD, offered a number of outcomes measurement strategies that address this need in her presentation at the Quality & Accountability Summit convened earlier this summer by the Institute for Behavioral Healthcare. Carise, who recently completed a postdoctoral fellowship at the University of Pennsylvania, began by listing public expectations for outcomes after substance abuse treatment:
- no return to substance use;
- safe, complete detox;
- reduced use of medical services;
- elimination of crime related to chemical dependency;
- return to employment and self-support; and
- minimal family disruption.

The top expectation for abstinence is asking too much, says Carise—a point we'll return to later. Moreover, abstinence rates alone don't tell us enough.

Research she had conducted with A. Thomas McLellan, PhD, and presented at the Summit relied on the Addiction Severity Index (ASI) to establish client profiles at treatment intake and to measure changes in problem severity over time. The ASI is administered by a trained interviewer and covers seven domains of clients' lives—medical status, employment/support status, family/social relationships, psychiatric status, drug use, alcohol use, and legal status.

Client Changes

The instrument's design allows providers to report changes in such variables as:
- number of days in the previous month that various substances were used;
- number of times the client had alcohol d.t.'s and/or drug overdoses;
- number of days employed and amount of income from work;

Source: Reprinted by permission of Manisses Communications Group, Inc. Originally published in Behavioral Health Outcomes September 1997; 2(9):4-5.

For more information on the ASI and TSR instruments, contact DeltaMetrics, One Commerce Square, 2005 Market Street, Suite 1120, Philadelphia, PA 19103; phone (800)238-2433; fax (215)665-2892; e-mail deltamet@aol.com.

- number of days involved in illegal activities and amount of illegal income;
- number of days experiencing serious family and other conflicts; and
- incidence of psychiatric symptoms.

Knowing such outcomes can provide powerful support for addiction treatment. However, there are other challenges to face in improving public opinion. For one thing, Carise says that providers need to provide comparative information and establish reasonable expectations.

For example, one University of Pennsylvania study tracked HIV infection rates among drug treatment clients only to find that the rate climbed from 13% to 18% over a three-year period. Many people would consider such an outcome to indicate failure. But when the investigators showed that the infection rate for an untreated control group rose from 21% to 39% over the same period, it was clear that the treatment group had better outcomes. Moreover, an expectation of slowing the growth rate was probably more reasonable than halting it altogether.

Then there are the skeptics who say that a major reason that addiction treatment works is not so much what providers do as it is motivation on the part of clients. A good response to such challenges, says Carise, is to compare your client outcomes with those of people on your wait list.

Service Needs

To convince the public to demand or support adequate funding for effective treatment, it is important to tie achievement of client outcomes to the services needed to produce them, according to Carise. (McLellan developed the Treatment Services Review [TSR] instrument to do just that.)

Numerous articles in past issues of *Behavioral Health Outcomes* have demonstrated that more is not necessarily better, but neither are severe limits on treatment and other services. The public and policy makers have the right to know how much each outcome costs to help them judge cost effectiveness and to conduct cost/benefit analyses.

Establishing realistic expectations for relapse is closely related to the question: How much is this going to cost? Carise recommends countering judgmental attitudes about relapse as evidence of character flaws by comparing chemically dependent clients with patients who have other chronic medical conditions (see table).

Behavioral Compliance Rates

Insulin dependent diabetics—
- compliance with medication regimen = < 50%
- compliance with diet and foot care = < 30%
- retreated within 12 months = 30-50%

Medication dependent hypertensives—
- compliance with medication regimen = < 30%
- compliance with diet = < 30%
- retreated within 12 months = 50-60%

Asthmatics—
- compliance with medication regimen = <30%
- retreated within 12 months = 60-80%

Source: National Center for Health Statistics, 13th edition.

Not only are the compliance rates cited here in line with those for chemically dependent clients, but denial appears to be just as rampant; Carise says that 50% of "medical" patients lie about their compliance.

"We don't tell diabetics who return for care: 'We won't treat you; we already treated you for this condition last year,'" says Carise. Yet that is precisely what people think we should tell alcoholics and drug addicts who slip or relapse.

With comprehensive, good quality outcomes data, providers might convince public stakeholders that such expectations are unreasonable.

Gambling Treatment Outcome Monitoring System (TOMS)

RANDY STINCHFIELD, PHD

Mission

The Gambling Treatment Outcome Monitoring System (TOMS) provides scientifically valid evaluations of the effectiveness of pathological gambling treatment programs for adolescents and adults. Addictions and mental health problems cause severe pain and suffering, as well as dramatic costs to society in terms of health care expenses and lost productivity. Treatment programs attempt to reduce both the human and economic costs of these disorders, and as a result are interested in their effectiveness in treating these disorders and how they may improve their effectiveness. The evaluation information is invaluable for developing a clearer picture of the types of clients served and for improving programs to better serve the needs of clients. Treatment programs are also interested in providing information about their effectiveness to potential consumers, third-party payers, and regulatory agencies. We are committed to providing evaluation services in a manner that is practical, user-friendly, non-intrusive and economical. It is also important that this information be provided by an objective research organization, rather than the treatment program itself.

Specific Aims

1. Describe the demographic and clinical characteristics of clients seeking treatment;
2. Measure the effectiveness of treatment;
3. Measure the level of client satisfaction with specific treatment components and the program in general; and
4. Identify variables that predict treatment completion, aftercare participation, and outcome.

Method

Treatment effectiveness is examined by comparing client data collected at admission, discharge, and follow-up. Outcome is assessed with a multidimensional assessment battery that includes measures of the following client variables: addiction problem severity, psychopathology, vocational/educational functioning, marital/family relations, criminal activity, peer and social relations, health care utilization, and select clinical problems. TOMS provides comprehensive written reports and face-to-face presentations may be arranged.

Treatment Outcome Monitoring System (TOMS)

TOMS provides you with all of the tools you need to measure the effectiveness of your treatment program. The tools include client consent forms, client admissions log, client tracking log, copies of intake, discharge, and follow-up questionnaires and answer sheets, computerized follow-up assessment mailings with cover letters, a step-by-step data collection manual, data collection and other technical support, computer data entry, computer data management and storage, statistical analyses, and semi-annual treatment outcome reports. Table 1 shows measurement points and content of questionnaires for the Gambling Treatment Outcome Monitoring System. With our assistance, you will set up the outcome monitoring system at your program, collect the data, and then send the data to us. We will then enter the data on computer, analyze your data, and write a treatment outcome report for you on a semi-annual basis. This system is our preferred mode of operation, but we are flexible and will adapt to the spe-

---

Source: Reprinted with the permission of the author.
   Randy Stinchfield, PhD, 689 Fairmount Avenue, St. Paul MN 55105. Tel: (612) 224-4152. E-mail: Randy.D.Stinchfield-1@tc.umn.edu. Web site: *www.cbc.med.umn.edu/~randy/gambling*.

cific needs of your program. Options include: (a) additional instruments; (b) additional measurement points; (c) additional data analyses; and (d) we collect the follow-up data. There is an added expense for each option. Costs can be controlled by working with us to develop a research design and sample selection procedure that is scientifically sound and cost-effective. A sample report is available upon request.

The treatment outcome report includes the following:
- executive summary,
- description of your treatment program,
- admission rates by month,
- client demographics and clinical history,
- gambling problem severity,
- substance use problem severity,
- treatment intensity,
- changes in psychosocial functioning between intake and discharge,
- changes in gambling problem severity (e.g., gambling frequency) between pretreatment and follow-up,
- comparison of your program outcome with similar programs,
- client ratings of treatment helpfulness and satisfaction with treatment,
- outcome of treatment noncompleters,
- comparison of treatment completers to noncompleters on outcome,
- posttreatment service utilization, and
- summary and recommendations.

Gambling Treatment Outcome Monitoring System
Measurement Points and Content of Questionnaires

Admission	Discharge	6-months Follow-up	12-months Follow-up
Demographics		Demographics	Demographics
Clinical and treatment history			
Gambling behaviors		Gambling behaviors	Gambling behaviors
Gambling frequency	Gambling frequency	Gambling frequency	Gambling frequency
Gambling Problem Severity		Gambling Problem Severity	Gambling Problem Severity
Financial problems		Financial problems	Financial problems
Legal problems		Legal problems	Legal problems
Problem recognition	Problem recognition		
Substance use frequency		Substance use frequency	Substance use frequency
Psychosocial problems		Psychosocial problems	Psychosocial problems
	Treatment component helpfulness		
	Client satisfaction		
	Discharge information		
		Posttreatment service utilization	Posttreatment service utilization

Treatment Outcome Study (TOS) Baseline Design

New York State Office of Alcoholism and Substance Abuse Services, Health and Planning Services Division, Evaluation and Program Monitoring Unit

The New York State Office of Alcoholism and Substance Abuse Services (OASAS) is about to implement a Treatment Outcome Study (TOS). The TOS seeks to assess the ability of OASAS-licensed programs to produce the desired treatment outcomes in the clients that they serve. The primary goals of the TOS are:
- to examine the relationship between types and intensity of services received and positive client outcome;
- to examine the effectiveness of different types of programs in producing positive outcomes in clients with similar presenting problems;
- to examine the cost-benefit of the New York drug and alcohol treatment system; and
- to determine the effectiveness of individual OASAS-licensed drug and alcohol treatment programs in producing positive client outcomes.

The New York State substance abuse and alcohol treatment system consists of over 1,200 operational programs. There are more than 530 licensed alcoholism treatment programs and over 740 licensed substance abuse treatment programs. Of those substance abuse and alcohol abuse programs, more than 700 are funded by OASAS. Average daily census figures reveal that, on a typical day, more than 123,000 individuals are enrolled in New York State's systems. There are more than 50,000 individuals enrolled in alcoholism programs at any given point in time, while more than 70,000 are enrolled in substance abuse programs. The number of annual admissions in each system differs significantly. The overwhelming majority of annual admissions occurs in alcoholism treatment programs. In 1994, there were approximately 191,000 admissions to alcoholism treatment programs and approximately 56,000 admissions to substance abuse treatment programs. In both the alcohol and substance abuse systems, outpatient programs comprise the largest proportion of program types. Likewise, the majority of clients axe found in outpatient programs; in 1994, approximately 90% of all enrollments occurred in various outpatient services.

The TOS will utilize a sample of alcohol and substance abuse treatment programs to conduct the evaluation. Detoxification programs and alcohol crisis centers are not included in the TOS because of the brief lengths of stay in those programs. Adolescent clients, 18 years of age and under, are also excluded because the TOS interview instruments are intended for adults only. The sampling methodology requires a 10% sample resulting in the selection of 119 programs. Within each program, 85 clients will be selected to participate on a voluntary basis resulting in a subject pool of approximately 10,000 clients.

OASAS randomly sampled programs to participate in the TOS based on program type, size and geographic location. Variations across programs in the rates of client admissions will result in varying dates for the completion of the sampling process. Thus, programs with lower admission rates are expected to take a longer period of time to complete their sampling. Programs will have up to two years to recruit their 85 clients.

Source: Treatment Outcomes Study (TOS) Baseline Design. *New York State Office of Alcoholism and Substance Abuse Services, Health and Planning Services Division, Evaluation and Program Monitoring Unit, October 1997. (Reprinted with permission.)*

OASAS has contacted programs by directly notifying them of their participation in the TOS and informing them of procedures to follow. Participating programs will select, for the client sample, the first 85 consecutive adult clients who are admitted into their program from a designated startup date, and who voluntarily consent to participate in the evaluation. For those clients who revoke their consent while in treatment, programs will be required to replace them with the next consenting, adult new admission. For a client to be included in a program's TOS sample, he/she must not have been previously included in any other program's TOS sample, and must have used alcohol or drugs in the past 30 days unless they are referred from the criminal justice system.

Once a client is selected for inclusion in the study, the program will obtain written client consent for participation. Since participation is voluntary, a client's refusal or acceptance to participate will in no way affect his/her access to treatment. Each client's consent form will be maintained at the program with the signed original forwarded to OASAS when the client leaves treatment.

When a client agrees to participate, the program must also obtain locator information. The locator form will be maintained at the program and updated regularly in conjunction with the three-month ASI interviews. This information will include the names, addresses and telephone numbers of up to three individuals who are most likely to know the whereabouts of the client once she/he has left treatment.

In addition, other forms of identification will be collected, e.g., driver's license number, social security number, Medicaid number. Clients who are homeless will also be asked to provide information on their places of residence during the prior six months. This information will be forwarded to OASAS and subsequently provided to the follow-up contractor.

Upon admission to the study, the programs will be required to record client-specific service data through the Client Services Reporting Form (CSRF) for each participating client. The CSRF system requires direct-care staff to record every service provided to the client, the duration of the service, the date the service was provided, and whether it was provided on-site or not. Information is recorded on the CSRF and is submitted to OASAS monthly. These data allows OASAS to examine the relationship between the type, frequency and intensity of services received, and client change while in treatment and after leaving treatment.

Within a week of admission, programs shall be required to administer an Addiction Severity Index (ASI) to each client participating in the study. The ASI is a widely used instrument that assesses client level of functioning in seven areas: medical status, employment status, drug and alcohol use, family history, family and social relationships, legal status, and psychiatric status. OASAS has made some modifications to the ASI primarily by integrating detailed instructions to the interviewer into the interview instrument and making both the client severity ratings and the family history grid optional. In addition, the client's motivation and readiness for treatment is assessed. For every three months that the client remains in treatment, the program will administer a shortened version of the ASI. All completed ASIs will be submitted to OASAS on a monthly basis. These data will permit OASAS to examine the progress clients make while in treatment.

As clients are discharged from the programs, OASAS will notify the follow-up contractor so that the six-month follow-up data collection dates may be determined and recorded. OASAS will forward to the contractor the necessary locator information. Six months following the client's termination from the program, the contractor will attempt to contact him/her by telephone using the locator information collected at admission. For clients who were admitted to, and remain in, a methadone maintenance program, follow-up will occur six months after the client has been in the treatment program for one year.

In order to protect client confidentiality during the follow-up segment of the TOS, the project is identified as the HOMES Project, i.e., Health Outcome Monitoring and Evaluation System Project. Therefore, when attempting to locate a client, the contractor's staff will identify themselves as HOMES Project staff and will not indicate any connection to the alcohol or substance abuse field. Note that, given the variations in the length of stay associated with different types of programs, there will be large variations across program types for the dates of client discharge. This results in a wide range of time during which six-month follow-up interviews by the contractor need to be conducted.

Once contacted, the client receives a telephone-administered follow-up ASI and is asked to provide other relevant information concerning his/her current status, activities since leaving treatment and satisfaction with the treatment received. This follow-up will be administered by the contractor utilizing a CATI system. For those clients who are homeless and cannot initially be contacted by telephone, attempts will be made to locate them in shelters and arrange for telephone interviews. The contractor must obtain training in the administration of the ASI for all staff who will administer the ASI to TOS clients. OASAS, while maintaining client confidentiality as specified in 42 CFR Part 2, will seek the cooperation of other state agencies (e.g., DMV, DCJS) in locating clients who could not be located by the contractor.

As follow-up interviews are completed, the contractor will forward all follow-up interview materials to OASAS on a monthly basis. Clients who complete the follow-up interview will be compensated ($20) for their participation, as research suggests that paying clients for their time increases the likelihood of client participation. Either upon completion of follow-up client interviews or upon determining that a client cannot be located, the contractor will return to OASAS all materials and forms with client identifying information.

OASAS will issue annual reports that describe the status of the project and the results of the analyses relating to the impact of client services on outcomes and the relative effectiveness of treatment types. As soon as this and the program specific data becomes available, they will be used to direct the provision of technical assistance and to inform OASAS funding and planning decisions.

Fact Sheet for Program Directors

Purpose

The Treatment Outcome Study (TOS) will examine:

1. The relationship between *types* and *intensity* of **services** received and positive **client outcomes**.

Services:
- refers to all services provided by the program's direct-care staff (e.g., nurses, doctors, counselors, social workers, psychologists, occupational therapists, aides and assistants of direct-care staff, etc.); this information will be recorded on the *Client Services Reporting Form (CSRF)*.
- types of services are found on the *Client Services Reporting Form (CSRF)* and mirror the services listed on the PPSI (see attached table entitled "*Service Categories from Client Services Reporting Form (CSRF)*").
- intensity of services: measured by the amount of time (i.e., # of minutes) and the frequency (# of times) that the service is provided.

Positive client outcomes will be based on analyses of measures from several instruments which will show the degree of client improvement over time. Baseline measures of client problems/conditions will be collected at admission and compared to similar outcome measures collected over time every three months while in treatment, at discharge, and six months after discharge:

Addiction Severity Index (ASI) Instruments: measures of improved

Table 1

Baseline Instruments	Outcome/Change Instruments
♦ Admission ASI	♦ In-Treatment (3-month) ASI
	♦ 6-Month Follow-up ASI
♦ Motivation and Readiness Scale	
♦ PAS-44 Client Admission form	♦ PAS-45 Client Discharge form
	♦ Client Satisfaction (6-Month Follow-up)

Chapter 5: Measuring the Outcome of Addictions Treatment

client outcomes will be based partly on changes over time in ASI composite scores in several major life areas (medical, employment/economic support, drug use, alcohol use, legal, family/social relationships, and psychiatric).

Motivation and Readiness Scale: since client motivation and readiness are likely to be highly associated with program retention, it is important to control for these factors when analyzing the effects of programs on successful client outcomes.

OASAS Client Admission/Discharge forms (pAS-44/45): measures of improved client outcomes might include, for instance, a reduction in the number of arrests, days incarcerated, hospitalizations (non-detox), inpatient detoxifications, emergency room visits, etc.

Client Satisfaction Instrument: provides information from the client's perspective with respect to the types of services received and their level of satisfaction with their treatment experience.

2) The relative effectiveness of different program types in producing positive client outcomes (e.g., do certain types of programs produce more positive improvements in certain types of clients?).

- Program type: programs are broken down into nine program type categories (see Participating Programs section).

3) The cost-benefit ratio of New York State's alcoholism and substance abuse treatment programs in producing positive client outcomes.

- After all data is collected, a cost offset analysis will be conducted, as in the CALDATA study.

4) The effectiveness of individual alcohol and substance abuse treatment programs in producing positive client outcomes.

- The ability to determine the effectiveness of individual programs on client outcomes will depend on the degree of change in client outcome measures combined with the final client sample sizes (i.e., if the sample is not large enough and the changes in outcomes are not strong enough, we may not be able to sufficiently detect the effects for individual programs); in order to ensure large enough sample sizes to detect program type effects, a large portion of the analysis will be based on pooling programs into the various program types and conducting aggregate-level analyses.

Participating Programs

- **Final Program Sample Size**: total of 119 programs
- **Funding Status**: includes 72 funded and 47 non-funded programs
- **Region**: includes programs from all major OASAS regions

Table 2

Region	# TOS Programs
Western	12
Finger Lakes	9
Central	7
Northeastern	12
Mid-Hudson	18
New York City	40
Long Island	21
TOTAL	119

- Randomly selected by *program type* (see Table 3), size (less than 50 clients, 50-150 clients, more than 150 clients), and *urbanicity* (NYC, NYC Suburban, Upstate Urban, Upstate Suburban)

Table 3

Program Type	# TOS Programs
Drug-Free and Medically Supervised Day Service	10
MMTP	16
Drug-Free Residential	12
Inpatient Rehabilitation	9
Outpatient Clinic with Module	16
Outpatient Clinic	15
Outpatient Drug-Free	16
Outpatient Medically Supervised	20
Outpatient Rehabilitation	5
TOTAL	119

Participating Clients

- Each client will be administered the following TOS interview instruments and related forms as shown below (where applicable):

Administered by:

	TOS Program Interviewer	Outside TOS Contractor
At admission	◆ Admission ASI ◆ Motivation and Readiness Scale ◆ Client Consent Form ◆ Client Locator Form	
Every 3 Months during treatment	◆ In-Treatment (3-month ASI) ◆ Client Locator Form (update only)	
6 months following discharge		◆ 6-Month Follow-up ASI ◆ Client Satisfaction

- Limited to the first 85 clients admitted consecutively into the program who:
  - are adults (18 years old and over)
  - AND consent to participate
  - AND either have used alcohol/drugs during the past 30 days (prior to admission) or are formally referred from the criminal justice system
  - AND are not already included in the TOS sample (through another program)

Program Responsibilities

Each of the 119 programs will do the following:

- *Assigning personnel* — each program will assign staff to the TOS as follows:
  - one TOS Program Coordinator will oversee and manage the data collection process and act as the main contact to the OASAS evaluation liaison assigned to that program.
  - one to three direct-care staff will be trained by Evaluation staff and by OASAS-certified ASI trainers to: 1) recruit the clients; 2) assist clients in filling out the Consent and Locator forms; 3) administer the Admission ASI and the Motivation and Readiness Scale at client admission, and 4) administer the In-Treatment ASI (and update the Client Locator Form) every 3 months that the client remains in treatment.
  - *Recruitment*: recruit the 85 TOS clients by explaining the purpose of the study and the client's role and rights in regards to their voluntary participation (a sheet entitled "Presentation to Clients" will be available as a guide in presenting the TOS to clients).
  - *Client Admission (PAS-44) and Discharge (PAS-45) Forms*
    - PAS-44: enter either a "10" (to indicate client participation in TOS) or an "18 (in NYC, to indicate both TOS and Workfare participation) in the upper right-hand corner of the PAS-44 (Special Project Code field) for each client who consents to participate in the TOS; this form should be completed on-line immediately for each client participating in TOS as he/she is admitted to the program so as to initiate the client tracking system.
    - PAS-45: these forms should also be completed on-line immediately when a TOS client is discharged so as to update the client tracking system which will notify the contractor regarding the six-month follow-up date.
  - *Consent Forms*: after recruiting each of the 85 clients, assist each in reading and signing a Client Consent Form (English or Spanish versions available) indicating their willingness to participate in the TOS and to be located and interviewed six months following discharge.
  - *Locator Forms*:
    - after a client consent form has been signed, obtain and fill out information on the Client Locator Form which is crucial to the success of the TOS, since it will provide the contact information necessary for the 6-month follow-up interview by an outside contractor.

Chapter 5: Measuring the Outcome of Addictions Treatment

- updating Client Locator Forms: updating should be done along with the administration of the In-Treatment ASIs and also when any new relevant locator information becomes available to the program staff.
- *TOS Interview Instruments*: administer a slightly modified OASAS version of the Addiction Severity Index (ASI) along with a short Motivation and Readiness Scale to each participating client at client admission, in addition to a briefer In-Treatment ASI version every three months that the client remains in treatment; to ensure the integrity of the data, these must be administered during acceptable time window dates which will be provided to the program (by the TOS On-Line Monitoring System) and will allow some flexibility in administering interviews.
- *Client Services and Reporting Form*: complete and submit reporting forms to document all services that the program's direct-care staff provide to the client.
- *TOS On-Line Monitoring System:* program coordinators will access the TOS system on a regular basis to do the following:
  1. **Retrieve OASAS reminder messages**: program coordinators will regularly check for various reminder and/or informational messages sent from OASAS evaluation staff; programs will be notified of any awaiting messages as soon as they sign onto the TOS system.
  2. **Enter TOS monitoring information**: program coordinators will enter applicable TOS client information and other changes regarding data collection as they occur (e.g., change in client TOS status, such as a client dropping out of TOS; dates that interviews are actually administered; changes in coordinator or interviewers and related requests for training of new interviewers).
  3. **View and print a variety of client tracking reports**: program coordinators will be able to obtain crucial tracking information (in addition to that described above in #2) that will aid in planning and monitoring their administration of interviews; this will be in the form of various viewable and printable reports, on all participating TOS clients, that will include information such as: client admission (and discharge) dates, TOS Status (of client), scheduled interview dates (and time window beginning and ending dates), ASI interview status (e.g., interview is due, late, done), dates that various ASI forms are due at OASAS and received, ASI Form status (e.g., form is due, late, received at OASAS), any major data collection form problems (e.g., Motivation and Readiness Scale is missing, legal section of ASI is blank).
- *MMTP Programs*: Clients who are admitted to MMTP programs and remain in treatment will be administered ASIs by program interviewers for 12 months, and follow-up by an outside contractor will occur 18 months following admission. Clients who drop-out of treatment or who are discharged before the 12 month period will be followed-up six months following the drop-out/discharge date.

Training

Training will be provided for TOS Coordinators and Interviewers for the following:
- ASI:
  - 2-day regional training on the ASI will be conducted by OASAS-certified trainers from the Academy of Addiction Studies who have received formal train-the-trainer training in the ASI.
  - OASAS will provide training for additional interviewers and coordinators (or retraining) over the course of the project as is deemed necessary.
- **TOS Procedures**: Evaluation staff will conduct regional one-day training sessions on TOS procedures and instructions on the completion of various data collection forms.
- **TOS On-line System**: Evaluation/MIS staff will conduct regional one-day training sessions on the use of the TOS On-Line System for aiding programs in planning and tracking data collection and monitoring each program's progress in the TOS.

- **OASAS On-line System**: MIS staff will conduct regional training sessions on the use of the OASAS Client Data System (CDS) for reporting admission, discharges, and monthly service delivery reports.
- **TOS Training Manual**: A comprehensive TOS User's Manual will be distributed to all TOS Program Coordinators and Interviewers on procedures to follow, how to complete data collection forms, and guidelines for submitting data collection forms to OASAS.

Evaluation's Role

- Development of the overall design of Treatment Outcome Study.
- Development of data collection forms.
- Development of training manuals for administering the ASI and for TOS procedures and issues.
- Development of design specifications for the TOS On-Line System.
- Daily monitoring of study progress (e.g., data collection):
  - conduct daily TOS On-Line System program monitoring and provide direct contact with TOS coordinators (as needed).
  - acting as program liaisons with Regional Office staff to ensure program compliance with study reporting requirements.
- Provide programs with feedback reports that include summaries of program and client performance.
- Management of an agency contract with an outside vendor to conduct the six-month telephone follow-up interviews.
- Conduct periodic regional meetings with TOS Program Coordinators to discuss progress of TOS, problems, issues, sharing of information, etc.

Critical Points

It is absolutely crucial to the success of the TOS that the following occurs:
- *Program Cooperation, Support, and Commitment*:
  - the support and cooperation of program directors.
  - the support and cooperation of program staff, in particular, those staff serving as TOS Program Coordinators and Interviewers.
  - participating programs will be expected to remain committed to the study for its duration. Active program participation ends when the last of their 85 clients is discharged.
- *Timely and Accurate Submission*:
  - **Instruments and Procedural forms**: ASIs, Client Services Reporting Forms, Consent and Locator forms must be completed accurately and submitted on a timely basis.
  - **TOS On-Line Monitoring System**: this system will require programs to sign on regularly to retrieve OASAS reminder messages, enter TOS monitoring information, and access the client tracking reports.
  - **OASAS' PAS-44's and PAS-45's (Admission and Discharge) forms**: must be submitted immediately (via the OASAS On-Line System) for TOS clients in order to keep the TOS On-Line System updated.
- *Client Confidentiality*: all data collection and procedural forms and client contacts will refer to the project as the HOMES (Health Outcome Monitoring and Evaluation System) Project so as to protect client confidentiality. While attempting to locate clients at the 6-month followup, the outside contractor will in no way associate the client with the substance/alcohol abuse treatment system to others.

Incentives for Participants

Both funded and non-funded programs that are selected to participate will receive:
- Top priority for on-line access to the OASAS Client Data System (CDS).
- On-line access to various OASAS data systems (e.g., CDS, Workscope, PPSI).
- CASAC credits for those program staff who serve as TOS Coordinators and those

who administer the ASIs (CASAC credits are contingent on a program's full compliance with all TOS requirements).

- Knowledge and documentation of the effectiveness of their program.

Service Categories from Client Services Reporting Form (CSRF)
for the Treatment Outcome Study

Drug and Alcohol Counseling
01 Individual Counseling
02 Group Counseling
03 Encounter Groups
04 Family Counseling
05 Family Group Counseling
06 Stress Management Counseling
07 Relapse Prevention Counseling
08 Aftercare Counseling

Vocational/Educational Services
09 Vocational/Educational Assessment
10 Individual Vocational/Educational Rehabilitation Counseling
11 Group Vocational/Educational Rehabilitation Counseling
12 Work Readiness and Employability Skills Training
13 Life Skills Training
14 English as a Second Language
15 Basic Education
16 Remedial Education
17 GED/High School Education
18 College Preparation
19 Vocational/Educational/Employment Referrals & Placements
20 Vocational/Educational/Employment Follow-Up & Support
21 Occupational Therapy
22 Chemical Dependency Training

Health-Related Services
23 Acupuncture
24 Detoxification
25 Medical Examination
26 Primary Medical Care
27 Emergency Medical Care
28 Nutritional Services
29 Pre/Post Natal Care
30 Pediatric Care
31 HIV Antibody Testing
32 Early HIV Primary Care
33 HIV Case Management
34 TB Testing
35 TB DOT/DOPT
36 Antabuse/Naltrexone Dispensed
37 Methadone/LAAM Dispensed
38 Psychotropic Medication Dispensed
39 Other Medication Dispensed (Not Methadone/Psychotropic Rx)
40 Urine Sampling
41 Breathalyzer
42 Blood Testing (Other than HIV)
43 Other Specialized Health-Related Services

Legal/Criminal Justice Services
44 Legal Counseling
45 Legal Representation
46 Reports to Court, DTAP, TASC, etc.
47 Reports to DMV's Drinking Driver Program

Social Services
48 Parent Training
49 Activities Therapies
50 Child Care
51 Housing Assistance
52 Recreational
53 Entitlement Assistance
54 Transportation

Mental Health Services
55 Individual Psychotherapy
56 Group Psychotherapy
57 Psychiatric Assessment
58 Psychological Assessment
59 Psychosocial Assessment
60 Psychotropic Medication Management
61 Psychiatric Crisis Intervention

Case Management
62 Formal Case Management Services
63 Crisis Intervention

QUICK-REFERENCE INSTRUMENT GUIDE

Instrument Name	Screening	Diagnosis	Assessment of Drinking Behavior	Treatment Planning	Treatment and Process Assessment	Outcome Evaluation
Adapted Short Michigan Alcoholism Screening Test for Fathers (F-SMAST) and Mothers (M-SMAST)	✿			☆		
Addiction Admission Scale (AAS)	✿					
Addiction Potential Scale (APS)	✿					
Addiction Severity Index (ASI)				✿		☆
Adolescent Alcohol Involvement Scale (AAIS)	✿					
Adolescent Diagnostic Interview (ADI)		✿		☆	☆	
Adolescent Drinking Index (ADi)	✿					
Alcohol Abstinence Self-Efficacy Scale (AASE)				✿		
Alcohol Clinical Index (ACI)	✿					
Alcohol Dependence Scale (ADS)	☆	✿		☆		
Alcohol Effects Questionnaire (AEFQ)				✿	☆	
Alcohol Expectancy Questionnaire (AEQ)				✿	☆	
Alcohol Expectancy Questionnaire - Adolescent (AEQ-A)				✿	☆	
Alcohol-Specific Role Play Test (ASRPT)				☆	✿	
Alcohol Timeline Followback Method (TLFB)			✿			
Alcohol Use Disorders and Associated Disabilities Interview Schedule (AUDADIS)		✿	☆			
Alcohol Use Disorders Identification Test (AUDIT)	✿					
Alcohol Use Inventory (AUI)				✿		☆
Brown-Peterson Recovery Progress Inventory (BPRPI)					✿	
CAGE	✿					
Chemical Dependency Assessment Profile (CDAP)		✿	☆	✿		
Clinical Institute, Withdrawal Assessment (CIWA)		✿		☆		
Composite International Diagnostic Interview (CIDI Core)		✿				
Comprehensive Drinker Profile (CDP)		☆	☆	✿		
Computerized Lifestyle Assessment (CLA)	✿		☆	✿		
Diagnostic Interview Schedule (DIS-III-R) (Alcohol Module)		✿				
Drinking Expectancy Questionnaire (DEQ)				✿	☆	
Drinker Inventory of Consequences (DrInC)		☆		☆		
Drinking Problems Index (DPI)		✿		✿		✿
Drinking Refusal Self-Efficacy Questionnaire (DRSEQ)				✿		
Drinking Related Internal External Locus of Control Scale (DRIE)				✿		
Drinking Restraint Scale (DRS)		✿		☆		
Drinking Self-Monitoring Log (DSML)			✿			
Drug Use Screening Inventory (DUSI) (revised)	✿			☆		

✿ Primary assessment domain usage; ☆ Secondary usage.

Source: A Quick-Reference Instrument Guide. In: National Institute on Alcohol Abuse and Alcoholism Treatment Handbook Series 4: Assessing Alcohol Problems: A Guide for Clinicians and Researchers, Allen and Columbus, Eds. NIH Pub. No. 95-3745, 1995 pp. 11-15.

QUICK-REFERENCE INSTRUMENT GUIDE (Continued)

Instrument Name	Screening	Diagnosis	Assessment of Drinking Behavior	Treatment Planning	Treatment and Process Assessment	Outcome Evaluation
Family Tree Questionnaire (FTQ) for Assessing Family History of Drinking Problems						
Followup Drinker Profile (FDP)				✿		✿
Impaired Control Scale (ICS)		✿				
Inventory of Drinking Situations (IDS)				✿		
Lifetime Drinking History (LDH)			✿			
MacAndrew Alcoholism Scale (Mac)	✿					
Michigan Alcoholism Screening Test (MAST) and variants	✿					
Brief MAST						
Malmo Modification of the MAST						
Short MAST						
Millon Clinical Multiaxial Inventory (MCMI-II)		✿				
Motivational Structure Questionnaire (MSQ)				✿		
Munich Alcoholism Test (MALT)	✿					
Negative Alcohol Expectancy Questionnaire (NAEQ)				✿	☆	
NET	✿					
Perceived Benefit of Drinking Scale (PBDS)	✿			☆		
Personal Experience Inventory (PEI)	☆			✿		
Personal Experience Screening Questionnaire (PESQ)	✿					
Problem Oriented Screening Instrument for Teenagers (POSIT)	✿			☆		
Problem Situation Inventory (PSI)		✿		☆	✿	
Psychiatric Research Interview for Substance and Mental Disorders (PRISM)		✿				
Quantity-Frequency (QF) Methods						
Composite Quantity Frequency (QF) Index						
Graduated-Frequency (GM) Measure						
NIAAA Quantity Frequency (QF)						
Quantity Frequency (QF)						
Quantity Frequency Variability (QFV) Index						
Volume-Pattern (VP) Index						
Volume Variability (V/V) Index						
Rand Quantity Frequency (QF)						
Readiness to Change Questionnaire (RTCQ)				✿		
Recovery Attitude and Treatment Evaluator (RAATE)		✿		✿		
Restrained Drinking Scale (RDS)						
Rutgers Alcohol Problem Index (RAPI)	✿					

✿ Primary assessment domain usage; ☆ Secondary usage.

QUICK-REFERENCE INSTRUMENT GUIDE (Continued)

Instrument Name	Screening	Diagnosis	Assessment of Drinking Behavior	Treatment Planning	Treatment and Process Assessment	Outcome Evaluation
Self-Administered Alcoholism Screening Test (SAAST)	❀					
Severity of Alcohol Dependence Questionnaire (SADQ)		❀				
Short Alcohol Dependence Data (SADD)		❀				
Situational Confidence Questionnaire (SCQ)				❀		
Steps Questionnaire						
Substance Abuse Subtle Screening Inventory (SASSI)	❀			☆	❀	
Substance Use Disorders Diagnostic Schedule (SUDDS)		❀		☆		☆
T-ACE	❀					
Teen-Addiction Severity Index (T-ASI)		❀		❀		
Temptation and Restraint Inventory (TRI)						
Treatment Services Review (TSR)					❀	
TWEAK	❀					
Veterans Alcoholism Screening Test (VAST)	❀					
Yale-Brown Obsessive Compulsive Scale—Modified (Y-BOCS-hd)		❀				
Young Adult Alcohol Problems Screening Test (YAAPST)	❀					
Your Workplace				❀		

❀ Primary assessment domain usage; ☆ Secondary usage.

Chapter 6

Children and Adolescents: Different Needs, Different Tools

The Santa Fe Summit on Behavioral Health, Final Report

A Special Section Which Addresses Outcomes Measurement for Children And Adolescents With Serious Emotional Disorders

This special section was developed after the initial Santa Fe Summit in recognition of the special methodological and other considerations necessary to address outcomes measurement in children, adolescents and families. This initial work focuses on the subpopulation of children most in need of mental health and substance abuse services.

This work grew out of the outcomes study panel at Santa Fe, and is included as a virtual stand-alone document. This section models the summit process from beginning to end, starting with values, identifying indicators for this risk-adjusted subpopulation, and then reviewing the relevant measures for this population.

In other sections of the report (process and access), the recommendations for children and adolescents are incorporated into the main text.

American College of Mental Health Administration (ACMHA) Proposed Child Outcomes

Introduction

The American College of Mental Health Administration (hereafter referred to as ACMHA) has endeavored to adapt, for children, adolescents, and their families, the values-based methodology for identification of service outcomes developed at the Santa Fe Summit in March of 1997. ACMHA is aware that numerous organizations (e.g., the Substance Abuse and Mental Health Services Administration, Center for Mental Health Services, National Alliance for the Mentally Ill, American Academy of Child and Adolescent Psychiatry, National Committee for Quality Assurance, American Managed Behavioral Healthcare Association, various foundation and corporate collaborators) are developing comprehensive access, performance and outcome standards for mental health and substance abuse services for adults and children. The ACMHA Child Outcomes Workgroup focused on outcomes but did not attempt to specify values, indicators and measures related to child service system access and performance during its short-lived tenure. For nearly two decades, federal, state, and foundation sponsored initiatives and policies have supported the development of a values-based and principle-driven model of service systems for children and their families known as a system of care (Stroul & Friedman, 1994). Efforts to measure access, structure, performance, and outcomes in systems of care continue as this report is written, and efforts of ACMHA and other groups to develop core performance measures for mental health and substance abuse care for children and families should incorporate aspects of system structure and coordination shown to improve access to an appropriate range of least restrictive services in such systems of care.

ACMHA gratefully acknowledges the feedback provided by the individuals convened by the Substance Abuse and Mental Health Services Administration (SAMSHA) to review a working draft of this document. Many of these individuals are participants in one of the aforementioned

---

Source: Excerpted from The Santa Fe Summit on Behavioral Health—The 1997 Final Report. American College of Mental Health Administration. March 1998 (Reprinted with permission.) For more on the Summit Final Report, see page 284.

group efforts to develop comprehensive performance and outcomes standards for child and family mental health and substance abuse services. Some of their recommendations were incorporated into the attached document; others were not. Rationale for non-inclusion generally revolved around the extent to which recommendations represented: (1) significant deviations from the values agreed upon at the Summit; (2) the concern of a single advocacy, administrative, or academic group (thus requiring deviation from the consensus process forged at the Summit); and/or (3) significant increases in data collection and response burden. The most vexing challenge faced by the Child Outcomes Work Group was that of reconciling measurement-related concerns with ACMHA's commitment to brevity, pragmatism, " simplicity and relevance"- attributes likely to be valued in the marketplace, where the burden and costs associated with the collection of outcome data will be borne by providers and consumers. Measurement in the field of child and adolescent mental health outcomes is still in an early stage. On the other hand, several symptom checklists, global rating scales, diagnostic interviews, and multidimensional functioning measures have been well validated. However, most are lengthy, require extensively trained interviewers, or rely exclusively on clinician judgment. Thus, the group has recommended subscales from instruments with demonstrated validity, despite the violation of psychometric rigor this strategy represents. Without support for further validation work, the ultimate value of outcomes standards will not be realized. In this vein, the "Methodological Standards for Outcome Measures" prepared by the CMHS Adult Outcome Measurement Standards Committee provides an excellent overview of the methodological issues to be addressed to develop outcomes standards that actually reflect treatment-related change (or maintenance of gains) in consumer populations.

In the material which follows, we have laid out; 1) working assumptions; 2) values; and, 3) indicators and suggested measures that index these values.

Child Outcomes Work Group Assumptions

The four assumptions that guided the group's work are enumerated below.

The target population is children and adolescents who exhibit symptoms and impairments sufficient to persistently and significantly interfere with functioning across multiple settings (e.g. school, home, and in community settings). These children might be described as having a serious emotional disturbance (SED) and also as a "risk adjusted" population. As such, they are distinguished from the general population of children and adolescents who, at various stages of development, exhibit problem behaviors and experience emotional distress that are transient in nature.

Child outcomes will reflect change at the client (child and family) level. This approach contrasts with a report card approach that reflects the status of a managed care entity with respect to certain indicators of an enrolled population at a single point in time. Assessment over time is essential to examining whether treatment delivered under the auspices of any care entity (managed or not), has an impact, and is particularly critical when dealing with children, for whom changes in behavior, stress, and distress vary (often considerably) over the course of normative development even in the absence of treatment. Thus, it is recommended that data pertinent to the indicators be collected at the outset of treatment, during the course of treatment, upon treatment termination, and up to 18 months year following treatment termination, for youth receiving treatment during any calendar year.

Data will be collected from multiple informants, including the child's caregiver and child, archival data from public agencies legally mandated to collect such data (e.g., schools, juvenile justice agencies, child protection agencies), and medical records.

Each indicator should be supported by some psychometric data, yet brief, thus requiring careful selection of subsets of items or scales rather than full measures. Although some valid and reliable measures of child and adolescent behaviors, symptoms, and functioning exist, and were reviewed by the work group, many of them require significant administration time and training. Research regarding the sensitivity of these measures to the experiences of the target (risk-adjusted) population of youth, and to treatment-related changes within such a population, is also limited. Moreover, there are no valid measures to

Chapter 6: Children and Adolescents: Different Needs, Different Tools   189 index some of the values articulated at the Summit as they relate to children. The group selected measures, subscales, and single-items supported by psychometric data whenever possible, views further psychometric work as essential to the identification of meaningful but pragmatic outcomes measures, and recommends that such work be supported once final consensus about the indicators to be measured is reached.

American College of Mental Health Administration Child Outcomes Work Group Consensus Values, Indicators, and Data Sources

Value 1: Youth Will Reside in the Homes of Their Families[1]

Indicator: Children and Adolescents Should Have a Stable Living Situation in a Home With a Family

Recommended Measures

1. Child's residence and the restrictiveness of the living environment rated in accordance with Robert Hawkins and colleagues' Restrictiveness of Living Environment Scales (ROLES; Hawkins, Almeida, Fabry, & Reitz, 1992).
2. Number of placement changes experienced by the child during treatment and at 6-month intervals following treatment termination, up to 18 months following treatment.
3. Number of days in out-of-home placement during treatment and at 6-month intervals following treatment termination, up to 18 months following treatment.

Data Sources
- Caregiver reports elicited at the outset and termination of treatment and at 6-month intervals during treatment and up to 18 months following treatment, the reporting window being the month prior to data collection.
- Archival data kept by placing agencies for placements occurring during treatment and at 6 month intervals up to 18 months following treatment, the reporting window being the previous 6 months. The ROLES rating scale can be distributed to these agencies, or to the managed care entity collecting the placement data from these agencies, so that restrictiveness of placements can be scored in a standardized manner.

Value 2: Youth Are Engaged In Productive Activity

Indicator: Youth Attend and Perform In School (Including Vocational)

Recommended Measures

Data regarding the following are collected from caregivers and school records.
1. Number of days absent
2. Incidents of truancy
3. Number of disciplinary incidents.
4. Expulsions
5. Pass/Fail within the last year

Caregiver reports are solicited at the outset and termination of treatment, and at 6-month intervals following treatment, the previous month being the time frame for reporting. Archival data regarding these items are obtained for the month prior to treatment, and for 6-month intervals up to 18 months after termination.

Value 3: Youth Have Good Physical and Mental Health And Substance Abuse

Indicator: Youth Maintain or Improve Health Status And Improve Mental Health And Substance Abuse Status

Recommended Measures

Physical Health:
1. Youth and caregiver response (about youth) on Item #1 of the Children's Health Questionnaire (CHQ; Landgraf

and Ware, 1991, 1996) at the outset, during, and upon termination of treatment, and at 6-month intervals up to 18 months following termination of treatment.
2. Youth pregnancy, as reported by youth and/or caregiver elicited at the outset and termination of treatment, and at 6-month intervals up to 18 months following termination of treatment.

Mental Health and Substance Abuse
1. Reports of suicide attempts made to caregiver, provider, or admitting hospital during treatment and at 6-month intervals up to 18 months following termination of treatment.
2. Symptoms related to mood (negative and positive) as described in CHQ Item 6.1.
3. Symptoms related to concentration, activity, eating, sleep, and antisocial behaviors, as described in the Adolescent Outcomes Module (ATOM; University of Arkansas for Medical Sciences, 1995).

Substance Abuse

Recommended: Drug Preference and Drug Involvement subscales of the Drug Use Screening Inventory adapted for adolescents (DUSI; Tarter & Hegedus, 1991).

Also proposed: Hair analysis to replace urine screens for youth involved in court-ordered substance abuse treatment, as hair analysis is less intrusive and offers more specific findings.

Value 4: Youth Are Safe From Criminal Victimization, Abuse, And Neglect

Indicator: Youth Will Not Experience Victimization, Abuse, or Neglect

Recommended Measures
1. Caregiver reports of criminal victimization of the youth prior to, during, and at 6 month intervals up to 18 months following termination of treatment.
2. Child Protective Service reports of abuse or neglect prior, during, and at 6 month intervals up to 18 months following termination of treatment.

Value 5: Youth Are Not in Trouble With the Law

Indicator: Youth in Treatment Will Not Be Arrested, Detained, Or Incarcerated

Recommended Measures

Data regarding the following are collected from youth and/or their caregivers and from the archives of county or state juvenile justice authorities/courts.
1. Number of arrests
2. Severity of crime coded in accordance with FBI Uniform Crime Reports
3. Number and length of incarcerations
4. Number and length of probation terms

For youth/caregivers and archival sources the reporting interval is the month prior to treatment, months during treatment, and month prior to 6 month intervals up to 18 months following termination of treatment.

Value 6: Youth Have Social Support

Indicator: Youth Have Prosocial Peers and Access To Support From Adults

Recommended Measures

Peers

Subscales from the Family, Friends, and Self (FFS) Assessment Scales (Simpson & McBride, 1992) that tap peer involvement, involvement with peers who get into trouble, and parent familiarity with peers. Responses follow a Likert type format ranging from "none" to "all." Youth responses are elicited at the outset, during, and at termination of treatment, and at 6-month intervals up to 18 months following treatment termination.

Adult (non parent) support

No valid measure of social support for youth from adults outside the family has been identified yet.

Value 7: Youth Perform Developmentally Appropriate Activities of Daily Living

Indicator: Youth Performs Developmentally Appropriate Self-Care and Life Skills

Recommended Measure

No valid measure spanning childhood and adolescence was identified; the Structured Vineland Scale for youth ages 4-5 and 6-12 has good psychometric properties but requires trained administrators and significant administration time.

Value 8: Youth Enjoy a Positive Quality of Life

Indicator: Youth Report Having A Positive Quality of Life

Recommended Measure:

No valid measure of the construct was identified, and downward extensions of adult quality-of-life measures were deemed inappropriate for youth, for whom the nature of the construct is yet to be defined. Thus, a range of constructs potentially related to a child's sense of well being (e.g., child's self-esteem or self-efficacy, positive family relations) and valid measures of them were considered. Most of these are quite lengthy. *Section #7 of the CHQ* (Landgraf & Ware, 1991, 1996) is relatively brief, and, although entitled "Self Esteem," it appears to tap a child's assessment of quality of life at home, school, and with friends and includes omnibus questions about life in general, and is offered as a potential starting point for measurement of the quality of life construct.

Acknowledgments

Members of the ACMHA Child Outcomes Work Group are:
Barbara J. Burns, Ph.D., Duke University
Robert Cole, Ph.D., Washington Business Group on Health
Connie Dellmuth, M.S.W., Washington Business Group on Health
Sonja K. Schoenwald, Ph.D., Medical University of South Carolina

Sybil Goldman, MSW, Georgetown Child Development Center, also provided assistance, and Kimberly Hoagwood, Ph.D., National Institute of Mental Health made excellent recommendations regarding measures of certain indicators and provided copies of measures and psychometric data for them. In the end, however, instrument length and administration training precluded their inclusion—and that of other well validated but lengthy instruments—in the current report.

The assistance of the Substance Abuse and Mental Health Administration in general, and of Eric Goplerud, Ph.D., and Dorothy Webman, Ph.D., in particular, in convening a review group and coordinating feedback mechanisms is gratefully acknowledged.

Notes

[1] Family is defined broadly to include relatives who are primary caregivers of youth and other guardians who provide a family environment (e.g., adoptive families, foster care families).

References

Center for Mental Health Services, Adult Outcome Measurement Standards Committee (1997) Methodological Standards for Outcome Measures (Draft). Rockville, MD: Author.

Hawkins, R.P., Alameida, M.C., Fabry, B., & Reitz, A.L. (1992). A scale to measure restrictiveness of living environment for troubled children and youth. *Hospital and Community Psychiatry*, 43, 54-58.

Langraf and Ware (1991, 1996). *Child Health Questionnaire—Child Self Report Form 87* (CHQ-CF87). Authors.

Simpson, D.D., & McBride, A.A. (1992). Family, friends, and self (FFS) assessment scales for Mexican American youth. *Hispanic Journal of Behavioral Sciences*, 14,1212-1216.

Stroul, B.A., & Friedman, R.M. (1994). *A system of care for children and youth with severe emotional disturbances*. Washington, DC: Georgetown University Development Center.

Tarter, R.E., & Hegedus, A.M. (1991). The drug use screening inventory. *Alcohol Health & Research World*, 15,65-75.

University of Arkansas for Medical Sciences (1995). *Adolescent Treatment Outcomes Module (ATOM)*. Little Rock: Author.

Use of the Child and Adolescent Functional Assessment Scale (CAFAS) As an Outcome Measure In Clinical Settings

KAY HODGES, PHD, MARIA M. WONG, PHD, AND MARK LATESSA, MSW

Abstract: *This article discusses how the Child and Adolescent Functional Assessment Scale (CAFAS) can be used as an outcome measure in clinical settings. Outcome data from two clinical samples are provided: a small community mental health center located in Michigan and a large referred sample from the Fort Bragg Evaluation Project. Outcome indicators for assessing change over time included overall level of dysfunction, percentage of respondents with severe impairment, mean total score, mean scores for individual CAFAS subscales, and change in total score at the client level. Implications of the findings were discussed from several perspectives: improving services to individual clients, developing databases at the local level that can be used for the agency's continuing self scrutiny, and pooling databases across sites that can be used to study broader issues within a managed care environment.*

The Child and Adolescent Functional Assessment Scale (CAFAS)[1] is used as an outcome measure by publicly and privately funded entities. Many states currently use the CAFAS to determine eligibility for state-managed programs or for measuring performance-based outcomes.[2-5] Individual agencies use the CAFAS to actively manage cases because it helps clarify treatment goals and track progress toward those goals over time. In addition, the CAFAS has been included as an outcome measure in two large studies: the Fort Bragg Evaluation Project (FBEP)[6] and the evaluation of the demonstration grants funded by the Center for Mental Health Services.[7,8]

In today's environment, use of measures is often mandated by oversight authorities or funding sources for the purposes of assessing outcome and determining client eligibility for specific levels of services. The individual agency is left to determine how the information can be used to benefit both the clients and the agency in general. It is critical that these measurements be clinically useful at the individual client level. Otherwise, it is likely that the instrumentation will not be applied reliably and, thus, will be unable to detect change over time.

In this article, information is presented on how to integrate the CAFAS into day-to-day clinical activities. Suggestions are also provided on how the information generated by the CAFAS can be used for the agency's internal evaluation. Data gathered by a small community mental health center (CMHC) in Michigan are used as a case example. The data were gathered as part of an informal pilot project that preceded a statewide evaluation effort. Indicators that can be used to

---

Source: Hodges K, Wong MM, and Latessa M. Use of the Child and Adolescent Functional Assessment Scale (CAFAS) as an Outcome Measure in Clinical Settings. The Journal of Mental Health Administration *August 1998*; 25(3):325-336. Copyright © 1998 by Sage Publications, Inc. Reprinted by permission of Sage Publications, Inc.

Address correspondence to Kay Hodges, PhD, Department of Psychology, Applied Research Unit, Eastern Michigan University, 102 King Hall, Ypsilanti, MI 48197. Maria M. Wong, PhD, is a postdoctoral fellow, Surrey Research Center, the Institute for Social Research, University of Michigan, Ann Arbor. Mark Latessa, MSW, is a research and quality assurance specialist, Quality Improvement Services, Livingston County Community Mental Health Services.

describe the youth served by the agency and to describe changes in client status over time are illustrated. In addition, the agency's data are compared to a large clinical sample collected in the FBEP for the purpose of external comparison. In the discussion, lessons learned are shared about how to maximize the accuracy and usefulness of the outcome data for internal evaluation.

Integration of the CAFAS In Clinical Care and Decision Making

In this section, the CAFAS, its psychometric properties, and ways in which the CAFAS can be integrated into routine clinical care are briefly described. A more detailed discussion is presented by Hodges.[9,10]

The CAFAS comprises a set of written items describing behavior that are organized into domains of functioning. Within each domain, behaviors are grouped into levels of impairment: severe, moderate, mild, and no or minimal impairment. For each scale, the rater determines the level of impairment that best describes the youth's most severe level of dysfunction during the time specified by the user (e.g., last month, last 3 months). The scores assigned to each of the categories are as follows: 30 for severe, 20 for moderate, 10 for mild, and 0 for minimal or no impairment.

The CAFAS is rated by a staff member based on information collected as part of the typical clinical services. The actual rating usually takes about 10 minutes. A structured 30-minute interview has been developed to obtain the information needed to rate the CAFAS,[11,12] although it is not necessary to use it. The 1989 version of the CAFAS, which was used by the CMHC and FBEP, consists of five scales for the youth and two for the caregiver. The scales used in this case study are as follows: Role Performance (i.e., how effectively the youth fulfills societal roles in school, home, and community), Behavior toward Self and Others (i.e., appropriateness of the youth's daily behavior), Moods/Emotions (i.e., modulation of the youth's emotional life), Thinking (i.e., ability of the youth to use rational thought processes), and Substance Use (i.e., youth's substance use and the extent to which it is inappropriate or disruptive). The total score refers to the sum of the five scales assessing the youth, with a range from 0 to 150. A higher score reflects greater impairment. The current version of the CAFAS[1] has eight youth scales (School Role Performance, Home Role Performance, Community Role Performance, Behavior Toward Others, Mood, Self-Harmful Behavior, Substance Use, and Thinking) and includes a list of strengths and/or goals appropriate to each scale.[9,10]

Satisfactory interrater reliability, test-retest reliability over a short time period, and internal consistency have been reported elsewhere.[11,13] Concurrent and predictive validity of the CAFAS was generated by the FBEP, in which youths referred for mental health services were assessed at intake, at 6 months, and at 12 months. High discriminant validity was demonstrated; inpatients (i.e., psychiatric inpatient, residential treatment center) scored higher on the CAFAS than youths in alternative care (i.e., alternative care to traditional residential, including home-based services, day treatment, specialized foster care, and group home), who in turn scored higher than youths in outpatient care. This finding was observed at intake and at 6 months and 12 months postintake.[13] As is desirable for a measure of outcome, the CAFAS proved to be sensitive to change. There was a significant main effect for time, with a reduction in CAFAS scores observed across time.[13] The CAFAS has also been useful in predicting service utilization and costs at 6 months and 12 months postintake. Higher impairment was significantly related to more restrictive care, higher cost, more bed days, and more days of services. In addition, when compared to other measures and to clinical diagnosis, the CAFAS score was the strongest predictor of subsequent service utilization and cost at 6 months and 12 months postintake.[14]

The CAFAS generates clinically useful information at three levels: individual item endorsement, level of impairment on each of the individual scales, and summary score indicating overall dysfunction. The items endorsed are descriptions (e.g., expelled from school) that can be useful in developing goals on the youth's treatment plan. In the scoring summary, critical items indicating risk behaviors toward others or the self are brought to the rater's attention (e.g., fire setting, aggression, suicidal risk). The impairment level for each scale (i.e., severe, moderate, mild, and no or minimal) is determined by the items endorsed. Specific profile patterns or high endorsements on specific scales may trigger an evaluative consultation or suggest a particular treatment protocol. The profile provides a format for organizing discussions with the youth, his or her caregivers, or other professionals.

A total score is generated by summing the youth scales. There are no cutoff scores for the CAFAS. However, a general framework for putting the CAFAS total score into context, referred to as Overall Level of Dysfunction, appears to be useful for laypersons.[9] For the 1989 version, the levels are as follows: 1 to 10 = none or minimal dysfunction, 20 to 30 = mild impairment (e.g., traditional outpatient services may suffice), 40 to 60 = moderate impairment (e.g., youths may be manageable with typical outpatient care or may need services beyond weekly outpatient visits), 70 to 90 = marked impairment (e.g., treatment that is more intensive than typical outpatient services would likely be warranted), 90 or higher = severe impairment (e.g., at minimum, an intensive intervention program would be indicated).

Case Study: Results for a CMHC

Procedures and Sample

A CMHC asked its staff to complete the CAFAS as part of a self-evaluation project. No extra funding or time was allotted to the clinicians, and since it was not required, there was no monitoring to determine compliance. Clients were to be rated on the CAFAS at their initial visit, after evaluation (if applicable), quarterly thereafter, and at discharge.

The sample presented in this article includes all cases for which there were at least two CAFAS ratings during a 15-month period. If there were more than two CAFAS administrations, the first and last CAFAS were used. For the purposes of this article, these two CAFAS administrations are referred to as the "intake" and the "last" CAFAS. As a result, the "last CAFAS" did not correspond to either a fixed time period or to the CAFAS done at discharge. However, the most frequent length of treatment was 6 months, and two-thirds of the cases only had two CAFAS ratings. The sample consisted of 179 youths, ranging in age from 5 to 17 years. The mean age was 11.15 years (SD = 3.47), with the breakdown of age categories as follows: 5 to 7 years old, 18.6%; 8 to 10, 26.6%; 11 to 13, 23.7%; and 14 and older, 31.1%. The sample was 66.5% boys and 33.5% girls. The only exclusions were to be emergency circumstances in which insufficient information to rate the CAFAS was available. Because data were not obtained on cases for which the CAFAS was not done, sample bias was unable to be examined.

Severity of Youths at Intake

The severity of the impairment of youths seen at intake can be summarized in three ways: (1) the mean for the total score; (2) Overall Level of Dysfunction, as indicated by CAFAS total score; and the (3) number of individual scales on which the youth was rated as severely impaired.

Mean, median, and mode for total score. The mean for the CAFAS total score was 60.78 (SD 25.01). The scores ranged from 10 to 130, with a median of 60 and a mode of 50. The distribution of total scores was positively skewed (skewness = .55, SE = .18; kurtosis = -.11, SE= .36), indicating a longer tail at the higher end of the impairment scale. Almost 70% of the sample scored between 40 and 80, inclusively. The typical client was clearly impaired and would likely involve more management than the traditional "once a week, seen in the office only" treatment protocol.

Overall level of dysfunction. Another way of evaluating the sample at intake is to examine the frequency of youths whose total score at intake fell into each of the five categories of general functioning described above. Of the 179 youths, less than 1% (n = 1) scored in the lowest category (0-10), indicating no treatment likely needed. Only 13% (n = 23) of their cases would definitely be expected to be treated on a nonintensive, outpatient basis (scores of 20-30). Half of the sample (n = 90) had scores ranging from 40 to 60. Depending on the situation, youths at this level could potentially be treated on numerous points along a continuum of restrictiveness of care. More than one-third of the clients fell into the two severest categories. For the 19% (n = 34) with scores of 70 and 80, treatment that is more intensive than typical outpatient services would likely be needed. The 17% (n = 31) of youths scoring in the 90 and above range are very impaired. Their CAFAS total scores were more than one standard deviation above the average youth being seen in the clinic. Residential care may be justified if there are few resources available for managing the youth's behavior. On the other hand, managing these youths in nonresidential care, with no serious or long-lasting negative side effects on the youth, family, or community, would likely indicate considerable resources and strengths within the youth's environment. In this case study, it was known that no youths were in inpatient settings, in residential treatment centers, or placed outside the community, which reflected well on the agency.

Frequency of individual scales rated at the severe impairment level. For each client, the number of individual CAFAS scales on which the youth was rated as severe impairment (i.e., received a score of 30) was summed. The frequency of cases were as follows: no severe ratings (n = 99), one (n = 43), two (n = 24), three (n = 12), and four (n = 1). Thus, 45% of the clients were rated as severely impaired on one or more scales. One-quarter of the clients were severely impaired on only one scale, and the remaining 20% were impaired on two or more scales.

Change Over Time

The indicators used to describe youth at intake can be used to assess change over time, comparing the first and last CAFAS rated.

Mean, median, and mode for total score. Change over time was assessed with a paired t-test that compared the first and last CAFAS. The test was significant, $t(178) = 10.79$, $p < .0001$. The average score at the last CAFAS was 38.60 ($SD = 25.74$), compared to 60.78 ($SD = 25.01$) at intake. The reduction in the CAFAS total score was almost one standard deviation. The effect size was .86, which is above the mean observed for one-group pre-post designs based on a meta-analysis reported by Lipsey and Wilson.[15] The median was reduced from 60 to 30, and the mode from 50 to 20. A score of 20 could be obtained by scoring mild on two scales, a condition that most parents probably would not consider serious enough to refer the youth for treatment. Thus, the modal score for the last CAFAS, which represents the most frequent score, would indicate a subclinical status.

Change in mean scores for individual scales. Using paired t-tests, the intake and last scores were compared for each of the five individual scales. Each of the t-tests was significant, except for the Substance Use scale. The results were as follows: Role Performance: $t(178) = 8.86$, $p < .0001$; Thinking: $t(178) = 4.53$, $p < .0001$; Behavior toward Self and Others: $t(178) = 8.31$, $p < .0001$; and Moods/Emotions: $t(178) = 9.16$, $p < .0001$. For each scale, there was a significant reduction in impairment as a function of time. The lack of significance for the Substance Use scale appears to reflect a floor effect in that there were very low impairment scores even at intake.

Overall level of dysfunction. If youths improved, an increase in the number of youths rated in the lowest levels of overall impairment (i.e., 0-10 and 20-30 groups) would be observed. For the remaining levels, all of which reflect a clinical level of impairment (i.e., the 40-60, 70-80, and 90 and higher groups), the number of youths should decrease. Figure 1 illustrates the change over time for each of the five levels of overall dysfunction. The solid lines show how the number of youths in the two lowest categories increased from first to last assessment, and the nonsolid lines show that the number of youths scoring in the higher levels of impairment at intake decreased from first to last CAFAS. The percentage of youths without impairment (0-10 scores) went from less than 1% at intake to 18% at last CAFAS, and the percentage of youths with mild impairment went from 13% at intake to 33% at last CAFAS. More than half of the cases had either no impairment or a low level of impairment (i.e., score of 30 or less) on their last CAFAS. At the other end of the continuum, the percentage of youths in the most severe category (i.e., scoring 90 or higher) was reduced by two-thirds (i.e., 17.3% to 5.6%), and in the next most severe category (i.e., 70-80), the percentage of youths was reduced by one-half (from 19.0% to 10.1%). This indicator provides a means of pinpointing cases for further scrutiny. Supervising clinical staff would likely want to review the 10 cases whose overall level of dysfunction was the highest level on their last CAFAS.

Frequency of individual scales rated at the severe impairment level. Figure 2 shows the change over time of the number of scales that were rated as severely impaired. If youths get better over time,

Figure 1. Change in Dysfunction Level From Intake to Last CAFAS in the CMHC Sample

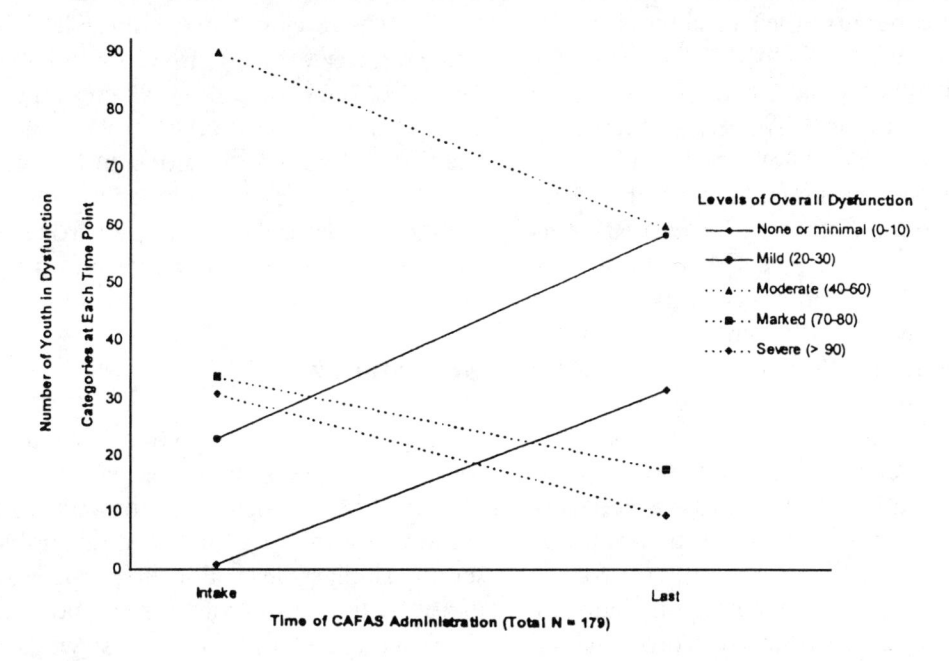

the number of youths having no scales rated as severe should increase, while the youths with one, two, or three scales rated as severe should decrease. In Figure 2, the solid line represents youths who had no scales rated as impaired and the nonsolid lines represent the other groups. A large majority of youths (87%) had no severe ratings of impairment on their last CAFAS. At the other extreme, only two youths had pervasive impairment, with three scales impaired. These two youths already

Figure 2. Change in Number of Youth Rated as Severely Impaired on the Five CAFAS Subscales in CMHC Samples

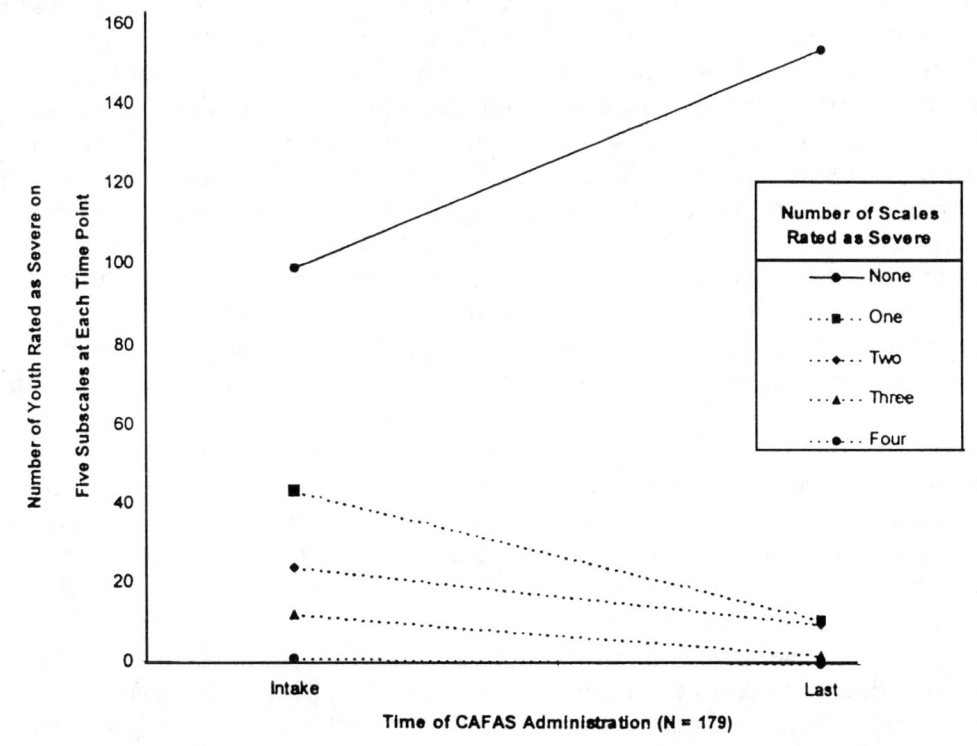

NOTE: CAFAS = Child and Adolescent Functional Assessment Scale; CMHC = community mental health center.

Chapter 6: Children and Adolescents: Different Needs, Different Tools

would have been identified for further scrutiny in the above analysis because their total score would have been at least 90.

Change in total score at the client level. Another way to examine change is to determine whether each youth's total score increased, decreased, or stayed the same. "Stayed about the same" was Change in Number of Youth Rated as Severely Impaired on the Five CAFAS Subscales in CMHC Samples defined as receiving the same score or a score within 10 points of the intake score. This definition would allow for some error in measurement given that the total score is measured in 10-point increments. Thus, a score that had increased was at least 20 points higher than the intake score, and a score was considered to have decreased if it was at least 20 points lower than the intake score. The majority of youths (59%) had lower impairment scores on their last CAFAS. About one-third (35%) scored in the same range. In all, 6% ($n = 11$) of the youths had higher impairment scores on their last CAFAS. Statistical testing could be conducted to test whether change in a particular direction (i.e., increased or decreased) was significant.

Record review of cases that appeared to deteriorate over time. The medical records for these 11 youths were reviewed. In this case study, there was no available Management Information System (MIS) that could be linked easily to the outcome data, so a qualitative review of the records was undertaken. The demographic characteristics of the youths were representative of the clinic, so there was no evidence that these youths disproportionately represented any subgroup of clients. For two cases, it appeared that the first CAFAS score may have been inaccurate in the direction of underestimating impairment. The clinic had a practice of rating the CAFAS at the first contact with the family (i.e., referred to as screening) and at the second contact (i.e., referred to as evaluation). Depending on the circumstances of the specific case and the flow of clients at the commencement of services, some clients were rated only once and others twice. Because of this practice, what appeared to be an obviously erroneous score given to two youths at screening could be identified. For 3 of the 11 cases, the clients had improved by the time the case was closed, which occurred after the ending date for the study. Two of the cases represented unsuccessful outcomes, despite considerable effort having been expended in both cases. The extensive clinical work included multiagency collaboration with intensive home-based services. Review of the clinical notes suggested that perhaps these two families felt unable to keep the youths in their home, despite the good intentions of everyone involved. For the remaining four cases, the family prematurely withdrew from treatment. These observations were very useful to the agency for its own self-corrective actions.

Summary

Overall, the findings from this case study appeared to be very favorable. However, for them to be considered meaningful, do they need to be compared to the performance of comparable agencies serving similar youth? For the purpose of self-evaluation within a clinical setting, the answer is no. The target goal for each youth would be a low total CAFAS score, ranging from a score of 0 (i.e., no impairment) to perhaps 30 (i.e., low to moderate impairment), provided that no individual scale was rated as severe. Certainly, a postintervention total CAFAS score of 30 or lower would be desirable for every youth, although perhaps not realistic for all. This goal also makes common sense from the perspective of the content of the CAFAS items at the different levels of severity for each individual scale. For example, a layperson would likely agree that a youth with occasional problems obeying school rules (i.e., rated as mild impairment on the School scale) is much better off than a youth who has been expelled (e.g., from the severe level) or has such persistent problems that school authority figures know the youth (i.e., from moderate level). As such, the CAFAS has a standard in terms of desirable clinical outcome, and comparative data are not essential.

However, to the extent that each youth cannot achieve a level of no impairment or that some situations are difficult to change, comparable data from similar agencies serving similar clients would be desirable. Given the lack of comparative data at the time of this study, existing research data were used to provide a ballpark figure of what might be a reasonable benchmark. The analysis that was conducted for the CMHC was replicated with data from the FBEP. These benchmark data were helpful when the CMHC administrative staff informally presented information to their board members.

Comparison to a Large Referred Sample

The first and second waves of the FBEP were chosen for comparison. The second wave, at 6 months, was chosen as opposed to the third wave, at 12 months, because more than two-thirds of the CMHC cases were closer to 6 months than to 12 months. A 6-month benchmark was thought to be the most useful comparison, since longer episodes of treatment under managed care will likely be the exception rather than the rule.

No statistical analyses were conducted comparing the two samples because the studies differ in many ways, making such analyses inappropriate. Examples of these differences include the timing of the second CAFAS rating (i.e., last vs. 6 months postintake), characteristics and training of the raters (i.e., clinicians vs. trained lay raters), economic incentives, and portal of entry procedures.[16,17] More detailed information on the sample and methods used in this study can be found in Breda,[16] Friedman,[18] and Hodges and Wong.[13]

Sample and Procedure

The 781 youths were evaluated at intake and 6-month postintake in the FBEP. The sample consisted of all youths who were referred for mental health services and agreed to participate in the study. They were from one of three army bases: Fort Bragg, North Carolina; Fort Stewart, Georgia; or Fort Campbell, Kentucky. Thus, the data from three sites were collapsed. It is worth noting that because the purpose of the FBEP was to evaluate the services at Fort Bragg by comparing them to two comparison sites (Fort Stewart and Fort Campbell), published articles have emphasized the lack of differences in outcome between the Fort Bragg and the comparison sites. However, there was a statistically significant reduction in impairment observed for both Fort Bragg and the comparison sites.[6]

Comparison on Severity Of Youth at Intake

The mean for the CAFAS total score at intake was 45.65 ($SD = 26.47$). The scores ranged from 0 to 140, with a median of 40 and a mode of 50. The percentages of cases scoring in the overall dysfunction categories for the CAPAS total score were as follows: none or minimal impairment (0-10), 11.9%; mild (20-30), 26.4%; moderate (40-60), 39.6%; marked (70-80), 14.6%; and severe (≥90), 7.6%. The percentage of cases that were rated as severe on the CAFAS individual subscales at intake were as follows: none rated as severe, 87.2%; one severe rating, 9.7%; two severe ratings, 2.7%; three severe ratings, 0.4%; and four severe ratings, 0.0%.

Comparison on Change Over Time

There was significant reduction in total CAFAS score from intake ($M = 45.65$, $SD = 26.47$) to 6 months postintake ($M = 31.39$, $SD = 26.03$), $t(780) = 14.33$, $p < .0001$. The effect size for change from intake to 6 months was .51. For the interval from intake to 12 months, the effect size was .67 ($t[616] = 16.67$, $p < .0001$), and for intake to 18 months, .78 ($t[372] = 15.00$, $p < .0001$). Paired t-tests were conducted for each of the individual CAFAS scales comparing intake to 6 months. Significant differences were observed on each of the five scales in the direction of less impairment at 6 months.

Change in overall level of dysfunction, as indicated by the impairment categories for the total CAFAS score, is depicted in Figure 3. The same pattern as was identified for the CMHC sample was observed. The number of youths scoring between 0 and 10 and between 20 and 30 increased, while the number of youths in each of the remaining categories (i.e., scores of 40 and higher) decreased. In the CMHC and FBEP samples, at the last (or 6-month) time point, 85% to 89% of the youths scored 60 or lower.

At 6 months, the data on percentages of youth rated as severely impaired on the five CAFAS subscales were as follows: none, 89.6%; one, 7.3%; two, 2.7%; three, 0.4%; and four, 0.0%. In both samples, at the last (or 6-month) CAFAS, about 85% to 87% of the youth were not severely impaired on any subscale. However, the data for FBEP were not as impressive as the data for the CMHC sample, because 87% of the FBEP sample had no severe impairments at intake.

Change in the total score at the client level for the FBEP was as follows: 45.7% had a lower impairment score 6 months later, compared to the

Figure 3. Change in Dysfunction Level From intake to 6-Month CAFAS in the FBEP Sample

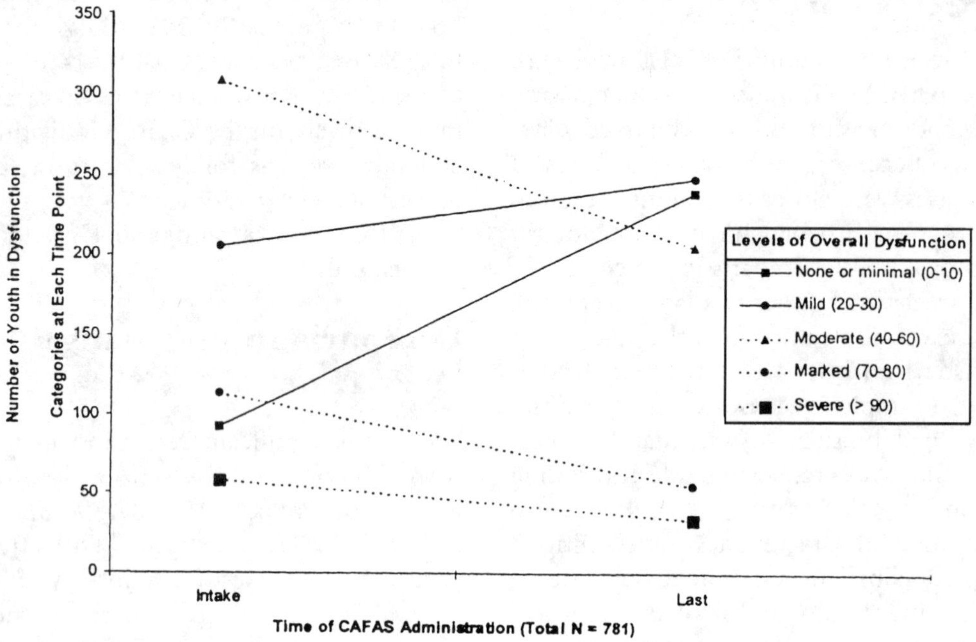

NOTE: CAFAS = Child and Adolescent Functional Assessment Scale; FBEP = Fort Bragg Evaluation Project.

intake total score; 42.1% scored within 10 points of the intake score when they were evaluated at 6 months; and 12.2% had a higher impairment score at 6 months, compared to intake.

Summary

Compared to this benchmark, the CMHC sample at intake was rated as more severe on each of the three indicators. This could be due to any number of factors, such as accuracy of the CAFAS ratings, influences that attracted less impaired youth for referral (i.e., no co-pay, all youth having to use one portal in the FBEP), and/or bias in sampling or attrition.

As for change over time, on each of the indicators, the CMHC performed as well or better than the FBEP. In part, this would be expected because the CMHC was rated as more impaired at intake. In presenting their statistics, CMHC staff could state that their 6% deterioration rate was less than the 12% observed in the FBEP, in which resources for treatment were extremely generous.

An important caveat is that no assumption about the causative factors for the reduction of impairment can be made for the case study or for the FBEP. There was no control group because no clients were denied treatment; nor were clients intentionally delayed in receiving treatment so that a waiting-list control group could be engineered. As a consequence, no unequivocal reason, such as effective treatment, can be attributed to change observed in the clients across time. However, this is the typical scenario in applied settings. In fact, it is hard to imagine that most funding sources for mental health services would want to pay for rigorous research or approve of conducting research on clients that includes denying or delaying treatment.

Discussion

This pilot study was initiated by the CMHC because the child and adolescent staff wanted to do a better job of assessing their effectiveness. To their credit, this was the first step in a process that has evolved into a statewide initiative. The result is a partnership in which local service providers, state administrators, and university researchers cooperate to generate an empirical basis that can hopefully influence policy decisions. The aim is to conduct mental health services research along the lines described by Speer and Newman.[19] The process by which this collaboration unfolded will be described briefly, followed by a discussion of specific suggestions regarding the use of the CAFAS as an outcome indicator.

Service providers wanted some help with assessing outcome, which was soon to be mandated at the state level, and with developing a data-based feedback loop with the aim of improving their services. As a result of consultation from the Research and Training Center of the University of Florida, various stakeholders around the state came to understand that for outcome data to be useful, a broader array of information needed to be collected (e.g., client characteristics, interventions offered).[20] This resulted in the providers of child services deciding to gather more data than required by the state and to pool information across sites. State administrators were being asked to generate a set of guidelines for determining levels of care within a managed care environment. To their credit, they wanted input from various stakeholders and welcomed the opportunity to empirically study any proposed guidelines. The availability of an automated version of the CAFAS made data collection and aggregation across sites feasible. The CAFAS program permitted computer scoring of the CAFAS as well as collection of other information about the youth, the youth's environment, and services offered. A state university had opened an applied research program and was eager to assist in aggregating and analyzing the data for the state administrators and the service providers. A pooled data set was generated for the purpose of developing an empirical basis for policy decisions. This statewide initiative is still ongoing; however, some suggestions based on experience with the case study are described.

Implications for Behavioral Health Services

Maximizing Credibility Of Ratings

In applied settings, it is seldom possible to have persons independent of the clinical services complete outcome measures. In fact, a strong case can be made that the treating clinician is the best person to make judgments about the client's growth. The clinician or case manager should be the professional who knows the most about the client. However, the credibility of the clinician's ratings may be questioned because of the obvious motive to show improvement in the client. Even so, from a practical and ethical perspective, the clinician may be the best judge. So, how can the veracity and credibility of the ratings be maximized given these constraints?

Probably the most important factor in reducing bias is the fact that each rating on the CAFAS must be supported by endorsement of at least one behavioral description of the youth. The CAFAS instructions stipulate this, and the form is designed to make justification easy to do. This is in contrast to global measures that do not require explicit justification of ratings. To maintain the integrity of the measure, it is critical that CAFAS ratings on each scale be supported by at least one specific item endorsement. Thus, requiring only scale scores for each scale would be unwise. This would endanger the accuracy of the rating. It is only human nature to allocate the least time and attention to a task that does not require justification or does not "really count' as part of the medical record. Clinicians are accustomed to the notion that notes in the medical records should be accurate; to do otherwise can be viewed as a fraudulent act. Thus, requiring the rater to specify which CAFAS items support the rating and incorporating the CAFAS form or profile into the medical record help reduce inaccurate ratings.

In addition, assessing interrater reliability and ensuring that all raters are satisfactorily trained will reduce rating error not due to demand characteristics. For this reason, the CAFAS training materials are designed so that they can be easily used and can be used to actually test the trainee's interrater reliability.[9,23] In fact, the CAFAS Self-Training Manual[23] is designed so that it can be done independently, although staff often enjoy group training because it provides an opportunity to discuss common concerns. Even very experienced raters need to establish interrater reliability because the important issue is that all raters follow the same rules. For example, is using extremely profane words an act of aggression toward an authority figure? No measure can be sensitive to true changes in performance unless it is reliably rated.

Other practices that should help reduce inadvertent and intentional rater bias include auditing and use of independent raters. From an administrative perspective, this issue is partly addressed via audits. For example, one state hired an auditing firm to examine a sample of the medical records to determine if there was support for the CAFAS ratings and for the measure being used for adults. Feedback was given to the individual sites so that they could improve their documentation. Another approach is to have independent CAFAS ratings done by trained raters. In fact, with a small sample of the CMHC clients, graduate students trained in the CAFAS conducted the CAFAS interview with a parent on the telephone.[12] The interview takes about 30 minutes and obtains all of the information needed to rate the CAFAS. The reason for the interview is that the independent rater does not have the same means of obtaining information as does the treating clinician. For example, a managed care company used the telephone interview approach to obtain CAFAS ratings on a sample of its clients whose services were being funded through the department of social services. The state required that providers report on outcome of services provided to their clients. This same approach can be used to conduct follow-up outcome studies for costly residential services in which the youth's behavior is constrained by external controls. Assessing outcome in the postdischarge time period after return to the community provides the most credible evidence.

Clinical Usefulness of the Outcome Data

Clients were to be evaluated at intake, every 3 months thereafter, and at discharge. The evaluations were to be used by frontline staff in making ongoing decisions about the client as treatment progressed. It was assumed that the CAFAS profile would be shared with caregivers, who were collaborators in shaping treatment interventions. Outcome assessment was conceptualized as a dynamic process that actually influenced treatment decisions, not as a measure to be done as pre- and post-events. As such, the measure becomes an actively used tool in the case management process. Assessment becomes part of the treatment in the hands of the clinician.

In the statewide initiative that evolved, this concept was preserved. The CAFAS computer program produced a client report each time a CAFAS evaluation was done, with a graph comparing the youth's intake and current CAFAS scores. Unless an outcome measure can be used for ongoing monitoring of the client's progress, it will be seen as an added paperwork burden with little redeeming value for the client or the frontline staff. Having the outcome measurement incorporated into the clinical routine in a meaningful way contributes to "buy in" on the part of frontline staff.

Quality Assurance

The CAFAS indicators that track change over time can identify youths who are not progressing well or who are functioning poorly even after some intervention. After identifying the types of cases that do not progress well, these cases can be monitored prospectively. The outcome indicators can be used to evaluate treatment protocols developed for specific client profiles. In fact, data can be pooled over sites to identify the strengths of various programs. Rather than compete, programs can cooperate around their areas of strength.

If the CAFAS indicators are linked to utilization data, then severity of the youth's impairment at intake can be compared to services offered, services received, and cost of services. Examining this relationship should indicate whether level of care received matched the apparent level of need. Exceptions to this expected pattern can be examined to see if customary care was offered. Cases that would warrant further scrutiny would be low-impairment cases with restrictive, out-of-community, or costly placements and high-impairment cases that use few resources or few liaisons with other service agencies.

This information can be used to develop realistic goals about treatment options for various types of client profiles. How much can a youth benefit and what is the typical course of change? When do the costs outweigh the marginal gains? These are difficult issues that deserve empirical investigation.[19]

Acknowledgments

The authors would like to thank the professional, support, and administrative staff of the Child and Adolescent Services of Livingston County Community Mental Health Services (LCCMH). In particular, we want to express appreciation to the members of the board of the LCCMH, Angus

M. Miller, executive director; Larry Newberg, associate director of clinical affairs; and Sherry Whalen, formerly program director of child and adolescent services. We also want to acknowledge the support of the Michigan Department of Community Health, especially Sherida K. Falvay, director of the Office of Children's Services, and Jim Wotring, director of Programs for Children with Emotional Disturbance.

References

1. Hodges K: *Child and Adolescent Functional Assessment Scale*. Ypsilanti: Eastern Michigan University, Department of Psychology, 1989, 1994, 1997.
2. Behar LB, Stelle L: Criteria for accessing child mental health and substance abuse services in North Carolina. In: Liberton CJ, Kutash K, Friedman RM (Eds.): *Proceedings of the Annual Research Conference: A System of Care for Children's Mental Health: Expanding the Research Base*. Tampa, FL: Research & Training Center for Children's Mental Health, 1997, pp. 262-264.
3. Irvin E, Hersch P: Proposed eligibility criteria and procedures for enrollment in Department of Mental Health continuing care. In: Liberton CJ, Kutash K, Friedman RM (Eds.): *Proceedings of the Annual Research Conference: A System of Care for Children's Mental Health: Expanding the Research Base*. Tampa, FL: Research & Training Center for Children's Mental Health, 1997, pp. 264-267.
4. Lemoine RL, Speier T, Ellzey S, et al.: Using the Child and Adolescent Functional Assessment Scale (CAFAS) to establish level-of-need for Medicaid managed care services. In: Liberton CJ, Kutash K, Friedman RM (Eds.): *Proceedings of the Annual Research Conference: A System of Care for Children's Mental Health: Expanding the Research Base*. Tampa, FL: Research & Training Center for Children's Mental Health, 1997, pp. 267-270.
5. Hodges K, Rosenblatt A, Irvin E, et al.: *Developing an Empirical Base for Managed Care in Public Mental Health Systems*. Symposium presented at the 10th Annual Research Conference: A System of Care for Children's Mental Health: Expanding the Research Base, Tampa, FL, February 1997.
6. Lambert WE, Guthrie PR: Clinical outcomes of a children's mental health managed care demonstration. *Journal of Mental Health Administration* 1996-,23(1):51-68.
7. Doucette-Gates A, Liao Q, Sondheimer A, et al.: *CMHS Evaluation: Model Changing-Metaphors and Meaning*. Symposium presented at the 10th Annual Research Conference: A System of Care for Children's Mental Health: Expanding the Research Base, Tampa, FL, February 1997.
8. Hodges K, Latessa M, Pernice F, et al.: *Practical Issues in Using the CAFAS for Clinical and Administrative Outcome*. Symposium presented at the 10th Annual Research Conference: A System of Care for Children's Mental Health: Expanding the Research Base, Tampa, FL, February 1997.
9. Hodges K: *CAFAS Manual for Training Coordinators, Clinical Administrators and Data Managers*. Ypsilanti: Eastern Michigan University, Department of Psychology, 1997.
10. Hodges K: Child and Adolescent Functional Assessment Scale. In: Maruish ME (Ed.): *The Use of Psychological Testing for Treatment Planning and Outcome Assessment,*in press. Liberton C, Kutash K, Friedman R: The 10th Annual Research Conference Proceedings, A System of Care for Children's Mental Health: Expanding the Research Base, 1998.
11. Hodges K: Psychometric Study of a Telephone Interview for the CAFAS Using an Expanded Version of the Scale. Paper presented at the 8th Annual Research Conference: A System of Care for Children's Mental Health: Expanding the Research Base, Tampa, FL, February 1995.
12. Pernice F, Gust J, Hodges K: *A Structured Interview for Collecting Objective Outcome Data in Clinical Settings*. Symposium presented at the 10th Annual Research Conference: A System of Care for Children's Mental Health: Expanding the Research Base, Tampa, FL, February 1997.
13. Hodges K, Wong MM: Psychometric characteristics of a multidimensional measure to assess impairment: The Child and Adolescent Functional Assessment Scale. *Journal of Child and Family Studies* 1996; 5:445-467.

14. Hodges K, Wong MM: Use of the Child and Adolescent Functional Assessment Scale to predict service utilization and cost. *Journal of Mental Health Administration* 1997; 24:278-290.
15. Lipsey MW, Wilson DB: The efficacy of psychological, educational, and behavioral treatment. *American Psychologist* 1993; 48:1181-1199.
16. Breda CS: Methodological issues in evaluating mental health outcomes of a children's mental health managed care demonstration. *Journal of Mental Health Administration* 1996; 23(1):40-50.
17. Foster EM, Summerfelt WT, Saunders RC: The costs of mental health services under the Fort Bragg demonstration. *Journal of Mental Health Administration* 1996; 23(1):92-106.
18. Friedman RM: The Fort Bragg Study: What can we conclude? *Journal of Child & Family Studies* 1996; 5:161-168.
19. Speer DC, Newman FL: Mental health services outcome evaluation. *Clinical Psychology Science and Practice* 1996; 3:105-129.
20. Hernandez M, Hodges S, Macbeth G, et al.: *Michigan Outcome Identification Project*. Tampa: University of South Florida, Florida Mental Health Institute, Department of Child and Family Studies, 1996.
21. Hodges K: *Measures for Assessing Impairment in Children and Adolescents*. Paper prepared for the U.S. Center for Mental Health Services. Rockville, MD: Department of Health and Human Services, Substance Abuse, and Mental Health Services Administration, 1994.
22. Hodges K, Gust J: Measures of impairment for children and adolescents. *Journal of Mental Health Administration* 1995; 22:403-413.
23. Hodges K: *The Child and Adolescent Functional Assessment Scale Self Training Manual*. Ypsilanti: Eastern Michigan University, Department of Psychology, 1994.

Fifth National Roundtable on Outcomes Measures in Child Welfare Services: Summary of Proceeedings

Emerging Trends in Child Welfare and Challenges Related To Outcome Measurement

PETER J. PECORA, PHD, MANAGER OF EVALUATION AND RESEARCH, THE CASEY FAMILY PROGRAM

Introduction

The conference organizers thought it would be useful to begin the Outcomes Roundtable with a review of some the major issues and developments facing the child welfare field. In the short time I will be speaking, it is impossible to cover them all, but we hope to share some of the lessons and developments from the managed care work underway in health care and behavioral health care, as well as highlight a few major trends in child welfare. I'll close by laying out some key questions that will be important to address as part of this conference and other work.

Program Challenges

Child welfare and mental health administrators, staff, parents, and youth are striving to focus on both the service delivery process and the results. But we have some serious problems in these fields from years of underfunding, underdevelopment, and use of poor information systems, among other factors. Many program areas in child welfare are experiencing significant service delivery problems, including large caseload sizes, insufficient staff training, inadequate funding for key family support services, and high turnover among top administrators and line staff. These and other administrative problems are resulting in unacceptable recidivism rates for child maltreatment, multiple child placements, and a backlog of youth who could be returned home or adopted with more intensive efforts. Some of these conditions are depicted in Figure 1 and a few will be discussed below.

For example, management approaches and consent decrees in some states are burying staff in process-oriented paperwork instead of allowing those systems to manage to outcomes. In contrast, other child welfare agencies are working hard to avoid this situation through streamlined practice guidelines and outcome-oriented case planning (Bruner, 1994; Traglia et al., 1996). The field also lacks good research data about what really works for whom in situations involving child maltreatment, provision of family support services, and helping youths achieve key developmental milestones in foster care. [Note 1.] Clearly, we will not be able to correct these conditions overnight, but there are many innovations being implemented across the country which provide hope for the future.

Source: Pecora PJ. Emerging Trends in child Welfare and Challenges Related to Outcome Measurement. Fifth National Roundtable on Outcomes Measures in Child Welfare Services: Summary of Proceedings. American Humane Association. (Reprinted with permission.)

*Revision of a paper presented at the fifth Annual Roundtable on Outcome Measures in Child Welfare Services, April 17, 1997. Peter Pecora is Manager of Research with The Casey Family Program and Associate Professor at the School of Social Work, University of Washington. Mailing address: The Casey Family Program, 1300 Dexter Avenue North, Suite 400, Seattle, Washington 98109-3547. Phone: (206) 270-4936. E-mail: ppecora@casey.org. Web address: **www.casey.org***

Figure 1. Sample Conditions Affecting Child Welfare

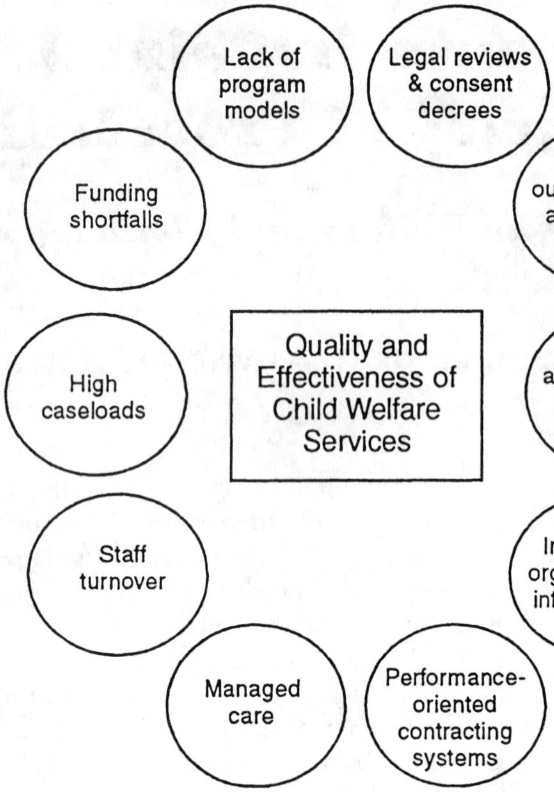

Quality and Effectiveness of Child Welfare Services
- Lack of program models
- Legal reviews & consent decrees
- Minimal outcome data about what works
- Complex and/or chronic youth/family problems
- Inadequate organizational infrastructure
- Performance-oriented contracting systems
- Managed care
- Staff turnover
- High caseloads
- Funding shortfalls

Trends in Child Welfare Related to Quality And Accountability

Some important trends in managed care and other areas in child welfare to be aware of include the following:

Consolidation of large managed care vendors in health care and behavioral health care. Value Behavioral Health was just purchased by Columbia HCA (the largest hospital corporation in the United States). A small core group of about eleven large managed care providers is forming due to mergers and acquisitions (Oss, 1997). Managed care behavioral health firms are moving from *purchasers* to becoming *providers* of service. Yet in some states, government agencies are setting up a kind of "fire wall" to prevent conflicts of interest from emerging where the managed care organization (MCO) has some provider networks bidding for contracts managed by the MCO.

Managed care and more heavily privatized systems in child welfare are actually being implemented. Kansas, Tennessee, and Massachusetts are the three states most commonly cited as currently implementing managed care initiatives, although in some jurisdictions the system is more of a performance contracting model. The capitated rate per child used in one of the states was about $14,000 per year. Hamilton County in Ohio has just completed negotiations with Magellan Solutions to be the management service organization (MSO) to deliver services to the Department of Human Services (e.g., child welfare), Community Mental Health Board, and the Alcohol and Addiction Services Board. Florida is privatizing services in four Districts.

Child welfare systems are beginning to outline key principles and ethics for managed care. Rather than have some managed care firm impose principles from health or behavioral health care, child welfare and other organizations are developing a service philosophy themselves. For example, Amy Winterfeld of the American Humane Association [AHA] outlined some proposed ethical principles at a recent AHA conference, and AHA has developed an ethics in managed care position paper (American Humane Association, 1996). In addition, practical papers are being written by child welfare and child mental health staff (e.g., Hernandez & Hodges, 1996) and by legal experts such as McHugh (1996).

Use of Logic Models. What complicates services refinement and outcome assessment is that many programs have not laid out a clear theory of change for major areas of service or client groups. (See Figure 2). This is a form of "logic model" that specifies who is being served with what services to accomplish what immediate and long-term outcomes. More programs such as Boysville of Michigan, Casey Family Services and others are developing logic models to provide a foundation for evaluation. Sue Ann Savas, Research Director for Boysville of Michigan, is one of the national leaders in implementing "Program Snapshots" or logic model summaries that help agencies outline who they are serving, community and other conditions affecting parent or child need, results desired and the program activities necessary to achieve those results. (Chen & Rossi, 1980, Committee on Prevention of Mental Disorders, 1995; Savas, 1996; Wholey, 1979.)

Outcomes assessment work is underway. Outcome frameworks or consumer report cards have been or are presently being developed by a number of health care and managed behavioral health care groups, including the following:

- **American Managed Behavior Health Association-AMBHA.** Their Quality and Access Standards Committee developed a report card of performance indicators-PERMS 1.0, but this report card focuses more on service delivery process and quality.
- **National Association for the Mentally Ill-NAMI.** Developing approaches to assessing service quality and some outcomes in behavioral mental health.
- **National Committee for Quality Assurance.** Promoting approaches to assessing service quality and some outcomes in health care primarily. Developed the Health Plan Employer Data and Information Set-the "HEDIS "instrument.

Figure 2. Steps for Developing Theories of Change

Developing a Theory of Change from Inside the Community

1. Identify key stakeholders.
2. Key stakeholders share their individual theories of change.
3. Build consensus among stakeholders:
   a. Prioritize outcomes and initial activities.
   b. Select indicators.
   c. Set thresholds (of expected results/outcomes).
   d. Map resources. (i.e., what will it take to accomplish this?)
4. Seek outside enrichment and critique. (Go after review by others.)
5. Make adjustments to the theory.
6. Develop the evaluation design and data collection plan.

Using a Theory of Change from Outside the Community

1. Identify key stakeholders.
2. Use opportunities to build knowledge and commitment to theory.
   a. Take stock.
   b. Provide opportunities for stakeholders to hear, engage, and critique.
   c. See, hear, and discuss theory of change based on real experience from people who are actually providing the intervention(s) and benefiting from it.
   d. See this as a set of conditions you seek, not a program per se.
   e. Emphasize that the theory of change can be revised.
3. Develop an implementation plan and build capacity to implement.
4. Develop a resource map and determine feasibility of this effort.
5. Develop the evaluation design and data collection plan.

Source: James P. Connell, Institute for Research and Reform in Education, and Evaluation Steering Committee of Roundtable for Comprehensive Community Innovation for Children and Families. (Phone: 215-242-2060). Presented at the Annie E. Casey Evaluating Community Change Research and Evaluation Conference, March 13, 1997, Baltimore, MD.

- **Outcomes Roundtable for Behavioral Health Care.** Developing standards for evaluating systems for assessing outcomes in health care and behavioral mental health for mental and addictive disorders.
- **Rehabilitation Counselors Association Outcomes Project.** Developing approaches to assessing service quality and some outcomes in health care and behavioral mental health.

Bridging Projects. Projects that might help bridge mental health and child welfare or clarify outcome frameworks for family services include the following:

- **The American Humane Association and the National Association of Public Child Welfare Administrators Outcomes Matrix.** These organizations have been cosponsoring a national meeting every year for the past five years to develop an outcomes framework for child welfare.
- **SAMSHA Center for Mental Health Services.** The Substance Abuse and Mental Health Services Administration (SAMHSA) is pilot-testing a new Mental Health Statistics Improvement Program "Consumer-Oriented Mental Health Report Card." Ron Manderscheid from SAMHSA is also convening meetings on measuring outcomes in public sector child and family services that are producing a number of products, including the following:
  a. Methodological standards for outcome measures (Center for Mental Health Services, 1997).
  b. A collection of papers produced by the Outcomes Roundtable for Child Services related to quality and accountability measurement in child and family services (e.g., child mental health, child welfare, juvenile justice) such as a conceptual model (Epstein, Hernandez, & Manderscheid, 1996); "Defining Populations of Children Served" (Doucette et al., 1997), "Intervention and Systems Organization" (Friedman et al., 1997). "Principles for Selecting Outcome Domains and Measures in Child Mental Health and Child Welfare Services" (Pecora et al., 1997).
  c. A survey of assessment measures being used in adult and child mental health (a joint effort between the CMHS Public Sector Outcome Measurement Group and the American College of Mental Health Administration); and a concept paper on "Person-Centered Outcomes Measurement."
- **Corporation for Standards and Outcomes.** This organization is implementing stakeholder surveys and systems of collecting outcome data through their SumOne for Kids^{SM} projects underway in Maryland and Pennsylvania. (www.standardsandoutcomes.com)
- **The Casey Outcomes and Decision Making Project.** This project involves a consortium funded by the Annie E. Casey Foundation/Casey Family Services and The Casey Family Program consisting of the funding agencies and the American Humane Association, American Bar Association Center on Children and the Law, and the Institute for Human Services Management. Spearheaded by the American Humane Association, the consortium will develop three major products that will serve as a part of a foundation for building a responsive managed care approach to child welfare:
  I. Philosophical and conceptual framework that identifies the common values and basic tenets of child welfare that will help frame the outcomes framework and decision making guidelines.
  II. Outcomes framework for child protective services, family-based services, family foster care, and residential treatment; and
  III. Conceptual framework and guidelines for making decisions about the level and type of out-of-home placement as applicable to child protective services, family-based services, family foster care and residential treatment, which could be used to set standards and guide case-level decisions within a managed care system (Annie E. Casey Foundation/Casey Family Services and The Casey Family Program, 1996).

Selected Challenges To Be Addressed

There are a number of key questions that need to be addressed by the field, including those described below.

How do we help establish a common nomenclature? I offer the list of definitions in Figure 3 as a starting point because we need to be clear in our terminology to maximize the effectiveness of this work. As McDonald, Allen, Westerfelt, and Piliavin (1996) and others have discussed, case outputs and statuses are very important information as they often lead to positive outcomes for youth and families, but they are different from outcomes and should be recognized as such. For example, an agency can reunify a high percentage of the children placed in foster care within one year of placement (a case output or status) and yet have 45% of these children re-reported for child neglect within 6 months of return home (an undesirable outcome).

How do we help establish a widely used set of core outcomes by major program area that are useful for fulfilling our accountability responsibilities to not only consumers, but for payers, program refinement, and for benchmarking programs with each other? The AHA Outcomes Roundtables, the SAMHSA products, and the Casey Outcomes and Decision Making Project referenced earlier are all examples of initiatives that can help with this challenge, along with the outcome database work of SumOne for Kids[SM].

How can we tailor various indicators of program performance by program area? While a core common set of outcome indicators would be helpful, it must be recognized that unique outcome indicators will be needed for special program areas such as child protective services, family-based services, short-term foster care, long-term foster care, group care, and adoption.

How will we use intranet and other more affordable information technology to build information systems that help us link data about who is served with what services, with what results, and at what cost? Without improved use of information technology, we will continue to emphasize administrative and output data rather than outcomes. Until practice-relevant MIS system technology is more available, some child welfare systems will continue to collect only selected outputs/case status variables (e.g., length of stay) which, while extremely important, do not capture some of the desired outcomes (e.g., child safety, school attendance, social skills).

States and counties feel that the mass of regulations and different requirements from various funding streams hamper their measurement efforts. If we are fortunate, states will clarify their terminology and begin to slowly capture more outcome data and move beyond just assessing outputs/case status variables, and do so in ways where the MIS data are produced as a natural by-

---

Figure 3. Outcome Monitoring Terminology

- **Service or intervention process:** Worker actions on behalf of children, youth, and families or the provision of services (e.g., crisis intervention, mental health counseling, social support groups, employment training).

- **Outputs/Case Status:** The instrumental or "status" results of certain services (e.g., the number of children reunited with birth family members, number of children adopted).

- **Outcome domain:** Major categories of outcomes for which there is more than one indicator of results (e.g., major areas of results for children, adults, families, or communities such as child safety, child functioning, parent/caregiver functioning, family functioning).

- **Indicator:** A measure, for which qualitative or quantitative data are available, which helps describe the degree of achievement of an outcome (e.g., child safety in terms of child abuse or neglect, parent functioning in terms of pro-social child discipline skills, or child-parent communication).

- **Performance measurement methods:** How the data on outcomes or outcome indicators are collected (e.g., worker observation, school report cards, standardized assessment instruments, medical examination reports, records of child abuse reports, juvenile arrest records).

Peter J. Pecora, The Casey Family Program and the University of Washington. Revised: June 14, 1997. Source: Adapted from Center for the Study of Social Policy. (December, 1994). *Results-based decision making and budgeting.* Washington, D.C.: Fiscal Policy Studies Institute, Center for the Study of Social Policy (Mimeograph), p. 2. Special thanks to Trina Osher of the Federation of Families for consultation regarding this terminology.

product of doing the actual work and not an afterthought or an "add-on" piece of work (e.g., see for example, Adams, 1996, 1997; Benbenishty & Osyerman, 1996).

How do we use Quality Improvement (QI) and other methods to help agencies use evaluation data beyond just telling them which program objectives have or have not been met? There is a form of "outcome mania" (Personal Communication, Mary Hargave, March 11, 1997) sweeping the field instead of a more balanced examination of who is being served, toward what result, and with what set of interventions. Outcome evaluation should not be isolated from other key agency quality assurance and QI functions, and should target achievement of practical results for people because this information can help guide QI methods (Hernandez & Hodges, 1996; Pecora et al., in preparation; Sechrest, McKnight, McKnight, 1996; Walton, 1986; Zirps & Cassafer, 1996).

Where will we find the funds to improve child welfare services, information systems, and outcome measurement methods? When a state or county agency chooses to contract with a private for-profit company, they may gain savings in MIS system development costs and administrative overhead, and yet may spend more funds per client on overhead due to the contractor's profit margin. One must determine how much money will be available for youth and families when the government is providing a profit to managed care companies for systems management or provision of direct services rather than community provider networks.

Because line staff and their supervisors are critical to implementing more of an outcome-oriented approach to service, how can we identify and then provide the necessary skills and supports for these staff? Outcome-oriented case planning and services are not easy to implement (e.g., Traglia et al., 1996). So who will provide the leadership and resources to make this happen across child welfare agencies in America? We need the equivalent of a "public health campaign" to bring to bear massive skill-building and support for a more rigorous approach to managing toward quality and increased accountability.

Conclusion

Child welfare has a limited database, wide variation in goals and values, limited public understanding and yet much public responsibility. Thus, during this current period of confusion and query, quality improvement, outcomes assessment, and managed care in child welfare are works in progress. The central challenge appears to be: will these strategies be an overlay on the existing child welfare system using concepts from business and industry or from the primary health care-behavioral health fields? Or will these strategies be redefined and reshaped to accommodate the change in population and needs, and used to create approaches which can achieve very real reforms-reducing fragmentation, creating wraparound services, and developing strength-based approaches which add value to families, neighborhoods and communities (Pecora, Massinga, & Mauzerall, 1997)? With careful program and outcome measures development, adherence to key professional ethics and standards, and broad commitment to both service quality and accountability, the latter vision might be reached.

Reference Notes

1. In contrast to recent critiques of child welfare, exemplary child and family social services agencies and promising interventions do exist. (See for example, Curtis, 1994; Fraser, Nelson, & Rivard, 1996; Fraser et al., 1996; and Schorr, 1988.)

References

Adams, W. (1996). *Questions and answers about the CIS.* Seattle, WA: The Casey Family Program.

Adams, W. (1997). *Intranet apps: Better, faster, cheaper.* Seattle, WA: The Casey Family Program.

American Humane Association and National Association of Public Child Welfare Administrators. (1996, May). *Matrices of indicators.* Presented at the Fourth Annual Roundtable on Outcome Measures in Child Welfare Services, San Antonio, Texas.

American Humane Association. (1996, June). *Ethical standards for the implementation of managed care in child welfare.* A product of the American Humane Association's Roundtable: Outcomes, Ethics, and Partnerships in a Managed Care Environment, Vail, Colorado.

Annie E. Casey Foundation/Casey Family Services, and The Casey Family Program. (1996). *Developing an outcomes framework and deci-*

sion making protocols for child welfare services. (A Request for Proposal issued by the Annie E. Casey Foundation/Casey Family Services and The Casey Family Program, October 31, 1996.) Baltimore, MD and Seattle, WA: Author.

Benbenishty, R., & Osyerman, D. (1996). How can Integrated Formation Systems (IIS) be a support? In: P.J. Pecora, W. Selig, F. Zirps, & S. Davis (Eds.), *Quality improvement and program evaluation in child welfare agencies: Managing into the next century.* Washington, D.C.: Child Welfare League of America.

Bruner, C. (1994). A framework for measuring the potential of comprehensive service strategies. In: N. Young, S. Gardner, S. Coley, L. Schorr & C. Bruner (Eds.), *Making a difference: Moving to outcome-based accountability from comprehensive service reforms.* Des Moines, IA: National Center for Service Integration, 29-39.

Center for Mental Health Services. (1996). *Consumer-Oriented Mental Health Report Card. The final report of the Mental Health Statistics Improvement Program (MHSIP) task force on a Consumer-Oriented Mental Health Report Card.* Washington, D.C.: U.S. Department of Health and Human Services, Substance Abuse and Mental Health Services Administration, Center of Mental Health Services.

Center for Mental Health Services. (1997). *Methodological standards for outcome measures.* (Draft). Prepared by Adult Outcome Measurement Standards Committee. Rockville, MD.

Chen, H-t, & Rossi, P. (1980). The multi-goal, theory-driven approach to evaluation: A model linking basic and applied social science. *Social Forces, 59*(September): 106-122.

Committee on Prevention of Mental Disorders. (1995). Division of Biobehavioral Sciences and Mental Disorders, Institute of Medicine. (1994). Appendix A—Summary. In P. J. Mraze, & R. Haggerty (Eds.), *Reducing risks for mental disorders—Frontiers of preventive intervention research.* Washington, D.C.: National Academy Press, p. 505.

Curtis, P. A. (Ed.) (1994). A research agenda for child welfare. *Child Welfare, 73*(5) special issue: 353-655.

Doucette-Gates, A., Katz-Leavy, J., Sondheimer, D., Biegel, A., Kingdon, D., & Schwartz, 1. (1997). *Defining populations of children served.* (Draft) Rockville, MD: SAMHSA Survey and Analysis Branch, Division of State and Community Systems Development, Center for Mental Health Services, Outcomes Roundtable for Child Services.

Epstein, I., Hernandez, M., & Manderscheid, R. (1996). Outcome Roundtable for Child Services conference paper. Rockville, MD: SAMHSA Survey and Analysis Branch, Division of State and Community Systems Development, Center for Mental Health Services; Outcomes Roundtable for Child Services, the National Resource Center on Permanency Planning; and the University of South Florida, Department of Child and Family Studies.

Feild, T. (1996). Managed care and child welfare: Will it work? *Public Welfare, 54*(3), 4-10.

Fraser, M.W., Nelson, K.E., & Rivard, J.C. (1996). The effectiveness of intensive family preservation services: A meta-analysis. Paper presented at the NIH-IASWR Conference, September 5-6, 1996, in Washington, D.C.

Fraser, M.W., Walton, E., Lewis, R.E., Pecora, P.J., & Walton. W.K. (1996). An experiment in family reunification: Correlates of outcome at one-year follow-up. *Children and Youth Services Review, 18*(4-5), 335-361.

Friedman, R., Crowe, C., Sanders, T., Webman, J., & Midman, J. (1997). Intervention and systems organization (Draft) Rockville, MD: SAMHSA Survey and Analysis Branch, Division of State and Community Systems Development, Center for Mental Health Services, Outcomes Roundtable for Child Services.

Hernandez, M., & Hodges, S. (1996). *The ecology of outcomes.* Tampa, FL: University of South Florida, Florida Mental Health Institute, Department of Child and Family Studies, The System Accountability Project for Children's Mental Health.

McDonald, T.P., Allen, R.I., Westerfelt, A., & Piliavin, I (1996). *Assessing the long-term effects of foster care: A research synthesis.* Washington, D.C.: Child Welfare League of America.

McHugh, L. (1996). Legal issues in managed care and permanency planning: An executive summary. *Behavioral Healthcare Tomorrow, 5*(6).

Oss, M. (1997, March). *Contracting with managed care entities: Tips for public agencies.* Presented at the Leadership Circle Symposium at the Child Welfare League of America's Managed Care Institute, Gettysburg, PA.

Pecora, P.J., Fluke, J., Bausell, C., Davis, C., Doucette-Gates, A., Koch, J.R., Mezera, M., Osher, T., & Rosenblatt, A. (1997). *Selecting outcome domains and measures in child mental health and child welfare services.* Rockville, MD: SAMHSA Survey and Analysis Branch, Division of State and Community Systems Development, Center for Mental Health Services, Outcomes Roundtable, Outcomes Work Group.

Pecora, P.J., Fraser, M.W., Nelson, K., McCroskey, J., & Meezan, W. (1995). *Evaluating family-based services.* New York: Aldine de Gruyter.

Pecora, P.J., Massinga, R., & Mauserall. H. (1997). Measuring outcomes in the changing environment of child welfare services. *Behavioral Healthcare Tomorrow, 6*(2). 2-6.

Pecora, P.J., Massinga, R., Nicoll, A., Marquart, J.C., Lightenberg, E., & Sandoval, T. (In preparation). *Beyond outcome mania: Quality and accountability in child welfare services.* Seattle, WA: The Casey Family Program.

Savas, S.A. (1996). What are we intending to do with those we work with? In P.J. Pecora, W. Selig, F. Zirps, & S. Davis (Eds.), *Quality improvement and program evaluation in child welfare agencies: Managing into the next century.* Washington, D.C.: Child Welfare League of America.

Schorr, L. (1988). *Within our reach: Breaking the cycle of disadvantage.* New York: Doubleday.

Sechrest, L., McKnight, P., & McKnight, K. (1996). Calibration of measures for psychotherapy outcome studies. *American Psychologist, 51*(10), 1065-1071.

Traglia, J.J., Pecora, P.J., Paddock G., &Wilson, L. (In press). Outcome-oriented case planning in family foster care. *Families in Society.*

Walton, M. (1986). *The Deming management method.* New York: Dodd, Mead & Company.

Wholey, J. (1979). *Evaluation: Promise and performance.* Washington, D.C.: Urban Institute.

Zirps, F., & Cassafer, D. (1996). Quality improvement in the agency: What does it take? In P.J. Pecora, W. Selig, F. Zirps, & S. Davis (Eds.), *Quality improvement and program evaluation in child welfare agencies: Managing into the next century.* Washington, D.C.: Child Welfare League of America.

Examining Outcome Across Service Systems and the Community

ERIC BJORKLUND, PRESIDENT,
UTAH YOUTH VILLAGE

Introduction And Overview

Discussion of Proposed Criteria

Recently there has been considerable interest in identifying criteria and procedures for the evaluation of adolescent out-of-home care programs. A number of different criteria have been recognized as important to outcome, and thus received the attention of researchers and program administrators. However, limited research or evaluation has been performed on the identified risk factors associated with recidivism among juvenile offenders.

The potential value of youth risk factors as the focus/criteria of evaluation research is obvious. If treatment can impact risk factors, the probability of recidivism would presumably also be impacted and reduced. If the impact of treatment on risk factors can be measured, researchers may have an immediate window into the effectiveness of treatment as it relates to preventing future difficulties. The above statements, while logically sound, certainly must be subjected to empirical scrutiny. The establishment of an ongoing evaluation program would provide the data necessary to address such questions further.

The factors identified through the research associated with recidivism among juvenile offenders—**family problems, negative peer influence, school difficulties, and substance abuse**—are frequently predictive of reoffending behavior.[1] We are suggesting measures that would indicate progress in negative peer influence and school difficulties and outcome measures that would show improvement in the competence of the youth to live with a family or to function more effectively in an alternative living arrangement.

We make no claim that these recommended outcome measures are perfect, however, we are hoping that they will prove to be useful indicators. We are confident, however, that we will not learn any more about our system unless we begin to measure outcomes. EXTREME CAUTION must be used to be careful about the conclusions drawn from this initiative. Providers which have comparatively small populations are at greater risk of being misrepresented by the data at first. Data should be interpreted with sensitivity to this issue. The data may only be useful after a year or two of study and interpretation.

By [and] large, the youth in custody of the Department have in common the first three of the four behaviors just mentioned: family problems, negative peer influence, and school difficulties. Because substance abuse is not a consistent problem among all DFS/DYC wards, and because it is a difficult and more expensive behavior to measure, we are not suggesting any measurement that would track a provider's ability to reduce the use of substance abuse. Of course, this is not to say that a Provider could not, on their own, track that data and use it effectively in representing their program to the divisions.

To identify a youth's susceptibility to negative peer influence, each provider would administer the Nowicki-Strickland Locus of Control test upon the admission and discharge of each youth in their program. It is our belief that the more a youth understands the consequences of the behavior, the less likely they will be to be at risk for negative peer influence. This belief has no basis in research and would be tested by this process.

We hope to measure the progress of children with regards to school difficulties by looking at the child's ongoing grades, citizenship, and attendance. However, given the fact that there are so many different types of systems between the several school districts, the various levels of class structure (mainstream, youth-in-custody, self-contained) it might be difficult to make meaningful comparisons.

With regards to teaching children to cope in family environments, we suggest that the

---

Source: Bjorklund E. *Examining Outcomes Across Service Systems and the Community.* Fifth National Roundtable on Outcome Measures in Child Welfare Services: Summary of Proceedings. *American Humane Association.* (Reprinted with permission.)

Department track children's movements to less restrictive environments, and their ability to maintain less restrictive environments after leaving the provider. This data can be obtained from the Department's own data system. All less restrictive environments are generally familylike in nature. Even independent living will usually involve living with other individuals and will necessitate sharing the refrigerator, the bathroom, and other activities that represent family dynamics.

Assessment of Difficulty

An overriding concern in an outcome measuring process such as we're proposing, is the ability to determine how difficult youth are when they are referred to a provider. We are convinced that it is important for the Department to attempt to ascertain in broad terms the difficulty of the child so as to make more meaning of the other outcome data.

To determine difficulty, we are suggesting three basic components. The first is identifying the period of time that the youth has received treatment of any kind, from the onset to the present. This treatment would be from a source external to his family. The second is the number of out-of-home placements the child has been placed in. Third, the Achenbach Child Behavioral Inventory would be administered to each youth upon admission into a program. The provider would provide to the State the scores of the child. The test will be administered by the immediate prior caregiver such as the parents or foster parents or by the current provider of services based on observations during the first few weeks of placement.

Test Instruments

You will note that a provider would be administering the Achenbach test and the Nowicki-Strickland Locus of Control tests when a youth is first admitted in a program. Because most providers are coordinating with Youth-in-Custody academic courses, the TABE test would probably already be provided by the Youth-in-Custody system. If it is not, however, it is a simple test for a provider to learn and administer.

In all, the Achenbach, Nowicki-Strickland, and TABE tests are not expensive tests to purchase nor are they difficult tests to apply. All of them could be applied by clerical staff. None of them require doctorate- or master-level individuals to interpret. While it will, unquestionably, be additional work for a provider to administer these tests, all (State and Private Providers) have agreed that the potential positive outcomes for the system warrant support, and that this testing will serve to educate the State and the system in general of the types of youth being treated by the provider's and the success that they are generally having with them.

Once the data from the youth admission and youth discharge sheets are in the system, together with the other information that DFS/DYC already have about the youth, the Divisions may be able to get a sense, over time, of the providers ability to increase academic competence, family living competence, and an internal sense of control in their life.

Moreover, the Department/Divisions will have a sense for the comparative difficulty of the youth that are being referred to the different providers. It is our belief that the data will show that the providers are generally successful in helping children make substantial changes in their lives. This success will be useful to the Divisions in relation to its consumers, the press, the legislature, the Governor, etc. Most importantly, it will benefit the children in the system by encouraging providers as well as caseworkers to make those decisions that will provide the best outcomes for children.

We anticipate that the data will not only be sorted in terms of providers and facilities, but could also be sorted in terms of caseworkers and units. This could become a very powerful tool in identifying those areas in the system where very excessive amounts of money are being spent with comparatively very little outcome to show for it. Lastly, it would be interesting and certainly possible to track the amount of money a child costs the system after receiving treatment from a provider.

Length of stay should not be considered as an outcome for purposes of this study. Looking at the overall cost of the youth in comparison to their difficulty would be a much better indicator of success. At least theoretically, the use of this data could encourage an evolution within the provider community that would develop treatment that moves children permanently out of the system quicker. This is a very different goal than simply looking at length of stay with a provider.

For example, if a child stays three extra months at a certain level of restrictiveness, perhaps the data will show over time that the child actually moves out of the child welfare system and costs less than a child who was substantially shorter in their stay with the provider.

Once you have data indicating comparative difficulty of youth, it allows the Department not only to sort the total overall cost of youth by providers but also by caseworkers, units and regions. How often have we heard that youth in the Wasatch front are more difficult than rural youth, or that the lack of facilities in the rural area make those youth more difficult and expensive to deal with, or that Youth Corrections youth are much tougher, or that children that get referred to psychiatric units are much more difficult.

The committee is hopeful that this data will give us a greater understanding of the type of dynamics in play in out-of-home care in the state. Understanding these dynamics would be the first genuine step towards controlling the costs of the system, while at the same time providing the care that is truly needed for the children.

Statement of Purpose

Even though millions of dollars are spent each year on residential care we have very little data to suggest that one provider or level of care is better (achieves the desired outcome for the child) than another. As a part of a continuing effort to focus on **outcome measures for children in State custody** it was determined that representatives from the Division of Family Services, the Division of Youth Corrections, the Youth Private Providers Association, the Department of Human Services, and the Bureau of Internal Review and Audit establish a project to begin to accomplish this. Critical variables need to be identified and measured that determine successful progress and/or program effectiveness in treating children in State custody who are placed in a residential program.

A complete plan would include:
1. An implementation schedule would need to be developed.
2. Agreement on the indicators to be measured would need to be reached primarily focusing in the area of the **"difficulty" of the child** and what constitutes **successful progress and/or program effectiveness**.
3. A process for collecting the data and a database would need to be established along with the necessary form for providers to use to submit the data.
4. Definitions would have to be agreed upon.
5. Testing instruments selected and other data collection requirements (from Education and the Juvenile Court) be established.
6. A training curriculum and schedule would need to be established, and
7. An "audit" process and responsibility assigned.

While we acknowledge that any effort to measure outcomes for children in residential programs would not be "perfect" it is noted that these beginnings would be a significant step forward for us as a Department (in a partnership with the providers) in establishing an ongoing evaluation program which will provide data necessary to address such questions further.

One other important note here is that two years ago during the 1994 Legislative Session, a bill was passed that mandated this kind of a process. The Governor vetoed the bill because he did not want such requirements in law, but at the same time committed the Department to such an effort. Until this project was begun, no such specific effort was underway to address these variables. The Private Provider Association President, Eric Bjorklund from Utah Youth Village, was the chief proponent of this legislation and has continued to provide leadership and support to the Department in these efforts. The Divisions of Youth Corrections and Family Services have been making efforts on outcome measures in other areas and this project complements that work and has fit in nicely with their goals.

Project Outline

The first task of the Project Committee was to agree on the variables to be used to give us an indication of successful progress and/or program effectiveness in treating children in State custody and placed in a residential program. While several viable approaches could be undertaken, it was critical to select an approach that was both useful in addressing our interests but at the same time would not be overwhelming and beyond the scope of available resources.

The following variables were discussed extensively and agreed upon as possible indicators of (1) child "difficulty," and (2) successful progress and/or program effectiveness.

Child "Difficulty" Indicators

- Achenbach Test—to determine child functioning; problem profile.
- Number of placements—restrictiveness of placement.
- Number of months it has been since treatment.
- Number of offenses (charged/convictions) (Matrix from the Juvenile Court).

Successful Progress and/or Program Effectiveness Indicators

- Family problems—Stability of next placement; less restrictive, less intensive.
- School problems—We would also look at grades and truancy.
- Peer relations-Nowicki-Strickland Locus of Control Test (pre and post).
- Substance abuse—(Although this was identified as an important variable we did not agree on a reasonable/workable method to measure this element.)
- Court involvement—Number of involvements, during and after custody.

General Project Objectives

It has been established by the Department of Human Services (DHS) that all programs providing out-of-home residential service to youth under State custody shall be evaluated to determine their outcomes. The following areas and methods have been identified for research purposes to encourage and determine successful progress and/or program effectiveness in treating children in State custody who are placed in a residential program. **The primary objective of the project is to measure outcome as stated above based on these variables and determine the viability of the variables in doing so.**

1. **Minimizing negative peer influence.** The potential impact of peer influence will be measured with the Nowicki-Strickland Locus of Control Test. This device is purported to measure the extent to which individual judgment is affected by external events (such as peers) as opposed to internal standards. Success is defined as change to a more internal standard.
2. **Ensuring adequate academic performance.** School performance will be measured by grades and attendance (to the extent available). Success is obtained if a youth's grades and attendance improve between the pre- and post-test.
3. **Minimizing future involvement of youth with the Juvenile Justice System.** This will be evaluated by accessing the Juvenile Information System which documents all criminal-type interactions youth have with the Juvenile Court. Success will be inversely proportional to the number of charges filed and charges found to be true (convictions) against a youth in the Juvenile Court.
4. **Improve the child's ability to function in a less structured setting.** This objective will be evaluated by determining the change in cost of treatment anytime changes are made in the physical location of a youth receiving residential treatment. This test will be applied whether the change is within or between service providers. Success is defined as a movement from a more to a less costly placement.

These variables have limitations and are subject to considerable interpretation but ultimately they have the potential of being an effective management tool in achieving our initial objective.

Project Implementation

The committee turned its attention to the implementation of the study. The following areas were identified to be addressed:

Group 1—(Members: Eric Bjorklund, Bob Lewis, John DeWitt, Dave Condie, Brad McGary, and others may be added as needed/indicated. Brad to chair.)

- Database establishment, components, location.
- Data analysis, study, report production, interpretation of data.
- Publishing the outcome results, format.

- Developing a form(s) on which to collect the data.

Group 2—Members: Eric Bjorklund, Lana Spivey, Gini Highfield, Chuck Parsons, Bob Lewis, Olivia Moreton, and others may be added as needed/indicated. Gini to chair.)
- Definition on # of placements (what constitutes a placement).
- Outline a "restrictiveness" continuum.
- Define "# of months since **treatment**."
- Define, in the area of Family Problems, what "stability of the next placement," "less restrictive/intensive."

Others—(Responsible parties for implementation, as indicated.)
- Achenbach Child Behavior Inventory Test-Providers will administer test, provide data and conduct training.
- TABE Academic Test (pre and post)—Providers will administer, provide data and conduct training
- Youth grades, citizenship and truancy scores—Department to secure from Education.
- Number of offenses (charged/convictions)—DYC to establish process for obtaining data, conduct training so that data can be collected/analyzed.
- Nowicki-Strickland Locus of Control Test (pre and post)—Providers to administer test, provide data, conduct training.
- Court involvement during and after custody—DYC to establish process for obtaining data, conduct training so that data can be collected/ analyzed.

Parameters of the Research (Definitions)

The research methods to demonstrate particular outcomes in the study, while straightforward, may not provide any conclusive evidence regarding the successful progress of children in particular programs, program effectiveness in treating children or other outcomes of critical interest to the Department and private providers. It has been agreed that these methods provide an important opportunity to move toward more effective outcomes. In gathering the data and evaluating the information, we will be better able to draw conclusions about its usefulness and be in a position to pursue other more effective avenues as indicated.

Testing will be administered to provide the following information:
- **Achenbach Child Behavior Inventory Test**—To determine child functioning and provide a problem profile. Test to be administered at the time of placement.
- **Nowicki-Strickland Locus of Control Test**—To measure the extent to which individual judgment is being affected by external events (peers) as opposed to internal standards. This test will be administered upon placement and at the conclusion of treatment in a program but not more than every 90 days.

The following definitions have been agreed upon:
- **Placement**—Out-of-home placement means that a child goes to a placement other than his/her natural home for more than three days for reasons relating to the child's or family's behavior. Natural home does not necessarily mean the home of the biological parents, although that will usually be the case. Running away or detention is not considered a placement.
- **Treatment**—When the child saw (first) a professional (social worker, psychologist, psychiatrist, specified licensed professional, not clergy) for purposes of changing the child's behavior.
- **Restrictiveness (of Placement)**—Successful movement to a *less restrictive* environment is when the child goes to another facility/placement that receives a lower payment rate from the State than the placement from which the child is leaving (costs include any wraparound services). Movement is based on going from one facility/home to another, even within the same provider system.

Other measures to be used in the research include:
- **Court Involvement**—Number of offenses including both charged offenses and convictions.
- **School Data**—Grades given in school, and attendance data will be gathered.

These are the identified elements to be used in this research. Other elements may be considered at some point in the future based on the information gathered or other factors of importance to the research.

Scope of Implementation

One of the concerns that the committee felt it needed to address was how these data will be applied in terms of the Department making placements, awarding contracts, or negotiate change. These indicators and outcomes are designed to ultimately produce data which the whole system can weigh, much like a consumer report. The data itself is to be the consequence or motivator of gathering and reporting of the data.

In other words, there is not intent or desire for this data to be used by statewide officials to decide that the whole state will use one particular model or not contract with a certain provider. We do not anticipate that the data will be accurate enough to make those types of global generalizations.

The Divisions have created a vendor system that reflects a free enterprise type of dynamic. By making this data available, we hope to better "round out" that free enterprise system.

Information System And Data Gathering

The Outcome Measures Project Committee has determined to use Microsoft ACCESS software in compiling research data. A program has been established and the forms developed...to manage data collection. Providers will be able to provide data on disk which will then be loaded into the program or by hard copy, sent to the project data entry staff who will complete data entry.

Data will be shared with participating agencies/providers. This will help us to determine that the system has received required information and that it is being accurately reflected in the database. Provider agencies will be in a position to raise issues and participate more fully in the process.

The Division of Family Services will be the "manager" of the information system for the project.

The committee has determined that clients involved in the project will be those coming into care starting in January 1996. These clients will be followed throughout the duration of their stay in a residential placement(s) and will have a six-month and one-year follow-up after leaving out-of-home placement. After the child turns eighteen years of age they will no longer be followed for purposes of this research. Additional follow-up could be done if indicated.

Data Analysis and Report Publication

As the reliability and validity of the proposed measures is yet to be established, the committee recommends that the distribution and use of the data be rigidly controlled in the first year of the project. During this time, test measurements will be forwarded to the Department **as they are collected**. Individual providers will receive monthly copies of material they submit to establish the accuracy of the processes for data reporting and storage. Reports summarizing the input also will be exchanged to begin the process of **developing summary formats for representing the data** that are understandable and useful to all parties involved. It must be clear to all that, during the first year of the project, Department administrators and case managers will make no conclusions about the effectiveness or lack of effectiveness of individual programs based on the data.

Beyond ensuring the accuracy and reliability of the process, efforts to analyze and understand the outcome measures, in the first year, should be focused on establishing (1) the **consistency or reliability of the measures** and (2) their **relationships to other, more traditional measures of success**, including the opinions of Department case managers, teachers, and parents.

Use and analysis of the data after the first year will depend, of course, on a number of things, including the feasibility of the data collection process and how sensible the findings seem to be. However, it is the committee's consensus that, if the process is continued past the first year, the data be opened to all parties. Taking proper care to guard client privacy, all providers should have access to information on all individual youth and any summaries describing individual programs. Further, any outcome-data-based decisions the Department makes about individual programs should be shared with any interested party.

Training of Project Participants

For the most part, training of project participants will be the responsibility of the Utah Youth Private Provider's Network. Initial training is scheduled to begin in January of 1996. Participating agencies will be trained on the goals of the project and the specific data elements to be reported and their definitions to insure maximum accuracy. Participants will be trained on how to submit data and where to direct information for the database.

Testing (Indicators And Limitations)

To our knowledge this is the first time these tests have been used across all the providers of the statewide system. These tests have not necessarily been created for this purpose and have not been tested in this type of process. Part of the project is to determine the validity of the tests to be accurate indicators of a child's successful progress. We believe, however, that the tests shall be valuable indicators of a child's progress.

None of the tests are to be administered more often than once every three months. This will minimize the possible effects of a test bias and also minimize the burdens of administering the tests.

Auditing of the Project/Process

It was determined by the project committee that periodic checks of the process need to be accomplished to determine the accuracy of the information being submitted to the system and that complete information is being provided. The integrity of the process is critical to the overall success and effectiveness of the research and any conclusions that may be drawn based on particular findings.

The Bureau of Internal Review and Audit will be responsible for this element of the project.

Conclusion

This project is a first step into looking at outcomes in residential settings, in terms of determining successful progress and/or program effectiveness in treating children in State custody. There are lots of questions to be asked in the process. We are confident that we will not learn any more about our system of residential care services unless we begin to measure in the ways we have proposed.

It is significant that agreement has been reached between the participating entities in the need for this project and the methods to be used. It should be noted that, as we are able to receive the data and analyze it, modifications and additional efforts are anticipated. This is an important beginning.

1. Alschuler, David M., and Armstrong, Troy L., *Intensive Aftercare for High-Risk Juveniles: An Assessment.* Submitted to Office of Juvenile and Delinquency Prevention, U.S. Department of Justice, 1990.

This paper was developed for the Utah Department of Human Services Outcome Measures Project (for children in State custody in residential settings). Committee members* include:

- Eric W. Bjorklund, Utah Youth Village, President, Utah Youth Providers (801) 272-9980
- Kathy Cooney, Director of Policy, Division of Child and Family Services (801) 538-4100
- John Dewitt, Division of Youth Corrections
- Virginia Highfield, Division of Youth Corrections
- Christene Jones, Division of Youth Corrections
- Robert Lewis, Division of Family Services
- Brad McGarry, Human Services
- Lynn A. Samsel, Human Services, Chair
- Lana Spivey, Valley Mental Health, ARTEC, Outcome Chair for Providers (801) 963-4206
- Mark Wensel, Research Analyst, Database Manager, DCFS (801) 538-4018

*There were many others that have assisted in the establishment of the project and participated in subcommittee work.

Multiagency Outcome Evaluation of Children's Services: A Case Study

SHIRLEY A. BECK, MSSA, PAMELA MEADOWCROFT, PHD, MATTHEW MASON, PHD, AND EDWARD S. KIELY, PHD

Abstract: *Outcome monitoring has become a focus of accountability for public and nonprofit human service agencies. Besides providing answers to funders' questions about the services' impact, outcome monitoring helps administrators improve program effectiveness. After a three-year development period and a one-year implementation experience, SumOne for Kids represents a technically advanced outcome-monitoring system for children's mental health and/or child welfare services. Initiated, designed, and tested by 31 children's service agencies throughout Pennsylvania, and with state bureaucrats' and policy makers' encouragement, SumOne for Kids represents an effort to create a bottom-up/top-down process for implementing a statewide outcome-monitoring system. This article describes the genesis of this outcome-monitoring system, primary design principles, use of social validation for outcome selection, resolution of methodological difficulties, and reasons for selecting functional over clinical outcomes. The article reviews lessons learned through the development experience instructive to children's service managers, program evaluators, and industry leaders interested in establishing outcome-monitoring systems.*

In recent years, measuring and monitoring outcomes has become a critical issue in the child welfare and mental health fields. Children are now entering the service system in larger numbers and with more severe disturbances.[1] Moreover, our most costly forms of mental health treatment (psychiatric hospitalization) and child welfare services (residential care) fail to provide payers or consumers with outcome accountability.[2] But, as the cost of services for these children continues to rise, service providers face increasing demands from legislators and government officials for data that provide evidence of service efficacy. Even the nonprofit, human service sector, through United Way policy directives,[3] is now receiving direct pressure to report on outcomes.

As Mary Jane England argues in Partnerships for Care, "Within the new health care system, the operative word will be value. Care will be provided-and paid for-on the basis of appropriateness and effectiveness as well as cost.., we need to define, measure, and use.., outcomes to determine the effectiveness of... care" (p. iii).[4] In addition, L. W. Kaplan of the United Way writes, "[W]e aren't as much concerned about what an agency says it's going to do, or how many people it is going to serve. We want to know how the client (the customer) will be better off: What will this person have learned; what will this person be better able to do" (p. 17).[3]

The general need for good information systems and the specific need for knowledge of

---

Source: Beck SA, Meadowcroft P, Mason M, and Kiely ES. *Multiagency Outcome Evaluation of Children's Services: A Case Study.* The Journal of Behavioral Health Services & Research May 1998; 25(2):163-176. Copyright 1998 by Sage Publications, Inc. Reprinted by permission of Sage Publications, Inc.

Shirley A. Beck, MSSA, was a research coordinator, Center for Research & Public Policy, The Pressley Ridge Schools, Pittsburgh, Pennsylvania at the time this article was written.

Pamela Meadowcroft, PhD, is deputy executive director, Center for Research & Public Policy, The Pressley Ridge Schools, Pittsburgh, Pennsylvania.

Edward S. Kiely, PhD, is a project associate, Center for Research & Public Policy, The Pressley Ridge Schools, Pittsburgh, Pennsylvania.

Address correspondence to Matthew Mason, PhD, Director, Center for Research & Public Policy, The Pressley Ridge Schools, 530 Marshall Avenue, Pittsburgh, PA 15214; e-mail: iammason@aol.com.

results is not new. Requests for increased accountability through good data management began as soon as government expenditures were allotted to the care of dependent children. Yet, the situation today is not markedly different from that in 1923:

> No one in Pennsylvania knows the extent of the expenditures of public funds for the care of dependent children, no one knows the number of such children now being maintained, no one knows the number of families involved, no one knows the extent of the turnover among the clients.., and no one knows the extent to which some of the expenditures have brought good or ill to the recipients, and certainly no one knows whether better service might not have been achieved for a smaller outlay more intelligently applied. The Children's Commission regards this as perhaps Pennsylvania's most serious situation affecting children. (p. 28)[5]

A software database program, SumOne for Kids,[6] is an outcome-monitoring system that measures the effectiveness of children's services in Pennsylvania.[7] Using SumOne for Kids, one can create a practical method to examine outcomes and, hence, affect the daily operations of services. The system was created with close attention to the data and reporting needs of agencies that provide direct care, supervision, mental health, education, and social services to children and their families. Over the course of three years, Pennsylvanians were surveyed to determine what outcomes to measure, data elements were developed and tested, and the database software was designed and tested.

The experiences gained from this effort should be instructive for any children's service manager, program evaluator, or industry leader who wants to establish an outcome-monitoring system. This article will describe the genesis and progress of SumOne for Kids and will pay special attention to design and guiding principles (both those adopted at the outset and those picked up along the way). SumOne for Kids remains a work in progress until it reaches its ultimate goal of implementation in large numbers of children's service agencies in Pennsylvania and the accompanying creation of a central database for benchmarking results in children's services. Apart from the public policy issues and political realities peculiar to this goal, the development and implementation of a widely used outcome-monitoring system lends itself as a representative case study of the generic issues that must be faced by outcome system designers.

Project Genesis

The focus on outcomes has been part of a sweeping national movement that was keenly felt in Pennsylvania as it struggled to adopt outcome-based education in 1993. Interest among the child-serving nonprofit agencies in Pennsylvania was initiated by John Pierce of the Pennsylvania Council of Children's Services (PCCS) and Clark Luster of The Pressley Ridge Schools (PRS), whose organizations were strategic in launching the effort.

The PCCS is a statewide association of nonprofit child-serving agencies. PCCS is made up of 85 agencies representing 70% of all private, nonprofit children's service agencies in the state. Collectively, these agencies serve approximately 20,000 children and their families on any given day with the full spectrum of children's services, including both in-home and out-of-home care.

The PRS is a 165-year-old, nonprofit, multi-state children's service agency that serves about 1,500 children and their families per day. PRS provides an array of social and mental health services and special education programs for troubled children and their families in Pennsylvania, West Virginia, Ohio, and Maryland. The array of services includes treatment foster care, educational programs, family preservation and in-home services, and residential services. For the past decade, PRS has conducted an annual outcome study to measure the effectiveness of the services provided to kids and families. Each year, staff members of PRS's Center for Research & Public Policy contact children (and their caregivers) who received at least 30 days of service and were discharged about one year earlier. Through the use of structured interviews with each child and her or his caregiver, outcome information is gathered.

PRS's outcome studies were originally designed to be a simple feedback system on a few socially significant outcomes (e.g., school attendance, restrictiveness of residential and educational environments, frequency of antisocial activities, satisfaction).[8] Demographic information from case records was included to create a "snapshot" of each child. PRS's cumulative efforts represent information from some 2,000 children. The most recent outcome study alone collected information from more than 700 discharged children who received services in the same year. The results of these outcome studies are used to evaluate the impact of PRS's programs, and to plan strategically for program improvement.

PCCS and PRS began discussions regarding the development of an outcome-monitoring system for all providers of children's services in Pennsylvania years before the actual development began. The key to launching the development was securing the approval of the PCCS Board; this approval was not automatic. Although most PCCS member agencies appreciated the merits of outcome measurement, there was no initial groundswell of support for the development of an outcome-monitoring system. PCCS support was nurtured over several years.

Many PCCS member agencies were unconvinced that the benefit of developing an outcome-monitoring system would be worth the development and implementation costs. Most felt that their mandated data reporting was already too extensive and too fragmented. Another source of resistance was based on the fear that the data collected could be used against member agencies. An outcome-monitoring system designed to report agency service results to funding entities is inherently threatening. Overall, these concerns generated passive, not active, resistance; a strong minority of the agencies were supporters, and most of the rest adopted a "wait and see" attitude. No member agency was diametrically opposed to the development of an outcome-monitoring system.

In 1989, the PCCS Board was finally persuaded to pursue the development of the outcome-monitoring system, with five arguments prevailing: (1) State legislation mandating outcome monitoring for children's services was imminent; the drive for cost control and accountability for the effective use of dollars made it so. Without answers about the empirical data on the actual information related to results of services, such a system would put funding for agency programs at risk. (2) Member agencies realized they would benefit more by participating in the development of an outcome-monitoring system that could be offered for statewide use, rather than have an outcome system designed and then imposed by the state. (3) Outcome monitoring was recognized as an important tool that could assist member agencies to better manage their resources. (4) Member agencies recognized the need for a multiagency system, which would help establish a central database of service outcomes and allow each member agency to compare their own service outcomes to those stored in the central database. (5) PRS had demonstrated, through its outcome studies, that outcome monitoring could be accomplished without using traditional, external, costly program evaluation models. Outcome measurement was a feasible answer to the call for accountability and management of results.

When the idea of creating an outcome-monitoring system was presented at a PCCS general membership meeting, 60 member agencies volunteered to participate in the development of such a system. Of these, 31 immediately pledged to commit staff time to the tasks involved in development and testing. With this show of support, PCCS leadership decided to create an outcome measurement system. Figure 1 summarizes the developmental process, which is explained in detail.

PCCS asked PRS to lead the design, testing, and implementation of a prototype outcome-monitoring system on the behalf of PCCS member agencies. PRS was charged to create an outcome-monitoring system that would (a) guide the collection of data in each participating agency and (b) aggregate the data into a central database. The outcome-monitoring system needed first to provide useful information to program managers, and second to meet the information objectives of the multiagency outcome system.

Since the ultimate sanction for a comprehensive statewide system would come from the state government, it was essential to involve state-level children's service officials from the beginning. A bottom-up/top-down model for planning and implementation was consequently adopted. This approach began by assembling a group of state-level bureaucrats, policy makers, educators, researchers, and practitioners to inform them of the purpose of the outcome-monitoring system, gain the support of their offices, and involve them in articulating a vision of what the system might look like. Those present gave high praise to the

Figure 1 Development Flow of Outcome-Monitoring System

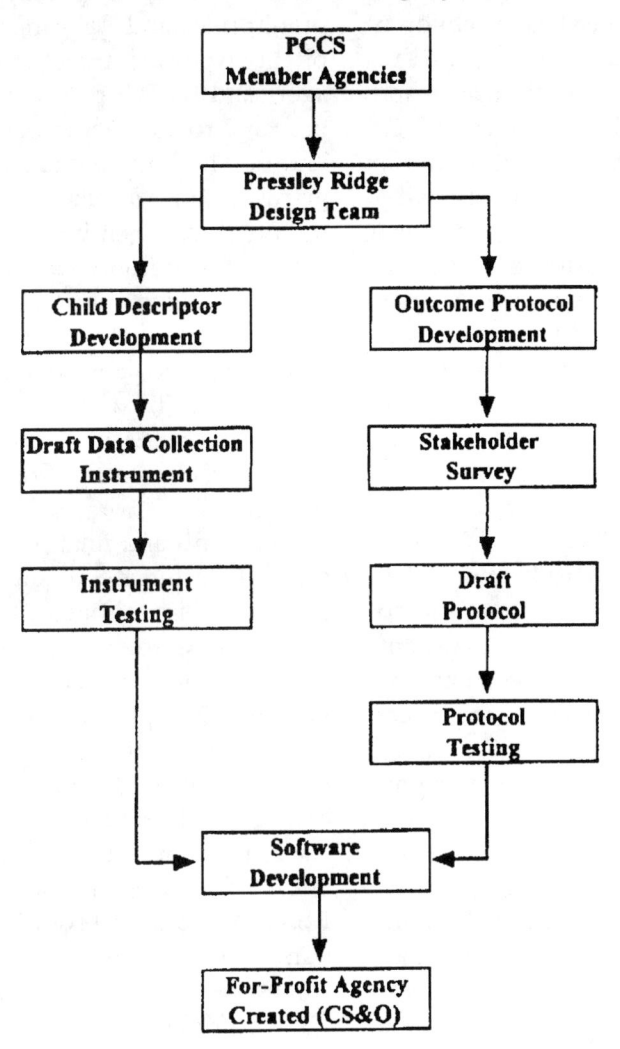

```
            PCCS
       Member Agencies
              |
              v
       Pressley Ridge
        Design Team
         /        \
        v          v
 Child Descriptor   Outcome Protocol
  Development        Development
        |                |
        v                v
 Draft Data Collection  Stakeholder
    Instrument           Survey
        |                |
        v                v
   Instrument          Draft
    Testing           Protocol
        |                |
        |                v
        |            Protocol
        |             Testing
        |                |
        v                v
           Software
          Development
              |
              v
       For-Profit Agency
        Created (CS&O)
```

concept, pledged their full support, and asked to be kept informed of progress. With this endorsement, the development of the outcome-monitoring system was launched in 1990 (initially called the Pennsylvania Outcome Project for Children's Services, and later renamed SumOne for Kids).

Development began by first learning about the 31 participating agencies and building a working relationship with them. The hope was that the agencies that volunteered for the development of SumOne for Kids would represent the diversity of child-serving agencies within the state. Such representation would maximize the generalizability of the outcome-monitoring system. Structured interview instruments were used to gather information at the agency and program level about history, funding sources, demographic makeup of the client constituency, average length of stay, admission and discharge criteria, program offerings, and services offered within each program.

These 31 agencies, in fact, represented the desired diversity. Geographically, they are located in 13 of Pennsylvania's 67 counties, covering all four regions of the state. The agencies range in age from 15 to 163 years. Most began by offering a single service or were an orphanage or other residential facility and now offer several programs with an average of 4.8 programs per agency. The most frequently operated program types are residential treatment facilities, foster family care, in-home and family preservation services, community-based group care facilities, partial hospitalization, special education (approved private schools for seriously emotionally disturbed children), and day treatment. More than two-thirds (67%) of the agencies provide mental health services in addition to their more traditional child welfare services. The number of Pennsylvania children served daily by the 31 agencies ranges from 44 to 595, with an average of 165. Although many agencies accept both boys and girls, the combined client population is approximately two-thirds male, one-third female. Nearly two-thirds (64%) of the agencies serve school-age children, whereas the remainder (36%) serve children of all ages. Funding and referrals for program services come primarily from the fields of child welfare, mental health, juvenile justice, and education.

System Design

Guiding Principles

From its inception, SumOne for Kids was guided by five basic principles. The first of these was to involve individuals in design and development who would eventually use the management system. The system development relied on these persons to articulate the technical specifications of the system, test the products, examine how system requirements could be built into ongoing program operations, and, ultimately, ensure that the system was user friendly and useful.

The second principle was to build on existing products. For example, PCCS had for some time required its member agencies to submit pen-and-paper information using its 31-item Child Profile Form. PRS was using its own pen-and-paper instrument, the Child Descriptor at Entry Form. An early decision in the life of the project was to build from these two instruments to create the project's child descriptor component.

When designing the system, project staff discarded such traditional program evaluation approaches as point-in-time measures of a particular program's or intervention's success, usually conducted by an external, objective evaluation researcher. Instead, the third design principle was to base the system on a self-evaluation model.[9] In this model, evaluation is not done to the program; rather, it is done with the program. Self-evaluation assumes that providers of services want to do a good job and that the purpose of an outcome evaluation system is to help them do so. According to Mathison, self-evaluating organizations are peopled by reflective individuals who have no particular expertise in program evaluation, but characteristically are interested in self-monitoring and self-improvement....Proponents of this type of internal evaluation perceive managers and service providers to be capable of and prepared to conduct evaluations of their own programs. The logic is that those who develop programs and provide services are in the best position to know what their intents are and have the greatest interest in improvement. (p. 160)[10]

The fourth principle involved articulating what a useful outcome evaluation system would include: (a) a detailed description of the client population; (b) a description and count of the types of services delivered; and (c) measures of outcomes, or results, of the services on the lives of the clients.[11]

The fifth and final principle was the emphasis on end or functional outcomes rather than on process or clinical outcomes.

Process outcomes reflect how services are delivered, or other key operational indicators of service. Examples of process outcomes might include length of stay, number of therapy sessions, cost per unit of service, and so on. Process outcomes are clearly important from a service delivery standpoint, but they offer no insight into the effect of services on consumers or communities. Rosenblatt and Atkisson[12] provide a conceptual framework for discussing various types of outcomes, including clinical and functional.

Clinical outcomes reflect psychological and physical changes related to signs or symptoms of disorders. Measurement of clinical outcomes might include the assessment of physical, emotional, cognitive, and behavioral signs related to a disorder. The reduction of symptoms of depression (evidenced by a change in score on a depression inventory, for example) would be one example of a clinical outcome. The value of clinical outcomes is in their individuality; however, they lack generalizability.

Functional outcomes reflect the effect of services on skills needed for an individual to succeed in his or her own community and lead a productive life (the end results). Examples of functional outcomes could include employment, school attendance, longevity of friendships, one's living situation, and so forth. Often, outcome measurement systems focus primarily on process or clinical, and not on functional, outcomes. In the development of SumOne for Kids, functional outcomes were emphasized over clinical because they are more universally measurable, more comparable across agencies, and provide data that can be readily understood by the public.

Formation of Development Groups

A consensus-building approach using small development groups of agencies to critique and test draft instruments was selected. Two functional development groups were created: (1) the identification and testing of a set of data elements to describe child and/or family clients and the services delivered to them (child descriptor database group) and (2) the development and testing of the outcome-gathering instruments (outcome protocol group). From the pool of 31 participating PCCS member agencies, 8 volunteered to participate in each area as a development group. PRS served as a pilot agency in both areas, and thus 17 agencies were involved in the development process. The remaining 14 PCCS member agencies were kept informed of developmental activities through a newsletter and by attending annual membership meetings.

Child Descriptor Database

The purpose of this development group was to identify a set of data elements to serve as descriptors of clients at point of entry, during treatment, and at discharge. These descriptive elements would be the foundation of the agency database from which a common multiagency database (central database) could be developed.

The first draft instrument was formed by the data elements in the existing pen-and-paper data-gathering forms used by PCCS and PRS, as well as other data elements from the outcome research literature. Building on existing data-gathering practices was useful because it both increased the speed of development and helped create consensus. From this first draft, a computerized prototype was created for demonstration purposes. Administrators and staff could actually see this early product in operation, which helped them remain committed to completing the laborious, detailed steps required to develop a final, reliable product.

After several iterations of agency feedback and revisions, a draft instrument emerged for formal testing. The instrument collected such information as the child's demographic characteristics, family characteristics, history of the child's residential and educational placements and their restrictiveness levels, psychiatric diagnoses and medications, insurance information, behavioral/physical problems, type of program serving the child, specific services provided, and permanency goals.

Three rounds of reliability testing were conducted involving staff from three different agencies per round. Staff participating in the test included intake workers, direct care/therapeutic staff, and middle managers. The testing involved two staff from each agency independently coding the same five cases using the draft instrument. Project staff reviewed their work to determine the nature and amount of coding differences. Analysis of each test led to a revised draft instrument to be used in the next test round. In every test round, the average time required to code the last case was less than half the average time required to code the first case. The pair-agreement rate on the 45 test cases ranged from a low of 66% in the first round to a high of 93% in the third round; overall agreement for the third round was 84%.

There were two results from this testing process: (1) a comprehensive child descriptor data-gathering instrument was produced that would form the basis of an electronic case file and (2) a standard was established that at least one staff member in each participating agency must meet. The standard is to achieve at least 85% agreement with project staff on the task of translating narrative case record information into code using a set of test cases.

Outcome Protocol

The purpose of this development group was to create an outcome measurement system. The first step in completing this task was to determine what outcomes the outcome-monitoring system (SumOne for Kids) would measure. This step was the most sensitive part of the development of the system. Because the ultimate aim was to collect data on common outcome measures, it was extremely important to minimize controversy in the selection of measures.

To ensure that the selection would be politically defensible, project staff decided that the measures should not simply be culled from the literature in order to avoid criticism on what literature was consulted, and should not be determined primarily by the opinions of "experts" (agency administrators, project staff) in order to avoid the criticism that the selection was skewed to make the programs appear successful. Instead, project staff decided that the outcomes selected for measurement would be first determined by use of social validation techniques,[12] a methodologically conservative approach for targeting such subjective issues as outcome definition. Such an approach allows issues of social importance to be judged by society, since these issues are based on subjective values.[13]

A social validation process polls members of society who are potentially most affected by the service.[14] These key members of society, or stakeholders, represent diverse societal groups (e.g., direct consumers of services; community members and leaders; community program personnel; advocacy groups; and local-, state-, and federal-level policy and political leaders).[15] Using social validation techniques, stakeholders can be asked what outcomes they expect of the services or program. The values of stakeholders make up the foundation on which the project is based.

Following specific criteria, the 31 agencies nominated potential survey responders in each of nine stakeholder groups: child clients (age 12 or older), parents of child clients, agency board members, school board members, community agency workers, poverty-level representatives, juvenile court judges, local legislators, and informal community leaders. This nomination process ensured that the stakeholders would represent the various regions of the state, different funding streams, and different program types. The final survey population included 700 children's service stakeholders across Pennsylvania.

The survey instrument was designed to gather ratings on 49 children's issues in terms of two dimensions: importance and satisfaction. The stakeholders used two 5-point scales to rate the importance of each issue and their satisfaction with the local services that addressed each issue. The issues were organized by life domain areas of educational, vocational, safety, living arrangements, family life, emotional/psychological, medical/psychiatric, social/recreational, cultural, spiritual, and legal. Stakeholders were also given the opportunity to add issues not included on the list and to rate those issues in terms of importance and satisfaction. A 90% response rate was achieved.[16]

Issues of high importance were identified when 90% or more of the stakeholders rated the issue a "5." Likewise, issues of low satisfaction were identified when 10% or more rated the issue a "1." Seven issues met the criteria for high importance; three of those seven also met the criteria for low satisfaction.

To ensure the buy-in of the project agencies, after informing the agency administrators of the results of the stakeholder survey, administrators were asked to rank order the same set of 49 issues. The top 10 from the administrators' ranking included six of the seven issues of high importance from the larger survey. Safe communities for raising children, the one high-importance criteria-level issue from the stakeholder survey, was not included among the administrators' top 10 because it was considered outside the realm of this set of agencies' services.

Six issues both met criteria for high importance in the stakeholder survey and were ranked among the top 10 of the agency administrators:
1. Children being taught the values of right and wrong, good and bad
2. Child neglect and abuse
3. Use of drugs and alcohol by children and teenagers
4. High school graduation
5. Parents being involved with their children in positive ways
6. Children attending school regularly.

The following four issues, although not meeting the criteria level in the stakeholder survey, were still of considerable importance, and were added by the administrators. The stakeholder survey rank ordering of these four issues is shown in parentheses following each issue:
1. Children having stable, long-term places to live (9th)
2. Children learning not to be aggressive (14th)
3. Children being protected from aggression or harm (8th)
4. Youth being taught skills for independent living (13th).

Project staff researched appropriate measures for each of the administrators' top 10 issues and developed a protocol for gathering the related outcome information. The protocol included (a) six draft interview instruments (three for use with children in age groups 3-6, 7-12, 13-18; the other three for use with the respective caregivers), (b) a monthly collection schedule for up to one year postdischarge, (c) a policy of confidentiality to child clients (except in instances of risk of harm to the child) in exchange for honest answers, (d) a policy on staff eligibility to conduct the outcome interviews, (e) a method for comparing an agency's or system's outcomes to existing norms, and (f) a component to determine the severity of a child's entering problem(s).

These materials were reviewed to determined whether implementation was possible using the existing agency staff. Since a primary goal of the project was to develop a low-cost, easy-to-use system, if agencies reported that they appeared to need additional staff for implementation, the protocol would be reduced in scope. As a result, the protocol was determined to be too large, complex, and burdensome. It was felt that 10 issues were too many to measure, the structured interviews should be more generic to eliminate the need for different instruments for children of different ages, and the frequency of collection should be reduced to fit an agency's existing routine. In response, the six instruments were reduced to two (one for the child and one for the caregiver), and the proposed interview frequency was reduced from monthly to quarterly throughout the duration of services and up to one year after discharge or completion of services.

Most significant, outcomes were consolidated into five major areas:
- *Productivity*: school attendance, graduation, and/or employment;
- *Antisocial activity*: drug and/or alcohol use;
- *Living environment*: stability and restrictiveness of the child's living environment;
- *Protection from harm*: frequency of injury or abuse by peers or adults and frequency of threats of harm from peers or adults;
- *Client satisfaction*: satisfaction with living arrangements, school or work, and with life in general.

For the most part, the first four outcome areas above abstract the larger themes in the administrators' top 10 list while retaining most of the criteria-level issues of importance of the stakeholder survey. The fifth outcome area, client satisfaction, while not a functional outcome, was added to supplement information on program effectiveness.

Two items from the review packet were tabled for future consideration: (1) norms for comparing results of agencies' outcomes and (2) severity rating of each child's disabilities or problems. Comparisons of agencies' outcomes with existing state or national norms on the above indicators would likely lead to erroneous conclusions because such norms are based on different child populations than those being served by the agencies. Because existing norms provide information on a representative sample of all children, the outcomes of agencies serving seriously troubled children would likely compare unfavorably. Educating policy makers on how to use norm comparisons would be too time consuming to consider at this stage in the development of SumOne for Kids. In addition, the ideal standard for comparisons should be based on the children served by participating agencies. However, such comparisons would be available only after the creation of a central database from which benchmarks or standards could be generated.

Severity of disturbance was seen as an important variable to include in the outcome evaluation system to ensure fair comparisons of outcomes across similar groups of children and, potentially, to use any change in severity as another measure of effectiveness. However, at the time of the review, existing instruments were considered too costly (required skill level and administration time) for large-scale use, and the methodology for developing severity levels based on the project's core data elements was not likely to be achieved quickly. Given the need for rapid development of useful products for agency managers, project staff decided to table the development of severity scales until the basic measurement systems and the software were produced.

Confidentiality of the children's answers to the outcome questionnaire produced the most disagreement. The policy was originally proposed to ensure honest answers to outcome questions. But some agency executives objected to granting children confidential interviews while in the custody of a treating agency. Their disapproval was primarily due to their desire to use outcome information for clinical purposes. Plus, the staffing patterns demanded by a policy of confidentiality created implementation problems. That is, confidentiality demanded case-neutral or nontherapeutically involved individuals to collect the outcome data if the child were being interviewed. Without confidentiality, caseworkers could collect the outcome information for their own clients. With confidentiality, the caseworker and all others directly involved in the case would not be permitted access to the outcome information except in aggregate form. Case-neutral persons could be caseworkers or other workers involved with children, but not with the children for whom they are collecting outcome information. Such sharing of responsibility between involved and noninvolved workers is common in the field of peer review. As is discussed below, the policy of confidentiality was ultimately adopted when, after four rounds of testing, it was demonstrated that confidentiality was essential in order to obtain honest answers from the children.

After revising the instruments, two levels of further testing were conducted. The first level was carried out in three rounds involving staff from three different agencies in each round. After a thorough review of the child and caregiver structured interview instruments and an opportunity to use each instrument in a role play interview, staff completed a questionnaire about each instrument. They answered questions such as (a) How clear are the instructions you will be expected to follow when you use these instruments?, (b) How clear is each question in the interview?, (c) How easy will it be for your clients (children and caregivers) to answer these questions?, (d) Will your clients be able to give real answers to these questions or will they say "don't know"?, and (e) How likely are your clients to give honest answers or will concerns about negative consequences affect their responses? Changes were made to the child and caregiver interviews following each test round for use in the next round. The final versions of the instruments took between seven and nine minutes to complete.

After completing the first level of testing with agency staff, participating members were sent revised instruments with introductory scripts for their use in a second level of testing, which was gathering feedback from a sample of child clients and respective caregivers. These respondents had been selected during the earlier rounds by use of a table of random numbers against numbered caseload lists. The questions agency staff asked were similar to those the children and their caregivers had answered earlier (i.e., clarity of the questions, ease of answering, likelihood of honest answers). Those responding included 37 children and 38 caregivers, which represented 97% and 95% of each sample, respectively.

This dual-level structured testing process allowed for the identification and correction of poorly worded instructions, questions, and other troublesome concepts with the instruments. For example, project staff members' earlier concern that confidentiality would be essential to obtain honest answers was confirmed by this process. Significant proportions of agency staff, child clients, and caregivers all indicated that some questions were not likely to be answered honestly unless the children were granted freedom from consequences. When the issue was revisited, administrators' concerns were eased in two ways. First, agency staff indicated that they, in essence, already knew the answers to the outcome questions, at least while children were in their care, so administrators were assured that important information of clinical significance would not be missed by granting confidentiality in exchange for a better chance at honest answers. Second, new instructions included stronger language to alert the interviewer and the child that any response that suggested the child may be at risk of harm could not be held in confidence. This dual-level testing process also revealed that the outcome-gathering instruments were best used with children aged seven or older, since participating staff consistently expressed the view that younger children would not be able to answer the questions.

Integrating and Launching The System

Following the testing of the child descriptors instrument and the outcome protocol, the combined set was converted into a PC-based database software system. Members of both development groups learned how to use the software in laboratory settings. Each agency received the software on computer disks to test at its own pace in its own setting. System modifications were made as user feedback was gathered from the on-site tests. Revised SumOne for Kids software and support manuals were distributed to the 17 agencies (those involved in the two development groups plus PRS) for their own use. This initial software, however, was not as flexible as was needed; the debugging process was time consuming and difficult. Although standard reports could be generated easily, they lacked the visual appeal that would encourage use of the data. At the same time, a change of leadership within PCCS led to lessened interest in the project. Finally, increasing amounts of time and costs were being devoted to the complex technology needed to summarize data and develop the central database. It appeared that SumOne for Kids was to be a prematurely completed project rather than a fully functioning outcome-monitoring system.

PRS realized that software improvement, ongoing enhancements, central database management, and distribution of SumOne for Kids would require specialized, technological expertise and resources. Instead of ending the project because of these barriers, PRS pursued additional foundation support to create a separate corporation, the Corporation for Standards & Outcomes (CS&O), for the continuation of SumOne for Kids. CS&O's sole purpose became the pursuit of technologically advanced methods for gathering, summarizing, and sharing information regarding the outcomes of human services. With its focus on technological improvements, CS&O redesigned the SumOne for Kids software to maximize flexibility within a few months' time; they began a replication of the initial project in Maryland and now have replications in Pennsylvania and other states.

Ensuring Data Integrity

As attention turned to implementation issues, the concern for data accuracy became paramount. Accuracy had been an explicit issue in the design of the system and drove decisions on such matters as the standard of accuracy in coding case information, confidentiality of client responses, and case-neutral staff. To ensure data integrity with new users, agencies will learn use of the system from packaged training materials that include a testing/certification process for staff involved in the task of coding case information. In addition, an audit program will be added to the outcome-monitoring system as a way to ensure data integrity on an ongoing basis.

CS&O will lead the development of the audit, and they have considered an array of alternatives for structuring it. A comprehensive audit system operating at the central database level will ultimately be necessary. Responsibility for the audit of an agency's data will reside with the agency itself. Agencies will be provided with an audit program that separates the process into an internal audit, conducted by agency staff or consultants, and an external audit, conducted by the agency's hired financial auditing firm as part of its annual engagement.

The internal audit will have two components, both of which will be documented in the agency's annual outcome report. The first component will be the agency's quality control of the outcome system (i.e., verification of compliance with the outcome protocol requirements and corrective actions taken as needed). The second component will be monitoring for data accuracy. Audit information will be compiled as part of the annual agency outcome report.

One or more of three methods will be employed to verify data accuracy. In the first method, an interviewer rating of each outcome interview will ensure that data entered into the automated system meet a certain criterion of believability. At the end of each outcome protocol, the interviewer uses a 5-point scale to rate the following factors, each of which relates to believability: (a) how well the child/caregiver understood the questions, (b) how cooperative the child/caregiver was, (c) how freely and comfortably the child/caregiver answered the questions, and (d) whether any of the responses were not fully believable. Interviews with an overall low rating (i.e., those considered "not believable") will be held in a separate file in the database and are not used as the basis for outcome reports. Thus, outcome reports will be based on information that has passed a level of rated believability. The number of nonbelievable interviews will be summarized in the agency's annual outcome report and will be reviewed as part of the agency's annual audit.

In the second method, a paired-agreement technique is used to monitor data accuracy. When the answers to the outcome questions posed to a child and his or her caregiver are the same (pair agreement), the information contained in both interviews will be considered accurate. When they do not agree, both interviews become suspect. The system will take the lower or worst case response as "the truth" when a child's and caregiver's responses differ. This default will serve to bias the reported data conservatively and will prevent the aggregated agency data from being inflated. A summary of the number of pair agreements/pair disagreements will also be part of the annual agency outcome report and will be reviewed as part of the annual audit.

In the third method, a sample of outcome reports is examined during the internal audit to determine how well the outcome reports reflect the actual responses from clients and caregivers. A case-neutral staff member or consultant will contact randomly selected child and caregiver respondents shortly after a regular protocol interview and query them again on selected elements of the original interview. The results of these tests will be summarized in the agency's annual outcome report and will be reviewed in the agency's annual audit.

The annual audit of financial statements in Pennsylvania is typically conducted by a CPA firm hired by the agency. SumOne for Kids will furnish an add-on audit program to be conducted by the agency's firm. The purpose of this audit program will be to review the agency's compliance with prescribed policies and procedures and their corrective actions, and to review the agency's monitoring of data accuracy. These reviews will serve as an evaluation of the agency's actual experience with collecting and reporting outcome information using the SumOne for Kids system.

Meshing With Concurrent Public Policy Initiatives

Much of the system's statewide implementation will depend on present and future circumstances in the public policy arena. Significant developments at all levels of government will affect the implementation opportunity. One development that has universal application to children's service agencies nationwide is the introduction of the Statewide Automated Child Welfare Information System (SACWIS).[17]

SACWIS is a federal matching grant program that helps states develop and operate comprehensive computer databases that integrate a number of existing state-operated children's service databases. However, SACWIS does not address functional outcomes. The Adoption and Foster Care Analysis and Reporting System (AFCARS) is one database in SACWIS. AFCARS lists its outcome categories as "reason for discharge" (reunification with parent, living with other relative, adoption, emancipation, guardianship, transfer to another agency, runaway, and death) and "date of discharge." Neither is an example of a functional outcome. SACWIS's current requirements do not address impacts or results after discharge, a deficiency addressed by SumOne for Kids. Nevertheless, many of the SACWIS data elements used to describe the population of children and families receiving welfare services will influence subsequent revisions to SumOne for Kids. The database developed through SumOne for Kids will need to be "nested" within the larger databases included in SACWIS to ensure that it is useful to state officials.

Another development at the federal level, in the form of the Government Performance and Results Act of 1993, is the legal requirement that U.S. government agencies must begin reporting on outcomes in their budget submissions. The outcome requirements by the federal government will affect programs at the state and local levels, and eventually all public and private agencies, that receive federal funding. General state legislation is also requiring information on human service outcomes. Furthermore, the Governmental Accounting Standards Board is going to require outcome reporting of all governmental units.[18]

For behavioral health and child welfare programs, which represent the largest and fastest growing costs for states, perhaps the most influential driving force for outcomes assessment is the adoption of managed care. As a means of controlling costs, managed care relies on predetermined standards to limit services to particular populations. Ultimately, standards must be based on the outcomes each service is expected to achieve. Child welfare and behavioral health outcome systems need to respond to funding streams and standard-setting organizations, but in time, these standards will become grounded in actual experience as recorded by outcome-monitoring programs.

Implications for Behavioral Health Services

Administrators of programs serving at-risk children and their families will be turning their attention to outcome measurement as the inducements grow. Whether systems are developed for a single agency, a group of agencies, or for a large system such as a county or state, outcome measurement will be on the frontier of social service evaluation. Ultimately, all efforts are largely idiosyncratic and depend on local circumstances. For outcome system designers at any level, it is far more useful to examine the decisions, assumptions, and principles that underlie the models than to emulate the features of the models. This article attempted to draw attention to some of the salient issues that led to the development of SumOne for Kids. The most important principles and observations to be gleaned from this effort include the following:

1. Involve stakeholders in the development of all aspects of the measurement system, including selection of outcomes.
2. Foster continued commitment to the long development process through any means possible, including group meetings, newsletters, communications regarding mandates for outcomes, and early products.
3. Measure a few things well, keep it simple, and build on what providers are already measuring. The involvement of many stakeholders in the development will naturally result in a system that is somewhat complicated and burdensome initially; realize that through testing and refinement, simplicity will result.
4. Design a system for agency self-evaluation, one that is built into ongoing program operations, and one in which agency staff routinely collect information for midstream correction. Moving toward a culture of outcome accountability requires that providers embrace self-evaluation as part of their program models,
5. Select outcomes based on social validation and ones that are immediately understandable and socially significant for both internal and external audiences. Such an emphasis will produce a greater reliance on functional outcomes.
6. Use rigorous testing procedures in the development of outcome measures, but recognize that naturalistic settings often require great flexibility in research design and methodology. Also, recognize that providers must be involved in product testing.
7. Work toward multiagency adoption of common outcome measures. The power of outcomes is the aggregate of many cases; thus, outcome measurement should increasingly focus on multiagency, multisystem data pools that can provide benchmarks for comparisons and answers to fundamental questions of children's services: which services work better than others, for which children, and at what cost.

Acknowledgments

The success of the SumOne for Kids effort was made possible by the generous funding of the Grable Foundation of Pittsburgh. We wish to also acknowledge the participating agencies for their forward thinking and willingness to participate in the development and testing of its products (pilot agencies noted by asterisks): Auberle Home, Bethany Children's Home*, Children's Aid Society of Somerset County*, Children's Home of Bradford*, Children's Home of Reading, Children's Home of York, Concern*, Craig House, Education Center at D. T. Watson, Friends Association for the Care and Protection of Children, Gannondale, George Junior Republic*, Hoffman Homes for Youth, Holy Family Institute*, Lourdesmont/Good Shepherd Youth and Family Services*, Lutheran Youth and Family Services*, New Life Youth and Family Services*, Northern Tier Youth Services, Perseus House, Pinebrook Services for Children and Youth*, Presbyterian Children's Village*, St. Gabriel's System, St. Michael's School*, Silver Springs-Martin Luther School*, Supportive Child/Adult Network, The Bait Foundation, The Pressley Ridge Schools*, The Wesley Institute*, The Whale's Tale*, Tressler Lutheran Services*, and Women's Association for Women's Alternatives.

References

1. United States House of Representatives Select Committee on Children, Youth, and Families:

No Place to Call Home: Discarded Children in America. Washington, DC: U.S. Govt. Printing Office, 1989.

2. Nadel MV: *Residential Care*. Report No. GAO HEHS 94 56. United States Government Accounting Office, Health, Education, and Human Services Division, Washington, DC, 1994.

3. Kaplan LW: *Making Quality Count: A New United Way of Allegheny County Program Review and Allocation System*. Pittsburgh, PA: Allegheny County United Way, 1993.

4. Cole RF, Poe SL: *Partnerships for Care: Systems of Care for Children With Serious Emotional Disturbances and Their Families*. Interim Report of the Mental Health Services Program for Youth. Washington, DC: Washington Business Group on Health, 1993.

5. Governor's Select Commission: *Memorandum on the Care of Dependent Children in Pennsylvania*. Commission report (suppl.), 1923.

6. *SumOne for Kids: An Outcomes-Based Measurement Software System*. Pittsburgh, PA: Corporation for Standards & Outcomes, 1994.

7. VanDenBerg J, Beck S, Pierce, J: The Pennsylvania outcome project for children's services. In: Kutash K, Liberton CJ, Algarin A, et al. (Eds.): *A System of Care for Children's Mental Health: Expanding the Research Base*. Tampa: Mental Health Institute, University of South Florida, 1992, pp. 233-238.

8. Fabry BD, Hawkins RE Luster WC: Monitoring outcomes of services to children and youths with severe emotional disorders: An economical follow-up procedure for mental health and child care agencies. *The Journal of Mental Health Administration* 1994; 21(3):271-282.

9. Usher L: Balancing Stakeholder Interests in Evaluations of Innovative Programs to Serve Families and Children. Paper presented at the annual meeting of the Association for Policy Analysis and Management, Washington, DC, October 30, 1993.

10. Mathison S: What do we know about internal evaluation? *Evaluation and Program Planning* 1991; 14:159-165.

11. Hawkins RP, Fremouw WJ, Reitz AL: A model useful in designing or describing evaluation of planned interventions in mental health. In: McSweeny A J, Fremouw WJ, Hawkins RP (Eds.): *Practical Program Evaluation in Youth Treatment*. Springfield, IL: Charles C Thomas, 1982, pp. 24-48.

12. Rosenblatt A, Atkisson CC: Assessing outcomes for sufferers of severe mental disorder: A conceptual framework and review. *Evaluation and Program Planning* 1993; 16:347-363.

13. Wolf MM: Social validity: The case for subjective measurement or How applied behavior analysis is finding its heart. *Journal of Applied Behavior Analysis* 1978; 11:203-214.

14. Barth RP: *Social and Cognitive Treatment of Children and Adolescents*. San Francisco: Jossey-Bass, 1986.

15. Gold N: Stakeholders and program evaluation: Characterizations and reflections. In: Bryk AS (Ed.): *Stakeholder-Based Evaluation*. San Francisco: Jossey-Bass, 1983, pp. 63-72.

16. VanDenBerg J, Beck S, Howarth D, et al.: *What Pennsylvanians Want From Children's Services: Summary Report on the Social Validation Study*. Pittsburgh, PA: The Pressley Ridge Center for Research and Public Policy, 1992.

17. Data collection for foster care and adoption; statewide automated child welfare information systems; final rule and interim final rule. *Federal Register* 1993; 58(244).

18. *Service Efforts and Accomplishments Reporting: Concepts Statement No. 2*. Governmental Accounting Standards Board No. 109-A. Norwalk, CT: Government Accounting Standards Board, April 1994.

Managing What You Measure: Creating Outcome-Driven Systems Of Care for Youth With Serious Emotional Disturbances

ABRAM ROSENBLATT, PhD, NORMAN WYMAN, MFCC, DON KINGDON, PhD, AND CRAIG ICHINOSE, PhD

Abstract: *This article presents the California System of Care Model for youth with severe emotional disturbances as an illustration of how ongoing assessment of the costs and outcomes of service delivery can be an integral part of a service delivery model. The core of this model, developed initially in Ventura County, California, is a five-step planning process that guides care system development and implementation. The implications of each stage of the planning process for evaluation and feedback at the child, family, and system levels are highlighted. A set of principles for selecting outcome measures deriving from the planning process are also presented that, in conjunction with the planning model, serve as guidelines for establishing outcome measures within care systems. The resulting specific plan for measuring system- and client-level outcomes deriving from this process, along with challenges to the implementation of the outcome management plan, is described.*

Social programs live and die as a consequence of swirling political, social, and economic winds. Changes in the political climate, in elected officials and their staffs, and in funding agency priorities can rapidly create, alter, and disband reforms in human service delivery. This process can lead to makeshift mechanisms of service delivery implementation that result in an array of complex, duplicative, and ineffective services. Over two decades ago, widely cited national reports began to document that the policy process had yielded an insufficient and unsuitable service system for youth with a range of emotional and behavioral problems.[1,2] As a consequence, efforts to reform services for youth with serious emotional disturbances (SED) began at both the federal and local levels. The resulting movement to create better integrated, more coordinated, family-centered systems of care for youth with SED[3,4] is gaining widespread popularity as it enters its second decade. The principles behind the movement drive the formulation and creation of service systems in an ever-increasing number of sites. The survival of the system of care movement, however, remains uncertain in a current political climate that emphasizes cost cutting; reallocation of

---

Source: Rosenblatt A, Wyman N, Kingdon D, and Ichinose C. Managing What You Measure: Creating Outcome-Driven Systems of Care for Youth With Serious Emotional Disturbances. The Journal of Behavioral Health Services and Research. *May 1998; 25(2):177-193. Copyright 1998 Sage Publications, Inc. Reprinted with permission by Sage Publications Inc.*

Address correspondence to Abram Rosenblatt, PhD, Associate Professor, Child Services Research Group, Department of Psychiatry, University of California, San Francisco, 44 Montgomery Street, Suite 1450, San Francisco, CA 94104; e-mail: abram@itsa.ucsf.edu.

Norman Wyman, MFCC, is chief of Children's System of Care, Santa Cruz County Mental Health, SantaCruz, California.

Don Kingdon, PhD, is chief of Children's Services, Ventura County Mental Health, Ventura, California.

Craig Ichinose, Ph.D., is an evaluation research specialist, Ventura County Mental Health, Ventura, California.

resources from federal, to state, to local levels; dramatic shifts in welfare policy; and the implementation of managed care in human services delivery. Consequently, proponents of the system of care approach find themselves in the dissonant position of watching a major service system reform movement expand and gain popularity while the long-term stability of the movement is threatened.

Systematic, ongoing research on and evaluation of the costs and outcomes of sites implementing the systems of care approach offers the promise of stabilizing the policy process by providing a cumulative record of successful strategies for service provision. Some enduring social programs, such as Head Start, owe at least some of their continued popularity to thorough research and evaluation. Nonetheless, programs of research and evaluation in applied settings are themselves subject to political and social forces and are difficult to design and implement. Evaluations can be ill conceived, or prematurely terminated for political or funding reasons. Even successful evaluations do not guarantee the survival of any given service innovation.

Results of the first generation of research on the effectiveness of systems of care for youth with SED are either unavailable, encouraging but still preliminary, or discouraging.[5,6] Although attempts to integrate services date to the 1970s, there remains precious little information on the costs and effects of these efforts.[7] The movement to create systems of care for youth with SED is one of a number of efforts representing a renewed interest in how to betterintegrate services for children and families with a variety of human service needs.

How can evaluation or research best inform system development and also inform policy development? Often, and ironically, evaluations of integrated and coordinated service systems are neither integrated nor coordinated with service delivery. Service systems are not created with measurable goals and outcomes in mind, and research programs do not take the information needs of service systems or policy makers into account. This article describes how research and evaluation can be an integral part of the creation, maintenance, and development of systems of care for youth with SED. The California System of Care Model is presented as an illustration of how evaluation and system development can coexist. This planning model for a system of care for youth with SED is based on the premise that establishing and continuously monitoring the desired outcomes of service delivery is an integral element of service system development and survival.

Outcome Assessment and the California System of Care Model

The California System of Care Model began in Ventura County in the early 1980s, and is now being implemented in 18 of California's 58 counties; 11 more counties are in the process of being added to this list. Fifty-nine percent of the 9.5 million children in California live in counties that are currently implementing the model.

The California System of Care Model fully embraces the principles of a system of care as elucidated by Stroul and Friedman,[3,4] but the way in which it implements these principles varies from county to county, depending on local needs. The original Ventura model[8] is a planning model that interweaves program development and evaluation research to create system- and consumer-related goals.

A description of the model system of care and results from the original demonstration and subsequent replications are presented elsewhere.[8-16] The model incorporates five planning steps for implementing an effective system of care in a specific community: (1) define the target population, (2) establish system of care goals, (3) build interagency coalitions, (4) design services and build in standards for quality care, and (5) monitor the system for client benefits and public cost-benefit.

Although the second and fifth planning steps most explicitly articulate the role of evaluation and research within the model, all of the planning steps address evaluation and feedback. Each planning step is evaluated, and feedback regarding the success of each step is provided.[17-19] At each planning step, researchers make choices regarding evaluation protocol based on outcome measures they develop and implement.

Step 1. Define the Target Population

The first step in the Ventura model is to define and establish the target population the system is designed to serve. These population groups can be large (e.g., all families in a county receiving Medicaid) or small (e.g., pregnant teens between the ages of 14 and 18). Consequently, the target population can be relatively heterogeneous or relatively homogeneous depending on its definition, and is likely to contain subpopulations of special interest and variable risk.

Evaluation and Feedback

The success of the system in providing equitable access to the intended target population can be evaluated early on in the implementation of the program and can continue throughout the life of the system. In the California System of Care Model, for example, the initial target population includes children and adolescents with a *DSM* diagnosis that results in significant functional impairment and risk of separation from family and community. A large proportion of these youth are legally mandated to receive some type of services through the juvenile justice, social welfare, or special education sectors. Presence or absence of diagnosis, level of functional impairment, legal mandates, and, to a somewhat more complicated degree, risk of separation from family can all be measured and assessed. Furthermore, the sociodemographic characteristics of the youth who receive care can be profiled to determine, for example, if certain ethnic, gender, or age groups are either over- or underrepresented in the care system.[13]

Multiple child serving agencies can serve specific target populations if they have data on the clinical and functional status, as well as utilization patterns, of a well-defined target population. The data also permit public sector agencies to document levels of need among the target population. Furthermore, the characteristics of the target population can reveal areas of unmet need, which can be developed as resources allow.

Implications for Outcome Evaluation

Choices regarding outcome measurement begin with the selection of the target population. Indicators appropriate to older children such as school performance, for example, are obviously not appropriate for younger, preschool-age children. More subtle examples exist. If the target population consists of youth who have relatively less functional impairment as a result of their distress, measures or indicators will need to be sensitive enough to detect relatively minor changes over time, since initial baselines may be so high as to create a ceiling effect. The ethnocultural characteristics of the target population have extremely important implications for outcome measure and indicator choice. Such measures must be suitable to the demographics of the target population, especially with respect to culture and age.

In large systems of care, subpopulations of youth may receive specific, targeted interventions. For example, youth who are in special education may receive enhanced services from a larger system of care that aims at improving overall educational achievement.[15] These targeted interventions are created based on the steps of planning model. Finally, the systems of care approach was designed specifically for youth with severe, multi-determined problems who require an interagency, often public sector based, service approach. Not all youth require all the services provided by a system of care. Consequently, defining a target population whose risk variables are well understood is an essential starting point for determining whether the full continuum of services provided by a system of care is even a desirable service delivery strategy.

Step 2. Establish System Of Care Goals

In the California System of Care Model, the service delivery goals are defined only within the context of a specific target population. All goals are designed with an eye toward how they will be evaluated and their importance to the stakeholders who are invested in the system. These stakeholders include family members, policy makers at various levels, consumers, community members, and care providers. System goals are designed to be consistent with the principles and values underlying systems of care nationwide.[3,20] Goals may exist at the system level or at the client level. System-level goals most often relate to the efficiency and operating characteristics of the care system and may include reducing rates of out-of-home placements, providing smooth transitions between levels and types of care, and providing culturally competent care. Client-level goals directly relate to positive changes in children and families such as improved social functioning, improved academic functioning, improved behaviors in the community, and consumer satisfaction.

Evaluation and Feedback
Although as many goals of a care system should be measured as possible, not all goals are easily operationalized. At this step, the evaluator can provide direction regarding which goals can or cannot be measured. In addition, feedback can be provided regarding how specific goals can be measured. An understanding of how specific goals can be measured will help service administrators understand which goals appeal to which stakeholders in the system. This process can help service providers more clearly focus and prioritize their goals. As an example, in the initial stages of service development, it may be more important to demonstrate that the system is efficient for purposes of gaining resources and political support for system development. Consequently, goals that appeal to policy makers, such as reducing costly placements, may gain initial priority in the development of the care system.

Implications for Outcome Evaluation
The goals of a care system are linked to the desired outcomes of the care system. To the degree possible, each goal will lead to a measurable outcome. The outcomes of each goal are monitored and feedback provided to those responsible for operating the system so that corrections can be made if goals are not being achieved. It is possible that an evaluator may want to measure a specific outcome but does not see a service system goal in place that can affect that outcome. In such a case, it is less likely that a service system will achieve success on that outcome, and so such discrepancies between the goals of the service system and the goals of the evaluator need to be resolved.

Step 3. Develop Necessary Interagency Partnerships

The third step in the planning model, the formation of partnerships, is designed to improve outcomes and reduce duplication of effort for a mutually defined target group of consumers. Partnerships may occur at different levels. They have existed for years at the service delivery level. Informal partnerships between a probation officer and a teacher or a protective service worker and a mental health therapist form the basis of teams that serve individual clients. At another level, agreement at the highest administrative levels that a defined group of children and families is a mutual public responsibility of specific agencies, regardless of the agency that serves them, forms the basis for institutionalized partnerships. The purpose of these partnerships is to improve the outcomes and manage risk for targeted children and families.

Forming interagency partnerships is obviously a complex and difficult task. Nonetheless, within the California System of Care Model, the goals of partner agencies—such as those in the juvenile probation, social services, and special education sectors—are considered equal to the goals of mental health.

Evaluation and Feedback
Forming partnerships may become a goal unto itself beyond the context of target population and mutually defined outcomes. Endless meetings may focus on developing and redeveloping written agreements to be reviewed by legal consultants, but they do not address the specific problems of children and families; until they do, they will fail to be productive. A continued focus on measurable outcomes in this step is essential if interagency partnerships are to result in more than good will and signed agreements. The evaluator can play an important role in ensuring a continued focus on the goals of the service system as the basis for all collaborative efforts.

Baseline information on the cost and functioning of the target population serves as the basis for interagency meetings and partnership developments. Often, a small group of adolescents who are using highly restrictive and costly levels of care becomes the focus of initial collaborative efforts. If agencies are able to succeed in managing the costs of care for these youth, and if outcomes are positive, then this success forms the basis for expanding the scope and intensity of interagency collaboration.

Implications for Outcome Evaluation
Part of the process of forming interagency partnerships involves the negotiation of how specific data elements related to outcome measurement will be

retrieved from partner agencies. Outcome information may reside in partner agency records or management information systems. Gaining access to these data raises all of the same collaborative problems as does providing interagency services. Technical difficulties in obtaining and understanding data systems are often far less problematic than collaborative difficulties, which include a sense of protection regarding data, lack of a shared mission that justifies data access, and concerns regarding how information will be used. The success of the service system in creating the necessary outcome-focused interagency partnerships will therefore affect the success of the evaluator in establishing access to needed data. Finally, the partnerships between the evaluator and the service systems need to be created at this step of the process so that the evaluator can find out which data are currently available for evaluating specific goals.

Step 4. Develop Services That Will Result in Achievement Of Goals for the Clients And the System

In many agencies, planning services is the first step in the process of developing a service array. In the California System of Care Model services are developed only after target populations, goals, and partnerships are negotiated. The foundation for effective service delivery is established by identifying target population, system and client service goals, and partnerships. A continuum of care initiated through services-driven design planning lacks the context of to whom, with whom, and to what outcomes are services delivered.

As an example, it is often tempting to plan services by location rather than the content of the intervention. Consequently, inpatient care may be considered the most intensive form of intervention for youth with the most uncontrollable levels of problematic behaviors. However, simply placing a youth in an inpatient setting will not produce positive change for the child. Rather, it is the content of the intervention that determines its ultimate intensity and success. The most intensive treatments are not necessarily linked to any specific treatment location. Targeting services to provide specific levels of intensity required to achieve outcomes for specific populations can help avoid the trap of implementing a continuum of service locations instead of a continuum of levels of intensity in service treatments.

The general principles of the planning model lead to a convergence on a common set of characteristics for Systems of Care. Service-level characteristics include (1) broad-based screening via a common screening protocol that all agencies use to refer youth to system of care services; (2) a multidisciplinary assessment of youth to determine needs and establish service plans; (3) family centered case management designed to coordinate and integrate care across agencies, including case management by multiagency teams for youth most in need; and (4) the careful and strategic use of out-of-home placements as a last resort, with extensive use of wraparound services, therapeutic foster care, in-home counseling, and day treatment to avoid more restrictive levels of care.

Specific program implementation varies from county to county. Intervention strategies include (1) emergency care and crisis intervention available 24 hours a day, seven days a week; (2) home-based services such as family preservation teams that rapidly respond to family needs in the field; (3) respite care for caregivers, including foster parents; (4) enriched foster care to help youth remain in high-quality foster home settings; (5) school-based programs run conjointly by education and mental health staff (these programs offer counseling, as well as creative arts, occupational therapy, and parental and group counseling); (6) juvenile justice programs that provide on-site crisis intervention and counseling, screening, and follow-up; (7) wraparound services backed by a flexible funding pool; (8) family involvement services such as parenting workshops, support groups and peer mentoring, peer counseling, caregiver training, and involvement of parents in policy setting; (9) minority outreach and recruitment to churches, businesses, and other neighborhood community organizations to recruit volunteers and secure institutional commitments of time and money; (10) resource development to obtain private sector support for public services; and (11) transitional services to work with older adolescents as they transition to adulthood.

Evaluation and Feedback

The evaluator can play a role in service design by making service planners aware of empirically effective programs. In addition, certain types of services are more or less likely to affect certain types of outcomes, and the evaluator can provide guidance regarding such relationships. A placement screening committee, for example, may reduce out-of-home placements but may have limited effect on psychosocial functioning. The evaluator can help maintain congruence between service system goals, the actual services implemented, and the desired system and client outcomes.

Implications for Outcome Evaluation

Specific services or programs will likely be associated with desired outcomes for specific groups of consumers. A program based in the juvenile hall, for example, will likely focus predominantly on controlling juvenile justice recidivism. Especially innovative or experimental programs may be the subject of more intensive evaluation efforts. Consequently, the choice of which services will be provided has direct implications for ongoing monitoring and feedback.

The development of a residential program in Santa Cruz County designed to provide services for juvenile offenders who are wards of the court illustrates the interplay between service development and evaluation data. In 1989, this residential program was developed specifically to increase family reunification, control group home placements, and reduce rearrest rates. After five years of implementation, the results appeared promising, leading to an expansion of the program from 12 to 18 beds. However, as this expansion was occurring, the long-term data on rearrests proved that the program was not as effective as early results had indicated. Consequently, an intensive interagency study was conducted, and the 18-bed program was modified significantly. Currently, rearrest rates for the program are once again back to lower, more desirable levels.

Step 5. Develop Methods for Monitoring Client and System Outcomes and Providing Feedback on These Outcomes For Client and Program Decision Making

The development of processes for collecting and reporting information on outcomes is the final step in the planning process. Just as developing services is often the first step for providers in program design, selecting outcome measures is often the first step for evaluators in the evaluation design. In this model, the step of establishing how the system will be monitored occurs after the groundwork for determining target populations, goals, partnerships, and services is established.

Outcome monitoring and feedback should take place at the system, program, and clinical levels.[6] Monitoring at the system level can provide information to groups that set policy and establish the direction and goals of the system. Programmatic feedback can be used by managers at the program level to fine tune services within a particular treatment modality or setting. Finally, feedback at the consumer and clinical levels can be used by line staff to produce consumer-level outcomes.

The success or failure of an intervention is most acutely felt by the children and families in the care system. The family, child, and clinician or caseworker require incremental feedback to sustain their efforts on a daily basis. Over time, information can be accumulated that allows children, families, and clinicians or caseworkers to see the big picture regarding improvement (or lack of improvement) over time. In Ventura County, for example, high levels of consumer satisfaction helped remind clinicians that families are appreciative of the supportive efforts of the system, even though the progress made by children can appear to be slow or nonexistent.

The California System of Care Model planning process has resulted in a set of outcome measurement principles and measures that can be implemented in care systems at any stage of development. The principles of outcome measurement tool selection are meant to operate in conjunction with the planning model as a guide to establishing outcome measures within a given community. These principles are as follows: (1) tool selection is based on the California System of Care Model and philosophy, (2) measures should have maximum value for all stakeholders, (3) measures should promote efficiency and effectiveness in implementation, (4) measures should have known psychometric properties, and (5) measures should yield clear and understandable results.

Tool Selection is Based on the California System of Care Model And Philosophy

The first principle emphasizes the need to integrate the selection of outcome measures with the underlying model for system design and service delivery. Much has already been detailed in this article regarding how the California System of Care Model guides the selection of outcome measures. It is, however, important to note that the principle is equally applicable to other service delivery models. This principle incorporates the tenets behind theory-based evaluations,[21] in which evaluations are guided by the underlying theory of how change is achieved within a service setting. This principle ensures that selected measures derive directly from the principles and values underlying a given care system.

Measures Should Have Maximum Value for all Stakeholders

Researchers, and scientific journals, do not constitute the primary outlet for dissemination of outcome results designed to drive system development and policy. Although publication of evaluation results are desirable, few real stakeholders in the delivery of mental health services read professional research journals. Rather, consumers, clinicians, administrators and managers, and policy makers need to be able to interpret research results. Each of these groups has varying information needs. In the California System of Care Model, the input of these stakeholders is obtained as a natural consequence of the planning process, through inclusionary rather than exclusionary practices in selecting target populations, goals, and services. It is also through the planning process that stakeholders can resolve conflicts that may arise when results are positive in one outcome domain but negative in another. A careful examination of less positive results is a cause for reexamination of the planning process that produced these results so that necessary changes in services can be made. Ultimately, the use of outcome results rests on matching the types of outcome data collected with the desired areas of impact.

Consumers, in this case children and families who are in need of, or who receive, services from the care system, are often invested in a range of outcome information. Satisfaction or dissatisfaction with services can, when voiced by consumers and consumer advocates, be a powerful agent for political change.[22] However, consumers are increasingly involved in more than one level of system development, including program planning and policy. Consequently, although consumers are primarily concerned with the fate of the individual receiving services, they are also often concerned about understanding and overcoming the political and programmatic barriers to improving services and the resources for funding these services. Whenever an outcome monitoring system is devised, consumer feedback is essential to the process. In addition, consumers are key evaluators of outcomes. Clinical staff may rate a child as showing improved functioning, whereas a parent may perceive the child as showing little or no improvement.

Clinicians often must work at the symptom level, attempting to reduce the occurrence of harmful behaviors and increase the occurrence of beneficial behaviors. Clinicians, especially those working within a strength-based model, are likely to be especially concerned about the ability of their clients to remain in school, to stay out of trouble, or to remain in the home. They are also likely to benefit from clinically oriented measures such as the Child Behavior Checklist, the Child and Adolescent Functional Assessment Scale, and other assessment devices that can help them understand the clinical profile and functional strengths and impairments of children and families.

Clinical status measures may also have some utility to *program administrators* if the data are quickly scored and analyzed. These data may help identify particular training or other programmatic and quality improvement needs. Administrators are also likely to find functional status data valuable. Information, for example, on work and school performance can point to specific academic programs that need to be better integrated with the care system. Finally, administrators are often concerned about the cost of services, and are likely to avoid costly and restrictive levels of institutional care.

Public perceptions of safety and public health undeniably drive part of the mental health policy debate. Interventions that are able to reduce public fears will likely be more easily embraced by *policy makers* from the grassroots to the elected level.

As a result, interventions that hope to affect policy need to strongly consider measuring variables such as arrest rates, suicide rates, and rates of comorbid conditions such as drug use. Cost of care is paramount in most public policy debates, and consequently data on the costs of services often take precedence over data on the effects of services when public policy at the local, state, and federal levels is determined.

Measures Should Promote Efficiency And Effectiveness in Implementation

Strategies for implementing ongoing outcome measures need to be considered in the context of funding, regulatory, and other paperwork-generating aspects of service delivery. It is often the case that initiatives for outcome measurement require the collection of data similar to those required for funding mechanisms or for quality improvement strategies. Outcome measures that can meet the multiple needs of a system are more likely to succeed. It is always important to take a streamlined, comprehensive approach to selecting outcome measures for ongoing use that eliminates duplication, maximizes revenue potential, and minimizes service disruption.

Measures Should Have Known Psychometric Properties

It is often tempting for states, localities, or even programs to create their own homegrown outcome measures. In the case of systems of care for youth with SED, this temptation is understandable, since few measures exist that focus on the strength-based approaches emphasized within many systems. Outcome indicators, such as arrest rates, school attendance and test scores, and information utilization may be collected directly from agency records and can be extremely valuable. In these cases, the question is one of accuracy of agency data collection. Outcome measures, however, designed to tap less direct indicators such as level of symptomatology, consumer satisfaction, or aspects of quality of life, need to have known psychometric properties. Developing good psychometric data on any outcome instrument is not a cursory task, and the effort required to do so can easily be underestimated. The danger of using an instrument that does not have known psychometric properties is straightforward: the users cannot be sure that they are measuring what they intend to measure (validity) or that the measurement is accurate (reliability), or sensitive to change over time. Consequently, a great deal of effort can be expended to collect data using homegrown measures that can yield virtually uninterpretable results. However, much work remains to be done to develop new outcome measures that are suitable for use within systems of care. The current selection of measures is extremely limited and greatly in need of expansion.[6,23]

Measures Should Yield Clear And Understandable Results

Outcome measures and indicators need to produce clear and understandable results. With respect to direct indicators such as arrests, costs, and grade level, the intelligibility of the results rests largely on how the results are presented. With respect to variables collected through assessment devices, the intelligibility of the results rests on both how the results are presented and on how the tool is scored. Outcome instruments that have no clear scoring scheme can yield a search for results at the individual item level, creating results of incomprehensible complexity. Similarly, well-standardized and normed instruments can provide a context in which to understand results. It is, for example, more advantageous to be able to say the average score indicates severity levels among the lowest 2% in the nation than to say the average score is 22.

Putting It Together: The Planning Process, Principles, and Outcomes

The core implication of the planning model approach for assessing outcomes is the need to clearly delineate consistency between choices at all five steps of the planning model. Table 1 draws from our experiences to illustrate how the target populations, goals, partnerships, programs or services, outcomes, and audiences or stakeholders can interrelate. Choices regarding the selection of any of these individual components affect other components. For example, if a care system is attempting to keep youth in school, there ought to be programs or interventions targeted specifically at helping a defined group of children reach that goal. Furthermore, measures need to be incorporated into an ongoing evaluation of the care system to ensure that the goal is met and that relevant audiences can be convinced of the utility of the program. In the case of keeping youth in school, such audiences might naturally include board of education members. Many measures may be suitable across a range of target populations and may have multiple impacts beyond those specified in Table 1.

The choice of which outcome measures to select will rest on some combination of the planning model process with the availability of measures, and available resources. However, the success of outcome studies relies on the congruence between goals, desired impacts, and the availability of quality measures or indicators. As care systems evolve, so too must measurement strategies. For example, system reform may begin by the creation of interagency teams and placement screening processes. The goal of these new interventions may be to reduce placements in restrictive levels of care. Consequently, the ability of youth in the care systems to remain in home becomes a critical measure of system outcomes given these new interventions. Although it may be desirable to measure other outcome domains, reductions in rates of placements may not translate into reductions in symptomatology. As the care system evolves, however, symptom measurement may become an important outcome assessment.

A specific case example from Ventura County shows the importance of measuring multiple variables at the child and family level. A young lady approaching her 18th birthday began to use increasing levels of inpatient care as her fear of transition to adulthood grew. Nonetheless, her level of academic achievement increased by two years over the same, one-year time frame. This helped the clinician and family to see the crisis as one of adjustment rather than the beginning of a pattern of deterioration, and they developed an intervention that enhanced and rewarded her considerable academic strengths, thereby building a sense of competency and capacity to deal with adulthood.

A Specific Plan for Outcome Measurement

Table 2 delineates the full range of outcome measurement strategies in use in counties implementing the California System of Care Model. Not all counties follow all the criteria; some counties receive funds through a grant from the Center for Mental Health Services and consequently have additional evaluation requirements as a part of their participation in the Children's Mental Health Initiative. Also included in Table 2 is a list of primary audiences for each measurement tool. Although many of the measures have multiple uses, each is specifically chosen to provide primary feedback to different levels of the care system. It is important to note that these indicators constitute a "least common denominator" outcome data set. Many counties use outcome assessment and other indicators that are tailored specifically to their own care systems.

The System-Level Measures and Outcomes section in Table 2, with the exception of "acute psychiatric hospital" and "restrictiveness of living environment," constitutes the initial core set of evaluation required by the original Ventura model expansion legislation for the funding of three additional system of care sites in California.[24]

Table 1. Example of Matching Goals, Populations, Measures, and Impacts

Step 1: Define Target Population	Step 2: Set Goals	Step 3: Create Partnerships	Step 4: Establish Services	Step 5: Establish Outcomes	Stakeholders
Youth at risk of out-of-home placement	In home	Mental health, social services, juvenile justice	Placement screening	Placements and expenditures in restrictive levels of care	Consumers, managers, policy makers
Youth enrolled in special education programs	In school	Mental health, education	Special day schools	School attendance, school achievement	Policy makers, teachers
Wards of the court	Out of trouble	Mental health, juvenile justice	Juvenile hall support	Rearrest rates	Policy makers, judges
Younger youth with multiple risk factors	Healthy	Mental health, primary health care	Assessment and Brief Therapy	Child Behavior Checklist	Clinicians, managers

Table 2. Full Ongoing Outcome Data Set for California System of Care Model Counties

What	Source	When	Primary Audience
Systems-level measures and outcomes			State and local policy makers, interagency partners, program managers
Placements			
State hospital: number, length of stay, cost	State data systems	Collected monthly	
Group Home: number, cost			
Foster homes: number, cost			
Acute psychiatric hospital: bed days, cost	County data	Collected monthly	
Restrictiveness of living environment (Restrictiveness of Living Environment Scale-ROLES)	Clinician/case manager	Entry, exit, annual	
Educational performance (for youth in select special education/mental health programs)		Ongoing	Program managers, interagency partners, local policy makers
School attendance	School records	Annually	
School performance	Achievement tests		
Juvenile justice (for youth in selected mental health, juvenile justice programs)	Court records	Ongoing, one-year pre- and post-program	
Recidivism: arrests and citations by type of offense			
Consumer-level measures and outcomes			
Functioning, competence, and impairment from caregiver, consumer, and clinician perspectives		Entry, six months,[a] annually, and discharge	Clinicians and consumers, program managers, local policy
Child Behavior Checklist	Caregiver		
Youth Self Report	Child		
Child and Adolescent Functional Assessment Scale	Clinician		
Satisfaction (Client Satisfaction Questionnaire-8)	Caregiver, child'	Sampled periodically	Consumers, program managers
Family Empowerment Scale'	Caregiver		

[a]. Required only for counties receiving a Children's Mental Health Initiative grant from the Center for Mental Health Services.

These measures, designed to tap whether youth are at home, in school, and out of trouble, have formed the basis of a number of published reports.[8-16] State legislation (AB377) specified effectiveness criteria for many of the outcomes, including lowering the rate of out-of-home placements and producing statistically significant improvements in academic achievement and reductions in juvenile arrests.

The system-level indicators have been used routinely for system management, program development, and policy purposes. They do not lend themselves to frequent use by clinicians, who may not have been aware of some of the indicators. Care systems use data regarding group home, foster home, state hospital, and hospital utilization as indicators. These indicators are used by the sectors of education and juvenile justice to create goals and assess the performance of programs.

The addition of consumer-level measures was prompted by the process of expanding the California System of Care Model from 3 to 10 counties through new legislation.[25] This legislation called for the measurement of child- and family-level outcomes within a care system. The measures selected for use are among the most popular in the research and clinical communities. Parents or caregivers complete the Child Behavior Checklist (CBCL), and children 12 years old and above complete the Youth Self Report (YSR). These measures provide data on social competencies (functional status) across a range of social contexts (school, home, community) and syndrome scales (clinical status).[26-28] Clinicians complete the Child and Adolescent Functional Assessment Scale,[29] a clinician rating scale that yields scores regarding the child's functioning in the domains of role performance (including school/work, home, and community subscales); thinking, behavior toward others; moods/self-harm (including moods/emotions and self-harmful behavior subscales); and substance use. These measures provide three perspectives on the functioning of the child: the caregiver, the child, and the clinician. State legislation (AB3015) specified that counties show "measurable improvement" in child and family functioning.

These three outcome measures represent a new level of development for ongoing evaluation within the California System of Care Model. They also signify a renewed focus within these care systems on improving the skills, training, and quality of the interventions provided by the clinical line staff within the care system. This renewed focus is another stage of development for care systems that demonstrated success in more system-level outcome indicators and are now ready to become more fully accountable for consumer-level outcomes. Clinicians are being trained on how to integrate information from these measures in order to develop plans of care for children and families. Over time, information on the progress of youth as measured by these instruments will be provided to clinicians to help them evaluate their success in meeting the clinical goals of the care system.

Finally, service satisfaction is assessed using the Client Satisfaction Questionnaire-8.[22] In addition, in counties funded by the Center for Mental Health Services, a newly developed measure of family empowerment, the Family Empowerment Scale, developed by the Research and Training Center on Family Support and Children's Mental Health at Portland State University, is completed by the parents or caretakers. This scale assesses parent or caretaker perceptions of roles and responsibilities within service systems and ability to advocate on behalf of the child.[30]

Challenges in Designing And Implementing an Outcome Management Plan

Implementing a core set of outcome measures across the 18 California System of Care Model counties is a complex task. The evaluation of the California System of Care Model is being conducted as a full partnership between the counties, the California Department of Mental Health, and the Child Services Research Group at the University of California, San Francisco (UCSF). Each county maintains locally hired and housed evaluation staff dedicated to collecting and analyzing data for county-specific purposes. In addition, each local evaluator provides a core set of data to the UCSF evaluation team. The UCSF evaluation team is funded by the California Department of Mental Health (Cal-DMH) and the Substance Abuse and Mental Health Services Administration, Center for Mental Health Services, to provide technical assistance to the sites and the department, to establish common measurement goals and strategies, to encourage and enhance communication between local-level evaluators, and to collect data across all sites for comparative and statewide policy development purposes. This arrangement is designed to facilitate the combination of local utilization of outcome information and statewide and national utilization of results.

Design Challenges

Designing an outcome management system for an integrated system of care for children with multiple system needs poses considerable challenges that derive from the interagency aspects of service delivery, the perspectives from which to assess outcomes, the multiple stakeholders concerned with outcomes of care, and a paucity of measurement tools and interagency information systems. In part, because of these challenges, the system in California was developed through a series of compromises. The goals of the care systems are, by definition, interagency goals, so that indicators of educational, placement, or arrest status are as important as clinical status. Unfortunately, information systems do not track youth across service sectors, and much fundamental information (such as arrests) is not routinely automated in some California counties. Even within a care sector, data collection is often fragmented. In the schools, for example, attendance records are frequently kept at a district level, and many counties have a dozen or more school districts. Consequently, although it would seem highly desirable to collect arrest, attendance, or placement data for all youth within a care system, such data are not readily available, and self-report data on these variables often are neither reliable nor convincing to local and state policy makers. For example, in California, juvenile justice and educational data are, in most cases, collected only on specific subpopulations of youth. Some counties have made exceptional strides in collecting these types of data for all youth enrolled in the system of care.

With respect to mental health outcomes, the most psychometrically developed scales (such as the CBCL) are not easy to administer and can be difficult for nonscientific audiences to interpret. Similarly, it is difficult to resolve whose perspective—the clinician's, parent's, or child's—best captures the actual fate of the family or child. Well-developed family functioning measures are even more cumbersome to administer. It is not surprising that many counties or states devise their own brief outcome measures even though the psychometric properties of these measures remain unaddressed. It is extraordinarily difficult, given the current state of measurement development, to strike a balance between practicality and rigor. Much more fundamental work is still needed in the development of relatively brief, but still meaningful, outcome measures that capture symptoms and functioning from multiple perspectives.

Implementation Challenges

A direct relationship exists between the ease of collecting outcome data and the level of development of the system of care. Often, difficulties in collecting outcome data reflect difficulties in collaborative efforts between agencies, as well as the orientation of clinical and administrative staff. It is simply easier to collect data from better integrated and coordinated service systems. Following the steps of the planning model to create a system of care requires a change in the culture of agencies, from clinical line staff to program managers to agency directors. New goals, new partnerships, and shared responsibilities for defined populations require agencies to shift from insular, protective modes of operation to open and collaborative efforts and information exchange.

Similarly, implementing outcomes, making agencies and line staff accountable for achieving goals, and modifying service delivery practices in order to better achieve goals requires extensive culture change at all levels of a care system. Historically, public agencies have invested more energy to demonstrate that sufficient numbers of youth are served rather than show that services are effective. Quality improvement efforts focus on accurate completion of clinical records and other indicators of process[31] rather than on outcomes. A myriad of billing reporting requirements, legacy information systems, and long-standing quality improvement mechanisms have resulted in considerable paperwork for clinical staff and program administrators. Finally, many clinicians are highly protective of their relationship with their clients, and may view outcome measurement of any type as intrusive.

Shifting attitudes toward viewing outcomes as helpful to management, as useful information for direct service providers, and as an essential part of a strategy for the ongoing sustainability of effective services, although integral to implementing the California System of Care Model, remains exceptionally difficult. An openness to change in the implementation process is essential for evaluators as well. Over time, outcome monitoring of the California System of Care Model has evolved and changed. Evaluation staff need to listen carefully to feedback provided by their service system partners if they are to understand outcomes and improve methods. This is an ongoing process that requires considerable trust between evaluators and service providers so that differences in opinion can be aired, discussed, and, when possible, resolved. The most potent weapon to date in helping systems view outcome information as valuable has been the presentation and feedback of evaluation results to line-level clinicians and program managers.

Challenges in Analysis and Use

Outcome measures need to be relevant and useful to a wide range of stakeholders. The usefulness of outcome results to different stakeholders depends in large part on how results are presented and analyzed as well as how measures are administered. It has frequently been the case that different levels of utility conflict with one another. For example, a well-constructed sample can be a much more efficient way to assess the outcomes of an entire system than giving measures to all youth who receive care. However, any sample means that certain children will not receive a set of outcome measures, thus limiting the utility of the outcome management system to clinicians who will only receive clinical feedback on a small portion of the youth they serve. In such scenarios, the goal of efficiency in implementing an outcome management system and the goal of providing information feedback to relevant stakeholders, such as clinicians, conflict. Similarly, although changes in a score on a standardized test are not likely to capture the attention of policy makers the way cost data or arrest data might, changes at the symptom level as reflected in standardized tests may best reflect the goals of a mental health clinician.

Technical analytic challenges result from the fundamental messiness of data collected in real world settings. Problems in the form of missing data, the meaning of statistical and clinical significance, measurable improvement, the representation and assessment of change, the comparability of data across sites, and a myriad of other analytic problems are raised whenever a large-scale outcome management system is implemented. Certainly, at the policy level in California, excessive complexity and the ambiguous presentation of results do not typically sway policy makers. Simple graphic representations have proven most useful to most of these stakeholders, although more complex statistical treatments may lie beneath the surface of the results.

Implications for Behavioral Health Services and Policy

This article emphasizes the use of outcome information to guide system development and produce fundamental, policy-relevant results. The current rush toward managed care in mental health services is continually drawing service outcomes and funding for services together.[32,33] These pressures have long existed in California. Public services have suffered because of economic recession, and voter initiatives have severely curtailed and limited the tax base for public services. These forces, in part, led to the development of a system of care model that integrates mental health treatment into existing child-serving systems to improve outcomes for a targeted group of children and families. The model acknowledges limited taxpayer tolerance for public spending by promoting efficient management of existing resources. Such a system reform requires a clear design that binds all participants into outcome-driven partnerships. In the model, change is accomplished by applying a planning model that moves participants through an often complex process in which each step leads to the next and in which no single step can achieve needed reforms sufficiently. The model thrives, in large part, because learning from mistakes and failures is an essential component of how services (and evaluation research) are developed within the model.

The implications for behavioral health policy and services in California have been profound. The California System of Care Model, with its outcome-driven approach, is the vehicle by which public services for youth with severe emotional disturbance grow and expand across a range of counties in California. Children's mental health programs in Santa Cruz County, for example, grew from 1.5 staff members in 1985 to more than 60 staff members in 1996. The model promotes experimentation and risk taking in service delivery approaches throughout the state. The counties implementing the model continue to set the standards for service delivery approaches in California. State mental health policy for children in California is built, in no small measure, on the planning model. As is the case nationwide, the sociopolitical context of the counties that are implementing the model are constantly changing, forcing continual evolution in service structures and outcome measurement strategies. The planning model, however, with its straightforward focus on achieving measurable goals for a specific target population, remains the same as it did a decade ago—a constant beacon in a sea of changes.

Acknowledgments

The authors acknowledge the many contributions of colleagues striving to implement outcome management systems in their counties: Alfredo Aguirre, Donna Dahl, Laura Fowler, Martin Giffin, Margie Helms, Pat Jordan, and Joan Luzney. We also appreciate the many contributions of colleagues in the California Department of Mental Health: Rachel Guerrero, Patrick Kelliher, and Vincent Mandella. We owe a special thanks to Randall Feltman of Ventura County for his inspiration and involvement and to Mario Hernandez for his guidance in developing the manuscript. Karla Kruse made valuable contributions to manuscript preparation. The views expressed in this manuscript are those of the authors.

References

1. Joint Commission on the Mental Health of Children: *Crisis in Child Mental Health: Challenge for the 1970s.* New York: Harper & Row, 1970.
2. Knitzer J: *Unclaimed Children: The Failure of Public Responsibility to Children and Adolescents in Need of Mental Health Services.* Washington, DC: Children's Defense Fund, 1982.
3. Stroul BA, Friedman RM: *A System of Care for Severely Emotionally Disturbed Children and Youth.* Washington, DC: Child and Adolescent Service System Program Technical Assistance Center, Georgetown University, 1986.

4. Stroul BA: *Children's Mental Health: Creating Systems of Care in a Changing Society.* Baltimore, MD: Paul H. Brookes, 1996.

5. Stroul BA: *Systems of Care for Children and Adolescents With Severe Emotional Disturbances: What Are the Results?* Washington, DC: CASSP Technical Assistance Center, Georgetown University Child Development Center, 1993.

6. Rosenblatt A: Assessing the child and family outcomes of systems of care for youth with severe emotional disturbance. In: Epstein MH, Kutash K, Duchnowski A (Eds.): *Community-Based Programming for Children With Serious Emotional Disturbance and Their Families: Research and Evaluations.* Austin, TX: PRO-ED, 1998.

7. Kagan SL, Neville PR: *Integrating Services for Children and Families: Understanding the Past to Shape the Future.* New Haven, CT: Yale University Press, 1993.

8. Feltman R, Essex D: *The Ventura Model: Presentation Package,* 1989. Available from Randall Feltman, Director, Ventura County Mental Health Services, 300 Hillmont Avenue, Ventura, CA 93003.

9. Attkisson CC, Rosenblatt A, Dresser KL, et al.: Effectiveness of the California System of Care Model for children and youth with severe emotional disorder. In: Nixon CT, Northrup D (Eds.): *Evaluating Mental Health Services: How Do Programs for Children "Work" in the Real World?* Thousand Oaks, CA: Sage, 1996, pp. 146-208.

10. Hernandez M, Goldman SK: A local approach to system development: Ventura County, California. In: Stroul BA (Ed.): *Children's Mental Health: Creating Systems of Care in a Changing Society.* Baltimore, MD: Paul H. Brookes, 1996, pp. 177-196.

11. Ichinose CK, Kingdon DW, Hernandez M: Developing community alternatives to group home placement for SED special education students in the Ventura County system of care. *Journal of Child and Family Studies* 1994; 3:193-210.

12. Jordan DD, Hernandez M: The Ventura Planning Model: A proposal for mental health reform. *The Journal of Mental Health Administration* 1990; 17:26-47.

13. Rosenblatt A, Attkisson CC: Integrating systems of care in California for youth with severe emotional disturbance 1: A descriptive overview of the California AB377 Evaluation Project. *Journal of Child and Family Studies* 1992; 1:93-113.

14. Rosenblatt A, Attkisson CC: Integrating systems of care in California for youth with severe emotional disturbance III: Answers that lead to questions about out-of-home placements and the California AB377 evaluation project. *Journal of Child and Family Studies* 1993; 2:119-141.

15. Rosenblatt A, Attkisson CC: Integrating systems of care in California for youth with severe emotional disturbance IV: Educational attendance and achievement. *Journal of Child and Family Studies* 1997; 6(l):113-129.

16. Rosenblatt A, Attkisson CC, Fernandez A: Integrating systems of care in California for youth with severe emotional disturbance II: Initial group home utilization and expenditure findings from the California AB377 Evaluation Project. *Journal of Child and Family Studies* 1992; 1:263-286.

17. Tharp RG, Gallimore R: The ecology of program research and evaluation: A model of evaluation succession. In: Sechrest L, West SG, Phillips MA, et al. (Eds.): *Evaluation Studies Review Annual.* Vol. 4. Beverly Hills, CA: Sage, 1979, pp. 39-60.

18. Hernandez M, Hodges S, Cascardi M: The ecology of outcomes: System accountability in children's mental health. *The Journal of Behavioral Health Services & Research* 1998; 25(2):136-150.

19. Weiss CH: Nothing as practical as good theory: Exploring theory-based evaluation for comprehensive community initiatives for children and families. In: Conell JP, Kubisch AC, Schorr LB, et al. (Eds.): *New Approaches to Evaluating Community Initiatives: Concept, Methods and Contexts.* Washington, DC: The Aspen Institute, 1995, pp. 65-92.

20. Stroul BA, Friedman RM: The system of care concept and philosophy. In: Stroul BA (Ed.): *Children's Mental Health: Creating Systems of Care in a Changing Society.* Baltimore, MD: Paul H. Brookes, 1996, pp. 3-22.

21. Chen HT: *Theory Driven Evaluations.* Newbury Park, CA: Sage, 1990.
22. Attkisson CC, Greenfield TK: Client Satisfaction Questionnaire-8 and Service Satisfaction Scale-30. In: Maruish ME (Ed.): *The Use of Psychological Testing for Treatment Planning and Outcome Assessment.* Hillsdale, NJ: Lawrence Erlbaum, 1994, pp. 402-422.
23. Heflinger CA: Client level outcomes of mental health services for children and adolescents. *New Directions for Program Evaluation* 1992; 54:31-45.
24. Children's Mental Health Services Act of 1987. California Welfare and Institutions Code 5565.10-5565.40.
25. Children's Mental Health Services Act of 1992. California Welfare and Institutions Code 5850-5883.
26. Achenbach TM, Edelbrock CS: *Manual for the Child Behavior Checklist and Revised Child Behavior Profile.* Burlington: Department of Psychiatry, University of Vermont, 1983.
27. Achenbach TM, Edelbrock CS: *Manual for the Teacher's Report Form and Teacher Version of the Child Behavior Profile.* Burlington: Department of Psychiatry, University of Vermont, 1986.
28. Achenbach TM, Edelbrock C, Howell CT: Empirically based assessment of the behavioral/emotional problems of 2 and 3 year old children. *Journal of Abnormal Child Psychology* 1987; 15:629-650.
29. Hodges K: *Child and Adolescent Functional Assessment Scale.* Ypsilanti: Department of Psychiatry, Eastern Michigan University, 1989, 1994.
30. Koren PE, De Chillo N, Friesen BJ: Measuring empowerment in families whose children have emotional disabilities: A brief questionnaire. *Rehabilitation Psychology* 1992; 37:305-321.
31. Stricker G, Rodriquez AR: *Handbook of Quality Assurance in Mental Health.* New York: Plenum, 1988.
32. Sabin JE: Psychotherapy and managed care. *The Harvard Mental Health Letter* 1995; 11:4-7.
33. Lambert MJ: Introduction to psychotherapy research. In: Beutler LE, Crago M (Eds.): *Psychotherapy Research: An International Review of Programmatic Studies.* Washington, DC: American Psychological Association, 1991, pp. 1-11.

Measuring Treatment Outcome and Client Satisfaction Among Children And Families: A Case Report

THOMAS G. PLANTE, CHARLES E. COUCHMAN, AND CONSTANCE A. HOFFMAN

> Formal assessment of client satisfaction and treatment outcome is more frequently being requested as a component of mental health services. This article outlines a treatment outcome and client satisfaction program implemented at the Children's Health Council, a private nonprofit mental health agency in Palo Alto, California, affiliated with the Stanford University Medical Center. The program was designed to be simple and inexpensive, and it is intended to serve as an example for other agencies and practicing professionals wishing to measure treatment outcome and client satisfaction.

Mental health professionals often struggle with developing methods to assess client satisfaction and outcome. Few have training and experience in this area of evaluation, and many are unsure how to obtain guidance. Few agencies and professionals have the financial resources to hire consultants or develop expensive and elaborate evaluation programs. These factors contribute to the extreme difficulty in developing, implementing, and supporting outcome and satisfaction assessment.

In response to the enormous pressures for providers of mental health services to demonstrate their effectiveness in an increasingly challenging consumer world (Coursey, 1977; Fabry, Hawkins, & Luster, 1994; Mirin & Namerow, 1991; Phillips & Rosenblatt, 1992; Plante, Couchman, & Diaz, 1995; Sheppard, 1993), the Children's Health Council (CHC), a private nonprofit agency that specializes in the assessment and treatment of children and families with mental health and educational problems, undertook the present study of treatment outcome and client satisfaction assessment. It was believed that this study would provide needed information to utilization review

---

Source: Plante TG, Couchman CE, and Hoffman CA. Measuring Treatment Outcome and Client Satisfaction Among Children and Families: A Case Report. Professional Psychology: Research and Practice 1998; 29(1):52-55. Copyright 1998 by the American Psychological Association. Reprinted with permission.

Thomas G. Plante received his PhD in clinical psychology from the University of Kansas in 1987. He is currently an associate professor of psychology at Santa Clara University and a clinical assistant professor of psychiatry and behavioral sciences at Stanford University School of Medicine. He is former director of mental health services and chief psychologist at the Children's Health Council, Palo Alto, California. He is a diplomate in clinical psychology of the American Board of Professional Psychology and maintains a private practice in Menlo Park, California. He teaches and writes on professional issues, clinical health psychology, intimate relationships, and psychological issues of Catholic clergy.

Charles E. Couchman received his BS in psychology from Santa Clara University in 1994 and is a former research assistant and teacher's aide at the Children's Health Council, Palo Alto, California. He is currently a graduate student in clinical psychology at the University of Rochester.

Constance A. Hoffman received her BS in psychology from Santa Clara University in 1994 and is a former research assistant at the Children's Health Council, Palo Alto, California. She is currently a research assistant at Santa Clara University and focuses on child development and abnormal psychology.

We would like to thank Carolyn Korbel, Michelle Deneau, and the clinicians, staff, and patients of the Children's Health Council for their assistance with and participation in this project.

Correspondence concerning this article should be addressed to Thomas G. Plante, Psychology Department, Santa Clara University, Santa Clara, California 95053-0333. Electronic mail may be sent via the Internet to tplante@mailer.scu.edu.

entities (Cummings, 1995; Dickey & Wagenaar, 1994; Kovacs, 1996) and help providers to easily collect and process the information.

The outcome and satisfaction assessment program presented here has been designed to be inexpensive and simple to implement, and it is intended to serve as an example for similar agencies interested in measuring treatment outcome and client satisfaction among children and family clients. In addition to a description of the program, the data collected during an 18-month period beginning at the onset of the project are presented. We hope that an examination of the CHC program will serve as a useful example for other agencies and practitioners wishing to design and implement similar treatment outcome and client satisfaction programs. The CHC program is presented not as a perfect or "gold standard" program but, rather, as an example of the type of program many agencies and private practitioners may find useful to implement and to learn from.

The Outcome—Satisfaction Demonstration Project

The assessment package consisted of four questionnaires: the Child and Adolescent Adjustment Profile (CAAP; Ellsworth, 1981), the Brief Psychiatric Rating Scale for Children (BPRS-C; Overall & Pfefferbaum, 1962), the Client Satisfaction Questionnaire-8 (CSQ-8; Nguyen, Attkisson, & Stegner, 1983), and a demographic questionnaire designed by the authors (Plante et al., 1995). These measures, described subsequently, were chosen after a comprehensive survey had been conducted of the treatment outcome and client satisfaction assessment measures available. With the exception of the demographic questionnaire, all have been shown to be adequately reliable and valid. They are appropriate for both children of elementary school age and adolescents, for all relevant *Diagnostic and Statistical Manual of Mental Disorders* (4th ed.; American Psychiatric Association, 1994) diagnoses, and for brief, long-term, individual, and group treatments. All of the measures are brief, inexpensive, accessible to the public, and simple to use.

The Child and Adolescent Adjustment Profile

The CAAP (Ellsworth, 1981) is designed to be completed by various adults working or living with the child or adolescent. These adults could include parents, teachers, treatment staff, and counselors. Parents were requested to complete the CAAP in this investigation. The scale is a 20-item self-report measure that assesses area of adjustment as defined by a factor analysis of five areas: Peer Relations (e.g., gets along with others), Dependency (e.g., wanted help but could have done on own), Hostility (e.g., upset if others don't agree), Productivity (e.g., works hard on assignments), and Withdrawal (e.g., daydreams). Behaviors are rated on a 4-point Likert-type scale ranging from *rarely* (1) to *almost always* (4). The score for each factor can range from a minimum of 4 to a maximum of 16. Higher scores indicate positive behaviors on the Peer Relations and Productivity factors, whereas high scores reflect negative behaviors on the Dependency, Hostility, and Withdrawal factors.

The Brief Psychiatric Rating Scale for Children

The BPRS-C (Gale, Pfefferbaum, Suhr, & Overall, 1986; Overall & Pfefferbaum, 1962) can be used by treating clinicians to assess general psychiatric symptoms. The 21 items measure seven areas defined by factor analysis: Behavior Problems (e.g., hostility), Depression (e.g., suicidal ideation), Thinking Disturbance (e.g., hallucinations), Psychomotor Excitation (e.g., hyperactivity), Withdrawal Retardation (e.g., blunted affect), Anxiety (e.g., tension), and Organicity (e.g., disorientation). The BPRS-C uses a 7-point Likert-type scale ranging from *not present* (1) to *extremely severe* (7). Each symptom group can range in score from a minimum of 3 to a maximum of 21, with higher scores indicating more severe behavioral symptoms. Total BPRS-C scores can thus range from 21 to 147.

Three questions were added to the BPRS-C form for this study to assess level of therapist perception of treatment success, therapist perception of cooperation of the family, and clinician satisfaction with treatment outcome. Each of these questions was scored on a 10-point Likert-type scale, with higher scores indicating higher levels of perceived success, cooperation, and satisfaction.

The Client Satisfaction Questionnaire-8

The CSQ-8 (Attkisson & Greenfield, 1994; Nguyen et al., 1983) is an 8-item abbreviated version of the 31-item Client Satisfaction Questionnaire developed by Larsen, Attkisson, Hargreaves, and Nguyen (1979). It is used to measure client satisfaction with treatment. Each item is rated on a 4-point Likert-type scale. The total for the 8 questions is calculated, resulting in a minimum score of 8 and a maximum score of 32. Higher scores indicate higher levels of satisfaction (Nguyen et al., 1983).

The Demographic Questionnaire

The demographic questionnaire (Plante et al., 1995) was designed to collect demographic data, such as age and gender of child, full-scale IQ, ethnicity, marital status of parents, birth order, religious affiliation and attitude, living situation, family and personal history, and diagnostic information.

Procedure

Treating clinicians were required to complete a BPRS-C shortly after their initial meeting with clients and then shortly after clients terminated therapy. An initial CAAP was delivered to clients' parents or guardians at their first visit to the CHC, along with standard agency intake forms. A form consisting of the CAAP and the CSQ-8 was delivered at 3-month intervals from this initial visit. Three-month intervals were used because many treatment plans, such as managed care contracts and state funding contracts, also use intervals of this length to evaluate services. The CAAP and the CSQ-8 were administered by the clinic receptionist when patients arrived for their appointments. Parents or guardians completed the forms while waiting in the lobby. This procedure maximized return rates (as compared with mail survey methods) and also reduced demand characteristics, because the therapists were not directly involved in patient data collection (Attkisson & Greenfield, 1994; Feifel & Eells, 1963). Therefore, as a means of encouraging honesty, client evaluations of therapists were not shown to therapists. Six months after termination of services, a follow-up form consisting of the CAAP and the CSQ-8 was administered to the parents or guardians by mail.

A cross section of patients treated at the CHC during the first 18 months of the program took part in the current demonstration project. The study consisted of 115 participants (79 boys and 36 girls), ranging from 6 to 17 years of age ($M = 10.5$, $SD = 3.1$). Of the 92 participants (80%) whose ethnicity was identified, 59 (64%) were described as Caucasian and 33 (36%) were described as being from an ethnic minority group (e.g., Asian, African American, Latin American, or of mixed ethnicity). There were completed demographic questionnaires for 94 participants, and, for these individuals, the primary psychiatric diagnoses included disruptive behavior problems ($n = 26$; 28%), depression and mood problems ($n = 20$; 21%), and posttraumatic stress disorder ($n = 17$; 18%). Twenty-five (27%) had experienced documented parental neglect, 20 (21%) had experienced documented physical abuse, and 14 (15%) had experienced documented sexual abuse. There were 35 (37%) documented cases of alcohol abuse within participants' immediate families. The number of treatment sessions ranged from 1 to 159, with a median of 7.5 and a standard deviation of 27.5.

Ninety-six initial CAAPs were completed. During subsequent 3-month periods, 36, 22, and 13 CAAPs were collected. It is important to note that, as time went on, fewer CAAPs were expected because treatment programs were short-term (and thus patients terminated before a 3-, 6-, 9-, or 12-month interval had expired) or because some newer patients were still in treatment as of the writing of this article. The mean initial CAAP scores rating symptom severity in five areas ranged from 9.7 to 11.7 ($SD = 2.7$ to 3.1), indicating moderate symptom severity. Later mean CAAP scores ranged from 9.0 to 12.1 ($SD = 2.4$ to 3.2), also indicating moderate symptom severity. The level of symptomology within each time period was not significantly different, and an examination of CAAP scores over time failed to indicate a significant change in severity of symptoms reported during treatment (all $ps > .05$).

An analysis of covariance (ANCOVA) with

repeated measures was conducted on the CAAP scores for the 36 participants who completed initial and 3-month CAAPs. Results of this analysis failed to reach statistical significance ($p > .05$), indicating that symptom scores on the CAAPs did not significantly decrease between the initial and 3-month assessments completed by the parents or guardians.

Ninety-four initial BPRS-Cs were completed by therapists, along with 39 terminal BPRS-Cs. The initial BPRS-Cs indicated moderate levels of symptomology, with a mean of 46.8 ($SD = 10.9$) of a maximum possible score of 147. The terminal BPRS-Cs showed a nonsignificant moderate decrease in symptoms (M score = 43.0, $SD = 10.7$). The therapists' ratings of treatment success revealed a mean of 5.9 ($SD = 1.9$) on a 10-point Likert-like scale ranging from 1 (*not at all*) to 10 (*very*). The mean therapist rating of family cooperation was 6.0 ($SD = 2.9$) on the same scale; the mean therapist rating of satisfaction with outcome was 5.7 ($SD = 2.4$). Thus, the BPRS-C indicated only moderate levels of treatment success, family cooperation, and treatment satisfaction as perceived by therapists.

An ANCOVA with repeated measures was conducted on the BPRS-C scores for the 39 participants who had pretreatment and posttreatment BPRS-C assessments completed by therapists. Results failed to reach statistical significance ($p > .05$), indicating that symptom scores on the BPRS-Cs did not significantly decrease between the initial and terminal assessments noted by treating therapists.

Throughout the study, client satisfaction remained high, with a mean score of 26.6 ($SD = 6.4$) of a possible 32 on the CSQ-8. Neither age nor gender was found to be associated with any of the relevant treatment outcome or client satisfaction variables (all $ps > .05$).

Discussion of Implications

The client satisfaction and treatment outcome program described is a simple and inexpensive program that uses reliable, valid, and brief assessment tools. The program may be useful to other agencies and private practices working with children and families around mental health issues. Effective data collection, analysis, and interpretation are challenging. Many obstacles must be overcome to obtain the maximum benefit of a treatment outcome and satisfaction evaluation program. This is especially true in large agencies in which many staff members, trainees, and clients are involved with the program.

Outcome evaluations may not reveal statistically significant reductions in symptoms over time, which is one reason it may be important to also collect satisfaction data. Stable reports of symptoms, combined with high satisfaction, may indicate that important "care" (as compared with "cure") is occurring. The lack of a noticeable reduction in symptoms also could be partially due to a decline in response rate over time as successfully treated patients finish their treatment and are no longer in the pool of patients completing the next round of 3-month forms. The lack of a reported reduction in symptoms during treatment may also be related to the modest level and range of severity of clients' symptoms; furthermore, short-term treatment patients may exhibit less severe symptomology, whereas long-term patients may tend to show more chronic, severe symptoms.

A limitation that emerged in our project related to the use of 3-month intervals to measure observations of the parents or guardians. Many therapy patients terminated before 3 months had passed, resulting in only two data points for such patients: an initial assessment and a follow-up assessment. Thus, changes observed by the parents or guardians during treatment were not measured, nor were changes observed during the 6 months between the termination of treatment and the administration of the follow-up assessment. Other programs may wish to consider using a "last day of treatment" administration of forms so as to capture more immediate evaluation data on shorter term cases.

Missing data can be a persistent and perhaps unavoidable problem. When trying to collect measures within specific time intervals, it becomes difficult if there are long intervals between appointments or if clients fail to attend sessions regularly. Cancellations, rescheduling, and failures to appear all can make reliable data collection an extremely difficult process. Also, any breakdown in the chain of assessment administration and collection will result in missing or late (and, hence, useless) data. Assessing treatment outcome and client satisfaction among clients from different cultural groups or among those who experience different psychiatric diagnoses poses another difficulty, depending on the ethnicity mix at a given clinic or practice.

Staff and client cooperation, as well as data collection and management, poses fundamental problems in securing useful client satisfaction and treatment outcome data. Staff and clients must be informed about the purpose and benefits of evaluation and must fully cooperate if the program is to be successful. Confidentiality must be considered carefully as well. Many of these problems can be overcome in private practice settings, where there are generally few staff members and few administrative obstacles.

References

American Psychiatric Association. (1994). *Diagnostic and statistical manual of mental disorders* (4th ed.). Washington, DC: Author.

Attkisson, C. C., & Greenfield, T. K. (1994). The Client Satisfaction Questionnaire-8 and the Service Satisfaction Scale-30. In M. Maruish (Ed.), *Psychological testing: Treatment planning and outcome assessment* (pp. 402-420). Hillsdale, NJ: Erlbaum.

Coursey, R.D. (1977). Basic questions and tasks. In R. D. Coursey (Ed.), *Program evaluation for mental health: Methods, strategies, participants* (pp. 1-8). New York: Grune & Stratton.

Cummings, N. A. (1995). Impact of managed care on employment and training: A primer for survival. *Professional Psychology: Research and Practice*, 26, 10-15.

Dickey, B., & Wagenaar, H. (1994). Evaluating mental health care reform: Including the clinician, client and family perspective. *Journal of Mental Health Administration*, 21, 313-319.

Ellsworth, R. B. (1981). *CAAP Scale: The measurement of child and adolescent adjustment.* Palo Alto, CA: Consulting Psychologists Press.

Fabry, B. D., Hawkins, R. P., & Luster, W. C. (1994). Monitoring outcomes of services to children and youths with severe emotional disorders: An economical follow-up procedure for mental health and child care agencies. *Journal of Mental Health Administration*, 21, 271-282.

Feifel, H., & Eells, J. (1963.). Patients and therapists assess the same psychotherapy. *Journal of Consulting Psychology*, 27, 310-318.

Gale, J., Pfefferbaum, B., Suhr, M. A., & Overall, J. E. (1986). The Brief Psychiatric Rating Scale for Children: A reliability study. *Journal of Clinical Child Psychology*, 15, 341-345.

Kovacs, A. (1996, March-April). Advice to the new professional. *The National Psychologist*, 5, 14.

Larsen, D.L., Attkisson, C.C., Hargreaves, W. A., & Nguyen, T D. (1979). Assessment of client/patient satisfaction: Development of a general scale. *Evaluation and Program Planning*, 2, 197-207.

Mirin, S. M., & Namerow, M. J. (1991). Why study treatment outcome? *Hospital and Community Psychiatry*, 42, 1007-1013.

Nguyen, T.D., Attkisson, C. C., & Stegner, B.L. (1983). Assessment of patient satisfaction: Development and refinement of a service evaluation questionnaire. *Evaluation and Program Planning*, 6, 299-313.

Overall, J. E., & Pfefferbaum, B. (1962). The Brief Psychiatric Rating Scale for Children. *Psychopharmacology Bulletin*, 18 (2), 10-16.

Phillips, K. A., & Rosenblatt, A. (1992). Speaking in tongues: Integrating economics and psychology into health and mental health services outcomes research. *Medical Care Review*, 49, 191-231.

Plante, T P., Couchman, C. E., & Diaz, A. R. (1995). Measuring treatment outcome and client satisfaction among children and families. *Journal of Mental Health Administration*, 22. 261-269.

Sheppard, M. (1993). Client satisfaction, extended intervention and interpersonal skills in community mental health. *Journal of Advanced Nursing*, 18, 246-259.

Measuring Outcomes in Children's Services: Appendix

> ### Sourcebook Editor's Note:
> Following is a list of outcomes instruments cited in *Measuring Outcomes in Children's Services* (Manisses, 1997). The list appears in the Appendix to that volume, which can be ordered from Manisses Communications Group, Inc., 208 Governor Street, Providence, Rhode Island 02906-3246; (800) 333-7771; (401) 831-6020; fax: (401) 861-6370; http://www.manisses.com

Anxiety

- Anxiety Disorders Interview Schedule for Children (ADIS-C)
  Citation: Silverman, W.K., Nelles, W.B. The Anxiety Disorders Interview Schedule for Children. *Journal of the American Academy of Child and Adolescent Psychiatry*, 27:772-778, 1988.

- Child Posttraumatic Stress Disorder Reaction Index
  Citation: Nader, K., Pynoos, R., *et al*. Children's PTSD reactions one year after a sniper attack at their school. *American Journal of Psychiatry*, 147:1526-1530, 1990.

- Children's Yale-Brown Obsessive Compulsive Symptom Checklist (CY-BOCS)
  Citation: Goodman, W.K., Rasmussen, S.A., *et al. Children's Yale-Brown Obsessive Compulsive Scale (CY-BOCS), ed. 1.* New Haven, CT: Yale University, 1986.

- Clinical Global Impression Scale
  Citation: Guy, W. ECDEU *Assessment Manual of Psychopharmacology*. DHEW publication ADM 76-338. Rockville, MD: National Institute of Mental Health, Psychopharmacology Research Branch.

- Daily diaries
  Citation: Beidel, D.C., Neal, A.M., Lederer, A.S. The feasibility and validity of a daily diary for the assessment of anxiety in children. *Behavior Therapy*, 22:505-517, 1991.

- Global Assessment Scale (GAS)
  Citation: Endicott, J., Spitzer, R.L., *et al*. The Global Assessment Scale. A procedure for measuring overall severity of psychiatric disturbance. *Archives of General Psychiatry*, 33:766-771, 1976.

- Leyton Obsessional Inventory—Child Version
  Citation: Berg, C.Z., Rapoport, J.L., Flament, M. The Leyton Obsessional Inventory—Child Version. *Journal of the American Academy of Child and Adolescent Psychiatry*, 25:84-91, 1986.

- Self-Assessment Manikin (SAM)
  Citation: Lang, P.J., Cuthbert, B.N. Affective information processing and the assessment of anxiety. *Journal of Behavioral Assessment*, 6:376-395, 1984.

- Social Phobia and Anxiety Inventory for Children (SPAI-C)

Source: Marshall Christner A (ed). Adapted from the appendix of Measuring Outcomes in Children's Services. Providence RI: Manisses Communication Group, Inc., 1998. (Reprinted with permission.)

Citation: Beidel, D.C., Turner, S.M., Morris, T.L. A new inventory to assess childhood social anxiety and phobia: The Social Phobia and Anxiety Inventory for Children. *Psychological Assessment*, 7:73-79, 1995.

- Yale-Brown Obsessive Compulsive Scale (Y-BO CS)
Citation: Goodman, W.K., Price, L.H. Rating scales for obsessive-compulsive disorder. In M.A. Jenike, L. Baer, W.E. Minichielli (Eds.), *Obsessive Compulsive Disorders: Theory and Management, ed. 2*. Littleton, MA: Year Book Medical Publishers, 1990.

Attention-Deficit Hyperactivity Disorder

- Attention Deficit Disorder Evaluation Scale (ADDES)
Citation: McCarney, S.B. *The Attention Deficit Disorder Evaluation Scale*, Technical Manual. Columbia, MO: Hawthorne Press, 1989.

- Home Situations Questionnaire (HSQ)
Citation: Barkley, R.A., Edelbrock, C.S. Assessing situation variation in children's behavior problems: The Home and School Situations Questionnaires. In R. Prinz (Ed.) *Advances in Behavioral Assessment of Children and Families, Vol. 3*. Greenwich, CT: JAI Press, 1987.

- Interaction Behavior Questionnaire (IBQ)
Citation: Robin, A.L., Foster, S. *Negotiating Parent-Adolescent Conflict*. New York: Guilford Press, 1989.

- Issues Checklist
Citation: Robin, A.L., Foster, S. *Negotiating Parent-Adolescent Conflict*. New York: Guilford Press, 1989.

- Locke-Wallace Marital Adjustment Test (LWMAT)
Citation: Locke, H.J., Wallace, K.M. Short marital adjustment and prediction tests: Their reliability and validity. *Journal of Marriage and Family Living*, 21:251-255, 1959.

- Parenting Stress Index
Citation: Abidin, R. *The Parenting Stress Index*. Charlottesville, VA: Pediatric Psychology Press, 1986.

- Peabody Picture Vocabulary Test, revised (PPVT-R)
Citation: Dunn, L.M., Dunn, L.M. *Peabody Picture Vocabular. Test (revised)*. Circle Pines, MN; American Guidance Service, 1981.

- The Pupil Evaluation Inventory (PEI)
Citation: Pekarik E., Prinz R., *et al.* The Pupil Evaluation Inventory: A sociometric technique for assessing children's social behavior. *Journal of Abnormal Child Psychology*, 4:83-97, 1976.

- Revised Conners Parent Rating Scale (RCPRS)
Citation: Goyette, C.H., Conners, C.K., Ulrich, R.F. Normative data for Revised Conners Parent and Teacher Rating Scales, *Journal of Abnormal Child Psychology*, 6:221-236, 1978.

- The Social Skills Rating Scale (SSRS)
Citation- Gresham, F.M., Elliott, S.N. Social Skills Rating System: Manual. Circle Pines MN: American Guidance Service, 1990.

Autism

- Leiter International Performance Scale
Citation: Leiter, R.G. Part I of the manual for the 1948 revision of the Leiter International Performance Scale: Evidence of the reliability and validity of the Leiter Tests. *Psychology Service Center Journal,* 11:1-72, 1959.

- Peabody Picture Vocabulary Test—Revised
Citation: Dunn, L.M. *Peabody Picture Vocabulary Test-Revised*. Circle River, MN: American Guidance Service, 1981.

- Personality Inventory for Children
Citation: Wirt, R.D., Lachar, D., et al. *Multidimensional Descriptions of Child Personality: A Manual for the Personality Inventory for Children.* Los Angeles: Western Psychological Services, 1977.

- The Vineland Adaptive Behavior Scales
Citation: Sparrow, S.S., Balla, D.A., Cicchetti, D.V. *Interview Edition Survey Form Manual.* Circle Pines, MN: American Guidance Service, 1984.

- Weschler Intelligence Scale for Children—Revised (WISC-R)
Citation: Wechsler, D. *Manual for the Wechsler Intelligence Scale for Children*—Revised. New York: Psychological Corp., 1974.

Child Abuse and Neglect

- Achenbach Child Behavior Checklist (CBC)
Citation: Achenbach, T.M., Edelbrock, C. *Manual for Child Behavior Checklist.* Burlington VT: Queen City Printers, 1983.

- Achenbach Teacher Rating Scale
Citation: Achenbach, T.M., Edelbrock, C. *Manual for the Teacher's Report Form. Burlington.* University of Vermont Department of Psychiatry, 1986.

- The Adult/Adolescent Parenting Inventory (AAPI)
Citation: Bavolek, S.J., Kline, D.F., McLaughlin, J.A. *Adult/Adolescent Parenting Inventory.* Logan: Utah State University, 1978.

- Bayley Scales of Infant Development
Citation: Bayley, N. *Bayley Scales of Infant Development.* New York: Psychological Corp., 1969.

- Child Behavior Checklist (CBCL)
Citation: Achenbach, T.M. *Manual for the Child Behavior Checklist/4-18 and 1991 Profile.* Burlington: University of Vermont. 1991.

- Child Depression Inventory
Citation: Kovacs, M. Rating scales to assess depression in school-aged children. *Acta Paedopsychiatrica, 46:305-315, 1981.*

- Children's Impact of Traumatic Events Scales-Revised (CITES-R)
Citation: Wolfe, V.V., Gentile, C., et al. The Children's Impact of Traumatic Events Scale: A measure of post-sexual abuse PTSD symptoms. *Behavioral Assessment, 13:359-383, 1991.*

- Child Sexual Behavior Inventory (CSBI)
Citation: Friedrich, W.N., Grambsch, P., et al. Normative sexual behavior in children. *Pediatrics, 88:456-464, 1991.*

- Family Risk Scales
Citation: Magura, S., Moses, B.S., et al. *Assessing Risk and Measuring Change in Families: The Family Risk Scales.* Washington, DC: Child Welfare League of America, 1987.

- Home Observation for Measurement of the Environment (HOME)
Citation: Caldwell, B., Bradley, R. *Administration Manual: Home Observation for Measurement of the Environment.* Little Rock: University of Arkansas, 1978.

- Magura and Moses Child Well-Being Scales
Citation: Magura, S., Moses, B.S. *Outcome Measures for Child Welfare Services, Theory, and Applications.* Washington, DC: Child Welfare League of America, 1986.

- The Parent Reaction to Incest Disclosure Scale (PRIDS)
Citation: Everson, M.D., Hunter, W.M., et al. Maternal support following disclosure of incest. *American Journal of Orthopsychiatry,* 59:197-207, 1989.

- Piers Harris Self-Esteem Inventory
Citation: Schwartz, M., Friedman, R., et al. The relationship between conceptual tempo and depression in children. *Journal of Consulting and Clinical Psychology*, 50:488-490, 1982.

- Problems and Conditions in the Life of the Family
Citation: Beck, D.F., Jones, M.A. *Progress on Family Problems: A Nationwide Study of Clients' and Counselors' Views on Family Agency Services*. New York: Family Service Association of America, 1973.

Conduct Disorders

- Achenbach's Child Behavior Checklist (CBCL)
Citation: Achenbach, T.M. *Manual fot the Child Behavior Checklist/4-18 and 1991 Profile*. Burlington, VT: University of Vermont, Department of Psychiatry, 1991.

- Achenbach Teacher Report Form
Citation: Achenbach, T.M. *Manual for the Teacher's Report Form and 1991 Profile*. Burlington: University of Vermont Dept. of Psychiatry, 1991.

- Children's Action Tendency Scale (CATS)
Citation: Deluty, R.H. Children's Action Tendency Scale: A self-report measure of aggressiveness, assertiveness, and submissiveness in children. *Journal of Consulting and Clinical Psychology*, 47:1061-1071, 1979.

- Conners Parent Teacher Questionnaire (PTQ)
Citation: Conners, C.K. *Conners Rating Scales Manual*. North Tonawanda, NY: Multi-Health Systems, Inc., 1990.

- Conners Teacher Questionnaire (CTQ)
Citation: Conners, C.K. *Conners Rating Scales Manual*. North Tonawanda, NY: Multi-Health Systems, Inc., 1990.

- Eyberg Child Behavior Inventory
Citation: Eyberg, S.M. Parent and teacher behavior inventories for the assessment of conduct problem behaviors in children. In L. WandeCreek and T.L. Jackson (Eds.) *Innovations in Clinical Practice: A Source Book*, Vol. 11. Sarasota, FL: Professional Resource Press, 1992.

- Family Environment Scale (FES)
Citation: Moos, R.H., Insel, P.M., Humphrey, B. *Family, Work, and Group Environment Scales*. Palo Alto, CA: Consulting Psychologists Press, 1974.

- Global Clinical Judgments (Consensus) Scale
Citation: Campbell, M., Small, A.M., et al. Behavioral efficacy of haloperidol and lithium carbonate: A comparison in hospitalized aggressive children with conduct disorder. *Archives of General Psychiatry*, 41:650-656, 1984.

- Ontario Child Health Study scales
Citation: Boyle, M.H., Offord, D.R., et al. Evaluation of the revised Ontario Child Health Study scales. *Journal of Child Psychology and Psychiatry and Allied Disciplines*, 34:189-213, 1993.

- Overt Aggression Scale (OAS)
Citation: Yudofsky, S.C., Silver, J.M., et al. Overt aggression scale for objective rating of verbal and physical aggression. *American Journal of Psychiatry*, 143(1):35-39, 1986.

- Parental Locus of Control Scale
Citation: Campis, L.K., Lyman, R.D., Prentice-Dunn, S. The parental locus of control scale: Development and validation. *Journal of Clinical Child Psychology*, 15:260-267, 1986.

- Parent-Child Rating Scale
Citation: Hightower, A.D. *The Parent-Child Rating Scale*. Rochester, NY: Department of Psychology, University of Rochester, 1990.

- Parenting Stress Index (PSI)

Citation: Abidin, R.R. *Parenting Stress Index Manual*. 3rd ed. Charlottesville, VA: Pediatric Psychology Press, 1990.

- POMS

Citation: Walker, M.K., Sprague, R.L., et al. Effects of methylphenidate hydrochloride on the subjective reporting of mood in children with attention deficit disorder. *Issues in Mental Health Nursing*, 9:373-385, 1988.

- Preschool Behavior Questionnaire (PBQ)

Citation: Behar, L.B., Stringfield, S. A behavior rating scale for the preschool child. *Developmental Psychology*, 10:601-610, 1974.

- Pupil Evaluation Inventory (PEI)

Citation: Pekarik, E.G., Prinz, R.H., et al. The Pupil Evaluation Inventory: A sociometric technique for assessing children's social behavior. *Journal of Abnormal Child Psychology*, 4:83-97, 1976.

- Risk Factor Interview

Citation: Kazdin, A.E., Mazurick, J.L., Bass, D. Risk for attrition in treatment of antisocial children and families. *Journal of Clinical Child Psychology*, 22:2-16, 1993.

- School Social Behavior Scale

Citation: Merrell, K.W. Using behavioral rating scales to assess social skills and antisocial behavior in school settings: Development of the School Social Behavior Scales. *School Psychology Review*, 22:115-133, 1993.

- Self-Report Delinquency Checklist (SRD)

Citation: Elliott, D.S., Dunford, F.W., Huizinga, D. The identification and prediction of career offenders utilizing self-reported and official data. In J.D. Burchard and S.N. Burchard (Eds.), *Preventing Delinquent Behavior*. Newbury Park, CA: Sage, 1987.

- Self-Report Delinquency Questionnaire (SRDQ)

Citation: LeBlanc, M., Fréchette, M. *Male Criminal Activity from Childhood Through Youth: Multilevel and Developmental Perspective*. New York: Springer-Verlag, 1989.

- Social Behavior Questionnaire (SBQ)

Citation: Loeber, R., Tremblay, R.E., et al. Continuity and desistance in disruptive boys' early fighting at school. *Developmental and Psychopathology*, 1:39-50, 1989.

- Social Interaction Observation System

Citation: Neckerman, H.J., Asher, K., Pavlidis, K. *Social Interaction Observation System*. Seattle, Wash: Harborview Injury Prevention and Research Center, 1994.

Cultural Competence

- Cultural Competence Self-Assessment Instrument

Cost: $25.95

Citation: Child Welfare League of America. *Cultural Competence Self-Assessment Instrument*. Washington, DC: Child Welfare League of America, 1993. Contact: (800) 407-6273 and refer to #5065 for more information.

Depression and Suicide

- Antisocial Behaviour Scale (ABS)

Citation: Olweus, D. Prevalence and incidence in the study of antisocial behaviour: Definitions and measurement. In M.W. Klein (Ed.), *Cross-National Research in Self-Reported Crime and Delinquency*. Dordrecht, the Netherlands: Kluwer, 1989.

- Beck Depression Inventory

Citation: Beck, A.T., Ward, C.H., et al. An inventory for measuring depression. *Archives of General Psychiatry*, 4:561-571, 1961.

- Children's Depression Inventory (CDI)

  Citation: Kovacs, M., Beck, F.T. An empirical clinical approach toward a definition of childhood depression. In J.G. Schulterbrandt, A. Raskin (Eds.) *Depression in Childhood: Diagnosis, Treatment and Conceptual Models.* New York: Raven Press, 1977.

- Depression Self-Rating Scale

  Citation: Asarnow, J.R., Carlson, G.A. Depression Self-Rating Scale: Utility with child psychiatric inpatients. *Journal of Consulting and Clinical Psychology,* 53: 491-499, 1985.

- Global Assessment Scale for children (C-GAS)

  Citation: Shaffer, D., Gould, M.S., *et al.* A children's Global Assessment Scale (CGAS). *Archives of General Psychiatry,* 40:1228-1231, 1983.

- Measure of Adolescent Potential for Suicide (MAPS)

  Citation: Eggert, L.L., Thompson, E.A., Herting, J.R. A measure of adolescent potential for suicide (MAPS): Development and preliminary findings. *Suicide and Life-Threatening Behavior,* 24(4):359-381, 1994.

- NIMH/Center for Epidemiological Studies-Depression Scale (CES-D)

  Citation: Radloff, L.S. The CES-D scale: A self-report depression scale for research in the general population. *Applied Psychological Measurement,* 1 (3):385-401, 1977.

- Revised Children's Manifest Anxiety Scale (RCMAS)

  Citation: Reynolds, C., Richmond, B. What I think and feel: A Revised Measure of Children's Manifest Anxiety. *Journal of Abnormal Child Psychology,* 6:271-280, 1978.

- Reynolds Adolescent Depression Scale (RADS)

  Citation: Reynolds, A. *The Reynolds Adolescent Depression Scale.* Madison, WI: University of Wisconsin, 1981.

- Rosenberg's Self-Esteem Scale

  Citation: Rosenberg, M. *Society and the Adolescent Self-Image.* Princeton, NJ: Princeton University Press, 1965.

- Schedule for Affective Disorders and Schizophrenia (K-SADS)

  Citation: Edelbrock, C., Costello, A. Structured psychiatric interviews for children. In M. Rutter, T. Hussain, I. Lann (Eds.) *Assessment and Diagnosis in Child Psychopathology.* London: Fulton.

- Social Adjustment Inventory for Children and Adolescents (SAICA)

  Citation: John, K., Gammon, D., *et al.* The Social Adjustment Inventory for Children and Adolescents (SAICA): Testing of a new semistructured interview. *Journal of the American Academy of Child and Adolescent Psychiatry,* 26:898-911, 1987.

- Streamlined Longitudinal Interval Continuation Evaluation

  Citation- Keller, M.B., Lavori, P.W., *et al.* The Longitudinal Interval Follow-up Evaluation: A comprehensive method for assessing outcome in prospective longitudinal studies. *Archives of General Psychiatry,* 44:540-548, 1987.

- Suicide Probability Scale (SPS)

  Citation: Cull, J.G., Gill, W.S. *Suicide Probability Scale: Manual.* Los Angeles: Western Psychological Services, 1982.

- Warr & Jackson's self-esteem inventory

  Citation: Warr, P., Jackson, P. Self-esteem and unemployment among young workers. *Travail Humain,* 46:355-366, 1983.

Eating Disorders

- Anoretic Outcome Scale

Contact: Eckert, E.D., Box 393 Mayo Building, University of Minnesota Hospitals, Minneapolis, MN 55455

- Body Shape Questionnaire

Citation: Cooper, P.J., Taylor, M.J., *et al.* The development and validation of the Body Shape Questionnaire. *International Journal of Eating Disorders,* 6:485-494, 1987.

- Camberwell Family Interview (CFI)

Citation: Vaughn, C.E., Left, J.P. The measurement of expressed emotion in the families of psychiatric patients. *British Journal of Social and Clinical Psychology,* 15:157-165, 1976.

- Eating Attitudes Test (EAT)

Use: Measures the frequency of 40 items representing common symptoms of anorexia.
Citation: Garner, D.M., Garfinkel, P.E. The eating attitudes test: An index of the symptoms of anorexia nervosa. *Psychological Medicine,* 9:273-279, 1979.
Time: 10 minutes.

- Eating Disorder Examination

Citation: Cooper, Z., Fairburn, C.G. The Eating Disorder Examination: A semi-structured interview for the assessment of the specific psychopathology of eating disorders. *International Journal of Eating Disorders,* 6:1-8, 1987.

- Eating Disorder Inventory (EDI)

Use: Assesses psychological and behavioral disturbances. 64-item self-report with eight subscales - drive for thinness, bulimia, body dissatisfaction, ineffectiveness, perfectionism, interpersonal distrust, interoceptive awareness, maturity fears.
Citation: Garner D.M. and Olmstead M.P.. *Eating Disorder Inventory Manual.* Psychological Assessment Resources Inc., 1984.
Time: Less than 20 minutes.

- The 'BITE'

Use: 30 items relating to symptoms, behavior, and dieting; second subscale measures severity.
Citation: Henderson M. and Freeman C.P.L. A self-rating scale for bulimia: The 'BITE.' *British Journal of Psychiatry,* 150:18-24, 1987.
Time: Less than 10 minutes.

- Morgan-Russell Outcome Assessment Schedule

Citation: Morgan, H.G., Hayward, A.E. Clinical assessment of anorexia nervosa: The Morgan-Russell Outcome Assessment Schedule. *British Journal of Psychiatry,* 152:367-371, 1988.

- Three-Factor Eating Questionnaire

Citation: Stunkard, A.J., Messick, S. The three-factor eating questionnaire to measure dietary restraint, disinhibition and hunger. *Journal of Psychosomatic Research,* 29:71-83, 1985.

Juvenile Delinquency

- Adolescent Behavior Checklist (ABC)

Citation: Demb, H., Brier, N., Huron, R. The adolescent behavior checklist. Unpublished manuscript, 1986.

- Behavior Frequency Scales

Citation: Tolan, P., Guerra, N. *What Works in Reducing Adolescent Violence: An Empirical Review of the Field.* Boulder, CO. The Center for the Study and Prevention of Violence, 1994.

- Beliefs Supporting Aggression

Citation: Farrell, A.D., Danish, S.J., *et al.* Evaluation of data screening methods in surveys of adolescents' drug use. Psychological assessment. *Journal of Consulting and Clinical Psychology,* 3:295-298, 1991.

- Brief Symptom Inventory

Citation: Derogatis, L.R. *Brief Symptom Inventory.* Baltimore: Clinical Psychometric Research, 1975.

Child Behavior Checklist (CBCL)

Citation: Achenbach, T.M., Edelbrock, C. *Manual for the Teachers' Report Form.* Burlington, VT: Department of Psychiatry, University of Vermont, 1986.

- Developmental Disability Screening

Citation: Brier, N., Carlson-Perez, E., Kaufman, J. The evolution and application of a screening instrument to identify adolescents with developmental disabilities. *Juvenile and Family Court Journal,* 40(1):35-42, 1989.

- Family Assessment Measure III

Citation: Skinner, H.A., Steinhauer, P.D., Santa Barbara, J. The family assessment measure. *Canadian Journal of Community Mental Health,* 2(2):91-105, 1983.

- Multidimensional Measure of Children's Perceptions of Control (MMCPC)

Citation: Connell, J.P. A new multidimensional measure of children's perception of control. *Child Development,* 56:1018-1041, 1985.

- Perceived Contingency Behavioral Domain Scale

Citation: Hartsfield, F., Licht, B.G., *et al.* Control beliefs and behavior problems of elementary school children. Paper presented at annual meeting of the American Psychological Association, New Orleans, LA, 1989.

- The Piers-Harris Self-Concept Scale

Citation: Piers, E.V. *Revised Manual for the Piers-Harris Self-Concept Scale.* Los Angeles: Western Psychological Services, 1984.

- Problem Behavior History

Citation: .Tolan, P., Guerra, N. *What Works in Reducing Adolescent Violence: An Empirical Review of the Field.* Boulder, CO: The Center for the Study and Prevention of Violence, 1994.

- Revised Behavior Problem Checklist

Citation: Quay, H.C., Peterson, D.R. *Manual for the Revised Behavior Problem Checklist.* Coral Gables, FL: University of Miami, 1987.

- Wide Range Achievement Test-Revised (WAT-R)

Citation: Jastak, S., Wilkinson, G.S. Wide Range Achievement Test-Revised, *Administration Manual.* Los Angeles: Western Psychological Services, 1984.

Miscellaneous Disorders

- Adolescent Problem Inventory (API)

Citation: Gaffney, L.R., McFall, R.M. A comparison of social skills in delinquent and nondelinquent adolescent girls using a behavioral role-playing inventory. *Journal of Consulting and Clinical Psychology,* 49:959-967, 1981.

- Behavior Symptom Inventory (BSI)

Citation: Derogatis, L.R., Spencer, P.M. The Brief Symptom Inventory (BSI) *Administration, Scoring, and Procedures Manual-I.* Baltimore: Clinical Psychometric Research, 1982.

- Brief Psychiatric Rating Scale (BPRS)

Citation: Overall, J.E., Gorham, D.E. The Brief Psychiatric Rating Scale. *Psychological Reports,* 10:799-812, 1961.

- Brief Psychiatric Rating Scale for Children (BPRS-C)

Citation: Overall, J., Pfefferbaum, B. A Brief Psychiatric Rating Scale for Children. *Innovations,* 3:264, 1984.

- Bunney-Hamburg Psychosis Rating Scale

Citation: Bunney, W.E., Hamburg, D.A. Methods for reliable longitudinal observation of behavior. *Archives of General Psychiatry,* 9:280-294, 1963.

- Child and Adolescent Functional Assessment Scale (CAFAS)

Citation: Hodges, K. *Child and Adolescent Functional Assessment Scales*. Nashville, TN: Vanderbilt Child Mental Health Services Evaluation Project, 1990.

- Client Description Form (CDF)

Citation: New York State Office of Mental Health. *Client Description Form*. Albany: Author, Bureau of Evaluation and Services Research, 1990.

- Devereux Rating Scale

Use: 40-item scale with four subscale areas including depression, physical symptoms and fears, interpersonal problems, and inappropriate behaviors and feelings. Oneversion for children, another for adolescents.
Cost: Complete kit - $95.
Time: 5 minutes to hand score.
Contact: The Psychological Corporation, Order Service Center, P.O. Box 839954, San Antonio, TX 78283-3954; (800) 228-0752.

- Devereux Scales of Mental Disorders (DSMD)

Use: 111-item child form and 110-item adolescent form measures a child's risk of emotional or behavioral disorders.
Cost: Complete kit - $130.
Training: Can be either a behavioral health professional, teacher, or parent.
Time: 15 minutes.
Contact: The Psychological Corporation, Order Service Center, P.O. Box 839954, San Antonio, TX 78283-3954; (800) 228-0752.

- Family Adaptability and Cohesion Evaluation Scale III (FACES III)

Citation: Olson, D.H., Portner, J., Lavee, Y. *Family Adaptability and Cohesion Scales III*. St. Paul: University of Minnesota, Family Social Science Department, 1985.

- The Global Assessment Scale (GAS)

Citation: Endicott, J., Spitzer, R.L., *et al*. The Global Assessment Scale: A procedure for measuring overall severity of psychiatric disturbance. *Archives of General Psychiatry,* 33:766-771, 1976.

- Parent Daily Report Checklist (PDR)

Citation: Chamberlain, P., Reid, J.B. Parent observation and report of child symptoms. *Behavioral Assessment,* 9:97-109, 1987.

- Personality Inventory for Youth (PIY)

Citation: Lacher, D., Gruber, C.P. *A Manual for the Personality Inventory for Youth (PIY): A Self-Report Companion to the Personality Inventory for Children (PIC)*. Los Angeles: Western Psychological Services, 1994.

- Revised Behavior Problem Checklist

Citation: Quay, H.C., Peterson, D.R. *Manual for the Revised Behavior Problem Checklist*. Published privately, 1987.

- Revised Symptom Checklist (SCL-90-R)

Citation: Derogatis, L.R. *SCL-90-R. Administration, Scoring and Procedures Manual, II*. Towson, Maryland: Clinical Psychometric Research, 1983.

- Scale for the Assessment of Negative Symptoms (SANS)

Citation: Andreasen, N.C. The Scale for the Assessment of Negative Symptoms (SANS). Iowa City, The University of Iowa, 1983.

- Scale for the Assessment of Positive Symptoms (SAPS)

Citation:. Andreasen, N.C. *The Scale for the Assessment of Positive Symptoms (SAPS)*. Iowa City: The University of Iowa, 1984.

Risky Behaviors

- Restrictiveness and Living Environments Scale (ROLES)
Citation: Hawkins, R.P., Almeida, M.C., *et al.* A scale to measure restrictiveness of living environments for troubled children and youths. *Hospital and Community Psychiatry,* 43:54-58, 1992.

- Sexual Risk Behavior Assessment Schedule-Youth
Citation: Meyer-Bahlburg, H.F.L., Ehrhardt, A.A., *et al. Sexual Risk Behavior Assessment Schedule-Youth.* New York: New York State Psychiatric Institute and Department of Psychiatry, College of Physicians and Surgeons of Columbia University, 1988.

- Suicide Probability Scale
Citation: Cull, J.G., Gill, W.S. *Suicide Probability Scale: Manual.* Los Angeles: Western Psychological Services, 1981.

- Taxonomy of Problematic Social Situations (TPOS)
Citation: Dodge, K.A., McClaskey, C.L., Feldman, E.L. A situational approach to the assessment of social competence in children. *Journal of Consulting and Clinical Psychology,* 53:344-353, 1985.

Substance Abuse

- Adolescent Drinking Index (ADI)
Use: 20 questions identify adolescents with problem drinking behaviors.
Cost: $48 for initial kit; additional per test cost. Discount for graduate students and training purposes with university.
Training: Must have a college degree in counseling, psychology, or related field and be approved (after training) by PAR, Inc.
Time: 5 minutes.
Contact: Psychological Assessment Resources Inc., P.O. Box 998, Odessa, FL; (800) 331-8378.

- Drug Abuse Screening Test (DAST)
Use: 28 items are used for clinical screening and treatment evaluation research.
Cost: Public domain — no fee.
Citation: Skinner, H.A. The Drug Abuse Screening Test. *Addictive Behaviors,* 7:363-371, 1982.
Sample question: No. 4—Can you get through the week without using drugs (other than those required for medical reasons)?

- Parent Satisfaction Scale
Citation: Besalal, V.A., Azrin, N.H. The reduction of parent-youth problems by reciprocity counseling. *Behaviour Research and Therapy,* 19:297-301, 1981.

- Quay Problem Behavior Checklist
Citation: Quay, H.C. Measuring dimensions of deviant behavior: The behavior problem checklist. *Journal of Abnormal Child Psychology,* 5:277-287, 1977.

- Youth Satisfaction Scale
Citation: Besalal, V.A., Azrin, N.H. The reduction of parent-youth problems by reciprocity counseling. *Behaviour Research and Therapy,* 19:297-301, 1981.

Chapter 7

Setting and Meeting Performance and Accreditation Requirements

Uncertain Outcome

Behavioral Health Care Organizations Are Viewing JCAHO's ORYX Initiative With Apprehension

Martin Sipkoff

An oryx is an African gazelle, known for speed and grace. In capital letters, it's also the name of the performance-based accreditation initiative launched by the Joint Commission on Accreditation of Healthcare Organizations (JCAHO) in February 1997. But for behavioral health organizations concerned about the cost and efficiency of the ORYX initiative, the name may be a misnomer. "We are finding the process complicated, time-consuming, and confusing," says a quality improvement manager for a stand-alone psychiatric hospital system who, like several representatives of behavioral organizations interviewed for this article, requested anonymity. "The problem is choosing measures that have meaning in a behavioral setting, let alone a (reporting) system that we can afford and understands our internal system."

JCAHO accredits hospitals and other health care organizations, like home care and outpatient providers, and makes its performance reports available to payers and the public. JCAHO accreditations traditionally have been conducted through triennial commission surveys and on-site visits. The ORYX initiative, by contrast, requires organizations to electronically report quarterly outcomes based on specific measures. The resulting accreditation process will be more detailed and meaningful to consumers, say JCAHO officials. They hope to begin releasing behavioral accreditation information containing ORYX data by 2001.

ORYX is important to health care organizations because nearly all MCOs require that their network providers be JCAHO accredited. "JCAHO is a presence that influences the organizations that provide services to many individuals. So it is important by its very existence," says Howard Waxman, research director of the Belmont Center for Comprehensive Treatment, the mental health facility of Albert Einstein Medical Center in Philadelphia. Waxman says Belmont has had an ongoing outcomes measurement program, and he applauds the ORYX initiative for "its potential to shift attention to those processes that determine the results of care." But Waxman, like other providers, has some apprehension. "At the same time, organizations are legitimately concerned about the added burden and expense of collecting the necessary data," he says.

Some behavioral health organizations may be concerned about the usefulness of the ORYX initiative because they habitually view the value of quality and outcomes measurements with some skepticism, say health care professionals. "Many behavioral health organizations are angry, scared, or confused by the ORYX initiative," says Joan Betzold, president of Professional Services Consultants Inc., a health care consulting firm in Bel Air MD. "Many view it as just another expense to be added to what they feel is the already high price of being accredited. Others feel it is just another attempt by regulators to tell them how to run their business."

Several representatives of behavioral health organizations questioned about ORYX said they did not wish to be quoted on their views about the initiative, citing concerns that it could cast doubt on their willingness to comply. "JCAHO is a powerful organization that is making a worthwhile attempt to make outcomes part of the accreditation process," says the director of a large inpatient psychiatric facility. "But we wonder how well they understand the complicated nature of behavioral health outcomes. The comparative outcomes data just doesn't exist in behavioral health care like it does in general medicine."

The lack of readily quantifiable performance measures is of concern to many behavioral health organizations. Many community mental health centers (CMHCs) are confused about what will be required under the ORYX initiative in order to maintain accreditation, says Lesa Yawn of the Yawn Consulting Group, Inc., a healthcare consulting firm in Virginia Beach VA, and a consultant with the National Council for Community Behavioral Healthcare in Rockville MD. "Organizations are concerned and unclear about where all this is headed," Yawn says. "Publicly funded organizations, like CMHCs, are particularly uncertain about what performance measurements will be required and how they are to report to JCAHO."

The Measures Predicament

Under ORYX, all 24-hour organizations will report their measurements through "performance measurement systems," which are data collection and reporting organizations like Access Measurement Systems, Inc., in Ashland MA, the Center for Healthcare Industry Performance Studies in Columbus OH, or the Gallup Organization in Lincoln NE. So choosing a system is the first hurdle being faced by behavioral health care organizations. That task is predicated on a determination of which measures to select to report to a chosen system and making certain the system is compatible with a organization's internal data collection system. Therefore, it is the issue of determining meaningful measures that most concerns organizations, says Yawn. "Choosing measures is what has organizations most concerned right now," she says. "The purpose and use of outcomes measurement is an ongoing issue in the behavioral health community, and the issue is made more urgent by the ORYX initiative."

Waxman agrees. "On the one hand, JCAHO has taken an enormous step in saying that we need to stop just looking at costs and start looking at outcomes," he says. "They are trying to integrate outcome monitoring with quality improvement. Unfortunately, we still need adequate software technology to make this function at the agency level."

The determination of valid and meaningful performance measures has been "an ongoing problem in the accreditation process for behavioral health organizations," says James Gallagher, chief executive officer of Charter Behavioral Health System of New Jersey, a 426-bed free-standing psychiatric hospital in Summit NJ. "The problem is quantifying measures," he says. "There has always been difficulty in this industry in agreeing upon meaningful objective measures."

For example, one performance indicator used by some measurement systems is psychiatric hospital readmissions. "Readmission rates may not be an especially good indicator of outcomes in terms of recovery because it is too hard to distinguish 'good' admissions from 'bad,' or unnecessary, admissions, and comparing readmissions across demographic groups can be misleading," says one provider.

Waxman says that "many of us are skeptical about the value of readmission rate as an indicator of quality," but adds that he "heard a medical director of a hospital claim that readmission rates were drastically lowered when case managers followed-up discharged patients to make sure that the first outpatient appointment was kept. This was an anecdotal account, but, if true, it suggests that readmission may be an indicator of good aftercare arrangements." If properly used, it could in fact be a meaningful ORYX indicator, Waxman says.

ORYX will serve "a useful purpose, if JCAHO picks performance indicators that function at the agency level," Waxman continues, "those that are used by the provider to measure effectiveness, such as enhanced functionality, and are actually helpful to enhance patient outcomes. But the problem is that many agencies and individual clinicians are not entirely thrilled with the choice of ORYX vendors or with the systems" because some providers "are not satisfied with the measurement process and others want systems that do more than just measure—that also provide useful diagnostic tools," says Waxman.

JCAHO Reassures Organizations

Sharon L. Sprenger, JCAHO's associate director for research and development, says that a Request for Indicators survey JCAHO conducted in late summer 1998 will facilitate the ability of behavioral health organizations to choose effective measures, but she says she understands that the issue is of concern to those organizations. She says that JCAHO reviews all measures prior to a system offering the measures for use in meeting ORYX requirements. "We appreciate the challenge organizations face in choosing measurements and systems," she says. "We are offering educational seminars and materials to organizations to help them select a performance measurement system that meets their needs."

JCAHO officials call ORYX the "Next Evolution in Accreditation," and say that once it is fully implemented, it will significantly enhance the current survey process through the use of an accurate and effective outcomes measurement. "We are aware there is concern among behavioral health organizations about the ORYX process, about how it will work and the choice of effective (performance) measures," says Mary Cesare-Murphy, executive director of JCAHO's behavioral health care accreditation program, "but we believe that once the process is in place, organizations will appreciate its effectiveness."

ORYX is a long-term, ongoing undertaking that "will establish a data-driven, continuous survey and accreditation process" that will complement the current more static process of periodic record harvesting, process evaluation, and on-site visits, say JCAHO officials. (On-site visits are scheduled to continue under ORYX.) "The ORYX initiative and its vision of a data-driven, more continuous accreditation process will increase the value of accreditation to all its users and provide greater stimulus to healthcare organizations to improve their processes," says Deborah M. Nadzam, JCAHO's vice president for performance measurement. "Through performance measurement and comparative analysis, the quality of care provided to the public can be improved and accountability for results can be demonstrated."

How ORYX Works for 24-Hour Health Systems

As of October 1998, JCAHO had accepted more than 200 systems for provider use, about a third with measures applicable to behavioral health performance. (A list of accepted systems is available at JCAHO's Web site, **http://www.jcaho.org**.)

Organizations will pay these vendors as much as several thousand dollars a quarter to process their measurement data and transmit that data to JCAHO. A performance measurement system must be chosen by 24-hour behavioral health organizations, such as freestanding psychiatric hospitals and community mental health centers with inpatient clinics, by March 1, 1999. (The deadline for hospitals and long-term care organizations was March 1, 1998.)

By March 1999, a 24-hour behavioral health facility must:
- select a performance measurement system and
- choose up to five clinical, patient perception of care, or health status measures, or enough measures to address 20 percent of the patient population, whichever is less. The minimum number of measures required is two.

An example of perception of care measures provided by JCAHO is patient satisfaction surveys that focus on the delivery of clinical care. "We are not looking for whether patients were satisfied with the attitude of the receptionist or the color of the treatment room, but measures related to actual delivery of health care services which may be condition specific, procedure specific, or address important functions of patient care, like medication use," says Sprenger. "We're not saying nonclinical perception of care measures aren't worthwhile for internal quality improvement, but they are not useful as the focus of the accreditation process." Health status measures address functional well-being of specific populations, both in general and in relation to specific conditions, and demonstrate change over time, for example, mental functioning, pain reduction or social functioning.

The initial quarter for which a provider must collect measurement data is the third quarter of 1999 and organizations must submit data through their performance measurement systems by March 31, 2000.

How ORYX Works for Non-24-Hour Programs

The ORYX requirements for behavioral health organizations that do not offer any 24-hour care are different. They are required to:
- Participate in a "Request for Indicators" survey project, which was completed in

fall 1998, in which the Joint Commission requested specific information about measures currently being used by the organizations to meet performance improvement standards. ("Indicators" is another word for performance measures.) The responses will be used to create a template of measures from which these types of behavioral health care organizations would then select measures.

- Select at least two measures from the resulting template and inform the Joint Commission of its selections by June 30, 1999.
- Begin collecting data for the selected template measures in the third quarter of 1999.
- Share measurement and improvement activities with surveyors during regular on-site surveys.

Sprenger says JCAHO plans to share the resulting template with non-24-hour behavioral health organizations in early 1999. Non-24-hour behavioral health organizations do not have to contract with a performance measurement system, "but in the future we may ask those organizations to contract with a system," Sprenger says. Organizations that offer both 24-hour behavioral health services and non-24-hour services at this time only need to meet the requirements for 24-hour organizations.

JCAHO requires that accredited organizations contract with only other organizations that "meet the intent of JCAHO standards and requirements." So CMHCs that contract with accredited hospitals that operate psychiatric units, which many do, must contract with organizations meeting ORYX requirements or they will fail to be in compliance. "It is this type of requirement that concerns CMHCs," says Yawn. "They will fail to be in compliance with the hospitals they contract with are not in compliance. So even if they themselves are not required to hire a performance system, the people they do business with are, and so they will need to be able to comply with the information requirements of those organizations. They will need to be able to supply the information the hospital requires in order for the hospital to be able to report its information to its system and then to the Joint Commission."

Choosing a System

By fall 1998, many behavioral health organizations reported forming committees to examine performance measurement systems. JCAHO defines a performance measurement system as "an interrelated set of process measures, outcome measures, or both, that facilitates internal comparisons over time and external comparisons of an organization's performance." "Performance measurement systems will meet JCAHO's accreditation needs by supplying comparative data for an organization within that system that can be incorporated into the survey and accreditation process and they will be used to monitor an accredited organization's performance between on-site surveys," Sprenger says.

"Simply stated, the process for selecting an ORYX vendor, or performance measurement system, is no different than selecting any other information vendor for the health care field," says Genie Skypek, a psychologist and behavioral healthcare consultant in Tampa FL. "An organization must fully understand its externally defined requirements as well as its internal needs and then must fully review the systems available to meet those requirements and needs, systematically eliminating those that cannot meet them."

"We are looking carefully at the costs of systems," says one provider, "but we also have to examine data system compatibility and reliability. One of the things that is making all that difficult is we're not sure which performance measures we're planning to use, which makes it hard to decide which system to use, and to date vendors can't give a lot of guidance on that."

JCAHO provides an outline, titled "Framework for the Selection of Performance Measurement Systems," that can help guide organizations in choosing a system. That document, and related materials, are available at the JCAHO Web site, **http://www.jacho.org/perfmeas**.

The value of the contribution of the ORYX enhancement to the JCAHO accreditation system will reflect the degree of commitment individual organizations make to the initiative, says Skypek. "For too long our field has been saying that we have no good outcome measures, so we should not begin the process of systematically measuring outcomes and comparing ourselves to other organizations. But at some point, we must begin to look more closely at what processes produce what outcomes. ORYX may well serve as a necessary catalyst for us to do what we should have been doing all along. Organizations who embrace the challenge and use the data they collect to improve the validity of the data and their outcomes while remaining efficient will have no difficulty complying with JCAHO's expectations from this new accreditation process. That is their expectation—that we will begin to find measures that help us in our efforts to achieve the best outcomes. Any data which reflects an organization's commitment to that process will only help their accreditation status."

New JCAHO Sentinel Event Policy Change Raises Concerns

The Joint Commission's decision to encourage health care organizations to report sentinel events or risk an Accreditation Watch designation raises concerns about both confidentiality and liability.

Health care providers may wonder what kind of confidentiality the Joint Commission will provide should they choose to self-report a sentinel event.

With privacy issues unclear, providers may also worry about the effect of self-reporting on their contracts, public image, and client base.

JCAHO Encourages Self-Reporting

The JCAHO changed its sentinel event policy last November to encourage all accredited organizations to self-report sentinel events within five business days of the incident.

A sentinel event is an unexpected occurrence involving death or serious physical or psychological injury. Serious injury includes the loss of limb or function. The JCAHO expanded the definition last November to include any process variance for which a recurrence would carry a significant chance of a serious adverse outcome.

In addition, an organization must conduct a root-cause analysis of the event and report its results to the JCAHO within 30 days. The Joint Commission will not place an organization on Accreditation Watch if it determines the root-cause analysis to be "thorough and credible."

But the Joint Commission will conduct an on-site visit if it finds out about the sentinel event five days after its occurrence from another source, such as a newspaper article. If surveyors confirm the incident is a sentinel event, the Joint Commission will place the organization on Accreditation Watch. The new policy will become effective on April 1, 1998.

Mixed Reactions To New Policy

The most common sentinel event the JCAHO investigates at behavioral health care facilities is inpatient suicides. Organizations must also take steps to prevent patient assaults on one another or staff, and patient escapes from the building or during trips, which all may fall into the Joint Commission's definition of a sentinel event.

Arthur Ring, senior consultant with Echo Management Group in Tampa, FL, has mixed reactions to the JCAHO policy change, which can benefit an organization by forcing it to examine its underlying assumptions about process stability. But, he says, self-examination isn't easy for health care organizations because of the accompanying baggage.

"It is a wonderful opportunity, if you can disengage yourself from the legal issues and the emotions," he says. "Here's an opportunity to know more about yourself."

He recommends that health care organizations consider hiring an independent, outside consultant to facilitate the root-cause analysis. That person will enter the process with an unbiased view and without the emotional involvement that staff may bring to the table. A hired consultant, he says, should be willing to challenge the underlying orthodoxies of the organization and be able to operate outside organizational assumptions.

Source: Reproduced from Briefings on Behavioral Health Accreditation, *© 1998 Opus Communications, P.O. Box 1168, Marblehead, MA 01945, (781) 639-1872. Used with permission.*

Liability Issues

The JCAHO policy change also raises concerns about confidentiality and liability if an organization chooses to report a sentinel event, Ring says. Reporting can raise malpractice questions, possibly endanger contracts, and potentially threaten a client base. "What kind of protection is the JCAHO going to offer regarding confidentiality?" Ring wonders. "I don't see any reassurance in writing that the JCAHO has thought this through." He recommends that organizations keep the names of patients and staff involved in the sentinel event out of the root-cause analysis. "The analysis focuses primarily on systems and process, not individual performance," according to the JCAHO's revised Sentinel Event Procedures of November 8, 1997.

While the Joint Commission doesn't publish the notification it receives of sentinel events or the root-cause analysis summaries it requires, the documents could be subject to legal discovery by lawyers.

The JCAHO won't announce the sentinel event publicly during the 30 days it allows the organization to perform the root-cause analysis.

But if someone calls and specifically inquires about the incident, it will acknowledge that it is aware of the sentinel event review process going on at the organization.

The JCAHO will issue the formal notification of any change in accreditation status, Type I recommendations, and follow-up requirements after reviewing the root-cause analysis and the results of its on-site visit (if it conducts one). Any change in status is public information.

Ring strongly advises health care facilities to consult with their legal counsel before reporting a sentinel event to the Joint Commission. Ring expects that attorneys for both health care providers and the JCAHO will continue to argue over the legal implications of the reporting requirements. "I see a lot of legal saber rattling going on," he says.

What To Do

The first thing Ring advises behavioral health care organizations to do is create a sentinel event policy immediately. "I would say that for an organization, if it doesn't have a policy in place, it needs to pronto," he says.

Each organization should involve clinical staff, board members, and its legal counsel in the policy creation, he says. Ring recommends that a policy spells out at least the following:

- The definition of a sentinel event, incorporating the JCAHO's elements
- The communication chain responsible for reporting a sentinel event
- The mechanism used to address the event (for example, an individual or a team)
- The resources staff will need to conduct an analysis, either internal or external (for example, an organization might use a state peer review board for assistance)
- A time frame for meeting the JCAHO's 30-day requirement for submitting a root-cause analysis.

Figure 1. What Should You Report?

Beginning April 1, the JCAHO wants health care organizations to report incidents that involve:
- an unanticipated death
- major permanent loss of bodily function
- infant abduction
- infant discharged to the wrong family
- rape (by another patient or staff member)
- hemolytic transfusion reaction
- surgery on the wrong patient or wrong body part

Figure 2. What Are the Most Common Types of Incidents?

The following list includes the most frequent types of sentinel events that the JCAHO investigated since 1996:
- Medication errors
- Inpatient suicides
- Surgery on the wrong side of the body
- Delays of treatment
- Patient restraint situations
- Transfusion errors
- Medical gases
- Infant abductions

Performance Measures Applicable To Behavioral Health Care Settings

Performance Measures

A performance measure or, as it is sometimes called, a performance indicator is a tool for generating clinical or nonclinical performance data. Clinical performance data are unbiased representations of client care processes or health outcomes.[1] Nonclinical performance data typically reflect the operation and outcomes of key support and administrative processes.

The following are among the multiple sources of performance measures: subject matter experts; professional literature; professional associations that may develop measures in relation to standards of practice or standards of care; behavioral health care facilities that define customized measures in tandem with the development of clinical guidelines or critical pathways; health systems that sometimes develop indicators to be used by their affiliated care delivery sites; and state mental health departments or other state authorities. Both public and private organizations with a vested interest in health care may develop performance measures and make those measures available.

Examples of Performance Measures

Many examples of performance measures are pertinent to behavioral health care settings. Some measures are clinical, whereas others may be administrative or operational. Some are robust, meaning that they are highly sensitive and specific so as to capture small degrees of change. Others are more general and are aimed at illustrating overall performance trends. Some examples follow.

Patrice Spath, ART, who works as a health care consultant, delineated a list of indicators that assess the quality of three aspects of behavioral health care: team treatment planning, implementation of the treatment plan, and documentation on the client record. Among the measures that she identified are the following:

- Percentage of suicidal clients placed on suicide precautions;
- Clients who are receiving lithium and whose vital signs are being recorded daily;
- Currency of treatment plans;
- Coordination of discharge planning;
- Development of aftercare plans; and
- Achievement of therapeutic recreation treatment goals.[2]

In 1996 the Maryland Quality Indicator Project identified four indicators for use by freestanding psychiatric hospitals and psychiatric acute care units in general hospitals. The measures capture data regarding the occurrence of specified critical incidents in relation to the total client population. These indicators are as follows:

- Injurious behaviors,
- Unplanned departures resulting in discharge,
- Transfers to an acute care (medical) unit, and
- Readmission within 15 days of discharge.[3]

Foundation Health PsychCare Services, a managed care provider with therapist affiliations across the country, developed a brief outcomes

---

Source: Using Performance Measurement to Improve Outcomes in Behavioral Health Care. Oakbrook Terrace IL: Joint Commission on Accreditation of Healthcare Organizations, copyright 1998, pages 15-26. Reprinted with permission.

> ### The National Library of Healthcare Indicators
>
> In 1997 the Joint Commission published the *National Library of Healthcare Indicators (NLHI): Health Plan and Network Edition*, a catalog of indicators that have been deemed by content experts to have face validity. It includes performance measures applicable to a wide variety of health care organizations.
>
> NLHI is a practical tool that organizes available, credible measures. NLHI's indicators are classified into four broad categories:
>
> 1. Clinical conditions;
> 2. Functional health status;
> 3. Satisfaction from the perspectives of consumers/enrollees, practitioners, and purchasers; and
> 4. Administrative and financial aspects of organizational performance.
>
> Each indicator in NLHI has its own profile that defines the measure, describes its focus and rationale, details its characteristics (including risk adjustment and stratification, if any), portrays its applicability to various health care delivery settings, and delineates the degree to which the indicator has been formally tested.
>
> NLHI is also available on the Joint Commission's Web site (**http://www.jcaho.org**).

tool called PROFILE. This tool consists of a small number of indicators designed to collect data on client functioning and problem resolution from both the consumer of service and therapist. Job, marriage/family, interpersonal relationships, and perception of current physical health are assessed via scaled questions. The degree of problem resolution for the precipitating problem is evaluated in the post-treatment period.[4]

Psychologists at the 1995 Annual Meeting of the American Psychological Association urged the development of new outcomes indicators for psychotherapy. It was recommended that performance measures examine therapeutic strategies targeted at promoting emotional and social support, cognitive restructuring, and training in coping skills as well as achieved outcomes such as changes in work product, lost days of work, and changes in social skills.[5]

Using Balanced Measures To Evaluate Organization Performance

A behavioral health care organization is a complex system performing interdependent clinical, support, administrative, and financial functions. These functions support the organization's mission through the accomplishment of key strategic and operational goals. Any effort to study and understand performance at the organizational level must also examine the performance of these various critical functions. For this reason, a behavioral health care facility should strive to develop and use a balanced performance measurement model.

A balanced performance measurement model is typically based on measures of outcomes, processes, and structures, as first described by Donabedian.[6] It also includes satisfaction measures to assess the perceptions and experiences of different vested parties, as discussed by Zastowny, et al.[7] The objective of a balanced measurement model is to evaluate organization performance by examining key functions from multiple critical perspectives. Input is sought from consumers, their significant others, staff, licensed independent practitioners, the surrounding community, purchasers, payers, and other interested parties. A balanced measurement model should elicit data and feedback about clinical performance, the performance of key administrative and business processes, the performance of employed staff and licensed independent practitioners, financial performance, and satisfaction levels. Table 1 provides a description of what a comprehensive, balanced measurement model for a behavioral health care organization should address.

Family of Measures

Sluyter and Martin endorse the balanced measurement model when they describe the need for behavioral health care organizations to develop and use a "family of measures," or in other words, a composite of individual measures that

Table 1. Components of a Balanced Measurement Model

1. **Health outcomes and functional status.** To what degree do the clients served
   - achieve clinical improvement, including symptom amelioration?
   - increase functional ability to maximal levels, return to usual routines of daily life, and self-report improvement?

2. **Satisfaction.** How satisfied are
   - consumers with their care experience, including the competence and compassion of staff, availability of needed care, and accessibility to essential services?
   - clients' significant others with the experiences of their loved one and with the education, support, and information offered to them?
   - payers and purchasers that the most comprehensive care is provided at the lowest cost and that service recipients return to a pretreatment level of functioning?
   - staff with the overall working environment?

3. **Clinical care processes.** Is the care provided
   - based on up-to-date practices?
   - reliably consistent?
   - appropriate and efficacious?
   - effective and efficient?
   - delivered competently?

4. **The operation of critical nonclinical processes.** Have the nonclinical processes that directly or indirectly support the delivery of care to consumers been identified and examined for
   - effectiveness?
   - consistency?
   - efficiency?
   - comprehensiveness?
   - currency?

5. **Resource management.** Is
   - staffing adequate?
   - necessary on-the-job-training provided?
   - essential capital equipment available?

6. **Financial performance.** Are
   - client lengths of stay and intensity of service levels acceptable?
   - operating costs at acceptable levels?
   - variances between projected and actual expenses acceptable?
   - revenue-to-expense ratios acceptable?
   - investments performing adequately?

describe an organization's performance from multiple perspectives: consumers, employees, suppliers, the external environment, and stakeholders. One of the expressed benefits of using a family of measures is that it facilitates a holistic view of organizational performance, thereby reducing the risks of focusing too much on individual measures.[8] Table 2 lists the characteristics of an effective family-of-measures performance measurement model.

Table 2. Characteristics of a Family-of-Measures Performance Measurement Model

An effective family-of-measures model should do the following:
1. Be linked to the organization's mission, vision, values, and strategic plan;
2. Be well communicated and understood throughout the organization;
3. Contain a focused, manageable number of measures that target key (strategic) performance areas;
4. Be technically sound, which is to say reliable, valid, and state of the art;
5. Be subjected to periodic systematic review and revision;
6. Provide information on performance levels and trends;
7. Be aligned with and reflective of the organization's reward and recognition systems;
8. Be developed with input from various stakeholders; and
9. Be pilot tested within the organization and revised based on the pilot experience before ongoing implementation.

Examples of Models of Balanced Measures of Performance

Significant efforts have been made to design balanced measures for behavioral health care. Many resources have been dedicated to the development and testing of individual performance measures and performance measurement systems.

The Institute for Behavioral Healthcare (IBH) collaborated with the University of Cincinnati on a project aimed at understanding the current use of performance indicators in mental health care delivery systems. This initiative, led by Teresa Kramer, research coordinator for the IBH project and director of research for University Managed Care/University Psychiatric Services at the University of Cincinnati, identified five general performance domains in the initial phase of the project: access and utilization, appropriateness, quality, outcomes, and prevention.

First, descriptive data about the types of indicators used in each of the performance domains were collected. Then, prevalence data were collected to determine the frequency of use of the different indicators for each of the five performance domains. Initial findings demonstrated the following:

1. The most common indicator used to evaluate access/utilization was "average number of sessions clients were given." Between 80% and 92% of respondents used this measure, depending on the type of treatment being monitored.
2. The indicator used most frequently to assess clinical appropriateness was "Percentage of inpatient cases reviewed for adequate documentation." This measure was used by 98% of respondents.
3. Five outcomes indicators were used by a majority of the respondents. These indicators and their rate of use by respondents were as follows:
   a. "Percentage of clients with improved functioning after treatment" (used by 75% of respondents);
   b. "Percentage of clients readmitted after a specific period of time" (used by 74% of respondents);
   c. "Percentage of clients with reduced symptoms after treatment" (used by 73% of respondents);
   d. "Percentage of clients with adverse outcomes" (used by 73% of respondents); and
   e. "Percentage of clients for whom post-treatment follow-up is conducted to evaluate outcomes" (used by 56% of respondents).[9]

In 1995 the American Managed Behavioral Healthcare Association released a performance report card format intended to aid data collection on quality and access in managed behavioral health care settings. Called PERMS 1.0 (Performance-Based Measures for Managed Behavioral Healthcare Programs), the performance measures were developed in accordance with three guiding principles: the indicators had to be meaningful, measurable, and manageable. The measures constituting the report card are divided into three broad categories: access to care, consumer satisfaction, and quality of care.[10] Table 3 lists the performance measures from PERMS 1.0. Currently all PERMS measures have been included, in some form, in the Health Plan Employer Data and Information Set (HEDIS).

In a similar effort, a consumer-oriented report card assessing the quality and cost of mental health and substance abuse services was developed by the Mental Health Statistics Improvement Program (MHSIP) Task Force of the Center for Mental Health Services in the U.S. Department of Health and Human Services. This report card is designed to assess behavioral health services from the consumer's perspective. Five critical domains of performance are evaluated by this report card:

- Access,
- Appropriateness,
- Outcomes,
- Consumer satisfaction, and
- Prevention.[8]

The Council of Behavioral Group Practices, a consortium of more than 70 group practices, was organized through the Institute for Behavioral Healthcare, which is a San Francisco-based education and advocacy organization. In 1992, the council began developing a full-service outcomes program. To ensure that this work would be part of multidisciplinary practice, managed care, and capitation, the council appointed two multidisciplinary behavioral groups-University Psychiatric Services at the University of Cincinnati and Mesa Mental

Table 3. Performance-Based Measures for Managed Behavioral Healthcare Programs (PERMS 1.0)

Category	Indicators
Access to care	Overall penetration rate (percentage of enrolled population that actually received services)
	Penetration rate by age, diagnostic category, treatment setting, and clinician type
	Outpatient, inpatient, and intensive alternatives to inpatient utilization
	Cost data for individuals with severe and persistent mental illness
	Structural issues (call abandonment rate, on-hold time, call answer time)
Consumer satisfaction	Satisfaction with wait time to first appointment
	Satisfaction with intake
	Satisfaction with clinical care provided by therapist
	Consumer-based self-assessment of outcomes
	Overall satisfaction rating
Quality of care*	Ambulatory follow up after hospitalization for major affective disorder (effectiveness)
	Treatment failure for substance abuse (effectiveness)
	Continuity of care (efficiency)
	Availability of medication management for schizophrenia (appropriateness)
	Family visits for children (appropriateness)
	Utilization of resources for adjustment disorders (appropriateness)

* The quality of care indicators assess effectiveness, efficiency, and appropriateness as aspects of care quality.

Table 4. Phases in the Development of the Integrated Outcomes Program Sponsored by the Council of Behavioral Practices

Phase	Work

1. Define the program's specific goals	The following goals were established:
	• Create a protocol for daily use as a quality improvement tool;
	• Acquire data to meet NCQA and Health Plan Employer Data and Information Set (HEDIS) 2.0 requirements;
	• Develop a psychometrically sound, comprehensive cost-effective protocol that measures
	   - mental health symptoms,
	   - substance abuse symptoms,
	   - daily functioning,
	   - clients' perceptions of their physical health and function, and
	   - client satisfaction;
	• Analyze client data related to treatment events (prescribed medications or number of psychotherapy sessions); and
	• Create a national benchmarking database for analysis of aggregate data from and feedback to participating practices.

2. Design the methodology for implementation	The following major challenges in designing a meaningful and durable methodology were identified:
	• How to regularly, and completely collect data from clients in office-based settings;
	• How to track clients over time, even after treatment termination; and
	• How to acquire a return rate of follow-up data that was adequate for methodological integrity,
	A protocol was selected that included the following:
	• Client completion of a pretreatment assessment battery (in the waiting area); and
	• Follow-up mailed assessments at
	   - 3 months,
	   - 6 months, and
	   - 12 months (regardless of whether the client remained in treatment).

3. Locate or develop the clinical instruments	The following instrument selection criteria were defined: • Psychometrically reliable and valid; • Not proprietary; • Able to assess both symptoms and function; and • Cost of less than $1.00 per administration. When instruments were evaluated against the selection criteria, three instruments met all criteria: • BASIS—32 (Behavior and Symptom Inventory Scale)—a screen for mental health and substance abuse symptoms and function; • PES (Progress Evaluation Scale)—a measure of daily functioning; and • SF—36 (also called HSQ or Health Status Questionnaire)—a widely-used instrument for measuring client perceptions of physical health and functioning. To meet HEDIS standards and project goals, three new instruments were developed: • Two client satisfaction and expectation instruments: the Beginning Services Survey and the Patient Satisfaction Survey; and • An instrument to collect data from the course of treatment: the Treatment Events Checklist.

Health in Albuquerque-to create and implement a national outcomes protocol.[11] Table 4 details the project's phases and the work accomplished in designing this integrated outcomes program.

Ambulatory behavioral health care is usually viewed as being significantly different from ambulatory care. The Association for Ambulatory Behavioral Healthcare (AABH) has committed to

Table 4. Phases in the Development of the Integrated Outcomes Program Sponsored by the Council of Behavioral Practices (continued)

Phase	Work
4. Develop or buy scoring and data analysis software	The following scoring and data analysis challenges were identified: Identifying and selecting a vendor who could provide a cost—effective, customized program for the designed protocol; • Defining the required data analyses and reports; and • Determining the best data entry method. The following data analysis decisions were made: Optically scannable forms were chosen for data entry; • A data analysis program with many clinician and aggregate data reports was created; and • The Outcomes Management Program (OMP) National Database was established in the Department of Psychiatry at the University of Cincinnati College of Medicine.
5. Run the pilot	The entire protocol was piloted by eight test group practices. They pilot tested the instruments, as well as the logistics and resources needed to maintain the outcomes program.
6. Revise the protocol based on the pilot test	Protocol revision took six months and included the following activities: • Modifying the instruments; • Building enhancements into the final software; and • Enumerating implementation criteria for participating practices.
7. Implement the program in a diverse set of group practices	Implementation occurred in spring 1995 and included 20 practices in 16 states. A full day of education on the protocol was conducted at the University of Cincinnati. Ongoing assistance was provided through frequent telephone technical support and written procedural updates. Further protocol adjustments were made based on this first implementation experience. New sites are in the process of coming on board. The OMP National Database wants to expand services into other areas.

8. Prepare for future program enhancements	Planned future enhancements include the following:
	• Expanding the protocol to include inpatients and children;
	• Enhancing the program by
	  - connecting participating sites to the national database via the Internet and
	  - using hand—held computers for the client—completed pretreatment assessment; and
	• Making modifications related to the introduction of HEDIS 3.0.

assembling a set of performance indicators for this subspecialty in ambulatory care. In 1993, the AABH assembled a task force to develop an outcomes measurement protocol. The goal of this project was to develop "a clinically sensitive way to influence patient care decision making." The hope was to build t national database to serve as a benchmarking resource. This protocol was anchored in measuring six crucial variables:

1. Demographics (client and family history, education, occupational performance, and referral and payment Sources);
2. Cost per client care episode (cost of the client's time);
3. Utilization of services;
4. Level of functioning (client's performance of activities entailed in daily living);
5. Severity of symptoms (duration and degree of distress of symptoms); and
6. Client satisfaction (evaluation of program services).[12]

Clinical Assessment Instruments as Sources of Behavioral Health Care Outcomes Measures

A large number of clinical instruments can be used for measuring outcomes achieved as a consequence of the provision of behavioral health care interventions. Many are used when completing client assessments and updating treatment plans, whereas others are used as part of ongoing performance improvement initiatives. By using existing clinical assessment instruments for measuring outcomes, organizations can collect performance data reliably and validly while shifting finite agency resources away from instrument design and testing to data collection, analysis, and improvement.

Smith et al characterize measurement instruments as either non-disorder specific or disorder specific. Non-disorder-specific instruments apply general outcomes measures to groups of consumers. Many such instruments have demonstrated reliability and validity. Often they are short. Examples of such instruments include the Client Satisfaction Questionnaire (CSQ8), which is an eight-item inventory on client satisfaction that is typically administered at the time of discharge front treatment, and the Behavior and Symptom Identification Scale (BASIS-32), which is a 32-item general inventory of symptoms and functioning that is commonly administered at the initiation and conclusion of treatment. Disorder-specific measurements are more narrowly focused on symptoms and functions that characterize a particular condition. They enable a more detailed and discriminating evaluation. Their greatest benefit is in fostering informed decisions about treatment and service efficacy. The approach used at the University of Arkansas for measuring outcomes in major depression, which assesses amount and frequency of treatment, medication dosage, adherence to treatment, and treatment delivery setting, is an example of a disorder-specific measurement.[13]

Sederer, Hermann, and Dickey identify the following characteristics of desirable assessment instruments for use in behavioral health settings:

- Validly and reliably assess the specific outcomes sought by service providers;
- Collect and analyze data, and generate reports simply and affordably; and
- Minimize response biases through careful design and administration.[14]

Sederer, Hermann, and Dickey also describe three types of clinical assessment instruments: symptom-based, function-based, and symptom- and function-based instruments.

Symptom-based instruments identify the presence of symptoms and evaluate their severity. A useful symptom-based instrument must be sensitive enough to discern changes in symptom severity as a result of treatment or natural progress of the disease. Two examples of symptom-based instruments are as follows:

1. Brief Psychiatric Rating Scale (BPRS), which is completed by the clinician in a very short time and consists of 18 symptom scores and one global impression of illness score; and
2. Beck Depression Inventory (BDI), a 21-item inventory of depressive symptoms presented on a Likert-type scale that can be quickly completed by the client.

Function-based instruments evaluate current functioning and capacity to conduct usual daily activities. Useful function-based instruments can detect changes in functioning over time. An example of a function-based instrument is the Medical Outcome Study 36 Item ShortForm Health Survey (SF-36). The SF-36 elicits the client's self-judgment regarding eight domains of health: physical functioning, mental health (distress and well-being), role limitation secondary to illness, role limitation secondary to emotional distress, body pain, social functioning, vitality, and perceptions of general health.

Symptom- and function-based instruments simultaneously evaluate the presence and severity of symptoms and functional capacity. Two examples of symptom- and function-based instruments are as follows:

1. Global Assessment of Functioning (GAF) scale, which assesses psychological, social, and occupational function along a continuum of mental health/illness. It does not evaluate impairment in function because of physical or environmental limitations. The clinician completes the instrument by assessing both symptoms and functioning on a severity scale. The GAF is axis V of the *Diagnostic and Statistical Manual of Mental Disorders* (DSM) and is, therefore, commonly known and easily integrated into the client's record.
2. BASIS-32, which is a 32-item self-administered measure of change in psychiatric disorders (including those with substance abuse comorbidity) that is applicable at

any level of care. The client uses a five-point scale to rate the degree of difficulty experienced with interpersonal relationships, daily living/role functioning, depression/anxiety, impulsive/addictive behavior, and psychosis.[14]

The desire to develop a fulsome understanding of client needs, problems, and progress have led to the development and use of a large number of clinical assessment instruments. These are valid, reliable, and often widely available population-based tools that help to accurately describe the individual client's status. Status, used in this way, may be broadly defined as symptoms, and level and state of functionality. Such instruments are valuable in aiding outcomes measurement and management initiatives.

Measuring Satisfaction With Behavioral Health Care Services

Satisfaction with health care services is one quality attribute of interest to multiple stakeholders, including consumers and their significant others, practitioners, providers, purchasers, accreditors, and regulators. The definitions of satisfaction as it relates to quality of care are numerous. Of particular interest is the categorization of client satisfaction articulated by Zastowny et al. They divide satisfaction into four dimensions:

1. Satisfaction with the processes of providing care;
2. Satisfaction with the health benefits that result from an episode of care;
3. Overall satisfaction with the global health care experience; and
4. Personal cost-benefit assessment, or the value of the specifically provided care processes and consequent outcomes.

Satisfaction is an important outcome that can and should be routinely evaluated. Measuring satisfaction is associated with several methodologic difficulties, including a limited number of reliable and valid measurement instruments and a lack of consensus regarding a definition of client satisfaction. Nevertheless, it is important to continue to strive to operationally define and assess satisfaction with behavioral health services.[7]

Satisfaction-based instruments in behavioral health care are not yet as universally accepted as symptom- and function-based instruments. Agencies often create their own satisfaction surveys to solicit information about clients' and significant others' satisfaction with the treatment experience.[14]

Ruggeri studied the "state of satisfaction measurement" in psychiatry with three goals in mind: to update work done on satisfaction assessment in mental health from the early 1980s through the early 1990s; to identify and describe the main instruments used to measure clients' and significant others' perception of care with behavioral health care services; and to provide guidelines for future development of instruments assessing satisfaction with mental health services.[15]

Summary

1. The multiple sources for behavioral health care performance measures include professional associations and organizations, the literature, NLHI, and health care delivery organizations and systems.
2. Performance measures useful in behavioral health care settings evaluate clinical and nonclinical functions, support and administrative processes, financial performance, and satisfaction of consumers and other interested stakeholders.
3. The use of a balanced model of performance measurement or a family-of-measures approach helps foster the holistic evaluation of organizational performance.
4. A large number of assessment instruments exist that have documented reliability and validity, and that can readily be used to measure clinical outcomes in individuals receiving treatment for psychiatric, psychological, substance abuse, and developmental disorders. These same instruments may be used with aggregate populations of consumers to assess performance trends and patterns at both the population and organizational levels.
5. Satisfaction with behavioral health care services is often underevaluated. However, assessment of satisfaction is an integral component of a balanced perfor-

mance measurement model. Although organizations may select one of the few standardized instruments, they often develop customized satisfaction questionnaires. When satisfaction is measured, feedback about the treatment outcome, care processes, overall treatment experience, and value of the service should be solicited.

References

1. O'Leary MR. *Clinical Performance Data: A Guide to Interpretation*. Oakbrook Terrace, IL: Joint Commission on Accreditation of Healthcare Organizations, 1996.
2. Spath,P: Be sure to monitor quality in your psychiatric unit. *Hospital Peer Review* 20:129-132, Sep 1995.
3. Morrissey J: Quality project expands to psych care. *Modern Healthcare* 26:49, Mar 1996.
4. Prager LO: Profile's behavioral outcomes: From brevity, knowledge. *Medical Outcomes & Guidelines Alert* 4:5-7, Mar 1996.
5. At annual meeting, psychologists grapple with outcomes mandate. *Medical Outcomes & Guidelines Alert* 3:2-3, Sep 1995.
6. Donabedian A: Quality assessment and assurance: Unity of purpose, diversity of means. *Inquiry* 25:173-192, Spring 1988.
7. Zastowny TR, et al: Patient satisfaction and experience with health services and quality of care. *Quality Management in Health Care* 3:50-61, 1995.
8. Sluyter GV, Martin MA: Measuring the performance of behavioral healthcare organizations: A proposed model. *Best Practices and Benchmarking in Healthcare* 1:283-289, Nov-Dec 1996.
9. Silverberg BA: Towards a common language. In Coughlin, KM (ed): *The 1997 Behavioral Outcomes & Guidelines Sourcebook*. New York: Faulkner & Gray, 1997, pp 73-74.
10. Report card allows managed care firms to collect basic behavioral care data. *BNA's Health Care Policy Report* 3:1459-1460, Sep 1995.
11. Zieman G, Kramer T: Implementing a practice-based outcomes program. In Coughlin KM (ed): *The 1997 Behavioral Outcomes & Guidelines Sourcebook*. New York: Faulkner & Gray, 1997, pp 93-95.
12. Report from the field: Indicators slowly penetrate ambulatory care. *Quality Management Update* 6:5-8, Sep 1996.
13. Smith RG, et al: Assessment tools in psychiatry. *Am J Med Qual* 11:S46-S49, Spring 1996.
14. Sederer LI, Hermann R, Dickey B: The imperative of outcome assessment in psychiatry. *Amer J Med Qual* 10:127-131, Fall 1995.
15. Ruggeri M: Patients' and relatives' satisfaction with psychiatric services: The state of the art of its measurement. *Soc Psychiatry Epidemiol* 29:212-227, 1994.

PERMS 2.0: A Step Toward Core Behavioral Measures?

RICHARD CAMER

Releasing its latest set of managed behavioral health care performance measures (PERMS 2.0) Sept. 1, the American Managed Behavioral Healthcare Association (AMBHA) said it hopes to continue to guide the entire behavioral health field in measuring access to care, quality, and consumer satisfaction. AMBHA is the trade group of large managed behavioral health care organizations.

"The whole reason that we are doing this is to evolve an actual benchmark," notes AMBHA executive director E. Clarke Ross. In releasing the updated measurement set, AMBHA hopes to reduce, though not eliminate, the wide variation in reporting that plagued PERMS 1.0. Groups will report data on a computerized template managed by Richard Frank, professor of health care policy at Harvard Medical School. AMBHA also will group the data by payer type to reduce the variation.

The second generation of PERMS was delayed by nearly two years, largely due to marked consolidation within the industry, acknowledges Ross. When PERMS 1.0 was released, 19 member organizations signed onto the process of developing and approving the measures. Considerable industry volatility meant that "both the measurement development process and member commitment to that process had to be postponed," Ross tells MOGA. While 19 member groups contributed to the first measurement set, consolidation resulted in an association of 11 members, with current members covering the behavioral health care of 112 million Americans, more than were covered previously.

With PERMS 1.0, AMBHA succeeded in getting the National Committee for Quality Assurance (NCQA) to beef up the behavioral health measures contained in HEDIS. Though PERMS 2.0 "borrows heavily" from HEDIS, AMBHA says its new suggested "leadership" measures "can serve as an instigator for change" for NCQA and the field at large, said Clarissa Marques, chair of AMBHA's committee on quality improvement and clinical services, at a Sept. 1 press conference in Washington. (See Table 1.)

"We wanted to be able to move from the foundation that we laid in PERMS 1.0 to adding some innovative features and taking a leadership position," said Marques, who is executive vice

Table 1. Suggested Leadership Measures in PERMS 2.0

1. Number and percent of inpatient mental health admissions that are involuntary.
2. Number and percent of patients who remain in treatment 60 and 90 days following admission into chemical dependency programs.
3. Number and percent of prescriptions of antipsychotic medications for non-psychotic conditions.
4. Number and percent of those older than 65 who receive prescriptions for two or more psychoactive drugs.
5. Percent of depressed patients who remain on antidepressants for 4 months or longer.
6. Utilization of behavioral health services provided by non-mental health/chemical dependency providers.
7. Utilization of psychotropic drugs by medical providers in patients with any diagnosis.

Source: American Managed Behavioral Healthcare Association (AMBHA).

Source: Camer R. PERMS 2.0: A Step Toward Core Behavioral Measures? Medical Outcomes & Guidelines Alert, *Faulkner & Gray, September 24, 1998; 6(18):6-8.*

president for clinical and quality improvement for Magellan Health Services in Columbia MD. "We also wanted to make sure that we are continuing to support report card initiatives in the broader health care field."

"Overall, it looks like a refinement with a few additions," John Morris, president-elect of the American College of Mental Health Administration (ACMHA), commented in a telephone interview. "I think it will be helpful in identifying those issues that a fairly large sector of the private behavioral health field considers important. And they are not inconsistent with the work that is being done by the rest of the field," said Morris, who chaired ACMHA's recent summit on performance measures in behavioral health.

Like its previous version, PERMS 2.0 contains measures on access to care, quality of care, and consumer satisfaction. AMBHA's dozen members have agreed to collect and report data quarterly on the core access, quality and consumer satisfaction measures. At least two AMBHA members will pilot test each of the seven "leadership" measures.

Changes in the new measurement set include:
- **Access.** Core access measures are drawn directly from HEDIS 3.0, a recognition of the fact that many organizations are already reporting these indicators, Marques said. Definitions of products and data collection methodologies were tightened, however, to enhance comparability between behavioral health organizations.
- **Quality.** PERMS 2.0 tracks follow-up for ambulatory mental health and substance abuse treatment at 7 days after discharge in addition to 30 days as measured in HEDIS 3.0. Similarly, readmission rates for mental health or substance abuse treatment are now tracked at 30 days after discharge, in addition to 90 and 365 days as measured in HEDIS 3.0. Two new quality items track board-certification among psychiatrists and the availability of bilingual providers.
- **Optional.** PERMS 2.0 includes five optional access and quality measures including the percentage of members seeking employee assistance program services, change in provider availability, and engagement rates for depression and substance abuse treatment. (See Table 2.)

PERMS 2.0 also contains 10 consumer satisfaction measures, three of which were drawn from PERMS 1.0 and the remainder from HEDIS and other report card initiatives by the federal Center for Mental Health Services and the Agency for Health Care Policy and Research.

"We recognized that there were already a number of different complementary report card initiatives underway," Marques said. "We took a look at the consumer-oriented initiatives that were out there and the reliability and validity of their items so that we did not have to go back and do a lot of item testing," Marques said.

The consumer satisfaction measures assess issues including patient satisfaction with mental health and other providers; patient involvement in treatment decisionmaking; comprehensibility of

Table 2. Changes in Core HEDIS-Type Measures in PERMS 2.0

Reporting Area	Measures
Access to Care	No new measures beyond those in PERMS 1.0. Methodology tightened to ensure greater comparability between health plans.
Quality of Care	Follow-up after discharge for mental health now measured at 7 days in additions to 30 days. Follow-up after discharge for substance abuse now measured at 7 days in addition to 30 days. Readmission rates for mental health now measured at 30 days in addition to 90 and 365 days. Readmission rates for substance abuse now measured at 30 days in addition to 90 and 365 days. Percent of psychiatrists who are board certified. Availability of providers with bilingual skills.

Source: American Managed Behavioral Healthcare Association (AMBHA).

provider explanations; and patient satisfaction with grievance procedures.

The seven "leadership" measures are intended to break new ground and track controversial issues such as the percentage of patients committed involuntarily, the use of antipsychotics in patients with no Axis I psychotic disorder, and the percentage of elderly patients who receive two or more prescriptions for psychoactive drugs.

"The criticism we heard in PERMS 1.0 is that it lacked depth and breadth," Marques said. "In terms of breadth I think we gave ourselves a lot of room for innovation in the leadership measures. It is probably an area where we are going to have to do quite a bit of piloting."

Marques said AMBHA members will begin collecting and reporting PERMS 2.0 data quarterly in 1999. Aggregate performance data for AMBHA members will probably not be available until "a sufficient degree of quarterly data is collected," probably in 2001, she said.

Whether a purchaser or consumer group then will be able to compare an individual AMBHA member's performance against the performance of other AMBHA members or the industry at large remains to be seen. AMBHA will only report the aggregate data; release of individual company data is at the company's discretion, Marques said.

It may become possible to compare AMBHA members with other companies in the industry on comparable HEDIS measures, she said. "There's not a lot of data out there. A lot more work needs to be done on norming the data."

National norms indeed are difficult to come by and the problem has only intensified with the proliferation of behavioral health performance measures produced by industry, government, and consumer groups. ACMHA convened a summit of payers, purchasers, and consumer groups in 1997 to try to reach some greater consensus on performance measures in the behavioral health field, said Morris, a professor of neuropsychiatry and behavioral science at the University of South Carolina School of Medicine.

In April, the group released its own core set of behavioral health performance measures, and is working with four accreditation groups, including NCQA and the Joint Commission on Accreditation of Healthcare Organizations, to try to build agreement "about what are the important measures and indicators that can help with that quality comparison question," Morris said.

"It is important to have at least a core set of indicators that is common among all the measuring strategies so at least you have a common platform for comparison," he said. "Until you have some kind of national benchmarking, I think it is going to be very confusing for purchasers and consumers."

The Santa Fe Summit on Behavioral Health, Final Report

Section II: The Key Indicators

> *Sourcebook Editor's Note:* In March 1996, the American College of Mental Health Administration (ACMHA) Board of Directors voted to serve as a neutral forum for development of consensus on challenging issues facing the field of mental health and substance abuse treatment and prevention. ACMHA then began hosting a series of mental health and substance abuse summits aimed at bringing together key leaders on targeted subjects. The first summit, held in Santa Fe NM, in 1997, was devoted to outcomes/performance measurement. The "Final Report" is the result of that initial venture. Leaders from all sectors of the mental health and substance abuse field were invited to attend a working meeting in March 1997 to see if consensus could be reached on core performance measures for mental health and substance abuse care. Approximately 100 individuals participated, including representatives of the Washington Business Group on Health, the American Managed Behavioral Healthcare Association (AMBHA), the National Alliance for the Mentally Ill (NAMI), the National Committee for Quality Assurance (NCQA), the Institute of Medicine (IOM), the Substance Abuse and Mental Health Administration (SAMHSA), the Council on the Accreditation of Rehabilitation Facilities (CARF), and the National Mental Health Association, along with ACMHA members. The College was assisted by an unrestricted educational grant from the Eli Lilly Company.
>
> Summit participants were divided into five working groups reflecting the domains targeted by those in attendance: prevention, access, process/performance, outcomes and structure. Each workgroup met over the course of two days in Santa Fe, at the end of which each produced a statement of core values for the domain, provisional indicators to capture success in that domain, possible measures and needed next steps. Participants continued to refine their work following the meeting. The moderators of the workgroups met in Washington, D.C., June 29-30, 1997, to review materials to be included in the first draft of the Summit's recommendations. The creators stress that the Final Report "is not intended so much as a cookbook as a set of guidelines and principles."

The Santa Fe Summit workgroups generated mountains of paper and logged hundreds of collective hours of conference calls. In order for this report to receive wide distribution, that level of detail is impossible. Therefore, the following indicators are much abbreviated and every effort has been made to keep the language simple and unambiguous. The indicators are grouped by four of the domains (outcomes, process, access, and structure). The domain of prevention is addressed in a separate section [Section IV], and there is a special section on outcomes for a riskadjusted group of children and adolescents [Section III].

ACMHA is using the definitions of **indicators** and **measures** developed as part of CARF's Strategic Outcomes Initiative.

An **indicator** is a "Domain (e.g., effectiveness, efficiency or satisfaction; either process or outcome) or variable used to point to program quality or performance.

A **measure** is a "Specific instrument or data element used to quantify or calibrate an indicator.

Source: The Santa Fe Summit on Behavioral Health: Preserving Quality and Value in the Managed Care Equation: Final Report. *The American College of Mental Health Administration. March 1998. Pages 13-18.* (Reprinted with permission.)

A. Outcome Indicators

The outcome indicators are broken into two sections: the first three indicators are appropriate for **all populations**, both the commercially insured and working populations, as well as persons with serious and persistent mental or addictive disorders. The remaining measures are seen as relevant primarily for individuals with serious disorders. The measures used to assess performance are different for the two populations.

All Adults

O-I-1. Adults [including those with serious and persistent mental or chemical dependency disorders] reside in their own homes or living arrangements of their own choosing.

ACMHA believes that the ability to choose and maintain a stable home environment is a useful indicator of the effectiveness of services for people with mental health and substance abuse disorders. Both types of disorders can expose the individual to the risk of homelessness, transience, or serial supervised living environments. This indicator is intended to capture individuals who are hospitalized, in jail for reasons directly related to their mental illnesses, or homebound. For employed populations, the measures can be less rigorous, but ACMHA believes that it should be part of a core set of domains.

O-I-2. Adults [including those with serious and persistent mental or chemical dependency disorders] are working.

For employed and commercially insured populations, absences from work and missed productivity are important indicators. For persons with serious and persistent mental and addictive disorders, this is increasingly seen as an essential element of recovery models. For some individuals "work" may be understood as meaningful daily activities (including job training, volunteer work, etc.), but consumer participants successfully urged the College to keep the language focused on **work**. Again, different measures are appropriate, but the indicator is part of the core set.

O-I-3. Adults [including those with serious and persistent mental or chemical dependency disorders] have good physical health and report good mental health [psychological well being].

It is vital that both general health and mental health be assessed in determining the effectiveness of interventions. Mental health and substance abuse services for all populations need to be integrated with primary health care to guarantee the best outcomes. There will be different measures for different population groups, but the value of general health is sufficient to place this indicator in the core set for all populations.

Indicators for Adults With Serious and Persistent Disorders

O-I-4. Adults with serious and persistent mental or chemical dependency disorders report feeling safe.

The issue of safety was highlighted in the work of the Summit. Persons with serious disorders can be at unusual risk for victimization, and often report feeling unsafe because of the reduced social and economic status that often accompanies a chronic illness. Consumers also express concerns about being victimized by public institutions and practices that deprive them of free movement and choices.

O-I-5. Adults with serious and persistent mental or chemical dependency disorders avoid trouble with the law.

Obviously, people with mental and addictive disorders can commit crimes and have criminal responsibility for the consequences of their actions. This indicator seeks to address the dangers of the use of jails and prisons as a de facto alternative to viable community services.

O-I-6. Adults with serious and persistent mental or chemical dependency disorders maintain a social support network.

The presence of social supports is well documented as enhancing the quality of life for persons with serious and persistent mental and addictive disorders, and these networks can play a pivotal role in relapse prevention and recovery.

O-I-7. Adults with serious and persistent mental or addictive disorders are able to manage their daily lives.

Consumers frequently report concerns about managing their daily lives effectively, including symptom management and conflict resolution. This indicator can help assess the effectiveness of a system's most basic interventions.

O-I-8. Adults with serious and persistent mental or addictive disorders report a positive quality of life.

Quality of life is the ultimate test of any health care intervention, and this indicator fits with the others as part of a comprehensive core set.

B. Process Indicators

The process indicators are designed to reflect on a system's performance in serving the needs of the individuals it serves. The essential role of the consumer in all aspects of care is highlighted in this section, reflecting emerging practice for both privately and publicly insured populations.

P-I-1. Consumers actively participated in decisions concerning their treatment.

This is a bedrock performance issue for ACMRA, and reflects the value statements of the Summit. Consumers are essential partners in all aspects of the therapeutic enterprise. In the case of individuals under 18, "consumer" should be understood to include family members or guardians actively participating in treatment. [See special section on children and adolescents in Section III.)

P-I-2. Consumers who receive inpatient services* receive face-to-face follow up care within seven days of discharge. [*"Inpatient services" are defined as 24-hour, medically supervised services for a primary mental or substance abuse diagnosis.]

There is face validity in the field for the importance of follow-up care for individuals whose mental and addictive disorders are so severe as to require intensive and restrictive levels of care. Failure to engage persons in ambulatory follow-up care after discharge from inpatient treatment is a powerful signal that continuity of care is not present.

P-I-3. Consumers with mental health and addictive disorders are engaged in treatment.

While it is possible that a single treatment or assessment visit is needed, the norm would be that continuing care is expected with a valid mental illness or substance abuse diagnosis. Failure to continue in regular treatment is especially highly correlated with unsuccessful outcomes for persons with substance abuse disorders and persistent mental health conditions.

P-I-4. Consumers receive adequate information to make informed choices.

This indicator is inextricably tied to indicator P-I-1 and indicator P-I-3; active participation in treatment can only be achieved when consumers are provided with useful information about those choices.

P-I-5. Consumers receive mental health inpatient services in a voluntary, noncoercive manner.

Some persons with mental illnesses may require involuntary hospitalization to protect themselves or others from harm. However, a well functioning service delivery system should be able to minimize unplanned, coercive hospital admissions through care management and effective alternative treatment resources. High rates of involuntary hospitalization may indicate inadequacies in ambulatory care services that are less intrusive/restrictive.

P-I-6. Consumers are satisfied with the services they receive.

Consumers of substance abuse and mental health services (and their families and guardians) are the best resources for determining whether or not systems are meeting their needs and expectations. It is especially important that clients with these disorders receive services that preserve the dignity and respect of the individual and family.

P-I-7. The system of care assumes responsibility for continuous and integrated care appropriate to the needs of children and families. [Also see Section IV, special section on children.]

Children with mental health and substance abuse problems are likely to be involved with many systems: schools, child welfare agencies, primary care and pediatric specialty care, juvenile justice, and others. Children's disorders often tend to have periodic changes and care can become episode-driven without consistency. Coordination and integration of care is essential across the developmental span.

C. Access Indicators

The Access indicators identified by the Summit reflect an attempt to move to more meaningful indicators of access than counts of phone rings or drop rates—although these have been useful proxies for access in systems that can track these data. The methodological issues in collecting and analyzing these data are considerable.

A-I-1. Consumer experiences of treatment (both positive and negative) are assessed on dimensions of appropriateness, timeliness and sensitivity of services delivered. [Also addressed in P-I-6]

Customer satisfaction is another bedrock indicator. The methodologies for measuring this variable are numerous, and need to also include measures of **dis**satisfaction.

A-I-2. Service denials, terminations, or refusals are assessed.

Denials, terminations or refusals for services (adjusted for benefits included in a service plan) can serve as a barometer of access. [Serious concerns have been raised about this indicator, because of the issue of the *clinical appropriateness* of some denials, e.g. the denial of a request for a more restrictive level of care than is indicated for a child, a request for a specific medication that is contraindicated medically, etc.]

A-I-3. Penetration rates demonstrate benchmarked levels of service delivery to like ovulations.

The attempt here is to insure that services are at expected levels, neither significantly higher nor lower than is the norm.

A-I-4. Access to a full range of services is demonstrable.

Easy access to a narrow range of services is not genuine access. (As the folk-adage puts it: "If all you have is a hammer, everything looks like a nail.") This indicator would encompass referral linkages and other strategies to offer a comprehensive array. This would have to be risk-adjusted for benefit packages that have limited scope.

A-I-5. Children and their families receive the appropriate services that they need, when they need them.

This indicator and A-I-6 below were developed and proposed to the Summit process by a group of child and adolescent experts convened by SAMHSA in late 1997. This indicator overlaps somewhat with other access indicators, but the special emphasis on child and family indicators is seen as essential.

A-I-6. Children and their families are being assessed for and offered services at appropriate levels.

This indicator seeks to highlight the importance of both penetration and proper matching of children and families to needed levels of care. Of special concern are children being under-identified and hence under-served, as well as children being over-served, for example in the instance of over or inappropriate utilization of out-of-home placements, restrictive settings, etc.

D. Structure Indicators

The structure indicators lend themselves more to traditional accreditation and survey techniques, as opposed to true "outcome" indicators, but are included as relevant to the over-all initiative.

S-I-1. The organization's structure is consistent with the delivery of mental and addictive disorder treatment, with effective consumer and professional representation in policy making.

In integrated systems, it is important to ensure that the special needs of persons with mental and addictive disorders are addressed by the structure. The involvement of consumers and professionals in policy is essential in all environments, whether private or public, managed or fee for service.

S-I-2. Consumer rights are clearly defined and procedures for resolution of complaints and grievances are in place and easy to use.

This is an essential element in most current certification protocols. ACMHA is especially concerned that measures reflect the system's capacities and performance in making complaint and grievance processes genuinely non-threatening and responsive.

S-I-3. Staffing levels and training are appropriate for delivery of the array of services and provide for meeting the diverse needs of the individuals served, including linguistic and cultural competence. The services delivered are based on scientific evidence of efficacy.
The issue of staffing is enormously complex, and is not responsive to a one-size-fits-all mentality. Increased attention to preprofessional and continuing educational strategies is essential if appropriate care is to be given in a field where rapid knowledge development is a byword; if staff are unprepared or basing interventions on unproven theoretical models, good care cannot result, and so treatment efficacy based on science is also critical under this element. Of special concern here is the cultural/linguistic element of this indicator given the diversity of people served by systems of care.

S-I-4. Data on clients is secure, available only to those who need to know.
Confidentiality remains an especially vexing concern in the mental and addictive disorders field, not least of all because of the multiplicity of laws (state and federal) and policies (federal, state and organizational) regulating access to consumer information. The system must demonstrate that it can protect confidentiality while enhancing communication of relevant clinical data among all providers of care.

S-I-5. There are appropriate linkages to other service systems with which consumers need to interact.
Persons with addictive and mental disorders frequently require services from more than one specialty service, and often need services from other social support systems. In the instance of children, adolescents and their families, this is even more of a need.

S-I-6. There is continuity of care within the organization and effective integration with external care-giving systems.
This indicator is a close corollary to **S-I-5**, but an indicator of both internal and external continuity of care is important.

S-I-7. There is a single fixed point of responsibility for each client.
All populations need this simple structural support. Consumers and families with complex service needs are better served when there is a single reference point.

S-I-8. There is a quality assurance system in place to examine adverse clinical events.
Systems need to be able to assess their own vulnerability to incidents such as suicide, multiple hospitalizations in a short time, etc. aggressive acts and other high-risk incidents.

S-I-9. Consumers and families are educated about their rights, the array of services available to them and likely outcomes of treatment interventions.
ACMHA is concerned here with improving the effectiveness of systems' communications with their service users. Again, this is a measure with high relevance for all populations.

Santa Fe Summit on Behavioral Health, Final Report

Section V: Measures

This section will include the proposed measures for each of the indicators selected for the core set. This was the part of the Summit's work that proved the most difficult for participants. There is considerable debate in the field about the efficacy of different measurement instruments, the burden of collecting data, data comparability, etc. ACMHA welcomes the work of our colleagues in refining and improving these recommendations. We propose that as the field accepts the values and indicators proposed in this document, that there will be a new consensus to tackle the methodological disputes in these targeted areas. The measures will follow the same order as the indicators.

In reviewing our work, HSRI offered some observations about issues that are cross-cutting for measurement:

(1) **For indicators/measures relying on survey data, what is an appropriate sample size?** Consensus needs to be reach about the size of differences that are sought, so that power analyses can be conducted and sample size determined.

(2) **How should the sample be drawn?** Before an indicator requiring a survey could be fully implemented, guidelines would need to be agreed upon regarding the survey administration (i.e., mailed? Phone? in-person?), minimum acceptable completion rates, and the larger sampling frame (i.e., all enrollees? All enrollees with at least one encounter? Etc.).

(3) **How will risk-adjusting and benchmarking be handled?** All measurement instruments will need to have demonstrable validity if they are to have utility across plans, populations and settings. (Dr. Joe Thompson of NCQA has made the important distinction between measures that are useful for internal quality improvement (QI) versus those that have reliability for quality comparison (QC), the latter having to meet a higher standard of scientific validity.)

There are tables in the appendix which give further detail. Measures have been selected based upon the judgement that they are **measurable**, **manageable** and **meaningful**.

Manageability reflects the relative ease/burden of collecting and analyzing the data collected.

Measurability refers to the extent to which a measure can give quantifiable and comparable expression of the domain being studied—the scientific dimension.

Meaningfulness refers to the relative utility of the measure to the mental health and substance abuse fields: Can the resulting information be useful to consumers and purchasers in making decisions? Can the information help providers manage better?

Outcome Measures

Indicator One. (O-I-1). Adults [including those with serious and persistent mental or chemical dependency disorders] reside in their own homes or living arrangements of their own choosing.

Proposed Measures: O-M-1. Consider categories from the Lehman Quality of Life Inventory (Brief version): (a) What is your current living arrange-

---

Source: The Santa Fe Summit on Behavioral Health: Preserving Quality and Value in the Managed Care Equation: Final Report. *The American College of Mental Health Administration. March 1998. Pages 37-41.* (Reprinted with permission.)

ment, and (b) How much choice did you have in selecting the place where you live. There is a rating scale from "Total" to "None" [Note: Use of these questions without checking for copyright and validity concerns is **not** recommended.]

O-I-2. Adults [including those with serious and persistent mental or chemical dependency disorders] are working.
Recommended Measure: O-M-2: For the risk-adjusted population of persons with severe and persistent mental illnesses, consider two items: (1) from the Lehman Quality of Life Scale (Brief version): (a) "What kind of work do you do at the present time?"; (2) from the International Association of Pyschosocial Rehabilitation (IAP-SRS) Programs "Toolkit for PsychoSocial Rehabilitation Outcomes: (b) "How many hours a week do you usually work?" [Note: Use of these questions without checking for copyright and validity concerns is **not** recommended.]

O-I-3. Adults [including those with serious and persistent mental or chemical dependency disorders] have good physical health and report good mental health.
Recommended Measure: O-M-3: Consider selected scales from the SF-12 (physical and mental component scales), BASIS 32 (depression and anxiety, psychosis, and impulsive addictive behavior scales), or MHSIP Report Card (symptoms, medications, and side effects questions). [Note: Use of these questions without checking for copyright and validity concerns is **not** recommended.]

O-I-4. Adults with serious and persistent mental or chemical dependency disorders report feeling safe.
Recommended Measures: Consider modified items from Lehman Quality of Life Inventory: (a) In the past <year> have you been a victim of a violent or non-violent crime?; (b) How safe do you feel where you live? [Note: Use of these questions without checking for copyright and validity concerns is **not** recommended.]

O-I-5. Adults with serious and persistent mental or chemical dependency disorders can avoid trouble with the law.
Recommended Measure: Consider adaptation from Lehman QOLI: In the past <year> have you been arrested or picked up for any crime? [Note: Use of these questions without checking for copyright and validity concerns is **not** recommended.]

O-I-6. Adults with serious and persistent mental or chemical dependency disorders maintain a social support network.
Recommended Measure: Consider multiple items from the Lehman QOLI: (a) In the past <year< how often did you: visit with a friend not living with you? Telephone a friend? Make a plan ahead of time to do something with a friend? Spend time with someone like a girlfriend or boyfriend? Talk with a member of your family on telephone? Get together with member of family? [Note: Use of these questions without checking for copyright and validity concerns is **not** recommended.]

O-I-7. Adults with serious and persistent mental or addictive disorders are able to manage their daily lives.
Recommended Measure: Consider selected items from the MHSIP Consumer Report Card Survey, specifically those relating to: "I deal more effectively with daily problems (Q26); "I am better able to control my life." (Q28); "I do better in my leisure time' "(Q34); "I have become more independent." (Q37); "I am more effective in getting what I 'want' [note: word is 'need' in MHSIP questionnaire]. (Q39); "I am better able to deal with crises: (modified from language in Q40: Original language: "I can deal better with people and situations that used to be a problem for me.")

O-I-8. Adults with serious and persistent mental or addictive disorders report a positive quality of life.
Recommended Measures: Consider single item from Lehman QOLI: "How do you feel about life in general?

Process/Performance Measures

P-I-1. Consumers actively participate in decisions concerning their treatment.
Recommended Measures: Consider two questions from MHSIP consumer survey: (a) I, not the staff decide my treatment goals (QI9); (b) I felt comfortable asking questions about my treatment and

medications (QI2). [Note: Use of these questions without checking for copyright and validity concerns is **not** recommended.]

P-I-2. Consumers who receive inpatient care* receive face-to-face follow up care within seven days of discharge. [* "Inpatient care" is defined as 24-hour, medically supervised care for a primary mental or substance abuse diagnosis.]
Recommended Measure: The total number of discharges from 24-hour, medically supervised care for a mental health or substance abuse diagnosis that were followed by at least one non-emergency, face-to-face mental health or substance abuse treatment visit within seven days, divided by all discharges from such settings, during a 12 month period.

P-I-3. Consumers with mental health and addictive disorders are engaged in treatment.
Recommended Measure: The total number of enrollees receiving one and only one mental health or substance abuse service in the past year, divided by the total number of enrollees receiving more than one mental health or substance abuse service in the same year.

P-I-4. Consumers receive adequate information to make informed choices.
Recommended Measure: Consider three questions from MHSIP survey: (a) I felt comfortable asking questions about my treatment and medication (Q12); (b) I was given information about my rights (modified from Q14); (c) I was told what side effects to watch for (modified from Q17). [Note: Use of these questions without checking for copyright and validity concerns is **not** recommended.]

P-I-5. Consumers receive mental health inpatient services in a voluntary, non-coercive manner.
Recommended Measure: Total number of admissions to 24-hour, medically supervised residential mental health and substance abuse treatment to which consumers are admitted (committed) involuntarily, divided by the total number of 24 hour, medically supervised admissions in a 12 month period.
[**Note: ACMHA acknowledges significant problems with data collection of this data** because of variability in plan design, methodology for coding encounters by individual versus family, variability in location of services, including primary care settings, etc.]

P-I-6. Consumers are satisfied with the services they receive.
Recommended Measure: Consider selected questions from the MHSIP Consumer Survey: (a) I like the services I receive from my mental health or substance abuse provider (modified from Q01); (b) I would recommend mental health or substance abuse provider to a family member or friend (modified from Q03); (c) I feel that I was helped by the services I received; (d) I feel that I was treated with dignity and respect (modified from Q20-n, Q14); (e) I feel that I was free to ask questions about my mental health and substance abuse treatment (modified from Q12); (f) I feel that my provider is sensitive to my cultural and ethnic background (Q20-n). [Note: Use of these questions without checking for copyright and validity concerns is **not** recommended.]

P-I-7. The system of care assumes responsibility for continuous and integrated care appropriate to the needs of children and families. [Also see Section IV, special section on children]
Recommended Measure: See special section on children, Section III.

Access Measures

A-I-1. Consumer experiences of treatment (both positive and negative) are assessed on dimensions of appropriateness, timeliness and sensitivity of services delivered
Recommended Measures: (a) Consider customer satisfaction with initial access measure from AMBRA PERMS: Was the amount of time you had to wait for your first appointment <not a problem>, <a small problem>, <a big problem>, <don't know>. [Note: Use of these questions without checking for copyright and validity concerns is **not** recommended.]
(b) Consider selected questions from MHSIP Consumer Survey: "I was unable to get the services I thought I needed"(Q09-n); "I was able to see a psychiatrist when I wanted to"(Q10); "Staff were

willing to see me as often as I felt it was necessary" (Q06); "Staff were not sensitive to my cultural/ethnic background" (Q 20-n); "The location of services was convenient" (Q05); "Services were available at a times that were good for me" (Q08); "I was unable to get some services I wanted because I could not pay for them. (Q04-n). [Note: Use of these questions without checking for copyright and validity concerns is **not** recommended.]

A-I-2. Service denials, terminations, or refusals are assessed

Recommended Measures: no measure identified. There are definitional, data source, and other problems with this indicator and its measurement. Considerable attention is being given to external review of this indicator.

A-I-3. Penetration rates demonstrate benchmarked levels of service delivery to like populations.

Recommended Measure: AMBHA PERMS I.0.

A-I-4. Access to a full range of services is demonstrable.

Recommended Measures: (a) MHSIP Report card measure of ready availability; requires more than one question; (b) review of contract provisions/external review protocols; (c) utilization rates by service type per administrative data base.

A-I-5. Children and families receive the appropriate services they need, when they need them.

Recommended Measures: The potential sources for this information include CAHPS, FSQ-R/YSQ-R, MHSIP Report Card, AMBHA PERMS, and YRBS. (a) Self/Family Report/Survey, which includes consideration of culture, geographic spread, clinical use and timeliness; and (b) information through service and administrative data bases retrieved through queries such as:

> Length of time from first appointment to second appointment by: (1) frequency distribution of % initial contact to first appointment; (2) % persons who show for first appointment within 30 days of initial contact. Length of time from first to second appointment by: (1) frequency distribution of % of initial appointment to second; (2) % of persons appearing for second appointment within 30 days of first.
> Percent of consumers identified via Geo-mapping to be within 30 mile radius of provider [NOTE: This would be a different measure for urban populations.]

(c) Information gathered through accreditation processes such as NCQA, CARF or JCAHO. An important variable accessible through this mechanism might be cultural competence/sensitivity as measured by provider offering translation or multilingual services if >10% are identified as non-English speaking.

A-I-6. Children and the families are being assessed for and offered services at appropriate levels

Recommended Measures: These measures could be gathered through service or administrative data base queries:

(a) penetration rate by age, sex, and population for services to clients with mental health and substance abuse primary diagnoses, as benchmarked against epidemiologically based predicted rates.

(b) Penetration rate in the primary health care system of clients by age, sex and population as compared to predicted rates;

(c) Follow-up and transition data monitoring the intervals of time between providers on referral; #days/referral, benchmarked against mean days for the system.

Structure Measures

As noted in the introduction, the structure measures tend to be the more traditional accreditation measures. In keeping with the ACMHA concept of not duplicating efforts of existing bodies, our recommendation in this area is that systems use those elements of existing accreditation surveys that address these indicators. CARF, NCQA, JCAHO, HCFA and others all have instruments or survey questions to assess these indicators.

It is the ACMHA position on these measures, that the standard should be: **A benchmarked or nationally accepted measure or survey that adequately supports a finding on the indicator in question.**

ACMHA believes that no survey system is adequate unless **all of the ACMHA indicators are covered.**

The Santa Fe Summit on Behavioral Health, Final Report

Section VI: Measures and Indicators

Considered But Not Recommended at This Time

Performance Indicator: P-I-5. Psychotherapeutic medications are used appropriately.
The misuse of psychotherapeutic agents is a source of grave concern for consumers, professionals and purchasers alike. The implications for ineffective (or worse, counter therapeutic or dangerous) treatments are significant.

Corresponding Measure: P-I-5. Psychotherapeutic medications are used appropriately.
Recommended Measure: None. Discussion: This is an important measure, which has face validity and is seen as an important quality of care indicator. However, an existing/established instrument for this indicator could not be found. Moreover, while the concept of "appropriateness of pharmacotherapy" is easy to appreciate, there are actually few, if any, established criteria for best practices and there is a wide range of "acceptable" practices. HEDIS 3.0 included a test measure regarding the use of antidepressant medications, but a concern of the workgroup was that this measure was narrow and addressed the issue of unnecessary prescription of medications, not the broader focus of use or lack of use of appropriate medications.

The workgroup is committed to the notion of monitoring and evaluation pharmacotherapy practice. Of special interest was the work of Lantz, Giambanco, and Buchalter in a recent issue of *Psychiatric Services* (47:9,951-55). The process work group recommends development of a measure based on this work, including a matrix of drug utilization sorted by major diagnostic categories. Other data variables (gender, ethnicity, age) were also proposed. This measure is seen as dependent on the existence of pharmacy data bases and electronic patient record technologies.

Source: The Santa Fe Summit on Behavioral Health: Preserving Quality and Value in the Managed Care Equation: Final Report. *The American College of Mental Health Administration.* March 1998. Page 42. *(Reprinted with permission.)*

The Santa Fe Summit on Behavioral Health, Final Report

Appendix 1
Comparison of Performance Indicators: NCQA/BHMAP—ACMHA—NASMHPD/NASADAD/APWA

PREPARED BY DR. ERIC GOPLERUD OF SAMHSA

Table 1 Comparison of Performance Indicators: Access

PERFORMANCE INDICATOR	NCQA/BHMAP	ACMHA	3 ASSNS
Penetration/utilization rates (by age, sex, race, setting)	✔	✔	✔
Consumer perception of access		✔	✔
Full range of services available: • weekend detox • new medications • in-home services for children	✔	✔	
Cultural accessibility	✔	✔	Dvpmnt set
Percent of members admitted to MH services that have inpatient services as their first encounter	✔		
Percent of elderly plan members screened for depression and substance abuse	✔		
Percent of alcohol/drug-related diagnoses that trigger alcohol or drug screening and percentage of positive screens that resulted in referral	✔		
Percent of enrolled population that lives within specified driving time of providers	✔		
Service denials, terminations or refusals		✔	Dvpmnt set

Source: The Santa Fe Summit on Behavioral Health: Preserving Quality and Value in the Managed Care Equation: Final Report. *The American College of Mental Health Administration. March 1998. Appendix 1, pages 59-61. (Reprinted with permission.)*

Table 2 Comparison of Performance Indicators: Quality/Appropriateness

PERFORMANCE INDICATOR	NCQA/BHMAP	ACMHA	3 ASSNS
Consumer participation in treatment planning (adults)		✔	✔
Consumers linked to primary health services			✔
Contact within 7 days following hospital discharge	✔	✔	✔
Adults with SMI receiving services that promote recovery			✔
Children receiving "best practice" e.g., in-home services			✔
Family involvement in treatment for children/adolescents	✔	✔	✔
Re-admissions within 30 days	✔		✔
Consumer perceptions of quality/appropriateness (or family proxy for children)	✔✔	✔✔	✔
Seclusion and restraint			✔
Medication used appropriately	✔	✔	✔
Incidence of diagnosis of depression, substance abuse	✔		
Use of standardized assessments and diagnostic procedures in guiding behavioral treatments	✔		
Engagement in treatment	✔	✔	
Rates of involuntary inpatient treatment in covered population	✔	✔	
Single point of responsibility for coordinating care across systems for children		✔	

Table 3 Comparison of Performance Indicators: Outcomes

PERFORMANCE INDICATOR	NCQA/BHMAP	ACMHA	3 ASSNS
Employment (adults)/school improvement (children)	✔	✔	✔
Level of functioning	✔	✔	✔
Symptom (substance use) reduction	✔		✔
Adverse outcomes • patient injuries • abnormal involuntary movements • elopement • out of home placements			✔
Consumer perception of outcomes	✔✔	✔	✔
Health status: morality	✔		✔
Recovery/hope/personhood	✔		✔
Reduced substance abuse impairment	✔		✔
Living situation		✔	✔
Criminal justice		✔	✔
Quality of life	✔	✔✔✔	

Appendix 2
ACMHA Process Group Indicators and Proposed Measures

PREPARED BY THE EVALUATION CENTER AT HSRI

ACMHA Process Group Indicators and Proposed Measures

INDICATOR	MEASURE	SOURCE	NUMERATOR	DENOMINATOR
1. Active consumer and family participation in decisions concerning treatments.	The percentage of consumers who actively participate in decisions concerning their treatment; as defined by the consumers response to survey questions regarding treatment: • I not staff, decided my treatment goals. • I felt comfortable asking questions about my treatments and medication. Note: This is based on a five point scale ranging from very satisfied to not satisfied.	MHSIP Report Card	The number of consumers who respond positively to those questions.	The total number of consumers who are surveyed.

INDICATOR	MEASURE	SOURCE	NUMERATOR	DENOMINATOR
3. Receipt of information to make informed choices.	The percent of consumers who receive adequate information to make informed choices; as defined by the consumer response to survey questions regarding adequate information: • I felt comfortable asking about my treatment and medication • I was given information about my rights • Staff told me what side effect to watch for. Note: This is based on a five point scale ranging from very satisfied to not satisfied.	MHSIP Report Card	The percentage of consumer who respond positively to those questions.	The total number of consumers surveyed.

INDICATOR	MEASURE	SOURCE	NUMERATOR	DENOMINATOR
3. Receipt of information to make informed choices.	The percent of consumers who receive adequate information to make informed choices; as defined by the consumer response to survey questions regarding adequate information: • I felt comfortable asking about my treatment and medication • I was given information about my rights • Staff told me what side effect to watch for. Note: This is based on a five point scale ranging from very satisfied to not satisfied.	MHSIP Report Card	The percentage of consumer who respond positively to those questions.	The total number of consumers surveyed.

INDICATOR	MEASURE	SOURCE	NUMERATOR	DENOMINATOR
4. Treatment (including prevention, assessment, intervention, rehabilitation, and habitation) follows best practice guidelines.	The total number of adults with a diagnosis of depression who received medication a the range specified by the American Psychiatric Association (APA) guidelines, divided by the total number of adults with the diagnosis who were prescribed medication.	MHSIP Report Card	The total number of adults with a diagnosis of depression who received medication at the range specified by the American Psychiatric Association (APA) guidelines.	The total number of adults with the same diagnosis who were prescribed medication.

Source: The Santa Fe Summit on Behavioral Health: Preserving Quality and Value in the Managed Care Equation: Final Report. *The American College of Mental Health Administration. March 1998. Appendix 2, pages 65-69. (Reprinted with permission.)*

INDICATOR	MEASURE	SOURCE	NUMERATOR	DENOMINATOR
5. Appropriate use of psychotherapeutic medications.	This measure tries to assess to what extent the plan uses psychotherapeutic medications appropriately by determining what percentage of enrollees given psychotherapeutic drugs were diagnosed with a condition that warrants such a prescription (including senile or presenile psychosis, alcoholic psychosis, drug psychosis, transient organic psychosis, chronic psychosis, schizophrenic psychosis, affective psychosis, paranoid states or other non-organic psychosis).	HEDIS 3.0	The number of enrollees who were prescribed a psychotherapeutic drug who had one of the following diagnosis: (senile or presenile psychosis, alcoholic psychosis, drug psychosis, transient organic psychosis, chronic psychosis, schizophrenic psychosis, affective psychosis, paranoid states or other non-organic psychosis).	The number of enrollees who were prescribed psychotherapeutic drug.

INDICATOR	MEASURE	SOURCE	NUMERATOR	DENOMINATOR
6. Family visits for children 12 years of age or younger.	Given any ambulatory treatment activity (claims, authorization, or encounter) for a child aged 12 years and younger, then also an activity (claims, authorization, or encounter) for a family visit. (The percentage of children for whom this is the case)	AMBHA PERMS	The number of children at least 12 years of age or younger who have received at least on ambulatory treatment or activity (claims, authorization, or encounter) in the first 11 months in a calendar year for whom there is at least 1 family visit in a calendar year.	The total number of children age 12 years and younger treated during the first 11 months of a calendar year.

INDICATOR	MEASURE	SOURCE	NUMERATOR	DENOMINATOR
7. Consumer satisfaction with services. (Outcome)	**(A)** AMBHA PERMS Access: Satisfaction with time interval to first appointment. Intake: Degree of satisfaction with intake worker. Clinical Care: • (a) Degree of satisfaction with therapist. • (b) Willingness to recommend therapist/program. Outcome: Consumer assessment of outcome. Global Satisfaction: Rating of overall satisfaction. **(B)** MHSIP Consumer Survey: To be determined. **(C)** CAHPS: To be determined.	(a) Consumer Satisfaction Survey Data (see attachments) (b) MHSIP Consumer Survey (see attachments) (c) CAHPS Behavioral Health Module (see attachments)		

INDICATOR	MEASURE	SOURCE	NUMERATOR	DENOMINATOR
8. Benchmarked and risk adjusted percentage of consumers who receive only one treatment visit. (Access)	(a) For each of the following age, sex, and ethnic grouping: the total number of enrollees receiving one mental health services in the past year, divided by the total number of enrollees. Age: 0-21, 22-64, 65+ Sex: Male, female Ethnicity: (1) White, African American, Asian, Other (2) Hispanic, non-Hispanic (b) For the same age, sex, and the ethnic grouping: the total number of enrollees receiving one and only one mental health service in the past year, divided by the total number of enrollees receiving one or more mental health services in the same year.	(a) MHSIP Report Card (b) MHSIP Report Card	The total number of enrollees receiving one mental health services in the past year. The total number of enrollees receiving one and only one mental health service in the past year.	The total number of enrollees. The total number of enrollees receiving one or more mental health services in the same year.

Appendix 4
Mental Health Statistical Improvement Program (MHSIP)

MHSIP Report Card Implementation Progress Report

- The MHSIP Task Force on a Consumer-Oriented Mental Health Report Card presented its report in April, 1996.
- Since that time—through a grant program developed by the Center for Mental Health Services (CMHS)—thirty-one states are working on implementing the report card or its component parts. Ten more states will be added this year.
- Besides the efforts of individual states, a five-state feasibility study sponsored by CMHS and coordinated by the NASMHPD Research Institute is testing the reporting of indicators across states in a standardized way. Issues related to standardized consumer surveys and methodologies, risk adjustment and data presentation are also being addressed.
- The MHSIP Report Card has made a significant contribution to other major national initiatives related to mental health performance measurement systems, including:
  - AMBHA PERMS 2.0
  - American College of Mental Health Administrators
  - NASMHPD Task Force on Performance Measures
  - National Committee on Quality Assurance
  - Performance Partnership grants
  - CMHS Mental Health Block Grant Performance Measures
- A short version of the MHSIP Consumer Survey was presented to NCQA's Committee on Performance Measurement and has been approved for inclusion in the 1999 HEDIS testing set. This survey will be used for adults with mental illnesses and adults with substance abuse. (This instrument has also been modified for use with children but this was not presented for approval.)
- The MHSIP Report Card measures of "follow up after hospitalization within seven days" was also adopted by NCQA replacing the previous similar measure of "follow up after hospitalization within 30 days."
- Human Services Research Institute (HSRI) is developing a toolkit for use of the MHSIP report card. HSRI is also working with the MHSIP Advisory Group to develop an Internet capability for communicating about the MHSIP report card.
- At its February, 1998 meeting, the MHSIP Advisory Group created a MHSIP Report Card Implementation Task Force that will coordinate report card implementation activities and will be responsible to the development of the next generation of the report card.

Source: The Santa Fe Summit on Behavioral Health: Preserving Quality and Value in the Managed Care Equation: Final Report. *The American College of Mental Health Administration. March 1998.* Appendix 4, pages 97-101. *(Reprinted with permission.)*

Figure 1 MHSIP Report Card Implementation Activities

```
                MHSIP Report Card --        →        MHSIP Report Card
                    April, 1996                      Implementation and
                                                         Version 2.0

        ┌───────────────────────┼───────────────────────┐
 41 state reform grants   NASMHPD President's    Other Performance
                              Task Force       Measurement Initiatives

 Activities:              Activities:            •ACMHA
  •MHSIP                   •Technical Workgroup  •AMBHA
  •CMHS                    •Five-state Feasibility Study  •NCQA
  •NRI                     •JCAHO ORYX           •PPG
  •HSRI                                          •CMHS Block Grant
```

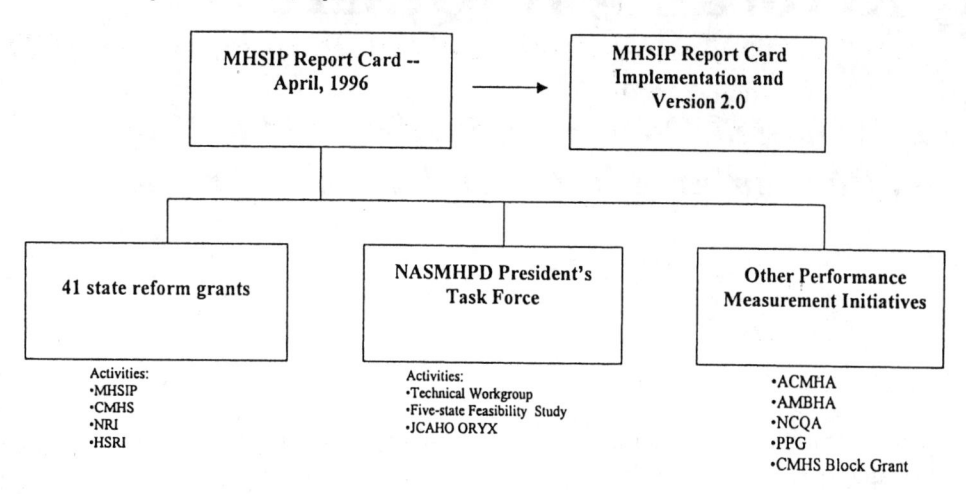

Table 12 Report Card Measures by Population

ACCESS	Children/ Adolescents with SED	Other Children/ Adolescents	Adults with SMI	Other Adults	Adults with Dual Diagnosis (MI and SA)	Total Population
Access 1: Average time from request to face-to-face meeting.	X	X	X	X	X	X
Access 2: Convenience of service location.			X	X	X	
Access 3: Convenient appointment times.			X	X	X	
Access 4: Easy access to therapist.			X	X	X	
Access 5: Average resources spent on services.	X	X	X	X	X	X
Access 6: Resources spent on consumer-run services.			X			
Access 7: Resources spent on sevices in natural settings.	X	X				
Access 8: Service availability.			X	X	X	
Access 9: Access to culturally competent provider.			X	X	X	
Access 10: Percent of persons receiving only one service.	X	X	X	X	X	X
Access 11: Percent of persons receiving SSI/SSDI and services.			X	X	X	
Access 12: Cost is obstacle to service.			X	X	X	
APPROPRIATNESS						
Appro 1: Active participation in decisions concerning treatment.			X	X	X	
Appro 2: Coercion into treatment options.			X	X	X	
Appro 3: Percent of involuntary admissions to inpatient treatment.			X	X	X	
Appro 4: Resource spent on services that promote recovery.			X			
Appro 5: Percent of consumers who receive services that promote recovery.			X			
Appro 6: Percent of persons discharged from inpatient care who receive services in 7 days.	X	X	X	X	X	X
Appro 7: Percent of persons discharged from emergency care who receive services in 3 days.	X	X	X	X	X	X
Appro 8: Percent of persons who change provider during year or term of treatment.	X	X	X	X	X	X

This table highlits specific populations for which each individual measure will be computed.

Chapter 7: Setting and Meeting Performance and Accreditation Requirements

Quality According to QISMC

HCFA's New Managed Care Standards Are Fueling Controversy, Particularly in the Behavioral Arena

JON HAMILTON

Behavioral health care organizations will have to offer objective evidence that they are helping Medicaid patients under the Health Care Financing Administration's (HCFA) latest quality initiative.

The Quality Improvement System for Managed Care (QISMC)—released in draft form in early 1998—declares that assessments of process and structure are no longer enough; all managed care plans with Medicare or Medicaid contracts must demonstrate improvement in patients' health and functional status.

Proposed regulations based on QISMC are expected in July 1998, final regulations in October. But because of QISMC's long phase-in period, lack of specifics, and efforts to give flexibility to both states and managed care plans, it may take years to determine the initiative's true impact. Also unclear is how QISMC requirements will mesh with existing government and private standards.

An All-Purpose Quality Tool

QISMC represents the government's ambitious effort to fashion a single, data-oriented system to ensure good care in virtually all government-funded managed care programs. It is intended to set the standards for both Medicare and Medicaid, and for both medical and behavioral care, whether carved out or integrated.

To create the system, HCFA hired the National Academy for State Health Policy (NASHP) to convene managed care organization representatives, state and federal purchasers and regulators, providers, and beneficiary advocates. Later, aided by special funding from the Substance Abuse and Mental Health Services Administration (SAMHSA), NASHP gathered a separate group of experts in mental health and substance abuse care. In early 1998, after considering input from these groups, NASHP distributed a "public review draft" of QISMC.

The draft defines quality as "the organization's objectively measured performance in protecting and improving the health, functional status, and satisfaction of its enrolled Medicare and Medicaid beneficiaries." The document does not endorse specific measurement systems, however, and gives both plans and states considerable leeway in implementation.

Under QISMC, every Medicaid MCO eventually will have to measure performance in 11 clinical "focus areas," including mental health treatment and substance abuse treatment. MCOs also will have to measure performance in six nonclinical areas, such as timeliness of services, complaint handling, and cultural competence. Choice of particular topics within each focus area is left to the managed care organization.

But organizations need not show improvement in any area until the end of the second year of review, and then need results in just two clinical and two nonclinical areas. Results for all focus

---

Source: Hamilton J. Quality According to QISMC. In: 1999 Medicaid Managed Behavioral Care Sourcebook, K Coughlin, ed. New York: Faulkner & Gray, pp. 368-370

Jon Hamilton, a writer based in Bellingham WA, was a 1997-1998 Media Fellow with the Henry J. Kaiser Family Foundation.

areas are not required until the end of the fifth year, which means an MCO could choose not to address mental health and substance abuse improvement until then.

Moreover, implementation could vary considerably from state to state. That's because setting minimum acceptable performance levels under QISMC will be left to state officials. States also will have the right to specify alternative focus areas if they're not satisfied with the ones on the list.

Areas of Uncertainty

HCFA officials say the new system is meant to address the confusion caused by multiple government assessment systems and a proliferation of private assessments and accreditation programs. The QISMC draft promises to "reduce duplicative or conflicting efforts and send a uniform message on quality to organizations and consumers."

So far, however, there has been considerable disagreement about what that message is. Backers of QISMC say it will set a new, higher standard for all managed care. Critics, though, say it lacks teeth and specificity, especially in the areas of substance abuse treatment, mental health care, and care of groups including the disabled.

NAHSP sent the draft to hundreds of organizations for comment. About 100 responses addressed behavioral care and substance abuse treatment, said Jeff Merrill, director of Economics and Policy Research at the University of Pennsylvania's Treatment Research Institute.

Merrill said respondents generally supported the QISMC effort, but added they had questions about certain aspects of the system. Among the questions, he said, were whether HCFA had the expertise to address mental health and substance abuse standards, whether MCOs are capable of carrying out the new performance measurements, how the system applies to carve-out plans, what role consumers play in quality assurance, and whether QISMC does enough to protect the privacy of mental health and substance abuse patients.

Despite such concerns, QISMC has some important backers, including SAMHSA.

"We're very enthusiastic," said Eric Goplerud, SAMHSA's associate administrator for managed care. "One of the things we've got to do is reduce the duplication and conflict between accrediting organizations and get a meaningful core set of quality standards. This looks like a really valuable engine for doing that."

Goplerud said the special panel on mental health and substance abuse greatly strengthened QISMC in those areas. Not only were mental health and substance abuse treatment included on the list of clinical focus areas, he said, but the draft document also took steps to address such issues as confidentiality and the adequacy of provider networks.

But some in the behavioral health field were less supportive.

"I hope HCFA reexamines the entire document with the idea of not issuing it at all," said Al Guida, vice president for Government Affairs of the National Mental Health Association.

Guida said HCFA is wrong to assume a single set of guidelines can assure quality care for special populations, including the disabled and mentally ill. Moreover the draft is "woefully inadequate" for these populations, he said, because it fails to specifically address issues such as adequate case management and appropriate referrals to adequate provider networks.

"HCFA has placed states' flexibility over the health concerns of people with disabilities in Medicaid," he said.

Claudia Schlosberg, staff attorney with the National Health Law Program, said she fears QISMC signals a move away from government enforcement.

"Quality improvement is not a substitute for regulatory oversight," she said. Schlosberg also thinks QISMC gives MCOs too much freedom in choosing which areas to focus on. She notes that a plan with a problem in one clinical area could avoid fixing it for five years under the proposed phase-in.

QISMC's Future

Although the QISMC document now in circulation is labeled a draft, there will be no final version released, HCFA officials said. Instead, comments on the draft are being used in shaping forthcoming regulations.

QISMC's ultimate manifestation also will be affected by the Balanced Budget Act of 1997, which came along after the QISMC project was

> ## QISMC's Charge
>
> "Under QISMC, a uniform set of quality standards will be used by HCFA and State Medicaid agencies in initial and ongoing determinations that an organization is eligible to enter into a Medicare or Medicaid contract. Each organization will:
> - Operate an internal program of quality assessment and performance improvement that achieves demonstrable improvements in enrollee health, functional status, or satisfaction across a broad spectrum of care and services.
> - Collect and report data reflecting its performance on standardized measures of health outcomes and enrollee satisfaction, and meet such minimum performance levels on these measures as may be established under its contract with HCFA or the State Medicaid agency.
> - Demonstrate compliance with basic requirements for administrative structures and processes that promote quality of care and beneficiary protection."
>
> *Source: Standards and Guidelines for Review of Medicaid and Medicare Managed Care Organizations, Public Review Draft, December 22, 1997.*

well under way. In fact, HCFA had not even finished analyzing the Amendment's implications for Medicaid when the QISMC draft was released.

Observers expect that QISMC will be tweaked to become consistent with the Act's new requirements to ensure quality in Medicaid managed care organizations. However, the QISMC draft concludes, "These requirements are substantially in accord with the directions HCFA was already taking under the QISMC process."

Performance Indicator Measurement In Behavioral Healthcare

Data Capture Methods, Cost-Effectiveness, And Emerging Stadards

Executive Summary

Many stakeholder and interest groups express concern publicly and frequently that aggressive cost containment efforts may be diminishing the access to and quality of behavioral healthcare services. Compelling anecdotes abound in support of this assertion, but objective data are necessary for purchasers and consumers to truly be able to hold organizations accountable for the accessibility and quality of their services. Data are also needed for purchasers and consumers of these services to make informed selection decisions based on criteria other than price.

A new approach to addressing this challenge is to measure and compare the performance of behavioral healthcare services and systems through standardized methods across similar types of organizations and report it openly in a "report card." This approach has already stimulated behavioral healthcare organizations to collect and report new types of data and to further develop their infrastructure of staff and information systems to support this capability. For most behavioral healthcare organizations, the cost of developing and maintaining this infrastructure is steep and is especially challenging to undertake in the current era of cost containment and downward price pressures.

In this context, the Institute for Behavioral Healthcare's National Leadership Council (NLC) decided to undertake a series of report card-related studies to determine the performance indicators that would provide the most value to the industry. The studies were based on detailed survey data collected from NLC member organizations. The NLC is a consortium of more than 300 of the leading behavioral healthcare organizations in the United States, which have joined forces to support and participate in projects to improve the behavioral healthcare field. This consortium includes group practices, community mental health centers, hospital-based systems, managed care organizations, pharmaceutical companies, professional and trade associations, and others. In aggregate, they cover behavioral healthcare benefits for over 110 million Americans and operate over 50% of the psychiatric hospital beds as well as a substantial percentage of the ambulatory and intermediate care services in the United States. The NLC's mission, size, and diversity position it to effectively undertake survey projects that provide unique and valuable information for the entire field.

The first phase of the NLC Performance Indicator Project was conducted to identify the performance indicators that are most widely used and valued by different types of behavioral healthcare organizations. The study also examined how these organizations rated the relative meaningfulness and validity of the information provided by different performance indicators, and how administratively feasible they regarded measurement of each indicator. This study, published in 1996, was the first of its kind to provide empirical data on the usefulness of the indicators from the organizations that actually measure them.

The second phase of the project, reported in this publication, is a natural extension of the first,

---

Source: Institute for Behavioral Healthcare Council. Performance Indicator Measurement in Behavioral Healthcare: Data Capture Methods, Cost-Effectiveness, and Emerging Standards; Phase II Survey Results and Future Implications. *Portola Valley CA: IBH, 1997. (Reprinted with permission).*

and provides the next step in gathering information needed by the field for comparative performance monitoring. Twenty-eight of the most widely used indicators, as determined in Phase I, were incorporated into a survey instrument that addressed organizations' experiences in actually measuring each indicator. Questions asked regarding measurement of each indicator included methods of data collection, costliness of data tracking, value for external reporting and for internal quality improvement, and performance standards set for each organization with regard to each indicator.

The data were analyzed in aggregate and separately for each of four main industry segments of behavioral healthcare: managed care organizations, group practices, community mental health centers, and specialty behavioral health facilities. Leaders from diverse behavioral healthcare organizations can find results described separately for their type of organization in the appendices. The results are described in detail with graphs and pie charts for each of the 28 indicators. The information includes the performance standards set by organizations of each type, providing an excellent resource for benchmarking.

The results of this study clearly indicate which performance indicators are perceived to provide the most and the least cost-effective information. Thus, for the first time, this study establishes a "relative value scale" for behavioral health performance indicators. The more cost-effective indicators focus primarily on access and utilization, although one of the consumer satisfaction measures and one of the outcome measures were also rated highly. Of the least cost-effective indicators, most involve traditional documentation review approaches to quality assurance, while others involve prevention services for which sufficient economic incentives do not exist.

The study reports several other important findings. A wide variability in methods used to measure a few of the indicators was revealed, so that variability in performance for these indicators probably reflects measurement method variance more than true differences in standards. This points to the importance of detailed instructions on measurement methods to ensure standardization and comparability of the data that are reported. This is an important responsibility for those organizations that undertake to develop and implement report cards.

Another important finding was a strong correlation between the types of performance data that organizations use the most for external reporting and for internal quality improvement. One interpretation of this finding is that purchaser requirements are increasingly influencing the kinds of performance upon which organizations focus.

Performance measurement is becoming widespread because of strong industry ideals and concerns regarding quality from consumers and purchasers that override challenging financial issues. To establish the ongoing capability to meet performance reporting requirements, behavioral healthcare organizations must develop a substantial information infrastructure, at considerable expense. To make these endeavors cost effective, those accrediting, quality assurance, and other organizations that develop performance reporting requirements and report cards are advised to select the most cost-effective indicators possible for use in performance measurement.

To accomplish this goal successfully, report card developers should also examine empirical data on the relative cost-effectiveness of each performance indicator they consider for selection and incorporation into report cards. Since cost-effectiveness ratings are likely to change over time as the field develops its information infrastructure further, empirical data on cost-effectiveness should be collected and examined regularly. The authors and the NLC Performance Indicator Task Force hope this study will help further the quality and accountability of our entire field in that positive direction.

Methodology

This phase of the Performance Indicators Study was conducted as a sequel to the last study published in July of 1996, which surveyed the industry on the current usage of 69 different performance indicators under the five domains of Access, Clinical Appropriateness, Quality, Outcomes, and Prevention. These domains are defined as follows:

- **Access:** The degree to which services and information about care are conveniently and easily obtained.
- **Clinical appropriateness:** The degree to which the type, amount, and level of clin-

ical services are delivered to promote the most positive clinical outcomes for the consumers.
- **Quality:** The extent to which excellence in care is a standard that is maintained and continuously reviewed.
- **Outcomes:** The extent to which services are cost effective and have a favorable effect on consumers' symptoms, functioning, and well-being.
- **Prevention:** The services and activities offered to reduce the prevalence, severity, or risk of mental health problems in a population.

For the purposes of the current study, 28 of the most commonly used indicators from the previous study were selected for inclusion in the survey. A task force of members representing behavioral group practices, managed care organizations, community mental health centers, and integrated delivery systems was convened to design the survey and develop the data collection methodology. Feedback on a draft survey was solicited from the NLC Roundtable participants at the Behavioral Healthcare Quality and Accountability Summit in June 1996 and incorporated into the final version.

Participants

All NLC members were surveyed; 106 responded, resulting in a return rate of 40%. The total number of respondents included 15 (14.20%) managed care organizations (MCOs), 17 (16.0%) behavioral group practices (BGPs), 54 (50.9%) community mental health centers/social and rehabilitation service agencies (CMHCs), 16 (15.1%) integrated delivery systems/specialty behavioral health facilities (IDS/SBFs), and 4 (3.8%) who identified themselves as belonging to an "other" category.

Additional information on the respondents was obtained and can be found in Table 1. As shown, respondents ranged in organization size, geographical location, capitation arrangements, and quality improvement staffing.

Survey Design

The survey consisted of three parts. Part I requested demographic information such as the industry segment the organization belonged to, its size, geographical location, primary business, and number of covered lives. The questions in Part II formed the main body of the survey and requested the following information on each indicator chosen for this survey:
- Whether the indicator was currently being used by the organization and, if not, whether it was planned to be used within the next year
- Primary data capture method for the indicator
- Number of indicators in the survey used in analyses with the indicator
- Frequency of data collection for the indicator
- Estimated level of staff time for tracking the indicator
- Estimated level of costs to track the indicator
- Estimated value of tracking the indicator for purposes of quality improvement
- Estimated value of tracking the indicator for external reporting purposes
- If the indicator was currently in use, whether there were specific standards established
- Reasons why the indicator was not currently in use, if applicable

Some of the questions requested categorical answers, while others required a 3-point or 4-point rating score from respondents. Care was taken to avoid open-ended answers, in order to elicit more quantifiable information.

Part III of the survey requested more specific information on the range of standards established for each indicator in use. Additional information regarding the methods of measurement, period of measurement, and sample size was requested on four outcomes indicators.

Procedure

The Institute for Behavioral Healthcare mailed surveys to all members of the National Leadership Council with instructions for completing them within a specified period of time. All surveys were coded so that anonymity of the respondents could be maintained. Data entry and analyses were subsequently performed by the authors of this report.

Table 1
Demographic Data on Respondents

Variable	Total (%)
Number of Sites	
1-5	28 (26.7%)
6-10	26 (24.8%)
11-25	30 (28.6%)
26-50	12 (11.4%)
More than 50	9 (8.6%)
Clinical Staff FTEs (excluding, provider network)	
1-50	42 (41.2%)
51-100	21 (20.6%)
101-500	33 (32.4%)
More than 500	6 (5.7%)
Provider Network Clinicians	
1-50	49 (53.3%)
51-100	10 (10.9%)
101-500	13 (14.1%)
501-1000	4 (4.3%)
More than 1000	16 (17.3%)
Geographic Location	
Single site	28 (26.4%)
Multiple sites in one state	54 (50.9%)
Multiple sites in more than one state	24 (22.6%)
Number of Covered Lives	
1-50,000	43 (44.8%)
50,001-250,000	24 (25.0%)
250,001-500,000	10 (10.4%)
More than 500,000	9 (9.3%)
Not applicable	10 (10.4%)
Total FTE Devoted to Quality Improvement Activities	
0-.5	8 (7.6%)
.6-1	14 (13.3%)
>1-2	26 (24.8%)
>2-5	35 (33.3%)
>5-10	13 (12.4%)
More than 10	9 (8.7%)

Results

Results for each item dimension across the 28 indicators are summarized in aggregate form in this section along with presentation of significant differences among the four industry segments where they exist. Significant differences were defined as those with a probability level of less than .05, using chi square analyses. Detailed results within each of the four industry segments are presented in Appendices B-E.

Data for four of the item dimensions were linear, allowing for correlational analyses. The four dimensions are estimated staff time and overall costs to track each indicator, and estimated value of each indicator for internal quality improvement and for external reporting. In addition to the summary, these results are reported in more detail in the following sections and in Appendices B-E. A composite "cost-effectiveness" score for each indicator was also derived and is listed in the section "Cost-Effectiveness of Indicators" with a brief summary.

Table 2. Usage Rates Varying by Industry Segment

Indicator	MCO Usage	BGP Usage	IDS/SBF Usage	CMHC Usage
Phone Response Time	86.5%	47.1%	40.0%	24.5%
Wait Time/Routine	93.3%	82.4%	37.5%	68.5%
Outpatient Visits/ 1000	86.7%	88.2%	62.5%	51.8%
Intensive Outpatient ALOS	60.0%	41.2%	37.5%	31.5%
Partial Hospitalization ALOS	60.0%	41.2%	37.5%	31.5%
Phone Abandonment	100.0%	37.5%	20.0%	13.9%
Inpatient Case Review for Adequate Documentation	50.0%	31.2%	93.8%	44.2%
Inpatient Cases Audited for Medical Necessity	50.0%	41.2%	87.5%	36.5%

Usage Rates

In general, MCOs were most likely to use all of the performance indicators included in this study, with the exception of performance indicators oriented toward inpatient care (e.g., inpatient Cases Audited for Medical Necessity and Percent of Inpatient Cases Reviewed for Adequate Documentation). These indicators were more likely to be used by the SBF/IDS respondents, as shown in Table 2.

Although CMHCs varied considerably as to whether they used various performance indicators, their responses most closely resembled those of the BGPs. However, the percentage of CMHCs that used each of these performance indicators was lower than the percentage of organizations within the other three segments surveyed.

Approximately 25% of the respondents overall indicated that they were planning to use the following indicators in the upcoming year:
- Percent of Patients Having Improved Functioning after Treatment
- Percent of Patients Whose Quality of Life Improved after Treatment
- Percent of Patients Having Reduced Symptoms after Treatment

Primary Data Capture Method

The primary data capture method used by most respondents depended upon both the performance indicator and industry segment using that indicator. For example, performance indicators pertaining to utilization of services were more likely to be captured vis-a-vis direct computer entry, whereas medical record reviews and audits were more likely to be tracked with paper and pencil methods. Managed care organizations were more likely to use direct computer entry methods, while CMHCs were more likely to use paper and pencil tracking systems as well as clerical entries.

Table 3 shows the 13 indicators for which there were significant differences among the four industry segments. For the most part, MCOs were most likely to use direct computer entry methods when compared to the other three groups. Methods for measuring accessibility (e.g., telephone response time, waiting times for appointments, etc.) were most likely to be direct computer entry.

Other Indicators Used in Analysis With Primary Indicator

The question of whether other indicators were used along with the primary indicator was designed to assess how data from the performance indicators are integrated into overall systems analyses for the purposes of quality improvement, accreditation, payor reporting, and so on. For example, are cost analyses integrated with utilization rates and clinical outcomes to provide more comprehensive data pertaining to clinical effectiveness? While this study did not determine which indicators were analyzed in conjunction with others, respondents were able to specify how many indicators are integrated in their respective data analyses.

The majority of respondents indicated that no more than 5 indicators were integrated in any overall data analysis, which remained fairly consistent across industry segments. Twenty percent or more of the respondents were integrating 11 or more other indicators with each of the following:

Table 3. Primary Data Capture Method by Industry Segment

Indicator	Industry Segment Results
Patient Satisfaction w/Access	More than 70% MCOs use scanning or direct computer entry; 66-91% BGPs, CMHCs, and IDS/SPFs use paper and pencil or paper to computer entry
Telephone Response Time	More than 75% BGPs and MCOs use direct computer entry; 60-80% IDS/SBFs and CMHCs use paper and pencil or paper to computer entry
Waiting Time/Routine Visit	50% MCOs use direct computer entry; 70-80% BGPs, IDS/SFBs, and CMHCs use paper and pencil or paper to computer entry
Waiting Time/Emergent Visit	40-50% MCOs and IDS/SBFs use direct computer entry; more than 70% BGPs and CMHCs use paper and pencil or paper to computer entry
Inpatient Days/1000 & Outpatient Visits/1000	93% MCOs use direct computer entry; 55-70% BGPs, IDS/SBFs, and CMHCs use paper and pencil or paper to computer entry
Outpatient Avg. Number of Sessions	87% MCOs use direct computer entry; only 40-50% BGPS, IDS/SBFs, and CMHCs use direct computer entry
Partial Hospitalization Average Length of Stay	86% MCOs use direct computer entry; 50-70% BGPs, IDS/SBFs, and CMHCs use paper and pencil or paper to computer entry
Telephone Abandonment Rate	80-100% MCOs, BGPs, and IDS/SBFs use direct computer entry; 67% CMHCs use paper and pencil
Written Plan for Quality	More than 25% MCOs and IDS/SBFs use computer entry; less than 2% BGPs and CMHCs use direct computer entry
Medical Records Audited	61% IDS/SBFs use paper and pencil or paper to computer entry; 70-75% MCOs, BGPs, and CMHCs use paper and pencil
Patients Readmitted	82% MCOs use direct computer entry; 67-88% BGPs, IDS/SBFs, and CMHCs use paper and pencil or paper to computer entry
Patients Improved Functioning	67% MCOs scan from paper to computer; 64-77% BGPs, IDS/SBFs, and CMHCs use paper and pencil or paper to computer entry

- Percent of Patients Satisfied with Access to Care
- Percent of Patients Reporting Overall Satisfaction with Quality of Care
- Written Plan for Monitoring Quality of Care
- Percent of Patients Whose Quality of Life Improved after Treatment
- Percent of Patients Having Reduced Symptoms after Treatment

Frequency of Data Collection

Frequency of data collection varied among indicators. For example, 50% of respondents indicated that they monitor phone response time daily, while

64.5% reported they monitor phone abandonment rates daily. However, the majority of respondents indicated they measure patient satisfaction on a quarterly basis, while they measure outcomes on anywhere from a daily to quarterly basis.

Differences were noted among industry segments on four indicators:

- Percent of Patients Reporting Overall Satisfaction with Quality of Care (BGPs, MCOs, and IDS/SBFs were more likely to monitor this indicator on a daily basis than CMHCs)
- Percent of Claims Paid within a Specified Period (50% of MCOs and IDS/SBFs monitor this indicator on a daily basis, while 70% of the BGPs and CMHCs monitor this indicator on a monthly basis)
- Percent of Patients Having Improved Functioning after Treatment (more MCOs and IDS/SBFs assess this indicator on a daily basis, while BGPs assess it on a monthly basis, and CMHCs assess it on a quarterly basis)
- Dissemination of Information on Behavioral Health and Prevention Issues (MCOs and BGPs were more likely to disseminate information on a quarterly basis)

Estimated Staff Time and Costs For Tracking Indicators

Tables 4 and 5 show indicators sorted according to the amount of staff time required to track them and average rated costliness to monitor. The ratings are aggregated for respondents throughout the behavioral healthcare industry. Appendices B-E also contain similar tables with data separated by each of the four main industry segments surveyed.

There was a .97 correlation between the amount of staff time required to track each indicator and the overall costliness of tracking. This suggests that management regards staff time as

Table 4. Averaged Ratings of the Staff Time Required for Tracking Each Indicator

Indicators (in rank order)	Rating
% of Inpatient Cases Reviewed for Adequate Documentation	2.22
% of Medical Records Audited for Quality	2.22
Written Plan for Monitoring Quality of Care	2.25
% of Inpatient Cases Audited for Medical Necessity	2.14
% of Providers Recredentialed	2.00
% of Patients w/Reduced Symptoms after Treatment	1.98
% of Patients w/Improved Functioning after Treatment	1.97
% of Inpatient Cases Reviewed w/Med. Director for Med. Necessity	1.95
Written Criteria to Determine Medical Necessity	1.92
% of Patients Whose Quality of Life Improved after Treatment	1.88
% of Patients w/Adverse Outcomes	1.85
Written Guidelines for High-Risk Procedures	1.81
% of Patients Reporting Overall Satisfaction w/Care	1.71
Psychoeducational Prevention Groups in Place	1.66
Dissemination of Info. on Behavioral Health and Prevention Issues	1.61
Waiting Time for Scheduling Emergent Visits	1.59
Outpatient Average Number of Sessions	1.59
% of Claims Paid within Specified Time	1.59
Waiting Time for Scheduling Routine Visits	1.56
% of Patients Readmitted after Specified Period	1.56
Acute Inpatient Average Length of Stay	1.52
Outpatient Visits/1000	1.52
% of Patients Satisfied w/Access to Care	1.45
Intensive Outpatient Average Length of Stay	1.41
Acute Inpatient Days/1000	1.41
Partial Hospitalization Average Length of Stay	1.41
Telephone Response Time by Staff	1.36
Telephone Abandonment Rate	1.22

1=Minimal, 2=Moderate, 3=High

Table 5. Averaged Ratings of the Costliness of Tracking Each Indicator

Indicators (in rank order)	Rating
% of Inpatient Cases Audited for Medical Necessity	2.18
% of Inpatient Cases Reviewed for Adequate Documentation	2.16
% of Medical Records Audited for Quality	2.13
Written Plan for Monitoring Quality of Care	2.11
% of Patients w/Reduced Symptoms after Treatment	2.00
% of Patients w/Improved Functioning after Treatment	1.98
% of Inpatient Cases Reviewed w/Med. Director for Med. Necessity	1.95
% of Providers Recredentialed	1.92
% of Patients Whose Quality of Life Improved after Treatment	1.88
% of Patients w/Adverse Outcomes	1.83
Written Guidelines for High-Risk Procedures	1.79
Written Criteria to Determine Medical Necessity	1.78
% of Patients Reporting Overall Satisfaction w/Care	1.71
Dissemination of Info. on Behavioral Health and Prevention Issues	1.68
Psychoeducational Prevention Groups in Place	1.63
% of Claims Paid within Specified Time	1.58
% of Patients Readmitted after Specified Period	1.56
Outpatient Average Number of Sessions	1.55
Outpatient Visits/1000	1.50
% of Patients Satisfied w/Access to Care	1.46
Waiting Time for Scheduling Emergent Visits	1.45
Telephone Response Time by Staff	1.45
Acute Inpatient Average Length of Stay	1.44
Telephone Abandonment Rate	1.44
Waiting Time for Scheduling Routine Visits	1.42
Acute Inpatient Days/1000	1.38
Intensive Outpatient Average Length of Stay	1.36
Partial Hospitalization Average Length of Stay	1.34

1=Minimal, 2=Moderate, 3=High

the primary cost factor in tracking these indicators. These correlations are discussed in the later section, "Interrelationships between Indicators."

Respondents gave a wide range of ratings to the indicators for the dimensions of staff time-intensiveness and costliness. The average rating on a 3-point scale for staff time ranged from a high of 2.2 for Percent of Inpatient Cases Reviewed for Adequate Documentation to a low of 1.22 for Telephone Abandonment Rate. For overall costliness, the highest average rating was 2.18 for Percent of Inpatient Cases Audited for Medical Necessity, and the lowest was 1.35 for Average Length of Stay in a Partial Hospital Program.

The indicators rated by the combined industry segments as requiring the most staff time and highest overall costs to monitor were primarily process indicators. They are typically found in accreditation standards, in contrast to outcome indicators usually found in report cards. These particular process indicators are categorized in domains that reflect the Appropriateness and Quality of Care domains:

- Percent of Inpatient Cases Audited for Medical Necessity
- Percent of Inpatient Cases Reviewed for Adequate Documentation
- Percent of Medical Records Audited for Quality
- Written Plan for Monitoring Quality of Care
- Percent of Inpatient Cases Reviewed with the Medical Director for Medical Necessity
- Percent of Providers Recredentialed Annually

The other indicators rated as staff time-intensive and costly were clinical outcomes. Because of their costliness to administer, they typically are not required in most report cards. They are:

- Percent of Patients Having Reduced Symptoms after Treatment

- Percent of Patients Having Improved Functioning after Treatment

All six indicators rated by the combined industry segments as requiring the least staff time and as least costly to track all reflect the domain of Access. They are performance outcome indicators commonly found in major report cards and in purchaser reporting requirements:
- Average Length of Stay in a Partial Program
- Average Length of Stay in an Intensive Outpatient Program
- Inpatient Days per Thousand (Enrolled Members)
- Waiting Time for Scheduling Routine Office Visits
- Telephone Call Abandonment Rate
- Average Length of Stay in an Inpatient Program

Estimated Value of Indicator for Internal Quality Improvement And for External Reporting

Tables 6 and 7 include information regarding the perceived value of each indicator for internal quality improvement and separately for external reporting purposes. The indicators are sorted in descending value with respect to their ratings on each of the two value dimensions. Appendices B-E contain four tables with the same type of data categorized by industry segments.

There was a .85 correlation between the perceived value of information provided by each indicator for internal quality improvement and for external reporting purposes. This indicates a strong convergence between what organizations find useful to improve their internal processes and what they need to report to external agencies. These correlations are discussed in the next section.

Respondents rated all of the indicators as moderate to high in value on both dimensions, but there was a substantial range. The average rating of an indicator's value for quality improvement on a 4-point scale ranged from a high of 2.95 for Inpatient Cases per Thousand to a low of 1.84 for Dissemination of Information on Behavioral Health and Prevention Services. For value of each indicator for external reporting requirements, the average ratings ranged from 2.88 for Percent of Patients Satisfied with the Overall Quality of Care to 1.93 for Dissemination of Information on Behavioral Health and Prevention Services.

The indicators rated by the combined industry segments as most valuable for either quality improvement or external reporting were all utilization and outcome-oriented measures, typically found in report cards. None were process indicators, more typically found in accreditation standards and procedures. These particular outcome-oriented indicators are best categorized in domains that reflect Access to Care, Quality of Care, and Outcomes of Care. They are:
- Acute Inpatient Days/1000 (Enrolled Members)
- Outpatient Visits/1000 (Enrolled Members)
- Percent of Patients Reporting Overall Satisfaction with Quality of Care
- Percent of Patients with Adverse Outcomes
- Average Length of Stay in an Inpatient Hospital Program
- Percent of Patients Having Improved Functioning after Treatment
- Percent of Patients Readmitted after a Specified Period of Time

The indicators rated by the combined industry segments as providing the least value for internal quality improvement and for external reporting purposes were the two indicators within the Prevention domain. This undoubtedly reflects a current state of affairs in which the industry does not have strong incentives for prevention and demand management programs. The indicators are:
- Dissemination of Information on Behavioral Health and Prevention Issues
- Psychoeducational Prevention Groups in Place

Other indicators rated as among the least valuable for both quality improvement and external reporting are:
- Percent of Inpatient Cases Reviewed for Adequate Documentation
- Average Length of Stay in a Partial Hospital Program

A few indicators were rated as among the least valuable for quality improvement but of somewhat more value for external reporting. They are:
- Percent of Providers Recredentialed Annually

Table 6. Averaged Ratings of the Perceived Value of Each Indicator for Internal Quality Improvement

Indicators (in rank order)	Rating
Acute Inpatient Days/1000	2.95
Outpatient Visits/1000	2.86
% of Patients Reporting Overall Satisfaction w/Care	2.83
% of Patients w/Adverse Outcomes	2.83
Acute Inpatient Average Length of Stay	2.78
% of Patients w/Improved Functioning after Treatment	2.77
% of Patients Readmitted after Specified Period	2.77
% of Patients w/Reduced Symptoms after Treatment	2.73
Written Plan for Monitoring Quality of Care	2.73
Written Guidelines for High-Risk Procedures	2.72
Outpatient Average Number of Sessions	2.71
% of Claims Paid within Specified Time	2.70
% of Medical Records Audited for Quality	2.69
Waiting Time for Scheduling Emergent Visits	2.69
% of Inpatient Cases Reviewed for Adequate Documentation	2.66
Waiting Time for Scheduling Routine Visits	2.63
% of Patients Satisfied with Access to Care	2.63
Intensive Outpatient Average Length of Stay	2.61
Written Criteria to Determine Medical Necessity	2.58
% of Inpatient Cases Audited for Medical Necessity	2.57
% of Patients Whose Quality of Life Improved after Treatment	2.54
Telephone Response Time by Staff	2.53
% of Inpatient Cases Reviewed w/Med. Director for Med. Necessity	2.51
Telephone Abandonment Rate	2.50
Partial Hospitalization Length of Stay	2.48
% of Providers Recredentialed	2.45
Psychoeducational Prevention Groups in Place	1.87
Dissemination of Info. on Behavioral Health and Prevention Issues	1.84

1=Low, 2=Moderate, 3=High, 4=Maximum

- Telephone Abandonment Rate
- Percent of Inpatient Cases Reviewed with a Medical Director for Medical Necessity

A few indicators were rated as among the least valuable for external reporting but of somewhat more value for internal quality improvement. They are:

   Written Criteria Available to Determine Medical Necessity for Each Level of Care
- Percent of Medical Records Audited for Quality
- Percent of Claims Paid within a Specified Number of Days

Interrelationships Between Indicators

The previous two sections review ratings for the indicators with respect to the four dimensions of Staff Time, Cost, Internal Quality Improvement, and External Reporting. These four dimensions were rated on a scale that can be considered linear and continuous, thereby permitting a correlational analysis. Table 8 summarizes the findings.

As was mentioned in the preceding two sections and indicated in Table 8, there is a highly significant correlation between staff time and overall costs involved in tracking the indicators and a similarly high correlation between the perceived value of the indicators for quality improvement and for external reporting purposes.

The most interesting finding in the table is the lack of significant positive correlations between the resources required to track these indicators and their perceived value. In fact, three of the four correlations are negative, although none significantly so. These findings have important implications for the industry, and they will be discussed in the concluding section of this report.

Table 7. Averaged Ratings of the Perceived Value of Each Indicator for External Reporting

Indicators (in rank order)	Rating
% of Patients Reporting Overall Satisfaction w/Care	2.88
Acute Inpatient Average Length of Stay	2.83
Outpatient Visits/1000	2.82
Acute Inpatient Days/1000	2.77
% of Patients w/Improved Functioning after Treatment	2.77
% of Patients Readmitted after Specified Period	2.73
Intensive Outpatient Average Length of Stay	2.67
Telephone Response Time by Staff	2.66
Waiting Time for Scheduling Emergent Visits	2.66
Telephone Abandonment Rate	2.65
% of Providers Recredentialed	2.65
Waiting Time for Scheduling Routine Visits	2.65
Outpatient Average Number of Sessions	2.65
% of Patients w/Reduced Symptoms after Treatment	2.65
% of Patients Satisfied with Access to Care	2.64
% of Inpatient Cases Reviewed w/Med. Director for Medical Necessity	2.60
% of Patients Whose Quality of Life Improved after Treatment	2.59
% of Patients w/Adverse Outcomes	2.58
% of Inpatient Cases Audited for Medical Necessity	2.55
Written Plan for Monitoring Quality of Care	2.54
Written Guidelines for High-Risk Procedures	2.54
% of Claims Paid within Specified Time	2.50
% of Inpatient Cases Reviewed for Adequate Documentation	2.46
Partial Hospitalization Length of Stay	2.43
% of Medical Records Audited for Quality	2.40
Written Criteria to Determine Medical Necessity	2.37
Dissemination of Info. on Behavioral Health and Prevention Issues	1.93
Psychoeducational Prevention Groups in Place	1.87

1=Low, 2=Moderate, 3=High, 4=Maximum

Correlation tables with the same data fields, disaggregated for the four industry segments surveyed, are included in Appendices B-E.

Cost-Effectiveness of Indicators

A composite "cost-effectiveness index" was derived by adding the rank order numbers for each indicator on the four item dimensions as follows:

1. Staff time for tracking the indicator (least time = 28, most time = 1)
2. Costs to track the indicator (least costly = 28, most costly = 1)
3. Value for internal quality improvement (most valued = 28, least valued = 1)
4. Value for external reporting (most valued = 28, least valued = 1)

Table 9 shows the relative cost-effectiveness of each indicator's rank ordered from most to least cost effective. The more cost-effective indicators were primarily in the Access domain and cover waiting time and utilization information. It is

Table 8. Correlations between Staff Time, Cost, Quality Improvement, and External Reporting

	Staff Time	Cost	Quality Improvement
Cost	.97		
Quality Improvement	.02	-.03	
External Reporting	-.17	-.18	.85

Table 9. Cost-Effectiveness Ranking of Indicators in Descending Value

Indicator	Cost-Effectiveness Score
Acute Inpatient Days/1000	104
Acute Inpatient Average Length of Stay	95
Outpatient Visits/1000	94
Intensive Outpatient Average Length of Stay	86
Percent of Patients Readmitted after Specified Period	82
Percent of Patients Reporting Overall Satisfaction with Quality of Care	80
Telephone Response Time by Staff Answering Calls	77
Telephone Call Abandonment Rate	76
Waiting Time for Scheduling Routine Office Visits	75
Outpatient Average Number of Sessions	74
Waiting Time for Scheduling Emergent Visits	72
% of Patients Satisfied with Access to Care	71
Partial Hospitalization Average Length of Stay	64
% of Patients Having Improved Functioning after Treatment	60
% of Patients with Adverse Outcomes	57
% of Claims Paid within Specified Period	53
% of Inpatient Cases Reviewed for Adequate Documentation	51
% of Cases Following Written Guidelines for High-Risk Procedures	50
% of Patients Having Reduced Symptoms after Treatment	47
% of Patients Whose Quality of Life Improved after Treatment	40
Written Plan for Monitoring Quality of Care	36
% of Inpatient Cases Reviewed with Medical Director for Medical Necessity	35
Written Criteria Available to Determine Medical Necessity for Each Level of Care	35
% of Providers Recredentialed	33
Psychoeducational Prevention Groups in Place	33
Dissemination of Information on Behavioral Health and Prevention Issues	31
% of Medical Records Audited for Quality	26
Inpatient Cases Audited for Medical Necessity	25

interesting to note that a patient satisfaction indicator (overall quality of care) and an outcome indicator (number of hospital readmissions) also ranked as among the most cost effective. Traditional documentation-oriented quality assurance indicators and prevention services ranked among the least cost effective.

Standards Established For Indicators

The majority of respondents have established performance standards for each indicator. More than 80% of respondents indicated they had established standards for the following indicators:

- Waiting Time for Scheduling Emergent Visits
- Telephone Call Abandonment Rate
- Percent of Inpatient Cases Reviewed for Adequate Documentation
- Inpatient Cases Audited for Medical Necessity
- Written Criteria Available to Determine Medical Necessity
- Percent of Medical Records Audited for Quality
- Percent of Patients Whose Quality of Life Improved after Treatment
- Percent of Patients Having Reduced Symptoms after Treatment
- Dissemination of Information on Behavioral Health and Prevention Issues
- Psychoeducational Prevention Groups in Place

There were no significant differences among industry segments as to whether standards had been established. Moreover, there were only four indicators for which there were significant differences in the specific standards established. These were:

- Acute Inpatient Days/1000 (MCOs and BGPs were more likely to report a standard of 11-20 days, while IDS/SBFs and CMHCs were more likely to report a standard of 1-10 days). Since this indicator refers to capitation contracts that do not pertain to many CMHCs, the meaning of these differences is open to question, and some of the responses may have been based on misunderstandings of the question.
- Partial Hospitalization ALOS (half of the MCOs established 11-15 ALOS, while 40-50% of the BGPs and IDS/SBFs established 6-10 days ALOS; CMHCs were much more variable across the ALOS range)
- Telephone Call Abandonment Rate (three fourths of the MCOs established a standard of 2-4% abandonment rate, while BGPs and CMHCs were more likely to have established a standard of less than 2% abandonment rate; IDS/SBFs were more variable in their responses). Since few of the BGPs and CMHCs use automated call distribution machines and, therefore, cannot measure abandonment rate precisely, the meaning of these differences is open to question and may in part be due to method variance.
- Percent of Claims Paid within a Specified Period (all of the MCOs reported they process 91-100% of claims within 30 days; other industry segments were more likely to process claims within 45 days)

More details regarding the specific standards set for each indicator by industry segment are available in Appendices B-E [not shown].

Reasons for Not Using Indicator

The most frequently cited reason for not using the indicator was its lack of relevance for that particular organization. Lack of technology was another reason respondents were not using a particular indicator. There were only two significant differences among industry segments for not using an indicator: IDS/SBFs were not as likely to track Intensive Outpatient Average Length of Stay because of budget constraints, while 100% of the IDS/SBFs were not as likely to track Percent of Patients Having Improved Functioning after Treatment because of limited resources.

Data on Special Indicators

Respondents varied considerably in the methods they used to assess patient satisfaction and patient improvement in symptoms, functioning, and quality of life. On-site administration of survey instruments was the most frequently reported assessment method for all the above items, although a large number of respondents also indicated that they contact patients by telephone, mail patients the surveys, and/or hold focus groups to obtain patient-related information.

Information on the time periods in which data are collected, the sample size studied to monitor each indicator, and specific survey instruments used is provided in Appendix F [not shown].

Conclusions

Provider and managed care organizations in both public and private sectors of the behavioral healthcare field are now routinely measuring their own performance and using the results for evaluation, reporting, and quality improvement. In doing so, they offer a particularly rich source of information on many aspects of organizational performance measurement. Their experience with these measurements can serve as an alternative or complement to expert consensus in formulating and evolving future performance indicators and measures for behavioral healthcare industry report cards.

Perhaps the most significant finding of this study is that organizations within our field are now able to make clear distinctions between more and less cost-effective performance indicators. At a time when many behavioral healthcare organizations are experiencing downward price pressures and declining profit margins, the recommendation or requirement to increase performance measurement can place a troublesome burden on organizations struggling to remain viable in the marketplace. In this context, ratings of the comparative cost-effectiveness of different performance indicators offer valuable information to guide the efforts of those who develop report card indicators and accreditation requirements. It is important that the indicators and requirements they select are ones that maximize the likelihood of quality improvement at the least cost.

Clear patterns are apparent in current industry ratings of the relative cost-effectiveness of performance indicators. Access (e.g., wait time) and utilization (average length of stay, days/1000) measures dominated the list of the most cost-effective indicators. An outcomes measure (inpatient readmission rates) and a measure of consumer satisfaction (with overall quality of care) were also among the top ten. The latter two indicators are more costly to measure but are clearly regarded as providing very valuable information.

Among the lowest on the list of cost-effectiveness ratings were traditional documentation review-oriented quality assurance indicators. This finding clearly suggests the importance of re-evaluating the appropriateness of traditional accreditation standards. Also among the least costeffective indicators were those related to education and prevention services. While preventive services are clearly worthwhile, the findings from this survey indicate that providers and managed care payors are not motivated to invest in prevention yet. Purchasers of behavioral healthcare services have yet to recognize the need to create strong incentives for developing behavioral health promotion, prevention, and risk management services.

This study confirmed the growing power of purchasers to drive the quality and accountability agenda. Respondents to the survey reported a strong relationship between the types of performance data they are required to report to external audiences (e.g., commercial and public purchasers, health plan payors, accrediting agencies and regulators), and the types of performance data they most use for their organizations' internal quality improvement efforts. As purchasers increase and refine their awareness of the types of performance data they can request from managed care and provider organizations, they will be in a better position to truly influence the behavioral healthcare market towards greater quality and accountability through the application of value-based purchasing methods.

There is a surprisingly high level of agreement among organizations, even across different segments of the behavioral healthcare industry, with regard to appropriate standards for some of the most commonly used performance indicators. It is doubtful that this would have been the case ten or more years ago. As purchasers form purchasing coalitions, and as provider and managed care industries consolidate, consensus on standards increases. This creates a basis for hope that our field can develop common measures and data collection methods, common standards from which to benchmark, and the capability of the industry to provide comparative data across similar types of organizations for selection decisions. This is essential if the behavioral healthcare field is to substantiate the value of their services to purchasers and consumers in a manner sufficiently compelling to circumvent the trend towards turning our professional services into a commodity. Comparable and objective data are required to make this shift so that purchasers and consumers can be assured of receiving accessible, appropriate, and high-quality care.

The variability in standards for a few of the indicators was clearly attributable to differences in how respondents measured them rather than to true differences between organizations in the standards they set for themselves. The behavioral healthcare field currently includes substantial diversity in approaches to interpreting and measuring performance indicators. Organizations within the field also differ widely in the degree to which they have developed their information systems and related infrastructure, and their consequent capability to measure performance with respect to certain specific indicators. Report card developers must address these disparities in interpretation and in measurement capabilities among organizations by providing clear, highly specific instructions to them on the measurement methods required to collect performance indicator data. This is crucial to assure comparability of performance indicator data across multiple organizations.

A further finding in this study was the variability of measurement instruments used and standards set with regard to consumer satisfaction and patient outcomes. Although consensus about which measures to use for evaluating performance with respect to these indicators was low, respondents confirmed the great importance of the indicators and standardized measurement methods. If we are to improve on effectiveness as a field and gain broader acceptance for the value of our behavioral health services, we must find ways to encourage widespread adoption of performance measures and standards in order to facilitate benchmarking and comparability. This presents a great opportunity for industrywide quality improvement through a consensus process that would result in the capability to compare performance data among organizations. We hope this study will help further others' efforts in that direction, for the betterment of our field and the health and well-being of our nation.

State Mental Health Directors Adopt a Framework of Performance Indicators For Mental Health Systems

May 1998

The National Association of State Mental Health Program Directors (NASMHPD) have developed a standardized framework for the evaluation of public mental health services across the country. This framework draws from the work of various other national initiatives, including the Mental Health Statistics Improvement Program (MHSIP), The National Committee on Quality Assurance (NCQA), the National Alliance for the Mentally Ill (NAMI), the American College of Mental Health Administrators, the Panel on Performance Partnership Grants, and the NASMBPD Research Institute initiatives.

At the NASMHPD Commissioners' Meeting, held in Washington, D.C., December 10-12, 1997, the SMFIA Commissioners/Directors voted unanimously to adopt and support the promotion of a standardized framework of performance measures and outcome indicators. The framework consists of five domains: access, quality/appropriateness, outcomes, structure/plan management, and early intervention/prevention. Within each domain, a set of performance measures is also identified. These domains and performance measures are attached.

This framework is intended to address the need for a standardized methodology for evaluating the impact of services provided through the public mental health system. The information collected in this system will increase accountability for mental health systems, will increase understanding of public mental health programs, and provide a basis for improving consumer outcomes achieved.

This set of indicators is a standardized framework and not a set of prescriptive measures. For some indicators, several options for measures are available. While the standardized framework consists of domains and indicators, proposed performance measures—consisting of specifications of numerators and denominators—have also been developed for most of these performance indicators. A technical workgroup will be completing the specifications for the performance measures in the next few months. The workgroup will also develop methods of risk adjustment so that appropriate comparisons among states can be made.

The standardized framework constitutes the consensual position of NASMHPD members regarding the performance indicators to be used in any comprehensive mental health service delivery system. State mental health agencies have agreed to advocate for the use of this framework in mental health initiatives in states. Also, NASMHPD and the NASMHPD Research Institute will promote these indicators and measures and their use with HCFA, NCQA, JCAHO, AMBHA, and other organizations and accreditation bodies which develop and implement performance measures.

NASMHPD, in collaboration with CMHS, SAMHSA, and other organizations, is pursuing the resources necessary to ensure the development, implementation, and promulgation of these measures and indicators.

For more information contact: Robert Glover, PhD (703-739-9333)

National Association of State Mental Health Program Directors, 66 Canal Center Plaza, Suite 302, Alexandria, VA 22314, 703-739-9333, FAX 703-548-9517

Source: National Association of State Mental Health Program Directors, 66 Canal Center Plaza, Suite 302, Alexandria VA 22314. Tel: (703) 739-9333; Fax: (703) 548-9517 (Reprinted with permission.)

NASMHPD President's Task Force on Performance Indicators and Outcome Measures: Framework of Mental Health Performance Indicators
Recommended by the Task Force, November 1997
Adopted by NASMHPD Membership, December 14, 1997

Domain: Access	Data Sources
Initial Set:	Type of Data System
• Penetration/Utilization rates (by age, sex, race, setting)	Enrollment/Encounter
• Consumer perception of access	Consumer Survey
Developmental Set:	
• Average time to first service	
• Denial of care	
• Homeless & rural access	

Domain: Quality/Appropriateness	Data Sources
Initial Set:	
• Consumer participation in treatment planning (Adults) *	Consumer Survey/Audit
• Consumers linked to primary health services	Encounter/Consumer Survey
• Contact within 7 days following hospital discharge	Encounter
• Adults w/ SMI receiving services that promote recovery (For example, adults receiving atypical medications*, adults receiving ACT, adults in supported employment, adults in supported housing)	Encounter
• Children receiving "Best Practice" (For example, children receiving in-home services)	Encounter
• Family Involvement in treatment for Children/Adolescents*	Family Survey
• Readmissions within 30 days*	Encounter
• Consumer perception of Quality/Appropriateness*	Consumer Survey
• Seclusion and Restraint*	MIS
• Medication errors*	MIS
Developmental Set	
• Follow-up after emergency services	
• Family involvement in treatment (Adults)	
• Screening for TB, HIV, etc	

Domain: Outcome	Data Sources
Initial Set	
• Employment (adults)/School improvement (Children)	Consumer Survey/Enrollment/Clinical
• Functioning*	Consumer Survey/Clinical
• Symptom relief*	Consumer Survey/Clinical
• Adverse outcomes:	MIS/Encounter
Patient injuries*	
Abnormal Involuntary Movements (AIMS)	
Elopement*	
Out of home placements	
• Consumer perception of Outcomes	Comsumer Survey
• Health status: mortality	Enrollment/MIS
• Recovery/Hope/Personhood (surrogate measures)	Consumer Survey
• Reduced substance abuse impairment	Consumer Survey/Clinical
• Living situation	Consumer Survey/Enrollment
• Criminal Justice	Consumer Survey/Enrollment linked/Encounter
Developmental Set	
• Recovery/Personhood/Hope	

Domain: Structure/Plan Management	Data Sources
Initial Set	
• Consumer/Family member involvement in policy development quality assurance & planning	MIS
• Proportion of expenditures on administration	Cost-Revenue Data
• Per member per month/average resources spent for MH	Cost-Revenue Data
Developmental Set	
• Stakeholder satisfaction	
• Cultural competence	

Domain: Early Intervention/Prevention	Data Sources
Initial Set	
None	
Developmental Set	
• Substance abuse screening	
• Use of self-help/self-management	
• Identification of high risk population	
• Psycho-educational programs	

* = Measures included in the Proposed NRI-Based JCAHO ORYX System

An Instrument To Evaluate The Process of Psychiatric Care In Ambulatory Settings

MICHAEL K. POPKIN, MD, ALLAN L. CALLIES, BA, NICOLE LURIE, MD, MSPH, JEFFREY HARMAN, MS, TAMARA STONER, BA, WILLARD G. MANNING, PHD

As part of an evaluation of the Utah Prepaid Mental Health Plan, the Process of Care Review Form was developed to assess the quality of the process of psychiatric care provided by Utah's community mental health centers (CMHCs) to clients with schizophrenia. This article briefly reviews issues in the measurement of quality of care and describes the development and implementation of the form. The 67-item form was designed for use by a trained abstracter to gather data from CMHC medical records in six areas: general management of the patient, medication management, medical management, social support, psychiatric hospitalization, and psychiatric assessment. A 59-item version of the form that omits the section on psychiatric assessment has been used in three waves of data collection to document data spanning five years (1990-1994) in the evaluation of the process of psychiatric care in the Utah plan. It is currently being used longitudinally to examine differences between Utah CMHCs receiving capitated payments and those paid on a fee-for-service basis by Medicaid. (*Psychiatric Services* 48:524-527, 1997)

In the drive to contain health care costs, many Medicaid programs are turning to managed care. The Health Care Financing Administration (HCFA) has granted waivers to several states to encourage innovation in the financing and delivery of care. In 1990 the state of Utah requested and received a freedom-of-choice waiver from HCFA, which allowed the state to develop the Utah Prepaid Mental Health Plan.

Under the plan, the state contracted with three of 11 community mental health centers (CMHCs) located in the state to provide mental health services on a capitated basis.[1,2] As part of an evaluation of the plan, we developed a method to assess the quality of the process of psychiatric care provided to clients with schizophrenia by Utah's CMHCs that were participating and not participating in the plan. This method was designed to make maximum use of data available in the medical records of clients of the CMHCs.

Implicit in the development of the instrument was the intent to explore the degree to which capitation was associated with a change in the process by which care was provided to persons with serious and persistent mental illness. A guiding principle was to determine if care was vigorous and

---

Source: Popkin, Michael K., et al. "An Instrument to Evaluate the Process of Psychiatric Care in Ambulatory Settings." Psychiatric Services, Vol. 48, . No. 4, April 1997, p. 524-527. Copyright 1997, the American Psychiatric Association. Reprinted by permission.

Dr. Popkin *is chief of psychiatry at Hennepin County Medical Center, 701 Park Avenue, Minneapolis, Minnesota 55415, and professor in the departments of psychiatry and medicine at the University of Minnesota Medical School. Mr. Callies is an administrative analyst in the department of psychiatry at the medical center.* Dr. Lurie *is professor of medicine and public health at the center and at the University of Minnesota School of Medicine and School of Public Health. Mr. Harman and Ms. Stoner are doctoral students and Dr. Manning is professor at the Institute for Health Services Research at the University Of Minnesota.*

proactive as opposed to passive and custodial—that is, whether the record reflected ongoing efforts to improve the patient's status and functioning or implicitly signaled acceptance that further gains were not likely.

Literature on assessment of the quality of care provided in CMHCs and other ambulatory settings that serve persons with serious and persistent mental illness is limited. The American Psychiatric Association has published a Manual of Psychiatric Quality Assurance,[3] which offers only general guidelines for examining quality assurance rather than specific operational criteria. Several authors have set forth theoretical and conceptual frameworks for quality of care in an ambulatory setting.[4-9] Donabedian[5] detailed a model for the examination of quality of care through the analysis of structure, process, and outcome. The model posits that the structural characteristics of the settings in which care is rendered influence the process of care. Similarly, changes in the process are construed as altering the effect of care on health status. Norquist and associates[10] noted that "Process relates to clinical treatment approaches and transactions between providers and patients, while outcome indicates patient status during or after treatment." Quality of care can be assessed by examining any (or all) of these three elements.

McGlynn and colleagues[7] noted the absence of conceptual frameworks about what constitutes acceptable processes of care and criteria defining high-quality mental health care. They recommended obtaining process information and information on symptomatology from clinical or medical records. Studies in medical (nonpsychiatric) care have demonstrated that the medical record very adequately represents what transpires in the course of treatment[11] and that there is a high concordance between documentation and actual medical performance.[12]

Keyes and Moynihan[13] suggested that criteria for high-quality care be developed through input from clinical specialists. With such input, they developed detailed criteria sets for the study of depression, which have not found wide acceptance to date. At present no standard instrument exists that can be readily implemented to gauge care received by persons with serious and persistent mental illness in CMHCs and other ambulatory settings.

The usefulness of "indicators" to gauge the extent to which standards of psychiatric care have been fulfilled has been underscored by Schaub (14), who has described them as well-defined and easy to measure variables related to the delivery and outcome of medical care." They represent only portions of a full standard; they can be obtained or employed in domains currently lacking formal standards.

Faumann[15] suggested that indicators of the quality of process of psychiatric care can be divided into three categories: condition, diagnosis, and treatment. Condition denotes the behavior of the patient—for example, acts of violence, failure to comply with directives, or the rate of substance use during treatment. Diagnosis is directed to the appropriate use of diagnostic systems, including the use of standardized diagnostic instruments, the neglect or detection of comorbid diseases, and the rate of not-otherwise-specified" diagnoses. According to Faumann, treatment indicators should cover all aspects of psychiatric treatment that might be problem-prone.

Schaub's examples[14] of treatment indicators included the use of neuroleptics among patients with schizophrenia, adequate information about effects and side effects of prescribed drugs, and change of medication without adequate cause. Schaub suggested that treatment failure might be identified by such indicators as the rate of discharge against medical advice and parasuicidal gestures or completed suicides.

In this paper, we describe the development of an instrument with which to examine the process of care rendered to persons with serious and persistent mental illness in ambulatory settings such as CMHCs, and we comment on our experience to date with the instrument's implementation in the Utah Prepaid Mental Health Plan.

Development of the Form

Cognizant of the virtues and limitations implicit in the use of medical records,[3,16] we drew on the work of Schaub[14] and Faumann,[15] as well as interviews with external consultants and the clinical experience of the study team, to identify five salient areas that encompass the principal elements of care in ambulatory settings such as CMHCs. These five areas are general management, medication management, medical management, psychiatric hospitalization, and psychiatric assessment.

Past efforts have often been restricted to examining psychotropic medication use as a proxy for care of this population. We consciously sought a broader approach for our analysis. We identified a series of specific elements to characterize the nature of care rendered in each of the five major domains. The group of elements for each domain constituted a separate section of the Process of Care Review Form, which was used to abstract data from CMHC medical records.

The first section of the instrument, general management, elicited information about the frequency of psychotherapy and crisis visits, the extent of use of case managers and day treatment, and the number of referrals to new programs. Information was also gathered about the number of specific treatment plan goals and the extent to which they are met. Other items in this section documented the patient's status with regard to independent living, whether scores on the Global Assessment of Functioning (GAF) were recorded, and whether the patient changed therapists or terminated treatment in the study interval.

The second section directed attention to medication management. Medical records are reviewed to identify the nature and extent of psychotropic drug protocols, doses below the lower limits of established normal ranges, monitoring of plasma levels, the frequency of medication visits, changes in medication, and the frequency and treatment of medication side effects.

The third section, medical management, examined the vigor of attention to patients' general medical status. Items explored the use of laboratory tests, the acknowledgment of accompanying axis III conditions, the frequency of investigations of the central nervous system, and the frequency and nature of nonpsychiatric hospitalizations.

The fourth section of the instrument characterized the psychiatric hospitalizations of CMHC patients. Elements addressed the frequency and duration of hospitalization, as well as the extent of communication between the CMHC and the inpatient psychiatric unit.

The final section of the instrument, psychiatric assessment, addressed whether DSM-III-R criteria for a diagnosis of schizophrenia were satisfied, whether the mental health discipline of the examiner was recorded, whether the patient's personal and familial psychiatric history (including hospitalizations and previous drug treatments and responses to treatment) was included, and whether a corroborative historian was used.

The resulting 54-item Process of Care Review Form listed each specific item and provided numerical codes for item responses to expedite subsequent computerization of data.

We developed a set of guidelines including explicit written directives for abstracters' collection of the requisite data. Abstracters were selected in part on the basis of past experience with medical records and CMHCs. Initial training lasted for eight hours on each of two consecutive days. The first four hours involved an item-by-item review of the instrument and guidelines with one of the instrument's authors. The remainder of the time was devoted to chart abstraction at two rural sites not affiliated with the Utah Prepaid Mental Health Plan and one urban center that was a plan member.

Each abstracter independently reviewed a series of approximately ten charts. The resultant data were compared with the trainer's abstracted data, and discrepancies were discussed and resolved. The discrepancies were largely restricted to the two items calling for subjective judgment—the comprehensiveness of the treatment plan and the extent to which treatment plan goals were achieved. Abstracters were not permitted to work independently until their abstracted data approximated that of the trainer. For items requiring counts, disparities greater than one were not acceptable.

For the two items of the instrument that involved subjective judgment, three options were available to the abstracter. To indicate whether the treatment plan was comprehensive, the options were "no," "yes, partially," and "yes, completely." The question about treatment goals was rephrased to indicate how many goals were set in the first three months of contact with the patient during the study year and how many of these goals were met, partially achieved, or not met during the study year. For these two items, it was not acceptable for the abstracter and the trainer to choose opposite-extreme options. Differences involving the use of the intermediate category were acceptable.

Each subsequent wave of data collection was preceded by an eight-hour one-day training session to reacquaint the same abstracters with the instrument and to abstract charts as described above. During the first wave, the trainer also conducted a spot check of abstracts midway through the data collection period and rerated five charts with each abstracter. No discrepancies outside the tolerances described above were identified.

Based on feedback from the on-site abstracters, commentary from external consultants, and compilation of data in the first review of records, we modified the instrument. We added a section to focus on assessment of social support. This section addresses the extent of involvement of the patient's family or other significant individuals in their care as documented in the record. It also examines the quality of the patient's housing, whether such housing has been visually inspected by CMHC personnel, and whether efforts have been made to change the patient's housing.

The final version of the Process of Care Review Form used in the Utah Prepaid Mental Health Plan consists of 59 items divided into five sections. The instrument is directed to information documented in the medical record; if care is not documented, we assumed for purposes of the study that it was not rendered. The section concerning psychiatric assessment was not used because few patients received new assessments in the study interval. The instrument is available from the first author.

Implementation Of the Form

The Process of Care Review Form has now been used in three waves of data collection to gather data spanning five years (1990-1994) in the evaluation of the process of psychiatric care in the Utah Prepaid Mental Health Plan. Four abstractors were trained to use the instrument and rapidly acquired familiarity and comfort with its application. Two of the abstracters participated for one year, and the remaining two participated in each of the three waves of the study. Each abstracter had to demonstrate the ability to abstract in accordance with the criteria previously discussed.

The instrument has permitted the retrieval of objective data documented by mental health professionals and workers. Data collection has proven feasible despite the absence of a standardized medical record format for Utah CMHCs. In one of the participating CMHCs, the structure of the medical records was revamped during the study interval. The instrument still permitted abstracters to collect the requisite data without difficulty.

Abstracters found that a working appreciation of the organization and structure of the medical record of a given CMHC enhanced the ease of identifying the requisite data. The time required to abstract data from a record using the form is highly dependent on the given structure of the medical record and has typically ranged from 45 to 60 minutes, varying with the complexity of the individual case. In addition, several items have consistently required more of the abstracters' time. They include the item about the extent to which treatment plan goals have been achieved, the item documenting whether the patient has received education about his or her illness, the item about the comprehensiveness of the treatment plan, and the items related to the extent of family involvement.

The instrument is arguably no better than the quality of documentation in the medical records of a given CMHC. Variation in documentation practices is common. Not all care is adequately or directly represented in the record. For example, the record may not reflect the tenor of interpersonal exchange or the level of the provider's resourcefulness and commitment to optimizing care. In addition, settings operating with a fee-for-service reimbursement structure may have an incentive to document services more thoroughly, because reimbursement is partly a function of the extent and caliber of documentation.

The emphasis in the instrument is on evidence of proactive, vigorous treatment. We presume that the frequency of referrals to other programs and efforts to advance patients to independent living are markers of appropriate care.

Because each abstracter was not permitted to abstract independently until he or she could demonstrate agreement with the trainer, formal interrater reliability was not assessed. Such formal assessment will be a necessary step before large-scale use of the instrument is implemented.

To date, use of the instrument has been restricted to patients diagnosed as having schizophrenia. Extending the review to other diagnoses seen among patients in CMHCs or to other kinds of clinical settings may require modification of the instrument.

It would be useful to obtain external corroboration of the data abstracted with the instrument. To this end, utilization, pharmacy, or laboratory claims data may provide insight. Also, longitudinal studies with identifiable outcomes would speak to the merits of the instrument's ability to identify optimal versus suboptimal care. In this light, we stress that process-of-care evaluation is one component of a more comprehensive view of quality being measured in the Utah Prepaid Mental Health Plan. Comparisons with data derived from patient surveys should prove instructive, and such analyses are in progress.

Conclusions

The Process of Care Review Form offers the opportunity for an instructive look at CMHC practice patterns. Such fundamental measures of the process of care have not routinely appeared in the literature. They form a meaningful reference point for gauging change that may result from shifts in reimbursement methods.

For the Utah Prepaid Mental Health Plan, we anticipate examining the instrument's items individually to preserve the richness of the resultant data set rather than imposing a weighting or scoring system that might obscure meaningful changes in practice patterns. The Process of Care Review Form is currently being used longitudinally to examine differences in the process of patient care at CMHCs in Utah receiving capitated payments and those paid on a fee-for-service basis for Medicaid.

References

1. Christianson JB, Gray DZ: What CMHCs can learn from two states' efforts to capitate Medicaid benefits. *Hospital and Community Psychiatry* 45:777-781, 1994
2. Christianson JB, Manning W, Lurie N, et al: Utah's Prepaid Mental Health Plan: the first year. *Health Affairs* 14(3):160-172, 1995
3. Mattson MR (ed): *Manual of Psychiatric Quality Assurance*. Washington, DC, American Psychiatric Association, 1992
4. McInnis T, Kitson L: Process and outcome evaluations in mental health systems. *International Journal of Mental Health*, 5(4); 58-72, 1977
5. Donabedian A: *The Definition of Quality and Approaches to Its Assessment*. Ann Arbor, Mich, Health Administration Press, 1980
6. Brook HB, Kamberg CJ, Lohr KN: Quality assessment in mental health. *Professional Psychiatry* 13:34-39, 1982
7. McGlynn EA, Norquist GS, Wells KB, et al: Quality of care research in mental health settings: responding to the challenge. *Inquiry* 25:157-170, 1988
8. Zusman J: Quality assurance in mental health care. *Hospital and Community Psychiatry* 39:1286-1290, 1988
9. Eppel AB, Fuyarchuk C, Phelps D, et al: A comprehensive and practical quality assurance program for community mental health services. *Canadian Journal of Psychiatry* 36: 102-106, 1991
10. Norquist GS. Wells KB, Rogers WH, et al: Quality of care for depressed elderly patients hospitalized in specialty psychiatric units or general medical wards. *Archives of General Psychiatry* 52:695-701, 1995
11. Lyons TF, Payne BC: The relationship of physicians' medical recording performance to their medical care performance. *Medical Care* 12:463-469, 1974
12. Kosecoff J, Fink A, Brook RH, et al: The appropriateness of using a medical procedure. *Medical Care* 25:196-201, 1987
13. Keyes MA, Moynihan C: Evaluation in mental health services: some quality of care criteria for CHAMPUS mental health services demonstration. *Quality Review Bulletin* 17:441-451, 1991
14. Schaub RT: Quality assurance in psychiatric care: the example of routine use of the AMDP system. *Pharmacopsychiatry* 17 (suppl):46-50, 1994
15. Faumann M: Quality assurance monitoring in psychiatry. *American Journal of Psychiatry* 149:1121-1130, 1989
16. Romm FJ, Putnam SM: The validity of the medical record. *Medical Care* 19:310-315, 1981

Chapter 8

Outcomes Management In the Public Sector

Help From Uncle Sam

A Federal Center Is Striving To Standardize and Improve Outcomes Measurement for the Public and Private Sectors

JON HAMILTON

In recent years the field of quality measurement in mental health has grown wildly and in every direction. Today, there are literally dozens of proprietary measurement systems—ranging from good to awful—vying for users. What most of the systems have in common is that they produce results that cannot be compared with those from other systems. The result is what mental health researchers have called the "Tower of Babel problem": a sudden proliferation of measurement languages that has stifled meaningful communication. The various performance and outcomes measurement systems also tend to emphasize the needs of providers or purchasers, rather than consumers, and to avoid the use of outcomes.

But amid the chaos, several groups are working to devise a common language by encouraging standards and benchmarks. These groups also want to improve quality measurement by addressing consumers' concerns and by including more outcome measures. Prominent among those seeking to advance the field is the Center for Mental Health Services (CMHS), an often overlooked branch of the federal Substance Abuse and Mental Health Services Administration (SAMHSA). Through a variety of initiatives, CMHS is helping to standardize and improve quality measurement systems, and ensure that they reflect the priorities of mental health consumers, as well as providers and payers. The agency also is trying to help purchasers and potential users evaluate quality measurement systems before selecting them.

The CMHS effort is led by Ron Manderscheid, chief of the Survey and Analysis Branch within the Division of State and Community Systems Development. Manderscheid has become a tireless advocate for improving mental health statistics, and has overseen dozens of grants to states to fund efforts to measure performance simply, reliably, and in ways that will allow comparisons with other states. He said such work is badly needed.

"States have no yardstick now," Manderscheid said. "We have seen a lot of shoddy products that in the end cannot produce good measurements. There have been many failed efforts."

Manderscheid believes both the public and private sector must quickly improve and standardize quality measurements in order to combat moves by payers to arbitrarily reduce spending on mental health services. Without widely supported outcome measures and report cards, he said, "the field cannot negotiate effectively with payers, for whom price is a primary, if not the only, consideration."

There are several major parts of the CMHS effort to improve quality measurement. The largest and best known is the agency's Consumer-Oriented Report Card project, which began in 1994. Under this initiative, CMHS has developed a report card and has funded testing of it in most states.

A CMHS project related to the report card effort involves trying to determine whether it's possible to report performance indicators in a standardized way across states. To this end, the agency has funded efforts in five states to look at the performance indicators they use and identify commonalties.

CMHS also has participated in several efforts to bring performance and outcomes players together to agree on standards. One such effort was the 1997 Santa Fe Summit, hosted by the American College of Mental Health Administration. The meeting sought to identify a core set of performance measures that many organizations would use, even as they added measures of their own to fill specific needs.

Finally, CMHS is working to help states, counties, and private entities assess various outcome measurement systems. The agency has completed a document that lays out the minimum methodological standards for such systems and hopes it will be used in both managed care contracting and in auditing mental health programs and plans. (See "Methodological Standards for Outcome Measures (Draft)," prepared by the Adult Outcome Measurement Standards Committee for the Center for Mental Health Services, January 1997.)

Manderscheid says the intent of all of these CMHS efforts is to help the people involved in quality initiatives get more for their money. And although CMHS as an agency focuses on public mental health care, he says, the outcomes work is intended to help private entities as well as public ones. Manderscheid says that's essential as more and more public mental health is being provided via contracts with private managed care companies.

A Report Card For Consumers

In April 1996, CMHS released the prototype of a report card designed to help consumers, providers, and payers assess the quality of services provided through managed mental health care plans. Other organizations had created report cards of their own. But most of these focused on the less severe mental illness commonly found in the private sector and were intended for providers or purchasers, rather than consumers. CMHS director Bernard Arons, MD, pronounced the CMHS report card "the first to measure key elements of recovery, such as choice and involvement in treatment options."

The report card, which grew out of the CMHS Mental Health Statistics Improvement Program (MHSIP), was designed by a group that included consumers, as well as providers, advocates, researchers, and policymakers. Their goal was to create a report card that was relatively inexpensive and easy to use while providing reliable answers to questions about care in four major areas:

- **Access**: Is it quick, convenient, and affordable? Are there cultural barriers? Do consumers have access to information, such as best practice guidelines?
- **Quality/Appropriateness**: Does the plan focus on consumers' strengths and involve them in developing policies and monitoring quality? Does it provide continuity of care?
- **Promotion/Prevention**: Does the plan take steps to detect mental illnesses before they become severe? Does it offer information about risk factors?
- **Outcomes**: Does treatment offered by the plan improve consumers' health and quality of life. Are consumers more productive and independent after treatment? Does treatment diminish psychological stress?

The report card relies on both objective measures, such as the resources devoted to mental health services, and consumer's subjective assessments of services and outcomes. It draws on encounter and enrollment data, and widely used instruments such as the SF-36 and the Abnormal Involuntary Movement Scale for adults with serious mental illnesses. CMHS tried to avoid creating new measures when existing ones would do the job. But full implementation of the report card does require use of a consumer survey designed by the task force.

The report card's emphasis on outcomes requires data elements that many mental health organizations do not collect—for example, the average change in days of work lost, or the percentage of children with serious emotional disturbances placed outside the home for at least one month during the year.

But the task force that guided development of the report card wanted to cover areas that should be measured, rather than limiting itself to available data. The assumption is that organizations eventually will begin collecting data that are important to quality assessments.

A Growing Impact

Initially, the report card was tested in a handful of states. But as it has been refined and gained acceptance, use has spread to more than 40 states, which have received grants from CMHS to aid in implementation. "My impression is there is strong support for this work and for us continuing this effort," Manderscheid says, adding, "We are still the only report card that contains outcome measures."

Many states use only portions of the report card. Even so, Richard H. Ellis, a mental health researcher for the Colorado Department of Human Services, calls the report card effort "a resounding success." In his state, he said, community mental health centers are judged using the composite score of several measures from the report card. The top scorers statewide are eligible for a bonus of about $50,000, he says, which has helped focus attention on the results.

Ellis says the report card has been effective in motivating the mental health centers because it measures things that they can improve. "The centers do pay attention to how they are doing because these are the kinds of measures that mental health centers have some power over," he says. "They can do things to improve community relations and outcomes."

The report card also has influenced other major initiatives on mental health performance measurement, including those of the National Committee for Quality Assurance (NCQA) and the American Managed Behavioral Healthcare Association (AMBHA). A version of the report card's consumer survey is likely to become part of NCQA's 2000 HEDIS testing set.

As its influence has spread, the CMHS report card has undergone a series of refinements, many suggested by outside groups. NCQA's Behavioral Health Measurement Advisory Panel, for example, suggested trimming the consumer survey portion from 40 questions to 21, and changing the wording of some questions to make them more applicable to health plans. The group in charge of the report card approved the shorter version, and CMHS has generally welcomed such suggestions. (See Appendix A for copies of the MHSIP consumer surveys.)

Measuring Across States

With its Consumer-Oriented Report Card in widespread use, CMHS has launched an effort to let states compare their results. The ultimate goal is to assemble a system that would produce a nationwide snapshot of mental health quality. But early results suggest that won't be easy because of major differences in states' ability to collect data, and the use of different measurement tools.

In 1997, the agency began funding a Feasibility Assessment Study in Colorado, Illinois, Massachusetts, South Carolina, and Texas. The study called on the states to assess the availability of data through statewide information systems and see whether they would be able to produce comparable quality measurements.

"What we found was that it's feasible, but you better pay attention to your data infrastructure and the definitions you use," Manderscheid reports. He says several states proved unable to produce data in at least one area.

Colorado was among the most advanced states in the study. Ellis says his state conducts client data collection at every admission into, and discharge from, the public mental health system, whether through a community mental health center, mental hospital, or any other point. The state also maintains encounter data, can analyze patterns in the use of services, and can track changes in patients' status over time. But Ellis says even his state was unable to report on two of 28 indicators in the study. Some other states were unable to report on as many as 14.

Comparing measurements proved even more challenging, Ellis said. Sometimes the problem was that one state used a 10-point scale while another used a five-point scale. Other times, subtle differences in the definition of a variable made things difficult. Moreover, there were methodological questions because, for example, some states conducted surveys by mail, while others used structured interviews.

Nonetheless, Ellis says he is encouraged by the results and by the improvements in data collection attributable to the Consumer-Oriented Report Card. "We're moving in the direction of comparability," he says. "All five states were able to report on at least 14 measures. A few years ago it would have been five measures."

Manderscheid says the next step is a three-year pilot project involving 10 states. They will attempt to assess quality statewide, not just in a county or region, and then see whether measurements are consistent from state to state, he says. Eventually, Manderscheid says, the project should involve all 50 states.

Establishing a Minimum Data Set

Efforts by CMHS to standardize quality measurement haven't been limited to public programs. The center has played a role in several projects that involved the private sector as well. Perhaps the most ambitious of these was the 1997 Santa Fe Summit on Behavioral Health, an effort to select a minimum set of the most useful performance and outcome measures from the major competing systems.

The meeting, held in March of that year, assembled about 100 mental health and substance abuse experts from groups including AMBHA, NCQA, SAMHSA, the Washington Business Group on Health, the National Alliance for the Mentally Ill, the Institute of Medicine, the National Mental Health Association, and the Council on the Accreditation of Rehabilitation Facilities (CARF). It was sponsored by the American College of Mental Health Administration (ACMHA), with assistance from CMHS.

"We came up with the notion that there was a huge proliferation of performance measures and indicator sets, and it would be a blessing to the field if some neutral body could come up with a core set to cross public and private sectors," says John Morris, incoming president of the ACMHA and who also holds posts at the University of South Carolina and the South Carolina Department of Mental Health. "We didn't know whether it would work."

At the meeting, participants broke into five working groups and spent two days discussing the best ways to measure success in five areas: prevention, access, process/performance, outcomes, and structure.

Although the meeting didn't produce a consensus, it began a process that allowed ACMHA to produce a report in March 1998 containing value statements and key indicators in each area. The report also includes proposed measures for each indicator, though, predictably, there was far less agreement on these.

So, for example, the section on process/performance measures offers as one indicator: "Consumers receive adequate information to make informed choices." For a recommended measure, however, the report asks that organizations merely to "consider" using several questions from the CMHS Consumer Survey.

But in spite of language intended to soft-pedal specific recommendations, the report does offer a set of measures culled from not only the report card, but the Lehman Quality of Life Inventory, the SF-12, AMBHA's PERMS, CARF, and others.

Manderscheid says CMHS enthusiastically supported the project because "we should all be measuring basic things the same way."

Morris says response to the report suggests many in the mental health field feel the same way. "I have been all over the country talking about this and the response is incredible," he says. "People are hungry for some simplification, some focus."

ACMHA initially printed 1,500 copies of the 140-page report, but was forced to order another 1,000 copies to meet demand. Interest from the public sector has come from places such as the New York Health Department, Morris says. In the private sector, he says, players such as CompCare in Lyndhurst NJ are using the document.

Looking Ahead

Next up for CMHS is a project to help organizations obtain the best quality measurement systems for their needs. In late 1998, the agency was preparing to release its Methodological Standards for Outcome Measures, a document that specifies minimum standards for outcome measurement systems. It is meant to serve as an aid in managed care contracting and in auditing of mental health programs and plans.

Organizations befuddled by sales pitches from various performance and outcome measurement systems should find the standards very helpful, Manderscheid says. "You have to show how proprietary systems measure up."

Other projects under way at CMHS include an effort to tailor outcome systems for children with emotional problems, a paper on how to effectively use outcomes in management decisions, and a paper on how to integrate the concept of "personhood" into outcomes work.

Down the road, Manderscheid says, CMHS hopes to study ways to create benchmarks that would allow direct comparison of results from one report card system to another. Despite the confusion caused by so many systems, he said, "there has been virtually no work in that area."

Development of Outcome Indicators For Monitoring the Quality of Public Mental Health Care

DEBRA SREBNIK, PHD, MICHAEL HENDRYX, PHD, JENNIFER STEVENSON, BA, SUSAN CAVERLY, ARNP, DENNIS G. DYCK, PHD, AND ANA MARI CAUCE, PHD

Objective: The study attempted to develop a brief and integrated set of reliable and valid outcome measures that could be used by both consumers and providers to assess the quality of public mental health care. *Methods*: A model of outcomes in four domains—consumer satisfaction, functioning, quality of life, and clinical status—was developed from the literature and from the priorities expressed by members of an advisory group of stakeholders. Based largely on extant measures, a consumer survey and a case manager survey were then created to assess these domains. A total of 236 adult consumers of mental health services from six community mental health centers in Washington State were surveyed. The four-item case manager survey to rate consumers' clinical status was completed by 163 of the participants' case managers. Scores and ratings on the survey were analyzed using correlational analysis and principal components analysis to determine whether the data provided empirical support for the four-domain model. *Results*: Principal components analysis demonstrated support for the four-domain model. Internal consistency of the outcome indicators was adequate, and their concurrent validity was partly supported. *Conclusions*: The described outcome measures provide a practical, empirically supported structure for monitoring and improving public mental health services. (*Psychiatric Services* 48: 903–909, 1997)

The quality of health and mental health care services has traditionally been defined on the basis of setting structure, service processes, and consumer outcome variables[1-8]. Outcomes are assessed and monitored more rarely than structure or process indicators because their measurement is considered to be costly and temporally removed from the point of service[4]. However, outcomes are a much more direct indicator of quality than either structure or process indicators.

The interplay between structure, process, and outcome variables is highlighted in the area of continuous quality improvement, in which improvement of poor outcomes occurs through understanding system processes and structure[9-11]. Outcome monitoring and continuous quality improvement have a heightened role within emerging managed care systems that may drive down costs and consequently put quality at risk.

Despite the importance of outcome monitoring, limited work has been done toward developing outcome assessment systems. Such systems have two components—a set of outcome assessment tools and a series of implementation mechanisms,

---

Source: Srebnik, Debra, et al. "Development of Outcome Indicators for Monitoring the Quality of Public Mental Health Care." Psychiatric Services. Vol. 48, No. 7, July 1997, p. 903–909. Copyright 1997, the American Psychiatric Association. Reprinted by permission.

Dr. Srebnik and Ms. Stevenson *are affiliated with the department of psychiatry and behavioral sciences at the University of Washington, Box 359300/CH-13, Seattle, Washington 98195. Dr. Hendryx and Dr. Dyck are with the Washington Institute for Mental Illness Research and Training and the department of psychology at Washington State University in Spokane. Ms. Caverly is affiliated with the department of Psychosocial nursing and Dr. Cauce is with the department of psychology at the University of Washington.*

including methods for sampling and data collection, analyzing and monitoring data, and providing feedback to stakeholders. This paper focuses on the first component, that of developing a comprehensive yet practical outcome assessment package to gather data on specific outcome indicators.

Outcome measures typically assess specific domains in detail—for example, a person's functioning, symptoms, and quality of life. However, when multiple domains must be assessed, the tools become too long and impractical. Agency administrators require brief user-friendly outcome measures that can be used repeatedly over time to monitor program quality[4]. Key outcomes must also be assessed by both service providers and consumers. A brief integrated package of outcome assessment tools that can be used by different raters to assess multiple domains has not been described. In the next section we introduce the conceptual framework for outcome domains on which measurement selection and outcome indicators are based. The remainder of the paper describes the reliability and validity tests of the indicators.

Outcome Priorities

To choose an appropriate set of outcomes, the consensus of "customers" is required[4]. However, gaining consensus about the most important outcomes to measure and how to measure them has been a challenge to the field, and no "gold standard" exists. Stakeholder groups, including mental health consumers, family members, providers, and administrators, often debate what service goals and outcome priorities should be (12; McGuirk F, Zahniser J, Bartsch D, et al., unpublished data, 1995).

Examination of frameworks that encompass the outcome priorities of many stakeholders[13-16] reveals four outcome domains: satisfaction, functional status, quality of life, and clinical status. These domains are conceptually supported by research reviewed below and by input from a stakeholder advisory committee established for this study, which was composed of consumers, family members, providers, administrators, and funders.

Stakeholder groups are all concerned about satisfaction with services (17; McGuirk F, Zahniser J, Bartsch D, et al., unpublished data, 1995). Important dimensions are general satisfaction, whether services meet stated needs, service context variables (accessibility, safety, friendliness, and facility environment), and appropriateness of services to persons with certain sociodemographic characteristics. Other key outcomes include whether consumers are involved in and influence service decisions[18-21].

Measures of functioning generally assess consumers' social and vocational role performance and their ability to perform activities of daily living. Service providers and administrators prioritize appropriate vocational and leisure activities[22], while researchers and administrators view positive interpersonal functioning as an important outcome[23]. Consumers have stressed the value of social support and a sense of belonging[24,25].

In the area of quality of life, both consumers and family members have identified adequate housing, employment or other meaningful activity, and sufficient finances as important outcomes[24-28]. Safety issues, including prevention of victimization and harm to others, are also important[29-32]. Quality of life can in part be viewed as the degree to which consumers are satisfied with their housing, activities, finances, and safety[21,23,33].

Researchers and service administrators are concerned with improved symptoms[24,32], knowledge of illness[31], and emotional well-being[29]. Self-management of illness, including compliance with treatment and medication, are also viewed as important issues by providers and administrators[26,32].

One of the most commonly reported outcomes for mental health care consumers is community tenure[23,31,34,35]. However, stakeholders do not agree about whether out-of-community care, such as hospitalization, is a positive or negative outcome[30]. Furthermore, episodes in institutions can be seen more as indicators of service responsiveness rather than as measures of consumer outcome. We have therefore chosen not to include community tenure as an outcome. Instead it was used as a general index against which the concurrent validity of our selected outcomes was evaluated.

Overall, the literature about the outcome priorities of various stakeholders supports a four-domain model of consumer outcomes. In the study reported here, empirical support for this model was provided through principal components analysis of surveys assessing these domains that were completed by 236 consumers and 163 of their case managers in Washington State.

Methods

Measures

Selection of measures was based on psychometric adequacy, brevity, ease of administration, and comprehensibility of items. Measures were reviewed by the study advisory committee and pilot tested by members of a consumer advisory committee. The surveys were completed in May and June 1995.

Consumer surveys. Consumer surveys included the eight-item Client Satisfaction Questionnaire (CSQ)[36] and the SF-12[37,38]. Seven items about residential arrangements, social and leisure functioning, family interactions, and safety were included from the Lehman Quality of Life Interview[39]. Three items were developed to assess consumer involvement in treatment—that is, the extent to which consumers feel they are part of decision making and planning—and two items assessed appropriateness of treatment for age and for ethnic and cultural background.

Four additional items from a California public mental health survey[40] assessed whether consumers work and education goals were attained. Four items assessed consumers' self-reported skills in handling stress and symptoms. Two items assessed whether consumers had been a victim of a crime in the past 12 months, and two items assessed concerns about their living condition.

Case manager surveys. Surveys were sent directly to the case managers. Case managers completed items about consumers' community tenure (including admissions to psychiatric and medical hospitals and jail episodes). They also completed the Four-Dimensional Classification Scale[41], which includes four single-item 7-point scales that assess symptoms, functioning, substance abuse, and treatment compliance.

Information systems. Regional management information systems were the source of sociodemographic data for the participants as well as information about their residential situations and daily activities.

Participants

A total of 236 consumers of mental health services were recruited by surveyors (see below) from six community mental health centers in two regions of Washington state. The regions encompass rural, suburban, and small urban centers. Regions were selected as part of a larger study evaluating the impact of replacing process regulations with clinical outcomes as a method of accountability.

Sixty percent of the sample were women. Ninety-one percent were Caucasian. The mean±SD age was 47.9±18.2 years. The incomes of most participants (79 percent) were below the poverty level, and most participants (89 percent) received Medicaid-funded services.

Eight percent of the participants were involved in paid work or in school. Most lived in their own residence or with parents (79 percent), while the remainder lived in supported housing or nursing homes. Diagnostic categories included schizophrenia (31 percent), major depression (18 percent), bipolar disorder (13 percent), dysthymia and minor depression (9 percent), adjustment disorder (6 percent), and dementia (3 percent).

The sample was representative of the regions mental health consumer population in gender, ethnicity, income, and residential situation. However, study participants were older, less likely to have meaningful daily activity, and more likely to have schizophrenia. Even though all study participants had case managers, case manager compliance was imperfect. Case manager surveys for only 163 of the participants were completed. Participants whose case managers completed the survey were younger than the full sample (t=5.1, df=108, p<.001), but they did not differ in ethnicity, gender, involvement in meaningful daily activity or diagnostic mix.

Consumer Data Collection

Consumers from service delivery systems adjacent to the study regions were hired as surveyors to facilitate self-administration of consumer surveys. Surveyors recruited consumers at agencies as they came in for appointments and on outreach appointments with case managers. Participants were generally able to complete the survey with little difficulty in 15 to 20 minutes.

Data Analyses

The analyses described below first examined within-domain and between domain correlations of the 13 scales in the four domains. A correlation matrix was created based on consumers' scores and case managers' ratings from the surveys. A principal components analysis was then conducted to determine whether the four domains could be empirically derived from the data in the correlation matrix. Finally, the 13 domain scales derived from the principal components analysis were tested for reliability and validity.

Results

Table 1 lists the 13 scales in the four domains that were examined in the surveys completed by consumers and case managers. (A copy of the full instrument is available from the first author.) The mean score or rating for each measure is reported, as are the number of items in each measure and the range of possible scores for each measure. Table 2 presents a correlation matrix showing the correlations between the measures listed in Table 1.

Correlations of Scales

Measures within a domain should correlate more highly with each other than with measures from other domains, which was borne out in the analysis. Within-domain correlations for satisfaction and functioning were moderately strong, indicating that the individual measures in each domain are related but also that each contributes some unique variance to the domain. For example, the intercorrelations of the measures related to satisfaction ranged from .24 to .58, and all were statistically significant (r > .18).

Most between-domain correlations were nonsignificant and lower than the within-domain correlations. For example, the functioning domain was distinct from the satisfaction domain, with no statistically significant correlations. Quality of life

Table 1. Mean scores of 236 mental health consumers on a survey measuring satisfaction, functioning, and quality of life and mean ratings of consumers' clinical status by 163 of their case managers

Domain and measure	Number of items in measure	Mean	SD	Possible score range
Satisfaction				
Client Satisfaction Questionnaire	8	3.29	.61	1–4
Involvement in treatment	3	3.98	1.03	1–5
Treatment appropriateness	2	3.98	1.07	1–5
Safety at the mental health center	1	.89	.32	0–1
Functioning				
Physical[1]	6	10.04	.74	—
Mental[1]	6	10.03	.66	—
Social and leisure	3	4.74	1.28	1–7
Skills for handling stress and symptoms	4	3.54	.87	1–5
Quality of life				
Safety	4	4.89	1.30	1–7
Concerns about living condition	2	.60	.38	0–1
Goal attainment	4	.73	.18	0–1
Victimization	2	1.82	.31	1–2
Clinical status				
Four-Dimensional Classification Scale	4	4.14	1.05	0–6

[1] *Because items from the SF-12 used to measure these constructs are rated on different scales, the standardized scale scores are shown.*

Table 2. Correlation matrix of data for 13 outcome measures in four domains obtained from a survey of 236 consumers and 163 case managers[1]

Domain and measure with Cronbach's alpha[2]	Satisfaction				Functioning				Quality of life			
	1	2	3	4	5	6	7	8	9	10	11	12
Satisfaction												
1. Client Satisfaction Questionnaire (.91)												
2. Involvement in treatment (.41)	.51											
3. Treatment appropriateness (.70)	.58	.39										
4. Safety at the mental health center	.46	.24	.33									
Functioning												
5. Physical (.80)	.05	.02	.00	-.05								
6. Mental (.77)	.17	-.02	.14	.16	.42							
7. Social and leisure (.64)	.21	.04	.10	.13	.17	.47						
8. Skills for handling stress and symptoms (.76)	.13	.05	-.02	.10	.33	.60	.42					
Quality of life												
9. Safety (.82)	.23	.10	.16	.30	.10	.20	.30	.16				
10. Concerns about living condition (.34)	.01	.03	-.10	.02	.05	.07	.14	.00	.27			
11. Goal attainment (.48)	.01	-.11	.06	-.01	-.11	.18	.14	.02	-.08	.25		
12. Victimization (.42)	.20	.07	.21	.25	-.05	.20	.22	.08	.26	.15	.20	
Clinical status												
13. Four-Dimensional Classification Scale (.61)	.15	.13	.30	.18	-.05	.03	.04	.06	.13	.10	.10	.14

[1] Correlations above .18 were significant at p<.05. Data on some items were missing for some consumers.
[2] Cronbach's alpha reflects the internal reliability of each measure (safety at the mental health center was measured by a single item and has no alpha).

was partly related to both functioning (four significant correlations) and satisfaction (five significant correlations). The clinical domain was more distinct from the other domains, with only one significant correlation.

Principal Components Analysis

Domains were derived from the principal components analysis based on a combination of eigenvalues greater than 1, relatively large positive eigenvectors or component loadings, and judgments about theory and interpretive clarity. The results are shown in Table 3. They were not surprising given the data in the correlation matrix, and they supported the four conceptually derived domains.

The satisfaction component included the CSQ and items about treatment involvement, appropriateness, and safety at the mental health center. This component accounted for 23 percent of the overall variance in consumers' scores on the survey; it had an eigenvalue of 3.01.

The functioning component included the SF-12 and items assessing social and leisure functioning and skills. This component accounted for 16 percent of the score variance and had an eigenvalue of 2.02. The quality of life component included items on safety, concerns about living condition, goal attainment, and victimization. This component had an eigenvalue of 1.47, accounting for 11 percent of the variance. The clinical status domain, measured by the four-item Four-Dimensional Classification Scale, had an eigenvalue of .94 and accounted for 7 percent of the variance.

Scale loadings on the satisfaction component were clearly distinct from other components. One measure from the functioning domain—social and leisure functioning—and one from the quality-of-life domain—safety—loaded higher on the satisfaction domain than on their respective domains. However, these measures were not included in the satisfaction domain because it made more interpretive sense to include them in their respective domains. Likewise, goal attainment was included in the quality-of-life domain for interpretive reasons, even though it also loaded on the clinical status domain.

Outcome Indicator Scores and Reliability

Outcome indicators were calculated as mean scores within each of the four domains derived from the principal components analysis—satisfaction, functioning, quality of life, and clinical status. Outcome indicators were scored so that positive values indicated more favorable status. Scores for

Table 3. Principal components analysis of 13 outcome measures, with component loadings on four outcome domains

Domain and measure	Component loadings[1]			
	Satisfaction (3.01)	Functioning (2.02)	Quality of life (1.47)	Clinical status (.94)
Satisfaction				
Client Satisfaction Questionnaire	.40	-.30	-.16	.06
Involvement in treatment	.35	-.34	-.23	-.03
Treatment appropriateness	.33	-.36	-.09	.16
Safety at the mental health center	.33	-.23	.01	-.13
Functioning				
Physical	.15	.35	-.35	-.09
Mental	.34	.42	-.10	.21
Social and leisure	.33	.30	.05	.01
Skills for handling stress and symptoms	.28	.40	-.22	.12
Quality of life				
Safety	.31	.03	.14	-.62
Concerns about living condition	.11	.12	.50	-.38
Goal attainment	.08	.11	.53	.54
Victimization	.27	-.03	.37	.01
Clinical status				
Four-Dimensional Classification Scale	.19	-.18	.20	.31

[1] *Eigenvalues are in parentheses below each domain.*

the domains of satisfaction, functioning, and quality of life were standardized for comparison around a mean of 10 and a standard deviation of 1.

For satisfaction, the mean±SD score for the sample of 236 participants was 9.94±.70; the internal reliability of the measures in this domain was high (Cronbach's alpha=.88). For functioning, the sample mean was 10.06±.74 (Cronbach's alpha=.85). For quality of life, the mean score was 9.93±.80 (Cronbach's alpha=.70). For clinical status, the mean rating was 4.15±1.05 (Cronbach's alpha=.61). The alpha values indicate that reliability was adequate.

Concurrent Validity

Because no standard exists by which to determine the concurrent validity of outcome indicators (that is, whether they measure what they claim to measure), we believe the key is to determine their relationship to more distal community-valued indicators, such as involvement in meaningful daily activity, residential independence, and community tenure. Meaningful activity was defined as involvement in any activity that was age appropriate and not treatment related. Residential independence was defined as residing in a stable location that was not linked with treatment or not a correctional facility. Community tenure was defined as the absence of a psychiatric or medical hospitalization or jail episode within the previous six months.

Parametric t tests were used to compare outcome indicators with distal indicator values. Two-tailed p values were set at <.05. As shown in Table 4, clinical status was significantly lower for participants without meaningful daily activity, those in dependent living situations, and those who had experienced an out-of-community episode. The relationship of consumer-reported satisfaction, functioning, and quality of life to validity indicators was more inconsistent. It is likely that residential situation, community tenure, and work involvement are strongly influenced by clinicians' decisions and their judgments about clinical status. A strong relationship, therefore, may not be as likely for the other outcome indicators, which are rated by consumers. Further, an anomaly of the data was that consumers living with their parents were considered to be "independent."

Table 4. Concurrent Validity of Four Outcome Domains Demonstrated by Their Associations With Three Community-Valued Outcome Indicators

Domain	Meaningful activity None N=112 Mean	SD	Any (N=89) Mean	SD	t	df	Living situation Dependent (N=49) Mean	SD	Independent (N=159) Mean	SD	t	df	Out-of-community episodes[1] Any (N=13) Mean	SD	None (N=51) Mean	SD	t	df[2]
Satisfaction	9.92	.80	10.10	.68	1.69	198	9.92	.86	10.01	.71	.82	203	10.60	.73	10.60	.69	.01	62
Functioning	9.96	.70	10.05	.55	.97	198	10.18	.67	9.95	.62	-2.18*	203	10.10	1.03	9.8	.82	-1.34*	61
Quality of life	9.88	.67	10.07	.59	1.99*	198	10.04	.65	9.94	.63	-.88	205	9.9	.67	9.8	.86	-.58	65
Clinical status	3.71	1.11	4.42	.95	3.90**	131	3.57	1.30	4.15	1.01	2.45*	134	3.2	1.09	4.2	.66	3.32**	14

[1] Admissions to psychiatric and medical hospitals and jail episodes.
[2] The df value for clinical status (df= 14) was estimated from samples with unequal variances.

* p<.05
** p<.01

Discussion

This study described the development of and empirical support for a set of practical yet comprehensive outcome indicators. Four outcome domains were identified from a theoretical framework, which was supported by stakeholder input. Brief measures, largely compiled from extant scales, adequately captured the content of each outcome domain: clinical status (four items), functioning (19 items), consumer satisfaction (14 items), and quality of life (12 items). Easily administered consumer and case manager surveys were developed.

The conceptually derived domains were empirically supported by the principal components analysis. Outcome indicators for each domain were found to have adequate internal consistency, and concurrent validity of the clinical status domain was supported. Researchers often feel torn between concerns for psychometric adequacy and administrative needs for very brief assessment tools. The results of this study are encouraging because they suggest that it is possible to have both.

The outcome indicators in this study lie within a growing body of work on outcomes and quality monitoring. Compendiums of outcome measures are popular, and methods for performance-based contracting and for designing provider "report cards" have been topics of recent industry conferences.[43-45] Measurement packages that assess relevant domains and that can be used by different raters [45-47] and separate consumer or clinician-rated measures [48,49] are also available. However, these tools are considerably longer than those described in this paper, and thus respondent burden is increased. Some are also proprietary,[45] making cost an additional consideration. Although each package and measure has strengths, we believe that the set of measures described in this study provides a unique combination of advantages in terms of brevity, cost, ease of administration, and psychometric promise.

Using Outcome Data

Discussion in this section focuses on use of the four outcome indicator scores shown in Table 2. However, one could also use raw individual scale scores (see Table 1) in similar ways.

It is important to recognize that the consumer population served in the public mental health system is clinically heterogeneous. Consumers' presenting problems range from mild anxiety to severe and persistent mental illness. The initial severity of illness is related to both the level of expected outcomes and the rate at which outcomes can be achieved. As such, it is critical to identify case-mix groups or risk groups that have similar expected outcomes.

Without such adjustment of expected outcome measures, providers may attempt through "skimming" or "dumping" to attract and serve consumers for whom positive outcomes are easier to achieve, particularly if providers' performance evaluation is tied to achievement of outcomes. Case-mix adjustment methods may be especially useful for capitated financing plans, in which both capitation rates and expected outcomes may be based on case-mix groups.

Stakeholder groups often have different uses for outcome data. For example, funders may want to use outcome indicators as the basis for contracting and accountability. Mean scores on the satisfaction indicator would be useful for this purpose. Risk-adjusted change in functioning or clinical status over a given period of time would also provide useful information. Fiscal incentives could then be based on the provider's performance relative to other providers or relative to that provider's previous performance. The choice of incentive structures is critical to the success of such an accountability system. Once an incentive structure is imposed, service providers will work toward obtaining the selected incentives, and other outcome goals may be compromised.

Service providers may want to use outcome indicators for quality improvement. They may, for example, be interested in examining risk-adjusted outcomes for different clinicians. Satisfaction ratings can be used to identify areas within a provider agency that may warrant further study for development of quality improvement projects. Consumers with scores at the extremes on any indicator can also be identified for the purpose of more intensive investigation, further clinical supervision of staff, or advocacy on behalf of the consumer.

Study Limitations

A limitation of the study is that the outcome indicators are relevant only to consumers already receiving mental health services. Stakeholders are also interested in understanding outcomes of consumers who may be in need of services but do not receive services or who prematurely terminate services.[27] Another limitation of the study was use of data from management information systems to determine concurrent validity. As discussed, certain variables, such as independent living, were defined in ways that hampered clear-cut conclusions.

Conclusions

This paper describes the development of outcome indicators related to consumer characteristics. Future research may expand this study into the area of indicators of system performance, such as service accessibility and responsiveness, staff satisfaction, and cost-efficiency.

Cultural differences in outcome indicators are another potentially fruitful area for research. Although some scales described here have been used with a variety of ethnic groups, their validity in capturing issues relevant to specific groups has yet to be established. Even if scales demonstrate such content validity, their relationship to distal community-valued variables may vary across groups. Research in this area might suggest adjustments of normative values for outcome indicators for different groups in a manner analogous to risk adjustment.

Overall, the outcome indicators discussed in this study provide a practical structure for mental health quality monitoring and improvement. Outcome indicators can be especially useful for mental health programs embarking on managed care where incentives may exist for decreasing service—and potentially service quality—in favor of cost savings. The outcome indicators discussed, based on stakeholder priorities, are assessed in a package that is brief, yet provides a rich array of information. As such, this set of empirically supported outcome indicators can serve as a critical and timely component of quality management in mental health care.

Acknowledgments

This research was sponsored by the Washington State Department of Social and Health Services, Mental Health Division. The authors thank John Whitbeck, Ph.D., for his guidance and critical comments on an earlier version of this paper.

References

1. Donabedian A: Explorations in Quality Assessment and Monitoring: Vol I. *The Definition of Quality and Approaches to Its Assessment.* Ann Arbor, Mich, Health Administration Press, 1980
2. Goldstein L: Linking utilization management with quality improvement. *Psychiatric Clinics of North America* 13:157–169, 1990
3. Evans ON, Faulkner L, Hodo G, et al: A quality improvement process for state mental health systems. *Hospital and Community Psychiatry* 43:465–469, 1992
4. McCarthy P, Gelber S, Dugger D: Outcome measurement to outcome management: the critical step. *Administration and Policy in Mental Health* 21:59–68, 1993
5. Pierson D: Quality assurance in the care of the disabled. *Health Marketing Quarterly* 1:125–180, 1984
6. Sederer L, St Clair RL: Quality assurance and managed mental health care. *Psychiatric Clinics of North America* 13:89–97, 1990
7. Sherman P: Simple quality assurance measures. *Evaluation and Program Planning* 10:227–229, 1987
8. Smukler M, Sherman P, Srebnik D, et al: Developing local service standards for managed mental health care systems. *Administration and Policy in Mental Health*, in press
9. Goonan K: *The Juran Prescription: Clinical Quality Management.* San Francisco, Jossey-Bass, 1995
10. Rago W, Reid W: Total quality management strategies in mental health systems. *Journal of Mental Health Administration* 18:253–263, 1991
11. Rosander A: *Deming's 14 Points Applied to Services.* New York, Dekker, 1991
12. Nelson G: The development of a mental health coalition: a case study. *American Journal of Community Psychology* 22:229–255, 1994
13. Ciarlo JA, Brown TR, Edwards DW, et al: *Assessing Mental Health Treatment Outcome Measurement Techniques.* National Institute of Mental Health Series FN. DHHS pub (ADM) 86-1301. Washington, DC, US Government Printing Office, 1986
14. Hargreaves WA, Shumway M: Effectiveness of mental health services for the severely mentally ill, in *The Future of Mental Health Services Research.* Edited by Taube CA, Mechanic D, Hohmann A. DHHS pub (ADM) 89-1600. Washington, DC, US Government Printing Office, 1989
15. Rosenblatt A, Attkisson CC: Assessing outcomes for sufferers of severe mental disorder: a conceptual framework and review. *Evaluation and Program Planning* 16:347–363, 1993
16. Ware JE Jr: Measuring health and functional status in mental health services research, in *The Future of Mental Health Services Research.* Edited by Taube CA, Mechanic D, Hohmann A. DHHS pub (ADM) 89-1600. Washington, DC, US Government Printing Office, 1989
17. Heflinger CA, Sonnichsen S, Brannan A: Parent satisfaction with children's mental health services in a children's mental health managed care demonstration. *Journal of Mental Health Administration* 23:69–79, 1996
18. Brown L, Thomas M, Allen DG, et al: Mental health reform: client and family member perspectives. *Evaluation and Program Planning* 17:81–92, 1994
19. Chamberlin J, Rogers J, Sneed C: Consumers, families, and community support systems. *Psychosocial Rehabilitation Journal* 12:93–106, 1989
20. Hanson J, Rapp C: Families' perceptions of a community mental health program for their relatives with a severe mental illness. *Community Mental Health Journal* 28:181–197, 1992
21. LaFave H, de Souza H, Prince P, et al: Partnerships for people with serious mental illness who live below the poverty line. *Psychiatric Services* 46:1071–1073, 1995
22. Solomon P, Beck S, Gordon B: *Barriers to Community Placement of Psychiatric Extended Care Facility Patients.* Columbus, Ohio Department of Mental Health, 1988
23. Jerrell J, Ridgely M: Evaluating changes in symptoms and functioning of dually diagnosed clients in specialized treatment. *Psychiatric Services* 46:233–238, 1995
24. Anthony W, Cohen M, Kennard W: Understanding the current facts and principles of mental health systems planning. *American Psychologist* 45:1249–1253, 1990

25. Chamberlin J, Rogers J: Planning a community—based mental health system. *American Psychologist* 45:1241–1244, 1990
26. Ford J, Youhng D, Perez B, et al: Needs assessment for persons with severe mental illness: what services are needed for successful community living? *Community Mental Health Journal* 28:491–503, 1992
27. Stockdill J: A government managers view of mental health advocacy groups. *Administration and Policy in Mental Health* 20:45–55,1992
28. Weisburd DE: Planning a community-based mental health system. *American Psychologist* 45:1245–1248, 1990
29. Kane R, Bartlett J, Potthoff S: Building an empirically based outcomes information system for managed mental health care. *Psychiatric Services* 46:459–461, 1995
30. Pulice T, McCormick L, Dewees M: A qualitative approach to assessing the effects of system change on consumers, families, and providers. *Psychiatric Services* 46:575–579, 1995
31. Solomon P, Draine J: The efficacy of a consumer case manager team: 2-year outcomes of a randomized trial. *Journal of Mental Health Administration* 22:135–146, 1995
32. Teague G: *Patterns of preferences for mental health outcomes among consumers, families, and providers*. Paper presented at annual conference on state mental health agency services research, San Antonio, Tex. 1995
33. Postrado L, Lehman A: Quality of life and clinical predictors of rehospitalization of persons with severe mental illness. *Psychiatric Services* 46:1161–1165, 1995
34. McGrew J, Bond G, Dietzen L, et al: A Multisite study of client outcomes in assertive community treatment. *Psychiatric Services* 46:696–701, 1995
35. Rapp C, Gowdy E, Sullivan WP, et al: Client outcome reporting: the status method. *Community Mental Health Journal* 24:118–133, 1988
36. Nguyen T, Attkisson C, Stegner B: Assessment of patient satisfaction: development and refinement of a service evaluation questionnaire. *Evaluation and Program Planning* 6:299–314, 1983
37. Bogaert-Martinez E, Caen E, Wilson W, et al: *The SF-36 as a measure of functioning and health-related quality of life in individuals with severe and persistent mental illness: psychometric properties and normative data*. Paper presented at the annual conference on state mental health agency services research and program evaluation, Alexandria, Va, 1996
38. McHorney C, Ware J, Raczek A: The MOS 36-item SF-36: II. psychometric and clinical tests of validity and measuring physical and mental health constructs. *Medical Care* 31:247–263, 1993
39. Lehman AF: *Quality of Life Interview Core Version*. Baltimore, University of Maryland, Center for Mental Health Services Research, 1991
40. Veit S: *California Mental Health Performance Outcome Project*. Report for the California State Department of Mental Health. Sacramento, California Department of Mental Health, 1995
41. Comtois KD, Ries R, Armstrong HE: Case manager ratings of the clinical status of dually diagnosed outpatients. *Hospital and Community Psychiatry* 45:568–573, 1994
42. *Consumer-Oriented Mental Health Report Card: The Final Report of the Mental Health Statistics Improvement Program (MHSIP) Task Force on Consumer-Oriented Mental Health Report Card*. Rockville, Md, Center for Mental Health Services, 1996
43. Cross T, McDonald E: *Evaluating the Outcomes of Children's Mental Health Services: A Guide for the Use of Available Child and Family Outcome Measures*. Prepared for the Technical Assistance Center for the Evaluation of Children's Mental Health Systems. Boston, Judge Baker Children's Center, 1995
44. *Behavioral Healthcare Outcomes: A Reference Guide to Measurement Tools*. Rockville, Md, National Community Mental Health Council, 1995
45. *Proprietary Outcome Measures*. King of Prussia, Penn, Compass, Inc, 1995
46. Dow M, Ward J, Thornton D: *User-friendly assessment of consumer satisfaction: touch screen and scanning methods for the BHRS*. Paper presented at the annual national conference on state mental health agency services research and program evaluation, Alexandria, Va, 1996

47. Ward J, Harrell T, Constantine R, et al: Increasing accountability for state-supported behavioral healthcare services. *Ibid*
48. Davis D, Fong M: Measuring outcomes in psychiatry: an inpatient model. *Journal on Quality Improvement* 22:125–133, 1996
49. Eisen S, Dill D, Grob M: Reliability and validity of a brief patient-reported instrument for psychiatric outcome evaluation. *Hospital and Community Psychiatry* 45:242–247, 1994

Implementing a Statewide Outcomes Management System for Consumers Of Public Mental Health Services

JAMES A. CLARDY, MD, BRENDA M. BOOTH, PHD, LESLIE G. SMITH, MD, CAROL R. NORDQUIST, MA, AND G. RICHARD SMITH, MD

The authors describe the development and implementation of an outcomes management system designed to measure outcomes and processes of care for public mental health consumers in Arkansas. The public-academic project was implemented in 1995 and is based on the Shewhart-Deming model of continuous quality improvement. All 15 community mental health centers (CMHCs) in the state participate in the project, which prospectively measures longitudinal outcomes of care for the tracer conditions of major depression and schizophrenia. Multiperspective measurement tools are used to measure patients' psychiatric status and general health status at periodic intervals; information is gathered on functioning, symptoms, severity of illness, social factors, demographic characteristics, and quality of life. A problem encountered during implementation was the relatively low rate of referral of patients with the tracer conditions for monitoring. Voluntary rather than mandatory participation in the outcomes management system by the CMHCs as well as clinicians' misperceptions about the system's purpose and concerns about confidentiality may have partly accounted for the low rate.

Compelled by numerous forces such as national health care reform[1] and managed care,[2] many states are undergoing reforms aimed at improving the organization and financing of public mental health services.[3-5] Issues such as access to care, continuity of care, and outcomes of care are also recent concerns for many states.[6-9] Although great interstate variation exists in accountability efforts,[10] documenting and improving the effectiveness of mental health services is clearly an urgent issue that has affected not only private payers, but public payers as well.

In the past, techniques such as utilization management and utilization review have been the primary methods for system accountability, with an emphasis on utilization of services.[11] However, the difficulty with using utilization review as the sole approach to assessing mental health services is the questionable assumption that service utilization is an adequate measure of treatment needs or effectiveness. In addition, utilization review typically examines only a few components of treatment—the location, amount, and, sometimes, type of care. Although utilization review was initially intended to improve the quality of care, it has resulted in the micromanagement of individual cases and often has left clinicians feeling frustrated that outside care reviewers unfamiliar with their patients are directing care.[12]

Current methods of accountability are much more focused on demonstrating how treatment affects outcomes, and these approaches include an increased role for consumers' perspectives of functioning and well-being.[13,14] For example, the state

---

Source: Clardy JA, Booth BM, Smith LG, Nordquist CR, and Smith GR. Implementing a Statewide Outcomes Management System for Consumers of Public Mental Health Services. *Psychiatric Services* February 1998; 49(2):191-195. Reprinted with the permission of American Psychiatric Press, Inc., 1400 K Street, NW, Washington, DC 20005.

The authors are affiliated with the National Institute of Mental Health's Center for Mental Healthcare Research and the department of psychiatry at the University of Arkansas for Medical Sciences, 4301 West Markham Street, Slot 589, Little rock, Arkansas 72205. Dr. Booth, Dr. G. Richard Smith, and Ms. Nordquist are also affiliated with the Health Services Research and Development Field Program of the Department of Veterans Affairs.

of Georgia has undergone a radical restructuring of its public mental health system, shifting from a centralized model of service delivery to one that is decentralized and consumer driven with regional boards whose membership is at least 50% percent consumers or family members.[13] These new approaches to accountability, particularly the use of outcomes management systems, promise to go beyond a narrow focus on service utilization to provide valid and reliable information on what types of care are most effective for whom and in what settings and circumstances.[15-19]

This paper describes a public academic collaboration to develop a statewide outcomes management system for measuring outcomes and processes of care for public mental health patients at risk for hospital admission. The system was also designed to provide information, such as about patients' satisfaction with their living situations, that could be used to shape policies. Other goals of the system were to promote successful treatment modalities, such as adequate medication dosing for chronically depressed patients, and to enhance continuous quality improvement initiatives.

Very little research has focused on efforts to achieve large-scale statewide system accountability such as the initiative described here, nor has research adequately addressed the effectiveness of such systems of care.[20] However, because of recent national trends to shift care from the hospital to the community[4,7] and local trends in Arkansas involving financial decentralization (21), questions about whether patients are receiving appropriate services and about the extent of these services are at the forefront of many stakeholders' agendas. It is hoped that the discussion of our approach, methods, data collection tools, and processes to facilitate continuous quality improvement, as well as issues encountered during implementation, will help others who are involved in clinical services research and accountability efforts in the public mental health system.

The Outcomes Management System

Background
Our working model for this considerable task relies heavily on the use of outcomes management consistent with the Shewhart-Deming conceptual model of continuous quality improvement (CQI).[22,23] This approach follows a cyclical process that begins with monitoring clinical performance to identify problems that influence clinical practice patterns and the causes of these problems. Once problems are identified, practice modifications can be recommended and introduced, and the results assessed. Most important, by using the CQI process, information can be fed back to clinicians and administrators to improve a system's clinical performance while also addressing issues of accountability.

Key collaborators in this public-academic venture to develop a statewide outcomes management system include the Health Care Financing Administration and the Arkansas Division of Mental Health Services (DMHS), agencies that both set policies and provide payments; the Center for Mental Healthcare Research, an academic institution that provided the implementation project team; and Arkansas community mental health centers (CMHCs), the provider agencies. The project was conceptualized in the winter of 1994 and implemented the following summer, in 1995.

The involvement of senior organizational leaders, particularly from the DMHS in our case, has been noted as a critical factor in the success of an outcomes management system.[17] To facilitate this involvement, before implementation of the system, the project team presented the proposed project to the executive directors of the CMHCs at a regular meeting in the spring of 1995. Voluntary support was necessary from each center director because CMHCs operate as private non-profit organizations in Arkansas and are not under the direct administrative control of the DMHS.

Clinician support, also an important element of success,[17] was fostered in the summer of 1995 by two days of intensive training for all CMHC clinicians participating in the project. The training was given by the project team from the Center for Mental Healthcare Research at a central site to allow the greatest attendance possible. Site-specific in-service training was provided on request, and the project team visited the facility to train CMHC clinicians to tailor data collection to their specific circumstances. Throughout the project, telephone consultation has been provided to CMHC clinicians as needed. The executive director at each CMHC selected a clinical staff member to provide additional training to all clinicians and to coordinate patient enrollment and data collection efforts throughout the project.

The scope and impact of this project is quite large in terms of dollars devoted to services and numbers of providers and patients. For example, although state and federal funds are not the only source of income for CMHCs in Arkansas, approximately $20 million of such funds were disbursed to the CMHCs in fiscal year 1996. Slightly more than 10 percent of this budget (approximately $2.6 million) was earmarked for alternatives to state hospitalization. All 15 CMHCs and their on-site staff throughout the state are involved in the project. In 1996, with a state population of 2,225,000, approximately 60,000 consumers received some type of CMHC service in Arkansas.

Project implementation costs are difficult to estimate, and costs of implementing such a project will vary greatly among different systems depending on the technology and resources that are available. Cost of maintaining the Arkansas outcomes management system will range from $100,000 to $175,000 a year, which is less than 1 percent of the state and federal funds spent annually in the CMHC system.

Some factors that would result in lower costs include care providers' collecting data from consumers at the point of service versus the use of special project assistants, less dependency on outside professional interpretation of data, less reliance on sources outside of the CMHC for providing technical support such as data entry, and sampling only as many consumers as are needed to provide an accurate appraisal of outcomes for the system.

System Design

A disorder-specific approach to sampling and assessment was used to examine how patient outcomes relate to treatment provided within the state's public mental health system. Consumers at CMHCs were selected to be monitored by the outcomes management system based on their psychiatric diagnosis. An assessment tool specifically designed to measure the salient aspects of their disease and its treatment was used.

This disease-specific approach, which is based on the tracer methodology, has been favored by others evaluating mental health services,[17,24] primarily because it provides relevant clinical and prognostic information for a particular disorder (tracer). Also, it uses specific tracers as an indicator of the overall quality and effectiveness of the system delivering that care;[25,26] thus this approach is more economical than one that monitors every condition and every patient.

For several reasons, schizophrenia and depression were chosen as tracer conditions in this outcomes management system to assess the quality and effectiveness of our public mental health services. Schizophrenia and depression have been rated as areas of primary professional concern by those involved in public-academic health linkages.[27] Depressive disorders in mental health settings are common.[28] In Arkansas the prevalence of schizophrenia and depression is quite high, as is the use of services by persons with these disorders compared with patients who have other diagnoses. For example, a 1994 study using a statewide database of patient characteristics and service use in Arkansas CMHCs showed that individuals with schizophrenia or with depression received 46.8 percent of all CMHC services provided (Zhang M, Smith GR, Heithoff K, et al, unpublished manuscript, 1996). Finally, the economic and social burdens associated with both of these disorders[29-32] make accountability and quality improvement efforts imperative.

Procedures

Recruitment of patients for monitoring and evaluation by the outcomes management system began in August 1995 and ended in December 1996. To be eligible, individuals had to have a diagnosis of major depression or schizophrenia, be 18 years of age or older, and be at risk for hospitalization, as initially determined by a clinician. Patients from each of the state's 15 CMHCs were considered for the depression tracer condition. However, a necessary component of our monitoring approach for patients with schizophrenia was a periodic face-to-face interview; given the costs and constraints involved in such interviews, patients with schizophrenia seen only in the eight CMHCs in central Arkansas were targeted for monitoring in the system.

To examine a relatively homogeneous patient population in terms of diagnosis, individuals with depression who were also known to have severe borderline personality disorder, antisocial personality disorder, or bipolar disorder were excluded from monitoring. Similarly, for the tracer condition of schizophrenia, individuals with schizoaffective disorder, organic psychosis, bipolar disorder, or depression with psychotic features were excluded.

Clinicians at each CMHC selected patients who met the above criteria. After appropriate diagnostic screening and patient consent, clinicians and patients completed the baseline portion of the Depression Outcomes Module[33] or the Schizophrenia Outcomes Module.[34] These instruments measure disorder-specific outcomes and prognostic case-mix characteristics as well as general health status, functioning, social factors, demographic characteristics, quality of life, and processes of care (for example, quantity and type of services). The modules are designed to measure outcomes from multiple perspectives and from several sources, including consumers' self-reports, clinicians' ratings, and medical records. They are also relatively brief and feasible to implement in routine mental health care settings.[26] To ensure patient privacy, the data collected for this project were secured as if they were research data, so they could not be readily linked to individual patients.

Collection of Follow-Up Data

The protocol for the outcome management system called for collecting follow-up data for patients with depression every four months after baseline for up to one year, or until the depressive disorder resolved, and for patients with schizophrenia every six months after baseline for one year The follow-up times were chosen based on clinical experience and on literature indicating that they would be reasonable periods for observing clinically meaningful changes.[35,36]

For individuals with depression, the follow-up forms were mailed to patients, administered by phone, or completed at the CMHC. For those with schizophrenia, face-to-face follow-up interviews were conducted by a trained research assistant at the CMHCs. The CMHCs provided temporary unused space for the interviews. They also helped locate patients and plan specific times for follow-up interviews.

Medical record review, one of the components of the modules, was performed after the last follow-up by trained research assistants. Diagnoses initially made by CMHC clinicians were verified using a clinician DSM-IV checklist diagnostic verification form, and any further questions about the diagnosis were resolved by a review of the patient's medical records by a research psychiatrist. Additional information collected by chart review included quantity and type of services utilized within the public mental health system, such as day treatment, or utilized elsewhere, such as emergency room services. Information on psychotropic medications prescribed was also obtained. Follow-up of service utilization ended in December 1997, one year after the final recruitment month.

Feedback for CQI

Perhaps the most important part of an outcomes management system is the feedback of information for continuous quality improvement. Not surprisingly, CQI is becoming a major goal in state mental health systems.[37] Our approach to CQI consisted of a twofold strategy. The first step involved a meeting between the project team and the CMHC directors to mutually decide how data could best be reported. The second step involved disseminating regular reports to participating stakeholders, starting in July 1996, so that they could conduct site-specific CQI initiatives, especially feedback of information to clinicians.

These regular reports provide a written and graphical summary of primary findings, including patient characteristics, changes in outcomes over time, and mental health services received. The reports are sent bimonthly to CMHC executive directors with a request for input on their concerns about patient care, managed care, and state policies. Regular reports are also sent to the director of the DMHS, the Arkansas Alliance for the Mentally Ill, and the Arkansas Mental Health Council.

When enough data are gathered, all individuals and groups that have been receiving regular reports will receive reports that will include comparisons between large subgroups of patients and analyses of patient and treatment characteristics associated with improved outcomes. It is anticipated that these reports will be ready by mid-1998.

Issues in Implementation

Others might benefit from a discussion of several issues related to our experiences in implementing a statewide outcomes management system in the public mental health setting. First, we believe a strength of our approach is that multiple perspectives and sources of outcome are taken into account over time and that all parties invested in the process of public mental health are represented. The people who can make a difference in improving the quality and effectiveness of care—consumers, clinicians, consumer advocates, DMHS administrators, CMHC directors, and other state policy makers—are all involved in the project. In addition, our disorder-specific design and measurement tools are economical and incorporate critical components of case-mix that provide sufficient differential data on which to base sound policy.

A limitation of our outcomes management system is that we have obtained fewer referrals for monitoring than were expected, given the number of known cases of schizophrenia and depression in the state. Although the limited number of referrals is a typical problem encountered in large-scale "real world" evaluations of this type,[38] the reasons for the low referral rate are not entirely clear. As in other studies of outcomes management systems, it is possible that referral rates are directly correlated with the number of clinicians at each site who are designated to make referrals and the number of staff in the outcomes management system responsible for data collection.[18]

However, other factors accounting for the relatively low number of referrals might include the stringent inclusion criteria, the fact that cooperation by CMHCs was voluntary, and concerns about confidentiality by both providers and consumers. Privacy in outcomes management systems is an ongoing concern. Although individual providers were not specifically monitored in this project, clinicians might have been hesitant to volunteer information they perceived could be used against them.

The CMHCs had no financial front-end investment in the outcomes management system and were strictly voluntary participants. Each CMHC agreed to designate time to enter a patient in the project, amounting to about one hour per participant. The CMHC also provided medical records so that service utilization data could be obtained. However, even though the project was described as an outcomes management system from the start, some CMHC staff members perceived that the data gathering was for academic research. This perception may have given the project lower priority in the CMHC system than if it had been viewed as a practical CQI tool. In light of these observations, it is clear that for an outcomes management system to operate to capacity, providers must value and incorporate it into the service delivery system as a necessary means of measuring the effectiveness of treatment. Research is needed to identify specific techniques for gaining providers' cooperation.

Limitations aside, we suggest that it is feasible to implement an outcomes management system in the public mental health setting, despite common perceptions noted by others that public mental health systems are complex and turbulent systems that do not support research efforts.[39] The application of clinical services research and outcomes management systems, such as the one described here, will become an increasingly important issue for political and clinical leaders in public mental health settings to consider.

Particularly as competition in the health care industry continues to intensify, public mental health systems must come to terms with these issues to survive. Not only do such state-of-the-art projects add to our current knowledge about processes of care and effectiveness of treatment, but they also provide guidance in solving practical problems such as case-mix adjustment, outcomes specificity, and quality improvement efforts. Thus they help reduce the burden on public mental health systems that many states currently face.

References

1. Ross EC, Mazade NA: The Clinton proposed health care reform: implications for persons with serious mental illness. *Administration and Policy in Mental Health* 21:251-261, 1994
2. Essock SM, Goldman HH: States embrace of managed mental health care. *Health Affairs* 14(3):34-44, 1995
3. Cuffel BJ, Snowden L, Green RS, et al: The California adult performance outcome survey: preliminary evidence on reliability and validity. *Community Mental Health Journal* 31:425-436, 1995

4. Dickey B, Cohen MD: Changing the financing of state mental health programs: using carrots, not sticks, to improve care. *Administration and Policy in Mental Health* 20:343-355, 1993
5. Gilchrist LD, Allen DG, Brown L, et al: A public-academic approach to designing a state mental health program evaluation. *Evaluation and Program Planning* 17:53-61, 1994
6. Glover R, Petrila J: Can state mental health agencies survive health care reform? *Hospital and Community Psychiatry* 45:911-913, 1994
7. Rapp CA, Moore TD: The first 18 months of mental health reform in Kansas. *Psychiatric Services* 46:580-585, 1995
8. Reinig SP, Hawley R: Realigning local-state relations: grassroots mental health restructuring in the Pacific Northwest. *Administration and Policy in Mental Health* 22:233-245, 1995
9. Brown L, Cox GB, Jones WE, et al: Effects of mental health reform on client characteristics, continuity of care, and community tenure. *Evaluation and Program Planning* 17:63-72, 1994
10. Davidson H, Schlesinger M, Dorwart RA, et al: State purchase of mental health care: models and motivations for maintaining accountability. *International Journal of Law and Psychiatry* 14:387-403, 1991
11. Tischler GL: Utilization management and the quality of care. *Hospital and Community Psychiatry* 41:1099-1102, 1990
12. Eddy DM: Clinical decision making: from theory to practice. *JAMA* 263:287-290, 1990
13. Elliott RL, Cohen MD, Evans DL: Reforming Georgia's mental health system. *Community Mental Health Journal* 31:413-423, 1995
14. Wells KB, Stewart A, Hays RD, et al: The functioning and well-being of depressed patients: results from the Medical Outcomes Study. *JAMA* 262:914-919, 1989
15. Ellwood PM: Outcomes management: a technology of patient experience. *New England Journal of Medicine* 318:1549-1556, 1988
16. Flynn L, Steinwachs D: Outcomes roundtable includes all stakeholders. *Health Affairs* 14(3):269-270, 1995
17. Smith GR, Fischer EP Nordquist CR, et al: Implementing outcomes management systems in mental health settings. *Psychiatric Services* 48:364-368, 1997
18. Steinwachs DM, Wu AW, Skinner EA: How will outcomes management work? *Health Affairs* 13(3):153-162, 1994
19. Wagner J, Gartner CG: Highlights of the 1995 Institute on Psychiatric Services. *Psychiatric Services* 47:13-20, 1996
20. Cutler DL, Bigelow D, McFarland B: The cost of fragmented mental health financing: is it worth it? *Community Mental Health Journal* 28:121-133, 1992
21. Cuffel BJ, Wait D, Head T: Shifting the responsibility for payment for state hospital services to community mental health agencies. *Hospital and Community Psychiatry* 45:460-465, 1994
22. Deming WE: *The New Economics for Industry, Education, Government.* Cambridge, Massachusetts Institute of Technology, Center for Advanced Engineering Study, 1993
23. Shewhart WA: *The Economic Control of Quality of the Manufactured Product.* Milwaukee, ASQC Quality Press, 1980
24. McGlynn EA, Norquist GS, Wells KB, et al: Quality-of-care research in mental health: responding to the challenge. *Inquiry* 25:157-170, 1988
25. Kessner DM, Kalk CE, Singer J: Assessing health quality: the case for tracers. *New England Journal of Medicine* 288:189-194, 1973
26. Smith GR, Rost KM, Fischer EP, et al: Assessing the effectiveness of mental health care in routine clinical practice: characteristics, development, and uses of patient outcomes modules. *Evaluation and the Health Professions* 20:65-80, 1997
27. O'Hare T Rodriguez R, Earls E: The current status of academic-mental health linkages in Rhode Island. *Community Mental Health Journal* 31:209-214. 1995
28. Rost KM, Smith GR, Burnam MA, et al: Measuring the outcomes of care for mental health problems: the case of depressive disorders. *Medical Care* 30(suppl 5):266-273, 1992
29. Health care reform for Americans with severe mental illness: report of the National Advisory, Mental Health Council. *American Journal of Psychiatry* 150:1447-1465, 1993
30. Eckett S: A commentary: measuring the health economics of depression. *Human Psychopharmacology* 10:33-37, 1995

31. Klerman GL, Weissman MM: The course, morbidity, and costs of depression. *Archives of General Psychiatry* 49:831-834, 1992
32. Cuffel BJ, Jeste DV, Halpain M, et al: Treatment costs and use of community mental health services for schizophrenia by age cohorts. *American Journal of Psychiatry* 153:870-876, 1996
33. Smith GR, Burnam MA, Burns BJ, et al: *Outcomes Module for Major Depression*. Little Rock, University of Arkansas for Medical Sciences, 1994
34. Cuffel BJ, Fischer EP, Owen RR, et al: An instrument for measurement of outcomes of care for schizophrenia: issues in development and implementation. *Evaluation and the Health Professions* 20:96-108, 1997
35. Prien RF, Carpenter LL, Kupfer DJ: The definition and operational criteria for treatment outcome of major depressive disorder: a review of the current research literature. *Archives of General Psychiatry* 48:796-800, 1991
36. Keitner GI, Ryan CE, Miller IW, et al: Recovery and major depression: factors associated with twelve-month outcome. *American Journal of Psychiatry* 149:93-99, 1992
37. Evans ON, Faulkner LR, Hodo GL, et al: A quality improvement process for state mental health systems. *Hospital and Community Psychiatry* 43:465-469, 1992
38. Cox GB, Allen DG, Brown L, et al: Recommendations for state-wide evaluations: lessons relearned. *Evaluation and Program Planning* 17:97-101, 1994
39. Hogan MF. Serving the seriously mentally ill: public-academic linkages in services, research, and training, in *Public Mental Health Systems and Research*. Edited by Wohlford P, Myers HF, Callan JE. Washington, DC, American Psychological Association, 1993

Michigan's Mission Based Performance Indicator System

For Persons With Mental Illness, Developmental Disabilities, And Emotional Disturbance

Introduction

"Delivering the Promise" & The Quality Management System for The Public Mental Health Services

In March of 1992, James K. Haveman, Jr. the Director of the Michigan Department of Community Health (MDCH) released to the people of the state of Michigan a report entitled: "Delivering the Promise—An Enhanced Model for Michigan's Public Mental Health System". As Director Haveman's cover letter indicated, this report was not the conclusion of a process, but a new beginning on the evolutionary path to a continuously improving mental health system in Michigan.

> "The system we seek to build will integrate the strengths of the present system with new structures and relationships to provide continuous improvement in quality of care to those who need mental health services."

That document established a new mission for the public mental health system and identified "meaningful accountability" as a critical characteristic of the public system.

> "Accountability is more than sending in reports. It means having rationale data available upon request which, properly presented and understood, gives evidence that outcomes are appropriate to the mission are being achieved at a frequency, quality and cost that are appropriate." (Pg. 9)

Based upon this vision, the Michigan Department of Community Health developed a set of performance indicator measures intended to provide meaningful accountability and a mechanism for continuous improvement within the public mental health system.

The Michigan Mission Based Performance Indicator System Development Process

Building upon the vision of "Delivering the Promise" and the previous efforts to introduce measures of quality into the public mental health system, MDCH staff and the Quality Improvement Council for Persons with Mental Illness, Developmental Disabilities and Severe Emotional Disturbance (hereafter referred to as the QI Council), established a process to identify and recommend performance measures for the public mental health system. The process included the identification of specific purposes for the effort, the establishment of a set of principles to guide the effort and the formation of work groups to propose the actual indicators. Ninety-one consumers, advocates, CMHSP staff and MDCH staff participated in the initial development effort and dozens more were involved in the actual implementation and refinement of the measures.

The purposes of the effort were to:
- Clearly delineate the dimensions of quality encompassed in the Mission Statement for the public mental health system;
- Develop a state wide aggregate status report to address issues of public accountability;

Source: Michigan Department of Community Health. (Reprinted with permission.)

- Provide a focus for the MDCH contract management process for CMHSPs; and
- Establish a link with existing health care reform planning efforts and establish a foundation for future quality management efforts.

Essential planning principles included:
- Keep it simple, useful, and truthful;
- Indicators must be "actionable". They must be amenable to intervention by CMHSPs;
- The indicators must be built upon accurate and uniform data;
- Indicators should reflect the perspectives of consumers, stakeholders and service delivery providers;
- The indicators should utilize and/or replacement of existing data reporting; and
- The number and complexity of indicators should be minimized.

MDCH staff and the QI Council, with the assistance of Dr. Edna Kamis-Gould from the Center for Mental Health Policy and Services Research at the University of Pennsylvania, subsequently identified three essential domains of quality contained in the mission statement for the public mental health system for which indicators were to be developed. These domains were: **Access, Efficiency & Outcome.**

Multiple workgroups consisting of 71 consumers, advocates, CMHSP staff, and MDCH staff were assembled in 1996 to develop the initial set of performance indicators within these domains. These work groups were facilitated by MDCH staff who used existing and proposed national performance measurement systems to act as a springboard for discussion. This included the National Committee for Quality Assurance's Health Plan Employer Data Set (HEDIS), the Center for Mental Health Services Consumer Oriented Report Card, and others. The result was the inclusion of 27 performance indicators, unique to Michigan, in the MDCH contracts with the CMHSP during the FY 97.

Michigan's Move to a Pre-Paid System of Speciality Services And Supports

In an effort to increase flexibility of the public system to provide more individualized supports and services of the scope, intensity and duration as desired and required by consumers, Michigan sought and received federal approval from the Health Care Financing Administration to create a pre-paid capitate system of care for Medicaid recipients. This premise was extended to all public funds given to forty-nine (49) Community Mental Health Service Programs (CMHSP), with an effective date of October 1, 1998.

As part of Michigan's effort to assure access and quality under the new system, a multi-dimension quality management system, within which the performance indicator system was incorporated, was developed. This quality management system included: 1) requirements that each CMHSP must have a local Quality Improvement Program which met MDCH defined standards; 2) prospective assurances of quality by the CMHSP (e.g. Certification/accreditation, licensure, responses to a Request for Information, etc.); 3) annual Site Visits to CMHSP to conduct: medical record reviews to assure that health and safety concerns are addressed, local systems implementation review, interviews/focus groups with consumers and local stakeholders, and verification of data collection and reporting methodologies; 4) the performance indicator data; 5) consumer characteristics and utilization data; 6) external evaluation and state-wide sampling data studies (e.g., consumer satisfaction & quality of life) and 7) reporting and tracking of sentinel events (e.g., death of recipients, accidents or physical illness requiring hospitalization, suspected abuse or neglect, incidents involving arrest or conviction, serious challenging behaviors, and medication errors.

Use of the Performance Indicator Data

Since the original focus of the data was to continually improve the performance of the CMHSP, the first sets of data was used primarily to improve the reliability and utility of the data while establishing a base line for future performance monitoring. While data was published from these initial efforts, some data was not used due to the start up issues of data reliability.

Under the pre-paid system of care, the performance data will be one aspect of the quality review of the CMHSP who will manage the funds. Contractual action will be taken for the failure to report data by the time frames established in contracts. With respect to performance level, the focus of quality improvement will be maintained initially. Data analysis will continue to include the use of a statistical procedure called a Tukey Box-and-Whisker Plot. This test determines if a CMHSP was a statistical outlier when compared to all other CMHSP. It is the intent of the department to engage in dialog with those CMHSP who were found to be statistical outliers for two consecutive reporting periods. Those who were statistical outliers with positive performance would be reviewed for possible best practice. Those who were statistical outliers withopportunities for improvement would begin a process of identifying causes and making improvements. Penalties during the first contract will likely be related to a lack of good faith efforts to make improvement.

As a result of the experiences with the initial set of indicators and the new concerns associated with a managed system of care, indicators from the original list of 27 were refined, deleted or expanded. The list to be part of the managed system of care contracts beginning October 1, 1998 are listed below. Questions regarding this performance system, the lessons learned, and the findings to date may be directed to:

Glenn A. Stanton, Director, Division of Quality Management and Service Innovation, Mental Health and Substance Abuse Services, Michigan Department of Community Health. e-mail: Stanton@State.MI.US

Judy Webb, Director Quality Improvement and Services Research Section, Division of Quality Management and Service Innovation, Mental Health and Substance Abuse Services, Michigan Department of Community Health. e-mail: Webb@State.MI.US

Michigan's Performance Indicators for the Managed System of Care To Be Implemented in 1998

I. Access

Penetration Rates of Under-Served Populations

1. Ratio of the percentage of persons 18 or younger in the area population receiving mental health services to the percentage of person 18 or younger in the area population.
2. Ratio of percentage of persons over age 65 in the area population receiving mental health services to the percentage of persons over 65 in the area population.
3. Ratio of percentage of ethnic minority persons in the area population receiving mental health services to the percentage of ethnic minority persons in the area population.
4. Ratio of percentage of persons 18 or older with serious mental illness in the area population receiving services to the percentage of persons 18 or older with serious mental illness in the area population
5. Ratio of the percentage of persons 18 or younger in the area population receiving substance abuse services to the percentage of person 18 or younger in the area population.
6. Percent of persons served for substance abuse who are women of child-bearing age (ages 11-44) divided by percent of area census who are women of child-bearing age.
7. Ratio of percentage of ethnic minority persons in the area population receiving substance abuse services to the percentage of ethnic minority persons in the area population.
8. Number of persons served who are injecting drug users divided by estimated number of area census of persons who are injecting drug users.
9. Persons served age 18 or older meeting a diagnosis of substance abuse or dependency divided by the projected substance abuse/dependence prevalence.

Penetration Rates of Medicaid Eligible Persons

10. Percentage of area Medicaid recipients having received CMHSP managed services.
11. Percentage of area Medicaid recipients having received CA managed services.

Timeliness

12. The percentage of persons receiving a pre-admission screening for psychiatric inpa-

tient care for whom the disposition was completed within three hours
Standard: 95%

13. The percentage of persons receiving a face-to-face meeting with a mental health professional within 14 calender days of a non-emergency request for service (reported for 3 sub-populations
Standard: 95%

14. Average Days between first non-emergent assessment with a mental health professional to the start of any needed on-going service (by 3 sub-populations)

15. The percentage of persons receiving a screening for emergency substance abuse services for whom the disposition was completed within three hours.
Standard: 95%

16. Average days between first non-emergent assessment with a substance abuse professional to the start of any needed ongoing service.

Continuity of Care—Mental Health

17. The percentage of persons who met the OBRA Level II Assessment criteria for specialized mental health services for persons residing in nursing homes, as determined by the Department, who received CMHSP managed mental health services.

18. The percentage of persons who met the OBRA Level II criteria determined to need nursing home care but less than specialized mental health services, as determined by the Department, who received CMHSP managed mental health services.

19. The percentage of persons discharged from a psychiatric inpatient unit who are seen for follow-up care within [30] days.

Denial/Appeals

20. Ratio of Sec.705 second opinions (denials of CMHSP access) which result in services

II. Efficiency

Utilization of Services

21. Days of 24-hour specialized residential care provided in a group home or institutional setting per thousand persons with developmental disabilities served.

22. Days of psychiatric inpatient care per thousand persons with mental illness served.

23. Percent of expenditures for persons with developmental disabilities used for 24-hour specialized residential care provided in a group home or institutional setting.

24. Percent of expenditures for persons with mental illness used for psychiatric inpatient care.

25. Percent of Medicaid eligible persons served who received inpatient, day/night care, and ambulatory services

Cost Per Case

26. Cost per case for adults with mental illness

27. Cost per case for children (age 17 or under) with a mental illness or severe emotional disturbance

28. Cost per case for persons with a developmental disability

29. Average cost per case for persons 18 and over with a substance abuse/dependence diagnosis, by service category.

30. Average cost per case for persons under age 18 with a substance abuse/dependence diagnosis, by service category.

III. Outcomes

Quality of Life—Employment (Mental Health)

31. Percentage of persons in Supported Employment (SE) working 10+ hours per week

32. Percentage of persons in SE earning minimum wage

33. Percentage of persons in SE continuously employed 6 months or longer

34. Percentage of persons with developmental disabilities receiving day or supported employment services who are working in integrated work settings

Quality of Life—Living Situation (Mental Health)

35. Percentage of children served living with their families

36. Percentage of adults served living in their own residence.

Satisfaction—Complaint/Dispute Resolution

37. Rates of substantiated mental health Recipient Rights complaints per thousand persons served in the category of "treatment suited to condition".
38. Rates of substantiated mental health Recipient Rights complaints per thousand persons served in the category of "dignity and respect".
39. The number of substantiated substance abuse recipient rights complaints per thousand persons served.
40. The percentage of persons 18 and over receiving substance abuse services who report satisfaction with services.
41. The percentage of persons receiving substance abuse services under age 18 and/or their families who report satisfaction with services.

Adverse Consumer Outcomes

42. Rates of suicides per thousand persons served.
43. Rates of substantiated recipient rights complaints per 1,000 persons served, in the categories of Abuse and Neglect I and II.
44. Readmission rates to inpatient psychiatric units within 15 days of discharge from a psychiatric inpatient unit.
    Standard: 95% or less.
45. The number of persons receiving substance abuse services whose reason for discharge was death.

[1] "Family" means natural or adoptive relatives (parents, grandparents, siblings, etc.)

[2] "Own residence" means lease, rental agreement, or deed/mortgage of home, apartment or condo is in individual's name.

A Multistakeholder-Driven Model For Developing an Outcome Management System

J. RANDY KOCH, PHD, ALLEN LEWIS, PHD, AND DWIGHT MCCALL, PHD

Abstract

Increasing demands for accountability in the delivery of public mental health services are engendering organized systems of treatment outcome monitoring. As such systems are designed and implemented, it is critical that key stakeholders be involved to the greatest extent possible in developing assessment instruments and methodologies so as to ensure relevance and acceptability of the outcome management system A multistakeholder-based initiative for developing standardized outcome assessment for public mental health services in Virginia is described. Key components of the initiative include the process by which stakeholders were enlisted, the identification of recommended assessment instruments, and a pilot project that began the evaluation of the feasibility, utility, and cost-benefit of using the instruments. To illustrate features of this initiative, the child/adolescent mental health pilot project is described in detail. Implications for behavioral health administrators and next steps for Virginia's outcome management system are discussed, highlighting the role of key stakeholders.

Public mental health services, no less than other governmental services, are being challenged by increasing demands for cost containment, continuous quality improvement, and accountability. In response, there has been ever greater attention devoted to the development of appropriate mechanisms for routine clinical assessment and monitoring of consumer outcomes, frequently as part of an overall strategy of "managed care." The past few years have seen a growing number of publications on the why and how of outcome assessment,[1] compendiums of outcome measures,[2-4] and conferences with a major focus on assessing the outcome of services (e.g., Mental Health Statistics Improvement Program, 1997; National Association of State Mental Health Program Directors, 1998; and Research and Training Center for Children's Mental Health, 1998).

A system for the routine assessment, analysis, and reporting of consumer outcomes, often referred to as an outcome management system (OMS), is one of several tools for managing care.* A well-designed OMS can serve multiple purposes.

For these and other reasons, health service systems in general are increasing their focus on outcome-based accountability.[5] In recent years, there has also been a growing emphasis in the mental health and substance abuse fields on measuring the outcomes of services.[6,7] Research on outcomes has been shown to enhance the ability of existing systems to monitor the quality of care.[8] A relationship between monitoring programs and the outcomes achieved by those programs has also been demonstrated.[9] Several states have recognized these advantages and have begun to make some effort to develop outcome management sys-

---

Source: Koch JR, Lewis A, McCall D. Multistakeholder-Driven Model for Developing an Outcome Management System. The Journal of Behavioral Health Services & Research May 1998; 25(2):151-162. Copyright © 1998 by Sage Publications, Inc. Reprinted by permission of Sage Publications, Inc.

Address correspondence to J. Randy Koch, Ph.D., Director of Research and Evaluation, Virginia Department of Mental Health, Mental Retardation, and Substance Abuse Services, P.O. Box 1797, Richmond, VA 23218.

Allen Lewis, Ph.D., is director of the Virginia Cancer Registry, Department of Health, Richmond, Virginia.

Dwight McCall, Ph.D., is a research and evaluation manager, Virginia Department of Mental Health, Mental Retardation, and Substance Abuse Services, Richmond, Virginia.

tems, including Colorado, Texas, Michigan, Vermont, Minnesota, California, Washington, Oregon, New York, North Carolina, and Virginia.

At a national level, evidence of this trend is seen in the creation of the Outcomes Roundtable for Children and Adolescents, a public-private partnership of consumers, families, public and private providers, researchers, and government agencies. The Outcomes Roundtable is developing strategies to assess the outcomes of services in order to improve the quality of care for persons with mental illness.[10] Similarly, the Report Card Task Force of the Mental Health Statistics Improvement Program, sponsored by the Center for Mental Health Services, represents a federally sponsored effort to systematically examine provider performance and consumer outcomes.[11]

Amid the recent efforts to examine the outcomes of all mental health services, the measurement of consumer outcomes is becoming a key area of focus in children's mental health services.[12-14] This trend has been accompanied by an increasing emphasis on developing common data sets, automated information systems, and regular feedback mechanisms for outcome data.[15] Several factors, including adoption of the systems of care model in providing children's mental health services,[16] the emphasis on more effective and less costly public services,[17] and general accountability concerns among state-level administrators,[18] have increased child and family service providers' attention on developing systems that promote accountability based on empirical outcomes.

The evaluation of children's mental health services is complicated, however, by the many facets of the comprehensive, coordinated systems of care model advocated for children's mental health services,[19] the intricacies of managed behavioral health care[20] and a history of evaluation based on data limited to service utilization and derived from inadequate reporting systems.[20]

These evolving efforts in the evaluation of children's mental health services have increasingly focused on the use of standardized outcome measures that have demonstrated both their psychometric soundness[8] and their practicality.[6] The use of standardized outcome assessments has numerous advantages, including established validity and reliability; more opportunity to compare results with those of other studies; and, in many instances, the availability of non-native data, training materials, and scoring software. Thus, it is no surprise that 16 states have been identified as routinely using standardized instruments to measure the degree of psychological impairment in children.[21]

Standardized Outcomes Assessment Initiative

Like most states, Virginia has experienced the demands for cost containment, quality improvement, and accountability. And, like other state mental health agencies, the Virginia Department of Mental Health, Mental Retardation, and Substance Abuse Services (DMHMRSAS) has mounted a concerted effort to build its capacity to assess the consumer outcomes of publicly funded services. In the recent past, these efforts have been in the form of the Evaluation of Community-Based Consumer Outcomes (ECCO) initiative. Through ECCO, the statewide network of providers of local, publicly funded services (i.e., community services boards [CSBs]†) conducted highly focused evaluations. The first three years of ECCO helped to demonstrate the importance of routinely assessing consumer outcomes, and the infrastructure necessary to accomplish this assessment. However, by focusing on narrowly defined target populations and specific types of services, this effort has proven to be too limited in scope to meet current needs in an era of managed care and increased accountability.

Although ECCO no longer fully meets the needs of Virginia's public mental health system, it did demonstrate the value of a multistakeholder evaluation process. To some extent, ECCO provided the impetus for its successor, the Standardized Outcomes Assessment Initiative, to involve stakeholders. All decisions made about evaluation design and implementation strategies were based on consensus of key stakeholders, including consumers, family members, community and facility providers, and central office staff. This approach greatly contributed to the success of ECCO.

Building on ECCO, a collaborative effort between the Administration Committee of the statewide association of CSBs (the Virginia Association of Community Services Boards [VACSB]) and the DMHMRSAS's Office of Research and Evaluation was initiated during the fall of 1994 to further enhance the public mental health, mental retardation, and substance abuse system's capacity to assess consumer outcomes. As part of this initiative, the state of Virginia articulated a goal of developing a system for measuring consumer outcomes that would be embraced by all constituencies. To achieve this goal, key stakeholders must be integrally involved in all developmental efforts. The inclusion of multiple stakeholders enhances the decision-making process and incorporates diverse perspectives.[22,23]

The remainder of this article presents the goals, design, and results of the initial steps of a major effort to design and implement an efficient system to monitor the consumer outcomes of services within Virginia's public system of services for persons with mental disabilities and substance abuse problems. The first steps in this effort were to (a) establish a process for multistakeholder involvement, (b) identify the outcome domains to be assessed, (c) select standardized outcome assessment instruments for future use, and (d) field test these instruments in pilot sites. This article will focus particularly on how a stakeholder-driven process can be used to identify outcomes to be assessed and measures to be used rather than on the analyses of findings from the field test.

Process for Multistakeholder Involvement

A work group process was utilized as the main vehicle for decision making in the Standardized Outcomes Assessment Initiative. The recognition that stakeholder involvement enhances the integrity of the decision-making process[24] reaffirmed the importance of including key stakeholders at the outset. Unfortunately, however, the published literature, including that of the mental health field, offers little information about this approach. Thus, with few resources to draw on, we embarked on our efforts to actively involve participants from a variety of stakeholders, including consumer and family advocacy groups, CSBs (both administrative and clinical staff), state facilities, and the DMHMRSAS central office. These stakeholders were included because they would either directly complete or administer the assessment instruments (e.g., clinical staff, consumers, and family members) and/or they would be primary consumers of the resulting information (e.g., clinical staff, advocacy organizations, provider administrative staff, and state administrators).

One of the challenges in forming the work groups was to represent the diversity of stakeholder perspectives while keeping the groups small enough to be able to efficiently handle the critical tasks of identifying, reviewing, and selecting recommended instruments in the time allotted. As a result, some stakeholders who could have made a contribution to this process were not recruited (e.g., local government officials, state legislative staff, and private payers).

In general, participants from the various stakeholder groups were recruited by a formal request to the leaders of relevant organizations. For example, a letter was written to the chairperson of the statewide council of CSB mental health directors asking for a representative from that group. Sometimes, a specific representative was recommended when a particular member of the organization was known to have an interest and expertise in this area.

Once convened, each work group was asked to select a leader. This person was responsible for convening and facilitating meetings, keeping the work groups on schedule and on task, and preparing the final report. In addition, each work group leader served on the steering committee, which was created to ensure coordination across the different work groups. Although each work group had a leader, all stakeholder representatives were fully engaged at the beginning of the work group process and were empowered to take ownership of the process through a consensus-driven model of decision making.

Identification of Recommended Instruments

The VACSB Administration Committee and the Office of Research and Evaluation jointly established several work groups to identify assessment and outcome instruments to be recommended to the field. Initially, four work groups were created, one for each population to be assessed: (a) adult mental health, (b) child/adolescent mental health, (c) mental retardation, and (d) adult substance abuse. A fifth work group was established later to address the assessment of consumer satisfaction for all populations. The initiative was led by the director of the Office of Research and Evaluation and a representative from the VACSB Administration Committee.

The specific charges to the work groups were as follows:
1. Identify dimensions/areas that should be addressed in assessing the outcomes of services for consumers receiving publicly-funded services (e.g., level of functioning, satisfaction, and symptom reduction).
2. Critically review existing instruments addressing each dimension.
3. Identify the "best" instruments for use in Virginia's system of public services.
4. Make recommendations regarding strategies to promote the use of the identified instruments throughout the public mental health, mental retardation, and substance abuse system.

The individual work groups were given great flexibility in the process they used to accomplish the assigned tasks. What was most important was that the groups, representing the perspectives of multiple stakeholders, arrive at a consensus regarding the recommended instruments.

In general, the work groups proceeded by reviewing the literature to help identify which dimensions or domains of outcomes should be assessed and to identify specific instruments for critical review. In addition, the work groups invited other individuals with experience and expertise with specific instruments to make presentations on those instruments. Although the specific domains selected to be the focus of outcome assessment varied somewhat across the individual target populations, they included (a) symptomatology, (b) level of functioning, (c) consumer satisfaction, and (d) quality of life.

Following these steps, the work groups identified several criteria for the selection of recommended instruments. The worksheet that was used to guide the evaluation of each instrument incorporated these criteria. Instruments were selected on the basis of their psychometric strengths and usefulness to stakeholders. Other considerations were the amount of training required, the level of difficulty of administering and scoring the instrument, the amount of time required to administer the instrument, and the costs associated with the instrument's use.

The work groups reviewed a wide range of potentially appropriate and useful instruments, and recommended several for further evaluation. Each recommended instrument was regarded as psychometrically sound and capable of providing useful data without being excessively burdensome on direct service staff.

Some work groups used a structured process in which each member rated the instruments on each criteria. The results of these ratings were then summarized and presented to the group to facilitate the decision-making process. Generally, using the criteria described above, the work groups were able to reach a consensus on the best instrument for each dimension/area to be addressed. In the rare instances in which a work group was not able to recommend a single instrument, a decision was made to field-test two alternative instruments and let the results of the field test inform the final decision. This proved to be a useful method for resolving differences of opinion in the identification of recommended instruments.

The Outcome Assessment Pilot Project

Following the identification of recommended instruments, a pilot project was designed to assess the feasibility, utility, and cost-benefit of using these instruments within the public mental health, mental retardation, and substance abuse system. The pilot project was recommended by the stakeholders represented in the initial work groups, who participated in its design. To help illustrate this stage of the initiative, the design and operation of the child/adolescent mental health pilot project will be described in detail.

The child/adolescent work group recommended four domains in which to assess consumer outcomes: (a) symptomatology, (b) level of youth functioning, (c) family functioning, and (c) parent satisfaction. This work group then reviewed 38 different instruments and reached consensus on one or more recommended instruments for each domain. The recommended instruments for child/adolescent mental health services and their associated assessment methods are summarized in Table 1.

The Child Behavior Checklist (CBCL)[25] is a well-established measure of behavior in children and adolescents aged 4-18 that addresses social competence as well as a wide range of behavior problems. The Child and Adolescent Functional Assessment Scale (CAFAS)[26] is completed by the

Table 1. Child/Adolescent Mental Health Instruments

Instrument	Domain	Data Source	Method
Child Behavior Checklist (CBCL)	Symptomatology	Parent/caregiver	Self-report questionnaire
Child and Adolescent Functional Assessment Scale (CAFAS)	Level of functioning	Case manager/clinician	Completed after interview with child or family member
Family Assessment Device (FAD)	Family functioning	Parent/caregiver	Self-report questionnaire
Consumer Satisfaction Questionnaire (CSQ-8)	Consumer satisfaction	Parent/caregiver	Self-report questionnaire
Family Satisfaction Questionnaire (FSQ)	Consumer satisfaction	Parent/caregiver	Self-report questionnaire

youth's case manager, or clinician, or by a trained staff person using a structured interview protocol. The instrument measures child functioning in role performance, thinking, behavior toward others, moods/self-harm, and substance abuse. The Family Assessment Device (FAD)[27] is a 60-item self-report instrument, completed by one or more family members, that assesses family functioning along six dimensions: problem solving, communication, roles, affective responsiveness, affective involvement, and behavior control. Two consumer satisfaction questionnaires were recommended. The eight-item version of the Client Satisfaction Questionnaire (CSQ-8)[28] is a global measure of satisfaction with mental health services. The Family Satisfaction Questionnaire (FSQ)[29] allows more focused assessment of parents' satisfaction with their children's services and progress as well as their own involvement in those services. Work group members felt that the CSQ-8, although developed originally for adult consumers, could be used appropriately with parents of child/adolescent consumers with some minor wording changes.

The project was designed to minimize the burden on the CSBs while still enabling a careful examination of key issues. The questions to be addressed through the pilot were as follows:

1. Are the instruments acceptable to CSB staff and consumers/family members?
2. Are the instruments relatively easy to administer?
3. Are the self-report instruments relatively easy to complete by parents?
4. Is the amount of time required to administer/complete the instruments acceptable to staff and parents?
5. Are the instruments appropriate for the population being assessed?
6. Do the instruments provide useful information to clinical staffs?

Methodology

Three CSBs were selected to pilot-test the child/adolescent mental health instruments from among those CSBs volunteering to participate in this effort. CSBs were selected based on their "organizational readiness" (including staff resources and expertise) to implement the required activities.

One staff person from each participating CSB served as a liaison ("project coordinator") between the CSB and the Office of Research and Evaluation. In this role, the Project Coordinator oversaw the implementation of the pilot activities at the CSB and served as the primary point of contact for the project.

Staff Selection

Four staff at each CSB were selected to complete/administer a package of instruments at each site. The project coordinators were instructed to ensure that, as a group, participating staff (a) provide services to a wide variety of consumers and (b) represent diversity in types of direct service staff (e.g., level of training and program area).

Training

Participating staff (project coordinators and clinicians) from each of the pilot sites attended a one-day workshop prior to implementing the pilot project activities. At this workshop, CSB staff were provided with a description of the history and goals of the pilot project and were instructed in the specific procedures to be carried out when conducting the project. At the workshop, staff were provided with all of the materials needed to complete the pilot project, including forms, scoring templates, and a manual with background reading on the instruments and the specific procedures to be followed when conducting the pilot. Staff were also trained in the use of each instrument. This training included a description of the purpose of the instrument, administration and scoring procedures, and guidelines for interpreting results of the assessments. For the one instrument that was not a self-report measure (i.e., the CAFAS), training included the completion of the instrument using several self-training vignettes. Staff were required to reach an acceptable level of reliability prior to using the CAFAS in this project.

Selection of Consumers

Each instrument was administered to a total of 16 consumers (4 per clinician) per CSB. Consumers were selected such that, as a group, they represented a wide range of consumer types served by the CSB. In particular, the youth in the child/adolescent mental health sites were selected to represent the diversity of child/adolescent consumers on the following dimensions: (a) race, (b) gender, (c) age, (d) level of functioning, (e) length of service, and (f) type of caregiver (e.g., both natural parents, foster parents, etc.).

Consumer Consent

Participation by consumers in the pilot project was voluntary. The purpose of the pilot project and the specific expectations of participants were explained to parents (or the youth's guardians, if applicable) prior to their agreement to participate. If the parents agreed to participate, a consent form was signed and witnessed. A copy of the consent form was given to the parents.

Assessment Protocol

The CAFAS was completed by staff on each child/adolescent participating in the project. In contrast, to reduce the burden on parents, not all self-report instruments were completed by all parents. Rather, one-half (i.e., two) of the parents for each staff person completed the CBCL and the CSQ-8, whereas the other half completed the FAD and the FSQ. Given this strategy, the total time required for any one parent to complete a set of assessment instruments was estimated to be approximately 30 minutes, a figure that was later confirmed through parent and staff reports.

Project Data Collection

Assessment logs, focus groups, and written reports were used to gather information to evaluate the individual instruments. Each of these methods of data collection is described below.

Assessment Log

After all instruments were completed for a given child/family, an assessment log was completed by the clinician. The assessment log served two purposes. First, it provided a means for tracking the types of consumers who participated in the pilot. This helped clinicians and project coordinators ensure that all types of child/adolescent consumers were represented by the participants in the pilot. Second, it allowed clinicians to record their observations and perceptions about the individual instruments, including the extent to which they provided useful information and any difficulties experienced during their administration. All completed assessment logs were submitted to the project coordinator. The project coordinator used the assessment logs to prepare a report on the pilot project.

Focus Groups

Two focus groups were conducted at each pilot site, one for CSB staff and one for parents of consumers. The focus groups were conducted by a staff member of the Office of Research and Evaluation.

The staff focus group at each CSB included the four clinicians and the project coordinator. These groups were used to determine staff opinions regarding the usefulness of the individual instruments, the ease with which they were administered, their appropriateness for the populations being served, and any other issues related to the use of the instruments.

The consumer focus groups were used to examine the instruments from the perspective of the parents. The discussion addressed such issues as the amount of time it took to complete the instruments and the extent to which the questions were understandable, relevant, and appropriate. A range of two to five parents per CSB attended the focus groups.

Written Reports

Each project coordinator prepared a brief report on his or her evaluation of the individual instruments. This report was to address the following:
- The usefulness of the information provided by the instruments for both clinical decision making and program management.
- The perceived cost (i.e., the amount of staff and consumer resources required to administer the instruments and manage the data collection process) versus the perceived benefits or usefulness of the data.
- Obstacles/issues that would have to be addressed if one were to administer the instruments on a routine basis and use the information for clinical and management decision making.

Pilot Results

Sample

A total of 48 consumers participated in the child/adolescent mental health services pilot. Of the youth, 53% were white and 60% were male. The youth ranged in age from 7 to 17 years; 34% were aged 10-12, and 30% were aged 13-15. The vast majority were rated by their clinician as having a level of functioning in the midrange of all youth served by that CSB, and 15% of the youth were rated as relatively low functioning when compared to other youth consumers. At the time of the assessment, the majority (58%) of the youth had been receiving CSB services for approximately one year, whereas very few (7%) had been receiving services for four weeks or less. Finally, 45% of the youth were living with their mother only, 20% were living with both natural parents, and 20% were living with a relative other than their parents.

Evaluation of Instruments

The results of this pilot project are consistent with the reported experiences of others who have used the instruments implemented in the pilot; that is, the instruments are generally easy to administer, provide useful information to clinicians, and are viewed positively by consumers. The results also validate the multistakeholder process used to identify recommended instruments for use in Virginia's public mental health system that are appropriate for the population being served, are feasible in terms of cost and ease of administration, and provide useful information.

The CAFAS appears to be a particularly valuable assessment device. One staff person stated that the CAFAS "gets our 'highest marks' in terms of its utility for both clinical and programmatic purposes." Clinicians reported that it provides the types of information that are most useful for treatment planning. It was also noted that this instrument would be especially useful within the context of an existing statewide, multiagency initiative because it assesses functioning in many different areas (i.e., it is not just a mental health instrument) and can be completed by nonclinicians. In addition, the CAFAS has direct application to managed care in that the total score can be related to the level of services needed for a given youth. The one disadvantage of the CAFAS is that it requires a moderate amount of training for raters to attain adequate levels of reliability.

The CBCL also appears to provide very useful clinical information. One of its main strengths is that national norms have been developed for different gender and age groups. This improves the usefulness of this instrument for both assessment and evaluation purposes. The two major drawbacks of this instrument are that (a) computer software for scoring the CBCL appears to be required to make the routine use of this instrument cost-efficient and (b) the self-report nature of the CBCL places an additional burden on consumers and requires additional staff time to read the instrument to parents with low levels of literacy.

The FAD provides useful information on family functioning but, given the format and focus of this instrument, it may be cost-beneficial in only limited situations (e.g., families receiving in-home or family therapy services). In addition, based on the reported difficulties in understanding certain items, the FAD should be used only when family members have at least a moderately high reading level. Finally, given the importance of assessing the impact of services on family functioning, an alternative instrument should be identified and tested.

Both the CSQ-8 and the FSQ provide useful feedback to program staff, are easy to administer, and are positively received by consumers. However, because the FSQ provides more detailed feedback to providers, it is more useful for quality improvement efforts.

Implications for Behavioral Health Services

The Standardized Outcomes Assessment Initiative was successful in (a) identifying appropriate and useful instruments for assessing consumer outcomes and (b) providing useful feedback on the implementation of these instruments in a public mental health service setting. A major factor in the success of this initiative was the involvement of multiple stakeholders in the process of selecting the recommended instruments, designing the pilot project, and providing feedback in the focus group process.

It was largely through such extensive stakeholder involvement that we were also able to identify and clarify the varying perspectives and needs of different stakeholders that must be addressed when developing an effective OMS. For example, clinical staff strongly advocated instruments that would help them assess treatment needs and track progress for individual consumers while not being overly time consuming. On the other hand, consumers wanted to ensure that the selected instruments provided them with an opportunity to report on their progress and not just rely on clinician ratings. Finally, accountability, planning, and marketing management staff emphasized the need for outcome data that could be aggregated, and hence indicate overall program performance.

The selection of specific outcome instruments, however, is only the first step in developing a fully operational OMS. Much work needs to be done to integrate these instruments into the day-to-day operation of service providers. Further, this must be accomplished in a manner that continues to involve key stakeholders, is most efficient, is least burdensome to staff, and provides the most useful information. If these objectives are not attained, the OMS will likely fail.

Next Steps

To continue our progress in the development of an OMS that will meet the needs of all stakeholders, another phase of pilot testing has been initiated. During this phase, the focus is on determining the infrastructure needed to support an OMS and the specific design features that will facilitate the most efficient and useful operation. Some of the particular questions being addressed are listed below.

1. Should outcome data be collected on the entire population of consumers, a representative sample, or a defined subpopulation?
2. At what time periods should outcome data be collected? Although assessments are typically made at admission into services and then again at discharge, should assessments be conducted at standardized intervals following admission, and if so, how frequently? Similarly, should follow-up assessments be conducted, and if so, how long after discharge?
3. Who should collect the data/administer the data collection instrument? Should assessments be conducted by (a) the consumer's therapist/case manager, (b) other agency staff, (c) or nonagency staff (e.g., consumers, private research firm)?
4. Where should the locus of responsibility be for data collection, management, analysis, and reporting? Should responsibility reside with the provider or should it be centralized at the state mental health agency or an organization with which it contracts?
5. What are the most efficient and effective mechanisms for data management, including data entry and transmission?
6. What mechanisms are most effective in ensuring complete, accurate, and timely data collection and reporting? (a) What

procedures should be used for data quality monitoring? (b) Would a system of positive and/or negative incentives improve data quality?
7. What are the most efficient mechanisms at the local and state levels for (a) data collection, (b) data entry/management, and (c) data analysis/reporting?
8. What resources are required for (a) data collection, (b) data entry/management, and (c) data analysis/ reporting?
9. What are the most useful reports for various stakeholders, including local providers, consumer/advocates, and state-level administrators/policy makers?
10. How frequently should reports be produced for various audiences to maximize their utility while containing costs?
11. What are the most appropriate and effective roles for different stakeholders in the continued operation of an OMS?

In addition to addressing these questions related to the design and operation of an OMS, the pilot is focusing on the development of several program management and accountability mechanisms. First, focus groups have been conducted with key stakeholders to determine their needs with respect to the reporting of data. Based on the results of these focus groups, draft reports (including graphical and tabular presentations of data, statistical analyses, etc.) have been generated for review by stakeholders as to utility and format. Based on this feedback, the reports were revised for final distribution. These reports will enable stakeholders to monitor the performance of the service delivery system with respect to desired clinical and administrative outcomes.

Second, each pilot site is being assisted in developing continuous quality improvement (CQI) mechanisms, utilizing OMS-generated data, to improve clinical and administrative procedures. A key component of this effort will be the creation of local "quality teams" whose task it will be to direct the application of OMS data to local program improvement.

Third, data from the first year of the pilot will be used to establish baselines for outcomes in the pilot sites. Along with data from other states and systems, these data will also be used to create benchmarks by which progress can be measured in later years.

Finally, data will be used at the state level to enhance accountability. The DMHMRSAS's current accountability system is based on a performance contract that emphasizes process and output data. In the future, an alternative accountability system may be explored. In particular, an outcome-based performance contracting system may be developed for piloting. Related to this effort will be the development of technical assistance and/or fiscal incentives designed to encourage improvement in the quality of data submissions as well as system performance and consumer outcomes.

Conclusion

The development and maintenance of an efficient and effective system for the routine monitoring of consumer outcomes and provider performance represents a significant challenge to the public mental health field. However, these challenges must be met in order to fulfill the promises of outcome-based accountability. Outcome-based accountability systems should serve at least three major stakeholders: the consumers of mental health services for whom such services have positive or negative effects; the general public, including families, advocacy groups, legislators, and other citizens who are concerned about the effectiveness and cost-benefit of such services; and those who fund and/or administer services, including state-level policy makers. Thus, public service delivery systems have an imperative to improve their ability not only to produce appropriate, desirable, and cost-effective outcomes, but to demonstrate such outcomes via systematic and rigorous assessment.

To ensure quality and acceptance of outcome measurement, all key stakeholders must be involved in developing, operating, and evaluating outcome management systems. The approach taken in this initiative of involving multiple stakeholders in the selection of instruments and in the design of implementation strategies contributes to project quality and acceptance because it ensures that the views of all stakeholders are heard, validated, and considered in the decision-making process. In addition, such a process enhances the probability of long-term support for the process and its products. Such support has already been demonstrated in Virginia by the high level of participation and investment by multiple stakeholders. Key stakeholders will continue to have a central role in future efforts to implement an outcome management system.

*Reliable and valid outcome measures are the critical component in a fully functioning OMS. Other key components are consumer information (e.g., demographic and clinical data) and service utilization information. Ultimately, each of these three types of information (and perhaps others) must be integrated to ensure maximal utility of the OMS.

Payer requirements: Many payers/managed care organizations require that providers routinely and systematically assess the consumer outcomes of their services.

Accountability: The routine collection, analysis, and reporting of outcomes data provides a mechanism for ensuring accountability to consumers and payers.

Clinical utility: Standardized data on individual consumers can be used by clinicians to develop treatment/rehabilitation plans and monitor consumer progress.

Quality improvement: Standardized data on program consumers may be used by managers to improve the effectiveness and efficiency of services.

Marketing: The results of outcome monitoring may be used to demonstrate the effectiveness of services to potential payers. In addition, the fact that a program has an OMS makes its services more marketable.

†Community-based mental health, mental retardation, and substance abuse services are provided in Virginia by a network of 40 CSBs, which provide services directly or through contracts with private providers.

References

1. Rounsalville BJ, Tims FM, Horton AH, et al. (Eds.): *Diagnostic Source Book on Drug Abuse Research and Treatment.* NIDA Publication No. 93-3508. Rockville, MD: National Institute on Drug Abuse, 1993.
2. Slayton LA (Ed.): *Behavioral Healthcare Outcomes: A Reference Guides Measurement Tools.* Rockville, MD: National Community Healthcare Council, 1995.
3. Young SC, Nicholson J, Davis M: *Guide to Instruments Assessing Consumer Satisfaction With Child and Adolescent Mental Health Services.* Working Paper No. 95-1. Worcester, MA: Center for Psychosocial and Forensic Services Research, University of Massachusetts Medical Center, 1995.
4. Sederer LI, Dickey B (Eds.): *Outcomes Assessment in Clinical Practice.* Baltimore, MD: Williams and Wilkins, 1996.
5. Relman AS: Assessment and accountability: The third revolution in medical care. *New England Journal of Medicine* 1988; 319:1220-1222.
6. Cross TP, McDonald E: *Evaluating the Outcome of Children's Mental Health Services: A Guide for the Use of Available Child and Family Outcome Measures.* Boston: Judge Baker Children's Center, 1995.
7. Graham K: Guidelines for using standardized outcome measures following addictions treatment. *Evaluation & the Health Professions* 1994; 17(1):43-59.
8. Rosenberg G, Holden G: Social work effectiveness: A response to Cheetham. Special issue on Research and Practice: Bridging the Gap. *Research on Social Work Practice* 1992; 2(3):288-296.
9. Schalock RL, Kiernan WE, McGaughey MJ, et al.: State MR/DD agency information systems and available data related to day and employment programs. *Mental Retardation* 1993; 31(1):29-34.
10. *Dialogue on Outcomes for Mental and Addictive Disorders.* Arlington, VA: National Alliance for the Mentally Ill, 1996.
11. *The MHSIP Consumer-Oriented Mental Health Report Card.* Washington, DC: Center for Mental Health Services, 1996.
12. Bickman L: Evaluation of demonstration programs: Measuring client outcomes. In: Stroul BA (Ed.): *Proceedings for the Children and Adolescents Service System Programs Technical Assistance Research Meeting.* Washington, DC: Children and Adolescents Service System Programs Technical Assistance Center, 1990.
13. VanDenBerg J, Beci S, Pierce J: The Pennsylvania Outcome Project for Children's Services. In: Kutash K, Liberton CJ, Algarin A, et al. (Eds.): *Children's Mental Health Services and Policy: Building a Research Base.* 5th Annual Research Conference Proceedings. Tampa: University of South Florida, Florida Mental Health Institute, Research and Training Center for

Children's Mental Health, 1992, pp. 233-238.
14. Schorr LB, Farrow F, Hornbeck D, et al.: *The Case for Shifting to Results-Based Accountability*. Boston: Judge Baker Children's Center, 1994.
15. Goerge RW: The promise of information systems. *Research and Evaluation in Group Care* 1993; 3:3-4.
16. Stroul BA, Friedman FM: *A System of Care for Severely Emotionally Disturbed Children & Youth*. Washington, DC: Children and Adolescent Service System Programs Technical Advisory Committee, 1986.
17. Horsch K: Results-based accountability systems: Opportunities and challenges. In: *The Evaluation Exchange: Emerging Strategies in Evaluating Child and Family Services*. Vol. 1. Boston: Harvard Family Research Project, 1996, issue 1.
18. Dunton N: Challenges to data capacity for outcome-based accountability. In: *The Evaluation Exchange: Emerging Strategies in Evaluating Child and Family Services*. Vol. 1. Boston: Harvard Family Research Project, 1996, issue 1.
19. Law CE: Evaluating children's managed mental health care. *Technical Assistance Brief 1996; 1(2):2-4.*
20. Burchard JD, Schaefer M: Improving accountability in a service delivery system in children's mental health. *Clinical Psychology Review* 1992; 12:867-882.
21. Hodges K, Gust BS: Measures of impairment for children and adolescents. *The Journal of Mental Health Administration* 1995; 22(4):403-413.
22. Robin G: Creating policy alternatives using stakeholder values. *Management Science* 1994; 40:1035-1048
23. Wallace GW: Balancing conflicting stakeholder requirements. *Journal for Quality and Participation* 1995.18(2):84-89.
24. Wallace D, White JB: Building integrity in organizations. *New Management* 1988; 6(1):30-35.
25. Achenbach TM: *Manual for the Child Behavior Checklist 14-18 and 1991 Profile*. Burlington: University of Vermont Department of Psychiatry, 1991.
26. Hodges K, Bickman L, Kurtz S, et al.: A multi-dimensional measure of level of functioning for children and adolescents. In: Algarin A, Friedman MR (Eds.): *A System of Care for Children's Mental Health*. Tampa: Research and Training Center for Children's Mental Health, Florida Mental Health Institute, University of South Florida, 1988.
27. Epstein NB, Baldwin LM, Bishop DS: The McMaster Family Assessment Device. *Journal of Marital and Family Therapy* 1983; 9:171-180.
28. Attkisson CC, Greenfield TK: The Client Satisfaction Questionnaire (CSQ) scales. In: Sederer LL, Dickey B (Eds.): *Outcome Assessment in Clinical Practice*. Baltimore, MD: Williams and Wilkins, 1995.
29. *Evaluation of the Comprehensive Mental Health Services Program for Children With Severe Emotional Disturbances*. Atlanta, GA: Macro International Inc. and University of South Florida, 1995.

Risk-Adjusting Mental Health Outcomes: Access and Quality Applications Under Managed Care*

Or, How Can Agencies Be Compared Fairly When They Treat Different Kinds of Clients?

Association for Health Services Research 15th Annual Meeting, Washington DC, June 1998

MICHAEL S. HENDRYX, PhD

Abstract
State mental health authorities (SMHAs) around the country are rapidly developing client outcomes monitoring systems. Outcomes are being used to compare the performance of publicly funded treatment agencies, publish comparative report cards, and award contracts or financial bonuses or sanctions to agencies. Comparing agencies or imposing financial consequences without taking into account agency-level differences in client severity is open to the legitimate criticism that some agencies treat riskier clients than others. Methods of risk-adjustment that take severity into account can potentially overcome this problem. This paper describes risk-adjustment and why it is important for SMHAs to examine. Three methods of doing risk-adjustment will be presented (difference scores, baseline stratification, and regression models). The strengths and weaknesses of each method will be summarized. Regression models are more valid and comprehensive, and are demographically unbiased, but are more technically demanding and expensive. Using data from 6 Washington mental health treatment agencies, it is shown that comparing agencies on unadjusted outcome performance leads to different conclusions about relative performance than when using risk-adjusted performance data. The particular method of risk-adjustment also influences conclusions about comparative agency performance. Issues in deciding which risk-adjustment method to use will be addressed, and strategies offered whereby a SMHA can implement and use a risk-adjustment method to compare agency outcomes fairly and to adjust capitation rates based on risk so as to encourage agencies to provide care for the highest risk clients.

Introduction

This paper addresses the question, "How can mental health agency performance be compared fairly when they treat different kinds of clients?" The purpose of this paper is to discuss risk-adjustment as state and local mental health authorities implement systems to monitor and improve outcomes of public mental health care. Risk-adjustment issues to be addressed include discussion of what it is, why it is important, alternative methods of doing it, and ways that it can be integrated into quality improvement activities and into access improvement efforts under managed care.

Source: Presented at the Association for Health Services Research, 15th Annual Meeting, Washington DC, June 1998. (Reprinted with permission.)

Address correspondence to Michael Hendryx, PhD, Associate Professor and Assistant Director, Washington Institute for Mental Illness Research and Training, Washington State University, 601 W. First Avenue, Spokane WA 99201. (509) 358-7624; (509) 358-7627 (fax); hendryx@wsu.edu.

What Is Risk-Adjustment?

Risk-adjustment refers to statistical corrections of outcome differences across treatment agencies. The statistical corrections take into account differences in risk that patients bring to treatment. The 'risk' in risk-adjustment refers to the risk of higher utilization or the risk of poorer outcomes that some clients bring to treatment. Although risk-adjustment can be done to predict future utilization, which will be briefly discussed toward the end of this paper, the focus in this paper is on predicting client treatment outcomes.

Why Do Risk-Adjustment?

Treatment outcomes may be used to guide quality improvement efforts, compare performance across agencies, impose financial incentives and sanctions based on performance, and refine capitation payment rates. Many state mental health authorities (SMHAs) are in fact developing outcomes monitoring systems for these purposes. However, comparisons of outcome performance that do not take risk differences into account are legitimately open to the criticism that some agencies treat riskier patients than others. Using unadjusted outcomes as the basis for financial rewards or penalties or performance-based contracting might provide agencies with an unintended incentive to avoid the highest risk clients. Publicly reporting unadjusted comparative agency outcome performance via "report cards" also disadvantages those agencies that treat the most difficult populations. Setting a capitation rate that is insensitive to severity differences encourages agencies to limit or deny care to the most severely-ill people.

There is a need to know whether outcomes are affected by risk variables, and to know which variables are important to include in a risk-adjustment model; only meaningful predictors should be included in order to make risk-adjustment as efficient and inexpensive as possible. Even if the risk-adjustment is only a partial correction for agency profile differences in risk, it can help to avoid penalizing agencies for treating higher risk clients (Iezzoni 1997) and can promote a dialogue between agency staff and administration focused on quality improvement. It can protect treatment access for high-risk clients, and even encourage access improvements if agencies are fairly compensated for serving the riskiest clients.

Does Risk-Adjustment Make a Difference in Examining Agency Level Mental Health Outcomes?

Yes, probably (Hendryx, Dyck and Srebnik, 1998). Unadjusted versus risk-adjusted comparative agency performance may lead one to make different conclusions about relative agency quality of care. The example below presents these results in more detail.

How Can Risk-Adjustment Be Done?

There is a need first to identify the important outcomes. Rosenblatt and Attkisson (1993) provide a framework to capture four important outcome dimensions. *Functioning* includes ability to function in community, work, and social roles, skills in handling symptoms, and includes discrete indicators of functional adaptation such as employment, hospitalization and incarceration. *Welfare and safety* addresses problems posed by severe mental illness including poverty, exposure to disease, adequacy of food and shelter, and safety from crime. *Life satisfaction* includes service satisfaction but also includes broader subjective well-being and happiness. *Clinical* outcomes include the classification and severity of both psychological and physical health impairments. These domains may be related to one another, but a single outcome indicator is probably not appropriate to use because agency performance varies by outcome, risk variables vary by outcome, and different stakeholders (consumers, providers, state administrators) may weight the relative importance of the various outcomes differently.

Second, the important risk variables or predictors must be identified. These may include baseline status of the outcome variable. Selection of relevant outcomes for public mental health outpatients, and selection of the appropriate candidate predictors, is an important but difficult issue. Stakeholder groups, including mental health consumers, providers and administrators often debate what constitutes service goals and outcome priorities (Nelson 1994). Our selection of outcomes for care of serious mental illness was based on the conceptual model of Rosenblatt and Attkisson (1993), and input from a multi-stakeholder advisory committee comprised of consumers, family members, providers, and regional and state administrators.

Appropriate predictors are those variables that relate to the outcome domains. These might include age, gender, race, and diagnosis, to the extent that they are demographic proxy measures for physiological health, population cohort, social roles, stress, discrimination, gender-related genetic factors, or other influences. To the extent that diagnosis also represents severity, chronicity, and symptoms, it may be predictive of functional or clinical outcomes. Level of substance abuse should be investigated, because substance abuse can impair medication effectiveness, compliance, and health. Because our focus is on a population that often receives ongoing care for serious and persistent mental illness, and because prior behavior is often a predictor of future behavior, taking into account the baseline or prior level of an outcome domain may also be important; such measures may capture some of the predictable individual differences in outcomes. Finally, if the outcome domains themselves are interrelated, a baseline score in one domain might be predictive of an outcome in another domain. As two hypothetical examples, if service satisfaction influences treatment motivation and compliance, satisfaction might be a predictor of later functional outcomes; also, a better functional capacity might improve one's chances for a better subsequent quality of life.

In sum, one can expect that multiple outcomes are important, and that specific predictors vary by outcome. But all predictors share common characteristics in that they have one or more potential conceptual impacts on the outcome domains. That is, factors that influence outcome *besides treatment* can be identified: prior functioning in the outcome of interest, substance abuse, prior health and severity of illness, satisfaction to the extent that it influences compliance, and stress and social relationships represented by demographic proxies. However, after testing the actual predictive power of variables, only the minimal set of important predictors should be retained in a final model in order to make data collection and analysis more efficient.

Third, issues of sampling and unit of analysis must be addressed. Some SMHAs track outcomes of every client who enters into service in the state, while others sample clients. If clients are sampled, the sampling should be randomized, and perhaps stratified by important subgroups defined by ethnicity, age, or other characteristics in order to represent these groups adequately. Sample sizes must be large enough that reliable estimates of performance can be made at the agency level. The unit of analysis is probably the client, followed over time.

Fourth, the timing of measures must be chosen. Clients should be assessed as they enter outpatient treatment, and at one or more later times to assess treatment progress. SMHAs vary in the collection schedules that they use, and follow-up assessments might be done at 90 days, quarterly, semi-annually, and/or annually. The costs of more frequent measurements must be weighed against the benefits of tracking the results of care. Serious attempts should also be made to find and assess clients at termination of treatment, to ascertain whether treatment has resolved successfully or whether termination is due to a hospitalization, incarceration, or clients simply "disappearing" from services without warning. The reason for termination then becomes an outcome in itself that may be predicted from the baseline measures and compared among agencies.

Once these choices have been made, there are three basic methods of doing risk-adjustment. Most state mental health authorities have not attempted risk-adjustment yet, and the few that have use a baseline stratification method or a baseline difference method. The difference method simply calculates the difference between an outcome score and a baseline score of the same measure. The stratification method categorizes clients into two or more groups based on baseline score (or some other baseline variable such as Medicaid category), and then calculates the outcome variable within each group. The third method is a statistical multiple regression model approach, predicting the outcome from a range of relevant indicators.

There are advantages to each approach. The stratification and baseline methods are simple and may capture the bulk of risk variance. The regression approach is comprehensive and may be more accurate or valid.

There are also disadvantages to each approach. The stratification method imposes arbitrary breaks in a baseline distribution, and creates outcomes in multiple strata that might aid internal quality improvement but will make cross-agency comparisons more complicated. To illustrate this, imagine three baseline strata of low-middle-high risk, formed by dividing the baseline distribution of the outcome variable into thirds. In this case the outcome will be a score or a percentage with a good or poor discrete outcome *in each stratum*, resulting in complex agency comparisons. Both stratification and difference methods are less accurate than a regression model to the extent that multiple variables at baseline predict outcomes. Baseline difference and stratification methods do not allow for statistical corrections for multiple vulnerable groups such as groups defined by race, gender and age. Because baseline difference and stratification methods are based on a single predictor, they are easier to manipulate to the advantage of the risk-bearer (e.g., if they are based only on a case manager report, that report can be easily inflated to make the clients look sicker.) Difference scores can be psychometrically unreliable. Difference scores also assume that the probability of positive change is equal across all baseline scores, which is probably not true. Some outcomes of interest (e.g., premature treatment drop-out, hospitalization) do not have a matching baseline unless prior records are available. The main disadvantage of the regression approach is its data collection, computation and reporting cost and complexity.

Example: Mental Health Outcomes In 6 Washington Agencies

The following example illustrates the effects of adjusted versus unadjusted results, and illustrates the conclusions that one might draw regarding comparative agency performance when using the three methods. The example is based on 289 adult clients from six mental health agencies in Washington State in 1996-97. The sample was divided into two cohorts of approximately equal size, cohort 1 measured at an earlier period of time than cohort 2. The agency-specific sample sizes are small and so these data should be considered suggestive and not definitive. The clients completed self-report instruments at two five-month intervals, to form a baseline and a follow-up observation. Case managers also completed ratings of client functioning, and demographic and diagnostic variables were collected from the management information systems databases. Three outcomes were examined: satisfaction with services, functioning, and welfare and safety.

First, the mean unadjusted agency outcome on each of the three measures was calculated at the follow-up period with cohort 2 data. The agencies were then ranked from best to worst outcome on each measure. Second, cohort 2 data were used to calculate the mean baseline to follow-up difference score for each agency, and agencies were again ranked. Third, cohort 1 data were used to conduct a multiple regression analysis to predict each outcome at follow-up from multiple baseline predictors, including baseline score in the same outcome but also diagnosis, age, race, gender, a case manager rating of substance abuse, and baseline scores in the cross domains (Hendryx et al. 1998). Using the resulting regression intercepts and coefficients, we calculated in cohort 2 the mean predicted score at follow-up for each agency. Then we calculated an observed/expected ratio (O/E ratio), as the observed or unadjusted score divided by the predicted score, O/E ratios greater than one indicate better than expected performance, and ratios less than one indicate worse than expected performance. Agencies were ranked using the O/E ratios.

Fourth, we examined the stratification method by dividing the cohort 2 baseline distributions into thirds, and calculating the agency mean outcome in each stratum for each of the three measures.

The results indicate that both the baseline difference method and the regression method result in different rankings of agency performance compared to the unadjusted rankings (Table 1). In other words, risk-adjustment makes a difference in conclusions about comparative agency performance. The baseline stratification method does not allow for easy visual comparison of relative agency performance, but suggests that there is wide variability in ranks across strata (Table 2).

The results from Table 1 also indicate that the regression model results in different ranks than

Table 1. A Comparison of Relative Agency Performance at Time 2 on Three Mental Health Outcomes Using the Unadjusted, Baseline Difference, and Regression Model Methods.

	Unadjusted rank	Baseline regression rank	Regression model rank	Baseline difference rank
Functioning				
Agency				
A	1	1	1	1
B	3	5	4	5
C	6	4	2	4
D	2	6	3	6
E	5	2	6	2
F	4	3	5	3
Satisfaction				
Agency				
A	1	4	1	4
B	4	5	3	5
C	6	1	4	1
D	3	2	5	2
E	2	3	2	3
F	5	6	6	6
Welfare and safety				
Agency				
A	3	6	3	6
B	5	2	4	2
C	6	5	6	5
D	2	4	5	4
E	4	1	2	1
F	1	3	1	3

the baseline model. Which approach should one use? The regression model that includes additional predictors is superior in terms of explained variance and other statistical criteria (Hendryx et al. 1998). It also includes age, sex and race corrections and so does not bias agencies that treat disproportionate shares of vulnerable people. Notice also that the regression model results in a more conservative "reshuffling" of agency ranks than the baseline difference model. This may be due to the fact that the psychometric reliability of change scores is often poor (Embretson 1991), and results in increased error or fluctuation in measurement. In another analysis (reported also in Table 1) we conducted a regression model using only the baseline score as a predictor; the resulting ranks more closely matched the present regression model results than the baseline difference model. For example, for the functioning outcome, the average deviation from unadjusted ranks for the baseline-only regression model was .8 rank, and for the full regression model was 1.3

Table 2. Ranked Agency Performance Using the Baseline Stratification Method. Cell Values Are Agency Ranks at Follow-Up Within Each Baseline Stratum

Agency	Baseline function Low	Mid	High	Baseline quality of life Low	Mid	High	Baseline satisfaction Low	Mid	High
A	2	1	1	3	6	3	3	1	1
B	4	5	3	2	5	5	2	6	6
C	5	4	5	5	4	6	5	4	5
D	6	2	6	6	2	1	4	2	4
E	3	6	4	1	3	4	1	3	3
F	1	3	2	4	1	2	6	5	2

ranks, while the average deviation for the non-regression baseline difference method was 2 ranks; the baseline difference method actually results in greater deviation, likely because it is inaccurate. The regression model is superior to the calculation of difference scores, and it is even possible that the simpler and more popular difference method might lead to gross errors in comparing agencies.

The drawback of the regression model is that it is more technically demanding. It may not be practical for all SMHAs to calculate regression models given their technical and professional resources. A cost-effectiveness analysis could illuminate whether it is worthwhile for an SMHA to use the regression method. Regression models require advanced software capacity, analytic expertise to run the initial regressions and compute O/E ratios, and collection of additional predictors beyond the baseline indicator. But even a difference model means that individuals need to be assessed at baseline and at least one additional time, data centralized and analyzed, and reports generated and disseminated.

If a SMHA Attempted To Implement Risk-Adjustment, How Would It Do It?

Baseline and follow-up data collection at treatment agencies, that includes reporting to the SMHA, would need to become routine, as it is in some states but not others. Issues regarding sampling and measurement as discussed earlier would need to be decided. Data collection might include a fairly brief yet psychometrically proven assessment tool that captures functioning, life satisfaction, welfare and safety, and clinical status. Outcomes that represent the domains need to be chosen with input from stakeholder groups. Data should be collected from at least two sources, such as consumers and case managers, so that the scores cannot be easily manipulated. Data reporting must result in useful and timely reports back to the agencies to make it worthwhile for them to oversee and invest in data collection.

Alternative regression models can be identified on a random half of an initial sample, and validated on the second half. "Alternative regression model" refers to a strategy to identify the most efficient model. This might be done by comparing a baseline-only regression model to a regression model identified through a stability analysis (Gruenberg et al. 1996.) The intent of a stability analysis is to avoid overfitting a model by choosing only the most stable predictors; it can be done by drawing repeated (e.g., 25) sub-samples from the larger sample, and conducting a regression analysis on each sub-sample using all possible predictors. Only predictors that pass a p-level criterion on a predetermined proportion of the analyses are retained in the final model. The cross-validation analysis then compares this reduced set model to the baseline-only model on a number of criteria including adjusted R^2, observed to predicted means and variances, intercept magnitudes, and residual error bias with respect to vulnerable groups.

Once a definitive model was chosen by a state, model validation could become an internal check and calculation of baseline expected scores and follow-up observed-to-expected (O/E) ratios could become routine. (O equals the observed follow-up outcome score, and E equals the expected score based on the regression model; O/E ratios greater than 1 indicate better than expected performance.) The results of the O/E ratios can be used to administer financial rewards or penalties and make re-contracting decisions, produce comparative outcome reports, and can be used internally by agencies to identify quality improvement opportunities. The expected scores at baseline can be used to adjust capitation rates to favor agencies with the highest baseline risk.

There is an important distinction between models that predict outcomes of treatment and those that attempt to predict future utilization of services. Utilization models can be developed to predict future use so as to estimate costs in setting appropriate capitation rates. Utilization models can use prior utilization statistics, client demographics, and diagnostic and clinical indicators to predict future levels of use. Unfortunately, attempts to predict mental health utilization have been largely unsuccessful (Ettner and Notman 1997; Brach 1995; Steams and Slifkin 1995). In any event, capitation rates paid to agencies based solely on their level of expected utilization might inadvertently reward overutilization. In addition, if clients are not followed over time there is no incentive to improve client status, especially if improvement makes the agency look like it has a less-sick population at the next payment cycle. Models should not award a higher capitation rate for a high-use agency unless that high use is legitimately needed for a sicker population: *this requires blending utilization and outcomes models.* A flat capitation rate that is the same regardless of risk differences might encourage agencies to rate fewer clients in need of services and more in need only of referral, but a graduated capitation rate that is determined only by the rating of a case manager might result in drift to higher rates. A preferred strategy will use a graduated rate, but will base the higher rate on a combination of data sources that is harder to manipulate.

A base capitation rate for an agency might be derived from the baseline expected utilization and expected severity scores. Then outcomes are monitored through dynamic models that follow individual clients over time, and awards/sanctions/contracts determined based on performance. A hospitalization, for example, can be a risk-adjusted outcome without assuming that hospitalization is bad, that compares each agency's success to others in limiting hospitalization through a risk-adjusted O/E ratio. Perhaps financial incentives could also be put into place for achieving favorable outcomes while also having less than expected utilization. By setting in place a graduated capitation rate, based on severity data that the agency cannot manipulate, costs can be reimbursed fairly and access for severely-ill clients encouraged. Then by rewarding favorable progress in treatment, incentives to improve quality of care are also in place.

Can the Regression Model Results Be Reported In a Non-Technical Way?

O/E outcome ratios are fairly easy to understand, as numbers greater than one are good and numbers less than one are bad. (Although if a goal is to reduce utilization, an O/E utilization ratio less than one might be good, if it occurs coincident with favorable outcomes.) Expected scores can be standardized to a common metric. So it seems that the answer is Yes, but this requires external validation.

How Can Multiple Outcomes Be Used To Encourage Access, Reward Good Performers, Publish Report Cards, Do Internal Quality Improvement, And Refine Capitation Rates?

The methods of setting and adjusting-rates based on performance should be done in a collaborative process involving administrators, providers, and consumer advocates. These stakeholders will need to decide how to assess multiple outcomes to come to a decision about overall quality and its financial consequences. They may decide to weight the various outcomes, and require multiple outcomes to be favorable in order for an agency to earn a reward. Results of the models should be reported to all stakeholder groups in a user-friendly format that helps to motivate their involvement. The final product put into practice by a SMHA should be a detailed strategy that specifies the steps in doing and using risk adjustment: sampling, measurement, design, analysis of static and dynamic models, use of model results to generate reports, methods to set capitation rates for an upcoming contract period based on static utilization and expected severity models, and methods to reward outcome performance based on dynamic outcome models with multiple outcome indicators.

In summary, the basic strategy is as follows. Baseline data are collected on all new consumers as they enter treatment. Dependent variables are utilization and outcome indicators. Independent variables are collected from multiple sources, and include prior use, demographic and diagnostic indicators, and baseline status in the Rosenblatt and Attkission (1993) outcome domains. There is an initial period in which models are developed and validated on samples of clients. Then, after model validation the risk-adjustment strategy is implemented. At implementation, each new consumer is measured at baseline and classified into one of a limited number of risk categories (e.g., 5) based on their expected utilization and outcome scores. Each category has a corresponding capitation rate per covered life per month. If there are, say, four outcome scores, the total agency payment per month equals: $\Sum$ (the rate per category times the number of clients per category) *times* .25, and then summed over outcomes. (Alternatively, a cost-utility approach might be used to weight each outcome rather than assuming equal weights [Hargreaves et al. 1988]. Also, whether or not this really works should be tested empirically.) To reduce the chances of manipulation, if at the agency level the case manager or agency recorded portion of the baseline severity is statistically higher than the self-report portion, the consumer is classified into the lower risk category (this sanction does not operate at the level of an individual client but only if case managers at an agency consistently rate severity to be higher than the consumers rate it). Payments to the agency are then made monthly or quarterly, so that quick turnaround time between agency reporting and calculation of severity is required. This strategy is intended to reward treating higher risk clients with a higher capitation rate, but attempts to avoid both artificial inflation or deflation of severity scores. (Artificial inflation occurs if case managers or agencies have predominant control over severity classifications and payments are higher for higher severity clients. Artificial deflation occurs if case managers or agencies have predominant control over classifying clients into active treatment versus brief intervention and flat capitated payments are made regardless of severity.)

Then, by following outcomes of the same clients over time, agencies may earn performance bonuses, such as a % of the monthly capitation rate, awarded at six or twelve month intervals. The bonus can be determined based on an O/E ratio algorithm that considers performance over multiple outcomes. This algorithm can be identified based on consensus methods involving state and local administrators, providers, and consumer advocates.

References

Brach, C. (1995). Designing capitation projects for persons with severe mental illness: A policy guide for state and local officials. Mental Health Policy Resource Center, Technical Assistance Monograph 3.

Embretson SE. (1991). Implications of a multidimensional latent trait model for measuring change. *Best Methods for the Analysis of Change*, Collins LM, Hom JL (eds), Washington DC: American Psychological Association, pp. 184-197.

Ettner SL, Notman EH. (1997). How well do ambulatory care groups predict expenditures on mental health and substance abuse patients? *Administration and Policy in Mental Health*, 24(4), 339-357.

Gruenberg L, Kaganova E, Hombrook MC. (1996). Improving the AAPCC with health-status measures from the MCBS. *Health Care Financing Review*, 17(3), 59-75.

Hargreaves W, Shumway M, Hu T, Cuffel B. (1998). *Cost-Outcome Methods for Mental Health*. San Diego: Academic Press.

Hendryx M, Dyck D, Srebnik D. (1998). Risk-adjustment outcome models for public mental health outpatient programs. Manuscript under review.

Iezzoni L.I. (1997). The risk of risk adjustment. *JAMA*, 278(19), 1600-1607.

Rosenblatt A, Attkisson CC. (1993). Assessing outcomes for sufferers of severe mental disorder: A conceptual framework and review. *Evaluation and Program Planning*, 16, 347-363.

Steams SC, Slifkin RT. (1995). State risk pools and mental health care use. *Health Affairs*, 14(3), 185-196.

Chapter 9

Selecting Meaningful Yardsticks

Guide to Behavioral Outcomes and Client Satisfaction Measurement Instruments

Once again, Faulkner & Gray presents its comprehensive survey of major outcome and satisfaction measurement tools. This year's survey encompasses 108 instruments and is based on questionnaires sent to instrument developers to elicit key data to aid in the instrument selection process. Developers of instruments included in last year's survey were invited to update their information and more than 20 new instruments have been added to the Guide, including the Severity of Psychiatric Illness, the Adolescent Treatment Outcomes Module, the Multnomah Community Ability Scale, and the Panic Outcomes Module.

Related Articles

- A "Global" Look at BASIS-32 (*McLean Reports*)
- Validation of the Panic Outcomes Module (*Evaluation & the Health Professions*)
- A Consumer-constructed Scale To Measure Empowerment Among Users of Mental Health Services (*Psychiatric Services*)
- Use of a New Outcome Scale To Determine Best Practices (*Psychiatric Services*)

Acuity of Psychiatric Illness—Adult Version

Developer's or distributor's description of instrument:	The Acuity of Psychiatric Illness is a brief outcome measure for use in acute psychiatric service settings. The measure allows for the reliable measurement of change within acute care treatment settings. It is quick to administer and can be used either prospectively or retrospectively.
Distributor information:	The Psychological Corporation, San Antonio TX, Phone: (800) 211-8378
Author:	John S. Lyons, PhD
Copyright status:	Copyright, The Psychological Corporation
Fees:	Per use or licensing fee available
Target population(s)/symptom(s):	Persons receiving acute psychiatric services. Assessing risk, symptom severity, need for monitoring and assistance, participation in treatment.
Clinical setting:	Acute psychiatric services including emergency departments, inpatient units, intensive outpatient, and partial hospital.
Primary use(s):	Change over time
Age group:	18 years and older
Domain(s):	Symptoms, Behavioral problems
Is instrument population-based or designed to measure change for individuals?	Measures change [for individuals]
Who completes instrument?	Any trained individual with experience with persons with acute psychiatric disorders.
Number of items:	11
Administration time:	1-2 minutes following standard assessment; 15 to 25 minutes as stand-alone measure
Administration options:	Paper/pencil or computer
Computer scoring possible?	Yes
Are norms available?	Yes
If so, normed on what groups?	Inpatient and older adult partial hospital
Reliability data:	Following training, the instrument can be used with good reliability. Kappa inter-rater reliability coefficients above .75 have been obtained routinely in reliability studies.
Validity data:	The API has been shown to be correlated with data collected using independent, standard interview-based assessments. Differential hospital and partial hospital outcome on the API has been shown to be correlated with other outcome indicators.
Key references:	• Lyons, JS, Howard, KI, O'Mahoney, MT, Lish, J (1997). The measurement and management of clinical outcomes in mental health. John Wiley & Sons, New York. • Yohanna, D,

Christopher, NJ, Lyons, JS, Miller, SI, Slomowitz, M, Bultemaa, JK (1998). Characteristics of short-stay admissions to a psychiatric inpatient service. *Behavioral Health Service and Research* (in press). • Leon, SC, Lyons, JS, Christopher, NJ, Miller, SI. (1998). Psychiatric hospital outcomes of dual diagnosis patients under managed care. *American Journal of Addictions*, 7, 81-86. • Lyons, JS, O'Mahoney, MT, Miller, SI, Neme, J, Kabot, J, Miller, F. (1997). Predicting readmission to the psychiatric hospital in a managed care environment: Implications for quality indicators, *American Journal of Psychiatry*, 154, 397-400. • Lyons, JS, Stutesman, J, Neme, J, Vessey, JT, O'Mahoney, MT, Camper, HJ. (1997). Predicting psychiatric emergency admissions and hospital outcomes. *Medical Care*, 35, 792-800. • Lansing, AE, Lyons, JS, Martens, LC, O'Mahoney, MT, Miller, SI, Obolsky, A. (1997). The treatment of dangerous patients in managed care: Psychiatric hospital utilization and outcome. *General Hospital Psychiatry*, 19, 112-118. • Lyons, JS, Thompson, BJ, Finkel, SI, Christopher, NJ, Shasha, M, McGivern, M. (1996). Psychiatric partial hospitalization for older adults: A retrospective study of case-mix and outcome. Continuum, 3, 125-132.

Acuity of Psychiatric Illness—Child And Adolescent Version

Developer's or distributor's description of instrument:	The Acuity of Psychiatric Illness' Child and Adolescent Version (CAPI) is a brief outcome measure for use in child mental health service settings. The measure allows for the reliable measurement of change within treatment settings. It is quick to administer and can be used either prospectively or retrospectively.
Distributor information:	The Psychological Corporation, San Antonio TX, Phone: (800) 211-8378
Author:	John S. Lyons, PhD
Copyright status:	Copyright, The Psychological Corporation
Fees:	Per use or licensing fee available
Target population(s)/symptom(s):	Children (over age 5) or adolescents receiving mental health services. Assessing risk, symptoms of SED, functioning, complications, and caregiver capacity.
Clinical setting:	Any mental health service setting for children and adolescents
Primary use(s):	Change over time
Age group:	5 to 18 years old
Domain(s):	Symptoms, Behavioral problems
Is instrument population-based or designed to measure change for individuals?	Measures change [in individuals]
Who completes instrument?	Any trained individual with experience with persons with children and adolescents' mental health services
Number of items:	20
Administration time:	3-5 minutes following standard assessment; 25 to 30 minutes as stand-alone measure
Administration options:	Paper/pencil or computer
Computer scoring possible?	Yes
Are norms available?	Yes
If so, normed on what groups?	Residential treatment center and intensive outpatient
Reliability data:	Following training, the instrument can be used with good reliability. Kappa inter-rater reliability coefficients above .75 have been obtained routinely in reliability studies.
Validity data:	The CAPI has been shown to be correlated with data collected using independent, standard interview-based assessments. Differential hospital and residential treatment outcomes on the CAPI has been shown to be correlated with other outcome indicators.
Key references:	• Lyons, JS, Howard, KI, O'Mahoney, MT, Lish, J (1997). *The measurement and management of clinical outcomes in men-*

tal health. John Wiley & Sons, New York. • Lyons, JS, Terry, P, Martinovich, Z, Peterson, J. (1998). *The trajectory of change for children and adolescents in residential treatment: A statewide study.* Working paper 98-004, Mental Health Services and Policy Program, Northwestern University. • Lyons, JS (1997). The evolving role of outcomes in managed mental health care. *Journal of Child and Family Studies*, 6, 1-8.

Addiction Severity Index (ASI)

Developer's or distributor's description of instrument:
The Addiction Severity Index (ASI) is a semi-structured instrument used in a face-to-face patient interview conducted by a clinician, researcher, or trained technician. It was developed by A. Thomas McLellan, PhD, and colleagues at the University of Pennsylvania in 1980. The ASI covers seven important areas of a patient's life: medical, employment/support, drug and alcohol use, legal, family/social, and psychiatric. The instrument is designed to obtain lifetime information about problem behaviors as well as focusing specifically on the 30 days prior to assessment. The ASI has high reliability and validity, as confirmed in studies published in leading journals. It is a widely used addiction assessment tool throughout the United States and other countries.

Distributor information: DeltaMetrics℠, 2005 Market Street, Suite 1120, Philadelphia PA 19103; Phone: (800) 238-2433 or (215) 665-2888

Author: A. Thomas McLellan, PhD and colleagues

Copyright status: Public domain (We charge $1 for postage and photocopying.)

Fees: [no answer]

Target population(s)/symptom(s): Substance abuse clients seeking treatment

Clinical setting: Is appropriate for substance abuse patients receiving treatment at all levels of care.

Primary use(s): Screening, Change over time, Post-treatment follow-up

Age group: 18 and up (no upper limit)

Domain(s): Life functioning (medical, legal, employment, drug/alcohol, family, psychiatric), Behavioral problems, Family environment, Severity and/or risk factors

Is instrument population-based or designed to measure change for individuals? For individuals

Who completes instrument? Clinician

Number of items: 155

Administration time: 45-60 minutes with training

Administration options: [no answer]

Computer scoring possible? [no answer]

Are norms available? [no answer]

If so, normed on what groups? N/A

Reliability data: Has demonstrated test-retest and interater reliability.

Validity data: Possesses discriminant, concurrent and predictive validity.

Key references:
• McLellan, A.T., Kushner, H., Metzger, D., Peters, R., Smith, I., Grissom, G., Pettinati, H., & Argeriou, M. (1992). The Fifth Edition of the Addiction Severity Index. *Journal of Substance Abuse Treatment*, Vol 9, 199-213. • McLellan, A.T.,

Luborsky, L., Cacciola, J., & Griffith, J.E. (1985). New Data From The Addiction Severity Index: Reliability And Validity In Three Centers. *Journal of Nervous and Mental Diseases*, 173, 412-423. • McLellan, A.T., Luborsky, L., O'Brien, C.P., & Woody, G.E. (1980); An Improved Evaluation Instrument For Substance Abuse Patients: The Addiction Severity Index. *Journal of Nervous and Mental Diseases*, 168, 26-33.

Adolescent Drinking Index (ADI)

Developer's or distributor's description of instrument:	This 24-item rating scale measures the severity of drinking problems, differentiating between alcohol use which is considered normal in adolescent development and that which is not normal. ADI items focus on the problems that arise from alcohol use, not on the amount or the frequency of consumption.
Distributor information:	PAR, Inc., P.O. Box 998, Odessa FL 33556, Phone: (800) 331-8378
Author:	Adele V. Harrell, PhD, and Philip W. Wirtz, PhD
Copyright status:	Copyrighted 1989
Fees:	ADI Introductory Kit (includes manual & 25 test booklets): $59.00. Package of 25 test booklets: $40.00
Target population(s)/symptom(s):	Adolescents
Clinical setting:	Individual or group settings
Primary use(s):	Screening, Post-treatment follow-up
Age group:	13-17
Domain(s):	Symptoms, Behavioral problems, Severity and/or risk factors
Is instrument population-based or designed to measure change for individuals?	Norm-based
Who completes instrument?	Self-report
Number of items:	24
Administration time:	5 minutes
Administration options:	Paper/pencil
Computer scoring possible?	No
Are norms available?	[no answer]
If so, normed on what groups?	N/A
Reliability data:	[no answer]
Validity data:	[no answer]
Key references:	[no answer]

Adolescent Treatment Outcomes Module (ATOM)

Developer's or distributor's description of instrument:	The Adolescent Treatment Outcomes Module (ATOM) is designed to be used in routine clinical care settings as part of an outcomes management system for continuous quality improvement by assessing patients' symptom severity and functioning over time. The module provides information on a comprehensive set of variables that are relevant to understanding how treatment affects outcomes in adolescents with various emotional and behavioral problems. The module is used to measure the process and type of care patients receive, the outcomes of that care, and the prognostic factors that influence either the types or outcomes of care.
Distributor information:	University of Arkansas for Medical Science, 4301 West Markham, Little Rock AR 72205, Phone: (501) 660-7550, Web: www.uams.edu/core/home.htm
Author:	James M. Robbins, PhD, J. Lynn Taylor, MD, Barbara J. Burns, PhD, Kathryn M. Rost, PhD, Terry Kramer, PhD, G. Richard Smith, MD
Copyright status:	Copyright © 1997 University of Arkansas for Medical Sciences, 4391 West Markham, Little Rock AR 72205
Fees:	The ATOM is protected under copyright and is available for unlimited free use, provided that there is no charge associated with its administration. To that end, UAMS permits unlimited reproduction and distribution of the module by the public for nonprofit, educational, or research purposes. However, any commercial use, including the creation of electronic versions or other derivative works of the module for sale, constitutes a violation of the copyright of the University, unless prior authorization has been granted in writing. A free internet-based resource to facilitate the use of the ATOM will be up and running by 12/31/98.
Target population(s)/symptom(s):	Adolescents 11 to 19 years of age, with moderate to severe impairment in functioning are the target population for the ATOM. Literacy above the fourth grade level is required for completion of self-report assessments. Users may consider the ATOM for children younger than age 11 provided a reader is available to administer instruments to the youth. A parent or caregiver who has had contact with the adolescent over the past 6 months must be available to complete the ATOM. The adolescent may not be actively psychotic or mentally retarded.

Clinical setting:	The ATOM is designed to be used in routine clinical care settings.
Primary use(s):	Diagnosis, Change over time, Post-treatment follow-up
Age group:	Adolescents ages of 11 to 19. (Children younger than age 11 may take this if a reader is available to administer instruments to the youth.)
Domain(s):	Symptoms, Life functioning, Client satisfaction, Behavioral problems, Family environment, Severity and/or risk factors
Is instrument population-based or designed to measure change for individuals?	The ATOM is both population-based and designed to measure change for individuals.
Who completes instrument?	**Parent Baseline & Follow-Up Assessments**: Completed by the parent or caregiver of the adolescent meeting eligibility requirements within 3 days of a visit for a new episode of an emotional or behavioral problem. **Patient Baseline & Follow-Up Assessments**: Completed by eligible adolescents (or a parent or guardian, if adolescent is illiterate or under the age of 11) within 3 days of a visit for a new episode of an emotional or behavioral problem. **Clinician Baseline Assessment**: Completed by the clinician immediately upon seeing the adolescent. **Medical Record Review:** Completed 6 months after the baseline assessment by a staff person. Modes of Collection include self-administration, personal interview, telephone interview and mail.
Number of items:	There are a total of 333 items, broken down as follows: Patient Baseline Assessment consists of 59 items; Parent Baseline Assessment 88; Clinician Baseline Assessment 9; Patient Follow-up Assessment 69; Parent Follow-up Assessment 95; and Medical Record Review 13.
Administration time:	**Parent Baseline & Follow-Up Assessments** take 25 minutes to complete; **Patient Baseline & Follow-Up Assessments** 22 minutes; **Clinician Baseline Assessment** 5 minutes; and **Medical Record Review** 10-15 minutes.
Administration options:	Currently, the administration options are paper/pencil. By 12/31/98, the ATOM will be online and can be administered by computer.
Computer scoring possible?	Computer scoring for the ATOM will be available by 12/31/98.
Are norms available?	No, not at the current time.
If so, normed on what groups?	N/A
Reliability data:	The reliability and validity of the prototype ATOM were tested against gold standard instruments to determine its sensitivity to clinical changes and determine its feasibility for use in routine clinical settings. Self-reported data were collected from 72 persons, aged 11 to 18 years, who received treatment at 2 inpatient and 2 outpatient units. Both adolescents and a parent were administered the ATOM and validating instruments within 3 days of start of treatment and at 6 months after baseline. Oppositional defiance, conduct, anxiety, depression, and attention deficit hyperactivity disorders were predicted by 10

self-reported symptoms. Test-retest correlations for 10 outcomes variables were excellent (r _0.70). Correlations of the ATOM with the expected direction of global measures of functioning were moderate for measures of functioning at home, in school, and in the community. The test-retest reliability coefficients and internal consistency alpha coefficients for key measures and correlations for caseness indicators and prognostic factors are available from developer.

Validity data: An expert panel evaluated the validity of the ATOM's content. Instruments used for criterion concurrent validity include the Child Behavior Checklist, the Diagnostic Interview Schedule for Children, and 17 others (list available from developer).

Key references:
- Brandenburg N, Friedman R, Silver S: The epidemiology of childhood psychiatric disorders. *Journal of the American Academy of Chlld and Adolescent Psychiatry* 29(1):76-83, 1990.
- Costello E: Developments in child psychiatric epidemiology. *Journal of the American Academy of Chlld and Adolescent Psychiatry* 28: 836-841, 1989.
- Saxe L, Cross T, Silverman N: Children's mental health: The gap between what we know and what we do not. *American Psychologist* 43: 800-807, 1988.
- Robbins J, Taylor J, Rost K, et al.: Measuring outcomes of care for adolescents with emotional and behavioral problems. Unpublished paper, Department of Pediatrics, University of Arkansas for Medical Sciences, 1997.
- Landgraf JM, Abetz L, Ware JE: *The CHQ User's Manual* Boston, MA: The Health Institute, New England Medical Center, 1996.
- American Psychiatric Association: *Diagnostic and Statistical Manual of Mental Disorders-IV (DSM-IV)—Fourth Edition*. Washington, DC: American Psychiatric Association, 1994.

The Alcohol/Substance Abuse Questionnaire (ASAQ)

Developer's or distributor's description of instrument:	The ASAQ is a paper-pencil self report drinking/drug use questionnaire that covers 15 sections of historical as well as current-use information. For example, such areas as "age of onset" of key symptoms, presence or absence of symptoms in a 30 day and lifetime window, quantity, frequency, and pattern of use, etc. Alcohol/drug use facilities use this instrument to standardize this information and to profile the severity of patients who seek services. A software program is being developed to simplify scoring and generate reports on either an individual or group basis.
Distributor information:	William J. Filstead, PhD, Performance-Based Outcomes, Inc., 5215 Old Orchard Road, Suite 700, Skokie IL 60077-1045; Phone: (847) 779-8550; Fax: (847) 965-0000; E-mail: pbo@mcs.com OR wsf@home.com; Web: www.consultnews.com
Author:	William J. Filstead PhD
Copyright status:	Copyrighted
Fees:	Fee is related to volume and scope of work
Target population(s)/symptom(s):	Alcohol and/or drug using populations
Clinical setting:	Across all levels of care
Primary use(s):	Diagnosis, Screening
Age group:	Adolescents through seniors
Domain(s):	Symptoms, Life functioning, Behavioral problems, Family environment, Severity and/or risk factors, Other (Quantity, frequency and pattern of alcohol/other drug use)
Is instrument population-based or designed to measure change for individuals?	Provides data on the individual—not intended to be used as a measure of change. Population profiles or comparisons across organizational sites are common.
Who completes instrument?	Self-report (Patient self-reports, post detoxification and prior to the start of treatment)
Number of items:	There are 15 sections to this instrument
Administration time:	30-40 minutes
Administration options:	Various hand-calculated templates to derive charts/graphs
Computer scoring possible?	In development
Are norms available?	Yes
If so, normed on what groups?	Patient type (alcohol, alcohol and drug, drug); Level of care (inpatient, outpatient)

Reliability data:	Test/retest reliability measured by Kappa and interclass correlation coefficients are well within the range reported by other investigators. across all items, symptom self report reliability was .76
Validity data:	Contrast group validity tests showed adequate validity—contrast as well as concurrent (across the various sections of the instrument)
Population sample(s) on which measure tested:	Alcohol/other drug using population in both outpatient/inpatient settings
Key references:	• Parrella, David and Filstead, Wm. "Self Report Reliability for Inpatient Alcoholics and Drug Abusers." Unpublished manuscript; *Journal of Studies in Alcohol* Vol 44, pp 85-92, 1988.

Alcohol Use Inventory (AUI)

Developer's or distributor's description of instrument:	The Alcohol Use Invetory test helps identify patterns of behavior, attitudes, and symptoms associated with the use and abuse of alcohol. The AUI test helps provide a basis for describing different ways in which individuals use alcohol, the major benefits derived from using alcohol, the negative consequences associated with it's use, and the degree of concern individuals express about the use of alcohol and it's consequences.
Distributor information:	Assessments Division of NCS, P.O.Box 1416, Minneapolis MN 55440, Phone: (800) 627-7271
Author:	J. L Horn, Ph.D., K.W. Wanberg, Ph.D., F.M. Foster, MS
Copyright status:	Copyright 1986
Fees:	AUI Manual $24.00, User's Guide $35.00, Test Booklets (10 per pkg) $30.00. Mail-in Scoring: Profile Report $7.25, Interpretive Report $14.50. Handscoring Starter Kit $100.00. Mircrotest Q Assessment System Software $89.00 license fee, Profile Report $6.25, Interpretive Report $13.50. For more information on pricing, contact NCS Client Relations at (800) 627-7271.
Target population(s)/symptom(s):	Adults and adolescents (age 16 and over) with known or suspected alcohol-related problems.
Clinical setting:	Psychologists, social workers, chemical dependency counselors, and physicians in alcohol treatment programs, community mental health centers, hospitals and general practice
Primary use(s):	Diagnosis, Change over time, Post-treatment follow-up
Age group:	16 and over
Domain(s):	Symptoms, Life functioning, Behavioral problems, Severity and/or risk factors, Drinking styles
Is instrument population-based or designed to measure change for individuals?	Instrument is designed to measure change for individuals.
Who completes instrument?	Client
Number of items:	228 multiple choice
Administration time:	35-60 minutes
Administration options:	Paper/pencil, Computer
Computer scoring possible?	Yes
Are norms available?	Yes
If so, normed on what groups?	1200 individuals who had been admitted to a public, inpatient alcohol treatment program
Reliability data:	Internal consistency ranges from .54-.93. Test—retest reliabilities range from .54-.89.

Validity data:	Nine of the AUI's scales are significantly correlated with the MAST. Research reported in outpatient, 1st admission inpatient, chronic severe inpatient, other alcohol use measures, AA attendence, predicting outcome.
Key references:	• AUI manual includes an extensive bibliograpy. • Horn, J.L., Wanber, K.W., and Foster, F.M. (1990). *Guide to the Alcohol Use Inventory.* National Computer Systems: Minneapolis

Ansell-Casey Life Skills Assessment 2.0 (ACLSA)

Developer's or distributor's description of instrument:	The Ansell-Casey Life Skills Assessment (ACLSA) addresses 18 life skill areas such as money management, decision making, and social relationships "status" indicators. There are three compatible versions of the ACLSA, each with forms for the youth and/or his or her caregiver to complete. The language of the ACLSA is clear and simple, which may account for a 25 to 40 minute completion time and original art adds to the user-friendly nature of the instrument. After youths and caregivers complete the instruments, they may be sent in for data capture, and an ACLSA Individual Report summarizing youth and caregiver responses will be returned to the agency.
Distributor information:	Developed by Dorothy I. Ansell and The Casey Family Program Dorothy I. Ansell: 3837 Northdale Blvd. #176, Tampa, FL 33624; (813) 264-1057. The Casey Family Program, Research Department: 1300 Dexter Avenue North, Suite 400, Seattle, WA 98109, attention Kimberly A. Nollan or Rachel Zachariah at (206) 282-7300.
Author:	The instrument was developed by Dorothy I. Ansell and The Casey Family Program. Dorothy I. Ansell, MSW, is president of Ansell and Associates, Inc.
Copyright status:	Copyrighted
Fees:	The ACLSA may be ordered in packets of 25 Youth or packets of 25 Caregiver forms from Bavendam Research Associates, 3010 77th Avenue SE, Suite 204, Mercer Island, WA 98040, (206) 232-3059. Forms are $6.00 per assessment, or $150 per packet. These costs include the forms, shipping, handling, scoring, and ACLSA Individual Reports.
Target population(s)/symptom(s):	The ACLSA was designed to assist various persons involved in child and family services (e.g., foster parents, service providers) to assess youth strengths and areas for additional development in relation to a wide variety of life skill competency areas.
Clinical setting:	While designed to be used with youths in out-of-home care, the ACLSA may be used with other youths as well (e.g., youths in a school setting).
Primary use(s):	Diagnosis, Screening, Change over time, Post-treatment follow-up
Age group:	There are three compatible versions of the ACLSA, each with forms for the youth and/or his or her caregiver to complete.

Domain(s):	The suggested age groups for each form are as follows: ACLSA-I for youths ages 8 to 11; ACLSA-II for youths ages 12 to 15; and ACLSA-III for youths ages 16 to 19. Life functioning, Other: Youth readiness for living in the community on his/her own
Is instrument population-based or designed to measure change for individuals?	Both. Norms are currently being developed based on a national sample of youths in out-of-home care and also with youths in school settings (mainstream). The ACLSA may be used to get a "snapshot" of how a youth is functioning, and may be used to monitor individual progress over time. In addition, the ACLSA may be used as a pre-post test to a clinical intervention, such as a group which targets life skill functioning.
Who completes instrument?	Self-report (both by the youth and his/her caregiver), and Clinician (if they know youths well)
Number of items:	ACLSA-I: 85 ACLSA-II: 115 ACLSA-III: 137
Suggested age range	ACLSA-I: 8-11 ACLSA-II: 12-15 ACLSA-III: 16-19
Administration time:	It takes approximately 20 to 40 minutes to complete, depending on the version and the reading ability of the person completing the ACLSA.
Administration options:	Paper/pencil
Computer scoring possible?	Instrument is computer scored as part of the purchase price. A summary report is issued after scoring.
Are norms available?	Instrument is being normed.
If so, normed on what groups?	N/A
Reliability data:	Internal Reliabilities for the ACLSA scales and sub-scales were assessed by employing coefficient alpha, which provides an index of the internal consistency of a scale. ACLSA-I: Most of the ACLSA scales have acceptable internal consistency. The reliability coefficients for scales ranged from 0.73 to 0.89 for caregivers and 0.75 to 0.87 for youths. The sub-scale reliabilities for caregivers ranged from 0.48 to 0.83 and from 0.48 to 0.75 for youths. Test-retest analyses: Overall findings indicate moderate (0.21) to high (0.89) correlations between administrations for all but one of the sub-scales. ACLSA-II: Internal reliabilities for the Casey sample scales ranged from 0.77 to 0.87 for caregivers and 0.72 to 0.75 for youths. The reliabilities for the sub-scales ranged from 0.56 to 0.78 for caregivers and 0.45 to 0.73 for youths sample. Test-retest analyses indicated moderate (0.40) to high (0.80) correlations between administrations for the sub-scales. ACLSA-III: Internal consistency scale reliabilities ranged from 0.83 to 0.93 for caregivers 0.83 to 0.91 for youths. The sub-scale reliabilities ranged from 0.65 to 0.93 for caregivers and 0.52 to 0.92 for youths. Test-retest analyses indicate moderate (0.47) to high (0.93) correlations between administrations for the sub-scales.

Validity data: Content-Related Evidence of Validity: The content validity of the ACLSA is quite strong. This confidence is based on involving youths, caregivers, child welfare professionals, and consultants as expert judges in selecting and refining the items that make up the ACLSA scales. Construct-Related Evidence of Validity: These analyses will be part of the analyses of normative data to be collected in 1997-1999. Predictive Validity based on Age and Gender Differences: The predictive validity of the ACLSA to date has focused on predictable differences in scale scores as a function of age and gender. Between groups Analyses of Variance (ANOVAs) were conducted to examine gender and age differences among the ACLSA-I scales. Significant differences were found based on gender and age group. (Contact publisher for details.)

Key references:
• Nollan, K. A., Pecora, P. J., Downs, A. C., Wolf, M., Horn, M., Martine, L., Lamont, E. (1997). Assessing life skills of adolescents in out-of-home care. *The International Journal of Child and Family Welfare*, 2(2):113-126.

AUDIT

Developer's or distributor's description of instrument: AUDIT is a brief structured interview that can be incorporated into a medical history. It contains questions about recent alcohol consumption, dependence symptoms and alcohol-related problems. The optional Clinical Screening Procedure consists of two interview items, a brief physical examination and a laboratory test. It is designed to complement the self-report AUDIT under conditions where additional clinical information is required.

Distributor information: World Health Organization, Programme for Substance Abuse, CH-1211, Geneva 27, Switzerland; or Dr. Thomas F. Babor, University of Connecticut Health Center, 263 Farmington Avenue, Farmington CT 06030-1910

Author: World Health Organization

Copyright status: Public domain

Fees: None

Target population(s)/symptom(s): AUDIT was developed by the World Health Organization to identify persons whose alcohol consumption has become hazardous or harmful to their health. Persons at high risk include medical patients, accident victims, suicidal persons, drunk driving offenders, and armed forces personnel. Screening with AUDIT can be conducted in a variety of health care settings.

Clinical setting: Primary care, Emergency Room, Hospital Admission

Primary use(s): Screening

Age group: Adults

Domain(s): Symptoms, Behavioral problems, Severity and/or risk factors

Is instrument population-based or designed to measure change for individuals? Individuals

Who completes instrument? Interviewer administered or self-reported

Number of items: 10

Administration time: 2 minutes

Administration options: Paper/pencil and computer

Computer scoring possible? Yes

Are norms available? [no answer]

If so, normed on what groups? [no answer]

Reliability data: [no answer]

Validity data: Based on the sample of 913 drinking patients, Saunders et al. evaluated the accuracy of AUDIT in detecting harmful and hazardous alcohol consumption by comparing the sensitivity and specificity for five different "gold standards:" (1.) hazardous alcohol consumption (defined as a typical daily intake exceeding 60g for a man and 40g for a woman) or recurrent intoxication; (2.) dependence symptoms (a positive response to at least one feature of the alcohol dependence syndrome); (3.) alcohol problems in the last year /a positive response to any of five questions on physical and psychosocial consequences); (4.) a combined index (which was a summation of all the evidence of harmful or hazardous alcohol consumption from the data set); and (5) Positive classification within groups of known alcoholics or abstainers. The cut-off points for the screening instrument were determined by examining the relationship between sensitivity and specificity for the first four conditions. Two cut-off points were determined, 8+ and 10+. Using the lower cut-off point the sensitivity for hazardous consumption and/or recurrent intoxication ranged from 95 to 100%. For dependence symptoms it varied from 93% to 100%, and for the problems in the last year from 91% to 100%. The sensitivity using the combined index ranged from 87 to 96%, with an overall value of 93%. When the cut-off point of 10 was taken, the sensitivities were lower, with an overall value of 80% for the combined index. The specificities were correspondingly higher: for the combined index values ranged from 95 to 100%, with an overall value of 98%.

Key references:
• Allen, J.P., Litten, R.Z., Fertig, J.B. and Babor, T. A review of research on the Alcohol Use Disorders Identification Test (AUDIT). *Alcoholism: Clinical and Experimental Research* 21(4): 613-619, 1997. • Saunders, J.B., Aasland, O.G., Babor, T.F., de la Fuente, J.R., and Grant, M. "Development of the Alcohol Use Disorders Identification Test (AUDIT): WHO collaborative project on early detection of persons with harmful alcohol consumption." II. *Addiction*, 88, 791-804, 1993.

Beck Anxiety Inventory (BAI)

Developer's or distributor's description of instrument: The BAI is a 21-item self-report measure that assesses the severity of an individual's anxiety. It can be administered in 5-10 minutes and scored by paraprofessionals, but should be interpreted by an appropriately trained clinician due to the frequent comorbidity of anxiety disorders. It is frequently used to measure treatment outcomes in outpatient settings for patients with mood or anxiety disorders.

Distributor information: The Psychological Corporation, 555 Academic Court, San Antonio TX 78204-2498, Phone: (800) 228-0752

Author: Aaron T. Beck, Robert A. Steer

Copyright status: Copyright (c) 1990 by Aaron T. Beck

Fees: A complete kit is $49.50, manual only is $24.00, 25 record forms are $27.50.

Target population(s)/symptom(s): Measures symptoms of anxiety in adults, adolescents, outpatients, inpatients and normals.

Clinical setting: Most appropriate use is with adult psychiatric outpatients.

Primary use(s): Diagnosis, Screening, Change over time, Post-treatment follow-up

Age group: 17+

Domain(s): Other: subjective, physiological, autonomic and panic-related symptoms of anxiety.

Is instrument population-based or designed to measure change for individuals? Individual-level change over time

Who completes instrument? Self-report (oral administration is acceptable if respondent needs assistance)

Number of items: 21

Administration time: 5-10 minutes

Administration options: [no answer]

Computer scoring possible? [no answer]

Are norms available? [no answer]

If so, normed on what groups? N/A

Reliability data: Internal Consistency: Cronbach coefficient alphas ranged from .85-.94 across various samples. Item Analysis: Corrected item-total correlations ranged from .18-.79 across samples. Test-Retest: Correlation between intake and one-week BAI scores was .75 p<.001.

Validity data: Content Validity: BAI content corresponds to DSM-III-R symptom criteria for anxiety disorders, particularly panic disorder and generalized anxiety disorder. Concurrent Validity: Correlations of the BAI with selected instruments (STAI Trait r=.58 p<.001, WRAD-Anxiety r=.54 p<.001, HARS-R r=.51

p<.001, CCL-Anxiety r=.51 p<.001, STAI State r=.47 p<.01). Construct Validity: BAI is correlated with measures of obsessive-compulsive disorder (MOC r=.41 p<.001). Discriminant Validity: A stepwise discriminant-function analysis, controlled for gender and age, indicated that the BAI differentiated between types of anxiety disorders [F(4,341)=11.57, p<.001)]. Factorial Validity: Four clusters have been identified with coefficient alphas significant at p<.001- Neurophysiological (.87), Subjective (.88), Panic (.73), Autonomic (.74).

Key references:
- Beck, A.T., Brown, G., Steer, R.A., Eidelson, J.I., & Riskind, J.H. (1987). Differentiating anxiety and depression: A test of the cognitive content specificity hypothesis. *Journal of Abnormal Psychology*, 96, 179-183.
- Beck, A.T., Epstein, N., Brown, G., & Steer, R.A. (1988). An inventory for measuring clinical anxiety: Psychometric properties. *Journal of Consulting and Clinical Psychology*, 56, 893-897.
- Beck, A.T., & Steer, R.A. (1990). *Manual for the Beck Anxiety Inventory*. San Antonio, TX: The Psychological Corporation.
- Fydrich, T., Dowdall, D., & Chambless, D.L. (1990, March). Aspects of reliability and validity for the Beck Anxiety Inventory. Paper presented at the National Conference on Phobias and Related Anxiety Disorders, Bethesda, MD.

Beck Depression Inventory—Second Edition (BDI-II)

Developer's or distributor's description of instrument: The BDI-II builds on 35 years of accumulated psychometric data and clinical experience with the BDI. It has been updated to include DSM-IV criteria for depression. The BDI-II is a 21-item self-report instrument which measures the severity of depression in adults and adolescents ages 13 years and older.

Distributor information: The Psychological Corporation, 555 Academic Court, San Antonio TX 78204-2498, Phone: (800) 228-0752

Author: Aaron T. Beck, Robert A. Steer, Gregory K. Brown

Copyright status: Copyright © 1996 by Aaron T. Beck

Fees: A complete kit is $53.00, manual only is $25.50, 25 record forms are $29.50.

Target population(s)/symptom(s): Primarily for adults, but has been used with adolescents in several studies.

Clinical setting: All (outpatient, inpatient, partial hospitalization)

Primary use(s): Screening, Change over time, Post-treatment follow-up

Age group: 13+

Domain(s): Other: cognitive, affective, somatic and performance-related symptoms of depression

Is instrument population-based or designed to measure change for individuals? Individual-based measure

Who completes instrument? Self-report (oral administration is acceptable if respondent needs assistance)

Number of items: 21

Administration time: 5-10 minutes

Administration options: [no answer]

Computer scoring possible? [no answer]

Are norms available? [no answer]

If so, normed on what groups? N/A

Reliability data: Internal Consistency: Coefficient alphas were .92 (outpatient sample), .93 (college students). Item Analysis: corrected item-total correlations ranged from .39-.70 (outpatient sample), .27-.74 (student sample), item-option characteristic curves are provided in the BDI-II manual. Test-Retest: Correlation between first and second sessions (approximately 1 week apart) was .93 p<.001 for a subsample of 26 outpatients.

Validity data: Content Validity: Items were reworded and added to the BDI-II to fully assess the DSM-IV criteria for depression. Construct Validity: The correlation between the BDI and BDI-II was .93 (p<.001) for 191 outpatients during initial evaluations. The correlation between take-home BDI forms and BDI-II forms completed approximately 1 week later during initial intake was .84 (p<.001) for 127 outpatients, 84 of which completed the take-home BDI. Correlations between BDI-II and selected instruments (BHS r=.68 p<.001, SSI r=.37 p<.001, BAI r=.60 p<.001, HRSD-R r=.71 p<.001, HARS-R r=.47 p<.001). Factorial Validity: Two factors were identified for psychiatric outpatients; a Somatic-Affective dimension of self-reported depression and a Cognitive dimension. The correlation between factors was .66 (p<.001). Two factors have also been identified for the college student sample; a Cognitive-Affective dimension and a Somatic dimension. The correlation between factors was .62 (p<.001). A factor-matching procedure revealed two highly correlated underlying cognitive-affective and somatic dimensions for both outpatients and students.

Key references:
- Beck, A.T., Rush, A.J., Shaw, B.F., & Emery, G. (1979). *Cognitive therapy of depression*. New York, Guilford Press.
- Beck, A.T., Steer, R.A., & Brown, G.K. (1996). *Manual for the Beck Depression Inventory—Second Edition*. San Antonio, TX: The Psychological Corporation.
- Beck, A.T., Steer, R.A., & Garbin, M.G. (1988). Psychometric properties of the Beck Depression Inventory: Twenty-five years of evaluation. *Clinical Psychology Review*, 8, 77-100.
- Steer, R.A., Beck, A.T., & Garrison, B. (1986). Applications of the Beck Depression Inventory. In N. Sartorius & T.A. Ban (Eds.), *Assessment of depression* (pp. 121-142). New York: Springer-Verlag.

Beck Hopelessness Scale (BHS)

Developer's or distributor's description of instrument:	The BHS is a 20-item scale for measuring the extent of negative attitudes about the future for adolescents and adults. It was originally developed to measure pessimism in psychiatric patients considered to be suicide risks, but it has been subsequently used with adolescent and adult normal populations. It has been used as an outcome measure to identify underlying suicide risk, even when suicidal ideation may be directly denied in a clinical interview.
Distributor information:	The Psychological Corporation, 555 Academic Court, San Antonio TX 78204-2498, Phone: (800) 228-0752
Author:	Aaron T. Beck, Robert A. Steer
Copyright status:	Copyright (c) 1988 by Aaron T. Beck
Fees:	A complete kit is $49.50, manual only is $24.00, 25 record forms are $27.50.
Target population(s)/symptom(s):	The BHS measures the extent of negative attitudes about the future in adolescents and adults in depressed and normal populations. It can be used as an indirect indicator of suicidal risk.
Clinical setting:	All (outpatient, inpatient, partial hospitalization)
Primary use(s):	Diagnosis, Screening, Change over time, Post-treatment follow-up
Age group:	13+ (most appropriate for those over 17 years old)
Domain(s):	Hopelessness, Pessimism, and Denial of optimism
Is instrument population-based or designed to measure change for individuals?	Individual-based measure
Who completes instrument?	Self-report (oral administration is acceptable if respondent needs assistance)
Number of items:	20
Administration time:	5-10 minutes
Administration options:	[no answer]
Computer scoring possible?	[no answer]
Are norms available?	[no answer]
If so, normed on what groups?	N/A
Reliability data:	Internal Consistency: Kuder-Richardson (KR-20) reliabilities for the suicide ideators, suicide attempters, alcoholics, heroin addicts, single-episode Major Depression Disorders, recurrent-episode Major Depression Disorders, and Dysthymic Disorders were .92, .93, .91, .82, .92, .92, and .87, respectively. Item Analysis: Corrected item-total correlations ranged from .24-.75 (suicide ideators), .32-.75 (suicide attempters), .18-.69 (alcoholics), .19-.57 (heroin addicts), .32-.71 (single-episode major depression), .26-.72 (recurrent-episode major depres-

sion), .06-.65 (dysthymic disorder) and are significant at p<.01. Test-Retest: For a sample of 21 outpatients tested at intake and 1 week later, the Pearson product-moment correlation was .69 (p<.001) between the test-retest scores. A sample of 99 outpatients who were tested at intake and 6 weeks later yielded a test-retest correlation of .66 (p<.001).

Validity data: Content Validity: The BHS items were selected to represent hopelessness as a system of negative attitudes concerning the person's future. They were chosen from a pool of statements made by patients who were asked to describe their expectancies when depressed and when not depressed. Concurrent Validity: Correlations of the BHS with the BDI for seven normative samples are significant at p<.001: .61 (suicide ideators), .70 (suicide attempters), .76 (alcoholics), .46 (heroin addicts), .51 (single-episode major depression), .64 (recurrent-episode major depression), .64 (dysthymic disorder). Construct Validity: Results indicate that the BHS is a better predictor of suicidal intent than is depression as measured by other instruments. Partial correlational analyses indicate that the relationship between hopelessness and suicidal intent (r=.47) was significantly higher than the relationship between depression and suicidal intent (r=.26). Factorial Validity: Different factor structures appear, depending on the type of population. (Contact publisher for details.) Predictive Validity: The BHS is a powerful indicator of eventual suicide. In one study, the mean BHS score was significantly higher in the suicide group (M=13.27, SD=4.43) than in the nonsuicide group (M=8.94, SD=6.05; t(163)=2.33, p<.05). The false-negative rate was 9.1%. In another study, the mean BHS score was significantly higher (p<.001) in the outpatient suicide group (M=15.13, SD=4.56) than in the nonsuicide group (M=9.99, SD=5.43). The false-negative rate for this study was 6.2%.

Key references:
• Beck, A.T., & Steer, R.A. (1988). *Manual for the Beck Hopelessness Scale*. San Antonio, TX: The Psychological Corporation. • Beck, A.T., Steer, R.A., Kovacs, M., & Garrison, B. (1985). Hopelessness and eventual suicide: A 10-year perspective study of patients hospitalized with suicidal ideation. *American Journal of Psychiatry* 142, 559-563. • Beck, A.T., Weissman, A., Lester, D., & Trexler, L. (1974). The measurement of pessimism: The Hopelessness Scale. *Journal of Consulting and Clinical Psychology*, 42, 861-865. • Johnson, J.H., & McCutcheon, S. (1981). Correlations of adolescent pessimism: A study of the Beck Hopelessness Scale. *Journal of Youth and Adolescence*, 10, 169-172.

Beginning Services Survey (BSS)

Developer's or distributor's description of instrument:	The Beginning Services Survey (BSS) was developed as a part of a large outcomes program (University of Cincinnati, Dept. of Psychiatry, Outcomes Management Project). The BSS gathers data from a patient immediately preceding outpatient treatment to assess satisfaction w/access to care (e.g. ease, convenience, time from calling to first appt., etc.) And expectations from care. Instrument is very useful for diverse outpatient populations and settings.
Distributor information:	N.A. Dewan, MD, Center for Quality Innovations & Research, 222 Piedmont Ave., Suite 8800, M.L. 665, Cincinnati OH 45219
Author:	Terry L. Kramer, PhD, Gayle L. Zieman, PhD
Copyright status:	Copyrighted
Fees:	No license fee
Target population(s)/symptom(s):	General population of inpatients and outpatients
Clinical setting:	Outpatient, inpatient and partial hospital
Primary use(s):	Screening
Age group:	14 and above
Domain(s):	Client satisfaction, Access to care
Is instrument population-based or designed to measure change for individuals?	Both
Who completes instrument?	Self-report
Number of items:	18
Administration time:	5 minutes
Administration options:	Paper/pencil
Computer scoring possible?	Yes
Are norms available?	Yes
If so, normed on what groups?	Outpatient adults, Managed care settings
Reliability data:	Comparative data available on all questions across multi-state treatment sites.
Validity data:	Data available on correlation between initial satisfaction and expectations with treatment outcomes and follow-up satisfaction.
Population sample(s) on which measure tested:	Behavioral Health, Outpatient (n=13,000) in 12 states
Key references:	[no answer]

Behavioral and Symptom Identification Scale (BASIS-32)

Distributor information:	Saeed Aminzadeh, Senior Director, Sales, HCIA-Response, 950 Winter Street, Waltham MA 02154, (781) 768-1805
Author:	Dr. Susan Eisen, McLean Hospital
Copyright status:	Copyrighted, McLean Hospital, 1985
Fees:	None ($50 for information packet)
Target population(s)/symptom(s):	Mental health patients
Clinical setting:	Inpatient and outpatient mental health settings
Primary use(s):	The BASIS-32 is used to assess the patient's own perception of his/her mental health status. The patient reports the degree of difficulty with symptoms or functioning that result in the need for psychiatric treatment. It is used to assess course and outcome of mental health treatment and services. Information is used by providers to assist in assessing outcomes, continuous quality improvement efforts, monitoring clinical decision-making and program planning. (Outcomes instrument, can be used to measure change over time and post treatment follow-up.)
Age group:	Mid-adolescents through adults (ages 14 and up)
Domain(s):	Relation to self and others, daily living and role functioning, depression and anxiety, impulsive and addictive behavior, psychosis.
Is instrument population-based or designed to measure change for individuals?	Both
Who completes instrument?	Patient Self-Report
Number of items:	32 symptom and problem items, 7 demographic items
Administration time:	5-10 minutes as self-report, 10-20 minutes as structured interview
Administration options:	Scanning, manual entry
Computer scoring possible?	Yes
Are norms available?	Yes
If so, normed on what groups?	Many groups. Please contact HCIA-Response
Reliability and Validity data:	Internal consistency for individual scales ranged from .63 to .80, and was .89 for the full scale. Test-retest ranged from .65 to .81. Concurrent and discriminant validity, and sensitivity to change, were tested based on hypotheses, which were supported.

Key references:
- Eisen, SV, Dill, DL, et al Reliability and Validity of a Brief Patient-Report Instrument for Psychiatric Outcomes Evaluation, *Hospital and Community Psychiatry*, 1994, 45(3):242-247.
- Eisen, SV Assessment of Subjective Distress by Patients' Self-Report versus Structured Interview, Psychological Reports, 1995, 76, 35-39; *Use of BASIS-32 for Outcome Assessment of Recipients of Outpatient Mental Health Services.*
- Eisen, S, Wilcox, M et al., March 1997.
- Russo, J, Roy-Byrne, P et al, The Relationship of Patient-Administered Outcome Assessments to Quality of Life and Physician Ratings: Validity of the BASIS-32, *Journal of Mental Health Administration*, 1997, 22:200-214.

Behavioral Healthcare Rating of Satisfaction (BHRS)

Developer's or distributor's description of instrument:	This is a 26-item consumer satisfaction scale that was designed with input from consumers, providers, and other interested stakeholders. The scale has a fourth grade reading level, is based on a 6-point Likert scale, and has good test-retest reliability and internal consistency. The questions concern five areas: satisfaction with staff relationships, perceived outcome, general satisfactions, environmental context of treatment, and negativity/coerciveness.
Distributor information:	A scannable version of the scale is available from Psychological Assessment Resources, Inc., Odessa FL.
Author:	Michael G. Dow and John C. Ward
Copyright status:	Copyrighted
Fees:	Scannable forms are available for $0.25 each from PAR, Inc. Other specialized uses should be discussed with Dr. Dow. Permission has been given in the past on a case by case basis for use as long as the scale remains intact and is identified as copyrighted and used with permission.
Target population(s)/symptom(s):	Adults receiving mental health and substance abuse treatment.
Clinical setting:	Mental health and substance abuse programs.
Primary use(s):	Post-treatment follow-up
Age group:	13 to elderly
Domain(s):	Client satisfaction
Is instrument population-based or designed to measure change for individuals?	Yes, in the sense that extensive norms are available. It is not designed to measure change.
Who completes instrument?	Consumer
Number of items:	26
Administration time:	10 minutes
Administration options:	Scannable; Paper/pencil; Computer (Microsoft Visual Basic Program has been developed which can use sound card and/or touchscreen if available.)
Computer scoring possible?	Yes—discuss with first author (dow@hal.fmhi.usf.edu).
Are norms available?	Yes
If so, normed on what groups?	Public mental health and substance abuse programs in Florida
Reliability data:	Test-retest reliability is .87
Validity data:	Items developed/selected by large group of consumers, professionals. Each item has been shown to discriminate across a range of programs and providers in FL.

Key references:
- Dow, M.G., & Ward, J. C. (1997). *Behavioral Healthcare Rating of Satisfaction.* Tampa, FL: University of South Florida, Florida Mental Health Institute, Dept. of Community Mental Health.

Brief Psychiatric Rating Scale (BPRS)

Developer's or distributor's description of instrument:	The BPRS is a psychiatric rating scale used to characterize manifest psychopathology observed in a semi-structured clinical interview. It consists of 18 symptom and behavior constructs, each rated on a 7-point scale of severity. It was originally designed to assess treatment response of psychiatric patients in controlled clinical trials. It has subsequently had wide use in characterizing patient populations, classification of patients according to phenomenological or syndrome type, and in documentation of clinical practice. Translated and used in countries from Europe to the Far East.
Distributor information:	John E. Overall, PhD, Department of Psychiatry and Behavioral Science, University of Texas Medical School, P.O. Box 20708, Houston TX 77225, Phone: (713) 500-2564
Author:	John E. Overall, Donald R. Gorham
Copyright status:	Original copyright Psychological Reports (1962) for first 16 items. Has been reproduced and widely distributed by drug companies, etc. Request permission approval J.E. Overall for publication, but no permission required for reproduction
Fees:	Reproduce no charge. Not available from publisher in commercial form
Target population(s)/symptom(s):	Major psychiatric disorders—schizophrenia, depression, general psychiatric
Clinical setting:	Inpatient or outpatient psychiatric
Primary use(s):	Diagnosis, Screening, Change over time, Post-treatment follow-up
Age group:	Adult
Domain(s):	Psychiatric symptoms
Is instrument population-based or designed to measure change for individuals?	Both—principal use in measuring change in clinical trials.
Who completes instrument?	Clinician
Number of items:	18
Administration time:	20 minutes for interview, 3 minutes to complete ratings
Administration options:	Clinician rated on paper/pencil form
Computer scoring possible?	Yes. The BPRS provides a "total pathology score" and 4 factor scores representing thinking disturbances, hostile suspiciousness, withdrawal-retardation and anxious depression. Profile patterns typical of major psychiatric diagnostic groups and patterns typical of patients treated with major classes of psychotherapeutic drugs can be used for probability diagnosis or treatment validation. Computer programs for factor scoring and patient classification can easily be written based on profile

	analysis or statistical probability models. Norms and (dated) computer programs are provided as examples in Overall and Klett (1983).
Are norms available?	Yes
If so, normed on what groups?	Major psychiatric diagnostic groups, Drug treatment prototypes, Phenomenological syndromes
Reliability data:	Reported in numerous publications and reviewed by Hedlund and Vieweg (1980). *J. Operational Research*, 11, 49-65. Interrater reliability for BPRS total score above .80 and median reliability for individual items .75.
Validity data:	Documented in hundreds of reports of clinical drug trials.
Key references:	• Overall, J.E. and Gorham, D.R. (1962). The brief psychiatric rating scale. *Psychological Reports*, 10, 799-812. • Overall, J.E. and Gorham, D.R. (1988). The brief psychiatric rating scale (BPRS): Recent developments in ascertainment and scaling. *Psychopharmacology Bulletin*, 24, 97-99. • Overall, J.E. and Klett, C.J. (1983). *Applied Multivariate Analysis*. Malabar FL: Krieger Publishing Company.

Brief Symptom Inventory™ (BSI)

Developer's or distributor's description of instrument:	The Brief Symptom Inventory™ (BSI) test is a self-report symptom inventory designed to measure psychological distress. It provides an overview of a patient's symptoms and their intensity. The BSI test also identifies the level of distress that a patient is experiencing at a specific point in time, as patients are asked to indicate whether they have experienced symptoms during a prescribed time period. "The last 7 days" is the standard normative period. Compared with the SCL-90-R test, the BSI test is most often used in situations where the brevity of the instrument is key to patient cooperation. When used for outcomes measurement, the BSI test is often administered at intake, during treatment, at discharge, and for follow-up.
Distributor information:	The BSI test is exclusively published and distributed by NCS Assessments, 5605 Green Circle Drive, Minnetonka MN 55343. It can be ordered by mail, by fax at (800) 632-9011, or by calling Customer Service at (800) 627-7271, ext. 5151. NCS publishes the BSI test in English, Hispanic, and French Canadian as standard products. In addition, there are numerous other foreign language translations which can be used for research purposes.
Author:	Leonard R. Derogatis, PhD
Copyright status:	The "Brief Symptom Inventory" is a trademark, and the "BSI" is a registered trademark of the test's author. Copyright © 1975
Fees:	Per use and site licenses available. Call or write for current catalog
Target population(s)/symptom(s):	The BSI test measures nine primary symptom dimensions: somatization, obsessive-compulsive, interpersonal sensitivity, depression, anxiety, hostility, phobic anxiety, paranoid ideation, and psychoticism. It also provides three global indices of distress including a Global Severity Index (GSI) that measures the current overall level of distress, a Positive Symptom Distress Index (PSDI) that measures the intensity of distress, and a Positive Symptom Total (PST) that indicates the number of patient-reported symptoms. The GSI is the single composite score most often used for measuring the outcome of a treatment program based on reducing symptom severity.
Clinical setting:	[no answer]
Primary use(s):	Screening, change over time, and post-treatment follow-up. Aggregating of data for continuous quality improvement
Age group:	13 years and older. The test is written at a 6th grade reading level

Domain(s):	Symptoms, Severity
Is instrument population-based or designed to measure change for individuals?	Measures change over time for an individual, but data can be agggregated for groups
Who completes instrument?	Self-report
Number of items:	53 items (short form of the SCL-90-R test)
Administration time:	8-10 minutes. Test can be done via paper and pencil, audio-cassette, or on-line computer administration
Administration options:	Computer, Fax-in, Mail-in, Site license
Computer scoring possible?	Yes
Are norms available?	Yes
If so, normed on what groups?	Inpatient psychiatric, Outpatient psychiatric, Community
Reliability data:	Internal consistency ranged from .71 to .85 for the 9 primary symptom dimension, and was calculated from the data of 719 psychiatric outpatients. Test-retest reliability ranged between .68 and .91 for a sample of 60 nonpatient individuals with a two week interval between tests.
Validity data:	There are over 335 studies attesting to the validity of the BSI. A BSI bibliography is available upon request.
Key references:	[no answer]

The Brown Assessment of Beliefs Scale

Developer's or distributor's description of instrument:	The Brown Assessment of Beliefs Scale is a seven-item clinician-administered semi-structured scale designed to assess delusionality of beliefs in a broad range of psychiatric disorders. To administer the scale, the dominant belief (obsession, concern, idea, worry, or delusion) that has preoccupied the patient during the past week is first established. For obsessions, the belief and associated consequences underlying the obsessional thought must be determined. The Brown Assessment of Beliefs Scale has specific probes and five anchors for each item, with descriptions corresponding to each anchor. The score for each item ranges from 0 (non-delusional, or least pathological) to 4 (delusional, or most pathological). Ratings represent an average score for the past week.
Distributor information:	Jane L. Eisen, MD, Butler Hospital, 345 Blackstone Blvd., Providence RI 02906
Author:	Jane L. Eisen, MD; Katharine A. Phillips, MD; Lee Baer, PhD; Douglas A. Beer, MD; Katherine D. Atala, MD; and Steven A. Rasmussen, MD
Copyright status:	Copyrighted
Fees:	None
Target population(s)/symptom(s):	Patients with obsessions, overvalued ideas or delusions. This may include patients with psychotic disorders (schizophrenia, schizoaffective disorder), mood disorders, obsessive compulsive disorder, body dysmorphic disorder, hypochondriasis, and anorexia nervosa.
Clinical setting:	Psychiatric inpatient, day hospital or outpatient setting
Primary use(s):	Change over time, Post-treatment follow-up
Age group:	Adults. A version has been developed for adolescents as well.
Domain(s):	Symptoms
Is instrument population-based or designed to measure change for individuals?	Change in individuals
Who completes instrument?	The clinician
Number of items:	7
Administration time:	5-15 minutes
Administration options:	Paper/pencil
Computer scoring possible?	No
Are norms available?	Mean scores are available for selected populations.
If so, normed on what groups?	Obsessive compulsive disorder, Body dysmorphic disorder

Reliability data:	Intraclass correlation coefficient for each item ranged from 0.78 to 0.96. Individual item test-retest ICCs ranged from 0.79 to 0.98.
Validity data:	*Discriminant Validity*: The total score on the Brown Assessment of Beliefs Scale was not significantly correlated with total score on the Beck Depression Inventory or the Yale-Brown Obsessive Compulsive Scale. The Brown Assessment of Beliefs Scale correlated only weakly with the BPRS, although this correlation reached statistical significance. *Convergent Validity* was demonstrated with the Characteristics of Delusions Rating Scale total score and the two items that assess delusional thinking on the Scale to Assess Unawareness of Mental Disorder. A high correlation was also found between the conviction item on the Brown Assessment of Beliefs Scale and conviction items on the Dimensions of Delusional Experience, the Fixity of Beliefs Scale, and the Characteristics of Delusions Rating Scale. *Sensitivity to Change*: The correlation between mean change in total Yale-Brown Obsessive Compulsive Scale score and mean change in total score on the Brown Assessment of Beliefs Scale was 0.43 ($p<0.008$), indicating that improvement in degree of delusionality as measured by the scale was correlated with but not identical to improvement in severity of OCD symptoms.
Key references:	• The Brown Assessment of Beliefs Scale: Reliability and Validity. *Am J Psychiatry* 1998; 155: 102-108.

Caregiver-Teacher Report Form For Ages 2-5 (C-TRF/2-5)

Developer's or distributor's description of instrument:	Contains 99 specific behavioral/emotional problem items and an open-ended item for adding problems to be rated as 0 = not true of the child, 1 = somewhat or sometimes true, 2 = very true or often true. Also has open-ended items for reporting illnesses, disabilities, raters' concerns, and best things about the child. Is used to obtain standardized description of problems. Is scored on a profile that compares child with normative samples of the same age and gender.
Distributor information:	Child Behavior Checklist, University Medical Education Associates, 1 South Prospect St., Burlington, VT 05401-3456
Author:	Thomas M. Achenbach, PhD
Copyright status:	Copyrighted
Fees:	Forms completed by day care providers and preschool teachers: 25 for $10. Profiles for hand-scoring C-TRF/2-5: 25 for $10. Computer scoring program $135.
Target population(s)/symptom(s):	Children 2 to 5 years old
Clinical setting:	All settings; ratings are based on child's behavior in daycare or preschool.
Primary use(s):	Assessment, Screening, Treatment planning, Change over time, Post-treatment follow-up
Age group:	2-5 years
Domain(s):	Symptoms, Behavioral and emotional problems
Is instrument population-based or designed to measure change for individuals?	Both
Who completes instrument?	Daycare providers and preschool teachers
Number of items:	100
Administration time:	self-administered in 10 minutes
Administration options:	Paper/pencil
Computer scoring possible?	Yes
Are norms available?	Yes
If so, normed on what groups?	National sample of 1,075 children in preschools and daycare
Reliability data:	Test-retest reliability over 8.7 days: correlation = .88 for total problems
Validity data:	Most scales discriminate significantly between referred and normative children.
Key references:	• Achenbach TM (1997). *Guide for the Caregiver-Teacher Report Form for Ages 2-5.* Burlington VT: University of Vermont Department of Psychiatry.

CERAD

(Consortium to Establish a Registry for Alzheimer's Disease) Clinical and Neuropsychology batteries; CERAD Neuropathology Assessment Forms

Developer's or distributor's description of instrument:	The CERAD Clinical and Neuropsychology batteries provide standardized reliable and valid assessments permitting the identification of Alzheimer's disease (AD) and other dementing disorders, and determination of level of severity of impairment. Information has been gathered on approximately 1200 patients with AD and 450 control subjects, re-evaluated annually for up to eight years. The CERAD Neuropathology Assessment has been completed for nearly 250 patients who have had brain autopsies. The measures have also been used to identify the presence and types of dementia in black and white elderly community residents. The measures are brief. Most information can be gathered by a trained paraprofessional, reducing clinician time. CERAD forms and data are available on CD-ROM. Foreign language versions are available (e.g., French, Spanish, Chinese).
Distributor information:	A. Heyman, MD, CERAD, Box 3203, Duke University Medical Center, Durham NC 27710, Fax: (919) 286-9219; email: stric007@mc.duke.edu
Author:	Clinical and Neuropsychology Battery: CERAD Steering Committee; Neuropathology Assessment: Suzanne Mirra, MD, et al.
Copyright status:	Copyrighted. For permission to use, write to A. Heyman, MD
Fees:	None
Target population(s)/symptom(s):	Middle-aged and elderly with severe cognitive impairment indicative of dementia
Clinical setting:	Tertiary care
Primary use(s):	Diagnosis, Screening, Change over time, Post-treatment follow-up. Also available for epidemiological surveys.
Age group:	50 years of age and older
Domain(s):	Symptoms, Dementia assessment
Is instrument population-based or designed to measure change for individuals?	Can be used at an individual level or in epidemiological surveys
Who completes instrument?	Clinician or trained paraprofessional
Number of items:	Clinical: 14 evaluation forms; Neuropsychology: 8 evaluation forms/tests
Administration time:	Clinical—varies, approximately one hour, Neuropsychology—approximately 40 minutes
Administration options:	In person, CAPI available for clinical assessment

Computer scoring possible?	Yes, for clinical section when used in epidemiological surveys
Are norms available?	Yes
If so, normed on what groups?	Tertiary care memory disorder clinic patients; representative community residents
Reliability data:	Neuropsychology: substantial interrater agreement (0.92-1.0) and high one-month test-retest reliability (0.53-0.91). See Welsh et al., CERAD Part V: A normative study of the neuropsychological battery. *Neurology* 1994;44:609-614. Neuropathology: Mirra et al, Interlaboratory comparison of neuropathology assessments in Alzheimer's disease: a study of the Consortium to Establish a Registry for Alzheimer's Disease (CERAD). *J Neuropath Exp Neurol* 1994;53(3):303-315.
Validity data:	Clinical: CERAD clinical diagnosis of AD confirmed at autopsy in 87 percent of cases. See Gearing et al., Neuropathology confirmation of the clinical diagnosis of Alzheimer's disease. *Neurology* 1995;45:461-466.
Key references:	Clinical and Neuropsychology Battery: • Morris et al, CERAD Part I: clinical and neuropsychological assessment of Alzheimer's disease. *Neurology* 1989;39:1159-1165. • Morris et al., CERAD Part IV: rates of cognitive change, a longitudinal assessment of probable Alzheimer's disease. *Neurology* 1993;43:2457-2465. • Welsh et al., CERAD Part V: a normative study of the neuropsychological battery. *Neurology* 1994;44:609-614. Neuropathology Assessment: Mirra et al., CERAD Part II: standardization of the neuropathological assessment of Alzheimer's disease. *Neurology* 1991;41:479-486. • Mirra et al., The neuropathology assessment of Alzheimer's disease and related dementias: the CERAD experience. In Coran et al., eds., *Alzheimer's Disease: Advances in Clinical and Basic Research*. John Wiley & Sons Ltd., 1993:207-211.

CERAD BRSD (Behavior Rating Scale For Dementia)

Developer's or distributor's description of instrument:	The BRSD assesses the presence, recency, and frequency of behavioral symptoms occurring in Alzheimer's disease. Factor analysis indicates that eight types of behavioral disturbances are assessed. It has been adopted for use in assessing drug interventions in Alzheimer's disease. The BRSD is also available in French and Spanish.
Distributor information:	A. Heyman, MD, CERAD, Box 3203, Duke University Medical Center, Durham NC 27710, Fax: (919) 286-9219, email: stric007@mc.duke.edu
Author:	Pierre Tariot, MD; James L. Mack, PhD; Marian Patterson, PhD
Copyright status:	Copyrighted
Fees:	No charge
Target population(s)/symptom(s):	Persons with dementia who have symptoms of behavioral pathology
Clinical setting:	Any
Primary use(s):	Evaluation of behavioral symptoms of dementia, Post-treatment follow-up
Age group:	50 years of age and older
Domain(s):	Behavioral problems
Is instrument population-based or designed to measure change for individuals?	Assessment at individual level
Who completes instrument?	Information obtained by interviewer from informant, typically caregiver
Number of items:	Full scale: 46 questions, Short form: 17 questions
Administration time:	30 minutes for full scale; 15 minutes for short form. Both in-person and telephone administration.
Administration options:	In person, Telephone
Computer scoring possible?	No
Are norms available?	Yes
If so, normed on what groups?	Patients with Alzheimer's disease attending tertiary care medical centers
Reliability data:	See journal references below
Validity data:	See journal references below
Key references:	• Tariot PH, Mack JL, Patterson MB, Edland SD, Weiner MF, Fillenbaum G, et al. The Behavior Rating Scale for Dementia of the Consortium to Establish a Registry for Alzheimer's Disease. *Am. J. Psychiatry* 1995;152:1349-1357.

Child and Adolescent Adjustment Profile (CAAP)

Developer's or distributor's description of instrument:	The purpose of the Child and Adolescent Adjustment Profile is to provide an easy to use, reliable and valid scale for measuring psychosocial adjustment of youth. The CAAP measures five factor analyzed areas of adjustment: Peer Relations, Dependency, Hostility, Productivity, and Withdrawal. It is designed to be rated by parents, counselors, teachers, and others who observe and work with children and adolescents.
Distributor information:	Ellsworth Krebs Associates, 3615 130th Ave NE, Bellevue, WA 98005, Phone: (425) 883-4762
Author:	Robert B. Ellsworth, PhD and Shanae L. Ellsworth, PhD
Copyright status:	Copyrighted
Fees:	Currently $10 per 25 scales, $5 per 25 profiles
Target population(s)/symptom(s):	Youth, variety of settings from schools, juvenile programs, mental health programs, anywhere interest in assessing psychosocial adjustment of youth
Clinical setting:	It has been used in both inpatient and outpatient settings.
Primary use(s):	Change over time
Age group:	6-18 years old
Domain(s):	Life functioning/adustment
Is instrument population-based or designed to measure change for individuals?	Has been used for both
Who completes instrument?	Clinician/Teacher/Parent/Others who work with or are familiar with child
Number of items:	20 items
Administration time:	10-15 minutes
Administration options:	Paper/pencil
Computer scoring possible?	No
Are norms available?	Yes
If so, normed on what groups?	Children ranging in age from three to nineteen who were not being seen for emotional or learning problems. Ratings were obtained from parents and teachers.
Reliability data:	Available
Validity data:	Available
Key references:	• Ellsworth SL, Ellsworth RB (1998). The CAAP: Measuring Child and Adolescent Adjustment. Bellevue WA: Institute for Program Evaluation.

Child and Adolescent Functional Assessment Scale (CAFAS)

Developer's or distributor's description of instrument:	The CAFAS scales, which rate the youth's degree of impairment, include: School/Work, Home, Community, Behavior Toward Others, Mood/Emotions, Self-Harmful Behavior, Substance Use, and Thinking Problems. The scale scores can be entered on a one-page Clinical Profile which provides a visual representation of how the youth functions across various settings. A total sore is also generated which provides an overall indicator of degree of dysfunction. The CAFAS user bases his or her rating on the information obtained during routine clinical procedures, such as the intake interview. However, a 30-minute telephone interview has been developed, which obtains all of the information needed to rate the CAFAS and which can be used by lay raters. Extensive validity and reliability data is available from the author. A Checklist for Caregivers, which can be completed by the parent, can also be used to obtain all of the information needed for rating the CAFAS.
Distributor information:	Kay Hodges, PhD, 2140 Old Earhart Rd., Ann Arbor MI 48105, Phone: (734) 769-9725, Fax: (734) 769-1434
Author:	Kay Hodges, PhD
Copyright status:	Copyrighted
Fees:	There is a charge which varies, depending on the type of form the user chooses. The formats available include: written form, clinical summary profile form, scannable answer form, and computerized CAFAS program.
Target population(s)/symptom(s):	Children and adolescents referred for mental health services
Clinical setting:	The CAFAS is for use with children at risk for psychiatric problems or referred because of behavioral, emotional, mental, psychiatric, psychological or substance use problems. It is used with youth being treated along the entire continuum of services, including outpatient, community-based programs, partial hospitalization and residential care, including inpatient units and residential treatment centers. It has also been successfully used with children in foster care.
Primary use(s):	Screening, Change over time, Post-treatment follow-up
Age group:	7-17 or school-aged children (1st-12th grade). There is a "downward" version of the CAFAS for children ages 4-6 years, referred to as the Preschool and Early Childhood Functional Assessment Scale (PECFAS)

Domain(s):	Life functioning, Behavioral problems, Family environment, Severity and/or risk factors, Degree of impairment in functioning due to emotional, behavioral, substance use, psychiatric or psychological problems
Is instrument population-based or designed to measure change for individuals?	Designed to measure change over time for individuals. The computerized version of the CAFAS generates a written report of the results on individual clients. The program also aggregates the data across clients and generates administrative and outcome reports.
Who completes instrument?	Clinician or lay interviewer. For doing independent or follow-up evaluations, trained non-professionals can be used to rate the CAFAS.
Number of items:	There are eight scales about the youth's functioning and two scales about the caregiver's functioning.
Administration time:	About 10 minutes. The CAFAS is not administered. The rater chooses from a list of behavioral descriptions, those which are true for the client being rated.
Administration options:	Written form, clinical summary profile form, Teleform® and NCS®, scannable answer form, computerized CAFAS program
Computer scoring possible?	Yes
Are norms available?	There are comparable data
If so, normed on what groups?	A large sample of seriously emotionally disturbed (SED) youth and a large sample of youth referred for mental health services.
Reliability data:	Data on the psychometric properties of the CAFAS have been produced from two large evaluations. One was of the Fort Bragg Evaluation Project (FBEP; Hodges & Wong, 1996; 1997) and the other from the national evaluation being conducted of the demonstration grants funded by the Center for Mental Health Services (CMHS; Hodges, Doutcette-Gates & Liao, 1996). The FBEP subjects were referred for mental health services, and the youth in the CMHS evaluation were most seriously emotionally disturbed youth. Reliability studies have demonstrated satisfactory internal consistency, test-retest reliability, and interrater reliability. Internal consistency has been demonstrated in both the FBEP and the CMHS evaluations. High interrater reliability has been reported for the CAFAS across different sites and with both lay and clinician raters. Satisfactory test-retest reliability was demonstrated in a study in which lay interviewers rated the CAFAS after administering the CAFAS interview via the telephone (Hodges, 1995).
Validity:	The items on the CAFAS have high content validity. Items refer to specific behaviors in specified domains of functioning. Contrast group validity has been demonstrated in both the FBEP and CMHS evaluations. Inpatients scored higher than youth in alternative care (e.g., home-based services, day treatment), who in turn scored as more impaired than youth in outpatient care. Predictive validity was demonstrated in the FBEP and CMHS studies. The CAFAS score at intake was found to

be related to services received over the subsequent year. Higher impairment, as measured by the CAFAS, was significantly related to more restrictive care, higher cost of services, more bed days, and more days of service. Furthermore, the predictive power of the CAFAS, assessed at intake, was compared to the presence of a variety of common diagnoses for children and to other commonly used assessment instruments. The CAFAS was the strongest predictor of costs and services at both 6 and 12 months. Sensitivity to change over time was found in both the FBEP and the CMHS evaluations.

Key references:
• Hodges, K., & Gust, J. (1995). Measures of impairment for children and adolescents. *Journal of Mental Health Administration*, 22, 403-413. • Hodges, K. & Wong, M.M. (1996). Psychometric characteristics of a multidimensional measure to assess impairment: The Child and Adolescent Functional Assessment Scale. *Journal of Child and Family Studies*, (5(4), 445-467. • Hodges, K. & Wong, M.M. (1997). Use of the Child and Adolescent Functional Assessment Scale to predict service utilization and cost. *Journal of Mental Health Administration*, 24(3), 278-290. • Hodges, K. (1996). CAFAS Manual for Training Coordinators, Clinical Administrators and Data Managers. Ypsilanti, MI: Eastern Michigan University, Department of Psychology. • Hodges, K., Wong, M., and Latessa, M. (1998). Use of the Child and Adolescent Functional Assessment Scale (CAFAS) as an outcome measure in clinical settings. *Journal of Behavioral Health Services & Research*, 25(3): 326-337.

Child Assessment Schedule (CAS)

Developer's or distributor's description of instrument:	The CAS is a structured diagnostic interview that generates the following information: presence or absence of diagnosis, number of diagnostically-related symptom scores for each diagnosis, and number of endorsements across various areas of life functioning (e.g., school, family, etc.). There are two versions of the CAS, one to be administered to the child and the other to be administered to the parent, inquiring about the child's symptoms and behavioral problems.
Distributor information:	Kay Hodges, PhD, 2140 Old Earhart Rd., Ann Arbor MI 48105, Phone: (734) 769-9725 Fax: (734) 769-1434
Author:	Kay Hodges, PhD
Copyright status:	Copyrighted
Fees:	There is a charge for the materials
Target population(s)/symptom(s):	Children and adolescents referred for mental health services
Clinical setting:	The CAS is for use with children at risk for psychiatric problems or referred because of behavioral, emotional, mental, psychiatric, psychological or substance abuse problems. It is used with youth being treated along the entire continuum of services, including outpatient, community-based programs, partial hospitalization and residential care including inpatient units and residential treatment centers.
Primary use(s):	Diagnosis, Screening, Change over time, Post-treatment follow-up
Age group:	The CAS is appropriate for youth 7-17 years old or school-aged children (1st-12th grade).
Domain(s):	Symptoms, Life functioning, Behavioral problems, Family environment, Severity and/or risk factors
Is instrument population-based or designed to measure change for individuals?	The information generated by the CAS can be aggregated across clients for research purposes
Who completes instrument?	Clinician or lay interviewer. There is an interview to be administered to the child as well as one to the parent. For doing independent or follow-up evaluations, trained lay interviewers can be used. The generation of diagnoses is done by computer or computer algorithm.
Number of items:	There are 12 sections or modules. Approximately half are related to diagnoses, with the remaining items inquiring about adjustment and functioning.
Administration time:	About 60 minutes. The interviewer asks the structured questions and based on the respondent's answer marks whether the item is true.

Administration options:	Paper/pencil
Computer scoring possible?	Via algorithm
Are norms available?	No
If so, normed on what groups?	N/A
Reliability data:	Information on reliability and validity of the CAS is summarized in Hodges (1993). There is evidence of internal consistency, test-retest reliability, and interrater reliability.
Validity data:	Contrast group and construct validity have been demonstrated in addition to sensitivity to change over time. In a study by Hodges, Kline, Stern, Cytryn and McKnew (1982), for each of these scales on the CAS, inpatients scored higher than outpatients, who in turn scored higher than controls. Significantly higher scores have been reported for psychiatric patients compared to nonreferred controls for each of the scale scores on the CAS (Thomson, Hodges and Hamlett, 1990). Contrast group validity was also reflected in two studies in which the CAS total scale score differentiated disturbed and nondisturbed children, as judged by an independent morbidity criterion (Verhulst, Bieman, Ende, Berden and Sanders-Woudstra, 1990; Verhulst, Althaus and Berden, 1987). Sensitivity to change over time, apparently related to interventions, was reported for children who were sexually abused (Runyan, Everson, Edelsohn, Hunter and Coulter, 1988) and for depressed children.
Key references:	Extensive reliability and validity data are available and summarized in Hodges, K. (1993). Structured interviews for assessing children. *Journal of Child Psychology and Psychiatry*, 34 (1), 49-68 (Other references available).

Child Behavior Checklist (CBCL) 2-3

Developer's or distributor's description of instrument:	The CBCL/2-3 obtains parent's ratings of 99 problem items; 59 items have counterparts on the CBCL/4-18. Profile includes 6 syndrome scales, Internalizing, Externalizing, and total problem scales based on 546 children. Normed on 368 nonreferred children. Hand-scored and computer-scored profiles are available.
Distributor information:	Child Behavior Checklist, University Medical Education Assoc., 1 South Prospect Street, Burlington VT 05401-3456, Fax: (802) 656-2602
Author:	Thomas M. Achenbach, PhD
Copyright status:	Copyrighted
Fees:	Classic forms completed by parents: 25 for $10. Profiles for hand-scoring of CBCL/2-3 (same for both sexes): 25 for $10. Templates for hand-scoring of CBCL/2-3 Profiles (same for both sexes): $7. Manual for the CBCL/2-3 and Profile, 210 pages: $25. Computer Program for scoring of CBCL/2-3, IBM Compatible 3.5": $135
Target population(s)/symptom(s):	Children aged 2-3 as seen by their parents
Clinical setting:	All settings
Primary use(s):	Assessment, Treatment planning, Screening, Change over time, Post-treatment follow-up
Age group:	2-3 years
Domain(s):	Symptoms, Behavioral and emotional problems
Is instrument population-based or designed to measure change for individuals?	Both
Who completes instrument?	Parents
Number of items:	100
Administration time:	10 minutes
Administration options:	Paper/pencil
Computer scoring possible?	Yes
Are norms available?	Yes
If so, normed on what groups?	National sample
Reliability data:	0.91 for total problems
Validity data:	All scales discriminate significantly between referred and non-referred children.
Key references:	• Achenbach TM (1992). *Manual for the Child Behavior Checklist/2-3 and 1992 profile.* Burlington VT: University of Vermont Department of Psychiatry.

Child Behavior Checklist (CBCL) 4-18

Developer's or distributor's description of instrument:	The CBCL/4-18 obtains parents' reports of children's competencies and problems. Profile for scoring the CBCL/4-18 includes 3 competence scales, total competence, 8 cross-informant syndromes, Internalizing, Externalizing, and total problem scales. Cross-informant syndromes scored from the CBCL/4-18, YSR, and TRF are: Aggressive Behavior, Anxious/Depressed, Attention Problems, Delinquent Behavior, Social Problems, Somatic Complaints, Thought Problems, and Withdrawn. Scales are based on parent's ratings of 4455 clinically referred children. Normed on 2,368 nonreferred children. Hand-scored and computer-scored profiles are available.
Distributor information:	Child Behavior Checklist, University Medical Education Assoc., 1 South Prospect Street, Burlington VT 05401-3456, Fax: (802) 656-2602
Author:	Thomas M. Achenbach, PhD
Copyright status:	Copyrighted
Fees:	Similar to "CBCL 2-3"
Target population(s)/symptom(s):	Parents' reports of a wide range of competencies and problems observed in their children
Clinical setting:	All settings
Primary use(s):	Assessment, Screening, Treatment planning, Change of time, Post-treatment follow-up
Age group:	4-18
Domain(s):	Symptoms, Life functioning, Behavioral problems
Is instrument population-based or designed to measure change for individuals?	Both
Who completes instrument?	Parents
Number of items:	120 problems items, 20 competence items
Administration time:	15-20 minutes
Administration options:	Paper/pencil, Machine-readable forms, Direct computer entry by patients
Computer scoring possible?	Yes
Are norms available?	Yes
If so, normed on what groups?	National sample
Reliability data:	0.93 for total problems
Validity data:	All scales discriminate significantly between referred and nonreferred children.
Key references:	• Achenbach TM (1991). *Manual for the Child Behavior Checklist/4-18 and 1991 profile.* Burlington VT: University of Vermont Department of Psychiatry.

Children's Depression Rating Scale, R (CDRS-R)

Developer's or distributor's description of instrument:	CDRS has long been used to diagnose depression and determine its severity. The CDRS-R is a brief rating scale based on a structured interview with the child (or an adult informant who knows the child well). The interviewer rates 17 symptom areas, including all those that serve as DSM-IV criteria for a diagnosis of depression.
Distributor information:	Western Psychological Services, 12031 Wilshire Blvd., Los Angeles CA 90025-1215, Phone: (800) 648-8857
Author:	Elva O. Poznanski, MD; Hartmut B. Mokros, PhD
Copyright status:	Copyrighted
Fees:	Kit, including 25 administrations: $57; Booklet (1 package of 25): $16.50
Target population(s)/symptom(s):	6-12 year olds with depression
Clinical setting:	Any hospital settings, pediatric clinics, or school settings
Primary use(s):	Diagnosis, Change over time
Age group:	6-12 years
Domain(s):	Symptoms, Life functioning, Severity and/or risk factors
Is instrument population-based or designed to measure change for individuals?	Standardized, not normed
Who completes instrument?	Clinician
Number of items:	40 +/-
Administration time:	15-20 minutes
Administration options:	Paper/pencil, Interview
Computer scoring possible?	No
Are norms available?	Yes
If so, normed on what groups?	Non-clinical sample of 6- to 12-year-old children
Reliability data:	See manual
Validity data:	See manual
Key references:	See manual

The Children's Global Assessment Scale (CGAS)

Developer's or distributor's description of instrument:	The CGAS is an adaptation of the GAS (Endicott, Spitzer, et al, Arch. Gen. Psychiatry 1976:766) designed to reflect the lowest level of functioning for a child or adolescent during a specified period of time. It allows the rater to assimilate and synthesize his or her knowledge about many different aspects of a patient's social and psychiatric functioning and condense it into a single clinically meaningful index of severity of disturbance. It has been used in numerous studies, as well as clinically, to classify overall severity of problems (and is very similar to the GAF in the DSM system).
Distributor information:	David Shaffer, MD, Division of Child and Adolescent Psychiatry, Columbia University/New York State Psychiatric Institute, 722 West 168th St., Unit 78, New York NY 10032
Author:	David Shaffer, MD; Madelyn Gould, PhD; Hector Bird, MD; Prudence Fisher, BA
Copyright status:	Public domain
Fees:	None
Target population(s)/symptom(s):	Children ages 4-16. Can be used in older children (up to 18) if in "childlike" setting (i.e., still going to high school, etc.).
Clinical setting:	Any clinical setting. Has also been used in community epidemiologic studies.
Primary use(s):	To classify overall severity of problems (degree of disability experienced by children because of their psychiatric symptoms)
Age group:	4-16, but see above
Domain(s):	Severity, Life functioning
Is instrument population-based or designed to measure change for individuals?	The scale has been used in numerous studies to classify overall severity of problems. It can also be used to look at change over time for an individual (it is very similar to Axis V in the DSM)
Who completes instrument?	A rating is assigned by a clinician after an interview with the child and/or after reviewing case materials
Number of items:	One. A single number (between 1 and 100) is assigned. There are 10 anchor points/descriptions to guide the clinician in making his assignment. Versions have also been developed for use by "lay interviewers" at the end of a diagnostic interview.
Administration time:	30 seconds up to 5-10 minutes, depending on familiarity with the scale
Administration options:	Paper/pencil
Computer scoring possible?	No

Are norms available?	No
If so, normed on what groups?	N/A
Reliability data:	Test-retest reliability—Intraclass correlation among clinicians is 0.83.
Validity data:	Has demonstrated good levels of concurrent validity correlating with Child Behavior Checklist Scores (Pearson r = -0.65) and Social competence scores (0.58). It has good discriminant validity with highly distinct score distinguishing referred and non referred subjects (p.<.001).
Key references:	• Shaffer et al. (1984) A Children's Global Assessment Scale (C-GAS) *Archives of General Psychiatry* 40(1):228-231. • Bird H. et al (1987) Further Measures of the Psychometric Properties of the Children's Global Assessment Scale. *Archives of General Psychiatry* 44:821-824. • Bird H. et al. (1996) Global Measures of Impairment for Epidemiologic and Clinical Use with Children and Adolescents. International *Journal of Methods in Psychiatric Research.* 6:295-307.

Clarity Health Assessment Scales™ Index Version

Developer's or distributor's description of instrument:	The Clarity Health Assessment Scales—Index Version is a questionnaire format instrument for use as a screening device to measure independently occurring components of well-being and distress. The instrument taps subjective well-being and distress on a co-equal status across the following six dimensions: (1) physical, (2) emotional, (3) mental, (4) social, (5) life satisfaction, and (6) life direction. Subjective well-being is defined as the individual's appraisal of their own status in terms of positive health functioning and life circumstances. Subjective distress is characterized as the individual's own response to conditions of symptoms, illness or disease. Respondents fill out the instrument using pen or pencil, which is then quickly hand-scored by the practitioner.
Distributor information:	Clarity Health Assessment Systems, Inc., 25 Garner Street, Norwalk CT 06854, Tel/Fax: (203) 852-8815
Author:	Barry Schlosser, PhD and Kevin L. Moreland, PhD
Copyright status:	Copyrighted, proprietary measure
Fees:	Contact Clarity for information
Target population(s)/symptom(s):	General U.S. population with a 5th to 7th grade reading level
Clinical setting:	All settings in which it is appropriate to monitor subjective health status
Primary use(s):	Screening and monitoring subjective health status
Age group:	14 years and up
Domain(s):	This instrument is used for behavioral health applications and provides screening measurement of subjective well-being and subjective distress. Domains include: Symptoms, Life Functioning, Severity and/or risk factors, and Well-being
Is instrument population-based or designed to measure change for individuals?	Population-based. This instrument can be used with individuals or for group aggregation purposes.
Who completes instrument?	Self-report
Number of items:	12
Administration time:	Approximately 5 minutes
Administration options:	[no answer]
Computer scoring possible?	[no answer]
Are norms available?	[no answer]
If so, normed on what groups?	N/A

Reliability data: Internal consistency information available to qualified users (e.g., from the generation 4.1 Adult Composite Database, the six-item well-being subscale reliability is .86 and the six-item distress subscale reliability is .76). Additional reliability information on test-retest is in preparation.

Validity data: Content and construct validity information available to qualified users. Additional validity information is in preparation.

Key references:
- Schlosser, B. (1996, Summer). New perspectives on outcomes assessment: The philosophy and application of the subjective health process model. *Psychotherapy*, Volume 33, Number 2, pp. 284-304.
- Schlosser, M.B. (1990, Spring). The assessment of subjective well-being and its relationship to the stress process. *Journal of Personality Assessment*, Volume 54, pp. 128-140.

Clarity Well-Being Scales™ Comprehensive Version

Developer's or distributor's description of instrument:
The Clarity Well Being Scales—Comprehensive Version is a questionnaire format instrument which provides detailed measures of well-being across the following six dimensions: 1) physical, 2) emotional, 3) mental, 4) social, 5) life satisfaction, and 6) life direction. A six-item component to screen for subjective distress and a fifteen-item paired comparison assessment are also included. The Clarity rationale regards the patient as a "whole person" who enters care not only with symptoms, but also with positive assets of well-being. Subjective well-being is defined as the individual's appraisal of their own status in terms of positive health functioning and life circumstances. Clinical research suggests that well-being data can accurately measure outcomes, provide decision support for therapeutic interventions and help track the course of care using growth criteria as benchmarks for treatment success.

Distributor information: Clarity Health Assessment Systems, Inc., 25 Garner Street, Norwalk CT 06854, Tel & Fax: (203) 852-8815

Author: Barry Schlosser, PhD, and Kevin L. Moreland, PhD

Copyright status: Copyrighted, proprietary measure

Fees: Contact Clarity for information

Target population(s)/symptom(s): General U.S. population with a 5th to 7th grade reading level

Clinical setting: All settings in which it is appropriate to monitor subjective health status

Primary use(s): Assessment and monitoring of subjective health status

Age group: 14 years and up

Domain(s): This instrument is used for behavioral health applications and provides measurement of subjective well-being, response style and screening measurement of subjective distress. Domains include Symptoms, Life Functioning, Severity and/or risk factors, Well-Being, and Response Portrayal

Is instrument population-based or designed to measure change for individuals? Population-based. This instrument can be used with individuals or for group aggregation purposes.

Who completes instrument? Self-report

Number of items: 112

Administration time: 20-30 minutes

Administration options: [no answer]

Computer scoring possible? [no answer]

Are norms available? [no answer]

If so, normed on what groups?	N/A
Reliability data:	Internal consistency information available to qualified users (e.g., from the generation 4.1 Adult Composite Database, the full scale reliability combining all six dimensions is .97; the six main subscale reliabilities range from .89 to .93). Additional reliability information on test-retest is in preparation.
Validity data:	Content and construct validity information available to qualified users. Additional validity information is in preparation.
Key references:	• Schlosser, B. (1996, Summer). New perspectives on outcomes assessment: The philosophy and application of the subjective health process model. *Psychotherapy*, Volume 33, Number 2, pp. 284-304. • Schlosser, M.B. (1990, Spring). The assessment of subjective well-being and its relationship to the stress process. *Journal of Personality Assessment*, Volume 54, pp. 128-140.

The Client Experience Questionnaire (CEQ)

Developer's or distributor's description of instrument:	The Client Experience Questionnaire (CEQ) is a way to evaluate client satisfaction with mental health services and the client's life satisfaction or quality of life. The CEQ is a selfc administered papercandcpencil q uestionnaire consisting of 42 questions and three scales: (1) The Satisfaction with Mental Health Services Scale (13 questions), (2) The Satisfaction with the Mental Health Program Scale (5 questions), and (3) The Quality of Life Questionnaire (QLQ) measuring the client's satisfaction with his or her living arrangements, finances, leisure, family relations, social life, health, and access to medical care (24 questions). The uses of the CEQ in client evaluations are many, including comparing clients in different treatment programs, understanding how clients respond to changes in services, and identifying differences between clients with different diagnoses. Normative data on over 2000 clients with serious mental illnesses being served in a range of mental health programs across the country are available.
Distributor information:	Jan Greenberg, PhD, University of Wisconsin, School of Social Work, 1350 University Ave., Madison WI 53706, Phone: (608) 263-4574, Fax: (608) 263-3836, E-mail: greenber@ssc.wisc.edu
Author:	James R. Greenley & Jan S. Greenberg
Copyright status:	Copyright James R. Greenley & Jan S. Greenberg
Fees:	None
Target population(s)/symptom(s):	Persons with severe and persistent mental illnesses (e.g., schizophrenia, major depression, bipolar disorder)
Clinical setting:	Inpatient and outpatient mental health settings; Community support programs
Primary use(s):	Change over time, Post-treatment follow-up
Age group:	18 years and older
Domain(s):	Client satisfaction, Quality of life
Is instrument population-based or designed to measure change for individuals?	Instrument can be used for either purpose.
Who completes instrument?	Individual with mental illness
Number of items:	42 items total
Administration time:	15 minutes
Administration options:	Paper/pencil
Computer scoring possible?	Yes
Are norms available?	Yes

If so, normed on what groups?	Persons 18 years and older with major mental illnesses (e.g., schizophrenia) who are living in the community and receiving publicly funded mental health services.
Reliability data:	Evidence for the reliability and validity of the CEQ is based on data gathered from 971 clients with serious mental illness who were receiving publicly funded community-based mental health services at the time of the study. The alpha reliability of the Satisfaction with Mental Health Services Scale is .96 and the Satisfaction with the Mental Health Program Scale is .88. The alpha reliability of the subscales of the Quality of Life Questionnaire are living arrangements (.88), finances (.88), leisure (.77), family relations (.91), social life (.89), health (.82), and access to medical care (.72).
Validity data:	A confirmatory factor analysis of the Satisfaction with Mental Health Services Scale indicated that a one factor solution provided a reasonably good fit (Standardized Root Mean Square Residual= .03; the Bentler-Bonnett Normed Fit Index= .94; Goodness of Fit Index= .91). A confirmatory factor analysis of the Satisfaction with the Mental Health Program Scale indicated an excellent fit for the hypothesized one factor structure. The results of a confirmatory factor analysis of the seven Quality of Life Questionnaires (QLQ) subscales using a random split-half procedure indicated that a seven-factor solution fit the data well (Greenberg, Greenley, & Brown, 1997). Scores on the quality of life scale also correlated significantly with the client's functioning and satisfaction with services, providing additional support for the validity of the QLQ.
Key references:	• Greenberg, J.S., Greenley, J.R., & Kim, H.W. (1995). The provision of mental health services to families of persons with severe mental illness (pp. 181-204). In J.R. Greenley (Ed.), *Research in Community and Mental Health*, Volume 8. Greenwich, CT: JAI Press. • Greenley, J.R., & Greenberg, J.S. (1997). Client experiences questionnaire: Introduction and Instructions. Mental Health Research Center, University of Wisconsin, Madison WI. • Greenley, James R., Greenberg, J. S., & Brown, R. (1997). Measuring quality of life: A new and practical survey instrument. *Social Work* 42 (3), 244-254. • Greenley, J.R., Schulz, R., Nam, S.H., & Peterson, R.W. (1985). Patient satisfaction with psychiatric inpatient care: Issues in measurement and applications (303-319). In J.R. Greenley (Ed.), *Research in Community Mental Health*, Volume 5. Greenwich CT: JAI Press.

The Client Satisfaction Questionnaire

(CSQ-8; also, CSQ-18-A and CSQ-18-B)

Developer's or distributor's description of instrument:	Since 1975, a team of investigators at the University of California, San Francisco (UCSF) has used standard scale development methods to construct measures for assessing consumer satisfaction with health and human services. The products of this research program, the CSQ scales, are direct measures of service satisfaction designed to be used with a wide range of client group and service types. The CSQ instruments are self-report questionnaires constructed to measure satisfaction with services received by individuals and families. The scales have been broadly adopted, nationally and internationally, by investigators and service program personnel who use the instruments for scientific work, evaluation research, and program planning. The most important of the early scales included the CSQ-8 and the CSQ-18 (the latter having parallel Forms A and B).
Distributor information:	Clifford Attkisson, PhD, Professor of Medical Psychology, Graduate Division, Millberry Union — 200 West, 500 Parnassus Avenue, University of California, San Francisco CA 94143-0244. Fax only: (415) 476-9690. Correspondents are asked to always provide mailing addresses, including U.S. post and electronic mail.
Author:	Clifford Attkisson, PhD and Daniel L. Larsen, PhD
Copyright status:	The Client Satisfaction Questionnaire, Copyright © 1989, 1990, 1997, Clifford Attkisson, PhD
Fees:	$250 for 500 uses ($.50 per use); $.30 per use in blocks of 100 for uses beyond 500; additional discounts and third party options for high-volume acquisitions.
Target population(s)/symptom(s):	The measures have been adopted in quality assurance, evaluation research, and services research studies across a wide range of health and human services settings, including outpatient and inpatient mental health facilities, public health center clinics, primary care health clinics, health maintenance organizations, employee assistance programs, mandatory short term alcohol abuse treatment programs, residential alcoholism treatment programs, community-based residential care, case management for the individuals with severe mental disorder, and with AIDS self-support and psycho-educational groups.
Clinical setting:	The CSQ is used in all levels of primary care, mental health care, and other human services.
Primary use(s):	Change over time, Post-treatment follow-up

Age group:	Direct reports are elicited from adolescents and adults. Parents and caretakers are often respondents about services provided to children.
Domain(s):	Client satisfaction
Is instrument population-based or designed to measure change for individuals?	While satisfaction scores have sometimes been treated as individual-level outcome measures, the usual application is to measure aggregate satisfaction levels of a group of consumers. The satisfaction scores have typically been employed as outcome performance indicators for a service organization, clinic, or system of care.
Who completes instrument?	Self-report (exclusively, except for parent or caretaker reports on services to children)
Number of items:	8 or 18 items. A longer 36-item experimental version is also available to investigators.
Administration time:	3 to 10 minutes depending on number of items used
Administration options:	Paper/pencil versions of the CSQ scales are available from Clifford Attkisson, PhD. Two options for computer assisted administration and scoring of the CSQ-8 scale are also available: (1) TELE*form*(r) for Windows(r)—English and Spanish language versions of the CSQ-8; and (2) the HCIA Response Products Division's system can be used for the English language scannable CSQ-8. Either of these computer administration/scoring options involves setup and equipment costs in addition to staff time.
Computer scoring possible?	Yes
Are norms available?	No, but see "Key References" below.
If so, normed on what groups?	Results from a variety of health and human service settings have been published.
Reliability data:	Research findings indicate that the CSQ scales are consistent and stable across a diverse range of sites, subject populations, and clinical or human service areas. Twelve published studies surveyed over 8000 subjects in the scale development and refinement phase. Several important findings emerged from the research program (Nguyen et al., 1983): 1. Internal Consistency. The CSQ-8 and the CSQ-18A and 18B have demonstrated very high levels of internal consistency as measured by Cronbach's alpha. Cronbach's alpha coefficients have ranged from .83 to .93. 2. Item-total Correlations. Moderately high item-total correlations were also reported and are consistent with the underlying single factor structure of the CSQ scales derived from factor analyses of the underlying data. These findings support the conclusion that the CSQ scales measure a global satisfaction construct. 3. Correlations among Scale Items. Inter-item correlations were only moderately high, suggesting that beyond the global satisfaction factor there is additional variance due to error of measurement and/or differential responses to item content detected by respondents.

Validity data: 1. Comparison with Other Measures and Methods. Various alternative methods were compared including: (a) ranking methodologies, and (b) indirect and direct approaches to assessing satisfaction (see, Attkisson & Pascoe, 1983). 2. Negatively Skewed Score Distributions. The CSQ scales almost always produce negatively skewed rating distributions when total raw scores or mean of item means are analyzed. Results indicate generally high satisfaction levels across sites and service types including mental health services and primary care services. These findings stimulated our interest in continuing to develop multifactorial satisfaction measures that yield bell-shaped score distributions within factorial components (Attkisson & Greenfield, 1994, 1995; Greenfield & Attkisson, 1989).

Key references:
- Attkisson, C.C., & Greenfield, T.K. (1996). The Client Satisfaction Questionnaire (CSQ) Scales. In L. L. Sederer & B. Dickey (Eds.), *Outcome assessment in clinical practice.* Baltimore, MD: Williams & Wilkins.
- Attkisson, C.C., & Greenfield, T.K. (1994). The Client Satisfaction Questionnaire-8 and the Service Satisfaction Questionnaire-30. In M.E. Maruish (Ed.), *The use of psychological testing for treatment planning and outcome assessment.* Hillsdale, NJ: Lawrence Erlbaum Associates.
- Attkisson, C.C., Greenfield, T.K., & Melendez, D. (1997). *The Client Satisfaction Questionnaire (CSQ) Scales: A history of scale development and a guide for users.* Available from: Clifford Attkisson, Ph.D.
- Attkisson, C.C., & Pascoe, G.C. (Eds.) (1983). Patient satisfaction in health and mental health services. A special issue of *Evaluation and Program Planning,* 6(3 & 4), 185-418.
- Attkisson, C.C., & Zwick, R. (1982). The Client Satisfaction Questionnaire: Psychometric properties and correlations with service utilization and psychotherapy outcome. *Evaluation and Program Planning,* 5, 233-237;

Client Satisfaction Survey (CSS)

Developer's or distributor's description of instrument: This instrument provides outpatient satisfaction measures on various quality issues. It has evolved over three years to its current form. It is self-administered and user-friendly.

Distributor information: Dr. Chris E. Stout, Forest Health System, Inc., 555 Wilson Lane, Des Plaines IL 60016, Phone: (847) 635-4100 ext. 580

Author: Dr. Chris E. Stout
Copyright status: Copyrighted
Fees: $100 annual license
Target population(s)/symptom(s): Outpatient psychiatric, All diagnoses
Clinical setting: Outpatient, Psychiatric
Primary use(s): Screening of quality/satisfaction
Age group: 12 years and up
Domain(s): Client satisfaction
Is instrument population-based or designed to measure change for individuals? N/A
Who completes instrument? Self-report
Number of items: 15
Administration time: 10 minutes
Administration options: Paper/pencil
Computer scoring possible? No
Are norms available? No
If so, normed on what groups? N/A
Reliability data: N/A
Validity data: N/A
Key references:
- Stout, C.E. (1996). Practical Clinical Management Tools for Practice Enhancement. In C. Stout, G. Theis, and J. Omer (Eds.) *The Complete Guide to Managed Behavioral Healthcare.* New York: John Wiley & Sons.

The Clinical Rating Scales (CRS)

Developer's or distributor's description of instrument:	The Clinical Rating Scales (CRS) is a therapist-completed instrument that provides a comprehensive biopsychosocial assessment of the patient's clinical status at any time in the course of care. It can be used with a broad patient population as a screening, assessment, and outcome tool. Adolescents through seniors are appropriate as are the range of clinical care services. It is easily completed (3 minutes) after the therapist has assessed the client. A computer software program exists for entering data, scoring this information, and generating an automated report. Any two reports can also be compared in a graphic format. Individual profiles as well as aggregate reports can be produced. Data can stay online so that care management and quality assurance activities can be easily performed.
Distributor information:	William J. Filstead, PhD, Performance-Based Outcomes, Inc., 5215 Old Orchard Road, Suite 700, Skokie IL 60077-1045; Phone: (847) 779-8550; Fax: (847) 965-0000; E-mail: pbo@mcs.com OR wsf@home.com; Web: www.consultnews.com
Author:	William J. Filstead, PhD
Copyright status:	Copyrighted
Fees:	There is an organizational user fee that, in part, is charged on volume
Target population(s)/symptom(s):	Behavioral health care patients; General medical patients
Clinical setting:	Full range of levels of care- can also be used in ER settings as well as phone crisis or hot lines.
Primary use(s):	Screening, Change over time, Post-treatment follow-up (There is a companion follow-up interview that covers the same items as the CRS).
Age group:	Adolescent thru senior citizens
Domain(s):	Symptoms, Life functioning, Behavioral problems, Family enviroment, Severity and/or risk factors, Other: Suggest plan of treatment/recommended seniors
Is instrument population-based or designed to measure change for individuals?	Individual changes over time; however, aggregate comparisons can be made across settings, diagnostic group, other clinical indicators, etc.
Who completes instrument?	Clinician (this is one of its strengths since it standardizes the psychosocial assessment process)
Number of items:	There are six sections: (1) symptoms covering four domains: physical functioning, role performance, interpersonal functioning, psychological signs (symptoms); (2) primary problem; (3)

	motivation; (4) global pathology; (5) functioning; (6) suggested services
Administration time:	This instrument is not administered. The therapist completes it after having seen the client and performing a psychosocial assessment. The CRS only takes a few minutes to complete.
Administration options:	Paper/pencil (hand scoring, plotting of data), Computer scoring, Fax-back service (form faxed to us, we score and produce report, and we fax the report back).
Computer scoring possible?	Software is available for automatic scoring; a report is produced along with a graph that plots impairment scores; faxed reports are produced.
Are norms available?	Yes
If so, normed on what groups?	Comparable program types (e.g., CMHC, inpatient psychiatric facilities, outpatient programs)
Reliability data:	Scale alpha coefficients: .70—.90; Inter-rater reliability: .77; Inter-rater agreement with other measures: .64 Brief Psychiatric Rating Scale, .71 Global Assessment
Validity data:	Concurrent validity with the CRS and the Brief Psychiatric Rating Scale: .75 and with the Global Assessment Scale: .59
Key references:	• Evaluation Review: *Journal of Applied Social Research.* Vol 6, No 2, pp 559-576, 1982.

Clinician Problem Scale (CPS-R), Clinician Functioning Scale (CFI)

Developer's or distributor's description of instrument:	These scales are designed to measure a full range of symptoms and role functioning in a full spectrum of behavioral health populations. They are specifically designed to assess change over time from a consumer perspective. They are coordinated with clinician rating scales. Subscales include depression, anxiety, substance abuse and impulsivity, cognitive difficulties, positive affect, psychotic symptoms, eating disorders, obsessive compulsive symptoms, somatic symptoms, major role, social role, and daily living.
Distributor information:	BHOS Inc., 689 Mamaroneck Avenue, Mamaroneck NY 10543; (800) 494-BHOS (2467)
Author:	William H. Berman, PhD and Stephen W. Hurt, PhD
Copyright status:	Copyrighted
Fees:	No per-use charge. $75 scale use registration fee for each scale. Additional fees for software applications
Target population(s)/symptom(s):	All
Clinical setting:	Inpatient, Outpatient, Day treatment
Primary use(s):	Screening, Change over time
Age group:	Adolescent, Adult, Geriatric
Domain(s):	Symptoms, Life functioning, Behavioral problems
Is instrument population-based or designed to measure change for individuals?	Both
Who completes instrument?	Clinician
Number of items:	CPS—30, CFI—14
Administration time:	5-10 minutes
Administration options:	Paper/pencil (which can be scanned or faxed into scoring software), Point of View palm-top box, Interactive voice response
Computer scoring possible?	Yes
Are norms available?	Yes
If so, normed on what groups?	Inpatients, Outpatients
Reliability data:	CPS subscale reliabilities range from 0.63 to 0.92; CFI ranges from 0.80 to 0.87.
Validity data:	Subscale convergent validity ranges from 0.44 to 0.81 with various scales.
Key references:	• Berman WH, Hurt SW, Bobadilla WV (1998). *Standardized clinician-related measures of symptoms and role function*. Symposium presented at the Society for Personality Assessment Annual Convention, Boston MA.

The Columbia Impairment Scale (CIS)

Developer's or distributor's description of instrument:	The CIS is a 13-item scale that can be administered by lay interviewers or clinicians to provide a global measure of impairment. The 13 items tap four major areas of functioning: interpersonal relations, broad psychopathological domains, functioning in job or schoolwork and use of leisure time. Items are scored on a spectrum ranging from 0 (no problem) to 4 (a very big problem) and a total score consisting of the additive sum of item scores is generated. A score of 16 or greater is suggested to discriminate between those who are definitely impaired and others. The parent administered instrument has better psychometric properties than the version administered directly to youth.
Distributor information:	Hector R. Bird, MD, N.Y. State Psychiatric Institute, (Unit 78), 722 West 168th Street, New York NY 10032
Author:	Hector R. Bird, MD, David Shaffer, MD, Prudence Fisher, MA
Copyright status:	Public domain
Fees:	NA
Target population(s)/symptom(s):	As a global measure of impairment for epidemiologic and clinical use
Clinical setting:	Can be used clinically as well as in community subjects
Primary use(s):	Diagnosis, Screening, Change over time
Age group:	Has been more thoroughly tested on subjects aged 9-17 years but is probably useful down to age 6 yrs.
Domain(s):	Life functioning, Behavioral problems, Other (Interpersonal relationships, use of leisure time, school/work functioning, overall problems with behavior at home and school, and with feelings).
Is instrument population-based or designed to measure change for individuals?	Both
Who completes instrument?	Self-report of youth or of parent about the youth. Parent and youth versions available
Number of items:	Thirteen (13)
Administration time:	2-3 minutes
Administration options:	Paper/pencil, computer
Computer scoring possible?	Yes
Are norms available?	No
If so, normed on what groups?	N/A
Reliability data:	Parent version: Internal consistency 0.89 (n=182), Internal consistency 0.82 (n=1,285), Test-retest intraclass correlation 0.89 (n=182) Youth version: Internal consistency 0.78 (n=182), Internal consistency 0.78 (n=1,285), Test-retest intraclass correlation 0.63 (n=182)

Validity data:	Correlation with a clinician's C-GAS Score Parent version: Pearson's r=-0.63, Youth version: Pearson's r=-0.50, Canonical correlation with other indicators of dysfunction (s.a. social competence, total symptom counts, mental health service use, school suspensions or expulsions, contact with the police, school performance) Parent version: Canonical correlation =0.70, Youth version: Canonical correlation =0.65
Population sample(s) on which measure tested:	Tested twice during the NIMH-MECA Study which initially involved a pilot study of both clinical and community subjects and subsequently included representative samples of four communities (Atlanta, New Haven, Westchester County in New York, and Metropolitan San Juan, Puerto Rico). Used in Spanish and English and the Spanish translation is also available.
Key references:	• Bird, H., Shaffer, D., Fisher, P., et al. (1993) The Columbia Impairment Scale (CIS): Pilot findings on a measure of global impairment for children and adolescents. *International Journal of Methods in Psychiatric Research* 3:167-176. • Bird, H., Andrews, H., Schwab-Stone, et al. (1996) Global measures of impairment for epidemiologic and clinical use with children and adolescents. *International Journal of Methods in Psychiatric Research* 6:295-307.

Compass® Treatment Assessment System:

Compass OP—Outpatient; Compass INT—Inpatient and partial hospital; Compass CD—Chemical Dependency

Developer's or distributor's description of instrument:	Compass® emerged in 1993 as the leading scientifically validated concurrent outcomes measurement system. Compass was developed to objectively measure the effectiveness of care during treatment. Concurrent measurement is the key; it allows the therapist, patient, and case manager to track the effectiveness of therapy, and to intervene if treatment veers off course. Compass provides feedback on the individual patient, provider, site and system-level to evaluate the effectiveness of care. Recent technological developments allow for flexibility in administration, including web-based, PC workstation and hand held devices in addition to traditional paper and pencil scannable forms. The Compass Suite of tools allows for a longitudinal record of patient progress across the continuum of behavioral health care.
Distributor information:	Integra, Inc., 1060 First Avenue, Suite 400, King of Prussia PA 19406
Author:	Kenneth I. Howard, PhD; Grant R. Grissom, PhD; Peter L. Brill, MD; Len Sperry, MD, PhD
Copyright status:	Proprietary system owned by Integra. Compass PC is owned by Bristol Myers Squibb.
Fees:	$1.00/administration. Project fee structure and subscription-based pricing also available
Target population(s)/symptom(s):	Adult mental health/ substance abuse patients
Clinical setting:	Compass OP—Outpatient; Compass INT—In-patient and partial hospital programs; Compass CD—Chemical dependency; Index Of Special Services (ISS)—Chemical dependency
Primary use(s):	Screening, Change over time, Post-treatment follow-up
Age group:	18-65
Domain(s):	Symptoms, Life functioning, Client satisfaction, Behavioral problems, Severity and/or risk factors, Subjective well-being
Is instrument population-based or designed to measure change for individuals?	Measures change for individuals
Who completes instrument?	Consumer and clinician
Number of items:	Varies with instrument: 16-96
Administration time:	15-20 minutes
Administration options:	Paper/pencil, PC workstation, Hand held POV, CD ROM, Web Based (Jan. 1999)
Computer scoring possible?	Yes

Are norms available?	Yes
If so, normed on what groups?	Adult patients within various levels of care
Reliability data:	Reliability of Compass subscale and full scale scores are generally good to excellent; both internal consistency and test-retest reliabilities have been published. Contact Integra for articles regarding the psychometric properties of Compass.
Validity data:	Compass validation techniques include "known groups" (patient vs. non-patient samples), construct validity, face validity and criterion validation against some of the most widely used mental health measures (e.g. BSI, SF-36, Beck Depression Inventory, Basis-32). Contact Integra for articles regarding the psychometric properties of Compass.
Key references:	• Brill, P. L. and Sperry, L. (1997). Using treatment outcomes information in clinical practice. *Psychiatric Annals*, 27:2, 124-126. • Grissom, G. R. (1997). Treatment outcomes in inpatient and substance abuse programs. *Psychiatric Annals*, 27:2, 113-118. • Grissom, G. R., Howard, K. I., Malcolm, D. J., & Brill, P. L. (1993). Integra's Compass® System: Developmental history and usefulness. Radnor, PA: Integra, Inc. • Kopta, S. M., Howard, K. I., Lowry, J. L., & Beutler, L. E. (1994). Patterns of symptomatic recovery in psychotherapy. *Journal of Consulting and Clinical Psychology*, 62, 1009-1016. • Howard, K. I., Martinovich, Z. & Black, M. (1997). Outpatient outcomes. *Psychiatric Annals*, 27:2, 108-112. • Howard, K. I., Moras, K., Brill, P. L., Martinovich, Z., & Lutz, W. (1996). Evaluation of psychotherapy: Efficacy, effectiveness, and patient progress. *American Psychologist*, 51, 1059-1064. • Howard, K. I., Brill, P. L., Lueger, R. J., O'Mahoney, M. T., & Grissom, G. R. (1992). Integra outpatient tracking assessment: Psychometric properties. Radnor, PA: Integra, Inc. • Howard, K. I., Kopta, S. M., Krause, M. S., & Orlinsky, D. E. (1986). The dose-effect relationship in psychotherapy. *American Psychologist*, 41, 159-164. • Howard, K. I., Lueger, R., Maling, M., & Martinovich, Z. (1993). A phase model of psychotherapy: Causal mediation of outcome. *Journal of Consulting and Clinical Psychology*, 61, 678-685. • Sperry, L., Brill, P. L., Howard, K. I., and Grissom, G. R. (1996). *Treatment Outcomes in Psychotherapy and Psychiatric Interventions*. New York: Brunner/Mazel.

Consumer Satisfaction Index (CSI)

Developer's or distributor's description of instrument:	The CSI is designed to measure behavioral health consumers' experience in treatment, across three domains: 1) system satisfaction-dissatisfaction with access, availability, responsiveness and cost; 2) treatment bond—satisfaction with the relationship with the provider; and 3) therapy alliance—satisfaction with goals, objectives, procedures, and process of care.
Distributor information:	BHOS Inc., 689 Mamaroneck Avenue, Mamaroneck NY 10543; (800) 494-BHOS (2467)
Author:	William H. Berman, PhD and Stephen W. Hurt, PhD
Copyright status:	Copyrighted
Fees:	No per-use charge. $75 scale use registration fee. Additional fees for software applications
Target population(s)/symptom(s):	All
Clinical setting:	Inpatient, Outpatient, Day treatment
Primary use(s):	Post-treatment follow-up
Age group:	Adolescent, Adult, Geriatric
Domain(s):	Client satisfaction
Is instrument population-based or designed to measure change for individuals?	Population-based
Who completes instrument?	Self-report
Number of items:	Short-form: 16, Long-form: 26
Administration time:	3 minutes
Administration options:	Paper/pencil (which can be scanned or faxed into scoring software), Point of View palm-top box, Interactive voice response
Computer scoring possible?	Yes
Are norms available?	Yes
If so, normed on what groups?	Outpatient psychiatric, Inpatient psychiatric
Reliability data:	Based on the 23 item scale, subscale reliability ranges from .63 to .95 and overall scale reliability is .95.
Validity data:	[no answer]
Key references:	• Berman WH, Hurt SW, McHenry S (1998). *Measuring satisfaction and treatment alliance: The Consumer Satisfaction Inventory*. Symposium presented at the Society for Personality Assessment Annual Convention, Boston MA.

The Depression Outcomes Module (DOM)

Developer's or distributor's description of instrument:	The primary goal of the Depression Outcomes Module (DOM) is to assess the patient characteristics, the processes of care, and outcomes of care for major depressive disorder (MDD). The DOM is designed to be used in routine clinical care settings as part of an Outcomes Management System for continuous quality improvement efforts such as the JCAHO's ORYX initiative. The DOM measures: (1) prognostic characteristics or casemix variables, including psychiatric and medical comorbidity, family history of depression or alcoholism, previous psychiatric hospitalizations and sociodemographic characteristics; (2) treatment for current depressive episode, including current psychotropic medication, psychotherapy, and location of treatment; and (3) outcomes of care, including severity of depressive symptoms, episode remission, suicidality, and bed days. The DOM identifies patients with MDD by determining whether the individual being assessed has a diagnosis of MDD as defined by DSM-IV criteria and assesses their symptom severity and functioning over time.
Distributor information:	Center for Outcomes Research and Effectiveness (CORE), Annette Marchitto, 5800 W. 10th Street, Suite 605, Little Rock AR 72204
Author:	G. Richard Smith, MD, Audrey Burnam, PhD, Barbara J. Burns, PhD, Paul Cleary, PhD, and Kathryn Rost, PhD
Copyright status:	The modules are copyrighted to the University of Arkansas for Medical Sciences (UAMS); however the modules are available for unlimited reproduction and distribution by the public for non-profit, educational or research purposes.
Fees:	The modules are available for a one time charge of thirty-five dollars ($35) per module or two modules for fifty dollars ($50).
Target population(s)/symptom(s):	Persons 18 years of age or older who are diagnosed with major depressive disorder
Clinical setting:	In addition to outpatient/inpatient/partial hospitalization environments, the modules can be utilized in day treatment and managed behavioral health care networks/health plans.
Primary use(s):	Diagnosis, Screening, Change over time, Post-treatment follow-up
Age group:	18 years of age or older
Domain(s):	Symptoms, Life functioning, Client satisfaction, Behavioral problems, Family environment, Severity and/or risk factors

Is instrument population-based or designed to measure change for individuals?	Data can be analyzed as an aggregate or on individual clients, providers, or sites.
Who completes instrument?	Self-report, clinician
Number of items:	Clinician Baseline Assessment—20 items, Optional Patient Screener—3 items, Patient Baseline Assessment—80 items, Patient Follow-up Assessment—83 items, Medical Record Review—11 items
Administration time:	Patient baseline assessment and follow-up assessments are self-administered and each require 25 minutes to complete. The medical record review requires 10 minutes.
Administration options:	Paper/pencil. Web site to be available for use by Fall 1998.
Computer scoring possible?	Computer web site/ scoring will be available by Fall 1998.
Are norms available?	No
If so, normed on what groups?	N/A
Reliability and validity data:	The diagnostic component of the DOM has been designed to provide the highest possible sensitivity and specificity when compared to the Depression Section of the Structured Clinical Interview for DSM-III-R (SCID). Early versions of the module achieved a 100 percent sensitivity with a specificity of 77.8 percent at baseline assessment in a specialty care population. In specialty care patients, test-retest reliability for severity of depression symptoms measured 1 week apart had a correlation co-efficient of $r=0.87$ ($p < 0.0001$). The two-item measure of suicidality was somewhat less reliable at retest ($r=0.56$). Internal consistency for the depression severity scale was high (alpha coefficient of 0.87). Two research assistants achieved 100 percent concordance for interrater reliability on the Medical Record Review. Depression severity correlated with clinician ratings of depression using the Hamilton-D ($r=0.41$, $p<0.01$), the number of depression symptoms on the SCID ($r=0.60$, $p<0.01$), and the number of depression symptoms on the Diagnostic Interview Schedule (DIS) interview ($r=0.56$, $p<0.01$). Changes in depression symptoms correlated strongly with three general measures of health: change in bed days ($r=0.56$, $p<0.005$), change in social functioning ($r=-0.52$, $p<0.01$), and change in emotional functioning ($r=-0.47$, $p<0.01$). One study comparing patients with and without pharmacotherapy treatment demonstrated a tendency for greater improvement in patients receiving pharmacotherapy.
Key references:	• Rost K, Smith GR, Burnam MA, Burns BJ. Measuring the outcomes of care for mental health problems: the case of depressive disorders. *Medical Care* 1992;30:MS266- MS273. • Rost K, Burnam MA, Smith GR. Development of screeners for depressive disorders and substance disorder history. *Medical Care* 31(3): 189-200, 1993

Derogatis Psychiatric Rating Scale™ (DPRS)

Developer's or distributor's description of instrument:
The Derogatis Psychiatric Rating Scale (DPRS) test, formerly known as the Hopkins Psychiatric Rating Scale, is a multidimensional psychiatric rating scale. The DPRS enables the clinician to rate his/her observations of a patient's psychological symptomatic distress on the same nine primary dimensional scales as measured by the SCL-90-R and BSI tests. It can be used alone for patients who are unable or unwilling to complete a self-report test or can be used in conjunction with the SCL-90-R and BSI tests to validate patient-reported results. The DPRS test can be scored via hand scoring or computer system software. At intake, the tests can reflect the severity-of-illness and establish a baseline for progress evaluation. During treatment, the test quantifies the effect of care on changes in symptom severity and supports decisions about continuing, changing, or terminating treatment. At discharge, the test assesses readiness for discharge based upon changes measured in symptom severity. It also establishes pre- and post-treatment comparisons for evaluation of outcomes and provider profiling. At follow-up, the test can measure the maintenance effect of care in evaluation of outcomes, medical cost offset, and provider profiling.

Distributor information:
The DPRS test is exclusively published and distributed by NCS Assessments, 5605 Green Circle Drive, Minnetonka MN 55343. It can be ordered by mail, by fax at (800) 632-9011, or by calling Customer Service at (800) 627-7271, ext. 5151

Author: Leonard R. Derogatis, PhD

Copyright status:
The "Derogatis Psychiatric Rating Scale" is a trademark and "DPRS" is a registered trademark of the test's author, Leonard R. Derogatis, PhD. Copyrighted © 1974, 1978

Fees: Per use and site licenses available. Call or write for current catalog.

Target population(s)/symptom(s):
The DPRS test measures the same nine primary symptom dimensions as the SCL-90-R and the BSI self-report tests: somatization, obsessive-compulsive, interpersonal sensitivity, depression, anxiety, hostility, phobic anxiety, paranoid ideation, and psychoticism. It also provides for rating on eight additional scales that are not amenable to self-report: sleep disturbance, psychomotor retardation, hysterical behavior, abjection-disinterest, conceptual dysfunction, disorientation, excitement, and euphoria. The DPRS also provides a Global Pathology Index

(GPI) for an overall rating of patient's current level of functioning.

Clinical setting:	[no answer]
Primary use(s):	Screening, Change over time, and post-treatment follow-up. Aggregating of data for continuous quality improvement
Age group:	Adolescents and adults
Domain(s):	Symptoms, Severity
Is instrument population-based or designed to measure change for individuals?	Measures change over time for an individual, but can be aggregated for groups
Who completes instrument?	Clinician rating form
Number of items:	17 scales and 1 global index
Administration time:	2-5 minutes
Reliability data:	[no answer]
Validity data:	[no answer]
Population sample(s) on which measure tested:	[no answer]
Administration options:	Hand score
Computer scoring possible?	Through site license only
Are norms available?	Yes
If so, normed on what groups?	See SCL-90-R norms
Key references:	[no answer]

Devereux Rating Scale—School Form (DSF)

Developer's or distributor's description of instrument:	The content of the DSF is derived from the federal definition of "Serious Emotional Disturbance." A Total Scale Score and four scale scores (Interpersonal Problems, Inappropriate Behaviors and Feelings, Depression, Physical Symptoms and Fears) are provided. The DSF utilizes a dual criterion of statistically reliable and clinically meaningful change to operationally define five treatment outcomes ranging from optimal to negative. These individual outcomes can then be aggregated for program evaluation and CQI/QA purposes.
Distributor information:	The Psychological Corporation, 555 Academic Court, San Antonio TX 78204, Key Contact: Paul LeBuffe, Devereux Institute of Clinical Training & Research, 444 Devereux Drive, PO Box 638, Villanova PA 19085, Phone: (610) 542-3057, Fax: (610) 542-3132
Author:	Jack A. Naglieri, Paul A. LeBuffe and Steven I. Pfeiffer
Copyright status:	Copyrighted
Fees:	Per use: manual—$50.00, 25 record forms—$22.50
Target population(s)/symptom(s):	Children and adolescents with emotional/behavioral disorders
Clinical setting:	[no answer]
Primary use(s):	Diagnosis, Outcome evaluation, Special education eligibility
Age group:	5-12 Child age level, 13-18 Adolescent age level
Domain(s):	Symptoms, Behavioral problems, Severity and/or risk factors
Is instrument population-based or designed to measure change for individuals?	Can be used at both individual and group level
Who completes instrument?	Parents or teachers
Number of items:	40
Administration time:	5 minutes
Administration options:	Paper/pencil
Computer scoring possible?	No
Are norms available?	Yes
If so, normed on what groups?	Children and adolescents from regular school classroom
Reliability data:	Total scale alpha reliability: .95; Test-retest reliability for 24 hour period: .75
Validity data:	6 criterion validity studies reported in manual. Mean predictive validity was 78 percent.
Key references:	• Nagliari, J.A., Bardos, A.N. & LeBuffe, P.A. (1995). Discriminant validity of the Devereux Behavior Rating Scale—School form for students with serious emotional disturbance. *School Psychology Review*, 24, 104-111. • Naglieri, J.A. &

Gottling, S.H. (1995). Use of the Teacher Report Form and the Devereux Behavior Rating Scale—School form with learning disabled/emotionally disordered students. *Journal of Clinical Child Psychology, 24,* 71-76.

Devereux Scales of Mental Disorders (DSMD)

Developer's or distributor's description of instrument:	The content of the DSMD is derived primarily from the DSM-IV. Results include total score, three Composite scores (Internalizing, Externalizing and Critical Pathology) and six scale scores (Conduct, Attention/Delinquency, Anxiety, Depression, Autism, Acute Problems). The DSMD was designed to measure outcomes in child and adolescent behavioral health care programs. Utilizing a dual criterion of statistically reliable and clinically meaningful change, the DSMD operationally defines five treatment outcomes ranging from optimal to negative. These individual outcomes can then be aggregated for program evaluation and CQI/QA purpose. A computerized scoring and interpretation program is available.
Distributor information:	The Psychological Corporation, 555 Academic Court, San Antonio TX 78204, Key Contact: Paul LeBuffe, Devereux Institute of Clinical Training & Research, 444 Devereux Drive, PO Box 638, Villanova PA 19085, Phone: (610) 542-3057, Fax: (610) 542-3132
Author:	Jack A. Naglieri, Paul A. LeBuffe and Steven I. Pfeiffer
Copyright status:	Copyrighted
Fees:	Per use: Manual—$50.00, 25 recorded forms—$40.00. Computer scoring and interpretation programs—$190.00
Target population(s)/symptom(s):	Children and adolescents (ages 5-18) with psychiatric disorder
Clinical setting:	[no answer]
Primary use(s):	Diagnosis, Treatment planning, Outcome evaluation
Age group:	5-12 Child age level, 13-18 Adolescent age level
Domain(s):	Symptoms, Severity and/or risk factors
Is instrument population-based or designed to measure change for individuals?	Can be used at both the individual and group level
Who completes instrument?	Parent and teacher
Number of items:	110
Administration time:	15 minutes
Administration options:	Paper/pencil
Computer scoring possible?	Yes. Scoring and interpretation.
Are norms available?	Yes
If so, normed on what groups?	Normative sample of 3,153 non-identified children and adolescents
Reliability data:	Total Scale alpha reliability: .97; Median scale alpha reliability: .89; Total scale test-retest reliability over a 24 hour interval: .76 for mental health staff and .90 for teachers

Validity data: Six criterion validity studies are reported in the manual. The mean predictive validity in these studies was 76 percent.

Key references:
- LeBuffe, P.A. & Pfeiffer, S.I. (1996). Measuring outcomes in residential treatment with the Devereux Scales of Mental Disorders. *Residential Treatment for Children and Youth*, 13, 83-91.

Direct Observation Form and Profile For Ages 5-14 (DOF)

Developer's or distributor's description of instrument:	The DOF is designed to score observations over 10-minute periods in classrooms and group activities. Has 96 problem items scored on 4-step rating scales. Provides for scoring on-task behavior at 1-minute intervals. The observer writes a narrative description of the child's behavior as it occurs over a 10-minute period and then rates problems observed during that period. Hand-scored and computer-scored profiles enable users to compare an observed target child with two observed control children for on-task, Internalizing, Externalizing, and total problems averaged for up to six observation sessions. The computer-scored profiles also include six syndrome scales derived from observations of 212 problem children aged 5-14. (The six syndrome scales are not scorable on hand-scored profiles.) Normed on 287 children observed as classroom controls for problem children. The CBCL/4-18 Manual reports DOF scale scores for referred and control children.
Distributor information:	Child Behavior Checklist, University Medical Education Assoc., 1 South Prospect Street, Burlington VT 05401-3456, Fax: (802) 656-2602
Author:	Thomas M. Achenbach, PhD
Copyright status:	Copyrighted
Fees:	Direct Observation Form for ages 5-14, completed by observer: 25 for $10. Profiles for hand-scoring of DOF (same for both sexes, no template needed): 25 for $10. Computer program for scoring of DOF, IBM Compatible 3.5": $135
Target population(s)/symptom(s):	Children aged 5-14 as seen by observers in classrooms and other group settings
Clinical setting:	Schools, Special education, Day treatment, Residential treatment settings
Primary use(s):	Assessment, Screening, Treatment planning, Change over time, Post-treatment follow-up
Age group:	5-14 years
Domain(s):	Symptoms, Life functioning, Behavioral problems
Is instrument population-based or designed to measure change for individuals?	Both
Who completes instrument?	Observer
Number of items:	97
Administration time:	10 minutes
Administration options:	Paper/pencil

Computer scoring possible?	Yes
Are norms available?	Yes
If so, normed on what groups?	Randomly selected children in 45 schools in Vermont, Nebraska and Oregon
Reliability and Validity data:	For DOF reliability and validity data, see McConaughy et al, *Journal of Abnormal Child Psychology.* 1988; 16:485-509.
Key references:	• Achenbach TM (1991). *Manual for the Child Behavior Checklist/4-18 and 1991 profile.* Burlington VT: University of Vermont Department of Psychiatry.

Family Empowerment Scale

Developer's or distributor's description of instrument:	The family empowerment scale is designed to assess empowerment in parents and other family caregivers whose children have emotional or behavioral disabilities. A 34-item, self-administered instrument, the FES provides three scores: empowerment within the family; empowerment with respect to obtaining services for one's own child; and empowerment with respect to advocacy on behalf of children with emotional disabilities. It has been used in exploratory and evaluation research.
Distributor information:	Research and Training Center on Family Support and Children's Mental Health, Attention: Denise Schmit, Portland State University, P.O. Box 751, Portland OR 97207-0751, Phone: (503) 725-4040. Technical questions key contact: Paul Koren, PhD, Phone: (503) 725-4162
Author:	Paul E. Koren, Neal DeChillo, Barbara J. Friesen
Copyright status:	Copyrighted (1992)
Fees:	No fees charged
Target population(s)/symptom(s):	Parents/family members/caregivers of children and youth with emotional and/or behavioral disabilities
Clinical setting:	"Outpatient" service settings
Primary use(s):	Change over time, Post-treatment follow-up
Age group:	Adults
Domain(s):	Family member/caregiver empowerment at conceptual levels of family, service system and community/political empowerment
Is instrument population-based or designed to measure change for individuals?	Measures change over time for individuals
Who completes instrument?	Self-report
Number of items:	34 items; 3 subscales
Administration time:	10 minutes or less
Administration options:	Paper/pencil
Computer scoring possible?	No
Are norms available?	No
If so, normed on what groups?	N/A
Reliability data:	Internal consistency: alpha coefficients .87 to .88 per scale. Test-retest: correlations .77 to .85 per scale.
Validity data:	Congruency with self-report behavioral indicators of empowerment
Key references:	• Koren, P.E., DeChillo, N., Friesen, B.J. (1992). Measuring empowerment in families whose children have emotional disabilities: A brief questionnaire. *Rehabilitation Psychology*.

37(4): 305-321. • See also: Singh, N.N., Curtis, W.J., Ellis, C.R., Nicholson, M.W., Villani, T.M., and Wechsler, H.A. (1995). Psychometric analysis of the family empowerment scale. *Journal of Emotional and Behavioral Disorders*, 3(2), 85-91.

Friedman Belief Scale

Developer's or distributor's description of instrument:	The Friedman Belief Scale has 20 positive (enhancing) and 20 negative (limiting) beliefs or cognitions and a comprehensive Research Bulletin with norms, reliability and validity data and correlations with over 100 other scales. The Friedman Belief Scale is easy to administer, score and interpret. It can easily be used to track changes over time in a clinical or research context in addition to its use as a powerful, clinical tool for change.
Distributor information:	Foundation for Well-Being, P.O. Box 627, Plymouth Meeting PA. 19462, Phone: (610) 828-4674, E-mail: PhilF101@aol.com, Web: http://www.philly.digitalcity.com/friedmanphilip/
Author:	Philip H. Friedman, PhD, Executive Director, Foundation for Well-Being
Copyright status:	Copyright 1993 by Philip H. Friedman, PhD
Fees:	The comprehensive Research Bulletin plus a copy of the Friedman Belief Scale is available for purchase. The "Permission Set" allows you to duplicate up to 200 copies of the Friedman Belief Scale within one year of purchase. It can be obtained for $98 plus $8 S & H or $106.
Target population(s)/symptom(s):	The Friedman Belief Scale can be used by anyone 16 years of age and older to assess their positive and negative beliefs (cognitions).
Clinical setting:	Outpatient mental health, managed care, community mental health, prisons, college clinics, executive coaching, health care environments, holistic health care, research and some inpatient populations with functional status.
Primary use(s):	Diagnosis, Screening, Change over time, Post-treatment follow-up
Age group:	16-80
Domain(s):	Symptoms, Life functioning, Client satisfaction, Severity and/or risk factors
Is instrument population-based or designed to measure change for individuals?	It is designed to measure change for individuals.
Who completes instrument?	The individual client or patient
Number of items:	40
Administration time:	About 5 minutes
Administration options:	Currently available as paper and pencil
Computer scoring possible?	Yes
Are norms available?	Yes
If so, normed on what groups?	Clinical and normal adults

Reliability data:	The Friedman Belief Scale has a cronbach alpha reliability score of .97. The test-retest reliability is .92 at 2 weeks, .82 at 3 weeks, .82 at 4 weeks.
Validity data:	The external or convergent validity correlation, i.e the correlation among the ratings of husbands and wives or couples living together filling out the scale on one person, is .62. The Friedman Belief Scale also correlates substantially in the expected direction with over 100 clinical, personality, attitudinal, stress (including depression & anxiety), relational, marital and interpersonal scales and subscales.
Key references:	• The Professional Research Manual summarizes the results of many studies using the Friedman Belief Scale.

Friedman Quality of Life Scale

Developer's or distributor's description of instrument:	The Friedman Quality of Life Scale has 12 items that assess a person's subjective experience of the quality of life. The items assess a person's ability to adjust to changes, enjoy themselves, handle problems that come up, feel free, accept and adapt to life etc.. The Friedman Quality of Life Scale is easy to administer, score and interpret and can easily be used to track changes over time.
Distributor information:	Foundation for Well-Being, P.O. Box 627, Plymouth Meeting PA. 19462, Phone: (610) 828-4674, E-mail: PhilF101@aol.com, Web: http://www.philly.digitalcity.com/friedmanphilip/
Author:	Philip H. Friedman, Ph D, Executive Director, Foundation for Well-Being
Copyright status:	Copyright 1994 by Philip H. Friedman, PhD
Fees:	A copy of the Friedman Quality of Life Scale plus the research norms are available for purchase. The "Permission Set" allows you to duplicate up to 200 copies of the Friedman Quality of Life Scale within one year of purchase. It can be obtained for $98 plus $8 S & H or $106.
Target population(s)/symptom(s):	The Friedman Quality of Life Scale can be used by anyone 16 years of age and older to briefly assess their subjective quality of life.
Clinical setting:	Outpatient mental health, managed care, community mental health, prisons, college clinics, executive coaching, health care environments, wholistic health care, research and some inpatient populations with functional status
Primary use(s):	Diagnosis, Screening, Change over time, Post-treatment follow-up
Age group:	16-80
Domain(s):	Symptoms, Life functioning, Client satisfaction, Severity and/or risk factors
Is instrument population-based or designed to measure change for individuals?	It is designed to measure change for individuals
Who completes instrument?	The individual client or patient
Number of items:	12
Administration time:	About 2-3 minutes
Administration options:	Currently available as paper and pencil
Computer scoring possible?	Yes
Are norms available?	Yes
If so, normed on what groups?	Normal adults, Clinically distressed adults beginning psychotherapy, and College students
Reliability data:	The Friedman Belief Scale has a cronbach alpha reliability score

	of .85. The test-retest reliability is .84 at 1 week, .81 at 2 weeks, .69 at 3 weeks and .55 at 4 weeks in a clinical population.
Validity data:	The Friedman Quality of Life Scale correlates .69 in a college sample, .55 in a clinical sample and .49 in a large sample of California employees with the Friedman Well-Being Scale. The Friedman Quality of Life Scale also correlates substantially in the expected direction with over 100 other clinical, personality, attitudinal, stress (including depression & anxiety), relational, marital and interpersonal scales and subscales.
Key references:	• The Quality of Life Scale Manual summarizes the results of the studies on clinicial, college and normal adult populations using the Friedman Quality of Life Scale.

Friedman Well-Being Scale

Developer's or distributor's
description of instrument: The Friedman Well-Being Scale consists of 20 bi-polar adjectives. It can be scored for an overall measure of well-being, the Friedman Well-Being Composite, and for 5 subscales: emotional stability; self-esteem/ self-confidence; joviality; sociability and happiness. Since it consists of bi-polar opposites the scale actually measures both directions, i.e. emotional stability-instability and happiness-unhappiness. Norms exist for a clinical, college and community population.

Distributor information: Foundation for Well-Being, P.O. Box 627, Plymouth Meeting PA. 19462, Phone: (610) 828-4674, E-mail: PhilF101@aol.com, Web: **http://www.philly.digitalcity.com/friedmanphilip/**

Author: Philip H. Friedman, Ph D, Executive Director, Foundation for Well-Being

Copyright status: Copyright 1992 by Philip H. Friedman, PhD

Fees: The comprehensive Professional Manual plus a copy of the Friedman Well-Being Scale is available for purchase. The "Permission Set" allows you to duplicate up to 200 copies of the Friedman Well-Being Scale within one year of purchase. It can be obtained for $98 plus $8 S & H or $106.

Target population(s)/symptom(s): The Friedman Well-Being Scale can be used by anyone 16 years of age and older to assess their state of emotional distress and well-being.

Clinical setting: Outpatient mental health, managed care, community mental health, prisons, college clinics, executive coaching, health care environments, wholistic health care, research and some inpatient populations with functional status.

Primary use(s): Diagnosis, Screening, Change over time, Post-treatment follow-up

Age group: 16-80

Domain(s): Symptoms, Life functioning, Client satisfaction, Severity and/or risk factors

Is instrument population-based
or designed to measure
change for individuals? It is designed to measure change for individuals

Who completes instrument? The individual client or patient.

Number of items: 20

Administration time: about 3-5 minutes

Administration options: Currently available as paper and pencil although a demo computer version is available.

Computer scoring possible? Yes

Are norms available? Yes

If so, normed on what groups? Normal adults, Clinically distressed adults beginning psy-

Chapter 9: Selecting Meaningful Yardsticks

	chotherapy, and College students
Reliability data:	The Friedman Well-Being Scale has an average cronbach alpha reliability score of .94 over a number of studies. The test-retest reliability is .85 at 3 weeks, .81 at 5 weeks, .81 at 10 weeks and .81 at 13 weeks for a clincial population and .73 at 4 weeks for a college population.
Validity data:	The external or convergent validity correlation, i.e the correlation among the ratings of husbands and wives or couples living together filling out the scale on one person, is .62. The Friedman Well-Being Scale also correlates substantially in the expected direction with over 100 clinical, personality, attitudinal, stress (including depression & anxiety), relational, marital and interpersonal scales and subscales.
Key references:	• The Friedman Well-Being Scale Professional Manual summarizes the results of 13 studies on clincial, college and normal adult populations using the Friedman Well-Being Scale. • California School of Professional Psyhcology Unpublished Norms for a Study of Normal Adults using the Friedman Well-Being Scale.

Functional Assessment Rating Scale (FARS)

Developer's or distributor's description of instrument: The Functional Assessment Rating Scale—FARS (Ward, J. & Dow, M, 1996) is a way of documenting and standardizing impressions from clinical evaluations or mental status exams that assess cognitive, social, and role functioning as well as some aspects related to quality of life. Earlier versions of the instrument were adapted from the Colorado Client Assessment Record (Ellis, Wackwitz & Foster, 1991). As a clinical tool, the FARS scales help identify and document (e.g. for charting or treatment plan development) an individual's current (within past three weeks) level of functioning. As a program management or outcomes monitoring tool, aggregated data can be used to (1) identify characteristics of people served; (2) develop risk adjusted norms to compare outcomes between programs, services, agencies, geographic areas, etc.; and (3) identify benchmark programs. It is currently in use in Wyoming (computerized version) and Florida (computerized version and scannable paper form) to monitor outcomes of state supported behavioral healthcare services.

Distributor information: The scannable paper form of the FARS is available from Psychological Assessment Resources (PAR) in Tampa, Florida at a cost of 20 to 25 cents per form (including shipping) depending upon order size. (Telephone 1-800-331-8378). Non-scannable versions of the scale are in the public domain. User's Manuals (clinical manuals and software manuals) and Computerized software for the Florida and/or Wyoming versions of the FARS are available free of charge on the internet at: http://outcomes.fmhi.usf.edu and http://outcomes.fmhi.usf.edu/wyoming.htm.

Author: John C. Ward, Jr., PhD, Associate Professor and Associate Chair, and Michael G. Dow, PhD, Professor and Research Director, Department of Community Mental Health, Louis de la Parte Florida Mental Health Institute University of South Florida, 13301 Bruce B. Downs, Blvd., Tampa FL 33612

Copyright status: The scales are copyrighted by the University of South Florida, the Florida Department of Children and Families and the authors. Computerized versions of the instrument may not be reproduced without permission of the authors and PAR. Non-scannable versions of the FARS are in the public domain.

Fees: Scannable forms printed by Psychological Assessment Resources (PAR) are available (see above) at 20 to 25 cents per

	form (depending on order size). There is no charge for use of non scannable versions. These are available from the authors or via the internet address listed above.
Target population(s)/symptom(s):	The FARS was developed for use in evaluating and monitoring progress and outcomes for individuals or aggregated groups of people recieving adult mental health and or substance abuse services.
Clinical setting:	The FARS was developed for use accross the full range of services within a continuity of care mental health or substance abuse service delivery system.
Primary use(s):	Diagnosis, Screening, Change over time, Post-treatment follow-up
Age group:	Adults, 18 years of age and older (a Children's Functional Assessment Rating Scale—CFARS, is available for evaluating children and adolescents).
Domain(s):	Symptoms, Life functioning, Behavioral problems, Family environment, Severity and/or risk factors
Is instrument population-based or designed to measure change for individuals?	The FARS was developed and evaluated for use in measuring change in individuals as well as use in population based program, service and state level outcome monitoring.
Who completes instrument?	The FARS was developed and evaluated for reliability and validity using clinicians ranging from Bachelor's level to Doctoral level as raters.
Number of items:	The FARS includes 18 problem severity rating areas of cognitive, social and role functioning. Brief (optional) checklist items are available within each area of functioning that allow the rater to document positive or negative symptoms or assets related to that specific domain. The usual areas of biographic and demographic identifiers are included (e.g., date of birth, gender, etc.) as well as some quality of life measures (e.g., income in past thirty days, days worked in last 30 days, days "in community" in last thirty days, etc.). A place to list diagnosis, purpose of evaluation (e.g. admission, discharge, etc.), level(s) or type(s) of care recieved, and rater identification are also included.
Administration time:	Five to fifteen minutes to complete form (depending on learning curve) after completion of interview. Although the FARS is not intended to be a structured interview, a brief interview format is also available from the authors.
Administration options:	Available in scannable forms, non-scannable forms, and computerized software. The computerized software allows the clinician or agency to print copies of individual evaluations or "histories" of an individuals evaluations to include in paper records. The software also includes menu options to create quality assurance and/or outcome monitoring reports on aggregated groups of individuals (e.g., program, service, agency, state level, etc.).
Computer scoring possible?	Yes
Are norms available?	Yes

If so, normed on what groups?	Adult Mental Health and Substance Abuse service recipients
Reliability data:	Acceptable ranges of interrater reliability have been demonstrated for use in both substance abuse and mental health services. Further information on reliability studies are available in the FARS User's Manual at http://outcomes.fmhi.usf.edu .
Validity data:	Evidence supporting face validity and construct validity is available in the FARS User's Manual at **http://outcomes.fmhi.usf.edu**. The FARS has been used extensively accross all levels of care in both Mental Health and Substance abuse services in Florida.
Key references:	A comprehensive research article on the FARS is in process. Additional information on development, evaluation and use of the instrument is available on the internet at: **http://outcomes.fmhi.usf.edu**.

Gambling Treatment Outcome Monitoring System (GAMTOMS)

Includes six instruments: Client Intake Questionnaire; Client Discharge Questionnaire; Client Follow-up Questionnaire; Staff Discharge Form; Significant Other Intake Questionnaire; and a Significant Other Follow-up Questionnaire

Developer's or distributor's description of instrument:	The Gambling Treatment Outcome Monitoring System is a multidimensional assessment method designed to evaluate the effectiveness of gambling treatment. The specific aims of the system are to describe the demographic and clinical characteristics of clients seeking treatment; measure the effectiveness of treatment; measure the level of client satisfaction with specific treatment components and the program in general; andidentify variables that predict treatment completion, posttreatment service participation, and outcome. Multidimensional assessments are administered at intake, discharge and follow-up. Variables assessed include client demographics, clinical and treatment history, gambling behaviors, gambling frequency, gambling problem severity, financial problems, legal problems, problem recognition, substance use frequency, psychosocial problems, treatment component helpfulness, client satisfaction, service utilization, discharge information, and posttreatment service utilization.
Distributor information:	Randy Stinchfield, PhD, 689 Fairmount Avenue, St. Paul MN 55105, Phone: (651) 224-4152, E-mail: Randy.D.Stinchfield-1@tc.umn.edu, Web: www.cbc.med.umn.edu/~randy/gambling
Author:	Randy Stinchfield, PhD and Ken Winters, PhD
Copyright status:	Not copyrighted at this time
Fees:	None
Target population(s)/symptom(s):	Clients admitted to treatment for pathological gambling
Clinical setting:	Gambling treatment programs and individual mental health practitioners providing treatment for pathological gambling
Primary use(s):	Diagnosis, Screening, Change over time, Post-treatment follow-up
Age group:	18-70+
Domain(s):	Symptoms, Life functioning, Client satisfaction, Behavioral problems, Family environment, Severity and/or risk factors, Gambling frequency, gambling problem severity, financial and legal problems related to gambling

Is instrument population-based or designed to measure change for individuals?	Designed to measure change for individuals
Who completes instrument?	The client completes the Client Intake Questionnaire, Client Discharge Questionnaire, and the Client Follow-up Questionnaire. The treatment staff completes the Staff Discharge Form, and the client's significant other completes the Significant Other Intake Questionnaire and the Significant Other Follow-up Questionnaire.
Number of items:	Client Intake Questionnaire: 91 items; Client Discharge Questionnaire: 63 items; Client Follow-up Questionnaire: 95 items; Staff Discharge Form: 12 items; Significant Other Intake Questionnaire: 38 items; Significant Other Follow-up Questionnaire: 44 items
Administration time:	Client Intake Questionnaire (45 minutes); Client Discharge Questionnaire (30 minutes); Client Follow-up Questionnaire (45 minutes); Staff Discharge Form (20 minutes); Significant Other Intake Questionnaire (20 minutes); Significant Other Follow-up Questionnaire (20 minutes)
Administration options:	Paper and pencil
Computer scoring possible?	No
Are norms available?	No
If so, normed on what groups?	[no answer]
Reliability data:	Reliability of specific scales within the GAMTOMS includes the following: *Coefficient Alpha*—South Oaks Gambling Screen (SOGS)=.85; DSM-IV Diagnostic Criteria=.89; Financial Problems=.78; Problem Recognition=.89; Recovery Orientation=.84; Psychosocial Problems=.90; Client Satisfaction=.84
Validity data:	Two types of validity are reported for two of the subscales within the GAMTOMS (SOGS and DSM-IV diagnostic criteria for pathological gambling): First, convergent validity for the South Oaks Gambling Screen (SOGS) was examined by measuring correlations between the SOGS and other measures of gambling problem severity. *Convergent Validity of the SOGS*: DSM-IV diagnostic criteria =.83; Gambling frequency =.49; Number of games played =.33; Recognition of a gambling problem =.65; Gambling-related debt =.49; Psychosocial problems =.57; Largest amount of money spent gambling in one day =.35; Number of days absent from work due to gambling =.44; Number of financial problems =.54. *Discriminant Validity of the SOGS* was examined by measuring correlations between the SOGS and variables that should not be related to gambling problem severity, such as client demographic variables: Age =.00; Gender =.12 ; Education =.11. *Convergent validity for the DSM-IV Diagnostic Criteria for Pathological Gambling* was examined by measuring correlations between the criteria and other measures of gambling problem severity: SOGS =.83; Gambling frequency =.43; Number of games played =.17; Recognition of a gambling problem =.78; Gambling-related debt =.41; Psychosocial problems =.62;

Largest amount of money spent gambling in one day =.41; Number of days absent from work due to gambling =.35; Number of financial problems =.40. *Discriminant Validity of the DSM-IV* was examined by measuring correlations between the DSM-IV and variables that should not be related to gambling problem severity, such as client demographic variables: Age =.02; Gender =.15; Education =.14.

Key references:
• Stinchfield, R., & Winters, K. (1996). *Effectiveness of Six State-Supported Compulsive Gambling Treatment Programs in Minnesota*. St. Paul: Minnesota Department of Human Services. • Stinchfield, R. & Winters, K. C. (1998). Client characteristics and predictors of attrition in Gambling Treatment. Manuscript submitted for publication. • Stinchfield, R. & Winters, K. C. (1998). Client outcomes of Minnesota's Gambling Treatment Demonstration Programs. Manuscript submitted for publication. • Stinchfield, R. (1998). Reliability, validity, and classification accuracy of the South Oaks Gambling Screen (SOGS). Manuscript submitted for publication. • Stinchfield, R. (1998). Reliability and validity of the DSM-IV diagnostic criteria for Pathological Gambling. Manuscript submitted for publication.

Global Assessment of Functioning (GAF) Scale

Distributor information:	Saeed Aminzadeh, Senior Director, Sales, HCIA-Response, 950 Winter Street, Waltham MA 02154, Phone: (781) 768-1805
Author:	Robert Spitzer
Copyright status:	Copyrighted
Fees:	None
Target population(s)/symptom(s):	Psychiatric patients
Clinical setting:	Admission to inpatient or outpatient facility
Primary use(s):	To assess patients at the time of admission to a mental health facility, as a part of a DSM-IV multiaxial assessment.
Age group:	18+
Domain(s):	Overall psychosocial health/sickness
Is instrument population-based or designed to measure change for individuals?	Individual
Who completes instrument?	Clinician
Number of items:	[no answer]
Administration time:	Only a few minutes, at most, after obtaining necessary information
Administration options:	Scanning, manual entry
Computer scoring possible?	Yes
Are norms available?	Yes
If so, normed on what groups?	Many groups. Please contact HCIA-Response.
Reliability data:	Intraclass correlation was .61 to .91, test retest was .62 to .82.
Validity data:	[no answer]
Key references:	• American Psychiatric Association. *Diagnostic and statistical manual of mental disorders.* 4th edition. Washington, DC: American Psychiatric Association, 1994. • Jones, SH, Thornicroft, G, et al A brief mental health outcome scale: reliability and validity. *British Journal of Psychology* 1995; 166:654-659

Revised Hamilton Rating Scale For Depression (RHRSD)

Developer's or distributor's description of instrument:	The RHRSD was developed in a medical setting and used concurrently with antidepressant medication to evaluate treatment response. The RHRSD contains both a self-report version and a WPS Auto Score Form which helps in ease of administration and efficiency. The test's new items help confirm diagnoses of depression by addressing DSM-IV's new criterion C for Major Depressive Episode.
Distributor information:	Western Psychological Services, 12031 Wilshire Blvd., Los Angeles CA 90025-1215, Phone: (800) 648-8857
Author:	W. L. Warren, PhD
Copyright status:	Copyrighted
Fees:	Kit, including 20 administrations: $72; Additional package of 25 forms: $32.50
Target population(s)/symptom(s):	Adult clinical populations
Clinical setting:	Outpatient, Inpatient, Partial hospitalization, Other
Primary use(s):	Screening, Change over time
Age group:	Adults
Domain(s):	Symptoms, Severity and/or risk factors
Is instrument population-based or designed to measure change for individuals?	Individuals
Who completes instrument?	Self-report and Clinician
Number of items:	76 items
Administration time:	5-10 minutes
Administration options:	Paper/pencil, Computer (disk)
Computer scoring possible?	Yes, via disk
Are norms available?	Yess
If so, normed on what groups?	See manual
Reliability data:	See manual
Validity data:	See manual
Key references:	See manual

Impact of Life Scale™

Developer's or distributor's description of instrument:	The Impact of Life Scale is a questionnaire format instrument which measures key life areas in which stress or pressure is felt, as opposed to the measurement of specific life events. The rationale is that in addition to a person's reaction to a specific event or events, the effects of such events can be characterized within thematic areas. The intent of the instrument is to portray these categories of experience on a subjective basis. Respondents fill out the instrument using pen or pencil, which is then hand-scored by the practitioner. The Impact of Life Scale is currently in its third iteration and contains items based upon clinical observation, research, and evaluation. Additional information about this instrument, including summary data, is available to qualified users.
Distributor information:	Clarity Health Assessment Systems, Inc., 25 Garner Street, Norwalk CT 06854, Tel/Fax: (203) 852-8815
Author:	Barry Schlosser, PhD
Copyright status:	Copyrighted, proprietary measure
Fees:	Contact Clarity for information
Target population(s)/symptom(s):	General U.S. population with a 5th to 7th grade reading level
Clinical setting:	All settings in which it is appropriate to monitor subjective stress status
Primary use(s):	Assessment of subjective stress in key thematic areas
Age group:	14 years and up
Domain(s):	This instrument is used for behavioral health applications and provides measurement of an individual's experience of stress and pressure. Domains include Symptoms, Life Functioning, Family environment, Severity and/or risk factors, and Stresses/Pressures.
Is instrument population-based or designed to measure change for individuals?	Population-based. This instrument can be used with individuals or for group aggregation purposes.
Who completes instrument?	Self-report
Number of items:	33
Administration time:	Approximately 10 minutes
Administration options:	[no answer]
Computer scoring possible?	[no answer]
Are norms available?	[no answer]
If so, normed on what groups?	N/A
Reliability data:	Internal consistency information available to qualified users (e.g., from the generation 4.1 Adult Composite database, the reliability is .93 for items 1-17; note: items 18-33 are present-

Chapter 9: Selecting Meaningful Yardsticks

ly "research" items added to enhance the scope of the prior version of this instrument).

Validity data: Content and construct validity information available to qualified users. Additional validity information is in preparation.

Key references:
• Schlosser, B. (1996, Summer). New perspectives on outcomes assessment: The philosophy and application of the subjective health process model. *Psychotherapy*, Volume 33, Number 2, pp. 284-304.

Managed Care Satisfaction Survey (MCO-SS)

Developer's or distributor's description of instrument:	This instrument provides managed care satisfaction measures on various quality issues. It has evolved over two years to its current form. It is self-administered and user-friendly.
Distributor information:	Dr. Chris E. Stout, Forest Health System, Inc., 555 Wilson Lane, Des Plaines IL, Phone: (847) 635-4100, ext. 580
Author:	Dr. Chris E. Stout
Copyright status:	Copyrighted
Fees:	$100 annual license
Target population(s)/symptom(s):	Managed care/utilization review/PPOs
Clinical setting:	Any managed care contracted treatment venue
Primary use(s):	Screening of quality/satisfaction
Age group:	N/A
Domain(s):	Client satisfaction
Is instrument population-based or designed to measure change for individuals?	N/A
Who completes instrument?	Self-report
Number of items:	24
Administration time:	10 minutes
Administration options:	Paper/pencil
Computer scoring possible?	No
Are norms available?	No
If so, normed on what groups?	N/A
Reliability data:	N/A
Validity data:	N/A
Key references:	• Stout, C.E. (1996). Practical Clinical Management Tools for Practic Enhancement. In C. Stout, G. Theis, and J. Omer (Eds.) *The Complete Guide to Managed Behavioral Healthcare.* New York: John Wiley & Sons.

Menninger Revision of Role Functioning Scale

Developer's or distributor's description of instrument: The instrument is designed to assess role functioning in four areas: Working/Productivity; Independent Living/Self-Care; Immediate Social Network Relationships; and Extended Social Network Relationships, primarily by means of a post-discharge follow-up interview. It can also be rated from an admission interview which includes the areas of functioning of the scale. Our revision has been used in several outcome studies at the Menninger Clinic.

Distributor information: Lolafaye Coyne, PhD, Director, Statistical Laboratory, Menninger, Box 829, Topeka KS 66601, Phone: (913) 350-5357

Author: [no answer]
Copyright status: Public domain
Fees: [no answer]
Target population(s)/symptom(s): Severely mentally ill
Clinical setting: [no answer]
Primary use(s): Change over time, Post-treatment follow-up
Age group: Adult
Domain(s): Life Functioning
Is instrument population-based or designed to measure change for individuals? Designed to measure change over time for individuals
Who completes instrument? Neutral clinical interviewer
Number of items: Four scales (not items) plus a summary scale
Administration time: The instrument is rated on the basis of a clinical interview with the patient which covers other areas in addition to role functioning. Altogether it takes three-fourths of an hour to one hour.
Administration options: [no answer]
Computer scoring possible? [no answer]
Are norms available? [no answer]
If so, normed on what groups? N/A
Reliability data: [no answer]
Validity data: [no answer]
Key references: [no answer]

Millon Adolescent Clinical Inventory™ (MACI™)

Developer's or distributor's description of instrument:	The MACI is a brief, self-report inventory that helps to assess an adolescent's personality along with expressed concerns and clinical syndromes. The test has a strong clinical focus, with the normative sample consisting of adolescents in various clinical treatment settings.
Distributor information:	Assessments Division of NCS, P.O. Box 1416, Minneapolis MN 55440, Phone: (800) 627-7271
Author:	Theodore Millon, PhD, DSc
Copyright status:	Copyrighted
Fees:	Varies with administration method
Target population(s)/symptom(s):	Adolescents in outpatient, inpatient, correctional, or residential treatment centers
Clinical setting:	Mental health and guidance professionals
Primary use(s):	Diagnosis, Screening
Age group:	13-19 years old
Domain(s):	Symptoms, Drinking styles
Is instrument population-based or designed to measure change for individuals?	Population
Who completes instrument?	Self-report
Number of items:	160 true/false
Administration time:	30 minutes
Administration options:	Paper/pencil, Audiocassette, and Computer
Computer scoring possible?	Mail-in service or on-site computer scoring via the MICROTEST Q assessment system software is available.
Are norms available?	Yes
If so, normed on what groups?	10,000 adolescents involved in inpatient or outpatient assessment or residential treatment programs.
Reliability data:	Internal consistency was measured via alpha coefficients, which ranged from .73 to .91 in the development sample. Test-retest reliability ranged from .57 to .92 for a sample of 47 adolescents with a test interval of 3-7 days.
Validity data:	Scales scores were validated using clinician judgments and collateral test instruments. Appendix F in the manual lists correlations between the MACI™ and the Beck Depression Inventory, Beck Hopelessness Scale, Beck Anxiety Inventory, Eating Disorder Inventory-2, and the Problem Orientation Screening Instrument for Teenagers. A bibliography of publications is also available upon request.
Key references:	• MACI™ Test Manual; bibliography of publications available upon request.

Millon Adolescent Personality Inventory (MAPI)

Developer's or distributor's description of instrument:	The MAPI is a brief, self-report inventory designed specifically for assessing adolescent personality characteristics, coping styles, expressed concerns and behavioral patterns. The MAPI was normed on both normal and adolescent patients.
Distributor information:	Assessments Division of NCS, P.O. Box 1416, Minneapolis MN 55440, Phone: (800) 627-7271
Author:	Theodore Millon, PhD, DSc
Copyright status:	Copyrighted
Fees:	Yes, varies
Target population(s)/symptom(s):	Adolescents in clinical, correctional and educational settings
Clinical setting:	Mental health and guidance professionals
Primary use(s):	Diagnosis, Screening, Treatment planning
Age group:	13-18
Domain(s):	Symptoms, Behavioral problems, Expressed concerns, Personality styles
Is instrument population-based or designed to measure change for individuals?	Population
Who completes instrument?	Self-report
Number of items:	150 True/False
Administration time:	20-30 minutes
Administration options:	Paper/pencil, Audiocassette, or Computer
Computer scoring possible?	Yes. Mail-in or on-site computer scoring is available (MICROTEST Q™).
Are norms available?	Yes
If so, normed on what groups?	430 adolescents involved in inpatient or outpatient psychological assessment or psychotherapy, plus 2,157 normal adolescents attending public or parochial junior and senior high schools.
Reliability data:	Internal consistency ranges from .67 to .84. Test-retest ranged between .53 to .82 for a sample of 105 adolescents with a test interval of 5 months.
Validity data:	MAPI Test Manual reports correlation data with 16PF, California Personality Inventory and Edwards Personal Preference Schedule. A bibliography is available upon request.
Key references:	• MAPI Test Manual. Bibliography available.

Millon Clinical Multiaxial Inventory III (MCMI)

Developer's or distributor's description of instrument:	The MCMI-III is a self-report instrument designed to assess DSM-IV related personality disorders and clinical syndromes. The instrument is based on the theories of Theodore Millon, PhD, DSc.
Distributor information:	Assessments Division of NCS, P.O. Box 1416, Minneapolis MN 55440, Phone: (800) 627-7271
Author:	Theodore Millon, PhD, DSc
Copyright status:	Copyrighted
Fees:	Yes, depends on method
Target population(s)/symptom(s):	Adults in IP/OP Therapy, Adults suspected of having personality disorder
Clinical setting:	Mental health and counseling settings
Primary use(s):	Diagnosis, Screening, Treatment planning
Age group:	18+ years
Domain(s):	Symptoms, Behavioral problems, Personality pattern, Severe personality pathology, Clinical syndromes, Severe syndromes
Is instrument population-based or designed to measure change for individuals?	Population-based
Who completes instrument?	Self-report
Number of items:	175 true/false
Administration time:	25 minutes
Administration options:	Paper/pencil, Audiocassette and Computer
Computer scoring possible?	Mail-in service or on-site computer scoring via Microtest Q(tm) available.
Are norms available?	Yes
If so, normed on what groups?	1,000 males and females representing a variety of diagnoses. These patients were from independent practice, clinics, mental health centers, residential treatment settings, and hospitals.
Reliability data:	Internal consistency ranges from .66 to .90. Alphas exceed .80 for 20 of the scales. Test-retest reliability ranged between .82 and .96 for a sample of 86 subjects with 5-14 days between tests.
Validity data:	Extensive bibliography available.
Key references:	• MCMI-III Test Manual (2nd edition). Bibliography available.

MOS-HIV Questionnaire

Developer's or distributor's description of instrument:	A population-specific health status questionnaire for those infected with the HIV virus or those with AIDS. Based on the SF 36 health survey.
Distributor information:	Medical Outcomes Trust, 8 Park Plaza, #503, Boston MA 02116, Phone: (617) 426-4046, Fax: (617) 426-4131, E-mail: MOTrust@worldnet.att.net
Author:	Albert W. Wu, MD, MPh
Copyright status:	(c) 1993 The Johns Hopkins University
Fees:	Distributed Royalty Free
Target population(s)/symptom(s):	HIV positive/AIDS populations, all symptoms associated with AIDS
Clinical setting:	[no answer]
Primary use(s):	Screening, Change over time, Post-treatment follow-up
Age group:	Adult
Domain(s):	Symptoms, Life functioning, Severity and/or risk factors
Is instrument population-based or designed to measure change for individuals?	[no answer]
Who completes instrument?	Self-report or Clinician
Number of items:	35
Administration time:	4-6 minutes
Reliability data:	[no answer]
Validity data:	[no answer]
Key references:	[no answer]

Multnomah Community Ability Scale

Developer's or distributor's description of instrument:	The Multnomah Community Ability Scale (MCAS) is a 17-item instrument, organized into four sub-scales, that efficiently measures the functioning level of adults with a severe and persistent mental illness (SPMI) who live in the community. The MCAS is designed to be completed by a case manager or other staff who work closely with the SPMI population. The instrument can be completed in 10 minutes and is supported by field-tested training materials, including a User's Manual and video. The authors and a research team are currently piloting related instruments, including a consumer self-report version, and an enhanced level-of-care assessment version.
Distributor Information:	Sela Barker, Network Behavioral HealthCare, Inc., 5415 S.E. Milwaukee Ave., Suite 3, Portland, OR. 97202, Phone: (503)238-0769 X24, E-mail: sela@nbhc.org
Author:	Sela Barker, LCSW and Nancy Barron, PhD
Copyright status:	Public domain. Future and enhanced versions will be copyrighted
Fees:	None. Training package available for $45 plus shipping, which includes User's Manual, training video, single-sheet version of the MCAS, and copies of 2 articles about the MCAS.
Target population(s)/symptoms(s):	Functioning of adults with severe and persistent mental illness, who reside in the community.
Clinical setting:	Programs that treat individuals with severe and persistent mental illness
Primary uses(s):	Change over time, Treatment Planning, Level of Care placement
Age group:	Adults, 18 and above
Domain(s):	Symptoms, Life functioning, Behavioral problems, Severity and/or risk factors, Social competence
Is instrument population-based or designed to measure change for individuals?:	Both
Who completes the instrument?	Primary clinician
Number of items:	17, organized in 4 sub-sections: Interference with Functioning, Adjustment to Living, Social Competence, and Behavioral Problems
Administration time:	10 minutes
Administration options:	Currently paper and pencil
Computer scoring possible?	Yes, when computer version complete
Are norms available?	Yes
If so, normed on what groups?:	Adults from urban and rural settings across the state of Oregon. Norms are organized by age and gender, by total score and by sub-scales.

Reliability data:	Inter-rater reliability of total score= .85; Test-retest reliability of total score + .83
Validity data:	Global rating as co-variate, MCAS total score = correlation of -0.78 (p less than .0001) Individual item and criterion variable comparison (age, hospital utilization, and outpatient utilization) shows high correlations, in expected patterns. Factor analysis shows that the scale's items formed 4 factors, consistent with the 4 sub-scales.
Key references:	Barker, S., Barron, N., McFarland, B.H., Bigelow, D.A. : A Community Ability Scale for Chronically Mentally Ill Consumers: Part I. Reliability and Validity, *Community Mental Health Journal*, Vol. 30, No. 4, August 1994.• Barker, S., Barron, N., McFarland, B.H., Bigelow, D.A., Carnahan, T.: A Community Ability Scale for Chronically Mentally Ill Consumers: Part II. Applications.

Neuropsychological Impairment Scale (NIS)

Developer's or distributor's description of instrument:	The NIS is a brief, self-report questionnaire which addresses both global impairment and specific symptom areas. The NIS brings up symptoms that patients often fail to mention in an informal clinical interview. Serving as an "early warning system," the NIS can identify areas for inquiry, focus treatment efforts, and help determine whether a patient will benefit from therapy. Specifically useful in assessing age- and AIDS-related dementia.
Distributor information:	Western Psychological Services, 12031 Wilshire Blvd., Los Angeles CA 90025-1215, Phone: (800) 648-8857
Author:	William E. O'Donnell, PhD, MPH; Clinton B. DeSoto, PhD; Janet L. DeSoto, EdD; Don MCQ Reynolds, PhD
Copyright status:	Copyrighted
Fees:	1 package, including 25 answer forms: $32.50; Complete Kit, including 50 administrations: $105
Target population(s)/symptom(s):	Adults with possible neuropsychological impairments
Clinical setting:	Outpatient, Inpatient, Partial hospitalization, Other
Primary use(s):	Diagnosis
Age group:	18-88 years
Domain(s):	Symptoms, Severity and/or risk factors; Subscale scores: Cognitive efficiency, Attention, Memory, Frustration tolerance, Learning-verbal, Academic skills, Critical items
Is instrument population-based or designed to measure change for individuals?	Based on norms
Who completes instrument?	Clinician
Number of items:	95 items
Administration time:	15-20 minutes
Administration options:	Paper/pencil, Computer
Computer scoring possible?	Yes—by 1999
Are norms available?	Yes
If so, normed on what groups?	(1) 1,000 nonclinical adults (aged 18-88); (2) Clinical norms drawn from 534 neuropsychiatric patients
Reliability data:	See manual
Validity data:	See manual
Key references:	See manual

Nowicki-Strickland Locus of Control Scales

Developer's or distributor's description of instrument:	The Nowicki-Strickland life span locus of control scales have been used to measure locus of control orientation in children and adults. It is easy to administer, has a low elementary school reading level and norms for literally thousands of subjects.
Distributor information:	Stephen Nowicki, PhD, Department of Psychology, Emory University, Atlanta GA 30322
Author:	Stephen Nowicki
Copyright status:	Public Domain
Fees:	$10 to cover mailing and copying
Target population(s)/symptom(s):	Scales are available for preschool through geriatric adults.
Clinical setting:	[no answer]
Primary use(s):	Diagnosis, Screening, Change over time, Post-treatment follow-up
Age group:	Three scales—child, adult, geriatric
Domain(s):	Symptoms, Life functioning, Client satisfaction, Behavioral problems, Family environment, Severity and/or risk factors
Is instrument population-based or designed to measure change for individuals?	Both
Who completes instrument?	Self-report, clinician if child is too young
Number of items:	Depends—anywhere from 26 for youngest to 40 for adults
Administration time:	5 minutes
Administration options:	[no answer]
Computer scoring possible?	[no answer]
Are norms available?	Yes
If so, normed on what groups?	Subjects from 7 years of age up
Reliability data:	Considerable—internal consistency and test-retest
Validity data:	Excellent predictive validity for personal, social and academic criteria
Key references:	• Nowicki SJ, Strickland BR (1973). *Journal of Consulting and Clinical Psychology* 40:148-155.

Ohio Youth Problems, Functioning, and Satisfaction Scales (Ohio Scales)

Distributor information:	Ohio Scales; c/o Ben Ogles, PhD; 241 Porter Hall; Ohio University; Athens OH 45701; (614) 593-1077
Author:	Ben Ogles, PhD
Copyright status:	Copyrighted
Fees:	Onetime fee per user which depends on the size of the organization and potential use (unlimited use thereafter). Fees are often waived for evaluation or research.
Target population(s)/symptom(s):	Children and adolescents with severe behavioral or emotional disorders.
Clinical setting:	Outpatient, Inpatient, Partial hospitalization, Other: Designed to track change for children and adolescents receiving a variety of mental health services with a primary focus on youth who receive services from various systems and programs.
Primary use(s):	Change over time
Age group:	5-18
Domain(s):	Symptoms, Life functioning, Client satisfaction, Behavioral problems, Other: Hopefulness
Is instrument population-based or designed to measure change for individuals?	Individuals?
Who completes instrument?	Self-report; Clinician, Case worker. There are three parallel versions (child 12-18; parent/primary caretaker; and agency worker).
Number of items:	Problems—44; Satisfaction—4; Hopefulness—4; Functioning—20; Total—72 (Note case worker does not complete satisfaction or hopefulness portions)
Administration time:	10-15 minutes
Administration options:	[no answer]
Computer scoring possible?	[no answer]
Are norms available?	[no answer]
If so, normed on what groups?	N/A
Reliability data:	Excellent internal consistency; (above .9 for functioning and problems) interrater and test-retest not currently assessed but studies are in progress.
Validity data:	Problems rated by parents correlated with the CBCL r= .89. Problems rated by youth correlated with the Youth Self report r=.82. Change over a four month time period on the agency worker rated problems and functioning scales correlated with changes on the Progress Evaluation Scales r=.47 and .38 respectively. Other studies are underway to assess construct validity.

Key references: Ogles, B. M., Lunnen, K. M., Gillespie, D. K., & Trout, S. C. (1996). Conceptualization and initial development of the Ohio Scales. In C. Liberton, K. Kutash, & R. Friedman (Eds.), *The 8th Annual Research Conference Proceedings, A System of Care for Children's Mental Health: Expanding the Research Base* (pp. 33-37). Tampa, FL: University of South Florida, Florida Mental Health Institute, Research and Training Center for Children's Mental Health.

Older Americans Resources And Services

Multidimensional Functional Assessment Questionnaire (OARS-MFAQ)

Developer's or distributor's description of instrument:	The OARS-MFAQ is a valid and reliable standardized questionnaire which, in part A, measures level of functioning in five areas (social, economic, mental health, physical health, activities of daily living). Information in each area can be summarized on unidimensional scales, and as 6-point ratings ranging from level of functioning excellent (1) to totally impaired (6). Part B is a service use and need assessment, providing information on 24 broadly encompassing, nonoverlapping, generically defined services. The OARS-MFAQ was designed to assess the impact of services on functional status. It permits clinical evaluation of individuals and assessment of populations, providing information on functional status and service need. Foreign language versions are available.
Distributor information:	Gerda G. Fillenbaum, PhD, Center for the Study of Aging and Human Development, Box 3003, Duke University Medical Center, Durham NC 27710, Fax: (919) 684-8569, E-mail: ggf@geri.duke.edu
Author:	Duke University Center for the Study of Aging and Human Development
Copyright status:	Copyrighted. For permission to use, write to: Director, Center for the Study of Aging and Human Development, Box 3003, Duke University Medical Center, Durham NC 27710
Fees:	None
Target population(s)/symptom(s):	Adult community residents, persons in institutions, clinic clients
Clinical setting:	Appropriate for any clinical setting where information on the patient's functional status is needed for assessment and/or planning.
Primary use(s):	Screening, Change over time, Post-treatment follow-up
Age group:	Adults particularly 65 years and over
Domain(s):	Life functioning, Functional status and service use
Is instrument population-based or designed to measure change for individuals?	Both
Who completes instrument?	Either self-report or clinician is feasible, but it is generally administered by a trained interviewer.
Number of items:	101 questions, several with sub-items
Administration time:	40 minutes
Administration options:	In person, Mail-in, Telephone, Paper/pencil
Computer scoring possible?	Yes

Are norms available?	Yes
If so, normed on what groups?	Community-representative sample (n = 2,146); Adult day care (random sample) (N = 119); Institutionalized (N = 100)
Reliability data:	Test-retest, average interval = 5 weeks, 90.7% of responses identical on both occasions. Inter-rater, intraclass correlation coefficient for summary scales for 11 raters and 30 questionnaires were: Social resources—.823; Economic resources—.783; Mental health—.803; Physical health—.662; Activities of daily living—.865 (all significant at p<\.001). Intra-rater, 7 raters, 12-18 month time interval, 17 questionnaires, ranged from .47-1.00. 80% of ratings were .80 or higher, only 3 were <.75. All statistically significant.
Validity data:	Content and consensual, assured by manner of development. Criterion, based on 33-49 subjects whose functional status covered the entire range. Summary ratings on: Economic resources, Mental health, Physical health, Activities of daily living compared with assessment based on an objective economic measure, evaluations made by geropsychiatrists, physicians' assistants and physical therapists. Agreement on summary score ratings (Spearman rank order correlations) were .68, .67, .82, and .89, respectively (all significant at p<.001).
Key references:	• Fillenbaum, G.G. *Multidimensional Functional Assessment of Older Adults: The Duke Older Americans Resources and Services Procedures.* Lawrence Erlbaum, Hillsdale NJ 1988. • Fillenbaum, G.G. & Smyer, M. The development, validity and reliability of the OARS Multidimensional Functional Assessment Questionnaire. *Journal of Gerontology*, 1981, 36, 428-434. • George, L.K. & Fillenbaum, G.G. The OARS methodology: A decade of experience in geriatric assessment. *Journal of the American Geriatrics Society*, 1985, 33, 607-615.

Outcome Questionnaire 45 Questions Version 2 (OQ-45.2)

Developer's or distributor's description of instrument:	The OQ-45.2 is a brief 45 item self report outcome/tracking instrument designed for repeated measurement of client progress through the course of therapy and at termination. The OQ-45.2 is the result of a unique partnership between behavioral health care administrators, practitioners, and academic researchers in response to the changing mental health arena and the accompanying demands for cost containment, quality care, reliable monitoring, and accountability for services provided. As continuous monitoring of outcome may be achieved by standardized data, Drs. Burlingame, Lambert, and Reisinger et al set out to design an instrument that would meet the needs of both providers and payers. The OQ-45.2, the product of intensive research, is an outcomes measure that meets multiple needs in today's market. Easy to score and interpret. Detailed Administration and Scoring Manual provided with each license. Windows software and fax to file versions are available for use in a variety of settings.
Distributor information:	Diana R. Maslauskas, DCSW, American Professional Credentialing Services LLC, P.O. Box 477, Wharton NJ 07885-0477, Phone: (500) 488-2727 or (410) 329-3777, E-mail: apcs@erols.com
Author:	Michael J. Lambert and Gary M. Burlingame
Copyright status:	Licensed and copyrighted
Fees:	For unlimited use by individuals, groups, fees begin at $40 for individual practitioners. Rate schedule available upon request.
Target population(s)/symptom(s):	Adults in any setting
Clinical setting:	[no answer]
Primary use(s):	Screening, Change over time, Post-treatment follow-up. Clinical QI studies
Age group:	17 and up
Domain(s):	Symptoms, Severity and/or risk factors, Subscales: Symptom Distress (SD), Interpersonal Relationships (IR), Social Role-Risk Screening (SR)
Is instrument population-based or designed to measure change for individuals?	Designed for individual but can be used for population and samples of populations
Who completes instrument?	Self-report
Number of items:	45
Administration time:	5 minutes

Administration options:	Fax back, IVR, paper/pencil
Computer scoring possible?	Yes. Multiple formats available.
Are norms available?	Yes
If so, normed on what groups?	Community (normal), EAP, Outpatient, Inpatient
Reliability data:	Test-Retest: .84; Internal Consistency: .93
Validity data:	Eleven estimates of concurrent validity reported. Comparisons range from .61 to .88.
Key references:	• Burlingame, et al. (1995) Pragmatics of Tracking Mental Health Outcomes in a Managed Care Setting. *Journal of Mental Health Administration*, Summer, 226-236. • Lambert, et al. (1996) The Reliability and Validity of the Outcome Questionnaire. *Clinical Psychology and Psychotherapy*, 3 (4) Summer, 249-258. • Lambert, et al. (1996) Data-Based Management for Tracking Outcome in Private Practice. *Clinical Psychology Science and Practice* 3, (2) Summer, 172-178. • Wells, et al. (1996) Conceptualization and Measurement of Patient Change During Psychotherapy: Development of the Outcome Questionnaire and Youth Outcome Questionnaire. *Psychotherapy*, 33, Summer, 275-283.

Panic Disorder Severity Scale

Developer's or distributor's description of instrument: The Panic Disorder Severity Scale developed by Shear and colleagues (Shear et al., 1997), is a seven-item interview designed to assess the overall severity of panic disorder severity. The interview assesses the following dimensions of panic disorder and associated symptoms: (a) frequency of panic attacks, (b) distress during panic attacks, (c) anticipatory anxiety, (d) agoraphobic fear and avoidance, (e) interoceptive fear and avoidance, (f) impairment of or interference with work functioning, and (g) impairment of or interference in social functioning.

Distributor information: [no answer]

Author: Shear, M.K., Brown, T., Sholomskas, D., Barlow, D.H., Gorman, J., Woods, S. and Cloitre, M.

Copyright status: Copyrighted 1992, Department of Psychiatry, University of Pittsburgh School of Medicine

Fees: None

Target population(s)/symptom(s): Persons with panic disorder, panic disorder symptoms

Clinical setting: The PDSS is to be used in clinical and research settings with persons for whom a diagnosis of panic disorder has been established.

Primary use(s): Change over time, Post-treatment follow-up

Age group: Designed for adults, but can also be used for adolescents

Domain(s): Symptoms, Life functioning (social and work)

Is instrument population-based or designed to measure change for individuals? Designed to measure change in individuals

Who completes instrument? An interviewer

Number of items: 7

Administration time: 10 minutes

Administration options: Interview version

Computer scoring possible? Not yet

Are norms available? For persons with panic disorder

If so, normed on what groups? Panic disorder outpatients (men and women, adults)

Reliability data: *Internal consistency*: Cronbach's alpha 0.65 (N =186 patients with Panic Disorder). *Test-retest reliability*: intraclass correlation coefficient 0.88 (n =24). *Inter-rater reliability*: 0.87 (n =24). *Inter-rater reliabiltiy for individual item*: ranged from 0.74-0.87.

Validity data: *Convergent*: Correlation with Anxiety Disorders Interview Scheduler r =.55 discriminant—article available.

Key references:
- Shear, M.K., Brown, T., Barlow, D.H., Money, R., Sholomskas, D.E., Woods, S.W., Gorman, J.M., and Papp, L.A. (1997). Multicenter collaborative Panic Disorder Severity Scale. *The American Journal of Psychiatry*, 154 (11), 1571-1575.

Panic Outcomes Module (POM)

Developer's or distributor's description of instrument:	The Panic Outcomes Module (POM) is designed to identify patients with panic disorder and to evaluate the outcomes of clinical care by measuring the types and extent of care delivered to patients, the outcomes of that care, and the patient characteristics that influence either the type or outcomes of care. The POM consists of 5 forms: the Patient Screener; Patient Baseline Assessment; Clinician Baseline Assessment; Patient Follow-up Assessment; and the Medical Record Review.
Distributor information:	University of Arkansas for Medical Science (UAMS), 4301 West Markham, Little Rock AR 72205
Author:	Kathryn Rost, PhD; G. Richard Smith, MD; Wayne Katon, MD; Jennifer Jones, PhD; Barbara Burns, PhD; Faye A. Luscombe, Dr PH; Audrey Burnam, PhD; and David Barlow, PhD
Copyright status:	Copyright © 1994 University of Arkansas for Medical Sciences, 4301 West Markham Street, Little Rock AR 72205
Fees:	The POM is protected under copyright and is available at a nominal fee for unlimited use, provided that there is no charge associated with its administration. To that end, UAMS permits unlimited reproduction and distribution of the module by the public for nonprofit, educational or research purposes. However, any commercial use, including the creation of electronic versions or other derivative works of the module for sale, constitutes a violation of the copyright of the University, unless prior authorization has been granted in writing.
Target population(s)/symptom(s):	Patients can enter the POM protocol in two ways: (1) after screening positive for panic disorder or (2) after a clinical diagnosis of panic disorder is made. If patients are illiterate or have impaired cognitive functioning, a decision will have to be made as to whether to include them.
Clinical setting:	The POM is designed for use in the general medical setting or in a health maintenance organization.
Primary use(s):	Diagnosis, Screening, Change over time, Post-treatment follow-up
Age group:	The POM can be used on all age groups.
Domain(s):	Symptoms, Life functioning, Client satisfaction, Severity and/or risk factors, Physical functioning
Is instrument population-based or designed to measure change for individuals?	The Panic Outcomes Module is both population-based and designed to measure individual change.

Who completes instrument?	The Patient Baseline and Follow-up Assessment Forms are both self-administered. The clinician completes the Clinician Baseline Assessment at the time of the baseline assessment. The Medical Record Review is completed for the patient at the same time the Patient Follow-up Assessment is completed and is done so by a staff member.
Number of items:	The POM has a total of 113 items, broken down as follows: The Patient Screener has 2 items; the Patient Baseline Assessment, 46; the Clinician Baseline Assessment, 8; the Patient Follow-up Assessment, 47; and the Medical Record Review, 10.
Administration time:	The Patient Screener takes 1 minute to complete, the Patient Baseline Assessment, 25 minutes, the Clinician Baseline Assessment, 5 minutes, the Patient Follow-up Assessment, 25 minutes, and the Medical Record Review, 15 minutes.
Administration options:	The POM is a paper/pencil instrument.
Computer scoring possible?	Currently, there is no computer scoring possible.
Are norms available?	No, not at the current time.
If so, normed on what groups?	[no answer]
Reliability and validity data:	Key constructs of the POM were divided into two domains for reliability and validity: outcomes and case-mix variables. The POM was validated in a longitudinal study of 73 patients receiving treatment in three settings for panic disorder over a 21-month period and a control sample of 24 patients who had never had a diagnosis of panic disorder, but were receiving treatment in the same setting for a different psychiatric disorder.

Intstruments used to validate the POM were: the Anxiety Disorders Interview (ADIS), the Diagnostic Interview Schedule (DIS), the Brief Symptom Inventory (BSI), the Acute Panic Inventory (API), the Agoraphobic Cognition Questionnaire (ACQ), the Body Sensations Questionnaire (BSQ), the Mobility Inventory (MI), Marks Subjective Symptom Scale (MSSS), the Sheehan Disability Scale (SDS), the Emotional Control Questionnaire (ECQ), the Marks Fear Questionnaire (MFQ), the Hamilton Anxiety Scale (HAS), the Hamilton Depression Scale (HDS) and the MS-PAS.

The patient-derived diagnosis demonstrated an unacceptable agreement with the ADIS (Kappa = 0.32), but an acceptable concordance between the clinician-derived diagnosis and the ADIS (Kappa = 0.61). The clinician-derived diagnosis has a sensitivity of 79 percent in patients with panic disorder and 92 percent specificity in the population without panic disorder.

Outcomes Measures: Internal consistency for outcomes measures was excellent: sensitivity to anxiety (Chronbach's a = 0.82); distress/avoidance (Chronbach's a = 0.86); and marital functioning (Chronbach's a = 0.89). Test-retest reliability ranging from 0.78 to 0.97 was strong for single item outcomes measures; however, sensitivity to anxiety and self-medication of alcohol and drugs showed significantly higher scores at test than at re-test. The validity of outcomes measures also had significant positive correlations with gold standard constructs. |

Case-Mix: The validity of many case-mix variables was excellent. The module measure of frequency of panic attacks correlated strongly (r = 71) with the ADIS measure of frequency. Patient self-report about current agoraphobia showed good agreement with the structured interview (k = 0.57), as did their report on lifetime depression and/or dysthymia (k = 0.55).

Prognostic Variables: The validity of prognostic variables was excellent. The POM-measured frequency of panic attacks was strongly correlated with the ADIS measure (r = 0.71). Structured interviews correlated with patient self-report on agoraphobia (k = 0.57) and lifetime alcohol and drug abuse/dependence were consistent with DIS measurements (k = 0.62, Yule's Q = 0.74, respectively).

Sensitivity to Change: Measures of change in the POM between baseline and follow-up in frequency of panic attacks, anticipatory anxiety, and avoidance/distress behaviors correlated with ADIS ratings (r = 0.47, 0.59 and 0.44, respectively).

Key references:
• Hollenberg J, Rost KM, Humphrey J, Owen RR, Smith GR: Validation of the Panic Outcomes Module. *Evaluation & The Health Professions* 1997;20(1):81-95. • Mosher LR, Keith SJ: Research on the psychosocial treatment of schizophrenia: A summary report. *American Journal of Psychiatry* 1979;136(5):1623-1631. • Odom SL, Strain PS: A comparison of peer-initiation and teacher-antecedent interventions for promoting reciprocal social interaction of autistic preschoolers. *Journal of Applied Behavioral Analysis* 1986;19:59-71. • Weissman MM, Klerman GL, Markowitz JS, Quellette R, Phi M: Suicidal ideation and suicide attempts in panic disorders and attacks. *New England Journal of Medicine* 1989;321(18):1209-1214.

Patient Satisfaction Survey—IV (PSS-IV)

Developer's or distributor's description of instrument: This instrument provides inpatient satisfaction measures on various quality issues. It has evolved over five years to its current form. It is self-administered and user-friendly.

Distributor information: Dr. Chris E. Stout, Forest Health Systems, Inc., 555 Wilson Lane, Des Plaines IL 60016, Phone: (847) 635-4100, ext. 580

Author: Dr. Chris E. Stout

Copyright status: Copyrighted, but can be used in public domain if proper citation to author noted.

Fees: $100 annual license

Target population(s)/symptom(s): Inpatient psychiatric, all diagnoses

Clinical setting: Inpatient, Psychiatric; Residential, Psychiatric

Primary use(s): Screening of quality/satisfaction

Age group: 12 years and up

Domain(s): Client satisfaction

Is instrument population-based or designed to measure change for individuals? N/A

Who completes instrument? Self-report

Number of items: 33

Administration time: 10 minutes

Administration options: Paper/pencil

Computer scoring possible? No

Are norms available? No

If so, normed on what groups? N/A

Reliability data: N/A

Validity data: N/A

Key references:
- Stout, C.E. (1996). Practical Clinical Management Tools for Practic Enhancement. In C. Stout, G. Theis, and J. Omer (EDS) *The Complete Guide to Managed Behavioral Healthcare*. New York: John Wiley & Sons.

Perceptions of Care (Inpatient And Outpatient)

Distributor information:	Saeed Aminzadeh, Senior Director, Sales, HCIA-Response, 950 Winter Street, Waltham, AM 02154, Phone: (781) 768-1805
Author:	Susan V. Eisen, PhD
Copyright status:	Public domain
Fees:	None
Target population(s)/symptom(s):	All inpatients or outpatients excluding children under 14 years old, 24 hours prior to discharge (for inpatients).
Clinical setting:	Inpatient or Outpatient (depending on version)
Primary use(s):	To evaluate patients' perceptions of the quality of interpersonal care they received during hospitalization. (Patient satisfaction tool).
Age group:	18+
Domain(s):	Professional relationship experienced with staff, quality of communication and information provided and overall experience of quality of care and services, including coordination of care after discharge
Is instrument population-based or designed to measure change for individuals?	Both
Who completes instrument?	Patient Self-Report
Number of items:	18
Administration time:	5 to 10 minutes
Administration options:	Scanning, manual entry
Computer scoring possible?	Yes
Are norms available?	For outpatient only. Inpatient norms are being developed.
If so, normed on what groups?	Many groups. Please contact HCIA-Response.
Reliability data:	[no answer]
Validity data:	[no answer]
Key references:	[no answer]

Personal Adjustment and Role Skills (PARS Scale)

Developer's or distributor's description of instrument:	The Personal Adjustment and Role Skills (PARS) Scale measures eight factor-analyzed areas of adjustment: close relations, alienation-depression, anxiety, confusion, alcohol/drug use, house activity, child relations, and employment. The scale is completed by a person close to the client.
Distributor information:	Ellsworth Krebs Associates, 3615 130th Ave, NE, Bellevue WA 98005, Phone: (425) 883-4762
Author:	Robert B. Ellsworth, PhD and Shanae L. Ellsworth, PhD
Copyright status:	Copyrighted
Fees:	$10 per 25 scales, $5 per 25 profiles
Target population(s)/symptom(s):	Adults receiving either inpatient or outpatient mental health services
Clinical setting:	It has been used in both inpatient and outpatient settings.
Primary use(s):	Change over time
Age group:	Adults
Domain(s):	Life-functioning/adjustment
Is instrument population-based or designed to measure change for individuals?	It has been used in both situations.
Who completes instrument?	Significant other
Number of items:	31 questions
Administration time:	10-15 minutes
Administration options:	Paper/pencil
Computer scoring possible?	No
Are norms available?	Yes
If so, normed on what groups?	Adults who had received inpatient or outpatient services
Reliability data:	Available]
Validity data:	Available
Key references:	• Ellsworth SL, Ellsworth RB (1998). *The PARS: Measuring personal adjustment and role skills.* Bellevue WA: Institute for Program Evaluation.

Personality Inventory for Children (PIC)

Developer's or distributor's description of instrument:	The PIC is one of the most widely used diagnostic instruments for children. The test assesses behavior, affect, and cognitive status in children 3-16 years of age. In addition to rich clinical material, it gives users a systematic way of obtaining useful intake and screening information.
Distributor information:	Western Psychological Services, 12031 Wilshire Blvd., Los Angeles CA 90025-1215, Phone: (800) 648-8857
Author:	Robert D. Wirt, PhD; David Lachar, PhD; James E. Klinedinst, PhD; Phillip D. Seat, PhD; William E. Broen, Jr., PhD
Copyright status:	Copyrighted
Fees:	Kit: $225, including 100 administrations; 100 answer sheets: $19.50
Target population(s)/symptom(s):	Children with observed personality problems
Clinical setting:	Home
Primary use(s):	Children's personality assessment
Age group:	3-16
Domain(s):	Symptoms, Behavioral problems, Family environment
Is instrument population-based or designed to measure change for individuals?	Population norms
Who completes instrument?	Mother or father
Number of items:	280 or 131
Administration time:	25-30 minutes
Administration options:	Paper/pencil, Computer (auto-score form)
Computer scoring possible?	Yes—via disk, mail-in or fax-in
Are norms available?	Yes
If so, normed on what groups?	See manual
Reliability data:	See manual
Validity data:	See manual
Key references:	See manual

The Personality Inventory for Youth (PIY)

Developer's or distributor's description of instrument:	The PIY assesses emotional and behavioral adjustment, family interaction, and academic functioning. The test is composed of 270 items covering 9 overlapping clinical scales and 24 non-overlapping clinical scales.
Distributor information:	Western Psychological Services, 12031 Wilshire Blvd., Los Angeles CA 90025-1215, Phone: (800) 648-8857
Author:	David Lachar, PhD; Christian P. Gruber, PhD
Copyright status:	Copyrighted
Fees:	Kit, including 100 administrations: $225; Answer sheet (package of 100): $18.50
Target population(s)/symptom(s):	Adolescents with personality disorders
Clinical setting:	School or home
Primary use(s):	Screening
Age group:	10-18 years
Domain(s):	Symptoms, Behavioral problems, Family environment, Severity and/or risk factors, Academic functioning
Is instrument population-based or designed to measure change for individuals?	Normed, Standardized
Who completes instrument?	Self-report
Number of items:	270 items
Administration time:	45 minutes
Administration options:	Paper/pencil, Computer (auto score)
Computer scoring possible?	Yes—via fax-in answer sheet, mail-in answer sheet or disk
Are norms available?	Yes
If so, normed on what groups?	Nationally representative sample of more than 2,300 students in grades 4 through 12
Reliability data:	See manual
Validity data:	See manual
Key references:	See manual

Personal Problem Scale (PPS) and Personal Functioning Index (PFI)

Developer's or distributor's description of instrument:	These scales are designed to measure a full range of behavioral health symptoms, problems, and role difficulties from the patient's perspective. They are designed to measure change during an episode of treatment. Subscales include depression, anxiety, impulsivity, psychosis, cognitive difficulties, major role, social role, and personal care.
Distributor information:	BHOS Inc., 689 Mamaroneck Avenue, Mamaroneck NY 10543; (800) 494-BHOS (2467)
Author:	William H. Berman, PhD and Stephen W. Hurt, PhD
Copyright status:	Copyrighted
Fees:	No per-use charge. $75 scale use registration fee for each scale. Additional fees for software applications.
Target population(s)/symptom(s):	All
Clinical setting:	Inpatient, Outpatient, Day treatment
Primary use(s):	Screening, Change over time, Post-treatment follow-up
Age group:	Adolescent, Adult, Geriatric
Domain(s):	Symptoms, Life functioning, Behavioral problems
Is instrument population-based or designed to measure change for individuals?	Both
Who completes instrument?	Patient self-report
Number of items:	PPS: 43; PFI: 14
Administration time:	3-5 minutes after experience
Administration options:	Paper/pencil (which can be scanned or faxed into scoring software), Point of View palm-top box, Interactive voice response
Computer scoring possible?	Yes
Are norms available?	Yes
If so, normed on what groups?	Psychiatric outpatient, Psychiatric inpatient, Healthy community sample
Reliability data:	PPS: subscale reliability ranges from .70 to .90; PFI: .83
Validity data:	PPS: subscale convergent validity with OQ-15 scales ranges from .52 to .85; PFI: convergent validity with SF-36 is .57
Key references:	• Hurt SW, Berman WH, Kolarz CM (1998). Self-reported symptoms and role functioning in behavioral health. Symposium presented at the Society for Personality Assessment Annual Convention, Boston MA. • Allard LP, Berman WH, Hurt SW, Greenberg J (1998). Using outcomes measures: Identifying and using risk adjusters of symptoms and role functioning. Symposium presented at the Society for Personality Assessment Annual Convention, Boston MA.

Piers-Harris Children's Self-Concept Scale (PHCSCS)

Developer's or distributor's description of instrument:	The Piers-Harris Children's Self-Concept Scale (PHCSCS) helps you evaluate the psychological health of children and adolescents, quickly identifying those who need further testing or treatment. And, unlike many other measures of self-concept, it is based on the child's own perceptions rather than the observations of parents or teacher.
Distributor information:	Publisher: Western Psychological Services, 12031 Wilshire Blvd., Los Angeles CA 90025-1251, Phone: (800) 648-8857
Author:	Ellen V. Piers, PhD and Dale B. Harris, PhD
Copyright status:	Copyrighted
Fees:	Kit (manual, 20 answer forms, 2 pre-paid computer scored answer sheets): $99.50. Components also available individually.
Target population(s)/symptom(s):	Children having emotional or behavioral difficulties
Clinical setting:	Schools and clinics
Primary use(s):	Diagnosis (in combination with other sources of information), Screening, Change over time, Post-treatment follow-up
Age group:	8-18 years
Domain(s):	Symptoms, Life functioning, Behavioral problems, Severity and/or risk factors, Physical appearance, Intellectual functioning, Popularity
Is instrument population-based or designed to measure change for individuals?	Designed to measure change over time for individuals
Who completes instrument?	Self-report
Number of items:	80
Administration time:	15 minutes
Administration options:	Paper/pencil, Computer
Computer scoring possible?	Yes—via disk, fax-in answer sheet, mail-in answer sheet
Are norms available?	Yes
If so, normed on what groups?	Updated norms for a diverse sample of 1,700 children ages 7 to 18 plus original norms
Reliability data:	Refer to manual
Validity data:	Refer to manual
Key references:	See manual

The Positive and Negative Syndrome Scale (PANSS)

Developer's or distributor's description of instrument:	The Positive and Negative Syndrome Scale (PANSS) has been specifically designed to assist in the assessment of schizophrenia. It provides a broad-based, standardized evaluation of psychopathology dimensions that helps to characterize the patient's clinical profile and to monitor changes with treatment.
Distributor information:	MHS, Inc., 908 Niagra Falls Blvd., North Tonawanda NY 14120-2060, Phone: (800) 456-3003, Fax: (416) 424-1736
Author:	Stanley R. Kay, PhD, Lewis A. Opler, MD, PhD, and Abraham Fiszbein, MD
Copyright status:	Copyright 1992 Multi-Health Systems Inc.
Fees:	PANSS complete kit (manual, 25 Quikscore forms, 25 structured clinical interview forms): $95
Target population(s)/symptom(s):	Schizophrenics
Clinical setting:	Primarily inpatient
Primary use(s):	Diagnosis, Screening, Change over time, Post-treatment follow-up
Age group:	Adults 18+
Domain(s):	Symptoms, Life functioning, Behavioral problems, Severity and/or risk factors
Is instrument population-based or designed to measure change for individuals?	Both
Who completes instrument?	Clinician
Number of items:	There are a total of 33 items: Positive Scale has 7 items; Negative Scale 7; General Psychopathology Scale 16; and Supplementary Items 3.
Administration time:	Completing the Quikscore requires 5-10 minutes, but also requires information gathering at interview, which can take 30-40 minutes.
Administration options:	Paper/pencil
Computer scoring possible?	No
Are norms available?	Yes
If so, normed on what groups?	Medicated schizophrenics
Reliability data:	Alpha coefficients ranged from .73-.83 ($p<.001$). The split-half reliability of the General Psychopathology Scale was .80 ($p<.001$). Test-retest reliability indexes for a subgroup of unremitted inpatients over a 3 to 6 month interval were .89, .82, .81 and .77 for the Positive, Negative, Composite and General Psychopathology Scales respectively.

Validity data:	The criterion-related validity of the PANSS as used for typological distinction was supported in two separate studies of 37 acute and 47 chronic schizophrenics. Significant inverse relationships between positive and negative items were obtained in both studies (r = -.62 and -.55 respectively, p<.01). The temporal stability of the PANSS has been demonstrated with a number of psychiatric samples. In a sample of 62 subacute schizophrenic patients, test-retest correlations after a 3-4 month period were r = .37 for the Positive and r = .43 for the Negative scales (Kay and Singh, 1989). Test-retest coefficients over a 3-6 month period were high in a sample of 15 chronic schizophrenic patients (Kay, Fiszbein and Opler, 1987): r = .80 (Positive), r = .68 (Negative) and r = .60 (General). In a group of 19 acute schizophrenia patients, the PANSS scales correlated r = .24 (Positive), r = -.13 (Negative) and r = -.18 (General) from baseline testing to a 2-year follow-up (Lindenmayer, Kay and Opler, 1986).
Key references:	• Kay, S.R., (1991). *Positive and Negative Syndromes in Schizophrenia: Assessment and Research.* New York: Brunner/Mazel. • Kay, S.R. (1990). Positive-negative symptom assessment in schizophrenia: Psychometric issues and scale comparison. *Psychiatric Quarterly,* 61, 163-178. • Kay, S.R., Fiszbein, A., and Opler, L.A. (1987). The Positive and Negative Syndrome Scale (PANSS) for schizophrenia. *Schizophrenia Bulletin,* 13, 261-276.

Problem Oriented Screening Instrument for Teenagers

Developer's or distributor's description of instrument:	The Problem Oriented Screening Instrument for Teenagers (POSIT) is a 139 yes/no item screening tool designed for adolescents 12-19 years to identify problems requiring an in-depth assessment and potentially a need for early intervention or treatment. The POSIT is a self-report questionnaire that assesses ten functional areas: substance use/abuse, physical health, mental health, family relationships, peer relationships, educational status (i.e., learning disabilities), vocational status, social skills, leisure/recreation, and aggressive behavior/delinquency. The POSIT is available in English and Spanish language versions, both of which come in paper-and-pencil, computerized, and audio-tape forms of administration. A POSIT Follow-up form is also available. The POSIT and POSIT Follow-up are suitable for use in hospitals, medical and mental health clinics, drug treatment programs, community service and correctional settings, school-based programs, and case management systems. And both are designed to gather case-level data for clinical decisions and/or aggregate data for needs-assessment surveys.
Distributor information:	Contact: Dr. Elizabeth Rahdert, Division of Clinical and Services Research, National Institute on Drug Abuse, Room 10A-10, 5600 Fishers Lane, Rockville MD 20857, Phone: (301) 443-0107. Or, National Clearinghouse for Alcohol and Drug Information, P.O. Box 2345, Rockville MD 20847-2345, Phone: (800) 729-6686
Author:	Elizabeth Rahdert, PhD, Editor
Copyright status:	The POSIT is in the public domain
Target population(s)/symptom(s):	Population: Adolescents (patients; clients; students; juvenile delinquents)
Clinical setting:	All medical and mental health settings; schools; juvenile court-sponsored centralized assessment centers; primary care office setting
Primary use(s):	The POSIT questionnaire is a screening instrument. The POSIT follow-up questionnaire can be used for post-treatment follow-up
Age group:	12 through 19 years
Who completes instrument?	The POSIT was designed as a self-report questionnaire, but can be administered by a clinician or by a second party who is not necessarily a clinician.
Number of items:	139 items

Administration time:	20-25 minutes
Administration options:	Paper/pencil, Computer with and without audio-assisted administration
Computer scoring possible?	Yes. For information on obtaining the computerized POSIT and POSIT Follow-up questionnaires with computerized scoring, contact PowerTrain, Inc. for software options and price list: PowerTrain, Inc., 8201 Corporate Dr., Suite 1080, Landover MD 20785. Phone: (301) 731-0900; Fax: (301) 731-0091; Web site: www.powertrain.com. Note: The POSIT questionnaire is in the public domain, and copyrighted software for administering and scoring the POSIT is available. If, however, a customer wants to write his/her own software to administer the POSIT, that is legal. They do not need to purchase or use the PowerTrain software.
Are norms available?	No
If so, normed on what groups?	N/A
Reliability and validity data:	The POSIT's test-retest reliability and internal validity have been established as have the discriminant, concurrent and predictive validity. See references.
Population sample(s) on which measure tested:	Inpatient/outpatient/residential mental and drug treatment populations and adolescent patients being seen in pediatric clinics; juvenile youths; students in public schools
Key references:	• Dembo, R. et al., Examination of the reliability of the POSIT among arrested youths entering a juvenile assessment center. *Substance Use & Misuse*, 31(7), 785-834, 1996. • McLaney, MA et al,. A validation study of the Problem Oriented Screening Instrument for Teenagers (POSIT). *Journal of Mental Health* 1994;3:363-376. • Babor, T.F. et al. Just say Y.E.S.: Matching adolescents to appropriate interventions for alcohol and other drug-related problems. *Alcohol Health & Research World* 1991;15(1):77-86. • Latimer, WW et al., Screening for drug abuse among adolescents in clinical and correctional settings using the Problem Oriented Screening Instrument for Teenagers. *American Journal of Drug and Alcohol Abuse* 1997;23(1):79-98.

Process of Care Review Form

Developer's or distributor's description of instrument:	The Process of Care Review form is a 59-item instrument divided into five sections. It was designed for use by trained abstractors to gather data from ambulatory medical records characterizing the general management of the patient, social support, medication management, psychiatric assessment and psychiatric hospitalization.
Distributor information:	Michael K. Popkin, MD, Chief of Psychiatry, Hennepin County Medical Center, 701 Park Avenue, Mail Code 844, Minneapolis MN 55415-1829, Phone: (612) 347-5764 or Allan L. Callies, Hennepin County Medical Center, 701 Park Avenue, Mail Code 84, Minneapolis MN 55415-1829, Phone: (612) 347-4054
Author:	Michael K. Popkin, MD and Allan L. Callies
Copyright status:	None
Fees:	None
Target population(s)/symptom(s):	Psychiatric outpatients, especially those with serious and persistent mental illness
Clinical setting:	Ambulatory clinics, Community mental health centers
Primary use(s):	Change over time, Post-treatment follow-up
Age group:	>18
Domain(s):	Life functioning, General management, Medication management, Social support, Medical management, and Hospitalization
Is instrument population-based or designed to measure change for individuals?	Measures change in individuals
Who completes instrument?	Trained abstractors
Number of items:	59
Administration time:	Variable. Approximately 30 minutes
Administration options:	Paper/pencil
Computer scoring possible?	Not applicable
Are norms available?	No
If so, normed on what groups?	[no answer]
Reliability data:	No formal studies performed to date
Validity data:	No formal studies performed to date
Key references:	• Popkin MK, Callies AL, Lurie N, et al. An instrument to evaluate the process of psychiatric care in ambulatory settings. *Psychiatric Services* 48:524-527, 1997.

Profile of Adaptation to Life (PAL Scale)

Developer's or distributor's description of instrument:	The purpose of the Profile of Adaptation (PAL Scale) is to provide an easy-to-use, reliable and valid scale for measuring psychosocial adjustment of adults. The PAL measures eleven factor-analyzed dimensions: negative emotions, psychological well being, income management, physical symptoms, alcohol/drug use, close relationships, relationships with children, social activity, self nurturing, personal growth, and nutrition and exercise.
Distributor information:	Ellsworth Krebs Associates, 3615 130th Ave, NE, Bellevue WA 98005, Phone: (425) 883-4762
Author:	Robert B. Ellsworth, PhD and Shanae L. Ellsworth, PhD
Copyright status:	Copyrighted
Fees:	$10 per 25 scales, $5 per 25 profiles
Target population(s)/symptom(s):	Adults, interest in assessing psychosocial adjustment
Clinical setting:	It has been used in inpatient and outpatient settings.
Primary use(s):	Change over time
Age group:	Adults
Domain(s):	Life-functioning/adjustment
Is instrument population-based or designed to measure change for individuals?	It has been used in both situations.
Who completes instrument?	Significant other
Number of items:	47 questions
Administration time:	10-15 minutes
Administration options:	Paper/pencil
Computer scoring possible?	No
Are norms available?	Yes
If so, normed on what groups?	National sample of adults representative of a broad range of age, educational and geographical characteristics
Reliability data:	Available
Validity data:	Available
Key references:	• Ellsworth SL, Ellsworth RB (1998). *The PAL: Measuring adaptation to life*. Bellevue WA: Institute for Program Evaluation.

PsychSentinel 3.0

Developer's or distributor's description of instrument:	PsychSentinel is an academic-based, behavioral health care outcome assessment system. The measure of outcome is based upon symptom reduction. Features include 13 symptom checklists, a severity of illness section which risk-adjusts the data, and a multi-site national reference database (over 14,000 cases) which provides norms for outcomes, length of stay and different levels of care. PsychSentinel can be used to reveal unrecognized problems, identify "best practices," provide data for marketing and to meet accreditation requirements.
Distributor information:	Hal Mark, PhD, University of Connecticut, School of Medicine, Department of Community Medicine, Farmington CT 06030-1910, Phone: (860) 679-3276 or (860) 679-3208
Author:	Hal Mark, PhD
Copyright status:	This is a non-proprietary system in the public domain. The forms are copy protected to insure standardization.
Fees:	There is an administrative fee, which includes scoring, data entry, analysis, and report preparation.
Target population(s)/symptom(s):	Children, adolescents, and adults in any level of behavioral health care treatment
Clinical setting:	Outpatient, inpatient, partial hospitalization, and Home Health Care
Primary use(s):	Diagnosis, Screening, Change over time, Post-treatment follow-up
Age group:	Children 6-12, adolescents 13-17, adults 18+ years old
Domain(s):	Symptoms, Life functioning, Behavioral problems, Family environment, Severity, and/or risk factors
Is instrument population-based or designed to measure change for individuals?	Both populations and individuals
Who completes instrument?	Clinician
Number of items:	There are nine severity of illness items and between 10 and 18 symptoms, depending on which symptom check list is used.
Administration time:	10 minutes
Administration options:	Paper/pencil
Computer scoring possible?	Yes
Are norms available?	Yes
If so, normed on what groups?	Sites that are using the system
Reliability data:	Interrater reliability Kappas range from .82 to .89 in studies at three sites
Validity data:	The validity of PsychSentinel is based upon the fact that the system is directly based upon DSM-IV criteria. As there are 13 diagnostically distinct symptom check lists, comparisons to

other measures which provide a single global score would be difficult to interpret.

Key references:
• Davis DF, Fong ML: Measuring outcomes in psychiatry: an inpatient model. *Joint Commission Journal on Quality Improvement* 22:125-133, 1996. • Mark H, Garet DE: Interpreting profiling data in behavioral health care for a continuous quality improvement cycle. *Joint Commission Journal on Quality Improvement*, Oct. 1997. • Roy-Byrne P, et al: A psychiatrist-rated battery of measures for assessing the clinical status of psychiatric inpatients. *Psychiatric Services* 46:347-352, 1995.

Quality of Life Inventory™ (QOLI)

Developer's or distributor's description of instrument:	Quality of Life Inventory (QOLI) test is a brief, yet comprehensive measure of life satisfaction, which reveals a respondent's satisfaction and dissatisfaction in 16 areas of life. It is useful in both the medical and mental health communities as it is non-offensive, providing a measure of positive mental health. The QOLI is often used as a screener to gather information at intake on "real world" aspects of a client's life and facilitate treatment planning. It is also used to assess a patient's progress during treatment and to measure outcomes. The overall Quality of Life score provides a single overall score for measuring the outcome of a treatment program. The QOLI test is often administered in conjunction with either the SCL-90-R or BSI test, which measures a patient's symptoms in order to determine what may be affecting his/her everyday functioning and response to treatment. When used for outcomes measurement, the QOLI test is often administered at intake, during treatment, at discharge, and for follow-up.
Distributor information:	The QOLI test is exclusively published and distributed by NCS Assessments, 5605 Green Circle Drive, Minnetonka MN 55343. It can be ordered by mail, by fax at (800) 632-901 or by calling Customer Service at (800) 627-7271, ext. 5151.
Author:	Michael B. Frisch, PhD
Copyright status:	The "QOLI" is a registered trademark of the test's author, Michael B. Frisch, PhD Copyright (c) 1988, 1994.
Fees:	Per use and site licenses available. Call or write for current catalog.
Target population(s)/symptom(s):	Measures 16 areas of life deemed potentially relevant to overall life satisfaction: health, self-esteem, goals and values, money, work, play, learning, creativity, helping, love, friends, children, relatives, home, neighborhood, and community
Clinical setting:	In clinics and hospitals for planning and evaluating medical and psychological treatment and at the conclusion of treatment. It is also used in non-health related settings such as college counseling centers and businesses with organizational development programs.
Primary use(s):	Screening, Change over time, and Post-treatment follow-up. Aggregating of data for continuous quality improvement
Age group:	Adults, 18 years and older. The test is written at a 6th grade reading level.

Domain(s):	Life functioning, quality of life
Is instrument population-based or designed to measure change for individuals?	Measures change over time for an individual, but data can be aggregated for groups.
Who completes instrument?	Self-report
Number of items:	32 items
Administration time:	5 minutes. Test can be done via paper-and pencil or on-line computer administration.
Administration options:	Paper/pencil and computer administration are available.
Computer scoring possible?	Yes
Are norms available?	Yes
If so, normed on what groups?	Normative data was drawn from a nonclinical population of 798 individuals from 12 US states. The racial and ethnic composition of the sample closely matches the 1990 US Census data and it is gender neutral. The age range was 17-80.
Reliability data:	Test-retest reliability coefficient of 0.73 over a two week interval. Internal consistency reliability was 0.79.
Validity data:	Validity data from Satisfaction With Life Scale (SWLS), Quality of Life Index and the Marlowe-Crowne Social Desirability Scale scores are presented in the QOLI manual along with information about repeated measure and treatment utility.
Key references:	• Frisch, MB 1993. The Quality of Life Inventory: A cognitive-behavioral tool for complete problem assessment, treatment planning, and outcome evaluation. *Behavior Therapist* 16:42-44. • Frisch, MB (1994b) *Manual and treatment guide for the Quality of Life Inventory (QOLI)*. Minneapolis MN: National Computer Systems. • Kazdin, AE (1993a) Evaluation in clinical practice: Clinically sensitive and systematic methods of treatment delivery, *Behavior Therapy*, 24:11-45

Quality of Life Interview

Distributor information:	Saeed Aminzadeh, Senior Director, Sales, HCIA-Response, 950 Winter Street, Waltham MA 02154, Phone (781) 768-1805
Author:	Dr. Anthony F. Lehman, University of Maryland
Copyright status:	Copyrighted
Fees:	None
Target population(s)/symptom(s):	Severely mentally ill individuals. Primarily used among schizophrenics and those with major affective disorder
Clinical setting:	Outpatient mental health settings
Primary use(s):	To assess the life circumstances of persons with severe mental illness both in terms of what they actually do and experience and life satisfaction. (Outcomes instrument; can be used to measure change over time and post treatment follow-up).
Age group:	18+
Domain(s):	Objective: Type of living situation, Types of productive activities, Number of days in productive activities, Frequency of family contacts, Frequency of social contacts, Amount of spending money, Adequacy of finances, Arrests during past month, Victim of violent crime during past month, Victim of non-violent crime during past month, and General health status. Subjective: Satisfaction with: Living situation, daily activities, family relations, social relations, finances, safety, and health.
Is instrument population-based or designed to measure change for individuals?	Both
Who completes instrument?	Patient Self-Report
Number of items:	[no answer]
Administration time:	Ten minutes
Administration options:	Scanning, manual entry
Computer scoring possible?	Yes
Are norms available?	Under development
If so, normed on what groups?	N/A
Reliability and Validity data:	Not yet been established, but this instrument has been extracted from a longer version that has had extensive validation.
Key references:	• Lehman, AF, Postrado, LT et al, Convergent Validation of Quality of Life Assessments for Persons With Severe Mental Illnesses, *Quality of Life Research*, Vol 2, 1993. • Lehman, AF, Measures of Quality of Life Among Persons With Severe and Persistent Mental Disorders, Soc Psychiatry *Psychiatr Epidemiol*, 1996, 31:78-88. • Lehman, AF, A Quality of Life Interview for the Chronically Mentally Ill, *Evaluation and Program Planning*, Vol 11, 51-62.

Quality of Well-Being Scale (QWB)

Developer's or distributor's description of instrument:	The QWB is an interviewer-administered instrument that measures well-being in individuals based on the social preferences that society generally associates with a person's level of functioning at a specific point in time. For each individual the scale averages values across three ratings of functioning: mobility, physical activity, and social activity and across one rating of symptomatic complaints that might inhibit function.
Distributor information:	Medical Outcomes Trust, 8 Park Plaza, #503, Boston MA 02116, Phone: (617) 426-4046, Fax: (617) 426-4131, E-mail: MOTrust@worldnet.att.net
Author:	John P. Anderson, PhD
Copyright status:	(c) 1991 Health Policy Project; School of Medicine, University of California, San Diego
Fees:	Distributed royalty free
Target population(s)/symptom(s):	General health questionnaire
Clinical setting:	[no answer]
Primary use(s):	Screening, Change over time, Post-treatment follow-up
Age group:	14 and up
Domain(s):	Symptoms, Life functioning, Severity and/or risk factors
Is instrument population-based or designed to measure change for individuals?	Population
Who completes instrument?	Clinician
Number of items:	132
Administration time:	25-30 minutes
Reliability data:	[no answer]
Validity data:	[no answer]
Key references:	[no answer]

Revised Behavior Problem Checklist

Developer's or distributor's description of instrument:	The RBPC is used to rate problem behaviors observed in adolescents and young children. The 6 RBPC subscales measure conduct disorder, socialized aggression, attention problems-immaturity, anxiety-withdrawal, psychotic behavior, and motor tension-excess. The RBPC has been used for a wide variety of purposes: to screen for behavior disorders in schools, as an aid in clinical diagnosis, to measure behavior change associated with psychological or pharmacological interventions, as part of battery to classify juvenile offenders, and to select subjects for research on behavior disorders in children and adolescents.
Distributor information:	PAR, Inc., P.O. Box 998, Odessa FL 33556, Phone: (800) 331-8378
Author:	Herbert C. Quay, PhD and Donald Peterson, PhD
Copyright status:	Copyrighted 1996
Fees:	RBPC intro kit (manual, 25 test booklets, and 25 profile sheets): $65.00. Package of 25 test booklets: $40.00. Package of 25 profile sheets: $12.00
Target population(s)/symptom(s):	Children & adolescents
Clinical setting:	Completed by teacher, parent or other observer
Primary use(s):	Diagnosis, Screening, Change over time, Post-treatment follow-up
Age group:	Ages 5-18
Domain(s):	Behavior problems
Is instrument population-based or designed to measure change for individuals?	Norm-based
Who completes instrument?	Clinician
Number of items:	89
Administration time:	20 minutes
Administration options:	Paper/pencil
Computer scoring possible?	No
Are norms available?	Yes
If so, normed on what groups?	Children ages 5-18
Reliability data:	[no answer]
Validity data:	[no answer]
Key references:	[no answer]

Saint Francis Academy Residential Program Follow-Up Form

Developer's or distributor's description of instrument: The Saint Francis Residential Program Follow-Up Form is an empirical and tested procedure to record the range of actual outcome performance of areas of progress and regression of former residents. A caring and apt interviewer telephones a parent at two and/or more years after each youth leaves treatment. Factors separately measured are: Family Interaction, Responsibility, Emotional Well-Being, Financial Independence, Legal Involvement, Abusiveness, and a second-order overall factor, Appropriate Adult Functioning. r. Forms and 1995 and 1996 reprints available from developer.

Distributor information: Ronald G. Force, MA, The Saint Francis Academy, P.O. Box 1340, Salina KS 67402-1340; (913) 825-0541

Author: [no answer]
Copyright status: Public domain
Fees: [no answer]
Target population(s)/symptom(s): Adolescents suffering from disruptive behavior disorder and attention deficit disorder
Clinical setting: [no answer]
Primary use(s): Post-treatment follow-up, Change over time
Age group: 14-24
Domain(s): Life functioning, Behavioral problems, Severity
Is instrument population-based or designed to measure change for individuals? Individuals
Who completes instrument? Parent
Number of items: 41
Administration time: 30 minutes
Administration options: [no answer]
Computer scoring possible? [no answer]
Are norms available? [no answer]
If so, normed on what groups? [no answer]
Reliability and validity data: Reliability and validity are above .85 r.
Key references: [no answer]

Satisfaction Survey (SS)

Developer's or distributor's description of instrument:	The Satisfaction Survey (SS) was developed as a part of a large outcomes program (University of Cincinnati, Dept. of Psychiatry, Outcomes Management Project). The SS assesses satisfaction with: clinician (MD and Psychotherapist separately), medication and psychotherapy effectiveness, reception staff, and billing processes as well as general satisfaction. Instrument is very useful for diverse outpatient populations and settings.
Distributor information:	N.A. Dewan, MD, Center for Quality Innovations & Research, 222 Piedmont Ave., Suite 8800, M.L. 665, Cincinnati OH 45219
Author:	Terry L Kramer, PhD, Gayle L. Zieman, PhD
Copyright status:	copyright
Fees:	No license fee
Target population(s)/symptom(s):	General population of inpatients and outpatients
Clinical setting:	Outpatient, inpatient and partial hospital
Primary use(s):	Post-treatment follow-up
Age group:	14 and above
Domain(s):	Client satisfaction
Is instrument population-based or designed to measure change for individuals?	Both
Who completes instrument?	Self-report
Number of items:	27 (optically scanned scoring)
Administration time:	5 minutes
Administration options:	Paper/pencil
Computer scoring possible?	Yes
Are norms available?	Yes
If so, normed on what groups?	Adult outpatients, Managed care settings
Reliability data:	Comparative data available on all questions across multi-state treatment sites.
Validity data:	Data available on correlation between satisfaction w/treatment outcomes and initial expectations from treatment
Population sample(s) on which measure tested:	Outpatient Behavioral Health (n=5000) in 12 states
Key references:	[no answer]

Sciacca Comprehensive Service Development

Client Progress Reviews for Mental Health Programs and Substance Abuse Programs (both with Program Review Readiness Scales)

Developer's or distributor's description of instrument:	The instruments are a component of Dual Diagnosis Treatment and Program Implementation Materials from the MIDAA Service Manual. They are used to assess the client's readiness (the readiness scales) to engage in treatment or services for Mental health and co-occuring Substance Disorder symptoms; Clients at all levels of readiness, including "denial" of symptoms, are engaged in services. These instruments measure and document progress from this starting point.
Distributor information:	Kathleen Sciacca, Sciacca Comprehensive Service Development for MIDAA, 299 Riverside Drive #3E, New York NY, Phone: (212) 866-5935
Author:	Kathleen Sciacca, MA
Copyright status:	Copyrighted
Fees:	Instruments are part of the "MIDAA Service Manual: A Step by Step Guide to Program Implementation for Multiple Disorders." Cost of Manual: $65.00.
Target population(s)/symptom(s):	Dual Diagnosis of Co-occurring mental illness and substance disorders. Includes severe mental illness and substance disorders. Substance disorders and personality disorders and other mental health symptoms.
Clinical setting:	Designed for all settings: Outpatient, Inpatient, Partial Hospital, Residential, ACT, PACT, Services for the Homeless, Shelters, Rehabilitation, Clubhouse models
Primary use(s):	Change over time
Age group:	Adolescents ages 12 years through 18 years. Adults ages 18 years and older
Domain(s):	Symptoms, Life functioning, Client satisfaction, Behavioral problems, Family environment, Severity and/or risk factors. Instruments measure client's readiness to engage in treatment and document progress in: client's ability to feel comfortable and trust the treatment setting; client's ability to acknowledge symptoms; to gain insight into interaction effects between mental illness and substance disorders; to address symptoms and engage in activities that lead to change; to reduce incidences of hospital and crisis service utilization; to change social network and symptom evoking behaviors; to improve functioning; to improve quality of living; to include family in services.

Is instrument population-based or designed to measure change for individuals?	Change over time for individuals
Who completes instrument?	Clinician
Number of items:	Sixteen
Administration time:	Fifteen minutes
Administration options:	[no answer]
Computer scoring possible?	[no answer]
Are norms available?	[no answer]
If so, normed on what groups?	N/A
Reliability data:	Empirical data, Computerized data, High Reliability.
Validity data:	Review of intrument for internal validity across providers. High.
Key references:	• Sciacca, K,Thompson, CM,Program Development and Integrated Treatment Across Systems for Dual Diagnosis: Mental Illness, Drug Addiction and Alcoholism (MIDAA). *The Journal of Mental Health Administration*, Vol.23, No.3., Summer 1996. pp. 288-297.

Self-Perception Profile for Adults

(Also Children, Adolescents, Learning-Disabled Students, and College Students)

Developer's or distributor's description of instrument:	The Self-Perception Profiles are instruments that tap self-perceptions across a range of domains. The Adult Profile assesses self-perceptions in the following domains: Intelligence, Job Competence, Athletic Competence, Physical Appearance, Close Friendship, Intimate Relationships, Morality, Sense of Humor, Nurturance, Household Management, and Adequacy as a Provider. The Adolescent Profile looks at the domains of: Scholastic Competence, Athletic Competence, Peer Likability, Close Friendship, Behavioral Conduct, Physical Appearance, Job Competence, and Romantic Appeal. In addition to the assessment of domain-specific self-concepts, the instruments include a separate subscale that taps global self worth—the extent to which the individual values him or herself as a person.
Distributor information:	Susan Harter, Department of Psychology, University of Denver, 2155 S. Race St., Denver CO 80208; Phone: (303) 871-3790
Author:	[no answer]
Copyright status:	Public domain
Fees:	$20 for manual
Target population(s)/symptom(s):	Depends on instruments (children, adolescents, learning-disabled students, college students, or adults)
Clinical setting:	[no answer]
Primary use(s):	Screening, Change over time, Post-treatment follow-up
Age group:	See above
Domain(s):	Self-concept
Is instrument population-based or designed to measure change for individuals?	Both
Who completes instrument?	Self-report
Number of items:	Depends on instrument
Administration time:	Approximately 20 minutes
Administration options:	[no answer]
Computer scoring possible?	[no answer]
Are norms available?	[no answer]
If so, normed on what groups?	N/A
Reliability data:	[no answer]
Validity data:	[no answer]
Key references:	[no answer]

Semi-Structured Clinical Interview for Children and Adolescents (SCICA)

Developer's or distributor's description of instrument:	The SCICA is designed for use by experienced interviewers. Instructions; protocol of questions and probes for ages 6-18; observation and self-report for rating what the child does and says during interview; profile for scoring ratings. Scorable by interviewer and observers. Scoring profiles are available for ages 6-12 only. Syndrome scales: Aggressive Behavior, Anxious, Anxious/Depressed, Attention Problems, Family Problems, Resistant, Strange, and Withdrawn, plus Internalizing, Externalizing, and separate total problem scales for Observation and Self-Report items. Hand-scored and computer-scored profiles are available.
Distributor information:	Child Behavior Checklist, University Medical Education Assoc., 1 South Prospect Street, Burlington VT 05401-3456, Fax: (802) 656-2602
Author:	Stephanie H. McConoughy, PhD, and Thomas M. Achenbach, PhD
Copyright status:	Copyrighted
Fees:	Semistructured Clinical Interview for Children & Adolescents: 25 for $10. Combined SCICA Observation & Self-Report Scoring Forms: 25 for $10. Profiles for hand-scoring of SCICA: 25 for $10. Manual for the SCICA: $25. IBM-compatible computer program for scoring the SCICA: $135. VHS video for practice scoring of SCICA interviews: $110
Target population(s)/symptom(s):	Children aged 6-18 as seen by clinical interview
Clinical setting:	[no answer]
Primary use(s):	Assessment, Screening, Change over time, Post-treatment follow-up
Age group:	6-18
Domain(s):	Symptoms, Life functioning, Behavioral problems
Is instrument population-based or designed to measure change for individuals?	Individuals
Who completes instrument?	Clinician
Number of items:	247
Administration time:	60-90 minutes, depending on whether achievement tests are included
Administration options:	Paper/pencil
Computer scoring possible?	Yes
Are norms available?	Yes
If so, normed on what groups?	Vermont children

Reliability data:	0.89 for observations; 0.73 for self-report
Validity data:	Most scales discriminate significantly between referred and nonreferred children.
Key references:	• McConaughy SH, Achenbach TM. *Manual for the Semistructured Clinical Interview for Children and Adolescents*. Burlington VT: University of Vermont Department of Psychiatry.

Service Satisfaction Scale (SSS-30)

Developer's or distributor's description of instrument:
The Services Satisfaction Scale-30 (SSS-30) is a multidimensional measure that assesses a number of empirical facets of satisfaction with health, mental health, or addictions-related services. The 30-item measure is supplemented with an optional group item and a section on personal characteristics and demographics. Two open-ended questions solicit additional comments. Two factor-based scales—Practitioner Manner and Skill (9 items) and Perceived Outcome (8-items)—have high internal reliability (see reliability section) and are well-replicated; two smaller scales Office Procedures (5-items) and Accessibility (4-items) supplement these (see reliability). The scale is typically administered as a paper-and-pencil self-report consumer satisfaction measure to waiting-room samples, often by receptionists during a typical two-week period (an item on number of sessions is included). Forms for case management and community-based residential services are available and have been administered in federally-funded randomized clinical trials.

Distributor information:
Thomas K. Greenfield, PhD, Senior Scientist, Western Consortium for Public Health, 2000 Hearst Ave., Suite 300, Berkeley CA 94709-2176; Fax: (510) 642-5208; E-mail: tgreenfield@arg.org

Author:
T.K. Greenfield, PhD, and C. C. Attkisson, PhD

Copyright status:
Copyrighted by Drs. T.K. Greenfield, C.C. Attkisson, and G.C. Pascoe

Fees:
$250 for first 500, $0.30 for use beyond 500. For placing orders, please make checks out to: Thomas K. Greenfield, Services Research, 6053 Ocean View Drive, Oakland, CA 94618. For ordering information, contact Dr. Greenfield by Fax at (510) 642-7175 or by e-mail: "tgreenfield@arg.org".

Target population(s)/symptom(s):
Primary care and mental health outpatients, substance abuse services/alcohol and chemical dependency treatments (versions for case management and residential services, e.g., SMI [seriously mentally ill] populations, available)

Clinical setting:
Outpatient (standard SSS-30 "practitioner" and "counselor" forms; SMI populations (SSS-Residential and SSS-Case Management forms). NOTE: The SSS-30 norm groups include primary care patients, mental health outpatients, EAP clients, and recipients of substance abuse services. Special versions have been used in studies of services for people with serious mental illness (SMI): the Residential and Case Management forms.

Primary use(s):	Post-treatment follow-up
Age group:	Adolescents and older (adults)
Domain(s):	Client satisfaction
Is instrument population-based or designed to measure change for individuals?	Has been used both service-wide, cross-sectional samples and over time, multiple measures (SMI Residential form)
Who completes instrument?	Self-report; has also been administered by interviewer for SMI clients.
Number of items:	30, plus one optional group item; and personal characteristics
Administration time:	5-10 minutes
Administration options:	[no answer]
Computer scoring possible?	[no answer]
Are norms available?	[no answer]
If so, normed on what groups?	N/A
Reliability data:	Two factor-based scales—Practitioner Manner and Skill (9 items) and Perceived Outcome (8-items)—have high internal reliabilities (average alpha = .88 & .83, respectively) and are well-replicated across studies; two smaller scales measuring Office Procedures (5-items, alpha = .74) and Accessibility (4 items, alpha = .67) supplement these. The SSS-30 composite score can serve as a general measure with high internal reliability (alphas = .93-.96 in several studies). A long-period test-retest correlation for the SSS-Case Management composite score was .57.
Validity data:	Experience with consumers and staff confirms that the SSS-30 has good face validity. In addition to the empirical and conceptual foundation for the scale, content validity is supported by content analyses of open-ended questions on best- and worst-liked service features. Multidimensionality of the scale helps assure its validity given the empirical distinctions service consumers have been found to make. The two main factor-based scales (Practitioner manner and Skill, and Perceived Outcome) have been repeatedly found in a series of studies with the SSS and so these subscales may be considered quite well established. The composite scale also has some value as a general satisfaction measure with excellent reliability (above). In one large-sample study, the correlation between the CSQ-8, a widely used unidimensional scale, and the SSS-30 composite score was .70 (p < .0001), adding to construct validity.
Key references:	• Attkisson, CC, and Greenfield, TK. (1995). The Client Satisfaction Questionnaire (CSQ) scales and the Service Satisfaction Scale-30 (SSS-30). In L.I. Sederer & B. Dickey (Eds.) *Outcomes assessment in clinical practice.* (pp. 120-127) Baltimore, MD: Williams & Wilkins. (SSS-30 in Appendix pp. 279-283). • Greenfield, T. K., and Attkisson, C. C. (in press) The UCSF Client Satisfaction Scales: II. The Service Satisfaction Scale-30. In M. Maruish (Ed.) *Psychological testing: Treatment planning and outcome assessment.* (2nd Ed) Mahwah, NJ: Lawrence Erlbaum Associates.• Attkisson, C. C., and Greenfield, T. K. (1994). The Client Satisfaction;

Questionnaire-8 and the Service Satisfaction Scale-30. In M. Maruish (Ed.) *Psychological testing: Treatment planning and outcome assessment*, pp. 402-420. Hillsdale, NJ: Lawrence Erlbaum Associates. • Greenfield, T. K., & Attkisson, C. C. (1989). Progress toward a multifactorial satisfaction scale for primary care and mental health services. *Evaluation and Program Planning*, 12: 271-278. • Greenfield, T. K. (in press). Client Satisfaction with Services for Substance Use Disorders: Part A: An Evaluation of Satisfaction with a State Drinker Driver Treatment Program; Part B. Client Satisfaction with Residential Substance Abuse Treatment Programmes. In *Evaluation of Treatment for Substance Use Disorders, Geneva: World Health Organization Programme on Substance Abuse.* • Greenfield, T. K. & Stoneking, B. C. (1993). *Service satisfaction with case management: An experimental test of augmenting staff teams with mental health consumers.* Paper presented at the Fourth Annual National Conference on State Mental Health Agency Services Research and Program Evaluation, National Association of State Mental Health Directors, Annapolis, MD, October 2-5. • Ruggeri, M. & Greenfield, T. K. (1995). The Italian version of the Service Satisfaction Scale (SSS-30) adapted for community-based psychiatric patients: Development, factor analysis and application. *Evaluation and Program Planning*, 18: 191-202.

Severity of Psychiatric Illness: Adult Version

Developer's or distributor's description of instrument:	The Severity of Psychiatric Illness is a decision support, case-mix descriptor measure for use in acute psychiatric service settings. The measure allows for the reliable predictor of level of care (e.g. inpatient, partial hospital) placement and predicts acute care resource use. It is quick to administer and can be used either prospectively or retrospectively.
Distributor information:	The Psychological Corporation, San Antonio TX, Phone: (800) 211-8378
Author:	John S. Lyons, PhD
Copyright status:	Copyright, The Psychological Corporation
Fees:	Per use or licensing fee available
Target population(s)/symptom(s):	Persons receiving acute psychiatric services. Assessing risk, symptom severity, complications to illness and complications to treatment.
Clinical setting:	Acute psychiatric services including emergency departments, inpatient units, intensive outpatient, and partial hospital.
Primary use(s):	Screening
Age group:	18 years and older
Domain(s):	Symptoms, Behavioral problems
Is instrument population-based or designed to measure change for individuals?	Population-based
Who completes instrument?	Any trained individual with experience with persons with acute psychiatric disorders.
Number of items:	14
Administration time:	1-2 minutes following standard assessment; 15 to 25 minutes as stand-alone measure
Administration options:	Paper/pencil or computer
Computer scoring possible?	Yes
Are norms available?	No, but normative decision-making algorithms are available
If so, normed on what groups?	[no answer]
Reliability data:	Following training, the instrument can be used with good reliability. Kappa inter-rater reliability coefficients above .85 have been obtained routinely in reliability studies.
Validity data:	The SPI has been shown to predict hospitalization decision, length of stay, in-hospital outcomes, and readmission. It has been shown to be correlated with data collected using independent, standard interview-based assessments.
Key references:	• Lyons, JS, Howard, KI, O'Mahoney, MT, Lish, J (1997). *The measurement and management of clinical outcomes in men-*

tal health. John Wiley & Sons, New York. • Yohanna, D, Christopher, NJ, Lyons, JS, Miller, SI, Slomowitz, M, Bultemaa, JK (1998). Characteristics of short-stay admissions to a psychiatric inpatient service. *Behavioral Health Service and Research* (in press). • Leon, SC, Lyons, JS, Christopher, NJ, Miller, SI. (1998). Psychiatric hospital outcomes of dual diagnosis patients under managed care. *American Journal of Addictions*, 7, 81-86. • Lyons, JS, O'Mahoney, MT, Miller, SI, Neme, J, Kabot, J, Miller, F. (1997). Predicting readmission to the psychiatric hospital in a managed care environment: Implications for quality indicators, *American Journal of Psychiatry*, 154, 397-400. • Lyons, JS, Stutesman, J, Neme, J, Vessey, JT, O'Mahoney, MT, Camper, HJ. (1997). Predicting psychiatric emergency admissions and hospital outcomes. *Medical Care*, 35, 792-800. • Lansing, AE, Lyons, JS, Martens, LC, O'Mahoney, MT, Miller, SI, Obolsky, A. (1997). The treatment of dangerous patients in managed care: Psychiatric hospital utilization and outcome. *General Hospital Psychiatry*, 19, 112-118. • Lyons, JS, Thompson, BJ, Finkel, SI, Christopher, NJ, Shasha, M, McGivern, M. (1996). Psychiatric partial hospitalization for older adults: A retrospective study of case-mix and outcome. *Continuum*, 3, 125-132. • Lyons, JS, O'Mahoney, M, Doheny, K, Dworkin, L, Miller, S. (1995). The prediction of short-stay psychiatric inpatients. *Administration and Policy in Mental Health*, 23, 17-25. • Lyons, JS, Colletta, J, Devens, M, Finkel, SI. (1995). The validity of the Severity of Psychiatric Illness in a sample of inpatients are a psychogeriatric unit. *International Psychogeriatrics*, 7, 407-416.

Severity of Psychiatric Illness—Child And Adolescent Version

Developer's or distributor's description of instrument:	The Severity of Psychiatric Illness—Child and Adolescent Version (CSPI) is a decision support and needs-based planning tool that can be used to describe the mental health needs of children age 5 and older. The measure supports ratings on symptoms of Serious Emotional Disorders, risk behaviors, functioning, complications, and caregiver capacity.
Distributor information:	The Psychological Corporation, San Antonio TX, Phone: (800) 211-8378
Author:	John S. Lyons, PhD
Copyright status:	Copyright, The Psychological Corporation
Fees:	Per use or licensing fee available
Target population(s)/symptom(s):	Child or adolescents receiving receiving mental health services. Assessing risk, symptom severity, functioning, co-morbidities, and caregiver capacity.
Clinical setting:	Any setting in which mental health services for children and adolescents are provided or in which screening or triage to such services is accomplished.
Primary use(s):	Screening, System planning
Age group:	5 to 18 years old
Domain(s):	Symptoms, Behavioral problems
Is instrument population-based or designed to measure change for individuals?	Population-based
Who completes instrument?	Any trained individual with experience with persons with children and adolescent mental health.
Number of items:	27
Administration time:	3-5 minutes following standard assessment; 20 to 30 minutes as stand-alone measure
Administration options:	Paper/pencil or computer
Computer scoring possible?	Yes
Are norms available?	No
If so, normed on what groups?	N/A
Reliability data:	Following training, the instrument can be used with good reliability. Kappa inter-rater reliability coefficients above .80 have been obtained routinely in reliability studies.
Validity data:	The CSPI has been shown to be correlated with data collected using independent, standard interview-based assessments. It has been shown to reliably predict residential treatment center placements, psychiatric hospitalizations and duration of care.

Key references:
- Lyons, JS, Howard, KI, O'Mahoney, MT, Lish, J (1997). *The measurement and management of clinical outcomes in mental health*. John Wiley & Sons, New York.
- Lyons, JS, Libman, L, Kisiel, CN, Shallcross, H. (1998). Understanding the mental health needs of children and adolescents in residential placement. *Professional Psychology: Research and Practice*, (in press).
- Lyons, JS, Kisiel, CL, Dulcan, M, Cohen, R, Chesler, P. (1997). Crisis assessment and psychiatric hospitalization of children and adolescents in state custody. *Journal of Child and Family Studies*, 6, 311-320.
- Lyons, JS (1997). The evolving role of outcomes in managed mental health care. *Journal of Child and Family Studies*, 6, 1-8.

SF-12™ Health Survey

Developer's or distributor's description of instrument:	A 12-item (two minute) version of the SF-36 Health Survey, designed for use in monitoring outcomes for general and specific populations. The survey can be self-administered by people 14 years of age and older, or administered by trained interviewers either in person or by telephone.
Distributor information:	Medical Outcomes Trust, 8 Park Plaza, #503, Boston MA 02116, Phone: (617) 426-4046, Fax: (617) 426-4131, E-mail: MOTrust@worldnet.att.net
Author:	John E. Ware, Jr., PhD, M. Kosinski and S.D. Keller
Copyright status:	© 1994 The Health Institute: New England Medical Center
Fees:	Distributed royalty free
Target population(s)/symptom(s):	General Health Survey
Clinical setting:	[no answer]
Primary use(s):	Diagnosis, Screening, Change over time, Post-treatment follow-up
Age group:	14 and up
Domain(s):	Life functioning, Severity and/or risk factors
Is instrument population-based or designed to measure change for individuals?	Both
Who completes instrument?	Self-report or clinician
Number of items:	12
Administration time:	2 minutes
Administration options:	[no answer]
Computer scoring possible?	[no answer]
Are norms available?	[no answer]
If so, normed on what groups?	N/A
Reliability data:	As documented in the user's manual and numerous publications, the reliability of SF-12 scores has been shown to be satisfactory using both test-retest and internal-consistency methods of estimation. Test-retest coefficients were nearly identical in the US and UK for the physical summary score (0.89 and 0.88) and for the mental summary score (0.76 and 0.78).
Validity data:	Because the SF-12 was constructed to reproduce the SF-36 summary measures of physical and mental health, the correlations between SF-12 summary measures and those "criteria" are most relevant to validity. On cross-validation these coefficients were 0.95 and 0.97, respectively, for physical and mental health.
Key references:	• Ware, J.E., Kosinski, M., and Keller, S.D. SF-12: *How to Score the SF-12 Physical and Mental Health Summary Scales*, Boston, MA: The Health Institute, New England Medical

Center (First Edition, March 1995; Second Edition, December 1995). • Ware, J.E., Kosinski, M., and Keller, S.D. A 12-item Short-Form Health Survey (SF-12): Construction of Scales and Preliminary Tests of Reliability and Validity. *Medical Care*, 1996:32(3):220-233. • Jenkinson, C., Layte, R. Development and testing of the UK SF-12. *Journal of Health Services Research and Policy, 1997, 2:14-18.* • Gandek, B., Ware, J.E., Aaronson, N.K. Cross-validation of item selection and item selection and scoring for the SF-12 Health Survey in nine countries: Results from the IQOLA Project. *Journal of Clinical Epidemiology, 1998* (in press).

SF-36™ Health Survey

Developer's or distributor's description of instrument:	A practical and valid instrument for measuring health status and outcome from the patient's point of view. Designed for use in surveys of general and specific populations, health policy evaluations, and clinical practice and research, the survey can be self-administered by people 14 years of age and older, or administered by trained interviewers either in person or by telephone. Measures eight health concepts, which are relevant across age, disease, and treatment groups.
Distributor information:	Medical Outcomes Trust, 8 Park Plaza, #503, Boston MA 02116, Phone: (617) 426-4046, Fax: (617) 426-4131, E-mail: MOTrust@worldnet.att.net
Author:	John E. Ware, Jr., PhD
Copyright status:	(c) 1992, Medical Outcomes Trust
Fees:	Distributed royalty free
Target population(s)/symptom(s):	General health survey
Clinical setting:	[no answer]
Primary use(s):	Diagnosis, Screening, Change over time, Post-treatment follow-up
Age group:	14 and up
Domain(s):	Life functioning, Severity and/or risk factors
Is instrument population-based or designed to measure change for individuals?	Both
Who completes instrument?	Self-report or clinician
Number of items:	36
Administration time:	5 minutes—self; 8-10 minutes—interviewer
Administration options:	[no answer]
Computer scoring possible?	[no answer]
Are norms available?	[no answer]
If so, normed on what groups?	N/A
Reliability data:	[no answer]
Validity data:	[no answer]
Key references:	[no answer]

Sickness Impact Profile™

Developer's or distributor's description of instrument:	A behaviorally based health status questionnaire. Everyday activities in 12 categories (sleep and rest, emotional behavior, body care and movement, home management, mobility, social interaction, ambulation, alertness behavior, communication, work, recreation and pastimes, and eating) are measured. Scoring can be done at the level of categories and dimensions as well as the total SIP level.
Distributor information:	Medical Outcomes Trust, 8 Park Plaza, #503, Boston MA 02116, Phone: (617) 426-4046, Fax: (617) 426-4131, E-mail: MOTrust@worldnet.att.net
Author:	Donald M. Steinwachs, PhD
Copyright status:	(c) 1977 The Johns Hopkins University
Fees:	Distributed royalty free
Target population(s)/symptom(s):	A general health questionnaire for ages 14 and up
Clinical setting:	[no answer]
Primary use(s):	Screening, Change over time, Post-treatment follow-up
Age group:	Adult
Domain(s):	Life functioning, Severity and/or risk factors
Is instrument population-based or designed to measure change for individuals?	Both
Who completes instrument?	Self-report or clinician
Number of items:	136
Administration time:	10-20 minutes
Administration options:	[no answer]
Computer scoring possible?	[no answer]
Are norms available?	[no answer]
If so, normed on what groups?	N/A
Reliability data:	[no answer]
Validity data:	[no answer]
Key references:	[no answer]

Stress Response Scale (SRS)

Developer's or distributor's description of instrument:	The SRS assesses the impact of stress on behavioral adjustment, and is useful in clinics, schools and community agencies as an element of a comprehensive assessment of life-stress. The instrument is based on a model that predicts five response styles: acting out, passive aggressive, overactive, repressed, and dependent.
Distributor information:	PAR, Inc., P.O. Box 998, Odessa FL 33556, Phone: (800) 331-8378
Author:	Lewis Chandler, PhD
Copyright status:	Copyrighted
Fees:	Introductory kit (manual and 25 rating forms, 50 scoring forms): $73
Target population(s)/symptom(s):	Children maladaptively coping with stressful situations
Clinical setting:	Individual administration
Primary use(s):	Diagnosis, Screening, Change over time, Post-treatment follow-up
Age group:	5-14 (experimental norms extend to 18)
Domain(s):	Symptoms, Life functioning, Behavioral problems, Severity and/or risk factors
Is instrument population-based or designed to measure change for individuals?	Norm-based
Who completes instrument?	Teacher, parent, or other adult
Number of items:	40
Administration time:	10-15 minutes
Administration options:	Paper/pencil
Computer scoring possible?	No
Are norms available?	Yes
If so, normed on what groups?	947 elementary school children ages 5-14 years (459 boys/488 girls)
Reliability data:	[no answer]
Validity data:	[no answer]
Key references:	[no answer]

The Substance Abuse Outcomes Module (SAOM)

Developer's or distributor's description of instrument:	The primary goal of the Substance Abuse Outcomes Module (SAOM) is to assess the patient characteristics, the processes of care, and outcomes of care for substance abuse. The SAOM is designed to be used in routine clinical care settings as part of an Outcomes Management System for continuous quality improvement efforts such as the JCAHO's ORYX initiative.
	The SAOM measures: (1) prognostic characteristics or casemix variables, including variables that predict treatment seeking, choice of treatment modality, and sociodemographic characteristics; (2) treatment for substance abuse including type, extent, and setting of treatment; and (3) outcomes of care, including the change in consumption, symptoms of dependence, and general functioning change over time. The SAOM identifies patients with substance abuse by determining whether the individual being assessed has a diagnosis of substance abuse as defined by DSM-IV criteria and assesses their symptom severity and functioning over time.
Distributor information:	Center for Outcomes Research and Effectiveness (CORE); Annette Marchitto; 5800 W. 10th Street, Suite 605; Little Rock AR 72204
Author:	G. Richard Smith, MD; Thomas Babor, PhD; Audrey Burnam, PhD; Kathryn Rost, PhD; Robert Drake, MD; and Kim Heithoff, ScD
Copyright status:	The modules are copyrighted to the University of Arkansas for Medical Sciences (UAMS); however the modules are available for unlimited reproduction and distribution by the public for non-profit, educational or research purposes.
Fees:	The modules are available for a one time charge of thirty-five dollars ($35) per module or two modules for fifty dollars ($50).
Target population(s)/symptom(s):	Persons 18 years of age or older with a diagnosis of substance abuse
Clinical setting:	In addition to outpatient/inpatient/partial hospitalization environments, the modules, can be utilized in day treatment and managed behavioral health care networks/health plans.
Primary use(s):	Diagnosis, Change over time, Post-treatment follow-up
Age group:	18 years of age or older.
Domain(s):	Symptoms, Life functioning, Behavioral problems, Family environment, Severity and/or risk factors

Is instrument population-based or designed to measure change for individuals?	Data can be analyzed as an aggregate or on individual clients, providers, or sites.
Who completes instrument?	Self-report and Clinician
Number of items:	Clinician Baseline Assessment—12 items, Patient Baseline Assessment—97 items, Patient Follow-up Assessment—75 items, Medical Record Review—6 items.
Administration time:	Patient baseline assessment and follow-up assessments are self-administered, and each require 25 minutes to complete. The medical record review requires 10 minutes.
Administration options:	Paper/pencil. Web site to be available for use by Fall 1998.
Computer scoring possible?	Computer Web site scoring will be available by Fall 1998.
Are norms available?	No
If so, normed on what groups?	N/A
Reliability and Validity data:	This module combines the most psychometrically sound and clinically relevant measures and scales from alcohol and drug abuse modules previously developed by the authors. The diagnostic component of the SAOM is consistent with the DSM-IV criteria, has good test-retest reliability (interaclass correlation coefficient [ICC] = 0.70), and good agreement with the Composite International Diagnostic Interview-Substance Abuse Module (18) (k = 0.95). The measure of alcohol consumption (quantity _ frequency of drinking in past month) incorporated into the module showed excellent test-retest reliability (ICC = 0.87) and concurrent validity using consumption estimates made using the Timeline Followback Assessment (Pearson r=0.74). The five subscales of the 20-item Consequences of Drug and Alcohol Use continued to demonstrate adequate test-retest reliability (ICCs ranging from 0.75 to 0.87) and internal consistency (coefficient % range from 0.72 to 0.94). The four-item Severity of Illness Scale, which assesses physical and social problems that have resulted from drug and alcohol use in the past three months, has good test-retest reliability (ICC=0.73) and internal consistency (Cronbach's % =0.72) and correlates highly with number of dependent symptoms (Pearson r=0.83). Similarly, the five-item Social Support Scale demonstrates adequate test-retest and internal consistency (ICC=0.67 and coefficient % = 0.87, respectively). Finally, although the SAOM attempts to measure support for sobriety as a prognostic indicator, the internal consistency of the items was found to be poor (% = 0.43) with marginal test-retest reliability (ICC=0.67).
Key references:	[no answer]

The Substance Abuse Subtle Screening Inventory (SASSI)

Developer's or distributor's description of instrument:	The SASSI is an empirically-derived addictions screening tool. It includes 26 face valid items and 67 subtle items that bear little apparent relationship to substance misuse. It yields 10 scales. 7 scales are used in decision rules that yield a dichotomous classification of high or low probability of having a substance dependence disorder. There is a scale that flags clients who did not respond to the items in a meaningful manner. Two additional scales provide supplementary clinical information. The instrument was designed to identify some substance dependent individuals who are unwilling to acknowledge relevant symptoms.
Distributor information:	The SASSI Institute, P.O. Box 5069, Bloomington IN 47407, Phone: (800) 726-0526, E-mail: sassi@sassi.com
Author:	Glenn Miller, Franklin Miller, Linda Lazowski
Copyright status:	Copyrighted
Fees:	From $1.50 per test (paper/pencil version) to $7.00 per administration (computerized versions) depending on quantity ordered and options selected
Target population(s)/symptom(s):	Substance-related disorders
Clinical setting:	Any human service setting that screens for substance dependence
Primary use(s):	Screening
Age group:	Adolescent version—ages 12-18, Adult version—ages 18 and up
Domain(s):	Addictions
Is instrument population-based or designed to measure change for individuals?	Normed screening measure
Who completes instrument?	Self-report
Number of items:	Adult Version 93; Adolescent Version 81
Administration time:	10 to 15 minutes
Administration options:	Paper/pencil, Computer, Optical scanning
Computer scoring possible?	Yes
Are norms available?	Yes
If so, normed on what groups?	Nonclinical samples
Reliability data:	Test-retest stability coefficient on the SASSI-3 scales range from .92 to 1.00
Validity data:	Overall accuracy 94%, Sensitivity 94%, Specificity 94%, Positive predictive power 98%, Negative predictive power 80%

Key references:
- Horrigan, T.J., Piazza, N.J., Weinstein, L. (1996). The Substance Abuse Subtle Screening Inventory (SASSI) is more cost effective and better selectivity than urine toxicology for the detection of substance abuse in pregnancy. *Journal of Perinatology*, 16(5), 326-330.
- Miller, F.G. (1997), SASSI: application and assessment for substance-related problems, *Journal of Substance Misuse*, 2, 163-166, Piazza, N.J. (1996), Dual diagnosis and adolescent psychiatric inpatients. Substance Use & Misuse, 31(2), 215-223.
- Risberg, R.A., Stevens, M.J., Graybill, D.F. (1995), Validating the adolescent form of the Substance Abuse Subtle Screening Inventory, *Journal of Child & Adolescent Substance Abuse*, 4(4), 25-41.

Substance Use Disorders Diagnostic Schedule (SUDDS-IV)

Developer's or distributor's description of instrument:	DSM-IV diagnostic tool for chemical dependency. Allows clinician to get DSM-IV diagnosis efficiently, defends clinical decisions and provides a complete patient diagnostic history.
Distributor information:	New Standards, Inc., 8441 Wayzata Blvd., Suite 105, Minneapolis MN 55426, Phone: (612) 797-9997 ext. 45, (800) 755-6299
Author:	Norman G. Hoffmann, PhD and Patricia A. Harrison, PhD
Copyright status:	Copyrighted
Fees:	$62.50 per 25
Target population(s)/symptom(s):	Chemically dependent
Clinical setting:	All
Primary use(s):	Diagnosis
Age group:	Primarily adult
Domain(s):	Symptoms, Life functioning, Severity and/or risk factors
Is instrument population-based or designed to measure change for individuals?	Individuals
Who completes instrument?	Clinician
Number of items:	63
Administration time:	30-40 minutes
Administration options:	Paper/pencil, Computer
Computer scoring possible?	Yes
Are norms available?	[no answer]
If so, normed on what groups?	N/A
Reliability data:	[no answer]
Validity data:	[no answer]
Key references:	[no answer]

Symptom Checklist-90-Revised™ (SCL-90-R)

Developer's or distributor's description of instrument:	The Symptom Checklist-90-Revised™ (SCL-90-R©) test is a self-report symptom inventory designed to measure psychological distress. It provides an overview of a patient's symptoms and their intensity. The SCL-90-R test also identifies the level of distress that a patient is experiencing at a specific point in time, as patients are asked to indicate whether they have experienced symptoms during a prescribed time period. "The last 7 days" is the standard normative period. Compared to the BSI test, the SCL-90-R test is most often used in situations where additional clinical information on patients is needed. When used for outcomes measurement, the SCL-90-R test is often administered at intake, during treatment, at discharge, and for follow-up. At intake, the tests can reflect the severity-of-illness and establish a baseline for progress evaluation. During treatment, the test quantifies the effect of care on changes in symptom severity and supports decisions about continuing, changing, or terminating treatment. At discharge, the test assesses readiness for discharge based upon changes measured in symptom severity. It also establishes pre- and post-treatment comparisons for evaluation of outcomes and provider profiling. At follow-up, the test can measure the maintenance effect of care in evaluation of outcomes, medical cost offset, and provider profiling.
Distributor information:	The SCL-90-R test is exclusively published and distributed by NCS Assessments, 5605 Green Circle Drive, Minnetonka MN 55343. It can be ordered by mail, by fax at (800) 632-9011, or by calling Customer Service at (800) 627-7271, ext. 5151. NCS publishes the SCL-90-R test in English, Hispanic, and French Canadian as standard products. In addition, there are numerous other foreign language translations which can be used for research purposes. All requests for foreign translations other than Hispanic or French Canadian should be made in writing to the Product Manager at NCS.
Author:	Leonard R. Derogatis, PhD
Copyright status:	The "Symptom Checklist-90-Revised" is a trademark and the "SCL-90-R" is a registered trademark of the test's author. Copyrighted (c) 1975.
Fees:	Per use and site licenses available. Call or write for current catalog

Target population(s)/symptom(s):	The SCL-90 test measures nine primary symptom dimensions: somatization, obsessive compulsive, interpersonal sensitivity, depression, anxiety, hostility, phobic anxiety, paranoid ideation, and psychoticism. It also provides three global indices of distress including a Global Severity Index (GSI) that measures the current overall level of distress, a Positive Symptom Distress Index (PSDI) that measures the intensity of distress, and a Positive Symptom Total (PST) that indicates the number of patient-reported symptoms.
Clinical setting:	[no answer]
Primary use(s):	Screening, change over time, and post-treatment follow-up. Aggregating of data for continuous quality improvement.
Age group:	13 years and older. The test is written at a 6th grade reading level
Domain(s):	Symptoms, Severity
Is instrument population-based or designed to measure change for individuals?	Measures change over time for an individual, but data can be aggregated for groups.
Who completes instrument?	Self-report
Number of items:	90 items (BSI test is the short form of the SCL-90-R test)
Administration time:	12-15 minutes. Test can be done via paper-and-pencil, audio-cassette or on-line computer administration.
Administration options:	Hand score, Computer, Mail-in, Fax-in, Site license
Computer scoring possible?	Yes
Are norms available?	Yes
If so, normed on what groups?	Inpatient psychiatric, Outpatient psychiatric, Community
Reliability data:	Internal consistency ranged from .77 to .90 for the 9 primary symptom dimensions, and was calculated from the data of 219 "symptomatic volunteers." Test-retest reliability ranged between .80 and .90 for a sample of 94 psychiatric outpatients with a one week interval between tests.
Validity data:	There are over 940 studies attesting to the validity of the SCL-90-R. An SCL-90-R bibliography is available upon request.
Key references:	[no answer]

Teacher's Report Form (TRF)

Developer's or distributor's description of instrument:	The TRF obtains teachers' ratings of many of the problems rated on the CBCL, plus additional items appropriate for teachers. Profile includes scales for academic performance, adaptive functioning, eight cross-informant syndromes, Internalizing, Externalizing, and total problems. Scales are based on 2,815 referred students. Normed on 1,391 nonreferred students. Hand-scored and computer-scored profiles are available.
Distributor information:	Child Behavior Checklist, University Medical Education Assoc., 1 South Prospect Street, Burlington VT 05401-3456, Fax: (802) 656-2602
Author:	Thomas M. Achenbach, PhD
Copyright status:	Copyrighted
Fees:	Teacher's Report Form for ages 5-18: 25 for $10. Profiles for hand-scoring of TRF:25 for $10. Templates for hand scoring of TRF Profiles: $7. Machine-readable TRF: 25 for $20. Manual for the TRF and Profile: $25. Computer program for scoring of TRF: $220
Target population(s)/symptom(s):	Children attending school, as seen by their teachers
Clinical setting:	[no answer]
Primary use(s):	Assessment, Screening, Change over time, Post-treatment follow-up
Age group:	5-18
Domain(s):	Symptoms, Life functioning, Behavioral problems
Is instrument population-based or designed to measure change for individuals?	Both
Who completes instrument?	Teacher
Number of items:	125
Administration time:	15-20 minutes
Administration options:	Paper/pencil, Machine-readable form, Direct computer entry by teachers
Computer scoring possible?	Yes
Are norms available?	Yes
If so, normed on what groups?	National sample
Reliability data:	0.95 for total problems
Validity data:	All scales discriminate significantly between referred and nonreferred children.
Key references:	• Achenbach TM (1991). *Manual for the Teacher's Report Form and 1991 profile*. Burlington VT: University of Vermont Department of Psychiatry.

Tennessee Self Concept Scale: Second Edition (TSCS:2)

Developer's or distributor's description of instrument:	The Tennessee Self-Concept Scale, the most popular measure of self-concept in adolescents and adults, can now be used with children, too. Restandardized, streamlined, and updated, the new TSCS:2 retains the clinical richness of the original test, while adding new norms (down to age 7), an additional scale, simplified scoring procedures, and more guidance in interpreting scores and designing therapeutic interventions. Though the test has been shortened, it includes most of the original Tennessee items. It gives you 15 scores, including the most useful from the previous edition, plus a new Academic/Work Score.
Distributor information:	Western Psychological Services, 12031 Wilshire Blvd., Los Angeles CA 90025-1251, Phone: (800) 648-8857
Author:	William H. Fitts, PhD and W.L. Warren, PhD
Copyright status:	Copyrighted
Fees:	TSCS:2 Kit (manual, 20 answer forms, 4 pre-paid computer scored answer sheets): $130. Components also available individually.
Target population(s)/symptom(s):	Clinical populations—individuals experiencing emotional or behavioral problems
Clinical setting:	Schools and clinics
Primary use(s):	Diagnosis, Screening, Change over time, Post-treatment follow-up
Age group:	7-90
Domain(s):	Life functioning, Behavioral problems, Self-concept
Is instrument population-based or designed to measure change for individuals?	Individuals
Who completes instrument?	Self-report
Number of items:	82
Administration time:	10 to 20 minutes
Administration options:	Paper/pencil, Computer
Computer scoring possible?	Yes—via disk, mail-in answer sheet or fax-in answer sheet
Are norms available?	Yes
If so, normed on what groups?	3,000 people from 7 to 90 years of age
Reliability data:	See manual
Validity data:	See manual
Key references:	See manual

Treatment Events Checklist (TEC)

Developer's or distributor's description of instrument:	The Treatment Events Checklist (TEC) was developed as a part of a large outcomes program (University of Cincinnati, Dept. of Psychiatry, Outcomes Management Project). The TEC gathers the following data regarding a patient's care: diagnoses initial and post-treatment, amount of care (e.g. number of individual psychotherapy sessions, or number of days in partial hospital care), levels of care used, medications used, and any adverse incidents during case. Instrument is very useful for diverse populations of outpatient and facility-based settings.
Distributor information:	N.A. Dewan, MD, Center for Quality Innovations & Research, 222 Piedmont Ave., Suite 8800, M.L. 665, Cincinnati OH 45219
Author:	Gayle L. Zieman, PhD, Terry L. Kramer, PhD
Copyright status:	Copyright
Fees:	Yes, per use $.35 ea.
Target population(s)/symptom(s):	General population of inpatients and outpatients
Clinical setting:	Outpatient, inpatient and partial hospital
Primary use(s):	Change over time
Age group:	14 and above
Domain(s):	Symptoms, Severity and/or risk factors, Other (Diagnoses, Amount & Level of care, Type of care)
Is instrument population-based or designed to measure change for individuals?	Both
Who completes instrument?	Clinician
Number of items:	27 (optically scanned scoring)
Administration time:	5 minutes
Administration options:	Paper/pencil
Computer scoring possible?	Yes
Are norms available?	Yes
If so, normed on what groups?	Adult outpatients, Managed care settings
Reliability data:	NA (is an abstraction of data from patient's treatment based on clinician's report or record review)
Validity data:	NA
Population sample(s) on which measure tested:	Behavioral Health Outpatients (n=6000) in 12 states
Key references:	[no answer]

Treatment Follow-Up Surveys (Child, Adolescent, Adult) IV

Developer's or distributor's description of instrument:	The instruments provide post-discharge data on symptoms, life functioning, client satisfaction, behavioral problems, family environment, and severity and/or risk factors from former inpatients. They have evolved over five years to their current form. they can be self-administered (we use them via telephone interview) and are user-friendly.
Distributor information:	Dr. Chris E. Stout, Forest Health System, Inc., 555 Wilson Lane, Des Plaines IL 60016, Phone: (847) 635-4100, ext. 580
Author:	Dr. Chris E. Stout
Copyright status:	Copyrighted, but can be used in public domain if proper citation to author noted
Fees:	$100 annual license
Target population(s)/symptom(s):	Inpatient psychiatric, all diagnoses
Clinical setting:	Inpatient, Psychiatric post-discharge, Residential
Primary use(s):	Post-treatment follow-up
Age group:	5-12 years, 12-17 years, 18 years and up
Domain(s):	Symptoms, Life functioning, Client satisfaction, Behavioral problems, Family environment, Severity and/or risk factors
Is instrument population-based or designed to measure change for individuals?	N/A
Who completes instrument?	Self-report
Number of items:	48-50
Administration time:	20 minutes
Administration options:	Paper/pencil
Computer scoring possible?	No
Are norms available?	No
If so, normed on what groups?	N/A
Reliability data:	N/A
Validity data:	N/A
Key references:	• Stout C.E. (1996), Practical clinical management tools for practice enhancement, in C. Stout, G. Theis and J. Oher (eds.), *The Complete Guide to Managed Behavioral Healthcare*, New York: John Wiley & Sons.

Treatment Outcome Package (TOP)

Developer's or distributor's description of instrument:
The TOP is designed to double as an assessment AND concurrent outcome tool capturing comprehensive symptom and functional data as well as extensive case-mix information. Countering industry trends toward shorter and less meaningful questionnaires, AMS has developed a tool that is clinically rich and has exceptional face validity for both consumers and providers. With the processing and delivery of comprehensive "lab test" reports within 15 minutes anywhere in the country, clients in both private and public settings have demonstrated an interest and ability to complete a more comprehensive questionnaire when they see its immediate and direct application to their care. As the medical industry attempts to compare one provider to another, it is essential for us to gather accurate, meaningful and fair comparisons. Client confidentiality is absolutely assured by a random code number assigned by the provider which only they can link back to a specific client.

Distributor information: Access Measurement Systems, Inc., 50 Main Street, Ashland MA 01721, Phone: (508) 881-4777, Fax: (508) 881-8777

Author: David R. Kraus, PhD, and John Jordan, PhD

Copyright status: Copyrighted

Fees: Costs are between $3 and $5 dollars per administration depending on volume for comprehensive questionnaires. Short (several subscales) versions range from $0.50 to $2.50. AMS only charges for data processing and immediate reporting via fax. Charges include cost of forms, faxback processing, individual patient reports and aggregate data reports.

Target population(s)/symptom(s): The TOP measures a full range of behavioral health symptoms on 13 subscales (functional domains: work, social, sex; and symptom domains: temper, sleep, generalized anxiety, depressions, anxiety, mania, paranoia, psychosis, self esteem, trauma, impulsive, and quality of life) along with patient satisfaction with treatment. It is used extensively with both public and private sector consumers and has become the standard for measurement in the Mass. Medicaid population.

Clinical setting: The TOP is currently being used in a full range of behavioral health care treatment settings including: outpatient, partial hospitalization, IOP, residential, crisis/respite and inpatient.

Primary use(s): Diagnosis, Screening, Change over time, Post-treatment follow-up, The TOP is designed to be used as an initial assessment and treatment outcome measuring tool. It can be administered at various points in or after treatment. It provides diagnostic suggestions based on DSM-IV algorithms.

Age group:	Adult version- 14 and older, Child version-3-18 years old
Domain(s):	Symptoms: Life Functioning, Client Satisfaction, Behavioral problems, Family environment, Severity and/or risk factors, Substance abuse, medical history, past psychiatric history, life stress and other case-mix variables.
Is instrument population-based or designed to measure change for individuals?	The TOP provides assessment and outcome reports with comparisons to the normal population and provides pre- and post-comparisons over time for individuals.
Who completes instrument?	The TOP is designed to be filled out by the client. It can be used however, as a structured interview, or when absolutely necessary, completed by the clinician. Each type of administration is handled differently. For child versions primary custodian, care-giver, clinician, social service worker, or the child him/herself can complete the form.
Number of items:	9-140 depending on short, medium or long forms used
Administration time:	Median time is 25 minutes for a psychiatric population. 15-30 minute range for private sector clients; 20-45 minute range for public sector clients.
Administration options:	Currently the TOP is administered as a paper and pencil questionnaire and is filled out by the client. After completion by the client, the TOP is faxed to AMS, scored, and returned to the provider in fifteen minutes. In addition, the TOP can be used as a structured interview or, if necessary, completed by the clinician. Each kind of administration is scored differently. The child TOP is completed by the primary custodian, care-giver, clinician, social service worker, or by the child. Computerized administration of the TOP will be available within the next year.
Computer scoring possible?	The TOP is scored by AMS using a computer program and then returned to the provider within fifteen minutes.
Are norms available?	Yes
If so, normed on what groups?	Norms were developed in three different ways: (1) General medical patients were sampled during routine medical visits with their primary care physician; (2) Random mailings were sent; and (3) AMS customers were asked to recruit subjects who were not clients or friends. In each case, subjects were asked to complete the TOP as well as the SF-36. This enabled us to check the TOP norming sample against the SF-36 norming sample. There were no differences in TOP scores in each of the three sampling groups, and comparing each TOP sample to the SF-36 indicated no significant differences in physical functioning or mental health functioning scores. In addition, the TOP has been validated on all sub-scales in four separate categories, including outcomes, assessment, stress and satisfaction.
Reliability data:	Internal consistency: .68-.85. Retest: .79-.91
Validity data:	SF36 variance predicted: Mental Health, .94; Social Functioning, .96. (others .76-.95); BASIS-36 variance predicted: Total Score, .96 (others, .87-.94); Brief Symptom

	Inventory, variance predicted: PST, .87, GSI, .95; Beck Depression Inventory, variance predicted: .98; MMPI variance predicted: 16-96 percent; CBCL variance predicted: 16-96 percent.
Key references:	• Kraus DR, Horan FP, Smith AM. Protecting client confidentiality and improving provider relations through a new form of managed care: collaborative care management. Submitted to *Behavioral Healthcare Tomorrow*, 1997. • Kraus DR, Jordan JR. Validation of a treatment outcome and assessment tool. Submitted to *Professional Psychology: Research and Practice*, 1997.

Treatment Satisfaction Survey

Distributor information: Saeed Aminzadeh, Senior Director, Sales, HCIA-Response, 950 Winter Street, Waltham MA 02154, Phone (781) 768-1805
Author: HCIA Response
Copyright status: Copyrighted
Fees: None
Target population(s)/symptom(s): Patients receiving mental health services
Clinical setting: Outpatient
Primary use(s): To assess treatment satisfaction of mental health services
Age group: 18+
Domain(s): Access to care, technical skills, interpersonal skills
Is instrument population-based or designed to measure change for individuals? Both
Who completes instrument? Patient self-report
Number of items: 9
Administration time: 5 minutes
Administration options: Scanning, manual entry
Computer scoring possible? Yes
Are norms available? No
If so, normed on what groups? N/A
Reliability data: [no answer]
Validity data: [no answer]
Key references: [no answer]

Y-OQ™2.01 (Youth Outcome Questionnaire Version 2.01)

Developer's or distributor's description of instrument:	The Y-OQ™2.01(Youth Outcome Questionnaire) is a brief 64-item parent report measure of treatment progress for children and adolescents (ages 4-17) receiving mental health intervention. It is the latest effort of a unique partnership between administrators, researchers, and practitioners, led by Drs. Burlingame, Lambert, and Reisinger, and seeks to fill a gap in outcome measurement for children and adolescents. Similar in its intent to the OQ™45.2, the tracking measure for adults, the Y-OQ™2.01 is meant to track actual change in functioning as opposed to assigning diagnoses. Through the use of cut-off scores and a reliable change index, the Y-OQ™2.01 allows the clinician to see the childs behavioral similarity at each treatment interval to inpatient populations, outpatient populations, and a large untreated community sample. It is easy to score and interpret. All licenses come with detailed Administration and Scoring Manual. Windows software and fax to file versions are available for use in a variety of settings.
Distributor information:	Diana R. Maslauskas, DCSW, American Professional Credentialing Services LLC, P.O. Box 477, Wharton NJ 07885-0477, Phone: (500) 488-2727 or (410) 329-3777, E-mail: apcs@erols.com
Author:	Gary M. Burlingame, H. Gawain Wells, and Michael J. Lambert
Copyright status:	Licensed and copyrighted
Fees:	For unlimited use by individuals, groups, fees begin at $40 for individual practitioners. Rate schedule available upon request.
Target population(s)/symptom(s):	Youth in any setting. Parent or guardian completes questionnaire.
Clinical setting:	[no answer]
Primary use(s):	Screening, Change over time, Post-treatment follow-up. Clinical QI studies
Age group:	4-17
Domain(s):	Symptoms, Behavioral problems, Severity and/or risk factors, Interpersonal distress, Somatic, Interpersonal Relationships, Critical items, Social problems, Behavioral dysfunction
Is instrument population-based or designed to measure change for individuals?	Either, but was primarily designed for individuals
Who completes instrument?	Parent or guardian
Number of items:	64

Administration time:	6-10 minutes
Administration options:	Fax back, IVR, paper/pencil
Computer scoring possible?	Yes. Multiple formats available.
Are norms available?	Yes
If so, normed on what groups?	Community (normal), EAP, Outpatient, Inpatient
Reliability data:	Internal Consistency: .97
Validity data:	One hundred and thirty three estimates of concurrent validity reported.

Key references:
- Burlingame, et al. (1995) Pragmatics of Tracking Mental Health Outcomes in a Managed Care Setting. *Journal of Mental Health Administration*, Summer, 226-236.
- Lambert, et al. (1996) The Reliability and Validity of the Outcome Questionnaire. *Clinical Psychology and Psychotherapy*, 3 (4) Summer, 249-258.
- Lambert, et al. (1996) Data-Based Management for Tracking Outcome in Private Practice. *Clinical Psychology Science and Practice* 3, (2) Summer, 172-178.
- Wells, et al. (1996) Conceptualization and Measurement of Patient Change During Psychotherapy: Development of the Outcome Questionnaire and Youth Outcome Questionnaire. *Psychotherapy* 33, Summer, 275-283.

Young Adult Behavior Checklist (YABCL)

Developer's or distributor's description of instrument:	Contains 13 socially desirable items, 105 specific problem items, and open-ended items for adding problems not already listed. Each item is scored 0 = not true, 1 = somewhat or sometimes true, or 2 = very true or often true. Items are aggregated on 8 empirically derived syndrome scales that have counterparts on the Young Adult Self Report, which is normed on the same national sample as the YABCL.
Distributor information:	Child Behavior Checklist, University Medical Education Associates, 1 South Prospect St., Burlington, VT 05401-3456
Author:	Thomas M. Achenbach, PhD
Copyright status:	Copyrighted
Fees:	Forms completed by parents and surrogates: 25 for $10, Profiles for hand-scoring YABCL: 25 for $10, Templates for hand-scoring: $7, Manual (also includes Young Adult Self-Report documentation): $25, IBM compatible computer scoring program (includes scoring of Young Adult Self-Report): $220
Target population(s)/symptom(s):	Behavioral/emotional problems of young adults aged 18-30
Clinical setting:	All settings
Primary use(s):	Screening, Change over time, Post-treatment follow-up
Age group:	18-30
Domain(s):	Symptoms, Behavioral problems
Is instrument population-based or designed to measure change for individuals?	Both
Who completes instrument?	Parents & others who know the subject well
Number of items:	105 specific problem items, plus open-ended items
Administration time:	10-15 minutes
Administration options:	Paper/pencil
Computer scoring possible?	Yes
Are norms available?	Yes
If so, normed on what groups?	National sample
Reliability data:	0.93 for total problems
Validity data:	All scales discriminate significantly (p<.01) between referred and nonreferred young adults.
Population sample(s) on which measure tested:	National sample of 1,074 parents who rated their young adult offspring
Key references:	• Achenbach et al., *Journal of American Academy of Child Adolescent Psychiatry*, 1995, 34, 658-669, Ferdinand & Verhulst, *American Journal of Psychiatry*, 1995, 166, 4480-488. • Stanger et al. *J. Ab. Child Psychol*, 1996, 24, 597-614

Young Adult Self-Report (YASR)

Developer's or distributor's description of instrument:	Problem items are scored on the same 8 empirically derived syndromes as the Young Adult Behavior Checklist. Computer program compares each individual's item and syndrome scores on up to 5 YASRs and YABCLs. Adaptive functioning items are scored on 5 scales; substance use on 3 scales.
Distributor information:	Child Behavior Checklist, University Medical Education Associates, 1 South Prospect St., Burlington, VT 05401-3456
Author:	Thomas M. Achenbach, PhD
Copyright status:	Copyrighted
Fees:	Forms completed by young adults: 25 for $10. Profiles for hand-scoring YASR: 25 for $10. Templates for hand-scoring: $7.00. Manual (also includes Young Adult Behavior Checklist): $220.
Target population(s)/symptom(s):	Adults ages 18-30; adaptive functioning in a school, job, family, marriage or partnership, friendships; behavioral and emotional problems; substance use (tobacco, alcohol, drug).
Clinical setting:	All settings
Primary use(s):	Screening, change over time, Post-treatment follow-up
Age group:	18-30
Domain(s):	Symptoms, Life functioning, Behavioral problems, Other (Substance use, adaptive functioning).
Is instrument population-based or designed to measure change for individuals?	Both
Who completes instrument?	Self-report
Number of items:	110 specific problem items, 14 socially desirable items, 26 adaptive functioning items, 3 substance use items.
Administration time:	15-20 minutes
Administration options:	Paper/pencil
Computer scoring possible?	Yes
Are norms available?	Yes
If so, normed on what groups?	National sample
Reliability data:	0.89 for total problems; 0.82 across all adaptive functioning scales; 0.92 across substance use scales.
Validity data:	Nearly all scales discriminate significantly between referred and nonreferred young adults.
Key references:	• Achenbach et al., *J. Am Academy of Child & Adolescent Psychiatry*, 1995, 34, 658-669, Ferdinand & Verhulst, *Am. J. Psychiatry*, 1995, 152, 1586-1594. • Ferdinand er al., *Brit. J. Psychiatry*, 1995, 166, 480-488. • Stanger et al., *J.Ab. Child Psychology*, 1996, 24, 597-614

The Youth Satisfaction Questionnaire (YSQ)

Developer's or distributor's description of instrument:	The YSQ is intended to be a brief, general measure of children's views of the services they receive and activities they are involved in. It has primarily been used in program evaluation.
Distributor information:	Research and Training Center on Family Support and Children's Mental Health, Attention: Denise Schmidt, Portland State University, PO Box 751, Portland OR 97207-0751, Phone: (503) 725-4040. Technical questions key contact: Paul Koren, PhD, Phone: (503) 725-4162
Author:	Denise Stuntzner-Gibson, MSW, Paul Koren, PhD, and Neal DeChillo, PhD
Copyright status:	Copyright 1992
Fees:	No fees charged per user/use.
Target population(s)/symptom(s):	Children and youth with severe emotional and/or behavioral disturbances or disorders requiring multiple services
Clinical setting:	All settings
Primary use(s):	Change over time, Post-treatment follow-up
Age group:	9-18 years
Domain(s):	Client satisfaction
Is instrument population-based or designed to measure change for individuals?	Currently used as a population-based measure, but could conceivably be used on an individual (single case study) basis.
Who completes instrument?	Self-report
Number of items:	5 general satisfaction items (3 point scale) plus variable (depending on number of service and activities) number of items to be "graded" (5 point scale)
Administration time:	5 minutes or less
Administration options:	Paper/pencil only
Computer scoring possible?	No
Are norms available?	No
If so, normed on what groups?	N/A
Reliability data:	Analysis of the five general satisfaction items at the top of the YSQ suggested that three items —measuring the extent to which youth liked the help they were getting, got the help they wanted, and felt that services helped in their lives—provided the most internally consistent composite score. The alpha coefficient associated with these three items was .80, which demonstrates substantial internal consistency.
Validity data:	No data available
Key references:	• Stuntzer-Gibson, D., Koren, P. E., & DeChillo, N. (1995). The Youth Satisfaction Questionnaire: What kids think of services. *Families in Society*, 76(10): 616-624.

Youth Self Report (YSR)

Developer's or distributor's description of instrument:	The YSR can be completed by youths having 5th grade reading skills, or administered orally. It has most of the same competence and problem items as the CBCL/4-18. Sixteen CBCL problem items are replaced with socially desirable items endorsed by most youths. Profile for scoring the YSR includes two competence scales, total competence, eight cross-informant syndromes, Internalizing, Externalizing, and total problem scales. Scales are based on 1272 clinically referred youths. Normed on 1315 nonreferred youths. Hand-scored and computer-scored profiles are available.
Distributor information:	Child Behavior Checklist, University Medical Education Assoc., 1 South Prospect Street, Burlington VT 05401-3456, Fax: (802) 656-2602
Author:	Thomas M. Achenbach, PhD
Copyright status:	Copyrighted
Fees:	Youth Self-Report for ages 11-18: 25 for $10, Profiles for hand-scoring of YSR: 25 for $10, Templates for hand-scoring of YSR profiles: $7. Machine readable YSR: 25 for $20, Manual for the YSR and profile: $25, Computer program for scoring of YSR: $195
Target population(s)/symptom(s):	Adolescents, as they see themselves
Clinical setting:	[no answer]
Primary use(s):	Assessment, Screening, Change over time, Post-treatment follow-up
Age group:	11-18
Domain(s):	Symptoms, Life functioning, Behavioral problems
Is instrument population-based or designed to measure change for individuals?	Both
Who completes instrument?	Self-report
Number of items:	102 problem items, 16 socially desirable items, 17 competence items
Administration time:	15-20 minutes
Administration options:	Paper/pencil, Machine-readable forms, Direct computer entry by youths
Computer scoring possible?	Yes
Are norms available?	Yes
If so, normed on what groups?	National sample
Reliability data:	0.79 for total problems
Validity data:	All scales discriminate significantly between referred and nonreferred youths.
Key references:	• Achenbach TM (1991). *Manual for the Youth Self-Report and 1991 profile.* Burlington VT: University of Vermont Department of Psychiatry.

A "Global" Look at BASIS-32

MCLEAN REPORTS

Winter 1998

Since it was first introduced at McLean in 1985, BASIS-32 has been used by hundreds of health care providers across the country, both large and small, to measure the effectiveness of psychiatric care. The following is a look at how several of those organizations have successfully integrated BASIS into their clinical care systems.

The **Council of Behavioral Group Practices** is a large consortium of independent behavioral health care practices affiliated with the Institute for Behavioral Health Care in Tiburon, California.

In 1994, the council began using McLean's BASIS-32 as part of an effort to evaluate the general health status of its patients. This initiative ultimately grew into what is today a comprehensive Outcomes Management Project (OMP), with BASIS-32 serving as the primary measurement tool for mental health care. The OMP currently provides outcomes data analysis and benchmark data to 19 practices in 12 states. To date, baseline data has been collected on more than 15,000 clients, including inpatients as well as outpatients.

Preliminary results suggest that greatest improvement occurs between intake and three-month follow-up, with continued but more gradual improvement at six-month follow-up, says Allen Daniels, EdD, one of OMPs founders.

"BASIS has a good set of measurement values. And although it was designed for hospitals, we're finding that it has good utility at all different delivery system sites," he notes.

The **Massachusetts Society for the Prevention of Cruelty to Children** (MSPCC) provides home- and clinic-based mental health services to children and adults throughout Massachusetts. The society's 12 clinic sites across the state handle 10,000 to 12,000 patient visits yearly.

In 1996, the society implemented an outcomes study using the BASIS-32 at intake and at two-month follow-up. Fifty-two percent of the study's sample population (414 adults and adolescents age 14 and over) were people of color (including 36 percent Latino, 10 percent African-American and 6 percent other populations of color). Preliminary results show the BASIS-32 appears to capture changes between intake and follow-up within each ethnic group (Latino, African-American and European descent).

According to Susan Eisen, PhD, assistant director, McLean Mental Health Services Research, these and other data collected on populations of color can be used to assess the validity of outcomes measurement instruments when used with minority groups. "This is important data because it shows that no matter what the patient's cultural background, BASIS is a useful tool for determining the results of psychiatric care."

According to Paul Youd, MSPCC utilization manager, the society now incorporates BASIS into every patient assessment and is hoping to use ongoing results in its future quality management plans. "It's certainly helpful to know that clients are improving as a result of care. Now, we'd like to go to the next step." That next step is to specifically address areas in which patients do not show improvement according to BASIS results. "We'd like to sort questionnaires that indicate no improvement in certain domains and take a look at why this may be occurring. It also would be helpful in looking for statewide pat-

---

Source: A "Global" Look at BASIS-32. McLean Reports *Winter 1998; Volume 5. Reprinted with permission from McLean Hospital, Belmont MA 02478.*

terns and, of course, for continuing to improve services."

Greenleaf Health Systems, based in Chattanooga, Tenn., has been using McLean's BASIS-32 for more than four years to assess adult inpatients and more recently, adult partial hospital patients, in both generic and specialty programs. "Even with the declines in length of stay, patients are still showing statistically and clinically significant behavior improvements following treatment. This is encouraging since the acuity of illness is going up," says Richard White, Greenleaf's vice president of Marketing.

After four years at Greenleaf, BASIS-32 has become an essential part of the organization's internal CQI efforts; additionally, it now is used for visits by the Joint Commission on the Accreditation of Healthcare Organizations. Finally, one of the first health organizations in the south to have clinical outcomes measures built into its care system, Greenleaf is using BASIS-32 in developing its managed care business.

In the future, White says Greenleaf hopes to add additional instruments to BASIS and to expand its use beyond the Tennessee border. As chairperson of the 11-hospital, statewide Georgia Behavioral Health Coalition, White is optimistic that he will be able to use BASIS in all hospitals in this provider system.

The **Departments of Mental Health in Los Angeles and San Francisco** counties are using the BASIS-32 in a collaborative project that began in September 1996. Along with other standardized measures, the BASIS-32 is being administered at intake and then again at six-month intervals to severely mentally ill adult and older adult outpatients at 25 program sites in the combined counties. By using a state-of-the-art, onsite scanning, system, immediate test results can be available for clinician and client.

According to Astrid Beigel, PhD, of the Los Angeles County Department of Mental Health, the two counties are in the process of analyzing, baseline data and soon will have sufficient numbers of clients who have completed two administrations to look at changes in client status over time. Beigel reports generally favorable responses from clinicians regarding BASIS' clinical usefulness. "Clinicians are reporting it is helpful in assessment and treatment planning. We do have to train and retrain the clinicians. We also have to reassure them that using BASIS is not intended to replace their clinical skills or judgement, but should be seen as a source of valuable information about the client's perception of his or her functioning."

McLean's BASIS Results

While the BASIS-32 originally was designed to assess inpatient care, the instrument now is being used to measure results of outpatient care and partial hospitalization as well. The following section presents McLean's 1995-1996 BASIS data for inpatients and outpatients.

Fig. 1 BASIS-32 Average at Admission: 1996 Patients

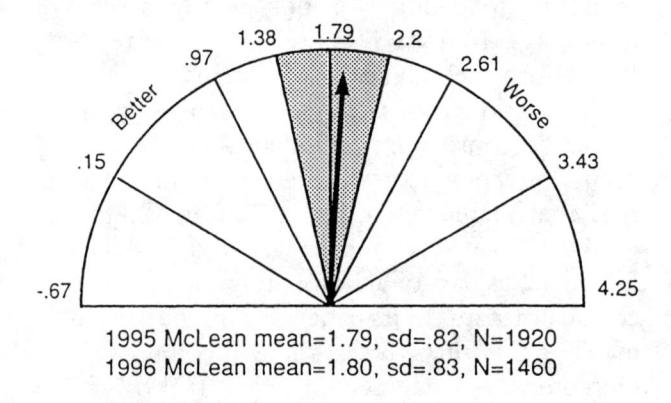

1995 McLean mean=1.79, sd=.82, N=1920
1996 McLean mean=1.80, sd=.83, N=1460

Fig. 2 BASIS-32 Average at Discharge: 1996 Patients

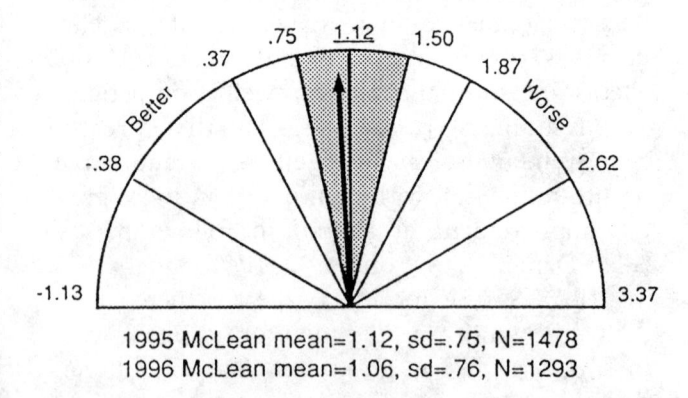

1995 McLean mean=1.12, sd=.75, N=1478
1996 McLean mean=1.06, sd=.76, N=1293

The instrument panels present the overall, mean BASIS-32 scores at admission and discharge for McLean patients discharged in 1996 compared to those discharged in 1995. The numbers at the apex indicate the mean 1995 scores, while the arrows indicate the mean 1996 scores. The

Fig. 3 Mean BASIS-32 Scores at Intake and Follow-up: McLean Outpatients, 1995-1996

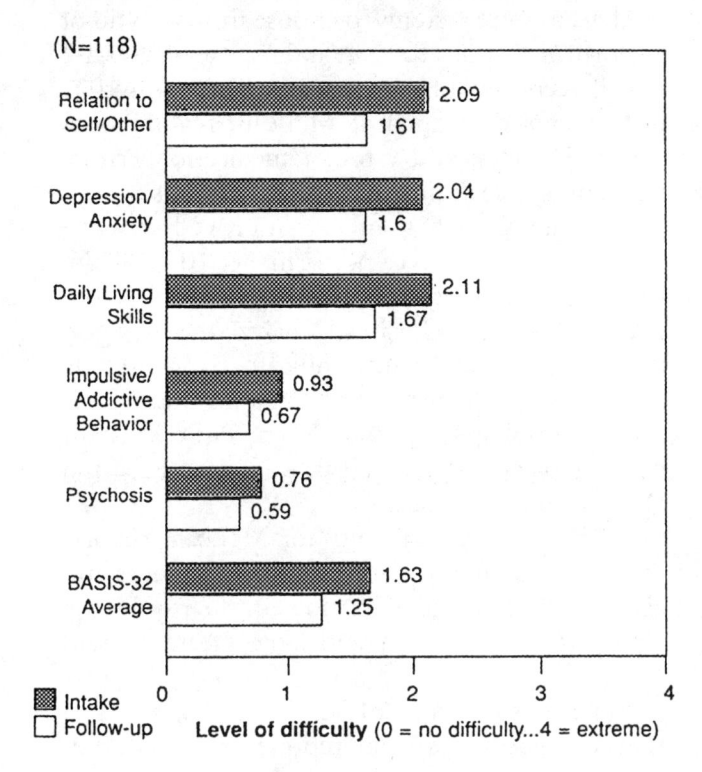

(N=118)

Subscale	Intake	Follow-up
Relation to Self/Other	2.09	1.61
Depression/Anxiety	2.04	1.6
Daily Living Skills	2.11	1.67
Impulsive/Addictive Behavior	0.93	0.67
Psychosis	0.76	0.59
BASIS-32 Average	1.63	1.25

Level of difficulty (0 = no difficulty...4 = extreme)

panels show that patient self-reported difficulty and degree of improvement in 1996 were very similar to those reported in 1995. In both years, patients showed statistically significant improvement across all BASIS results.

The graph represents mean BASIS-32 scores at intake and at four-to-eight-week follow-up for 118 patients treated through the McLean Outpatient Psychiatry Service. Change over time was statistically significant for each of the BASIS-32 subscales and for the overall mean score.

Predictors of Improvement

BASIS-32 scores at admission and discharge indicate that the great majority of patients (about 80 percent) show clinical improvement over the course of hospitalization. However, some patients improve much more than others, while a few patients worsen or improve much less than others.

In order to use clinical outcomes data to improve quality of care, it is helpful to identify the factors that may predict who will improve less than the expected mean. The McLean outcomes database includes demographic and clinical information, such as diagnosis and length of stay, as well as information on satisfaction as measured by McLean's patient self-report survey, Perceptions of Care (PoC).

Controlling for severity at admission, McLean has identified several variables as being statistically significant predictors of worse than the expected mean of clinical improvement:

- comorbid Axis 11 diagnosis (personality disorder)
- low socioeconomic status
- living in a half-way house or other treatment setting prior to admission
- lower perceived satisfaction as measured by the PoC survey

Diagnosis, socioeconomic status and housing, arrangements are pre-existing factors over which clinicians have limited control. However, because patients' perception of care can be within clinicians' control, improving patient satisfaction might have a positive impact on clinical outcomes.

BASIS-32 as an Alliance Builder

Clinicians and clinical administrators sometimes question the "validity" of patient self-report instruments, like the BASIS-32 and McLean's Perceptions of Care (PoC), particularly when they are used with acutely or severely ill patients and when the clinician's assessment differs significantly from that of the patient.

At McLean, we regard differences in perspective as genuine, but a potential impediment to effective treatment. Unless the patient's perspective, and distress, is understood and recognized, a treatment alliance may elude the treating clinician. McLean clinicians hope to expand the uses and usefulness of BASIS-32 by highlighting patient and clinician differences.

"Our thought is that the BASIS-32 might serve as a tool to uncover differences and thereby build upon patient-treater alliances and enhance treatment outcome and patient satisfaction," says Lloyd Sederer, MD, medical director and executive vice president for McLean.

In a pilot study, McLean used matched patient groups to determine the outcome of meeting or not meeting with a patient to review his/her BASIS-32 scores and validate his/her experience and expectations. "Our clinical hypothesis is that a review with the patient of the patient's self report at admission will enable the patient to feel better understood, help the clinician better establish a treatment alliance and better bridge differences in the patient's and clinician's goals. Outcome and satisfaction thereby can be enhanced," says Sederer.

Preliminary results show important statistical evidence to support the use of BASIS-32 to enhance alliance and patient satisfaction.

McLean's Performance Measurement System Wins JCAHO Approval

McLean's BASIS-32 Plus Performance Measurement System has received the endorsement of the nation's largest hospital accrediting body.

The Joint Commission on Accreditation of Healthcare Organizations (JCAHO) has given its nod of approval for "BASIS-32 Plus" to become a JCAHO-endorsed performance measurement system through its newly established ORYX initiative.

Under the JCAHO's ORYX program, all behavioral health care facilities wishing to attain JCAHO accreditation will have to adopt a JCAHO-endorsed, clinical performance measurement system by 1998 or 1999, when the new standards are expected to take effect.

"BASIS-32 Plus represents an important resource for psychiatric facilities and services that are seeking an effective, affordable, risk-adjusted outcomes assessment system," said Lloyd Sederer, MD, McLean's medical director and executive vice president. "We are delighted to be chosen for inclusion by the JCAHO."

BASIS-32 Plus is a comprehensive performance measurement system that enables behavioral health care systems to choose from a menu of performance indicators, including the BASIS-32 and Perceptions of Care, two patient self-report instruments developed at McLean; readmissions within 30 days; and rates of medication errors, restraint and seclusion and patient assaults.

As the provider of an approved system, McLean will receive performance data from behavioral health care organizations that choose BASIS-32 Plus. McLean will analyze their data on their chosen performance indicators and provide reports as well as benchmark data on the organization's results, said Susan Eisen, PhD, assistant director of the Mental Health Services Research Department at McLean.

"This is an opportunity for McLean Reports to extend its outcomes measurement services and expertise to other organizations in the psychiatric field. We are honored and very pleased," said Eisen.

The designation of BASIS-32 Plus as a JCAHO-accepted system represents yet another distinction for McLean in the outcomes assessment arena. BASIS-32, requested for use by more than 1,500 health care providers across the country, earned the New England Healthcare Assembly's 1996 Blue Ribbon Award for innovation in health care; was recognized by the National Alliance for the Mentally Ill/Johns Hopkins Outcomes Roundtable Steering Committee as an exemplary outcomes program; and was accepted into the Medical Outcomes Trust library of internationally available outcomes measurement instruments.

Validation of the Panic Outcomes Module

JAN HOLLENBERG, KATHRYN M. ROST, JOYLYN HUMPHREY, RICHARD R. OWEN, JR, G. RICHARD SMITH, JR.

This article discusses the validation of a module designed to evaluate the outcomes of clinical care for panic disorder. The research utilized a longitudinal design to examine cross-sectional relationships and change over time within and between subjects. Baseline, follow-up, and test-retest data were collected on 73 patients. The initial field test indicates that the Panic Outcomes Module measures outcomes and case-mix characteristic with acceptable levels of measurement error for group data. The module's measure of change in panic severity demonstrated encouraging agreement with the structured judgment of change. This module, completed in approximately 20 minutes, is short enough to incorporate into outpatient mental health settings. We recommend that providers and administrators interested in monitoring the outcomes of specialty care for panic disorder seek assistance from health services researchers to use the Panic Outcomes Module. Further research is needed to validate this module for use in primary care populations

Recent community studies estimate that 3.5% of the general population (Kessler et al., 1994) meet lifetime criteria for panic disorder as defined by the Diagnostic and Statistical Manual of Mental Disorders-III-Revised (American Psychiatric Association, 1987). An additional 3.6% of the population report having one or more panic attacks in their lifetime (Klerman, Weissman, Ouellette, Johnson, & Greenwald, 1991). Efficacious treatments for panic disorder utilizing psychopharmacologic agents (Ballenger et al., 1988; Chouinard, Annable, Fontaine, & Solyom, 1982; Lydiard et al., 1992; Ravaris, Friedman, Hauri, & McHugo, 1991) and cognitive behavioral therapies (Barlow, 1992; Beck, 1988; Beck, Sokol, Clark, Berchick, & Wright, 1992; Klosko, Barlow, Tassinari, & Cerny, 1990) have been developed to treat patients with this debilitating condition. We have very little information on the proportion of panic patients who receive effective treatment when they seek care from mental health professionals, nor do we understand much about the outcomes of care routinely provided for panic disorder. To address these questions, there is a need for data collection procedures to be created to collect reliable and valid information about disease-specific outcomes of panic disorder. Such an instrument (or instruments) could be used in conjunction with existing measures, such as the Health Status Questionnaire (McHomey, Lu, & Ware, 1991), which measure general health status.

Following the direction provided by a nine member, multi-institutional panel, we created a series of four instruments known as the Panic

---

Source: Hollenberg J, Rost KM, Humphrey J, Owen RR, and Smith GR. Validation of the Panic Outcomes Module. Evaluation & the Health Professions 1997; 20(1):81-95. Copyright © 1997 by Sage Publications, Inc. Reprinted by permission of Sage Publications, Inc.

Authors' Note: This work was supported in part by the NIMH Center for Rural Mental Healthcare Research (P50MH48197). The authors gratefully acknowledge help from Andrea Waller, Carl Elliot, Cindy Mosley, Debbie Hodges, Melonie Shelton, Dan Ranieri, Shelly Alberts, Pat Barber, Cathy Gerrol, Thomas Babor, David Barlow, Audrey Burnam, Barbara Burns, Jennifer Jones, Wayne Katon, Faye Luscombe, and the clinicians and who participated in the study. The research here was supported by the Upjohn Company. Address correspondence and requests for reprints to Jan Hollenberg, M.S., Department of Psychiatry and Behavioral Sciences, 4301 West Markham, Slot 554, Little Rock, AR 72205, (501) 686-5600.

Outcomes Module. The module was designed to evaluate the outcomes of clinical care by measuring the types and extent of care delivered to patients with panic disorder, the outcomes of that care, and the patient characteristics that influence either the type or outcomes of care. The specific objectives of this project include (a) determination of the accuracy of the diagnosis of panic disorder made by self-report in the outcomes module compared to psychiatric assessment, (b) investigation of the reliability and validity of key constructs in the module, (c) the examination of the module's sensitivity in measuring important clinical changes, and (d) exploration of the feasibility of administering the module to a representative group of patients in a routine care setting.

Method

Design

The research utilized a longitudinal design to examine cross-sectional relationships and change over time within and between subjects. A cohort of 73 patients beginning treatment for an episode of panic disorder who met the eligibility criteria outlined below were referred to the study by clinicians conducting initial evaluations and treatment in three managed mental health care programs over a 21 month period. Baseline data were collected from patients using self-administered instruments and personal interviews. Baseline data also were collected from the clinician using self-administered instruments. Follow-up data, including test-retest information, were collected from patients using self-administered instruments and personal interviews.

Control subjects also were needed to evaluate the concordance between a diagnosis of panic disorder based on the self-administered module and a diagnosis based on a structured psychiatric interview. To meet this need, a referred sample of 24 patients who were without a lifetime diagnosis of panic disorder and were beginning treatment in the same mental health settings for any other psychiatric disorder also completed self-administered instruments and personal interviews at baseline.

Recruitment of Subjects

A research assistant instructed all clinicians in the three treatment settings on the eligibility requirements at the beginning of the study, informed them that they would be paid $50 for each subject they referred, and reviewed the criteria multiple times with each clinician during the recruitment phase. Eligible patients were defined as patients who met the following criteria in the judgment of the clinicians: primary or secondary diagnosis of current panic disorder, first visit for panic disorder or current exacerbation of panic disorder, 18 years of age or older, able to follow written instructions in English, no psychotic episode in past year, sufficient cognitive function to report about the past 6 months, and a telephone at home—with no hearing impairment that would preclude telephone interview.

Initial eligibility criteria also required that subjects were not currently on any anti-anxiety drugs (e.g., prescribed by primary care provider before referral to specialty care) to maximize our ability to examine change in anxiety over time; however, this requirement was dropped early in recruitment when we discovered it eliminated the vast majority of otherwise eligible patients.

Clinicians in the same treatment settings also referred an additional 24 subjects to serve as controls. The research team determined that control patients had no lifetime history of panic disorder by a structured psychiatric interview. Control subjects met all other criteria listed above. In addition, the protocol required that they be 65 years of age or younger, because panic disorder is more prevalent in younger cohorts (Robins et al., 1984).

According to the protocol approved for human subjects research, a representative in each treatment setting met with each newly referred patient to explain the purpose of the study and the estimated time involved in the initial assessment, a follow-up assessment, and a test-retest assessment. Subjects were assured that all information collected from self-administered instruments and personal interviews at baseline and follow-up would not be shared with the treatment team unless that patient requested, that results of the study would be presented for groups of patients only, and that their course of treatment would not be affected by their participation in the study. Each participant was told that completion of the follow-up assessment was crucial to the study regardless of success with treatment. Only one eligible panic patient refused to participate after referral. One control patient was eliminated when the structured psychiatric interview indicated the patient met criteria for panic disorder in remission.

Data Collection

Subjects completed the Patient Baseline Assessment of the Panic Outcomes Module and accompanying validation instruments the day of or the day after referral. They also completed a structured psychiatric interview an average of 3.3 days after referral (range 0-25). The interview was administered over the telephone by an experienced mental health research clinician. Clinicians completed the Clinician Baseline Assessment and three validation instruments on average the day of referral (range 0-6). After the completion of all baseline interviews, panic patients and control subjects were reimbursed $50. Clinicians were paid $50 for completing baseline data collection for each patient referred.

Follow-Up Subjects

The research assistant called panic subjects 2 months after their index visit. Patients were reminded that no information would be shared with the treatment team unless the patient requested. Following this telephone call, two sets of self-administered forms were sent to each subject. The first set of forms consisted of the Patient Follow-up Assessment of the Panic Outcomes Module and accompanying validation instruments. Patients were instructed to complete these immediately on arrival. The second set of forms included only the Patient Follow-up Assessment that was administered to establish test-retest reliability. Subjects were instructed to complete the second set of forms 3 days after completing the first set and return all forms in the mail to the research assistant. Within 3 days of receiving these forms, a mental health research clinician contacted each subject to administer a structured psychiatric interview over the telephone. When this interview was completed and all forms had been returned, the subject received a second check for $75.

Instruments Used in the Study

Panic Outcomes Module

The Panic Outcomes Module consists of the Patient Baseline Assessment, the Clinician Baseline Assessment, the Patient Follow-up Assessment, and the Medical Record Review. The self-administered Patient Baseline Assessment was designed to establish a diagnosis of panic disorder based on patient self-report to examine change in outcomes over time by measuring baseline levels of relevant outcomes, and to measure patient case-mix characteristics that previous research has shown to affect outcomes. The Clinician Baseline Assessment includes the assessment of eligibility criteria to participate in outcomes monitoring, questions that establish a diagnosis of panic disorder, and initial treatment recommendations. The self-administered Patient Follow-up Assessment provides outcomes data on the same constructs measured at baseline. It also contains patient reports about treatment received from sources other than the major provider or payer of care. The Medical Record Review provides information regarding treatment received for panic disorder by measuring both pharmacologic and psychotherapy treatments. The self-administered Health Status Questionnaire (HSQ) (McHomey et al., 1991) is a 36-item instrument administered at baseline and follow-up measuring health status dimensions that complement the outcomes m the Panic Outcomes Module.[1]

Validation Instruments

The mental health research clinician administered the Anxiety Disorders Interview Schedule (ADIS) (DiNardo, Moras, Barlow, Rapee, & Brown, 1990) and the Diagnostic Interview Schedule (DIS) (Robins & Helzer, 1982) (Somatization Disorder, Generalized Anxiety Disorder, Major Depression and Dysthymia, Alcohol Abuse and Dependence, Drug Abuse and Dependence). The patient completed the Brief Symptom Inventory (BSI) (Derogatis & Melisaratos, 1983), the Acute Panic Inventory (API) (Dillon, Lorman, Leibowitz, Fyer, & Klein, 1987), the Agoraphobic Cognition Questionnaire (ACQ) (Chambless, Caputo, Bright, & Gallagher, 1984), the Body Sensations Questionnaire (BSQ) (Chambless et al., 1984), the Mobility Inventory (MD (Chambless, Caputo, Jasin, Gracely, & Williams, 1985), the

Sheehan Disability Scale (SDS) (Leon, Shear, Portera, & Klerman, 1992), the Emotional Control Questionnaire (ECQ) (Rapee, Craske, & Barlow, 1989), and the Marks Fear Questionnaire (MFQ) (Marks & Mathews, 1979). The treating clinician completed the Hamilton Anxiety Scale (HAS) (Hamilton, 1959), the Hamilton Depression Scale (HDS) (Hamilton, 1960), and the MC-PAS (Shear, Sholomskas, & Cloitre, 1993).

Results

Subject Description

For the 73 subjects recruited, the mean age was 36.7 years (SD = 9.5, range 21 to 71), 52 (71%) were female. Sixty-four (88%) were Caucasian, 2 (3%) were African American, and 7 (10%) were of other racial backgrounds. Forty-seven subjects (64%) were currently married. Sixty-six subjects (90%) had graduated from high school. Sixty-three subjects (86%) had annual incomes of greater than $20,000; 7 (10%) had incomes between $10,000 and $20,000; and 3 (4%) had incomes of less than $10,000. All subjects were diagnosed as meeting DSM-III-R (American Psychiatric Association, 1987) criteria for current panic disorder by the ADIS. Sixty subjects (83.3%) also met DSM-III-R criteria for current agoraphobia on the ADIS.

ADIS interviews indicated that subjects had experienced on average 8.9 full panic attacks (SD = 12.8, range 0-60) in the last month and, on average, 18.6 limited panic attacks (SD = 33.6, range 0-150). Structured psychiatric diagnoses of co-occurring lifetime psychiatric disorders using the Diagnostic Interview Schedule showed that 13 subjects (17.8%) met criteria for gene anxiety disorder, 39 subjects (53.4%) met criteria for major depression or dysthymia, 7 subjects (9.6%) met criteria for alcohol abuse and/or dependence, 11 subjects (15.1%) met criteria for drug abuse and/or dependence, and 1 subject (1.4%) met criteria for somatization disorder. No subjects reported any lifetime psychotic symptoms. We obtained information on 70 subjects after discharge (95.9%), an average of 2.3 months after their index visit (SD = 0.6, range 1.1-4.8 months).

Twelve clinicians in the three treatment settings participated in the study. Three were psychiatrists, 5 were Ph.D. psychologists, and 4 were masters level psychologists or social workers.

Accuracy of Patient Reports About Diagnostic Criteria

The first objective of the study was to compare the agreement between the 1 month diagnosis derived from the Patient Baseline Assessment with the 1 month diagnosis made in the structured psychiatric interview. The patient-derived diagnosis demonstrated unacceptable agreement with the ADIS diagnosis of current panic disorder (K =.32). However, there was good concordance between the clinician-derived diagnosis based on two items in the Clinician Baseline Assessment and the ADIS diagnosis (K = .61). The clinician diagnosis in the module has 79% sensitivity in the panic population and 92% specificity in the nonpanic populations.

Reliability and Validity of Key Constructs in the Module

The second objective of the study was to determine the reliability and validity of key constructs in the outcomes module. Key constructs were divided into two domains: outcomes and case-mix variables.

Outcomes: Reliability

The three outcomes measured by scales demonstrated excellent internal consistency: .82 for sensitivity to anxiety, .86 for distress/avoidance, and .89 for marital functioning. Strong test-retest reliability was demonstrated for the remaining single item outcomes measures, ranging from .78 to .97. Only two measures, sensitivity to anxiety and self-medication of alcohol or drugs, showed differences on test-retest comparisons; both had significantly higher scores at test.

Outcomes: Validity

We validated outcomes measures in the module by examining the relationships between module measures and gold standard measures of overlapping constructs, as shown in Table 1. The majority of the outcomes scales were compared with multiple gold standard measures because there was not a single gold standard measure that measured the exact construct we were trying to tap.

Table 1. Validity of Outcomes Measures

Module Outcomes Measure	Standard	Correlation
Frequency of panic attacks	ADIS[a]	.71
Number of symptoms during the panic attack	ADIS	.60
Sensitivity to anxiety	Acute Panic Inventory	.72
	Agoraphobic Cognition Questionnaire Subscales	.45–.67
Anticipatory	Emotional Control Questionnaire	.41
	ADIS	.61
	Hamilton Anxiety	.27
Avoidance/distress	ADIS	.62
	Hamilton Anxiety	.26
	Marks Fear Questionnaire	.68
	Mobility Index Inventory for Agoraphobic Subscales	.74–.76
	Body Symptom Questionnaire	.58
Suicidality	Hamilton Depression Item	.56
Occupational functioning	Sheehan Scale Item	.60
	Marks Subjective Symptom Scale Item	.53
	MC-PAS Scale Item	.54
Marital functioning	Marks Subjective Symptom Scale	.40–.56
	Sheehan Scale	.56
Sexual functioning	Marks Subjective Symptom Scale Item	.39
	Sheehan Scale Item	.36
	Hamilton Depression Item	.39
	Hamilton Anxiety Item	.42
Life satisfaction	Brief Symptom Inventory Subscales	.41–.75
	Sheehan Scale Item	.45–.54
	ADIS	.40
	Hamilton Depression Scale	.56
	Hamilton Anxiety Scale	.45
Self-medication		
Smoking	Severity of Panic on ADIS	.24
Alcohol/Drugs	Severity of Panic on ADIS	.27
Social functioning	Marks Subjective Symptom Scale Item	.67
	Sheehan Scale Item	.61
	MC-PAS Item	.45
Bed days	Severity of Panic on ADIS	.22
	Severity of Agoraphobia on ADIS	.36

[a] ADIS = Anxiety Disorders Interview Schedule

All module measures maintained significant positive correlations with the gold standard constructs. These correlations ranged between .22 and .76.

Case-Mix Variables: Validity

As shown in Table 2, the validity of many case-mix variables was excellent. The module measure of frequency of panic attacks correlated strongly (r = .71) with the ADIS measure of frequency. Patient self-report about current agoraphobia showed good agreement with the structured interview (K = .57), as did their report on lifetime depression and/or dysthymia (K = .55). Both measures of lifetime alcohol and drug abuse/dependence from the module demonstrated encouraging concordance with the DIS (K = .62 and Yule's Q = .74, respectively). The lifelong worry question used to assess lifetime generalized anxiety disorder in the module did not compare well with the DIS diagnosis. Somatization disorder was dropped from consideration as a case-mix measure due to its low prevalence rate (1.4%).

Sensitivity to Change

The third objective of the study was to examine the module's sensitivity to clinically relevant change. Specifically, we were interested in evaluating the extent to which changes in frequency of panic attacks, anticipatory anxiety, and avoidance/distress patients reported between baseline and follow-up on the Outcomes Module correlated with a psychiatric interviewer's ratings of changes of these measures. Our analyses indicated that module measure of these constructs correlated .47, .59, and .44, respectively, with change in ADIS ratings of the same constructs.

Feasibility

The fourth objective of the study was to gather information about the feasibility of outcomes monitoring in routine clinical situations. We divided our investigations of feasibility into three areas: missing data, length of time needed to fill out forms, and following a representative group of patients with panic disorder.

First, using the protocol we described, there was little missing data on outcomes forms. Less than 1% of the data were missing, on average, from the Patient Baseline Assessment (range across patients 0-18%). Similarly, there were low levels of missing data on the Clinician Baseline Assessment across patients (x 0.7%, range across patients 0-13%). Predictably, there was substantially more data missing from the Patient Follow-up Assessment. Of the 70 subjects (95.9%) contacted at follow-up, 5% of the data were missing on average (range 1-10%). The scoring included in the manual provides instructions that score the nonmissing items for a given scale, so that the patient does not drop out of the analysis if they are missing a limited amount of data.

Second, patients on average took 18.5 minutes to complete the Patient Baseline Assessment (range 5-45 minutes). Clinicians on average took 8.6 minutes to complete the Clinician Baseline Assessment (range 3-45 minutes). The Patient Follow-up Assessment took 19.5 minutes on average to complete (range 9-85 minutes). Because many items have been eliminated from each instrument in the module, we expect completion times for the revised Panic Outcomes Module to be substantially shorter.

Third, the largest feasibility issue in implementing an outcomes management system for panic disorder is following a representative group of patients with the tracer condition in the treatment setting. We could not judge this because we were studying a referred cohort rather than a consecutive cohort of patients with panic diagnosis. We did, however, find it was feasible to follow 95.9% of referred patients who were being reimbursed for their participation 2 months after their index visit.

Table 2

Validity of Case-Mix Measures

Module Case-mix Measure	Standard	Correlation
Frequency of panic attacks	ADIS	.71
Psychiatric		
Agoraphobia	ADIS	(.57)
Lifetime depression/		
dysthymia	Diagnostics Interview Schedule	(.55)
Generalized anxiety disorder	Diagnostics Interview Schedule	(.08)
Lifetime alcohol abuse/		
dependence	Diagnostics Interview Schedule	(.62)
Lifetime drug abuse/		
dependence	Diagnostics Interview Schedule	(.74)[a]
Personality disorder	None available	
Medical comorbidities	None available	
Duration of panic disorder	None available	

NOTE: ( ) = κ
[a] Nonprevalence dependent concordance measure Yule's Q.

Discussion

The results from this initial field test indicate that the Panic Outcomes Module measures the outcomes and most case-mix constructs suggested by our expert panel with levels of measurement error acceptable for the analysis of group data. The major outcomes measures demonstrate good to excellent reliability, validity, and sensitivity to change over time. Patients cooperated in completing the module so that relatively little data were missing. Both patient and clinician components of the module appear to be short enough to incorporate into routine clinical settings. However, our results may overstate the feasibility of conducting outcomes monitoring in the larger group of patients because our sample was clinician-referred and well-compensated for their participation.

The strengths of this study include the careful execution of the protocol, high rates of follow-up (95.9%), the construction of outcomes measures with good reliability and validity, and the demonstration of criterion and concurrent validity for case-mix variables. The weaknesses of the study include the lack of information to determine the representativeness of this group to panic patients in these treatment settings, missing test-retest reliability estimates for case-mix variables, limited reliability or validity testing of the treatment variables in the module, and limited information to address questions on combining case-mix variables to allow statistical adjustment for between-group comparisons. Studies in larger populations of panic patients are needed to create and test various approaches to case-mix adjustment before cross-site comparisons can be meaningfully made. These studies need to determine whether case-mix variable adjustment can best be accomplished by latent variable approaches, analysis of covariance approaches using multiple covariates, or the use of a single covariate (e.g., severity). Validation studies addressing the specific aims we have outlined here in primary care populations also are needed before the module can be meaningfully used in these settings.

Based on these findings, we recommend that providers and administrators interested in monitoring the outcomes of care for panic disorder in specialty care settings seek assistance from health services researchers to develop a site-specific protocol using the Panic Outcomes Module to add to the knowledge base established by this initial study. Our experience indicates that clinicians in mental health care settings should refer all patients they suspect as having panic disorder into an outcomes management protocol. Patients who do not meet diagnostic criteria on the Physician Baseline Assessment can then be excluded, leaving the outcomes management team with a relatively diagnostically homogeneous group of patients to follow over time. The protocol should include the identification of staff whose primary responsibility is to recruit a representative sample of patients into the protocol and conduct follow-up interviews within a specified window, regardless of whether patients complete the program. Administrators also should seek assistance from investigators in the analysis and interpretation of the nonexperimental data generated by this protocol. The addition of sufficient resources to conduct outcomes monitoring will provide previously unavailable insights to clinicians and program administrators about practice variation and the relative effectiveness of various treatments provided patients with panic disorder.

Note:[1] The module and accompanying manual are available free of charge by writing Suzanne McCarthy, Center for Outcomes Research and Effectiveness, 4301 W. Markham, Slot 554, Little Rock. AR 72205 or by calling (501) 686-5600.

References

American Psychiatric Association. (1987). *Diagnostic and statistical manual of mental disorders* (3rd ed.). Washington, DC: Author.

Ballenger, J.C, Burrows, G.D., DuPont, R.L., Jr., Lesser, I.M., Noyes, R., Jr., Pecknold, J.C., Rifkin, A, & Swinson, R.P. (1988). Alprazolam in panic disorder and agoraphobia: Results from a multi center trial: I. Efficacy in short-term treatment. *Archives of General Psychiatry*, 45, 413-422.

Barlow, D.H. (1992). Cognitive-behavioral approaches to panic disorder and social phobia. *Bulletin of the Menninger Clinic*, 56(2 Suppl A), A14-A28.

Beck, A.T. (1998). Cognitive approaches to panic disorder. Theory and therapy. In S. Rachman

& J. D Maser (Eds.), *Panic: Psychological Perspectives* (pp. 91-109). Hillsdale, NJ: Lawrence Erlbaum.

Beck, A.T. Sokol, L.. Clark, D.A., Berchick. R., & Wright, F. (1992). A crossover study of focused cognitive therapy for panic disorder. *American Journal of Psychiatry,* 149, 778-783.

Chambless. D.L. Caputo, G.C., Bright, P., & Gallagher, R. (1994). Assessment of fear in agoraphobics: The Body Sensations Questionnaire and the Agoraphobic Cognitions Questionnaire. *Journal of Consulting and Clinical Psychology,* 52, 1090-1097.

Chambless, D.L, Caputo, G.C., Jasin, S.E., Gracely, E.J., & Williams, C. (1985). The mobility inventory for agoraphobia. *Behaviour Research & Therapy,* 23, 35-44.

Chouinard, G, Annable, L, Fontaine, R., & Solyom, L (1982). Alprazolam in the treatment of generalized anxiety and panic disorders: A double-blind placebo-controlled study. *Psychopharmacology,* 77, 229-233.

Derogatis, L.R., & Melisaratos, N. (1983).The brief symptom inventory: An introductory report. *Psychological Medicine,* 13, 595-605.

Dillon, D.J., Lorman, J.M., Leibowitz, M.R., Fyer, A.J., & Klein, D.F. (1987). Measurement of panic and anxiety. *Psychiatry Research,* 20, 97-105.

DiNardo, P.A., Moras, I.C., Barlow, D.H., Rapee, R.M., & Brown, TA. (1990). Reliability of DSM-III-R anxiety disorder categories: Using the Anxiety Disorders Interview Schedule Revised (ADIS-R). *Archives of General Psychiatry,* 50, 251-256.

Hamilton. M. (1959). The assessment of anxiety states by rating. *British Journal of Medical Psychology,* 32, 50-55.

Hamilton. M. (1960). A rating scale for depression. *Journal of Neurology, Neurosurgery, & Psychiatry,* 23, 56-62.

Kessler, R.C., McGonagle, K.A., Zhao, S., Nelson, C.B., Hughes, M., Eshleman, S., Wittchen, H., & Kendler, K.S. (1994). Lifetime and 12-month prevalence of DSM-III-R psychiatric disorders in the United States: Results from the national comorbidity survey. *Archives of General Psychiatry,* 51, 8-19.

Klerman, G.L, Weissman, M.M., Ouellette, R., Johnson, J., & Greenwald, S. (1991). Panic in the community: Social morbidity and health care utilization. *Journal of the American Medical Association,* 265, 742-746.

Klosko. J.S., Barlow, D.H., Tassinari, R., & Cerny, J.A. (1990). A comparison of Alprazolam and behavior therapy in treatment of panic disorder. *Journal of Consulting and Clinical Psychology,* 58, 77-84.

Leon, A.C., Shear, M.C., Portera, L., & Klerman, G.L. (1992). Assessing impairment in patients with panic disorder: The Sheehan Disability Scale. *Social Psychiatry & Psychiatric Epidemiology,* 27, 78-82.

Lydiard, R.B., Lesser, I.M., Ballenger, J.C., Rubin, R.T., A.M., & Dupont, R. (1992). A fixed-dose study of alprazolam 2 mg, alprazolam 6 mg, and placebo in panic disorder. *Journal of Clinical Psychopharmacology,* 12, 96-103.

Marks, I.M, & Mathews, A.M. (1979). Brief standard self-rating for phobic patients. *Behaviour Research & Therapy,* 17, 263-267.

McHorney, C., Lu, R., & Ware, J. (1991). *36-Item Short Form Survey: III. Preliminary tests in patients with medical and psychiatric conditions.* Unpublished manuscript.

Rapee, R.M., Craske, M.G., & Barlow, D.H. (1989, November). *The Emotional Control Questionnaire.* Poster session presented at American Association of Behavioral Therapies Annual Meeting, Washington, DC. Unpublished manuscript.

Ravaris, C.L., Friedman, M.J., Hauri RJ., & McHugo, G.J. (1991). A controlled study of alprazolam and propanolol in panic-disordered and agoraphobic outpatients. *Journal of Clinical Psychopharmacology,* 11, 344-350.

Robins, L.N., & Helzer J.E. (1982). Diagnostic interview schedule. *Archives of General Psychiatry,* 39, 1442-1445.

Robins, L.N., Helzer, J.E., Weissman, M.M., Orvascbel, H., Gruenberg, E., Burke, J.D., & Regier, D. (1994). Lifetime prevalence of specific psychiatric disorders in three sites. *Archives of General Psychiatry,* 41, 949-958.

Shear, M.K., Sholomskas, D., & Cloitre, M. (1993). *Information on reliability and validity of the MC-PAS.* Unpublished manuscript.

A Consumer-Constructed Scale To Measure Empowerment Among Users Of Mental Health Services

E. SALLY ROGERS, ScD, JUDI CHAMBERLIN, MARSHA LANGER ELLISON, PhD, AND TIM CREAN, BA

Objective: A scale to measure the personal construct of empowerment as defined by consumers of mental health services was developed and field tested. *Methods*: After extensive development, pilot testing, and analyses, a 28-item scale to measure empowerment was tested on 271 members of six self-help programs in six states. Factor analyses were used to identify the underlying dimensions of empowerment. To establish the scale's reliability and validity, responses were factor analyzed, and other analyses were conducted. *Results*: Analyses revealed five factors: self-efficacy—self-esteem, power—powerlessness, community activism, righteous anger, and optimism—control over the future. Empowerment was related to quality of life and income but not to the demographic variables of age, gender, ethnicity, marital status, education level, or employment status. Empowerment was inversely related to use of traditional mental health services and positively related to community activism. *Conclusions*: The findings set a framework for a clearer understanding of the imprecise and overused concept of empowerment. The scale demonstrated adequate internal consistency and some evidence for validity. Further testing must be done to establish whether it has discriminant validity and is sensitive to change.

Despite the burgeoning use of the term "empowerment" in the lexicon of mental health programs, few researchers or service providers have attempted to define, operationalize, or measure it.[1,2] Early definitions of empowerment grew out of studies conducted by Rappaport,[3,4] who defined psychological empowerment as "the connection between a sense of personal competence, a desire for and a willingness to take action in the public domain."

McLean[1] noted that empowerment is often defined as the action of those who are disempowered and acting to become empowered. Furthermore, Segal and his colleagues[2] described empowerment as a process of "gaining control over one's life and influencing the organizational and societal structure in which one lives." Staples[5] described empowerment as "a process by which power is developed, facilitated, or sanctioned [allowing] subordinate individuals to build capacities to act on their own behalf."

In the mental health literature, empowerment appears most prominently in relation to the function or mission of self-help programs[6-8] and to how mental health professionals or services can promote empowerment.[9-11] Empowerment has been extensively discussed in several fields other than mental health, including social work, community psychology and case management. It has been appropriated by so many other fields that it has been referred to as a "buzzword" with little meaning. Simon[12] stated that the roots of empowerment lie in the "self-help and mutual aid

---

Source: Rogers ES, Chamberlin J, Langer Ellison M, and Crean T. A Consumer-Constructed Scale To Measure Empowerment Among Users of Mental Health Services. Psychiatric Services August 1997; 48(80:1042-1047. (Reprinted with permission.)

The authors are affiliated with the Center for Psychiatric Rehabilitation at Boston University, 930 Commonwealth Avenue, Boston, Massachusetts 02215.

tradition of the United States" and that "not a single constituency, or client population of the human services professions has failed to join the empowerment movement." Empowerment has also been studied in relation to family concerns[13-17] and to persons who are homeless and mentally ill.[18-21]

Despite this growing emphasis on empowerment as the goal of mental health services and self-help involvement, few empirical studies of empowerment as a construct, a process, or an outcome have been done. One qualitative inquiry has been conducted to examine empowerment from the consumer's perspective.[22] Rosenfield and her colleagues[23] have also attempted to define and study empowerment within the context of a psychosocial rehabilitation clubhouse program. Using a 21-item scale to measure empowerment, they found that it was associated with many aspects of quality of life but was unrelated to members' satisfaction with their employment or financial status. Similarly, Segal and associates[2] developed scales to measure the personal, organizational, and extraorganizational aspects of empowerment, which they tested on members of four client-run self-help agencies.

Although these studies have shed light on the construct of empowerment, more research is needed to develop a reliable and valid measure. The purpose of this study was to further define and operationalize the construct of personal empowerment from the perspective of consumers, survivors, and former patients and to construct and validate a scale that can be used in a variety of settings.

Methods

The survey was designed with the assistance of a consumer research advisory board, under the direction of the second author. At the outset of the project, the second author selected for the board ten individuals who were leaders in the consumer-survivor movement, who were able to represent various factions of that movement, and who were diverse in gender, ideology, ethnicity, and the area of the country in which they resided. Three meetings were held with the board to design and plan the study. The use of such a board is encouraged by proponents of participatory action research,[24,25] who assert that for evaluation to be meaningful and credible, constituents of that research must be involved.

Sample

Using various resources, the board developed a list of 200 self-help programs across the country, and letters were sent to each program requesting its participation. Based on the responses to the initial recruitment letter, final site selections were made. They included six self-help programs, one in each of six states: New Hampshire, New Jersey, Indiana, Arkansas, Washington, and California. Program selection was based on geographical and ethnic diversity; various types of consumer-run programs were chosen.

Each site identified an individual to act as a liaison. The second author visited all but one site to discuss the project further (the remaining site was contacted by telephone). On these visits she discussed the logistics of project implementation, met members, and secured the final agreement for participation.

Instruments

Instruments were developed using standard guidelines for paper-and-pencil surveys.[26,27]

Empowerment Scale. The board delineated 15 attributes of empowerment based on its definition of psychological empowerment (see box). The need for this process became apparent when the board reviewed and then rejected several standard psychological instruments as measures of empowerment. The board felt that no existing instrument captured the dimensions of empowerment in relation to persons with mental illness. Furthermore, board members feared that study participants might find these instruments offensive.

Then began the process of developing the scale by asking the board members to arrive at a consensus about a definition of empowerment that was relevant for persons with mental illness. Several dimensions of empowerment related to the definition, such as control over one's life, achievement of goals, self-esteem, and self-efficacy, were identified and agreed on.

Using these dimensions, items for the scale were modeled after the Rotter Internal-External Locus of Control Instrument,[28] the Self-Efficacy Scale,[29] and the Rosenberg Self-Esteem Scale.[30]

> **Attributes of Empowerment Developed By an Advisory Board Of Leaders of the Self-Help Movement**
>
> Having decision-making power
> Having access to information and resources
> Having a range of options from which to make choices (not just yes-no and either-or)
> Assertiveness
> A feeling that one can make a difference (being hopeful)
> Learning to think critically; unlearning the conditioning; seeing things differently. For example, learning to redefine who one is (speaking in one's own voice), learning to redefine what one can do, and learning to redefine one's relationships to institutionalized power
> Learning about and expressing anger
> Not feeling alone; feeling part of a group
> Understanding that a person has rights
> Effecting change in one's life and one's community
> Learning skills (for example, communication) that one defines as important
> Changing others' perceptions of one's competency and capacity to act
> Coming out of the closet
> Growth and change that is never-ending and self-initiated
> Increasing one's positive self-image and overcoming stigma

The initial scale consisted of 48 items, rated on a four-point Likert scale ranging from strongly agree to strongly disagree. It was tested on a sample of 100 subjects in two self-help programs in New Hampshire. Factor and reliability analyses were conducted, and 28 items having the highest factor loadings were retained.

The final items of the scale did not address all aspects of the board's original definition of empowerment; however, the board was satisfied that most aspects were addressed and that the items captured the essence of empowerment as they perceived and defined it.

Other instruments. In addition to the Empowerment Scale, seven brief instruments were developed for use in this study. They included a checklist of 22 traditional mental health services on which respondents indicated whether they had used each service in the past year; a five-item scale to assess the effect of self-help on social supports; an 11-item scale to assess the effect of self-help on quality of life; a five-item scale to assess the effect of self-help on self-esteem; a 19-item scale to assess participants' satisfaction with their self-help program; a 16-item community activity checklist; and a demographic questionnaire. The questionnaire asked respondents about the length of time they had been involved in self-help and how many hours on average they attended their program each week, as well as requesting as their demographic characteristics, vocational and residential status, and psychiatric history.

The final version of the Empowerment Scale and other instruments used in this study were pilot tested with a local self-help program that did not participate in the study. (The instruments are available from the first author.)

Survey Procedures And Data Analysis

Data were collected between March and August 1992. All instruments and procedures were approved by the institutional review board. Informed consent was obtained from all participants. The liaison at each program site was responsible for recruiting individual members at the program for participation, ensuring the anonymous handling of the instruments, and returning the instruments to the center. A total of 271 usable questionnaires were returned.

To examine the validity of the instrument, we used correlations, t tests, regressions, and descriptive statistics. We used analyses of variance to test for differences among programs and to examine differences in respondent characteristics. To examine the psychometric properties of the scale, we used factor analysis and statistics to examine internal consistency. Several demographic variables were dummy coded for the multiple regressions. They were marital status (single, not married, and married), housing status (independent housing supervised housing, and homeless or other housing), and ethnic status (minority and non-minority).

Results

Empowerment Scale

The 28 items of the Empowerment Scale were summed and averaged to arrive at an overall empowerment score. Out of a possible score of 4, the mean ± SD score was 2.94 ±.32 (range, 1.82 to 3.79). These results suggested that respondents scored somewhat above the middle range of the scale. Analysis of variance indicated that empowerment scores did not differ significantly between the six self-help programs. Mean scores at the six sites ranged from 2.75 to 3.02.

Cronbach's alpha suggested a high degree of internal consistency (alpha = .86, N = 261). Results of a factor analysis using principal components analysis and oblique rotation suggested a somewhat satisfactory factor solution. Five factors were extracted, accounting for 54 percent of the variance in scores. Table 1 shows the items that loaded on each factor. The skree test and conceptual clarity of the factor solution were used to determine the final number of factors as well as the method of rotation.

Construct Validity

Despite our prediction that self-help involvement and empowerment would be positively related, no significant correlations were found between the total Empowerment Scale score and hours spent in the self-help program per week or the total number of years of involvement in self-help. The mean ± SD number of hours spent in the program was 15.34 ± 15, and the mean number of years of involvement was 4.70 ± 4.73.

We also examined the relationship between Empowerment Scale scores and the demographic characteristics of respondents. A t test indicated that males and females did not differ significantly in their feelings of empowerment. Analysis of variance suggested no significant differences by race (white, black, or other racial status) or by marital status (married; single; or divorced, widowed, or separated). No significant correlation was found between empowerment and educational level achieved or total number of previous psychiatric hospitalizations.

As might be expected, a small but statistically significant relationship was found between the number of community activities engaged in and empowerment (r = .15, N = 261, p = .02). A small but statistically significant inverse correlation was found between use of traditional mental health services and empowerment (r = -.14, N = 256, p = .02)

Respondents were categorized by whether they were working in a "regular" job (N = 43); those who were doing sheltered or volunteer work or who were retired, in school, or unemployed were classified as not working (N = 210). The mean Empowerment Scale score was 3.01 for the working respondents and 2.92 for the nonworking respondents, a nonsignificant difference. They were also categorized by whether they were engaged in any productive activity that is, in a regular job, a sheltered workshop, volunteer work, or school (N = 104) or not so engaged (N = 149). No significant difference in empowerment scores was found between these groups.

Although no differences in empowerment were found between working and nonworking respondents, a significant relationship was noted between total monthly income and respondents' scores on the Empowerment Scale (r = .24, N = 234, p < .001). Furthermore, among the respondents who were en-aged in productive activity, a significant positive relationship was found between the number of hours engaged and empowerment (r = .34, N = 98, p = .001).

In addition, we found significant positive correlations between empowerment and quality of life (r = .36, N = 254, p < .001), social support (r = .17, N = 253, p = .002), and self-esteem (r = .51, N = 258, p < .001). The correlation with self-esteem may be explained, at least in part, by the fact that items explicitly tapping self-esteem were included in the Empowerment Scale. A significant positive correlation between empowerment and respondents' satisfaction with their self-help program was also found (r = .28, N = 255, p < .001).

Predictors of Empowerment

Two stepwise multiple regressions were conducted to determine the best predictors of empowerment. First used were respondents' characteristics, including age, gender, educational status, ethnicity, age at first psychiatric contact, work status, housing status, marital status, total monthly income, and total number of lifetime psychiatric

Table 1: Factors Derived From the Empowerment Scale

Factor and scale item[1]	Loading
Factor 1: Self-esteem-self-efficacy[2]	
I generally accomplish what I set out to do	.79
I have a positive attitude about myself	.74
When I make plans, I am almost certain to make them work	.72
I am usually confident about the decisions I make	.70
I am often able to overcome barriers	.56
I feel I am a person of worth, at least on an equal basis with others	.47
I see myself as a capable person	.46
I am able to do things as well as most other people	.41
I feel I have a number of good qualities	.41
Factor 2: Power-powerlessness[3]	
I feel powerless most of the time	.69
Making waves never gets you anywhere[4]	.66
You can't fight city hall	.66
When I am unsure about something, I usually go along with the group	.66
Experts are in the best position to decide what people should do or learn	.63
Most of the misfortunes in my life were due to bad luck	.62
Usually, I feel alone	.60
People have no right to get angry just because they don't like some things	.43
Factor 3: Community activism and autonomy[5]	
People have a right to make their own decisions, even if they are bad ones	.68
People should try to live their lives the way they want to	.64
People working together can have an effect on their community	.62
People have more power if they join together as a group	.53
Working with others in my community, can help to change things for the better	.52
Very often a problem can be solved by taking action[4]	.41
Factor 4: Optimism and control over the future[6]	
People are limited only by what they think possible	.78
I can pretty much determine what will happen in my life	.62
I am generally optimistic about the future	.58
Very often a problem can be solved by taking action[3]	.42
Factor 5: Righteous anger[7]	
Getting angry about something is often the first step toward changing it	.73
People have no right to get angry just because they don't like some things	.52
Getting angry about something never helps	.48
Making waves never gets you anywhere[4]	.40

[1] Items that are negatively worded were recoded for consistency before the factor analysis.
[2] Eigenvalue=6.85, variance explained=24.5 percent
[3] Eigenvalue=3.48, variance explained = 12.4 percent
[4] This item loaded on more than one factor.
[5] Eigenvalue=2.13, variance explained =7.6 percent
[6] Eigenvalue = 1.5, variance explained = 5.4 percent
[7] Eigenvalue = 1.12, variance explained = 4 percent

hospitalizations. Only total monthly income emerged as a significant predictor of empowerment, explaining 5 percent of the variance in empowerment scores (adjusted $R^2 = .048$, $F = 14.71$, $df = 1,271$, $p < .001$).

The second regression was conducted using several of the other measures, including quality of life, number of community activities engaged in, satisfaction with the self-help program, number of traditional mental health services received, and social support items. This multiple regression was considerably more successful in explaining the variability in empowerment scores, accounting for 22 percent of the variance (adjusted $R^2 = .22$, $F = 20.19$, $df = 4,268$, $p < .001$). The most useful predictors were items measuring quality of life, number of traditional mental health services received, number of community activities engaged in, and overall life satisfaction. The items measuring satisfaction with the self-help program and satisfaction with social supports were not useful predictors of empowerment in this multivariate analysis.

Known-Groups Validity

The Empowerment Scale was administered to two other groups for additional validation. One group consisted of 56 patients hospitalized at a state facility (mean length of stay = 4.3 years; range = three months to 22.6 years) (31), and the other of 200 college students (32). In the former group, the mean ± SD scale score was 2.29 ± .24, and in the latter group, it was 3.16 ± .24. The first mean is approximately two standard deviations below the mean in this study, and the second is about two standard deviations above it. These results lend credence to the scale's ability to discriminate among groups of respondents whose feelings of empowerment are different from those of participants in self-help programs.

Discussion

Clarifying the Construct Of Empowerment

Our attempt to develop and validate a scale measuring the construct of empowerment, as defined by consumers and former patients themselves, was successful. The scale has high internal consistency, and analyses produced a somewhat satisfactory five-factor solution.

Furthermore, the findings of this study set a framework for understanding the imprecise concept of empowerment. Using a tripod metaphor, there are three legs or supports that constitute empowerment. The first is self-esteem—self-efficacy, and optimism and control over the future; it can be thought of as a sense of self-worth and a belief that one can control one's destiny and life events. The self-esteem—self-efficacy factor was one of the strongest and most consistent produced by the factor analysis. It is partly equivalent to the idea of internal locus of control as described by Rotter (33) and to other definitions and scales measuring self-efficacy and mastery.

The second leg of empowerment is actual power, another consistent factor in the scale. The remaining two factors of the scale constitute the third support. These factors are righteous anger and community activism. They imply the ability and willingness to harness anger into action and a sociopolitical component of empowerment that is evident in both community activism and righteous anger factors.

This framework of empowerment was supported by the additional analyses conducted in this study. As predicted, a positive relationship was found between empowerment scores and the number of community activities engaged in (for example, writing to a public official and voting), which buttresses the idea of action as a component of empowerment. The inverse relationship between empowerment scores and use of traditional mental health services is somewhat difficult to tease out from a causal perspective given the ex post facto nature of this study.

A significant relationship was found between number of hours worked (among those working) and empowerment. Monthly income was also a predictor of empowerment, which differs from Rosenfield's finding.[23] In this society, income and earning power are often linked to actual power, the second leg of empowerment; thus the relationship between income and empowerment seems reasonable.

Like Rosenfield, we found that empowerment was related to quality of life but unrelated to employment status. Although empowerment was related to income, when monthly income was combined with other variables such as quality of life and life satisfaction, it lost its predictive power. This finding suggests that income may play a mediating role in empowerment by increasing quality of life, which in turn affects feelings of empowerment.

The absence of a relationship between the total empowerment score and the host of demographic variables tested shows that empowerment is not limited to the privileged, the educated, the majority race, or the employed; it is an "equal opportunity" personal state.

Our initial hypothesis that empowerment would be positively related to the length and intensity of involvement with a self-help program was not borne out by the data. Empowerment was correlated with satisfaction with the self-help program when those variables were examined in a bivariate correlational analysis. However, satisfaction with the self-help program lost its predictive power in the multivariate analysis.

Conclusions

This study yielded a valid and reliable measure of empowerment that was developed from the perspective of consumer activists, and it further served to clarify the components of empowerment and its relationship to other factors. Results of this study suggest that programs wishing to promote empowerment among their members must focus on increasing self-esteem and self-efficacy, decreasing feelings of powerlessness, and increasing feelings of power especially by increasing financial resources. They must also focus on heightening sociopolitical consciousness and community activism.

It should be noted that the persons selected to construct this scale can be considered leaders of the self-help movement. As such, it may be argued that they represent a higher-functioning and more educated group than would a random selection of consumers of mental health services. Consequently, the empowerment scale constructed by this sample may look different from one constructed solely by users of mental health services. On the other hand, the persons who served on this advisory board are active in shaping policy and defining new directions in mental health services, so their voices deserve our attention.

The framework for empowerment developed by this study is consistent with the definitions offered by Rappaport[3], Staples[5], and McLean.[1] Our results provide empirical support for at least part of the advisory board's initial definition of empowerment. Results of our study suggest that an empowered person is one who has a sense of self-worth, self-efficacy, and power. The empowered person recognizes use of anger as a motivating force to instigate social change and is optimistic about the ability to exert control over his or her life. He or she recognizes the importance of the group or community to effect change, but the empowered person also values autonomy.

Further testing of the empowerment scale will yield additional information about the psychometric properties of the scale and, in turn, the construct of empowerment. For example, evidence for known-groups validity could be strengthened by administering the scale to additional samples suspected of having lower or higher empowerment scores. It would also be useful to determine if the scale is both sensitive to change and stable over time. Administering the scale to new participants of a program thought to promote empowerment may yield evidence of its sensitivity (and indeed may suggest whether empowerment is a changeable trait), while additional studies examining test-retest reliability would yield evidence of its stability. In addition, it may be useful to administer the scale along with other standardized measures of psychological functioning to gather more evidence of the scale's convergent and divergent validity. Unfortunately, these assessments were beyond the scope of this initial study, and the results are correspondingly limited.

References

1. McLean A: Empowerment and the psychiatric/expatient movement in the United States: contradictions, crisis, and change. *Social Science in Medicine* 40:1063-1071, 1995
2. Segal S, Silverman C, Temkin T: Measuring empowerment in client-run self-help agencies. *Community Mental Health Journal* 31:215-227, 1995
3. Rappaport J: Terms of empowerment/exemplars of prevention: toward a theory for community psychology. *American Journal of Community Psychology* 15:121-142, 1987
4. Zimmerman M, Rappaport J: Citizen partici-

pation, perceived control, and psychological empowerment. *American Journal of Community Psychology* 16:725-750, 1988

5. Staples L: Consumer empowerment in the Massachusetts Mental Health System: A Comparison of Attitudes, Perceptions, and Opinions Within and Between Provider Groups. Doctoral dissertation. Boston. Boston University, School of Social Work. 1993

6. Chamberlin J: The ex-patient's movement: where we've been and where we're going. *Journal of Mind and Behavior* 11:323-336, 1990

7. Segal SP, Silverman C, Temkin T: Empowerment and self-help agency practice for people with mental disabilities. *Social Work* 39:727-735, 1993

8. Chamberlin J, Rogers ES, Ellison M: Self-help programs: a description of their characteristics and their members. *Psychiatric Rehabilitation Journal* 19(3):33-42, 1996

9. Freund PD: Professional role(s) in the empowerment process: "working with" mental health consumers. *Psychosocial Rehabilitation Journal* 16:65-73, 1993

10. O'rear G, O'rear TM: Way Station: a comprehensive approach to residential services for and with people with serious mental illness. *Psychosocial Rehabilitation Journal* 13:77-90, 1990

11. Ellison ML: Empowerment and Demedicalization in Mental Health Case Management: Meaning and Measurement. Doctoral dissertation. Boston, Boston University, Department of Sociology, 1996

12. Simon B: Rethinking empowerment. *Journal of Progressive Human Services* l(l): 27-40, 1990

13. Hatfield AB: Consumer issues in mental illness. *New Directions for Mental Services*, no 34:35-42, 1987

14. Battaglino L: Family empowerment through self-help groups. *New Directions for Mental Health Services*, no 34:43-51, 1987

15. Kassia JP, Boothroyd P, Ben Dror R: The family support group: families and professionals in partnership. *Psychosocial Rehabilitation Journal* 15:91-96, 1992

16. East E: Family as a resource: maintaining chronically mentally ill members in the community. *Health and Social Work* 17:93- 97, 1992

17. Pfeiffer EJ, Mostek M: Services for families of people with mental illness. *Hospital and Community Psychiatry* 42:262-264, 1991

18. Cohen CI, Thompson KS: Homeless mentally ill or mentally ill homeless? *American Journal of Psychiatry* 149:816-823, 1992

19. Susser E, Goldfinger SM, White A: Some clinical approaches to the homeless mentally ill. *Community Mental Health Journal* 26:463-480, 1990

20. Cohen MB: Social work practice with homeless mentally ill people: engaging the client. *Social Work* 34:505-509, 1989

21. Cheung FM: People against the mentally ill: community opposition to residential treatment facilities. *Community Mental Health Journal* 26:205-212, 1996

22. Connolly LM, Keele BS, Kleinbeck SV, et al: A place to be Yourself: empowerment from the client's perspective. *Image: Journal of Nursing Scholarship* 25:297-303, 1993

23. Rosenfield S: Factors contributing to the subjective quality of life of the chronic mentally ill. *Journal of Health and Social Behavior* 33:299-315, 1992

24. Whyte WF (ed): *Participatory Action Research*. Newbury Park, Calif, Sage, 1991

25. Rogers ES, Palmer-Erbs V: Participatory action research: implications for researchers in psychiatric rehabilitation, *Psychosocial Rehabilitation Journal* 18:3-12, 1994

26. Dillman D: *Mail and Telephone Surveys: The Total Design Method*. New York, Wiley, 1978

27. Fink A, Kosecoff J: *How to Conduct Surveys*. Newbury Park, Calif, Sage, 1985

28. Rotter JB: Generalized Expectancies for Internal Versus External Control of Reinforcement. *Psychological Monographs*, vol 80, 1966

29. Sherer M, Adams C: Construct validation of the Self-Efficacy Scale. *Psychological Reports* 53:899-902, 1983

30. Rosenberg M: *Society and the Adolescent Self-Image*. Princeton, NJ, Princeton University Press, 1965

31. Sharkey D: *Validation of the Empowerment Scale With a Hospital Population*. Medfield, Mass. Medfield State Hospital, 1995

32. Nuthall R: *Validation of the Empowerment Scale With a College Population*. Boston, Boston College, Department of Counseling and Developmental Psychology 1995

33. Rotter JB: *Social Learning and Clinical Psychology*. Englewood Cliffs, NJ, Prentice-Hall, 1954

Use of a New Outcome Scale To Determine Best Practices

WILLIAM R. HOLCOMB, PHD, MPA, BERNARD D. BEITMAN, MD, CHERYL A. HEMME, MD, ALEX JOSYLIN, BA, AND SHANNON PRINDIVILLE, BA

Efforts to control health care costs and to encourage health care reform have led to increasing demand for quantitative measurement of the effectiveness of behavioral health treatment. Outcomes must be used to inform stakeholders, including consumers, clinicians, and managers, about treatment-related gains to be useful in improving patient services. Best-practices benchmarking using outcome data has become important for both clinical practice and policy making in the U.S. and in other countries.[1-6]

The program evaluation described in this paper assessed treatment outcomes in the areas of quality of life, symptomatology, and level of functioning for a cohort of outpatients one year after they began treatment at a university psychiatric clinic. The patients' satisfaction with treatment was also assessed, and data on several demographic and clinical variables were collected to explore possible contributing factors to treatment gains.

Few follow-up studies describing the gains patients make in naturalistic treatment settings have been done.[7] The quasiexperimental design without a control group and without random assignment used in this study does not allow conclusions to be drawn about causes of gains, but it can assess whether gains are made in important life areas and how these gains are related to patients' satisfaction with the services they received.

Evaluation Procedures

All new patients who came to the University of Missouri psychiatric outpatient clinic during 1995 (N = 200) were given the Treatment Outcome Profile at intake. The patients were mailed a follow-up profile form to complete about one year later. The profile form completed at admission contained 27 self-report items, divided among three major scales that measure quality of life, symptomatology, and level of functioning. Responses to items were marked on 5-point Likert-type scales, on which higher scores indicated better quality of life, reduced symptoms, and better functioning. The form used at follow-up measured these three major areas and also included a scale that measured patient satisfaction. Responses to items associated with the satisfaction scale were marked on a 5-point scale on which higher scores indicated more satisfaction. (A copy of the Treatment Outcome Profile is available from the first author.)

Each of the major scales encompassed two to four subscales (see Table 1). Details about the internal reliability and criterion validity of the Treatment Outcome Profile for use with psychiatric and substance abuse inpatients are published elsewhere.[8] The Beck Depression Inventory (BDI)[9] and the Zung Anxiety Scale[10] were also given at intake but not at follow-up.

Source: Holcomb WR, Beitman BD, Hemme CA, Josylin A, and Prindiville S. Use of a New Outcome Scale To Determine Best Practices. Psychiatric Services May 1998; 49(5):583-595. (Reprinted with permission.)

William R. Holcomb is President and CEO of Behavioral Health Concepts, Inc., 2716 Forum Blvd., Suite 4, Columbia MO 65203. Tel: (573) 446-0405. Cost for users of treatment outcome profile system: $495 (includes survey tool and software).

Dr. Holcomb, Dr. Beitman, and Dr. Hemme are affiliated with the department of psychiatry and neurology at the University of Missouri-Columbia. Mr. Josylin and Ms. Prindiville are graduate students in psychology at the University of Missouri-Columbia. Address correspondence to Dr. Holcomb at Behavioral Health Concepts, Victoria Park, 2716 Forum Boulevard, Suite 4, Columbia, Missouri 65203.

Table 1

Scores, on scales and subscales of the Treatment Outcome Profile at intake and at one-year follow-up for 100 new outpatients treated at a university psychiatric clinic in 1995[1]

Scale or subscale	Intake Mean	SD	Follow-up Mean	SD	F2	p
Quality of life	2.98	.73	3.32	.90	23.69	<.001
Self-esteem	2.63	.97	3.09	1.09	19.39	<.001
Social support	3.56	.87	3.73	.92	3.83	.053
Health	3.01	1.07	3.24	1.16	6.80	.011
Work and leisure	2.86	.95	3.37	1.02	27.76	<.001
Symptomatology	3.04	.75	3.59	.94	36.75	<.001
Depression	2.65	1.06	3.32	1.19	27.95	<.001
Anxiety	2.79	.93	3.39	1.14	28.47	<.001
Hostility or paranoia	3.68	.91	4.05	.91	15.98	<.001
Level of fiinctioning	3.61	.64	3.91	.75	17.48	<.001
Disruptive behavior	3.73	.74	4.04	.74	17.23	<.001
Community skills	3.49	.82	3.78	.92	9.11	.003
Total 3	3.19	.61	3.59	.80	36.12	<.001
Patient satisfaction	-	-	3.68	.90	-	-
Treatment	-	-	3.49	1.10	-	-
Staff	-	-	3.48	1.05	-	-
Environment	-	-	3.93	.79	-	-

1 All variables except patient satisfaction were measured on a 5-point scale on which higher scores indicate better outcome or more satisfaction. Based on multivariate analysis of variance using a within-subject design and repeated measures on one factor, Hotellings Lawley Trace=1.03, F=4.84, P<.00l
· df= 1,99 for all conpari sons
· Total for qualitv-of-life, svmptomatology, and level-of-functioning scales

Of the original sample of 200 new patients, 144 had legitimate addresses on record at the time of follow-up. One hundred forms were returned after three mailings plus telephone calls asking for help in returning the forms. Therefore, a return rate of 69 percent of those with legitimate addresses was achieved, with a 50 percent overall return rate. No statistical differences on dependent variables were found between patients who returned forms and those who did not, except that those who returned forms had more health concerns, as measured by the health subscale of the Treatment Outcome Profile.

At the time of the study, the university clinic that was the study setting provided about 450 adult treatment episodes of care per month. The majority of patients were employees of the university or government agencies who were provided outpatient psychiatric services under managed care contracts.

Of the 100 subjects with follow-up data, 71 were women, and 29 were men. Ninety-one percent were Caucasian. The average age was 43 years. The average number of visits per subject during the study period was 5.6. Patients were seen by attending psychiatrists, resident psychiatrists, and doctoral-level psychologists. The primary modes of treatment were psychotherapy, pharmacotherapy, and referral to other agencies for supportive social services.

The most frequent *DSM-IV* primary diagnosis was major depression, for 40 patients, followed by dysthymia, for 24 patients, and panic disorder, for 14 patients. Other diagnoses included adjustment disorder, six patients; anxiety, six patients; bipolar disorder, five patients; alcohol and drug abuse, three patients; and schizophrenia, two patients.

Results

Total scores on the BDI and the Zung Anxiety Scale at intake were highly correlated with all scales and subscales of the Treatment Outcome

Profile at intake, thus demonstrating the profile's construct validity. The BDI correlated most highly with the symptomatology scale (r = -.66), the total score for the profile (r = -.69), and the depression subscale (r = -.58). The Zung Anxiety Scale had high correlations with the total score for the profile (r = -.61), the symptomatology scale (r = -.58), and the anxiety subscale (r = -.64).

Table 1 presents comparisons of measures of dependent variables at intake and one-year follow-up. All scales and subscales of the Treatment Outcome Profile showed significant gains over the study period. Seventy-three patients reported positive gains in total scores on the profile one year after receiving treatment. (Scores on the satisfaction scale were not included in figuring the total scores for the Treatment Outcome Profile at follow-up.) The most sensitive measures— those with high F values and largest gains—were the symptomatology scale, the total score, the anxiety subscale, the depression subscale, the work and leisure subscale, and the quality-of-life scale.

To further explore variables related to one-year follow-up, stepwise multiple regression was used to predict the overall gain in total scores.[11] Thirteen independent variables were included in the multiple regression. They were number of treatment sessions, whether the patient saw only a psychiatrist or a psychiatrist and a psychologist, satisfaction with treatment, satisfaction with staff, satisfaction with the treatment environment, time between the intake and follow-up measures, a diagnosis of depression, a diagnosis of panic disorder, the clinician's level of experience, source of referral (self or a physician), whether the patient was prescribed medications, gender, and age.

Only satisfaction with treatment (p = .003) and age (p = .01) were significant and were retained in the final model (F = 7.43, p = .001, R^2 = .138). Patients who had higher satisfaction ratings and who were younger tended to report greater overall treatment gains. Patients who were self-referred tended to have greater self-reported gains, but the difference was not significant. This model accounted for only 13.8 percent of the total variance of overall treatment gain. Clearly changes in the person's life, such as marriage, work, and traumatic stresses, may have had additional influences on psychological well-being of the patients during treatment, but these variables were not assessed in this study.

Because satisfaction with treatment was directly related to treatment gain, stepwise multiple regression was again used to explore variables that could predict satisfaction with treatment. All of the clinical and demographic variables previously mentioned were included in the analysis except the satisfaction variables. A one-variable model was produced, with number of treatment sessions as the only significant predictor of satisfaction (F = 10.11, p = .002, R^2 = .10). A larger number of sessions was associated with greater satisfaction. Even though the number of sessions was not directly related to treatment gains, it may have been indirectly related through its influence on satisfaction with treatment. However, the model could account for only 10 percent of the variance. Other possible sources of variance, not measured in this analysis, could include many variables related to the relationship of the clinician and patient and variables related to past treatment history.

A more detailed analysis of satisfaction scores and their relationship to whether subjects had improved over the study period was done. Subjects whose total score on the Treatment Outcome Profile at follow-up was greater than the total score at intake categorized as "improved." Scores on the overall satisfaction scale and the three satisfaction subscales were recoded into three possible responses, with responses marked 1 or 2 considered dissatisfied, those marked 3 considered neutral, and those marked 3 or 4 considered satisfied. Thus the total number and percentage of satisfied, dissatisfied, and neutral subjects in the follow-up sample were determined (see Table 2).

Overall, 65 percent of the follow-up sample reported satisfaction with services, 9 percent expressed dissatisfaction, and 26 percent were neutral. Chi square analysis revealed that overall satisfaction with services and satisfaction with staff were directly related to whether the subjects reported improvement on the Treatment Outcome Profile.

Discussion

One year after beginning treatment in an outpatient setting, patients reported reduced symptomatology and trains in quality of life and level of functioning. Those who reported the greatest gains also reported the greatest satisfaction with treatment. The strong relationship between treat-

Table 2

Satisfaction with outpatient services among patients who did and did not report overall improvement in total score on the Treatment Outcome Profile at one-year follow-up[1]

Satisfaction variables	Not improved (N=27) N	%	Improved (N = 73) N	%	Total (N 100) N	%	X2	p
Satisfaction with treatment							5.73	ns
Dissatisfied	7	25.9	8	11.0	15	15.0		
Satisfied	12	44.4	51	69.9	63	63.0		
Neutral	8	29.6	14	19.2	22	22.0		
Satisfaction with staff							8.89	.012
Dissatisfied	9	33.3	8	11.0	17	17.0		
Satisfied	10	37.0	49	67.1	59	59.0		
Neutral	8	29.6	16	21.9	24	24.0		
Satisfaction with environment							3.50	ns
Dissatisfied	1	3.7	5	6.8	6	6.0		
Satisfied	20	74.1	62	84.9	82	82.0		
Neutral	6	22.2	6	8.2	12	12.0		
Overall satisfaction							6.68	.035
Dissatisfied	4	14.4	5	6.8	9	9.0		
Satisfied	12	44.4	53	72.6	65	65.0		
Neutral	11	40.7	15	20.5	26	26.0		

1 Likelihood-ratio clii square analysis was used to test for significant differences between observed and expected frequencies.
† df=2 for all comparisons

ment gain and satisfaction with treatment suggests that the patients themselves attribute their gains to treatment received.

It was surprising to find that variables hypothesized to have an effect on treatment gains were not shown to influence treatment. These variables included whether psychiatric medications were prescribed, clinicians' level of experience, whether the patient saw both a psychiatrist and a psychologist, patients' gender, and diagnosis. Younger patients were more likely to have greater treatment gains.

Relatively low levels of patient satisfaction with services were obtained in this sample, compared with samples of inpatients assessed at discharge,[12] other samples of outpatients in mental health settings,[13,14] and samples of recipients of other types of human services.[15]

Several explanations for these findings are possible. The university clinic where the study was conducted was going through a stressful transition from a fee-for-service system to a capitated managed care system. Under the new system, patients were required to have a referral from their primary care physician before intake. Patients who were already in treatment were referred back to their insurance companies to clarify benefits before treatment could continue. Some of these procedures were cumbersome to the emotionally distraught persons who sought treatment.

The clinic has improved its intake procedures and has more recently adapted to managed care priorities. It is anticipated that this improved administrative effectiveness will be reflected in higher patient satisfaction ratings in the next follow-up study.

The Treatment Outcome Profile showed good sensitivity and predictive validity in revealing statistically significant gains one year after patients began treatment. Seventy-three percent of the subjects in the study reported overall improvement, with gains in quality of life, symptomatology, and level of functioning. On average, the sample gained .65 of a standard deviation from intake total scores. These one-year treatment gains serve as an internal benchmark for future comparative studies.

Likewise, the patient satisfaction ratings provide internal benchmarks for future comparisons. Subjects distinguished between their satisfaction with the environment and their satisfaction with overall treatment and treatment staff. Subjects who received more treatment sessions reported higher satisfaction. The practical meaning of patients' ratings of neutral and dissatisfied should be explored in future research. However, a high frequency of neutral and dissatisfied responses could indicate disgruntlement with administrative and financial hassles associated with receiving services in a managed care environment.

These findings are being used by administrators at the university clinic to target quality assurance efforts to improve patient satisfaction ratings and overall treatment gains. Data are also being collected from other public and private outpatient settings serving patients with different levels of functioning and different diagnoses to help establish external best-practice benchmarks using the Treatment Outcome Profile.

Acknowledgments

The authors wish to thank Debbie Dow, Gretchen Herr, Christy Lemery, Melanie Burns, and Sherry Wagner.

References

1. Epstein AM: The outcomes movement: will it get us where we want to go? *New England Journal of Medicine* 323:266-269, 1990
2. Flynn L, Steinwachs D: Special report: outcome round table includes stakeholders. *Health Affairs* 14(3):269-270, 1995
3. Lohr KN: Outcome measurement: concepts and questions. *Inquiry* 25:37-50, 1988
4. Andrews C: Best practices for implementing outcomes management. *Behavioral Healthcare Tomorrow* 4:19-21, 1995
5. Thorton PH, Goldman HH, Stegner BL, et al: Assessing the costs and outcomes together: cost-effectiveness of two systems of acute psychiatric care. *Evaluation and Program Planning* 13:231-241, 1990
6. Smith GR, Fisher EP, Nordquist CR, et al: Implementing outcome management systems in mental health settings. *Psychiatric Services* 48:364-368, 1997
7. Speer DC, Newman FL: Mental health services outcome evaluation. *Clinical Psychology* 3:105-129, 1996
8. Holcomb WR, Parker JC, Leong GB: Outcomes of inpatients treated on a VA psychiatric unit and a substance abuse treatment unit. *Psychiatric Services* 48:699-704, 1997
9. Beck AT, Steer RA: *Beck Depression Inventory Manual.* San Antonio, Tex, Psychological Corp, 1987
10. Zung W: A rating scale for anxiety disorders. *Psychosomatics* 12:371-379, 1971
11. Norusis MJ: *SPSS for Windows: Base System User's Guide, Release 6.0.* Chicago, SPSS Inc, 1993
12. Holcomb WR, Adams NA, Ponder HM, et al: The development and construct validation of a consumer satisfaction questionnaire for psychiatric inpatients. *Evaluation and Program Planning* 12:189-194, 1989
13. Lebow JL: Client satisfaction with mental health treatment. *Evaluation Review* 7: 729-752, 1983
14. Tanner BA: Factors influencing client satisfaction with mental health services: a review of quantitative research. *Evaluation and Program Planning* 4:279-286, 1981
15. Fornell C: A national customer satisfaction barometer, in *Performance Measurement and Evaluation.* Edited by Holloway J, Lewis J, Mallory G. London, Sage, 1995

Chapter 10

Practicing What You Preach: Creating and Implementing Behavioral Guidelines

Devising Depression Guidelines For Primary Care Physicians

HMO Administrators Are Refining AHCPR's 1993 Parameters

CYNTHIA WASHAM

When the Agency for Health Care Policy and Research (AHCPR) issued its guidelines on depression in 1993, the managed care industry rejoiced. The lengthy directive helped explain why so few cases of major depression were accurately diagnosed and suggested that the best place to detect and treat depression was also the cheapest.

According to the agency guidelines, 15 percent of Americans have a major depressive disorder sometime during their lives. Yet fewer than a third are accurately diagnosed.

A major reason is that few seek psychiatric care, often out of fear of the stigma of mental illness. Research conducted by Group Health Cooperative of Puget Sound indicates only 50 percent of patients with a major depressive disorder seek treatment. Many who are unwilling to visit a psychiatrist, however, will accept treatment from their primary care physician.

"At least half of patients prefer treatment from a primary care physician," said Dr. Jeff Mitchell, associate medical director at Laureate Psychiatric Clinic and Hospital in Tulsa OK. Mitchell developed depression guidelines for New Mexico's Lovelace Health Plan and is refining those of Laureate's HMO.

Although some may not complain of sadness, depressed patients visit their primary care practitioner two to three times as often as other patients. Those suffering from major depression make up an estimated 5 to 9 percent of primary care patients.

Primary care physicians, then, have the greatest opportunity to detect and treat depression. Yet, the guidelines emphasized, too many depressed patients in primary care were not getting the treatment they needed.

The AHCPR guidelines were embraced by managed care because they justified treating one of the country's costliest illnesses in the primary care setting, rather than in the more expensive specialist's office. Some HMOs adopted the guidelines in full, while others used them as a template to design their own.

Five years later, administrators of many HMOs are rethinking their depression guidelines. They know primary care cuts the cost of treatment. But can costs be reduced further without compromising care? Are primary care physicians preventing relapses as well as specialists? Are they saving patients' overall health costs? Are they spotting more cases of major depression? Or are they perhaps over-diagnosing and treating mildly depressed patients who would recover on their own?

These are among the questions HMO managers are asking today as they fine-tune their approach to depression.

HMOs Disagree on Merits Of Increasing Detection

Because primary care practitioners miss so many cases of depression, guidelines typically include a section on diagnosis. There's little agreement, however, on how to spot these hidden cases. Studies have shown that depressed patients often complain of somatic problems including sexual dysfunction, headaches, stomach aches, and chest pains.

"Patients who are heavy users of medical services often have high rates of depression," Laureate's Jeff Mitchell says.

One school of thought is that spotting these hidden cases of depression will save money on needless diagnostic tests for physical problems. Mitchell is among the believers. He adopted the Zung Depression Scale screening questionnaire for primary care physicians to give any patient they suspect might be depressed. Prozac manufacturer Eli Lilly & Co. supplies the questionnaires to the HMO. "Doctors like it because they can ask patients to fill it out and go do something else," Mitchell said.

Training physicians to use the questionnaire boosted the percentage of Lovelace HMO patients diagnosed with depression from just over 4 to 7 percent, Mitchell says.

Some patients were taken aback when told they suffered from depression, but Mitchell says the scale, with it's black-and-white results, helped physicians explain the diagnosis to patients and the need for treatment.

Other HMOs, however, eschew depression screening. One of those is Group Health Cooperative of Puget Sound in Seattle WA. Administrators of the 600,000-member HMO avoid screening tools because they're only 80 to 90 percent sensitive. They indicate many false positives and patients with only minor depression.

The AHCPR and other guidelines recommend aggressive treatment only for patients suffering from debilitating major depression. Minor depression is a temporary bout of sadness that often affects people following divorce, a death in the family, or other traumatic event. Patients normally recover from minor depression without medical treatment.

Screening a large number of patients whose symptoms merely suggest the possibility of depression will boost the number of diagnoses, says Marvin Rosenberg, Group Health's depression road-map coordinator. Yet he believes that patients with no clear symptoms of depression are unlikely to benefit from treatment.

"There is a group of people who come in with somatic complaints masking the real disorder (depression)," he said. "Studies show those people have poor response to treatment."

Group Health advises its physicians instead to perform more comprehensive and accurate diagnostic exams on patients reporting symptoms of major depression. Treatment is recommended for those with moderate or severe major depression, as defined in the *Diagnostic and Statistical Manual of Mental Disorders* (*DSM*).

Another criticism of widespread screening is that it threatens patients' privacy. "I would advocate patients not filling out these screening questions," said William Golden, MD, associate professor of general internal medicine at the University of Arkansas and a member of the committee that wrote the AHCPR guidelines. "They have no idea what's going to happen to that data."

Psychiatrists, Nurses Improve Patient Compliance

A key message of the AHCPR guidelines is that within 12 weeks, two-thirds of patients with major depression improve.

In reality, success rates are often lower, because patients don't comply. A study conducted by Group Health Cooperative of Puget Sound showed that without any treatment, 30 percent of patients with a major depressive disorder improved. Among depression patients being treated by a primary care doctor, the rate climbed to just 40 percent.

Antidepressants are highly effective in treating major depression when used for six to nine months. Yet a third of all patients stop taking them during the first month. Some 44 percent stop within three months, according to Rosenberg. This raises their risk of relapse, and possibly their long-term health-care costs.

To promote patient compliance, Group Health in 1994 began altering its primary care model. Traditionally, most patients were treated only by their primary care practitioner. Some physicians referred patients to psychiatrists, but rarely followed up on their care. Studies have shown, however, that 40 to 60 percent of patients never go to the specialist.

Group Health's experimental "collaborative model" brought psychiatrists into the primary care clinic to work closely with the primary care physicians.

The HMO began the pilot program by offering primary care physicians a half-day workshop on diagnosing and treating depression. Participating primary care doctors then were paired with psychiatrists at the same clinic. During the first six weeks of treatment, patients alternated visits to their primary care provider and a psychiatrist, seeing each twice.

Patients in the collaborative model also received more than the usual amount of patient education. Each watched a 20-minute video explaining depression and its treatment. They also were given pamphlets and urged to ask questions.

Group Health's collaborative approach was a huge success. Approximately 70 percent of the patients showed at least a 50 percent improvement in their scores on the Hamilton Depression Rating Scale after four months. Only 40 percent of a control group receiving customary primary care showed the same level of improvement.

Rosenberg attributes the model's success to the combination of collaborative physician care, depression training for primary care physicians and patient education.

The collaborative approach initially costs more, although Group Health reports that it creates long-term savings because more patients complete their treatment. Group Health reported an average cost of $1,700 to $1,800 for collaborative-care treatment of major depression. Usual-care treatment typically costs $1,950 to $2,150. For patients suffering from minor depression, however, collaborative care increased costs without improving outcomes.

Group Health researchers now are experimenting with limiting the collaborative model to patients least likely to improve under primary care alone. According to a company report, about 40 percent of patients with major depression respond well to usual care. The 60 percent most likely to need specialized care are those with more severe symptoms and high neuroticism scores.

"We're looking at holding off on collaborative care for six to eight weeks and then identifying patients who are not doing well," explains Michael VonKorff, senior investigator with Group Health.

If the model proves effective, it will further reduce the cost of depression treatment.

Another technique a number of HMOs are using to enhance patient compliance is follow-up telephone calls from nurses. HMO giant Kaiser Permanente four years ago discovered that having nurses regularly check on patients significantly improved compliance at little cost.

The company trained primary care nurses to call patients between visits to inquire about their medication usage, symptoms and any problems. During the first two weeks following diagnosis, nurses called depressed patients two to four times. They continued calling regularly, though less frequently, during the following weeks. Patients received an average of 11 calls during the course of their treatment, each one lasting approximately six to seven minutes. Nurses kept detailed logs of their phone calls and reviewed them with the primary care physicians.

"At the six month point, patients who receive telephone follow-up are doing significantly better (on the Hamilton scale) than those who don't," said Enid Hunkeler, senior investigator at Kaiser Permanente's research division in northern California. "Patients develop close rapport with the nurses."

She said the company is now studying the effects of cutting down on the number of physician visits while increasing the length of nurse calls.

Group Health began telephone follow-ups recently and Mitchell hopes to introduce a similar program at Laureate.

"It doesn't require a physician to ask basic questions of a patient," Group Health's Rosenberg said. "A lot of nurses make these calls."

Some Patients Treated Too Much, Others Too Little

Few doubt that managed care has succeeded in improving the diagnosis and treatment of depression in the primary care setting. But some wonder whether efforts to minimize the cost of treatment have gone too far. In their report on collaborative care, researchers from Group Health admit that depressed patients receiving routine primary care were seen an average of twice during their first eight weeks of drug treatment, far below the four visits recommended in the AHCPR guidelines.

William Golden, one of the AHCPR guidelines' framers, fears some patients are being shortchanged.

"Most HMOs feel they'll save money by treating depression as long as they keep a lid on the number of visits," he said. "I think some of these patients will end up consuming more resources."

While the number of patient visits for major depression is being curtailed, use of antidepressants is on the rise, particularly the heavily marketed selective serotonin reuptake inhibitors (SSRIs). A study conducted at the University of Minnesota found a 20 percent increase in the number of doctor visits leading to the prescribing of psychotropic drugs in the last decade. The majority of the drugs are antidepressants.

Golden suspects that many of the prescriptions are being used to treat minor depression, in spite of the recommendation against it by the AHCPR and many HMO guidelines. He believes physicians are over-prescribing the drugs to appease patients influenced by advertising.

"I think SSRIs (Prozac, Zoloft, and Paxil) are being over-prescribed," he said. "Patients are asking for them. For a lot of physicians, it's easier to write the script than fight."

Group Health's VonKorff also sees many physicians straying from the guidelines in prescribing antidepressants. "There's a lot of money being spent on medications," he said. "When you look at the percentage of patients who meet the strict criteria for major depression, it's about half (of those on antidepressants)."

Costly SSRIs have become the most commonly prescribed antidepressants in the United States. A study conducted by Group Health showed, however, that they're no more effective than the considerably cheaper tricyclic drugs (Elavil, Tofranil, Sinequan). (Simon, et al., *Journal of the American Medical Association*, Vol. 275, June 26, 1996.) One apparent benefit of SSRIs is that patients reported fewer adverse reactions and were more likely to continue the medication than those taking other antidepressants. Although SSRIs cost 10 to 20 times more than tricyclic drugs, the overall cost of depression care was similar for both patient groups because even among SSRI users, medication made up only 11 percent of the total treatment cost.

Physicians' Behavior Tough To Change

But how far should HMOs go in directing physicians' care of patients?

Group Health's Rosenberg believes guidelines should appeal to a physician's appreciation of scientific research. "Nowhere in the guidelines do we tell practitioners they can't do something," he said.

Instead, the guidelines present research, some by Group Health, some by others, supporting certain practices. "We go to the literature," Rosenberg said. "We put together scientific review committees to analyze the evidence and then we come to some consensus about the validity of the conclusions. We're evidence driven."

VonKorff admits that often even scientific evidence isn't enough to persuade many physicians to follow guidelines. "I don't know anybody who really knows how to make doctors change their ways," he said.

Alan Ehrlich, MD, chairman of the practice-guidelines committee for Fallon Community Health Plan in Massachusetts, believes physicians will follow guidelines if they're specific. "There are a lot of primary care doctors looking for specific directions," he said. "You need to state up front the key objectives."

The 205,000-member HMO has been using depression guidelines for primary care since 1995. But Ehrlich readily admits they have been useless. Three years later, a psychiatric group working with the HMO told him major depression is still underdiagnosed.

Ehrlich attributes the guidelines' failure to their lack of specific recommendations and the absence of any measurements. Fallon in 1998 was revising its guidelines and expected to release the new version early in the fall.

Rather than advise physicians to "treat with antidepressants for six months," as the old guidelines did, the new will specify a class of antidepressants and a set number of patient visits over a given time period. Fallon also will provide physicians with screening questionnaires to give patients they suspect may be depressed.

Along with the guidelines, practitioners will receive a letter from Ehrlich explaining the reason for the guidelines and the importance of following them. Ehrlich expects to review charts and computer data to measure compliance within six to nine months. If goals are not being met, he will consider more physician education.

"You need to know what you're trying to measure before you develop guidelines," he said. "If you put together something very usable and very clear, it will work."

A Decisive Year Ahead
For the Practice Guidelines Coalition

DAVID STRICKLAND

In the field of behavioral health care—where treatments are seldom backed by science and practitioners are often divided along discipline lines—the creation of industrywide, evidence-based practice guidelines seems an unlikely rallying point.

Despite these challenges, a few of the field's bellwethers have launched a national effort to conceive behavioral care guidelines borne of consensus. Leaders of the project, known as the Practice Guidelines Coalition (PGC), are forging a guidelines strategy they hope will establish common ground among the diverse associations, societies, schools of thought, and constituencies within the coalition's tentative ranks.

PGC's goal is to produce clinical practice guidelines for behavioral health providers "that are based on a broad consensus about the best available evidence...readily understandable by practitioners, focused on core clinical processes and measurable outcomes, nationally disseminated, multidisciplinary, and available in the public domain."

But without the explicit support of two of the field's most powerful associations, the fledgling PGC's search for common ground may already be on shaky ground. The American Psychological Association and the American Psychiatric Association—who are often at odds—agree that PGC's guidelines development effort merits a "wait and see" approach rather than an endorsement.

According to PGC steering committee member Steven Hayes, the wait will be over in late 1998. That's when PGC plans to release its first two guidelines, he says. These two "demonstration project" guidelines will address panic disorder and the behavioral management of pain.

Panic disorder was selected "because it is a syndrome with a good deal of scientific and clinical literature pertaining to its diagnostic and comorbidity features, as well as literature pertaining to the efficacy and effectiveness of pharmacological and psychosocial treatments," states a PGC letter soliciting input on the guidelines.

Behavioral management of pain was selected "because of the coalition's stated interest in developing practice guidelines that bridge physical health and behavioral health issues and that deal with clinical problems that are not well-defined syndromes," and because "there is a good deal of clinical and scientific literature about pain management that could support development of a scientifically sound practice guideline."

Early on, PGC decided to focus on "high frequency and/or high impact" conditions, including:
- *behavior disorders*, such as bulimia, depression, bipolar affective disorder, and substance abuse;
- *clinical problems that don't necessarily involve behavior disorders*, such as marital distress and work stress;
- *clinical risk situations*, such as suicidal crisis; and
- *behavioral aspects of acute and chronic illness, health promotion, and disease prevention*, such as smoking cessation and weight reduction.

The coalition also hopes to address several other issues, such as assessing whether the guidelines have a positive impact on clinical and func-

---

Source: Strickland D. A Decisive Year Ahead for the Practice Guidelines Coalition. In: 1999 Medical Outcomes & Guidelines Sourcebook, L Newman, ed. New York: Faulkner & Gray, 1998, pp.237–241.

tional outcomes; whether they promote more cost-effective care; and whether the program is effective in "removing extremes in unexplained variability" and providing a "floor" for industry-wide quality improvement efforts, he says.

The coalition was launched during the National Planning Summit on Scientifically-Based Behavioral Health Practice Guidelines meeting, held November 1996 in Orlando FL, and June 1997 in Minneapolis MN. This summit brought together providers, researchers, consumers, and government officials.

Funded by grants from the federal Substance Abuse and Mental Health Services Administration (SAMHSA) and the National Institutes of Health's Office of Behavioral and Social Sciences Research (OBSSR), the planning summit was sponsored by the Association for Advancement of Behavior Therapy (AABT) and the American Association of Applied and Preventive Psychology (AAAPP.)

Hayes is president of AABT and immediate past president of AAAPP. Other PGC steering committee members include Ian Shaffer, MD, of Value Behavioral Health, a Virginia-based managed care provider network, and Kirk Strosahl of Group Health Cooperative of Puget Sound, a Seattle WA-based HMO.

Several Stakeholders, A Single Tent

Like the summit that spawned it—but unlike most other efforts to develop practice guidelines for clinicians—PGC strives to include "all the major stakeholders" in behavioral health care, namely the "associations and agencies representing the behavioral sciences and professions, behavioral health providers, behavioral health care systems, behavioral health care managers, consumers of behavioral health services, purchasers of behavioral health services, accrediting bodies in the behavioral health industry, and interested parties from government or society at large," state the PGC bylaws.

Hayes diplomatically refers to PGC as "an exercise in coalition building." He recognizes that behavioral health field has been rife with conflict and draws attention to the ongoing philosophical "war" between psychologists and psychiatrists as one source of friction. Hayes says his experience developing "scientific standards" for AAAPP taught him that any attempt to foster industry-wide consensus on the practice of care won't move forward without the collaboration of several key—and often opposing—groups heading in the same direction at the same time. "You can't get the ball going by working discipline-by-discipline and area-by-area," he says.

"One of the attractive things about the Practice Guidelines Coalition is its attempt to break down some of the disciplinary barriers," says OBSSR director Norman Anderson. Its explicit focus on the scientific and clinical evidence, rather than on the disciplines that generated it appeals to Anderson, who calls PGC "an unprecedented coalescing of the diverse groups" within the field of behavioral care.

From another vantage point, some PGC participants see coalition building as a way to fend off guidelines that don't reflect industry consensus that are being handed down by outside accrediting organizations. For example, anticipating that accreditation of managed behavioral organizations by National Committee for Quality Assurance will soon be contingent on implementation of evidence-based guidelines, board members say that this was a "key factor" in forming PGC.

A Tough Sell

Drawing from a list of over 60 nominations, PGC's steering committee appointed its first two guideline panels in May 1998. As dictated in the PGC "Administrative Framework for Practice Guideline Development and Approval," each panel is composed of two scientists, two practitioners, two industry representatives, and two consumer advocates.

Consumer advocates have equal say in PGC's guidelines development process because the "core purpose of behavioral health care systems is to enhance the behavioral, psychological, and physical health and well-being of consumers," says PGC's Statement of Operating Principles, "Given that purpose, the structure of these systems must be guided primarily by what is in the best interest of the consumer, rather than by the interests of the industry, the professions or the providers."

The panels' structure "doesn't let scientists override the process," Hayes says, "You can't build consensus over a right-wing, hard-core researcher or clinician agenda." Yet it's likely that turf battles will be "left at the door," Hayes insists, because PGC's guidelines aren't intended for specific specialties or disciplines.

Instead, the guidelines "will focus on core assessment or intervention procedures that can be implemented by any appropriately trained behavioral health provider," states PGC's constitution. "In cases where different disciplinary expertise may be required, guidelines will offer basic decision rules for determining when to involve another behavioral health professional."

Feuds among various "schools of thought" and the major professional societies could make reaching consensus difficult, warns steering committee member Tom Trabin, director of the Institute for Behavioral Healthcare and vice president for CentraLink. The Institute and CentraLink are educational organizations based in Tiburon CA.

For example, Trabin cites two schools of thought on the treatment of depression. One school wants depression to be treated exclusively with psychotherapy, while the other stresses pharmaceutical therapy. Subgroup "extremists" exist within these camps, he warns.

Psychiatrists Are Skeptical

The American Psychiatric Association (APA) "won't spend lots of time" assisting PGC's effort because it won't agree with hard and fast statements on drug treatment, warns William Ayers, MD, who until recently served as the APA and American Academy of Child and Adolescent Psychiatry representative to PGC. He doubts that consensus is possible. "The groups [involved] are so splintered and different from each other," observes Ayers, who is also clinical associate professor of psychiatry at the University of California at San Francisco CA.

The association has decided to wait until PGC produces its first guidelines before deciding whether to continue with any level of participation in the "highly ambitious program," notes Ayers. "We won't walk out entirely, but we don't think it's a viable effort."

Aside from its view that the coalition's attempt to achieve widespread consensus over practice guidelines is ill-advised and impractical, the American Psychiatric Association has other concerns, according to Ayers. It is also critical of PGC's liberal definition of "evidence," the relatively brief amount of time allotted for weighing evidence and drafting guidelines, with each panel including just two practitioners and two researchers, Ayers says.

Although PGC vows to include the best available evidence in its guidelines and give more weight to empirical evidence, "All reasonable sources of evidence are relevant...Expert opinion and clinical experience will be employed as a source of evidence," according to PGC's Statement of Operating Principles.

Armed with summary tables detailing evidence submitted by coalition members and experts in the field, each PGC guideline panel "will meet intensively for one or two three-day retreats" to develop a guideline draft.

In contrast, the American Psychiatric Association's "science-based medical practice guidelines" development process typically involves large groups of clinicians and researchers engaged in lengthy discussions over a two-year period, Ayers says.

Until 1998, Ayers was a member of the American Psychiatric Association's oversight committee on practice guidelines. He is also former president of AACAP who has been active in that organization's guidelines program.

Psychologists Fear Focus On Empirical Evidence

The American Psychological Association is also reluctant to buy into the process. The psychologists' group is most concerned that they might be stung by panels' over-reliance on empirical evidence.

The relatively few studies of therapeutic techniques employed by psychologists tend to focus on the treatments' "efficacy" rather than their "effectiveness," says Geoffrey Reed, the American Psychological Association's executive director for professional development. These studies don't adequately capture the true nature of these treatments as delivered in the field, Reed says. They fail to take into account real-world factors such as non-fixed durations of treatment, patients being treated for multiple conditions, self-correcting behaviors, and ongoing adjustments to treatment strategies for individual patients who often don't fit the neat profiles outlined in research protocols, he says.

In a February report to the American Psychological Association's board of directors, Reed warns that PGC documents used terms like "'empirical evidence' in such a way as to suggest that these terms were meant to reflect the narrowest interpretation of allowable evidence." It questions whether this "lays the foundation for a bias toward treatments that have been manualized and tested in randomized, controlled treatment trials, and the conclusion that interventions for a wide range of disorders that have not been (or cannot be) tested in this way are not supported by evidence," he wrote.

Taking the high road, the psychologists' society Board of Professional Affairs (BPA) and Committee for the Advancement of Professional Practice (CAPP) argue that "a treatment's clinical basis, theoretical basis, experiential basis, and the evidence of its effectiveness may be equally or even more important considerations in the selection of a particular treatment than its 'empirical' basis as it is narrowly conceptualized in efficacy research," says Reed.

Researchers are especially concerned about the view that to be deemed valid, guidelines must be based on trial data, says Don Routh, representative to PGC from the Society for a Science of Clinical Psychology, an offshoot of the American Psychological Association's clinical psychology division. Routh is president of that division, which creates and publishes treatises on "empirically supported guidelines" in lieu of practice guidelines.

Researchers and academics in the field of psychology have a vested interest in determining "what works and what doesn't," but they also view efforts to steer practitioners away from therapies "not yet studied and proven effective" as a "threat to their livelihood" says Routh, a professor of psychology at the University of Miami in Florida. They also worry that such efforts could cause research funds to dry up, he observes.

However, Hayes insists that PGC purposely "defines 'evidence' broadly, because so many organizations fear that if we go too far in defining evidence," guidelines won't reflect that "some well-established, traditional clinical practices have withstood the test of time."

The American Psychological Association also has concerns about PGC's guidelines development and ratification process, Reed says. Specifically, the psychologists' group is concerned that consumer and industry representatives could have undue influence in weighing clinical and empirical evidence. "There needs to be a firewall" between these constituencies and the decision-making process that ultimately judges the strength of evidence generated by, and ultimately dictating proper care by, behavioral health professionals, Reed says.

The association also takes issue with PGC's plan to approve and disseminate guidelines based on endorsement by 75 percent or more of all coalition members, as determined by a vote. "They [PGC] talk about consensus, but a majority vote is not consensus," Reed says.

Confronting Doubts About Guidelines

As a matter of policy, the American Psychological Association is wary of practice guidelines in general. A formal examination, conducted by its BPA, "indicates that many treatment guidelines in mental health are medically biased in ways not supported by available evidence...Worse, many treatment guidelines produced by managed care organizations appear to be vehicles for cost-motivated restrictions of treatment disguised in the language of empiricism and clinical quality," Reed says, summarizing the association's official position on guidelines.

In particular, the association's BPA and CAPP are concerned PGC's guidelines effort "would play into the hands of organized health care delivery systems that seek to implement arbitrary and reductionistic treatment criteria and clinical protocols that further erode the influence of professional judgment on the treatment process...that interventions for mental health conditions, psychiatric disorders, emotional problems, and psychosocial aspects of physical disorders would be held to a higher and more restrictive standard than interventions considered 'medical,' further restricting access to appropriate treatment," he says.

Rather than institute a program to produce guidelines intended for its members and other providers in the field, like the American Psychiatric Association has done, the American Psychological Association has produced a "template," which incorporates its stance on guidelines, for guiding the guidelines development efforts of others, and for evaluating the resulting guidelines. The association's template says guidelines "should be based on careful, judicious, and systematic weighing of research data *and* clinical expertise."

Hayes says PGC's leadership is very aware of various individual—and influential—organizations' distrust and disdain for practice guidelines. He says that awareness has impacted most of the coalition's activities since its inception and is reflected in PGC's governing principles and membership policy.

As proof, he points to early correspondence from the steering committee inviting participants in the planning summit to nominate panel members and submit evidence. "Any collaborative effort raises fears and entails risk," the letter states, "But many of the strongest fears are associated not with the coalition per se, but with practice guidelines more generally."

Tentative Participation

The letter outlines how the group's coalition-building strategy depends on potential members' acceptance of the first two "pilot" guidelines and how there is no obligation to join the coalition before the participants examine the guidelines as a group. "Until that time it was agreed that there would be no formal membership in PGC, and thus that organizations could participate actively in the development process without yet having to decide whether participation in the coalition would ultimately be in their best interests," the letter explains, adding that the pilot guidelines "will give concrete form to the hopes and fears of participants as they consider their formal participation in the coalition."

As plans are being made to convene the first two guidelines panels, Hayes is optimistic. Since the planning summit, the number of organizations actively participating in PGC has grown from fewer than 45 to approximately 65, he says. The increase in participating organizations signals PGC is experiencing "clear momentum," Hayes says, "No one has walked away from the table yet."

Steering committee member Trabin sounds a bit more cautious. "The politics are sensitive. We're trying to institute a huge social change and we must move slowly and very delicately," he says, "The coalition still needs to coalesce."

Practice Guidelines Coalition: Administrative Framework for Practice Guideline Development and Approval

Goal: To quickly and efficiently develop practice guidelines that are scientifically sound, clinically useful, consumer focused and usable in the context of daily practice.

Announcement of Guideline Project

The goal of this phase is to announce the start of a guideline project, normally 3-6 months before the panel is actually convened, to begin to gather evidentiary input from interested stakeholders and to recruit the guideline panel.

1. Coalition members are asked to nominate panel members and to provide a supporting rationale to the PGC central office.
2. The PGC central office will provide Coalition members with the core assessment and treatment questions that are to be addressed in the guideline.
3. Coalition members are asked to submit either a) a narrative evidence summary, along with original research reports and associated evidence tables that conform to the Institute of Medicine evidence rating system, or b) up to 10 unreviewed empirical reports; and c) a statement of clinical expert opinion or best practice innovation in areas where clinical practice may be ahead of science. Normally, these documents will need to be received within three months of the date of the announcement. For "a" and "c" above, the PGC central office will distribute forms that will allow for some standardization in the submissions received.

Convening the Guideline Panel

The goal of this phase is to select and convene the guideline panel, to identify roles and responsibilities of panel members and to formulate an overall work plan.

1. The guideline panel is selected by the steering committee based upon a review of the nominations and other input from Coalition members.
2. The guideline panel consists of the following members:
   - Two respected scientists who are not strongly identified with a treatment or assessment model in the area of the guideline. They function more like "jurors" as in the NIH consensus conference model. Their role is to sort through the evidentiary summaries, articles and narrative summaries and organize their response to the core clinical and assessment questions, along with a statement of scientific confidence in each recommendation. Normally, one of these scientists will be non medically trained; the other will be medically trained. These scientists will expected to seek counsel from their colleagues in the event critical data is missing from the evidence reviews or when the evidence is hard to sort out and more expertise may be required.

Source: Practice Guidelines Coalition.

- Two behavioral health practitioners from different disciplines, whose role is to review and incorporate statements of expert opinion/best practice innovation into the guideline, to provide the panel with perspective about the likely practice impacts of scientific recommendations, to review their ease of application during a normal behavioral health service, and to review the user friendly attributes of the guideline format. These representatives should not represent an association point of view, but rather the practitioner point of view. To this end, it is expected that these representatives will engage in active outreach to the practitioner groups in the Coalition to obtain the best possible input.
- Two behavioral health industry representatives, one public sector and one private sector, whose role is to address the implementation aspects of the guideline as it is being developed. This may involve questions around comparative costs of two treatments with equal efficacy, feedback when recommendations are becoming too esoteric or specialized to be feasible in a typical delivery system, etc. In their industry representation role, these individuals should interact with industry members in the Coalition to assure that all viewpoints are being considered.
- Two consumer advocates, one representing direct recipients and one representing significant others impacted by a behavioral health condition and the demands of treatment, whose role is to keep the panel focused on consumer and family needs and preferences, to help construct meaningful consumer information that would be attached to the guideline, to look at feasibility in terms of personal cost, retention in treatment, burden of care placed on the family and so forth. Since there are many consumer constituencies with possibly differing points of view, it is important that the consumer panelists interface with other consumer groups in the Coalition so as to represent the widest range of perspectives.
- One PGC staff facilitator, who is not a "panel member," but whose role is to keep the panel on track, to establish a viable work plan with the panel, to help panel members maintain clarity about their roles and responsibilities, to establish meeting agendas, to convene meetings and phone conferences and to provide focused facilitation. The facilitator maintains an ongoing link with the steering committee regarding the progress of the panel and any questions the panel has regarding the process and the mission. The facilitator decides if the panel is at impasse about a particular clinical recommendation and activates the steering committee to resolve the impasse.

The Process of the Guideline Panel

The goal of the guideline panel is to initiate an organized, structured process for completing evidentiary review and making clinical recommendations, crafting the guideline product attending to stakeholder requirements and submitting the product to the PGC steering committee for review and approval. This process is designed to be as brief, efficient and least costly as possible.

1. The guideline panel will not be convened until the "cut-off date" for evidentiary submissions has passed and the panel facilitator has organized all submissions.
2. The scientist panel members will then have these evidentiary documents forwarded to them for review prior to the panel meeting. They will review them with respect to answering the following questions, which relate to the content of the practice guideline. These questions are as follows:
   - What is the best established and most appropriate method of assessment for this condition? Are there assessment methods that should not be used?
   - Are there any age, sex, racial, ethnic, religious, economic, disability, social/

familial or work setting factors that might mitigate how this problem presents or might influence treatment selection, likelihood of response or retention in treatment? Are there functional outcomes in any of these areas that should be measured?
- What treatments have been shown to be effective with this problem? What core interventions in this treatment that are most associated with positive clinical response? Is there evidence regarding the acceptability of recommended treatments with providers? What is the probability of positive treatment response based upon a review of "completers" data? Are there treatments with more variable or poorer outcomes that should not be employed? If there is more than one effective treatment, is there a significant cost differential between the two? Is this cost differential mitigated by other factors, for example, reduced relapse rates?
- What are the consumer acceptance data like with the recommended treatment(s)? Are there differential drop out rates that might effect the population effectiveness of the treatments? What information should consumers receive regarding the risks and benefits of this treatment? Are there potential side effects that might effect treatment acceptability?
- What is the estimated time frame for positive clinical response? What assessment procedure is recommended for measuring clinical response and when should it be used? What should be done if a patient is not responding as expected to the treatment? When should an alternative treatment be added or substituted for the existing treatment?
- What are the most commonly occurring co-morbid conditions? How do they influence treatment selection and prognosis? Are there functionally distinct subgroups within this problem area, either diagnostically or in terms of underlying etiological or maintaining processes? Are there differential treatment considerations related to subgroups?
- Is this a recurring problem that is subject to relapse? What is the relapse rate in patients who have responded to the preferred treatment(s)? What methods should be employed to prevent relapse?
- Is there evidence that primary prevention or health promotion interventions can forestall the appearance and/or progression of this condition? If so, what are the core components of such effective interventions?

1. The guideline panel will meet intensively for one or two three-day retreats. The goal of these intensive meetings is to get the rough draft of the guideline done.
2. The first phase is scientific input. The goal is to define the areas where the science seems to answer the core clinical questions and what the specific evidence based recommendations will be. This process should also reveal which areas lack sufficient data or have contradictory data such that expert opinion will be required.
3. Once the science input is finished, the other panel members will begin a review of the potential strong points and weak points of the data. At this point, statements of expert opinion and/or practice innovation will be introduced relative to the empirically based recommendations. The guideline will be crafted through these discussions into a form that is consistent with the operating principles of the Coalition.
4. In the event an impasse is reached within a panel about a particular issue, the facilitator will declare an impasse, make sure he/she has captured the essence of the opposing points of view, and, will move the panel on to the next element of the work plan. In the event an impasse cannot be resolved over time, the draft document will be distributed with the opposing points of view contained in the impasse.
5. Once the guideline structure/recrafting discussions have concluded, the facilitator is responsible for getting the product into semi-final form. This will be sent to all panel members, with a short turn around

Chapter 10: Creating and Implementing Behavioral Guidelines

requirement. The facilitator will make note of requested changes and make them if they are routine or small issues. In the event of a big change, the facilitator will convene a phone conference of the panel members and attempt to resolve the potential problems. If this cannot be achieved, the facilitator will declare an impasse and move the issue to the steering committee for a final decision.
6. Drafts of the guidelines will be distributed to all PGC members including practicing clinicians, with the request that they provide feedback to the panel on the draft document.
7. When the feedback has been assimilated and a near final draft is supported by the panel, the guideline is passed on to the steering committee for review. The panel remains empowered until the final product has been approved by the Coalition, then it is disbanded.

Steering Committee Review Process

The goal of the steering committee review process is to do a due diligence check on the semi-final guideline drafts. Here, the purpose is to review the format, more than the content, of the drafted product. Is it short? Does it appear user friendly? Is it graphically easy to take in? Have scientific recommendations and expert opinion been clearly differentiated Have all the clinical content questions been answered or at least addressed?
1. Only in the rarest of circumstances will the steering committee find itself unable to support a particular guideline recommendation. Ordinarily, if there is a red flag of that magnitude, the draft will be sent back to the panel with a request for clarification or to address the issue of concern.
2. The steering committee will approve a guideline by consensus. If it is unable to reach consensus, the guideline will be returned to the panel for modification. If consensus is reached in the steering committee, the guideline draft will be ready for review and approval by the Coalition members.

Coalition Review Process

The goal of the Coalition review process is to endorse the practice guideline, so that it can be disseminated. The Coalition membership must vote to approve a practice guideline and to have it released to the general public.
1. The draft guideline is disseminated to all PGC members (by mail, e-mail or fax). A minimum 30 day period of review is allowed for input on final modifications that might be made. The PGC membership will vote on whether to approve and distribute each guideline product, either at the annual meeting of the membership or through a mail or e-mail ballot process.

A 75% affirmative majority vote is required to approve a guideline and to allow it to be disseminated. Rarely should a guideline be voted down at the general Coalition level. However, in the event it is, the steering committee will attempt to capture the essence of the problems that led to a failure to support the guideline. The panel will be reconvened to address the problem. At that point, the review and approval cycle articulated above will be repeated.

Ethical and Political Issues in Practice Guidelines Implementation: A Dialogue

DANIEL J. ABRAHAMSON, PHD, DANIEL FISHER, MD, PHD, AND IAN A. SHAFFER, MD

Public and private sector policies that are requiring accountability for quality treatment recently developed a new focus: implementation of practice guidelines. From reports and books and books resting unnoticed on bookshelves, they are now being reformulated and rewritten for everyday use. With seeming suddenness, the controversies regarding these guidelines have acquired an immediacy they never had before. Public and professional forums are needed for a full discussion of the issues regarding their content and the manner in which they are implemented.

Many stakeholder and interest groups are involved in these developments, with a lot at stake. In this dialogue section, perspectives from three such groups are represented: consumers of mental health services, clinicians, and managed care organizations. There are, of course, many differences within these three groups, so that no one person can represent the entire range of opinions. However, the three opinion leaders featured here give a strong portrayal of the differing vantage points from which the issues are reviewed.

Several challenges, major themes, and consequent recommendations arise from this dialogue section which reflect an increasingly heated nationwide discussion. Guidelines should be developed with input from many stakeholder groups, including consumers. The behavioral healthcare field must agree on a hierarchy of types of evidence with which to weigh the value of competing guidelines. They must be neutral with regard to the turf battles between professional disciplines. Less traditional interventions, such as self-help methods and peer support groups, must also be included.

Where strong evidence exists for best practices, they should be disseminated and used more widely so there is less variability in treatment approaches. However, especially in areas where such evidence is not substantial, room must be maintained for consumer choice. Clinicians and care managers must inform consumers of their choices and the relative risks of different approaches.—
Tom Trabin, PhD, MSM

Source: Reprinted with permission by Manisses Communications Group, Inc. Originally published in Behavioral Healthcare Tomorrow *June 1998; 7(3):32-38.)*

Daniel J. Abrahamson, PhD, is the administrative director of the Traumatic Stress Institute/Center for Adult & Adolescent Psychotherapy in South Windsor, Connecticut. He was a member of the American Psychological Association's Task Force on Psychological Intervention Guidelines and currently chairs that association's Template Implementation Work Group on practice guidelines.

Daniel Fisher, MD, PhD, has recovered from schizophrenia, and is executive director of the National Empowerment Center, Inc., in Lawrence, Massachusetts. He is a board certified psychiatrist who is medical director of E. Middlesex Outpatient Center, and a former neurochemical researcher at the National Institute of Mental Health (NIMH).

Ian A. Shaffer, MD, is executive vice president and chief medical officer for Value Behavioral Health, Inc. Its offices are in Falls Church, Virginia.

Political Issues in Practice Guidelines Implementation

Daniel J. Abrahamson, PhD

During the past several years there has been an unprecedented proliferation of clinical practice guidelines pertaining to mental health. These guidelines have been generated by managed care organizations (MCOs), professional associations, government agencies, and various health-care-related consortiums. The form and substance of these guidelines is remarkably variable. In fact, the most comprehensive analysis of mental health treatment guidelines to date concluded, "The guidelines reviewed vary greatly in quality, scope, focus, and degree of empirical grounding."[1]

Despite the confusion generated by the variability in practice guidelines, there is no evidence that the situation will improve anytime soon. Adding fuel to the fire is the requirement by the National Committee for Quality Assurance (NCQA) that for MCOs to receive accreditation, they must develop and disseminate practice guidelines. Without clear direction from the NCQA as to what these guidelines should look like, there will inevitably be more variability and confusion in the guideline proliferation gold rush.

Given the current state of affairs in guideline development, it is not surprising that efforts at implementation have been abysmal. The whole issue begins to take on an "emperor's new clothes" feeling, as everyone points to their own guidelines as "state of the art." Unfortunately, there is little evidence to support the validity or utility of most treatment guidelines.

The problem with most available guidelines is that they do not explicitly address the political and ethical issues inherent to the process of guideline development and implementation. Additionally, there is far too little attention paid to evaluating the quality and integrity of clinical practice guidelines that are being developed. It starts to feel as though there are more people involved in developing guidelines than there are those using them.

In the remainder of this article a number of political and ethical issues relevant to guideline implementation will be discussed. It is being argued that until such issues are addressed openly and appropriate emphasis is placed on evaluating their validity, guidelines in the mental health arena will be far more image than substance.

The most profound political/ethical issue related to guidelines involves their overreliance on pharmacological interventions relative to other psychotherapeutic modalities. Even relatively well-researched guidelines are not immune to this bias. The Agency for Health Care Policy and Research (AHCPR) guidelines for treatment of depression have been criticized for reflecting a biomedical bias.[2] Despite the fact that the empirical literature supports psychotherapy as being at least as effective as pharmacotherapy in the treatment of depression, this guideline has patients being treated pharmacologically. In most cases a referral for psychotherapy is triggered only after repeated failures with different medications.

It is not difficult to surmise the basis for this bias. Pharmaceutical companies stand to gain from this misrepresentation, as do many MCOs. The MCOs assume they will save money based on the faulty logic that pharmacotherapy is less expensive than psychotherapy. When the cost of long-term maintenance on drugs is factored into the equation, psychotherapy is often less expensive. To the extent, however, that psychopharmacological costs are paid for by the medical or prescription benefit, MCOs may still stand to gain by requiring medication trials where they may not be justifiable on the basis of the evidence.

A second trend in guideline development with significant political and ethical implications is the increasing emphasis on including only "empirically validated" treatments in the guidelines. On the surface this does not appear to be highly problematic. Who, one might argue, would disagree with the need to include only empirically validated treatments in a practice guideline? The problem emerges when one starts delving into a more detailed analysis of what is meant by "empirically validated." The Task Force on Promotion and Dissemination of Psychological Procedures requires that a treatment approach be validated with two randomly controlled trials or a large series of well-designed, single-case designs in order to be considered a "well-established" treatment.[3] In either case the studies must be conducted with treatment manuals. Since a definition of this type can have significant impact on those developing treatment guidelines, it is important to note a major limitation to the narrowly defined approach to clinical science reflected in this over-reliance on efficacy research.

Seligman points to the importance of effectiveness research to demonstrate that well-established treatments that have not been empirically validated can still be highly effective. He asserts that it is an erroneous assumption that a treatment does not work if it has not been validated with traditional efficacy research. The following quote from Seligman demonstrates the absurdity of placing too much emphasis on efficacy research:

> It is hard to imagine how one could ever do a scientifically compelling efficacy study of a treatment which had variable duration and self-correcting improvisations and was aimed at improved quality of life as well as symptom relief, with patients who were not randomly assigned and had multiple problems.[4]

The relative roles of efficacy and effectiveness research for clinical practice guidelines have been thoroughly addressed in the Template for Developing Guidelines.[5] The Template requires that treatment guidelines be constructed on the basis of two simultaneous considerations or dimensions: treatment efficacy and clinical utility. The document provides considerable detail as to how these dimensions are defined and measured for the purpose of developing treatment guidelines. It is essential to note that for a recommendation to be included in a guideline, the Template stipulates that there must be sufficient evidence in both realms. Adherence to the standards set forth in the Template can help to reduce the unnecessary clutter of invalid guidelines that currently exists in the field.

Public availability of guidelines is another central issue to any discussion of the ethical and political landscape of practice guidelines. For too long MCOs hid behind the contention that their practice guidelines were proprietary and as such were not made public. Surprisingly, given NCQA requirements for dissemination of guidelines, some MCOs continue to work under this premise. Worse yet, while some MCOs publish their practice guidelines, they maintain unpublished utilization review criteria that serve as the basis for decisions about authorizing or discontinuing treatment. What begins to happen is that guidelines are shaped to mimic the benefit rather than being independently validated on the basis of the best available evidence. While cost containment based on benefit design may be a legitimate function for MCOS, it should not be confused with the identification of optimal care. Such "truth in advertising" is a core issue in the guidelines arena.

The meager available evidence points to the fact that, despite their widespread proliferation, clinical practice guidelines are being used minimally. This is unfortunate given the potential benefit that can be derived from useful practice guidelines. Unless those who develop guidelines pay attention to the political and ethical realities for those who are expected to use those guidelines, the waste will continue. Tremendous resources will be pumped into generating guidelines that nobody will use. It is not enough for everyone to nod their heads in agreement as the emperor's new guidelines go by.

References

1. Science Applications International Corporation (1994), *Side by Side Comparison of Mental Health Practice Guidelines*, Beaverton, Oregon.
2. Munoz, R.F., Hollon, S.D., McGrath, E., Rehm, L.P., and VandenBos, G.R.(1994). On the AHCPR depression in primary care guidelines: Further considerations for practitioners. *American Psychologist*, 49, 42-61.
3. Task Force on Promotion and Dissemination of Psychological Procedures (1995). Training in and dissemination of empirically-validated psychological treatments: Report and recommendation. *The Clinical Psychologist*, 48, 3-23.
4. Seligman, M.E.P. (1995). The effectiveness of psychotherapy: The Consumer Reports study. *American Psychologist*, 50, 965-974.
5. American Psychological Association, Task Force on Psychological Intervention Guidelines (1995). Template for developing guidelines: Interventions for mental disorders and psychosocial aspects of physical disorders. Washington, DC: American Psychological Association.

Recovery: The Behavioral Healthcare Guidelines Of Tomorrow

Daniel Fisher, MD, PhD

Whereas the behavioral healthcare practice guidelines of today are maintenance-based, the guidelines of tomorrow will be recovery-based. Whereas the guidelines of today are written by maintenance experts, the guidelines of tomorrow will be written by recovery experts. Whereas the practice guidelines of today are a reflection of the interests of the parties sponsoring them, the guidelines of tomorrow will reflect the interests of people recovering. Whereas the guidelines of today are based on a static view of people as chemical machines whose emotional disorders are lifelong chemical imbalances needing lifelong chemical regulation, the guidelines of tomorrow will be based on a dynamic view of people as fully human beings whose emotional disorders are temporary imbalances of mind, body, and social role from which one can fully recover by self-managed care.

Maintenance-Based Guidelines

Guidelines by the American Psychiatric Association (APA) for schizophrenia reflect the present underlying societal treatment goal for people labelled with mental illness: maintenance. They narrowly define the problem as biological, the treatment as mostly medication, and the practitioners as mostly psychiatrists. As the following quote from the APA shows: "[Schizophrenia] is considered a brain disease...it is one of the most debilitating and misunderstood illnesses known. Unfortunately it is a chronic illness that affects most sufferers over a lifetime. However, its symptoms generally can be controlled with treatment [medication]."[1]

To discover the present state of practice guidelines, we searched the Internet and found The Doctor's Guide to the Internet on top.[2] The Guide places a heavy emphasis on medication with information sponsored by 30 pharmaceutical companies. The third item cited was generated by a private group, Expert Knowledge Systems, whose guidelines for schizophrenia and obsessive-compulsive disorder were also very medication-oriented. The group is funded by four drug companies. There is a link under obsessive-compulsive disorder (OCD) to another Web site, the OCD Resource Center.[3] Once again, for OCD we find a biological description with a medication prescription in a site sponsored by the manufacturer of a medication for OCD. Another site, called Webtrack in Schizophrenia, had its own summary of the recently released American Psychiatric Association Practice Guidelines for Schizophrenia with repeated emphasis on a particular antipsychotic.[4] Webtrack is sponsored by the manufacturer of that particular drug.

The Center for Mental Health Service Research at the University of Maryland, under contract with the Agency for Health Care Policy and Research (AHCPR), is generating a new set of guidelines for schizophrenia. Although these guidelines include more of the psychosocial aspects of treatment, they, like all the rest, have not included primary consumers on their review panels nor have they included literature about consumer-run services or recovery. These sources of knowledge were omitted because they were instructed by their funders only to include controlled research studies appearing in peer reviewed journals. These requirements are a barrier to the use of most consumer writings and studies. The omission of consumer participation also leaves this group with maintenance-based guidelines.

Recovery-Based Practice Guidelines

Practice guidelines of tomorrow need to be based on the recent findings that many people fully recover from major mental illness.[5,6,7] Dr. Courtenay Harding and colleagues found that the recovery rate was uniformly better in Vermont than in Maine. The authors concluded that the biggest difference between the two states lay in the values underlying their policies. "Perhaps the most important value was that the [Vermont] program had a pervasive attitude of hope and optimism about human potential through the vision that if given the opportunity persons with mental illness could become self-sufficient."[7] In contrast, Maine had maintenance and stabilization as its goals.

According to rehabilitation professionals, recovery means recovery of a person's functioning without ever recovering from their underlying mental illness.[8] In contrast, research at the National Empowerment Center (NEC) has found that most consumer/survivors who have recovered from mental illness emphasized that they were motivated to recover when they and the people around them believed in their capacity to do so. This finding is consistent with that of the Vermont study.

We propose a new vision of recovery upon which to base the guidelines of tomorrow. Since the label mental illness supersedes all individual diagnoses, we propose a set of guidelines for recovery from mental illness in general. We suggest these take precedence over those developed for individual diagnoses. It is well known that once someone has suffered a loss of social role due to severe emotional problems he or she is often given a variety of diagnoses.

As seen in this figure, it is recommended that all practice be directed toward the goal of returning a person to a meaningful social role in which they can control their own life. Overcoming the misperception by staff and public that people with mental illness are permanently incapable of living a full social life is an essential step. Until it is undertaken, professionals will continue to believe that anyone labeled with mental illness is incapable of recovering a membership in society because they will never again be fully human. As long as people not yet labeled with mental illness deny their own inadequacies, fears, anger, and sadness, they will insist that only the mentally ill are sad (depressed), frightened (paranoid), and mad (angry). To acknowledge the parallel to other "isms", Chamberlin has characterized this attitude of discrimination towards people with mental illness as mentalism.[5] The best way to become more aware of one's own mentalism is by entering into dialogue with people who have been so labeled.

Self-Managed Care Planning is an example of recovery-based care planning developing through the NEC. Self-managed care is consumer-directed, multilevel, strength-building planning to genuinely assist a person to gain a meaningful role in society. This planning is contrasted to maintenance-based treatment planning which by its nature is professionally directed to correct pathology.

Self-Managed Care Planning

Self-to-Self Level: Self-Help And Coping Strategies

- Help the person, and the people around that person, to believe in the capacity to recover through use of self-help manuals,

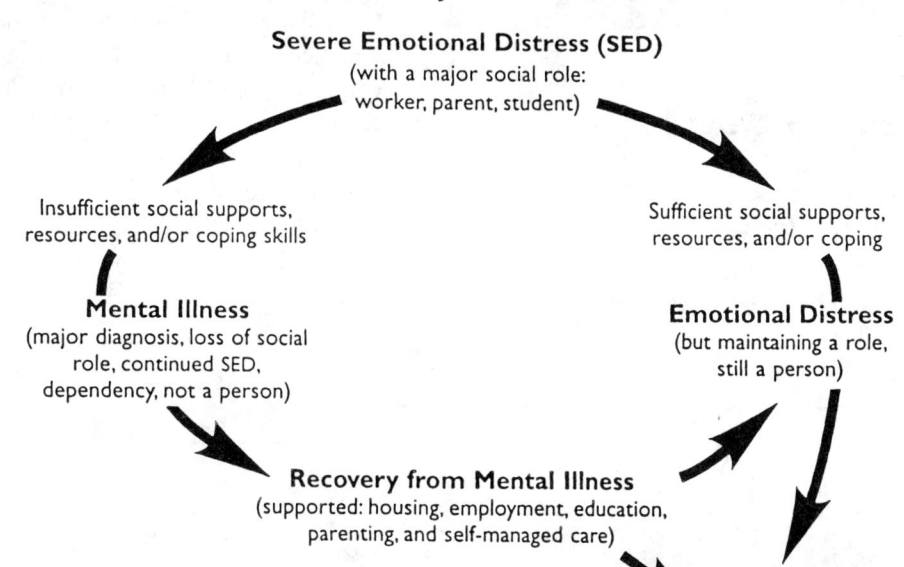

Figure 1. Empowerment Vision of Recovery from Mental Illness

Severe Emotional Distress (SED)
(with a major social role: worker, parent, student)

Insufficient social supports, resources, and/or coping skills

Sufficient social supports, resources, and/or coping

Mental Illness
(major diagnosis, loss of social role, continued SED, dependency, not a person)

Emotional Distress
(but maintaining a role, still a person)

Recovery from Mental Illness
(supported: housing, employment, education, parenting, and self-managed care)

Healing Emotionally

Chapter 10: Creating and Implementing Behavioral Guidelines

tapes, and videos produced by people in recovery on topics such as coping with voices, for example.
- Help the person to develop an individual plan for exercise, diet, meditation, biofeedback, visualization, and other forms of self-care. Encourage self-expression through writing, music, arts, and dance.

Self-to-Helper Level

- Consumer-directed services such as client-centered psychotherapy, informed use of medication, self-directed rehabilitation, advance directives in crisis planning, and member-run psychosocial clubs.
- Complementary medicine: acupuncture, herbs, and others.

Consumers Working As Providers

- Consumers experience acceptance and inspiration in working with providers who have recovered from mental illness. Information on this area can be obtained through the NEC.

Self-to-Peer Level

- Self-help groups: running the gamut from broad-based mutual support, to support by diagnoses, warm lines, and consumer-run social clubs.

Self to the Greater World

- Groups outside the mental health system: peer groups, churches, dance groups, bowling, and others.
- Supported work through a job coach, supported housing, supported education, supported parenting.
- Training in cultural competence.

Conclusion

Existing practice guidelines are based on continuing institutionalized thinking that people never recover from mental illness, and that the goal of treatment should be maintenance. Therefore, the hope-robbing nature of existing guidelines is interfering with recovery and as such is more damaging than useful. We recommend a delay in the implementation of existing maintenance-based practice guidelines for mental illness until up-to-date recovery-based guidelines can be developed. This would be best done by meaningful participation of consumer/survivors and use of our writings at all levels of guideline development and implementation. This will require a shift in social policy as well as in societal attitudes. With resources and determination, the state mental health authorities, in conjunction with national consumer/survivor groups, could carry out this shift to recovery-based guidelines.

References

1. APA news release (March 1997).
2. www.pslgroup.comdoc/guide.htm
3. www.ocdresource.com
4. www.futur.com/webtrack/arc96.htm
5. Chamberlin, J. (1978) *On Our Own*. New York: McGraw-Hill.
6. Fisher, D. (1994) Hope, humanity, and voice in recovery from psychiatric disability. *The CAMI Journal*, 5:3, 13-15.
7. DeSisto, et al. (1995) The Maine-Vermont three decade studies of serious mental illness: matched comparison of cross-sectional outcome, *Br Jrn of Psychiatry*, 167, 338-342.
8. Blanch, A., Fisher, D., et al. (1993) Recovery dialogues. *Disabilities Studies Quarterly*. Spring issue. Riverside, California: Self-Help Committee, California Network of Mental Health Clients.

Accountability And Variability

IAN A. SHAFFER, MD

Managed care has required increased accountability on the part of all healthcare providers. With this accountability has come an increased awareness of some of the variability in clinical practice. With the desire to limit inappropriate variability and improve our understanding of treatments that are effective through the use of practical outcomes measurements, there has been an explosion of new practice guidelines. These guidelines may take the form of a decision tree based on clinical information, a clinical treatment protocol that may be utilized for a specific diagnosis at a specific level of care, or a comprehensive treatment guideline related to a specific illness. All of these guidelines present a series of challenges, both in development and implementation.

Webster's notes that ethics are "Principles of right or good behavior" and politics involve "the study, structure, or affairs of state." In looking at these two terms, it becomes clear that applying these issues to guidelines will impact various constituencies, all of whom wish to do the best they can for beneficiaries seeking care.

The development of guidelines presents challenges. Clinicians with various orientations may interpret clinical evidence differently. For some guidelines such as panic disorder and obsessive-compulsive disorder, the treatments that are most effective are more readily known. But there are a number of areas of treatment in behavioral disorders for which specific hard, clinical evidence is not yet available. In these areas, the orientation of the clinician begins to influence the guideline design, and potentially, its use.

At the same time, consumers have become more active in the development of treatment plans for the disorders from which they suffer. From their experience as consumers and as the people afflicted, they bring a unique understanding of the impact of treatment on the disorder. They raise important questions about guidelines and may in fact challenge some of the scientific evidence. Further, consumers are very concerned about maintaining choice within treatment. Guidelines must therefore speak not only to the treatments that are appropriate for the disorder but also to choices that can be made from among those potential treatments.

Once a choice has been selected, the guidelines must speak to timeframes for which a specific treatment can remain unchallenged before the absence of progress prompts reappraisal.

Practicing clinicians are ethically bound to advocate for their patients, even in the face of allocation issues. It is important, however, for clinicians to recognize that resources for healthcare are finite. This raises an ethical dilemma as clinicians advocate for the individuals they see, requiring treatment on the one hand, and the recognition of the need to provide healthcare for an entire population on the other. Universal access to care is a principle that all clinicians hold dear and must be balanced with recognition of finite resources. As the American Medical Association points out, decisions regarding resource allocations must not be made at bedside, but through high-level policy decisions that must be made much earlier.[1]

Guideline development, as the first step in implementation, must recognize the need for standardization of care while at the same time recognizing and allowing for potential variations based on patient need. Consumer choice and resource allocations remain important components of the overall process.

Guidelines present challenges to all three parties concerned with healthcare: specifically, the consumer, the provider, and the payor. Much of the time, the interest of all parties is similar. However, there are times when the focus of these three groups diverge.

Consumers want guidelines to present cost-effective methods of treatment that can maximize the potential for a positive outcome. Speed of treatment and the ability to continue to make choices about their own care are very important. Guidelines must therefore allow for variation on two levels. The first level involves the recognition that, in many cases, there may not be an absolute number one treatment. There must therefore be room for choosing which treatment will be started and when changes should take place. At the same time, consumers should be informed of the potential risks and benefits of the choices they make in order to allow for an informed choice.

Finally, a critical component of any guideline is its acceptance by the consumer group. In order to obtain such acceptance, appropriate consumers should be included in guideline implementation, from the inception of its development to implementation, and from monitoring of treatment outcomes to modification of the guideline over time.

Providers of care must also buy in to the guideline if they are expected to use it. The guidelines must have a solid clinical base, readily understood by practitioners. Guidelines raise several additional challenges for providers within a managed care setting. Providers are not only asked to choose treatments that are effective, but also to attend to cost effectiveness. Clinical practice guidelines rarely address this issue directly. Further, providers are faced with situations where a guideline may have several procedures to choose from, in a situation where not all procedures are covered. The issue of so-called gag clauses in provider contracts can present an ethical dilemma for providers in the acceptance of the guidelines if they conflict with benefit coverages. It is important to note that a recent study by the American Managed Behavioral Healthcare Association (AMBHA) has indicated that the leading managed behavioral healthcare organizations do not have such gag clauses.[2]

Another key issue for providers is a recognition that the guidelines must allow for decisions that need to be made when the individual practitioner is one-on-one with the consumer. If resource allocation choices are to be made, they must occur prior to the moment of care delivery. Therefore, in order to obtain provider acceptance of practice guideline implementation, the provider must be a part of the development team, understand the clinical underpinnings and resource allocation principle of the guideline, and have room to make appropriate alternative decisions when individual situations present themselves.

Payors also have a strong interest in practice guidelines. Benefit managers of major companies are frequently attempting to understand the variations that may occur in treatments. Moreover, they are anxious to obtain outcomes information that will help them understand the treatment selected and the value of the resources extended for such treatment. Payors are being asked to consider full parity for mental illness and substance abuse. To accept that request, payors will need to be reassured that treatments provided are clearly justified and that decisions are based on sound clinical rationale. They recognize that guidelines by themselves are only one component of what is required. The guideline must be a tool to assist in the measurement of outcomes. The tool must be modified on a regular basis, following the merging clinical research and information obtained from ongoing outcomes studies.

In conclusion, it is important to recognize the value of well-developed and updated clinical practice guidelines based on clinical research and treatment information. In and of itself, however, the research and treatment data will be insufficient to obtain significant guideline implementation. Participation of the key groups—consumers, providers, and payors—is essential in meaningful guideline activity. The guidelines must recognize the context in which they are to be used. Various individuals and groups bring multiple perspectives to the practice of healthcare. We must ensure that the guidelines recognize these variations while retaining the scientific rigor that is needed for them to be meaningful.

References

1. American Medical Association (January 25, 1995) Ethical Issues in Managed Care, prepared by the Council on Ethical and Judicial Affairs, *JAMA*, Volume 23, Number 4, 330-335.
2. American Managed Behavioral Healthcare Association (August 5, 1996), Performance-based Accountability, Managed Care, and the Concerns of Psychiatry and Psychology, Survey of AMBHA Members.

At Issue: Translating Research Into Practice

The Schizophrenia Patient Outcomes Research Team (PORT) Treatment Recommendations

ANTHONY F. LEHMAN, DONALD M. STEINWACHS, AND THE CO-INVESTIGATORS OF THE PORT PROJECT

The At Issue section of the *Schizophrenia Bulletin* contains viewpoints and arguments on controversial issues. Articles published in this section may not meet the strict editorial and scientific standards that are applied to major articles in the *Bulletin*. In addition, the viewpoints expressed in the following articles do not necessarily represent those of the staff or the Editorial Advisory Board of the *Bulletin*.—The Editors.

Abstract

Beginning in 1992, the Agency for Health Care Policy and Research and the National Institute of Mental Health funded the Schizophrenia Patient Outcomes Research Team (PORT) to develop and disseminate recommendations for the treatment of schizophrenia based on existing scientific evidence. These Treatment Recommendations, presented here in final form for the first time, are based on exhaustive reviews of the treatment outcomes literature (previously published in *Schizophrenia Bulletin*, Vol. 21, No. 4, 1995) and focus on those treatments for which there is substantial evidence of efficacy. The recommendations address antipsychotic agents, adjunctive pharmacotherapies, electroconvulsive therapy, psychological interventions, family interventions, vocational rehabilitation, and assertive community treatment/intensive case management. Support for each recommendation is referenced to the previous PORT literature reviews, and the recommendations are rated according to the level of supporting evidence. The PORT Treatment Recommendations provide a basis for moving toward "evidence-based" practice for schizophrenia and identify both the strengths and limitations in our current knowledge base.
Key words: Mental health services, quality of care.
Schizophrenia Bulletin, 24(1):1-10, 1998.

In 1992 the Agency for Health Care Policy and Research (AHCPR) and the National Institute of Mental Health established a Patient Outcomes Research Team (PORT) for Schizophrenia at the University of Maryland School of Medicine and the Johns Hopkins University School of Public Health. This PORT combines the expertise of three major research centers at two universities: the Center for Research on Services for Severe Mental Illness (Johns Hopkins University and the University of Maryland), the University of Maryland Center for Mental Health Services Research, and the Maryland Psychiatric Research Center (at the University of Maryland). The prime objective of the PORT is to develop recommendations for the treatment of persons with

---

Source: Lehman AF, Steinwachs DM. At Issue: Translating Research Into Practice. Schizophrenia Bulletin 1998; 24(1): 1-10.
  Editor's Note: According to AHCPR, this journal article serves as the final report for the Schizophrenia Patient Outcomes Research Team.

schizophrenia based on a synthesis of the best scientific evidence, with the ultimate goal of improving the quality and cost-effectiveness of care for persons with this diagnosis.

The PORT Treatment Recommendations are statements about the care of persons with schizophrenia based on substantial scientific evidence. They begin with the assumption that an accurate diagnosis of schizophrenia has been made. They also recognize that treatment for an individual will depend on a variety of factors other than a diagnosis of schizophrenia, such as the presence of other psychiatric and medical conditions, personal and social circumstances, and individual variations. By nature of the fact that the Treatment Recommendations are based on scientific studies, they reflect what is known from well-controlled research. However, this requirement that recommendations be based on substantial scientific evidence means they are silent about or may appear to understate the importance of other aspects of treatment that have not been evaluated adequately. Therefore, there are many more recommendations about pharmacotherapies than about psychosocial treatments. This does not mean that psychosocial treatments are less important than medications, but reflects the fact that we know much less about which psychosocial treatments are helpful. Future research may shed light on these other aspects of care that are often viewed by practitioners, consumers, and families as vitally important, but for which we lack adequate scientific evidence for efficacy and effectiveness at the present time. Even with these limitations in mind, it is hoped that the PORT Treatment Recommendations will be used to enhance the treatment currently being offered to persons with schizophrenia.

The PORT Treatment Recommendations are organized according to categories of interventions, consistent with the framework of the recently completed review of the treatment literature by the PORT—see *Schizophrenia Bulletin*, Vol. 21, No. 4, 1995. The intervention categories are (1) antipsychotic medications; (2) adjunctive pharmacotherapies for anxiety, depression, and aggression/hostility; (3) electroconvulsive therapy; (4) psychological interventions; (5) family interventions; (6) vocational rehabilitation; and (7) assertive community treatment/assertive case management. For each recommendation, a brief rationale and annotations to the above referenced issue of *Schizophrenia Bulletin* are provided. These earlier literature reviews offer extensive bibliographies for the interested reader.

The level of evidence for each recommendation is also provided. In writing the recommendations, the PORT investigators adopted the criteria on levels of evidence used for development of the AHCPR Depression Guidelines, as follows:

Level A: Good research-based evidence, with some expert opinion, to support the recommendation

Level B: Fair research-based evidence, with substantial expert opinion, to support the recommendation

Level C: Recommendation based primarily on expert opinion, with minimal research-based evidence, but significant clinical experience

We sent initial drafts of these recommendations to experts for review. The experts were asked to rate their level of agreement with each recommendation based on their knowledge of the literature and to provide citations of studies that would argue for revision of the recommendations. Recommendations were modified based on this feedback only if supporting data from published research were provided; that is, opinion alone was not considered adequate to modify a recommendation.

Treatment Recommendations

Pharmacotherapies: Treatment Of Acute Symptom Episodes

Recommendation 1. Antipsychotic medications, other than clozapine, should be used as the first-line treatment to reduce psychotic symptoms for persons experiencing an acute symptom episode of schizophrenia.

Rationale. Over 100 randomized double-blind studies consistently support the efficacy of antipsychotic medications relative to placebo in the reduction of the acute positive symptoms (hallucinations, delusions, thought disorganization, bizarre behavior) of schizophrenia. Approximately 50 to 80 percent of persons will improve signifi-

Table 1. Chlorpromazine (CPZ) Equivalences and PORT Recommended Dosing Of Antipsychotic Medications

Medication	CPZ equivalence[1]	CPZ-equivalence multiplier[2]	PORT recommended total daily dose range (mg/day) Acute therapy	PORT recommended total daily dose range (mg/day) Maintenance therapy
Chlorpromazine	100	1	300-1000	300-600
Triflupromazine	25	4	75-250	75-150
Mesoridazine	50	2	150-400[3]	150-300
Thioridazine	100	1	300-800[3]	300-600
Acetophenazine	20	5	60-200	60-120
Fluphenazine HCl	2	50	6-20	6-12
Perphenazine	10	10	30-100	30-60
Prochlorperazine	15	6	50-150	50-100
Trifluoperazine	5	20	15-50	15-30
Chlorprothixene	100	1	300-1000	300-600
Thiothixene	5	20	15-50	15-30
Haloperidol	2	50	6-20	6-12
Loxapine	10	10	30-100	30-60
Molindone	10	10	30-100	30-60
Clozapine	50	2	200-600	200-800
Risperidone	1	100	4-10	4-10

Note: PORT = Patient Outcomes Research Team. HCl = hydrochloride. Adapted from Zito 1994 and Kane 1996.
[1]Approximate dose equivalent to 100 mg of chlorpromazine (relative potency); may not be the same at lower versus higher doses.
[2]This number multiplied by the dose of antipsychotic medication results in the chlorpromazine-equivalent dose.
[3]To avoid the risk of retinopathy, doses of 400 mg (mesoridazine) and 800 mg (thioridazine) should not be exceeded.

Table 2. Chlorpromazine (CPZ) Equivalencies and Dosing of Fluphenazine Decanoate

Q every week FPZ-DEC (mg)	Oral FPZ HCl (mg)	CPZ-EQ (mg)	Q every 2 weeks FPZ-DEC (mg)	Oral FPZ HCl (mg)	CPZ-EQ (mg)	Q every 3 weeks FPZ-DEC (mg)	Oral FPZ HCl (mg)	CPZ-EQ (mg)	Q every 4 weeks FPZ-DEC (mg)	Oral FPZ HCl (mg)	CPZ-EQ (mg)
6.25 (.25 cc)	10	500	6.25 (.25 cc)	5	250	6.25 (.25 cc)	3.3	165	6.25 (.25 cc)	2.5	125
12.5 (.50 cc)	20	1000	12.5 (.50 cc)	10	500	12.5 (.50 cc)	6.6	333	12.5 (.50 cc)	5.0	250
18.75 (.75 cc)	30	1500	18.75 (.75 cc)	15	750	18.75 (.75 cc)	10.0	500	18.75 (.75 cc)	7.5	375
25 (1.0 cc)	40	2000	25 (1.0 cc)	20	1000	25 (1.0 cc)	13.3	665	25 (1.0 cc)	10.0	500
37.5 (1.50 cc)	60	3000	37.5 (1.5 cc)	30	1500	37.5 (1.50 cc)	20.0	1000	37.5 (1.5 cc)	15.0	750
50 (2.0 cc)	80	4000	50 (2.0 cc)	40	2000	50 (2.0 cc)	26.3	1315	50 (2.0 cc)	20.0	1000

Note: Q = quantity. Fluphenazine decanoate (FPZ-DEC) doses are converted to daily oral fluphenazine hydrochloride (oral FPZ HCl) doses and to estimated daily chlorpromazine-equivalent (CPZ-EQ) doses. Decanoate conversions are based on an empirical rule suggested by Kane (25 mg every 3 weeks of decanoate is equivalent to 665 CPZ-EQ per day). These are theoretically determined values and should be interpreted as approximations only. Therefore, comparisons of daily CPZ-EQ doses derived from these values with Patient Outcomes Research Team (PORT)-recommended oral dosing ranges should not be made. However, decanoate doses below the bold line are NOT recommended. Adapted from Zito 1994 and Kane 1996.

Chapter 10: Creating and Implementing Behavioral Guidelines

Table 3. Chlorpromazine (CPZ) Equivalencies And Dosing of Haloperidol Decanoate

HPL-DEC	Q every month	HPL Q every day	CPZ-EQ
50 mg	(1.0 cc)	5 mg	250 mg
100 mg	(2.0 cc)	10 mg	500 mg
150 mg	(2.5 cc)	15 mg	750 mg
200 mg	(3.0 cc)	20 mg	1000 mg

Note: Q = quantity. Haloperidol decanoate (HPL-DEC) doses are converted to daily oral haloperidol (HPL) doses and to estimated daily chlorpromazine-equivalent (CPZ-EQ) doses. Decanoate conversions are based on the following rule: 5 mg oral HPL per day is equivalent to 50 mg HPL-DEC every month. These are theoretically determined values and should be interpreted as approximations only. Therefore, comparisons of daily CPZ-EQ doses derived from these values with Patient Outcomes Research Team (PORT)-recommended oral dosing ranges should not be made. Adapted from Zito 1994 and Kane 1996.

cantly with this treatment compared with about 5 to 45 percent on placebo. (Review references: Dixon et al. 1995, p. 568; Umbricht and Kane 1995, p. 603; Level of evidence: A)

Recommendation 2. The dosage of antipsychotic medication for an acute symptom episode should be in the range of 300-1,000 chlorpromazine (CPZ) equivalents per day for a minimum of 6 weeks. Reasons for dosages outside this range should be justified. The minimum effective dose should be used. (Cross-reference tables of CPZ dose equivalents of various antipsychotic agents are included in tables 1-3.)

Rationale. Randomized clinical trials have consistently found that acute positive symptoms in most persons respond to a daily dose of an antipsychotic medication between 300 and 1,000 CPZ equivalents administered for a minimum of 6 weeks. The risk of suboptimal response increases substantially below this range, and there is little evidence of further benefit above this range. Higher doses also carry an increased burden of side effects. (Review reference: Dixon et al. 1995, p. 569; Level of evidence: A).

Recommendation 3. Persons experiencing their first acute symptom episode should be treated with an antipsychotic medication other than clozapine, but dosages should remain in the lower end of the range mentioned in Recommendation 2 (300-500 mg CPZ equivalents per day).

Rationale. Recent studies indicate that persons experiencing their first episode of acute symptoms of schizophrenia respond as well or better to antipsychotic medications in terms of symptom reduction than persons experiencing a recurrent episode., They may also respond to somewhat lower doses. Although "watchful waiting" is an alternative approach raised by concerns about medication side effects, this option is mitigated by concerns that persistent psychosis may complicate the subsequent course of illness. (Review reference: Dixon et al. 1995, p. 574; Level of evidence: B)

Recommendation 4. Massive loading doses of antipsychotic medication, referred to as the practice of "rapid neuroleptization," should not be used.

Rationale. Rapid loading doses of antipsychotic medications have shown no general advantage over more moderate dosing approaches (see Recommendation 2). They also carry a significant side-effect burden. Rapid initiation of antipsychotic treatment is important at the onset of an exacerbation, but not a rapid loading dose. (Review reference: Dixon et al. 1995, p. 569; Level of evidence: A)

Recommendation 5. Since studies have found no superior efficacy of any antipsychotic medication over another in the treatment of positive symptoms, except for clozapine in treatment-refractory patients, choice of antipsychotic medication should be made on the basis of patient acceptability, prior individual drug response, individual side-effect profile, and long-term treatment planning.

Rationale. As above, studies have found no superior efficacy of any of the antipsychotic medications relative to each other in the treatment of positive symptoms. (Review reference: Dixon et al. 1995, p. 573; Level of evidence: A for equivalent efficacy; C for other factors affecting medication choice)

Recommendation 6. Monitoring of plasma levels of antipsychotic medications should be limited to the following circumstances: (1) when patients fail to respond to what is usually an adequate dose; (2) when it is difficult for the clinician to discriminate drug side effects—particularly akathisia or akinesia-from symptoms of schizophrenia such as agitation or negative symptoms (a high blood level might be associated with increased adverse effects); (3) when antipsychotic drugs are combined with other drugs that may affect their pharmacokinetics; (4) in the very young, the elderly, and the medically compromised in whom the pharmacokinetics may be significantly altered; and (5) when noncompliance is suspected. Plasma levels are most useful when using haloperidol, which has only one active metabolite.

Rationale. In general, there is at best a moderate correspondence between plasma drug level and clinical response to antipsychotic medications. Studies suggest an inverted-U or therapeutic window response curve such that persons with moderate plasma levels of haloperidol show a better clinical response than those with low or high levels. The upper end of this therapeutic window is often defined by side effects. Inadequate clinical response to apparently adequate dosages of antipsychotic medications warrants assessment of plasma levels to rule out unusual or altered drug metabolism or noncompliance. (Review references: Baldessarini et al. 1990; Kane and Marder 1993; Level of evidence: B)

Recommendation 7. Prophylactic use of anti-Parkinson agents to reduce the incidence of extrapyramidal side effects (EPS) should be determined on a case-by-case basis, taking into account patient and physician preferences, prior individual history of EPS, and other risk factors for both EPS and anticholinergic side effects. The effectiveness of and continued need for anti-Parkinson agents should be assessed in an ongoing fashion.

Rationale. Although the data are clear that anti-Parkinson agents are effective in reducing or eliminating the EPS of antipsychotic medications, experts disagree about the advisability of using these agents prophylactically. The controversy arises in weighing the risks of EPS against those of the side effects of anti-Parkinson agents. Prophylaxis may be especially important among persons with a prior history of noncompliance or drug discontinuation related to EPS and among persons for whom even mild EPS may lead to drug aversion (e.g., among patients with paranoia or somatic delusions). Avoidance of anticholinergic effects may be especially important in the elderly and in individuals with a history of anticholinergic crises. (Review references: Rifkin and Siris 1987; Davis et al. 1989; Level of evidence: B)

Pharmacotherapies: Maintenance Pharmacotherapy

Recommendation 8. Persons who experience acute symptom relief with an antipsychotic medication should continue to receive this medication for at least 1 year subsequent to symptom stabilization to reduce the risk of relapse or worsening of positive symptoms.

Rationale. More than 30 clinical trials have confirmed that maintenance therapy with an antipsychotic medication after an initial positive response during an acute symptom episode significantly reduces the risk of symptom relapse during the first year after the acute symptom episode. On average, persons on maintenance therapy experienced symptom relapse over a follow-up year at a rate of about 20 to 25 percent compared with about 55 percent for those on placebo. The value of maintenance therapy beyond the first year has not been studied extensively. (Review reference: Dixon et al. 1995, pp. 569-570; Level of evidence: A)

Recommendation 9. The maintenance dosage should be in the range of 300 to 600 CPZ equivalents (oral or depot) per day. If the initial dosage to relieve an acute symptom episode exceeds this range, efforts should be made to reduce the dosage gradually to this range, such as a 10 percent reduction in dosage every 6 weeks until either early signs of relapse begin to emerge or until the lower level of this recommended range is achieved (see Recommendation 2). The new maintenance dosage should be at the last level at which symptoms were well controlled. Dosages in excess of 600 CPZ equivalents per day should be avoided unless symptom control and patient comfort are clearly superior at these higher dosages. The lowest effective dose should be used.

Rationale. Maintenance therapy trials have found that maintenance doses below 300 mg CPZ equivalents per day carry an increased risk of relapse, although a substantial proportion of persons (up to 50%) can be maintained successfully at these lower doses, warranting a gradual and carefully monitored effort to reduce dosage over time. There is no evidence that maintenance doses above 600 mg CPZ equivalents per day confer any additional advantage in general. (Review reference: Dixon et al. 1995, pp. 570-572; Level of evidence: A)

Recommendation 10. Reassessment of the dosage level or the need for maintenance antipsychotic therapy should be ongoing. Patients who have had only one episode of positive symptoms before initiation of antipsychotic therapy and who have experienced no positive symptoms during the year of maintenance therapy should be given a trial period off medication, assuming they are aware of the potential risk of relapse and agree to this plan. For patients with more than one prior episode who have experienced good symptom control on the medication during the preceding year, maintenance therapy should be continued unless unacceptable side effects or some other contraindications to antipsychotic treatment have developed. If the maintenance dosage has been high (>600 CPZ equivalents) during the past year, attempts to lower the dosage as described in Recommendation 9 should be considered. Reasons for not attempting to lower dosage should be clearly indicated, such as patient preference in the face of concerns about symptom relapse or life stressors that militate against attempts to lower medications.

Rationale. Clinical trials of maintenance antipsychotic therapy have generally not followed patients in maintenance therapy beyond 1 year, and thus evidence regarding long-term maintenance is lacking (see also rationale for Recommendation 8). (Review references Kissling 1992; Dixon et al. 1995, pp. 570-571; Level of evidence: C)

Recommendation 11. Targeted, intermittent dosage maintenance strategies should not be used routinely in lieu of continuous dosage regimens because of the increased risk of symptom worsening or relapse. These strategies may be considered for patients who refuse maintenance or for whom some other contraindication to maintenance therapy exists, such as side-effect sensitivity.

Rationale. The relatively few studies of targeted, intermittent dose strategies suggest that the relapse rate is higher than for continuous maintenance therapy. Therefore, this approach is recommended only for the circumstances identified above. (Review reference: Dixon et al. 1995, pp. 570-571; Level of evidence: B)

Recommendation 12. Depot antipsychotic maintenance therapy should be strongly considered for persons who have difficulty complying with oral medication or who prefer the depot regimen. Depot therapy may be used as a first-option maintenance strategy.

Rationale. Controlled trials have produced inconsistent results with regard to whether depot medication reduces the risk of relapse in comparison with oral medication. However, the design of these studies, which by definition include persons willing to accept medication in a clinical trial, may bias against any advantage of depot medication. Further, the duration of these studies has been inadequate to demonstrate a strong advantage for depot medication. In persons for whom compliance is a problem, depot medication offers clear advantages if it is accepted by the patient. If acceptable to the patient, depot medication is just as appropriate as oral medication as the first-line maintenance therapy strategy. (Review reference: Dixon et al. 1995, p. 573; Level of evidence: B)

Pharmacotherapies: New Antipsychotic Medications[1]

Recommendation 13. A trial of clozapine should be offered to patients with schizophrenia or schizoaffective disorder whose positive symptoms do not robustly respond to adequate trials of two different classes of antipsychotic medications. Exceptions include patients who cannot receive clozapine due to a history of blood dyscrasia or cardiac arrhythmia. Lack of response to previous antipsychotic trials is defined by persistent symptoms after two 6-week trials of up to 1,000 CPZ equivalents of antipsychotic agents from two different chemical classes (e.g., phenothiazines and butyrophenones). An adequate clozapine trial should last at least 3 months at a dosage from 300 to 800 mg per day. Dosages should reflect the lowest possible effective dose. If patients do not respond, a blood level should be obtained and dosages slowly increased to 800 mg to the extent that side effects are tolerated. If effective, clozapine should be continued as maintenance therapy.

Rationale. Controlled clinical trials have found that clozapine produces significant clinical improvement in at least 30 percent of patients who fail to achieve an adequate response to or cannot tolerate conventional antipsychotic medications. It should be considered only after other antipsychotic medications prove inadequate because of its low but significant risk of agranulocytosis, complexity of management (weekly white cell count reports), and cost. The level of evidence for the differential effectiveness of clozapine among outpatients is limited by the low number of studies of outpatients. (Review reference: Buchanan 1995, pp. 580-584; Level of evidence: A for inpatients; B for outpatients)

Recommendation 14. A trial of clozapine should be offered to patients with schizophrenia or schizoaffective disorder who have repeatedly displayed violent behavior and persistent psychotic symptoms that have not been responsive to trials of at least two different types of antipsychotic medications (as defined in Recommendation 13).

Rationale. Randomized clinical trials, as well as nonrandomized studies, suggest that clozapine significantly reduces hostility among treatment-refractory patients. It should only be considered after other antipsychotic medications prove inadequate. (Review reference: Buchanan 1995, p. 582; Level of evidence: B)

Recommendation 15. A trial of clozapine should be offered to patients who require antipsychotic therapy, but who experience intolerable side effects to other antipsychotic agents, including severe or very distressing tardive dyskinesia, persistent dystonia, and neuroleptic malignant syndrome.

Rationale. A limited body of evidence suggests that clozapine causes substantially less tardive dyskinesia than antipsychotic medications, although there are reports of cases in which tardive dyskinesia has worsened on clozapine. For the patient with severe tardive dyskinesia for whom ongoing treatment with another antipsychotic agent poses a substantial risk of continuation or further progression of the movement disorder, but for whom antipsychotic therapy is essential to prevent serious relapse, a trial with clozapine is indicated. (Review reference: Buchanan 1995, p. 587; Level of evidence: B)

Recommendation 16. Persons who achieve an adequate reduction in positive symptoms on conventional antipsychotic medications, but who have significant EPS that do not respond adequately to anti-Parkinson agents, should be offered a trial of risperidone. An adequate risperidone trial for this purpose should last from 6 to 12 weeks at a dosage from 4 to 10 mg per day. Dosages should reflect the lowest possible effective dose. Per Recommendation 1, risperidone also can be used as a first-line medication.

Rationale. In clinical trials, risperidone has been found to be at least as effective as other antipsychotic medications in reducing the positive symptoms of schizophrenia. Its major potential advantage over other antipsychotic medications is that it produces fewer EPS at the lower end of its effective dose range (4-10 mg · per day). Therefore, for patients on the older antipsychotic agents and in whom EPS is a significant problem, risperidone offers an alternative. (Review reference: Umbricht and Kane 1995, pp. 602-604; Level of evidence: B)

Pharmacotherapies: Adjunctive Pharmacotherapies

Recommendation 17. Persons who experience persistent and clinically significant, associated symptoms of anxiety, depression, or hostility, despite an adequate reduction in positive symptoms with antipsychotic therapy, should receive a trial of adjunctive pharmacotherapy. A trial of a benzodiazepine or propranolol is merited for persistent anxiety. An antidepressant trial should be considered for persistent depression. Adjunctive therapy with lithium, a benzodiazepine, or carbamazepine should be considered for persistent hostility or manic-like symptoms. The reasons for the absence of such trials for appropriate patients should be documented. Certain adjunctive medications should be avoided in patients currently receiving clozapine to avoid synergistic side effects; for example, respiratory depression with benzodiazepines and bone marrow suppression with carbamazepine.

Rationale. Anxiety and tension may respond to treatment with adjunctive benzodiazepines, although a few studies reported a waning effect of these agents, perhaps due to tolerance, after a few weeks of treatment. Disruptive, dangerous, or assaultive behavior may be modified by the addition of benzodiazepines or carbamazepine to an antipsychotic regimen. Evidence of the usefulness of benzodiazepines for this indication comes from open or retrospective studies, and no double-blind studies have thus far addressed its efficacy. Similarly, these behaviors are cited as potentially responsive to adjunctive carbamazepine, although most evidence is from open studies, with only one positive double-blind study. Excitement and irritability (often classified as "affective symptoms") seem to benefit from adjunctive lithium treatment, with a small amount of evidence that benzodiazepines and carbamazepine also might be useful. Antidepressants seem to benefit patients who have episodic signs and symptoms of depressive illness in addition to schizophrenia, if they are administered in phases of illness other than the active, psychotic exacerbation phase. Antidepressants can be efficacious without exacerbating psychotic symptoms when used adjunctively with antipsychotics. Most studies of adjunctive treatments for schizophrenia were done with patients who had chronic schizophrenia and who were often designated as treatment refractory. Little is known about the efficacy of adjunctive agents for first-episode schizophrenia, for patients experiencing acute episodes of psychosis, or for stable patients receiving maintenance antipsychotic therapy. Little is known about the long-term effectiveness of adjunctive agents. (Review reference: Johns and Thompson 1995, pp. 612-613; Level of evidence: B)

Recommendation 18. Persons who experience persistent and clinically significant positive symptoms despite adequate antipsychotic therapy, including trials with the newer antipsychotics (clozapine or risperidone), should receive a trial of adjunctive pharmacotherapy as described in Recommendation 17.

Rationale. No adjunctive agent has demonstrated clear and consistent benefit in a majority of persons with schizophrenia. However, the most promising agents are the benzodiazepines (which may be useful in as many as 50% of patients with schizophrenia), lithium, and carbamazepine (which may be of mild or modest value to treatment-nonresponsive patients). Very little evidence supports a role for adjunctive propranolol. Valproate, calcium channel blockers, antidepressants, clonidine, and dopaminergic agents have no demonstrated use in terms of global improvement, although they may be useful for individual symptom complexes. Positive symptoms may improve when benzodiazepines, carbamazepine, lithium, or propranolol are added to antipsychotics. Adjunctive benzodiazepines produced significant improvement of positive symptoms in about half the double-blind studies that addressed this question. Adjunctive carbamazepine produced significant improvement in only a fraction of double-blind studies. Adjunctive lithium seems to alleviate, to some degree, positive symptoms in a subgroup of patients. Finally, adjunctive propranolol produces only slim evidence of a therapeutic effect on positive symptoms in a minority of double-blind studies. (Review reference: Johns and Thompson 1995, pp. 611-612; Level of evidence: C)

Electroconvulsive Therapy (ETC)

Recommendation 19. Patients who have not responded to recommended antipsychotic therapy should be considered for a trial of ECT alone or in combination with an antipsychotic if (a) the person has been ill for less than 1 year or, if ill for more than 1 year, is in the early phase of an acute exacerbation or (b) affective or catatonic symptoms are predominant.

Rationale. There are scientifically sound studies that show that ECT reduces acute symptoms in schizophrenia. Some authors dispute this finding, however, with several pointing to the problem of affective symptoms in schizophrenia and the diagnostic confounding of schizophrenia with affective disorders. The majority of authors indicate that a secondary role is most appropriate, and there is a general consensus that the effects of ECT on schizophrenia are short lived. A few studies with minimal data show continued improvement at follow-up of several years when ECT is followed by maintenance antipsychotic therapy. Catatonic schizophrenia and schizoaffective disorder seem to be most responsive to ECT, and in general the affective symptoms respond selectively to it. (Review reference: Johns and Thompson 1995, pp. 610-611; Level of evidence: B)

Recommendation 20. The dosage of ECT (i.e., number of treatments) used to treat patients with schizophrenia should be comparable to that used for patients with affective disorders (about 12 treatments).

Rationale. Three controlled studies found definite improvement after 12 or fewer treatments, and another study indicates that the average number of treatments needed for improvement is 13.6. (Review reference: Johns and Thompson 1995, pp. 610-611; Level of evidence: B)

Recommendation 21. Regressive forms of ECT are not recommended for persons with schizophrenia.

Rationale. Most reviewers indicate that selected patients with severe and chronic schizophrenia may benefit from modified ECT, but others indicate that the procedure is "drastic," "experimental," and "controversial." (Review reference: Johns and Thompson 1995, pp. 610-611; Level of evidence: C)

Psychological Treatments

Recommendation 22. Individual and group psychotherapies adhering to a psychodynamic model (defined as therapies that use interpretation of unconscious material and focus on transference and regression) should not be used in the treatment of persons with schizophrenia.

Rationale. The scientific data on this issue are quite limited. However, there is no evidence in support of the superiority of psychoanalytic therapy to other forms of therapy, and there is a consensus that psychotherapy that promotes regression and psychotic transference can be harmful to persons with schizophrenia. This risk, combined with the high cost and lack of evidence of any benefit, argues strongly against the use of psychoanalytic therapy, even in combination with effective pharmacotherapy. (Review reference: Scott and Dixon 1995b, p. 623; Level of evidence: C)

Recommendation 23. Individual and group therapies employing well-specified combinations of support, education, and behavioral and cognitive skills training approaches designed to address the specific deficits of persons with schizophrenia should be offered over time to improve functioning and enhance other targeted problems, such as medication noncompliance.

Rationale. Although the scientific data for this recommendation are limited and flawed, controlled studies have found some additional benefit when a supportive form of psychotherapy is added to pharmacotherapy for persons with schizophrenia. The most effective forms and doses of these therapies and their modes of action remain unknown. (Review reference: Scott and Dixon 1995b, pp. 623-627; Level of evidence: B)

Family Treatments

Recommendation 24. Patients who have ongoing contact with their families should be offered a family psychosocial intervention that spans at least 9 months and provides a combination of education about the illness, family support, crisis intervention, and problem-solving skills training. Such interventions should also be offered to nonfamily caregivers.

Rationale. Randomized clinical trials have repeatedly demonstrated that family interventions that provide some combination of illness education, support, problem-solving training, and crisis intervention, in combination with appropriate pharmacotherapy, reduce 1-year relapse rates from a 40 to 53 percent range to a 2 to 23 percent range. (Review reference: Dixon and Lehman 1995, p. 639; Level of evidence: A)

Recommendation 25. Family interventions should not be restricted to patients whose families are identified as having high levels of "expressed emotion" (criticism, hostility, overinvolvement).

Rationale. Although the earlier controlled trials of family psychoeducation programs focused on the variable of family expressed emotion as a mediator of the impact of this intervention on outcomes, more recent studies have found that these interventions offer substantial benefit to patients and families regardless of the level of expressed emotion. (Review reference: Dixon and Lehman 1995, p. 639; Level of evidence: B)

Recommendation 26. Family therapies based on the premise that family dysfunction is the etiology of the patient's schizophrenic disorder should *not* be used.

Rationale. Research has failed to substantiate hypothesized causal links between family dysfunction and the etiology of schizophrenia. Therefore, therapies specifically designed from this premise are not empirically founded. Although there has been little or no randomized, controlled research on the impact of family therapies arising from this orientation, experts in the field have expressed strong caution against the use of these techniques. The presumption that family interaction causes schizophrenia, especially as an alternative to biological risk factors, has led to serious disruption in clinician/family trust without any evidence of therapeutic effectiveness. The repudiation of the theoretical premise of these therapies, the lack of empirical studies, and the strong clinical opinion raising concerns about the potential harm caused by these approaches lead to this recommendation. (Review reference: Dixon and Lehman 1995, p. 631; Level of evidence: C)

Vocational Rehabilitation

Recommendation 27. Persons with schizophrenia who have *any* of the following characteristics should be offered vocational services. The person (a) identifies competitive employment as a personal goal, (b) has a history of prior competitive employment, (c) has a minimal history of psychiatric hospitalization, and (d) is judged on the basis of a formal vocational assessment to have good work skills.

Rationale. Controlled studies of vocational rehabilitation interventions for persons with schizophrenia have not shown consistent or significant impacts on outcomes other than those directly related to involvement in the rehabilitation program (e.g., increased involvement in sheltered work). However, these studies have been flawed by the failure to control for individual characteristics that may alter a person's vocational potential. They have identified subgroups of recipients post hoc who benefited from the interventions. The above characteristics have been found to be predictive of better vocational outcomes in persons with schizophrenia, and therefore persons with these characteristics should be offered such services. (Review reference: Lehman 1995, pp. 647-653; Level of evidence: C)

Recommendation 28. The range of vocational services available in a service system for persons with schizophrenia living in the community who meet the criteria defined in Recommendation 27 should include (a) prevocational training, (b) transitional employment, (c) supported employment, and (d) vocational counseling and education services (job clubs, rehabilitation counseling, postemployment services).

Rationale. Recent controlled studies have reported significantly improved vocational outcomes for the supported employment model, which emphasizes rapid placement in a real job setting and strong support from a job coach or other employment specialist to adapt to and sustain the job. Therefore, unless ongoing research fails to substantiate these early findings, supported employment should definitely be available to persons meeting the aforementioned criteria. Scientific data supporting the effectiveness of the other forms of vocational services mentioned above are lacking, but some persons who are good candidates for supported employment may benefit from the addition of these services as well, so they are mentioned in the recommendation. (Review reference: Lehman 1995, pp. 647-653; Level of evidence: B)

Service Systems

Recommendation 29. Systems of care serving persons with schizophrenia who are high service users should include assertive case management (ACM) and assertive community treatment (ACT) programs.

Rationale. Persons with disabling schizophrenia who are at high risk for discontinuation of treatment or for repeated crises require an array of clinical, rehabilitation, and social services to address their needs. Coordination, integration, and continuity of services among providers over time can be substantially enhanced through ACM and ACT. Randomized trials have demonstrated consistently the effectiveness of these programs in reducing inpatient use among such high-risk patients. Several studies also support improvements in clinical and social outcomes. These studies suggest that both ACT and ACM are superior to conventional case management for high-risk cases. (Review reference: Scott and Dixon 1995a, pp. 659-664; Level of evidence: A)

Recommendation 30. Assertive community treatment programs should be targeted to individuals at high risk for repeated rehospitalizations or who have been difficult to retain in active treatment with more traditional types of services.

Rationale. The original ACT studies reporting efficacy for these approaches targeted these high-risk persons. The efficacy of either model with lower risk patient groups has not been established. The high cost of ACT therefore warrants careful targeting for cost-effectiveness. (Review reference: Scott and Dixon 1995a, pp. 659-664; Level of evidence: B)

Discussion

The PORT Treatment Recommendations represent a concerted and systematic effort to develop guidelines about the treatment of persons with schizophrenia distilled narrowly from available scientific evidence. As such, they reflect both the strengths and limitations of this knowledge base. Such recommendations are useful from at least two major perspectives.

First, they form a basis for disseminating current knowledge into practice. The Treatment Recommendations provide focal points or benchmarks for asking whether current practices measure up to what is known to be helpful based on the best scientific evidence available. Such questions about the quality of care should be asked by treatment practitioners, patients, families, service system planners, and health care payers. Are we providing care based on the best knowledge available? These recommendations can challenge practitioners and service systems to do better and can challenge patients and families to expect better services. The recommendations are recommendations, not mandates, because individual patient needs vary considerably from the average. However, the Treatment Recommendations should stimulate close examination of practices at both the aggregate and the individual patient levels to ensure that treatments are offered in the most effective manner.

Second, they serve to highlight what we do not know. Not all of the gaps in our knowledge about treatment can be filled by evidence developed in clinical trials. Clinical wisdom can and should be accumulated and shared directly from practical experience. But there are many aspects of treatment for schizophrenia that need careful, ongoing scientific scrutiny to ensure that, whenever possible, objective evidence of effectiveness is the basis for practice. It should be good news that treatment recommendations such as those presented here will be outdated in the not too distant future and that new knowledge will require their modification, as well as the addition of new recommendations. In short, we should practice what we know today while we are continually learning to change practices for tomorrow.

The Authors

Anthony F. Lehman, M.D., Principal Investigator of the Schizophrenia Patient Outcomes Research Team, is Professor of Psychiatry, University of Maryland School of Medicine and Co-Director of the Center for Mental Health Services Research, University of Maryland, Baltimore, MD. Donald M. Steinwachs, Ph.D., Co-Principal Investigator, is Professor of Health Policy and Management and Chair of the Department of Health Policy and Management, The Johns Hopkins University School of Hygiene and Public Health, Baltimore, MD. Co-Investigators at the Center for Mental Health Services Research, University of Maryland School of Medicine include Lisa B. Dixon, M.D., M.P.H.; Howard H. Goldman, M.D., Ph.D.; Fred Osher, M.D.; Leticia Postrado, Ph.D.; Jack E. Scott, Sc.D.; and James W. Thompson, M.D. Co-Investigators from the Department of Health Policy and Management, The Johns Hopkins University School of Hygiene and Public Health include Maureen Fahey, M.A.; Pamela Fischer, Ph.D.; Judith Ann Kasper, Ph.D.; Alan Lyles, Sc.D.; and Elizabeth Ann Skinner, M.S.W. Co-Investigators from the Maryland Psychiatric Research Center include Robert Buchanan, M.D.; William T. Carpenter, Jr., M.D.; and Jerome Levine, M.D. The Co-Investigator from the RAND Corporation is Elizabeth Ann McGlynn, Ph.D. The Co-Investigator from the Department of Veterans Affairs Northeast Program Evaluation Center and Yale University is Robert Rosenheck, M.D. The Co-Investigator from the University of Maryland School of Pharmacy is Julie Zito, Ph.D.

Note

1. As of the writing of these recommendations (September 1996), additional antipsychotic agents were expected to reach the market within the next 1 to 2 years. These agents include olanzapine, quetiapine, sertindole, and ziprasidone. No recommendations specific to these newer compounds are included because the level of data on them is more limited than clozapine and risperidone. Until proven otherwise, the use of these newer compounds, when marketed, should follow the recommendations for antipsychotic agents other than clozapine.

References

Baldessarini, R.J.; Cohen, B.M.; and Teicher, M. Pharmacologic treatment. In: Levy, S.T., and Ninan, P.T., eds. *Schizophrenia: Treatment of Acute Psychotic Episodes*. Washington DC: American Psychiatric Press, 1990. pp.61-118.

Buchanan, R.W. Clozapine: Efficacy and safety. *Schizophrenia Bulletin*, 21(4):579-591, 1995.

Antipsychotic drugs. In: Kaplan, H.I., and Sadock, B.J., eds. *Comprehensive Textbook of Psychiatry*. Baltimore, MD: Williams & Wilkins, 1989. pp. 1591-1626.

Dixon, L.B., and Lehman, A.F. Family interventions for schizophrenia. *Schizophrenia Bulletin*, 21(4):631-643, 1995.

Dixon, L.B.; Lehmán, A.F.; and Levine, J. Conventional antipsychotic medications for schizophrenia. *Schizophrenia Bulletin*, 21(4): 567-577, 1995.

Johns, C.A., and Thompson, J.W. Adjunctive treatments in schizophrenia: Pharmacotherapies and electroconvulsive therapy. *Schizophrenia Bulletin*, 21(4):607-619, 1995.

Kane, J.M. Schizophrenia. *New England Journal of Medicine*, 334:34-41, 1996.

Kane, J.M., and Marder, S.R. Psychopharmacologic treatment of schizophrenia. *Schizophrenia Bulletin*, 19(2): 287-302, 1993.

Kissling, W. Ideal and reality of neuroleptic relapse prevention. British *Journal of Psychiatry*, 161 (Suppl.): 133-139, 1992.

Lehman, A.F. Vocational rehabilitation in schizophrenia. *Schizophrenia Bulletin*, 21(4):645-656, 1995.

Rifkin, A., and Siris, S. Drug treatment of acute schizophrenia. In: Meltzer, H., ed. *Psychopharmacology: The Third Generation of Progress*. New York, NY: Raven Press, 1987. pp. 1095-1101.

Scott, J.E., and Dixon, L.B. Assertive community treatment and case management for schizophrenia. *Schizophrenia Bulletin*, 21(4):657-668, 1995a.

Scott, J.E., and Dixon, L.B. Psychological interventions for schizophrenia. *Schizophrenia Bulletin*, 21(4):621-630, 1995b.

Umbricht, D., and Kate, J.M. Risperidone: Efficacy and safety. *Schizophrenia Bulletin*, 21(4):593-606, 1995.

Addressing Issues of Face Validity in The Application of a Clinical Guideline

JAMES WESTPHAL, SANJAYA KUMAR, JILL RUSH, AND ILA C. SARKAR

Clinical guidelines and task force recommendations have varying degrees of acceptance and application in local settings (Lobach 1995). Guidelines are usually made available to help clinicians and patients choose the best approaches to care based on benefits, risks, and cost to the system (Shapiro et al. 1993). Implementing and adopting practice guidelines to current practices can be a slow process, involving a multifaceted approach to behavior modification through information dissemination. Guidelines can also have differing levels of face validity for clinicians. This report illustrates a management approach when a guideline lacks face validity for the clinicians involved in an evaluation.

The context of this report is a collaborative, statewide mental health quality improvement project for the practice of electroconvulsive therapy (ECT) among Medicare patients in Louisiana. Objections from the clinician participants caused the project coordinators to use a different approach in the use of medications considered detrimental to ECT, proposed by the American Psychiatric Association's (APA) task force recommendations (Weiner et al. 1990). Presented here are findings from the baseline data and the evaluation methodology that will be used to evaluate the applicability of the controversial task force recommendation.

In 1992, the Health Care Financing Administration (HFCA) changed their approach to

---

Source: Westphal J, Kumar S, Rush J, and Sarkar LC. Addressing Isues of Face Validity in the Application of a Clinical Guideline. Evaluation Review June 1997; 21(3):379-387. Copyright © 1997 by Sage Publications, Inc. Reprinted by permission of Sage Publications, Inc.

James Westphal is the deputy chair and director of consultation and liaison for the Department of Psychiatry at the Louisiana State University Medical Center in Shreveport. He is currently working on medical informatics, outcome research, and quality improvement projects. He has developed an integrated statewide mental health utilization database for the Louisiana State Department of Mental Health.

Sanjaya Kumar is currently a clinical project specialist with Louisiana Health Care Review, Inc., in Baton Rouge, Louisiana.

Jill Rush is an assistant professor in the Department of Psychiatry, Louisiana State University Medical Center, Shreveport. She is currently working on outcome studies in mental health.

Ila C. Sarkar is currently a statistician with Louisiana Health Care Review, Inc., in Baton Rouge, Louisiana.

Authors' note: This cooperative project was coordinated by staff at Louisiana Health Care Review, Inc. (LHCR). Opinions expressed and methods used are those of the authors, and do not necessarily reflect Health Care Financing Administration (HCFA) policy. The authors assume all responsibility for the accuracy and completeness of the data used. Work was performed under Contract No. 500-93-0707 between Louisiana Health Care Review, Inc. and the Health Care

Financing Administration/Department of Health and Human Services, in the course of fulfilling contractual obligations in the Peer Review Organization's 4th Scope of Work. The authors thank Madelyn Rappaport, project manager, LHCR, for coordinating and facilitating various activities for the project; Ronald Horswell, director of applied research, LHCR, for statistical consultation and analytical methodology; Marion Harrison, data analyst, LHCR, for conducting the required data analysis; and Ali H. Rashidee, project coordinator, LHCR, for his assistance in reviewing and editing the manuscript. Address correspondence and requests for reprints to James Westphal, Department of Psychiatry, Louisiana State University Medical Center, 1501 Kings Highway, P.O. Box 33932, Shreveport, LA 71130-3932.

improving the quality of care for Medicare beneficiaries by establishing the Health Care Quality Improvement Program (HCQIP; Grant et al. 1996). Emphasis was removed from evaluating individual cases with poor outcomes and sanctioning doctors and hospitals (quality assurance) and redirected toward promotion of universally accepted quality improvement processes (Jencks and Wilensky 1992). HFCA contracted with state peer-review organizations (PROs) in each state to develop statewide collaborative quality improvement projects for elderly inpatients (Grant et al. 1996).

Quality improvement consists of a cycle of five phases for improving performance (Joint Commission on Accreditation of Healthcare Organizations [JCAHO] 1996): design, measurement, assessment, improvement, and evaluation and redesign. The design phase usually consists of conceptualization of the problem, hypotheses generation, setting of objectives, developing methods to obtain reliable data, and developing an analytical plan to define indicators. This is followed by the collection of required data using a structured methodology and interrater reliability testing in the measurement phase. The assessment phase follows with the analysis of baseline data and development of comparative indicator reports for providers participating in the study. Improvement then consists of delineation of action plans based on baseline indicator performance. The cycle is completed with the evaluation and redesign phase consisting of analysis of follow-up data, postimplementation of action plans, and dissemination of comparative indicator reports, including redefining project objectives.

The Louisiana Medicare ECT Project

ECT was developed in 1938, and was widely used in the 1950s and 1960s, mostly for schizophrenia. The advent of modem psychopharmacology and a public backlash about "brain damage" resulting from unregulated ECT use precipitated a decline in ECT utilization (Kaplan, Sadock, and Grebb 1994). This trend also stimulated clinical research to define the appropriate scope of practice for ECT and the needed adjustments to the procedure to balance effectiveness and the transient cognitive impairment secondary to ECT. In 1990, the APA published the task force report on ECT (Weiner et al. 1990) that comprehensively reviewed 428 references through 1988 and included input from over 90 professional and patient advocate groups. The report included recommendations on the institutional aspects of ECT administration and clinical process aspects, such as patient selection, work-up, and the required documentation of ECT procedures.

QI Project Development

The design phase of the project calculated the variation in patient ECT admissions and developed the indicator areas and the data-gathering methodology. Medicare claims data for fiscal years 1992 to 1994 were used to map the prevalence of inpatient ECT admissions in the Medicare population of each parish (county). The results indicated ECT practice to be highly variable within the state ($SCV^1 = 1.34$) in comparison to other med-

TABLE 1: Baseline ECT Indicators

Indicator	Desciption
1	Documentation of a pro-ECT psychiatric evaluation
2	Documentation of a pre-ECT medical evaluation including recommended laboratory and EKG
3	Documentation of a pre-ECT anesthesia evaluation
4	Presence of a signed ECT informed consent
5	Documentation of appropriateness of ECT for patient
6	Administration of detrimental modications within 48 hours before ECT administration
7	Documentation of electrode placement at each ECT administration
8	Adequate seizure duration for each ECT administration
9	Monitoring of cognitive side effects of ECT after each administration
10	Monitoring of depressive target symptoms after each ECT administration
11	Documentation of discharge plan and referrals

ical and surgical procedures. These findings were in agreement with a national survey reported by Herman et al. (1995). Eleven indicator areas were developed (see Table 1) from the APA ECT task force recommendations (Weiner et al. 1990).

The measurement phase consisted of a retrospective baseline chart review using an instrument developed to measure the indicators, performed on all Medicare patients who received inpatient ECT in the fiscal year 1994. A total of 184 medical records and 945 ECT procedures were reviewed.

The assessment phase analyzed abstracted information and computed compliance rates for both provider and statewide indicators. A report of the statewide baseline results was developed and disseminated to provider hospitals, including an invitation for participation on the collaborative mental health quality improvement (QI) project with Louisiana Health Care Review, Inc. (LHCR).

The improvement phase started with the first meeting of the provider group in August 1995. Using the baseline information both statewide and for their hospitals, the providers were able to focus their quality improvement efforts and decide whether systemic or educational interventions were appropriate to their settings. Baseline results indicated uniform statewide compliance (>90%) for pre-ECT psychiatric evaluation, pre-ECT medical and laboratory evaluation, presence of signed ECT consent forms, documentation of seizure duration, and posthospitalization treatment plans and referrals. The provider group decided not to pursue monitoring of these indicators.

Significantly, low compliance (<90%) was found for pre-ECT anesthesia evaluation, documentation of appropriateness of ECT, administration of medication considered detrimental to ECT, documentation of electrode placement, monitoring of cognitive status changes, and monitoring of depressive target symptoms. For these indicators, improvement strategies were discussed and plans were put forth for implementation. A uniform recording sheet for ECT patient work-up and administration including weekly MiniMental State (Folstein, Folstein, and McHugh 1975) and Hamilton Melancholia Scale (Bech et al. 1981) scores were adopted. A follow-up data tool was designed to check for compliance with these indicators. Indicator six, which reports the use of medications considered to be detrimental to ECT treatment, was identified by the provider group as controversial, and a different strategy was adopted.

Evaluation of the Detrimental Medication Recommendation

At the initial project meeting, the clinicians voiced strong concern that the detrimental medication recommendations for ECT were based on weak scientific evidence. Several suggested that if the recommendations were followed completely, quality of care and patient comfort would be compromised, especially for agitated patients receiving ECT. The clinicians suggested deleting this indicator area with continued data collection and regular discussions with the study group on the use of detrimental medications. The provider group decided to include 10 specific complications potentially linked to the detrimental medications on the project data collection tool.

The LHCR study coordinators, taking a collaborative approach, agreed with this strategy. They decided to further analyze the baseline data to determine if the local use of medications detrimental to ECT provided data that supported the task force recommendations. The coordinators hoped to make this area of controversy an exercise in learning QI methods through the analysis of clinical data.

A literature review on concurrent use of lithium and benzodiazepines during ECT found that the evidence in this area was conflicting, predominantly retrospective, and limited by small sample sizes. In a 1980 study by Stromgren et al., a retrospective design was employed to study 43 patients treated with ECT and benzodiazepine concurrently with a primary diagnosis of depression. They measured the duration and number of seizures, but no clinical outcome measures were obtained. The concurrent use of ECT with benzodiazepines was not advised due to a hypothesized decreased effectiveness from shortened seizure duration (Stromgren et al. 1980). In 1982, a contradictory study was published by Johnstone et al. that showed that patients treated with bilateral ECT had no adverse effects with concurrent benzodiazepine treatment. In 1985, Standish-Barry, Deacon, and Snaith published a theoretical paper proposing caution when ECT and benzodiazepines were used simultaneously due to decreased seizure duration. A 1990 retrospective study by Pettinati evaluated the effect of benzodiazepines on unilateral ECT. The study population consisted of 48 patients, with 94% having a diagnosis of major depression. They reported increased therapeutic failures for unilateral ECT with concurrent use of benzodiazepines, based on the Hamilton Rating Scale for Depression. A case report by Cohen and Lawton (1992) noted that a 67-year-old anxious and depressed female showed no improvement with benzodiazepines given concurrently with bilateral ECT. However, ECT treatments following discontinuation of benzodiazepines yielded marked improvement. These authors proposed that the concomitant use of ECT and benzodiazepines decreased the effectiveness not only of unilateral but also bilateral ECT.

The literature on lithium's adverse effects on ECT is also conflicting and predominantly retrospective. Small and Milstein (1990) published a review that cited eight case studies and two retrospective surveys: Small et al. (1980), with 25 lithium and ECT treated patients, and Penny et al. (1990), who studied 76 lithium and ECT treated patients. The major findings were impaired neuropsychological testing and increased confusion post-ECT, respectively. Two other studies conducted by Krishna, Taylor, and Abrams (1978) and Kukopulos et al. (1987) found no adverse effects of combining lithium and ECT.

Further analysis of the statewide baseline focused on the use of detrimental medications. First, an analysis of administration of the medications considered detrimental by provider was completed. No statewide patterns were found; individual provider hospitals had unique patterns of administering these medications. Second, an analysis to identify the frequency and type of detrimental medications that were administered concurrently with ECT was completed. Both benzodiazepines and lithium were administered frequently enough for further analysis. A third analysis focusing on impaired cognitive function and the administration of benzodiazepines and lithium was completed. No statistical association was found between the administration of either medication and cognitive complications. Analysis was done comparing early readmission in the benzodiazepine and nonbenzodiazepine groups. A statistically significant difference was found in the early readmission rate in the benzodiazepine group.

The methodology and results of all the discussed baseline analyses were discussed in the monthly study group meetings. The clinicians had opportunities to discuss concerns and questions and give their input to the study coordinators and statisticians. Over several months, the study group clinicians became involved and supportive in this part of the QI project.

Future Analysis

The use of both benzodiazepines and lithium will be correlated with changes in weekly Mini-Mental State examinations and Hamilton ratings, length of stay, and time to readmission. This data will be pertinent to the hypothesized adverse effect of lithium on cognition and the proposed effect of benzodiazepines on decreasing the effectiveness of ECT. The Mini-Mental exam will allow a quantitative analysis of change in cognitive function. The addition of length-of-stay and time-to-readmission data will provide a better measure of effectiveness than change in a depressive rating scale alone (the predominant outcome measured in the reviewed literature). In addition, each patient will be severity adjusted, which will partially compensate for the possibility that the lithium and benzodiazepine treated patients may have higher cognitive complications and decreased effectiveness because of more severe psychiatric illness and/or medical comorbidity.

Conclusion

Resistance to a clinical guideline because of lack of face validity by clinicians was used as an opportunity to involve clinicians in using data to evaluate their clinical practices. The early experience of this project's coordinators found clinicians open to feedback when they were involved with the analytic decisions, and the data originated from their colleagues' and their own practices. Unexpectedly, the local data supported the task force recommendations on benzodiazepines, but did not support the recommendations on lithium. Future project data will be used to quantitatively evaluate the applicability of these task force recommendations to current ECT practice in Louisiana. No matter what the results, the QI project's clinician participants will benefit from participating in an objective and systematic evaluation of their clinical practice.

Footnotes

1. SCV, known as the statistical component of variance, is the measure of the magnitude of geographic practice pattern variation for a specific procedure, based on defined provider service areas.

References

Bech, P., et al. 1981. The Hamilton Depression Scale. Evaluation of objectivity using logistic models. *Acta Psychiatrica Scandinavia* 63:290-9.

Cohen, S.L., and C. Lawton. 1992. Do benzodiazepines interfere with the action of electroconvulsive therapy? *British Journal of Psychiatry* 160:545-6.

Folstein, M.F., S.E. Folstein, and P.R. McHugh. 1975. "Mini-Mental State": A practical method for grading the cognitive state of patients for the clinician. *Journal of Psychiatric Research* 12:189-98.

Grant, J.B., et al. 1996. HCFA's Health Care Quality Improvement Program: The medical informatics challenge. *Journal of the American Medical Information Association* 3:15-26.

Herman, R.C., et al. 1995. Variation in ECT use in the United States. *American Journal of Psychiatry* 152:869-75.

Jencks, S.F. and G.R. Wilensky. 1992. Health care quality improvement initiative: A new approach to quality assurance. *Journal of the American Medical Association* 268 (7): 900-3.

Johnstone, E.C., et al. 1982. The Northwick Park electroconvulsive therapy trial. *Lancet* 2:1317-20.

Joint Commission on Accreditation of Healthcare Organizations (JCAHO). 1996. *A guide to performance improvement in behavioral health care organizations. Cycle for improving performance-Measure.* Oakbrook Terrace, IL: JCAHO.

Kaplan, H., B. Sadock, and J. Grebb. 1994. *Synopsis of psychiatry.* Baltimore, MD: Williams and Wilkins.

Krishna, N.R., M.A. Taylor, and R. Abrams. 1978. Response to lithium carbonate. *Biological Psychiatry* 13:601-6.

Kukopulos, A., et al. 1987. Electroconvulsive therapy. In *Depression and mania: Modern lithium therapy*, edited by R N. Johnson, 177-80. Washington, DC: IRL Press.

Lobach, D.F. 1995. A model for adapting clinical guidelines for electronic implementation in primary care. In *Proceedings of the Annual Symposium on Computer Applications in Medical Care*, 581-5. Durham, NC: Duke University Medical Center.

Penny, J.F., et al. 1990. Concurrent and close temporal administration of lithium and ECT. *Convulsive Therapy* 6:139-45.

Pettinati, H.M., et al. 1990. Evidence for less improvement in depression in patients taking benzodiazephines during unilateral ECT. *American Journal of Psychiatry* 147(8):1029-35.

Shapiro, D.W., et al. 1993. Containing costs while improving quality of care: The role of profiling and practice guidelines. *Annual Review of Public Health* 14:219-41.

Small, J.G., et al. 1980. Complications with electroconvulsive treatment combined with lithium. *Biological Psychiatry* 15:103-12.

Small, J.G., and V. Milstein. 1990. Lithium interactions: Lithium and electroconvulsive therapy. *Journal of Clinical Psychopharmacology* 10:346-50.

Standish-Barry, H.M., V. Deacon, and R.P. Snaith. 1985. The relationship of concurrent benzodiazepine administration to seizure duration I ECT. *Acta Psychiatrica Scandinavia* 71:269-71.

Stromgren, L.S., et al. 1980. Factors influencing seizure duration and number of seizures applied in unilateral electroconvulsive therapy. *Acta Psychiatrica Scandinavia* 62:158-65.

Weiner, R.D., et al. 1990. *The American Psychiatric Association Task Force on Electroconvulsive Therapy. The practice of electroconvulsive therapy: Recommendations for treatment, training and privileging.* Washington, DC: American Psychiatric Association.

Routine Treatment of Adult Depression

MARK OLFSON, MD, MPH, TERRI L. TANIELIAN, MA, BRENNAN D. PETERSON, BS, AND DEBORAH A. ZARIN, MD

Although an estimated 5.7 million visits are made to psychiatrists each year for the treatment of depression,[1] much of the information about such treatment is derived from patients in university-based research studies.[2] To better understand how psychiatrists in the community treat major depression, we surveyed a convenience sample from the American Psychiatric Association's Practice Research Network. The study served as a baseline assessment of psychiatrists' adherence to treatment recommendations in APA's *Practice Guideline for Major Depressive Disorder in Adults*[3] in preparation for a quality improvement program.

The sample consisted of 210 psychiatrists, of whom 189, or 90 percent, responded. The psychiatrists were presented with case vignettes of several patients with major depression of varying severity and asked to answer specific questions about how they would manage such patients. The questions, which covered such areas as selection of initial treatment or length of maintenance therapy, were based on recommendations in the practice guideline.

As Figure 1 shows, the initial treatment selected varied with severity of illness. Severity of illness was also linked to how long the psychiatrists generally waited to see if a patient selected for psychotherapy alone would respond before initiating a trial of medication. The average wait was 5.1 weeks in mild cases and 3.3 weeks in moderate

Figure 1. Percentage of Patients Receiving Three Types of Initial Treatment for Major Depression, Categorized by Severity of Illness

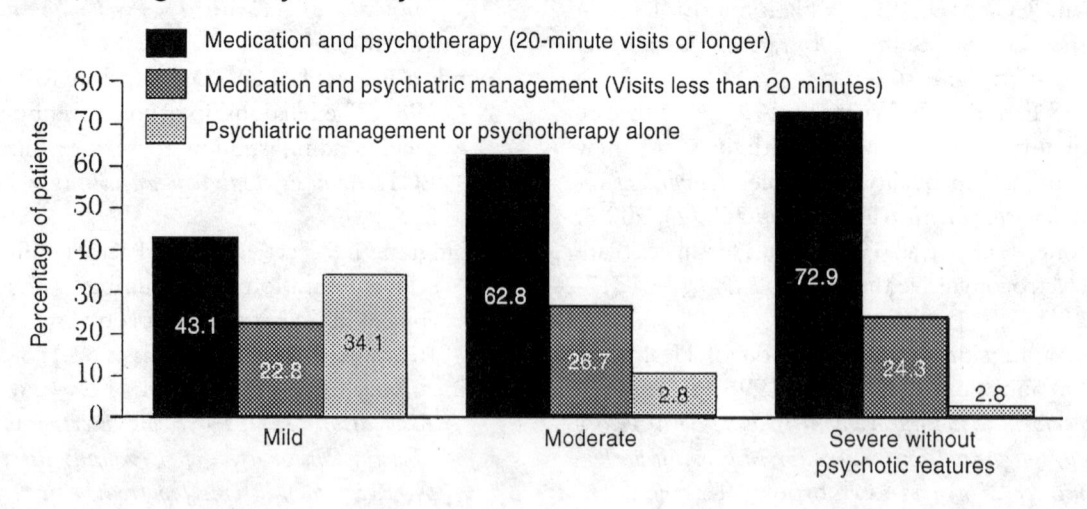

Severity	Medication and psychotherapy (20-minute visits or longer)	Medication and psychiatric management (Visits less than 20 minutes)	Psychiatric management or psychotherapy alone
Mild	43.1	22.8	34.1
Moderate	62.8	26.7	2.8
Severe without psychotic features	72.9	24.3	2.8

Source: Olfson M, Tanielian TL, Peterson BD, and Zarin DA. Routine Treatment of Adult Depression. *Psychiatric Services* March 1998; 49(3):299.

Dr. Olfson is with the New York State Psychiatric Institute, 722 West 168th Street, New York, New York 10032, and the College of Physicians and Surgeons of Columbia University. Ms. Tanielian, Mr. Peterson, and Dr. Zarin are with the office of research of the American Psychiatric Association in Washington, D.C.

cases. Almost 52 percent reported waiting four weeks or less to see if a patient responded to an antidepressant before recommending another medication or treatment. A third waited five or six weeks, and the remainder (16 percent) waited more than six weeks. Figure 2 shows how long the psychiatrists maintained first episode patients on antidepressant medication following full recovery.

The survey findings reflect a consensus among psychiatrists on combining medication and psychotherapy in the treatment of major depression, particularly in its most severe forms. In keeping with the APA practice guideline, a majority of psychiatrists wait no more than six weeks before declaring a medication trial a success or a failure, and they maintain first-episode patients on medication for at least six months following full recovery.

References

1. Olfson M, Pincus HA: Outpatient mental health care in nonhospital settings: distribution of patients across provider groups. *American Journal of Psychiatry* 153:1353-1356, 1996
2. Kupfer DJ, Freedman DX: Treatment of depression: "standard" clinical practice as an unexamined topic. *Archives of General Psychiatry* 43:509-511, 1986
3. Practice Guideline for Major Depressive Disorder in Adults. *American Journal of Psychiatry* 150 (Apr suppl):1-26, 1993

Figure 2. Average Duration of Maintenance Drug Treatment for Major Depression Following Recovery, by Percentage of Psychiatrists Responding to Survey (N = 189)

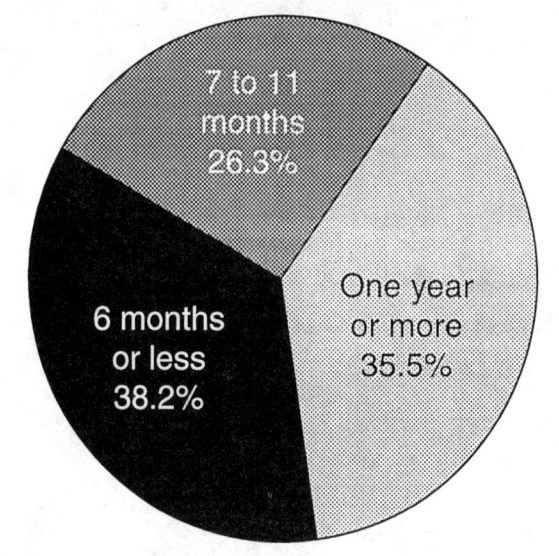

- 7 to 11 months 26.3%
- One year or more 35.5%
- 6 months or less 38.2%

Directory of Behavioral Practice Guidelines

American Academy of Child & Adolescent Psychiatry

AACAP Public Information Office
P.O. Box 96106
Washington DC 20090-6106
(800) 333-7636
(202) 966-7300
Fax: (202) 966-2891
Virginia Q. Anthony, Executive Director

Practice Parameters for the Assessment and Treatment of Children and Adolescents with Attention Deficit Hyperactivity Disorder (October 1997)
Price: $20

Practice Parameters for the Assessment and Treatment of Children and Adolescents with Anxiety Disorders (October 1997)
Price: $20

Practice Parameters for Child Custody Evaluation (October 1997).
Price: $20

Practice Parameters for the Assessment and Treatment of Children and Adolescents with Conduct Disorder (October 1997).
Price: $20

Practice Parameters for the Assessment and Treatment of Children and Adolescents with Substance Use Disorders (October 1997)
Price: $20

Practice Parameters for the Assessment and Treatment of Children and Adolescents with Bipolar Disorder (January 1997).
Price: $20

Practice Parameters for the Forensic Evaluation of Children and Adolescents Who May Have Been Physically or Sexually Abused (March 1997).
Price: $20

Practice Parameters for the Psychiatric Assessment of Children and Adolescents (October 1995).
Price: $20

Practice Parameters for the Psychiatric Assessment of Infants and Toddlers (0-36 months) (October 1997).
Price: $20

Practice Parameters for the Assessment and Treatment of Children and Adolescents with Schizophrenia (June 1994).
Price: $20

Supplement to the Journal of the American Academy of Child and Adolescent Psychiatry (October 1997) (Contains complete set of 10 Practice Parameters listed above).
Price: $60

Criteria for Short-Term Treatment of Acute Psychiatric Illness. (1997).
Price: $30

Source: Faulkner & Gray's Healthcare Information Center, 1998.

Best Principles for Managed Care Medicaid RFPs: How Decision-Makers Can Select and Monitor High Quality Programs (1996).
Price: $20

Guidelines for Training Toward Community-Based Systems of Care for Children with Serious Emotional Disturbances (1996).
Price: $10

American Medical Directors Association

10480 Little Patuxent Parkway, Suite 760
Columbia MD 21044
(800) 876-2632
(410) 740-9743
Fax: (410) 740-4572
http://www.amda.com/home.htm

Depression (1996)
Cost: $8

Pharmacotherapy Companion to Depression (1998)
Cost: $8

American Psychiatric Association

1400 K Street, N.W.
Washington DC 20005
(202) 682-6842
Fax: (202) 789-1874
Deborah A. Zarin, M.D., Leslie Seigle, Karen Cooper, Office of Quality Improvement and Psychiatric Services
To order: 800-368-5777

Practice Guideline for Eating Disorders (1993) (anticipated update, late 1998)

Practice Guideline for Major Depressive Disorder in Adults (1993) (anticipated update, late 1998)

Practice Guideline for Treatment of Patients with Bipolar Disorder (1994) (anticipated update, 1999)

Practice Guideline for Treatment of Patients with Substance Use Disorders: Alcohol, Cocaine, Opioids (1995) (anticipated update, 1999)

Practice Guideline for Psychiatric Evaluation of Adults (1995)

Practice Guideline for the Treatment of Patients with Nicotine Dependence (1996) (anticipated update, 2000)

Practice Guideline for the Treatment of Patients with Schizophrenia (1997) (anticipated update, 2001)

Practice Guideline for the Treatment of Patients with Alzheimer's Disease and Other Dementias of Late Life (1997) (anticipated update, 2001)

Practice Guideline for the Treatment of Patients with Panic Disorder (1998) (anticipated update, 2003)
Price: For each of the above: $22.50
Compilation of five completed guidelines: Eating Disorders, Major Depressive Disorder, Bipolar Disorder, Substance Use, and Psychiatric Evaluation of Adults (1996)
Price: hardcover: $49.95; paperbound: $39.95

Forthcoming APA Guidelines:

Delirium (anticipated publication, winter 1999)

Geriatric Care (anticipated publication, summer 1999)

HIV/AIDS (anticipated publication, summer 2000)

Obsessive Compulsive Disorder (no date set)

Post-Traumatic Stress Disorder (no date set)

Personality Disorders, (no date set)

American Psychological Association

Practice Directorate
750 First Street, N.E.
Washington DC 20002-4242
(800) 374-2723
(202) 336-5800
Fax: (202) 336-5797
Order Dept.: (202) 336-5510
Suzanna Hicks, Administrative Assistant, Board and Committee Operations, Practice Directorate
The first three guidelines are also available on the Web at: http://www.apa.org/practice/prof.html

Guidelines for Child Custody Evaluations In Divorce Proceedings (1994)
Price: No cost

Guidelines for Psychological Evaluations in Child Protection Matters (1998)
Price: No cost

Guidelines for the Evaluation of Dementia and Age-Related Cognitive Decline (1998)
Price: No cost

APA General Guidelines for Providers of Psychological Services
Price: No cost

Parameters of Managed Mental Health Care: Legal, Ethical, and Professional Guidelines
Price: No cost

Template for Developing Guidelines: Interventions for Mental Disorders and Psychological Aspects of Physical Disorders (1995)
Price: No cost

RecordKeeping Guidelines (1993)
Price: No cost

American Society of Addiction Medicine

4601 North Park Ave, Upper Arcade
Suite 101
Chevy Chase, M.D. 20815
(301) 656-3920
(800) 844-8948
Fax: (301) 656-3815
Online address: ASAMOffice@AOL.com
http://www.asam.org/
ASAM Publications Distribution Center: (800) 844-8948

ASAM Clinical Practice Guideline: *The Role of Phenytoin In The Management of Alcohol Withdrawal Syndrome*
Price: No cost (see http://www.asam.org/)

ASAM Clinical Practice Guideline: *Pharmacological Management of Alcohol Withdrawal*
Price: No cost (see http://www.asam.org/)

Patient Placement Criteria for the Treatment of Substance-Related Disorders (Second Edition) (1996)

The ASAM PPC-2 provides two sets of guidelines, one for adults and one for adolescents, and five levels of service for each group. It is available at a cost of $85 for ASAM members and $100 for non-members. A hypertext software version is also available.

Detoxification: Principals and Protocols (in *Topics in Addiction Medicine*, Vol. 1, No. 2)
Price: $20 nonmembers

Association for Ambulatory Behavioral Healthcare

301 North Fairfax Street, Suite 109
Alexandria VA 22314-2633
(703) 836-2274
Fax: (703) 836-0083
Joe Piontkowski, Communications Associate

Standards and Guidelines for Partial Hospitalization Adult Programs, Second Edition (1994)
Price: $20

Standards and Guidelines for Partial Hospitalization Child and Adolescent Programs, Second Edition (1995)
Price: $20

Standards and Guidelines for Partial Hospitalization Geriatric Programs (1997)
Price: $20

Standards and Guidelines for Partial Hospitalization Chemical Dependency Programs (1996)
Price: $20

Standards and Guidelines for Level II (Intensive Outpatient Programs) (1998)
Price: $20

The Expert Consensus Guideline Series

Expert Knowledge Systems, LLC
P.O. Box 804
Fairfield, CT 06430
The Expert Consensus Guidelines are available on the World Wide Web at:
http://www.psychguides.com/index.htm

Treatment of Bipolar Disorder (1996)

Treatment of Schizophrenia (November 1996) (revised edition to be released late 1998)

Treatment of Obsessive-Compulsive Disorder (1996)

Treatment of Agitation in Older Persons with Dementia (1998)

Institute for Clinical Systems Integration

8009 34th St. South
Suite 1200
Bloomington MN 55425
(612) 883-7999
http://www.icsi.org
To order guidelines:
ICSI Publications Fulfillment Center
c/o the ARDEL Group
13355 10th Ave. North, Suite 108
Minneapolis MN 5541
(612) 545-1919
Fax: (612) 545-0335

Major Depression, Panic Disorder & Generalized Anxiety Disorder
Price: $25

Major Depression in Specialty Care Adults
Price: $25

Tobacco Prevention & Cessation
Price: $25

Diagnosis and Management of Attention Deficit Hyperactivity Disorder
Price: $25

Domestic Violence
Price: $25

Technology Assessment:
Acupuncture for Treatment of Chemical Dependency
Price: $25

Institute for Healthcare Quality

Institute for Healthcare Quality
10900 Hampshire Avenue South
Minneapolis MN 55438-2306
(800) 824 3882, ext. 7536
(612) 946 7536
Fax: (612) 829-3578

QualityFIRST Behavioral Health Guidelines
(A risk management tool for managing behavioral care, covering more than 77 mental health and chemical dependency disorders and used by managed care organizations, mental health county boards, and third party managed care programs.)
Price: Call

International Association Of Psychosocial Rehabilitation Services

10025 Governor Warfield Parkway, #301
Columbia MD 21044-3357
(410) 730-7190
Fax: (410) 730-5965

Practice Guidelines for the Psychiatric Rehabilitation of Persons with Severe and Persistent Mental Illness in a Managed Care Environment (1997)
Price: $8 for non-members

International Society for The Study of Dissociation

4700 W. Lake Avenue
Glenview, IL 60025-1485
(847) 375-4718
The guidelines are available on the World Wide Web at:
http://www.issd.org/isdguide.htm

Guidelines for Treating Dissociative Identity Disorder (1994, 1997).
Price: No cost

The National (Australian) Health and Medical Research Council

The Australian Government Publishing Service
GPO Box 84
Canberra, ACT, 2601
Australia
Fax: 61 2 6295 4888

Depression in Young People: Clinical Practice Guidelines (Cat. No. 9609296) (1997)
Cost 16.95 (Aus. dollars)

Depression in Young People: A Guide for Mental Health Professionals (Cat. No. 9609342) (1997)
Cost 10.55 (Aus. dollars)

Depression in Young People: A Guide for General Practitioners (Cat. No. 960927) (1997)
Cost 11.95 (Aus. dollars)

National Clearinghouse For Alcohol and Drug Information

(800) 729-6686
Fax: (301) 468-6433
Web address: http://www.health.org/pubs/catalog/

Selected guidelines from the Treatment Improvement Protocol (TIP) Series, produced by the federal Center for Substance Abuse Treatment (all guidelines are free of charge):
State Methadone Treatment Guidelines. Treatment Improvement Protocol (TIP) Series 1 (1993). 393 pp. BKD98

Pregnant, Substance-Using Women. Treatment Improvement Protocol (TIP) Series 2 (Reprint 1995) 90 pp. BKD107

Screening and Assessment of Alcohol and Other Drug-Abusing Adolescents. Treatment Improvement Protocol (TIP) Series 3 (Reprint 1995). 270 pp. BKD108

Guidelines for the Treatment of Alcohol and Other Drug-Abusing Adolescents. Treatment Improvement Protocol (TIP) Series 4 (1993). 188 pp. BKD109

Improving Treatment for Drug-Exposed Infants. Treatment Improvement Protocol (TIP) Series 5 (Reprint 1995). 94 pp. BKD110

Screening for Infectious Diseases Among Substance Abusers. Treatment Improvement Protocol (TIP) Series 6 (Reprint 1995). 160 pp. BKD131

Screening and Assessment for Alcohol and Other Drug Abuse Among Adults in the Criminal Justice System. Treatment Improvement Protocol (TIP) Series 7 (1994). 129 pp. BKD138

Intensive Outpatient Treatment for Alcohol and Other Drug Abuse. Treatment Improvement Protocol (TIP) Series 8 (1994) 114 pp. BKD139

Assessment and Treatment of Patients with Coexisting Mental Illness and Alcohol and Other Drug Abuse. Treatment Improvement Protocol (TIP) Series 9 (Reprint 1995). 114 pp. BKD134

Assessment and Treatment of Cocaine-Abusing, Methadone-Maintained Patients. Treatment Improvement Protocol (TIP) Series 10 (1994). 129 pp. BKD157

The Role and Current Status of Patient Placement Criteria in the Treatment of Substance Use Disorders. Treatment Improvement Protocol (TIP) Series 13 (1995). BKD161

Treatment for HIV-Infected Alcohol and Other Drug Abusers. Treatment Improvement Protocol (TIP) Series 15 (1995). BKD163

Matching Treatment to Patient Needs in Opioid Substitution Therapy. Treatment Improvement Protocol (TIP) Series 20 (1995). BKD168

A Guide to Substance Abuse Services for Primary Care Clinicians. Treatment Improvement Protocol Series 24 (1997). 168 pp. BKD234

Substance Abuse Treatment and Domestic Violence. Treatment Improvement Protocol Series 25 (1997, CSAT). 152 pp. BKD239

Substance Abuse Among Older Adults. Treatment Improvement Protocol Series 26 (1998) 173 pp. BKD250

National Community Mental Healthcare Council

12300 Twinbrook Parkway, Suite 320
Rockville MD 20852
(301) 984-6200
Fax: (301) 881-7159
Jose Escalante, Editorial Associate

Community Mental Healthcare Organization Adult Partial Hospitalization Program Standards and Guidelines (1995)
Price: $10

Preferred Clinical Practices Guide of Behavioral Health Network of Vermont, Version 2 (1995)
Price: $125 nonmembers (see below)

The Oak Group

888 Worcester Street, 3rd Floor
Wellesley MA 02181
(781) 237-6822
Fax: (617) 237-6535

Managed Care Appropriateness Protocol, Behavioral Health Module (1997)
Price: Negotiated

Practice Guidelines Coalition

Jennifer Gregg
Department of Psychology / 296
University of Nevada
Reno, NV 89557-0062
Fax: (702) 784-1126
E-mail: jeng@scs.unr.edu

Panic Disorder (forthcoming)

Behavioral Aspects of the Management of Chronic Pain (forthcoming)

Preferred Clinical Practices Guide of Behavioral Health Network of Vermont

Distributed by the National Council for Community Behavioral Healthcare
12300 Twinbrook Parkway
Suite 320
Rockville MD 20852
(301) 984-6200
Fax: (301) 881-7159

Preferred Clinical Practices Guide of Behavioral Health Network of Vermont
Guide includes guidelines on:
- Conduct/Oppositional Defiant Disorders
- Attention-Deficit Hyperactivity Disorder
- Eating Disorders
- Psychotic Disorders
- Anxiety Disorders in Adults
- Anxiety Disorders in Children and Adolescents
- Mood Disorders
- Adjustment Disorders
- Substance-Related Disorders

Price: $75 for NCMHC members/$125 for non-members

The Psychological Corporation

555 Academic Court
San Antonio TX 78218-2498
(800) 228-0752
Fax: (800) 232-1223
Customer Service Department

The Psychological Corporation publishes a variety of manuals of empirically-validated treatments for specific disorders through its Graywinds Publication Division.
Cost varies by treatment manual.

U.S. Agency for Health Care Policy and Research (AHCPR)

2101 East Jefferson Street
Rockville, MD 20852
(301) 594-1364

To order guideline products or to obtain further information on their availability, call the AHCPR Clearinghouse at 800-358-9295, or write to:
AHCPR
Publications Clearinghouse
P.O. Box 8547
Silver Spring MD 20907.

AHCPR's guidelines are available on the World Wide Web at: **http://www.ahcpr.gov/clinic/**

AHCPR statement on guidelines' availability: "The contents of these Clinical Practice Guidelines are in the public domain within the United States only and may be used and reproduced without special permission in America, except for those copyrighted materials noted for which further reproduction, in any form, is prohibited without the specific permission of copyright holders. Citation as to source is appreciated."

Depression in Primary Care: Volume 1. Detection and Diagnosis
AHCPR Publication No. 93-0550 (April 1993)

Depression in Primary Care: Volume 2. Treatment of Major Depression
Clinical Practice Guideline Number 5
AHCPR Publication No. 93-0551 (April 1993)

Smoking Cessation
Clinical Guideline Number 18
AHCPR Publication No. 96-0692 (April 1996)

Recognition and Initial Assessment of Alzheimer's Disease and Related Dementias
Clinical Practice Guideline No. 19
AHCPR Publication No. 97-0702 (November 1996)

West Virginia Office of Behavioral Health Services

State Capitol Complex
Building 6, Room B-717
Charleston WV 25305
(304) 558-0627
Fax: (304) 558-1008
Division of Mental Health and Community Rehabilitation Services

Practice for Adults with Serious Mental Illness (1996)
Price: No cost

Managed Behavioral Healthcare Organizations

(Some of the following MBHOs make their guidelines available to the greater professional community, while others restrict them to network providers only.)

Comprehensive Behavioral Care, Inc.

4200 West Cypress Street, Suite 300
Tampa FL 33607
(813) 876-5036, (813) 872-1561
Tracey Smithey, MD, Medical Director

CBC Best Practice Guidelines (1995)
Price: No cost

ComPsych Behavioral Health Corporation

NBC Tower
455 North Cityfront Plaza Drive, 24th Floor
Chicago IL 60611-5506
(312) 595-4033
Fax: (312) 595-4055
Desiree Ross, Provider Relations

Best Practices Guidelines (1995)
Price: No cost

First Mental Health

501 Great Circle Road, Suite 300
Nashville TN 37228
(615) 256-3400
Fax: (615) 256-0786
Executive Director

Best Practices Guidelines (1995)
Price: No cost

Horizon Behavioral Services (formerly ACORN Behavioral Healthcare Management Corp. and FPM Behavioral Health, Inc.)

ACORN
134 North Narbeth Avenue
Narbeth PA 19072-2299
(800) 223-7050
Fax: (610) 664-8373
Quality Assurance Department

Clinical Criteria (1995)
Price: No cost

FPM

1276 Minnesota Avenue
Winter Park FL 32789
(407) 647-6153
Fax: (407) 647-0668
Gordon L. Steinhauer, Senior Vice President, Operations

Provider and Orientation Manual (1995)
Price: No cost

Integra, Inc.

1060 First Avenue, Suite 400
King of Prussia PA 19406
(610) 992-7000
Fax: (610) 992-7046
Provider Service Department

Best Practices Guidelines (1995)
Price: No cost

Magellan Health Services

P.O. Box 5040
Columbia MD 21046
(800) 788-4005
(410) 953-1000

Human Affairs International, Green Spring, and Merit are now part of Magellan Health Services. Eventually, Magellan will create a single set of guidelines, but for now each of the three companies is using its own guidelines.

Human Affairs International

10150 South Centennial Parkway
Sandy UT 84070
(801) 256-7300
Fax: (801) 578-7191
Gerard Niewenhous, (801) 256-7045

Best Practices Guidelines (1995)
Price: No cost

Green Spring

(410) 953-1000
Provider Relations Department

Best Practices Guidelines (1995)
Price: No cost

Merit Behavioral Care Corporation

One Maynard Drive
Park Ridge NJ 07656
(800) 999-9772, ext. 2992
Fax: (314) 595-3810
Provider Relations Department

Best Practices for Assessing and Managing the Suicidal Patient (1996)
Price: No cost:

MCC Managed Behavioral Care, Inc.

11095 Viking Drive, Suite 350
Eden Prairie MN 55344
(612) 996-2799
Fax: (612) 943-9579
Roger Anderson, Director of Quality Management

MCC Clinical Guidelines for Mental Health and Substance Abuse Treatment (1996)
Price: $35 hardcover, $10 disk.

ValueOptions, Inc. (formerly FHC Options and Value Behavioral Health)

P.O. Box 4080
Virginia Beach VA 23454
(800) 397-1630 (Provider Line)
Deb Adler, Vice President for Network Management

ValueOptions is in the process of merging the two companies' guidelines. Projected date of completion for the merged guidelines is February 1999. Until that time, the two different networks' guidelines will be used:

Options: *Best Practices Guidelines* (1995)

Value: *VBH Clinical Criteria & Protocols* (1995)

Chapter 11

Recent Mental Health And Substance Abuse Research Findings

Review of Recent Outcomes Literature

JOHN J. MCGINLEY

A "Systems of Care" Approach Fails To Boost Clinical Outcomes

Bickman L, Summerfelt WT, and Noser K. Comparative Outcomes of Emotionally Disturbed Children and Adolescents in a System of Services and Usual Care. Psychiatric Services *1997; 48:1543-1548.*

A "systems of care" approach to providing mental health services to families with seriously emotionally disturbed children and adolescents afforded better system-level outcomes (e.g., access, cost), but demonstrated no difference in clinical outcomes (e.g., functioning, symptoms), when compared to a "traditional care" approach.

In a randomized longitudinal study, a comprehensive and integrated "systems of care" approach was compared to a "traditional care" approach to mental health services. The study involved 350 families with a seriously emotionally disturbed child or adolescent aged 9 to 17. System-level outcomes (e.g., access, cost) and clinical outcomes (e.g., functioning, symptoms) were examined at six-month follow-up. Clinical outcomes were assessed with the Child Assessment Schedule (CAS), the Child Behavior Checklist (CBCL), and the Child and Adolescent Functional Assessment Schedule (CAFAS), for example. Results indicated that although there was an increased access to care and amount of care in the "systems of care" approach, there were no differences in the clinical outcomes among the two approaches. It was concluded that the effectiveness of a "systems of care" approach was mostly limited to system-level outcomes.

Address reprint requests to: Leonard Bickman, PhD, Center for Mental Health Policy, Vanderbilt Institute of Public Policy Studies, Vanderbilt University, 1207 18th Avenue South, Nashville, TN 37212.

CBT More Effective in Treating Adolescent Depression

Brent DA, Holder D, Kolko D, Birmaher B, Baugher M, Roth C, Iyengar, and Johnson BA. A Clinical Psychotherapy Trial for Adolescent Depression Comparing Cognitive, Family, and Supportive Therapy. Archives of General Psychiatry *1997; 54:877-885.*

In a comparison of three psychosocial therapies, cognitive behavioral therapy was demonstrated to be more efficacious with depressed adolescents in a clinical setting.

A randomized clinical trail examined the efficacy of three psychosocial therapies for the treatment of adolescent depression. Clinically referred adolescent patients (N = 107) with DSM-III-R major depressive disorder were randomly assigned to cognitive-behavior therapy (CBT), nondirective supportive therapy (NST), or systematic behavior family therapy (SBFT) for 12 to 16 sessions once a week. Study measures included the Beck Depression Inventory (BDI) and the Children's Global Assessment Schedule (CGAS). Results indicated that patients who received CBT showed a

---

John J. McGinley, MS, is special assistant for Program Evaluation and Research at Project Return Foundation, Inc., in New York, and a PhD student in the Clinical Health Psychology Program, Ferkauf Graduate School of Psychology/Albert Einstein College of Medicine, Yeshiva University in the Bronx NY.

decreased rate of major depressive disorder at the end of treatment, with a higher rate of remission, and more rapid relief of self-reported and interviewer-rated depression. CBT was determined to be more efficacious than NST or SBFT for depressed adolescents in clinical settings.

Address reprint requests to: David A. Brent, MD, University of Pittsburgh School of Medicine, Western Psychiatric Institute and Clinic, 3811 O'Hara Street, Pittsburgh, PA 15213.

CBT for Depressed Alcoholics Yields Better Results Than RT

Brown RA, Evans DM, Miller IW, Burgess ES, and Mueller TI. Cognitive-Behavioral Treatment for Depression in Alcoholism. Journal of Consulting and Clinical Psychology *1997; 65:715-726.*

Significantly better alcohol use outcomes (i.e., days abstinent, total abstinence, and drinks per day) were noted for depressed alcoholics receiving eight sessions of cognitive-behavioral therapy (CBT) compared with a relaxation training (RT) control treatment.

Alcoholics with comorbid depression received eight sessions of cognitive-behavioral therapy (CBT; n = 19) or a relaxation training control (RT; n = 16) in conjunction with their standard alcohol treatment. All patients had a DSM-III-R diagnosis of alcohol dependence or abuse and a Beck Depression Inventory (BDI) depressive symptoms score of >10. Additional measures included the modified Hamilton Rating Scale for Depression (HAM-D) and the Profile of Mood States (POMS). Results indicated that during treatment, patients who received CBT had more reductions in their somatic depressive symptoms and in their anxious and depressed mood, compared with patients who received RT. At the 3-month follow-up CBT patients had a greater percentage of abstinent days and by the 6-month follow-up had a significantly better percentage of abstinent days (90 vs. 68 percent), total abstinence (47 vs. 13 percent), and drinks per day (.5 vs. 5.7). Further, it was observed that patients who received CBT also had more frequent AA meeting attendance. Clinical applications and future research directions are discussed.

Address correspondence to: Dr. Richard A. Brown, Butler Hospital-Brown University School of Medicine, 345 Blackstone Boulevard, Providence, RI 02906; Richard_Brown@Brown.edu

MICA Clients Show Improvement in a Modified Therapeutic Community

Carroll JFX and McGinley JJ. Managing MICA Clients in a Modified Therapeutic Community With Enhanced Staffing. Journal of Substance Abuse Treatment *(in press).*

Mentally ill chemical abusers showed significant improvement on Tennessee Self Concept Scale scores across diagnostic groups between admission to a modified therapeutic community and six to seven months later.

A prospective pre-post research design was used to evaluate the effectiveness of "a modified therapeutic community (TC) with enhanced mental health staffing" in treating mentally ill chemical abusers (MICA). Client admissions (N = 438) were screened for DSM-IV diagnoses and placed into one of three operationalized conditions: (1) non-MICA (no comorbid diagnosis of mental illness, n = 135); (2) general MICA (a comorbid diagnosis of mental illness without psychotropic medication, n = 245); and (3) severe MICA (a comorbid diagnosis of mental illness with psychotropic medication, n = 58). The Tennessee Self Concept Scale (TSCS) was administered to residents "after admission and at six-month intervals thereafter." Results indicated that: (a) at initial TSCS testing the three diagnostic groups differed significantly, with the non-MICA group scoring better (i.e., highest in self-esteem and lowest in psychopathology), the severe MICA group scoring worst (i.e., lowest in self-esteem and highest in psychopathology), and the general MICA group scoring in between the other two groups; (b) after six to seven months of treatment, all three diagnostic groups evidenced "significant improvement in their TSCS scores"; (c) when baseline TSCS admission scores were taken into account (i.e., controlled for), no significant differences were noted between the three diagnostic groups at the six-month TSCS testing (i.e., all three groups achieved a similar amount of progress); (d) several TSCS scales noted significant gender differences, in that women scored lower than men in self-esteem and higher than men in psychopathology. Clinical observations (e.g., importance of interdisciplinary treatment team integration) and research limitations (e.g., no control group) are discussed.

Address correspondence to: Jerome F. X. Carroll, PhD, Vice-President, Clinical Operations, Project Return Foundation, Inc., Ten Astor Place, New York, NY 10003.

Six Factors Predict Outcomes in First-Episode Psychosis

Cohen BM, Tohen M, Yurgelen-Todd D, Renshaw PF, and Hennen J. Predictors of Outcome in First-Episode Psychosis. Paper presented at the annual meeting of the American Psychiatric Association, San Diego CA, May 1997.

Six factors, including diagnosis of a non-affective psychosis, predict poor outcomes for patients with first-episode psychosis and patients diagnosed with a first-episode non-affective psychosis.

In a prospective study, clinical predictors of poor outcomes in patients with first episode psychosis were examined. Subjects included 342 patients "with a first-episode of psychosis and 107 patients with a diagnosis of first-episode, non-affective psychosis (i.e., schizophrenia, schizoaffective disorder, delusional disorder, schizophreniform disorder or brief psychosis)." Only 9 percent of subjects were reported lost to follow-up. Researchers found that six factors predicted poor outcomes: (1) diagnosis of a non-affective psychosis; (2) occurrence of a comorbid psychiatric diagnosis; (3) insidious onset of the illness; (4) medication non-compliance; (5) minority group membership; and, (6) being male. It was concluded that as newer medications offer better symptom alleviation, with better tolerance and greater patient satisfaction, outcomes and treatment compliance may improve. The authors' use of magnetic resonance brain imaging was also described; early findings "suggest an association between neurochemical and functional changes in the brain and outcome, both before and after medication treatment."

Address correspondence to: Bruce M. Cohen, MD, PhD, Department of Psychiatry, McLean Hospital, 115 Mill Street, Belmont, MA 02178-1048.

Strength of Therapeutic Alliance Predicts Alcoholism Treatment Outcome

Connors G J, Carroll KM, DiClemente CC, Longabaugh R, and Donovan DM. The Therapeutic Alliance and Its Relationship to Alcoholism Treatment Participation and Outcome. Journal of Consulting and Clinical Psychology 1997; 65:588-598.

The therapeutic alliance is a significant predictor of increased treatment participation and improved drinking outcomes among outpatients, but not among aftercare clients.

Two large multisite clinical trials (i.e., Project Match) examined the contribution of the therapeutic alliance in alcoholism treatment. Alcoholic outpatient (Study 1, N = 952) and aftercare (Study 2, N = 774) clients were randomly assigned to one of three treatment modalities: cognitive-behavioral therapy (CBT), 12 Step Facilitation (TSF), or Motivational Enhancement Therapy (MET). The Working Alliance Inventory (WAI) was completed by clients and therapists on the second or third treatment session and at 12-month post-treatment follow-up. Results indicated that both client and therapist WAI ratings significantly predicted participation in treatment and drinking outcomes in the outpatient sample (Study 1) at both the beginning of treatment and at 12-month follow-up. Ratings of the working alliance by aftercare clients (Study 2) were not predictive of participation in treatment or drinking behavior, whereas therapist ratings only predicted one measure of drinking behavior (percentage of days abstinent) during treatment and at 12-month follow-up. The authors concluded that the working alliance contributed to an increase in treatment participation and improved drinking outcomes for alcoholic outpatients.

Address correspondence to: Dr. Gerard J. Connors, Research Institute on Addictions, 1021 Main Street, Buffalo, NY 14203.

Fluoxetine Use Results in Lower Net Costs

Croghan TW, Lair TJ, Engelhart L, Crown WE, Copley-Merriman C, Melfi CA, Obenchain RL, and Buesching DP. Effect of antidepressant therapy on health care utilization and costs in primary care. Psychiatric Services *1997; 48:1420-1426.*

Among four types of antidepressant medications, fluoxetine appeared to provide the best adherence to medical guidelines with no increase in costs.

A retrospective analysis of medical and pharmacological records for 1,242 patients diagnosed with depression (without comorbid psychotic or substance use disorders) in primary care settings was conducted. Patients had initial prescriptions in one of four antidepressant medication cohorts: (1) fluoxetine; (2) trazodone; (3) tricyclics amitriptyline or imipramine; and (4) secondary amine tricyclics desipramine or nortriptyline. The main outcome measures were total health charges, total mental health charges, and antidepressant use patterns. Results indicated that patients treated with fluoxetine had higher six-month continuous use rates. Further, when statistically adjusted for selection bias (i.e., non-random assignment to treatments) using a multivariate "sample selection models" technique, no differences in total medical charges were observed among the four medication cohorts. It was concluded that fluoxetine, which has a higher price, can be used to treat depression without a higher cost.

Address correspondence to: Thomas W. Croghan, MD, Lilly Research Laboratories, Eli Lilly and Company, Lilly Corporate Center, Indianapolis, IN 46285.

Fluoxetine Effective For Depressed Children And Adolescents

Emslie GJ, Rush AJ, Weinberg WA, Kowatch RA, Hughes CW, Carmody T, and Rintelmann J. A double-blind, randomized, placebo-controlled trial of fluoxetine in children and adolescents with depression. Archives of General Psychiatry *1997; 54:1031-1037.*

A comparison of fluoxetine versus a placebo in the treatment of depressed children and adolescents found better treatment responsiveness and lower depressive scores in the fluoxetine group.

Researchers evaluated the efficacy of fluoxetine in the treatment of children and adolescents ages 7 to 17 with nonpsychotic major depression. Subjects (N = 96) were stratified by age (i.e., 12 or less; 13 or more) and gender and randomly assigned to an 8-week double-blind trial of fluoxetine (n = 48) or placebo (n = 48). The primary outcome measures included the Clinical Global Impressions (CGI) scale and the Children's Depression Rating Scale-Revised (CDRS-R). Results noted significant overall improvement (i.e., responsiveness to treatment) on the CGI scale for the fluoxetine group (56 percent) compared with the placebo group (33 percent), when the full intent-to-treat sample was examined at exit from the study (i.e., at eight weeks or less). However, results of overall improvement on the CGI scale were not significantly different by group for subjects who completed the eight-week trial. The fluoxetine group also had significantly lower depression scores on the CDRS-R after five weeks of treatment. The authors concluded that "fluoxetine was superior to placebo in the acute phase treatment of major depressive disorder in child and adolescent outpatients with severe, persistent depression."

Address reprint requests to: Graham J. Emslie, MD, Department of Psychiatry, University of Texas at Dallas, Southwestern Medical Center, 5323 Harry Hines Boulevard, Dallas, TX 75235-9070.

Intensive Use of Inpatient Services Under Managed Care Examined

Geller JL, Fisher WH, McDermeit M, and Brown JM. (1998). The Effects of Public Managed Care on Patterns of Intensive Use of Inpatient Psychiatric Services. Psychiatric Services *1998; 49:327-332.*

A study examined the characteristics of patients with frequent hospital admissions under Massachusetts public sector managed care and offered recommendations, among them that public sector managed care contracts should provide special attention to subpopulations at high risk for multiple hospital admissions.

Researchers utilized a state tracking system under public sector managed care to evaluate the characteristics of patients with frequent inpatient hospital admissions (i.e., five or more admissions within one of four fiscal years). Frequent hospital users were then compared to those admitted to inpatient units who did not meet frequent hospital user criteria. Results indicated that frequent hospital users tended to be younger Caucasian women with a personality disorder and a substance use background. Frequent admittees were also more likely to be lower functioning and to have increased levels of distress. Although the frequent admissions group accounted for 6 to 8 percent of psychiatric admissions involved in case management, they represented 21 to 27 percent of all inpatient admissions. Frequent hospital users also had longer lengths of stay in hospitals they had not been admitted to in the last 12 months. The authors concluded that public-sector managed care contracts should be developed or revised to provide special attention to subpopulations at high risk for multiple hospital admissions. The development of inpatient provider networks that would empower frequent users to return to the facility that discharged them was also recommended.

Address correspondence to: Jeffrey L. Geller, MD, MPH, Professor of Psychiatry, Director of Public-Sector Psychiatry, University of Massachusetts Medical School, 55 Lake Avenue North, Worcester, MA 01655.

Amphetamine Superior To Placebo in ADHD Treatment Over 15 Months

Gillberg C, Melander H, Von Knorrig AL, Janols LO, Thernlund G, Hagglof B, Eidevall-Wallin L, Gustafsson P, and Kopp S. Long-Term Stimulant Treatment of Children With Attention-Deficit Hyperactivity Disorder Symptoms: A randomized, double-blind, placebo-controlled trial. Archives of General Psychiatry 1997; 54:857-864.

The efficacy of amphetamine versus placebo in children with attention deficit disorder was evaluated in a long-term controlled clinical trial. Results indicated that amphetamine was superior to placebo in the maintenance of better outcomes over 15-months of treatment.

An 18-month controlled clinical trial of amphetamine versus placebo was conducted with children aged 6 to 11 years (N = 62) diagnosed with attention-deficit hyperactivity disorder (ADHD). In the study, subjects received: (1) single-blind treatment with amphetamine the first three months; (2) randomized double-blind treatment with amphetamine or placebo stratified by age (i.e., 6 to 8 years and 9 to 11 years) the next twelve months; and, (3) single-blind placebo the last three months. The primary efficacy measures were the length of randomized double-blind treatment and the Conners Parent (and Teacher) Rating Scales, which measure behavioral abnormality. Results indicated that all subjects had significant improvement on the Conners scales (compared with baseline) in the first three months of the single-blind amphetamine treatment. In the next twelve months of double-blind randomized treatment, the placebo group was significantly more likely than the amphetamine group to be withdrawn from randomized treatment and to show increases in deviance levels. Improvements on the Wechsler Intelligence Scale for Children-Revised (WISC-R) were also noted for the amphetamine condition. Adverse effects of amphetamine were reported to be relatively mild and few. The authors concluded that amphetamine was superior to placebo in the treatment of children with ADHD and that positive effects remained evident after 15 months of treatment.

Address reprint requests to: Christopher Gillberg, MD, PhD, Department of Child and Adolescent Psychiatry, University of Goteborg, Annedals Clinics, S 413 45 Goteborg, Sweden; christopher.gillberg@pediat.gu.se

Psychotherapy Reduces PTSD Symptoms of Adolescent Earthquake Victims

Goenjian AK, Karayan I, Pynoos RS, Minassian D, Najarian LM, Steinberg AM, and Fairbanks LA. Outcome of Psychotherapy Among Early Adolescents After Trauma. American Journal of Psychiatry 1997; 154:536-542.

The efficacy of a school-based trauma/grief-focused psychotherapy intervention was demonstrated with adolescents traumatized by an earthquake. At post-follow-up adolescents who received a school-based psychotherapy intervention (compared to adolescents who did not) had less severe posttraumatic stress symptoms, as well as depressive symptoms that did not worsen.

The effectiveness of a school-based trauma/ grief-focused psychotherapy intervention used to treat early adolescents traumatized by an Armenian earthquake was evaluated. In this natural quasi-experiment the severity of posttraumatic stress symptoms and depressive reactions were compared for a psychotherapy (n = 35) and control (n = 29) condition at preintervention (one-and-a-half years after the earthquake) and postintervention (3 years after the earthquake). (Because of the limited number of mental health personnel, not all schools could receive the intervention.) Results indicated that the severity of posttraumatic symptoms increased significantly for the adolescents in the control schools and decreased significantly for the adolescents who received the psychotherapy intervention. Further, although there were no changes in depressive symptoms for the psychotherapy group, the depressive symptoms in the control group significantly worsened. The authors concluded that: (1) trauma/grief-focused psychotherapy was efficacious in reducing PTSD symptoms and preventing depressive symptoms from getting worse; (2) results support the use of school-based interventions following major disasters; and, (3) Western approaches to psychotherapy can be applied cross-culturally.

Address reprint requests to: Armen K. Goenjian, MD, 4510 East Pacific Coast Highway, Long Beach, CA 90804.

Combining Psychotherapy and Pharmacotherapy Lowers Costs

Goldman W, McCulloch J, Cuffel B, Zarin DA, Suarez A, and Burns BJ. Outpatient Utilization Patterns of Integrated and Split Psychotherapy and Pharmacotherapy for Depression. Psychiatric Services *1998; 49:477-482.*

Utilization and costs are lower when psychotherapy and pharmacotherapy for depressed outpatients is provided by the same psychiatric provider compared with "split" treatment (i.e., a psychiatrist for pharmacotherapy and a nonphysician psychotherapist for psychotherapy).

A quasi-experimental retrospective analysis was performed on claims data from a managed care company over an 18-month period. The utilization and costs of treating depressed patients with "integrated" (n = 191) versus "split" treatment (n = 1,326) were compared. Integrated treatment was defined as when a psychiatrist provided both the psychotherapy and pharmacotherapy, whereas split treatment was defined as when a nonphysican psychotherapist provided psychotherapy and a psychiatrist provided pharmacotherapy. Patients with comorbid bipolar disorder, schizophrenia, and psychotic disorders were not included in the study. Results indicated that patients who received integrated treatment had, on average, significantly fewer outpatient sessions with significantly lower treatment costs. Integrated treatment was also viewed as associated with more treatment episodes over a briefer period of time than was split treatment. Treatment effectiveness and quality of care were not considered. It was concluded that the results do not support the prevailing belief that integrated treatment is more costly than split treatment.

Address correspondence to: William Goldman, MD, United Behavioral Health, 425 Market Street, 27th Floor, San Francisco, CA 94105-2426; bgoldma@uhc.com

Social Disability Is Strong Predictor of Outcomes In ADHD Boys

Greene RW, Biederman J, Faraone SV, Sienna M, and Garcia-Jetton J. Adolescent Outcome of Boys With Attention-Deficit/Hyperactivity Disorder and Social Disability: Results From a 4-Year Longitudinal Follow-Up Study. Journal of Consulting and Clinical Psychology *1997; 65:758-767.*

Social disability (SD) is a strong predictor of poor psychiatric (e.g., anxiety) and social (e.g., substance use) outcomes in boys with attention-deficit/hyperactivity disorder (ADHD).

A longitudinal 4-year follow-up study examined: (1) whether boys with attention-deficit/hyperactivity disorder (ADHD) identified as being "socially disabled" had different longitudinal outcomes than boys with ADHD who were not socially disabled; and (2) whether social disability was a long-term predictor of severe outcomes (e.g., substance use). The sample consisted of 119 boys with ADHD and 107 comparison boys without ADHD between the ages of 6 and 17 years. Social disability (SD) was assessed by maternal ratings on the Social Adjustment Inventory for Children and Adolescents (SAICA). Measures of family functioning, behavior problems, and cognitive and academic functioning were also examined. Results of the four-year follow-up indicated that boys with ADHD + SD had significantly poorer psychiatric (i.e., mood and anxiety disorders) and social (i.e., substance use and disruptive disorders) outcomes, compared with ADHD boys without SD or non-ADHD comparison boys. Further, baseline social disability was a strong predictor of later conduct disorder and substance use disorders in boys with ADHD + SD. The authors concluded that the present longitudinal study confirmed and extended the validity and usefulness of the social disability construct.

Address correspondence to: Dr. Ross W. Green, Pediatric Psychopharmacology Unit, Massachusetts General Hospital, ACC-725, Boston, MA 02114.

Childrens' Day Treatment Gains Maintained at Five Years

Grizenko N. Outcome of Multimodal Day Treatment for Children With Severe Behavior Problems: A Five-Year Follow-Up. Journal of the American Academy of Child and Adolescent Psychiatry *1997; 36:989-997.*

An evaluation of multimodal day treatment for children with severe behavior problems found that program completers maintained improvements in global functioning (i.e., behavior, peer relations, self-perception, and academic performance) at five-year follow-up.

Based on a prospective study, "the long-term outcome of a multimodal day treatment for children with severe behavior problems" was evaluated. Children (N = 33) who had completed a day treatment program were assessed with several standardized measures (e.g., the Revised Child Behavior Profile (RCBP) and the Hare Self-Esteem Scale) at intake, discharge, and five-year follow-up. Parents' willingness to participate in family therapy was required for admission into the study. Results indicated that improvements were maintained in several areas of global functioning, including: behavior, peer relations, self-perception, and academic performance. Stepwise regression analysis demonstrated that four predictors (i.e., parental cooperation, RCBP total and externalizing scores, and problem pregnancy) accounted for 92 percent of the adjusted variance (variance accounted for) in children's behavioral functioning. Parental cooperation was observed to be the most important predictor of children's positive outcomes.

Address reprint requests to: Natalie Grizenko, MD, FRCP, Lyall Pavilion, Douglas Hospital, 6875 Lasalle Boulevard, Verdun, Quebec, Canada H4H 1R3.

Assertive Community Treatment Engages and Retains SPMI

Herinckx HA, Kinney RF, Clarke GN, and Paulson RI. Assertive Community Treatment Versus Usual Care in Engaging and Retaining Clients With Severe Mental Illness. Psychiatric Services *1997; 48:1297-1306.*

Compared to usual care, assertive community treatment demonstrated a greater ability to engage and retain clients with severe mental illness.

In an observational study that used random assignment, two assertive community treatment teams (n = 116) were compared to usual care (n = 58) for clients with serious and persistent mental illness. Assertive community treatment was designed to improve client engagement and retention through assertive outreach, small caseload ratios, shared caseloads, and participation by the consumer in treatment. In this study one of the assertive community treatment teams was staffed by "self-identified mental health consumers with a DSM-III-R axis I diagnosis, [whereas] members of the other assertive community treatment team reported no diagnosable mental illness." Results indicated that the assertive community treatment teams had significantly better retention (68 percent) than usual care (43 percent). There were no significant differences in client retention between the two assertive community treatment teams. Further, in both treatments clients were followed for up to 870 days, and the first nine months were associated with the greatest risk for client dropout. Dissatisfaction with treatment was twice as likely to be related to client dropout in the usual care treatment condition. Lastly, it was observed that each night clients spent homeless in the last six months prior to admission was related to a 14 percent increase in the chances of dropout. It was concluded that engagement and retention in community mental health care was better demonstrated through assertive community treatment.

Address correspondence to: Heidi A. Herinckx, MA, Regional Research Institute,

Portland State University, P.O. Box 751, Portland, OR 97207.

Personal Therapy for Schizophrenia Most Effective With Stable Home Life

Hogarty GE, Kornblith SJ, Greenwald D, DiBarry AL, Cooley S, Ulrich RF, Carter M, and Flesher S. Three-Year Trials of Personal Therapy Among Schizophrenic Patients Living With or Independent of Family, I: Description of Study and Effects on Relapse Rates. American Journal of Psychiatry 1997; 154:1504-1513.

The effectiveness of "personal therapy" in the treatment of patients with schizophrenia or schizoaffective disorder was evaluated in two concurrent three-year therapy trials. Results observed that patients who lived with their families (Trial 1) and received personal therapy had fewer relapses. However, patients who lived alone or with non-relatives (Trial 2) and received personal therapy had significantly more relapses.

Two concurrent three-year randomized therapy trials were conducted to evaluate the effectiveness of "personal therapy" (e.g., an approach developed to reduce late-relapse) in hospital patients discharged with a diagnosis of schizophrenia or schizoaffective disorder. Antipsychotic medication was prescribed to all patients in both trials and adjusted to the minimal effective dose. In Trial 1, patients who lived with family (N = 97) were randomly assigned to one of four conditions: personal therapy; family therapy; combined personal and family therapy; or supportive therapy. In Trial 2, patients who lived alone or with non-relatives (N = 54) were assigned randomly to personal therapy or supportive therapy. Significant differences between the two study groups were noted in age, gender, race, marital status, and psychiatric history. Relapse was the main outcome measure in this study. Over the course of the three-year study, 29 percent of patients (N = 151) experienced a psychotic relapse and 16 percent had a nonpsychotic affective relapse. Results indicated that patients who lived with their families (Trial 1) and received personal therapy had fewer relapses than did patients who received family therapy or supportive therapy. However, patients who lived alone or with non-relatives and received personal therapy (Trial 2) had significantly more relapses than did patients who received supportive therapy. It was concluded that personal therapy reduced relapse more effectively in patients who lived with their family, but increased relapse in patients who lived alone or with non-relatives. The authors suggest that personal therapy might be best initiated with patients who evidence greater stability in their symptoms and residential circumstances.

Address reprint requests to: Professor Gerard E. Hogarty, MSW, Western Psychiatric Institute and Clinic, 3811 O'Hara Street, Pittsburgh, PA 15213.

Study Questions Effectiveness of Brief Treatment for Schizophrenia

Hogarty GE, Greenwald D, Ulrich RF, Kornblith SJ, DiBarry AL, Cooley S, Carter M, and Flesher S. Three-Year Trials of Personal Therapy Among Schizophrenic Patients Living With or Independent of Family, II: Effects on Adjustment of Patients. American Journal of Psychiatry 1997; 154, 1514-1524.

Examined the effects of psychosocial treatment (i.e., personal therapy, supportive therapy, and family therapy) on the social and personal adjustment of patients with schizophrenia and schizoaffective disorder. Results indicated that patients who received "personal therapy" had more improvements in their social adjustment (i.e., role performance).

The second part of this three-year randomized therapy trial (see above) attempted to examine the independent effects of psychosocial treatment on patients' social and personal adjustment. In order to maximize the independent effects of treatment, relapsed patients were reentered into their original treatment condition upon recovery. Assessments of social adjustment (i.e., role performance) and personal adjustment (i.e., residual symptoms) were completed by clinicians, patients, and (where applicable) families at baseline and at six-month intervals thereafter. Measures of social adjustment included: The Social Adjustment Scale II and the Major Role Adjustment Inventory. Personal adjustment was measured with the Brief Psychiatric Rating Scale (BPRS) and the Raskin Depression Scale, for example. Families rated patient adjustment with the Katz Adjustment

Scale. Results were as follows: (1) overall, patients who received "personal therapy" (Trial 1 & 2) had more improvement in their role performance, but not much improvement in their symptoms; (2) patients who received personal therapy and lived with their family (Trial 1) had the best overall performance outcomes; (3) patients who received family therapy (Trial 1) had more improvements in their residual symptoms; and (4) patients who received personal therapy and lived alone or with non-relatives (Trial 2) had more improved work performance and relationships (outside the home). The authors concluded that personal therapy showed broad improvements in social adjustment (i.e., role performance) and that these improvements continued through the second and third years of the study. The effectiveness of brief treatments for schizophrenia was questioned in light of the continued improvements patients made in long-term personal therapy.

Address reprint requests to: Professor Gerard E. Hogarty, MSW, Western Psychiatric Institute and Clinic, 3811 O'Hara Street, Pittsburgh, PA 15213.

Self-Report Outcome Tool Is Reliable and Valid for Inpatients

Holcomb WR, Parker JC, and Leong GB. Outcomes of Inpatients Treated on a VA Psychiatric Unit and a Substance Abuse Treatment Unit. Psychiatric Services 1997; 48:699-704.

The utility of an outcome measurement tool, the Treatment Outcome Profile (TOP), in documenting treatment effectiveness in two inpatient hospital units (i.e., psychiatric and substance abuse) was evaluated. Results indicated significant treatment gains in both units. Support for the reliability and validity of the TOP was demonstrated.

A pre-post research design was used with an inpatient psychiatric unit (n = 66) and an inpatient substance abuse unit (n = 88) to evaluate the utility of the Treatment Outcome Profile (TOP). The TOP is a self-report instrument containing four outcome scales: "quality of life, symptoms, level of functioning, and patient satisfaction with services (at discharge only)." Patients in both inpatient units indicated significant treatment gains. Improvements were obtained by both groups in symptoms, quality of life, and level of functioning.

It was also noted that patients in the psychiatric unit self-reported more impairment at admission and evidenced less therapeutic gain at discharge, when compared to patients in the substance abuse unit. Both the psychiatric and substance abuse groups reported high patient satisfaction (80 and 91 percent) and low dissatisfaction (7.5 and 2 percent), respectively, relative to other service industries (e.g., general medical care, department stores). The authors concluded that the TOPS scales "demonstrate acceptable overall levels of internal reliability" and that "the instrument demonstrates both content and predictive validity [and] is a valid and sensitive outcome measurement tool."

Address correspondence to: William R. Holcomb, PhD, Behavioral Health Concepts, Inc., 1001 Cherry Street, Suite 207, Columbia, MO 65201.

Persons With Panic Symptoms Have Higher Health Care Utilization

Katerndahl DA and Realini JP. Use of Health Care Services by Persons With Panic Symptoms. Psychiatric Services 1997; 48:1027-1032.

Subjects from a community-based sample who had panic symptoms used health care services at a significantly higher rate than those without such symptoms, and the difference was attributed to help-seeking for the panic symptoms.

A randomly selected community-based sample of subjects with panic symptoms (n = 97) was compared to a matched group (i.e., age, gender, and race) of control subjects (n = 97) without panic symptoms. Information about health care utilization was collected over a two-month period (i.e., health care sources, barriers to access, and levels of medical insurance coverage). Results indicated that "subjects with panic symptoms had [significantly] higher utilization rates for the services of psychiatrists and psychologists and for ambulance services than control subjects." Both groups had similar barriers to health care access, but the control group had more types of services covered by their medical insurance. It was noted that although subjects with panic symptoms had less medical insurance coverage and similar barriers to access, they had a higher rate of health care usage compared to the control subjects. The increased utilization of health care by subjects with panic symptoms was noted to be due "to help seeking specifically for symptoms of panic."

Address correspondence to: David A. Katerndahl, MD, MA, Department of Family Practice, University of Texas Health Science Center at San Antonio, 7703 Floyd Curl Drive, San Antonio, TX 78284.

Exposure and Cognitive Restructuring Are Effective in Treating PTSD

Marks I, Lovell K, Noshirvani H, Livanou M, and Thrasher S. Treatment of Posttraumatic Stress Disorder by Exposure and/or Cognitive Restructuring. Archives of General Psychiatry 1998; 55:317-325.

Three types of therapeutic interventions (i.e., prolonged exposure, cognitive restructuring, and relaxation) were used over 10 sessions to treat patients with posttraumatic stress disorder (PTSD). Results indicated that prolonged exposure and cognitive restructuring were therapeutically effective in improving PTSD symptoms through six-month follow-up, whereas relaxation demonstrated only moderate improvements.

A controlled study of the effectiveness of cognitive restructuring, prolonged exposure, and relaxation was conducted with patients (N = 87) diagnosed with posttraumatic stress disorder (PTSD). Patients were randomly assigned to 10 sessions in one of four conditions: (1) cognitive restructuring alone; (2) prolonged exposure alone (live or imagined); (3) cognitive restructuring and prolonged exposure; or (4) relaxation alone. PTSD was measured with the Clinician-Administered PTSD Scale (CAPS 2), the Impact of Events Scale (IES), and PTSD Symptoms Scale. Results indicated that cognitive restructuring, prolonged exposure, and their combination were therapeutic in improving PTSD symptoms through six-month follow-up. Relaxation demonstrated only moderate improvement in PTSD symptoms.

Address reprint requests to: Isaac Marks, MD, Institute of Psychiatry, London SE58AF, England; I.Marks@iop.bpmf.ac.uk

SSRI Improves Symptoms of Chronic Posttraumatic Stress Disorder

Marshall RD, Schneier FR, Fallon BA, Knight CBG, Abbate LA, Goetz D, Campeas R, and Liebowitz MR. An Open Trial of Paroxetine in Patients With Noncombat-Related, Chronic Posttraumatic Stress Disorder. Journal of Clinical Psychopharmacology 1998; 18, 10-18.

The selective serotonin reuptake inhibitor paroxetine resulted in significant reductions in symptoms of patients diagnosed with chronic posttraumatic stress disorder (PTSD) unrelated to combat. There also was a negative correlation between positive responsiveness to paroxetine and cumulative childhood trauma.

The efficacy of a 12-week open trial of paroxetine (Paxil; a selective serotonin reuptake inhibitor or SSRI) for patients (N = 19) diagnosed with "noncombat-related, chronic posttraumatic stress disorder [PTSD]" was examined. The physician, the patient, and an independent evaluator made assessments. PTSD symptoms were primarily assessed with the Davidson Trauma Scale (DTS) and the Impact of Event Scale (IES). Established rating scales for anxiety, depression, and general symptoms were also used. Results indicated significant improvements in all three PTSD symptom clusters (i.e., intrusive, avoidance, and arousal), as well as in anxiety, depression, and dissociative symptoms. There were reductions of 48 percent noted in PTSD symptom scores. Further, a negative correlation was observed between the effectiveness of the pharmacological response to paroxetine and the patients' cumulative childhood trauma. Based on these findings the authors recommend that a placebo-controlled clinical trial of paroxetine be conducted.

Address reprint requests to: Randall D. Marshall, MD, Director of Trauma Studies, Anxiety Disorders Clinic, Unit 13, New York State Psychiatric Institute, 722 West 168th Street, New York, NY 10032.

Affiliation With AA Following Treatment Improves Outcomes

Morgenstern J, Labouvie E, McCrady BS, Kahler CW, and Frey RM. (1997). Affiliation With

Alcoholics Anonymous After Treatment: A Study of Its Therapeutic Effects and Mechanisms of Action. Journal of Consulting and Clinical Psychology 1997; 65:768-777.

Increased Alcoholics Anonymous (AA) affiliation post-treatment predicts less substance use and is related to better sustained motivation, self-efficacy, and more active coping.

In a prospective correlational study, the efficacy of Alcoholics Anonymous (AA) after formal treatment was evaluated. Participants included 100 individuals admitted to a chemical dependency program at two private hospitals and diagnosed with a current DSM-IV drug use disorder (27 percent), alcohol use disorder (43 percent), or both a drug and alcohol use disorder (30 percent). Participants were assessed at baseline, spent an average of 21 days in intensive treatment, and were followed-up at one and six months after discharge. AA attendance and four processes of change were assessed: (1) self-efficacy, with the Situational Confidence Questionnaire (SCQ); (2) commitment to abstinence, with a subscale of the Addiction Treatment Attitude Questionnaire (ATAQ); (3) cognitive and behavioral coping, with a modified version of the Processes of Change (POC) Questionnaire and, (4) primary appraisal of harm, with the Primary Appraisal Measure (PAM), developed by the authors. The main outcome measure was the percentage of days a substance was used at one and six months. Results indicated that better outcomes (e.g., less substance use) were predicted by increased AA affiliation. AA affiliation was also related to maintenance of motivation and self-efficacy and to an increase in active coping efforts. The authors point out "the value of embedding a test of explanatory models in an evaluation study."

Address correspondence to: Dr. Jon Morgenstern, Department of Psychiatry, Mount Sinai School of Medicine, Box 1230, One Gustave L. Levy Place, New York, NY 10029-6574; jon_morgenstern@smtplink.mssm.edu

Higher Costs Associated With ECT May Be Result Of Selection Bias

Olfson M, Marcus S, Sackeim HA, Thompson J, and Pincus HA. *Use of ECT for the Inpatient Treatment of Recurrent Major Depression.* American Journal of Psychiatry 1998; 155:22-29.

When patient, diagnostic, and hospital differences are controlled, prompt use of electroconvulsive therapy in the first five days of admission resulted in shorter stays at a lower cost.

A retrospective analysis of national data from the 1993 Healthcare Cost and Utilization Project examined the frequency and distribution, as well as the cost and treatment length, of electroconvulsive therapy (ECT) for hospital inpatients (N = 1,754) diagnosed with recurrent major depression. Results indicated that 9 percent of inpatients with recurrent major depression received ECT and 59 percent of these patients "received their initial ECT session within the first five days after hospital admission." Patients who were older, white, had private insurance, and lived in wealthier areas were significantly more likely to have received ECT. These patients tended to have longer and more costly hospital admissions. When several demographic, diagnostic, and hospital characteristics were controlled for, prompt ECT within the first five days of admission was associated with significantly shorter stays at a lower cost. The authors concluded that the longer stays and higher costs of ECT observed in inpatient hospital settings may be the result of patient selection.

Address reprint requests to: Mark Olfson, MD, MPH, New York State Psychiatric Institute, 722 West 168th Street, New York, NY 10032.

Paroxetine (Paxil) May Be Important Alternative for Treatment of Depression With Anxiety

Ravindran AV, Judge R, Hunter BN, Bray J, and Morton NH. *A Double-Blind, Multicenter Study in Primary Care Comparing Paroxetine and Clomipramine in Patients With Depression and Associated Anxiety.* Journal of Clinical Psychiatry 1997; 58:112-118.

A comparison of paroxetine and clomipramine for treating depression with associated anxiety found no significant differences in efficacy, although patients receiving paroxetine were better able to tolerate adverse experiences.

The efficacy of a 12-week comparative, double-blind clinical trial of paroxetine (Paxil, a selective serotonin reuptake inhibitor or SSRI; n = 500) and clomipramine (Anafranil, a tricyclic antidepressant; n = 502) was conducted with 1,002 depressed patients with associated anxiety. Patients in this multicenter study were drawn from 121 primary care facilities from 10 countries. After an initial screening into the study, "clinical assessments were made at baseline and after two, four, six, eight, and 12 weeks of active treatment." Assessments were made with the Montgomery-Asberg Depression Rating Scale (MADRS), the Clinical Anxiety Scale (CAS), and the Clinical Global Impressions (CGI) scale. Results indicated no significant differences in the efficacy of paroxetine and clomipramine. However, paroxetine was better tolerated in terms of treatment-emergent adverse experiences. The authors concluded that paroxetine's better tolerability may make it an important alternative for the treatment of depression with associated anxiety.

Address reprint requests to: Arun V. Ravindran, MB, PhD, Royal Ottawa Hospital, Research Department, 1145 Carling Avenue, Ottawa, Ontario, Canada, K1Z 7K4.

Clozapine More Effective and Costs Less Than Haloperidol

Rosenheck R, Cramer J, Xu W, Thomas J, Henderson W, Frisman L, Fye C, and Charney D. A Comparison of Clozapine and Haloperidol in Hospitalized Patients With Refractory Schizophrenia. New England Journal of Medicine 1997; 337:809-815.

In a comparison of clozapine and haloperidol in treating refractory schizophrenia, clozapine resulted in more consistent long-term use with fewer symptoms and fewer days of psychiatric hospitalization. Overall costs appeared similar when per capita costs to society were compared to per capita drug costs.

The effectiveness and cost of clozapine (Clozaril, n = 205) and haloperidol (Haldol, n = 218) were compared in a one-year randomized double-blind study of hospitalized patients with refractory schizophrenia. Patients were drawn from one of 15 Veterans Affairs (VA) medical centers and had been hospitalized for schizophrenia for more than 30 days in the previous year. Several measures were used to assess outcome, including the Structured Clinical Interview for the Positive and Negative Syndrome Scale. Social-rehabilitation and case-management services were provided as indicated. Results observed that patients assigned to the clozapine group were significantly more likely to remain on this medication for the year (57 percent), as compared to the haloperidol group (28 percent). Patients in the clozapine group also evidenced significantly lower symptom levels, had fewer days of psychiatric hospitalization, and had more units of outpatient services than the haloperidol group. In terms of cost, the clozapine group had a significantly lower per capita cost to society (i.e., $2,734), but a significantly higher per capita cost for medication (i.e., $2,832). Finally, the clozapine group had fewer side effects and less tardive dyskinesia, but did have three patients who developed and fully recovered from agranulocytosis (a white blood cell disorder). The authors concluded that clozapine was "somewhat more effective" with less side effects and similar in cost to haloperidol.

Address reprint requests to: Robert Rosenheck, MD, Northeast Program Evaluation Center (182), VA Connecticut Healthcare System, 950 Campbell Avenue, West Haven, CT 06516.

Study Fails To Support Imipramine in Treating Social Phobia

Simpson HB, Schneier FR, Campeas RB, Marshall RD, Fallon BA, Davies S, Klein DF, and Liebowitz MR. Imipramine in the Treatment of Social Phobia. Journal of Clinical Psychopharmacology 1998; 18:132-135.

The efficacy of imipramine for patients with a primary diagnosis of social phobia was not supported in an eight-week open trial.

This study examined the efficacy of imipramine for patients (N = 15) with a primary diagnosis of social phobia. Patients received one-week of placebo followed by an eight-week open trial of imipramine. The open trial was completed by nine patients (60 percent), while six patients (40 percent) dropped out of the trial early due to adverse side effects. The Clinical Global Impression (CGI) scale, the Liebowitz Social Anxiety Scale (LSAS), the Hamilton Rating Scale for Depression (HAM-D), and the Liebowitz Social Phobic Disorders (LSPD)-Overall Severity scale were used to evaluate efficacy outcomes. Results indicated that reductions in outcomes with imipramine were comparable to those of placebo. Further, all patients had a significant problem with the side effects of imipramine. The efficacy of imipramine in treating social phobia was not supported. "The utility of a small open-pilot trial in psychopharmacology research" was noted.

Address reprint requests to: H. Blair Simpson, MD, PhD, New York State Psychiatric Institute, Anxiety Disorders Clinic, 722 West 168th Street, Unit 13, New York, NY 10032.

Intensive Case Management of SPMI Older Adults Evaluated

Speer DC and Stiles PG. Severely and Persistently Mentally Ill Older Adults and Case Management. Continuum *1997; 4:13-25.*

Despite an intensive case management program over a two-year period, older adults with severe and persistent mental illness (SPMI) were consistently rated by case managers as moderate in role functioning (e.g., involvement, communication) and the consumers rated themselves moderate in stress, depression, and physical symptoms.

An outcomes evaluation of 20 older adults with SPMI who received intensive case management (i.e., aggressive outreach with in vivo services) in a supported housing program was conducted. Consumers were assessed for stress, depression, and physical symptoms (e.g., The Perceived Stress Scale) every six months over a two-year period. Case managers also rated consumers on several scales of role-functioning (e.g., involvement, communication). Results indicated that stress, depression, and physical symptoms were present for consumers in moderate degrees over the two-year period without much change. Likewise, consumers were rated moderate in their "involvement and communication with others, taking care of household maintenance tasks, and participating in outside social activities." The evaluation noted two additional observations in regards to stress: (1) although consumers scored moderately on the Perceived Stress Scale, half of the sample reached the age-stratified criterion for pathological stress at least once, and yet functioned reasonably well; and (2) the consumers who chose to live in a foster home (n = 4) reported stress levels that were notably lower than the stress levels reported by consumers who decided to live independently.

Address correspondence to: David C. Speer, PhD, Associate Professor, Department of Aging and Mental Health, Louis de la Parte Florida Mental Health Institute, University of South Florida, Tampa, FL.

Study Finds Link Between High-Volume Providers and Shorter Inpatient Stays

Thomas MR, Fryer GE, Rosenberg SA, Kassner C, Dubovsky SL, and Shore JH. Examining the Link Between High-Volume Providers and Shorter Inpatient Stays. Psychiatric Services *1997; 48:1396-1398.*

Patients treated by high-volume psychiatric providers had significantly shorter lengths of inpatient psychiatric stays than those treated by low-volume psychiatric providers.

The study investigated whether there were differences in inpatient lengths of stay between patient admissions (N = 1,397) treated by high-volume versus low-volume psychiatric providers in a retrospective analysis of hospital records. Inpatient psychiatric admissions between 1985 and 1992 were examined, and due to hospital restructuring, divided into two time periods: the traditional psychiatric unit (1985-1989) and the alternatives program (1990-1992). High-volume psychiatric providers were defined as the fewest number of psychiatrists who in total "served half of all admissions that year." When combined by time period, results indicated that the length of stay for patients with high-volume providers (i.e., 11.3 days) was significantly shorter than the length of stay for patients with low-volume providers (i.e., 16.2 days). When examined separately, both the traditional psychiatric unit (i.e., 17.4 vs. 23.4 days) and the alternatives program (i.e., 5.6 vs. 11.3 days) were also significantly different, with shorter lengths of stay for patients with high-volume providers.

Address correspondence to: Marshall R. Thomas, MD, Assistant Professor, Director of Acute Care and Inpatient Services, University of Colorado Health Sciences Center, 4455 East 12th Avenue, Denver, CO 80220.

International Trial Concludes Olanzapine Superior to Haloperidol

Tollefson GD, Beasley Jr. CM, Tran PV, Street JS, Krueger JA, Tamura RN, Graffeo KA, and Thieme ME. Olanzapine Versus Haloperidol in the Treatment of Schizophrenia and Schizoaffective and Schizophreniform Disorders: Results of an International Collaborative Trial. American Journal of Psychiatry 1997; 154:457-465.

Olanzapine had greater efficacy than haloperidol with significantly fewer side-effects in the treatment of schizophrenia and related psychotic disorders.

A prospective double-blind six-week clinical trial compared the efficacy and safety of an atypical anti-psychotic (i.e., olanzapine, n = 1,336) and a conventional (i.e., haloperidol, n = 660) anti-psychotic in the treatment of schizophrenia and related psychotic disorders. The trial took place over 14-months at 174 sites in 17 countries throughout Europe and North America. Changes in baseline to endpoint total scores on the Brief Psychiatric Rating Scale (BPRS) were used as the primary measure of efficacy. Secondary measures included negative and positive symptoms, depression, drug side-effects, and overall drug safety, and were measured with the BPRS, the Montgomery-Asberg Depression Rating Scale, and the Clinical Global Impression (CGI) scale. Results indicated that olanzapine was clinically superior to haloperidol on all primary and secondary efficacy measures. Further, patients who received olanzapine were more likely to complete the six-week clinical trial (i.e., 66 vs. 47 percent) and to experience significantly fewer disruptions in treatment due to adverse drug reactions or lack of drug efficacy. It was concluded in terms of efficacy and safety that olanzapine was superior to haloperidol.

Address reprint requests to: Gary D. Tollefson, MD, PhD, Lilly Research Laboratories, Eli Lilly and Company, Lilly Corporate Center, Drop Code 0538, Indianapolis, IN 46285.

Olanzapine More Effective With Fewer Side-Effects Than Risperidone

Tran PV, Hamilton SH, Kuntz AJ, Potvin JH, Andersen SW, Beasley Jr. C, and Tollefson GD. Double-Blind Comparison of Olanzapine Versus Risperidone in the Treatment of Schizophrenia and Other Psychotic Disorders. Journal of Clinical Psychopharmacology 1997; 17:407-418.

In an international clinical trial, olanzapine had greater efficacy than risperidone with significantly fewer side-effects in the treatment of schizophrenia and related psychotic disorders.

A prospective double-blind 28-week clinical trial compared the efficacy and safety of olanzapine (n = 172) and risperidone (n = 167) in the treatment of schizophrenia and related psychotic disorders. The trial involved 35 investigational sites in nine countries. Treatment efficacy was measured with the Brief Psychiatric Rating Scale (BPRS) and its related or extracted subscales, the Clinical Global Impression (CGI) scale, and the Scale for the Assessment of Negative Symptoms (SANS). Several measures were also used to assess adverse events. Results indicated that olanzapine and risperidone were both effective and safe. However, compared to risperidone, olanzapine showed: (1) significantly greater efficacy with negative symptoms; (2) a better overall response rate to positive and negative symptoms; and, (3) significantly fewer adverse events (e.g., sexual dysfunction and other drug side-effects). The authors concluded that "olanzapine seemed to have a risk-versus-benefit advantage."

Address reprint requests to: Pierre V. Tran, MD, Lilly Research Laboratories, Eli Lilly and Company, Lilly Corporate Center, Drop Code 0538, Indianapolis, IN 46285.

Study Reveals Predictors Of Suicidal Intent in Depressed Patients

Van Gastel A, Schotte C, and Maes M. The Prediction of Suicidal Intent in Depressed Patients. Acta Psychiatrica Scandinavica 1997; 96,:254-259.

Depression severity, previous psychiatric hospitalizations, and lower global functioning in the previous year are significantly related to suicidal ideation, but not to attempted suicide, in depressed inpatients. The presence of a comorbid personality disorder is a significant predictor of both suicidal ideation and attempted suicide.

The study examined predictors of suicidal ideation or attempted suicide in 338 depressed inpatients admitted into a 30-bed psychiatric unit between 1986 and 1994. Patients received a diagnosis based on the Structured Clinical Interview for DSM-III (SCID) Patient Version, and were classified into one of five groups: major depression without melancholia (n = 152); major depression with melancholia (n = 79); adjustment disorder with depressed mood (n = 52); dysthymic disorder (n = 41); and, psychotic depression (n = 14). Severity of illness was assessed with: the Hamilton Depression Rating Scale (HDRS); the Beck Depression Inventory (BDI); the Zung Self-Rating Depression Scale (SDS); and, the Zung Self-Rating Anxiety Scale (SAS). Suicide attempts that occurred during the SCID index period that were serious enough to require hospitalization were counted. A composite of the BDI and the SDS was used to measure a Suicidal Ideation Score (SIS). Results observed that suicidal ideation was related significantly to: (1) depression severity; (2) previous psychiatric hospitalizations; and (3) the presence of a lower global assessment of functioning (GAF) in the year prior to hospitalization. More specifically, the strongest predictors of suicidal ideation were: feelings of guilt, depressed mood, hopelessness, loss of interest, and low self-esteem. A higher SIS for patients with a more severe subtype of depression (e.g., psychotic depression) was also noted. Although none of the above predictors of suicidal ideation were related to attempted suicide, depressed patients with a comorbid personality disorder had significantly more suicide attempts and evidenced more suicidal ideation.

Address correspondence to: Dr. Michael Maes, Clinical Research Center for Mental Health, University Department of Psychiatry, AZ Stuivenberg, 267 Lange Beeldekensstraat, 2060 Antwerp, Belgium.

Introduction of Risperidone Shifts Use of Mental Health Resources

Viale G, Mechling L, Maislin G, Durkin M, Engelhart L, and Lawrence BJ. Impact of Risperidone on the Use of Mental Health Care Resources. Psychiatric Services 1997; 48:1153-1159.

A study of health care utilization and costs both before and after the introduction of risperidone in patients with treatment-refractory schizoaffective disorder or schizophrenia found that risperidone was associated with less use of inpatient and residential services. Although pharmaceutical care offset the decreased provider-delivered costs, overall costs were not raised significantly.

Researchers conducted a retrospective analysis of a county's pharmacy and mental health care services databases to evaluate the effectiveness of risperidone for "patients with treatment-refractory schizophrenia or schizoaffective disorder." Changes in economic outcomes (e.g., drug costs versus the cost offset of reduced utilization of other services) and psychiatric health care utilization (e.g., number of hospitalizations) were examined for patients (N = 139) at least six months prior to and six months following risperidone treatment. Results noted reductions in the number days in acute care inpatient facilities (26 percent less) and in the number of days in residential treatment (57 percent less) after the introduction of risperidone. Reductions were complemented by increases in treatment planning (52 percent more visits) and day treatment (89 percent more visits). Overall, treatment costs were slightly higher (3.4 percent) after risperidone was initiated, with an average increase of $373 per patient per year. The authors concluded that risperidone treatment decreased the utilization of provider-delivered services (- $1,210) through the increased utilization of pharmaceutical care (+ $1,583), without a significant increase in health care costs.

Address correspondence to: Gary Viale, PharmD, (Assistant Clinical Professor, University of California, San Francisco) Director of Pharmacy, Department of Mental Health, Santa Clara Valley Health and Hospitals System, 2221 Enborg Lane, San Jose, CA 95128.

Collaborative Care Pays Off in Treatment of Major Depression

Von Korff M, Katon W, Bush T, Lin EHB, Simon GE, Saunders K, Ludman E, Walker E, and Unutzer J. Treatment Costs, Cost Offset, and Cost-Effectiveness of Collaborative Management of Depression. Psychosomatic Medicine 1998; 60:143-149.

Primary care patients with major depression who received Collaborative Care had more cost-effective treatment than those who received usual care.

Two randomized, controlled trials evaluated the "treatment costs, cost-offset effects, and cost-effectiveness" of Collaborative Care versus Usual Care for patients with major or minor depression in primary care. In Trial 1 (N = 217), Collaborative Care was provided by a consulting psychiatrist (in co-management with a primary physician) through "enhanced management of pharmacotherapy and psychoeducational interventions to enhance adherence." In Trial 2 (N = 153), Collaborative Care was provided by a consulting psychologist (in co-management with a primary physician and in consultation with a psychiatrist for medication management) in the form of "brief cognitive-behavioral therapy and enhanced patient education." Interventions in both trials were provided over a four- to six-week period. Results indicated that the increased treatment costs of Collaborative Care were mainly due to the intervention visits provided by psychiatrists (Trial 1) and psychologists (Trial 2). A cost-offset effect was observed, in that patients with major depression (not minor depression) used less specialty mental health services with Collaborative Care. Further, cost-effectiveness increased for patients with major depression (not minor depression) in Collaborative Care treatment. When the cost per patient treated successfully (i.e., at least a 50 percent decrease in depressive symptom scores at four-month follow-up) was examined, Collaborative Care was less costly than Usual Care. It was concluded that patients with major depression may receive more value from their treatment services through the provision of Collaborative Care.

Address reprint requests to: Michael Von Korff, ScD, Center for Health Studies, Group Health Cooperative of Puget Sound, 1730 Minor Avenue, Suite 1600, Seattle, WA 98101.

Anticonvulsant Has Modest Effect on Subjects With Bipolar Depression

Young LT, Robb JC, Patelis-Siotis I, MacDonald C, and Joffe RT. Acute Treatment of Bipolar Depression With Gabapentin. Biological Psychiatry 1997; 42:851-853.

The anticonvulsant gabapentin was administered to 15 patients with bipolar disorder, yielding a significant yet modest reduction in symptoms among those subjects who responded to the medication.

Researchers examined the efficacy of gabapentin, a novel anticonvulsant, in the treatment of bipolar depression with a six-week open-label case series of 15 patients. Subjects had been treated unsuccessfully with at least two mood stabilizers in the past and met criteria for DSM-IV bipolar disorder I or II based on the Structured Clinical Interview. Both the Young Mania Rating Scale and the Hamilton Depression Rating Scale were used to rate mood at baseline and weekly. Results indicated a modest but significant reduction in depressed mood on the Hamilton. Responders to the medication included 53 percent of the sample. A dose-response relationship was not demonstrated. The authors concluded that the antidepressant effects of gabapentin were supported by a subgroup of responders.

Address reprint requests to: L. Trevor Young, MD, Room 3G57, Health Sciences Center, 1200 Main Street W., Hamilton, Ontario, Canada, L8N 3Z5.

Appendix A
Selected Instruments

MHSIP Consumer Survey

In order to improve mental health services we need to know what you think about the treatment you receive, the people who provide it, and the results of this treatment.

DEMOGRAPHICS

Age _____   Male _____   Female _____

Race/Ethnicity   African American _____   Asian _____   Native American _____
                 Caucasian _____   Hispanic/Latino _____   Other _____

Do you currently receive Medicaid? Yes _____   No _____

Please indicate your agreement with each of the following statements by circling the number that best represents your opinion. If the question is about something you have not experienced, circle the number 9, to indicate that this item is "not applicable" to you.

		Strongly Agree	Agree	I am Neutral	Disagree	Strongly Disagree	Not Applicable
1	I liked the services that I received here.	1	2	3	4	5	9
2	If I had other choices, I would still get services from this agency.	1	2	3	4	5	9
3	I would recommend this agency to a friend or family member.	1	2	3	4	5	9
4	I was able to get the services I needed even if I couldn't pay for them.	1	2	3	4	5	9
5	The location of services was convenient (parking, public transportation, distance, etc).	1	2	3	4	5	9
6	Staff were willing to see me as often as I felt it was necessary.	1	2	3	4	5	9
7	Staff returned my calls within 24 hours.	1	2	3	4	5	9
8	Services were available at times that were good for me.	1	2	3	4	5	9
9	I was able to get the services I thought I needed.	1	2	3	4	5	9
10	I was able to see a psychiatrist when I wanted to.	1	2	3	4	5	9
11	Staff here believe I can grow, change and recover.	1	2	3	4	5	9
12	I felt comfortable asking questions about my treatment and medication.	1	2	3	4	5	9
13	I felt free to complain.	1	2	3	4	5	9
14	Staff respected my rights.	1	2	3	4	5	9
15	I was given information about my rights.	1	2	3	4	5	9
		Strongly Agree	Agree	I am Neutral	Disagree	Strongly Disagree	Not Applicable

Source: Mental Health Statistical Improvement Program: MHSIP Consumer Survey.

16	Staff encouraged me to take responsibility for how I live my life.	1	2	3	4	5	9
17	Staff told me what side-effects to watch for.	1	2	3	4	5	9
18	Staff respected my wishes about who is, and is not to be given information about my treatment.	1	2	3	4	5	9
19	I, not staff, decided my treatment goals.	1	2	3	4	5	9
20	Staff were sensitive to my cultural/ethnic background.	1	2	3	4	5	9
21	Staff helped me obtain information so that I could take charge of managing my illness.	1	2	3	4	5	9
22	Staff believe that I can choose what is best for me.	1	2	3	4	5	9
23	I was encouraged to use consumer-run programs (support groups, drop-in centers, crisis phone line, etc.).	1	2	3	4	5	9
24	Some of the services I received were not helpful.	1	2	3	4	5	9
25	Staff I worked with were competent and knowledgeable.	1	2	3	4	5	9

AS A DIRECT RESULT OF SERVICES I RECEIVED:

26	I deal more effectively with daily problems.	1	2	3	4	5	9
27	I feel better about myself.	1	2	3	4	5	9
28	I am better able to control my life.	1	2	3	4	5	9
29	I experienced harmful medication side-effects.	1	2	3	4	5	9
30	I am better able to deal with crises.	1	2	3	4	5	9
31	I am getting along better with my family.	1	2	3	4	5	9
32	I do better in social situations.	1	2	3	4	5	9
33	I do better in school/work.	1	2	3	4	5	9
34	I do better in my leisure time.	1	2	3	4	5	9
35	My housing situation has improved.	1	2	3	4	5	9
36	My symptoms are not bothering me as much.	1	2	3	4	5	9
37	I have become more independent.	1	2	3	4	5	9
38	The medication I am taking help me control symptoms that used to bother me.	1	2	3	4	5	9
39	I have become more effective in getting what I need.	1	2	3	4	5	9
40	I can deal better with people and situations that used to be a problem for me.	1	2	3	4	5	9

Mental Health Statistical Improvement Program (MHSIP) Consumer Survey (Short Version)

MHSIP Short Form

Based on your care received last year from [health plan name], please indicate your agreement/disagreement with each statement by circling what best represents your opinion. Response options for all questions are: **I Strongly Agree / Agree / I am Neutral / I Disagree / Strongly Disagree / Not Applicable.**

1) I liked the services that I received.
2) If I had other choices, I would still choose to get services from this health plan.
3) I would recommend this health plan to a friend or family member.
4) The location of services was convenient.
5) My caregivers were willing to help as often as I felt was necessary.
6) My calls were returned within 24 hours.
7) Services were available at times that were good for me.
8) I was able to get all the services I thought I needed.
9) My caregivers believed that I could grow, change and recover.
10) I felt free to complain.
11) I was told what side effects to watch for.
12) My wishes about who is and is not to be given information about my treatment were respected.
13) My caregivers were sensitive to my cultural/ethnic background.
14) My caregivers helped me obtain the information needed so I could take charge of managing my illness.

As a direct result of the services I received:

15) I deal more effectively with daily problems.
16) I am better able to control my life.
17) I am better able to deal with crisis.
18) I am getting along better with my family.
19) I do better in social situations.
20) I do better in school and/or work.
21) My symptoms are not bothering me as much.

Source: Excerpted from The Santa Fe Summit on Behavioral Health; Preserving Quality and Value in the Managed Care Equation: Final Report. *The American College of Mental Health Administration. March 1998. Page 106 (Behavioral Health Map Recommendation).*

Solution-Focused Recovery Scale For Abuse Survivors

YVONNE DOLAN, MA, AND LYNN JOHNSON

Name_____
Date_____

Circle the number that applies to you today: 0 = Not at all, 1 = Just a little, 2 = Occasionally, 3 = Some of the time; a fair amount of the time; 4 = Frequently or most of the time.

| 0 | 1 | 2 | 3 | 4 | A. I am able to think/talk about the abuse or the sexual abuse when it is appropriate.
| 0 | 1 | 2 | 3 | 4 | B. I am able to think/talk about things other than the abuse or sexual abuse.
| 0 | 1 | 2 | 3 | 4 | C. I sleep adequately; I don't feel unusually sleepy in the daytime.
| 0 | 1 | 2 | 3 | 4 | D. I feel part of a supportive family.
| 0 | 1 | 2 | 3 | 4 | E. I stand up for my self (I am reasonably assertive).
| 0 | 1 | 2 | 3 | 4 | F. I maintain physical appearance (weight, hair, nails etc.)
| 0 | 1 | 2 | 3 | 4 | G. I go to work; I am on time, I am reasonably productive.
| 0 | 1 | 2 | 3 | 4 | H. I am satisfied with my work.
| 0 | 1 | 2 | 3 | 4 | I. I engage in social activities outside the home.
| 0 | 1 | 2 | 3 | 4 | J. I have a healthy appetite.
| 0 | 1 | 2 | 3 | 4 | K. I care for child, loved ones, pets. (I can take care of others.)
| 0 | 1 | 2 | 3 | 4 | L. I adapt to new situations.
| 0 | 1 | 2 | 3 | 4 | M. I initiate contact with friends, loved ones.
| 0 | 1 | 2 | 3 | 4 | N. I show a sense of humor.
| 0 | 1 | 2 | 3 | 4 | O. I am interested in future goals.
| 0 | 1 | 2 | 3 | 4 | P. I pursue leisure activities.
| 0 | 1 | 2 | 3 | 4 | Q. I exercise regularly.
| 0 | 1 | 2 | 3 | 4 | R. I take sensible protective measures inside and outside house.
| 0 | 1 | 2 | 3 | 4 | S. I choose supportive relationships over non-supportive ones.
| 0 | 1 | 2 | 3 | 4 | T. I am able to relax without drugs or alcohol.
| 0 | 1 | 2 | 3 | 4 | U. I seem to tolerate constructive criticism well.
| 0 | 1 | 2 | 3 | 4 | V. I seem to accept praise well. I thank the person giving the praise.
| 0 | 1 | 2 | 3 | 4 | W. I enjoy a healthy sexual relationship. I can give and accept intimacy.

Source: Yvonne Dolan, MA. In: Resolving Sexual Abuse by Y. Dolan, W.W. Norton, 1992. [See http://www.xmission.com/~rebling/pub/sfrs.html.] (Reprinted with permission.)

Children's Functional Assessment Rating Scale™ (CFARS™) - Florida Version
(Please use a number 2 pencil.)

SOCIAL SECURITY NUMBER OF CHILD/YOUTH BEING RATED	DATE OF BIRTH (MO./DAY/YEAR)	PROVIDER AGENCY TAX ID#	SITE ID	EVALUATION DATE (MO./DAY/YEAR)	DISTRICT OF PAYER / SERVICE

Population Certification (Children's Categories Mark one if applicable):
○ SED ○ Emotional Disturbance ○ At Risk of Developing an Emotional Disturbance ○ SA Certification

Gender of Person Being Rated: ○ Male ○ Female

Child/Youth has Medicaid Coverage: ○ Yes ○ No ○ Could not be determined

Child/Youth has Title 21 Coverage: ○ Yes ○ No ○ Could not be determined

Purpose of Evaluation

Provider Agency Evaluation (Mark One)
○ Admission to Provider Agency
○ Every 3 Month Interval After Admission to Provider Agency
○ Discharge from Provider Agency
○ None of the Above

Program/Service Evaluation (Mark One)
○ Admission to Program or Service
○ 6 Months After Admission to Program or Service
○ Annually After Admission to Program or Service
○ Planned Discharge from, or Transfer to, Program or Service Within Agency
○ Administrative Discharge
○ None of the Above

Level of Care
Current Level of Care, or if "Admission", indicate admission level(s) of care: (Mark all that apply)
○ Addictions Receiving Facility   ○ Medication Clinic
○ Targeted Case Management   ○ Outpatient
○ FSPT Case Management   ○ Residential Level (mark one): ① ② ③ ④
○ CRC Case Management   ○ Respite/Mentoring
○ CSU/CCSU/Inpatient   ○ Pre-Independent Living
○ Day Treatment   ○ Other
○ In Home and On-Site Services

For "Discharge" or "Transfer", indicate the level(s) of care the individual is being discharged or transferred to: (Mark all that apply)
○ Addictions Receiving Facility   ○ Medication Clinic
○ Targeted Case Management   ○ Outpatient
○ FSPT Case Management   ○ Residential Level (mark one): ① ② ③ ④
○ CRC Case Management   ○ Respite/Mentoring
○ CSU/CCSU/Inpatient   ○ Pre-Independent Living
○ Day Treatment   ○ Other
○ In Home and On-Site Services   ○ None

DSM-IV Diagnosis Axis I or II
Optional Code	Primary	Secondary (Optional)

Days spent in community in the last 30 days: (maximum = 30):
(Do not count days spent in non-community settings such as: jail/detention, CSU/SRT/Inpatient, mental health hospital, children's residential treatment, wilderness camp, homeless or runaway)
0 1 2 3 4 5 6 7 8 9 10 11 12 13 14 15 16 17 18 19 20 21 22 23 24 25 26 27 28 29 30

Total School Days Available in last 30 days (Maximum = 22):
0 1 2 3 4 5 6 7 8 9 10 11 12 13 14 15 16 17 18 19 20 21 22

Legal Status (Mark One)

Adjudicated Children
○ Delinquent, in physical custody
○ Delinquent, not in physical custody
○ Dependent, in physical custody
○ Dependent, not in physical custody
○ Dependent & Delinquent, in physical custody
○ Dependent & Delinquent, not in physical custody
○ CINS, not in physical custody

Non-Adjudicated Children
○ Other children & families program
○ Under custody & supervision of family, relatives or guardian

School Days Attended in last 30 days (Maximum = 22):
0 1 2 3 4 5 6 7 8 9 10 11 12 13 14 15 16 17 18 19 20 21 22

Was the child committed or recommitted to DJJ in the last 90 days?
○ Yes ○ No

Adapted from the Colorado Client Assessment Record (CCAR) and Functional Assessment Rating Scale (FARS)
J. Ward, M. Dow, T. Saunders, S. Halls, K. Musante, K. Penner, R. Berry, N. Sachs-Ericcsson
1996, 1997, 1998, USF/FMHI/ Fla. Dept. Children and Families, ADM D7

(Over)

Source: Children's Functional Assessment Rating Scale™ (CFARS™) — Florida Version. Copyright John C. Ward, PhD, and Michael G. Dow, PhD, University of South Florida and the Florida Department of Children and Families. (Reprinted with permission.)

Problem Severity Ratings

Use the scale below to rate the child/youth's current (last three weeks) level of severity for each category. To rate a category, fill in a numbered circle on the line next to the category. Also, fill in the circle next to each word or phrase that describes the person's problems or assets.

1	2	3	4	5	6	7	8	9
No Problem	Less than Slight Problem	Slight Problem	Slight to Moderate Problem	Moderate Problem	Moderate to Severe Problem	Severe Problem	Severe to Extreme Problem	Extreme Problem

Depression ① ② ③ ④ ⑤ ⑥ ⑦ ⑧ ⑨
- ○ Depressed Mood ○ Happy ○ Sleep Problems
- ○ Sad ○ Hopeless ○ Lacks Energy/Interest
- ○ Irritable ○ Withdrawn ○ Anti-Dep. Meds.

Anxiety ① ② ③ ④ ⑤ ⑥ ⑦ ⑧ ⑨
- ○ Anxious/Tense ○ Calm ○ Guilt
- ○ Phobic ○ Worried/Fearful ○ Anti-Anx. Meds.
- ○ Obsessive/Comp. ○ Panic

Hyperactivity ① ② ③ ④ ⑤ ⑥ ⑦ ⑧ ⑨
- ○ Manic ○ Inattentive ○ Agitated
- ○ Sleep Deficit ○ Overactive/Hyperactive ○ Mood Swings
- ○ Pressured Speech ○ Relaxed ○ Impulsivity
- ○ ADHD Meds. ○ Anti-Manic Meds.

Thought Process ① ② ③ ④ ⑤ ⑥ ⑦ ⑧ ⑨
- ○ Illogical ○ Delusional ○ Hallucinations
- ○ Paranoid ○ Ruminative ○ Command Hallucinations
- ○ Derailed Thinking ○ Loose Associations ○ Intact
- ○ Oriented ○ Disoriented ○ Anti-Psych. Meds.

Cognitive Performance ① ② ③ ④ ⑤ ⑥ ⑦ ⑧ ⑨
- ○ Poor Memory ○ Low Self-Awareness
- ○ Poor Attention/Concentration ○ Developmental Disability
- ○ Insightful ○ Concrete Thinking
- ○ Impaired Judgement ○ Slow Processing

Medical/Physical ① ② ③ ④ ⑤ ⑥ ⑦ ⑧ ⑨
- ○ Acute Illness ○ Hypochondria ○ Good Health
- ○ CNS Disorder ○ Chronic Illness ○ Need Med./Dental Care
- ○ Pregnant ○ Poor Nutrition ○ Enuretic/Encopretic
- ○ Eating Disorder ○ Seizures ○ Stress-Related Illness

Traumatic Stress ① ② ③ ④ ⑤ ⑥ ⑦ ⑧ ⑨
- ○ Acute ○ Dreams/Nightmares
- ○ Chronic ○ Detached
- ○ Avoidance ○ Repression/Amnesia
- ○ Upsetting Memories ○ Hypervigilance

Substance Use ① ② ③ ④ ⑤ ⑥ ⑦ ⑧ ⑨
- ○ Alcohol ○ Drug(s) ○ Dependence
- ○ Abuse ○ Over the Counter Drugs ○ Cravings/Urges
- ○ DUI ○ Abstinent ○ I.V. Drugs
- ○ Recovery ○ Interferes w/Functioning ○ Med. Control

Interpersonal Relationships ① ② ③ ④ ⑤ ⑥ ⑦ ⑧ ⑨
- ○ Problem w/Friends ○ Diff. Estab./Maintain Relationships
- ○ Poor Social Skills ○ Age-Appropriate Group Participation
- ○ Adequate Social Skills ○ Supportive Relationships
- ○ Overly Shy

Behavior in "Home" Setting ① ② ③ ④ ⑤ ⑥ ⑦ ⑧ ⑨
- ○ Disregards Rules ○ Defies Authority
- ○ Conflict w/Sibling or Peer ○ Conflict w/Parent or Caregiver
- ○ Conflict w/Relative ○ Respectful
- ○ Responsible

ADL Functioning ① ② ③ ④ ⑤ ⑥ ⑦ ⑧ ⑨
- ○ Handicapped   **Not age appropriate in:**
- ○ Permanent Disability ○ Communication ○ Self-Care
- ○ No Known Limitations ○ Hygiene ○ Recreation
- ○ Mobility

Socio-Legal ① ② ③ ④ ⑤ ⑥ ⑦ ⑧ ⑨
- ○ Disregards Rules ○ Offenses/Property ○ Offenses/Person
- ○ Firesetting ○ Community Cntrl./Reentry ○ Pending Charges
- ○ Dishonest ○ Use/Con Other(s) ○ Incompetent to Proceed
- ○ Detention/Commitment ○ Street Gang Member

Work ○   or School ○ ① ② ③ ④ ⑤ ⑥ ⑦ ⑧ ⑨
- ○ Absenteeism ○ Poor Performance ○ Regular Attendance
- ○ Dropped Out ○ Learning Disabilities ○ Seeking Emp.
- ○ Employed ○ Doesn't Read/Write ○ Tardiness
- ○ Defies Authority ○ Not Employed ○ Suspended
- ○ Disruptive ○ Terminated/Expelled ○ Skips Classes

Danger to Self ① ② ③ ④ ⑤ ⑥ ⑦ ⑧ ⑨
- ○ Suicidal Ideation ○ Current Plan ○ Recent Attempt
- ○ Past Attempt ○ Self-Injury ○ Self-Mutilation
- ○ "Risk-Taking" Behavior ○ Serious Self-Neglect ○ Inability to Care for Self

Danger to Others ① ② ③ ④ ⑤ ⑥ ⑦ ⑧ ⑨
- ○ Violent Temper ○ Threatens Others
- ○ Causes Serious Injury ○ Homicidal Ideation
- ○ Use of Weapons ○ Homicidal Threats
- ○ Assaultive ○ Homicidal Attempts
- ○ Cruelty to Animals ○ Accused of Sexual Assault
- ○ Does Not Appear Dangerous to Others ○ Physically Aggressive

Security/Management Needs ① ② ③ ④ ⑤ ⑥ ⑦ ⑧ ⑨
- ○ Home w/o Supervision ○ Suicide Watch
- ○ Behavioral Contract ○ Locked Unit
- ○ Protection from Others ○ Seclusion
- ○ Home w/Supervision ○ Run/Escape Risk
- ○ Restraint ○ Involuntary Exam/Commit.
- ○ Time-out ○ PRN
- ○ Monitored House Arrest ○ One-to-One Supervision

CURRENT LEVEL OF FUNCTIONING RATING

CGAS SCALE RATING: ⓪ ① ② ③ ④ ⑤ ⑥ ⑦ ⑧ ⑨

Use the Children's Global Assessment Scale (CGAS) to indicate your overall rating of this child/youth's current level of functioning.

Type of Rater ID#
- ○ SSN
- ○ Employee ID#
- ○ Other

RATER ID#: ⓪ ① ② ③ ④ ⑤ ⑥ ⑦ ⑧ ⑨ (×8 columns)

Adapted from the Colorado Client Assessment Record (CCAR) and Functional Assessment Rating Scale (FARS)
J. Ward, M. Dow, T. Saunders, S. Halls, K. Musante, K. Penner, R. Berry, N. Sachs-Ericcsson 1996, 1997, 1998, USF/FMHI/ Fla. Dept. Children and Families, ADM D7

CP98-0938 (C1.F3) Printed in U.S.A.   0987654321

Functional Assessment Rating Scale™ (FARS™) - Florida Version
(Please use a number 2 pencil.)

SOCIAL SECURITY NUMBER OF PERSON BEING RATED | **DATE OF BIRTH** (MO. DAY YEAR) | **PROVIDER AGENCY TAX ID#** | **SITE ID** | **EVALUATION DATE** (MO. DAY YEAR) | **DISTRICT OF PAYER / SERVICE**

Population Certification

Adult Mental Health Categories (Mark one if applicable):
- ○ Forensic
- ○ Severe and persistent mental illness
- ○ Crisis
- ○ Other

Adult Substance Abuse Categories (Mark one if applicable):
- ○ Parents Putting Children at Risk
- ○ Involved in Criminal Justice System
- ○ Dually Diagnosed
- ○ Intravenous (IV) Drug User
- ○ Other SA Diagnosis

Gender of Person Being Rated: ○ Male ○ Female   Person being rated has Medicaid Coverage ○ Yes ○ No ○ Could not be determined

Purpose of Evaluation

Provider Agency Evaluation (Mark One)
- ○ Admission to Provider Agency
- ○ Every 3 Month Interval After Admission to Provider Agency
- ○ Discharge from Provider Agency
- ○ None of the Above

Program/Service Evaluation (Mark One)
- ○ Admission to Program or Service
- ○ 6 Months After Admission to Program or Service
- ○ Annually After Admission to Program or Service
- ○ Planned Discharge from, or Transfer to, Program or Service Within Agency
- ○ Administrative Discharge
- ○ None of the Above

Level of Care

Current Level of Care, or if just admitted, indicate admission level(s) of care: (Mark all that apply)
- ○ CSU/Inpatient ○ Vocational ○ Intensive C.M. ○ Detox. ○ PHP
- ○ Day Treatment ○ State Hosp ○ Outpatient ○ Other
- ○ Case Mgmt. ○ Residential Level (mark one) ① ② ③ ④

For "Discharge" or "Transfer", indicate the level(s) of care the individual is being discharged or transferred to:
- ○ CSU/Inpatient ○ Vocational ○ Intensive C.M. ○ Detox. ○ PHP
- ○ Day Treatment ○ State Hosp ○ Outpatient ○ Other ○ None
- ○ Case Mgmt. ○ Residential Level (mark one) ① ② ③ ④

Does the individual report a history of (mark all that apply):
- Sexual abuse as a: ○ Child   Physical abuse as a: ○ Child
- ○ Adult   ○ Adult
- ○ Elder   ○ Elder

Days spent in community in the last 30 days:
(Do not count days spent in non-community settings such as: jail/detention, CSU/SRT/Inpatient, mental health hospital, children's residential treatment, wilderness camp, homeless or runaway)

Total days of paid work in the last 30 days
(Most full time positions involve 22 days)

Monthly Income (from each source in the last 30 days): Consumer's Paid Employment | Consumer's Govt Subsidies | Other Income

DSM-IV Diagnosis Axis I or II: Primary | Secondary (Optional) | Optional Code

Legal Status (Mark One)
Note: These legal status codes are taken from the IDS Manual dated 7/1/1996

No Court Jurisdiction
- ○ = Competent, no charges
- ○ = Civil incompetence of person or property.

Criminal Competent
- ○ = Incarcerated
- ○ = Release pending hearing

Criminal Incompetent
- ○ = Release pending hearing
- ○ = Invol. hospitalization (direct commit)
- ○ = Incarcerated
- ○ = Invol. hosp.-revoc. of cond. release
- ○ = Conditionally released

Not Guilty by Reason of Insanity
- ○ = Involuntary hospital-direct commit
- ○ = Invol. hosp.-revoc. of cond. release
- ○ = Released pending hearing
- ○ = Conditionally released
- ○ = Incarcerated

Adapted from the Colorado Client Assessment Record   **(Over)**   J. Ward & M. Dow, 1994, 1996, 1997, 1998, USF, FMHI / Fla. Dept. Children and Families / HRS D7

Source: Functional Assessment Rating Scale™ (FARS™) — Florida Version. Copyright John C. Ward, Phd, and Michael G. Dow, PhD, the University of South Florida, and the Florida Department of Children and Families. (Reprinted with permission.)

Problem Severity Ratings

Use the scale below to rate the individual's current (last 3 weeks) level of severity for each category.
To rate a category, fill in a numbered circle on the line next to the category. Also, fill in the circle next to each word or phrase that describes the person's problems or assets.

1	2	3	4	5	6	7	8	9
No Problem	Less than Slight Problem	Slight Problem	Slight to Moderate Problem	Moderate Problem	Moderate to Severe Problem	Severe Problem	Severe to Extreme Problem	Extreme Problem

Depression ① ② ③ ④ ⑤ ⑥ ⑦ ⑧ ⑨
○ Depressed Mood ○ Worthless ○ Lonely
○ Anhedonic ○ Hopeless ○ Sleep Problems
○ Sad ○ Happy ○ Anti-Dep. Meds.

Anxiety ① ② ③ ④ ⑤ ⑥ ⑦ ⑧ ⑨
○ Anxious ○ Calm ○ Guilt
○ Tense ○ Fearful ○ Anti-Anx. Meds.
○ Obsessive ○ Panic

Hyper Affect ① ② ③ ④ ⑤ ⑥ ⑦ ⑧ ⑨
○ Manic ○ Elevated Mood ○ Agitated
○ Sleep Deficit ○ Overactive ○ Mood Swings
○ Pressured Speech ○ Relaxed ○ Anti-Manic Meds.

Thought Process ① ② ③ ④ ⑤ ⑥ ⑦ ⑧ ⑨
○ Illogical ○ Delusional ○ Hallucinating
○ Paranoid ○ Ruminative ○ Intact
○ Derailed Thinking ○ Loose Associations ○ Anti-Psych. Med.

Cognitive Performance ① ② ③ ④ ⑤ ⑥ ⑦ ⑧ ⑨
○ Poor Memory ○ Low Self-Awareness ○ Impaired Judgement
○ Short Attention ○ Developmental Disability ○ Slow Processing
○ Insightful ○ Poor Concentration ○ Orientation x 4
○ Not oriented to person ○ Not oriented to place ○ Not oriented to time ○ Not oriented to circumstance

Medical/Physical ① ② ③ ④ ⑤ ⑥ ⑦ ⑧ ⑨
○ Acute Illness ○ Hndcp. or Perm. Dis. ○ Good Health
○ CNS Disorder ○ Chronic Illness ○ Need Med. Care
○ Eating Disorder ○ Poor Nutrition ○ Enuretic./Encop.

Traumatic Stress ① ② ③ ④ ⑤ ⑥ ⑦ ⑧ ⑨
○ Acute ○ Dreams/Nightmares
○ Chronic ○ Detached
○ Avoidant ○ Repression/Amnesia
○ Upsetting Memories

Substance Use ① ② ③ ④ ⑤ ⑥ ⑦ ⑧ ⑨
○ Alcohol ○ Drug(s) ○ Dependence
○ Abuse ○ Family History ○ Cravings/Urges
○ DUI ○ Abstinent ○ Med. Control
○ Recovery ○ Interferes w/Duties ○ I.V. Drugs

Interpersonal Relationships ① ② ③ ④ ⑤ ⑥ ⑦ ⑧ ⑨
○ Problems w/Friends ○ Difficulty Establishing Relationships
○ Poor Social Skills ○ Difficulty Maintaining Relationships
○ Adequate Social Skills ○ Supportive Relationships

Family Relationships ① ② ③ ④ ⑤ ⑥ ⑦ ⑧ ⑨
○ No Contact w/Fam. ○ Poor Parenting Skills ○ Supportive Family
○ Difficulty w/Partner ○ Acting Out ○ No Family
○ Difficulty w/Relative ○ Difficulty w/Child ○ Difficulty w/Parent

Family Environment ① ② ③ ④ ⑤ ⑥ ⑦ ⑧ ⑨
○ Fam. Instability ○ Separation ○ Custody Prob.
○ Family Legal ○ Stable Home ○ Divorce
○ Single Parent ○ Birth in Family ○ Death in Family

Socio-Legal ① ② ③ ④ ⑤ ⑥ ⑦ ⑧ ⑨
○ Disregards Rules ○ Offense/Property ○ Offense/Person
○ 916 Cond. Release ○ Probation ○ Pending Charges
○ Dishonesty ○ Use/Con Other(s) ○ Reliable

Work ○ or School ○ ① ② ③ ④ ⑤ ⑥ ⑦ ⑧ ⑨
○ Absenteeism ○ Poor Performance ○ Attends School
○ Termination(s) ○ Learning Disabilities ○ Seeking Employ.
○ Employed ○ Doesn't Read/Write ○ Tardiness
○ Disabled ○ Not Employed

ADL Functioning ① ② ③ ④ ⑤ ⑥ ⑦ ⑧ ⑨
Problem Areas:
○ Money Management ○ Meal Preparation
○ Personal Hygiene ○ Transportation
○ Obtain/Maintain Employment ○ Obtain/Maintain Housing

Ability to Care for Self ① ② ③ ④ ⑤ ⑥ ⑦ ⑧ ⑨
○ Able to Care for Self ○ Risk of Harm
○ Suffers from Neglect ○ Refuses to Care for Self
○ Not Able to Survive w/o Help ○ Alt. Care Not Available

Danger to Self ① ② ③ ④ ⑤ ⑥ ⑦ ⑧ ⑨
○ Suicidal Ideation ○ Current Plan ○ Recent Attempt
○ Past Attempt ○ Self-Injury ○ Self-Mutilation

Danger to Others ① ② ③ ④ ⑤ ⑥ ⑦ ⑧ ⑨
○ Violent Temper ○ Threatens Others
○ Physical Abuser ○ Homicidal Ideation
○ Hostile ○ Homicidal Threats
○ Assaultive ○ Homicide Attempt
○ Does Not Appear Dangerous to Others

Security/Management Needs ① ② ③ ④ ⑤ ⑥ ⑦ ⑧ ⑨
○ Home w/o Supervision ○ Suicide Watch
○ Behavioral Contract ○ Locked Unit
○ Protection from Others ○ Seclusion
○ Home w/ Supervision ○ Run/Escape Risk
○ Restraint ○ Involuntary Exam/Commit.

CURRENT LEVEL OF FUNCTIONING RATING

GAF SCALE RATING — Use the Global Assessment of Functioning (GAF) Scale from the DSM-IV (American Psychiatric Association, 1994) to indicate your overall rating of this individual's current level of functioning.

⓪⓪ ①① ②② ③③ ④④ ⑤⑤ ⑥⑥ ⑦⑦ ⑧⑧ ⑨⑨

RATER ID#

⓪⓪⓪⓪⓪⓪⓪⓪
①①①①①①①①
②②②②②②②②
③③③③③③③③
④④④④④④④④
⑤⑤⑤⑤⑤⑤⑤⑤
⑥⑥⑥⑥⑥⑥⑥⑥
⑦⑦⑦⑦⑦⑦⑦⑦
⑧⑧⑧⑧⑧⑧⑧⑧
⑨⑨⑨⑨⑨⑨⑨⑨

Type of ID# ○ SSN
○ Employee ID#
○ Other

CP98-0937 (C1.F3) Printed in U.S.A.   0987654321   J. Ward & M. Dow, 1994, 1996, 1997, 1998, USF, FMHI / Fla. Dept. Children and Families / HRS D7

CHILD AND ADOLESCENT STRENGTHS ASSESSMENT

Name _____ ID _____ Date _____

FAMILY STRENGTHS

	No Evidence	*Interest/Potential*	*Yes, Definitely*
1. Has strong positive relation with at least one parent	☐	☐	☐
2. Has strong positive relation with at least one adult relative (non-parent)	☐	☐	☐
3. Has strong positive relation with at least one brother or sister	☐	☐	☐
4. Strong positive relations exist among relatives	☐	☐	☐
5. Family has reliable communication	☐	☐	☐
6. Has a sense of belonging to a family	☐	☐	☐

SCHOOL/VOCATIONAL STRENGTHS

	No Evidence	*Interest/Potential*	*Yes, Definitely*
7. Excels in at least one subject	☐	☐	☐
8. Likes to write (e.g. keeps a diary, etc)	☐	☐	☐
9. Reads for pleasure	☐	☐	☐
10. Has done well for at least one year during schooling	☐	☐	☐
11. Has a particular vocational skill (e.g. auto repair, electronics)	☐	☐	☐
12. Is articulate in speech (e.g. speaks well)	☐	☐	☐
13. Is a hard worker	☐	☐	☐
14. Has identified career goals for adulthood	☐	☐	☐

Source: Copyright 1998 John S. Lyons. Reprinted with permission. The Child and Adolescent Strengths Assessment was developed by John S. Lyons, PhD, of the Mental Health Services and Policy Program at Northwestern University. Further information is available by contacting him at jsl329@nwu.edu or (312) 908-8972.

Appendix A: Selected Instruments

PSYCHOLOGICAL STRENGTHS

	No Evidence	*Interest/Potential*	*Yes, Definitely*
15. Has a sense of humor	☐	☐	☐
16. Has the ability to adapt to stressful life circumstances	☐	☐	☐
17. Has the ability to enjoy positive life experiences	☐	☐	☐
18. Is able to express emotions accurately	☐	☐	☐
19. Has the ability to trust others	☐	☐	☐

PEER STRENGTHS

	No Evidence	*Interest/Potential*	*Yes, Definitely*
20. Has close friend(s)	☐	☐	☐
21. Negotiates appropriately with peers	☐	☐	☐
22. Is well liked by peers	☐	☐	☐

MORALITY/SPIRITUALITY

	No evidence	*Interest/Potential*	*Yes, Definitely*
23. Has developed values/morals (e.g. honesty, respect)	☐	☐	☐
24. Has expressed religious/spiritual beliefs	☐	☐	☐
25. Attends religious services regularly	☐	☐	☐
26. Participates in church youth groups	☐	☐	☐

EXTRACURRICULAR STRENGTHS

	No evidence	*Interest/Potential*	*Yes, Definitely*
27. Has artistic/creative talent	☐	☐	☐
28. Has a hobby or hobbies	☐	☐	☐
29. Participates in a community service youth group	☐	☐	☐
30. Participates in organized sports	☐	☐	☐

McLean Hospital Outpatient Perceptions of Care

OPOC   **FOR OFFICE USE ONLY**   Site code   ☐☐☐

INSTRUCTIONS TO STAFF: Please write the respondent's Identification Number and Visit Number, one digit in each box. Fill in the Visit Type and Level of Care using the code numbers below.

Identification Number   ☐☐☐☐☐☐☐☐

Visit Number   ☐☐☐☐☐☐☐

Visit Type
  1 = Mid-Treatment
  2 = End of Treatment
  3 = Post-Treatment Follow-up.   ☐

PERCEPTIONS OF CARE

INSTRUCTIONS TO RESPONDENT: We would like to know your views about the mental health services you have been receiving as an outpatient at this facility. We will use this information to improve our quality of care. Your responses are confidential and will not be identified by name to the clinicians involved in your treatment or in any report that is prepared from your answers to these questions.

Please fill in the circle that corresponds to your answer to each of the questions below. Please answer every question.

#	Question	(1)	(2)	(3)	(4)
1.	When you called the outpatient department, did you get an appointment as soon as you needed it?	Yes	No		
2.	Were you referred to a clinician who met your needs?	Yes completely	Partially	Not at all	
3.	When you call or check in for appointments, are you treated with courtesy and respect?	Never	Sometimes	Usually	Always
4.	How long do you usually wait to be seen beyond your appointment time	Less than 10 minutes	10–20 minutes	20–30 minutes	More than 10 minutes
5.	When you call your clinician, how long does it usually take for your calls to be returned?	I have not called my clinician	Less than 4 hours	4–24 hours	More than 24 hours
6.	Does the clinician you see explain things in a way you can understand?	Never	Sometimes	Usually	Always
7.	Does the clinician you see listen carefully to you	Never	Sometimes	Usually	Always
8.	Does the clinician you see treat you with respect and dignity?	Never	Sometimes	Usually	Always
9.	Does the clinician you see give you reassurance and support?	Never	Sometimes	Usually	Always
10.	Does your clinician help you learn how to deal with your problems yourself?	Never	Sometimes	Usually	Always
11.	Are you involved as much as you want to be in decisions about your treatment	Never	Sometimes	Usually	Always
12.	How much does your clinician involve your family in your treatment?	Never	Sometimes	Usually	Always

Source: Instrument developed at McLean Hospital as part of the McLean BASIS-32 Plus Performace Measurement System. (Reprinted with permission.)

		More than I want	Less than I want	About the right amount	No involvement, which is what I want
13.	Have you been informed about the benefits and risks of the medication you are taking	(1) Yes	(2) No	(3) I am not taking medication	
14.	Have you been told what to do in case of side effects or emergency	(1) Yes	(2) No		
15.	How much have you been helped by the care you received at the outpatient service?	(1) Not at all	(2) Somewhat	(3) Quite a bit	(4) A great deal
16.	Is the space where you see your clinician clean and comfortable?	(1) Never	(2) Sometimes	(3) Usually	(4) Always
17.	Using any number from 0 to 10, what is you overall rating of the care you received at the outpatient service	(1) (2) (3) (4) (5) (6) (7) (8) (9) (10) Worst possible case .... Best possible case			
18.	Would you recommend the outpatient services at this facility to someone who needed mental health or substance abuse treatment	(1) Yes	(2) Unsure	(3) No	

19. Please fill in today's date [ ] MONTH [ ] DAY [ ] YEAR

What services are you receiving at the outpatient department of this facility?

		Yes	No
20.	Medication	(1)	(2)
21.	Individual Therapy	(1)	(2)
22.	Group Therapy	(1)	(2)
23.	Other Treatment	(1)	(2)

24. Please identify staff whom you feel deserve special recognition.

25. Is there anything else you would like to tell us about your care?

Rhode Island Outcome Evaluation Instrument: Instructions

This survey has been developed by consumers, family members, and mental health professionals who want to know how the mental health system works for you. Your participation in this survey is completely voluntary. However, your opinions, feelings, and thoughts are very important to us, and can make a difference in the future quality of services delivered. Your answers to these questions will be used as part of an evaluation of mental health services at your center and in Rhode Island.

Instructions for Completing the Survey

- The survey usually takes less than half an hour to complete.
- Please take some time to read each question carefully, and answer it by filling in the circle or the boxes provided.
- For each question, use a dark pen or pencil to completely shade in the appropriate circle or fill in the box with the appropriate number.
- For the best results, please avoid marking outside of the circles and boxes.
- It is important that you answer each question as frankly and honestly as you can.
- If you do not understand a question, or if you need help filling out the questionnaire, feel free to ask for assistance.

Instructions for Returning The Survey

Whether you choose to complete the survey or not, please do the following:
- When you are finished with the survey, fold it up, and place it in the envelope provided.
- Seal the envelope and sign your name across the back flap.
- Return the envelope to agency staff.

The signed and sealed envelope will be given to management staff who will remove the envelope with your name on it, and then deliver the forms to the State offices. This process ensures that your individual answers will remain completely confidential. Staff members who provide you with services at this agency will not see your individual answers (unless you have asked them for help in filling out the survey). They will only see summary reports on the entire agency.

Thank you for your help!

Source: Rhode Island Department of Mental Health, Retardation, and Hospitals, Integrated Mental Health Services, Office of Managed Care Monitoring and Decision Support Systems.

RHODE ISLAND OUTCOME EVALUATION INSTRUMENT

A. Section to be completed by STAFF:

Please use a dark pen or pencil to shade in the circle next to the response that best represents your answer, or to fill in the blank provided.
Note: Please enter the client's MHSIP unique ID in the spaces provided at the top of each page before distributing pages 2-4 to the client.
**Thank you for your assistance!

Shade circles like this: ●
Not like this: ⊗ ⌀

1. This evaluation is for the 12 month period ending:

				Year:	
○ January	○ April	○ July	○ October	○ 1998	○ 2001
○ February	○ May	○ August	○ November	○ 1999	○ 2002
○ March	○ June	○ September	○ December	○ 2000	

2. MHSIP unique ID of <u>staff</u> completing this evaluation: [ ][ ][ ][ ][ ][ ][ ]

3. MHSIP unique ID of <u>client</u> completing this evaluation: [ ][ ][ ][ ][ ][ ][ ]

4a. Agency:
○ NRI ○ MHS ○ EBAY ○ FHR
○ CCC ○ KENT ○ NEWP ○ NAFI
○ PROV ○ SHORE ○ RWOOD

4b. Program:
○ MTT
○ MHPRR
○ CPST

5. Indicate the number of times the client used an Acute Inpatient Psychiatric Service in the 12 month review period: (e.g., 5 = "005") [ ][ ][ ]

6. Indicate whether the client used any of the service categories listed below in the 12 month review period:

   a. Mental Health Crisis Service or Respite Service   ○ Yes ○ No
   b. Eleanor Slater Hospital Psychiatric Service   ○ Yes ○ No
   c. Non-Psychiatric Hospital Emergency Room Service   ○ Yes ○ No
   d. Non-Psychiatric Hospital Emergency Room Service (resulting in Admission) ○ Yes ○ No
   e. Substance Abuse Detoxification Service   ○ Yes ○ No
   f. Correctional Facility   ○ Yes ○ No

7. How would you describe the client's general physical health?
   ○ Excellent ○ Poor
   ○ Good   ○ Very Poor
   ○ Fair

Staff Comments:

8. Indicate the type of client participation:
   ○ The client completed his/her section of the survey alone.
   ○ The client completed his/her section of the survey with staff assistance.
   ○ The client refused to complete his/her section of the survey.
   ○ Unknown

Please add any other comments you may have here:

RHODE ISLAND OUTCOME EVALUATION INSTRUMENT

B. *Section to be completed by CLIENT:*   MHSIP unique ID ☐☐☐☐☐☐☐

Please use a dark pen or pencil to shade in the circle next to the response that best represents your situation, or to fill in the blank provided.
****Thank you, in advance, for your help!*

Shade circles like this: ●
Not like this: ⊠ ✓

1. How satisfied are you with your current housing arrangement?	○ Very Satisfied ○ Somewhat Dissatisfied ○ Somewhat Satisfied ○ Very Dissatisfied ○ Neither Satisfied Nor Dissatisfied
2. How safe do you feel in your home/neighborhood?	○ Very Safe ○ Somewhat Unsafe ○ Somewhat Safe ○ Very Unsafe ○ Neither Safe Nor Unsafe
3. In general, to what extent do you experience difficulty in getting to the places you want to go (work/school, health services, shopping, etc.)?	○ No Difficulty ○ Quite a Bit of Difficulty ○ A Little Difficulty ○ Extreme Difficulty ○ Moderate Difficulty
4. Is there a physical health care provider that you usually use when you have a physical health problem?	○ Yes ○ No
5. How would you describe your general physical health?	○ Excellent ○ Poor ○ Good ○ Very Poor ○ Fair
6. Have you had a complete physical exam in the last 12 months?	○ Yes ○ No
7. <u>During the last 12 months</u>: a. Have you ever felt you ought to cut down your drinking? ○ Yes ○ No b. Have people annoyed you by criticizing your drinking? ○ Yes ○ No c. Have you ever felt bad or guilty about your drinking? ○ Yes ○ No d. Have you ever had to take a drink first thing in the morning to steady your nerves or to get rid of a hangover? ○ Yes ○ No	
8. <u>During the last 12 months</u>: a. Have you ever felt you ought to cut down your drug use? ○ Yes ○ No b. Have people annoyed you by criticizing your drug use? ○ Yes ○ No c. Have you ever felt bad or guilty about your drug use? ○ Yes ○ No d. Have you ever had to take a drug first thing in the morning to steady your nerves or to get rid of a hangover? ○ Yes ○ No	
9. Have you been arrested in the past 12 months?	○ Yes ○ No
10. In the past 3 months, did you work at a paid job? ○ Yes ○ No <u>If yes</u>, for how many weeks? ☐☐ (e.g., 4 weeks = "04") How many hours per week? ☐☐ (e.g., 5 hours = "05") Hourly pay? (e.g., $6.00/hour = "06.00") $ ☐☐.☐☐	
11. If you answered "Yes" to the above question, how satisfied were/are you with that job?	○ Very Satisfied ○ Somewhat Dissatisfied ○ Somewhat Satisfied ○ Very Dissatisfied ○ Neither Satisfied Nor Dissatisfied
12. In the past 3 months, were you a student attending a high school, vocational training, college, or graduate degree program?	○ Yes ○ No
13. Do you belong to any social clubs, special interest/activity groups, self-help groups, support groups, etc., sponsored by your <u>mental health agency</u>?	○ Yes, to two or more ○ No ○ Yes, to one
14. Do you belong to any social clubs, special interest/activity groups, self-help groups, support groups, etc., sponsored by your <u>community</u>?	○ Yes, to two or more ○ No ○ Yes, to one
15. To what extent do you have regular emotional support from family, friends, or people outside the mental health agency?	○ A Great Deal ○ Very Little ○ Quite a Bit ○ Not at All ○ A Moderate Amount
16. How satisfied are you with your participation in the life of the community?	○ Very Satisfied ○ Somewhat Dissatisfied ○ Somewhat Satisfied ○ Very Dissatisfied ○ Neither Satisfied Nor Dissatisfied

B. *Section to be completed by CLIENT (continued):*   MHSIP unique ID ☐☐☐☐☐☐☐

17. How frequently do you participate in the activities of a spiritual/religious group?	○ Daily ○ Once a Week ○ Once a Month	○ Occasionally ○ Never
18. In the past 12 months, to what extent did you actively participate in developing and evaluating your treatment plan?	○ A Great Deal ○ Quite a Bit ○ A Moderate Amount	○ Very Little ○ Not at All
19. In the past 12 months, to what extent have you been better able to control your life?	○ A Great Deal ○ Quite a Bit ○ A Moderate Amount	○ Very Little ○ Not at All
20. In the past 12 months, to what extent have you felt better about yourself?	○ A Great Deal ○ Quite a Bit ○ A Moderate Amount	○ Very Little ○ Not at All

Please indicate your agreement/disagreement with each of the following statements by shading in the circle under the response that best represents your opinion. If the question is about something you have not experienced, shade in the circle under "Not Applicable" to indicate that this item does not apply to you.

#	Statement	Strongly Agree	Agree	I am Neutral	Disagree	Strongly Disagree	Not Applicable
21.	I like the services that I received here.	○	○	○	○	○	○
22.	If I had other choices, I would still get services from this agency.	○	○	○	○	○	○
23.	I would recommend this agency to a friend or family member.	○	○	○	○	○	○
24.	I was able to get the services I wanted even if I could not pay for them	○	○	○	○	○	○
25.	The location of services was convenient (parking, public transportation, distance, etc.).	○	○	○	○	○	○
26.	Staff were willing to see me as often as I felt it was necessary.	○	○	○	○	○	○
27.	Staff returned my call within 24 hours.	○	○	○	○	○	○
28.	Services were available at times that were good for me.	○	○	○	○	○	○
29.	I was able to get all the services I thought I needed.	○	○	○	○	○	○
30.	I was able to see a psychiatrist when I wanted to.	○	○	○	○	○	○
31.	Staff here believe that I can grow, change, and recover.	○	○	○	○	○	○
32.	I felt comfortable asking questions about my treatment and medication.	○	○	○	○	○	○
33.	I felt free to complain.	○	○	○	○	○	○
34.	Staff respected my rights.	○	○	○	○	○	○
35.	I was given information about my rights.	○	○	○	○	○	○
36.	Staff encouraged me to take responsibility for how I live my life.	○	○	○	○	○	○
37.	Staff told me what side effects to watch for.	○	○	○	○	○	○
38.	Staff respected my wishes about who is, and is not, to be given information about my treatment.	○	○	○	○	○	○
39.	I, not staff, decided my treatment goals.	○	○	○	○	○	○
40.	Staff were sensitive to my cultural background (race, religion, language, etc.).	○	○	○	○	○	○
41.	Staff helped me obtain the information I needed so that I could take charge of managing my illness.	○	○	○	○	○	○
42.	Staff believe that I can choose what is best for me.	○	○	○	○	○	○

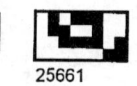

B. Section to be completed by CLIENT (continued): MHSIP unique ID ☐☐☐☐☐☐☐

	Please indicate your agreement/disagreement with each statement by shading in the circle under the response that best represents your opinion.	Strongly Agree	Agree	I am Neutral	Disagree	Strongly Disagree	Not Applicable
43.	I was encouraged to use consumer-run programs (support groups, drop-in centers, crisis phone line, etc.)	○	○	○	○	○	○
44.	All of the services I received were helpful.	○	○	○	○	○	○
45.	Staff I worked with were competent and knowledgeable.	○	○	○	○	○	○
	AS A DIRECT RESULT OF SERVICES I RECEIVED:						
46.	I deal more effectively with daily problems.	○	○	○	○	○	○
47.	I feel better about myself.	○	○	○	○	○	○
48.	I am better able to control my life.	○	○	○	○	○	○
49.	I experienced no harmful medication side effects.	○	○	○	○	○	○
50.	I am better able to deal with crisis.	○	○	○	○	○	○
51.	I am getting along better with my family.	○	○	○	○	○	○
52.	I do better in social situations.	○	○	○	○	○	○
53.	I do better in school/work.	○	○	○	○	○	○
54.	I do better with my leisure time.	○	○	○	○	○	○
55.	My housing situation has improved.	○	○	○	○	○	○
56.	My symptoms are not bothering me as much.	○	○	○	○	○	○
57.	I have become more independent.	○	○	○	○	○	○
58.	The medications I am taking help me control symptoms that used to bother me.	○	○	○	○	○	○
59.	I have become more effective in getting what I need.	○	○	○	○	○	○
60.	I can deal better with people and situations that used to be a problem for me.	○	○	○	○	○	○

61. I have been a consumer of mental health services for:
  ○ Less than 6 months   ○ Between 2 and 5 years
  ○ Between 6 months and 1 year   ○ Between 5 and 10 years
  ○ Between 1 and 2 years   ○ More than 10 years

Comments:
Please add any other comments you may have here:

Appendix A: Selected Instruments

Appendix B
Outcomes Measurement System Vendors

Access Measurement Systems, Inc.

50 Main Street
Ashland MA 01721
Tel: (800) 329-0949
Fax: (508) 881-8777
E-mail: Jcrawford@AMS-outcomes.com

Contact
Jeanne Crawford, MA, MPH, Associate Vice President

Year company founded
1993

Targeted treatment setting(s)
All settings

Targeted patient populations
All patient populations

Domains measured
Psychiatric symptoms, Social functioning, Quality of life, Patient satisfaction, Health status, Extensive case-mix—life stress, co-morbid medical conditions, demographics, language spoken, payer of treatment, etc.
Instrument(s) employed
  We will use virtually any questionnaire, including BASIS-32, SF-36 and OQ-45, as well as any others that an organization receives permission to use and for which they have interest in the added credibility of a neutral, third party processing organization and extensive comparison data. Our proprietary Treatment Outcome Package (TOP) looks at a full range of functional, symptom, medical, quality of life, and case-mix variables in one questionnaire.

System cost
$2-$5/administration, depending on volume. Price includes: questionnaire forms (3 color); immediate scoring and reporting via fax; clinically useful individual assessment reports; database management; and aggregate satisfaction and outcome reports.

Can other instruments be integrated?
Absolutely. We help many organizations customize, modify and develop their own tools.

Customizable in other ways?
We can customize the tools, process and reports to fit anyone's unique needs.

Benchmark database available? If so, how large?
Monthly or quarterly access to a large, accurate comparative database is our specialty. The database is growing by thousands each month, and we also have the most stringent data accuracy requirements in the industry, which ensures the accuracy of these comparisons. Rather than relying on caregivers to honestly report their data to us, we process each and every client encounter in real-time, and can ensure that the data is not biased, self-selected or modified.

Computer-based?
Our high-tech QuickAccess^{SM} system is only high-tech on our end. Providers need only a fax machine to gain access to an immediate scoring and reporting system. Aggregate and raw data can be delivered in any frequency interval for a wide

variety of standard database, spreadsheet, statistical and csv formats. Hardware for those who are interested will be available soon.

Availability on Internet
Transfer of data can be

How users record data
Paper and pencil, scannable forms

Real-time reports?
Absolutely

Customer support?
"800" number tech and customer support

Number of installations
Over 15,000 clinicians are using the system nationwide.

Patients in system
Over 30,000 as of October 1998

Names of large clients (up to four)
Mental Health Corporations of Massachusetts; Washington State Community Mental Health Council, Harvard Teaching Hospitals, University of Massachusetts Medical School

Special or unique features
The system incorporates features to address many of the problems that plague outcomes measurement. These include: a neutral third-party processing organization to deal with data credibility and reporting accuracy-useful when an organization wishes to employ the data for contracting, accreditation or other "external" uses; a fax-based processing system utilizing QuickAccessSM technology; real-time data access and decision support tools; fairer comparisons, which are achieved by measuring more of the factors outside of provider and/or payer control that influence outcomes; and extensive data accuracy protections that eliminate most fraudulent, unscientific or distorted results.

AdvantaCare, Inc.

85 Constitution Lane, Suite 100F
Danvers MA 01923
Tel: (978) 777-7887; (877) Go AdvantaCare ((877) 462-3826)
Fax: (978) 777-6446
E-mail: info@advantacare.com
Internet: www.advantacare.com

Contact
Michael D. McGee, MD, Chairman and Chief Clinical Officer
Robert L. Keener, Vice President of Sales and Marketing

Year company founded
1991

Targeted treatment setting(s)
All health and human service settings

Targeted patient populations
Behavioral Health and Human Service Populations

Domains measured
Clinical outcomes, Satisfaction (Patient, Family, Referral Source, Provider), and performance indicators.

Instrument(s) employed
Short Form, 12 items (SF-12)
Behavior and Symptom Impairment Scale, 32 items
(BASIS-32) Outcomes Questionnaire, 45 items (OQ-45)
Youth Outcomes Questionnaire (YOQ)
OASIS-B
SSS-30 Satisfaction Assessment
SSS-Residential Satisfaction Assessment Life Skills Profile
Perceptions of Care Satisfaction Assessment (From McLean Hospital)
Problem Frequency Index-B for Substance Abuse (PFI-B) (This is a self-report version of the ASI).
Other tools available upon request

System cost
Per-patient and administrative fees as follows:
$4/patient/year, excluding phone charges (these are ~$5/patient/year). Includes up to 4 assessments/year/patient. Additional assessments are billed at $2.5/assessment, (including phone charges).
$200/month administrative fee for organizations $50/month administrative fee for small group practices $10/month administrative fee for individual providers

Can other instruments be integrated?
Yes. Quickly, easily, and inexpensively. Advant Assess comes with a customizing feature, StudyBuilder (available 4/99), which allows users to input and implement any quality measure or instrument on line via the Internet.

Can the system be customizable in other ways?
AdvantAssess is an automated quality assessment work environment that has virtually unlimited customizability. With AdvantAssess, users can create their own assessments, studies, and reports.

AdvantAssess comes with an online clinical assessment and treatment reporter. Users can specify which clinical, demographic or treatment variables are required for a given study. Users can add custom clinical, demographic or treatment variables. Users can create their own assessments, group assessments into custom assessment events, and arrange assessment events along timelines to create their own custom Studies. Users can then use AdvantAssess's online multidimensional data analysis tool and report generator (available 3/99) to perform unlimited analyses of individual, organization, and benchmark performance. Users can create custom reports for repeated use.

Is a benchmark database available? If so, how large?

AdvantAssess is a performance database available nationally (even globally) by telephone or Internet browser. Benchmark data is available online, real-time, from anywhere in the world, 24 hours a day, seven days a week.

Is the system computer-based?
Yes.

Available on the Internet?

Yes. Users interact with AdvantAssess via telephone or Internet browser.

By browser, AdvantAssess has the look, feel, and behavior of a client-server software system. Users can register patients, input clinical and demographic data, open and episodes of care, record treatment information, enroll subjects in studies, complete assessments, and view performance and management reports. The Internet is especially suited for online data analysis and report generation, and for inputting text-based information, such as names.

AdvantAssess does not require the Internet, however, for routine daily use. Users can register patients, open and close episodes of care, enroll patients in studies, administer assessments, and request reports in just a few seconds with the telephone. AdvantAssess automatically faxes assessment results, performance reports, and management reports. AdvantAssess will even call study subjects to remind them when their assessments are due.

How do users record data?

All data input by all users (patients, administrators, providers, others) is directly into AdvantAssess by telephone or Internet browser.

Are real-time reports possible?
All reports are real time

Customer support?
24/7 by telephone. Assess to a host of nationally known consultants within one to three business days.

Number of installations?
Ten

Number of patients in system?
~1000 to date since launch of AdvantAssess in August 1998.

Names of large clients (up to four)
Adcare Hospital

Special or unique features

Online StudyBuilder for creating custom assessments and studies. Online unlimited analytic capabilities by clinical, demographic and treatment variables.

Online report generation, including automatic recurrent reports

Use of IVR (telephone interactive voice response) for daily activities. Users need only a telephone and a fax to use the system.

Instant receipt of clinical assessment results.

System reminds users to take assessments that are due.

Global performance database available by telephone or Internet. Users can begin using system immediately with little or no training.

Ultra-secure and confidential system actually decreases risks of data loss or breaks in confidentiality.

No need for up-front hardware or software expenditures.

Less expensive than any competing systems while offering much greater value and flexibility.

IVR assessment administration preferred by patients over paper and pencil assessments. Assessments can be completed conveniently at home.

BHOS, Inc. (formerly Behavioral Health Outcomes Systems)

689 Mamaroneck Avenue
Mamaroneck NY 10543
Tel: (800) 494-BHOS (2467)
Fax: (914) 381-1725
E-mail: billb@bhos.com
Internet: www.bhos.com

Contact
William H. Berman, President

Year company founded
1994

Targeted treatment setting(s)
All settings: Outpatient, Inpatient, Partial Hospitalization

Targeted patient populations
All patient populations: Adults, Adolescents, Children, Geriatric, Substance abusers

Domains measured
Psychiatric symptoms (rated by patient and/or clinician), Social functioning (rated by patient and/or clinician), Quality of life (optional), Patient satisfaction, Health status SF-36/SF-12 (standard scorer), Work functioning, Daily functioning

Instrument(s) employed
The SF-36, SF-12, the BHOS Patient Problems Scale, the Clinician-Rated Problems Scale, the Patient Functioning Index, the Clinician-Rated Functioning Index, the Consumer Satisfaction Index (Inpatient and Outpatient), the Substance Abuse Inventory, GHAA and NCQA Satisfaction Surveys, the Geriatric Depression Scale, and the Mini-Mental State Exam. A wide range of other outcomes instruments are available for custom-designed outcomes measurement.

System cost
HealthScore™ has several versions ranging from $249 for a hand-entered SF-12 or SF-36 software, to $4,000 for the HealthScore Basic (note prices subject to change). Large volume pricing, and custom system design costs are available on request.

Can other instruments be integrated?
Virtually any measure, scale, interview, or data capture form can be easily integrated into the system. Other instruments already in the system include the BASIS-32, the BPRS, the Devereux Scales, the Beck Depression Inventory, and the GHAA and NCQA member satisfaction surveys.

Customizable in other ways?
HealthScore allows the user to custom design outcomes modules, including measures, time-points for data collection, and reports. Multiple data entry methods are also possible, including manual entry, flat-bed scanner, direct-fax, IVR, and palm top box. HealthScore has been integrated into the UNI/CARE Systems, Inc. For pricing, including additional reports and instruments, contact Michelle Means at 919-467-9295.

Benchmark database available? If so, how large?
Benchmark data is available on all scales, with different database sizes for each scale. Sample sizes for the BHOS PPS and PFI are approximately 5,000. Comparison data for the SF-12 is is growing by approximately 750 records per month.

Computer-based?

The software requires a Pentium processor with 32 megabytes of RAM, 100 megabytes of hard drive space, and Windows 95. A flat-bed scanner is required for scannable entry; a fax card is required for fax entry.

Availability on Internet

Not at the present, but development is under way.

How users record data

Users may choose paper forms, which are either scanned or faxed into the databases, palm top box, or IVR.

Real-time reports?

The system provides real-time individual case reports that include both numeric and graphic data along with normative comparison tables. The standard software allows real-time aggregate reports for data averaged by clinician, by site, by diagnostic category, by age, gender, payer organization, and for the total sample.

Customer support?

Training is available as needed. Telephone and e-mail customer support are also available.

Number of installations

60 single measure applications; 28 multistudy, multimeasure applications of July 1998.

Patients in system

Comparison databases vary depending on measures. Examples include: SF-12~5,000; SF-36~4,000; BASIS-32 (through U. Cincinnati) ~8,000; BHOS Scales~2-4,000

Names of large clients (up to four)

Kaiser-Permanente of Northern California; Group Health Cooperative of Puget Sound; University of Miami Behavioral Health (through UNI/CARE); PRO Behavioral Health

Special or unique features

The system is integrated as a module into UNI/CARE Systems, Inc's Behavioral Health Information System and can be purchased through UNI/CARE as part of an integrated information system. The data table structure is non-proprietary and can be accessed through or input to through other database applications. BHOS is a Joint Commission ORYX approved listed vendor. All standard BHOS measures for the adult substance abuse, child and adolescent and geriatric modules are ORYX approved.

Corporation for Standards & Outcomes (CS&O)

101 Emerson Avenue
Pittsburgh PA 15215
Tel: (800) 587-7861; (412) 781-5480
Fax: (412) 781-5482
E-mail: driggscso@aol.com
Internet: www.standardsandoutcomes.com

Contact
Gerald E. Driggs, President & CEO

Year company founded
1995

Targeted treatment setting(s)
All settings; child welfare, juvenile justice and substance abuse also covered.

Targeted patient populations
Adolescents, Children; families can be applied to other populations.

Domains measured
Social functioning, Quality of life, Patient satisfaction, Functional outcomes derived from stakeholder survey process.

Instrument(s) employed
CS&O Outcome Interview (child & adult versions); numerous severity assessment tools; incorporates IQ, diagnosis and educational testing information.

System cost
Annual subscription fee varies with size of installation. Average cost is $3,500 per agency (eight users). Additional users can be added.

Can other instruments be integrated?
Yes

Customizable in other ways?
Yes

Benchmark database available? If so, how large?
Yes. We have 42,000 client records as of September 1997, and it is growing quarterly at a rate of approximately 5,000 records.

Computer-based?
Yes. It is cross-platform. The client server version requires Windows 95, a 100 megahertz (minimum), pentium processor-based PC with 16 megabytes RAM and adequate storage.

Availability on Internet
Many CS&O services are available through the Internet.

How users record data
Electronic data input

Real-time reports?
Yes

Customer support?
Yes

Number of installations
Available on request

Patients in system
Available on request

Names of large clients (up to four)
Available on request

Special or unique features
System is used in conjunction with full-blown outcomes methodology for defining, tracking and comparing outcomes. CS&O has a growing national collaborative and a database for benchmarking purposes.

DeltaMetrics

Assessment and Treatment Outcomes Management System (ATOMS)

2005 Market Street, Suite 1120
Philadelphia, PA 19103
Tel: (800) 238-2433
Fax: (215) 665-2892
E-mail: HYPERLINK mailto:deltamet@aol.com deltamet@aol.com

Contact
Richard V. Weiss, PhD, Research Psychologist

Year company founded
1994

Targeted treatment setting(s)
All settings

Targeted patient populations
Adults, Adolescents (under development)

Domains measured
Psychiatric symptoms, Social functioning, Quality of life, Patient satisfaction, Health status, Substance abuse

Instrument(s) employed
Problem Frequency Index—B (PFI-B), Risk Adjustment Scale (RAS), ATOMS Clinical Tracker

System cost
Varies according to size and organizational structure of client.

Can other instruments be integrated?
Yes. Specifically, the system has been designed with the BASIS-32 and SF-12 available for client use.

Customizable in other ways?
Yes. Report formats can be tailored. There are multiple methods of data entry available.

Benchmark database available? If so, how large?
Yes. The ATOMS includes a growing national database. Currently, the database consists of approximately 1,000 cases.

Computer-based?
Yes. The ATOMS computer application requires hardware that is 486 or better with 16 megabytes of RAM and 15 megabytes of hard disk space. The software runs on Windows 3.1 and Windows 95.

Availability on Internet?
No.

How users record data
The ATOMS is flexible. Data can be collected via patient self-report or interview. Patients can enter their responses into PC workstations using touch screen, mouse, or keyboard. Data can also be recorded by administrative staff via scannable forms, touch screen, mouse, or keyboard.

Real-time reports?
Yes. Four types of reports can be generated on demand: (1) Intake Profiles, which are a concise summary of the information collected using baseline instrumentation; (2) Individual Treatment

Progress Reports, which display patient progress over time; (3) Aggregate Management Reports, which profile a patient population; and (4) JCAHO/ORYX Reports, which present data on approved performance indicators.

Customer support?
Technical assistance and outcomes design and reporting consultation are available.

Number of installations
Five

Patients in system
Approximately 1,000

Names of large clients (up to four)
Short-term. John's Mercy; The Arbour Health System; Members of Indiana Council of Community Mental Health Centers.

Special or unique features
The ATOMS consists of a core intake battery and a core tracking instrument as well as optional supplementary instruments. The core intake battery creates a minimum data set that contains sufficient information for risk adjustment and multidimensional symptom and function severity profiling. The core tracking instrument creates a minimum data set that profiles outcome status and change, and provides summary measures of patient satisfaction with treatment, and medication compliance.

The ATOMS and a number of its measurement domains (e.g., reduction in psychiatric severity, reduction in substance abuse severity, medication compliance) have been accepted by the JCAHO for accreditation purposes in connection with the ORYX initiative. The instrumentation and software were developed after thorough research into existing instrumentation and management information systems. The ATOMS was initially piloted by eight member hospitals of the National Association of Psychiatric Health Systems (NAPHS) whose feedback was incorporated into subsequent versions of the systems. The instruments were further developed by DeltaMetrics researchers and tested in a variety of treatment settings and patient populations.

Three design principles distinguish the ATOMS: 1) a multidimensional approach to patient assessment, 2) patient self-report, and 3) problem frequency as a measurement strategy.

Multidimensional Approach
The ATOMS relies on the principle that assessment of psychiatric symptoms alone provides information of marginal value. Based on a growing body of research, DeltaMetrics believes that a multidimensional profile is necessary for valid treatment planning, treatment assessment, level of care decisions, and outcomes evaluation. Only with multidimensional information can treatment be truly individualized and progress be meaningfully measured.

Patient Self-Report
The assessment approach relies largely on patient self-report. DeltaMetrics selected a patient self-report approach for two reasons. First, it is the most cost-efficient way of gathering the type of data needed for an initial assessment, level of care decisions, and outcomes. Clinician time is minimized because extensive and valuable information is obtained directly from the patient. Second, with many types of patients and under many circumstances, research has consistently shown that patient reports of their own problems and functioning can be valid indicators of status and progress.

Problem Frequency
Biopsychosocial evaluations generally employ one of two general strategies to assess patient status: problem severity, in which patients are asked how much of a bother a particular problem is; and problem frequency, in which patients are asked how frequently a problem occurs. The ATOMS describes patient status with a problem frequency measurement approach. Treatment facilities that piloted early versions of the ATOMS reported that our problem frequency approach to patient status description was highly-valued and easily-understood. Also, over the past 15 years, our experience with substance abusers has shown that frequency of target behaviors is both well-related to other parameters (e.g., number of symptoms, maximum severity, duration of problem) and very sensitive to change over time. Through subsequent testing with the ATOMS, we have replicated such findings with general psychiatric patients.

HCIA's Response

950 Winter Street, Suite 3450
Waltham MA 02154
Tel: (617) 768-1800
Fax: (617) 768-1811
Internet: http://www.hcia.com

Contact
Content and Sales: Saeed Aminzadeh, Senior Director, Sales, [Tel: (617) 768-1805]

Year company founded
1989

Targeted treatment setting(s)
All settings

Targeted patient populations
All patient populations

Domains measured
Psychiatric symptoms, Social functioning, Quality of life, Patient satisfaction, Health status

Instrument(s) employed
BASIS-32, QLI, CBCL, and YSR, Client Satisfaction Questionnaire (CSQ-8), Treatment Satisfaction Survey, Global Assessment of Functioning (GAF), Perceptions of Care (Inpatient and Outpatient)

System cost
System cost: Release 2.5 is currently being released. Please contact Saeed Aminzadeh, Senior Director, Sales.

Can other instruments be integrated?
Yes. We currently have the SF-36, SF-12, Health Risk Profiler, Senior Health Tool, and other disease specific modules.

Customizable in other ways?
Yes. We have Survey Designer™ for use with our software which enables the user the ability to develop their own surveys. In addition to standard survey forms, HCIA/Response supports clients with the design and automation of risk screening tools, disease specific instruments and multidimensional instruments for use in QI programs that are integrated into our data collection platforms. Over 50 percent of HCIA/ RESPONSE's projects for clients involve the design and automation of customized or public domain instruments.

Benchmark database available? If so, how large?
Benchmark data is available for certain survey instruments.

Computer-based?
Yes. Minimum system requirements are 8 megabytes of RAM (16 megabytes preferred) on a 486 machine.

Availability on Internet
Will be available by the end of 1998.

How users record data
Scannable survey cards, fax-based data capture

Real-time reports?
Yes

Customer support?

A customer service "800" phone number is available for technical support.

Number of installations

Approximately 2,000

Patients in system

Our outcomes warehouse, which includes several hundred survey administrations, is available to clients.

Names of large clients (up to four)

City of San Francisco; City of Los Angeles; Kaiser Permanente.

Special or unique features

A client/server system is available for clients that wish to collect data from a variety of different locations and store the data on a central server.

Integra, Inc.

Compassᴿ Treatment Assessment System

1060 First Avenue, Suite 400
King of Prussia Pa 19406
Tel: (610) 992-7000
Fax (610) 992-7046
E-mail ed@integra-ease.com

Contact person
Edwin Edghill
Rick Jackson

Year company founded
1977

Parent company
Integra, Inc.

Targeted treatment setting(s)
Outpatient, Inpatient, Partial Hospital

Targeted patient populations
Adult mental health/chemical dependency outpatient, inpatient and partial hospital populations

Domains measured
Outpatient: Mental Health index, Current Symptoms (several subscales including depression, anxiety, phobia, substance abuse, etc.), Current Life Functioning (including Work, Family, Health Status, etc.), Current Well-Being, Presenting Problems (with several subscales) Scales.

Inpatient/Partial Hospital: Overall Symptoms (Patient and Staff Report), Assaultiveness (Patient & Staff Report, Lifetime & Past 24 Hours), Mania, Suicidality (Patient & Staff Report, Lifetime & Past 24 Hours), Overall Functioning, Activities of Daily Living (Patient and Staff Report), Social Functioning, Well-Being, Anxiety, Depression, Substance Abuse, Family Functioning, Task Performance, Treatment Participation, Psychosis Scales.

Chemical Dependency: Severity of Alcohol, Drug, Psychiatric, Employment/Support, Family/Social, Legal, and Medical Problems Scales.

System cost
Compass pricing:
Compass OP (outpatient): 1/administration may also be purchased on a subscription basis.
Compass INT (intensive-in-patient, partial) for JCAHO Oryx initiative: $7,000-$15,000 per facility.
The full Compass suite and systems may be purchased on a project basis for those whho desire a fully integrated outcomes management system.

Can other instruments be integrated
Yes

Customizable in other ways
Yes

Benchmark database available? If so, how large?
70,000

Computer-based?
Yes

Available on Internet
January 1999

How users record data
Multiple Administration Platforms: including paper-and-pencil scannable forms, PC Workstation, Web-based, Point-of-View hand held device.

Real-time reports?
Yes

Customer support?
Yes

Number of installations
Integra has been utilizing the COMPASS System since its inception in 1993 with 30+ nationwide accounts.

Patients in system
Varies due to product

Names of large clients (up to four)
InfoMc, Innovative Systems, Askesis Development Group, Pitney Bowes

Special or unique features
COMPASS PC for use in primary care settings is owned by Bristol Myers Squibb. Flexibility in administration due to recent technological developments.

Mental Health Outcomes, Inc.

1500 Waters Ridge Drive
Lewisville TX 75057-6011
Tel: (800) 266-4440
Fax: (972) 420-8215
E-mail: billed@psinet.com
Internet: www.mhoutcomes.com

Contact
William S. Edell, PhD, Senior Vice President, Clinical Development
Jeff Maynard, Vice President, Market Development

Year company founded
1995

Parent company
Horizon Health Corporation

Targeted treatment setting(s)
Inpatient, Partial hospital, Intensive outpatient, and Outpatient

Targeted patient populations
All patient populations

Domains measured
Psychiatric symptoms, Social functioning, Quality of life, Patient satisfaction, Health status, Program characteristics, Maladaptive behaviors, Cost-effectiveness

Instrument(s) employed
Health Status Questionnaire (HSQ); SF-36; Behavior and Symptom Identification Scale (BASIS-32); Brief Psychiatric Rating Scale (BPRS); Global Assessment of Functioning (GAF); Geriatric Depression Scale (GDS); Mini-Mental State Exam; Psychogeriatric Dependency Rating Scale; Medication Usage Questionnaire; Admission and Follow-up Questionnaires; Medical Record Information Forms; Patient Satisfaction Form

System cost
$830-$2,950 per month, depending on specific outcomes modules selected.

Can other instruments be integrated?
Yes

Customizable in other ways?
Yes. Depth of measurement, training, reports, examination of specialty track within program, specific treatments and staff elements.

Benchmark database available? If so, how large?
Yes. Over 20,000 psychiatric participants (as of August 1998).

Computer-based?
Computerized processing for automated data entry, statistical analyses, and reporting

Availability on Internet
As needed

How users record data
Scannable (optical mark read) instruments

Real-time reports?
No

Customer support?
Dedicated clinical and data management personnel, on-site training, toll-free support line (unlimited access during business hours)

Number of installations
The CQI+SM Outcomes Measurement System is currently operational in 71 facilities, with contracts to implement CQI+SM and signed at an additional 15 facilities, as of July 15, 1998.

Patients in system
Over 20,000 patients

Names of large clients (up to four)
Reference list provided upon request.

Special or unique features
The CQI+SM Outcomes Measurement System views outcomes from a multidimensional perspective, understanding that no single number or brief instrument can capture the complexity of the overall functioning of the individual for all interested parties. There is a strong emphasis on the training of staff involved in the actual data collection, and there is unlimited client access to a toll-free hot line. Weekly data integrity audit reports are provided to each site to keep staff abreast of their progress in obtaining required information from patients, and all follow-ups are conducted by the professional staff at MHO, Inc. to insure the integrity of data collection "post discharge" from the program. CQI+SM uses a variety of valid and reliable instruments tailored specifically to the target populations. The CQI+SM Outcomes Measurement System is included on the ORYX (JCAHO) list of acceptable performance measurement systems.

OQ Systems, Inc.

34 Wall Street, P.O. Box 2054
Norwalk, CT 06852-2054
Tel: (203) 838-6003
Fax: (203) 866-9614
E-mail: algobc@mindspring.com
Internet: www.oqsystems.com

Contact person
Geoffrey V. Gray, PhD

Year company founded?
1992

Targeted treatment setting(s)
All mental health and substance abuse treatment settings

Targeted patient populations?
All mental health and substance abuse patient populations, including children adolescents and adults served by HMO, EAP, college counseling center, community mental health center, medicaid/medicare, SPMI, etc.

Domains measured?
Adult: Symptom Distress, Interpersonal Relations, Social Role, Well Being Children/Adolescent: Intrapersonal Distress, Somatic, Interpersonal Relations, Critical Items, Social Problems, Behavior Dysfunction

Instrument(s) employed
OQ-45.2, Y-OQ-2.0

System cost
Depends on system: client server systems come with a variety of data capture methodologies: IVR (with fax-back), Scan, Fax, Manual, Internet

Can other instruments be integrated?
Yes

Can the system be customizable in other ways?
Yes

Is a benchmark database available? If so, how large?
Yes. 30,000 plus records

Is the system computer-based?
Yes

Available on the Internet?
Yes

How do users record data?
Database

Are real-time reports possible?
Yes. They are an essential part of the system.

Customer support?
Yes

Number of installations?
60 plus

Number of patients in system?
Several million

Names of large clients (up to four)?
Magellan, United Health Care, Kaiser-Permanente, Intermountain Health

Special or unique features?
Multiple data capture methods, including IVR allows for seamless integration into any system. Data hosting available.

Parrot Software

P.O. Box 250755
West Bloomfield MI 48325
Tel: (800) 727-7681
Fax: (248) 788-3224
E-mail: parrot@mcs.net
Internet: http://www.parrotsoft.com

Contact
Fred Weiner

Year company founded
1981

Targeted treatment setting(s)
All settings

Targeted patient populations
All patient populations

Domains measured
You enter the ones you want to evaluate.

Instrument(s) employed
You enter the ones you want to use.

System cost
$499

Can other instruments be integrated?
Yes

Customizable in other ways?
All aspects

Benchmark database available? If so, how large?
No

Computer-based?
Windows 3.x or 95 and 8 megabytes of RAM

Availability on Internet
Demo is available.

How users record data
Easy input screen

Real-time reports?
Yes. Reports can be generated at anytime for any period of time.

Customer support?
"800" number is available from 8:30 AM to 5:30 PM Eastern Time.

Number of installations
More than 300

Special or unique features
Generates any type of report required. Demo disk available.

Performance-Based Outcomes, Inc.

5215 Old Orchard Road, Suite 700
Skokie IL 6007-1045
Tel: (847) 779-8550
Fax: (847) 965-0000
E-mail: pbo@mcs.com
Internet: pbo-outcomes.com

Contact
William J. Filstead, PhD, President

Year company founded
1993

Targeted treatment setting(s)
Behavioral health and general health care settings

Targeted patient populations
Adolescents and adults

Domains measured
Psychosocial, health status, CD issues, satisfaction

Instrument(s) employed
Clinical Rating Scale; Alcohol Substance Abuse Questionnaire; various standardized measures

System cost
Costs vary based on measures used, applications, nature of our participation, and volume.

Can other instruments be integrated?
Yes

Customizable in other ways?
Yes. We are able to link site-specific information to these measures and/or add additional survey type questions to these measures.

Benchmark database available? If so, how large?
Database/benchmarking is possible for some measures like the FIM/FAM, SCL-90 or SF-36.

Computer-based?
Some of the applications require a 386 or higher IBM-compatible machine running DOS 3.3 or later and Microsoft Windows 3.1 or later. The best configuration is a 486-class machine running DOS 6.0 with 4 megabytes RAM and a hard disk with 2 megabytes of free disk space.

Availability on Internet
At the Web site, one can download a demo disk of applications.

How users record data
Users can send data electronically, via diskettes, or as paper/pencil forms.

Real-time reports?
Yes. Some applications print and store information once it is entered; these data also remain online for management/clinical use.

Customer support?
Yes. Technical/consulting support is part of the contractual agreement.

Number of installations
22

Patients in system
It is hard to estimate, due to different applications being used by various clients. It could be as high as 32,000.

Names of large clients (up to four)
Parkside Seniors; Merit Behavioral Care Corp.; Hazelden/Betty Ford; CMHCs

Special or unique features
Easily adaptable to sites; tailored information possible; very few expenses associated with hardware/software-start-up experiences.

Strategic Advantage Systems Corporation

2125 E. Hennepin Avenue
Minneapolis MN 55413
Tel: (612) 331-8700
Fax: (612) 331-8181
E-mail: info@stradv.com
Web: www.stradv.com

Contact
Bill Keenan, National Program Director

Year company founded
1986

Parent company
Magellan Health Services

Targeted treatment setting(s)
All settings

Targeted patient populations
Adults, Adolescents, Elderly

Domains measured
Psychiatric symptom severity, Psychological well-being, Physical well-being, Daily role functioning, Living conditions, Occupational functioning, Treatment motivation, Resource utilization, Social functioning, Patient satisfaction, Health status, Length of stay, Discharge disposition

Instrument(s) employed
SF-12, Symptom Assessment-45™ (SA-45™), Symptom Assessment-24™ (SA-24™), Decision Care™ System 3.1 Clinical Intake Questionnaire, DecisionCare™ System 3.1 Clinical Discharge Questionnaire, DecisionCare™ System 3.1 Patient Intake Questionnaire, DecisionCare™ System 3.1 Patient Discharge Questionnaire (includes satisfaction questionnaire), Decision Care™ System 3.1 Family/ Friend Satisfaction Questionnaire

System cost
Depends on size of population to be measured and number of instruments included. Ranges from $1,000 to $10,000 per program.

Can other instruments be integrated?
Yes

Customizable in other ways?
Yes. While the system relies on a generic product, the data collected, the method of data collection, analysis and reporting can be customized to meet the end user's needs.

Benchmark database available? If so, how large?
Yes. The database has 30,000 cases as of August 1997, with an additional 5,000 to 6,000 added each month.

Computer-based?
Data input and output is fax-based for the end-user, with a sophisticated computer-based system to support the input, data analysis and fax output process. This system is housed at Strategic Advantage Systems Corporation.

Availability on Internet
Data collection of the SA-45™ via the Internet is in development.

How users record data
Number-two pencil bubble forms

Real-time reports?
The SA-45™ InfiniFax provides real-time reporting via a low-burden, low-cost, fax-based data input/output system. A one-page instrument is sent to SAI for analysis and scoring via the end user's fax machine, and a patient profile is

returned to the sender via fax within 5 to 15 minutes of the original submission. The SF-12 will be available via InfiniFax in the fourth quarter of 1997. Additional instruments can be delivered via the InfiniFax, at the customer's request, making real-time reporting possible on a variety of public domain or customer proprietary instruments.

Customer support?

Hotline assistance is available during business hours, 9:00-4:00 CST. Self-study training materials are part of every purchase.

Number of installations

Over 90 facilities use the DecisionCare System, and more than 200 use the SA-45 InfiniFax.

Patients in system

30,000+ with an additional 5,000 to 6,000 added each month

Names of large clients (up to four)

Charter Behavioral Health Systems (USA); Homewood Health Center (Canada); Greenspring Health Services (USA)

Special or unique features

Strategic Advantage Systems Corporation has met the initial criteria for inclusion in the future accreditation process and is included on the Joint Commission's list of acceptable systems. A one-page instrument provides real-time results in 5 to 15 minutes that can be used to streamline the authorization and treatment planning process. All the benefits of the SA-45 InfiniFax System-low-burden, real-time reports via a fax machine-can be applied to other instruments, and any public domain or customer-owned instrument can be delivered via InfiniFax.

Velocity Healthcare Informatics

8441 Wayzata Blvd., Suite 105
Minneapolis MN 55426
Tel: (612) 797-9997
Fax: (612) 797-9993
Web: www.velocity.com

Contact
Penelope Frohardt, Corporate Communications Specialist

Year company founded
1993

Parent company
Object Products, Inc.

Targeted treatment setting(s)
All settings: Outpatient, Inpatient, Partial Hospitalization, Disease Management for Chronic Conditions

Targeted patient populations
All patient populations: Adults, Elderly, Substance abusers, Patients with Depression

Domains measured
Psychiatric symptoms, Social functioning, Quality of life, Patient satisfaction, Health status

Instrument(s) employed
SF-36, HSQ, SF-12, Depression, Alcohol and Substance Abuse

System cost
Packages start at $5,000 and up.

Can other instruments be integrated?
Yes

Customizable in other ways?
Yes

Benchmark database available? If so, how large?
Yes. Currently, over 4,000 patients are included in the reference data set.

Computer-based?
Yes. The minimum system requirements are: a 386sx IBM-compatible personal computer with 8 megabytes RAM and a 60 megabyte hard drive with 12 megabytes of free disk space, a monochrome monitor, mouse, 9-pin dot matrix printer (Windows-compatible), 2400 baud modem, and Windows 3.1.

Availability on Internet
No

How users record data
Data Entry: Manual, Fax in/Fax back, Scanning, Service Bureau

Real-time reports?
Yes

Customer support?
Yes

Number of installations
Over 100

Patients in system
Over 4,000 in reference data

Names of large clients (up to four)
Dean Medical Center, WI; Washington University School of Medicine, MO; St. Josephs Hospital, NC

Appendix C
Behavioral Benchmarks

OMP Has System for Comparing Provider Outcomes

BARBARA BENGEN-SELTZER, MBA, MA

Clinicians may be asking outcomes proponents: "Even if you could quantify my results with patients, how would you really know whether these results are good or bad?" One way to give some perspective or meaning to clinician "scores" is to compare them with those of clinicians in other group settings.

This is the premise of the Outcomes Management Project (OMP), initially sponsored by the national Council of Behavioral Group Practices. Established in 1995, OMP is now housed in the Department of Psychiatry at the University of Cincinnati College of Medicine. Co-founded by Allen S. Daniels EdD, director of University Psychiatric Services in Cincinnati, and Gayle L. Zieman, PhD, chief clinical officer of Mesa Mental Health in Albuquerque, OMP coordinates and analyzes data from 20 participating group practices and integrated delivery systems nationally.

OMP providers collect data according to a standard protocol and then funnel the data back to OMP to create benchmarking "norms." Reports and national aggregate data are issued quarterly to participant groups. OMP now has pretreatment assessment data on 15,000 patients in 12 states and follow-up data at 3 and 6 months on more than 7,000 patients.

"An individual result means very little unless you can compare it against a national benchmark," notes Daniels. "One of the strengths of the OMP system is

that it drives empowerment back to the provider. We give the data back to the providers so they can analyze it and make changes in their own operations." This allows providers to answer questions such as: "Why do we seem to have more of a problem with patient access than other group practices nationally?"

An unusual feature of the OMP is that each participating group licenses the OMP software so that each site scores its own results and keeps its actual data. "This allows each participating provider group to conduct its own analysis and to ask the questions it considers important," said Mesa's Zieman. "Our participating clinics have something they value—they can slice the data in their own way and pump it back through their own software package."

Answers to Clinical Practice Questions

What tools does the OMP system give participating providers? Perhaps its most useful function is

---

Source: Barbara Bengen-Seltzer. OMP Has System for Comparing Provider Outcomes. Behavioral Health Outcomes. 1998 Vol. 3(1):4-5. Reprinted with permission.

Ms. Bengen-Seltzer is consulting editor of Behavioral Health Outcomes and principal of Strategic Health Care Consulting, 215 Corey St., Boston, MA 02132-2328; phone (617) 327-7092; fax (617) 327-7672; e-mail bbengenseltzer@mindspring.com.

Dr. Daniels can be reached at (513) 475-8710.

Dr. Zieman can be reached at (505) 828-9297, x1004; fax (505) 858-1779.

to address long-standing questions about the efficacy of different treatment options. A medical director from a local health plan asked University Psychiatric Services (UPS) in Cincinnati which kind of model provides the best care for therapy patients who also need medications. Is it:

- one in which the therapist does therapy while a psychiatrist handles medications?
- one where the psychiatrist handles both the therapy and medications? or
- one in which the therapist provides therapy and the primary care physician handles medication?

According to UPS data, the most effective model in its practice turned out to be situations where the therapist works with the primary care physician. Since there are factors specific to the UPS practice that might influence this finding, a next step would be to see whether this result is confirmed in the other 19 OMP sites, says Daniels.

In the second example, UPS administrators discovered that for patients in therapy for depression, its clinicians were prescribing fewer medications than clinicians at the 20 OMP sites overall. This was true even though the UPS patients had scored in the same range as the national OMP norm for depression severity, Daniels says.

UPS staff wanted to know whether their patients might be undermedicated, so they compared their group outcomes for depressed patients against the OMP average. The findings showed that UPS had better outcomes than the OMP average, suggesting that psychotherapy was an effective choice, and that the smaller reliance on medications was not harmful.

Meanwhile another project member—the Mesa Health group in Albuquerque—tackled other questions about relative efficacy of treatment modalities. For example, administrators wanted to know whether depressed patients do better if their initial treatment was to receive medications or to receive psychotherapy. The group's data indicated that while long-term outcomes for both groups were comparable, the patients who started with medications had a shorter length of treatment overall than the patients who began with psychotherapy, even if medication was added later, says Zieman.

Mesa examined early indicators for high-need patients, based on trends spotted in OMP aggre-

> ### Application to Smaller Provider Systems
>
> A key aspect concerning outcomes analysis of the type being done by OMP is the need for sufficient patient volume to make the findings reliable. According to Zieman, a provider group should be able to collect initial pretreatment data on at least 200 to 300 a patients a year.
>
> A smaller group could look at its aggregate data with even 150 or fewer patients but might not be able to subdivide the data further by diagnostic category or specific clinician. Alternatively, several smaller groups could form a cooperative, buy one software license and house the software data at one location. A location coder would allow each provider to track its own data and still keep the costs manageable, says Zieman.

gate data. Mesa's data indicate that two patient scores on subscales of the pretreatment assessment tool correlate highly with the amount of treatment that a patient seems to need. They are the patient's reported level of:

1) social functioning in relationships with the family, at work, in school, etc.; and
2) difficulty in completing physical activities of daily living.

Mesa is refining these findings for use as red flags in daily operations; if a patient's scores on pretreatment assessment fall outside a designated range, Mesa clinicians would order more intensive up-front treatment and case management. Zieman says that a next step would be to track patients receiving this more intensive service to see whether their outcomes are more positive than similar high-risk patients treated under the regular regimen.

Cost for Participants

As of January 1998, annual OMP costs to participant provider groups, who must pay to license the OMP software and get access to the aggregate national data, will vary according to their chosen level of data analysis. A provider group that merely wants to measure its level of patient satisfaction against national aggregate data, for example, would pay $3,500-4,000 a year. A provider group that wants to measure satisfaction as well as clinical outcomes against national data on patients before treatment and at follow-up would pay around $8,000 a year.

The Outcomes Management Project is a work in progress and faces some challenges ahead. It is important to note, for example, that OMP's aggregate numbers are really averages from 20 provider systems that reflect current practices, rather than normative standards based on consensus about best practices. Even a common practice among the systems might not be a best practice. However, the OMP venture represents an important step toward national benchmarking.

In order to develop more sophisticated data analyses, an OMP goal is to cluster similar provider systems, so that a specific group practice could compare its results to similar groups, where variables such as patient access might be comparable. However, this may require a larger number and variety of participating provider systems and a larger patient volume than OMP now has to make the subcategories meaningful.

A final challenge to participating provider groups is making organizational shifts so that their staff who work with the quality and outcomes data have access to operations. Daniels says, "if quality isn't an integral part of operations, you have fundamental problems."

Behavioral Benchmarks: Results From the National Outcomes Management Project

The goal of the National Outcomes Management Project (National OMP) is to aid behavioral healthcare sites in implementing quality and performance improvement activities and support accreditation efforts through pragmatic local and national data. The project, established in 1993 represents a consortium of behavioral healthcare leaders from across the nation. The National OMP was a 1997 winner of the National Outcomes Roundtable. Members of the National OMP have immediate access to data compiled over several years of national benchmarking. Measurements have been designed to address accreditation activities, clinical effectiveness, and payer relations.

The National OMP facilitates cost effective and efficient quality and performance improvement activities in managed care and provider based settings. The database includes results regarding satisfaction, outcomes, health status and treatment patterns. It provides a psychometrically sound, comprehensive, and cost effective outcomes management protocol for outpatient and inpatient treatment with a reliable and valid core data assessing:

- The short and long term effectiveness of mental health and substance abuse (MH/SA) treatment provided (symptom cessation or reduction, and functional change).
- The impact of MH/SA treatment on physical health status.
- The patients' satisfaction with the care provided and care delivery system.
- The practice specific data about interactions between care provider, symptom or functional change and demographic factors (e.g. change among adolescent ADHD patients who received medication only compared to those who also had psychotherapy).

Once the data is collected locally analysis can be accomplished using staff at the provider's site or it can be sent directly to the National OMP Service Bureau at the Center for Quality Innovations & Research, which is associated with the Department of Psychiatry, University of Cincinnati where data entry and scanning are completed promptly. Quarterly, aggregate analysis of data is performed regarding symptom levels and their change over time based on treatment modality and length. Reports are produced and forwarded to all members summarizing local and national results. local data sent to the Service Bureau is returned to the provider allowing additional analysis.

Continual technical support is provided on survey instruments, methodological issues, and implementation. Communication is augmented with quarterly user-group teleconferences, annual user-group references, and the Benchmarking and Behavioral Healthcare newsletter. Members are encouraged to learn from one another, sharing answers and solutions for managing costs and quality in behavioral healthcare.

The National OMP is a clinically sound, cost effective, outcomes measurement system suitable for an entire continuum of care with a national benchmarking database. This collaborative service is an affordable solution for managing cost and quality of behavioral healthcare.

Source: Behavioral Benchmarks: Results from the National Outcomes Management Project. © *Center for Quality Innovations & Research, Department of Psychiatry, University of Cincinnati. (Reprinted with permission.)*

Table 1. Pre-Treatment Demographic Information

DEMOGRAPHIC VARIABLE		NATIONAL AGGREGATE (JAN. 1998 REPORT)	
		N	PERCENT
GENDER	Male	5533	35.4
	Female	10117	64.6
RACE	African American	788	5.1
	Caucasian	12676	81.6
	Asian/Pacific Islander	169	1.1
	American Indian/Alaskan	156	1.0
	Other	1741	11.2
AGE GROUP	14-18	1059	7.0
	19-24	2122	14.0
	25-34	4094	27.0
	35-44	4251	28.0
	55-54	2529	16.7
	55-64	746	4.9
	65-74	281	1.9
	75 or more	99	0.7
MARITAL STATUS	Married	7558	48.5
	Widowed	287	1.8
	Separated	1060	6.8
	Divorced	2317	14.9
	Never Married	4367	28.0
EDUCATIONAL LEVEL	Less than High School Graduate	2016	12.9
	High School Graduate	3473	22.3
	Some College	5203	33.4
	College Graduate	2929	18.8
	Post Graduate	1956	12.6

Table 2. Source of Referral

	National Aggregate (Jan. 1998 Reports)	
	N	PERCENT
Primary Care Physician	5835	36.7
Work/Employee Assistance	1651	10.4
Insurance Company	2642	16.6
Teacher/School	112	0.07
Self	3102	19.5
Friend	1016	6.4
Court	225	1.4
Other	2511	15.8

Table 3. Problems Presented by Patients

PROBLEMS PRESENTED BY PATIENTS	NATIONAL AGGREGATE (JAN. 1998 REPORT)	
	N	PERCENT
Family Problems	6711	42.2
Depression	9088	57.2
Work/School Problems	2959	18.6
Anxiety	5378	33.8
Anger	3618	22.8
Alcohol	1371	8.6
Behavior Problems	1864	11.7
Other	2584	16.2

Table 4. Treatment Needs Identified by Patients

TREATMENT IDENTIFIED BY PATIENTS	NATIONAL AGGREGATE (JAN. 1998 REPORT)	
	N	PERCENT
Individual Therapy	9249	58.1
Medication	4356	27.4
Relationship Therapy	3307	20.8
Crisis Intervention	543	3.4
Family Therapy	1820	11.4
Hospitalization	154	1
Group Therapy	761	4.8
Psychological Testing	886	5.6
Other	492	3.1
Do not know	4038	25.4

Appendix C: Behavioral Benchmarks

Table 5A. Mean Scores for BASIS-32 National Sites. Sites N = 15
January 1998 Report—Pre-Treatment

SUB-SCALE[1]	PRE-TREATMENT NATIONAL MEAN N=16800
Relation to Self & Others	1.66
Depression/Anxiety	1.74
Daily Living Skills	1.59
Impulsive/Addictive	0.69
Psychosis	0.53
Total Mean	1.28

[1] Rated as a 5 point scale ranging from 0, no difficulty in the symptom or behavior area, to 4, extreme difficulty

Table 5B. Mean Scores for BASIS-32 National Sites. Sites N = 14
January 1998 Report—3 Month Follow-up

SUB-SCALE[1]	N=2958
Relation to Self & Others	1.19
Depression/Anxiety	1.15
Daily Living Skills	1.11
Impulsive/Addictive	0.40
Psychosis	0.35
Total Mean	0.87

[1] Rated as a 5 point scale ranging from 0, no difficulty in the symptom or behavior area, to 4, extreme difficulty

Table 5C. Mean Scores for BASIS-32 National Sites. Sites N = 11
January 1998 Report—6 Month Follow-up

SUB-SCALE[1]	NATIONAL MEAN N=831
Relation to Self & Others	1.11
Depression/Anxiety	1.06
Daily Living Skills	1.04
Impulsive/Addictive	0.39
Psychosis	0.32
Total Mean	0.81

[1] Rated as a 5 point scale ranging from 0, no difficulty in the symptom or behavior area, to 4, extreme difficulty

Table 6A. Mean Scores for SF-36 National Sites. Sites N = 14
January 1998 Report—Pre-Treatment

SUB-SCALE[1]	NATIONAL MEAN N=17047
Physical Functioning	83.82
Role Physical	66.82
Bodily Pain	67.89
General Health	65.12
Vitality	40.16
Social Functioning	55.05
Role Emotional	44.10
Mental Health	48.44

[1] Rated as a 0 to 100, with 0 indicating the least favorable health status, 100 the most favorable

Table 6B. Mean Scores for SF-36 National Sites. Sites N = 13
January 1998 Report—3 Month Follow-up

SUB-SCALE[1]	NATIONAL MEAN N=2619
Physical Functioning	83.10
Role Physical	71.78
Bodily Pain	70.35
General Health	67.08
Vitality	49-15
Social Functioning	70-08
Role Emotional	60.90
Mental Health	61.90

[1] Rated on a scale of 0 to 100, with 0 indicating the least favorable health status, 100 the most favorable

Table 6C. Mean Scores for SF-36 National Sites. Sites N = 11
January 1998 Report—6 Month Follow-up

SUB-SCALE[1]	NATIONAL MEAN N=711
Physical Functioning	81.59
Role Physical	71.41
Bodily Pain	70.42
General Health	67.29
Vitality	51.14
Social Functioning	71.79
Role Emotional	64.73
Mental Health	64.11

[1] Rated on a scale of 0 to 100, with 0 indicating the least favorable health status, 100 the most favorable

Appendix C: Behavioral Benchmarks

Table 7A. Mean Scores for General Satisfaction National Sites. Sites N = 11 January 1998 Report—3 Month Follow-up

SUB-SCALE[1]	NATIONAL MEAN N=4791
Quality of Service	3.26
Received Right Kind of Service	3.27
Program Met Needs	3.03
Recommend to Friend	3.37
Amount of Help	3.20
Helped Deal with Problem	3.30
Overall Satisfaction	3.25
Come Back to program	3.37
Emergency Assistance	3.05

[1] *Rated as a 4 point scale ranging from 1, the least general satisfaction to 4, the most satisfaction*

Table 7B. Mean Scores for General Satisfaction National Sites. Sites N = 11 January 1998 Report—6 Month Follow-up

SUB-SCALE[1]	NATIONAL MEAN N=999
Quality of Service	3.27
Received Right Kind of Service	3.32
Program Met Needs	3.10
Recommend to Friend	3.41
Amount of Help	3.24
Helped Deal with Problem	3.38
Overall Satisfaction	3.31
Come Back to program	3.39
Emergency Assistance	3.08

[1] *Rated as a 4 point scale ranging from 1, the least general satisfaction to 4, the most satisfaction*

Table 8A. Mean Scores for Psychotherapy Satisfaction National Sites. Sites N = 11 January 1998 Report—3 Month Follow-up

SUB-SCALE[1]	NATIONAL MEAN N=3981
Confidence in Therapist	3.90
Understanding and Concerti	4.01
Explanation of Problem/Tx Plan	3.65
Promptness of Therapist	3.97
Improvement by Psychotherapy	3.26

[1] *Rated as a 5 point scale ranging from 1, the least general satisfaction to 5, the most satisfaction*

Table 8B. Mean Scores for Psychotherapy Satisfaction National Sites. Sites N = 11 January 1998 Report—6 Month Follow-up

SUB-SCALE[1]	NATIONAL MEAN N=828
Confidence in Therapist	3.90
Understanding and Concern	3.99
Explanation of Problem/Tx Plan	3.67
Promptness of Therapist	3.97
Improvement by Psychotherapy	3.35

[1] *Rated as a 5 point scale ranging from 1, the least general satisfaction to 5, the most satisfaction*

Appendix C: Behavioral Benchmarks

**Table 9A. Mean Scores for Medication Satisfaction National Sites. Sites N = 11
January 1998 Report—3 Month Follow-up**

SUB-SCALE[1]	NATIONAL MEAN N=2378
Confidence in Physician	3.93
Understanding and Concern	3.88
Explanation of Medication	3.90
Explanation of Effects	3.75
Promptness of Physician	3.85
Improvement by Medication	3.50

[1]*Rated as a 5 point scale ranging from 1, the least general satisfaction to 5, the most satisfaction*

**Table 9B. Mean Scores for Medication Satisfaction National Sites. Sites N = 11
January 1998 Report—6 Month Follow-up**

SUB-SCALE[1]	NATIONAL MEAN N=529
Confidence in Physician	3.99
Understanding and Concern	3.89
Explanation of Medication	3.91
Explanation of Effects	3.73
Promptness of Physician	3.90
Improvement by Medication	3.61

[1]*Rated as a 5 point scale ranging from 1, the least general satisfaction to 5, the most satisfaction*

Table 10A. Mean Scores for Office Functioning Satisfaction National Sites. Sites N = 11 January 1998 Report—3 Month Follow-up

SUB-SCALE[1]	NATIONAL MEAN N=4663
Courtesy of Reception Staff	3.90
Promptness of Office Telephones	3.82
Help in Insurance Questions	3.79
Waiting Area comfort & Appearance	3.85
Accuracy & Clarity of Bill	3.69
Courtesy of Billing Staff	3.77

[1] *Rated as a 5 point scale ranging from 1, the least general satisfaction to 5, the most satisfaction*

Table 10B. Mean Scores for Office Functioning Satisfaction National Sites. Sites N = 11 January 1998 Report—6 Month Follow-up

SUB-SCALE[1]	NATIONAL MEAN N=969
Courtesy of Reception Staff	3.90
Promptness of Office Telephones	3.81
Help in Insurance Questions	3.78
Waiting Area comfort & Appearance	3.81
Accuracy & Clarity of Bill	3.61
Courtesy of Billing Staff	3.70

[1] *Rated as a 5 point scale ranging from 1, the least general satisfaction to 5, the most satisfaction*

* Significant at 0.05 level

Table 11. Six-Month Treatment Events Checklist Data

TREATMENT VARIABLES	NATIONAL AGGREGATE (JAN 1998 REPORT)	
	N	PERCENT
TREATMENT STATUS		
Currently Receiving Psychotherapy	1484	18.50
Currently Receiving Medication Management	1901	23.70
Has Discontinued Treatment	4958	61.80
Mutual Agreement with Therapist	1337	16.70
Referral to Another Clinician/Facility	386	4.80
Discharge from Hospital Without Follow-up	6	0.10
Terminated Without Therapist Agreement	2054	25.60
Other Reason	1200	14.90
OUTPATIENT TREATMENT SESSIONS		
Number of Individual/Family Sessions		
No sessions	1991	24.80
1–3 sessions	3403	42.40
4–6 sessions	1309	16.30
7–9 sessions	623	7.80
10–12 sessions	328	4.00
> 12 sessions	373	4.70
Number of Group Therapy Sessions		
No sessions	7604	94.70
1–3 sessions	157	1.90
4–6 sessions	130	1.60
7–9 sessions	63	0.80
10–12 sessions	36	0.40
> 12 sessions	35	0.40

Table 11. Six-Month Treatment Events Checklist Data (Continued)

TREATMENT VARIABLES	NATIONAL AGGREGATE (JAN 1998 REPORT)	
	N	PERCENT
Number of Medication Evaluation Sessions		
No sessions	4581	57.10
1–3 sessions	2255	28.00
4–6 sessions	832	10.40
7–9 sessions	241	3.00
10–12 sessions	69	0.90
> 12 sessions	49	0.50
Number of Other Outpatient Therapy		
No sessions	7853	97.80
1–3 sessions	149	1.80
4–6 sessions	14	0.20
7–9 sessions	3	0.10
10–12 sessions	3	0.10
> 12 sessions	5	0.10
INPATIENT / ALTERNATIVE DAYS		
Number of Days of Inpatient Hospitalization		
No sessions	7830	97.50
1–3 sessions	68	0.80
4–6 sessions	54	0.60
7–9 sessions	25	0.40
10–12 sessions	21	0.30
> 12 sessions	29	0.40
Number of Days of Outpatient Hospitalization		
No sessions	7938	98.90
1–3 sessions	53	0.70
4–6 sessions	14	0.20
7–9 sessions	5	0.10
10–12 sessions	9	0.10
> 12 sessions	8	0.10

Appendix C: Behavioral Benchmarks

Table 11. Six-Month Treatment Events Checklist Data (Continued)

TREATMENT VARIABLES	NATIONAL AGGREGATE (JAN 1998 REPORT)	
	N	PERCENT
Tx		
No sessions	7979	99.40
1–3 sessions	16	0.20
4–6 sessions	6	0.10
7–9 sessions	2	0.10
10–12 sessions	6	0.10
> 12 sessions	18	0.20
Number of Days of Other Facility Program		
No sessions	8005	99.70
1–3 sessions	6	0.10
4–6 sessions	5	0.10
7–9 sessions	9	0.10
10–12 sessions	2	0.00
> 12 sessions	0	0.00
Diagnosis-Axis I-Primary-Pre-Tx		
Depression	2255	32.30
Adjustment Disorder	2173	31.10
Bipolar Disorder	245	3.50
Alcohol / Substance Abuse	230	3.30
Dysthymia	657	9.40
Anxiety / Panic Disorder	508	7.30
Miscellaneous	808	11.60
Medications Prescribed		
Anti-anxiety / Tranquilizer	928	11.60
SSRI Antidepressant	2800	34.90
Tricyclic Antidepressant	667	8.30
NLI\O Antidepressant	32	0.40
Antipsychotic	239	3.00
Stimulant	175	2.20
Anticonvulsant	189	2.40
Other	1213	15.10
Critical Events		
Self-injurious	56	0.70
Threatened harm to others	30	0.40
Harmed others	17	0.20
Suicide attempt	27	0.30
Suicide	19	0.30

Beginning Services Survey Responses

BEGINNING SERVICES RESPONSES	NATIONAL AGGREGATE (JAN. 1998 REPORT)	
	N	PERCENT
No. of Treatment Visits Needed as Identified by Patient		
1–visit	912	5.8
2–5 visits	2117	13.5
6–10 visits	1008	6.4
11–15 visits	277	1.8
> 15 visits	479	3.1
Don't Know	10884	69.4
Number of Working Days Between 1st Call & 1st Appointment		
0–2 days	4323	28
3–5 days	3191	20.7
6–9 days	2911	18.9
10–19 days	3210	20.8
20–29 days	1156	7.5
>30 days	621	4
Promptness with Which 1st Appointment Was Made		
Very Prompt	90.52	58.9
Somewhat Prompt	3852	25.1
Somewhat Delayed	1823	11.9
Very Delayed	634	4.1
Ease of Scheduling 1st Appointment		
Very Easy	10628	69.5
Somewhat Easy	3223	21.1
Somewhat Difficult	1132	7.4
Very Difficult	310	2
Convenience of Office location		
Very Convenient	7147	45.6
Somewhat Convenient	5778	36.8
Somewhat Inconvenient	2145	13.7
Very Inconvenient	610	3.9
Ease of Obtaining Referral from PCP/EAP		
Very Easy	6018	40.5
Somewhat Easy	1851	12.4
Somewhat Difficult	455	3.1
Very Difficult	171	1.2
Was Not Required	6374	42.9

Appendix C: Behavioral Benchmarks

Appendix D
Sources

Martha Beattie, PhD
1742 Hudson Drive
San Jose CA 95124-1736
(408) 266-5228

Astrid Beigel, PhD
Chief
Quality and Outcome Bureau
Los Angeles County Department
of Mental Health
550 South Vermont Avenue
Los Angeles CA 90020
(213) 738-3290

Lee Bennett
Program Director
Horizons South
650 S. Bascom Avenue
San Jose CA 95218
(408) 295-6675

William Berman, PhD
CEO
BHOS, Inc.
689 Mamaroneck Avenue
Mamaroneck NY 10543
(914) 381-7784
Fax: (914) 381-1725
E-mail: billb@bhos.com

Joan Betzold
President
Professional Services Consultants Inc.
1147 Starmount Court
Suite B
Bel Air MD 21015
(410) 569-6106

Ray Brien
Director
Mental Health and Substance Abuse Services
of the Berkshires
33 East Street
Pittsfield MA 01201
(413) 499 0412

Benjamin Brodey, MD, MPH
Director of Research
Medassure IVR Systems, Inc.
4558 Fourth Avenue, NE
Seattle WA 98105
(206) 917-6076
Fax: (206) 548-9575
E-mail: brodey@u.washington.edu

Mary Cesare-Murphy, PhD
Executive Director
Behavioral Health Care Accreditation Program
Joint Commission on Accreditation
of Healthcare Organizations
One Renaissance Boulevard
Oakbrook Terrace IL 60181
(630) 792-5791

William Coleman
QI Director
Montana Community Partners
P.O. Box 2510
Billings MT 59102
(888) 599-2233
Fax: (888) 685-7657
E-mail: bcoleman@magellan.com

Bruce Copley
Deputy Director
Department of Alcohol & Drug Services
Park Alameda Health Facility
976 Lenzen Avenue
Third Floor
San Jose CA 95126-2737
(408) 299-6141

Jeanne Crawford, MA, MPH
Associate Vice President
Access Measurement Systems
50 Main Street
Ashland MA 01721
(508) 881-4777
Fax: (508) 881-3777
jcrawford@ams-outcomes.com

Les DelPizzo
Vice President
Marketing
CMHC Systems
570 Metro Place North
Dublin OH 43017
(614) 764-0143

Bill Edell, PhD
Senior Vice President for Clinical Development
Mental Health Outcomes
1500 Waters Ridge Drive
Lewisville TX 75057
(972) 420-8200
Fax: (972) 420-8215
E-mail: billedell@psinet.com

Alan Ehrlich, MD
Chairman
Practices-Guidelines Committee
Fallon Community Health Plan
176 West Street
Milford MA 01757
(508) 852-0600
Fax: (508) 634-3216

Richard H. Ellis, PhD
Researcher, Mental Health Services
Colorado Department of Human Services
3824 Princeton Circle
Denver CO 80236
(303) 866-7415
Fax: (303) 866-7428

Elizabeth Funk
Executive Director
Mental Health Corporations of Massachusetts
182 Central Street
Suite 203
Natick, MA 01760
(508) 647-8311

James Gallagher
Chief Executive Officer
Charter Behavioral Health System of Summit, NJ
19 Prospect Street
Summit NJ 07901
(908) 522-7011

William Golden, MD
Associate Professor
General Internal Medicine
Department of Medicine
University of Arkansas for Medical Sciences
Slot 641
4301 West Markham
Little Rock AR 72205
(501) 686-5000

Geoffrey Gray, PhD
President
OQ Systems, Inc.
34 Wall Street
Suite G
Norwalk CT 06850
(203) 838-6003
Fax: (203) 866-9614
E-mail: algobc@mindspring.com

Grant Grissom, PhD
Vice President
Research and Development
Field Diagnostic Services, Inc.
North American Technology Center
680 Jacksonville Road
Warminster PA 18974
(800) 966-9700
Fax: (215) 672-9560

Appendix D: Sources

Lawrence A. Heller, PhD
Executive Director
The American College
  of Mental Health Administration
7625 West Hutchinson Avenue
Pittsburgh PA 15218-1248
(412) 244-0670
Fax: (412) 244-9916

Sean Hill
Manager of Quality Management
Eastway Corporation
12 West Wenger Road
Englewood OH 45322
(513) 937-2200

Enid Hunkeler
Senior Investigator
Kaiser Permanente
Division of Research
3505 Broadway
Oakland CA 94611
(510)450-2232

Kevin Kearney
Point of View Survey Systems, Inc.
1380 Lawrence Street
Suite 820
Denver CO 80204
(303) 534-3044
Fax: (303) 623-5426
E-mail: POVSS@aol.com

David Kraus, PhD
President
Access Measurement Systems
50 Main Street
Ashland MA 01721
(508) 881-4777

Donald Kreeger
Director of Program Development
Institute for Behavioral Health Care
4370 Alpine Road
Suite 209
Portola Valley CA 94028
(650) 851-6735
Fax: (650) 851-0406

Tom Lambric
Stark County Community Mental Health Board
800 Market Avenue North
Canton OH 44702
(330) 455-6644

John S. Lyons, PhD
Director
Mental Health Services and Policy Program
Department of Psychiatry and Behavioral Sciences
Northwestern University Medical School
Ward 0-200
303 East Chicago Avenue
Chicago IL 60611
(312) 908-8968
E-mail: jsl329@nwu.edu

Jerry Mahoney
Director
Sales and Marketing
International Voice Technologies Corporation
1230 Route 34
Abnerdeen NJ 07747
Fax: (732) 441-9895
Internet: http://www.ivoice.com

Ronald Manderscheid, PhD
Chief
Survey and Analysis Branch
Division of State and Community Systems
Development
Center for Mental Health Services
5600 Fishers Lane 15 C-04
Rockville MD 20857
(301) 443-3343

Zachary Meyer
Vice President
Corporate Medical
MCC Behavioral Care
11095 Viking Drive
Eden Prairie MN 55344
(612) 996-2732
Fax: (612) 996-2722

Jeff Mitchell, MD
Associate Medical Director
Laureate Psychiatric Clinic and Hospital
6655 S. Yale Avenue
Tulsa OK 74136
(918) 491-5677
Fax: (918) 481-4065

John Morris, MSW
Director of Interdisciplinary Studies
South Carolina Department of Mental Health
Professor of Neuropsychiatry
   and Behavioral Science
University of South Carolina School of Medicine
3555 Harden Street Extension
Suite 104-A
Columbia SC 29203
(803) 434-4225
Fax: (803) 434-4277

Dennis Morrison, PhD
Center for Behavioral Health
645 S Rogers Street
Bloomington IN 47403
(812) 337-2302
Fax: (812) 337-2438
E-mail: dennym@kiva.net

Martin Nankin
CEO
Field Diagnostic Services, Inc.
North American Technology Center
680 Jacksonville Road
Warminster PA 18974
(800) 966-9700, ext. 423
Fax: (215) 672-9560

Joseph P. Naughton-Travers, EdM
Principal
Behavioral Health Advantage
1521 Bridford Parkway
Suite 11-H
Greensboro NC 27407
(336) 294-5161
E-mail: joent@aol.com

Abdin Noboa, PhD
Program Development Specialist
Office of Consumer Services
Department of Mental Health
30 East Broad Street
Columbus OH 43266-0414
(614) 644-5297

Jordan A. Oshlag, MSW, LICSW
243 Hudson Road
Sudbury MA 01776-1624
(978) 443-7574
E-mail: SLTJAO@Sprynet.com

Curtis Reisinger, PhD
Senior Vice President
American Professional Credentialling Services
P.O. Box 477
Wharton NJ 07885
Phone/Fax: (973) 366-8665
E-mail: apcs@erols.com

Marvin Rosenberg
Depression Road-Map Coordinator
Group Health Cooperative of Puget Sound
CP & I, Second Floor
521 Wall Street
Seattle WA 98121
(206) 448-4437
Fax (206) 448-2420

Dee Roth
Chief
Office of Program Evaluation and Research
Ohio Department of Mental Health
30 East Broad Street
Columbus, OH 43266-0414
(614) 466-8651

Grace Rowan-Szal, PhD
Research Scientist
Institute of Behavioral Health Research
Texas Christian University
Fort Worth TX 76129
(817) 921-722
Fax: (817) 257-7290
E-mail: g.szal@tcu.edu

Appendix D: Sources

Ida Santos
Quality Improvement Manager
Quality Improvement/Managed Care
    Coordination Office
Department of Alcohol & Drug Services
Park Alameda Health Facility
976 Lenzen Avenue
3rd Floor
San Jose CA 95126-2737
(408) 299-6141

Genie Skypek, PhD
Psychologist
2528 W. Tennessee Avenue
Tampa FL 33629
(813) 254-3926
E-mail: skypek@mindspring.com

Thomas Slaven, PhD
National Director
Behavioral Health Division, CARF
4513 East Grant Road
Tucson AZ 85712
(520) 335-1044
Fax: (520) 318-1129

Sharon Sprenger
Associate Director for Research and Evaluation
Joint Commission on Accreditation
    of Healthcare Organizations
One Renaissance Boulevard
Oakbrook Terrace IL 60181
(630) 792-5968
Fax: 630-792-4081
E-mail: ssprenger@jcaho.org

Kurt Strosahl, PhD
Research Evaluation Manager
Group Health NW
Group Health Permanente Medical Group
1730 Minor Avenue
Suite 1400
Seattle WA 98101
(206) 287-2588
Fax: (206) 287-2656

Christine Torre
Manager
Quality and Outcome Bureau
Los Angeles County Department
    of Mental Health
550 South Vermont Avenue
Los Angeles CA 90020
(213) 738-3290

Michael VonKorff
Senior Investigator
Group Health Cooperative of Puget Sound
1730 Minor Avenue
Suite 1600
Seattle WA 98101
(206) 287-2900

Howard Waxman, PhD
Research Director
Belmont Center for Comprehensive Treatment
4200 Monument Road
Philadelphia PA 19131
(215) 581-9176
Fax: (215) 581-3777

Lesa Yawn, PhD
c/o National Council for Community
    Behavioral Healthcare
12300 Twinbrook Parkway
Suite 320
Rockville MD 20852
(301) 984-6200
Fax: (301) 881-7159

Gayle Zieman, PhD
Vice President
Mesa Mental Health
6723 Academy Road, NE
Albuquerque NM 87109
(505) 858-1585
Fax: 505-858-1779
E-mail: glzieman@earthlink.net

Appendix E
Other Resource Organizations And Periodicals

Administration and Policy in Mental Health
Human Sciences Press
233 Spring Street
New York NY 10013
(212) 620-8000
Fax: (212) 807-1047

Agency for Health Care Policy and Research (AHCPR)
2101 East Jefferson Street
Rockville MD 20852
(301) 594-1364

American Academy of Child & Adolescent Psychiatry
3615 Wisconsin Avenue, NW
Washington DC 20016-3007
(202) 966-7300
Fax: (202) 966-2891

American Accreditation Healthcare Commission/URAC
1275 K Street, NW
Washington DC 20005
(202) 216-9010
Fax: (202) 216-9006

American Association of Health Plans
1129 20th Street, NW, Suite 600
Washington DC 20036
(202) 778-3200
Fax: (202) 331-7487

American Managed Behavioral Healthcare Association
700 Thirteenth Street, NW
Suite 950
Washington DC 20005
(202) 434-4565
Fax: (202) 434-4564

American College of Medical Quality
P.O. Box 34493
Bethesda MD 20827-0493

American Public Welfare Association
810 First Street, NW
Suite 500
Washington, D.C. 20002

American Psychiatric Association
1400 K Street, NW
Washington DC 20005
(202) 682-6142
Fax: (202) 682-6255

American Psychological Association
750 First Street, NE
Washington DC 20002-4242
(202) 336-5500

American Society of Addiction Medicine
4601 North Park Avenue
Arcade Suite 101
Chevy Chase, MD 20815
(301) 656-3920
Fax: (301) 656-3815

Association for Ambulatory Behavioral Healthcare
301 North Fairfax Street
Suite 109
Alexandria VA 22314-2633
(703) 836-2274
Fax: (703) 836-0083
Internet: aaph@pie.org

Bazelon Center for Mental Health Law
1101 15th Street, NW
Suite 1212
Washington DC 20005-5002
(202) 467-5730
Fax: (202) 223-0409

Behavioral Health Care Update
5215 Old Orchard Road
Suite 700
Skokie IL 60077-1045
(847) 779-8550
Fax: (847) 965-0000
E-mail: wjf@pbo-outcomes.com

Behavioral Health Outcomes
Manisses Communications Group
208 Governor Street
P.O. Box 9758
Providence RI 02906
(401) 831-6020
(800) 333-7771
Fax: (401) 861-6370
E-mail: kstove@manisses.com

Behavioral Healthcare Tomorrow
Manisses Communications Group
208 Governor Street
P.O. Box 9758
Providence RI 02906
(401) 831-6020
(800) 333-7771
Fax: (401) 861-6370

Behavioral Health Treatment
Manisses Communications Group
P.O. Box 9758
Providence RI 02940-9758
(401) 831-6020
(800) 333-7771

Business & Health
5 Paragon Drive
Montvale NJ 07645
(201) 358-7200

Center for Health Policy Research
The George Washington University
Medical Center
2021 K Street. NW
Suite 800
Washington DC 20006
(202) 296-6922
Fax: (202) 296-0025

Center for Mental Health Policy
Vanderbilt University Institute
for Public Policy Studies
1207 18th Ave South
Nashville TN 37212
(615) 322-8694
Fax: (615) 322-7049

Center for Mental Health Services
Substance Abuse and Mental Health
Services Administration
5600 Fishers Lane
Room 13-103
Rockville MD 20857
(301) 443-2792
(Knowledge Exchange Network (800) 789-2647)

Center for Outcomes Research (CORE)
5800 West 10th Street
Suite 605
Little Rock AR 72204
(501) 660-7550
Fax: (501) 660-7543
E-mail: sheltonmelonies@exchange.uams.edu

Center for Quality Innovations & Research
222 Piedmont Avenue, Suite 8800
Cincinnati, OH 45219-4218
(513) 558-8353
E-mail: Wilton@uc.campus.mci.net

Center for Substance Abuse Prevention
Substance Abuse and Mental Health
 Services Administration
5600 Fishers Lane
Rockwall 2, 9th floor
Rockville MD 20857
(301) 443-0365

Center for Substance Abuse Treatment
Substance Abuse and Mental Health
 Services Administration
5600 Fishers Lane
Rockwall 2, 6th floor
Rockville MD 20857
(301) 443-5052

CentraLink
1110 Mar West Street, Suite E
Tiburon CA 94920
(415) 435-9821
Fax: (415) 435-9092

Consumer Managed Care Network
66 Canal Center Plaza
Suite 302
Alexandria VA 22314
(703) 739-9333

Employee Benefit Resource Institute
2121 K Street, NW
Suite 600
Washington DC 20037-1893
(202) 659-0670
Fax: (202) 775-6312

The Evaluation Center@HSRI
 (Human Services Research Institute)
2336 Massachusetts Avenue
Cambridge MA 02140
(617) 876-0426
Fax: (617) 492-7401
Internet: hughes@hsri.org

Family Services Research Center
Dept. of Psychiatry and Behavioral Science
Medical University of South Carolina
171 Ashley Avenue
Charleston SC 29203

Federation of Families for Children's Mental Health
1021 Prince Street
Alexandria VA 22314
(703) 684-7710

Foundation for Accountability (FACCT)
520 SW Sixth Avenue
Suite 700
Portland OR 97204
(503) 223-2228
Fax: (503) 223-4336

Health Care Financing Administration
Office of Managed Care
Room S-32607
6500 Security Blvd.
Baltimore MD 21244-1850
(410) 786-7817
(410) 786-3000 (HCFA main number)

Health Policy Tracking Service
National Conference of State Legislatures
444 No. Capitol Street, NW
Suite 515
Washington DC 20001
(202) 624-5400

Health Resources and Services Administration
Bureau of Primary Care
4350 East-West Highway
Bethesda MD 20814
(301) 594-4060

Human Service Collaborative
2262 Hall Place, NW
Suite 204
Washington DC 20007
(202) 333-1892
Fax: (202) 333-8217

Institute for Behavioral Healthcare
1110 Mar West Street
Suite E
Tiburon CA 94920
(415) 435-9821
Fax: (415) 435-9092

Institute of Medicine
Neuroscience and Behavioral Health Division
2101 Constitution Avenue, NW
Washington DC 20418
(202) 334-3387
Fax: (202) 334-1317

International Association of Psychosocial
   Rehabilitation Services
10025 Gov. Warfield Parkway
Suite 301
Columbia MD 21044-3357
(410) 730-7190

InterStudy
2901 Metro Drive
4th Floor
Bloomington MN 55425
(800) 844-3351
(612) 858-9291
Fax: (612) 854-5698

Henry J. Kaiser Family Foundation
Kaiser Commission on the Future of Medicaid
1450 G Street, NW
Suite 250
Washington DC 20005
(800) 656-4533 (Publications Request Line)
(202) 347-5270

Joint Commission on Accreditation of
   Healthcare Organizations
1 Renaissance Plaza
Oakbrook Terrace IL 60181
(630) 792-5800

*The Journal of Behavioral Health Services
   & Research*
Louis de la Parte Florida Mental Health Institute
University of South Florida
13301 Bruce B. Downs Boulevard
Tampa FL 33612-3807
(813) 974-6400
Fax: (813) 974-6257

Journal Watch for Psychiatry
Massachusetts Medical Society
1440 Main Street
Waltham MA 02154-1600
(800) 843-6356
Fax: (781) 893-0413

Legal Action Center
236 Massachusetts Avenue, NW
Suite 505
Washington DC 20002
(202) 544-5478
Fax: (202) 544-5712

Managed Behavioral Health News
Atlantic Information Services, Inc.
1100 17th Street, NW Suite 300
Washington DC 20036
(800) 521-4323
(202) 775-9008
Fax: (202) 331-9542

Managed Care News
National Federation of Societies for Clinical
Social Work
P.O. Box 3740
Arlington VA 22203

Manisses Communications Group
208 Governor Street
P.O. Box 9758
Providence RI 02906
(401) 831-6020
(800) 333-7771
Fax: (401) 861-6370

Mental Health News Alert
8204 Fenton Street
Silver Spring MD 20910
(800) 666-6380

Mental Health Report
Business Publishers, Inc.
951 Pershing Drive
Silver Spring MD 20910-4464
(301) 589-5103

Mental Health Weekly
Manisses Communications Group
P.O. Box 9758
Providence RI 02940-9758
(401) 831-6020

National Academy of State Health Policy
50 Monument Square
Room 502
Portland ME 04101
(207) 874-6524
Fax: 207-874-6527

National Alliance for the Mentally Ill
200 North Glebe Road
Suite 1015
Arlington VA 22203-2754
(800) 950-6264
(703) 524-7600
Fax: (703) 524 9094

National Association for Rural Mental Health
3700 W. Division Street
Suite 105
St. Cloud MN 56301
(320) 202-1820

National Association of Alcoholism and Drug Abuse Counselors
3717 Columbia Pike
Suite 300
Arlington VA 22204
(703) 741-7686

National Association of County Behavioral Health Directors
(technical assistance division: The County Behavioral Health Institute)
1555 Connecticut Avenue, NW
Suite 200
Washington D.C. 20036
(202) 234-7543, ext. 29

National Association of Psychiatric Health Systems
1317 F Street, NW
Suite 301
Washington DC 20004
(202) 393-6700
Fax: (202) 783-6041

National Association of Social Workers
750 First Street, NW
Suite 700
Washington DC 20002-4241
(800) 638-8799
(202) 408-8600

National Association of State Alcohol & Drug Abuse Directors
4444 North Capitol Street, NW
Washington DC 20001

National Association of State Mental Health Program Directors
66 Canal Center Plaza
Suite 302
Alexandria VA 22314
(703) 739-9333
Fax: (703) 548-9517

National Attention Deficit Disorder Association
9930 Johnnycake Ridge Road
Suite 3E
Mentor OH 44060
(216) 350-9595
"Fax On Demand" service: (313) 769-6729

National Clearinghouse for Alcohol and Drug Information
11426 Rockville Pike
Suite 200
Rockville MD 20852
(800) 729-6686
(301) 468-2600

The National Center On Outcomes Research
100 West Road
Suite 406
Towson MD 21204
(410) 583-0060
Fax: (410) 583-0063
E-mail: natcente@ncor.org

National Coalition of Mental Health Professionals and Consumers
PO Box 438
Commack NY 11725-0438
(888)-SAY-NO-MC
(516) 424-5232
Fax: (516) 549-3942
E-mail: NCMHPC@aol.com

National Committee for Quality Assurance
2000 L Street, NW
Suite 500
Washington DC 20036
(202) 955-3500
Fax: (202) 955-3599

National Council for Community Behavioral Healthcare
12300 Twinbrook Parkway
Suite 320
Rockville MD 20852
(301) 984-6200
Fax: (301) 881-7159

National Empowerment Center
20 Vallard Road
Lawrence MA 01843
(800) 769-3728

National Governors Association
Health Policy Studies Division
444 North Capitol Street, NW Suite 267
Washington DC 20001
(202) 624-5300
Fax: (202) 624-5313

National Health Policy Forum
2021 K Street, NW Suite 800
Washington DC 20006
(202) 872-1390
Fax: (202) 862-9837

National Institute of Mental Health
Parklawn Building
5600 Fishers Lane
Room 10-130
Rockville MD 20857
(301) 443-3648

National Institute on Alcohol Abuse and Alcoholism
Parklawn Building
5600 Fishers Lane
Rockville MD 20857
(301) 443-0786

National Institute on Drug Abuse
Parklawn Building
5600 Fishers Lane
Room 10A-30
Rockville MD 20857
(301) 443-4060

National Managed Health Care Congress
70 Blanchard Road Suite 4000
Burlington MA 01803
(617) 270-6000
Fax: (617) 270-6004

National Mental Health Association
1021 Prince Street
Alexandria VA 22314-2971
(703) 684-7722

National Mental Health Consumers' Self-Help Clearinghouse
1211 Chestnut Street
Suite 1000
Philadelphia PA 19107
(800) 553-4539

National Resource Center on Homelessness and Mental Illness
262 Delaware Avenue
Delmar NY 12054
(800) 444-7415
Fax: (518) 439-7612

National Technical Assistance Center
Georgetown University
Child Development Center
3307 M Street, NW
Suite 400
Washington DC 20007
(202) 687-5000

OC (Obsessive-Compulsive) Foundation
P.O. Box 70
Milford, CT 06460-0070
(203) 878-5669
http://pages.prodigy.com/alwillen/ocf.html

Practice Strategies
P.O. Box 79445
Baltimore MD 21279-0445
(919) 553-0637 (editorial)

Psychiatric Practice & Managed Care
Office of Psychiatric Services
American Psychiatric Association
1400 K Street, NW
Washington DC 20005
(202) 682-6142

The Rehabilitation Accreditation Commission (CARF)
4891 East Grant Road
Tucson, AZ 85712
(520) 325-1044
Fax: (520) 318-1129

Research Center for Managed Care and Drug Abuse Treatment
Heller Graduate School of Advanced Studies in Social Welfare
Brandeis University
Mail Stop 035
Waltham MA 02254-9110
(617) 736-3951

Research and Training Center for Children's Mental Health
Florida Mental Health Institute
University of South Florida
13301 Bruce B. Downs Blvd.
Tampa FL 33612-3899
(813) 974-7184

Robert Wood Johnson Foundation
PO Box 2316
Princeton NJ 08543-2316
(609) 452 8701
Fax: (609) 452 1865

Society of Behavioral Medicine
401 East Jefferson Street
Suite 205
Rockville MD 20850
(301) 251-2790

Technical Assistance Collaborative
1 Center Plaza
Suite 310
Boston MA 02108
(617) 742-5657
Fax: (617) 742-0509

Albert E. Treischman Center
1968 Central Avenue
Needham MA 02192
(617) 449-0626
Fax: (617) 449-9074
(The Center mounts an annual "Clinical Technologies" conference focusing on outcomes and quality measurement)

Washington Business Group on Health
777 North Capitol Street, NW
Suite 800
Washington DC 20002
(202) 408-9320
Fax: (202) 408-9332

Appendix F
Further Reading

(See also Chapter 11, "Recent Mental Health and Substance Abuse Research Findings")

Allen & Columbus, eds. *Assessing Alcohol Problems: A Guide for Clinicians and Researchers.* NIAA Treatment Handbook Series 4. Bethesda MD: 1995.

Association for Ambulatory Behavioral Healthcare, The. *Implementing Outcomes Measurement in Behavioral Healthcare.* Alexandria VA: 1996.

Barrows and Clayton. Privacy, Confidentiality, and Electronic Medical Records. *Journal of the American Informatics Association* 1996; 3(2):139-148.

Behavioral Health Outcomes: A Reference Guide to Measurement Tools. Rockville MD: National Council for Community Behavioral Healthcare, 1995.

Bell D, Richard A, and Feltz L. Mediators of drug treatment outcomes. *Addictive Behaviors* 1996; 21(5)597-613.

Bengen-Seltzer B. Fourth Generation Managed Behavioral Health: What Does It Look Like? *Part 1: Managed Medicaid, Outcomes, and Integrated Delivery Systems.* Providence RI: Manisses Communications Group, 1995.

Bengen-Seltzer B. Fourth Generation Managed Behavioral Health: What Does It Look Like? *Part 2: Integration of Primary Care and Behavioral Health; Residential Behavioral Services; and Accreditation and Performance Measures.* Providence RI: Manisses Communications Group, 1997.

Bergmann PE, Smith MB, and Hoffmann NG. Adolescent treatment: Implications for assessment, practice guidelines, and outcome management. *Substance Abuse* 1995; 42(2):453-472.

Brugha TS and Lindsay S. Quality of mental health service care: the forgotten pathway from process to outcome. *Social Psychiatry and Psychiatric Epidemiology* 1996; 31(2):89-98.

Buck JA and Umland B. Covering mental health and substance abuse services. *Health Affairs* 1997; 16(4).

Burlingame GM, Lambert MJ, Reisinger CW, et al. Pragmatics of tracking mental health outcomes in a managed care setting. *Journal of Mental Health Administration* 1995; 22(3):226-236.

CARF (The Rehabilitation Accreditation Commission). *Managing Outcomes: Customer-Driven Outcomes Measurement & Management Systems, A Guide to Development and Use.* Tucson AZ: 1997

Center for Substance Abuse Treatment. *Guidelines for the Treatment of Alcohol and Other Drug Abuse.* Rockville MD: U.S. Department of Health and Human Services, Public Health Service, Substance Abuse and Mental Health Services Administration, 1993.

Center for Substance Abuse Treatment. *Developing State Outcomes Monitoring Systems for Alcohol and Other Drug Abuse Treatment. Treatment Improvement Series (No. 14).* Rockville MD: U.S. Department of Health and

Human Services, Public Health Service, Substance Abuse and Mental Health Services Administration, 1995.

Chandler, Daniel. Client Outcomes in a Three-Year Controlled Study of an Integrated Service Agency Model. *Psychiatric Services* December 1996; 47(12):1337-1343.

Chisholm, et al. Quality indicators for primary mental health within managed care: a public health focus. *Archives of Psychiatric Nursing* 1997; 11(4):1671-1681.

Coughlin KM (ed.). *The 1999 Medicaid Managed Behavioral Care Sourcebook*. New York NY: Faulkner & Gray, 1998.

Coughlin KM (ed.). *The 1997 Guide to Behavioral Resources on the Internet*. New York NY: Faulkner & Gray, 1997.

Coughlin KM (ed.). *The 1998 Behavioral Outcomes & Guidelines Sourcebook*. New York NY: Faulkner & Gray, 1997.

Coulehan, et al. Treating Depressed Primary Care Patients Improves Their Physical, Mental, and Social Functioning. *Archives of Internal Medicine*, May 26, 1997; 157(10):1113-1120.

Cross T, McDonald E., and Lyons H. *Evaluating the Outcome of Children's Mental Health Services: A Guide for the Use of Available Child and Family Outcome Measures: Volume II.* Boston MA: Technical Assistance Center for the Evaluation of Children's Mental Health Systems, Judge Baker Children's Center, 1997.

Crott and Gills. Economic Comparisons of the Pharmacotherapy of Depression: An overview. *Acta Psychiatr. Scand* April 1998; 97(4):241-52

Daniels A, et al. *The Behavioral Healthcare Quality & Accountability Tool Kit*. Version One. Portola Valley CA: CentraLink, 1997.

Derrick and Kushner. Outcome Studies: Can In-House Studies Be Performed Reliably and Inexpensively? *Treatment Today*. Winter 1997.

Dobson KS and Craig KD (eds.) *Empirically Supported Therapies*. Thousand Oaks CA: Sage, 1998.

Drake, et al. Using Clinician Rating Scales To Assess Substance Abuse Among Persons With Severe Mental Illness. In *Sederer & Dickey Outcomes Assessment in Clinical Practice*. Baltimore MD: Williams & Wilkins, 1996.

Evaluation Center@HSRI. *The Toolkit for Measuring Psychosocial Rehabilitation Outcomes (PN-4)*. Cambridge MA: Evaluation Center@HSRI.

Evaluation Center@HSRI. *Stakeholder Perspectives on Mental Health Performance Indicators: Working Papers Prepared for the MHSIP Phase*. Cambridge MA: Evaluation Center@HSRI , 1995.

Evaluation Center@HSRI. *The Toolkit on Evaluating Substance Abuse in Persons With Severe Mental Illness (PN-6)*. Cambridge MA: Evaluation Center@HSRI.

First Steps: A Guide to Integrating Information Systems Evaluation of Children's Mental Health Services. The Technical Assistance Center for the Evaluation of Children's Mental Health Systems, Judge Baker Children's Center. 2nd Ed., January 1996.

Fisher, et al. *Methodoligical Standards for Outcome Measures*. Adult Outcome Measurement Standards Committee. Rockville, MD: Center for Mental Health Services, January 1997.

French MT, et al. A Structured Instrument for Estimating the Economic Cost of Drug Abuse Treatment. The Drug Abuse Treatment Cost Analysis Program (DATCAP). *Journal of Substance Abuse Treatment* Sept./Oct. 97:445-455.

Flynn LM, Manderscheid RW, Smith GR, and Steinwachs DM. Principles for Assessment of Patient Outcomes in Mental Health Care. *Psychiatric Services* 1997; 48(8).

George RA, McFarland BH Angell RH, and Pollack DA. *Guidelines and Standards of Care for Mental Health Treatments in the Oregon Health Plan.* Portland OR: 1994.

Gilbert et al. Texas Medication Algorithm Project: Definitions, Rationale, and Methods to Develop Medication Algorithms. *Journal of Clinical Psychiatry* 1998;59(7):345-351.

Gill KJ, Pratt CW, and Librera LA. The effects of consumer vs. staff administration on the measurement of consumer satisfaction with psychiatric rehabilitation. *Psychiatric Rehabilitation Journal* 1998; 21(4):365-370.

Gotheil, McLellan, and Druley. Length of stay, patient severity and treatment outcome: An example from the field of alcoholism. *Journal of Studies on Alcohol.* In press as of 1997.

Hall LL. National Report Card: The Impact Of Managed Care On People With Severe Mental Illness. *Behavioral Healthcare Tomorrow.* April 1997.

Harrison and Asche. Comparison of Substance Abuse Treatment Outcomes For Inpatients And Outpatients. *Journal of Substance Abuse Treatment.* In press.

Hendryx M, Dyck D, and Srebnik D. *Risk-Adjusted Outcome Models for Public Mental Health Outpatient Programs.* Health Services Research. In Press.

Hirschfeld, et al. The National Depressive and Manic-Depressive Association Consensus Statement on the undertreatment of Depression. *Journal of the American Medical Association* 1997; 277:333-340.

Hodges K, Wong MM, and Latessa M: Use of the Child and Adolescent Functional Assessment Scale (CAFAS) as an Outcome Measure in Clinical Settings. *The Journal of Behavioral Health Services & Research* August 1998; 25(3):326-337.

Howard KI, et al. Evaluation of Psychotherapy: Efficacy, Effectiveness, and Patient Progress. *American Psychologist* 1996; 51:1059-1064.

Hughes D (ed.). *Evaluating Managed Mental Health Care: A Sourcebook.* Cambridge MA: The Evaluation Center@HSRI, 1995.

Inch, et al. Use of the Brief Psychiatric Rating Scale To Measure Success in a Psychosocial Day Program. *Psychiatric Services* September 1997; 48(9):1195-1197.

Imhof and Hirsch. Treatment Protocol Effectiveness Study. A White Paper of the Office of National Drug Control Policy. *Journal of Substance Abuse Treatment* 1997; 13(4).

Institute for Behavioral Healthcare. *Performance Indicator Measurement in Behavioral Healthcare: Data Capture Methods, Cost-Effectiveness, and Emerging Standards; Phase II Survey Results and Future Implications.* Portola Valley CA: Institute for Behavioral Healthcare, 1997.

International Association of Psychosocial Rehabilitation. *Outcome Measures for Psychosocial Rehabilitation.* Columbia MD: 1995.

Kane RL, et al. Building an Empirically Based Outcomes Information System for Managed Mental Health Care. *Psychiatric Services* 1995; 46(5):459-461.

Katon W, et al. Collaborative Management To Achieve Treatment Guidelines. *Journal of the American Medical Association* 1995; 273(13):1026-1031.

Kearney W. The Central Ethical Issues for Large-Scale Outcomes Databases. *Behavioral Healthcare Tomorrow* April 1997.

Kimmich M. Implementing Quality Assurance Techniques and Measuring Outcomes in a Managed Care Approach to Child Welfare. In *Second National Roundtable on Managed Care in Child Welfare Services: Summary of Proceedings.* Englewood CO: American Humane Association, 1997.

Kocsis JH. Practice Guidelines and Professional Challenges: What Psychotherapists Need To Do. *Archives of General Psychiatry* 1996; 53(4):303-304.

Kramer K, Daniels A, Mahesh N, et al. *Performance Indicators in Behavioral Healthcare: Measures of Access, Appropriateness, Quality, Outcomes, and Prevention.* Portola Valley CA: Institute for Behavioral Healthcare, 1996.

Kurland D. Review of quality evaluation systems for mental health services. *American Journal of Medical Quality* 1995; 10(3):141-148.

LaFond JQ. Toward a Working Model of Outcome Measures for the Public Welfare Domain. *Schizophrenia Bulletin.* NIMH, 1992.

Leon, et al. Psychiatric Hospital Outcomes of Dual Diagnosis Patients Under Managed Care. *American Journal of Addictions,* 1997; 7:81-86.

Lyons JS. The Evolving Role of Outcomes in Managed Behavioral Health Care. *Journal of Child and Family Studies* 1997; (6):1-8.

Lyons JS, Howard KI, O'Mahoney MT, and Lish J. *Measurement and Management of Clinical Outcomes.* New York: John Wiley and Sons, 1997.

Magura and Moses. *Outcome Measures for Child Welfare Services: Theory and Applications.* Washington DC: Child Welfare League of America, 1986.

Maruish ME (ed.). *The Use of Psychological Testing for Treatment Planning and Outcome Assessment.* Hillsdale NJ: Lawrence Erlbaum Associates, 1994.

Mayo-Smith, et al. Pharmacological management of alcohol withdrawal: a meta-based practice guideline. *Journal of the American Medical Association* July 9, 1997:144-151.

McLellan, et al. Evaluating the Effectiveness of Addictions Treatments: Reasonable Expectations, Appropriate Comparisons. *The Milbank Quarterly* 1996; 74(1):51-85

McLellan AT, Grissom G, and Brill P. Problem-Service "Matching" in Addiction Treatment: A Prospective Study in 4 Programs. *Archives of General Psychiatry* August 1997; 54(8):730-735.

McLellan and Hunkeler. Patient Satisfaction and Outcomes in Alcohol and Drug Abuse Treatment. *Psychiatric Services* May 1998; 49(5):573-575.

Milrod B and Busch F. Long-Term Outcome of Panic Disorder Treatment. *The Journal of Nervous and Mental Disorders* 1996; 184:723-730.

Morrissey JP, Johnsen MC, and Calloway MO. Evaluating Performance and Change in Mental Health Systems Serving Children and Youth: An Interorganizational Network Approach. *Journal of Mental Health Administration* 1997:24(1).

Moynihan MH, et al. *Colorado Mental Health Institute at Fort Logan Child and Adolescent Tracking and Treatment Outcome Study.* Unpublished manuscript. University of Colorado at Boulder.

Mundt JC. Interactive Voice Response Systems in Clinical Research and Treatment. *Psychiatric Services* May 1997; 48(5):611-612.

Muñoz R, Hollon S, McGrath E, Rehm L, and VandenBos G. On the AHCPR Guidelines: Further Considerations for Practitioners. *American Psychologist* 1994; 49:42-61.

National Association of State Mental Health Program Directors Research Institute. *Five State Feasibility Study on State Mental Health Agency Performance Measures.* Draft Executive Summary. Alexandria VA: National Association of State Mental Health Program Directors Research Institute, May 1, 1998.

National Committee for Quality Assurance. *Health Plan Employer Data and Information Set (HEDIS) 1999.* Vols. 1-6. Washington DC: National Committee for Quality Assurance, 1998.

National Council for Community Behavioral Healthcare. *Behavioral Healthcare Outcomes: A Reference Guide to Measurement Tools*. Rockville MD: National Council for Community Behavioral Healthcare, 1995.

Newman, et al. *Indiana Hoosier Assurance Plan Packet: Report on Research/Implementation Strategy & Assessment Instruments to Support Level of Care Determination*. Cambridge MA: The Evaluation Center@HSRI, July 29, 1997.

Nuttbrock, et al. Outcomes of Homeless Mentally Ill Chemical Abusers in Community Residences and a Therapeutic Community. *Psychiatric Services* January 1998; 49(1):68-76.

Office of Ethnic Minority Affairs. Guidelines for Providers of Psychological Services to Ethnic Linguistic and Culturally Diverse Populations. *American Psychologist* 1993; 48(1):45-48.

Ohio Mental Health Outcomes Task Force. *Vital Signs: A Statewide Approach to Measuring Consumer Outcomes in Ohio's Publicly-Supported Community Mental Health System*. Ohio Department of Mental Health. Columbus, Ohio: March 1998.

Outcomes Evaluation: A Manual for Behavioral Health Care Providers, 2nd Ed. Providence RI: Manisses Communications Group, 1996.

Pickett S. et al. Factors Predicting Patients' Satisfaction With Managed Mental Health Care. *Psychiatric Services* 1995; 46(7)722-723.

Plante TG, Couchaman CE, and Diaz AR. Measuring Treatment Outcome and Client Satisfaction Among Children and Families. *Journal of Mental Health Administration* 1995; 22(3):262-269.

Pallak MS and Cummings NA. Outcomes Research in Managed Mental Health Care: Issues, Strategies, and Trends. In: *Managed Behavioral Health Care: A Search for Precision*, Shueman SA, Mayhugh SL, Gould BS, eds. Springfield MA: Charles C Thomas, 1994.

Perloff E. *Health and Psychosocial Instruments (HAPI)*. Pittsburgh PA: Behavioral Measurement Database Services, 1991.

Persons JB, et al. The Role of Psychotherapy in the Treatment of Depression: Review of Two Practice Guidelines. *Archives of General Psychiatry* 1996; 53:283-290.

Phillips, et al. Measuring Program Performance in Methadone Treatment Using In-Treatment Outcomes: An Illustration. *Journal of Mental Health Administration* 22(3).

Pincus, Zarin, and West. Peering Into the Black Box: Measuring Outcomes of Managed Care. *Archives of General Psychiatry* 1996; 53:870-877.

Popkin, et al. An Instrument To Evaluate the Process of Psychiatric Care in Ambulatory Settings. *Psychiatric Services* 1997; 48:524-527.

Raskin, et al. A Model for Evaluating Intensive Outpatient Behavioral Health Care Programs. *Psychiatric Services* 1996; 47(11).

Robinson G. *Mental Health Measures in Medicaid HEDIS*. Rockville MD: Center for Mental Health Services, 1996

Roy-Byrne, et al. Evidence for Limited Validity of the Revised Global Assessment of Functioning Scale. *Psychiatric Services* 47(9):864.

Sederer and Dickey, eds. *Outcomes Assessment in Clinical Practice*. Baltimore MD: Williams & Wilkins, 1996.

Science Applications International Corporation. *Side-by-Side Comparison of Mental Health Practice Guidelines*. Beaverton OR: November 30, 1994, 159 pages.

Science Applications International Corporation. *Outcome Management Systems for Mental Health and Chemical Dependency Services*. Beaverton OR: April 30, 1996, 155 pages.

Sexton. The Relevance of Counseling Outcome Research: Current Trends and Practical Implications. *Journal of Counseling and Development* 1996; 74:590-600.

Simon GE, et al. Predictors of Outpatient Mental Health Utilization by Primary Care Patient in a Health Maintenance Organization. *American Journal of Psychiatry* 1994; 151(6):908-913.

Simon GE and VonKorff M. Recognition, Management, and Outcomes of Depression in Primary Care. *Archives of Family Medicine* 1995; 4:99-105.

Simonson W. Algorithmic Depression Treatment Guidelines for Consultant Pharmacists. *Consultant Pharmacist* 1996; 11(Suppl A):27-34.

Spath PL. *Practice Guidelines for Mental Health and Substance Abuse Treatment Providers.* American Health Information Management Association, Behavioral Health Section, June 21, 1997.

Sperry L and Fink P, eds. Treatment Outcomes in Clinical Practice. (A special section devoted to outcomes). *Psychiatric Annals* 1997; 27(2):94-133.

Stinchfield RD, Niforopulos L, and Feder SH. Follow-Up Contact Bias in Adolescent Substance Abuse Treatment Outcome Research. *Journal of Studies on Alcohol* 1994a; 55:265-289.

Stout C, Theis G, and Omer J, eds. *The Complete Guide to Managed Behavioral Healthcare.* New York NY: John Wiley & Sons, 1996.

Task Force on Principles and Recommendations for Outcomes. *Using Outcomes To Improve Care: Quality Assessment of Mental Health and Substance Abuse.* Arlington VA: National Alliance for the Mentally Ill, 1995.

Teague GB, Bond GR, and Drake RE. Program Fidelity in Assertive Community Treatment: Development and Use of a Measure. *American Journal of Orthopsychiatry* April 1998; 68(2):216-232.

Trabin T and Freeman M. *Inside Outcomes: The National Review of Behavioral Healthcare Outcomes Management Programs* (Revised and Expanded). Portola Valley CA: CentraLink, 1995.

VA [Veteran's Administration] Pilots Major Depressive Disorder Pathway. *Issues & Outcomes* March-April 1997; 3(2):4-6.

Wedding, et al. Maintaining the Confidentiality of Computerized Mental Health Outcome. *Journal of Mental Health Administration*; 22(3).

Wells KB, Astrachan BM, Tischler GL, and Unutzer J. Issues and Approaches in Evaluating Managed Mental Health Care. *Milbank Quarterly* 1995; 73(1):57-75.

WICHE Mental Health Program. *Consumer Report Card.* Boulder CO: WICHE Mental Health Program, 1995.

Wilson GT. Treatment Manuals in Clinical Practice. *Behaviour Research and Therapy* March 1997; 35(3):205-10.

Woody and Kihlstrom. Outcomes, Quality and Cost: Integrating Psychotherapy and Mental Health Service Research. *Psychotherapy Research* 1997; 7(4):365-381.

Woody SR and Sanderson WC, eds. Manuals for Empirically Supported Treatments: 1998 Update. *The Clinical Psychologist* 1998; 51:17-21.

Young NK, Coley SM, and Gardner SL. *Getting to Outcomes in Integrated Service Models.* Irvine CA: Center for Collaboration for Children, 1994.

Zarin, et al. Practice-Based Research in Psychiatry. *American Journal of Psychiatry* 1997; 154:1199-1208.

Appendix G
Key Internet Resources

About the SF-36
http://www.mcw.edu/midas/health/SF-36.html

Alberta Clinical Practice Guidelines
http://www.amda.ab.ca/general/clinical-practice-guidelines/index.html

Alcoholism Treatment Assessment Instruments
http://silk.nih.gov/silk/niaaal/publication/instable.htm

American Academy of Child and Adolescent Psychiatry
http://www.aacap.org/

American Academy of Psychiatry and the Law
http://www1.cc.emory.edu/appl

Bazelon Center for Mental Health Law
http://www.bazelon.org

Bluestem Health for Kansas
http://www2.kumc.edu/bluestem/

Center for Health Care Strategies
http://www.chcs.org

Dual Diagnosis Web Site
http://pobox.com/~dualdiagnosis

Dr. Ivan's Depression Central
http://www.psycom.net/depression.central.html

The Evaluation Center @ HSRI
http://www.hsri.org/eval/eval.html

Evidence-based mental health
http://www.bmjpg.com/data/ebmh.htm

Evidence-Based Health Informatics
Health Information Research Unit
McMaster University
http://hiru.hirunet.mcmaster.ca/

Florida Mental Health Institute
University of South Florida
http://www.fmhi.usf.edu/

Healthcare Quality Assessment
http://www.qserve.com/hcass/

Internet Mental Health
http://www.mentalhealth.com

Knowledge Exchange Network (KEN)
http://www.mentalhealth.org/
Sponsored by the Center for Mental Health Services, part of the Substance Abuse and Mental Health Services Admnistration (SAMHSA), KEN is a multifaceted information resource for both mental health practitioners and consumers of mental health services.

Manuals for Empirically Supported Treatments: 1998 Update
http://www.sscp.psych.ndsu.nodak.edu/

Medline Access Sites:
http://www.healthgate.com
http://igm.nlm.nih.gov
http://www.medscape.com

Mental Health InfoSource
http://www.mhsource.com/

Mental Health Meetings
http://users.interport.net/~mpulier/psyjumps.html

Mental Health Net
http://cmhc.com/

Mental Health Statistics Improvement Program
http://www.mhsip.org/home.html

National Alliance for the Mentally Ill
http://www.nami.org/

National Association of Psychiatric Health Systems
http://www.naphs.org

National Council for Community Behavioral Healthcare (formerly the National Community Mental Healthcare Council)
http://www.nccbh.org

National Health Law Program, Inc.
http://www.healthlaw.org/

National Institute on Alcohol Abuse and Alcoholism
http://www.niaaa.nih.gov/

National Institute on Alcohol Abuse and Alcoholism
Alcohol and Alcohol Problems Science Database (ETOH)
http://etoh.niaaa.nih.gov/

National Technical Assistance Center for State Mental Health
http://www.nasmhpd.org/ntac/

Net Outcomes
An Internet-based treatment outcomes management system created by the Center for Outcomes Research and Effectiveness (CORE).
http://www.netoutcomes.net

Obsessive Compulsive & Spectrum Disorders Association
http://www.ocdhelp.org

Outcomes Assessment and Research
http://www.sph.uth.tmc.edu/www/res/outcomes/outcomes.htm

Quality Resources Online
http://www.casti.com/qc/

PIE Online
http://www.mimh.edu

Practice Guidelines Coalition
http://www.unr.edu/psych/pgc/

PsychLink's Outcomes and Satisfaction Measurement Tools
http://www.psychlink.com/news/prcstrat/art11.html

Psychotherapy Finances Online
http://www.psyfin.com

Quality in Therapy ("A slowly growing assortment of ideas, links, tools, and references for providing high-quality therapy")
http://www.xmission.com/~rebling/pub/sft.html

Reuters Health Information Services
http://www.reutershealth.com

Substance Abuse and Mental Health Services Administration
http://www.samhsa.gov/

SAMHSA's National Directory of Drug Abuse and Alcoholism Treatment and Prevention Programs
Developed by SAMHSA's Office of Scientific Analysis
http://www.health.org/search/treatdir96.htm

U.S. Department of Labor—Substance Abuse Information Database (SAID)
http://www.dol.gov:8001/said.nsf

Texas Medication Algorithm Project (TMAP): An Evaluation of the Clinical and Economic Impact of Medication Algorithms in Public Sector Patients with Severe and Persistent Mental Illnesses
An Interim Progress Report
October 20, 1997
http://www.mhmr.state.tx.us/meds/interim.htm

TMAP 3 Algorithms
http://www.mhmr.state.tx.us/meds/app4.htm

Lists of Links

beeHive
http://watarts.uwaterloo.ca/~bee/remotepsych.html

Behavioral Healthcare Resources on the Web
http://www.umdnj.edu/psyevnts/pointers.html

Dr. Bob's Mental Health Links
http://uhs.bsd.uchicago.edu/dr-bob/mental.html

Yahoo! Mental Health Links
http://www.yahoo.com/Health/Mental_Health/

Mailing Lists

MBHEVAL (Topical Evaluation Network National Health Care List)
This mailing list is established and maintained by the Evaluation Center@HSRI, a grant program of the Center for Mental Health Services funded to provide technical assistance related to the evaluation of adult mental health system change. The Human Services Research Institute is a nonprofit research and planning organization based in Cambridge MA. Mailing list archives at: http://maelstrom.stjohns.edu/archives/mbheval.html. As of September 30, 1998, MBHEVAL had 457 subscribers.

To subscribe to MBHEVAL, send the following command in the BODY of mail to LISTSERV@SJUVM.STJOHNS.EDU: Subscribe MBHEVAL; [your first name; your last name].

OUTCMTEN (Mental Health Outcomes Evaluation)
The purpose of the OUTCMTEN mailing list is to develop a broad collective expertise with respect to problems of assessing and analyzing outcomes of interventions aimed at improving mental health systems. The existence of such a network will both foster and facilitate communications among all mental health system stakeholders to improve measurement and, consequently, understanding of interventions and their effects. Mailing list archives at: http://maelstrom.stjohns.edu/archives/outcmten.html. As of September 30, 1998, OUTCMTEN had 1,150 subscribers.

To subscribe to OUTCMTEN, send the following command in the BODY of mail to LISTSERV@SJUVM.STJOHNS.EDU: Subscribe OUTCMTEN; [your first name; your last name].

Public Sector Outcomes Mailing List
puboutcm@world.std.com
Majordomo@world.std.com
subscribe: puboutcm

Managed Behavioral Healthcare (252 subscribers)
listserv@sjuvm.stjohns.edu
subscribe: mbhc name

Mailing list archives at
MAELSTROM.STJOHNS.EDU
http://maelstrom.stjohns.edu/archives/index.html

Interwork Institute (list of behavioral mailing lists)
http://interwork.sdsu.edu/resources/listserv_info.html

Appendix H
Acronyms

ABD:	aged, blind, and disabled	**FFS:**	fee-for-service
ADC:	Alcohol and Drug Counselor	**GAD:**	Generalized Anxiety Disorder
AFDC:	Aid to Families with Dependent Children	**GAF:**	Global Assessment of Functioning
AHCPR:	Agency for Health Care Policy and Research	**HCFA:**	Health Care Financing Administration
AMBHA:	American Managed Behavioral Healthcare Association	**HEDIS:**	Health Plan Employer Data and Information Set
AOD:	alcohol and other drug	**HHS:**	Department of Health & Human Services
ASO:	administrative services only	**HMO:**	health maintenance organization
BBA:	Balanced Budget Act	**IDS:**	integrated delivery system
BHO:	behavioral healthcare organization	**IMD:**	Institution for Mental Diseases
CBT:	cognitive behavioral therapy	**IOP:**	intensive outpatient
CD:	chemical dependency	**IP:**	inpatient
CME:	care management entity	**JCAHO:**	Joint Commission on Accreditation of Healthcare Organizations
CMHC:	community mental health center		
CMHS:	Center for Mental Health Services (part of SAMHSA)	**LCSW:**	Licensed clinical social worker
CQI:	Continuous Quality Improvement	**LOS:**	length of stay
CQIS:	Clinical Quality Information System	**LPC:**	licensed professional counselor
		LTC:	long-term care
CSAP:	Center for Substance Abuse Prevention (part of SAMHSA)	**MAOI:**	Monoamine oxidase inhibitor
		MBHO:	managed behavioral healthcare organization
CSAT:	Center for Substance Abuse Treatment (part of SAMHSA)	**MCO:**	managed care organization
D&A:	drug and alcohol	**MH:**	mental health
DD:	developmentally disabled	**MHSIP:**	Mental Health Statistics Improvement Program
DRG:	Diagnosis-Related Group		
DSM:	Diagnostic and Statistical Manual of Mental Disorders	**MICA:**	mentally ill chemical abusing
		MIS:	Management Information System
EAP:	employee assistance program	**MR/DD:**	mentally retarded/developmentally disabled
ECT:	Electroconvulsive Therapy		
EPO:	exclusive provider organization	**MSO:**	management services organization (or, rarely, medical staff organization)
EPS:	extrapyramidal symptoms		
EPSDT:	early periodic screening, diagnosis and treatment		
		NCQA:	National Committee for Quality Assurance
ERISA:	Employee Retirement Income Security Act of 1974	**NIDA:**	National Institute on Drug Abuse

NIH:	National Institutes of Health	**QI:**	quality improvement
NIMH:	National Institute of Mental Health	**SA:**	substance abuse
NOS:	not otherwise specified	**SAMHSA:**	Substance Abuse and Mental Health Services Administration (part of the U.S. Department of Health and Human Services)
OCD:	Obsessive-Compulsive Disorder		
OP:	outpatient		
PCCM:	primary care case management	**SED:**	severely emotionally disturbed
PCP:	primary care physician	**SF-36:**	RAND Short Form 36
PD:	Panic Disorder	**SMI:**	serious mental illness
PERMS:	Performance Measures for Managed Behavioral Healthcare Programs	**SPMI:**	seriously and persistently mentally ill
		SSRI:	selective serotonin reuptake inhibitor
PHO:	physician-hospital organization		
PHP:	prepaid health plan	**TANF:**	Temporary Assistance for Needy Families
PMPM:	per-member, per-month		
PPO:	preferred provider organization	**TPA:**	third-party administrator
PTSD:	Posttraumatic Stress Disorder	**UR:**	utilization review
QARI:	Quality Assurance Reform Initiative		